TO

Dave

With thanks for all your help - and the gigs!!

Alos R

BRITISH SINGLE-SEATER FIGHTER SQUADRONS ON THE WESTERN FRONT IN WORLD WAR I

BRITISH SINGLE-SEATER FIGHTER SQUADRONS

ON THE WESTERN FRONT

IN WORLD WAR I

Alex Revell

Schiffer Military History
Atglen, PA

Acknowledgments

Firstly I would like to thank my fellow researchers, members of Cross and Cockade Great Britain/ International, Cross and Cockade USA and Over the Front, whose researches over the last forty years have resulted in such a vast fund of knowledge of the war in the air in 1914-1918. I often feel that in their love and enthusiasm for their hobby they perhaps tend to overlook the valuable histori- cal contribution they have made – and are still making – for the benefit of future generations of aviation enthusiasts. This is especially true of those of us lucky enough to have had many of the participants of that first war in the air as personal friends, now sadly no longer with us.

My heartfelt thanks to those friends who answered, as always, so promptly and generously my request for photographs: Frank Cheesman, Barrington Gray, Norman Franks, Phil Jarrett, Bob Jones, Bob Lynes, Neal O'Connor, Les Rogers, Margaret Stanbury, Bill Vandersteen and Mike Westrop. A special thank you to Dave Robinson for his computer skills in rescuing old photographs, and to my wife Linda, for her photographic skills, patience, and so much else.

Alex Revell
Nancledra, Cornwall
2005

Dedication
To the officers, NCOs, men and ratings who served in the Royal Flying Corps, Royal Airforce and the Royal Naval Air Service in the war of 1914-1918.

Book design by Robert Biondi.

Printed in China.
ISBN: 0-7643-2420-9

We are always looking for people to write books on new and related subjects. If you have an idea for a book, please contact us at the address below.

Published by Schiffer Publishing Ltd.
4880 Lower Valley Road
Atglen, PA 19310
Phone: (610) 593-1777
FAX: (610) 593-2002
E-mail: Info@schifferbooks.com.
Visit our web site at: www.schifferbooks.com
Please write for a free catalog.
This book may be purchased from the publisher.
Please include $3.95 postage.
Try your bookstore first.

In Europe, Schiffer books are distributed by:
Bushwood Books
6 Marksbury Ave.
Kew Gardens
Surrey TW9 4JF
England
Phone: 44 (0)20 8392-8585
FAX: 44 (0)20 8392-9876
E-mail: Bushwd@aol.com.
Free postage in the UK. Europe: air mail at cost.
Try your bookstore first.

CONTENTS

INTRODUCTION

The aim of this book is to give an overall picture of the activities of the single-seater fighter squadrons of the Royal Flying Corps, later the Royal Air Force, over the Western Front in the war of 1914-1918. This gives rise to the danger of giving an incomplete and fragmented view of the air war in that it does not cover – other than in a peripheral way – the all important role played by the gallant crews of the reconnaissance aeroplanes of the Corps Wings and the two-seat fighter/reconnaissance aeroplanes of the Army Wings RFC/RAF: they too had their victories and defeats. Both the remit and size of this book precludes detailing their onerous and exacting work, and I would ask the reader to bear in mind that the daily flying and fighting of the single-seater fighter squadrons, although vitally important, was a relatively smaller role – however gallant – in the air over the Western Front during the tragic years of 1914-1918.

Because of the sheer proliferation of the scale of air combats from the spring of 1917, space also precluded the detailing of the majority of daily combats, which had been possible up to the end of 1916. I have therefore detailed only those combats which I feel are of particular interest or importance, especially those for which there are first hand accounts. There were of course were many more actions, no less worthy, that fully deserve to have been recounted, but as with the hundreds of actions by the Royal Navy in the Napoleonic wars, these have now passed into history, preserved only in the yellowing combat reports of the era or in the recollections of former RFC/RAF pilots.

PROLOGUE

The war of 1914-1918 – the Great War – saw the advent of a new type of warfare. For the first time in history the aeroplane was to play an important and vital role in the pursuit of war. The advantage of the aeroplane over cavalry in reporting the position of enemy troops had been realised before the war – speed of reporting was essential – and during the first days of the war of movement in France the aeroplanes of the opposing armies carried out important reconnaissance flights. However, with the impasse of a static war reached on the Western Front, with trenches stretching from the Belgian coast to the borders of Switzerland, it became imperative to reconnoitre the activities of an adversary behind his trenches – to see over 'the other side of the hill.' The aeroplane was the solution.

From the earliest days of trench warfare the antagonists made full use of their two-seater aeroplanes – crewed by a pilot and observer – to reconnoitre the activities of the opposite side: photographing defences; trench systems; the disposition of forces; to give warning of a coming offensive by observing the build up of troops and *matériel* in back areas.

The use of artillery also became a major factor in trench warfare. It was soon realised that the use of aeroplanes for spotting the fall of shot and relaying the results and corrections by wireless to the artillery batteries was of utmost importance.

It therefore became essential to prevent the reconnaissance aeroplanes from carrying out their tasks – in effect, to deny the enemy his 'eyes'. The solution was the fighter aeroplane, the sole purpose of which was to destroy the two-seater reconnaissance aeroplanes of the enemy. This in turn led to the each side seeking to protect their reconnaissance aeroplanes by the deployment of fighter aeroplanes, either in close escort, or by seeking out the enemy fighters and destroying them before they could interfere with the work of the two-seaters. The concept of the fighter aeroplane was born.

CHAPTER ONE

EARLY DAYS

In 1908 the pioneer aviator and aeroplane designer Alliott Verdon Roe attended a meeting at the British War Office. Along with other prominent designers and manufacturers he hoped to persuade the British Government to support the embryo British aeroplane manufacturing industry by the placement of government orders.

'We were received by Mr R B Haldane, who was secretary of State for War at that time, and after we had placed our case before him we were replied to by Colonel J E Seeley, his secretary, who spoke on his behalf, saying: "Gentlemen, much as I would like to help you by placing orders, we regret we cannot do this as we are trustees of the public purse and we do not consider that aeroplanes will be of any possible use for war purposes."'

Only four years later, during the 1912 Army manoeuvres, General Grierson, commanding the defending force, was in no doubt that the seven aeroplanes allotted to him from the newly-formed Royal Flying Corps had enabled him to defeat the attacking force under Sir Douglas Haig. Grierson's cavalry commander had informed him that with the opposing forces so far apart it was impossible for the cavalry to give him the position of Haig's force in under 24 hours. Captain H R M Brooke-Popham, commanding 3 Squadron RFC, undertook to carry out a reconnaissance and his aeroplanes left the ground at 6.00am. In less than three hours Brooke-Popham gave Grierson a complete, accurate and detailed picture of the disposition of Haig's forces. Grierson later commented, with remarkable prescience: 'Personally, I think there is no doubt that, before land fighting takes place, we shall have to fight and destroy the enemy's aircraft. It seems to me impossible for troops to fight while hostile aircraft are able to keep up their observation. That is to say, warfare will be impossible unless we have mastery of the air.'

At the outbreak of war in 1914 the role of the aeroplane was still seen purely as one of reconnaissance, a natural extension of the cavalry, and opinion remained divided as to whether it was absolutely necessary to arm aeroplanes; indeed many people still persistently held the view that the aeroplane would have no practical use in warfare. Although some thought had been given to the potential of the aeroplane as an offensive weapon – notably by manufacturers such as Sopwith, Vickers, Avro and the Royal Aircraft Factory, with their respective gunbus designs – the development of a fighting aeroplane was not pursued with any sense of urgency.

Consequently, not one of the 64 aeroplanes that the Royal Flying Corps took to France with the British Expeditionary Force on 14 August 1914 was armed for fighting in the air. The aeroplanes which equipped the four squadrons of the RFC in 1914 were a varied collection of two-seater types: Nos 2 and 4 Squadrons were equipped with the Royal Factory designed BE2; 3 Squadron with Bleriots, Henry Farmans and a single BE8; and 5 Squadron operated Henry Farmans, Avros and two BE8s.

The RFC had only four single-seater aeroplanes on charge: Sopwith Tabloids, crated at the Aircraft Park at Amiens. The first of a long line of Sopwith fighters, the Tabloid had a top speed of 92mph and could climb at the rate of 1,200 feet per minute – an impressive performance for those days. An order for 12 Tabloids had been placed for use as high-speed reconnaissance scouts and message carriers, the term 'scout' later becoming synonymous with any single-seater fighter. On August 28 the Tabloids were unpacked and erected and two were issued to 3 Squadron, to be flown by Lieutenants Norman Spratt and Gordon Bell, two Special Reserve officers attached to the Aircraft Park. Initially the Tabloids were unarmed, but Spratt experimented with various offensive weapons, including a revolver, flechettes – small pointed darts to be dropped on enemy troops – and, bizarrely, a hand grenade on a long cable.

On August 16 all four squadrons flew from Amiens to their aerodrome at Maubeuge, south of Mons and ten miles behind the line designated to be held by the BEF. On August 19 Capt P B Joubert de la Ferté of 3 Squadron and Lt G W Mapplebeck of 4 Squadron flew the RFC's first reconnaissance of the war. It was not a success. The weather was cloudy and both pilots lost contact. Mapplebeck returned to Maubeuge at noon, having seen only a small body of cavalry at Gembloux, but Joubert was lost for two hours in the heavy cloud and finally landed at Tournai, where he attempted to ascertain the location of the Belgian army. Nothing was known in Tournai and Jourbert left, only to again lose his way, landing at Courtrai two hours later. At Courtrai a local *gendarme* was able to tell him that the HQ of the Belgian flying corps was at Louvain. Joubert finally landed back at Maubeuge at 5.30pm, eight hours after his departure, with very little of consequence to report.

The First Hostile

At about 2.30pm on the afternoon of August 22 the first hostile aeroplane to be seen by the RFC flew over Maubeuge aerodrome at 4,000ft. Two BEs and a Henry Farman at once took off in an effort to intercept the intruder. Major C A H Longcroft, a supernumerary attached to 2 Squadron, flying one of the BE2as, intended to drop hand grenades on the enemy machine, but before the BE could climb to his height the German pilot turned east and escaped. The Henry Farman from 5 Squadron, flown by Lt Louis Strange with Lt L da C Penn-Gaskell as his observer, was armed with a Lewis gun, but the added weight so impaired the performance of the Farman that it had reached only 1,000ft, and was still labourously climbing, half an hour after the German machine had gone. Major Higgins, Strange's commanding officer, ordered him to dispense with the Lewis gun and revert to the customary rifle, despite Strange pointing out that the BE2s had also failed to reach the German machine.

Twelve reconnaissance flights on August 22 revealed large bodies of enemy troops moving towards the British held positions at Mons, and the next day British troops were in action against an enemy force vastly superior in numbers.[1] At Maubeuge, heavy gunfire could be heard and that evening the sky to the north-east was illuminated by the flash of gunfire and burning villages.

On 24 August 1914 the retreat of the British Army from Mons began. In the morning, at 8.00am, the squadrons of the RFC received orders to evacuate Maubeuge. James McCudden, then a mechanic in 3 Squadron, later to become one of the most successful fighter pilots of the war, left in a Bleriot piloted by Philip Joubert and his last view of the RFC's first aerodrome in France was a Henry Farman, which had refused to start because of engine trouble, burning on the ground.

Over the following 12 days the RFC squadrons moved almost daily. The first stop after Maubeuge was Le Cateau. The next day they moved again, to St.Quentin, flying on again the following day to La Fère. They stayed at La Fère a day, before moving on to an aerodrome on Compiègne racecourse on August 28, and then to Senslis on August 30. The squadrons were at Juilly on August 31, Serris on September 2, Touquin the next day and, finally, at Melun on September 4.

The location of new aerodromes during the retreat from Mons presented no problems. As early as 1911 Capt Frederick Sykes, who was later to become Commanding Officer of the Military Wing of the RFC on its formation in 1912, had cycled the countryside of northern France to select possible landing grounds, but the strain, so early imposed on the transport and servicing facilities of the RFC, the youngest corps in the British Army, was a severe test. That the RFC came through such a test with flying colours, even learnt valuable lessons from the retreat, is testimony to the improvisational skills of both officers and men. Billets were found in farmhouses, private houses, barns, haystacks; even, when the weather was bad, under the wings of their aeroplanes. Unfortunately the weather was not always kind. McCudden recorded that during the first days of the retreat it was hot and dry, and had not rained for over a fortnight, but on Wednesday, August 26, it was raining 'very hard.' Conditions were so bad that although all the machines reached La Fère, only two landed on the actual aerodrome. McCudden's charge, Bleriot Parasol No.616, had landed in a very muddy ploughed field. 'I filled up with petrol and oil and had a look round the engine and machine and then tied it down for the night. It was raining very hard and as there were six inches of mud under the machine I decided not to sleep under the wing that night, so I slept in the pilot's seat with a waterproof sheet over me.'[2]

It was not until August 31 that the personnel of 3 Squadron enjoyed the luxury of their first bath since leaving England on August 12. At Juilly there was a deserted convent with an ornamental lake and McCudden and several of his fellow mechanics in 3 Squadron went down to bathe. 'We spent a very pleasant afternoon there and we also found some very nice apples in the grounds as well.'[3]

Food was short during the retreat, augmented by apples – scrumped from the convent and wayside orchards – and blackberries, which the French peasants considered poisonous. Officers and men shared their provisions, one officer providing the milk for tea by milking a cow in a nearby field.

The First Aerial Victories

During the retreat, operations were still flown, and on August 26 the first enemy aeroplane was brought down. The German machine, 'a Rumpler Taube monoplane', flew over the airfield at La Fère at 11.00am. Everyone had a shot at the enemy – McCudden standing on a petrol tin in an attempt to increase the trajectory of his Webley revolver – and several BE2as and an Avro took off in intercept the intruder. The Rumpler was flying at only 1,000ft and was intercepted by Lts C W Wilson and C E C Rabagliati of 5 Squadron in the Avro. Rabagliati, in the front cockpit, opened fire and forced the enemy machine to land in a field edged by a large wood. Lt. Harvey-Kelly and Sergeant-Major Street, in one of 2 Squadron's BE2as, landed beside the German machine and chased the pilot and his observer into the wood, where they made good their escape. Harvey-Kelly removed a plaque from the machine and proudly displayed it as a trophy of war, but later happily gave it to Wilson, who claimed it as a victory for 5 Squadron. Another enemy machine was captured during the day, near Le Quesnoy.

Three days later, at Compiègne, a German machine flew over the aerodrome and dropped three bombs. Spratt took off in a Tabloid, armed with flechettes, and gave chase. Quickly gaining on the enemy machine, Spratt circled it and threw his flechettes, forcing the enemy pilot to land. McCudden recorded that these visits from German machines were common and took place at nearly every aerodrome the RFC occupied during the retreat.

Even though Sir John French, commanding the BEF in France, had been warned of the heavy concentration of German troops on his front at Mons – and the various attempted enveloping movements on his flank by von Kluck's First Army – in the early days of the retreat French's HQ had been still a little dubious of the worth of air reconnaissance. However, the valuable reports given to him by the RFC during the retreat had dispelled these reservations, especially on September 1 at Juilly: German cavalry was reported by the RFC to be in the thickly wooded area to the north, only two miles from French's HQ and with no British troops between. HQ hastily decamped. French had also been well served throughout the retreat by the harassment of the advancing German army by the RFC – small and crude as these attempts were. Louis Strange recalled that the daily routine for the squadrons during the retreat was one of dawn reconnaissance and the dropping of hand grenades and petrol bombs on the advancing enemy troops.

The German forces were finally halted by the battle of the Marne and it was after the successful conclusion of the battle that Sir John French, in his despatch of 7 September 1914, made the first official mention of fighting in the air.

'I wish particularly to bring to your Lordships' notice the admirable work done by the Royal Flying Corps under Sir David Henderson. Their skill, energy, and perseverance have been beyond all praise. They have furnished me with complete and accurate information, which has been of incalculable value in the conduct of operations. Fired at constantly by both friend and foe, and not hesitating to fly in every kind of weather, they have remained undaunted throughout. Further, by actually fighting in the air, they had succeeded in destroying five of the enemy's machines.'

The Beginnings of Air Combat

In the autumn of 1914, during the battles of the Aisne and the first battle of Ypres, there were occasional fights in the air and the combatants began to give serious thoughts to the arming both of their reconnaissance machines and the faster, more agile, single-seater scouts. In September, 4 Squadron was already fitting each of its Henry Farmans with a Lewis gun, and during the month two Bristol Scouts were taken on charge by the RFC, one going to 3 Squadron, to be flown by Lt R Cholmondeley, and the other to 5 Squadron, where it was flown by the CO, Major J F A 'Josh' Higgins. Although, like the Tabloid, the little Bristols had been conceived as single-seater reconnaissance scouts, they were quickly armed. As no synchronising or interrupter gear – which would allow a gun to be fired through propeller in the line of flight, enabling the aeroplane to be aimed like a gun – was available at this time, 3 Squadron fitted two rifles, one on each side of the fuselage, angled outwards at approximately 45 degrees to enable the gun to fire clear of the propeller. In 5 Squadron a single rifle was fitted, a revolver was carried and a quantity of hand grenades. 'Josh' Higgins loved his Bristol and its armament, but his eyesight was so poor that he could never get near enough to an opponent to use it to advantage. In October the single SE2, built by the Royal Aircraft Factory at Farnborough, was also issued to 3 Squadron and armed in a similar fashion to the Bristol.

With the ending of the first battle of Ypres in November 1914 the war of movement stagnated to one of entrenched positions, with the opposing forces facing each other in trenches that ran from the Belgian coast to Switzerland. Despite the onset of winter, combats in the air were becoming more frequent as each side attempted to interfere with the other's reconnaissance machines, which were now also being used to range for the artillery.

A typical example of the type of combat that was now taking place occurred on November 22, when an Avro 504 of 5 Squadron, flown by the aggressive and inventive Louis Strange, with Lt Freddy Small in the observer's cockpit, attacked a German two-seater Aviatik at 7,000ft near St.Omer. The Avro was armed with a Lewis gun carried on a mounting of Strange's own design, consisting of a length of rope, a steel tube and a pulley. Strange dived on the Aviatik from a height advantage of 500ft, at right angles to its line of flight, turned underneath it and flew in the same direction, a little in front and less than a hundred feet below. The German pilot turned twice, followed by the Avro, and Small emptied a drum of ammunition into the enemy machine. The enemy observer fired back at the Avro with a pistol. His aim was good. Strange saw Small grimace with surprise and blood began to run out of his gloved right hand. Despite this, Small changed the drum and again emptied the entire contents into the German machine. The German pilot put his machine into a steep side-slip and landed behind the British lines near Neuve-Église. Strange landed at a nearby aerodrome, saw Small to a first aid post, then borrowed a motor cycle to ride to the scene of the

Germans' forced landing, intending to claim them as prisoners. On his arrival at the scene he found that both were unwounded, although there were some twenty bullet holes in their machine. To Strange's astonishment, the German observer, a commissioned officer, was so incensed at his NCO pilot having given up the fight while still uninjured that he fought off his captors, dragged his unfortunate pilot from the cockpit, knocked him down and began to kick him about the body.

By the end of 1914, after four and a half months of war, the RFC had seen a great deal of fighting: a pattern was beginning to emerge from 'the fog of war' and 1915 was to see rapid development in both equipment and tactics, with the squadrons being called upon to undertake new tasks and duties.

NOTES

1. The second machine to return from these flights contained the RFC's first casualty by enemy action. Sergeant-Major D S Jillings, flying as an observer to Lt. M W Noel of 2 Squadron, had been hit in the leg by a rifle bullet, the first British soldier to be wounded in an aeroplane. The RFC's first casualties of the war were Lt.Skene and Air Mechanic Keith Barlow of 3 Squadron, killed when taking off for France on 12 August 1914.

2. *Five Years In The Royal Flying Corps.* James McCudden. The Aeroplane and General Publishing Co. London 1918.
3. *Ibid.*

CHAPTER TWO

1915: NEW TASKS

In 1915, with the combatants in entrenched positions along the entire Western Front, and with the war no longer one of movement, the role of the aeroplane took on a new significance. It was no longer seen as an extension of the cavalry – for cavalry has no place in static warfare – but reconnaissance still played a vital, if slightly changed role. Aeroplanes were now the only means of penetrating behind the enemy's front line trenches in order to oversee his troop movements and concentration of reserves; his build up of forces for offensives; train movements; rolling stock; the location and stockpiling of ammunition and *matériel* dumps: a thousand and one details to build an accurate and detailed picture of operations in the enemy's back areas, not only to foresee his intentions but to plan one's own. During the battle of the Aisne in the late autumn of 1914, the RFC had also begun to observe for the artillery, and with the beginning of trench warfare, with the artillery taking up static positions behind the front line trenches, the aeroplane had begun not only to report on the fall of shot but to discover and map the opposing gun batteries for counter-battery work.

The role of the reconnaissance aeroplane therefore became one of prime importance and it was necessary for each of the combatants to destroy them – in essence, to deny the enemy his eyes. It naturally followed that the task would fall to fast, well-armed aeroplanes, in effect, fighters. Each side had therefore to protect its reconnaissance aeroplanes from fighter attack by attacking and destroying the enemy's fighters with its own. It followed logically that the fighter aeroplane had three main tasks: to destroy the enemy's observation machines; to protect its own by attacking and destroying the enemy fighters; and to escort its own observation machines to protect them from attacks by any enemy aeroplanes which had evaded its patrols. The age of the fighter aeroplane had arrived.

At the beginning of 1915 the RFC still had only four single-seater aeroplanes on charge: the SE2 with 3 Squadron; two Martinsyde S1s with 5 Squadron, and another with 4 Squadron; and 6 Squadron, which had arrived at St.Omer on 21 October 1914, had the fourth. Of the four Sopwith Tabloids issued to the squadrons, two had been wrecked and struck off strength at the beginning of September 1914 and two more – one had arrived at the Park on 15 January 1915 – were sent back to England on 4 February 1914. The sole remaining Tabloid on active service at the beginning of the year was with 4 Squadron, but it was struck off strength on January 22. The SE2 and the Martinsydes were armed in various extempory ways to act as escorts to the reconnaissance aeroplanes of their squadrons.

In February 1915, Lt.Col. Brook-Popham distributed a set of notes and recommendations on air fighting to the flight commanders of the squadrons under his command in 2 Wing. He pointed out that, 'the moral effect of a fast machine, however, skilfully manoeuvred, will be very small if no weapon of offence is carried.' Among Brooke-Popham's more fanciful ideas of what should constitute a 'weapon of offence' were dropping steel darts, bombs, and even, as presumably a last resort, that of charging the enemy and colliding with him – hardly a valid option for pilots not equipped with parachutes. However, Brooke-Popham did recognise the importance of the gun as the most effective means of attacking the enemy, although his recommendations were that a pistol in single-seater aeroplanes and a rifle in two-seaters, should be carried, arguing that the weight of a machine gun would adversely affect the performance of the aeroplane carrying it. Despite this reservation by Brooke-Popham, a Lewis gun expert was appointed to tour the squadrons to instruct pilots and observers in the art of deflection shooting and other skills.

With the opening of the battle of Neuve Chapelle on the morning of 10 March 1915, the war in the air increased in both momentum and pace. From what in 1914 had been mainly a passive role, the RFC began to take a more directly offensive part in the operations: spotting for the artillery, working with the attacking troops and, for the first time on an organised scale, bombing railway junctions, stations and troop positions.

During the spring of 1915, combats in the air became more frequent, although in some instances these could be frustratingly inconclusive. On the afternoon of April 28, for example, Malcolm Bell-Irving, flying 1 Squadron's Martinsyde S1., armed with two automatic pistols, attempted to intercept a number of enemy machines over the Ypres Salient. Over a period of nearly an hour, and in the course of seven separate attacks, all Bell-Irving's attempts were frustrated by the superior speed and climb of the enemy aeroplanes. Bell-Irving was of the opinion that even if the Martinsyde had been armed with a machine gun it would have been of little use in attacking a faster aeroplane. Although he had seen a total of nine enemy machines and had attacked, or attempted to attack, all of them, he felt sure that there were only three of four and that they were merely playing with the slow-climbing Martinsyde.[1]

As the war progressed, through the spring and summer, combats became more common and, although perhaps not typical of these early combats, that fought by Capt Louis Strange of 6 Squadron graphically illustrates one of the more unusual dangers of fighting in the air in 1915. On May 10, Strange, flying the Squadron's Martinsyde S1. No.2449, armed with a Lewis gun mounted on the top wing to fire above the arc of the propeller, took off to intercept an Aviatik. Over Menin both machines were close to their respective ceilings, with the Martinsyde closing fast. As the range closed the German observer began firing a Parabellum pistol at the pursuing Martinsyde. Strange later wrote: 'as some of his bullets came unpleasantly close I thought it high time to retaliate and gave him a drum from my Lewis gun, but without much effect. But when I wanted to take off the empty one and replace it with a full one it seemed to jam, and as I was unable to remove it with one hand I wedged the stick between my knees and tugged at the obstinate thing with both hands.'

Strange stood up in his seat to get a better purchase on the recalcitrant drum. As he pulled, his safety belt slipped down, his knees lost their grip on the control column and the Martinsyde, already climbing at its maximum angle, stalled and flicked over in a spin. 'As I was half out of the cockpit at the time, the spin threw me clear of the machine, but I still kept both my hands on the drum of the Lewis gun. Only a few seconds previously I had been cursing because I could not get that drum off, but now I prayed fervently that it would stay on for ever.'

The little Martinsyde was now inverted, in a flat spin, and Strange, hanging in space from the top plane, knew that the drum could come loose at any moment. It was imperative that he gain a hold on a more permanent part of his aeroplane.

'The first thing I thought of was the top of the centre section strut, which was behind and below the Lewis gun, but as the machine was now flying upside down I had sufficient wits left to realise that it was above and behind me, though where it was exactly I could not tell. Dare I let go the drum with one hand and make a grab for it? Well, there was nothing else for it but to take the risk; I let go and found the strut all right; then I released my other hand and gripped the strut on the other side.'

Although in a far less dangerous situation, Strange was still in an extremely precarious position: his chin was jammed hard against the centre section of the top wing, his feet still kicked in space, and the propeller seemed dangerously close to his face. He realised that his only chance of survival was to somehow get his feet back into the cockpit.

'I kept on kicking upwards behind me until at last I got one foot and then the other hooked inside the cockpit. Somehow I got the stick between my legs again and jammed on full aileron and elevator; I do not know exactly what happened then, but somehow the trick was done. The machine came over the right way up and I fell off the top plane into my seat with a bump.'

But Strange's troubles were not yet over. When he tried to regain control he found that the control column was immovable; the force of his precipitate re-entry into the cockpit had smashed the wooden seat and he was now sitting on the floor of the Martinsyde's cockpit, effectively jamming the controls.

'Something had to be done quickly, as although the engine had stopped through lack of petrol when the machine was upside down, it was now roaring away merrily and taking me down in a dive which looked likely to end in a wood to the north of Menin. So I throttled back and braced my shoulders against the back of the cockpit; then I pulled out the bits of broken seat and freed the controls. Luckily I found them working all right so I was able to pull the machine's nose up and open the throttle again. I flattened out, clearing the trees on the Menin road with very little to spare.'

Strange flew back along the Menin road, ruefully surveying the smashed instruments, mute testimony of his frantic efforts to regain control with his feet. 'I went to bed early that night and slept for a good solid twelve hours, but oh! how stiff I was the next day.'[2]

After the war, Strange learnt that the observer of the Aviatik had claimed a victory over a British scout, which had gone down in a spin into a wood on the north side of Menin.

The observer reported that he had seen the pilot of the scout thrown out of his machine, although he had not fallen clear. On the strength of this evidence the Germans spent half a day vainly searching the wood for the wreckage.

Hawker VC

On the evening of July 25, Capt Lanoe G Hawker of 6 Squadron took off in the Squadron's Bristol Scout. The Bristol, No.1611, was armed with a Lewis gun firing forwards at an angle to miss the propeller, a device which called for considerable skill on the part of the pilot, in both flying and marksmanship. Although Hawker had had several combats while flying the Bristol, forcing down a number of enemy machines, some smoking, he had gained no definite victories while flying it. As Hawker approached the Ypres Salient he saw two enemy observation machines and immediately attacked the nearest, emptying a whole drum of Lewis into it before turning his attentions to its companion. Hawker succeeded in firing another drum into the second machine before both Germans dived away. Hawker climbed to regain his height and continued his patrol at 11,000ft. Half an hour passed before he saw another opponent: a two-seater at 10,000ft over Hooge. Hawker was determined to destroy this machine and placed himself with the glare of the evening sun behind him before he attacked. The surprise was complete. Hawker opened fire from 100 yards.

The black-crossed machine went down out of control, turned upside down and burst into flames before hitting the ground in the British Lines east of Zillebeke. A map was later found on the body of the observer on which he had pinpointed the positions of various British batteries. As a bonus the map also gave the location of a troublesome German gun that had long eluded detection: mute testimony to the importance of Hawker's victory, the most successful yet fought by a single-seater scout of the RFC.

An anti-aircraft battery later reported that one of the machines Hawker had first attacked over the Salient had force landed in its own lines. Hawker received a congratulatory telegram from General Plummer, the Army Commander. For the actions on July 25 and for his tireless and courageous work since his arrival in France the previous October, Hawker was awarded the Victoria Cross, the first to be awarded for a combat in the air between opposing aeroplanes.

On 1 April 1915, nearly four months before Hawker's action in July, the era of the true single-seater fighter had begun when Lt Roland Garros, a member of *Escadrille de chasse NS12*, flying a Morane- Saulnier Type L., had shot down an Albatros two-seater. The Morane's propeller was protected by steel deflector plates, enabling Garros to fire through the propeller and aim the entire aeroplane as a gun. Exploiting his initial success, Garros shot down five enemy aeroplanes in 18 days before the Morane was hit by groundfire on April 18, forcing Garros to land behind enemy lines. He attempted to set fire to the Morane, but was only partially successful and the Germans were quick to realise the potential of a fighter aeroplane which could fire through its propeller along its line of flight.

The first attempt by the Germans to copy the deflection blade device was unsuccessful. They quickly realised, however, that at best it was a makeshift solution to the problem and they issued a Parabellum LMG14 machine gun to Antony Fokker, the Dutch aeroplane designer and manufacturer, with instructions to design an efficient interrupter gear.

It had long been realised that for the aeroplane to have any use as a true fighter a device would have to be found to enable its gun, or guns, to be fired through the arc of the propeller. The obvious solution to the problem was to arm the pusher design of aeroplane, where the propeller was behind the pilot, giving an uninterrupted field of fire, but the tractor types were faster and more effective aerodynamically. Many people had foreseen this potential problem and in July 1913 a Swiss-born engineer, Franz Schneider, technical director and chief designer of the LVG Company, had patented a design in Germany for an interrupter gear, details of which were given in the September issue of the German aviation magazine *Flugsport*. Fokker's engineers, Luebbe and Heber, were conversant with Schneider's work – his conception being that the firing of the gun should be interrupted if a propeller blade was in the line of fire – had seen the superiority of his solution over that of the crude deflection plates system and had developed a gun synchronisation gear at the Fokker works at Schwerin. Therefore, less than a week later, after modifications had been made to take into account the firing mechanism of the Parabellum, Fokker was demonstrating a gun synchronisation gear fitted to a Fokker M5K, a single-seater tractor monoplane of his own design, with the intention of selling both aeroplane and gun gear to the German High Command. The *Feldflugchef* was impressed and placed an immediate order for fifty of the new Fokker monoplanes equipped with the synchronisation gear. Fokker was urged to complete the order as quickly as possible as it was intended to issue single Fokkers to the *Feldflieger Abteilungen* units operating in the areas where allied aeroplanes had taken command of the air. By July 12, eleven especially selected pilots from the *Feldflieger Abteilungen* were flying the new fighters: the 'Fokker Scourge' was about to begin.

The Fokker Scourge

On 1 August 1915, a Fokker pilot with *Feldflieger Abteilung 62*, *Ltn* Max Immelmann scored his first victory flying the new type when he shot down a BE2c from 2 Squadron piloted by 2Lt William Reid, who was flying without an observer on a bombing raid to Vitry[3] After some ten minutes of manoeuvring and the expenditure of nearly 500 rounds of ammunition – perhaps demonstrating Immelmann's initial lack of expertise with the new fighter – the BE was finally forced to land and the wounded Reid was taken prisoner.[4]

Immelmann's companion Fokker pilot in *Feldflieger Abteilung 62* was *Ltn* Oswald Boelcke, later to emerge as the first 'ace' of the German Army Air Service, with a final score of forty victories and the acknowledged 'father' of German fighter tactics.

Despite its successes, the Fokker monoplane – the E1 and its later variants – had a poor performance and was far from an ideal fighter aeroplane, but in the hands of the emerging German fighter pilots its gun synchronisation gear transformed it into a highly effective fighter. The slow, poorly armed and unmanoeuvrable reconnaissance machines of the RFC were no match for the agile monoplanes. By October the Fokkers had begun to inflict heavy casualties and the air superiority that the RFC had enjoyed during the later spring and early summer of 1915, with the almost complete domination of the Arras front by the Vickers FB5, had effectively ended.

The attrition rate of aeroplanes had been high in the first months of the war. In August 1914 the RFC had commenced operations on the Western Front with 64 aeroplanes. By the beginning of October, 40 machines had been struck off strength and at the end of the year, after four and a half months of active service, the RFC had 61 aeroplanes of charge, but this had been achieved only by the expedient of depleting Home Establishment of men and machines.

At the end of the first full year of war the British Expeditionary Force in France had been expanded from four divisions to 30, but only seven squadrons had been added to the strength of the RFC. This shortage was exacerbated by the complication of more diverse and additional duties having been added to the Corp's original role of reconnaissance. By the early autumn of 1915 the success of the Fokkers had shown that control of the air was essential if the RFC was to meet the requirements of the army commanders. New tactics were called for. Major General Hugh Trenchard, who had taken command of the RFC from Sir David Henderson on 19 August 1915, put forward a programme of expansion to solve this and other problems. Trenchard's proposals included the formation of specialist single-seater fighter squadrons, but pending the arrival of these it was necessary to formulate a strategy to combat the deprecations of the Fokkers. By January 1916 these had reached an unacceptable level and the situation became so desperate that on 14 January 1916, RFC.HQ. issued an order that effectively reduced its strength.

'Until the Royal Flying Corps are in possession of a machine as good or better than the German Fokker it seems that a change in the tactics employed becomes necessary. It is hoped very shortly to obtain a machine which will be able to successfully engage the Fokkers at present in use by the Germans. In the meantime, it must be laid down as a hard and fast rule that a machine proceeding on reconnaissance must be escorted by at least three other fighting machines. These machines must fly in close formation and a reconnaissance should not be continued if any of the machines becomes detached. This should apply to both short and long reconnaissances. Aeroplanes proceeding on photographic duty any considerable distance east of the lines should be similarly escorted. From recent experience it seems that the Germans are now employing their aeroplanes in groups of three or four, and these numbers are frequently encountered by our aeroplanes. Flying in formation must be practised by all pilots.'

In the event the superiority of the Fokkers was not to last. In 1916, with additional squadrons arriving in France equipped with aeroplanes capable of dealing with the Fokkers, the pendulum of air superiority was to swing once more in favour of the RFC.

NOTES

1. Malcolm Bell-Irving was a Canadian from Vancouver. All six Bell-Irving brothers served in the war; two others – Alan and Richard – in the RFC. Two of the four Bell-Irving sisters also served.

2. Extracts from 'My Most Thrilling Flight' *Popular Flying* 1932. Strange had another thrilling flight in another war. In 1940, when the German Army was overrunning France and the RAF was evacuating, Strange took off in an unarmed Hawker Hurricane to fly it back to England. The lone Hurricane was attacked by two Messerschmitt 109s. Strange took the only evasive action tactic open to him: he went down to ground level and contour-chased to the coast, at one time flying between an avenue of trees leading to a chateau, zooming over the house at the last minute. The young Messerschmitt pilots acknowledged Strange's flying skills and gave up the chase.

3. It is believed that this is the first official victory to be gained by a Fokker E Type, although *Ltn*. Kurt Wintgens of *Feldflieger Abteilung 6b,* had forced a French Morane to land on 1 July 1915.

4. Reid, a Canadian, was repatriated to Switzerland on 30 May 1916.

CHAPTER THREE

THE YEAR OF THE FIGHTERS

On 23 January 1916, 20 Squadron landed in France, the first squadron to be equipped with the FE2b. The FE2b was a sturdy two-seat pusher fighter/reconnaissance aeroplane which was to play no small part in combating the menace of the German Fokkers, but it was not until February 7, when 24 Squadron landed its little DH2 pushers at St.Omer, that the RFC's first true single-seater fighter squadron arrived in France.

Twenty-four Squadron had been formed at Hounslow on 1 September 1915 from a nucleus of 17 Squadron. On September 28 Major Lanoe G Hawker took command. The Squadron was equipped with a varied collection of aeroplanes: Avros, Martinsydes, Curtiss, Caudron and Farman types, with only a single Bristol Scout, but on 10 January 1916 the first DH2s began to arrive and by February 7, when the squadron left for France, it had its full complement of 12.

On its arrival in France, 24 Squadron found that the compact little DH2 was not without its faults. The first casualty suffered by the squadron was on February 9, when its C Flight Commander, 2Lt E A C Archer, spun into the ground on returning from patrol. There appeared to be no reason for this accident and the general opinion of the pilots was that Archer's legs were numb from the intense cold and that he had lost control. Four days later 2Lt E A Cave was killed in similar circumstances, spinning into the ground on 11 Squadron's aerodrome. These two fatalities caused a great deal of speculation and disquiet among the pilots of 24 Squadron; they felt that their aeroplanes were unsafe and that recovery from a spin was difficult, if not impossible. Hawker took immediate action. He took a DH2 up to 8,000 feet and came down in a succession of left and right hand spins. After landing Hawker explained the procedure for recovery from a spin and Lt Cowan was the first of his pilots to take off and emulate Hawker's example. Other pilots followed suit and thereafter had more confidence in their machines.

The Gnôme Monosoupape rotary engine, which powered the DH2, in addition to being unreliable to the extent of one flight in every three suffering from an engine defect, also had an unpleasant tendency to shed one or more of its cylinders. At best this caused excessive vibration until the unbalanced engine could be switched off; at worst the shed cylinder smashed or even severed a tailboom, causing the aeroplane to break up in mid-air. This condition was known as 'Cylindritis' and was caused by a worn cylinder fracturing around the ring of small inlet holes around its base. Before the summer of 1916, when 'Cylindritis' was cured by better engine maintenance, several pilots in 24 Squadron and other squadrons flying the DH2 lost their lives, and many had narrow escapes.

Another cause of contention was the method of mounting the Lewis gun. The swivel mounting, which in theory gave a pilot a field of fire in a wide arc in front of the aeroplane, or, by elevating the gun, to fire both forwards and upwards, was soon found to be impracticable. It was difficult to fly the aeroplane with one hand while aiming and firing the gun with the other, and when elevated the gun fouled the control column. The whole mounting was simply *too* moveable and the pilots soon nicknamed it 'the wobbly mounting'.

Hawker, who had an extremely inventive mind and was a fine practical engineer, very quickly devised a clamp to hold the gun in a single fixed position, but this was forbidden by HQ and Hawker temporised by designing a spring clip, which although holding the gun firmly enabled it to be released if necessary.

After Archer's death, and its probable cause, Hawker also turned his attention to the problem of the DH2 being an extremely cold little machine to fly, the pilot gaining no warmth from the engine mounted behind him.[1] Hawker designed and had made special boots in an attempt to alleviate this problem. Fur lined, reaching up the outside of the thighs and under the crotch, these boots became universally known throughout the RFC as 'fug boots' and later became standard issue.

While at St.Omer, 24 Squadron was under the command of RFC.HQ. and its orders were to carry out daily patrols between Bollezelle and Therouanne with the object of preventing any enemy machines from approaching RFC Headquarters. In addition to this duty, two machines were to be in constant readiness to take off and intercept any intruder that had evaded the standing patrol. On February 9 the Squadron was ordered to fly to Bertangles, on transfer to 13th Wing, 3rd Brigade, to come under the orders of the Third Army, but ten days of appalling weather kept it on the ground at St.Omer and it was not until February 20 that all the Squadron's DH2s were at their new base.

At Bertangles war flying commenced in earnest, but it was April 2 before 24 Squadron gained its first decisive victory, when 2Lts Tidmarsh and Sibley shot down an Albatros two-seater. Sibley, flying a DH2 unusually armed with two Lewis guns, attacked first, half a mile south of Baizieux. Tidmarsh then joined in the attack and the two DH2s forced the enemy machine down between Grandcourt and the River Ancre.

On the morning of April 25 the pilots of 24 Squadron had their first combats with the Fokker monoplane. The day was bright and clear and five BE2cs from 15 Squadron set off on a reconnaissance for 4th Army, escorted by three DH2s from 24 Squadron flown by Lts J O Andrews, D Wilson and N P Manfield. Over Bapaume at 9,000 feet the first Fokker was seen, a thousand feet higher, the thin but menacing silhouette rapidly approaching the British formation. Closing to within attacking distance a Fokker dived on a BE, but Andrews quickly intercepted it and fired half a drum of Lewis into it. The German pilot immediately broke off his attack and dived away with Andrews in pursuit. The Fokker outdived the DH2 and Andrews gave up the chase and returned to his charges. Another Fokker then appeared and dived on Manfield, overshooting the DH2 and missing in its pass. Manfield turned and fired half a drum at the Fokker as it flashed by. At 10.00am another Fokker, flown by *Ltn* Max Immelmann, who at this time had fourteen victories, came up to the British formation from behind and made an attack on Andrews, who turned quickly out of the line of fire. Immelmann followed the DH2 and the two machines circled each other, looking for an opening, Immelmann keeping up an almost continuous fire. Andrews finally turned inside Immelmann, got on the Fokker's tail and fired into the monoplane. Immelmann dived away from this attack but was then tackled by Manfield, who followed him down and fired half a drum. Immelmann dived steeply and flattened out lower down. That night Immelmann wrote home that the two DH2s had 'worked splendidly together' and during the fight had put 11 shots into his machine, hitting the petrol tank, the fuselage and undercarriage struts and the propeller. 'I could only save myself by a nosedive of 1,000 metres. Then at last the two of them left me alone. It was not a nice business.'

While Andrews and Manfield were fighting with Immelmann, 2Lt S E Cowan was flying an escort to a single BE2c of 9 Squadron. The reconnaissance had been successfully completed and the two British machines were flying back to the lines when they were attacked by a Fokker over Flers at 9,000ft. The German pilot attacked Cowan from behind and above, his bullets appearing to Cowan to explode as they hit the DH2. Cowan flew an upward spiral to reach the Fokker five hundred feet above him. When he was within a 100ft he pulled up the nose of the DH2 and fired half a drum. The engine of the DH2 was missing badly, but despite this Cowan held it in the climb and was able to reach the Fokker's height. Outmanoeuvring the enemy pilot, Cowan got on his tail and at a distance of 'two lengths' – presumably of a DH2 – finished his first drum. Because his gun was clamped rigid, Cowan was able to quickly replace his empty drum with a fresh one. Getting still closer to his opponent, so that the DH2 was thrown about by the slipstream of the Fokker, making his aim 'erratic', Cowan fired the whole of the fresh drum. The Fokker pilot took violent evasive action but failed to shake off the tenacious Cowan. As a last resort he put the Fokker into a vertical bank, sideslipped 500ft and went down in a nosedive, flattening out further down. Cowan fired at the Fokker as it dived away, then rejoined the BE2c and finished his escort. The comment was later added to Cowan's combat report that the Fokker pilot appeared to have using explosive bullets, expressly forbidden under pre-war treaty obligations because of the horrific wounds such ammunition could cause. The report ended with the comment that in spite of his engine running badly, Cowan had experienced no difficulty in outmanoeuvring the Fokker.

Five days after these first actions against the Fokkers, 2Lt D M Tidmarsh destroyed a Fokker over Bapaume. Tidmarsh and two other DH2s of 24 Squadron were escorting a Flight of FE2bs of 22 Squadron on a reconnaissance to Péronne, when a Fokker monoplane was seen coming from the direction of Bapaume, flying west of the British formation to cut off its possible retreat. Tidmarsh, flying DH2 No.5965, was at 7,000ft and waited until the Fokker, 3,000ft lower, was nearly underneath his DH2, 'then I turned off the petrol and dived straight down at him.'

The German pilot dived steeply to evade Tidmarsh's attack, but at 1,000ft he lost control and crashed into the roofs of the houses of Bapaume, both wings of his machine breaking off. Tidmarsh, who had not fired a single shot, climbed back to rejoin his companions. German records show one aeroplane missing in the area, from *Feldflieger Abteilung 32*, possibly that flown by a *Ltn* Schmedes. It was obvious from these first combats with the Fokkers that the German monoplanes were no match for the agile DH2s and easily outmanoeuvred by the little pushers, a point that had been by no means certain up to that time.

The pilots of 24 Squadron fought an increasing number of successful combats during May – Tidmarsh shot down an LVG in flames over Pozières and Contalmaison on May 20, and later, in the same patrol, Lt. D Wilson shot down an Albatros two-seater in flames to crash south of Maricourt. On May 23, Hawker wrote home with news of these victories and to proudly announce that Cowan and Tidmarsh had both been awarded the Military Cross. On the same day, General Sir Henry Rawlinson, commanding 4th Army, reported that while escorted by the DH2s his reconnaissance machines, unmolested by the Fokkers, were once more able to photograph the German trench systems on his front.

'I cannot speak to highly of the work of these young pilots, most of whom have recently come out from England and the de Havilland machine has unquestionably proved itself superior to the Fokker in speed, manoeuvrability, climbing and general fighting efficiency.'

The Fokker menace had been well and truly met and beaten.

Reinforcements

Two additional fighter squadrons had been added to the strength of the RFC in March 1916. The first of these, 27 Squadron, which had been formed from a nucleus of 24 Squadron on 5th November 1915, arrived at St.Omer on 1 March 1916, flying on to Treizennes the next day. Although its intended role was that of fighter/ reconnaissance duties the squadron was equipped with the Martinsyde G100, a powerful but rather large and unwieldy aeroplane – it later acquired the unflattering nickname of the 'Elephant' – and early operational experience quickly highlighted its faults as a possible fighter; it was not only less manoeuvrable than the contemporary DH2, Bristol and Morane scouts, but the view from the cockpit was restricted, an obvious disadvantage in a fighter. In April, General Trenchard changed the squadron's rôle to that of bombing and reconnaissance.

The second single-seater fighter squadron to fly to France was 29 Squadron, equipped with the DH2. Formed at Fort Grange, Gosport, on 7 November 1915 from a nucleus of 23 Squadron, 29 Squadron began to receive its DH2s in February 1916, but although its transport and groundcrews left for France on 14 and 16 March, the squadron's aeroplanes were not ready to leave until March 24.

Hawker's 24 Squadron had flown to France with the loss of only three of its DH2s on the way – all in take off and landing crashes due to the high winds in February – but 29 Squadron failed to match this success. Three DH2s at Gosport on the morning of March 24 refused to start owing to engine trouble, but the remaining nine aeroplanes left for Dover, flying a little inland and parallel to the coast. Engine failure on this first stage of its journey to France robbed the squadron of another DH2 when Capt L G Sweet was forced to land at Shoreham. The already inclement weather then deteriorated into a snowstorm, forcing four more machines down en route and only four DH2s survived to land at Dover. Only three of these DH2s left for St.Omer later the same day and one of these crashed on landing, fortunately with no extensive damage to either pilot or machine.

Because of these accidents and forced landings a number of pilots had no aeroplanes in which to fly to France and there was a two-week delay in their departure while replacement DH2s were being delivered. Before the entire squadron was safely in France on April 14 it had lost another two machines: one ditched in the English Channel and another crashed due to engine failure while flying from St.Omer to its base at Abeele on March 30. A later inquiry into this disastrous debut of 29 Squadron reported that in delivering 12 machines to France, 26 or 27 machines were 'consumed'. Fortunately this heavy expenditure of aeroplanes had not been accompanied by any loss of life, only two pilots being slightly injured. The inquiry was of the opinion that the losses had been caused by the snowstorm, the inexperience of the pilots with the DH2, and an outbreak of measles among the squadron's groundcrew in the immediate period before the squadron left for France, implying that the serviceability of the engines had been adversely affected.

Twenty-nine Squadron flew to its base at Abeele on April 15 and came under the orders of 11th Wing, 2 Brigade: it was to fly over the Second Army Front, covering the Salient at Ypres. At this stage of the war the Ypres Front was relatively quiet, the offensives being further south. Lt Geoffrey Bowman, who joined 29 Squadron in July 1916 recalled: 'Nothing much happened in 29 Squadron during 1916. We were in the Ypres Salient and all the Huns had gone down to the Somme.' Nevertheless, the squadron scored its first victory on May 1 when Lt H O D Seagrave forced a two-seater – described as an 'Aviatik' – to land near Gheluvelt. Seagrave was patrolling over the Salient early in the morning when he first saw the enemy machine and he attacked from above and behind, firing three drums of Lewis from a range of 80 yards. The gunner of the hostile two-seater had failed to see the DH2 and only managed to get off seven shots at Seagrave before his pilot put their aeroplane into a steep left-hand spiral dive. Seagrave followed it down to 500ft and saw it make a forced landing in a field.

On May 17, patrolling over Ypres at 13,000ft, J Noakes, a sergeant pilot with the squadron, attacked an LVG that was ranging for its artillery. Noakes first saw the enemy machine flying north at 10,000ft over Bixshoote and he flew east, over the enemy lines, towards Langemarck, to cut off its retreat. The enemy pilot and observer failed to see the little DH2, turned, and flew towards Noakes, who shut off his engine and dived to attack them from a height advantage of 3,000ft, firing a complete drum in the dive. Pulling out of his dive, Noakes changed his Lewis gun drum and turned to renew his attack, but could not see the enemy machine. The DH2 then came under AA fire from the ground and Noakes climbed to regain his height. Noakes believed that he had shot down the LVG but although he returned to the area twice during the remainder of his patrol he failed to locate a crash.

On May 25 Major Eric Lewis Conran took command of 29 Squadron, replacing Major Dawes; on the same day the squadron's compliment of DH2s was increased from 12 to 18. Production DH2s were now coming on stream – approximately 445 were finally built – and 24 Squadron's strength was also increased.

The third DH2 squadron to arrive in France, however, had only 12 DH2s on charge, augmented by two Vickers ES1 scouts. Thirty-two Squadron had been formed at Netheravon on 12 January 1916, and on February 1 Major Lionel Wilmot Brabazon Rees MC., took command. Lionel Rees had learnt to fly in 1913 at his own expense and had served as a flying instructor at Upavon before going to France as a senior flight commander in 11 Squadron in July 1915. Flying a Vickers FB5 he made many reconnaissance flights and had a number of combats while flying with the squadron and in October 1915 he was awarded a Military Cross for 'conspicuous gallantry and skill on several occasions.' A young pilot who flew out to France with 32 Squadron on 28 May, Lt Gwilym Lewis, regarded Rees as a 'prince'. Writing over sixty years later he remembered Rees as: 'quiet, delightful and brave, with the heart of a fighting lion' adding that Rees also knew the inside of a Mono engine 'thoroughly'.[2] In a letter home in 1916 Lewis showed a remarkable prescience: commenting on Rees's MC, he wrote: 'I shouldn't be surprised if he came home with a VC.'

Still in England, 32 Squadron's first DH2 arrived on February 13, but owing to the casualties sustained by 24 and 29 Squadrons, in both men and machines, DH2s and pilots of 32 Squadron were sent to France as replacements. In addition, Rees later commented that his squadron had to train all its pilots and mechanics on the DH2, none of whom, with the exception of one of his flight commanders, Capt Gilmore, had had any previous experience with either the DH2 or its powerplant, the 100hp Gnôme Monosoupape.[3]

Under these restraints 32 Squadron was not up to its full strength of 12 DH2s until May 20. Orders were received on May 18 that the Squadron would leave for France ten days later and on the morning of May 28 all the squadron's aeroplanes were lined up and ready to go, with the exception of Lt J C Simpson who had collided with a tractor the previous day. Mist precluded an early start but the DH2s finally left the ground at 11.00am and set course for Folkestone – a flight of 125 miles – led by Rees flying one of the Vickers.

Although it would have been expected that 32 Squadron would have gained some benefit and expertise in the servicing and maintenance of their aeroplanes from the hard won experience of 24 and 29 Squadrons, it had a similar series of mishaps on its flight to join the BEF in France. Two DH2s forced landed with the ever-present engine trouble on the way to Folkestone, and a third only managed to complete the flight with a propeller damaged by a broken rocker arm. After lunch, and with their aeroplanes refuelled, the pilots took off for the cross-channel flight to St.Omer.

The day was fine, visibility was good and the squadron flew out over the sea at 6,000ft. However, not long into the flight, engine trouble forced one DH2 to return to Folkestone and as the remainder of the DH2s approached Cape Gris Nez the engine of another seized up. The pilot, Lt C L Bath, attempted to land on top of the cliff but overshot. Luckily the drop over the edge of the cliff enabled the DH2 to pick up enough flying speed to enable Bath to make a safe landing on the beach. The following day, after a replacement engine had been fitted, Bath took off to rejoin the rest of the squadron at St.Omer, but lost his way and landed to ask for directions. Taking off again he ran into a barbed wire fence, writing off the DH2. Four out of the twelve DH2s that had left Netheravon had failed to reach St.Omer, a third of the Squadron strength. On June 7 the squadron moved into its aerodrome at Treizennes and came under the orders of 10th (Army) Wing, 1st Brigade, sharing the aerodrome with 25 Squadron flying FE2bs.

During the first weeks of June 1916 the weather was bad, restricting flying, but 32 Squadron suffered its first casualty from enemy action in the early morning of June 8. Lt R A Stubbs, who had been heavily 'archied',[4] while on patrol, crashed while attempting to land on the aerodrome at Erevin-Capelle. As the DH2 made its approach at 100ft it was seen to zoom, then dive into the ground. Stubbs was killed instantly and a later post mortem showed only superficial wounds caused by AA fire. The pilots of 32 Squadron believed that he had lost consciousness while coming in to land.

Later that same morning eighteen year old 2Lt Gwilym Lewis had 32 squadron's first combat when he attacked a Roland C.II while patrolling the Loos-Souchez area. Lewis left the ground at 6.45am, climbed to 6,000ft and followed the canal to Bethune before heading south. Apart from seeing several friendly FEs and observing the 'mess' north of Loos, Lewis sighted no other aeroplanes and by 8.00am was both bored and cold. Fifteen minutes later he saw a machine in the distance, coming towards him, and he flew to meet it. As he got nearer Lewis positioned himself between the other machine and the trenches and saw that it was an enemy two-seater: 'painted pale blue green underneath and looking quite a speed merchant. One pair of struts each side and an observer sitting behind his swivel gun ready for use.'[5] Lewis turned and attacked the enemy, a Roland, from the side, firing off a few shots. The Roland pilot turned sharply and Lewis followed, later observing that he had never banked his DH2 so suddenly, but he was determined not to be outmanoeuvred. However, the Roland pilot was more experienced than Lewis; coming out of his turn he put his nose down and dived for the safety of his own Lines. Lewis attempted to follow but the Roland was faster and he gave up the pursuit after three-quarters of a mile. An FE pilot who had witnessed the fight later reported that Lewis had opened fire at too long a range, and had missed the chance of a victory, but Lionel Rees assured his inexperienced young pilot that he had done his best.

On 28 May 1916 another fighter squadron had arrived in France. Sixty Squadron, which was to become one of the RFC's most successful fighter squadrons, had been formed at Gosport on 15 May under the command of Major F Waldron – universally known as throughout the RFC as 'Ferdy' – from No.1 Aeroplane Reserve Squadron. Unlike its fellow squadrons, which received their aeroplanes in England and flew them to France, 60 Squadron was to be equipped with French Morane-Saulnier types and the entire squadron crossed to France by boat and took up its quarters at St.Omer.

A few days later the squadron's aeroplanes began to arrive: one Flight had nine Morane-Saulnier Type N monoplanes; another, four Type BB biplanes; and the third Flight was allocated three Type L and LA Parasol monoplanes. The Parasols were replaced in the middle of June by more Type N monoplanes and by the time the squadron had moved to its first base at Boisdinghem on May 31, 'A' and 'C' Flights were equipped with Morane Ns – known as 'Bullets' – with 'B' Flight keeping its Morane biplanes.

The Morane N1 'Bullet' was a monoplane with a monocoque type fuselage, powered by an 80hp Le Rhône 9C rotary engine and armed with a single Lewis gun firing through the propeller, the blades being protected – it was hoped – by metal deflector plates. With its heavy control system of wing warping, allied to the disproportionate sensitiveness of its elevators, the Morane N was not an easy machine to fly. With its high wing loading it had, in the words of one pilot, 'the gliding angle of a brick,' and above 10,000ft it was difficult to turn sharply without stalling. Despite these faults, in the hands of an experienced pilot the Morane was a match for the German Fokker monoplane, one of which had been captured intact on 8 April. In an evaluation combat flown against the Fokker it quickly became obvious that the Morane was superior.

On 10 June 60 Squadron moved to its base at Vert Galant, an aerodrome on the Doullens to Amiens road, and came under the orders of Ninth (HQ) Wing. Ninth (HQ) Wing was a tactical Wing, not tied to any Army, and provided a tactical reserve that could be moved to any part of the British Front as needed. Sixty Squadron's companion squadrons in the Wing were: 21 Squadron (RE7 and BE2s), 27 Squadron (Martinsyde G100), and two Flights of 70 Squadron (Sopwith 1 1/2 Strutter). Sixty Squadron's duties were offensive patrols, reconnaissance and, later in the year, the landing of spies behind the enemy lines. The squadron's area of operations covered the Albert-Arras sector of the Front and patrols were flown in Flight strength. From the earliest patrols the squadron's Morane 'Bullets', with their close resemblance to the Fokker E III, were fired at by British anti-aircraft batteries and on July 19 permission was given by Wing HQ to paint red the black spinner and engine cowlings of the Moranes. This was successful and the red was later extended to include the undercarriage and cabane.

Reorganisation

Contemporary with developments in the specialist fighter squadrons, equipped mainly with one type of aeroplane, the RFC still had a number of single-seater fighters of various types attached to reconnaissance squadrons for escort work and fighting, and these also saw an increasing amount of combats in the early months of 1916. In October 1914 the RFC had been organised into Wings, to work with the various army corps, and as early as April 1915, as combats in the air became more frequent, Sir David Henderson, then commanding the RFC, had put forward the view that fighter aeroplanes should be concentrated into specialist squadron. However, Wing Commanders were reluctant to give up the leavening of single-seater fighters on their squadron strength and Henderson bowed to their views. In January 1916, with the rapid expansion of the RFC – both actual and planned – it became necessary to reconstitute the Wings into Corps and Army Wings: the Corps Wings to carry out reconnaissance, artillery spotting and photography on the immediate front of its Army Corps; the Army Wings to undertake deeper reconnaissance and bombing as ordered by the Army Commander. The nature of the work carried out by the Army Wings called for an aeroplane capable of fighting for its information and with a superior performance to those machines used by the corps squadrons.

The German *Feldflieger Abteilungen*, the equivalent of the RFC's corps squadrons, also carried two or three Fokker and Pfalz monoplane fighters on their strength, but soon after the opening of the battle of Verdun in February 1916 it had been found that the Fokkers and Pfalz were more effective when grouped together in *Kampfeinsitzer Kommandos* (single-seater fighter units) and 21 Fokker and Pfalz E types were grouped into three *Kommandos*. In April, Trenchard, profiting from the lessons of Verdun, decided to concentrate into the Army Wings those single-seater fighters still attached to the corps squadrons and by the end of August 1916 the corps squadrons no longer had any single-seater fighters on their strength.

Before the arrival in France of the fighter squadrons proper, the pilots who had flown the single-seat fighters on the strength of their corps squadron were all volunteers and, by temperament and talent, those most suitable to become fighter pilots. These like-spirited men – and later, those of the first fighter squadrons proper – were a tightly knit hierarchy within the RFC, a small band of men all known to each other, either personally or by reputation: the RFC's first fighter pilots.

A typical example of these early pilots was Lt William Mays Fry. In 1916 Fry had been flying 12 Squadron's BE2cs on bombing raids since the beginning of July. On July 12, LtCol Gordon Shepherd asked Fry if he would like to transfer to single-seater scouts. Fry admitted to Shepherd that the idea of flying these fast machines rather frightened him, but thinking that nothing could be worse than bombing raids in a BE2c, he agreed. Later that same day Fry was told to report to 11 Squadron at Savy Berlette, some five miles from 12 Squadron's aerodrome at Avesnes-le-Comte. On arrival at 11 Squadron Fry found that it 'was something of a hybrid, even for those days.' Its machines consisted of two Flights of Vickers FB5 pushers, with the third Flight equipped with a mixture of single-seat tractors: two or three Bristol Scouts, a Vickers ES1 Bullet; a Spad, flown in the squadron by Capt Leslie Foot; and a Nieuport, this last being flown at the time of Fry's arrival by Lt Albert Ball, later to become the RFC's first 'ace'.

Fry was taken out to a Bristol Scout by Foot – known throughout the RFC as 'Feet' – and the C.O. of 11 Squadron, Major T O'B Hubbard, and given some 'casual' instruction on the controls. He was then asked to fly the Bristol for half and hour or so, both Foot and Hubbard imploring him not to crash it as it was the only serviceable Bristol remaining in the squadron. Fry took off successfully but found the light controls of the Bristol 'rather frightening' after the larger and heavier BE2c. The throttle control of the 80hp Le Rhône engine, with its fine adjustment for air intake was a complete mystery to Fry and he was extremely nervous at having to land the little scout, especially as he could see a group of pilots and mechanics watching his progress from the edge of the aerodrome. Plucking up his courage, Fry made his approach, shut off the engine and glided in to land. Unfortunately he came in too fast and overshot the aerodrome into a field of standing corn, turning the Bristol over onto its back. Fry felt sure that this would be the end of his chance to be a fighter pilot, but both Foot and Hubbard were sympathetic and told him he could try again as soon as another machine was serviceable.

'I returned to 12 Squadron almost at once, or within a day or two, to carry on until there was a serviceable scout in 11 Squadron for me to fly. There was no question of being sent to 11 Squadron to *learn* to fly the Scout. If I had negotiated that first flight successfully I should have commenced flying operationally at once, probably the next day. That is how things were at that time. You were just dumped into a Scout Flight and had to pick it up as you went along. One thing about 11 Squadron at that time was that for Ball to be in a squadron commanded by Major Hubbard was an astonishing juxtaposition, almost as strange as for Major Hubbard to have in his squadron the RFC's first full Flight of tractor scouts. "Mother" Hubbard was by nature so gentle that, literally, he would not hurt a fly and it was inconceivable that he should be responsible for organising the shooting down of German aeroplanes. On top of this, the flight commander, Leslie Foot, was not what one would call an aggressive type. He was a beautiful pilot and fought like a tiger, but one could not imagine him bearing any animosity towards his opponent or opponents or in fact towards anyone at all. After a fight nothing would have given him more pleasure than to sit down with his opponent over a drink, or several drinks, and discuss the fight all over again. He was one of those to whom aerial fighting was in the nature of a sport, and he was a wonderful flight commander. Pilots like him were of great value at this time of the great surge of airfighting as they taught the finer points of flying and, they themselves, by practice and experiment in action, evaluated the capabilities and best way of fighting their machines. There was no one else and no textbooks or manuals.'[6]

In April, in accordance with Trenchard's instructions, the single-seater scouts on the strength of the corps squadrons had been transferred to the two-seater fighter/reconnaissance squadrons of the new Army Wings. To fly these scouts, the pilots of the corps squadrons – such as Fry – who had shown suitable aptitude and aggressive qualities, were also attached to the Army Wing squadrons. Typical of these transfers, in both men and machines, was that of the two Nieuports and a Bristol Scout received by 11 Squadron at Savy, and Lt Albert Ball. Ball was in 13 Squadron, also stationed at Savy and flying BEs, and on the evening of May 7 – exactly a year before his death – Ball walked over to report to his new squadron. He carried a note from his CO. to say that he should do well: he was keen, conscientious, and had been flying 13 Squadron's Bristol Scout without breaking it.

Albert Ball was destined to become the leading fighter pilot in 1916 and in one short year to capture the imagination of the British public. Born in 1896 in Nottingham, Ball joined the Nottingham and Derbyshire Regiment at the outbreak of war, and in June 1915, while stationed at Perivale in north London, only a short distance from Hendon aerodrome, learnt to fly there at his own expense. In January 1916, Ball was seconded to the RFC, and on 17 February was posted to 13 Squadron in France to fly BE2cs. Ball flew his first patrol over the Lines four days later.

In addition to his normal duties with 13 Squadron of reconnaissance and ranging for the artillery, Ball had several combats, notably one on April 29 when, undeterred by the odds, Ball and his observer attacked a formation of five Albatros C.IIIs, forcing one to land with a wounded observer. This aggressiveness brought Ball to the attention of HQ. He was earmarked as a pilot suitable to fly the new scouts and sent to St.Omer to fly a Morane Bullet. Back at 13 Squadron after successful completing this test of his flying abilities, Ball constantly pestered his CO., Major Marsh, to allow him to fly the Squadron's Bristol Scout D. Ball only made a few flights in the Bristol before it was crashed by another pilot. A replacement Bristol was received by May 5 and Ball's only flight in it nearly ended in disaster: the gun interrupter gear was faulty and firing a burst to warm his gun, Ball nearly shot off his propeller. Two days later he walked across the aerodrome to join 11 Squadron's tractor scout flight.

Ball scored his first victory in his new squadron on May 16. Flying the squadron's Bristol Scout he attacked an Albatros two-seater over Givenchy and shot it down out of control. Ball failed to see the enemy machine crash, but it was awarded as his first official victory. At this time, 11 Squadron had three Nieuport 16s on charge and Ball was allocated Nieuport 5173. Ball flew this machine almost exclusively for the next few weeks, scoring his next two victories while flying it on May 29.

Other pilots in 11 Squadron who flew the Nieuports at this time were Capts Pattison, Crook and Cooper. Cooper was very short and found it difficult to change the drum of the Lewis gun, mounted above the top wing of the Nieuports to enable it to be fired clear of the propeller. In the squadron's workshops, Sergeant R G Foster designed a curved rail mounting which enable the gun to be pulled down into a vertical position in front of the pilot and the drum changed. This mounting was later officially adopted and known as the Foster Mounting.

In June 1916 preparations for the Battle of the Somme were in full swing; the tempo of the air war increased, and when weather conditions permitted the squadrons of the RFC were in almost daily combat with the German Army Air Service. The Fokker pilots were still aggressive. On May 31, Max Immelmann, promoted to *Oberleutnant* in April and now the leading Fokker pilot, accompanied by *Oblt.* Max Mulzer and *Unteroffizier* Wolfgang Heinemann, all from *Feldflieger Abteilung 62* based at Douai, attacked four FE2bs and two Martinsydes of 23 Squadron over Adinfer Wood at 9.15am.

As the Fokkers came out of the morning sun, Lt. L C Powell shouted to his pilot, 2Lt. E F Allan, to stall, so that he could get in a shot at their attacker by firing back over the top plane of the FE, but he was almost immediately hit in the head and killed. The Fokker pilot then pulled away and Allen flew FE2b 5235 back to base. The official RFC Communique gives FE2b 6345 – flown by 2Lt. A Cairne-Duff and Corporal G Maxwell, both wounded in action and taken prisoners of war – as also being in this fight, but the casualty report gives this crew as having last seen out of control 'in a dive' west of Cambrai at 7.05am, nearly two and a half hours before the reports of the combat by the other FEs with Immelmann and his companions.

During this combat Max Immelmann's twin-gunned Fokker E.IV suffered severe damage. As Immelmann opened fire on one of the FEs the interrupter gear failed and shot off one of the Fokker's propeller blades. Before Immelmann could switch off the ignition the unbalanced engine had torn the engine bed from its mounting, throwing the engine forward. Luckily the violent jerking of the Fokker then threw the engine back into position, restoring the centre of gravity, and Immelmann was able to regain control and land the badly damaged fighter.

On the evening of June 18 Immelmann was not so lucky. After a combat in the late afternoon, in which he shot down FE2b 6940 from 25 Squadron, crewed by Lt. C E Rogers and Sgt. H Taylor – Rogers was killed and Taylor wounded and taken POW – Immelmann was relaxing in the Mess when he received a report that enemy aeroplanes were again over the German Lines. Other Fokker pilots of *KEK Douai*[7] were already on patrol, but Immelmann took off in Fokker E.III 246/16 accompanied by Wolfgang Heinemann.

As Immelmann and Heinemann approached the scene of the action they could see that four other Fokkers were already attacking four British machines, with an additional two Fokkers in combat with another group of four. Further off still, two other Fokkers were tackling three more hostile machines. By the standards of the day a very large airfight was developing. Surprisingly, in view of the large number of Fokkers present, the German anti-aircraft guns were still firing at the British formations and Immelmann fired a white signal flare to order them to stop firing before he commenced his attack on one of the FEs of 25 Squadron. It was 8.45pm (British time). Immelmann's shots wounded both 2Lt J R B Savage and his observer 2nd Air Mechanic P Robinson. Savage, although mortally wounded, managed to land FE2b 4909 and Robinson was taken prisoner.

As Immelmann attacked Savage he was in turn attacked by Lt G B McCubbin and his observer Corporal J H Waller, flying FE2b 6346. As McCubbin closed with the Fokker, Immelmann realised his danger and began to turn. Waller opened fire and the Fokker immediately went down out of control and crashed.[8]

The Germans later claimed that Immelmann's death had been caused by structural failure of his Fokker, similar to that of May 31, and perhaps the truth will never be firmly established, but Max Immelmann, 'Eagle of Lille' was dead and the GAAS had suffered a severe blow.

The end of June saw a brief respite for the combatants before the opening of the Allied offensive on the Somme. During the last four days of June the weather was bad and little flying was done, but dawn on Sunday 1 July 1916 was fine, with the promise of a perfect summer's day. It was to be the last few hours of life for nearly 20,000 British soldiers.

NOTES

1. James McCudden, flying DH2s in 29 Squadron in December 1916, later wrote in his autobiography: 'I did not care whether I was shot down or not, I was so utterly frozen'.

2. Letter to the author.

3. Historian Barrington-Gray, who has made a detailed study of the DH2, has pointed out that no official maintenance handbook on the DH2 had been issued by Airco, the makers, and no technical information was readily available until Major Rees wrote a handbook, which was published in June 1916.

4. RFC slang for anti-aircraft fire, reputedly from a popular music hall song of the day: 'Archibald, certainly not!'

5. Cross and Cockade International.

6. Letter to the author.

7. The Fokkers with *Feldflieger Abteilung 62* had been detached on 12 June and redesignated *Kampfeinsitzer Kommando III* (Douai) with Immelmann in command.

8. McCubbin was awarded a Distinguished Service Order and Waller a Distinguished Conduct Medal for the action of 18 June. On 26 June they were in combat with a Fokker near Beuvry. Waller sent their attacker down out of control, but the FE was badly shot up and McCubbin wounded in the arm.

CHAPTER FOUR

THE SOMME

The primary British objective in the battle of the Somme was a thrust towards the German positions on Pozières Ridge. On securing the Ridge it was intended to push on to the enemy positions in front of Bapaume; the extent of the main attack was an 18-mile front from Gommecourt to La Boiselle. The Fourth Army, commanded by Sir Henry Rawlinson was to bear the brunt of the attack, supported by one Corps from Third Army. The newly-formed Fourth Army had been moved into the Front Line in late February, taking up positions from Gommecourt to Curlu, and to serve its air needs an additional RFC brigade was needed. On 1 April 1916, the new brigade was formed by 3rd (Corps) Wing; 14th (Army) Wing, and No.1 Kite Balloon Wing. This new brigade was designated 4th Brigade and placed under the command of Brigadier-General E B Ashmore. Third (Corps) Wing, under the command of LtCol E R Ludlow-Hewitt MC., was made up of 3 Squadron (Moranes); 4 Squadron (BEs); 9 Squadron (BEs); 15 Squadron (BEs) and No.1 Kite Balloon Squadron. The Fourteenth (Army) Wing, under LtCol C G Hoare, consisted of two fighter squadrons: 22 Squadron (FE2bs) and 24 Squadron (DH2s with three Bristol Scouts and two Morane Bullets attached from squadrons of Third [Corps] Wing). In March 1916 it had been decided to increase the strength of RFC squadrons from 12 to 18 aeroplanes and the squadrons of 4th Brigade were the first to benefit from this decision, five of its squadrons being up to the new establishment figure by the middle of June and the sixth by the first week of July. As further support for the squadrons of 4th Brigade during the coming battle, 9th Headquarters Wing, Commanded by LtCol H C T Dowding and which consisted of 21 Squadron (RE7s and BEs); 27 Squadron (Martinsyde G.100) 60 Squadron (Moranes) was moved to Fienvillers (21 and 27 Squadrons); and Vert Galant (60) during June, plus three Flights of 70 Squadron (Sopwith 1 1/2 Strutter) also at Fienvillers.

At the opening of the battle of the Somme the squadrons of 4th Army had 167 aeroplanes on charge; in addition the BE2cs of 8 Squadron were detailed to support a subsidiary attack on Gommecourt. The total strength of the RFC at the opening of the battle of the Somme was 27 squadrons, with a strength of 421 aeroplanes and four Kite Balloon squadrons.[1]

Opposing the squadrons of the RFC at the opening of the battle were the squadrons of the German 2nd Army with a total of 104 aeroplanes and six observation balloons. This force consisted of five *Feldflieger Abteilungen,* four *Artillerie Flieger Abteilungen*; two *Kampfeinsitzer Kommandos* (with sixteen single-seater fighters on charge); *Kampfgeschwader 1*; and three *Feldluftschiffer Abteilungen* (balloons).[2] In addition to its overwhelming numerical superiority the RFC now also had technically superior fighter aeroplanes.

The task of the RFC fighter squadrons in the Army Wings was the protection of the corps squadron aeroplanes, working in close support of the ground forces. This was achieved by continuous Line and Offensive Patrols and escort work, negating the efforts of the Fokker and Pfalz E Types, which could no longer operate over the main battlefront, leaving the corps aeroplanes of the RFC free to work unmolested.

On the morning of July 1 the first offensive patrol flown by 24 Squadron left Bertangles at 6.45am to patrol a line from Péronne, then through Pye to Gommecourt. These patrols were kept up throughout the day, the last leaving the Front Line only as night fell.

The first 24 Squadron pilot to have any success was 2Lt S E Cowan, flying a patrol with four other DH2s and a Bristol Scout from the Squadron. Cowan's first opponent was described by him as a fast machine, somewhat like a Bristol Scout – probably a Fokker D1 or D11 – flying over Péronne. Cowan dived at the hostile machine and fired half a drum of

Lewis at it, but the enemy scout dived away very fast and left the DH2 behind.

It was twenty minutes before the patrol saw any further action. Two LVGs were seen flying east between Courcellete and Bapaume. Cowan dived on the rearmost machine, firing half a drum into it before he came up to the second. He fired the remainder of the drum into this LVG and the enemy observer dropped down into his cockpit and ceased to return Cowan's fire. The other LVG was now on Cowan's tail and he broke off the combat and climbed away. Gaining his height, Cowan changed his Lewis gun drum and returned to the attack, driving the LVG down out of control through the clouds. A little over ten minutes later Cowan attacked a twin-tailed machine, possibly an Ago, and fired a couple of bursts at it. The enemy machine dived away to the east and Cowan lost sight of it. Cowan was later credited with two enemy machines crashed and an observer wounded from these actions.

Twenty-four Squadron kept up its patrols throughout the day. On a mid-day patrol by five DH2s, a Morane Type N and a Bristol Scout, three enemy machines were attacked. Lt T H Bayetto, flying the Morane, forced one of the enemy to land near Biefvillers and Lt. G A Knight chased the others towards Bapaume. Bayetto and Lt Sibley later attacked hostile observation balloons but the attacks failed due to lack of suitable incendiary ammunition.

Hawker did not fly in any of the squadron patrols during the day but flew two valuable reconnaissance flights, reporting on the progress of the ground attack, which was not going well. At the end of the first day of the battle, the total British casualties were appalling: 19,240 killed or died of wounds; 35,493 wounded; 2,152 missing; 585 prisoners of war; a total casualty cost of 57,470. On the right of the line there had been small gains in ground won, but these were untenable after nightfall and the troops withdrew. The attack had been a costly failure, the British Army suffering the worst casualties in its history. The RFC had had almost complete control of the air above the fighting, but had lost five BEs, and two FE2bs from 22 Squadron.

On the second day of the offensive the RFC lost only two aeroplanes – an FE2b and a BE – although another BE landed with a wounded observer and an RE7 and a Martinsyde were damaged and forced to land. In the late afternoon Albert Ball escorted four FEs across the Lines and attacked six Roland C.IIs. An FE shot down one of the German two-seaters and Ball another. Half an hour later Ball shot down an Aviatik by diving underneath the enemy machine, pulling down his Lewis gun and firing into the belly of his opponent which went down to crash in a field. This was the first time Ball had used this method of attack, which was later to become almost his trademark.

The other fighter squadron in action over the battle front, 60 Squadron, had no casualties on the first day of the offensive but on 3 July the squadron suffered a severe blow when its popular CO., Major 'Ferdy' Waldron, was shot down and killed, the first of the squadron's pilots to be killed in action.

On 3 July Waldron, who had been awarded a victory over an LVG on 1 July, led an offensive patrol of four Morane Bullets flown by Capt Smith-Barry and Lts H H Balfour, J N Simpson and D V Armstrong. Simpson and Armstrong's Bullets developed engine trouble and they returned, but Waldron carried on with Balfour and Smith-Barry, flying along the Arras to Cambrai road. As the three Moranes approached Cambrai a formation of enemy two-seaters, led by a Fokker E Type was seen. This formation was followed by two additional Fokker monoplanes, bringing the number of enemy machines to around a dozen. Undeterred by these odds, Waldron immediately led Balfour and Smith-Barry in an attack. Balfour later wrote. 'I'm sure they were not contemplating war at all but Ferdy pointed us towards them and led us straight in. My next impressions were rather mixed. I seemed to be surrounded by Huns in two seaters.'[3]

Waldron was outmanoeuvred by a Fokker pilot who gained a position on the tail of the Morane. Balfour saw that his CO was in trouble and succeeded in driving off the Fokker, but the damage was done. Waldron had been badly wounded by the enemy pilot's fire and although he managed to land his damaged Morane he died of his wounds that night. Smith-Barry and Balfour dispersed the enemy formation before returning to Vert Galant, Smith-Barry with a badly shot up Morane. Waldron, who had flown at least one patrol a day as an example to his pilots, was a pilot of great experience, experience which the RFC was greatly in need of at this time of expansion, and his loss brought an order from RFC.HQ: that squadron commanders should no longer fly over the Lines.

Bad weather on July 4 brought a welcome respite for two days, but operations recommenced on July 6, with a 3 Squadron Morane L Type being forced to land with a wounded pilot (2Lt T A Tillard) and observer (Flt Sgt Hall) after a combat with five LVGs. The Morane was escorted by Lt Wood in a DH2 of 24 Squadron and Lt Goodrich flying the squadron's Morane. The formation was surprised by the five LVGs and one shot the Parasol down. Wood then attacked this LVG and sent it down to crash.

Four DH2s from 24 Squadron had combats while on patrol on July 9. Anti-aircraft bursts over Achiet pointed out a Fokker monoplane to Lt F W Honnet. Honnet dived, and unseen by the Fokker pilot got on his tail and fired a whole drum into the enemy machine that sideslipped and went down to crash east of Bihucourt.

One of the other DH2s on patrol, Lt S E Pither, after unsuccessfully chasing an enemy scout near Arras, attacked a Roland two-seater flying at 9,000ft from the direction of Bapaume. Pither opened fire from 40 yards, coming under continuous return fire from the Roland's observer. Before Pither had fired a complete drum of Lewis, the observer ceased firing and the Roland went down out of control.

These combats were typical of those fought by the fighter squadrons of the RFC over the Somme during the first days of the battle, with only a brief rest on the 4th and 5th of July. On July 9 there was an increase of enemy air activity along the entire Front and twenty-four combats were fought, some of the enemy reconnaissance aeroplanes penetrating up to ten miles behind the British back areas on the 1st Army Front. The German effort on the Verdun Front was no longer one of offensive and air formations were being moved to counter the RFC's superior strength on the Somme.

Lionel Rees VC

During the early days of the Somme battle the fighter squadrons on the Army fronts not directly involved had not been inactive. On the opening day of the Somme battle the DH2s of 32 Squadron flew successful escorts to bombing raids on the railway station at Don and the town of Lille. These actions saw no enemy aeroplanes and brought back valuable information on enemy railway and troop movements. After one of these raids an action was fought that would result in the award of a Victoria Cross to 32 Squadron's CO., Major Lionel Wilmot Brabazon Rees.

Major Rees and Lt J C Simpson, a Canadian, took off at 5.55am. Simpson's orders were to patrol the area of La Bassée, Loos and Souchez, while Rees patrolled the Front Lines to observe the return of the bombers and their DH2 escorts. A force of ten German aeroplanes – Rumplers and Albatros two-seaters of *Kagohl 3,* commanded by *Ltn* Erich Zimmerman – was seen crossing the Lines and despite the odds against him Simpson immediately attacked it. Three of the enemy machines broke away from their formation and gave the DH2 their undivided attention. Simpson was shot eight times in the head; his DH2 crashed in the Loos Salient and was later destroyed by German artillery.

A few moments after Simpson's fall, Major Rees also sighted the enemy formation. At first Rees mistook them for a British formation, perhaps some of the bombers returning home, but as he drew closer one of the group left the formation, turned and dived towards him, firing its gun. Rees later wrote: 'I waited until he came within convenient range and fired one drum … after the 30th round I saw the top of the fuselage splinter between the pilot and observer.' The enemy machine turned and dived east, Rees noting that it was marked with a large '3' and a small cross on its fuselage.

Rees then attacked another two-seater. Seeing the DH2 approaching the observer fired red Very lights, calling for assistance, and three machines broke away from the remainder of the formation to come to its aid. 'They fired an immense amount of ammunition, but were so far away that it had no effect.' In their haste to come to the aid of their companion, the three enemy machines overshot the DH2 and went down out of the scene of the action. Rees closed on the lone two-seater and fired a drum into it. 'After about 30 rounds a big cloud of blue haze came out of the nacelle in front of the pilot. The machine turned and wobbled, and I last saw him down over the Lines under control. It looked either as if a cylinder was pierced, knocked off, or else the petrol tank punctured.'

Rees then saw that the five remaining enemy machines were in a tight bunch and made towards them. These also opened fire on the DH2 at long range. Rees returned their fire, aiming into the centre of the formation in an effort to disperse it. His tactic was successful. The enemy formation scattered 'in all directions.' Rees saw the enemy leader and two others flying west, with the intention of carrying on with their mission, and he gave chase, rapidly overhauling them. As he came up to the lower of the enemy machines it turned sharply and dropped a bomb, opening fire at its pursuer from long range. Rees closed the distance, but before he could open fire a bullet from the enemy observer's gun hit him in the upper leg, temporarily paralysing it.

Despite his wound, Rees fired a drum of Lewis at the two-seater, but with his leg still numb he had no control of his rudder and the DH2 swept 'backwards and forwards'. Rees was within ten yards of the enemy before he stopped firing and he could see the observer sitting back in his cockpit, firing his gun straight up into the air instead of at his attacker. Having expended his drum, Rees pulled out his pistol, but in his haste he dropped it and it fell to the front of his nacelle by his feet. Rees turned away and found that feeling in his leg had returned. Seeing that the leader of the German formation was now flying east towards his own lines, Rees again gave chase.

'I got within long range of him. He was firing an immense amount of ammunition. Just before he reached the lines, I gave him one drum. I was using the Beliene sight fixed to the gun, but as the sun had only just risen it was not shining on the cross wires. Even without the cross wires the tracers appeared to be going very near the target, simply through looking through the tube which is aligned with the axis of the gun.' Rees fired a full drum at the two-seater before giving up the chase; he could not climb to its height and it was impossible to close the range.

Having completely dispersed the enemy formation and forcing them to return to their own lines, Rees turned for base. His leg was now becoming very painful, but he made a good landing at Treizennes and taxied the DH2 to the sheds, where he climbed painfully from his cockpit and sat on the grass to await the arrival of transport to take him to a casualty clearing station. Gwilym Lewis was there and later wrote home: 'I told you he was the bravest man in the world. He landed in the usual manner, taxied in. They got the steps for him to get out of his machine. He got out and sat on the grass and calmly told the fellows to bring him a tender to take him to hospital.'[4]

Rees had fought these actions against *Kaghol 3* at 9,000ft, the German machines initially being two thousand feet above him. He reported that the enemy crews followed their usual tactics of circling and firing at about 45 degrees between their tailplanes and wings. The *Kaghol* lost two aeroplanes in the fight: the machine that Rees had sent down with blue smoke pouring its nose, and the third machine he had attacked. The observer in this machine was the *Staffelführer, Ltn* Zimmermann. Zimmermann was killed and his pilot *Ltn* Wendler wounded by Rees' fire and they crashed by the little hamlet of Petit Hantay, near La Bassée.

The award of a Victoria Cross for Rees' action was gazetted on 5 August 1916 and Rees received his medal at the hands of King George V on December 14.

Unfortunately, Rees' leg wound was more serious than at first supposed; he had to relinquish command of 32 Squadron and was invalided home to England. Capt S G Gilmour replaced Rees, taking acting command of the squadron, but was wounded in the evening of the same day while flying as an escort to the FEs of 25 Squadron on a bombing raid. Gilmour was attacked by a Fokker monoplane near Annoeullin and in a single burst of fire the enemy pilot's bullets grazed his head in three places, one going through his ear. Luckily the enemy pilot then withdrew and Gilmour was able to land at La Gorgue. His wounds were not serious but he was a week in hospital.

The fighter squadrons on the First Army Front suffered no casualties on July 2 but the next day 2Lt J Godlee's DH2 of 32 Squadron crashed on takeoff due to engine failure. Godlee was unhurt but the DH2 was wrecked. Later that day Capt. H von Poellnitz and Lt Hunt attacked a Roland two-seater over Bethune, but although Hunt pressed home his attack the Roland was faster and dived away.

Thirty-two Squadron had a successful day on July 9. After completing an escort for the FEs of 25 Squadron and seeing them safely back across the Lines, the three DH2s went to the aid of a BE2c being attacked by two Fokkers from a group of four. 2Lt P B G Hunt dived at one of the Fokkers and fired half a drum. The Fokker turned and dived away. Hunt was then attacked by its companion, but he succeeded in driving this one off as well, allowing the BE to escape back across the British Lines.

By July 7 the first phase of the Battle of the Somme was over. The rôle played by the RFC in the battle had been of considerable value to the ground forces – help made possible by its numerical and technical superiority over the enemy – but air reinforcements for the German 2nd Army were arriving and on 19 July two new *Kampfeinsitzer Staffeln* had been formed. From 19 July the GAAS was constantly reinforced on the 2nd Army Front and fights with enemy fighters became more frequent.

NOTES

1. These numbers were to be augmented further as the battle wore on; an additional four RFC squadrons arrived from Home Establishment in July and August, three more in October and an RNAS squadron flew into Vert Galant from Dunkirk on 26 October.

2. *Pictorial History of The German Air Service 1914-1918*, Alex Imrie.
3. Later Lord Balfour of Inchrye. Lord Balfour died in 1988.
4. Cross and Cockade International.

CHAPTER FIVE

NEW ARRIVALS

Despite its rapid rate of expansion the RFC in July 1916 was in many ways still a refreshingly informal organisation. One young pilot's account of his first posting to a squadron on active service during the Battle of the Somme, gives an evocative picture of his casual, almost offhand acceptance by his fellow pilots.

'The Crossley tender was bumping and banging along a vile road under the afternoon sun, raising a cloud of white dust which eddied and swirled back inside and vied with the fumes of the exhaust in choking the solitary occupant, who sat looking at his valise on the seat opposite. He cared nothing for the jolting or suffocation, for he was thinking of the squadron he was on his way to join – a scout squadron, the summit of his ambition. For months he had lived through this moment in anticipation, but now that it had arrived he found himself unable to realise it. His mind was filled with a strange blend of curiosity and apprehension.

The tender stopped and he jumped out. The driver pulled out his valise. There was the aerodrome. He saw a lot of little huts in a wood – no doubt these were the officers' quarters. Now that the tender had stopped he could hear the rumble of the guns. He saw the squadron office and, suddenly, all confidence deserted him. He walked up to the office feeling nervous and self-conscious. The Recording Officer was there, very busy with his maps and papers, and he tried diffidently to attract his attention. The Recording Officer looked up. "Oh" he said. "You are Smith! Come along down to the Mess and have some tea. We can fill up the forms afterwards." And down they walked to the Mess.

Almost before Smith realised what was happening he was being introduced to the CO. He was surprised to see how young he looked and how full of energy and enthusiasm. He could hardly wait for any tea in his eagerness to go up to the aerodrome and watch the flying. As soon as he could he walked up to the sheds. Aeroplanes were dropping into the aerodrome straight from the battle itself. Somehow this seemed odd. Others were taking off, the pilots with unconcerned faces and in methodical orderly manner. A message arrived telling him to report to OC. 'A' Flight. He reported and was given a machine: DH2 No.5967.

"A" Flight had red wheels and red outer struts with white bands on them that denoted the individual machine. Smith noticed that his number was four. He was almost painfully anxious to know his fitter, his rigger and his machine. He spent an hour or more in conversation with the men, or sitting in the machine, trying the controls and gun trigger. He had never before seen a gun fitted to a DH2. He knew soon, perhaps this very evening, he would have to make a trial flight, under the critical eye of the flight commander or even the CO. He was quite determined to put up a good show. With this in his mind he walked around the aerodrome, noting the bad patches and making up his mind where he would try to land. But the summons did not come that evening.

After dinner he went to bed early. But not to sleep. What a plaque of insects! His hut was an Armstrong one, and he shared it with another pilot. This officer had a mosquito net and other elaborate precautions. Just when he had counted his 276th earwig he fell asleep.

He was awakened in the morning by a stunning roar. He sat up in the creaking camp bed. The early morning patrol was taking off and the first off the ground had just skimmed over the top of his hut. He heard then go off one after the other, one, two, three four. Four of them. The air was full of the throbbing of four Mono engines. A deeper roar broke out as the FE2bs on the aerodrome the other side of the railway burst into life. The whole morning sky was rent with the sound of roaring engines. Engine after engine being tested on the ground. Presently and gradually the noise died down, until only the distant humming of the patrol could be heard. Even that died away and he heard only the bell of the village church proclaiming early Mass.

What a strange was this he was entering upon. So full of delightful novelties. He had forgotten for the moment that this was war. He had still to make his first flight and do that first patrol. But no one could be other than optimistic on such a beautiful morning; Smith got up and looked at his watch – 5.30am. Well, he might as well get up and see what was doing. He got out of bed and poured some cold water into a canvas basin. The noise awoke his companion, though the aeroplanes did not. He glanced at Smith with mild astonishment and fell asleep again.

Smith got up quietly, shaved in cold water and dressed in his aerodrome everyday kit. While he is thus engaged I will tell you something about him. He was twenty and a half years of age, fairly normal, a Territorial infantry officer of eighteen months service, very keen on flying, a little nervous, rather imaginative, and of average intelligence. He was a good pilot, though he did not know it then. He knew he had never crashed, but put that down to luck, in which he was, no doubt, very nearly right.

He left the hut and walked up to the aerodrome. No one seemed to be about. He walked into 'A' Flight sheds. All the machines were there so it was not 'A' Flight that was out. He went and looked at his aeroplane again, examined turnbuckles, controls, pulleys, everything. He looked with awe at the flight commander's machine, with its coloured streamers on the outer struts. He examined it closely. Its planes, he noticed with a thrill, were covered with patches of fabric, repairing bullet holes. He wondered if he would ever rise to lead a Flight in the air. Somehow he felt sure he would, but he knew that, even with luck, the way was one of hard work and perseverance. A dreadful thought had been in his mind for some days now, though he kept it sternly in the background. What would he be like under fire? This unpleasant question would obtrude itself on his thoughts this morning; he could not keep it back, though he knew the question could only be answered by the test itself.

He turned for relief to the Flight Sergeant, who had just come into the shed, and started a technical discussion with him. The Flight Sergeant, a busy man, was polite, and stood it for five minutes; then he excused himself and disappeared into a sort of dog kennel that was his office. In a minute he appeared again and ordered two of the machines to be taken outside. A defensive patrol was going off in half an hour. As Smith watched the preparations, fascinated, the two pilots who were going on patrol appeared walking up from the Mess. They nodded to Smith then went into the Flight Office and put on great leather coats and mufflers and all the paraphernalia of the active serve pilot. They then went out and, after a short look over the machines, climbed into their seats. To do this they had to use a step ladder, as it was not possible to get in by the ordinary way with all their flying clothes on.

They started their engines almost at the same moment, and tripped them on the switch. Each the tested his engine and waved away the chocks. They taxied slowly out on to the aerodrome and Smith noticed that one of the machines carried one solitary black streamer. He began to feel hungry now, but just as he was thinking of going down to the Mess he heard the hum of returning aeroplanes. The early patrol of four machines was coming back. He could see them – one, two, three specks against the sky. Where was the fourth? He could not see him anywhere. One after the other they shut off their engines and gliding down into the wind, alighted carefully. Smith's professional interest was aroused and he admitted to himself that fellows out here could fly all right. He started to walk towards the machines and nearly bumped into the CO. He saluted and got a smile and a "Good morning". The pilots one by one got out of their machines and clustered around the CO., all were talking at once. Smith hung about shyly and tried to understand what they were saying, but it was beyond him. Their conversation seemed to be something like this.

"Yes, sir, quite different, long nose, sort of pale green …with a great streamer…I saw two fellows all right. After that we could not catch them,… I did not see that fellow…where did Brown get to?…I think they were some sort of Rolands, sir…came right out of the sun over Achiet….two thousand feet above us. Never saw them until they were on us. Buckingham (ammunition) jammed again, no damned use…Very few artillery machines…You got that one all right Bill, I saw him. Did that BE get away all right? The mist put 'em off, I expect…miles below us, most of it…. Lots of clouds coming up from the sou'west…Did you see that balloon over Moislains? Quite low….yes….old Brown's all right. I saw him land at Baisieux…. Did you notice that third Fokker? What height did you make them, Bill?….Very few trains about ….By Jove! Did you see the way that fellow turned?"

Smith was reassured. Any fool could see that these pilots were happy. Their faces shone and they never stopped laughing. Was this the war? Smith felt more than ever anxious to get the preliminaries over and become a useful pilot in the squadron. He felt quite impatient. Would they ever let him fly?'

New Opponents

Throughout the rest of July the fighter squadrons of the RFC fought an increasing number of combats; in addition, the number of aeroplanes involved in the daily fights now began to increase On the evening of July 20 an offensive patrol of four DH2s of 'B' Flight, 24 Squadron, met and engaged a formation of five LVGs, three Rolands and three Fokkers over Bapaume.

Capt R E A W Hughes-Chamberlain led Lts C M B Chapman and Evans in the attack. Hughes-Chamberlain first engaged one of the LVGs, but it dived away east and he turned his attention to a Fokker flying below it. After half a drum from Hughes-Chamberlain's Lewis the Fokker pilot also dived away, but flattened out at lower level. Hughes-Chamberlain was then attacked from behind by a Roland, but he escaped by a steep climbing turn, outmanoeuvred the enemy machine and fired the rest of his drum into it. The Roland went down but Hughes-Chamberlain was too busy changing his Lewis gun drum to see what happened to it.

Evans had attacked one of the other Rolands, firing half a drum at it from only 25 yards. The Roland went down out of control, but Evans was attacked from behind by two Fokker monoplanes. In their haste to shoot down the DH2 the Fokker pilots nearly collided and Evans evaded them and attacked an LVG.

Chapman had tackled two of the enemy formation, but he then drove off a Fokker and an LVG that were attacking Evans, whose Lewis gun had jammed. Evans cleared the jam and attacked another LVG, which cleared east.

The fourth member of the Flight was Lt McKay, but the engine of his DH2 had been running badly and he had been forced to remain at 8,500ft, fifteen hundred feet below the patrol at the start of the fight. A Roland dived at him and opened fire but McKay outmanoeuvred it and returned its fire. The Roland stopped firing and went down in a spin. McKay then came under attack from a Fokker monoplane; he could not evade this attack because of his failing engine and he put the DH2 into a steep spiral in an attempt to throw off the enemy pilot. Chapman saw McKay's predicament and dived to attack the Fokker, 1,000ft over High Wood. The Fokker went down, spinning, hit the ground and burst into flames.

After more combats and manoeuvring for favourable positions, the British fighters finally drove the enemy machines back to their own Lines, patrolling for another 15 minutes before returning to Bertangles.

The entire fight had been witnessed by British anti-aircraft batteries, an observer in a 9 Squadron BE., and 4th Army observers. The British AA reported three enemy machines and one DH2 driven down; the observer confirming that three EA had gone down, one bursting into flames. The 4th Army reports gave one enemy machine falling in flames, one burning on the ground and two or three falling out of control.

It was considered that the victories should go to Evans, a Roland; McKay, another Roland; Chapman, whose Fokker was seen to burst into flames on hitting the ground; and Hughes-Chamberlain, a Fokker or a Roland, or possibly both. The DH2 seen going down by the AA was McKay, who returned safely. The pilots of 24 Squadron received a telegram the next morning from General Trenchard.

'Well done 24 Squadron in the fight last night. Keep it going. We have the Hun cold.'

Twenty-four Squadron's DH2s were in action again the following morning. The FEs of 22 Squadron led them on an Offensive Patrol to the east of Péronne, nearly as far as Roisel, where they were attacked by ten enemy machines – Rolands and Fokkers. In the fierce fighting a Fokker was forced to land by Lt Andrews and was attacked on the ground by Lt Pither. The enemy formation was finally driven off but two of the FEs had been badly shot about and had to return. One of the DH pilots, Lt Honnet, reported that one of the Fokkers was flown by a very skillful pilot and was painted a 'butcher' blue with white crosses. The DH2s carried on with their patrol, were joined by Major Hawker, and at 8.15am attacked another enemy formation. Hawker was first to see and attack the enemy machines, opening fire at 100 yards, but his Lewis gun came loose on its mounting, spoiling his aim. These enemy machines were thought to be Ago C types, all dispersed by the DH2s, although no victories were gained.

A midday patrol by the squadron had two combats: first driving a formation of seven enemy machines back over the Lines over Martinpuich, then another formation of five from over Morval. Some of these enemy machines were flying at 15,000ft. and the DH2s could not climb to their height. In the late afternoon the squadron flew an escort for attacks on the enemy balloon line, but the proposed attackers failed to put in an appearance. Later, at 8.25pm, Lt H C Evans with two other DH2s and a pair of FEs from 22 Squadron had a more positive result. The British force was patrolling east of Combles when it sighted a lone Morane flying towards a formation of German machines. The Morane was from 3 Squadron, crewed by the colourful combination of Lt Green, pilot, and Lt Brown, observer, who were flying an artillery patrol when they had seen the enemy machines 5,000ft. above them. The Morane was joined by the DH2s and the FEs and the entire formation climbed to attack the enemy force, which had been reinforced by five LVGs and two Fokkers.

The first attack by the British machines succeeded in breaking up the enemy formation, which scattered. The Morane and two of the DH2s, flown by Lt Andrews and Sergeant W Piercy, attacked one of the Fokkers which crashed near Warlencourt,[1] and two more were forced to land near Transloy.

Evans engaged one of the two-seaters, firing a drum into it from 75 yards range, forcing it to dive east with its engine full on, and it was seen by other members of the patrol to fall out of control into Combles village. Evans had lost sight of this machine while he was changing his drum but he engaged another, which he drove down. One of the FEs attacked another of the enemy force, which crashed in a field near Beaulencourt. The entire fight lasted over half an hour, resulting in all the enemy machines diving away, back over their own lines, in twos and threes.

It was during the day that the new double drum for the Lewis gun was tried out. Hawker wrote: 'The double drums worked perfectly and were easier to change than the single (47 round Lewis gun drum).'

Thirty seven year old Henry Evans, a veteran of the Boer war, who had been ranching in Alberta, Canada, at the outbreak of war, and who had served in France with the Alberta Dragoons before transferring to the RFC, was one of the most successful pilots in 24 Squadron. Evans had joined the squadron on 4 July and had gained his first victory on 20 July: a Roland sent down out of control over Flers. He followed this with a C Type two-seater the next day over Combles.

During August the airfighting continued with even greater intensity, with the main concentration of German air strength still over the 4th Army Front. The GAAS was undergoing a period of reorganisation and reviewing its tactics in the light of the RFC's continued control of the air above the Somme battlefield. The operations of the *Flieger Abteilungen* were to be overseen by a *Gruppenführer der Flieger* to employ them to the best tactical advantage. The second change, the most important one was the formation of the first *Jagdstaffeln* – literally 'hunting squadrons' These were formed in the field and utilised the pilots who had been flying the single-seater fighters in the *Kampfeinsitzer Kommandos*. These *Jasta* – as they were abbreviated – were each to be equipped with fourteen of the new 'D' Type fighters, developed to replace the now obsolete 'E' Type monoplanes. As historian Alex Imrie has remarked: 'These units became the main aerial weapon, the elite of the German Army Air Service.'[2]

The pilots of the RFC fighter squadrons were in almost daily combat during August and casualties began to mount. The RFC was to lose nearly forty aeroplanes to enemy action during the month, even though bad weather restricted flying for nine days during the period. Only five of these losses were single-seater fighters and the casualties suffered by the corps squadrons are indicative of the gathering strength of the GAAS.

On August 3 the DH2s of both 24 and 32 Squadron were in combat with large formations of enemy aeroplanes.[3] Four DH2s of 24 Squadron were the first in action, in the early afternoon, attacking seven enemy machines over Flers. In the course of the action Lt Cowan drove off one of the enemy, which was on the tail of a DH2, then chased two others towards Velu. Overtaking these, Cowan opening fire on the rear machine. The leading machine immediately fired a white light and both enemy machines landed. Returning from this action Cowan attacked another two-seater from above and behind. After several bursts from Cowan's Lewis gun, the enemy observer stopped firing and Cowan could see that he was hanging head downwards over the side of his cockpit. Cowan fired a few more bursts and the enemy machine went down in a spiral, which gradually became steeper and faster.

While Cowan was attacking these various enemy machines, Capt John Andrews and Lt A E Glew had chased the others, finally engaging them over Sailly. Glew send one down and Andrews, firing a double drum into another, saw the observer collapse into his cockpit.

An evening patrol from 32 Squadron, sent out to ascertain the damage inflicted by a bombing raid earlier in the day on Grevillers, sighted an enemy formation consisting of six LVGs, a twin-engined machine and two Fokker monoplanes. A general combat ensued, but there were no casualties on either side. Although all the hostile machines directed a very heavy fire on the three DH2s, Capt.Wilson's was the only one to sustain any damage.

On August 6, Capt. Henry Evans of 24 Squadron shot down an LVG and two days later he shot down a Roland from a group of four. Evans had attacked these Rolands over Bapaume and during the fight they had shot away the aileron control of the DH2, holed the petrol tank and stopped its engine.

'I saw that petrol was running out of the safety bag, so I turned on the emergency supply. The engine picked up but the machine having no aileron control I could only fly in small circles, firing a few shots when the gun passed in the direction of any of the HA (hostile Aircraft). There were three of them all around me, but they turned east and dived. I noticed that petrol was running over the floor of the machine so immediately switched off. The machine gradually straightened up and I was able to glide west with the wind and land at Baizieux.'

The DH2 was badly shot about, not repairable in the Squadron's workshops, and was sent back to 2AD.[4]

Two additional fighter squadrons arrived in France during August. Nineteen Squadron, equipped with the ill-fated BE12, arrived at Fienvillers on 1 August and came under the orders of 9th Wing. The BE12 was an unsuccessful attempt to modify the basic BE two-seater design into a single-seater fighter, despite the inherent stability of the BE design making it completely unsuitable for the rôle, with its essential requirement of manoeuvrability. The BE12 was quickly found to be useless as a fighter aeroplane and was relegated to bombing duties.[5]

On August 2 a Flight of 40 Squadron arrived at Treizennes and came under the orders of Tenth (Army) Wing, I Brigade. The squadron had been formed at Gosport on 26 February 1916 under the temporary command of Capt R G Howard DSO, but Major Robert Lorraine MC. assumed command in March. Before the war Lorraine had been a successful actor and was also a pilot of some repute. As such he had hoped to join the RFC at the outbreak of war, but on reporting to Farnborough on 12 August 1914 he had crashed two aeroplanes on landing from his first two flights. The RFC could ill afford to lose machines at this time, and even though Lorraine was considered a pioneer aviator he went to France on September 3 as an observer with 3 Squadron. Lorraine was wounded in the lung by anti-aircraft fire on 22 November 1914, the wound serious enough for him to receive the Last Sacrament two days later. However, he made a slow but steady recovery and on 11 December arrived back in England.

In July 1915 Lorraine was back in France, this time as a pilot, and on September 15 was posted to 5 Squadron as 'B' Flight Commander. During September, Lorraine and his observer, the Honourable Eric Lubbock, shot down an Albatros from *Feldflieger Abteilung 33*. The pilot was mortally wounded and died soon after coming down just behind the British Lines, but the observer was only slightly wounded and made a prisoner of war. Lorraine and Lubbock were both awarded a Military Cross.

On 19 August 1916 'B' and 'C' Flights of 40 Squadron landed at St.Omer, rejoining 'A' Flight at Treizennes on August 25. The squadron was equipped with the FE8, another single-seater pusher type, very similar to the DH2 in configuration, and it commenced operations on the Front from Armentières to just north of Arras.

In August an NCO pilot who was to become one of the RFC's most successful fighter pilots and patrol leaders joined 29 Squadron. As previously noted, James Thomas Byford McCudden had gone to France as an air mechanic with 3 Squadron at the outbreak of war; he had flown as an observer in the squadron's various aeroplanes during 1915 and in January 1916, had been promoted to Flight Sergeant and sent back to England to train as a pilot. His first posting as a pilot to France in July that year was with 20 Squadron, flying FE2bs, but on August 3 he achieved his ambition to fly scouts and was posted to 29 Squadron to fly DH2s. McCudden's new squadron was in the north, away from the main Somme battlefield, but he was to gain valuable experience in the coming months.

The RFC's First Ace

August 10 saw the return of Albert Ball to duty as a fighter pilot. Since his first victory while flying 11 Squadron's Bristol Scout on May 16, Ball had steadily increased his victories to four before going on leave on June 10. On this return to 11 Squadron on June 23, Ball entered the most successful period of his career as an airfighter, scoring his next victory – a balloon – on June 25. In the morning Ball's first attack on the selected balloon had been unsuccessful and he took off again in the afternoon determined to destroy it. Pressing home his attacks, Ball finally set the balloon on fire with phosphorus bombs, but his Nieuport was badly shot about and Ball had to nurse the damaged fighter for eight miles before he crossed the British Front Line trenches to safety. Ball thought destroying balloons ' a rotten job' but he was awarded a Military Cross for his work on the afternoon of June 25.

On June 27, Ball and three other pilots flying with 11 Squadron were concentrated into 'B' Flight, to form the squadron's 'scout' Flight of single-seaters. The day was not a good one for Ball: taking off on patrol at 7.00am he saw a concentration of enemy troops and transport in a wood. Going down for a closer look, the Nieuport was hit by anti-aircraft fire; one of the engine cylinders was smashed and a piece of shrapnel narrowly missed Ball's leg. Ball was forced to land behind the British trenches.

Ball was to reach his zenith during the Somme battles. From the beginning of the offensive on July 1, until he was posted to Home Establishment in October, Ball scored 26 victories, making him the RFC's premier fighter pilot and, in the words of the official history, 'the spearhead of the achievement of Flying Corps over the Somme.' But the tempo of the fighting during the first two weeks of the battle taxed Ball's nerves to such an extent that on July 16 he wrote to his mother that he had had twelve fights during the day and was feeling 'a bit poo-poo just now.' Two days later he asked his CO., Major Hubbard, if he might have a rest from flying for a few days. Hubbard, instead of quietly resting Ball, referred his request to General Higgins, commanding 3rd Brigade. Higgins – colloquially known throughout the RFC as 'all bum and eyeglass' – had Ball transferred to 8 Squadron to fly BE2cs on general reconnaissance and artillery co-operation work. These duties were far from a rest and Ball was extremely upset, writing home to his father. 'This is thanks after my work. Oh, I am feeling down in the dumps.'

Ball's posting may have been Higgins' way of disciplining him a little. Ball was known to be outspokenly intolerant of senior officers, commenting unfavourably to them of the poor aeroplanes he and his fellow pilots were being asked to fly – asked by Trenchard of his opinion of the BE12, Ball had reputedly told the General: 'it's a bloody awful machine, – but it is also true that many other fighter pilots had seen a great deal more action than Ball, not to mention the hard-pressed pilots and observers of the corps squadrons. It is probable that Higgins wished to show Ball the other side of the coin.

While with 8 Squadron Ball resolved to make the best he could of his 'rest'. In addition to his normal squadron duties he volunteered for the hazardous job of landing a spy behind the German lines after dark. The unarmed BE was chased by three Fokkers – evaded only by the gathering dusk – and heavily archied. On landing the spy determinedly refused to leave the BE, even though Ball had landed three times before finally giving up and returning. This aborted mission put Ball back into Higgins' good books – if he had ever been out of them – and he was returned to duty with 11 Squadron on 10 August. Six days after his return Ball wrote home, this time in a more cheerful mood. 'Dearest people, Hallo. I am back in my dear old hut. All is OK and my garden is fine, You will be surprised to hear that I have started with luck. I went up this morning and attacked five Hun machines. One I got and two forced down. After this I had to run for all my ammunition was used. However, I got back OK with only two hits on my machine.'

Ball was only awarded one victory from this combat, a Roland C.II, bringing his official victory score to eight, but six days later he destroyed three Roland C.IIs in forty-five minutes. It was the first 'hat trick' to be scored by an RFC pilot in a single day.

Ball had now perfected his technique of gaining a favourable position underneath an enemy machine, pulling down his Lewis gun and firing up into its underside, and used this method to score the three victories on August 21. Attacking seven Rolands over Bapaume, Ball closed to within fifteen yards before opening fire, sending one down to crash west of the town. Regaining his height, Ball attacked five more Rolands coming south from the direction of Vaulx. Undetected by the German pilots, Ball took up position under one Roland and opened fire from thirty feet before they were aware of his presence, shooting down two before running out of ammunition and being chased back to the Lines. Ball landed at 8 Squadron for more ammunition and returned to his patrol area. He attacked several more enemy formations, but was again driven back to the British Lines with his Nieuport badly shot about. This was Ball's last patrol as a member of 11 Squadron. The following day he was transferred to 60 Squadron.

During the intensive fighting in July, 60 Squadron had suffered very heavy casualties. It had lost its CO, Major Waldron on July 3, but although there was then a lull in its casualties until July 21, when it lost a pilot killed, and five

days later an observer wounded, the last day of the month brought a portent of things to come when two Moranes were lost, one crew being wounded, the other killed. On August 2, two additional Moranes were lost, with both crews killed in action, and the next day a pilot dropping a spy was forced to land with engine trouble and taken prisoner. Included in these casualties were two of the squadron's flight commanders. Major R Smith-Barry, who had taken command after Waldron's death, was appalled at the casualty rate and informed LtCol Hugh Dowding, commanding 9th Wing, that he could not send into action any more new pilots with less than seven hours total flying time. Dowding agreed with Smith-Barry and informed Trenchard, who withdrew the squadron from operations on August 3, writing to Haig:

'I have had to withdraw one of the GHQ fighting squadrons from work temporarily, and have sent it to St.Andre-aux-Bois. This squadron, since the battle began, has lost a squadron Commander, two flight commanders and one pilot, (all) killed and missing and yesterday it lost two more machines with two pilots and observers to AA fire. Besides this they have had several officers wounded. They have a difficult machine to fly, and I think a rest away from work is absolutely essential.'

It would seem that of equal importance in Trenchard's decision to rest 60 Squadron was the quality of its equipment. The Morane BB biplanes, of which the squadron had one Flight, were outclassed even by the almost obsolete Fokker *eindekkers* and although 'B' Flight continued to fly the 80hp Morane Type N Bullet, on 29 July 'C' Flight had begun to be re-equipped with the 110hp Le Rhône-powered Bullet, the Type I and V. If the Morane N had been unpopular with the 60 Squadron pilots, the new type was feared and detested by all.

The idea to re-engine the 80hp Bullet with a larger engine is reputed to have been Trenchard's, who thought that re-engined and re-armed with an interrupted Vickers gun firing through the propeller arc, the Bullet would be 'the best machine in the air.' It has been said that when the idea was put to the French manufacturers they agreed to build the new type but only on condition that they should be test flown by the RFC, as they would not allow their own test pilots to fly them.

Lt. Willie Fry, who joined 60 Squadron on 1 October, remembered in his autobiography his first flight in one of the 110hp Bullets.[6]

'I was numbed and almost speechless with fear at having to take the machine into the air, but I wasn't going to show it.' The Morane had a balanced elevator and wing warping control for banking, both worked from the control column. This made the machine very light on fore and aft control but stiff and heavy laterally. Warping the wings to bank was by 'brute force', whereas the balanced elevator control was very light, making it easy, in Fry's recollection, to pull the control column right back until the tailplane was at right angles to the line of flight, pulling the tail off.'[7]

While at St.Andre, 60 Squadron posted out its observers; by August 12 they had all been sent to squadrons operating with two-seater aeroplanes. It had become apparent that stronger patrols of fighters, flying both offensive patrols and escorts, were essential to maintain air superiority over the battle front and it had been decided to transfer those Nieuports and their pilots attached to Nos. 1, 3 and 11 Squadrons – squadrons flying two-seater aeroplanes – into 60 Squadron. On August 16 Lts Douglas Latta MC., Tony Waters and Sidney Parker flew in from 1 Squadron, and Frank Goodrich, an American serving in 3 Squadron, was transferred, promoted to captain and given command of 'A' Flight. Over the next few days, six additional pilots, the entire scout Flight of 11 Squadron, would arrive, flying in three Type 16 and three Type 17 Nieuports.

On August 23, its three weeks of training completed, 60 Squadron flew to its new base at Izel-le-Hameau, coming under the orders of 13 (Army) Wing, III Brigade. On the same day, Ball and Foot flew into Izel to join the squadron, Ball bringing his Nieuport and Foot his Spad. The squadron now had two Flights of Nieuports and one of Morane Bullets.

Ball's score now began to mount rapidly. Two days after his arrival he shot down a Roland C.II out of control south of Arras, following this victory with another treble on 28 August when he shot down two Rolands and a 'C' Type during the day. The first Roland, which was from *Feldflieger Abteilung 207,* was shot down just after 7.00am. Ball's fire killed the pilot, *Ltn* Joachim von Arnim, but the observer, *Ltn.* Böhne managed to land the damaged machine near Transloy.

That evening, flying an escort duty, Ball forced two enemy machines to land, then attacked four flying south-east of Adinfer, shooting down the nearest, a Roland, from his favourite position of underneath. The Roland crashed just east of Ayette. Ball was awarded one victory, forced to land, from the first fight of the evening and the Roland destroyed from the second.

Major Smith-Barry, commanding 60 Squadron, asked Ball to submit a list of his victory claims and combats: these amounted to 84 combats; eleven machines and one balloon brought down and seen to crash; twelve machines forced down and damaged, plus a further five machines forced down but not seen to crash. This total made Ball the leading British pilot of the time, with 15 officially confirmed victories over aeroplanes, plus a balloon, in 84 fights, although Ball himself wrote home that he thought it to be only 12 machines crashed and the balloon. By the end of August Ball's official score stood at 17.

The First Albatros Fighters

By the end of August 1916 the superiority of the RFC over the Somme was coming to an end. Seven of the new *Jagdstaffeln* had been formed in late August and by the end of the month two were in action over the Somme, equipped with the new Halberstadt D.I and D.II and Fokker biplane 'D' types, all of which were superior to the pusher fighters of the RFC, the DH2 and FE8. On the last day of the month the pilots of 24 Squadron fought their first action with another new type of enemy fighter that was to become the mainstay of the *Jagdstaffeln,* the D series Albatros. Only two or three of the Albatros fighters were at the Front by the end of August, but John Andrews and Glew met these and fought them for half an hour.

At ten minutes after midday, Andrews and Glew of 'A' Flight were on patrol over Ginchy when they were attacked by three enemy fighters: 'They were a new type, extremely fast and climbing quickly. Biplane with propeller boss, apparently single-seater but firing both in front and over the tail from what appeared to be a rear mounting on the left hand side. The tailplane was very large and rounded, like a fishtail.'

The German pilots, perhaps not yet accustomed to their new aeroplanes, kept above the DH2s, diving, firing, and then climbing again. Andrews and Glew found that they could not climb to the enemy fighters and managed to get off only a few shots during each attack. After thirty minutes the enemy machines withdrew, having inflicted no damage on the DH2s. Ten minutes later one Albatros returned and the DH2s attacked it at 7,000ft over Curlu, Andrews diving at it and firing a double drum of Lewis at 100yards range. The Albatros pilot put his aeroplane into a steep dive and disappeared into a cloud, closely pursued by Andrews. Glew, who had stayed above Andrews, dived under the cloud and waited until the Albatros emerged, still in a steep dive. Glew had time to fire only half a drum before the enemy scout dived away towards Clery.

Despite the puzzling reference to the rear-firing gun – the 24 Squadron pilots may have confused it with a signal gun mounted on the side of the cockpit of the Albatros, as was common with German aeroplanes – from the general description, and especially that of the tailplane, these enemy fighters were the new Albatros D.Is, almost certainly from *Jasta 1.* Although clearly outclassed by the new Albatros fighters in speed and rate of climb, the DH2 was very manoeuvrable in the hands of experienced pilots of the calibre of Andrews and Glew, and they undoubtedly owed their survival to these two factors, set against the relative inexperience of the *Jasta* pilots in fighting with their new machines.

The two *Jasta* operating over the Somme area were *Jagdstaffeln 1* and 2. *Jasta 2* was under the command of *Hptm*

Oswald Boelcke, the foremost German fighter pilot with 19 victories, all but the first scored on the Fokker E Type monoplanes. Boelcke's grasp of airfighting tactics and his personal tuition of the hand-picked pilots of his new command, were to instil great confidence into the pilots of the new *Jagdstaffeln* and earn him the reputation as the father of German fighter tactics. Pilots picked by Boelcke, who were later to become highly successful fighter pilots, included Erwin Böhme (24 victories) Max Müller (36 victories) and the most successful of them all, Manfred von Richthofen (80 victories).

During August the RFC fighter squadrons engaged over the Somme had fought an increasing number of combats against growing opposition from the *Jagdstaffeln.* Twenty-Four Squadron's historian later wrote: 'The offensive patrols were continued daily, and although escorts were provided to photographic and reconnaissance machines, offensive work became the principal duty of the squadron; individual fighting gave place to formations of machines indulging in aerial combat which sometimes lasted for nearly an hour.'

Further north the fighter squadrons of I and II Brigades were not inactive on the Ypres front, although McCudden, flying with 29 Squadron, commented in his autobiography that in early September 'there seemed to be something radically wrong with the German air service.' Reporting on a bombing raid which had met with no resistance he wrote: 'Here were about twenty British machines at all heights from 8,000 to 14,000 feet roving just as they pleased eight miles behind the enemy trenches and not a single German machine up to molest them at all.' This scarcity of opposition was because the RFC and RNAS had overwhelming numerical superiority on the Ypres front, with more than double the strength of the German units opposing them. Even so there were combats taking place. Twenty-nine Squadron claimed two victories in August, but lost a pilot wounded early in the month, a pilot fatally wounded on August 24 and another shot down and captured.

Although NCO pilots in the fighter squadrons were a rare breed, 29 Squadron had two outstanding sergeant pilots: James McCudden and Jack Noakes.[8] Noakes was an exceptional pilot. Full of confidence in his ability; he threw the DH2 about the sky in a way which horrified his flight commander, Capt Latch, who remonstrated with Noakes many times. Even if his engine were not running as smoothly at it might, Noakes would take off at the steepest possible angle of climb. A receipt for disaster which earned the description: 'his angle of climb varied inversely with the "square" of the "rise" of his engine.' Noakes

and McCudden were placed in C Flight and Noakes introduced McCudden to the DH2 on the morning of his arrival, impressing upon the new arrival that the defects of the little pusher were more imagined than real.[9]

Another new arrival at 29 Squadron during August was Geoffrey Hilton Bowman, 'Beery' to his friends on account of his florid complexion. On September 3 Bowman was involved in a fight that nearly ended his career. While on escort duty Bowman saw a BE2c under attack by a Fokker. Bowman later wrote in his logbook: 'Went on bomb raid and saw a 2c being attacked by Fokker. Dived on Fokker who left 2c. I was then attacked by a Roland scout and while flying nose on to each other I shot him. Being out of control HA came straight on and took off his right hand top plane on my R. wing. My lateral control was Na Poo. HA went down over Zinsilles. I came back to Lines at 2,000ft.'

September 1916 was a hectic month for Bowman, who had another narrow escape at the end of the month. On September 27 he was flying an offensive patrol. 'While at 12,000ft saw a Hun balloon at 14,000ft over Hun lines. One plug cut out so could not climb. Came back to get new machine. Set balloon on fire over Kemel (sic) Hill. Engine cut out so had to land. Hit telegraph pole and crashed completely in same field as balloon. Captured Hun officer in balloon.'

Before this adventure of Bowman's McCudden had opened his eventual score of 57 victories, On September 6, on patrol between Armentières and Ypres, McCudden saw an enemy two-seater, white in colour, approaching the British Lines over Messines. McCudden gave chase, and the enemy machine immediately turned and made for its own Lines, nose down. The speeds of the two combatants were almost equal and McCudden could come no closer than 400 yards so he opened fire with a drum of Lewis. The two-seater continued to dive and McCudden changed drums to renew the attack. After another drum of Lewis, McCudden's opponent dived even more steeply and there was still no reply from the gunner. McCudden put a third drum on his Lewis and fired it into the fleeing enemy machine. Both McCudden and the two-seater were now down to 4,000ft, 'well east of the Lines'. McCudden considered that he was too low over hostile territory and turned away as the enemy machine went down through the clouds at 2,000ft over Gheluve, still diving steeply. Three days later a report was received from an agent behind the German Lines that a German machine had crashed on the Menin road at the time of McCudden's combat, 'so that was my first Hun.'

NOTES

1. *Ltn.* Otto Parschau, a Fokker pilot commanding *FFl.Abt.32*, landed mortally wounded on 21 July after a combat over Grevillers.

2. *Pictorial History of the German Air Service*, Alex Imrie.

3. On the afternoon of Friday 21 July 32 Squadron had left 10th (Army) Wing, flown to its new aerodrome at Vert Galant and came under the orders of 9th Wing.

4. When Evans was shot down and killed by anti-aircraft fire on 3 September 1916 he had five victories and had been awarded a DSO and a Mention in Despatches.

5. On 28 July, 21 Squadron, equipped with BE2s, had been withdrawn from 9th Wing and posted to Boisdinghem to be re-equipped with the BE12.

6. *Air Of Battle*. Wing Commander W M Fry. William Kimber. 1974.

7. Fry served many years in the RFC and RAF, in both world wars and the inter-war period, and flew many types of aeroplane, but he once confided in the author that the 110hp Morane was the only aeroplane he ever flew which he felt was actively trying to kill him.

8. Noakes was commissioned in the field. After the war he originated the concept of 'crazy flying'.

9. McCudden also had a penchant for taking off in this manner. It was almost certainly the reason for his death in a flying accident in 1918.

CHAPTER SIX

THE FINAL PHASE

The third and last phase of the Battle of the Somme opened on September 15. The main attacks were again carried out by the British 4th Army, its objectives being the German third line trench system between Morval and Le Sars. The Reserve Army was to attack Courcelette and the high ground northeast of Thiepval to secure the flank of 4th Army. For the first time tanks were to support the infantry with 42 going into action with 4th Army and seven with the Reserve Army.

In the war above the battlefield the RFC corps squadrons flew bombing, reconnaissance and artillery ranging missions. In addition to their usual duties, orders from Wing had specified that German observation balloons were to be attacked on the day before the opening of the offensive and Alan Bell-Irving and Ball had attacked two balloons at Avesnes-le-Bapaume with Le Prieur rockets, Bell-Irving setting one balloon alight. On the morning of the offensive three balloons were in positions to oversee British tanks taking part in the offensive and Trenchard visited 60 Squadron, asking for volunteers to destroy them. Ball, now a captain, 2Lts A M Walters and Euan Gilchrist, and Capt A S M Summers, all took off in Nieuports armed with Le Prieur rockets.

Ball and Walters found that their allotted balloons had been taken down, and they attacked a formation of LVGs and Fokker D Types to the northeast of Bapaume. Ball fired all eight of his rockets at one of the Fokkers from a range of 200 yards, but missed. He then closed to fifty yards and fired half a drum of Lewis. The Fokker went down to crash just east of Beugny. Walters had better luck with his rockets, hitting one of the LVGs in the fuselage and setting it alight. The burning machine finally crashed by Bapaume.

Euan Gilchrist had destroyed his balloon and another was also burnt. This was credited to Capt Summers, who was shot down in flames and killed by the anti-aircraft batteries defending the balloon.

Ball forced a two-seater to land near Nurlu during the afternoon and destroyed a Roland C.II. northeast of Bertincourt in the evening.

The pilots of 24 Squadron also had some success during the day. While flying a morning offensive patrol Lts Patrick A Langan-Byrne, W E Nixon, A E McKay and A G Knight attacked a hostile formation of 17 machines over Morval. Langan-Byrne shot one down in flames and Knight sent another down to crash near Flers. 2Lt M J J G Mare-Montembault of 32 Squadron was attacked by a Roland but he turned, got on its tail and shot it down in flames.

The *Jadgstaffeln* had been highly aggressive on the days leading up to the offensive, and on the first day of the battle mounted a spirited counterattack. There was a great deal of fiercely contested airfighting during the day and the RFC casualties were correspondingly heavy, with seven aircrew killed in action and eight wounded. It was a particularly bad day for 70 Squadron, which lost four of its Sopwith 1 1/2 Strutters in combat with Boelcke's *Jasta 2*. The Squadron had lost an aeroplane to Boelcke the previous day, September 14. Boelcke, flying a Fokker D.III, had shot down the 1 1/2 Strutter, which broke up in mid air, and shortly afterwards he forced 2Lt J V Bowring of 24 Squadron to land his damaged DH2. In the combat with 70 Squadron the next day, Boelcke, accompanied by Manfred von Richthofen, shot down one Sopwith to crash near Hesbécourt. He chased another back to the Lines and saw it crash five hundred metres behind the British front line trenches. The pilot was unhurt but the observer was killed in the crash. Although Boelcke claimed only two 70 Squadron Sopwith 1 1/2 Strutters from this fight, a third was lost and another badly shot up and forced to land on 15 Squadron's aerodrome. In the evening of the following day *Jasta 2* scored another victory when *Ltn* Höhne, flying one of the new Albatros D.IIs, which had arrived during the day, shot down an FE2b from 11 Squadron. Additional victories for the GAAS were a BE2c of 15 Squadron, forced to land near Albert with a dying observer; another BE2c, from 2 Squadron, shot down by a Fokker; and a Morane and three FE2bs were shot up and badly damaged. Worse was to follow.

By September 17 *Jasta 2* had six Albatros D.IIs on charge and in the afternoon, Boelcke, flying with von Richthofen and Reimann, attacked a formation of eight BE2cs from 12 Squadron escorted by FE2bs from 11 Squadron. Boelcke forced the leader of the FE2bs to land behind the German lines, where the crew set fire to their machine. *Ltn* Hans Reimann shot down another of the FEs, wounding the pilot and killing the observer with his fire. Manfred von Richthofen scored the first of his eighty victories by shooting down another FE from 11 Squadron, crewed by L B F Morris (pilot) and Tom Rees (obs). Morris, dying of his wounds, managed to land the FE on the German aerodrome at Flesquières. Richthofen, still excited by his first victory, made a bad landing nearby and watched as the dying pilot and dead observer were taken from their cockpit.

During the fight *Ltn* Frankl of *Jasta 4* had arrived, shooting down another of the FEs, and 2 BEs from 12 Squadron were also lost during the action to AA fire. A patrol from 60 Squadron finally appeared and helped the remaining FEs to disperse the German fighters.

Ltn Erwin Böhme of *Jasta 2* had shot down a Sopwith 1 1/2 Strutter of 70 Squadron flying a long reconnaissance earlier in the morning and the victories in the afternoon made it a good day for *Jasta 2*. During the day's fighting the RFC had again suffered heavy casualties, losing ten aeroplanes with 16 crew killed, wounded or prisoner of war.

The weather broke on September 18 and there was little flying, but in the early evening of the following day a reconnaissance by FE2bs of 11 Squadron, escorted by a mixed formation of Morane Bullets and Nieuports from 60 Squadron, was attacked by twenty enemy fighters over Bapaume. Some of the enemy machines were from *Jasta 2* and Boelcke shot down Capt H C 'Jimmy' Tower, flying one of the Moranes. Boelcke got on the Morane's tail over Achiet le Grand and shot one of its wings off. The Morane burst into flames and crashed in a wood near Grévillers.

Under the aggressive attack by the German fighters, the reconnaissance was abandoned. Three of the FEs were badly shot up, one force landing near Delville Wood with a wounded observer, where it was destroyed by shell fire, and a crew member of another was wounded. One of the Moranes, flown by Lt L S Weedon, was badly damaged by fire from a 'small biplane', which shot away the outer warp control wire on the port side of the Morane. As a consequence, Weedon could only make turns to starboard and when he landed back at base – a smooth landing luckily – it was found that his port wing was

so badly damaged that it could have broken off at any time. Two Fokkers were claimed as seen to crash during the fight, one as a result of a collision with a Morane.

The weather was bad for the next two days and there were only two casualties: a crew from 22 Squadron taken prisoner on the 20th and a pilot from 3 Squadron wounded in the arm. But the next allied attack was planned for the 25th of the month and it was necessary to register the enemy guns, photograph their positions and generally reconnoitre the area of the coming attack. The corps squadrons flew over three hundred hours over the enemy lines on September 22 and casualties were again heavy with six machines lost and nine crew members killed, wounded or prisoners of war. The *Jagdstaffeln* were again successful with *Ltn* Walter Höhne, *Ltn* Hans Reimann, and *Offstv.* Leopold Reimann from *Jasta 2* shooting down three BE12s from 19 Squadron, with Rudolf Berthold of *Jasta 4* claiming a BE12 from 21 Squadron, which he shot down in flames to crash in the forest of St.Pierre. In addition, two FE2bs from 18 Squadron were shot down by *Jasta 4;* an observer from 22 Squadron was killed; an FE. crew from 25 Squadron was taken prisoner and a Martinsyde of 27 Squadron was shot up and badly damaged.

The next day was little better. A formation of six Martinsydes of 27 Squadron flew a morning patrol to Cambrai and was attacked by the *Jagdstaffeln.. Jasta 2* added to its rapidly mounting victory score, Hans Reimann, Böhme and von Richthofen each shooting down a Martinsyde. After shooting down his opponent, Hans Reimann collided with another Martinsyde, flown by 2Lt L F Forbes, and crashed to his death. Forbes tried to land his damaged machine at 24 Squadron's aerodrome, but landing at a slower speed the Martinsyde became uncontrollable. Forbes hit a tree, crashed and was severely injured.

RFC.HQ. decided that something had to be done about its continued losses to the determined pilots of the *Jagdstaffeln* and in the afternoon of September 24 a special offensive sweep was flown to attack the aerodromes of the *Jagdstaffeln* around Cambrai. Sixty machines took part in the attack, including five BE12s from 19 Squadron, six Martinsydes from 27 Squadron and six FEs from 22 Squadron. Two of the BE12s were shot down by *Ltn* Kurt Wintgens of *Jasta 1* – aided in one instance by a two-seater crew from *FeldFliegerAbteilung 22* – and a Martinsyde from 27 Squadron was shot down and its pilot captured. One of the FE crews claimed a Roland out of control over Bertincourt.

In view of the rough handling the BE12 had so far received at the hands of the German fighter pilots, it seems the height of folly to have sent them into the very heart of the enemy fighter concentration. After the events of September 24, Trenchard at last realised the unsuitability of the type as a fighter and withdrew them from that duty: 'I have lost a very large number of them,' he wrote, 'and I am afraid that we are losing more of these machines than we can afford in pilots and certainly more, I am afraid, than they bring down. Although I am short of machines to do the work that is now necessary with the large number of Germans against us, I can do nothing else but to request that no more be sent out to this country.' Trenchard's solution to this problem of supply could hardly have endeared him to the unfortunate pilots of the squadrons flying the BE12: they were switched to a bombing role.

Monday September 25 was a bright, cloudless day, but again there was a ground mist. The British infantry were to attack towards Gueudecourt, curving round to the north of Flers. The *Jagdstaffeln* were out in force but made little attempt to interfere with the corps aeroplanes. Forty Squadron's FE8s flew an escort for the FE2bs of 25 Squadron which were to bomb enemy aerodromes in preparation for a later raid by seven BE2cs of 16 Squadron on the railway station at Libercourt, also to be escorted by 40 Squadron. During the attacks on the aerodromes only one German fighter managed to get into the air and this was ineffective. Casualties were light during the day with only two men wounded – one slightly – and an observer of a BE2c dying of his injuries after his machine had been forced to land. One of 40 Squadron's FE8s had its propeller shot off by AA fire, was also forced to land and was wrecked.

The pilots of the *Jagdstaffeln* were strangely inactive on the 25th and 26th of the month, but on September 27 *Jasta 2* attacked the Martinsydes of 27 Squadron, claiming two: Boelcke shot down one, which crashed near Ervillers, then attacked another. After firing into this Martinsyde, Boelcke observed that it no longer attempted to evade his fire, but continued to circle. He flew closer and saw that the pilot was dead. Boelcke noted the number of the Martinsyde – 7495 – and when he landed he claimed it as his second victory of the action. However, Boelcke found that one of his young pilots, *Offstv* Leopold Reimann had fired at the Martinsyde and had also claimed it. Boelcke had the victory awarded to Reimann.

Conditions on the September 28 were hazy, the weather was again deteriorating, but the day was noteworthy for the first victory to be scored by an RFC Spad 7 when Captain Leslie Foot shot down an Albatros from a formation of four over Avesnes-les-Bapaume.

There was no war flying on September 29, but the last day of the month was fine and warm and 12 and 13 Squadrons, escorted by Morane Bullets and Nieuports from 60 Squadron and the FEs of 11 Squadron, bombed Lagnicourt, the home of *Jasta 2*. The attackers were met by nine enemy fighters and von Richthofen shot down one of the FEs of the escort for his third victory. Another of the escort FEs was badly shot about

and forced to land; a Morane from 60 Squadron was badly damaged and also forced to land, and a pilot of a DH2 from 24 Squadron, who had wandered into the fight, was wounded. On the credit side for the RFC, Ball and the crew of one of the FEs shared an Albatros C Type destroyed, and Ball claimed two 'Rolands', one of which was *Ltn.d.R*. Ernst Diener of *Jasta 2*, who was killed.

During September the full impact of the *Jagdstaffeln* had made itself felt and there had been a dramatic increase in the casualties suffered by the squadrons of the RFC. It had clung doggedly to its command of the air, but the Moranes and pusher aeroplanes were now completely outclassed by the new Albatros fighters, and although the Nieuport could hold its own in manoeuvrability, it carried only one gun – as did the pusher aeroplanes – against the two carried by the German fighters. The pendulum of air superiority had now begun to swing back in favour of the GAAS, and after only two years of war the importance of that superiority had become only too apparent

Trenchard wrote to Haig on 30 September advising him of the position. Haig reported to the War Office that an immediate increase in fighter squadrons would be needed to contain the new *Jagdstaffeln*, 'the enemy has made extraordinary efforts to increase the number and develop the speed and power of his fighting machines. He has unfortunately succeeded in doing so … it is necessary to realise clearly, and at once, that we shall undoubtedly lose our superiority in the air if I am not provided at an early date with improved means of retaining it.' Haig also pointed out the technical inferiority of the RFC's fighter aeroplanes, comparing all but the FE2b, the Nieuport and the Sopwith Pup unfavourably with the new German fighters equipping the Jagdstaffeln – 'all other fighting machines at my disposal are decidedly inferior.'

The *Luftstreitkräfte*

Weather conditions were bad throughout most of October 1916. This hiatus in the ground war allowed the German armies to regroup, and the GAAS was reorganised on 8 October into the formal establishment of the *Luftstreitkräfte* under the command of *Generalleutnant* von Hoeppner as *Kommandierenden General der Luftstreikräfte (Kogenluft)* The *Kogenluft* was to be responsible to the Chief of the general staff of all the German armies in the field and for the operations of the German air service, both at the front and for training units in Germany. This reorganisation involved the renaming of the *Feldflieger Abteilungen* as *Flieger Abteilungen,* some being designated *Artillerie Flieger Abteilungen.* Thirty *Schutzstaffeln* were formed, and thirty *Jagdstaffeln* were planned, each with a complement of 16 fighters.

Each of these units had clearly defined roles: the *FL.Abt.* were to carry out long range reconnaissance; the *Fl.Abt (A)*

worked in close co-operation with the infantry and artillery; the *Schusta* were to provide escorts to the *Fl.Abt.(A)* and undertake short range reconnaissance as required; and the *Jagdstaffeln* were concerned exclusively with aerial fighting: to find, engage and destroy the enemy observation machines and fighters.

The *Jagdstaffeln* continued to inflict heavy casualties on the RFC throughout the remainder of the month, *Jasta 2* alone claiming another 25 victories.[1] On October 22 they fought an action with the newly-arrived 45 Squadron, equipped with Sopwith 1 1/2 Strutters. In a fight over the Bapaume-Péronne area, 45 Squadron lost three crews killed in action to Boelcke, Böhme and Reimann, plus another aeroplane forced to land with a wounded observer. In addition to the continued successes of *Jasta 2*, the other *Jasta 1, 4, 5* and *8* also began to score more frequently.

Between October 20 and 22 nearly 200 combats were fought and although the RFC squadrons met with some success, claiming over 50 aeroplanes destroyed, sent down out of control or forced to land during the fighting, casualties were heavy with 17 aeroplanes lost or damaged and 31 aircrew killed or wounded. On October 23, Trenchard reinforced the RFC squadrons on the Somme: three corps squadrons were moved into the area and two fighter squadrons. 29 Squadron flew down to Izel-le-Hameau and 32 Squadron moved to Léalvillers on October 25.

On October 17, as additional reinforcement to the hard-pressed RFC squadrons on the Somme, the War office had requested that the Royal Naval Air Service should form a new squadron from its forces at Dunkirk. This squadron, under the command of Squadron Commander G R Bromet, and designated Naval 8, was based at Vert Galant and the first of its aeroplanes arrived on October 26, a mixed complement of Nieuports and Sopwiths: six two-seater Sopwith 1 1/2 Strutters, six Nieuport 17s and six Sopwith Pups. The Sopwith Pup, a highly manoeuvrable rotary-engined single-seater fighter, had up to this time been used exclusively by the RNAS and had scored some initial successes with 1 (Naval) Wing since its issue in early September. The initial six Pups with Naval 8 came from 1 (Naval) Wing; additional Pups would arrive by 16 November to replace the Sopwith 1 1/2 Strutters and more to replace the Nieuports by the end of the year. From April until the end of 1916 naval fighter pilots would claim 22 victories over enemy aircraft.

Two additional squadrons also came out from England during October. Forty-one Squadron had arrived on October 15 and 46 Squadron on October 20. Equipped with the FE8, a type already virtually obsolete, 41 Squadron, under the command of Major J A H Landon, flew into Abeele aerodrome

on October 21 to commence operational flying under the orders of 11th Wing, II Brigade. 46 Squadron, commanded by Major P Babington, and equipped with Nieuport 20 two-seaters, was based at Droglandt with 2nd Wing.

On October 25 *Jasta 2* continued its successful month, shooting down three BEs. The first, a BE12 from 21 Squadron, fell to von Richthofen for his sixth victory; the second, a BE2c from 4 Squadron, to his *Jasta* companion *Ltn* Walter Höne. The third, a BE2d from 7 Squadron, was shot down in flames by Boelcke for his 39th victory.

The morning of October 26 saw the first of the two large air battles that took place during the day. At 7.25am, near Bapaume, five DH2s of 24 Squadron fought nearly 20 enemy fighters, most of them Halberstadts. The 24 Squadron pilots found that although the Halberstadts were faster, with a better climb, they lost height in turns. Making full use of this the British pilots managed to continue the fight without loss until half of the enemy fighters had withdrawn. The fighting was fiercely contested with no positive result for either side. Finally, running low on fuel, the DH2s turned for base but were impeded by the strong westerly wind. The remaining German pilots pressed home their attacks but met with no success and the DH2s returned to their aerodrome at Bertangles with only one pilot slightly wounded.

In the afternoon a second fight showed a more positive result for the German fighter pilots. Eight Albatros D.IIs of *Jasta 2*, led by Boelcke, attacked four BE2cs engaged in artillery co-operation, Boelcke shooting down one from 5 Squadron and *Oblt* Stefan Kirmaier another from 7 Squadron. Kirmaier then tackled a BE2c – reported to be armoured – from 15 Squadron and shot this down. Capt. Leslie Foot of 60 Squadron, flying a Nieuport 16, saw the fight in progress and dived to the assistance of one of the BEs under attack by an Albatros flown by Hans Imelmann. Foot got in one burst at the Albatros, but Imelmann turned to meet the threat, got above the Nieuport, and an accurate burst hit the wing mounting of Foot's Lewis gun., putting it out of action. Foot endeavoured to out turn the German fighter but Imelmann got on the Nieuport's tail, staying there despite all Foot's efforts to shake him off. As a last resort, Foot dived almost to ground level, but Imelmann followed him down and another burst set fire to the Nieuport's petrol tank. Luckily, by this time Foot was very low and the Nieuport crashed almost at once, burning itself out. Foot escaped without injury.

A patrol of DH2s from 32 Squadron had also seen the action with the BEs and came to their aid, shooting down one of the enemy fighters, which crashed in the German Lines, close to the wreckage of one of the BEs.

The Master Falls

At the height of these continued successes, the *Luftstreitkräfte* suffered a severe blow. On October 28 Lts Knight and McKay of 24 Squadron were flying a defensive patrol over the Pozières-Bapaume area at 8,000ft, McKay, who had been delayed earlier with engine trouble, flying 1,500ft below Knight. Six enemy fighters were seen at 10,000ft over Pozières, but they hesitated five minutes before attacking the DH2s, one Albatros diving under Knight, presumably to attack McKay, while the others dived on Knight. During the fight the six enemy fighters were reinforced by a further six, some of which went down to attack McKay. By this time those pilots flying the DH2 had learnt that their best tactic in fighting the higher performance Albatros D.II was to keep turning and rely on their superior manoeuvrability to avoid being shot down. The Albatros pilots dived in turn under the tails of the DH2s, before climbing back for another pass, but the British pilots resisted the temptation to dive after each opponent and kept turning, firing short bursts at any enemy fighter which came into their sights. These tactics were effectual and the DH2s held their own against the heavy odds. After five minutes of strenuous fighting two of the German fighters were seen to collide. One had dived at Knight, who had turned hard to the left to evade the attack. The Albatros zoomed to the right and collided with another, which was also diving on Knight. 'Bits were seen to fall off; only one EA was seen to go down, and it glided away east, apparently under control, but was very shortly lost to sight as the DHs were too heavily engaged to watch it.'

The fight continued for another fifteen minutes, the enemy fighters driving the two DH2s down to 5,000ft over Bapaume before breaking off the action and flying east. Knight and McKay returned to Bertangles.

The two Albatros that had collided were flown by Oswald Boelcke and Erwin Böhme, Böhme's undercarriage striking Boelcke's left top wing. Boelcke began to glide down, but there were clouds at lower level and in the increased turbulence the damaged Albatros became uncontrollable and Boelcke crashed near a German gun battery and was killed. Böhme attempted to land nearby but the area was full of shell holes and broken ground and he flew back to Lagnicourt and landed, turning his Albatros over. Böhme was so distracted by the loss of his friend and his part in the collision, that he was unaware that he had crashed and went with the other pilots in a car to the scene of Boelcke's crash. Böhme later wrote that he felt that Boelcke would have survived the crash if he had been wearing a crash helmet and had been firmly strapped in, as the actual impact had not been very great. On October 31 Böhme wrote to his girlfriend: 'now everything is empty for us. Only gradually are we beginning to realise the void Boelcke leaves behind, that without him the soul of the whole squadron

is lacking. In every relation he was our unparalleled leader and master.'

Boelcke, a brave and chivalrous man, much admired and respected in the RFC, was the leading fighter pilot of the *Luftstreitkräfte* at the time of his death, with forty victories. As an innovator and teacher of fighter tactics his death came at an inopportune time for the emerging *Jagdstaffeln*. But the tradition was well founded and in capable hands. In less than six months from Boelcke's death, one of his pupils, Manfred von Richthofen, had equalled his master's score.

Between October 22 and 31, a period that included five days when no flying was possible because of the bad weather, the RFC lost 18 aeroplanes. Twenty-four aircrew had been killed, six wounded and six taken prisoner. The fighter squadrons of the RFC, hard pressed and fighting with inferior aeroplanes, were failing in their task of protecting the corps aeroplanes. The offensive patrols of the fighter squadrons, flown in attempts to contain the *Jagdstaffeln,* had cost heavily in losses with little of the desired result: the two-seater squadrons had casualties of almost 40% and almost 90% of all casualties had been caused by the *Jagdstaffeln*.

November 1916 opened with a day of high winds, low clouds and rain. The coming winter was to be the worst suffered by Europe for many years. There was some airfighting in the first four days of the month, the BE squadrons losing four aeroplanes with four crew killed and three wounded; 22 Squadron lost three FEs, with two pilots killed, one wounded and captured, and two observers taken prisoner, wounded or injured. An FE of 18 Squadron was also shot down and its crew killed by von Richthofen for his seventh victory, his *Jasta* comrade, Hans Imelmann, shooting down a Nieuport of 60 Squadron for his fourth.

Although a BE was lost to AA fire on November 5, there was no flying of any significance until November 9, when weather conditions improved sufficiently to allow a bombing raid to be flown to the German ammunition dump at Vraucourt by the BEs of 12 and 13 Squadrons, escorted by 11, 29 and 60 Squadrons.

Soon after crossing the Front Lines at 9.00am. a large force of enemy fighters attacked the British formation, intensifying its efforts as the bombers and their escorts approached the target area. The German tactics were effective, breaking up the British formation, and 12 Squadron lost two of its BEs to *Jasta 2*. Eleven Squadron lost one of its FEs on the German side, its pilot wounded and his corporal observer killed, and the observer in another was wounded. Of the escort, 29 Squadron lost two of its DH2s: one to *Jasta 1* and another to *Jasta 4*.

Another patrol from 29 Squadron, for some reason not involved in the escort, had left Izel-le-Hameau at 7.30am and included James McCudden. The three DH2s had just flown over Achiet-le-Grand when McCudden saw six enemy fighters in the distance. He pointed these out to Noakes, who was leading the Flight, and being a long way east of the Lines the DH2s retreated westwards, with the German fighters in pursuit, finally catching them before they reaching the safety of the British Front Line. It was James McCudden's first sight of the new Albatros D.II.

'One Hun came down at me nose on but then turned away, and in doing so I got a good view of a Hun which I had never seen before. It had a fuselage like the belly of a fish. Its wings were cut fairly square at the tips, and had no dihedral angle. The tailplane was of the shape of a spade.'

The three DH2s – McCudden, Noakes and Lt. Ball (no relation to Albert Ball) – were in the middle of the six enemy fighters and, as McCudden later wrote, 'were having rather a bad time of it, for we were a long way east of the Line, so we all knew that we had to fight hard or go down.' McCudden wrote that the Albatros pilots operated very well, their main tactic being the same as the Albatros formation that had fought with Knight and McKay on October 29: one to dive from the front and then turn away, inviting its opponent to follow, then flying straight to give one of its *Jasta* comrades the chance of a shot. But the DH2s stuck together and because of their manoeuvrability and the skill of their pilots – Ball is an unknown quantity, but Noakes and McCudden were both superb pilots – fought their way back to the Lines. By this time McCudden had used all his ammunition and had to 'chase around after Huns without firing at them.' As the DH2s reached the Front Line, the German pilots broke off the action and flew east.

As the enemy machines withdrew, McCudden had time to inspect his machine. It was badly damaged. 'My tailplane was a mass of torn fabric, and various wires were hanging, cut by bullets.'

After he had landed McCudden 'had a good look round my machine and found that the Huns had scored twenty-four hits. This was the greatest number I have ever had. I do not believe in being shot about. It is bad or careless flying to allow one's self to be shot about when one ought usually to be able to prevent it by properly timed manoeuvres.' McCudden was perhaps being unduly harsh with his self-criticism, considering that he had fought against aeroplanes of superior performance, armed with twin guns to his single Lewis gun.

In addition to the two DH2s lost on the morning's escort duty, 29 Squadron lost two others from a patrol that had taken off at 11.30am. Luckily none of the casualties was fatal: three pilots were wounded and taken prisoner, and 2Lt N Brearley, who was wounded in the lung and crashed in No Man's Land, lay in a shell hole until dark before crawling back to the British trenches.

Despite the fact that only fifteen days saw any flying during the month, losses had begun to escalate in those squadrons flying the DH2 and FE8 pushers. Both were now hopelessly outclassed by the new German fighters; heavily armed and with their superior speed they could, and did, exploit the tactical advantages of being either to initiate or evade a combat and, importantly, when to withdraw.

On November 23 Major Lanoe Hawker VC., DSO., was shot down and killed by Manfred von Richthofen for his eleventh victory. Hawker, flying the more manoeuvrable but slower aeroplane, fought superbly, with all his great skill, but his engine began to run badly and he was finally forced to break off the action and dive for the safety of the British Lines. Richthofen followed, firing burst after burst at the fleeing DH2 and Hawker fell, shot through the head, only 150 ft above the ground and a few hundred yards from safety.

Hawker's death was as great a blow to the RFC as Boelcke's had been to the *Luftstreitkräfte*. Both were teachers, innovators of fighter tactics, and superb and charismatic leaders.

The last battles of the Somme had opened on 18 November, but a thaw had turned the ground into a sea of mud and the attacks died out in the atrocious weather conditions, snow and blizzards finally bringing the fighting to a halt. So ended 'the greatest continual battle which the world had yet seen'.[2]

From November 28 to December 4 there was no war flying, fog keeping the aeroplanes of the combatants on the ground. Operations recommenced on December 4 but the weather clamped down again the following day. Only limited flying was possible until December 11, when a BE was lost by 10 Squadron; 32 Squadron lost a DH2 to Richthofen for his twelfth victory, and 60 Squadron's Capt E O Grenfell was wounded in action and forced to land his Nieuport 17 near Arras. There was then little flying until December 20, when Richthofen, Hans Imelmann and *Ltn.* Wortmann of *Jasta 2* shot down three FEs from 18 Squadron, two of the crews being killed and the other captured. The FE claimed by Richthofen was his fourteenth victory. The next day *Ltn* Werner Voss of *Jasta 2* shot down a BE from 7 Squadron for the third of his eventual 48 victories.

General Winter

As winter set in over the Western Front, airfighting gradually died down, flaring only spasmodically when the weather permitted. A brief improvement in conditions on December 24 enabled the corps squadrons to resume work, and although there was no flying on Christmas day. Boxing Day, December 26, saw a number of fiercely fought combats with seven losses going to the *Jagdstaffeln*. There were 21 combats fought the next day. In the early afternoon a patrol of six DH2s of 29 Squadron were on patrol from Arras to Monchy. Three of the DH2s returned with engine trouble leaving Capt J D Payne, McCudden, and Lt Jennings. At 3.00pm McCudden saw several enemy scouts leaving their aerodrome at Croisilles. These climbed quickly to the height of the three DH2s and Payne attacked the nearest. Another of the Albatri then fastened onto Payne's tail, but this was driven off by Jennings, who in turn came under the fire of two more. McCudden could see that Jennings was 'having a bad time', and went to his aid, firing at one of Jennings' attackers that was flying black and white streamers. The Albatros immediately turned to face McCudden, coming at the DH2 'nose on'. Albatros and DH2 were firing simultaneously as they closed the distance, but McCudden's Lewis gun stopped with a bad double feed. Now in the middle of the Albatri, McCudden half-rolled and dived away for several hundred feet, but as he pulled out of his dive he was attacked again, 'by my old friend with the black and white streamers.' McCudden spun and dived several times, making for the safety of the British lines, but the enemy pilot drove him down to 800 feet, only leaving him when his Albatros came under fire from British anti-aircraft guns. McCudden rectified his stoppage and followed the Albatros back across the trenches but the enemy pilot outclimbed the DH2 and rejoined his *Jasta* companions at 5,000 feet over Ronsart. McCudden returned to Le Hameau. On landing, his return was greeted with some surprise by his fellow pilots who had been sure he had been shot down. Manfred von Richthofen claimed his fifteenth victory on 27 December, a FE two-seater south of Arras. There were no losses of FE2bs which fit the time and place of Richthofen's claim and it has recently been suggested that his 'victory' was McCudden. Although there is some merit to this theory – Richthofen and McCudden's account of their combats have similarities, and time and location fit – Richthofen claimed a 'Vickers' two-seater. Although the FE2b and DH2 were both pusher aeroplanes of the same configuration, it is hard to understand why Richthofen would have confused the two types during the fairly extended combat, the single seat DH2 being considerably smaller than the two-seat FE2b.

From December 29 until the end of the year the weather effectively stopped nearly all flying.

Despite the emergence of the *Jagdstaffeln* – there were 25 in existence by the end of 1916 – the RFC had managed to cling tenaciously to the command of the air, but it had not been without heavy cost. Between July 1, at the beginning of

the Somme battles, until they ended on November 18, the RFC had lost 308 pilots and 109 observers, killed, wounded or missing, and over 800 aeroplanes had been struck off strength. The number of squadrons had been increased from 27 on July 1 to 38 by the end of the year. The RFC now had eight single-seater fighter squadrons plus the services of Naval 8, but of these eight squadrons, five – Nos. 24, 29, 32 and 41 – were still equipped with the obsolete DH2 and FE8 pushers, and only two squadrons, 60 Squadron with its Nieuport 17s, and Naval 8 with its Sopwith Pups, were effective against the Albatros D.IIs and Halberstdt D series which now equipped the *Jagdstaffeln*.[3] These German fighters, although lacking the overall manoeuvrability of the Pup and Nieuport 17, were both better armed and, importantly, faster at operational height. This gave the German fighter pilots the distinct advantage of being able to both initiate a combat and terminate it, an advantage ideally suited to the defensive policy pursued by the *Luftstreitkräfte*. This was to have disastrous consequences for the RFC in the opening months and spring of 1917.

But these trials still lay in the future. In the winter of 1916 the weary and battle-worn pilots and observers blessed the inclement weather, grateful for the rest from the gruelling round of daily offensive patrols, escort duties and reconnaissance. They had fought hard and well. In the words of the official historian: 'They were not a melancholy company. Fighting to them was sport, a grim one, but still a sport, and they relived their adventures in the Mess with a zest that borrowed something from the playing field dressing room. They did not belittle their risks. Rather they accepted them as a price to be paid for the joy of the new life that was theirs. They met in the air an enemy who lived under similar conditions, and their combats were clean rapid contests in which brain and artistry were exalted above mere muscle. Many of the squadrons had suffered grievous losses, but they came from the battle strong in the knowledge that they had been called upon to play a big part and they had not failed.'

It is doubtful if the pilots and observers would have subscribed wholeheartedly, if at all, to the post-war rhetoric of the official historian. They had all seen men – friends – fall to their death in blazing and broken aeroplanes; had helped to take others from bloodstained and shattered cockpits. If the naïve conception of airfighting as a sport – albeit a dangerous one – still lingered faintly at the end of 1916, the coming year was to see the end of that misconception. In 1917 the war in the air was to develop into a long, bloody and protracted struggle.

NOTES

1. On October 16 Boelcke shot down Lt. Patrick Langan-Byrne of 24 Squadron for his 34th victory. Langan-Byrne had scored ten victories with 24 Squadron, had been awarded the DSO and was 24 Squadron's B Flight Commander. Hawker later wrote: 'I haven't recovered from the blow of losing him, he was such a nice lad as well as the best officer I have ever met.'

2. *The War in The Air,* Raleigh and Jones. Oxford University Press.

3. 54 Squadron, equipped with Sopwith Pups, had arrived in France on December 25 but was not yet operational. Nineteen Squadron had six Spad V11s on charge in December but would not be up to full strength until February 1917.

CHAPTER SEVEN

A NEW YEAR - A TERM OF TRIAL

From the lessons of the Somme battles in 1916 it had become obvious that control of the air above the battlefield was prerequisite in both strategic and tactical planning. Prior to his letter to the War Office in September 1916, Haig had written the previous June, asserting – on advice from Trenchard – that the number of RFC squadrons in France should number 56 by the spring of 1917. This estimate of the BEF's needs had been met with some alarm in Whitehall, an alarm exacerbated in November 1916 when Haig had written again, augmenting his requirements by an additional twenty fighter squadrons, no doubt due to the deprecations of the new German *Jagdstaffeln*. On 12 December 1916 the Army Council had formally approved the expansion of the RFC to 106 active squadrons, plus a further 95 in reserve. A few days later two night flying squadrons were added. The importance of protecting the aeroplanes of the corps squadrons in their vital tasks of reconnaissance and artillery spotting was reflected in the proportion of two fighter squadrons to every corps squadron.

Despite these promised reinforcements, Haig wrote again in January 1917. Bearing in mind the curtailment of flying during the winter months, neither he nor Trenchard envisaged losing control of the air during the first months of 1917, but Haig warned that even with the promised replacements the RFC would still have insufficient men and machines to support a spring offensive; that it would have lost control of the air by April. Despite these warnings the RFC was still seriously under strength at the beginning of 1917.

The first three days of the New Year saw little aerial activity – the weather was bad, with gale force winds – but on January 4 Naval 8 were in action in the afternoon. FltCom C R Mackenzie leading FltSubLts E R Grange, A S Todd, J C Croft and R A Little attacked seven Albatros scouts of *Jasta* Boelcke near Bapaume.[1] Grange led the attack followed by Little. During the fighting Little saw Todd being attacked by three of the Albatros and went to his assistance, but the left wings of Todd's Sopwith Pup broke away and the Pup went down. The Albatros pilots broke off the action and dived away. Little went down to view Todd's crash, which was surrounded by troops. Allan Todd, a Canadian – at 30 years of age rather old for a fighter pilot – was Manfred von Richthofen's 16th victory. Croft had also been shot down and taken prisoner.[2] These were von Richthofen's first encounters with the Sopwith Pup and he commented in his combat report that 'the enemy plane was superior to ours.' The following day the DH2s of 24 Squadron were in fierce combat with eight enemy scouts and Lt. W James was wounded in the thigh. He landed his DH2 behind the British lines at Le Forest and was taken to hospital.

Naval 8 and 32 Squadron were in action on January 7. R A Little of Naval 8 went to the assistance of a BE2 that was being attacked by a German scout over Grevillers. Little fired sixty rounds into the hostile aeroplane and it turned over on its back and fell out of control. Albatros scouts from *Jasta B* were in the area and FltSubLt A Lawson of 8 Naval was wounded in combat; his Pup badly shot about. A morning patrol from 32 Squadron was also in this action and 2Lt E Wagner was shot down and killed by *Ltn* Erwin Böhme of *Jasta B* for his ninth victory. The weather now clamped down, with snow, freezing conditions and high winds. On the January 8, taking off from 29 Squadron's aerodrome at Le Hameau, the DH2 of 2Lt. A N Benge was blown over by the strong winds. The DH2 was a write off but Benge was unhurt.

The weather now progressively deteriorated, with frequent snow showers and high winds; by the 14th of the month flying was impossible. On January 21 weather conditions were better but hazy, which precluded the pilots of 60 Squadron flying patrols. Most of the pilots were taking the day off in Amiens but a few were making practice flights in the vicinity of their aerodrome at Le Hameau. To their astonishment a German Rumpler suddenly appeared out of the mist and landed on the field. The Rumpler was from *KG4/KS24* and the crew had become lost. *Oblt* Schumacher, the observer, had earlier ordered his pilot, *Vzfw* Thurau, to land so that he could attempt to asertain their position. Unfortunately they were at Tinques, behind the British lines, and Schumacher was taken prisoner. Thurau hastily took off again, but still lost, landed at Le Hameau. Realising his mistake, and possibly fed up with the whole situation, he set fire to the Rumpler and was taken prisoner. He and his officer were later reunited at Le Hameau, Schumacher soundly remonstrating with his pilot on becoming lost. Schumacher was given tea in the 60 Squadron Officers' Mess, with Thurau being entertained by the 60 Squadron sergeants. Active war flying began again on January 23, although the snow was thick on the ground and it was still extremely cold – 12 degrees of frost – with a biting east wind. A patrol from 40 Squadron left the ground after lunch. Almost at the end of their patrol time, just to the west of Lens, Lt E Benbow saw eight enemy aeroplanes 2,000 feet below the FE8s. Benbow dived to attack these but his gun jammed and he was attacked by a red Albatros. Benbow dived and managed to shake off his attacker. During the action Manfred von Richthofen had attacked the FE8 flown by Lt John Hay. Hay had that morning shot down an Albatros two-seater for his third victory, but Richthofen quickly gained a favourable position and shot the FE8 down in flames for his seventeenth victory, Hay jumping from his blazing aeroplane. It was Richthofen's first victory while flying a newly issued Albatros D III. Forty-One Squadron also lost a pilot killed, near Boesinghe: 2Lt S F Cody, shot down by *Ltn*. Walter von Bülow-Bothkamp of *Jasta 18* for his sixth victory. However, not all went the way of the *Jasta* pilots. The Corps squadrons also had their share of successes. *Ltn* von Bülow was forced to land by Williams and Spenser of 45 Squadron and *Jasta B* lost two pilots in the afternoon in the vicinity of Miraumont: Lt E Pashley of 24 Squadron went to the aid of a BE which was being attacked by an Albatros flown by *Vzfw* Ostrop. Either under Pashley's fire, or due to structural failure, the wings of Ostrop's Albatros D.III broke away and he was killed. At the same time, *Ltn* Hans Imelmann, one of the early *KEK* Fokker pilots, who had been personally picked by Boelcke for his new *Jasta,* and who had scored six victories since the previous October, was attacking a BE crewed by Captain McMillan and Lt. Hopkins of 4 Squadron. Well-placed shots by Hopkins hit Imelmann's machine in the petrol tank and it burst into flames. Imelmann was killed.

Twenty-nine Squadron were also in action during the day. In the morning Capt Hill led his flight down to attack a German two-seater over Monchy-le Preux, but a formation of German scouts intervened and the DH2 pilots had to fight their way out. McCudden was firing at an Albatros when he was attacked by a 'Fokker biplane' passing just in front of him and slightly above. McCudden pulled his Lewis gun up and fired at the Fokker, but there was a sudden vibration and noise. Some of his spent cartridges had fallen into his propeller, breaking the blades. McCudden immediately switched off his engine and dived for the safety of the British lines. The enemy scout followed the DH2 down but broke off his pursuit at 2,000 feet and cleared east. McCudden landed in a field behind Arras, walked to an artillery battery nearby and telephoned his squadron for a replacement propeller. McCudden was in action again in the afternoon, attacking a two-seater south of Arras. He fired a whole drum of Lewis at the enemy machine but as he turned away to replace the drum the two-seater dived steeply east and made its escape. Forty-One Squadron lost a sergeant pilot on January 24. C S Tooms was shot down west of Wytschaete during the afternoon by *Vzfw* Ulmer of *Jasta 8.* 2Lt A Denison of the squadron was also in action and was forced to land, wounded in the arm. It was also a bad day for Naval 8. The commander of A Flight, C R Mackenzie was shot down by *Ltn* Hans von Keudell of *Jasta 1* for his eleventh victory. Mackenzie was seen flying over the German lines, dead in cockpit of his Sopwith Pup (N5198). He crashed fatally and was buried with full military honours. 'So passed a born leader and a brave man.'

The day had not been without its successes however. Capt H Wood and Lt E McKay of 24 Squadron attacked a two-seater over Fins. The enemy machine turned towards the British Lines and landed. The German pilot held off the approaching troops with his revolver until his observer had set fire to their machine. *Ltn* Ernst Bury and *Uffz* Max Delklock were taken POW. Their machine was designated G9.

On 25 January there was a good deal of fighting. Lt H Pell of 40 Squadron attacked a machine from *Fl.Abt (A)235* over Lens. Pell wounded the pilot, *Vzfw* Adolf Niess, forcing him to land. At 10.30am, on patrol at 16,000ft over Clery sur Somme, Capt A Lees of 54 Squadron claimed an Albatros D.111 and twenty minutes later drove down a hostile two-seater. At 10.30am, northeast of Moislains, *Flgmt* Gustav Kinkel of *Jasta B* was shot down and taken POW by Lt McKay of 24 Squadron. Kinkel's Albatros, D.111.No.1982/16, was evaluated by the British and numbered G5.

After lunch a patrol from 24 Squadron led by Capt Long attacked an LVG of *Fl Abt (A)216.* Long shot the LVG down in flames, the pilot, *Ltn d Res* Ewald Erdmann and the observer, *Ltn d Res* Günter Kallenbach both jumping to their deaths.

The DH2s of 29 Squadron were on patrol on the morning of 26 January when they sighted a German two-seater, very low, flying north from Adinfer Wood. McCudden opened fire from 200 yards, closing to 100 yards to finish his Lewis gun drum. The two-seater rolled over on its right wing tip and went down in a side-slipping dive through a layer of mist, 300ft above the ground. Because of the mist it was impossible to see the enemy crash. McCudden was credited only with an out of control, but he felt that because of the low height, 'he undoubtedly must have crashed.' It was McCudden's second victory.

The pilots of the DH2 squadrons continued their successes on January 27. Capt S Long of 24 Squadron attacked a hostile two seater from *Fl Abt(A)233* and shot it down over Morval, killing *Ltn* Brandt and *Vzfw* Lang. A patrol from 32 Squadron attacked two enemy machines near Ervillers and shot one down to crash near St.Leger. The Sopwith Pups of 54 Squadron were also in action. Lt F Hudson shot down a machine from *FlAbt (A)239* crewed by *Vzfw* Erich Blume and Kurt Wöhler, which fell in No Man's Land near Courcelette.

The fighter squadrons suffered only one combat casualty on January 28: 2Lt A Barker of 41 Squadron who was wounded. The weather was again extremely windy and there was little flying. The next day, January 29, saw a combat between 12 Halberstadts and five FE2bs of 25 Squadron, which were escorted by three FE8s from 40 Squadron. In the fierce fight Lt A V Blenkiron of 25 Squadron was wounded in the thigh but stood up, fired at one of the German machines, and sent it down out of control, trailing smoke and flames. Three more Halberstadts were driven down and the remaining German pilots broke off the action.

During the day a patrol from 60 Squadron fought a combat with Albatri from *Jasta 11*. Capt. 'Duke' Meintjes, Lt Keith Caldwell – known throughout the RFC as 'Grid' because of his allusion to all aeroplanes as 'Grids'– and Lt William Fry were a few miles behind the German lines, just east of Gommecourt, flying at 13,000ft. Conditions were perfect. The Nieuports were in a sunlit, bright blue sky, large cumulus clouds below them. Suddenly, Meintjes saw eight Albatros scouts a few hundred feet below, the bright colours of the enemy scouts – 'all the colours of the rainbow and led by a blood-red plane'– showing up vividly against the snow-white cloud, their black crosses 'startlingly clear.' Meintjes manoeuvred into a favourable position with the sun at his back, then dived to attack the Albatri. The three British pilots were unaware that they were attacking the experienced pilots of *Jasta 11* flying their new Albatros D IIIs.

In his autobiography,[3] Fry recalled that he had no time to feel fear as he followed Meintjes and Caldwell into the fight. 'All was chaos for a few seconds. Meintj shot one down in our first attack.[4] I think we surprised them by coming round the side of a cloud.' Fry escaped with only a few bullet holes through his machine, 'after seeming to have an Albatros on my tail shooting at me every time I looked round.' Caldwell was attacked by several of the Albatri, his machine riddled with bullets, and he was lucky to make a forced landing behind his own Lines. Fry was of the opinion that they were fortunate to have escaped as lightly as they did. 'The speed and tempo of the fight was something none of us had experienced before and it was a foretaste of what air fighting was going to be like in the future.' Nearly fifty years later, writing from his native New Zealand, 'Grid' Caldwell recalled the fight.

'We were a happy gang with old Meintj as leader. I remember a pretty hectic little do, Meintjes, you and I had early in '17 when we changed a line patrol into an offensive patrol and ran into 8 good Hun Albatri led by a red fellow which could well have been our friend Richthofen. Meintj shot one down, I was chased home with a riddled Nieuport and you survived too. I remember the CO seemed happy about it and gave us his Crossley car and a day off.'

Fry's combat report gives a more detailed picture.

'While on an OP with Captain Meintjes and Lieut Caldwell we met a formation of 8 Albatros scouts east of Gommecourt and dived on the formation, having manoeuvred for position between the sun and the H.A. Two turned slightly northeast and Captain Meintjes took one and I took the other, the rest of the formation breaking up. Lieut Caldwell selected one of the rest. I got on the H.A's tail and fired about thirty rounds at short range. It dived steeply east and I did not follow as there were others nearer. I then got on the tail of another H.A. and followed it down to about 3,000 feet firing all the time at very close range. It went very low and I did not watch it any further as I turned to change drums. Captain Meintjes and I then met and recrossed the lines and climbed to 11,000 feet and attacked the remaining 5 machines of the hostile formation east of Adinfer. I got on the tail of two machines in succession firing at close range, both dived east steeply, the whole formation being broken up. I then returned to the aerodrome for more ammunition.'

Writing in 1973, Fry commented on the report, which he had not seen since that day in 1917. 'The report seems highly coloured to me now. I was unquestionably glad of the excuse to cross back to our lines to change ammunition drums and gain a little respite, but cannot see myself looking for another fight with that crowd even though Meintj naturally did so and

I had to follow him. Compared to that fight, all that had gone before was preliminary sparring.'

On the first day of February, 29 Squadron lost Lt A P V Daly, who was shot down by Werner Voss for his fourth victory. The DH2s had attacked the pilots of *Jasta B* over Achiet-le-Petit. Daly was intent on chasing one of the Albatri when Voss attacked him from behind. His first burst hit the engine of the DH2, his second wounded Daly in the shoulder. Daly managed to land the DH2 near Essarts and was taken POW.[5]

The next day 29 Squadron evened up the score. McCudden was leading a patrol over Monchy-au-Bois at 11,000ft when a German two-seater was seen flying towards the Lines, 8,000ft below the DH2s. All the British pilots dived to intercept the enemy machine. Seeing the danger, the enemy pilot turned east, towards his own lines. McCudden followed his usual practise at the time: opening fire at 200 yards and closing to 100 yards. As he narrowed the range he nearly collided with another DH2 and had to turn sharply away to avoid a collision. The two-seater went down to crash and was awarded jointly to Major W A Grattan-Bellew, 29 Squadron's Commanding Officer, and McCudden. McCudden was 'positive that the C.O. got the Hun' but Grattan-Bellew insisted that it was credited to McCudden.

The pilots of 32 Squadron were also in action during the day, attacking nine enemy machines over Bapaume. One enemy machine was driven down and another seen to land, but the Squadron lost 2Lt H Blythe, claimed by *Ltn* Gutermuth of *Jasta 5* for his first victory. Blythe had been wounded and taken POW but he died of his wounds eight days later.

Naval 8 had also been in action during the day losing a pilot in combat with a two-seater. FltSubLt. W E Traynor was shot down by *Offst* Kosmahl and *Ltn* Schulz of *Fl Abt (A)261* and crashed at Hermies. This was Naval 8's last action in the area. The Squadron was relocated to Furnes for a six-week rest and to have its Sopwith Pups replaced by Sopwith Triplanes. The Squadron's place at Vert Galant was taken by Naval 3 who took over Naval 8's Pups. Eight pilots from Three Naval Wing had been transferred to Naval 3, including the Canadians: Raymond Collishaw, Whealy, McNeil, Armstrong, Wigglesworth, Glen, Fall and Molone, who joined the Canadians already with the Squadron. More Canadians were to arrive during the following weeks. With the Squadron's commanding officer, Redford H (Red) Mulock, also a Canadian, Collishaw observed that Naval 3 was 'pretty much a Canadian show at this time.'

The fourth day of the month saw a great deal of fiercely contested fighting by the scout squadrons. Capt H W von Poellnitz, Lts E C Pashley and R H M S Saunders of 24 Squadron were all in action, sending one enemy machine down out

of control and destroying another. Pashley and Saunders had gone to the aid of five 22 Squadron FE2bs under attack from eight Albatri of *Jasta B*. *Ltn* Christian von Scheele of *Jasta B* was shot down by Pashley and a crew of one of the FE2bs and crashed near Le Mesnil.

A patrol from 32 Squadron attacked a hostile formation over Achiet during the afternoon. Capt W G S Curphey MC drove one down, but sustained some combat damage and he returned to his aerodrome at Léalvillers. Several of the DHs had been badly shot about in the combat and Curphey and 2Lt.A C Randall took up replacement DH2s to return to the fight. They had several combats, forcing one machine down, but Curphey's DH2 was badly shot up again and he was hit in the head, possibly by *Ltn* Bôhme of *Jasta B*. Despite his wound Curphey managed to return to Léavillers.

Thirty-two Squadron were again in action the next day. A patrol attacked nine enemy machines near Grevillers and Capt H W G Jones sent one down out of control, possibly *Vzfw* Thiel of *Jasta B* who was lightly wounded in action on February 5.

On February 6 a patrol from 41 Squadron on patrol over St.Eloi spotted an Albatros two-seater a thousand feet below them. The Albatros pilot saw the threat and turned for his own lines, but 2Lt E B W Bartlett caught the fleeing two-seater and opened fire from 150 yards. The enemy observer returned Bartlett's fire, but his pilot put their machine into a vertical dive only 1,000 feet from the ground. Bartlett's engine had cut out during his attack, his attention was focused on restarting it and he failed to observe if the two-seater crashed. There were no German casualties for the day so the crew of the Albatros must have forced landed and escaped injury.

McCudden was flying a lone patrol when he saw an Albatros two-seater flying east over Berles-au-Bois at 7,000 feet. The enemy was two miles west of the front line and had apparently been photographing the British back areas. McCudden attacked at 200 yards range, just west of Monchy-au Bois. The German observer returned his fire, 'we both blazed away at one another.' The Albatros pilot dived steeply and McCudden was hopeful that he would land in the British lines, but he managed to edge east. McCudden put on a fresh drum and attacked again. The Albatros gave 'an unmistakable plunge' and finally landed in the northeastern corner of Adinfer Wood, gracefully subsiding on its back in the snow. McCudden was disappointed that he had not succeeded in bringing the Albatros down in the British lines: 'of course it is the ambition of every youthful pilot to down a Hun in our lines.'

Thirty-two Squadron were in action early on the morning of February 7, 2Lt C.E.M Pickthorn and Lt A C Randall, driving down a hostile machine to a forced landing. Later in the day, another patrol from the Squadron was attacked by nine enemy aeroplanes. Curphey, now apparently recovered from his slight head wound of three days previously, claimed one victory from the fight and 2Lt H.D.Davies claimed another.

The next six days were relatively quiet for the scout squadrons. On 8 February Lt G F Hasler forced an Albatros two-seater from *Fl Abt (A)235* to land behind its own lines, the enemy machine turning over onto its back. Two days later Capt L P Aizlewood of 32 Squadron claimed an out of control victory, but was wounded in the combat, behind the British lines south west of Serre. Werner Voss of *Jasta B* claimed a 'Vickers' – the generic name given to the German pilots to the DH2 and FE pushers – forced down behind the British lines at Puisieux, west of Serre, but Aizlewood had managed to return to Léavillers safely.

A patrol from 60 Squadron forced an enemy machine down on 14 February, and FltLt R G Mack of Naval 3 claimed another. There were no German casualties but 2Lt J V Fairbairn of 54 Squadron had the dubious honour of being the first Sopwith Pup pilot to be lost in action by the RFC. He was wounded, crash landed, and taken POW. Fairbairn was claimed by *Ltn*. G Schlenker of *Jasta 3* for his second victory.[6]

There was an increase of fighting by the scout squadrons on February 15. Newly reconstituted as a scout squadron, No.1 Squadron had their first combat flying their Nieuport scouts. Lts P M Le Gallais and J A Slater were on patrol near Ploegsteert and attacked a German two-seater coming from the direction of Menin. Slater fired half a drum of Lewis into the enemy machine from a range of 60 yards. The German pilot attempted to dive away but Slater emptied the rest of his drum into it and it went down vertically out of control over Frelinghien. Further to the north, east of Ypres, Le Gallais and Slater, Capt J M E Shepherd and 2Lt H Welch later fought three enemy scouts. Shepherd was shot down near Gheluvelt and killed, the second victory of *Vzfw* Glasmacher of *Jasta 8*. Shepherd was the Squadron's first casualty as a scout squadron.

Second Lt Victor Collins of the squadron had better luck. In the afternoon he had chased an enemy machine back over its own lines and on returning to the British lines saw four Albatri flying west. In spite of the odds he attacked these from the rear. Two of the enemy scouts turned to face him, their fire hitting his engine and stopping it. Collins turned sharply to the left and fired half a drum of Lewis into the nearest Albatros. It burst into flames and crashed behind the British Lines. The dead pilot was *Ltn* Hans von Keudell, the *Staffelführer* of *Jasta 27*, with 12 victories. He had been in command of the *Jasta* for only ten days. His Albatros D III No.2017/16 was designated G11

After unsuccessfully attacking a two-seater, Collishaw of Naval 3 had better fortune in a later combat with two enemy scouts. Collishaw fired several bursts into one enemy machine and it went down in a spin. Collishaw attempted to follow the scout down but his engine had been hit in the fight. It finally cut out completely and Collishaw was forced to land just north of Albert. In combat with several enemy aeroplanes Capt H W G Jones of 32 Squadron was wounded twice, but managed to drive down one of the enemy machines. Jones returned to Léalvillers, but 2Lt C H March was wounded, shot down and taken POW, claimed by *Vzfw* Heinrich Büssing of *Jasta 5* for his third victory.

McCudden was also in action on 15 February. Sighting a pair of two-seaters over Adinfer Wood, McCudden attacked one, firing a complete drum into it from 200 yards. McCudden turned away to change his Lewis gun drum but came under attack from his rear from the other two-seater's front gun. McCudden evaded the two-seater – 'a funny little fat fellow that I had not previously seen' – and turned west, climbing to rejoin his patrol over Blainville. A little later McCudden saw the two-seater again, very low and flying back to the British lines. McCudden dived to attack it, catching it over the trenches at Monchy. He expected the enemy pilot to turn away east, 'as per usual' but the two-seater began to circle at 1,500 feet. 'I got directly behind at 50 yards, and the Hun gunner and I had a shooting match.' The German pilot steepened his circle and McCudden saw that the gunner was having hold on to the fuselage with one hand while pointing his gun 'very erratically at me with the other.' McCudden saw his chance, 'banged' on a fresh drum and fired the whole of it into the two-seater, which was now down to 300 feet. The enemy machine went down in a steep dive, attempted to land, but smashed its lower wing before standing up on its nose. It then fell back onto its tail. The 'funny little fat fellow' was a Roland C.II. McCudden recorded that in the afternoon the C.O of 29 Squadron took a patrol out to Monchy to each fire three drums of Lewis into 'my wrecked Hun' from a thousand feet.

Against these successes the scout squadrons suffered two additional casualties to those already noted. A patrol of Pups from 54 Squadron was severely handled by some enemy scouts from *Jasta 1*. *Ltn* von Stenglin shot down one of the Pups, flown by 2Lt E H Hamilton, and another, piloted by N A Phillips, was badly shot up and forced to land at 3 Squadron's aerodrome at Laviéville. A third Pup from the Squadron flown by Capt C L M Scott was hit by anti-aircraft fire and Scott was killed.

The weather had been generally good since late January: McCudden noted on February 16 that there had been clear skies since January 20, and that he had flown over the German lines every day. But in the late afternoon of February 16 the sky clouded to the south, with the high herringbone sky that precludes a break up of fine weather. It now rained day after day along the entire front and there was no flying for the next eight days.

The early afternoon of February 25 saw a fight over Arras between the DH2s of 29 Squadron and *Jasta B*. *Ltn* Voss attacked DH2 A2557 flown by Lt Reginald Lund, severely wounding him, and the DH2 crashed in the British lines close to Arras.[7] Voss then turned his attention to another DH2 flown by Capt Harold Payn, badly damaging the little pusher with accurate bursts. Payn dived steeply in an attempt to evade Voss and two of his squadron comrades came to his aid, forcing Voss to break off his attack. Voss claimed both DH2s but Payn was an experienced pilot and managed to fly the badly damaged DH2 back to his aerodrome at Le Hameau. Twenty-nine Squadron were again in action the following day. Lt L.L.Carter was wounded in the leg, but returned safely. The scout squadrons recorded no combats on February 27. The next day the weather again deteriorated and 'no work was possible.'

NOTES

1. In December 1916 *Jasta 2* had been renamed *Jasta* Boelcke in honour of its former commander.

2. Croft's Sopwith Pup A626 was the first Pup to be captured by the Germans.

3. *Air of Battle*, W M Fry, William Kimber, 1974.

4. *Ltn* Georg Simon *Jasta 11*, was wounded on this day.

5. Daly was repatriated to Holland in May 1918.

6. Fairbairn was repatriated to Holland in April 1918.

7. Lund eventually recovered from his wounds.

CHAPTER EIGHT

THE HINDENBURG LINE

In September 1916 the German Supreme Command of the Army (OHL) had begun to formulate plans for the construction of extremely strong defensive positions on the Western Front. In five sections, these would run from the Belgian coast to Pont-à-Mousson on the Moselle. The section between Arras to a point six miles east of Soissons was considered the first priority, to be completed as quickly as possible. This would cut off the salient held by the German First, Second and Seventh Armies, shortening the front by twenty-five miles. To the Germans these fortifications were named *Siegfriedstellung*, to the British they were known as the Hindenburg Line. Completion of the fortifications was to be by the beginning of March 1917, with a staged withdrawal to begin on the 16th of the month. In October 1916 the British had been aware that construction work was being carried out some way behind the German front lines, but no attention had been paid to the information, which was uncertain and vague. By January 1917 reports from prisoners and deserters revealed that new defensive positions were in fact being built, although details of its strength and exact position were still uncertain.

The activities of the *Jagdstaffeln*, plus the adverse weather conditions had curtailed the long range reconnaissance work of the RFC Corps squadrons, which had limited their work to the German front line and the three reserve trenches directly behind them, to the west of the Hindenburg Line. By the middle of February 1917, however, reports began to come in that a staged local withdrawal was being planned by the German Army, possibly only to its first reserve line. This belief was fortified when the British Fourth Army attacked Miraumont on 17 February. Although the attack met with only limited success, continued British pressure caused the Germans to withdraw to their first reserve line. It was not until 25 February that the British learnt that the intended withdrawal was to

be to the Hindenburg Line, but they still had no positive information as to its extent, course, or how far it extended into the French held part of the line.[1] Intelligence sources then uncovered more indications that the withdrawal was to be in one fast operation, but by then it was too late to formulate plans for an effective interference.

At the beginning of March, however, it was not on the Somme that the airfighting grew in intensity during the month, but further north, around Arras, where the British First Army was preparing for a spring offensive.

On the first day of March there was little activity, although a Sopwith Pup of 9 Naval, damaged in combat, was forced down into the sea off the Dutch coast and the pilot interned.

There was no flying the next two days but on March 4 there was a great deal of fighting. In the morning the Pups of 54 Squadron were in action with elements of *Jasta 3* in the vicinity of St.Quentin and *Ltn* Schlenker wounded Capt A Lees, forcing him to land and be taken prisoner. The DH2s of 29 Squadron and 11 Squadron's FEs had a combat over Tilloy with *Jasta 5* and 2Lt A J Pearson of 29 Squadron and Lts Braham and Boddy of 11 Squadron forced down *Ltn* Max Böhme. Böhme was taken prisoner and his Albatros D II 910/16 was given the number G14.

The Nieuports of 1 Squadron were also active during the day. After a number of indecisive combats, Lt T F Hazell left the patrol with a failing engine. The remaining two Nieuports, flown by Lts C J Q Brand and V G A Bush, carried on and later attacked an Albatros C type, hitting the German pilot. The Albatros stalled, rolled over into an inverted position, fell for several thousand feet, then began to dive and break up. Several large pieces were seen to fall off and the Albatros finally crashed near a wood. To add to this squadron success, Lt. E S T Cole also destroyed an LVG during the day.

On March 4 Naval 3 had what Raymond Collishaw described as one of its 'more memorable days.' Late in the morning, two Flights from the squadron were detailed to escort the FE2bs of 18 Squadron to Cambrai. During a combat with Halberstadt scouts over Hermies, Collishaw, John Malone and H Wiggleworth each sent an Halberstadt down out of control, but during the fight FltLt Hank Wambolt, was shot down and killed by *Ltn* Schröder for his first victory, and FltSubLt L A Powell was wounded in the stomach. Powell crash landed on the British side and was taken to hospital, but died of his wounds three days later. FltSubLt J P White had also been shot down in the fight, claimed by *Oblt* Hans Kummetz of *Jasta 1* for the first of his seven victories.

FltLt R G Mack and FltSubLt Leonard 'Tich' Rochford of Naval 3 also flew an escort during the morning. After flying to Laviéville for a briefing with their charges, two Moranes of 3 Squadron, they took off and crossed the lines at 13,000 feet. The photo-reconnaissance successfully completed the Moranes and Pups turned for home, but over Manancourt they were attacked by five Albatros scouts. Rochford later wrote: 'for the first time I was in a scrap with German fighters. They were very close and just above me. I heard the rat-tat-tat of their Spandau guns and felt frightened as I manoeuvred my Pup to prevent one getting his sights on me.'

A mottled brown and black Albatros dived from Rochford's right hand side, straight across the path of his Pup, intent on attacking Mack. Rochford fired quick burst into it: 'he fell away sideways.' The Albatros pilots then broke off their attack and cleared east. Mack and Rochford joined up with the Moranes and escorted them back to Laviéville, where they had lunch in 3 Squadron's mess. Mack confirmed that the Albatros shot at by Rochford had gone down completely out of control. It was the first of Rochford's eventual 29 victories.

Two pilots from 41 Squadron, Lts R H M S Saundby and Andrew Fraser were on patrol when they saw a flight of three Nieuports attacking a formation of Albatri. This combat was 2,000 feet above the FE8s and before they could climb into the fight the Nieuports broke off the action. Ten minutes later, however, one of the Nieuports again attacked one of the Albatri, which dived across the front of Saundby. Saundby fired a burst of 25 rounds at this Albatros, but it was outdiving the FE8 and the range rapidly increased from 40 to 100 yards. Fraser, below Saundby, fired a full drum into the Albatros as it flashed by and it went down to crash east of Polygon Wood.

The pilots of 40 Squadron claimed two enemy machines forced down in the general fighting during the day, as did Lt Hazell of 1 Squadron, but Lt C O Usborne's FE8 was badly shot about in combat and he was forced to land.

There was no flying on March 5 due to bad weather, but the next day, in the words of the official communiqué: 'Hostile aircraft were exceptionally active during the day and a great number of combats took place.' Over 70 enemy aeroplanes were seen over the First Army front and 23 crossed the lines.

Lieutenant Benbow of 40 Squadron attacked an enemy scout and sent it down in flames near Givenchy for his eighth victory.[2] Capt S H Long and Lt Pashley of 24 Squadron attacked a two-seater. They reported that their fire had hit the enemy observer, but the pilot must have also have been hit for a report later confirmed that the two-seater had crashed.

These victories however were scant compensation for the casualties suffered by the scout squadrons, with two pilots killed and two taken prisoner. Thirty-two Squadron, in a fight with *Jasta B* above the Bapaume to St Quentin road, lost three of their FE8s. Second Lt Maximillian John Jules Gabriel Mare-Montembault was shot down by Adolf von Tutschek for the first of his 27 victories. The DH2 crashed between the villages of Beugny and Beugnatre and Mare-Montembault – not surprisingly known to his fellow pilots as 'Monty' – was taken prisoner. Monty was no novice: he had joined 32 Squadron the previous August and had scored six victories. This was not the first time he had been shot down by a pilot of *Jasta B*. On 10 October 1916 his controls had been shot away by Erwin Böhme and he had crashed by Mouquet Farm in the British lines.

Captain H G Southon of 29 Squadron also fell to a pilot of *Jasta B*. Werner Voss chased the DH2 a little further north and finally shot it down to crash at Favreuil, just north of Bapaume. Southon had been badly wounded by Voss' fire and was made POW.[3] Another pilot of 32 Squadron, Lt C E M Pickthorn, was wounded slightly during the day while on a Line patrol.

On March 6, however, Manfred von Richthofen was shot down by Capt L E Claremont, the observer in a BE2e of 16 Squadron. Richthofen had just shot down another BE of the squadron when Claremont's accurate fire hit his Albatros in the petrol tank and the engine. Petrol poured into his cockpit and Richthofen – fearful of fire – forced landed in a small field.[4]

Sixty Squadron lost two of their pilots during this day of continued success for the *Jagdstaffeln*. The corps squadrons were finding that the *Jagdstaffeln* were making photo-reconnaissance work extremely difficult and some 60 Squadron's Nieuports were fitted with cameras. On 6 March 2Lt Philip Joyce of 60 Squadron had taken photographs of the area around Cambrai and was being escorted back to the British lines by C Flight: Lts Caldwell, F Bower and L S Weedon. Reaching the supposed safety of the line, and within sight of their aerodrome at Filescamp Farm, the three escorts left Joyce, and returned to engage some enemy aircraft they had seen earlier near Cambrai. When C Flight returned to Filescamp Farm they were astonished to learn that Joyce had not returned and his body was never recovered. Joyce's fate remained a mystery for many years but recent research has suggested the possibility that he was brought down by *Oblt* Kummetz of *Jasta 1*, who claimed a 'Sopwith' one seater at Achiet-le-Grand. Achiet-le-Grand is directly west of Cambrai, en route for the shortest way back to the front line for the Nieuports, but some distance southeast of Filescamp Farm.

During the day Major E P Graves, CO of 60 Squadron, was leading a patrol of three Nieuports towards the lines when he saw an FE2b being attacked by eight Albatri of *Jasta 1* south west of Arras. This was some distance west of the British front line, an indication of the growing confidence of the pilots of the *Jagdstaffeln*. Graves went to the aid of the FE, but was shot in the eye and his Nieuport burst into flames and crashed north of Rivière. Major Graves was the victim of *Ofstvz* Cymera of *Jasta 1* who claimed a 'Sopwith' single-seater at Agny, which is just north of Rivière.

The obsolescence of the FE8 and DH2 was now becoming ever more obvious. The offensive policy of the RFC, advocated by Trenchard, was unsustainable by a force equipped with inferior aeroplanes to those of the enemy. The corps squadrons were sustaining heavy losses to the *Jagdstaffeln* pilots, now fully experienced on their Albatros and Halberstadt D types, and the scout squadrons of the RFC were almost powerless to stop their operations. The casualties suffered by the fighter squadrons on March 6 illustrated this only too well. On March 6 the RFC had lost ten aircrew killed, seven wounded and six taken prisoner. In addition seven aeroplanes were damaged and forced to land.

On March 9 no Corps aeroplanes were lost but the pilots of the *Jagdstaffeln* cut a swathe through 40 Squadron, equipped with the now hopelessly outclassed FE8 pushers. Eight FE8s from the squadron left at 9.20am on an offensive patrol. In the vicinity of Bailleul they were attacked by five Albatri of *Jasta 11*. One of the FE8s, flown by Lt L B Blaxland, had just turned back with engine trouble and he could only watch the combat as he nursed his machine back to the lines. The ensuing fight lasted half an hour.

The first FE to fall was flown by 2Lt R E Neve, who had taken off twenty-five minutes earlier than the other FE8s. *Ltn* Karl Allmenroder shot Neve's FE down in flames to crash in the British lines at 9.30am. Neve jumped clear just before the crash, and survived, although injured. Three more FE8s were shot down in quick succession. *Ltn* Karl Schäfer shot down 2Lts W B Hills and G F Haseler to crash behind the German

lines and be made POWs. Kurt Wolff shot down 2Lt T Shepard near Annay, and he was also taken prisoner. 2Lt H C Todd had his engine shot up and had to force land at 2 Squadron's aerodrome, and Lt W Morrice, his engine also put out of action, force landed by the La Bassée Canal. A patrol of DH2s from 29 Squadron, which had been flying an early morning escort, and which attempted to come to the aid of the 40 Squadron pilots, lost Lt Arthur John Pearson, shot down in flames by Manfred von Richthofen for his 25th victory. In view of these losses the pilots of 40 Squadron were no doubt relieved to hear that they were to be re-equipped with Nieuport scouts in the near future, but the first Nieuports were not received until the end of the month.

On March 10 no flying was possible due to bad weather, no doubt to the relief of the hard pressed aircrews of the RFC, but March 11 saw a return to operations and an increase in casualties. During the day eight aircraft were lost and a further 12 either forced to land or return badly damaged. During the morning it was the turn of 32 Squadron, another of the fighter squadrons equipped with the obsolete pusher types, to suffer unacceptable casualties. Luckily none of the pilots was killed, but four were wounded in combat and forced to land, and another was injured in a crash landing.

Six DH2s of 32 Squadron were flying a line patrol when they were attacked by nine enemy aircraft east of Bapaume. During the fighting Lt Pickthorn wounded *Ltn* Erkenbrecht of *Jasta 12*, who crash landed his Albatros by Grévillers. Second Lt G Howe fired a full drum of Lewis into one enemy scout from very close range. The pilot was seen to throw up his hands and fall forward onto his controls. The Albatros went down out of control and crashed.[5] To offset these successes, all the DH2s were badly damaged and either crash landed or were forced to land, luckily in their own lines: Lts Howe, A C Randall and Capt J M Robb had been wounded and Lts W A Young and J H Cross were injured in their crashes. Only Pickthorn, forced to land near Bapaume, escaped injury, but his DH2 overturned on the wet ground and was wrecked.

In the afternoon two Nieuports of 60 Squadron were escorting a flight of BE2s to Bailleul when they dived to attack a lone enemy scout below them. It was the classic decoy trap. The Nieuports were immediately jumped by four Albatri from *Jasta B*. Werner Voss wounded Lt A D Whitehead in the knee, the bullet coming out through his right thigh. Whitehead lost control of his Nieuport and it fell into a spin. After spinning for several thousand feet Whitehead recovered control, pulled out into a dive and made for the safety of the British lines. Voss immediately resumed his attack, his shots hitting Whitehead's engine and destroying his elevator controls. The Nieuport again went into a spin. Whitehead fainted from shock and loss of blood and the Nieuport – the official casualty report states that it then burst into flames – spun into the ground near Bailleul. Miraculously, Whitehead survived the impact and woke up a week later in hospital in Douai.[6]

Naval 3 pilots were also in action during the day, FltSubLts B C Bell and HG Travers each claiming a victory.

On March 15 a patrol from 1 Squadron led by Capt C J Q Brand saw a good deal of action. Brand first attacked a Albatros C Type from *Fl Abt (A)250* and killed *Ltn* Pop and *Gefr* Werner von Schlichting. The Flight then reformed and later fought six enemy scouts. One of the Albatri was claimed by Lt C C Clark as destroyed and the Flight claimed another out of control and two driven down.

Although the FE2bs of 25 Squadron and the Sopwith 1 1/2 Strutters of 43 Squadron flew an offensive patrol near Lens on March 16, and were in combat for over twenty minutes with sixteen enemy scouts, claiming three down out of control, with no loss to themselves, the single-seater scout squadrons saw no action during the day.

On March 17 British troops began to move forward to occupy the areas abandoned by the German forces that had retired to the prepared positions of the Hindenburg Line. The Corps squadrons of the RFC, keeping open communications with the British troops who were advancing into areas ruthlessly devastated by the retiring German forces, met no opposition from the *Jagdstaffeln*. German reconnaissance aircraft had seen preparations for an attack by the British First and Third armies in the Vimy Ridge-Arras sector and the *Luftstreitkräfte* was conserving its forces for the coming British offensive.

Three Nieuports of 1 Squadron, led by Lt J A Slater, flew an escort to the FE2ds of 20 Squadron on the morning of March 17, joining up with the large pushers over Bailleul at 11,000 feet. A number of Albatros scouts were seen but these did not attack until they were joined by four more in the vicinity of Lille. The enemy scouts then dived on the formation and shot down one of the Nieuports, flown by 2Lt A J Gilson.[7] Slater and 2Lt C C Clark then tackled the Albatri, but after a brief fight the German pilots broke off the action and climbed to regain their height. From this height advantage they carried out dive and zoom attacks on the FEs for the remainder of the patrol time, only breaking off the fight at the front line. Only one of the 20 Squadron's FEs was lost, hit by *Flak* over Lomme.

Naval 3 pilots were also in action during the morning, flying an escort to the FE2ds of 18 Squadron on the 5th Army front. Unlike the escort from 1 Squadron, Naval 3 used all three of its Flights: A Flight flew just above the FEs, with B and C Flights stacked above them at 17,000 feet. This combined offensive patrol and escort saw a great deal of combat with enemy scouts. Two were claimed shot down in flames

and three out of control. Two FEs were lost in the fights: one crash landed injuring its observer; the second was badly shot about and crash landed in the front line trenches. One pilot from Naval 3, FltSubLt F D Casey, his Pup damaged during the one of the combats, crashlanded near Contalmaison. The Pup was a total wreck but Casey was unhurt. The following day, none the worse for his crash landing, Casey forced down an enemy machine.

On 18 March 66 Squadron, which had been at St.Omer since March 3, flew its Sopwith Pups into Vert Galant aerodrome on the Albert to Doullens road to join the fighter squadrons of 9th Wing. There was little action during the day, the weather still being unsettled. The next day, 19 Squadron flying its new Spad V11s, which had replaced its ineffectual BE12s, were in action for the first time. It was an inauspicious beginning. In combat with *Jagdstaffeln 12* and *5* the Squadron lost three of its Spads. In the area of Bourlon Wood, Capt W J Cairnes was hit in the engine and forced to land behind the British lines at Ginchy. Lt A T Hope's Spad was also hit in the engine and he force landed behind the British lines at Melicocq. The third Spad lost was 2Lt S Purves, who was attacked near Roisel by *Hptm* von Osterroht of *Jasta 12*. Purves escaped the attentions of von Osterroht but then flew further southeast, possibly lost. Ten minutes later, over Homblières, east of St Quentin, he was attacked by *Ltn* Schneider of *Jasta 5*. The Spad was now out of petrol; Purves was forced to land and was taken prisoner.

No flying was possible on March 20 owing to the bad weather. The next day 24 Squadron lost Capt H W G Jones. A patrol from the squadron came under attack and Jones was last seen going down in a spin over over Roupy. He had been wounded and landed near Aubigny. Lt E L Benbow of 40 Squadron was wounded by anti-aircraft fire during the day.

On patrol on March 21 Lt C E M Pickthorn of 32 Squadron attacked an Albatros D I near Lagnicourt. Pickthorn's fire wounded the pilot and he force landed behind the British lines at Vaulx-Vraucourt. The pilot was *Rittmeister* Prinz Friedrich Karl of Prussia. Prinz Karl was deputy leader of *Fl Abt (A) 258* but often volunteered his service as a fighter pilot. On this occasion he was flying an old Albatros D I borrowed from *Jasta B*. Karl was taken to hospital but died of his wounds on 7 April. The Albatros D I 410/16 was designated G17.

RFC communiqué No.80 states there was little aerial activity on March 22, with only two indecisive combats, but 2Lt S J Stocks was wounded in the stomach, making the second casualty for 40 Squadron in two days. The next day's activities were similar: the Corps squadrons carried out their work, but enemy activity was noted as 'below normal.' In contrast, March 24 saw a great deal of activity and the scout squadrons were in combat throughout the day.

A patrol of three Spads from 19 Squadron was patrolling in the area of Lens when they were attacked by *Jasta 11*. Lt H A Orelbar claimed an 'Halberstadt' out of control, but 2Lt F L Harding had a severe gun stoppage and had to leave the fight; The third Spad, flown by Lt R P Baker, was attacked by Manfred von Richthofen. Baker was wounded in the knee by von Richthofen's fire and his Spad hit in the petrol tank. Baker force landed near Givenchy, his Spad turning over in a shell hole. Baker was made POW, Manfred von Richthofen's 30th victory.

At five minutes past seven in the early morning of March 25 two Nieuports of 29 Squadron took off from their aerodrome at Le Hameau on an escort patrol. One of the Nieuports turned back with engine trouble but the other, flown by Lt C G Gilbert, carried on. Another escort patrol left Le Hameau twenty-five minutes after the first pair. These patrols were possibly an escort for the FE2bs of 11 Squadron. If so, they were totally inadequate. An hour and fifteen minutes after taking off, Gilbert was attacked by Manfred von Richthofen. Richthofen's fire hit the Nieuport in the petrol tank and shot away its controls. Gilbert survived the crash at Tilloy and was taken prisoner – in his pyjamas! Thinking the patrol would only be of short duration he had simply rolled out of bed and not bothered to dress before takeoff. Why he should have neglected to dress more warmly in March, other than a greatcoat, is inexplicable.

March 25 was another disastrous day for 70 Squadron. On a deep reconnaissance to the Hindenburg Line, they were attacked by *Jasta 5* and lost all five Sopwith 1 1/2 Strutters. In two days the Squadron had suffered four pilots and observers killed; two pilots died of wounds; three observers died of wounds; a pilot and an observer POW and a pilot and observer injured. The effect on the morale of the squadron must have been devastating. The RFC communiqué for March 25 noted: 'The photographs of the Hindenburg Line were of much value,' with no hint of the cost in casualties.

The pilots of A Flight 60 Squadron were in action in the late afternoon when they attacked three Albatros scouts near St.Leger. Sixty Squadron records give that Lts A Binnie, F Bower and W Bishop were each credited with an Albatros: the pilot of Binnie's victory as being taken prisoner. Bower was credited with an out of control and Bishop was awarded the third Albatros crashed for his first victory. Despite these claims the *Jagdstaffeln* had only two casualties on March 25: *Ltn* Mallinckrodt of *Jasta 20* and *Gefr* Berkling of *Jasta 22*, both wounded in action.

Bad weather conditions curtailed flying for the next two days. On March 27 Naval 8 returned on attachment to the hard-pressed squadrons of the RFC, flying their newly issued Sopwith Triplanes into Auchel. On March 28 Lts S Cole, H Welch and C C Clark of 1 Squadron were in combat with the Albatros scouts of *Jasta 30*. Cole and Clark each claimed an Albatros driven down out of control, but 2Lt Welch was shot down and killed by *Oblt* Bethge of the *Jasta.*

The weather on March 29 was 'unfavourable for air work' On March 30 a patrol from 60 Squadron took off to patrol the area of Arras, led by Lt W Bishop. Conditions were unfavourable, with a strong westerly wind taking the Nieuports further into German territory. Seeing no enemy aircraft over Arras, the inexperienced Bishop led the Flight still further into hostile territory. Over Vitry, east of Arras, Bishop saw a solitary Albatros and led the patrol down to attack it. It was a decoy and they were jumped by ten Albatri from *Jasta 11*. The fight drifted northwards and over Fouquières *Ltn* Wolff was attacked by 2Lt Bower. *Ltn* Allmenroder saw Wolff's danger and attacked Bower taking the Nieuport off Wolff's tail, but he was then attacked by another of the Nieuports. Wolff attacked this Nieuport, flown by Lt W P Garnett, and it went down to crash behind the German lines at Fresnoy. Garnett was killed. Frank Bower was hit in the back by an explosive bullet and lost control of his machine, which fell into a spin. In a state of shock, blood pouring from his wounds and holding his intestines in with one hand, Bower regained control and flew west until he could no longer hear AA fire, finally landing at Chipilly. Bower climbed out of his Nieuport and walked forty yards before collapsing. His Nieuport was undamaged and was flown back to the Squadron the next day, the same day that Bower died in hospital.

Jasta 11 were in action again during the afternoon, with the Nieuports of 40 Squadron. Capt R Gregory shot down and killed *Ltn* Hans-Georg Lübbert, but *Ltn* Allmenroder shot down Lt D M F Sinclair, who was taken POW. Gregory's victory was the first to be scored by the squadron since its re-equipment with Nieuport Scouts.

In the early morning on the last day of the month 60 Squadron flew a strong escort for the FE2bs of 11 Squadron: Major A J L Scott, the Squadron CO, leading Capt C T Black and Lts W Bishop, E J D Townesend, L H Leckie, Molesworth and Binnie. A group of Albatri were sighted and Black led the attack. Scott and Black shared credit for one of the enemy scouts sent down to crash, and Bishop claimed another shot down. Their escort's attention being elsewhere, one of the FEs was shot down by *Ltn* Wolff of *Jasta 11* and the pilot and his observer captured. The observer later died of his wounds. A quarter of an hour later Molesworth and Binnie forced a Rumpler to land near Queant. This was possibly from *Fl Abt (A) 256* which had an observer wounded in action on 31 March. Binnie later drove down an Albatros east of Roclincourt and Townesend claimed another enemy machine late in the day near Arras.

March 1917 had been a disastrous month for the RFC. The corps had suffered heavily in casualties to personnel, killed wounded and taken POW, and over a hundred and twenty aeroplanes had been lost, damaged or destroyed. Worse was to come.

For two weeks since March 17 the British forces had been moving steadily forward into the areas laid waste by the enemy, but there was no question of launching an all out offensive: the German troops were falling back on well fortified positions and could have counter attacked at any time from a position of strength. Conversely, the British armies were moving further and further from their prepared positions: a temporary defensive line had always to be organised to safeguard against a sudden attack by the enemy, and communications links had to be set up and maintained. As the British cavalry and small detachments of troops moved forward, probing the latest positions of the retiring German army, the main body of the infantry moved to each new line, securing it to ensure that it was capable of being well defended.

The main concentration of the RFC was now in progress further north, behind the Arras-Vimy front in preparation for the coming offensive. Although Trenchard could ill afford to split his available air strength, he instructed his Brigade Commanders to exploit the German retirement on the Somme as much as possible.

The essentials were:

1. To keep those enemy forces who were in immediate contact with British troops under constant observation.

2. To harass the withdrawal of the enemy troops by 'every means in their power.'[8]

3. Aerial reconnaissance to asertain any indication of a withdrawal further east of the Hindenburg Line: burning villages; road and rail movements of troops and supplies; new aerodromes; the condition – whether or not they had been damaged or destroyed – of cross-roads, bridges, culverts etc.

The Army wings of the RFC were to carry out deeper reconnaissance. To photograph and reconnoitre both the Hindenburg Line itself and the areas to its east. To facilitate this, in addition to the two seat fighter-reconnaissance aeroplanes of the Army wings, some single-seat fighters were also fitted with cameras: the Nieuports of 60 Squadron – as already stated – the DH2s of 32 Squadron and the Spads of 23 Squadron. For the reasons already given, these duties were carried out with little interference by the *Jagdstaffeln*.

NOTES

1. On February 25 a patrol of Sopwith Pups from 54 Squadron reported fires burning in villages well behind the German lines and a reconnaissance by 18 Squadron the following day returned with details of the German defences.

2. This victory made Benbow the highest scoring RFC pilot flying the now virtually obsolete FE8. His victory was probably *Ltn* Hübbert of *Jasta 11* WIA on 6 March.

3. Southon was repatriated to Switzerland in late December 1917.

4. The official history, *War In The Air* is in error in dating this incident as 9 March.

5. Possibly *Ofstv* Alfred Behling of *Jasta 1*, killed between Biefvillers and Bihucourt.

6. Whitehead sustained serious injuries, including a fractured skull, but he eventually recovered and was repatriated to Switzerland in January 1918.

7. Gilson was claimed by *Ltn* Strähle of *Jasta 18* for his third victory.

8. Despite this injunction there seems to have been little or no attempt to harass the retreating German troops by ground strafing by fighters.

CHAPTER NINE

BLOODY APRIL

The immediate objective of the offensive at Arras, due to begin on April 9, was the capture of Vimy Ridge, but its main purpose was to distract German attention from preparations for the large scale offensive to be launched on April 16 on the Aisne by French forces under General Nivelle. The Germans were fully aware of the French plans, having captured a French Sergeant Major who was carrying full details of the coming attack, and knew exactly where to concentrate their available air forces. These needed to be carefully conserved. Although the *Jagdstaffeln* had inflicted heavy losses on the RFC during March, in reality the number of fighters employed was relatively small. Most *jasta* were still well below establishment in both pilots and aeroplanes. Alex Imrie, noted historian of the German Air Force, has pointed out that the nominal strength of a *jasta* was 12 aeroplanes but some had so recently been formed that they carried only seven aeroplanes and pilots on strength. The RFC had numerical superiority but it was not enough. The technical superiority of the German fighters and the ever-growing confidence of their pilots in exploiting their aircraft to full potential amply compensated for their numerical inferiority.

Weather conditions on the first day of April 1917 were bad, with low cloud, wind and rain, but during the morning there was a small amount of artillery spotting by the corps squadrons. Flying one of these sorties, a BE2c of 15 Squadron was shot down in the vicinity of St Léger by Werner Voss for his 23rd victory, the only RFC machine lost to enemy action during the day. It is perhaps ironical, in view of coming events, that it was the *Jagdstaffeln* which suffered the first fighter pilot casualty of the month: a BE2c of 12 Squadron shot down the *Staffelführer* of *Jasta 3, Ltn* Alfred Mohr.

The weather on the morning of April 2 was little changed and most of the aerial activity took place in the morning. A force of four Nieuports of 60 Squadron left the ground at 7.15am: Lts Black, Hall and Williams flying an escort for Lt Molesworth, whose Nieuport was fitted with a camera. Half an hour after taking off they attacked a formation of Albatros scouts from *Jasta 2* over Fontaine-les-Croisilles. One of the enemy scouts was sent down out of control, but while 2Lt V F Williams was engaged with another he was attacked by *Ltn* Bernert. Bernert's fire killed Williams; his Nieuport burst into flames and crashed.

An early morning photo-reconnaissance patrol of 22 Squadron was attacked by *Jasta 5* over Gouzeaucourt Wood. One of the FE2bs was shot down in flames by *Offstv* Nathanael for his fifth victory, but some DH2s of 24 Squadron then joined the fight and claimed one of the Albatri, seen to catch fire and crash, and another sent down out of control. One of the 22 Squadron's crews also claimed an Albatros as driven down and seen to crash. Against these claims, neither *Jasta 5* nor any other *Jasta* reported casualties for the time and place in question. The two victories claimed by the British pilots as out of control are understandable, the enemy pilots in both instances may have survived the crashes uninjured, but why the first of these claims, the Albatros seen to catch fire before crashing, is not reflected in the German losses for the day is hard to understand.

Williams of 60 Squadron was the only fighter pilot lost during the day but the corps squadrons had lost a BE2d to Richthofen for his thirty-second victory and a Sopwith 1 1/2 Strutter for his thirty-third. Another three BEs were badly damaged. Twenty-two Squadron lost an FE2b with the crew both killed, but although 57 Squadron lost two FE2ds in combat with *Jasta B* they shot down and killed two of the *Jasta B* pilots: *Ltn* König and *Ltn* Wortmann.

On April 3 the DH2s of 32 Squadron were in combat with *Jasta 5* near Lagnicourt and lost Lt E L Heyworth, who was shot down by *Offst* Nathanael for his sixth victory. During the action Lt L W Barney's DH2 was badly shot up. Barney turned for the British lines, pursued by an Albatros, but managed to crash land near Vaulx Vraucourt. *Vzfw* Eisenhuth of *Jasta 5* was awarded an FE2b near Hendecourt, but in all probability his victory was Barney. Forty Squadron lost 2Lt S A Sharpe in the afternoon, brought down and made POW by *Ltn* Nernst of *Jasta 30*.

The air offensive for the forthcoming battle of Arras opened on April 4, but low clouds wind and rain limited the amount of flying. Snow was also moving in from the east and was reported by several squadrons to be falling on their aerodromes. Despite these adverse conditions, *Jasta 4* and *10* were in action, shooting down a BE2f of 12 Squadron, forcing an FE2b from 11 Squadron to land behind the British lines and destroying a balloon.

Three Sopwith Pups of C Flight 54 Squadron were detailed to attack kite balloons, with three other Pups flying top cover. On arrival at Gouy, the area where the balloons had been reported, only one was found to be up. F N Hudson, R G H Pixey and R M Charley attacked this balloon and the German observer took to his parachute. A return attack by all three Pups finally caused the balloon to burst into flames. The Pups were now flying at low level and made for the British lines. Going still lower they strafed enemy troops and positions. Pixey fired at a horseman and Hudson attacked a large group of troops unloading railway trucks.

A patrol from 40 Squadron took off on a line patrol during the morning. Lt Benbow's Nieuport was hit in the petrol tank by ground fire and he was forced to return, but the fighter squadrons had no casualties.

An improvement in the weather the next morning saw a great deal of fighting during the day. Offensive patrols by the fighter squadrons were successful in keeping the *jagdstaffeln* well east of the front lines and the corps aeroplanes were able to work unmolested.

A patrol of DH2s of 24 Squadron were on patrol in the late morning when they spotted a two-seater of *Fl Abt (A) 210* in the vicinity of Douai. The two-seater was escorted by three Albatros scouts and in the ensuing fight, 2Lt J K Ross was wounded, his DH2 going down in a spin over Honnecourt. Ross was claimed by the crew of the two-seater: he died of his wounds four days later. Lt Henry W Woollett attacked one of the Albatri and claimed it as destroyed, crashing a mile and a half east of Honnecourt for the first of his 35 victories.

Sixty Squadron's Nieuports had earlier been fitted with Le Prieur rockets in anticipation of being ordered to attack kite balloons during the air offensive. The first attacks on balloons were ordered for April 5 and just after midday Lts Bishop and E J D Townesend took off to attack two balloons near Cambrai. Bishop's target was not aloft and Townesend was intercepted by *Jasta 11*. Accurate fire from *Vzfw* Festner wounded Townesend in both legs and forced him to crash land behind the German lines. The young Canadian was thrown out of the cockpit on impact and was taken prisoner.

During the late evening 29 squadron claimed its first victory of the month – the first flying its newly issued Nieuports. The Nieuports attacked *Jasta 3* over Vitry en Artois and although Lt C V de Rogers and 2Lt E J Pascoe shared one Albatros as out of control, Lt N A Birks was wounded, forced to land behind enemy lines and was made POW by *Vzfw* Menckhoff of *Jasta 3* for his second victory. Sixty Squadron were out again at the end of the day, this time flying a defensive patrol: Lts Langwill, Robertson, Hervey and Elliott and Hall, led by 2Lt G Pidcock. They attacked two enemy aeroplanes, one of which was a red Albatros, and sent one down out of control near Riencourt at 6.45pm. At about the same time and in the same general area as this action by 60 Squadron, Naval 6 was in combat with German fighters. FltCom E W Norton claimed one down in flames, another out of control west of Douai, and FltSubLt Thorne another out of control. On the debit side, FltSubLt R K Slater was seen going down in a spin over Arras and was subsequently taken POW. Some researchers have awarded Slater to *Ltn* E Voss of *Jasta 20* (no relation to Werner Voss) but Voss' claim was at Omissey, just north of St.Quentin, some thirty-six miles further south of Arras.

FltCom R S Dallas of Naval 1 also scored during the day. At this time Naval 1 was based south of Albert at Chipilly. The Squadron had been re-equipped with Sopwith Triplanes in December 1916 and were to fly the highly successful little Sopwith until the following December. On April 5 Dallas wrote: 'we start the big show properly and everybody is indeed a little anxious to see what things are really like. I lead the formation, Teddy being good enough to come with me.[1] As we climbed towards the lines we felt secure and were proud of our mounts. We soon got intimation that Fritz dwelt below, for from our high and lofty position we could look down with scorn on our baffled pursuers.[2] Several times Huns put themselves in our path but we were cute and accepted not of their kind offer, till one, not knowing the sting of the Tripod fell victim to his horrid ways. We landed at Ham short of gas.'

The one 'not knowing the sting of the Tripod' (the nickname Dallas had given to the Triplane) was described by him as an Albatros D III, the first he had met in combat, its fuselage and one of its wings coloured light brown, the other wing red. Dallas sent it down in a spin over St.Quentin. Other than a pilot of *Jasta 18* who was wounded and taken prisoner, the

Jagdstaffeln had no losses during the day. The German pilot had taken the evasive action of a spin out of trouble, a common ploy.

Gordon Taylor of 66 Squadron took off alone to look for German two-seaters, but sighted five or six Albatros scouts strafing the British trenches near Cambrai. Taylor had complete confidence in the manoeuvrability of his Pup and dived to attack the German scouts. 'I selected one, a red machine with some chequered marks on the fuselage, and started to turn in behind him as he was soaring round for another dive on the trenches. I don't think he saw me for he made no attempt to evade the attack and I got a good burst into him, saw him rear up in a terrific zoom, fall over the top and dive for the near earth. But if he had not seen me, one of the others had; as I pulled out there was the sound of machine gun fire close behind my tail. My machine swept into a climbing turn before I knew my hand had moved the controls even. I was aware of a Hun going by, so close that I instinctively shrank back from the threat of collision. But he passed and another was on my tail instead. Again the instant evasion. I was suddenly conscious of the shark-like creatures closing in on me.'

Taylor tried to climb away from the Albatri, but they kept above him. 'They had me cold. I couldn't reach them to attack, and couldn't climb away to escape. The instant I flew straight they would nail me.

There was only one remaining possibility, a move which I had always avoided and from which there was no turning back. I decided to dive right down on the deck, and hare off home below the trees and the church towers. There were only a thousand feet to lose. I shook off a Hun with a sideways loop, ruddered down off the top and dived for the earth. This manoeuvre gave me a few seconds start. I remember the broken earth, with the shell holes, my wheels only a few feet off the ground. A Hun began to overtake me, diving, turning to get me in his sights. I had to watch him, and also to avoid flying into the ground. I swerved away as his nose was coming on, and he was forced to pull out to avoid crashing. If I could get through without colliding with some obstruction I'd be all right. A broken village came rushing up and I went skating round the ruined houses, past some splintered trees, and once more down flat against the earth. Then there were fields, green and brown, behind the lines, and a fold in the ground. I poured the Pup down the low valley, almost brushing the grass that flattened itself below my wings. A quick look behind. The Huns had gone, the air was clear.'

Good Friday, April 6, was a day of continued successes for the pilots of the *Jagdstaffeln*; they inflicted heavy losses both on the corps squadrons and the two-seater fighters of the RFC. Twenty aeroplanes were lost in action; 23 crewmembers were killed and 14 were taken POW, of whom three were wounded, including one who died of his wounds.

The fighter squadrons were in action early. At 7.30am Capt K C McCallum of 23 Squadron destroyed an Albatros two-seater, the first victory for the Squadron's new Spads.

The first fighter casualty of the day was a Sopwith Triplane of Naval 1. A patrol had taken off from Chipilly just after 6.30am. It is not clear from available records if they had been in combat, but at 8.00am FltSubLt N D M Hewitt's Triplane was seen circling over Doignies before coming down behind the German lines near Mons. *Ltn* Schäfer of *Jasta 11* claimed a Sopwith west of Vimy during the morning, but this is too far north to have been Hewitt. *Flakbatterie 505* claimed a victory at Lagnicourt, only 2 1/2 miles from Doignies, but its claim was for an FE.

The Nieuports of 40 Squadron flew special missions to attack the German balloon line during the morning. From 8,000 feet 2Lt H C Todd dived on one balloon tethered 500 feet above the ground over Neuvireuil. Closing to ten yards Todd fired three Le Prieur rockets. The balloon burst into flames. Todd came under heavy fire from the balloon's ground defences – AA, flaming onions and rifle fire – but he escaped and recrossed the lines over Arras at 2,000 feet. A little further north 2Lt H S Pell was not so lucky in his attack on a balloon at Sallaumines, just to the south east of Lens. His Nieuport was hit by groundfire and Pell was killed.

The triplanes of Naval 1 were action again just before noon. FltSubLt L M B Weil was attacked by two Halberstadt scouts, but another triplane drove them off. A little later, however, he was attacked by *Hptm* Osterroht of *Jasta 12* and shot down. Weil's crash is given in the German victory lists as being at 'Malakow' railway station. Although the serial number of Weil's triplane is correctly given (5448) Malakow may be incorrectly spelt. It does not appear to be on any modern map of the area and sounds very unlike a French place name.

April 6 saw 66 Squadron's first serious combat. Lt F Williams of C Flight fired a long burst at an enemy two-seater, causing the observer to fall from the aeroplane to his death.

Sixty and 29 Squadrons were also in action during the day, as were the Naval Squadrons, 1, 3 and 6, but no definite victories were claimed.

The Pups of 54 Squadron were flying an escort for the FE2bs of 22 Squadron in the area of St.Quentin when they were attacked by enemy fighters. One, described as 'a very fast scout,' was flown by a German pilot who was very skillful and manoeuvred well. He attacked Lt S G Rome, but Lt Oliver Stewart got behind him and shot the enemy machine down to crash near St.Quentin. During this escort Lt F N Hudson shot down a two-seater over Le Catelet.

In the morning 2Lt R M Foster of 54 Squadron had a lucky escape when he was attacked near Lagnicourt by Werner Voss of *Jasta B*. Voss had just shot down a BE2e of 15 Squadron for his twenty-fourth victory and was intent on making Foster's Pup his twenty-fifth. After a brief fight Voss' fire damaged the Pup, and Foster was forced to land at Lagnicourt, in the British lines, close by the crash of the BE2e. Foster was uninjured.[3]

On April 6 the *Jagdstaffeln* lost five pilots: two from *Jasta 5* were killed in a collision while in combat with the FE2ds of 57 Squadron; *Jasta 3* had a pilot wounded in action, as did *Jasta 12*, and a pilot of *Jasta 20* was shot down in flames.

April 7 was a day of low cloud wind and rain, a welcome respite for the aircrews. Nevertheless, the all important work of reconnaissance and artillery spotting still had to undertaken, and the destruction of enemy kite balloons was seen as being of prime importance in view of the imminent offensive, now only two days away.

Four Nieuports of 1 Squadron took off to deal with balloons in the vicinity of Ypres. On sighting the balloons, however, Slater and E D 'Spider' Atkinson saw that they were protected by several enemy scouts and wisely decided against an attack. One of the Nieuports was flown by Lt R J Bevington. From a letter he later wrote to his brother from a prison camp it seems that he did not have a chance to locate the balloons before he was attacked by *Jasta 8* and shot down. *Hptm* von Hünerbein hit the Nieuport in the engine and wounded Bevington in the foot. While Bevington was attempting to restart his engine his left wing hit a tree. The right bottom wing then hit the ground and the Nieuport stood up on its nose leaving Bevington hanging from his seat strap.[4]

The weather cleared towards the afternoon; the rain stopped and conditions were better. Just before 3.00pm Lt W Bishop of 60 Squadron took off alone to attack a balloon at Ecourt St.Quentin. As Bishop began his dive he was intercepted by an Albatros. Bishop pulled up into a loop, got behind the Albatros and a burst of fire sent it down. Bishop then resumed his attack on the balloon, diving to within five hundred feet of the ground, but the long dive choked his engine. Bishop prepared to make a forced landing behind enemy lines, but at fifteen feet the engine restarted. Bishop made for the British lines in a hail of ground fire. He was awarded both the balloon and an Albatros D III as destroyed.

A patrol from 60 Squadron left Filescamp Farm at twenty minutes to five: six Nieuports flown by Lts G Smart, C S Hall, H Hervey, C Patteson, D N Robertson and J M Elliott. Over Arras they were attacked by four Albatros scouts of *Jasta 11* led by Richthofen. The highly expert *Jasta 11* pilots made short work of the relatively inexperienced British pilots. *Ltn* Schäfer

and *Ltn* Wolff were each credited with a Nieuport and Richthofen shot down a third in flames, flown by Lt G O Smart. 2Lt Hervey's Nieuport was hit in the engine and badly damaged but he managed to return to Filescamp Farm. His guns had frozen during the fight and he had been unable to defend himself. Robertson had been wounded in the hand and his Nieuport badly shot about, but he and Elliott, also with a badly damaged Nieuport, returned to base. Hopelessly lost after the fight, Cyril Patteson landed at an RNAS aerodrome.

George Smart's blazing Nieuport had crashed just behind the British lines. Smart had burnt to death and was buried in a shell hole by front line British troops. The squadron later erected a cross over his grave.

As the remnants of this Flight landed at Filescamp Farm another four Nieuports took off: Lts Leckie, Pidcock, Kirton and Langwill, led by Capt M Knowles. The combat reports filed later suggest that only one enemy aeroplane had been engaged but Capt Knowles failed to return. He had been shot down south east of Fampoux by *Ltn* W Frankel, the *Staffelführer* of *Jasta 4*, and taken prisoner.[5]

It had been a bad day for 60 Squadron, but while the first Flight had been in action with *Jasta 11* a patrol of Nieuports from 29 Squadron had also lost two of their number. *Ltn* Bernert of *Jasta B* shot down and killed 2Lt J H Muir at Roeux, just east of Arras and *Vzfw* Paterman of *Jasta 4* killed Capt A Jennings at Fresnes. The German victory lists correctly give the serial numbers of each Nieuport.

During the afternoon the indefatigable Lt Todd, C Flight Commander of 40 Squadron, decided to repeat his balloon victory of the previous day. He attacked a balloon over the Sallaumines – Noyelles area, diving from 8,000 to 3,000 feet and opening fire at close range. Todd destroyed the balloon, but the Nieuport came under very heavy anti-aircraft fire, was badly damaged, and Todd was lucky to be able to return.

A patrol from Naval 8 were in action during the afternoon, in the vicinity of Arras. Shell bursts from anti-aircraft fire attracted Robert Little's attention to three Albatros D IIIs flying at the same level as himself – 7,000feet. He immediately attacked the nearest Albatros, painted bright red with blue wings, but was attacked by its companion, coloured green. Little managed to outmanoeuvre the green scout and sent it down in a steep spiral to hit the ground near the trenches north east of Arras. Intent on watching the green scout, Little was attacked by the red Albatros, which hit his oil tank. Little broke off the combat and returned.

During the day 56 Squadron flew its SE5s into Vert Galant, an aerodrome abreast the Doullens to Amiens road. The squadron shared the aerodrome with 66 and 19 Squadrons and came under the orders of 9th Wing. Fifty-six Squadron had been working up to strength at London Colney since the previous July and was the first squadron to be equipped with the SE5, a new fighter from the Royal Aircraft Factory.

In the SE5 the RFC at last had an aeroplane that was more than a match for the German Albatros. It was strong, fast, a steady gun platform and, importantly, was armed with two guns: a Vickers firing through the propeller arc and a Lewis gun mounted on the top wing. However, despite the coming offensive at Arras and the urgent requirement for command of the air, necessary modifications to both aeroplanes and guns kept the squadron on the ground at Vert Galant and they were not to fly their first patrol until April 22. Even then they were forbidden to cross the front lines.

Easter Sunday, 8 April, was generally fine, although there was some cloud and scattered snow showers.

At 8.15am it was snowing at Filescamp Farm when Major Scott, the CO of 60 Squadron, took off, leading a patrol of five Nieuports on an offensive patrol. Near Douai, Major Scott attacked an Albatros two-seater, which dived away from his fire. Bishop followed it down and shot at it again, but the enemy machine was already going down out of control. The Nieuports were then attacked by *Jasta 11*. *Ltn* Fester almost immediately shot down and killed Major J A A Milot, a French-Canadian who had been with the squadron since March 13. Hamilton Hervey had a bad gun jam and managed to escape into the cloud cover. 'I was making my solitary way back to Arras, hoping to pick up the rest of the Flight there, when an anti-aircraft gun opened up on me, and a large fragment of shrapnel passed through my bottom plane and lodged in my engine. At first I had a faint hope that I should be able to glide back over our lines, but I had not sufficient height, and eventually finished up on top of a well-camouflaged German artillery dugout.'[6]

Harvey was hauled out of his Nieuport before he had a chance to destroy it and taken off to the officers' billet, where he was given lunch. After lunch Hervey was interrogated by a German intelligence officer. Hervey quickly realised that the officer was very astute and decided the best course of action was to keep completely silent. After telling Hervey the number of his squadron and where it was based – both correct – the officer explained that the previous day he had examined another pilot of 60 Squadron, Captain Knowles. This surprised Hervey, who was a particular friend of Knowles, and who he had understood to have been killed. Hervey hid his interest and kept a blank face. He was later taken to the Caserne at Douai, the temporary accommodation for POWs, and spent the rest of the war in captivity, escaping once but recaptured.

The rest of the formation had escaped into the heavy clouds. Bishop, flying alone, later claimed two Albatros D IIIs as out of control: the first north east of Arras at 9.30am and another near Vitry en Artois forty minutes later. He also claimed

the Albatros C type from the first encounter, and a balloon as 'wound down.' The balloon was not allowed.

An Albatros scout was claimed from the encounter with *Jasta 11* as having gone down out of control. This was possibly *Vzfw* Festner, who force landed his Albatros with a cracked wing.

The pilots of 1 Squadron carried out more successful attacks on balloons in the morning, shooting down two in flames, one each to Capt C J Quintin-Brand and Lt E S T Cole.

The fighter squadrons flew deep offensive patrols during the morning in an attempt to stop the *Jagdstaffeln* interfering with the work of the corps aeroplanes. This was successful. A Sopwith 1 1/2 Strutter of 43 Squadron was brought down in the morning (Richthofen's 38th victory) but there were no further losses until the afternoon.

Naval 8 pilots were out during the day, two enemy machines were claimed as driven down out of control by FltSubLt F D Casey and FltLt H G Travers. Roderic Dallas of Naval 1, on patrol with FltSubLt Culling, found an Albatros two-seater, painted dark green with a red nose, and shot it down out of control east of Cambrai.

The pilots of Naval 3 also claimed two out of control victories, near Pronville.

In the afternoon an offensive patrol of B Flight from 66 Squadron attacked six Halberstadts and Capt G W Roberts and Lts C C S Montgomery and A J Lucas each claimed an out of control. C Flight were also out and Lt J T Collier damaged an enemy machine, driving it down.

Late in the evening 29 Squadron were in action in the Croisilles area and 2Lt T J Owen was shot down and killed by *Ltn* G Schlenker of *Jasta 3*. Owen was the last fighter casualty of the day.

The *Jagdstaffeln* lost four pilots during the day. *Ltn* Frankl of *Jasta 4*; a pilot from *Jasta 6* killed on the French front, and a pilot from *Jasta 8* wounded in action.

During the five days before the opening of the battle of Arras, from 4 to 8 April, 75 British aeroplanes had been lost in action, with a personnel loss of 19 killed, 13 wounded and 73 missing. There were also a high number of flying accidents, in which 56 aeroplanes had been struck off strength. The pilots and observers of the corps and army squadrons were finding the strain of daily fighting against an enemy equipped with superior equipment was becoming intolerable: nerves were frayed and morale was affected. Now, with the addition of the heavy losses in March, was surely the time for Trenchard to temper his offensive policy with a degree of caution and economy: a continuous offensive policy is unsuited to a technically inferior side. In addition, to offset their numerical inferiority, the Germans had instituted a system of ground observance officers (*Flugmeldedienst)* along the entire front.

These advised the *Jagdstaffeln* of the position of the RFC's standing fighter patrols and, when they had passed, directed their operations to the British corps aeroplanes working above the trenches – a tactic which has been likened to that of a burglar waiting until a patrolling policeman has left the area. This conserved and concentrated the strength of the *Jagdstaffeln*. In those instances where the corps aeroplanes were provided with escorts they were able to work unmolested, but these escorts were arranged at Wing or squadron level and were not a result of orders from the GOC.

The Battle of Arras

The British front of the attack ran from Givenchy-Gohelle at its northern point to near Croisilles in the south. The objective of the main and most important thrust in the north was the capture of Vimy Ridge by the First Army. The fighter strength of the First Army – the Tenth Army Wing – comprised four squadrons, only two of which were single-seat fighter squadrons: 40 Squadron (17 Nieuport scouts) and Naval 8 (18 Sopwith Triplanes). The strength of the single-seater fighter squadrons was augmented by those of the Ninth Headquarters Wing: 19 Squadron (18 Spads) 27 Squadron (18 Martinsyde scouts) 56 Squadron (13 SE5s) 66 Squadron (18 Sopwith Pups) On the periphery of the main thrust at Vimy was the Thirteenth Army Wing of the Third Army, which was comprised of four single-seater fighter squadrons: 29, 60 and Naval 6 Squadrons (16,18 and 18 Nieuport scouts). An overall total for the two armies of 141 fighter aircraft.[7]

The Fifth and Fourth Armies, not directly involved with the offensive, had another eight squadrons of single-seater fighters on strength. The entire air strength of the four British armies, the First, Third, Fifth and Fourth, on a front stretching approximately from Lille in the north to Péronne in the south, was 41 squadrons consisting of 754 aeroplanes, of which 296 were single-seater fighters. The German air strength opposing the British armies at Arras consisted of 264 aeroplanes, only 114 of which were single-seater fighters: the main concentration of the German air forces was opposite the French armies on the Aisne, where nearly 240 fighters were employed.

The frontage of the main assault at Arras was some 7,000 yards and 2,000 guns – a third of them heavies – had been moved into the sector to punch a hole through the German wire. The artillery bombardment had opened on April 4 but the persistent falls of snow had obscured any observation of results and the gunners had no idea of how effective their fire had been in cutting the wire, or how much was still intact. When the appaling weather conditions postponed the attack for twenty-four hours the gunners had heaved a sigh of relief. In fact, their fire had been extremely effective: the opposing Germans troops were either dead or isolated, sheltering as best they could in countless overlapping shell holes in the devastated landscape.

The battle of Arras opened at 5.30am on April 9. The wind direction had changed during the night, bringing still colder conditions, and the troops of the British First and Third Armies advanced through snow and sleet.

If weather conditions were difficult for the advancing troops on the ground, their heavy packs and equipment – half their body weight – now heavier still with moisture, it rendered air operations almost impossible. In addition to the snow there was a southwesterly gale blowing at high altitudes: both bombing attacks, and offensive patrols by the fighter squadrons, were curtailed. Nevertheless, despite the high wind, sixty-one targets were dealt with by artillery co-operation aeroplanes and a further 55 by observation balloons. Fighter patrols were flown behind the line of the battle to protect the corps aeroplanes and the balloons but there was little interference from the *Jagdstaffeln*. Only *Ltn* Schäfer of *Jasta 11* scored a victory: a BE2d of 4 Squadron.

Naval 6 and Naval 8 flew long distance patrols during the day, the only fighter squadrons to do so, and lost two pilots to the weather. Returning from a fight over the Cambrai area at noon, two Nieuports crashed due to the gale conditions. FltSubLt J deC Paynter had previously been wounded in a combat, but survived his crash. The other pilot, FltSubLt A L Thorne, was killed.

The weather worsened still further on April 10. Despite the conditions the Nieuports of 60 Squadron flew reconnaissance patrols but were forced to fly at only 200 feet. Naval 8 also attempted a patrol in the afternoon. The five triplanes became separated in the heavy snowstorms. Coming out of the storm, E D Crundall was completely lost. 'After a while I saw a Triplane following me so I realised that if I made a mistake in my direction both of us would be lost. I eventually saw an aerodrome, so I circled it, and and landed and the other Triplane landed behind me. Cuzner was flying it. There was nobody on the aerodrome and the hangars were empty. We pushed our Triplanes into a hangar.'[8] Crundall and Cuzner found a Frenchman who told them that they were at the abandoned aerodrome of St.Leger, but that there was a British aerodrome at Marieux, about three miles away. The duo walked to Marieux, which housed Naval 3, and found that another member of the patrol, Booker, had just landed there.

The next day the weather improved and it was a day of intense fighting, with many casualties. Nine BE2s were lost during the day, the Richthofen brothers, Lothar and Manfred, claiming one each.

Of the single-seater fighters, Naval 3 bore the brunt of the main fighting during the day. The squadron was detailed to escort BE2cs to bomb Cambrai. Approaching the target they

Above: The Maurice Farman S7 Longhorn. Many of the first fighter pilots of the RFC learned to fly on this type of machine.

Right: A Sopwith Tabloid, the type in which Lts Norman Spratt and Gordon Bell armed in various ways and flew while attached to the Aircraft Park in August 1914.

Right: This BE2b of 4 Squadron at St.Omer is typical of the type flown by the RFC in the early days of the war.

Top left: Lt Norman C Spratt. As was Gordon Bell, his contemporary in 3 Squadron, Spratt was a pre-war pilot.

Top right: Lt Charles Gordon Bell. C G Grey, the editor of the Aeroplane, wrote of Bell. 'Everyone who knew him well lived in a continual state of exasperated affection towards him. At times people who did not know him thought he was mad, but it was his exuberant sense of humour that really upset the stolid Englishman. Somehow Bell's quaint sayings were made funnier still by his queer little stutter which always seemed to add point to his remarks. His Dalmatian and beautiful white Hispano car were all part of the accoutrements of this vivid, irritating, loveable personality.' Bell scored five victories in 1915, before being returned to HE because of ill health. Bell was killed while test flying a Vickers FB16E on 29 July 1918.

Below: Lt Louis Strange. 5 Squadron 1914. This photograph was taken at Hendon in 1914 during a flying meeting.

A Henry Farman F 20. The type of machine in which Louis Strange and Penn Gaskell attempted to intercept the German aeroplane on 22 August 1914.

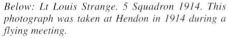

At the end of the retreat from Mons RFC HQ occupied the French aerodrome at Melun where this photograph was taken. This group of 3 Squadron NCOs enjoying tea and Crawford's biscuits includes FltSgt William McCudden (in braces) and Sgts A Kidd, H Robbins, E McEvoy and Corp G H White.

Above: A Bleriot Parasol.

Far left: Flt Sgt William Thomas James McCudden. The eldest of the McCudden brothers, Bill McCudden transferred from the Royal Engineers to the RFC in May 1912 (No.61) and was the fourth NCO pilot of the RFC to gain his Wings, taking his Royal Aero Club Certificate No.269 on 13 August 1912. At the outbreak of war McCudden was with 3 Squadron, but the squadron had a full complement of officer pilots and he was put in charge of the squadron's motor transport in France. William McCudden was killed in a flying accident on 1 May 1915 while serving as a flying instructor in 13 Squadron.

Left: Major Hubert Harvey-Kelly. Harvey-Kelly died of wounds on 29 April 1917.

Left: During the first days of the RFC in France a number of civilian vehicles were impressed into service. In 1914-1915, this Thornycroft van, belonging to a famous sauce manufacturer, was used by 3 Squadron as an ammunition carrier.

Above: The Bristol Scout C, powered by a 80hp Gnome engine.

Right: An Avro 504.

Right: An SE2.

Above: A Martinsyde S1. The type in which Louis Strange had his 'adventure' on 10 May 1915.

Left: Lanoe Hawker demonstrating how to keep warm in the air during the winter of 1914-1915. In March 1915 Hawker was serving with 6 Squadron, stationed at Poperhinghe, sharing the aerodrome with the French Escadrille MF 33. All the French pilots wore goatskin coats in an attempt to keep out the bitter cold and their British counterparts quickly followed suit, but retaining their very British balaclava helmets. Hawker is also wearing leather trousers and personal non-standard goggles.

Below: Bristol Scout type C No.1611. On 7 June 1915 Lanoe Hawker wrote home: 'I have a beautiful little toy, a new Bristol Scout that goes at 80 and climbs at five or six hundred feet a minute.' Hawker won the VC for his action on 25 July 1915 while flying this aeroplane.

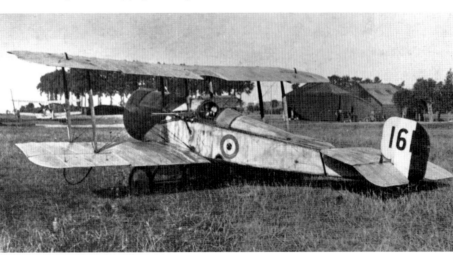

Above: A Fokker E III in flight. Despite its technical shortcomings the Fokker was an effective weapon in the hands of men such as Immelmann and Boelcke.

Right: A Vickers Gunbus from 16 Squadron in German hands.

Right: Oswald Boelcke and Max Immelmann. Two exponents of the Fokker Eindecker are the subjects of this contemporary German postcard Unsere Flieger-Helden (Our Flier Heroes). Immelmann's career was brief, albeit meteoric, but Boelcke was later to die in a mid-air collision after having brought down 40 allied aeroplanes.

Right: The FE2d. This aeroplane A 6516 is a presentation aeroplane The Colony of Mauritius No.13, powered by a 275hp Rolls Royce engine, and was flown by 20 Squadron in the summer of 1917. Although often depicted as 'easy meat' for the fighters of the Jagdstaffeln, and many were shot down, in capable hands the FE could still give a good account of itself and several high scoring German pilots were shot down by their crews. Max Immelman was shot down and killed by an FE crew of 25 Squadron and both Karl Schäfer and Manfred von Richthofen were shot down by crews of 20 Squadron. Richthofen was wounded in the head and crashlanded, but Schäfer was killed.

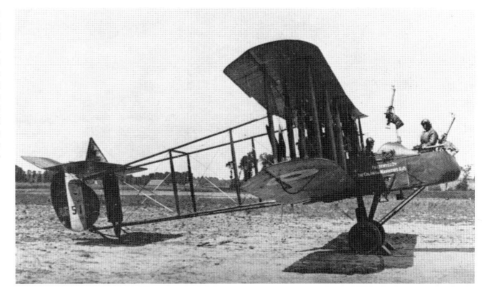

Right: A DH2 of 24 Squadron at Bertangles.

Below: Line up of 24 Squadron's DH2s at Bertangles July 1916. The red and white strut markings to differentiate the different Flights can be clearly seen. The aeroplane at the extreme right is a Morane-Saulnier N Type.

This Morane Bullett No.5069 from 1 Squadron was shot down on 9 March 1916. The pilot, 2Lt R P Turner, was killed.

2Lt David M Tidmarsh MC. 24 Squadron. On 2 April 1916, Tidmarsh and S J Sibley shot down an Albatros two-seater for 24 Squadron's first victory.

Pilots of 3 Naval Wing under instruction at Redcar. L to R Front Row: Arthur Dissette. unknown instructor. Gerald Nash. Back Row. L to R: John Sharman. Harold Edwards. Nash scored six victories with Naval 10 until he was shot down and taken prisoner on 25 June 1917. John Sharman became a flight commander in Naval 10 and was credited with eight victories until he was shot down and killed on 22 July 1917. He was posthumously awarded a DSC+Bar. Harold Edwards served as an Air Marshal in the RCAF in World War II.

Left: 2Lt S J Sibley. Sibley flew DH2s with 24 Squadron until injured in an accident on 25 August 1916.

Right: R H B Ker (left) and S E Cowan. One of 24 Squadron's original pilots, Cowan served with the squadron until posted to 29 Squadron as a Flight Commander on 1 October 1916. Attacking an enemy aeroplane on 17 November 1916 Cowan collided with the DH2 flown by 2Lt W S F Saundby and both men were killed.

Far right: 2Lt David Mary Tidmarsh MC stands by his shell damaged DH2 5929. On 21 April 1916 Tidmarsh was on patrol at 10,000ft when a howitzer shell reached its apogee and smashed through the nacelle of the DH2 without exploding, narrowly missing Tidmarsh's legs.

Right: The exit hole in the nacelle of DH2 5929. Tidmarsh later commented that he thought his knees had been 'decapitated.'

Below: DH2s of 29 Squadron on Abeele aerodrome 1916.

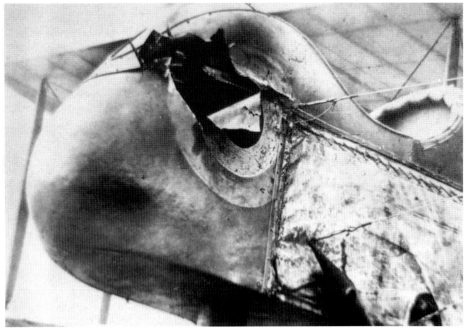

Above: Major William John Charles Kennedy-Cochran-Patrick DSO.MC+Bar in Nieuport 16 No.5172. This photograph was taken on 26 April 1916 after Kennedy-Cochran-Patrick had shot down an LVG C Type, the first of his 21 victories. At the time Kennedy-Cochran-Patrick was stationed at No1 AD at St Omer and the Nieuport was allocated to him for the defence of the Depot. Kennedy-Cochran-Patrick later served with distinction in 70, 23 and 60 Squadrons. Known throughout the RFC/RAF as simply 'Major Pat' Kennedy-Cochran-Patrick survived the war but was killed in a flying accident on 26 September 1933.

Right: Major Eric Lewis Conran. Conran commanded 29 Squadron from 25 May to 4 September 1916.

Far right: Sgt O G 'Jack' Noakes A brilliant pilot, Noakes flew DH2s with 29 Squadron from May 1916 to 20 January 1917.

Below: DH2s of 32 Squadron on Vert Galant aerodrome July 1916. The Squadron CO Major T A E Cairnes is standing on the far right.

Above: In June 1916 60 Squadron used a number of Morane-Saulnier Type BB biplanes powered by a 110hp Le Rhône engine.

Right: Naval pilots at Luxieul. Front Row. L to R: Thought to be FlCom J D Newberry. G R S Fleming. A W Carter. C Draper. D Masson. Back Row. L to R: P E Beasley. Unknown. W M Alexander.

Right: Francis 'Ferdy' Waldron.

Far right: William Mays Fry MC. Fry flew with 12, 11, 60, 23 and 79 Squadrons. Fry scored a total of 11 victories, one of which was Ltn Walter von Bülow Staffelführer of Jasta B with 28 victories. Fry returned to the RAF after the war and was a Wing Commander in World War II. 'Willie' Fry died on 4 August 1992.

Above: Bristol Scout Type D No.7053. This machine was one of the third production batch. It is armed with a synchronised Vickers gun firing through the propeller arc. On the port side is a chute for clearing spent cartridges.

Right: Capt Ernest Leslie Foot. 'Feet' Foot served in 11 and 60 Squadrons in 1916. He scored five victories until he was shot down in flames on 26 October 1916. Foot survived this crash but was posted to HE on 3 November 1916.

Far right: Embryo fighter pilot. Albert Ball at Hendon on 15 October 1915, the day he gained his Royal Aero Club Certificate No.1898.

Right: A Nieuport 16 of 60 Squadron. Late 1916.

Right: Lt T P H Bayetto, seen here with a Morane-Saulnier Type N, was a popular officer in the RFC. Bayetto's father was head chef at one of London's leading hotels and was always happy to give any of his son's RFC friends a superb meal free of charge.

Right: Lt Sidney Edward Cowan MC+2Bars. Serving in 24 Squadron flying DH2s, Cowan scored six victories between 4 May and 16 September 1916, becoming one of the first 'aces' of the RFC. Cowan transferred to 29 Squadron as a flight commander on 1 October 1916, scoring one more victory on 17 November 1916, but was killed in a mid-air collision later in the day.

Far right: Major F F Waldron (left) and Cap R R Smith-Barry of 60 Squadron in 1916. Smith-Barry took over the command of 60 Squadron after the death of Waldron on 3 July 1916. Smith-Barry was later the founder of the School of Special Flying at Gosport.

Below: After his crash on 3 July 1916 Major F 'Ferdy' Waldron's Morane Bullet A 175 was crudely reconstructed by the Germans.

Right: Lionel Wilmot Brabazon Rees VC. OBE. MC. AFC.

Far right: Capt L P Aizlewood MC. 32 Squadron.

Right: An aggressive Lt G H Bonnell in the cockpit of his DH2 in 32 Squadron in 1916.

Below: Pilots of 32 Squadron, Vert Galant aerodrome, September 1916. L to R: Lt G H Bonnell. Lt C T Inman (equipment officer). Lt M J Mare-Montembault. Lt F H Coleman. Capt J M Robb. Capt L P Aizlewood MC. Capt H W G Jones. Lt R H Wallace. Capt C H Nicholas. Capt E Henty. Capt C N Martin. Major T A E Cairnes. Capt G Allen. Lt C R Bath. Capt H W von Poellnitz. Lt O V Thomas. Lt G H Lewis. Lt P Hunt.

Right: Capt R E A W Hughes-Chamberlain. 24 Squadron 1916. Hughes-Chamberlain was wounded on 16 August 1916.

Far right: Squadron Commander Redford Henry Mulock DSO+Bar DSC+Bar LdeH. Mulock was a Canadian who joined the Canadian Field Artillery in 1911, transferred to the RNAS in 1915 and was the first commanding officer of Naval 3 in France.

Right: Capt John Oliver Andrews while flight commander of A Flight 24 Squadron 1916.

Far right: Capt Albert Ball with his Nieuport in 60 Squadron.

Above: The cockpit of Ball's Nieuport 16.

Right: One of the earliest Nieuport 16s to be transferred from the RNAS to the RFC was this machine A126. It was issued to 11 Squadron on 26 April 1916 and flown by Lt Albert Ball.

Right: Pilots of 32 Squadron. Vert Galant 1916. L to R: W G S Curphey. E Henty. F H Coleman. M J Mare-Montembault. R E Wilson. Wilson was shot down and taken POW by Boelcke on 2 September 1916; Curphey was shot down in flames on 14 May 1917 and died of his wounds the next day; Mare-Montembault was shot down and taken prisoner on 6 March 1917 by Tutschek of Jasta B, and Coleman was injured in a flying accident on 7 August 1917.

Right: Capt. James Douglas Latta MC. Latta flew Nieuports in 1 and 66 Squadrons, scoring five victories. Latta was wounded in combat on 8 June 1917. He is seen here while a fighting instructor at the Ayr.

Below: The Albatros D I first began to appear over the Western Front in mid-September 1916. This D I. No.391/16 was shot down by Captains Parker and Hervey of 8 Squadron on 16 November 1916. The pilot was Ltn Karl Büttner of Jasta B.

Right: This DH2 5994 from 29 Squadron was shot down on 25 August 1916. Lt K K Turner was taken prisoner.

Right: Lt W A C Morgan (left) and Lt S J Sibley with his head bandaged after crashing his DH2 on 25 August 1916 after a fight with an enemy two-seater.

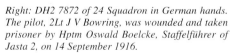

Above: Lt R E Wilson (left) and Hptm Oswald Boelcke after Wilson's capture on 2 September 1916.

Right: DH2 7872 of 24 Squadron in German hands. The pilot, 2Lt J V Bowring, was wounded and taken prisoner by Hptm Oswald Boelcke, Staffelführer of Jasta 2, on 14 September 1916.

Left: K H Riversdale-Elliot. S E Cowan. S J Sibley and R H B Ker of 24 Squadron examining a machine gun taken from an enemy two-seater shot down on 20 May 1916 by Lt D Wilson.

Opposite
Top: 'A' Flight of 41 Squadron on 10 October 1916, five days before leaving for France. On the extreme right, wearing a forage cap, is Capt H Jackson, who was hit by anti aircraft fire on the morning of 7 June 1917 and later died of his wounds after his FE8 6437 crashed in the British lines.

Center left: Oswald Boelcke. Boelcke commanded Jasta 2 from July 1916 until his death in action on 28 October when he collided with another Albatros of his Jasta flown by Erwin Böhme. In December 1916 Jasta 2 was renamed Jasta Boelcke in Boelcke's honour.

Center right: Nieuport 16 A 125, marked B 4 on the top decking, was shot down on 3 November 1916. The pilot Lt J M J Spenser of 60 Squadron is variously reported to have been killed, or died of his wounds while in captivity.

Bottom: DH2 A 2543. 2Lt I Curlewis of 29 Squadron was wounded and shot down while flying this machine on 9 November 1916.

Far left: Capt Alan Duncan Bell-Irving. A Canadian from Vancouver, Bell-Irving was wounded on 14 December 1915 while flying as an observer with 7 Squadron. After recovering he trained as a pilot and joined 60 Squadron in May 1916. He opened his score on 18 August, shooting down a Roland C type and by 15 October had been awarded seven victories, including a balloon. He was shot down on 21 October, and survived uninjured, but on 9 November he was wounded in the left thigh and crashlanded. Bell-Irving was awarded a MC+Bar and a CdeG for his work in 60 Squadron.

Left: DH2 A 2542 in a German scrapyard. Lt P A Langan Byrne of 24 Squadron was shot down and killed on 16 October 1916 by Oswald Boelcke for his 34th victory.

Left: A Sopwith Pup. Often described as the most delightful flying machine ever made, the Sopwith Pup was operational with two RFC squadrons by the end of 1916.

Right: A leader of men who combined modesty with courage, gentleness with a steely determination and unselfishness with a most human understanding.' Capt Lanoe G Hawker VC, DSO, Royal Engineers and RFC.

Far right: Capt Norman Brearley DSO.MC. 29 Squadron 1916. An Australian, Brearley was wounded in action on 9 November 1916. He crashed behind enemy lines but escaped overnight to the British trenches.

Right: 2Lt Deane of 41 Squadron was last seen over Picanton on 26 November 1916 flying this FE8 No.6454 '6'. The machine suffered engine failure and Deane was forced to land behind enemy lines.

Right: On leave. Flt Sgt James McCudden 3 Squadron. The pillion passenger is his sister Mary.

Right: Lt R H Soundy of 41 Squadron fully attired to combat the bitter winter cold of 1916-1917 in the exposed open cockpit of an FE8.

Far right: 60 Squadron's Christmas card for 1916, designed by Capt Roderic Hill.

Right and below: Two views of Sopwith Pup A 626 from Naval 8. This machine was shot down near Bapaume on 4 January 1917 and FltSubLt J C Croft was made POW. This victory has been credited to Ltn Mallinckrodt of Jasta 10 but his claim is too far south, at Neuchatel near Rheims.

Above: Nieuports of A Flight 60 Squadron on Izel-le-
Hamel aerodrome in the winter of 1917. L to R: Lt C
S Hall. Capt H Kirton. Lt G O Smart. Hall and Smart
were both shot down on the afternoon of 7 April 1917
by Jasta 11. Smart, flying Nieuport 17 A6645, was
Manfred von Richthofen's 37th victory and Hall, in
Nieuport 23 A6766, was either the 12th victory for
Ltn Karl Schäfer or the 7th victory of Ltn Kurt Wolff.
In a later patrol the same evening, 60 Squadron lost
Capt M B Knowles, taken POW by Jasta 4, and
although Lt H Hervey returned safely his Nieuport
was shot about and badly damaged.

Two at right: The Opposition. The Albatros D III
(above) began to appear at the front in January 1917,
replacing the earlier variants, the DI and DII. The
next development of the type, the DV (below) began
to equip the jagdstaffeln in July 1917, followed by a
further development the DVa. The Albatros scouts were
the mainstay of the German jagdstaffeln until the
introduction of the Fokker D VII in the spring of 1918,
but there were still large numbers of Albatros still in
service at the end of the war. The Albatros scout was
referred to as a 'V' Strutter by the pilots of the RFC,
and the plural was 'Albatri' a term much preferred to
the 'verbal atrocity of Albatrosess'.

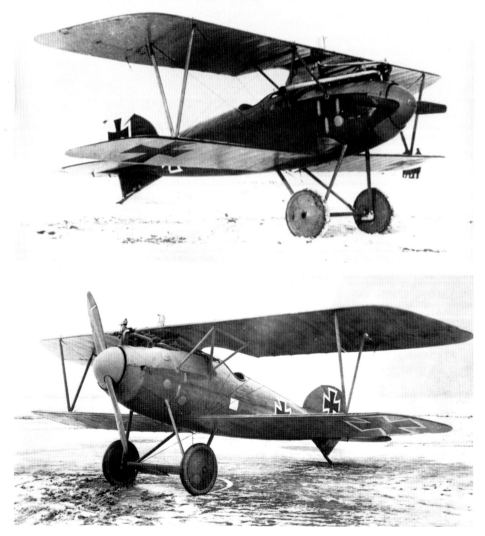

Right: Sgt Pilot Cecil Stephen Tooms. 41 Squadron. Tooms brought down an Albatros scout for 41 Squadron's first victory on the morning of 24 January 1917. Only four hours later, while flying an afternoon patrol, Tooms was shot down and killed by Vzfw Ulmer of Jasta 8.

Far right: Squadron Commander Christopher Draper DSC. Draper was a pre-war pilot, gaining his Royal Aero Club Certificate in October 1913. Draper joined the RNAS in January 1914 and served with 3 Wing, Naval 6, Naval 8 and commanded 208 Squadron RAF in 1918. Draper is credited with nine victories. His autobiography is entitled The Mad Major. Draper died in 1979.

Right: Pilots of C Flight 60 Squadron at Savy, December 1916. L to R: Lt A D Whitehead. Lt L S Weedon. Capt H Meintjes (Flight Commander). Lt K L Caldwell. Capt A Binnie. Lt W M Fry.

Below: Nieuport 16 A201 of A Flight 60 Squadron at Izel-le-Hameau in January-March 1917. L to R: Lt H Hamer. Lt H Kirton. Lt G Smart. Albert Ball scored 11 of his 44 victories flying this Nieuport. He first flew it in 11 Squadron, scoring his 8th victory while flying it on 16 August 1916. On 23 August 1916, Ball was transferred to 60 Squadron and he took this Nieuport with him, scoring his 29th victory with it on 30 September 1916.

Above: Nieuports of C Flight 60 Squadron at Izel-le-Hameau, January 1917. The Nieuport on the extreme right, A274, marked C2, was flown by Lt William Fry. The airman standing on the left, in front of Nieuport A6646 C5, is Sgt Day.

Right: Capt Hubert Wilson Godfrey Jones (left) and Lt B P G Hunt of 32 Squadron. Jones scored seven victories while with 32 Squadron. On 11 March 1917 he transferred to 24 Squadron as commander of C Flight, but was wounded ten days later, coming down in the British lines.

Right: Lt S Hay in FE8 7616 of 41 Squadron on patrol over the Ypres Salient in early 1917. Note the Flight Commander's streamers flying from both wingtips.

Above: Nieuports of C Flight 60 Squadron at Filescamp Farm aerodrome in early 1917.

Right: A Spad VII. Spads were flown on the Western front by 19 and 23 Squadrons. The Spad VII was first ordered by the Admiralty for use by the RNAS squadrons, but on 26 February 1917 the Admiralty agreed to exchange all its Spads for Sopwith Triplanes, then on order for the RFC. Subsequently, the naval pilots flew the Sopwith Triplanes with great success.

Above: Capt Robert Henry Magnus Spenser Saundby MC. Saundby flew DH2s with 24 Squadron in 1916 and scored three victories while with the squadron. In January 1917 Saundby was posted to 41 Squadron to fly FE8s and he scored another victory in March 1917 before being posted to HE. In the early hours of the morning of 17 July 1917 Saundby was one of three aircraft of 37 Home Defence Squadron which individually attacked Zeppelin L 48 and brought it down in flames in Suffolk. Saundby remained in the RAF after the war and in 1946 retired as Air Marshal Sir Robert Saundby KCB. KBE. MC. DFC. AFC. MC. DFC.

Center right: The fuselage of Albatros D III 910/16 '8' being taken away for examination. This machine was being flown by Ltn Max Böhme of Jasta 5 when he was shot down and taken prisoner by Lt Pearson of 29 Squadron and Lts Graham and Boddy of 11 Squadron on 4 March 1917. The Albatros was given the captured number G 14. Right: FE8 A 4874 '4'. 2Lt G F Haseler of 40 Squadron was forced to land and taken POW on 9 March 1917. Haseler's FE8 was one of six lost by 40 Squadron in the morning patrol on this date. Three pilots were taken POW and three forced to land with badly damaged aircraft. One wounded pilot, 2Lt R E Neve, survived by jumping clear of his burning machine before it crashed.

Above: FE8 A 6456.Another of the FE8s lost by 40 Squadron on 9 March 1916. 2Lt T Shepard was taken POW.

Above: Major Evelyn Paget Graves. Graves was appointed to the command of 60 Squadron just before Christmas 1916. He was shot down in flames and killed on 6 March 1917.

Left: Capt Kenneth Leaske in FE8 7626 of 41 Squadron over the Ypres Salient in early 1917.

Left: Nieuport A 6617 was shot down on 17 March 1917 by Ltn Paul Strähle of Jasta 18. 2Lt A J Gilson of 1 Squadron was killed.

Left: Spad A 6706. Lt R P Baker of 19 Squadron was wounded and taken POW in this Spad on 24 March 1917.

Above: The fuselage of Albatros D I 410/16. This Albatros was flown by Rittmeister Prinz Friedrich Karl of FlAbt (A) 258 who was shot down and taken prisoner on 21 March 1917 by Lt Pickthorne of 32 Squadron. Karl died of his wounds on 7 April.

Above: Major William Arthur Grattan-Bellew. Commanding Officer 29 Squadron from 5 September 1916 to 21 March 1917. Grattan-Bellew was fatally injured in a flying accident while ferrying the last of 29 Squadron's DH2s back to No.2 Aeroplane Depot.

Left: Capt William Bishop with his Nieuport in 60 Squadron.

The wreckage of Nieuport 17 A 6615. Lt Hugh Welch of 1 Squadron was killed on 28 March 1917 by Oblt Bethge of Jasta 30. Above left can just be seen Bethge's Albatros, upended in a muddy field after he attempted to land close by.

Above: Roderic Stanley Dallas. Dallas served in 1 Naval Wing in 1916, scoring six victories. When 1 Naval Wing became Naval 1 Squadron in 1917, equipped with Sopwith Triplanes, Dallas added another sixteen victories and became a flight commander with a DSC. On the formation of the RAF on 1 April 1918, Dallas was given command of 40 Squadron, where he scored another nine victories, bringing his total to 32.

A contemporary German postcard of 1917 by Sanke, publicising the fighter pilots of Richthofen's Jasta 11. L to R: Vzfw Sebastian Festner. Ltn Karl Schäfer. Rittmeister Manfred von Richthofen. Ltn Lothar von Richthofen. Ltn Kurt Wolff. Only Lothar von Richthofen survived the war. He was killed in a flying accident in 1922.

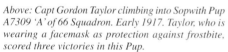

Above: Capt Gordon Taylor climbing into Sopwith Pup A7309 'A' of 66 Squadron. Early 1917. Taylor, who is wearing a facemask as protection against frostbite, scored three victories in this Pup.

Right: Nieuport 'VI' of 40 Squadron at Bruay. 1917.

Below: Nieuport A 6605 '3' of 1 Squadron has collected a crowd of curious German troops. Its pilot, Lt R J Bevington, was taken POW on 7 April 1917. A Lewis gun drum can be seen on the tailplane.

Right: Lt Oliver 'Stewpot' Stewart of 54 Squadron with his personally monogrammed Sopwith Pup in 1917. This is almost certainly Sopwith Pup A 6156 in which he scored three of his five victories.

Below: The SE5s of 56 Squadron lined up on London Colney aerodrome on the morning of 7 April 1917 just about to leave for France.

Bottom: Pilots of 56 Squadron at London Colney aerodrome in April 1917 just before leaving for France. Back Row. L to R: G J Constable Maxwell. W B Melville. H M T Lehmann. C R W Knight. L M Barlow. K J Knaggs. Front Row. L to R: C A Lewis. J O Leach. R G Blomfield (CO). A Ball. R T C Hoidge.

Top: On leaving England the pilots of 56 Squadron were issued life belts for the flight across the Channel. Lt Kenneth Knaggs is wearing his on the morning of 7 April at London Colney.

Bottom: FltSubLt Thomas Grey Culling. A New Zealander, Culling flew with 1 Naval in the April and May of 1917. He was credited with six victories.

Top: Capt Ernest Foot in the cockpit of an SE5. Posted to 56 Squadron in March 1917, Foot was injured in a car accident the evening before the squadron left for France. Foot was killed flying a Bristol M 1C on 23 June 1923 while taking part in The Grosvenor Trophy Race.

Bottom: Pilots of 1 Squadron. Spring 1917. L to R: E S T Cole. Lionel Mars. James Slater. P M Le Gallais.

Top: Lts H E Hervey MC+Bar (60 Sqdn). Leslie M Mansbridge (C Flight Commander 1 Sqdn). Arthur P F Rhys Davids (56 Sqdn). This photograph was taken while training at the Central Flying School in early 1917.

Bottom: FltLt C D Booker. Naval 8. Spring 1917.

Above: Lt Edwin Stuart Travis Cole in Nieuport A 6603 of 1 Squadron. One of the first Nieuport 17s to be issued to 1 Squadron in January 1917, Cole scored two of his eight victories in this machine.

Right: Spad A 6690 of 23 Squadron, shot down on 11 April 1917 by Ltn Frommherz of Jasta B for his first victory. The pilot, 2Lt S Roche, was taken prisoner.

Right: FltCom R G Mack of Naval 8 was flying his personally named Sopwith Pup N 6172 'Black Tulip' when he was shot down and taken POW on 12 April 1917 by Hptm Paul von Osterroht, Staffelführer of Jasta 12. Osterroht was shot down and killed eleven days later by pilots of Naval 8.

Top left: FltCom Edward Duncan Crundall in his Sopwith Triplane 'Whitfield', named after his home village.

Above: Capts Geoffrey Pidcock (left) and Keith 'Grid' Caldwell. 60 Squadron.

Left: Ltn Hanko of Jasta 28 shot down Nieuport A 313 of 1 Squadron on 22 April 1917. Lt A W Wood was wounded and taken POW.

Below: Sopwith Triplanes of Naval 8. Spring 1917. N 5468 'Angel' was flown by FltLt C H B Jenner-Parson; the next Triplane N 5465 was flown by FltSubLt E D Crundall.

were attacked by Albatros and Halberstadt scouts. FltLt Breadner, leading the patrol, shot one of the enemy scouts down in flames, but other enemy scouts went down to attack the BEs. Breadner drove off an Albatros, then attacked another which spun down, one wing breaking off. FltSubLt J S T Fall attacked another and sent it down in flames, but he then became separated from the rest of the Pups and attacked by three aggressive Albatros pilots, who forced him down to 200 feet. Manoeuvring to evade their attacks, Fall suddenly found one of the Albatri to his right, flying so close that as he turned to attack it the pilot's head filled the small ring of his Aldis sight. Fall saw his tracers hit the German pilot in the head and the Albatros spun into the ground. No doubt shaken by the loss of their comrade, the remaining two Albatri cleared east. Coming under fire from German cavalry and machine guns, Fall flew towards the British trenches at 200 feet. Just before he reached them, he was attacked by an Halberstadt. The enemy pilot made a quick pass, broke away, then returned. Fall evaded this second attack, looping straight over the Halberstadt and firing a long burst into it. The enemy scout went down and crashed. Crossing the German trenches, Fall again came under heavy fire from the ground, but he landed safely on 35 Squadron's aerodrome at Savy with his Pup badly shot about. All the remaining Pups returned safely, although Flt Sub-Lt Bennett's aeroplane was also badly damaged, probably from ground fire as some of the fighting had taken place at only 50 feet.

The Spads of 23 Squadron were also in the action near Cambrai and lost one of their number during the fighting: 2Lt S Roche, forced to land at Cuvillers and taken POW by *Ltn* H Frommherz of *Jasta B*. The squadron lost another Spad later in the day. At half past twelve, in the vicinity of Noreuil, *Ltn* F O Bernert of *Jasta B* shot down a Morane Parasol of 3 Squadron then turned his attention to a Spad from 23 Squadron flown by Lt F C Troup. Bernert's accurate fire shot away Troup's control wires and he was forced to land at Ecoust-St Mien.

The bad weather returned the next day, April 12, with snow blizzards. What reconnaissance work that could be carried out showed the German forces retreating. A vast gap had been pushed through the German defensive positions in front of Arras and it would be some time before reinforcements could be brought up. North of the Scarpe, however, the Germans were holding firm and the British troops penetrated only as far as the village of Monchy.

The extreme weather curtailed air operations. The only casualty for the fighter squadrons was a Sopwith Pup of Naval 3. FltLt Robin Mack led an escort for the FEs of 18 Squadron and the formation was attacked by *Jasta 12* in the vicinity of Queant-Pronville. During the fighting one of the enemy scouts was seen to go down with its wings broken off, and another

three seen to fall out of control, but Mack failed to return. He had been wounded in the leg and forced to land by *Hptm* von Osterroht for his fifth victory. Mack managed to land his Pup (named Black Tulip) undamaged, but his foot was later amputated in a German hospital. On their return no one claimed the Albatros going down with its wings broken off and it was assumed that it had been shot down by Mack, but it was in all probability that flown by *Ltn* Schulte who had collided with one of the FEs.

The pilots of C Flight Naval 3 all gave their Pups 'black' names. As well as Robin Mack's Black Tulip, Leonard Rochford flew Black Bess, Art Whealy flew Black Prince and Raymond Collishaw, Black Maria. The cowlings of the C Flight Pups were all painted black, with B Flight favouring red and A Flight blue.

April 13 was the first day since the beginning of the offensive that the weather conditions were good enough for a full day's work in the air. The *Luftstreitkräfte* were concentrating in an attempt to protect their retreating ground forces, flying low-level operations over the battlefront.

It was a bad day for 19 Squadron. Detailed to escort six RE8s of 59 Squadron they took off too late to meet the two seaters at the rendezvous and failed to find them. The RE8s were on a photo-reconnaissance mission of the front line from Quiery-la-Motte to Etaing, dangerously close to *Jasta 11*'s aerodrome at Douai. Within the space of a few minutes all the RE8s were shot down by the pilots of *Jasta 11*, Manfred von Richthofen claimed one, his brother Lothar another, with *Ltn* Wolff and *Vzfw* Festner claiming one each. The remaining two RE8s were not credited to individual pilots of *Jasta 11* but they failed to return and their crews were reported killed in action. In total, 59 Squadron lost ten aircrew killed in action from this engagement, with only Festner's victory surviving to be wounded and taken POW.

In another close escort, this time to 12 Martinsydes of 27 Squadron, 19 Squadron had more success. They failed to save one Martinsyde, which was shot down by *Ltn* Kurt Wolff of *Jasta 11,* but they saw the remaining eleven safely back over the Lines, then went back to tackle the enemy scouts. An Albatros was claimed as out of control near Brebières by Lt G S Buck of the squadron; possibly *Uffz* Simon Ruckser of *Jasta 37,* wounded in action on April 13.

In the evening, attacks were carried out on the railway centre at Hénin-Liétard in an attempt to stop German reinforcements arriving for the battle of Arras. The FE2bs of 25 Squadron were escorted by Nieuports of 40 Squadron, but after the two-seaters had dropped their bombs the Nieuports left their charges and the pushers were attacked by *Jasta 11*. Manfred von Richthofen shot down one FE – his second victory of the day over the type – and *Vzfw* Festner shot down another.

Jasta 4 were also in the action and another FE was claimed by *Ltn* Klein.

April 13 was a day of heavy casualties for the RFC. Seven FEs failed to return and another was badly shot up. Six RE8s were lost, plus a Morane, a Martinsyde, a Bristol F2a. and a Nieuport 12. In addition a BE was shot up and badly damaged with 29 hits. The fighter squadrons had only one casualty, a Nieuport of 23 Squadron: 2Lt B Scott-Foxwell, who was wounded and shot down over Monchy-le-Preux by *Ltn* Kurt Wolff of *Jasta 11*. The day had seen 20 RFC personnel killed in action; seven wounded and six POW, three of whom were wounded.

As the heavy ground fighting continued on the Arras front massive German reinforcements were thrown into the battle, bringing the number of troops employed to almost double those at the outset of the British offensive. The *Luftstreitkräfte* was also reinforced: four additional *Flieger Abteilung*, both for reconnaissance and artillery work; a *Schutzstaffel (Schusta)* for the protection of the *Flieger Abteilung,* and two *Jasta* – 12 and 33 – were moved into the area.

The *Luftstreitkräfte* had also modified its tactics. The pilots of the *Jagdstaffeln* were no longer flying high patrols. They were now flying low to evade the high British fighter patrols and attacking the corps aeroplanes working at lower levels. The *Jagdstaffeln* were also conserving their strength by the intelligent of the *Flugmeldedienst* officers, operating only when British fighters were not in the immediate area, when their attacks would have the maximum effect.

The Sopwith Pups of 54 Squadron took off at dawn on Saturday April 14 to patrol the Cambrai area. Lt R N S Smith was wounded in a fight with enemy scouts but returned safely. Lt M B Cole attacked a two-seater over Gonnelieu and killed or wounded the observer who was seen hanging over the side of the fuselage.

Later in the morning another attempt was made to photograph the front line from Quiery-la-Motte to Etaing. To forestall a repetition of the disastrous losses of the previous day, suffered by the RE8s of 59 Squadron, the FE2bs of 11 Squadron were used, escorted by Nieuports from 29 Squadron. The photo-reconnaissance machines and their escort took off at 8.40am and were intercepted by *Jasta 4* over Vitry. The Nieuports successfully prevented the *Jasta* pilots from getting among the FEs – only one of which was shot up, with its observer Corporal W Hodgson killed – but lost 2Lt E J Pascoe who was shot down and killed over Fresnoy by *Oblt* von Döring for his first victory.

B Flight of 60 Squadron – Capt A Binnie, leading Lts W Russell, L Chapman, G Young and J Cock – had also taken off in the early morning to patrol the Douai area. Binnie and Russell dived to attack a pair of hostile two-seaters near Douai but return fire from the observer of one hit Russell's Nieuport in the petrol tank. Petrol poured over Russell's legs and his engine stopped. At this juncture *Jasta 11* also attacked the patrol. Manfred von Richthofen attacked the disabled Russell and shot the Nieuport down to crash just south of Bois Bernard. Russell was made POW. Binnie was hit in the shoulder by Lothar von Richthofen while changing a drum on his top wing Lewis gun. The Nieuport caught fire. Binnie sideslipped down and managed to put out the fire, but then fainted with the pain from his shoulder. Luckily Binnie regained consciousness in time to land the damaged Nieuport behind the lines, but it ran into a shell hole and turned over, again catching fire. German troops pulled Binnie, again unconscious, from the blazing wreckage and he came to in a German hospital where his arm was later amputated.[9]

Ltn Kurt Wolff shot down the New Zealander John Cock, who was killed, and *Vzfw* Festner shot down Lewis Chapman. Chapman was made POW but had been wounded by Festner's fire and died of his wounds two days later. Lt Graham Young was the only pilot to return from this patrol. He had turned to attack two of the Albatri but his gun jammed after only five shots. Turning quickly away, he stalled and the Nieuport went into a spin. When Young finally managed regain control he was alone in the sky and could see no sign of the others. After patrolling over Arras for a time, he returned to Le Hameau.

Led by FltLt Charles Booker, C Flight of Naval 8 took off from Auchel at 8.00am as escort for the FEs of 25 Squadron flying a photo-reconnaissance mission. The engine of FltSubLt Crundall's triplane was running badly and he could not keep up with the formation. An hour after takeoff, a long way east of the lines, Crundall saw two aeroplanes of a type he had not seen before. 'They looked somewhat like Nieuports but much bigger.' Crundall was 'a bit scared.' Not only was he alone with a badly running engine, but the aeroplanes, which he suspected were German, were between him and the safety of the British lines. He realised that he had to make a decision. The thought of being taken prisoner terrified him, so he decided to 'have a go and sell my life as dearly as possible if I had to fight.' Crundall climbed as steeply as his faulty engine would allow. The strange aeroplanes also climbed, confirming Crundall's suspicions that they were hostile. When they were about three to four miles away, Crundall turned and approached them. At a hundred yards Crundall saw that they were two-seaters, the black crosses clearly visible on their top wings, and one of the enemy observers opened fire. This made Crundall furious. 'I literally saw red and dived on the tail of the nearest, firing my gun all the time. I got closer and closer to his tail until I was almost touching it, and I could see the pilot's and observer's heads and every detail of the machine.' The two-seater went over on one wing and went down in a steep nosedive. Crundall was thrilled by this unexpected success, relaxed his vigilance, and was attacked by the other two-seater. Crundall again 'saw red.' He turned quickly got onto his attacker's tail and fired a long burst at close range. The enemy went down in a step dive with Crundall following, but he realised, as the dive steepened, that the triplane's wings were in danger of breaking off and he shut off his engine and eased out of his dive. Levelling out he found that the triplane was flying left wing heavy and he had to hold his control column fully over to the right to maintain level flight.

The fight had started at 14,000 feet, but Crundall was now down to 7,000 feet, well east of Douai, the home of *Jasta 11*. Crundall made for the safety of the British lines, but the strong westerly wind hampered his progress and it took him thirty minutes to reach the front line trenches, heavily archied all the way. He landed at the first friendly aerodrome, filled up with petrol and oil, ascertained his position and flew back to Auchel. After having made out his combat report Crundall inspected his triplane. It was badly damaged. All the flying wires were stretched and slack, and one of the centre section struts had cracked and was bent out of straight. Only one bullet hole was found, in the lower left hand wing. All the other damage was the result of the prolonged dive. A more detailed inspection later found the triplane to be even more badly strained than at first thought, and also located another bullet hole: a round had penetrated the engine cowling, just missing the petrol tank.

Both the enemy two-seaters had been seen to crash by independent witnesses and Crundall was awarded two Albatros C types as destroyed.

In the evening, Spads from 19 Squadron took off on an offensive patrol along the line Bailleul-Vitry-Sains. In the vicinity of Bailleul they were attacked by *Jasta 11*. Lt Edward Capper engaged *Ltn* Kurt Wolff, but the highly experienced Wolff quickly reversed the position and shot Capper's Spad down in flames. Lothar von Richthofen also claimed a 'Sopwith' down from this fight, but the squadron lost only Capper, killed in action, and Lt J W Baker wounded.

The weather was bad on April 15, with rain and low clouds all day, the rain constant until 4 o'clock in the afternoon. Only a few sorties were flown by the Corps squadrons, which had one casualty: a BE of 2 Squadron was badly shot up by archie, wounding the pilot.

During the day Haig informed his army commanders that he proposed a pause of several days before launching any further attacks on the Arras front. In place of the local attacks, which had been made to consolidate the early successes of the first phases of the battle and to insure the forward positions were more tenable, his aim was now to prepare for a large-scale, well co-ordinated attack

April 16 saw only a little improvement in the weather, with a few clear spells during the day. However, it was essential that air operations on the Arras front should still be carried out if at all possible and the corps squadrons were fully engaged. Another attempt was made to photograph the important part of the line between Drocourt and Queant. This time the FEs of 18 Squadron were heavily escorted to protect them from the *Jagdstaffeln* and none were lost.

A patrol of six Nieuports of 60 Squadron took off on an offensive patrol at 8.00am. Yet again the squadron was to suffer heavily at the hands of the highly experienced pilots of *Jasta 11*. An hour and a quarter after taking off the Nieuports were attacked by von Richthofen's pilots over Plouvain and four were shot down. 2Lt G H Pidcock, leading the patrol succeeded in driving down two of the Albatri, but Lt John MacC Elliott, a Canadian, was killed, crashing near Vitry, and 2Lt R E Kimbell was shot down near Roeux by Kurt Wolff. Lothar von Richthofen claimed Lt D N Robertson, who came down near Rouex. Robertson, from Glasgow, was wounded and taken prisoner, but later died of his wounds. 2Lt Trevor Langwill was also wounded. He came down at Biache St.Vaast and was taken POW but died of his wounds the next day in Douai hospital. Langwill was claimed by *Vzfw* Festner, whose engine was hit in the fight, forcing him to make an emergency landing.

Only Pidcock and Leckie returned from this patrol. Sixty Squadron had lost eight pilots in three days. Major Scott, commanding the squadron, was forced to suspend patrols until replacement aeroplanes and pilots had been obtained. Luckily, the weather conditions deteriorated so much that no flying was possible for the next four days, enabling the squadron to replace its aeroplanes and attempt to train its new pilots.

At 6.00am the French opened their planned offensive in the south. At first all went well, but German reinforcements poured into the battle and at the end of the first day's fighting none of the objectives had been achieved.[10]

On the Arras front the weather was bad for the next three days and there was very little flying. Although Bishop of 60 Squadron claimed a two-seater, shot down in flames near Biache St.Vaast on April 20, the *Luftstreitkräfte* reported no losses in the area.

There was a general improvement of the weather on April 21, but mist and low cloud over the front lines hampered the work of the RFC, not clearing until late in the afternoon. At 4.30pm six Nieuports from 29 Squadron took off on an Offensive Patrol. The Flight had no sooner crossed the lines than they were attacked by *Jasta 11* just east of Fresnes. Second Lts C V deB Rogers, F Sadler and A B Morgan were all shot down and killed by Lothar von Richthofen, Kurt Wolff and Karl Schäfer.

The Pups of Naval 3 were in action just after 5.30pm with four Albatros D IIIs in the Cagnicourt area. FltSubLt Hubert Broad sent one down out of control, which was seen to crash, and Irishman, FltLt Francis Casey, also sent two down out of control. It was a successful evening for Naval 3, the Canadian John Malone also claimed a two-seater in the evening, possibly from *Schusta 11*, and H G 'Tiny' Travers also claimed a victory.[11]

Later in the afternoon the FE2bs of 25 Squadron were carrying out a photo-reconnaissance when they were attacked by *Jasta 30*. The Sopwith Triplanes of Naval 8 were nearby, at 12,000 feet over Oppy, and hurried into the fight. Robert Little had seen the enemy scouts while they were climbing west with the intention of attacking the FEs and as they began their attack Little dived on the nearest, opening fire from 20 yards. The unfortunate German pilot was caught between two fires, from the gunner of the FE and Little. The Albatros dived away, out of control, nearly colliding with the FE, which had been hit and was gliding down. Little left the fight with a jammed gun and landed beside the FE to see if he could help. The FE had crashlanded near Bouvigny Wood, badly shot about, but the crew were unhurt. The Albatros attacked by Little, crashlanded but the pilot, *Ltn* Oscar Seitz, was uninjured.

Another member of Little's patrol also claimed a victory from the fight. Despite having a gun jam in his first attack on the enemy scouts, FltLt A Arnold stayed in the fight, hampering them in their attacks on the FEs. However, his first attack had been successful and he saw one of the Albatri going down with its wings broken off, hit both by his fire and the gunner of the FE it had been attacking. This was Albatros D III 2147/16 which fell in the British lines and was given the number G22. Its pilot, *Ltn* Gustav Nernst was killed.

German two-seaters were claimed during the day by the pilots of 23 Squadron. A patrol from the squadron engaged three in the vicinity of Cambrai. Lt R H Stoken attacked one over Sauchy Lestree, forcing it down to within 800 feet of the ground and firing over 200 rounds into it. In the words of the RFC communiqué: 'This HA was seen to disappear into a small wood.' Two other 23 Squadron pilots also claimed victories. Lt R Keller drove another two-seater down, and Capt K McAllum either killed or wounded the observer in another.

Sunday, April 22 was fine but cloudy. Attacks were made in the morning on German observation balloons along the entire front. Although three balloons were brought down in flames and a further four hauled down emitting smoke, these brought retaliatory attacks on British balloons and three were shot down in flames by Gontermann and Schneider of *Jasta 5*.

Sixty Squadron pilots had been involved in these attacks. A few minutes after 7.00am, Lts H Ross and G Wood each shot a balloon down in flames over Drury and Boiry Notre

Dame respectively, and Lt W Moleswoth sent a third down smoking. Half an hour later, over Vis-en-Artois, Lt A Penny sent another down in flames.

While the German balloons were being attacked, seven formations of single-seater fighters and three of two-seater fighters from the Army Wings – a total of 50 aeroplanes – were patrolling the battle front: an area roughly twenty miles long by six miles deep. In the face of this opposition the German fighter pilots dived away east on being attacked, and regained their height, waiting their chance to return to the front lines and attack the aeroplanes of the Corps squadrons working over the battle front. These tactics were highly successful and the *Jagdstaffeln* claimed nine victories during the day.

Three Sopwith triplanes of Naval 1 took off at 4.30am: FltLt Roderic Dallas leading FltSubLts T G Culling and R G Carr. Carr was forced to return with a 'dud' engine but Dallas and Culling attacked a large formation of enemy two-seaters and scouts over Vitry-en-Artois. Dallas later wrote:

'April 22 1917. Big scrap, met the Travelling Circus and Culling, my valuable comrade in the air went with me into a formation of fourteen of them. We revved round and counterattacked so to speak, and in the general mix up Culling got one and I got two.'

This combat against superior numbers demonstrated the excellent performance of the Sopwith Triplane. With their higher speed and rate of climb, the British pilots kept up continuous dive and zoom attacks on the enemy formation for forty five minutes, keeping it split up and finally forcing it to retreat eastwards, frustrating its mission.

A patrol of nine Nieuports from 1 Squadron, led by Capt E D Atkinson, left the ground at five minutes to six to patrol a line Lille-Seclin-Carvin-La Bassée. One of the Nieuports turned back with engine trouble and Lt E S T Cole escorted it back to the safety of the front line trenches. Returning to rejoin the patrol, Cole saw a balloon, and despite heavy ground fire and and a guardian enemy scout, dived to attack it. The balloon was being rapidly hauled down, but Cole's fire set it alight when it was within twenty feet of the ground. The engine of the Nieuport engine was then hit by ground fire and began to run badly. Cole turned west for safety of the British trenches. His wheels several times touched down on the German side, but he finally skimmed over the trenches at 50 feet.

The remainder of the patrol from 1 Squadron had meanwhile attacked eight Albatri of *Jasta 28* to the east of Lille. Two of the enemy scouts were claimed as out of control by Atkinson and 2Lt E M Wright, but Lt A W Wood was seen spinning down to crash land behind the German lines. Wood injured his foot in the crash but was otherwise unhurt and was taken prisoner. Wood was claimed by *Ltn* August Hanko for his first victory.

Three Spads of 19 Squadron, led by Lt W Reed, took off at ten minutes after six to patrol from Bailleul to Bullecourt. One of the pilots, Lt Applin, lost the formation, but Reed and Lt Hamilton attacked three Albatros two-seaters in the vicinity of Courcelles. Hamilton's gun jammed, forcing him to break off his attack, but Reed shot down one of the two-seaters over Quiery. The pilot of the two-seater, *Ltn* Mobius, of *FlAbt (A) 211*, had been wounded by Reed's fire but managed to land safely. His observer *Ltn* Goldhammer was unhurt.

The morning's fighting ended with Lt.W Bishop of 60 Squadron claiming an Albatros east of Vimy.

After lunch, the FEs of 11 Squadron flew a photo-reconnaissance of the Drocourt-Queant line, taking off at 2.40pm. The squadron had already flown a reconnaissance of the same line in the morning, at the cost of two aircrew wounded: the afternoon was to prove more costly. Just over an hour after take off the FEs were attacked by *Jasta 11* east of Bapaume. Kurt Wolff and Manfred von Richthofen each shot down an FE, Richthofen's victim falling in the British lines at Lagnicourt, Wolff's at Hendecourt. All of the FEs were badly shot about, one coming down close to the front line with a mortally wounded observer. Three other observers were also wounded.

The FEs of 18 Squadron, taking off on a bombing raid in the evening, were more fortunate; they were escorted by the Spads of 23 Squadron and the Sopwith Pups of Naval 3 and had only one pilot wounded in the knee by a shell splinter from anti-aircraft fire. After the FEs had dropped their bombs, the formation was attacked by four enemy scouts, but the Pups had no difficulty in driving these off and seeing the bombers safely back to the front lines.

The Spads, however, had become separated from the FEs and Pups and mistook a combined force of Albatri from *Jagdstaffeln 5* and *12* for a British formation and climbed to join it. Paul von Osterroht, the *Staffelführer* of *Jasta 12,* shot down 2Lt F C Craig, who was taken POW, and *Offst* E Nathanael of *Jasta 5* claimed 2Lt K R Furniss, who was also taken prisoner but later died of his wounds. A third Spad was claimed by *Vzfw* Jorke of *Jasta 12*, but it returned safely, although its pilot, Capt K C McCallum, had been wounded in the foot.

At 4.45am on April 23 the ground offensive recommenced, with the infantry of the British First and Third Armies attacking a line from Gavrelle to Croiselles. The fighting was continuous throughout the day with the German troops counterattacking in some strength. The contact patrols flown by the corps squadrons of the RFC had no success in establishing the extent of any advance, being constantly interrupted in their work by the low flying *Schutzstaffeln*, operating in sections of two or three aircraft. It had been intended that the troops would show

their positions with flares, but they were understandably reluctant to reveal their positions to the German airmen. For the first three and three quarter hours of the attack there were forty eight single-seater fighters patrolling the area above the battle, but these failed to curtail the operations of the *Schutzstaffeln*.[12]

During the early morning a combined reconnaissance and bombing operation was carried out by squadrons of Ninth Wing. The Sopwith 1 1/2 Strutters of 70 Squadron were detailed to photograph the Mons-Condé canal. The Sopwiths were to reach the area by flying north of the main battle area and return by flying to its south. Following closely behind the Sopwiths, five Martinsydes of 27 Squadron and four DH4s of 55 Squadron were to diverge to bomb the sugar factory at Lecelles (Martinsydes) and the railway station at Valenciennes (DH4s). On their return, all the disparate formations were to rendezvous over Beauvois with the returning Sopwiths.

On the outward journey an escort was provided by six Pups of 66 Squadron, to wait in the area of Orchies until the Martinsydes and DH4s had passed. For the return journey an additional four Pups of 66 Squadron and three Spads of 19 Squadron were to wait east of Cambrai to escort the combined formations home. Despite the fact that on the outward journey four of the six Pups had to turn back with engine or gun troubles the whole operation was carried out with no opposition and all the aircraft returned safely.

There were no doubt good tactical reasons for this operation but the impression remains that it added nothing to the immediate effort of the offensive: without it, fifteen additional fighters would have been released to operate over the battle area. The official history states that Close Offensive patrols by the Army Wings of the I and II brigades, and Ninth Wing were flown throughout the day over the battle area, but these did little to protect the Line Patrols of the Corps squadrons from the *Schutzstaffeln*. There were many encounters with German aircraft, which developed into combats involving large numbers, but the tactically aware German units often broke off these combats, returning east, and there were few decisive results.

The pilots of Naval 1 and 3 were in action early in the morning. Naval 3 attacked a formation of Albatri flying in the vicinity of Havrincourt and in a running fight claimed one destroyed and four out of control. Further north, to the west of Douai, four Sopwith Triplanes of Naval 1, including Dallas and Culling, were fighting nine enemy scouts. Several of the enemy were seen to be hit but there were no decisive results and Dallas and Culling broke off the action to attack a pair of two-seaters west of the town, sending both down out of control.

In the morning, Capt Albert Ball of 56 Squadron claimed the squadron's first victory. Ball had taken off at 6.00am flying his personal Nieuport. He had little regard for new SE5 which equipped 56 Squadron, preferring the more manoeuvrable Nieuport, the type in which he had scored so many of his victories in 1916. He patrolled the Douai-Cambrai area knowing that the area was full of enemy aerodromes and that any enemy aeroplanes would have to pass him on their way back to their base. At 6.45 he saw two Albatros C.IIIs below him and dived to attack them. The first evaded his attack, but Ball secured his favourite position underneath the other, firing half a drum of Lewis gun into it. The Albatros went down to crash by the side of the Tilloy to Abancourt road, just beyond some houses. Nobody got out. A few minutes later Ball attacked another Albatros from underneath, but the pilot throttled back and Ball overshot, coming into range of the pilot's front gun. A well-aimed burst hit the Nieuport and Ball dived away. On his return it was found that the Albatros pilot had put 15 rounds into wing spars.

An unusual event took place later in the morning. At 10.00am the pilots of Naval 3 at Marieux were astonished to see a large German bomber flying west, 12,000 feet above their aerodrome. Several pilots took off to intercept the bomber but it was Lloyd Breadner who finally reached its height. Closing to within 50 yards, Breadner succeeded in firing only a hundred rounds before his gun jammed. But he had hit the bomber's engines and it forced landed in a field near Vron, turning up on to its nose.

Although his gun was out of action, Breadner dived at the crew in an attempt to frighten them away from their machine before they could destroy it, then landed close by and walked to the scene of the crash. On his arrival he found that the three-man crew – *Ltns* Schweren, Wirsch and *Offizierstellverteter* Hecher – had already been arrested but had successfully detonated all but one of the bombs they had been carrying. Despite this, much of the machine – a Gotha IV (610/16) of *Kagohl III/15* – was still intact and Breadner returned in triumph to the mess at Marieux wearing the German pilot's hat, and with several souvenirs, including the black crosses, which were pinned up in the Squadron's Mess.[13]

Later in the morning Ball was again in action, this time flying an SE5, his Nieuport of the morning needing new bottom wings. He attacked an Albatros C.III over Adinfer but his Vickers gun jammed and he landed at 60 Squadron's aerodrome to rectify the fault. Taking off again he flew to the Cambrai area and attacked five Albatros scouts over Selvigny, firing 150 rounds into the nearest. The Albatros went down out of control and burst into flames before reaching the ground. The remaining Albatri put some bullets into the SE but using his superior speed Ball shook them off. Fifteen minutes later he attacked another Albatros C.III just to the north of Cambrai. The two-seater dived steeply away and made a good landing,

the pilot, *Vzfw* Ebert of *FlAbt 7* helping his observer, *Ltn* Berger, who was suffering from a severe neck wound, out of their machine.

On patrol in the afternoon, Lts K Mackenzie, Ellis and W Bond of 40 Squadron attacked a pair of two seaters over Lens. Bond had a gun jam and was forced to break off his attack on one, but MacKenzie and Ellis shot the other down out of control.

During the afternoon the DH4s of 55 Squadron and Martinsydes of 27 Squadron flew a bombing raid escorted by four Nieuports from 29 Squadron. On their return, in the vicinity of Vadencourt, they were attacked by *Jagdstaffeln* 26 and 12. In the fierce fighting the Nieuports had two pilots wounded and another crashed his aeroplane on landing, writing it off. The DH4s had a pilot killed and two wounded, with two observers also wounded. Another DH4 crashlanded with no injury to its pilot or observer. The Martinsydes of 27 Squadron had only one casualty: Lt M H Coote wounded in the leg.[14]

Two of the Nieuports force landed at Rochincourt, near enough to the front line for them to be shelled and destroyed by German artillery fire. The other pilot, Capt E F Elderton, although wounded in the leg, managed to return, but all three Nieuports were struck off squadron strength.

In the early evening the FE2bs of 22 Squadron flew a photo-reconnaissance mission, escorted by the DH2s of 24 Squadron. The formation was attacked by *Jasta 5,* Kurt Schneider diving on a DH2 flown by 2Lt M A White. Turning quickly to evade Schneider, White collided with a FE and both machines crashed near Le Verguier. Schneider was credited with two victories.

The FEs of 18 Squadron, escorted by five Sopwith Pups of Naval 3, took off at 5.30pm to bomb Epinoy. Approaching the target the formation was attacked by *Jasta 26.* The fighting was so intense that the bombers were forced to turn back, but not before *Ltn* Göring of the *Jasta* had shot one of the FEs in the radiator and wounded the pilot, forcing him to land behind the British lines. *Jasta 26* was then reinforced by *Jagdstaffeln* 12 and 23 and a large scale dogfight began, the FEs edging towards the British lines. The Naval pilots managed to shepherd their charges safely back to the lines and then returned to the fight. The Pup pilots claimed several Albatri down out of control, but the *Jagdstaffeln* lost only two pilots: *Uffz* Nauczak of *Jasta 33* was severely wounded, and the *Staffelführer* of *Jasta 12, Hptm* Paul von Osterroht was shot down and killed.

The pilots of the fighter squadrons made several other claims during the day. Seven pilots from Naval 3 claimed victories: Jack Malone attacked three scouts, hitting the pilot in one and sending it down. He drove another down out of control and the third made off. Out of ammunition, Malone then landed at a nearby RFC aerodrome, rearmed and recrossed the lines, attacking and driving down two more enemy aeroplanes before returning to Marieux.

The Commanding Officer of 19 Squadron, Major H D Harvey-Kelly, one of the most popular men in the RFC, attacked an Albatros D.III near Graincourt at 7.10pm, closing to within 50 yards before firing. The Albatros went down steeply. The pilot attempted to flatten out when near the ground but it was too late and he crashed a mile outside the town of Cambrai. Another pilot of 19 Squadron, 2Lt J M Child, claimed a two-seater, shot down to crash northwest of Douai.

The pilots of 29 Squadron also claimed victories during the day. Capt A G Jones-Williams claimed an enemy machine crashed and another out of control; R N Upson and Rutherford each claimed an out of control. These successes were offset by the loss of two pilots wounded and a Nieuport shot down and wrecked, although the pilot was unhurt.

The weather continued fine the next day and the ground fighting continued, with heavy German counterattacks.

The Sopwith 1 1/2 Strutters of 70 Squadron left Fienvillers at half past five in the morning on a reconnaissance to the Cambrai area, escorted by the Pups of 66 Squadron. Approaching Cambrai the formation was attacked by *Jasta B* and elements of *Jasta 33*. *Ltn* Bernert of *Jasta B* shot down one of the Sopwiths and *Oblt* Lorenz of *Jasta 33* shot down 2Lt R S Capon of 66 Squadron. Capon was wounded and taken prisoner, the first 66 Squadron combat casualty since it had arrived in France at the beginning of March. Two other Pups returned to their base at Vert Galant, badly shot up from this action. The Sopwith 1 1/2 Strutters and Pups claimed three of the enemy shot down out of control, but the *Jagdstaffeln* had no reported losses.

Offensive and Line Patrols were flown throughout the day by 56 Squadron and Naval 1, 3 and 8 Squadrons. In the morning Naval 8 were in action with *Jasta 5* and lost FltSubLt E B J Walter, killed in action by *Ltn* Gontermann. Walter had not been with Naval 8 for very long, was small, boyish looking, and had been nicknamed 'The War Baby.' Before leaving on his last patrol Walter, the third man in a group, had defied superstition, accepting a light for his cigarette: 'Why waste another match, your suspicion is tommy-rot. Give me a light.' Flying his Sopwith Triplane named 'Mincol', he had become separated from the rest of the Flight and was attacked by three Albatri. Walter crashed in the British lines and was found to have been shot through the heart.

Roderic Dallas of Naval 1 flew a patrol in the early morning and claimed an enemy scout. He fired 30 rounds into it at point blank range and it went down vertically until it was lost to view in the haze.

A patrol of three SE5s from 56 Squadron took of at 7.00am. They had several combats with two-seaters and scouts east of Arras but had to break off the combats due to continual gun jams. A second patrol took of at 10.00am. A pair of enemy two-seaters was sighted between Gavrelle and Bullecourt, three thousand feet below the SEs. Capt C M Crowe led Lts L Barlow and M Kay down to attack these, but his Vickers only fired a few shots before it jammed. Maurice Kay closed to within 50 yards before opening fire but the Constantinesco gear of his Vickers failed. Kay came under heavy fire from the enemy observer and he was forced to dive below the enemy machine. Securing a position underneath, Kay pulled down his top wing Lewis gun and fired 20 rounds into the two-seater.

Leonard Barlow had closed with the other two-seater and fired both guns from 50 yards until the Constantinesco pipe of his Vickers gun burst. Undeterred by this he fired a complete drum of Lewis into the enemy machine before turning away. The two-seater went down completely out of control and hit the ground near Bellone. This machine was possibly from *FlAbt (A) 224*, flown by *Vzfw* Schleichardt, who managed to force land. Both he and his observer were unhurt. Ten minutes later the SEs sighted five Albatri, all with bright red tails and fuselages, flying over Douai. Crowe attacked one from 100 yards range until forced to turn away with yet another jam in his Vickers. Kay took over from Crowe, firing his Lewis – his Vickers still being inoperative – and following the enemy scout down to 6,000feet, where he came under heavy and accurate AA fire. Climbing back to 11,000 feet, Kay saw two Nieuports fighting with one of the red-nosed Albatri but he could do nothing to help them as both his guns were now out of action. These Albatri, by their colour and location were most probably from *Jasta 11*. It would have been the first time they had been attacked by SE5s.

At noon a DFW CV was seen flying over Naval 8's aerodrome at Auchel. Crundall and Booker rushed to their triplanes and took off, but the enemy machine was very high and they lost sight of it when they were still 10,000 feet below it. Robert Little, who seems to have been warned before Crundall and Booker of the approach of the DFW, gained its height and attacked it as it turned east. Two Nieuports from 40 Squadron were also attacking, and the DFW turned north. Little followed, firing whenever an opportunity presented itself. He saw that the enemy observer was not returning his fire so he closed the range. The DFW was now steadily losing height and a mile east of Bethune, Little closed the range to within 10 to 15 yards, watching his tracers going into its fuselage. The DFW was hit in the oil tank, the propeller jerked to a stop, its nose it went down and it made a perfect landing in a field. Little followed it down, but his engine lost pressure in the dive and he was forced to land, ran into a ditch and turned the triplane over onto its back. One of the German crew came over and helped Little out of his triplane. The DFW was from *FlAbt 18*, crewed by *Ltn* Freidrich Neumüller and *Ltn* Hans Huppertz, and was given the number G.24. Crundall later wrote

'The three of them went to lunch and soon they were the best of pals, exchanging souvenirs and relating their various experiences. The Germans spoke good English and both of them had been awarded the Iron Cross. The Germans were very surprised when large plates of meat were served to them because, in Germany, they said, meat was very scarce.'

After the war, Neumuller wrote to Little, only to learn that he had been killed. Somehow he obtained the address of Little's widow and wrote: 'Because he was so amiable to me on the darkest day of my soldier's life, I will never forget him. He was in every respect a knightly adversary of the air.' Neumüller never did forget: every year, until his own death, he sent Mrs Little a Christmas card, only interrupted during the years of World War II.

During the day, Booker of Naval 8 also attacked a two-seater in the vicinity of Auchel. Archie pointed out this aeroplane to him over the 'drome and he followed it to Arras. He then lost sight of it for a time, but Archie pointed it out again and he finally attacked it east of Arras. The enemy observer and Booker exchanged fire, until Booker's fire hit the observer, who fell down into his cockpit. The two-seater went down towards Douai, trailing smoke, but under control. Booker had no wish to poke his nose into Douai, so he returned.

Capt T F Hazell and 2Lt L M Mansbridge of 1 Squadron were flying a lunchtime patrol when they spotted an pair of Albatros two-seaters 4,000 feet below them. Hazell dived, came up in the blind spot under the tail of one of the Albatri and opened fire. Smoke immediately came out of the two-seater's fuselage and it went down in a steep dive, the brave observer hanging over the side, firing a pistol at Hazell. The Albatros finally burst into flames and fell in the German lines. This Albatros was from *Fl Abt (A) 227*, crewed by *Uffz* Otto Haberland and *Ltn de R* Heinrich Klose, both killed.

After lunch, further attacks were made on enemy balloons. Observation was still of utmost importance and it was imperative that they should be destroyed. An attack was made on all the balloons along the entire front, but only two were destroyed. Sixty Squadron carried out attacks on the balloons over Arras: Bishop shot at one which was already on the ground, but 'Moley' Molesworth was more successful, setting his target on fire. Attacking his allotted balloon east of Arras, 2Lt Reginald Clark was attacked by an enemy two-seater. Clark returned the attack, hitting the enemy observer, who stopped firing, but before he could follow up this advantage Clark was attacked by four Albatros scouts, their fire wounding him twice

in his leg, breaking it. Clark turned for home but another burst holed his petrol tank and petrol soaked him from his thighs down. Despite his injuries, Clark returned the attacks, firing half a drum of Lewis at one Albatros, but another shot away his controls and set the Nieuport on fire. Clark crashlanded in the front line trenches and was pulled from the wreckage of his Nieuport by a Corporal Summers of the 1st Canadian Pioneer Battalion. Clark refused to have his wounds attended to until he had submitted his report. He was taken to the nearest casualty clearing station and then to hospital but died of his wounds on May 1.

The pilots of 29 Squadron also attacked balloons: Lts Le Gallis and L M S Essell were both successful.

Capt Albert Ball took out a patrol of three SE5s at 1.00pm. Ball was forced to return with gun trouble, but Lts Gerald Maxwell and Clarence Knight carried on alone, despite their lack of experience. Over Douai they saw a green Albatros D.III. Maxwell came up under its tail and fired a complete drum of Lewis into it from ten yards. The enemy scout went down near Hamel. The SEs followed it down, firing all the time, until they came under heavy AA fire at 1,500 feet. That night Maxwell wrote in his diary. 'Got my first Hun. Single seater Albatros scout. Came up under his tail to about ten yards and loosed off. EA dived to earth and crashed.'

Another patrol from 56 Squadron took off at 3.00pm. Almost at the end of their endurance they sighted five Albatros scouts over Fresnoy. 2Lt Kenneth Knaggs shot a green painted Albatros down in a spin over the Arras to Douai road, just east of Fresnes. Lts John Leach and Cecil Lewis both attacked a red Albatros, but it evaded their attacks and the SEs cleared. As they did so they saw the green Albatros shot down by Knaggs flatten out near the ground, the pilot recovering from his evasive spin and climbing to rejoin his *Jasta* companions.

Naval 3 pilots were in action at ten minutes to five. FltLt Travers and FltSubLts F D Casey and Malone attacked a DFW CV from *Fl Abt 26* between Morchies and Louverval. Both Travers and Casey had gun jams and turned away. Malone then attacked. After his first burst the enemy observer dropped down into his cockpit but then re-emerged and fired at Malone, who had closed to within 20 yards. The observer again disappeared and Malone forced the DFW to land just behind the British front line at Doignies. Malone's engine, which had been running badly throughout the patrol, now refused to open up and he was forced to land beside the DFW. Malone helped the German pilot, *Uffz* Max Haase – slightly wounded in the head – to remove his badly wounded observer, *Ltn* Karl Keim, from his cockpit before the German artillery began to shell the two machines, completely destroying both. Malone and his two erstwhile opponents were forced to take cover in a shell hole until they could be rescued. Keim died of his wounds ten minutes later.

Max Haase was taken to Naval 3's mess at Marieux and stayed with the squadron for a few days. 'Tich' Rochford later recalled, 'He was a pleasant, friendly little man with a sense of humour. He was also something of an artist and drew several pencil sketches for us. I remember one of them was of a very full-breasted woman under which he wrote in German the caption "Double-seater." On his departure he said he had enjoyed staying with us very much.'

Just after 5.00pm a patrol of six Nieuports from 60 Squadron led by Lt William Mays Fry saw six Albatri attacking a BE over Vis-en-Artois. Three of the Nieuports, joined by a Sopwith Triplane, dived to the aid of the BE, which had been driven down to 1,500 feet. The Albatri, all with red fuselages and wings – with the exception of one which had green wings – were from *Jasta 11*, but quickly disengaged and dived east. German pilots at this time were very wary of any Sopwith Triplane they encountered – a combination of respect both for its performance and the aggressiveness of the Naval pilots who flew them.

The skies were heavy with cloud the next day – April 25 – but the corps squadrons were out in force, taking advantage of the conditions. The fighter squadrons flew closer to the front lines where they were more able to protect the allied two-seaters from the *Jagdstaffeln* and casualties were fewer. 'Tich' Rochford and E Pierce of Naval 3 flew to an advanced landing ground at Beugnatre, much closer to the lines than Marieux, and stood by to takeoff and attack any enemy aeroplanes reported to them by field telephone in an army observation post. During the evening Colonel Vesey-Holt arrived. Not content with there being no reported activity, the colonel ordered them into the air to check that enemy aircraft working not over the lines. The two Pups flew along the front lines at 3,000 feet – no doubt cursing the Colonel – but saw no enemy aircraft, only large numbers of BEs and FEs. As dusk fell they flew back to Marieux.

Despite the closer patrols flown by the fighter squadrons, some enemy fighters, no doubt taking advantage of the low cloud, managed to shoot down two BEs – one of which managed to return to base – an RE8, an FE2b, and a Bristol F2a. The *Jagdstaffeln* paid dearly for these victories. On patrol over Oppy *Jasta 11* attacked the Sopwith 1 1/2 Strutters of 43 Squadron. During the fight *Vzfw* Sebastian Festner was shot down and killed by 2Lt J L Dickson, the gunner of one of the Sopwiths. This was a heavy blow to the *Jasta*. Festner was one of their most promising pilots; he had scored 12 victories since February 5, ten of them in April.

The low cloud continued the following day, only clearing in the evening. The *Jagdstaffeln* took full advantage of the improved weather conditions, and inflicted heavy casualties on the corps aeroplanes. *Jasta 11* shot down two BEs from 16 Squadron and another from 5 Squadron; *Jasta 30* claimed another BE from 10 Squadron, and *Jasta 5* shot down two FEs from 22 squadron, badly damaging another.

During the morning Naval 8 had flown a Line Patrol but the low cloud kept them at 2,000 feet and they saw nothing. Later in the afternoon six triplanes from the squadron – Crundall, Booker, S W McCrudden in one flight, with Knight leading another two – flew an escort for two FEs of 25 Squadron. The Flight led by A R Knight became separated from the others and as the two FEs and the remaining triplanes approached Douai they were attacked by *Jasta 11*. At first Crundall did not realise what was happening: 'until I saw Booker dive at an Albatros scout. Then another Albatros dived on Booker so I attacked it at very close range and watched my tracer bullets hitting the fuselage. I got so close to its tail that I could hardly miss doing considerable damage when, suddenly, the Albatros went down in a vertical spiral dive.' Looking around Crundall then found that he was alone in the sky. He flew west, not knowing where he was, expecting any minute to be attacked. Eventually he saw an aerodrome and landed to find his bearings. He was at Marieux, the home of Naval 3. On his return to Auchel, Crundall found that he had been credited with the Albatros, which had been seen to dive into the ground by the pilot of one of the FEs. Booker had shot another down in flames and the FEs had claimed another.

The SEs of 56 Squadron were also in action during the evening. Ball led Lts Lehmann, Melville and Barlow on a patrol at 6.15pm. Soon after takeoff the patrol split up. Ball flew to his favourite hunting ground to the west of Douai and Barlow detached himself from Lehmann and Melville.[15] Barlow attacked a pair of two-seaters south of Lens but suffered the ever present gun trouble and broke off the attack, landing at Savy to clear his guns before returning the Vert Galant. Lehmann and Melville also returned having seen no enemy aeroplanes, but to the south Ball was fighting for his life.

After leaving the patrol he had seen a formation of FEs flying west from Cambrai, with five enemy scouts from *Jasta 3* climbing from their aerodrome at Awoingt to intercept them. Ball, 'went and sat' over Cambrai. Waiting until the enemy scouts had climbed to 6,000 feet he dived on the nearest, closed to within 20 yards and fired a drum of Lewis and 50 rounds of Vickers into it. The white painted Albatros went down to crash in a small wood to the northeast of Cambrai. Ball then turned west for the Lines but found his way blocked by the remaining five Albatri.

Ball made straight for them, firing as he went, but the German pilots refused to scatter and effectively boxed in the SE. Ball broke away and fled to the southeast, the Albatri in hot pursuit, anxious to avenge their Jasta comrade. One Albatros outdistanced the others and Ball turned to face it, firing both guns. The Albatri, flown by *Vzfw* Emil Hisenhuth of *Jasta 3* burst into flames and went down. The rest of the Albatri were now near enough to attack the SE but Ball managed to evade their fire and again dived to the southeast. He returned to Vert Galant at dusk.

Sometime in the evening a patrol from 19 Squadron was attacked by several Sopwith Triplanes from a Naval squadron – most probably Naval 8. Lt J M Child's Spad was damaged by the triplanes' fire and he was forced to dive with his engine full on to escape them, force landing at Bellevue. Lt J D V Holmes was also attacked by two of the triplanes but managed to evade them and return. Later that evening there were no doubt angry telephone calls to all the naval squadrons in the area.[16]

During the evening FltLt Travers led A Flight from Naval 3 in an Offensive Patrol. From 17,000 feet Travers led the formation down on an Albatros 4,000 feet below them, but was forced to break off his attack with a gun jam. Jack Malone continued the attack, pushing the Albatros down to 7,000 feet, but was then attacked by three others. He saw the first Albatros crash in a field near Cambrai, but the remaining Albatri were persistent, continuing to attack him. Malone was now very low and decided that the only way to shake off the enemy scouts was to pretend to land. As his wheels touched the ground he saw that all three Albatri were also intending to land. Malone opened up his engine and climbed away into the sun, closely followed by the frustrated enemy pilots. They could not catch him and Malone crossed the Lines at 2,000 feet, ground fire forcing the enemy pilots to give up the chase. FltLt F D Casey and Jack Malone each claimed an enemy scout shot down from this action.

One of the few actions by the fighter squadrons during the morning had been flown by Lt A V Burbury of 1 Squadron. He took off at noon to intercept an enemy two-seater reported to be working over the Lines. He failed to find the enemy so he attacked a balloon in the vicinity of Wervicq and shot it down in flames. His blood now up, Burbury flew to attack another balloon near Quesnoy. However, he had not regained his height after his attack on the first balloon and flying at only a hundred feet he was hit by Archie near Comines. The Nieuport crashed behind the German lines and Burbury was taken prisoner.

Another casualty of the morning was 2Lt N D Henderson of 60 Squadron. While on patrol his Nieuport was hit by Archie and he crashed into a lake between Fauchy and Fampoux.

Henderson was seriously injured in the crash and was taken to hospital.

Low cloud persisted for the whole of April 27 and there was a slackening of activity in the air war. One BE and a Sopwith 1 1/2 Strutter were shot down by ground fire and *Jasta 11* claimed two FE2bs from 11 Squadron. Bishop of 60 Squadron and H Ellis each destroyed a balloon during the morning. The only casualty from the fighter squadrons was a Nieuport of 60 Squadron. Ferrying a new Nieuport 17 from 2 ASD at Candas to the Squadron's aerodrome at Le Hameau, 2Lt F Steadman became hopelessly lost, landed behind the German lines and was made POW.

The low clouds continued next day, April 28. The ground attacks were resumed at 4.25am: German trenches along a two-mile front at Arleux-en-Gohelle were taken: ground was won at Oppy and on the slopes of Greenland Hill. Flares were initially used to successfully to mark the advance to the aeroplanes of the corps squadrons but as the German counter attacks developed the deployment of flares ceased and no progress could be see from the air. The *Jagdstaffeln* pilots, aided by the low cloud, concentrated on the corps machines working over the trenches: two 5 Squadron BEs were badly shot up – one by Wolff of *Jasta 11*, who also claimed another from 16 Squadron; Manfred von Richthofen claimed another BE from 13 Squadron; and another five were badly shot up either by ground fire or hostile fighters.

Despite the forlorn plea of the pilots of 54 Squadron in their squadron song, sung to the old tune of *'Somerset,'* the German pilots were concentrating on their duty of destroying the strategically important aeroplanes of the corps squadrons:

> *'Oh, we've come up from Fifty-Four;*
> *We're the Sopwith Pups you know,*
> *And wherever you dirty swine may be*
> *The Sopwith Pup will go.*
> *And if you want a proper scrap,*
> *Don't chase 2cs any more;*
> *For we'll come up and do the job,*
> *Because we're Fifty-Four.'*

Naval 8 flew an offensive patrol at dawn: six triplanes led by Little climbed up through the clouds until they emerged into the clear air at 4,000 feet. Crundall turned back with engine trouble, but the others carried on. This patrol seems to have seen no action but just after noon Little shot down a two seater over Oppy.

It was not until its third patrol of the day that 56 Squadron saw any action. A Flight, led by Ball, took off at 4.50pm and sighted three Albatros two-seaters at 7,000 feet over Cambrai. Ball led the Flight down through the cloud cover but his guns jammed after only a few shots. Ball climbed back into the cloud cover, retified the jams and returned to the attack, sending down one of the two-seaters down, although under control. He then attacked another. This time his guns worked perfectly and he sent it down to crash at Fontaine. Ball had now lost contact with his Flight, which had become split up in the heavy cloud and he, in his own words, 'sat above the clouds until a two seater Albatros came up above the clouds at Épéhy.' Ball chased this enemy machine to within five hundred feet of the ground, so intent on the chase that he came under heavy and accurate fire from the ground. The controls of the SE5 were hit and it fell into a spin. Ball managed to regain control and flew gingerly back to Vert Galant, only his left elevator fully working, with only a single top wire still intact.

As the SE came in to land at Vert Galant the watching pilots could see that the elevators were flapping loose and that the nose of the machine was covered in oil from a riddled oil tank. Ball climbed shakily from the SE, called angrily for a rag to wipe the oil from his face and shoulders and literally stamped to the sheds. Twenty minutes later he flew off in his Nieuport, still furious. After an hour and thirty-five minutes he returned to Vert Galant. He had seen nothing on which to vent his anger.

While Ball had been fighting to regain control of his SE5, Gerald Maxwell had also been hit by Archie. Maxwell had become separated from his companions – Knight and Knaggs – and although flying at 10,000 feet his SE5 was hit in the radiator and elevators by very accurate fire. His engine finally seized over the trenches and he forced landed at Station 126 on the Decauville railway. Maxwell's diary entry read: 'Complete wreck. Engine fell out of machine and machine turned right over. Me no hurt. Hit ground at about 140mph.' He was sufficiently shaken to enter the incident in the wrong day.

Just after 5.00pm 56 Squadron flew an escort for Sopwith 1 1/2 Strutters that had been forced to turn back from their objective because of the bad weather. Having seen the two-seaters safely to Albert, the SE5 formation, led by Capt Cyril 'Billy' Crowe, went down through the clouds to 3,000 feet and patrolled over Douai, but the *Jagdstaffeln* refused the bait. Another patrol took off twenty minutes after the escort, but visibility was now so bad that they emptied their guns into the enemy trenches around Arras and returned.

The weather showed some improvement on the morning of April 29. Visibility was bad between 2,000 and 3,000 feet but good between 10 and 12,000 feet. The ground fighting continued in intensity with British troops fighting furiously around Oppy. The airfighting began early. Two Nieuports of 40 Squadron were on patrol at 6.45am: Capt W Bond and Lt J A G Brewis. Bond later wrote to his wife.

'At 6.30 am I was out on an OP with another fellow. I was leading and after we had been over the lines half an hour, getting 'Archied' very badly, we lost each other in the mist, which was very thick. There were no Huns about, so at the end of an hour I started to return to the new aerodrome and, through carelessness, took the wrong direction and went south.[17] After twenty minutes I failed to recognise the country and turned north on chance, struck an aerodrome and found I was nearly forty miles away from here. The fellow who went out with me is posted as missing. He must have had engine trouble or lost his way and been taken prisoner.'[18]

Capt H Meintjes took C Flight of 56 Squadron off the ground at 9.00am to patrol from Vitry to Villers. At 10.00am, as the SEs were passing between the villages of Hamel and Récourt, the patrol was attacked by six Albatros scouts, grey in colour, which came at them from out of the bright morning sun. The experienced Meintjes went into a steep climbing turn, evading the attack, but looking down he saw that 2Lt W Melville was spinning down with two of the enemy scouts on his tail. Meintjes dived onto one of the Albatri, took it off Melville's tail and fought it down to 6,000 feet, just above the cloudbank. The Albatros turned over onto its back and went down through the cloud out of control. Meintjes regained his height but the enemy scouts had cleared east. Melville had spun down into the cloud and shaken off the other Albatros.

In their first pass the Albatri had hit the SE5 of the third member of the patrol, Lt. R T C Hoidge, in the elevators, ailerons and back spar, one burst hitting the top of the fuselage just behind Hoidge's head. Hoidge had no guns; the wire control of his Vickers had broken on crossing the lines early in the patrol and he now had a jam in his Lewis. Hoidge was inexperienced, but he kept calm and used the superior speed of the SE to outclimb the enemy scouts. Getting above them, and despite his lack of armament, he dived at the nearest. The Albatri broke off the action and cleared east.

A formation of FEs from 57 Squadron had seen this action and had dived to get into the fight, but they were too late. They arrived after the SEs had cleared and ran into the grey Albatri. One of the FEs was shot down but one Albatros went down out of control, the pilot falling from his machine. The remaining Albatri then broke off the action and a little later formed up with six Albatri from *Jasta 11*, led by Manfred von Richthofen. Above the German scouts were three Spads of 23 Squadron, led by their CO Major Harvey-Kelly and he took them down to attack. In view of the odds this was perhaps a foolish action and all three Spads were shot down in the fight. Lothar von Richthofen shot down Lt W N Hamilton who was taken prisoner; Manfred von Richthofen killed 2Lt. R Applin and *Ltn* Kurt Wolff wounded Major Harvey-Kelly who crashed near Sailly-en-Ostrevent. Harvey-Kelly survived the crash but died of his wounds in a German hospital three days later. Harvey-Kelly was a great loss for the RFC: he had been a pre-war pilot, had been the first British airman to land in France in August 1914 and was extremely popular throughout the corps.

The fight with the Spads had been seen by a flight of Naval triplanes – perhaps Harvey-Kelly had seen these and counted on their support in his attack – and the Naval pilots later claimed three of the enemy scouts out of control, one of which was seen to crash, but no *Jagdstaffeln* losses were reported which fit for time and place. While following the Sopwith Triplanes back to the lines the enemy fighters were seen by Bishop of 60 Squadron who claimed to have attacked one and sent it down in flames.

Nieuports from 29 Squadron were out in the morning, strafing enemy troop positions. Two were hit by *Kraffwagenflak 63* (anti-aircraft gun mounted on a lorry chassis) brought down and taken prisoner: Lt H B Milling and Sgt G Humble.

The Naval squadrons fared badly during the day. Crundall, Booker and McCrudden of Naval 3 took off in the morning to escort FEs taking photographs in the Lens-Gavrelle area. Conditions were very misty and the formations had difficulty in keeping together. For most of the time they were flying at 5,000 feet and 'flaming onions and shells were coming up around us.' The same three pilots took off again at 3.00pm and were attacked by six Albatri over Vitry/Henin-Lietard at 12,000 feet. Crundall fired at one which went down with black smoke coming from it. Booker's gun had jammed and the Triplanes returned.

Naval 1 were in action just before noon. FltSubLt H V Rowley and Flt Lt C B Ridley shared an enemy machine down out of control. Rowley's engine failed after this action and he was forced to land on rough ground near Bethune, overturning his triplane.

Ten Sopwith Pups of Naval 3 flew an escort for the FEs of 18 Squadron in the morning. Eleven enemy scouts attacked the formation, but the Pups successfully defended their charges and saw them safely back over the Lines without loss before turning back to re-engage the enemy fighters. At 10.35am over Elincourt the Pups were attacked by eight enemy scouts, probably from *Jasta 5*. In the fighting FltSubLt S L Bennett was shot down and killed by *Ltn* Kurt Schneider of *Jasta 5*. The Naval pilots claimed three of the enemy scouts as out of control but the *Jasta* had no losses, the German pilots using their usual evasive tactic of spinning down out of trouble.

After lunch, Nieuports of Naval 6 were in action with 12 enemy scouts at 1.15pm and H V Fletcher was wounded, crashed behind the German lines and taken POW.

A patrol of SE5s from 56 Squadron took off from Vert Galant at 1.00pm to patrol from Epinoy to Cambrai. Led by

Capt Crowe, the Flight spotted an Albatros C type over Bugnicourt. All three SEs fired at this machine, Jack Leach following it down to 2,000 feet before it turned over and went down through the clouds. Crowe reformed the patrol, climbed to 8,000 feet and flew to Cambrai. Over the town they saw five enemy scouts, but these had a height advantage of 3,000 feet and Crowe turned his pilots west, climbing hard to put the SEs on an equal level. The German scouts attacked in formation. Crowe had time to notice that their black crosses were on white square backgrounds – perhaps a sign that they were older type Albatros or Halberstadt machines – and that they were all silvery-grey in colour. There were several minutes of confused fighting, Crowe forcing an enemy down to 3,000 feet until fell out of control over Waziers. Although inexperienced pilots, Leach and Lt M Kay had contained the enemy scouts, who made off east, taking advantage of the cloud cover. Crowe again reformed the patrol and led them over Douai, the base of *Jasta 11*. Signalling Leach and Kay to remain at 5,000 feet, Crowe coolly went down to 2,400 feet to have a look at the enemy aerodrome. He later reported its position, the number of the hangars, and a large wooden shed with a new roof. Crowe saw only four machines on the ground and none came up to challenge the British scouts. After unsuccessfully chasing a two-seater, the patrol returned.

Capt Ball took out the next patrol from the squadron. British anti-aircraft fire pointed out a two-seater to them at 13,000 feet over Adinfer. While the SEs were climbing for height the two-seater pilot saw them coming and dived east for the safety of his own lines, but the SEs finally caught the enemy machine over the trenches north of Lens.

The two-seater was now very low. Despite coming under heavy ground fire Ball attacked it, but his Vickers jammed after only two shots. He fired a green light for Knaggs and Knight to continue the attack, but they had gone in pursuit of a pair of two-seaters over Vendin-le-Vieil, to the north of Lens. Both these machines escaped.

At 3.00pm *Jasta 11* shot down two FE2bs of 18 Squadron on a photo-reconnaissance. Manfred von Richthofen shot down one FE, Kurt Wolff the other. A third escaped into the cloud cover, badly shot up, and forced landed with a wounded observer. At 6.15pm *Jasta 11* were again in action, the Richthofen brothers attacking two BE2es of 12 Squadron. A patrol of Naval 8 triplanes were in the area; Robert Little saw a red Albatros attacking one of the BEs and dived on the enemy scout, flown by Lothar von Richthofen. Little was followed down by Flight Commander A R Arnold but the two triplanes came under heavy ground fire and were forced to break off the action. They had not been in time to save the unfortunate BE which was claimed by Lothar for his 14th victory.

Little and Arnold regained their height and flew towards Droucourt. Over Douai aerodrome they saw five Albatri below them and dived to attack, joined by a triplane from Naval 1 flown by FltSubLt R P Minifie. Little saw Minifie's triplane, with a large numeral 16 on the fuselage, fighting with three of the enemy scouts and he dived to assist. Both the Naval pilots hit one Albatros that went down to crash on the aerodrome. The remaining Albatri continued to fight the triplanes, but the Naval pilots all managed to extricate themselves and fly west. Minifie later recalled. 'Yes, they nearly had me down on Douai aerodrome, about 200 to 300 feet off it, but luckily my triplane was just that little shade faster then they were. I was going low for home, and they let me go and get a lead of about 500 yards on them. So that was that, they just couldn't catch me.'

After this action, Little and Arnold reformed with the rest of the patrol – Knight, Johnson, McDonald and Cuzner – and twenty five minutes later attacked a formation of Albatros scouts, again over Douai, possibly the same scouts fought earlier. Naval 1 were also in this fight. FltSubLt A P Heywood, force landed his badly shot up triplane behind the British lines, but thinking he was in German territory, burnt it. FltSubLt H Wallace, wounded in the arm, managed to force land behind the British lines south of Bapaume, and Rowley, hit in his engine, also force landed near Bapaume. Naval 8 lost FltSubLt Albert Cuzner, claimed by Manfred von Richthofen for his 52nd victory.

During the evening's fighting, 40 Squadron lost Capt F L Barwell, possibly the last loss for the fighter squadrons during a day of intense and confused fighting.

The last day of April saw a change in the tactics of the *Luftstreitkräfte*. The deployment of the *Jagdstaffeln* within the organisation of the German Army had never been fully established and in late April it was decided that the various *Jagdstaffeln* should be divided amongst the Army Group HQs (*Gruppenkommandos*). Owing to the concentration of *Jagdstaffeln* in the German armies during the Arras battles it had become possible to allocate several *Jagdstaffeln* to each Army Group. Ideally these combined *Jagdstaffeln* should be under one leader, but these early leaders were pilots of limited experience in aerial fighting who seldom flew, and the grouping was in effect only a temporary measure to enable more fighters to be employed at any one time to combat the larger formations now being flown by the RFC. Over the next month, however, it became obvious that such units lacked both positive leadership in actual combat, and any cohesive operational plan, and this was to lead to the formation of permanent groups of *Jagdstaffeln* (*Jagdgeschwader*) under experienced and active commanders. In the interim, *Jagdstaffeln 3,4,11* and *33* were combined and flew their first operation on April 30, twenty fighters setting out from Douai in the morning.

The first combat was with a line patrol of FE2bs from 57 Squadron, escorted by Sopwith Triplanes of Naval 8. Two of the FEs were shot down in the German lines and a third crashed in the British lines with a wounded pilot and a dying observer. The Naval pilots managed to extricate the remaining FEs, saw them back to the lines, and the German scouts broke off the action.

Little was one of the pilots of Naval 8 involved in the intense fighting. He attacked one Albatros from a group of five that was attacking an FE, but saw another FE going down with an Albatros on its tail. Little broke off his attack and dived to assist this FE, but before he could close the range it went down, flattened out and landed. Little then climbed back to 7,000 feet, joined another FE and together they fought off an attack by seven enemy scouts. Little sent one down in a spin and the FE's observer put a burst through the fuselage of another, which went down out of control. Four additional FEs then joined Little and the FE, but they were attacked by another nine Albatri. One of these dived on Little from out of the bright, early morning sun. Little turned to engage the enemy scout but his gun jammed. Little attempted to turn away from the attack but the enemy pilot stuck with him, hitting the triplane in the wings and petrol pump. Little used the Sopwith's manoeuvring abilities to get behind and under the tail of the Albatros and stayed there, clearing his gun jam. With his gun now working, Little opened fire at the Albatros, only ten feet above him, and it went down in a slow spiral into ground mist at 1,000 feet, where Little lost sight of it.

A patrol of three SEs of 56 Squadron took off at 6.15am as an escort for DH4s, but failed to make contact with the bombers at the designated rendezvous over Carvin. After chasing an enemy two-seater east, Cecil Lewis, leading the patrol, decided to fly a normal offensive patrol and headed towards Douai. Over the town they were attacked by an enemy scout – described as an HA Nieuport – coloured silver with a yellow nose. After an amount of indecisive manoeuvring for position, the enemy scout made off east, gained some extra height and returned to attack the SEs. They saw him coming, pulled down their top wing Lewis guns, and fired at him from below. This method of dealing with his attack seems not to have have been experienced before by the German pilot and he broke off the action and dived away, followed by Lewis, who gave him a short burst from his Vickers gun. The enemy pilot steepened his dive and made off in the direction of Corbeham.

The next patrol flown by 56 Squadron was to see the Squadron's first casualty. Capt Crowe, Lt J O Leach and 2Lt M A Kay took off at 8.05am to patrol between Vitry and Villers. As he was about to turn the patrol north Crowe saw a group of enemy fighters manoeuvring to attack a formation of FEs patrolling 3,000 feet below them and he led the SEs down to intercept the enemy fighters, which were coloured silver with green wingtips. In Crowe's own words 'a very stubborn, ding-dong fight ensued, some HA (hostile aircraft) being above and some below the SEs.'

Seeing Maurice Kay in trouble with an Albatros on his tail, Leach dived to Kay's assistance, getting good bursts into his attacker, overshooting in his eagerness to help his comrade. Zooming away and looking down Leach saw both Kay and the Albatros hit the ground near Villers-au-Tertre and burst into flames. The Albatros pilot, *Ltn* Friedrich Mallinckodt of *Jasta 20* was severely wounded, either in the crash or by Leach's fire. Kay was killed.

Crowe had a long fight with another of the Albatri, finally sending it down to crash south of Lens. He then had several skirmishes with enemy scouts and two-seaters before returning, landing on 8 Squadron's aerodrome on the last of his petrol before refuelling and returning to Vert Galant.

Captain C J Quintin-Brand of 1 Squadron took off early to intercept two enemy machines that had been reported as working over the lines. Over Wytschaete he found a pair of two-seaters and he attacked the nearest, painted a reddish brown, closing to within a hundred yards. Quintin-Brand's fire hit the enemy observer who fell back into his cockpit and Quintin-Brand, the threat of the rear gunner removed, closed to 70 yards and fired the rest of his Lewis gun drum into the two-seater. The enemy machine went down in a near vertical dive, hit the ground in the British lines near Houplines and burst into flames. Although little was left of it, the two-seater, a DFW C.V of *Fl Abt (A)204* was given the British number G 27. The crew, *Vzfw* Max Baatz and *Ltn* Alexander Schlieper were both killed.

In the middle of the morning the pilots of Naval 1 provided an escort for six Bristol Fighters of 48 Squadron on a reconnaissance of the German trench system east of Douai. Enemy fighters, which a little earlier had been in action with the FEs of 57 Squadron and their escort of triplanes from Naval 8, had broken off the combat, and had then joined up with some two-seaters. This combined force of 15 now attacked the Bristols and the Sopwith Triplanes of Naval 1. A long fight ensued, with the German machines making repeated and determined attacks, and the Bristols were forced to abandon their task and fight their way back to the lines. Dallas and Culling were heavily engaged with the German fighters – Dallas at one point fighting seven on his own – but succeeded in their efforts to protect the Bristols and none were lost.

Although being 'busy' with the enemy scouts Dallas had spotted a Rumpler. Leaving Culling to see the Bristols on the last leg of their journey home, Dallas intercepted it over Haynecourt and shot it down. Dallas then went to the aid of

some FEs which were being attacked, sending one of the enemy scouts down with a thirty round burst.

FltLt R J O Compston, C D Booker and A R Knight of Naval 8 were also out in the area east of Douai. Compston was at 15,000 feet when he sighted an Albatros climbing for height. He dived to attack this machine, closing to within 50 yards, the enemy pilot's head in his sights. Compston fired a long burst. The Albatros turned over onto its side and went down out of control. A little later, having climbed back to 13,500 feet, Compston attacked a two-seater, which turned across his front. Compston opened fire from a hundred yards range, his bullets transversing along the fuselage of the enemy machine which went down out of control. Compston was then attacked by a white Albatros. This pilot was very skilful and he and Compston fought for some considerable time without result. Compston later wrote: 'He was a better pilot than the other two and as my gun jammed once, and my petrol was getting low, I left for home.'

Booker and Knight had also been involved in several combats, Booker claiming an Albatros out of control over Douai.

Two Spads of 19 Squadron, Capt D A L Davidson and Lt J M Child flying an offensive patrol in the area of Lens, had a fight with three enemy aircraft over Vitry but were forced to break off the action because of continual gun jams. They returned to their aerodrome at Vert Galant to rectify the jams, took off again and sighted a two-seater of *Schutzstaffel 19* low over the lines. Both Spads dived to attack the enemy machine but Davidson's aeroplane was hit, either by ground fire or by the enemy gunner, and it exploded in midair – Child later described it as 'blown up in air.'

During the day the *Schusta* had been stepping up their low level attacks on the British ground troops and 29, 60 and 19 Squadrons were detailed to fly line patrols at low height to attack these aeroplanes. These tactics met with little success: despite many combats none were conclusive and no *Schusta* machines were brought down.

Naval 3 left the ground at 4.15pm to provide an escort for the FEs of 18 Squadron and were attacked by enemy scouts from *Jasta 12*. John Malone had earlier left the formation and had flown off in the direction of Cambrai. In his autobiography Leonard Rochford of Naval 3 later wrote that Malone was in the habit of leaving the formation to hunt alone and that it was ultimately his undoing.[19] Malone was shot down and killed over Rumaucourt by *Ltn* Paul Billik of *Jasta 12* for the first of his eventual 31 victories. The Germans later reported that Malone had been buried at Epinoy. Collishaw claimed an Albatros destroyed during the fighting.

In the early evening the Nieuports of 29 Squadron were in action with *Jasta 3* and 2Lt R H Upson was shot down by

Vzfw Carl Menckhoff of the *Jasta* and taken prisoner. A patrol of Nieuports from 60 Squadron were also in action. *Jasta 6* attacked them over Roupy and Major Scott's Nieuport was hit in the engine, forcing him to land near Monchy le Preux. Scott was unhurt.

Other claims by the fighter pilots during the day were an Albatros two-seater shot down over Brebieres-Fresnes by Capt J O Andrews of 66 Squadron for his eighth victory; and Lt W Bishop of 60 Squadron claimed a two-seater destroyed south east of Lens at 11.15, and another forced to land a short time later. Early in the morning the aerodrome of Naval 8 had been bombed. The Naval pilots took off in pursuit of the intruders. Compston and Little claimed two each and Booker another.

The Cost

During April 1917 the RFC suffered its heaviest casualties of the war to date, earning the month the sobriquet of 'Bloody April.' Exact figures are difficult to finalise, but 404 aircrew had been lost during the month, two hundred and sixty-four of whom had been killed or taken prisoner east of the lines, with an additional 30 who died of their wounds in captivity. Seventy-six aircrew were unwounded prisoners of war and 28 wounded POWs. Of these totals: 28 fighter pilots were killed; 8 wounded; 29 taken prisoner, of whom six were wounded, with another eight dying of their wounds in captivity. One pilot died of his wounds west of the lines.

Due to many factors it is not possible to compute with any reasonable accuracy the number of aeroplanes lost: the majority were a direct result of enemy action, shot down either behind the German or British lines; some returned to their aerodromes badly shot up and had to be struck of the strength of the squadrons, while others could be repaired, either in the squadrons' workshops or at the aircraft repair depots.

There can be no doubt that as casualties mounted during the month the morale of pilots and observers of the RFC had taken a severe blow. Young men are resilient, but the daily toll, the absence of friends and comrades at dinner in the Mess each night, undoubtedly had an adverse effect. Oliver Stewart, a pilot with 54 Squadron, later wrote: 'Our casualties mounted alarmingly. There was hardly an evening when the same people gathered in the mess. It was here that a certain amount of frank and free comment on our casualty rate could be heard.' Major K K Horn, the Commanding Officer of 54 Squadron, discouraged these discussions, but they continued. Stewart again:

This feeling, although officially looked on as defeatist, was prevalent among operational pilots for part of the 1914-1918 war. The British airservices, both the Royal Naval Air Service and the Royal Flying Corps – more particularly the latter – were often wastefully used. Officers of the higher command, from Major-General Hugh Trenchard as he was then, down to the commanders of wings, according to the critics, were throwing away aircraft and lives for no distinguishable purpose. At any rate they did not convince their pilots that there was a purpose. The aim seemed to be to contrive the greatest number of confrontations of British and German aircraft and to have the greatest number of battles in the air. To us junior officers there was no discernible military objective.' [20]

Stewart was, of course, talking from the prospective of a fighter pilot and there can be no doubt that the tactics employed by the Army wing commanders were inefficient and wasteful of men and machines. Trenchard's policy of being always on the offensive had been influenced by naval doctrines: to seek out and destroy the enemy; that the British front lines were the enemy coasts. Trenchard applied these doctrines to the airwar, failing to appreciate that the air is a three dimensional sphere, making these doctrines largely irrelevant. Trenchard's policy had two main flaws: he saw British aircraft ten miles over the enemy back areas as being ten times more offensive as those aircraft one mile over the trenches. His offensive strategy was in effect a territorial strategy. The tactics of offensive patrols, deep into enemy territory, with the handicap of the almost constant prevailing westerly wind in France, resulted in the RFC fighting at a huge disadvantage. A large number of aircrew, disabled by wounds, or with damaged machines, struggling unsuccessfully to reach the safety of the British front lines, came down behind the enemy lines. Air Vice-Marshal Gould Lee, in 1917 a young fighter pilot on the Western Front, wrote in his book *No Parachute:*

'The direct losses were augmented by the wear and tear on pilots and planes in chasing the mirage of air ascendancy over the Lines by continuous standing patrols of fighters along the entire British front, regardless of the needs of the tactical situation, ground or air. While we thus dissipated our strength, more often than not merely beating the empty air, the Germans, in their so-called defensive strategy, concentrated forces superior in numbers or equipment and engaged our scattered line patrols in turn, and our Distant Offensive Patrols as and when it suited them. The result was that in 1917 British air losses were at times nearly four times as great as the German.' [21]

Gould Lee goes on to say that the real criterion of an offensive policy is not *place*, but *aggressiveness,* and here he touches on the second fallacy in Trenchard's policy: an aggressive policy is useless against a technically superior enemy – in Gould Lees' words, 'the most rashly aggressive pigeon won't get far with a hawk.' In the spring of 1917 the pilots and observers were asked to fight – and die – in technically obsolete aeroplanes. The various types of BE2 which equipped the luckless corps squadrons of the RFC had long been outclassed, the Sopwith 1 1/2 Strutters were little better and the RE8 was viewed by many of its pilots as a death trap, with a tendency to spin, which was not cured until May 1917. Even the FE2bs, sturdy and strong aeroplanes that they were, were no match for the German Albatros and Halberstadt fighters. The DH2s and FE8s, which had effectively defeated the Fokker scourge, had become outclassed by the end of 1916 by the latest Albatros and Halberstadt fighters of the emerging *Jagdstaffeln*. Only the excellent Sopwith Pup and Sopwith Triplane (this last type being used exclusively by the Naval squadrons), the various Nieuport types and the Spad could meet the new German fighters on anything approaching equal terms. But even though these aeroplanes were, in the main, more manoeuvrable than the German scouts, their armament of a single Vickers or Lewis gun, against the twin Spandau guns of the German scouts, and their lower top speed, which enabled the German pilots to avoid, initiate or break off combat at will, placed the pilots of the RFC at a serious tactical disadvantage.

To the pilots and observers of early 1917, the persistence of their commanders in sending patrols deep into enemy territory in obsolete machines, despite the high loss of men and machines, was incomprehensible: as irrational as General Haig's unyielding adherence to a war of attrition, also with its total disregard of casualties.

Apart from the casualties they inflicted, the success of the *Jagdstaffeln* had another, far more reaching effect. The most critical time in the life of a fighter pilot was undoubtedly his first month or six weeks of combat. If he could survive this period, become completely orientated in the air and absorb the basic skills of this trade, he stood a good chance of surviving his first tour of duty – usually six months – and becoming a successful, or at least experienced, fighter pilot. The embryo RFC fighter pilot in the period of late 1916 to the June of 1917 would have been flying an aeroplane inferior in most respects to the German Albatros and Halberstadt fighters, a serious and often fatal disadvantage.

The pilots of the first *Jagdstaffeln* were fortunate in two respects: firstly they were almost without exception experienced pilots, having already served in two-seater units; secondly, and of prime importance, they were able to learn their trade when the fighter aeroplanes of the *Luftstreitkräfte* were overwhelmingly superior to those of their opponents, which enabled them to survive that important initial period of combat. When the pendulum of technical air superiority swung once again in favour of the RFC and RNAS, with the introduction of the SE5 and Sopwith Camel, those early pilots of the *Jagdstaffeln* were experienced enough to weather the storm. Despite often being outnumbered, the *Jagdstaffeln* fought superbly until the very end of the conflict. That they did so was in no small measure due to the experience gained during the period of their technical superiority, from the winter of 1916 to the spring of 1917.

NOTES

1. 'Teddy' was T F N Gerrard DSC and Croix de Guerre. Gerrard scored a total of nine victories. He survived the war but died in a polo accident in the early 1920s.

2. The Sopwith Triplane had a ceiling of 20,500 feet. On 22 January 1917 Dallas had reached an altitude of 26,000 feet in Sopwith Triplane N5436. In contrast, the 'baffled pursuers,' were probably flying the Albatros D III, which had a ceiling of approximately 18,500 feet.

3. Foster later served in 209 Squadron and scored a total of 16 victories before the end of the war. He served in World War II in Bomber Command and finally retired as Air Chief Marshal Sir Robert Foster, KCB, CBE, DFC.

4. Bevington was repatriated in December 1918.

5. Knowles was the last of Frankel's twenty victories. Frankel was killed the next day in a fight with the Bristol Fighters of 48 Squadron.

6. *Cage Birds*, H E Harvey, Penguin Books, 1940.

7. The SE5s of 56 Squadron are not included in this total. The Squadron was not operational until 23 April.

8. *Fighter Pilot on the Western Front*, Wing Commander E D Crundall, William Kimber, London. 1975.

9. Lt.Col Alan Binnie was killed in World War II while serving in the Australian army. He was flying as a passenger in a Bristol Beaufort when it crashed in Japanese held territory in New Guinea.

10 Only twenty-four hours after the first attacks, General Nivelle abandoned his original conception of a strategic exploitation northwards in combination with the British armies. At the end of April the French Government ordered Nivelle to abandon the attacks scheduled for early May. Some ground had been gained, but between April 16 and April 25, the French armies lost 30,000 men killed, 100,000 wounded and 4,000 taken prisoner. Almost 80% of these losses were on the first day of the offensive. These heavy losses were to have serious consequences for the French, leading to the mutinies of 1917.

11. *Uffz* Johann Brosius and *Ltn.d R* Köhler of *Schusta 11* were both made POWs on April 21.

12. 15 Sopwith Triplanes of Naval 1; five additional Triplanes from Naval 8; seven SE5s of 56 Squadron; seven Spads from 19 Squadron; eight Nieuports of 29 and a further Squadron and a further six Nieuports from 60 Squadron.

13. The Gotha was given the number G23 in the British captured aircraft lists.

14. After recovering from his wound, Coote was to join 56 Squadron in the following June.

15. That Ball allowed the patrol – apart from himself inexperienced fighter pilots – to separate is indicative of how out of touch Ball was with the change in tactics since he had last been in France and how unsuited in temperament he was to be a Flight Commander.

16. The mistake by the Naval pilots is perhaps understandable. Only two squadrons were equipped with Spads at this time, 19 and 23 Squadron, and many RFC pilots thought the Spad 'a very Hunnish looking machine.'

17. Forty Squadron had moved from Auchel to Bruay on April 29.

18. Lt J A G Brewis had been shot down and killed by *Flak 28,40,61* and *68* east of Hendecourt.

19. *I Chose the Sky,* Leonard H Rochford DSC and Bar, DFC, William Kimber, London 1977.

20. *Words and Music for a Mechanical Man*, Oliver Stewart, Faber & Faber, London 1967.

21. *No Parachute,* Arthur Gould Lee, Jarrolds, London 1968.

CHAPTER TEN

THE PENDULUM SWINGS

May was to see the beginning of a reverse swing in the pendulum of air superiority in favour of the RFC. During the month the obsolete BE types were finally phased out and the corps squadrons re-equipped with the Armstrong Whitworth FK8 and the RE8. Both these types were sturdy, robust aeroplanes, a great improvement on the BE's, and in the hands of an aggressive crew were more able to defend themselves. Although the RE8 had a disastrous operational debut – notably on April 6 when three from 59 Squadron were lost in one operation, and on April 13, when a further six from the squadron were shot down by *Jasta 11* – the type was still a vast improvement on the BEs. With the arrival of the superb Sopwith Camel in June, allied to the SE5 and its later variant the SE5a, the RFC and RNAS at last had two fighters that were more than a match for the Albatros fighters of the *Luftstreitkräfte.*

On the first day of May 1917, there was a lull in the ground fighting while the ground forces were re-organised and the artillery prepared. The weather was good and the corps aeroplanes were out in force above the lines, co-operating with the artillery batteries. The new German tactics of concentrating large numbers of fighters had the effect of localising their efforts and made them easier to find and bring to combat. Paradoxically, this aided Trenchard's wasteful offensive strategy. Although some squadrons found themselves facing large formations of enemy fighters, to the pilots and observers of the corps squadrons the sky suddenly seemed clearer of enemy machines.

Another factor was the tremendous daily effort that the pilots of the *Jagdstaffeln* had made during April. Despite their superior equipment, they too were tired. Manfred von Richthofen, now Germany's leading fighter pilot, with 52 victories, went on leave on the evening of April 30 and much of the impetus of the German fighter effort seemed to go with him. RFC casualties in May were to be much lower than those in April.

If the pilots and observers viewed the onset of the fine spring weather with mixed feelings, meaning as it did that more patrols were able to be flown, they nevertheless welcomed the feeling of renewal that spring always brings and began to enjoy their off duty hours.

The pilots of 56 Squadron at Vert Galant were now well settled into their new base. Writing home to his mother, Arthur Rhys Davids described his Nissen hut living quarters:

'We have four of them, side by side, and they are made of wood with circular corrugated iron roofs. Each is divided into four compartments, usually one half from the other and across the middle and one half bisected again by a partition up the centre. All the partitions are a kind of brown canvas, floors just boards, but I have bought a straw mat and also a *"descent delit"* in other words a get-out-of-bed, alias a very nice quite ordinary little flooring of carpetlet.'

Rhys Davids 'little den' was about 12 feet long by 9 feet wide. He had the sunny side of the hut, looking out across the aerodrome. He had put up some shelves for his books, hung his photographs on the walls and had a small fold up wicker table. Outside he had a small 'suburban garden,' with a few bedraggled plants and some 'choice weeds.' The squadron also had badminton and croquet courts and a cinder tennis court, which the pilots had made themselves with the aid of some German prisoners, 'a healthy looking lot who work well and seem quite happy if sullen.' For entertainment in the evenings the pilots had the choice of Amiens, only a short distance away, but more frequently went into Doullens, a pleasant little town six miles from the aerodrome. There was a little restaurant in Doullens, the *Hotel des 4 Fils Aymon,* which served excellent food.

On May 1, three SE5s of 56 Squadron took off at 8.30am on its first patrol of the day. The patrol drove off a pair of enemy two-seaters working over the lines between Arras and Cambrai, but fifteen minutes later one persistant crew was back. This time 2Lt Kenneth Knaggs made no mistake and sent the brown Albatros from *Schusta 30(B)* down to crash near Roeux. The pilot, *Unteroffizier* Adam Föller, a Bavarian from Schwetzinger, was killed in the crash and the observer *Flg* Sandtner was wounded.

During the day's fighting, 1 Squadron lost two Flight Commanders. The South African, Capt Quintin-Brand, shot down an Albatros C type over Warneton at 9.15am and another over Ploegsteert three quarters of an hour later. The observer of the second Albatros must have got in some good shooting at the Nieuport: it was badly damaged and Quintin Brand was hit in the hand. He was sent to hospital the next day. Capt E D 'Spider' Atkinson took a patrol of Nieuports out at 9.45. One pilot crashed on takeoff and another dropped out with engine trouble. Returning from the patrol the Flight attacked four enemy scouts of *Jasta 28* at 12,000 feet over Ypres. These were led by the *Staffelführer* Karl Emil Schäfer. Schäfer had been promoted to the command of *Jasta 28* from *Jasta 11* only five days previously and was still flying an all red Albatros. Schäfer and Atkinson fought for several minutes until Schäfer hit the Nieuport in the carburettor. Atkinson spun out of the fight and force landed near Elverdinghe. Atkinson was awarded to Schäfer as his 25th victory.[1]

Lieutenant E S T Cole had a more positive result. He fought his opponent down from 12,000 to 800 feet. A final burst from Coles sent the Albatros down in flames and it fell into a small pond. Cole landed nearby and helped extricate the pilot from the wreckage. Among the troops attracted to the scene of the crash was a doctor and he found that the pilot, *Ltn* Alexander Kutscher, had been hit five times in the heart. Kutscher's Albatros was given the number G 30.

The FE8s of 41 Squadron lost a pilot to three Albatri during the afternoon. 2Lt E C H R Nicholls was wounded in the head and right heel and sent to hospital.

At 6.00pm Capt Ball led 56 Squadron's last patrol of the day. Ball shot down a pair of two-seaters, one crashing near Marquion, the other into the trenches southwest of Cambrai.

The Sopwith Pups and Triplanes of the Naval squadrons were in action during the day. Three Flights of Pups from Naval 3 took off to fly an escort to the FEs of 18 Squadron on a photo-reconnaissance to Cambrai. SqdnCom L S Breadner led B Flight as close escort with F D Casey and A Flight above them. C Flight, led by F C Armstrong were higher still, at 12,000 feet. Soon after crossing the lines, C Flight were attacked by a number of Albatros scouts. 'Tich' Rochford and Armstrong fought one Albatros down to 8,000 feet then broke off to pick up the FEs again. 'However they were miles ahead of us and we could not catch up and eventually lost them completely because the EA were diverting our attention all the time.'

Some confusion seems to have taken place in the tactics employed by the Naval pilots. B Flight were chased back to the lines by 14 enemy scouts and Casey and A Flight picked up the FEs from another squadron. On their return to Marieux there was 'much argument' over the mixup. All the FEs had returned safely but the squadron had lost FltSubLt A S Mather, who had been shot down by *Oblt* Adolk von Tutschek of *Jasta 12* and taken POW. Mather was von Tutschek's third official victory. During the fighting, FltSubLt. J S T Fall of B Flight had shot down *Ltn* Gerhard Strehl of *Jasta 12*, the Albatros falling in flames to crash near Epinoy.

Naval 8 were also flying an escort to FEs in the morning. FltSubLt D M Shields was shot down while fighting seven Albatri, elements of *Jasta 4* and *11*. Shields succeeded in shooting down one of the enemy out of control before he was himself shot down, crashing just inside the British lines near Vimy Ridge. Donald Shields broke a leg and dislocated his shoulder in the crash and was forced to hide in a nearby shell hole while German artillery fire destroyed his triplane. Shields was awarded to *Ltn* Kurt von Döring of *Jasta 4* for his second victory.

Thirty minutes after this fight, *Ltn* Kurt Wolff of *Jasta 11* shot down and killed FltSubLt E D Roach of Naval 8 flying Sopwith Triplane N5474, marked 'Gwen,' for his 28th victory.

The weather continued fine on May 2. The ground offensive was scheduled to begin again on May 3, but before then enemy observation balloons had to be dealt with. A plan had been formulated by LtCol W R Freeman, commanding Tenth Wing: artillery were to put down a special barrage on the German trenches in the area of the balloons while the pilots of 40 Squadron hedge-hopped at fifty feet towards their targets.

The barrage opened at 9.00am and six Nieuports of 40 Squadron took off. William Bond of 40 Squadron wrote home to his wife the next day. 'It was an experiment in balloon strafing and it came off. Six of us attacked six balloons and we destroyed five. One fellow failed because his gun jammed like mine did that day, you remember? I had eleven bullet holes in my machine and some of the others were nearly as bad.'[2] All the Nieuports returned, but all had sustained considerable damage from ground fire.

The first patrol from 56 Squadron left the ground at 6.00am. Flying a patrol line further north than previously, the SEs saw nothing until 7.30am: a pair of Albatros two-seaters over Vitry and 3,000 feet lower than the SEs. Capt Henry 'Duke' Meintjes closed to within 100 yards before opening fire and sent one enemy machine down in a slow, wide spiral.

Meintjes followed it down, firing again from 25 yards before turning away. The green and brown Albatros finally hit the ground just west of Corbehem.

In the evening there was a large fight east of Arras involving over forty aeroplanes, twenty five of them British: Sopwith Pups of 66 Squadron, Bristol Fighters from 48 Squadron, the FE2ds of 20 Squadron, and two SEs – Ball and Kenneth Knaggs – from 56 Squadron. Although the individual fights were inconclusive, the German pilots were gradually driven back to Douai, being outnumbered and out manoeuvred. Just before the main fight began, Capt Ball had attacked the nearest of four red-painted Albatri. As Ball went into his attack he was jumped from the rear by four others. Ball turned steeply, causing the first enemy scout to overshoot. As the Albatros flashed by, Ball pulled down his top wing Lewis gun and fired fifty rounds into it. Following it down, firing all the time, he finally left the Albatros at 2,000 feet and it crashed into rough ground between Halte and Vitry.

After the large fight – there were no British casualties – Ball flew south towards Cambrai. He fired at a white two-seater but lost sight of it in the deepening dusk and landed back at Vert Galant at 8.30pm.

On an escort patrol during the day, Lt W Fry of 60 Squadron forced an enemy scout to land, but in the combat the right hand bottom wing of his Nieuport broke free from its strut fixing – a common fault of the Nieuport. The Nieuport went into a spin, but Fry managed to recover and flew back to Filescamp Farm. Major Scott commented in his report to Wing: 'This is the fourth Nieuport Scout to break in the air in 35 days. Luckily Lt Fry is a good and fearless pilot.'

The ground attack recommenced at 3.45am on the morning of May 3, extending for 16 miles along the fronts of the British First, Third and Fifth Armies. Early successes were short-lived. New counter attack tactics, copied from the British and French, were used by the German Armies involved, the so called 'elastic defence.' The front line was lightly held while the mass of troops remained in support in the rear, poised to deliver rapid counter attacks. These tactics had been anticipated and the corps aeroplanes were ordered to fly from dawn to dusk over the captured positions and report on the massing of any enemy troops for counter attacks. However, the chaos of the ground fighting made this almost impossible. Only the Sopwith 1 1/2 Strutters of 43 Squadron reported any build up of enemy troops and five of the Sopwiths attacked them at heights of from 50 to 300 feet.

There was little air fighting during the day but the Martinsydes of 27 Squadron twice bombed Don: in the early morning and after lunch. On each of these bombing raids the Martinsydes were escorted by SEs of 56 Squadron. In the morning raid, after seeing the bombers safely back across the

lines, the SEs flew a normal offensive patrol south of Douai. Lts Lewis and Knight attacked six enemy scouts just to the east of Saudemont but without any positive results. Both Knight's guns jammed and he was attacked by two of the Albatri, but he zoomed, and easily outclimbed them. While tackling one Albatros, Lewis was twice attacked from the rear by four others, with the added advantage of height. Lewis easily evaded these attacks, each time diving, turning underneath the enemy scouts, then zooming away. Outflown by the brilliant flying of Lewis, using the power of his SE to advantage, the German pilots broke off the action and flew east. It was an indication that the SE5 was a superior aeroplane to the German Albatros.

During an evening patrol 41 Squadron lost two pilots. Seven FE8s left their aerodrome at Hondschoote at 4.30pm. Over Roulers the FE8s were attacked by seven Albatri. Hopelessly outclassed in performance the little pushers formed a defensive circle and the fight drifted towards Houthulst Forest. The initial seven enemy scouts were joined by another six and one dived onto the tail of Capt S F Browning's FE. Lt C E V Porter attempted to save Browning but was cut off by the enemy scouts and Browning went down in a spin to crash near Draaibank, west of Houthulst Forest. Four more enemy scouts then came up from the direction of Lille. Lts Porter and E D MacKay each claimed an Albatros out of control, MacKay's seen as being forced to land, but Lt Fraser was wounded and went down. Macgown followed Fraser down but Fraser waved him away and finally crashed at Bultehock, the next village to Browning's crash. Fraser was pinned under the wreckage of his FE8 and was fired at by the Albatros pilots until he was removed from the aeroplane by German troops. Fraser spent two days with his captors, *Jasta 8*, stationed at Rumbeke, and one of the enemy pilots showed him the damage that his Albatros had taken during the fight. Despite the overall superiority of the Albatros over their FE8s, five of the seven pilots returned without further damage.

The spring weather continued to improve the next day – May 4. It was fine and warm and the *Jagdstaffeln* were out in considerable force. The Naval squadrons were out early, Naval 3 taking off at 5.30am. Led by Armstrong, the Flight crossed the lines at 17,000 feet and west of Cambrai they spotted an Albatros two-seater flying west to the British lines. Each time the Pups tried to close the range, the enemy pilot retreated to the east, but eventually they caught the Albatros and Armstrong and A T Whealy shot it down.

Just after mid-day 56 Squadron flew an escort for the Martinsydes of 27 Squadron. The SEs saw the bombers back to the lines then returned to the Douai area, intending to escort a formation of DH4s from 55 Squadron, which was returning from bombing the German aerodrome at La Brayelle. The patrol failed to find the DH4s, but sighted a group of four Albatri at 12,000 feet over Férin. 'Billy' Crowe attacked the nearest enemy machine but the pilot evaded his attack: he zoomed, turned sharply, got behind the SE and hit it in the wings and tail with a quick burst of fire. Crowe dived quickly away to the left. The enemy pilot neglected to follow up his advantage and cleared east.

The pilots of 60 Squadron were at lunch when a message came through that a German two-seater was working at artillery co-operation over the lines and William Bishop and Fry took off to attack it. Archie bursts pointed out the enemy machine to the two Nieuports and as they approached Bishop and Fry saw that there were, in fact, a pair of two-seaters. Bishop later reported that he attacked the nearest, firing twenty rounds before turning away; and that Fry followed his attack, also firing at the two-seater. As Fry turned away Bishop renewed his attack, firing 40 rounds into the enemy machine which did two turns of a spin and went down to crash. The other machine made off. Fry only remembered that both enemy machines cleared east and he did not see the two-seater claimed by Bishop crash. When Bishop and Fry returned their lunches had been kept hot for them. They had been only an hour in the air.

Albert Ball took two SEs – Gerald Maxwell and Knaggs – on an early evening patrol, taking off at 5.30pm and flying to an enemy aerodrome south of Cambrai. The SE pilots noted the number of sheds and that several aeroplanes were taking off, before flying back to the lines. Ball then saw eight Albatros scouts over Riencourt at 12,000 feet. The SEs climbed for a little extra height, picked an Albatros each and went down. Ball's first opponent dived away towards Douai; Ball let it go and attacked another. This also dived away, but in a straighter line and Ball followed it down, getting underneath it and firing half a drum of Lewis into its underside. The enemy scout went down and crashed near Graincourt, the crash witnessed by nearby AA batteries. Maxwell fastened on the tail of one Albatros and fired a long burst from both guns, closing the range from 50 to 20 yards. The enemy pilot slumped forward and the Albatros crashed near Sauchy-Lestrée.

Both Maxwell and Knaggs had gun jams and Ball led them to 23 Squadron's aerodrome at Baizieux, where they landed and cleared the jams. When the SEs were ready to leave, the engine of Knagg's SE refused to start. Leaving Knaggs behind, Ball and Maxwell took off and climbed hard towards Douai. Flying along the Arras to Doaui road the SEs spotted a pair of two-seaters from a *Flieger Abteilung (A)*. These machines were nearly always to be found flying at 4,000 feet in the vicinity of Vitry, working with the German artillery. Ball and Maxwell, three thousand feet above the two-seaters, went down to attack them but were met by four red-painted Albatri of *Jasta 11*.

There were several minutes of confused fighting before the German pilots broke off the combat and made off. Ball looked round for Maxwell and saw him low down, pulling out of a dive and 'apparently alright.' Ball turned for the front lines but was attacked by a large number of enemy machines – Maxwell later gave their number as 30. Ball fired at several of his attackers but his guns jammed and putting down the nose of his SE he made use of its superior speed, outdistancing the enemy machines. Maxwell had still not returned to Vert Galant at 10.30pm and it was feared that he had been shot down, but he had forced landed at Bruay and stayed the night there with 40 Squadron.

On a late evening patrol in the Ecourt – St.Quentin area, Naval 3 lost FltSubLt H S Murton. The patrol was attacked by *Jasta 12* and *Oblt* von Tutschek shot down Murton – flying his triplane named 'Black Bess.' – who crashlanded at Fresnes-Vitry on the Arras to Douai road and was taken POW.

On May 5 many of the RFC squadrons were given a rest, although aeroplanes of the corps squadrons flew artillery co-operation flights against 89 targets. Of the fighter squadrons only 56,40 and 23 are mentioned as having been in action by the RFC communiqué for the day.

The day was fine and warm and Capt Crowe took a patrol of five SEs out at 5.00am, making for the area of Cambrai. Seeing no activity there, the Flight turned back and flew to the Douai area. Passing between Estrées and Courchelettes they saw what they took to be a formation of three Nieuports, 500 feet above them. However, as the SEs flew under the Nieuports, they were attacked. These 'Nieuports' were Siemens-Schuckert D Is. With its rotary engine and Nieuport tail and rudder the Siemens was an almost exact copy of the Nieuport 17, which led the experienced Crowe to mistake them for friendly aeroplanes. Luckily, no damage was done. Crowe turned the formation to meet the attack and after a brief skirmish the enemy scouts made off, the element of surprise lost.

The SEs they turned west and attacked a two-seater over Noyelles. All the SEs attacked this machine but they all overshot in their passes and the enemy pilot dived away east. The sun was now high in eastern sky, blinding the pilots, and a ground mist made visibility very poor. The SEs again patrolled to Cambrai before returning.

It was not until the evening that another patrol was flown. Ball led Lewis, Melville, Hoidge, Broadberry and Maxwell off the ground at 6.00pm. The SEs headed for the area of Douai-Cambrai – Ball's favourite hunting ground – but both Broadberry and Maxwell turned back with engine trouble. Flying to Arras the remaining SEs split up; Ball flying towards Lens where the sky was clearer; Lewis leading the others towards Douai.

Crossing the lines, Ball saw a pair of Albatros scouts flying towards Carvin. Ball turned away and climbed hard to close the height advantage held by the enemy scouts, but as he reached 11,000 feet one of the enemy pilots got on his tail and opened fire. Ball turned quickly, saw the other Albatros was still some distance away, got underneath his attacker and fired two drums of Lewis into it at very close range. The Albatros dived with Ball following. The enemy pilot made no attempt to evade Ball, who followed close behind, firing another drum of Lewis into his machine. The Albatros went down out of control but its companion had now closed the distance and attacked Ball. After a brief period of manoeuvring for position, SE and Albatros flew head on towards each other, both firing as the distance between them closed. The SE was hit in the engine and Ball was covered in oil from the punctured oil tank. Ball zoomed away. His engine was still giving full power but his oil pressure was nil. He could see no sign of either of the Albatri but he went down to 3,000 feet and saw them both lying in a field within 400 yards of each other. The SE's Hispano-Suiza ran for another three quarters of a hour, getting very little oil under hardly any pressure, but it saw Ball safely home to Vert Galant.

This combat and near escape left Ball shaken and physically exhausted. T B Marson, the 56 Squadron recording officer, recalled in his memoirs:

'Flushed in the face, his eyes brilliant, his hair blown and dishevelled, he came to the squadron office to make his report, but for a long time he was in so an over-wrought a state that dictation was an impossibility to him.'[3]

Ball firmly believed that the pilot of the Albatros had meant to ram him; that he owed his escape to divine intervention. 'God is very good to me,' he is reported to have said. 'God must have me in his keeping.' Unlike many of his fellow pilots Ball's religious beliefs were unshaken by the daily killing he witnessed.[4]

After Ball had left the other SEs Cecil Lewis led them towards Douai. Melville became separated from his companions in the clouds over the town, but Lewis and Hoidge attacked a formation of red Albatri from *Jasta 11* over Montigny. After a brief indecisive fight the SEs regained their height and reformed. Seeing a formation of Naval Triplanes in the vicinity and feeling sure of their support, Lewis led Hoidge down to attack the red Albatri again. In the fierce fight, Hoidge shot one down out of control with a burst of fire directly under the pilot's seat. Lewis was attacked by six of the enemy scouts, but he evaded their attacks using the superior speed and zoom of his SE5 and sent one down out of control with a burst from 20 yards range.

The evening was a successful one for Lt Herbert Ellis of 40 Squadron. Flying a lone patrol he crossed the lines high above Douai, then returned at low level. Over the enemy aerodrome he attacked three Albatros scouts as they were landing. The first sideslipped into the ground; Ellis then attacked the other, which landed on its nose on the aerodrome and turned over. The third Albatros landed safely. Flying low for the lines, Ellis was attacked by another Albatros. He outmanoeuvred this scout and got into a good attacking position, but his gun jammed. Ellis drew his Colt automatic and fired at the enemy pilot. The Albatros spun down and broke up in mid air.

Lt W T Walder of 40 Squadron also claimed an enemy machine out of control during the day's fighting, but in the morning 23 Squadron lost 2Lt C C Cheatle, whose Spad was last see going east across the Bapaume to Cambrai road.

May 6 was also fine and sunny. A high wind hampered flying to some extent in the morning, but it dropped in the evening and Ball, flying his Nieuport, took a patrol out at 7.00pm. Over Arras, Ball left the SEs, flew towards Douai, and soon sighted four red Albatros scouts, flying towards Cambrai and a thousand feet below him. Ball, in his usual impetuous manner, attacked at once, firing two and a half drums of Lewis into the nearest which went down to crash near the crossroads and railway, just to the south of Sancourt. The remaining enemy pilots seemed little inclined to return Ball's attack and kept well clear of him until he turned west for the lines. They then attacked the Nieuport, but Ball easily outmanoeuvred the enemy scouts, which he found were particularly slow in turns. Ball was now out of ammunition and he returned. The SEs had landed ten minutes before him having seen no action.

Forty Squadron were also in action. Capt R W Gregory flew a mid-morning patrol with Lt W Bond and they shot down a two-seater that was confirmed by the artillery. Four more Nieuports from the squadron went out again in the evening. Gregory shot down another two seater and Lt L L Morgan (nicknamed 'The Air Hog' because he seemed to always be in the air) shot down an Albatros. Returning from patrol, Ellis made a bad force landing at the advanced landing ground and suffered a severe concussion. Lt K MacKenzie was attacked by some red-painted Albatri and forced to land behind the British lines. Lt E Mannock of 40 Squadron also made a bad landing on returning to the aerodrome turning his Nieuport upside down: 'Just a bump under the wing at the wrong moment and over she went. These buses are very light.'

Sixty Squadron supplied an escort for photo-reconnaissance in the Cambrai area. At 6.00pm they were attacked by six yellow-painted Albatri of *Jasta 5*.

Lt Spenser 'Nigger' Horn shot one down out of control, but 2Lt C W McKissock was shot down by *Offst* Edmund Nathanael to be taken POW, and 2Lt G D Hunter was wounded and taken prisoner by *Ltn* Kurt Schneider. Hunter had been hit in the back by an explosive bullet; gangrene set in over the next few days and Hunter's arm had to be amputated just above the elbow.

On May 7 the day was again fine and warm but there was a hint of thunder in the air.

Meintjes led 'C' Flight of 56 Squadron on patrol, taking off at 8.00am. An hour later the Flight had a short and indecisive skirmish with four enemy scouts before sighting a hostile two-seater south of Lens. Cecil Lewis and 'Duke' Meintjes both attacked this machine and finally sent it down over Quiéry. Two more enemy two-seaters were driven east, without result, but 'Georgie' Hoidge chased them down to 6,000 feet and when he regained his height he had lost the other SEs. Hoidge later attacked a lone Albatros scout over Cambrai but four others came to its assistance and Hoidge wisely turned west and outdistanced them. Before returning, Meintjes unsuccessfully attacked a balloon over St Quentin.

At 12.30pm Ball, Maxwell and Knaggs flew an escort for the Sopwith 1 1/2 Strutters of 70 Squadron, whose orders were to photo the German aerodromes at Caudry and Neuvilly. Arriving over the enemy aerodromes they appeared to be deserted and the formations turned for home. A number of enemy scouts and two-seaters came up after the British formation but only one came close enough to pose a thread. Ball drove this off. This concentration of enemy machines shadowed the SEs and Sopwiths back to the lines, keeping a thousand yards to the rear, sheering off each time the SEs turned back to attack them.

Flying an offensive patrol in the morning, E D Crundall of Naval 8 attacked an Albatros scout over Douai, getting onto its tail and firing from close range. He later wrote in his diary: 'he went down in a vertical dive. I thought I saw black smoke and flames but I am not sure. I find it very difficult to watch a machine go right down to the ground. I always seem to lose it in the conglomeration of objects on the surface.' FltSubLt H A Pailthorpe of Naval 8 was credited with a hostile scout destroyed, possibly from this same patrol.

Another attack on balloons, the second in a week, was carried out by 40 Squadron. At breakfast William Bond was sitting next to his CO Major L A Tilney. Bond had flown in the previous balloon attack and Tilney asked him if he would again take part. Bond readily agreed, but his Flight Commander, Gregory, objected, saying that nobody should fly such a dangerous mission twice. Gregory did however, suggest that the remainder of the Squadron should fly over the balloons, at a safe height from Archie, to distract attention from the actual attack.

The Nieuports left the ground at 8.58am, but Bond was late in getting off and the other Nieuports were over the lines before he saw them. From three miles away Bond saw three of the balloons start to burn. Turning away, he saw three additional balloons to the south and he flew to investigate. Arriving over the balloons he found that three enemy two-seaters were flying behind them. Bond had the advantage of height and spiralled down to have a nearer look at the enemy machines, but as he approached he heard one of the enemy gunners firing at him. Bond changed his spiral into a dive and attacked the nearest enemy machine. The gunner fired a burst at the Nieuport but all three two-seaters suddenly dived east. They had seen five SEs diving on them. Bond watched as all eight machines disappeared from sight.

The main attack on the balloons had been successful, with seven destroyed, falling to Lts Morgan, Hall, Cudemore, Redler, Nixon, Parry and Mannock. The cost was one of 40 Squadron's Flight Commanders, Capt W E Nixon, who was shot down and killed. All the Nieuports sustained heavy damage from groundfire: 2Lt Parry's fuel tank was shot up, forcing him to land near Camblain L'Abbé. The balloon shot down by Lt. Edward Mannock was the first of the 16 victories he was to score while serving in 40 Squadron.

An additional Nieuport lost during the day was from 29 Squadron: 2Lt G S Gaskain of 29 Squadron was shot down and killed in the late afternoon by Lothar von Richthofen of *Jasta 11* for his 19th victory.

During the afternoon the weather deteriorated. It became very dark and storm clouds began to build up. The pilots of 56 Squadron fully expected that there would be no further flying, but while they were at tea orders came from Wing to fly the scheduled evening patrol in the Douai-Cambrai area. At 5.30pm eleven SE5s – an unusually large patrol – took off and made for the patrol area. The weather was very bad. Thick layers of cumulus cloud ranged from 2,000 to 10, 000 feet with gaps of varying sizes between them. Ball, leading Maxwell and Knaggs crossed the front lines south of the Bapaume to Cambrai road, flying at 7,000 feet, just below the higher clouds and flying a course to take them to the north of Cambrai. The remainder of the SEs, 'C' Flight – Meintjes, Hoidge, Lewis and Melville – climbed to 9,000 feet and went north east towards Cambrai, with 'B' Flight: Crowe, Leach, Rhys Davids and Chaworth-Musters, passing over them a thousand feet higher, making towards the south of Cambrai.

Over the Bois-de-Bourlon area 'B' Flight ran into a very thick cloud. Just before the Flight entered the cloud Chaworth-Musters left the formation to investigate an aeroplane, although whether this was hostile or friendly was not known. Chaworth-Musters was not seen again: he was shot down by Werner Voss of *Jasta B* for his 25th victory.

Crowe, Leach and Rhys Davids finally came out of the cloud over the railway station at Sauchy-Lestrée and Crowe and Leach attacked an enemy scout south of Vitry. Crowe overshot in his first pass and had a gun stoppage in his second attack, but Leach shot the scout down to crash just east of Vitry.

Rhys Davids had been about to join in the attacks on this scout when he was attacked from the rear by another, coloured red with a green band behind the pilot's cockpit. This Albatros was flown by *Ltn* Wolff of *Jasta 11*. Rhys Davids was unaware he was being attacked until he saw Wolff's tracers, but although he survived Wolff's first pass his SE had been hit in the engine, undercarriage and wings:

'I had heard one bullet go into my undercraige with the deuce of a whonk, one or two others were making themselves unpleasant by spoiling the appearance of my immaculate planes, and the tiresome young man in the red bus finally was unkind enough to plonk one into my engine, which we found afterwards made a hole six inches square in the water jacket.'

Rhys Davids was in trouble, but while he was considering how best to extricate himself from the attentions of the 'tiresome young man in the red bus' Wolff broke off the action and made off towards Douai. Rhys Davids turned for the lines, but two miles west of Arras his engine finally seized and he force landed in a field near La Herlière.

After shooting down the first Albatros, Leach became separated from Crowe and was attacked by another. A burst of fire hit the SE in the petrol tank, one bullet ricocheting off the tank and hitting Leach in the leg. Leach fainted from the pain of his wound and the SE went into a spin. Petrol from the ruptured tank blew back into Leach's face, revived him in time, and he regained control and landed among the trenches on Vimy Ridge. Canadian troops lifted him from the cockpit and he was taken to No.4 Canadian Hospital. His leg was later amputated.

Crowe, after a brief combat with another enemy scout flew to the pre-arranged rendevous at Arras and was joined by Cecil Lewis.

Meintjes and 'C' Flight destroyed an enemy machine described as being of 'the Nieuport type' and coloured white. All the Flight had shot at this aeroplane and after reforming they flew northwest over the Arras to Cambrai road. Here they were attacked by four red Albatri from *Jasta 11*. Meintjes was engaged by a persistent Albatros and had to go into a spin to shake off the enemy pilot. Regaining his height, Meintjes saw a red Albatros over Férin. He attacked this Albatros, shooting it down to crash just to the east of Gouy-sous-Bellone. The pilot, *Ltn* Wolfgang von Pluschow of *Jasta 11* was injured in the crash.

Meintjes was next in action east of Lens, attacking an Albatros 9,000 feet below him. The enemy pilot saw the threat and evaded Meintjes with a steep climbing turn. He then completely out-manoeuvred Meintjes, shot him through the wrist and blew off the top of his control column. Meintjes dived away and landed near Sains-en-Gohelle. As the SE rolled to a stop Meintjes finally lost consciousness. He was lifted from the SE5 by troops of the 46th Division whose HQ was nearby.

The heavy clouds had split up the SEs in the evening sky and various isolated and individual actions were fought. After one such, Crowe found himself alone, flew towards Arras and attacked an Albatros scout. The enemy pilot turned to meet Crowe's attack and the two machines flew straight at each other in the gathering dusk. Crowe zoomed over the enemy scout, turning as he did so to get on its tail, but the enemy pilot turned quicker, got on the tail of the SE and shot Crowe's goggles off his helmet. Crowe, considerably shaken by this, climbed hard, managed to evade any further attacks from the lone scout, but came under attack from another formation of red Albatri. Crowe turned west, outdistanced them, and flew towards Fresnoy, where he joined up with Ball who was flying towards Lens.

With the combination of the heavy clouds and the gathering darkness visibility was now very bad. Ball fired two red Very lights as a signal that he had seen hostile machines, and Crowe, although he could see no aeroplanes of any description, followed Ball who was now flying towards Loos. Suddenly, Ball dived and attacked an Albatros, followed by Crowe. As Crowe turned for another pass he saw Ball again attacking the Albatros, almost certainly flown by Lothar von Richthofen, and also saw a Naval Triplane and a Spad some 500 feet above the action. Ball and the Albatros, still fighting, then flew into a heavy thundercloud and Crowe lost sight of them. Knowing his petrol was now almost exhausted, and having no wish to fly into the dangerous cloud, Crowe flew west and landed at Naval 8's aerodrome at Auchel.

Ltn Hailer, a German officer, was the next person to see Ball alive. Ball's SE5 emerged from the thick cloud only two hundred feet above the ground. It was inverted and the propeller was stationary. In this position the SE5 hit the ground, the tailplane breaking off with the impact. Hailer and two other officers hurried to the scene of the crash. Ball was dead, but Hailer and his companions could see no evidence of wounds on his body, nor any combat damage on the wreckage of the SE5 to denote that it had been shot down as the result of an airfight. They concluded that Ball had died as a result of the crash. This was confirmed by a doctor who later examined Ball's body, and found that Ball had sustained a broken back and leg.

Lothar von Richthofen was later credited with having shot down Ball, but Lothar's claim was for a triplane, and no naval triplanes were lost on the evening of May 7. This is not the place to enter into the controversies and many theories that have been put forward over the years to explain Ball's death. From the known facts, the logical explanation is that Ball became disorientated in the extremely thick cloud and the SE5 became inverted. H N Charles, the 56 Squadron engineering officer at the time, has stated that the early model of the SE5 could not be flown inverted: the large float chambered carburettor of the early Hispano-Suiza engine would immediately flood the air intake, choking and stopping the engine. When Ball emerged from the thundercloud the SE was inverted, had a dead engine, and was only 200 feet above the ground. The resultant crash was inevitable.

The loss of Ball, its leading fighter pilot, was a heavy blow to the entire RFC, even more so to the pilots of 56 Squadron. They had been confident of the ability of their SE5s to match the German fighters in performance, but Ball's dislike of the type was now remembered and enlarged upon. Crowe would have none of this: he knew the SE5 was a fine aeroplane and forcibly defended its potentiality as a fighter. With the loss of his fellow Flight Commanders, Meintjes and Ball, Crowe single-handedly ran all three Flights of the squadron until replacements arrived and was largely responsible for upholding the squadron's morale during this period.

There were low clouds and rain on the morning of May 8. Although it cleared a little towards the evening there was still haze and low clouds over the lines. Some patrols were attempted but returned because of the conditions.

The weather had cleared by the morning of May 9: the 9th Wing War Dairy recorded 'Fine all day.'

Naval 8 were out in the early morning. Robert Little with FltSubLt L E B Wimbush and another Sopwith Triplane from the Squadron were on patrol over Lens and attacked a pair of two-seaters flying to the east of the town. Before the triplanes could press home their attacks they were attacked by a number of Albatros scouts from *Jasta 3*. One Albatros passed close by Little and dived on Wimbush who was slightly lower. Wimbush and the Albatros pilot fought for sometime until the triplane was hit in the engine and Wimbush slightly wounded in the leg. Wimbush disengaged from the fight by spinning down over Farbus. He flattened out lower down and returned to his aerodrome at Furnes. Crundall recalled: 'We lifted him out of the machine and he was taken to hospital. Luckily it is only a slight wound.' Wimbush was credited to *Vzfw* Karl Menckhoff of *Jasta 3*.

Little had dived into the enemy formation, firing at several, one of which spun away. The enemy scouts then broke off the action and dived east but returned to attack a DH4 that had joined the triplanes. Outnumbered, the British formation retreated to the lines and the naval pilots returned to Furnes.

Little took off again at 9.25am to intercept two LVGs that had been reported working over the Lines. Forty-five minutes later he found the enemy machines flying at 10,000 feet near Lens. Little drove one east of the town, put a burst through its centre section and it went down out of control. Little was then attacked by its companion that had been joined by two others. While fighting these, Little found he was also below a formation of Albatri. One of these attacked him, but dived past the triplane; Little got onto its tail and fired into its cockpit at such close range that he felt sure he must have hit the pilot.

Fifty-four Squadron flew an escort for 22 Squadron during the afternoon, taking off at 2.25pm. The formation was attacked by a large number of enemy aeroplanes, including elements from *Jasta B. Ltn* Werner Voss sent 2Lt G C T Hadrill down in a flat spin and he forced landed behind the German lines at Lesdain. One of the German machines was reported to have been forced down by one of the FE2bs, crash landing close by Hadrill's Pup.

Pilots from 54 Squadron claimed two victories. 2Lt M B Cole sent a white two-seater down to crash, which was confirmed by the other members of the patrol and Lt E J Y Grevelink drove down a black and white scout, which was also seen to crash.

On May 9 Trenchard put forward his proposals for the redistribution of the RFC for the coming British offensive in Flanders. The fighting on the Arras front was coming to its conclusion, although there would still be ground fighting there until the end of the month. On May 17, for instance, British troops captured Bullecourt and there were to be several minor attacks in which, for the first time, fighter aeroplanes were to directly assist the ground troops.

The fine weather continued on May 10. Two pilots of 66 Squadron were lost in the morning's fighting. 2Lt D J Sheehan was shot down between Sailly and Vitry by Lothar von Richthofen for his 22nd victory and Lt T H Wickett was wounded, forced to land behind enemy lines and taken POW. An Offensive Patrol from 54 Squadron lost a pilot when Capt R G H Pixley was forced to land after being shot up; his Pup came down in a shell hole and Pixley was injured in the crash. Twenty-four Squadron suffered its first casualty for some time, losing Lt H C Cutler, who was shot down just east of Epéhy. The two squadrons flying the outdated DH2 – 24 and 32 Squadrons – were stationed a little to the south of the main battle area of Arras, and 41 Squadron, flying the equally obsolete FE8, was stationed further the north at Abeele. This was possibly to conserve their strength until they could be re-equipped with more modern aircraft.[5]

An early morning patrol by 60 Squadron, led by William Fry, chased two enemy aircraft, but failed to get close enough to attack them. Fry went out alone on a High Offensive Patrol after lunch. He several times attacked three Albatros scouts over Vitry, but without success. [6]

William Bond of 40 Squadron wrote home to his wife the following afternoon:

'Dearest One,

I got a Hun yesterday afternoon. It was a great scrap and I was fearfully pleased, because for the first time in a scrap I tried a pukka Immelmann turn and brought it off. I was with Romney (Capt Gregory. Author) and when we were at 16,500, about five miles over the lines, he dived on two Hun two-seaters at about 14,000. I saw him go down and pass right underneath and then I went for the other. It was a big bus with polished yellow wooden body and green wings. At about 100 yards I started firing, and the Hun, who was going across me, turned and climbed round as if to get on my tail. Then came my Immelmann! With engine full on, I pulled the machine up hard and nearly vertical. When she was almost stalling I kicked her left hand rudder hard and the machine whipped over on one wing, turned her nose down, and came out in exactly the opposite direction. The Hun was now dead in front of my gun about 200 feet below me. I opened on him again and almost immediately he started diving and slowly spinning. To keep my gun on him I had to go down absolutely vertical, and eventually went beyond the vertical and found myself on my back with the engine stopped through choking. When at length I fell into a normal attitude again, the Hun had disappeared. One of our patrols which had come over in time to see the scrap says he went down spinning and crashed.' [7]

An excited FltSubLt. Oliver B Ellis of Naval 1 also wrote home on May 11:

'At last I can claim a Hun. Last night I drove two down, and with the help of another man crashed a third. It was a glorious scrap but one doesn't often get such a chance. I fought a Hun down 5,000 feet and eventually saw him off, not crashed, but driven down. Then I found six on my tail, so the only thing to do was to fight them until something happened. Luckily the something was another of our lot and while he was there I drove another Hun down, then my partner had a gun jam and I had four to keep going until another of my lot turned up at which three of the four Huns thought fit to go. This other man dived on the Hun and pumped quite a lot into him, and drove him below me, so, as my partner had drawn off, I attacked and finished off the unfortunate Hun, who crashed. We were then at 15,000 feet, 10 miles the wrong side of the lines and had Archies the whole way home. I found I had one strut nearly shot through and two hits from Archies, one within half an inch of my petrol tank. It's a great war isn't it. It's raining like fun tonight.' [8]

On May 10 Naval 8 was in the process of moving from Auchel to a new aerodrome at Mont St Eloi. Booker led C Flight to the new base in the morning and after they had landed Crundall asked if he might fly a lone patrol. Booker agreed and Crundall took off at 9.15am. Crundall flew along the Hindenburg Line from Vitry to La Bassée at 10,000 feet, coming under heavy Archie. A new German aerodrome had been reported as being the area and Crundall went down to 4,000 feet, found it and marked its position on his map. Flaming onions were coming up at the triplane and Crundall regained his height, climbing to 9,000 feet, where he saw an enemy two-seater. The enemy machine was climbing almost as fast as the triplane and pulling his machine up into a near stalling position Crundall fired a long burst at it. The triplane stalled, lost 1,000 feet of height and the two-seater made good its escape, climbing out of range.

The German *Flak* batteries now had the Crundall's height; a shell burst close to the triplane and a piece of shrapnel hit Crundall.

'I felt a violent stab in the back as though someone had struck me a heavy blow with a hammer, and the engine stopped.' Petrol poured out over Crundall's flying boots, draining his tank in half a minute; he was six miles over the German side with 8,000 feet of height. He knew he had been wounded, probably seriously, and he decided to make for Bethune, assuming that there would be a hospital there. However, he had first to cross the front lines and he glided towards them, losing height all the time and under a 'terrific bombardment.' Thankfully, as he crossed the trenches at 3,000 feet the groundfire ceased, but he now felt very faint. He set the tail trim to give him the flattest glide angle possible and made for Bethune, selecting a field close to the town.

As Crundall came in to land he suddenly saw that there were some telegraph wires in front of him, but he was now losing consciousness too quickly to worry about them. As the ground approached Crundall eased the control column back and felt his wheels gently touching the ground. He fainted before the triplane had stopped its landing run.

When Crundall regained consciousness he was lying on the ground beside his triplane surrounded by troops. Luckily there was a road nearby and he was taken to a car and driven to a Casualty Clearing Station. It was later found that the piece of shrapnel in his back was within a tenth of an inch of his spine, severing the metal ring of his trouser braces on its entry. Three days later Crundall was on a hospital ship to England. He rejoined Naval 8 on July 13. [9]

The War Diary of 9th Wing recorded the weather on May 11 as being 'fine and very warm.' A patrol of six SE5s from 56 Squadron left the ground at 6.00am. Led by Cyril Crowe their orders were to patrol a line ten miles east of the Lens-La Bassée Canal to Vimy. A formation of Albatros scouts was seen near Lens, but these refused to fight and dived away. Crowe then returned with engine trouble and Cecil Lewis took command of the Flight, taking it in a northerly direction. Over Pont-a-Vendin the SEs attacked four Albatros scouts, but these also dived away after a short skirmish. The patrol then flew north to Vimy and attempted to bring yet another formation of enemy scouts to combat, but again, although they had the advantage of height, the German pilots cleared to the north. Below the SE formation a corps aeroplane was under heavy anti-aircraft fire, but as the SEs watched the shell bursts ceased: four red Albatri were diving to attack the British two-seater. The SEs dived to intercept them. The fight was short and sharp: Lewis and Maxwell both attacked the same Albatros from thirty yards, Lewis from below, Maxwell from above. The enemy machine went down out of control followed by Maxwell. At 7,000 feet the Albatros turned over onto its back. The remaining Albatri had cleared and the SEs reformed and returned to Vert Galant.

Fifty-four Squadron were in action with *Jasta 6* during the morning, and lost 2Lt H C Duxbury killed south of Lesdain by *Vzfw* Fritz Krebs of the *Jasta*. On the plus side for the Squadron, Capt W V Strugnell shot down a two-seater over Walincourt and an Albatros scout near Beaurevoir.

An Australian pilot, Lt A S Shepherd of 29 Squadron, claimed an Albatros destroyed over Sailly at 10.15am for the first of his eventual ten victories.

The naval squadrons were also in action. Naval 3 were in combat with *Jasta 12* over Bourlon in the early afternoon, losing FltSubLt J Bampfylde-Daniel to either *Oblt* Tutschek or *Vzfw* Reissinger. Bampfylde-Daniel was wounded in the fight and taken POW. FltSubLt H S Broad was wounded in the face during the fighting.

In the late evening FltSubLt O J Gagnier of Naval 6 was in a fight with four enemy machines and was forced to land in No Man's Land by *Ltn* Küppers of *Jasta 12*.

At 7.15pm, over Bourlon Wood, Capt W J C K Cochrane-Patrick of 19 Squadron shot down and killed *Ofst* Edmund Nathanael of Jasta 5 for his ninth victory. Nathanael was one of the rising stars of *Jasta 5*; he had scored 15 victories in two months since joining the *Jasta*.

On the evening of May 11 troops of the British Third Army attacked and captured enemy positions on both banks of the river Scarpe. The troops left their trenches at 7.30pm and attacked under a creeping barrage, proceeded by low flying FE2bs of 11 Squadron and the Nieuports of 60 Squadron, strafing the enemy positions.

The Nieuports of 60 Squadron were led by Lt Willie Fry, who recalled in his autobiography that these attacks required a great degree of accuracy, both in the timing of the attacks and their location. Ordinary maps were of no use because of the devastated nature of the terrain, a mass of shell holes and trenches, and the pilots had to rely on aerial photographs, studied earlier. Orders were that the enemy trenches should be attacked as the troops went over the top and watches were carefully synchronised with those of Third Army HQ. Five Nieuports arrived over the area before the ground attack and flew to and fro above the front lines. Everything was quiet below. Then, at five minutes before zero hour, the artillery began their barrage, compounded by return fire from the German batteries. Fry later wrote:

'The thought of having to shortly dive down into the middle of it all was not pleasant. I looked round to see the others following me in close formation. Then, at the exact moment, we turned parallel to the lines, peeled off and dived one after the other, concentrating our fire on the German trenches as shown on the maps we had studied so carefully. The sky must have been teeming with shells and before we dived we all caught sight of some in the air and now and then saw the curve of the top of the trajectory of some of them.'

The Nieuports went down to within 300 feet of the ground, picked out their targets, using a railway cutting as a guide, and fired into and along the German trenches. Reaching the end of the target area they turned and renewed their attacks, repeating them until their ammunition was exhausted.

'The din was tremendous and we were bumped about by air disturbance caused by shells passing near by.' The pilots turned off individually to change their Lewis gun drums – 'there was no question of replacing the empty ones in the cockpit, they just went overboard.'

The pilots, exhilarated by the success of their attacks, but with their ammunition exhausted, flew straight back to Filescamp farm, only a short flight of a few minutes. Here they rearmed with fresh Lewis gun drums, and with Major Scott's approval and encouragement went back.to renew their attacks. This time even more care was called for; it was not certain which of the enemy trenches the British troops had already taken, and the Nieuports attacked only those trenches further back, which they knew the troops could not possibly have reached. They again used all their ammunition and escaped with no loss. It was nearly dark as the last Nieuport landed back at Filescamp Farm. Fry was awarded a Military Cross for his leadership in this action.[10]

On May 12 the fine weather continued. The Spads of 19 Squadron and the Nieuports of 29 Squadron were over the lines early in the morning. 19 Squadron lost Capt W D Bransby-Williams in a fight with hostile scouts over Fresnoy and 2Lt C R Sloan of 29 Squadron was shot down and killed over Inchy by *Uffz* Friedrich Gille of *Jasta 12*. During this fight with *Jasta 12*, Lts W V Sherwood and A M Wray each claimed an Albatros and 2Lt J D Atkinson later claimed a two-seater as driven down and a balloon as destroyed.

The Nieuports of 1 Squadron flew an escort in the morning for the FE2ds of 20 Squadron on a bombing raid. In a running fight with hostile scouts the B Flight Commander, Capt F W Honnet, sent an Albatros scout down out of control and was attacked by seven others. He outmanoeuvred the enemy scouts and returned safely.

Other victories claimed during the day were an Albatros two-seater out of control to Capt A W Keen of 40 Squadron and a two-seater shot down by a patrol from 54 Squadron. Shortly after this action Capt W V Strugnell and 2Lt M B Cole of 54 Squadron each claimed victories, Strugnell's was seen to crash in a small pond by pilots of 29 Squadron.

An evening patrol by 56 Squadron lost Lt. A J Jessop to anti-aircraft fire. The SE5 received a direct hit and went down in a spin before breaking up in mid-air. Jessop was claimed by *Kflabattr.101* and *U Flakzug 159*.

May 13 was mainly fine but with thunder and heavy rainstorms throughout the day.

The fighter squadrons lost three pilots. At 8.30pm, in a combat with *Jasta 11* in the Fresnes area, 29 Squadron lost 2Lt A M Sutherland and Sgt W H Dunn, both surviving as POWs. Earlier in the day 40 Squadron had lost Lt A B Raymond, also taken prisoner. Raymond, whose nickname was 'Rastus' was on patrol with Capt Keen when he was lost. Edward Mannock, who had met Raymond during training, wrote in his diary the next day. 'Rastus missing. Went out yesterday on second patrol, lost leader in the clouds and hasn't been seen since. I feel awfully miserable about it. My special chum. His loss is felt throughout the squadron. Everyone liked him. Kismet!'

On the credit side for the day, Lt Fry of 60 Squadron destroyed an Albatros over Dury at 2.30pm for his third victory, and four pilots of 23 Squadron claimed two hostile aircraft in flames. A patrol of 29 Squadron was attacked by eight Albatros scouts and A M Wray added to his success of the previous day by shooting one down to crash.

Thirty-two Squadron were detailed to attack balloons on May 14. Capt W G S Curphey led two DH2s in the attack, and the balloons were hauled down, the observers taking to their parachutes. The little pushers were then attacked by *Jasta B* and *Hptm* Franz Walz shot down Curphey, his DH2 falling in flames near Vis en Artois. Curphey died of his wounds the next day.

Second Lieutenant C C Tayler claimed one Albatros from the fight; his machine was badly shot up but he managed to return. Wright, the third member of the patrol also returned safely.

Naval 3 also lost a pilot. In action with *Jasta 33*, FltSubLt W R Walker was shot down and captured by *Obltn* Heinrich Lorenz.

There was a little flying the next day but the weather then finally broke. Low clouds wind and rain made flying impossible for two days.

May 18 dawned fine and bright but the weather gradually deteriorated again during the day and there were low clouds and rain by the evening. At 8.15am six Nieuports of 1 Squadron took off: their orders were to attack enemy balloons. It was to be a disastrous morning for the squadron. The Nieuports, all armed with rockets, crossed the lines very low, hoping to approach unseen, but the balloons were rapidly hauled down and only two were destroyed. Second Lieutenant T H Lines sent his target down in flames, but was then hit by ground fire. Lines forced landed his damaged Nieuport and was taken POW. Lieutenants L Drummond and 2Lt M G Cole were also hit by ground fire and both crashed and were killed. Lt H J Duncan destroyed his balloon, but although wounded in the thigh he managed to return.

There were further casualties for the fighter squadrons. Attacking an enemy two-seater over Oppy, 2Lt R J Grandin of 60 Squadron was hit by the observer's return fire; his Nieuport went into a dive and broke up in mid-air. The Spad of 2Lt Lieutenant J D V Holmes, 19 Squadron, had engine failure and he forced landed behind the German lines to be taken prisoner.

Nineteen Squadron suffered another casualty the next day: 2Lt S F Allabarton was last seen east of Arras and it was later learned that he had been hit by anti-aircraft fire and forced to land behind the German lines.

The Spads of 23 Squadron were in combat with *Jasta 3* in the Sailly area in the morning and Sgt C J Abrahams was killed by *Ltn* Julius Schmidt for his third victory.

At Filescamp Farm the pilots of 60 Squadron were preparing to set off on a morning patrol, either sitting in their Nieuports or standing nearby, when they were astonished to see an Albatros suddenly appear out of the cloud a thousand feet above the aerodrome: 'there was considerable excitement with mechanics running about and pointing upwards.' The German pilot realised his mistake and quickly climbed back into the cloud cover. Those pilots who were not yet in their machines hurriedly climbed into their cockpits. One pilot, a Scotsman, G C Young, was so excited that in his hurry he forgot to wave for his chocks to be taken away from under his wheels before he opened up his engine. The tail of the Nieuport immediately went up, it stood on its nose, then went over onto its back.

The other pilots took off and flew up through the cloud looking for the enemy scout. William Fry, after flying around for sometime, finally spotted it and gave chase, firing a few bursts, but in his own words 'too excited at first to take proper aim through the sight.' The Albatros pilot, *Ltn* Georg Noth of *Jasta B*, decided that discretion was the better part of valour and crash landed in the nearest open space, turning the Albatros over. Both Noth and Fry were very low when Fry attacked and Fry had to pull up sharply to avoid a collision with the Albatros. Fry put his Nieuport down close by, ran to the scene of the crash and shook hands with Georg Noth, who admitted that he had become lost. A battalion of Somerset Light Infantry – Fry's regiment before he had been seconded to the RFC – who were in rest nearby, had surrounded the Albatros and their adjutant telephoned Major Scott for a car to be sent for Noth to be taken back to Filescamp Farm. Fry flew back to the aerodrome.

Noth was taken into 60 Squadron's mess for lunch. Fry recalled that although plied with drink, Noth said very little and gave nothing away, but he did volunteer the information that he was with *Jasta* B and a Cambrai theatre ticket was found in his tunic for the previous night's performance. Fry later commented: 'the whole affair was no achievement on my part as it was pure luck to come across him in the clouds, there was no fight, and once I got on his tail he gave up.'

Noth's Albatros D III No. 796/17 was designated G 39 and sent to England for evaluation.[11]

The Sopwith Triplanes of Naval 1 were in action in the late evening with a combined force of *Jagdstaffeln 12* and *4*. FltSubLt G G Bowman and FltSubLt O B Ellis (who had written home so excitedly on May 11) were both shot down and killed: Bowman claimed by *Oblt* Tutschek of *Jasta 12*; Ellis, who was seen to fall out of his machine, by *Ltn* Groos of *Jasta 4*.

The ground strafing tactics of May 11 by 60 Squadron Nieuports and FEs of 11 Squadron were repeated on May 20 when the British ground forces attacked the Hindenburg Line between Bullecourt and the British front line west of Fontaine-les-Croisilles. As the attacking infantry left their trenches at 5.15am six Nieuports and seven FEs flew to a line two miles behind the German trenches and attacked detachments of enemy infantry and gun crews.

The fighter squadrons had five casualties on May 20. An FE8 of 41 Squadron was hit by Archie and forced to land, turning turtle and throwing out the pilot. Another 41 Squadron pilot was wounded in the arm, also by anti-aircraft fire. Naval 10 had a pilot wounded in combat and forced to land, and von Tutschek shot down a Spad from 23 Squadron. Fifty-six Squadron lost Lt C E French who was shot down by *Flakbattr 527* and was awarded to *Hptm* Holzer. It would appear to have been a good day for the German *Flak* batteries.

The area of operations was now to be further north. On May 21 the first bombardments began in preparation for the forthcoming battle of Messines. The ground fighting on the Arras front was now 'desultory,' although fighting in the air seems to have still been intense. There were low clouds and rain throughout the day and there was little flying. Weather conditions were similar the next day but some patrols were flown.

An early afternoon patrol from 56 Squadron on the morning of May 23 found conditions were still bad – a morning patrol had been attempted, but the SEs had returned after an hour due to the bad weather – but Lt Cecil Lewis shot down a two-seater out of control over Beaumont. During the evening another patrol from the squadron had better luck. Capt P Prothero sent a green scout down out of control; Arthur Rhys Davids drove another scout down and Cyril Crowe, joining up with some Sopwith Pups, Spads and Bristol Fighters, sent a two-seater down out of control over Tilloy. Lt A H Orlebar of 19 Squadron claimed an Albatros in flames east of Douai, and Lt L F Jenkin of 1 Squadron sent an Albatros scout down out of control south of Becelaere.

Casualties in the fighter squadrons were light. Forty-six Squadron, which had gone to France equipped with Nieuport two-seaters, began its transition from a Corps to an Army Squadron when it began to re-equip with Sopwith Pups in April. The Squadron's first Pup casualty was in the evening of May 23 when *Ltn* Schäfer of *Jasta 28* shot down 2Lt J P Stephen over Wytschaete.

The morning of May 24 was cloudy, but with large clear patches. The first casualty for the fighter squadrons was a DH5 of 24 Squadron, flown by J H H Goodall who was shot down and taken POW. Goodhall was the first DH5 casualty for 24 Squadron.

Lt L L Morgan of 40 Squadron, the 'Air Hog,' was hit by Archie and his Nieuport crashed a mile behind the front line trenches. Padre Keymer – whose nickname in the Squadron was the 'Odd Man – later found Morgan in a CCS. He had a compound fracture of the right leg and his left ankle was smashed, but was he was conscious and told the Padre exactly what had happened. William Bond reported to his wife:[12] 'His machine had been hit when he was flying low at about 4,500. feet. A gas attack and a big bombardment was on at the time. The shell hit the engine and burst on percussion. It blew out part of the engine, tore off the undercarriage and made a big hole in the bottom of the fuselage. The 'Air Hog' was hit in the legs by fragments of shell. He found himself sitting in an open framework with one leg dangling down useless. With the other, the left, although the ankle was smashed, he managed to steer. Though the balance was all wrong, he forced his machine down in a steady glide, avoiding some trees and chose a clear place to land. He crashed on landing, of course, but crawled out of the hole in front and was found by the ambulance men a few minutes later. He was perfectly conscious and never lost consciousness the whole time. It was a wonderful performance and a miracle too, to have a direct hit and still be alive. He may be badly crippled, but he is in no serious danger. No more "jolly old patrols" for him, however!'[13]

A Sopwith Pup from 66 Squadron, and a Sopwith Triplane from Naval 8 were both lost in the morning, but on the credit side, FltCom C D Booker of Naval 8 shot down *Ltn d R* Hans Hintsch of *Jasta 11* for his 24th victory.

An escort for the DH4s of 55 Squadron, bombing the railway station at Busigny, was flown by 56 Squadron in the morning. The formations were shadowed by twenty enemy machines. An attempt by the SEs to engage five resulted in a sharp but indecisive fight before the enemy machines cleared east. Cyril Crowe led another patrol in the evening, flying ten miles behind the enemy lines. South of Douai they engaged a formation of enemy scouts. All the SEs attacked and Crowe sent one Albatros, possibly *Ltn* Ernst Bauer of *Jasta 3,* down in a slow spiral and it was seen to crash.

The SEs were now very low, a long way over the German lines, and Crowe led them towards the west, climbing to 11,000 feet. They next sighted an enemy two-seater, below the SEs, but escorted by five Albatros scouts above. Hoidge and Rhys Davids dived to attack the two-seater, the rest of the Flight staying up to protect them from its escort. The escorting Albatri had made no attempt to interfere, sheering off on seeing the SEs climbing to their height, and Hoidge and Rhys Davids shot the two-seater down in flames over Gouy-sous-Bellone.

The SEs later caught another two-seater over Sains and Rhys Davids attacked it, wounding or killing the enemy observer before it went down, smoking badly. While attacking the two-seater, Rhys Davids was attacked in turn by an Albatros with a red nose and tailplane, but Hoidge took this Albatros off Rhys Davids tail and it spun away.

Lieutenant O M Sutton of 54 Squadron had a lucky escape. Fighting with an Albatros over Premont he collided with the enemy scout, but managed to return to his aerodrome with a damaged wing, claiming the Albatros as destroyed.

There were two further casualties during the morning: Captain L A Smith of 66 Squadron was shot down and taken POW and FltSubLt H L Smith of Naval 8 was shot down and killed over Flers by *Ltn* Maashoff of *Jasta 11*.

May 25 was mainly clear although there were clouds at varying levels. In the words of the RFC communiqué for the day: 'Machines of 56, 66 and 19 Squadrons had considerable fighting.' During the 'considerable fighting' 19 Squadron had a pilot, the Australian Lt H G P Okenden, wounded, and their fellow Spad Squadron, 23, also had a pilot wounded, 2Lt E W Hallam, possibly by *Unteroffizier* Gille of *Jasta 12*.

During a morning Offensive Patrol 1 Squadron lost a pilot when they were attacked by four Albatri. Lieutenant J R Anthony was wounded, shot down and taken prisoner, but later died of his wounds. Anthony was awarded to *Ltn* Paul Strähle of *Jasta 18* for his sixth victory.

Nieuports of 60 Squadron, led by Lt 'Grid' Caldwell, saw a great deal of fighting in the morning. Twenty enemy aeroplanes were seen over Louvain in various groups, and some inconclusive dogfighting went on for over half and hour. The Nieuports, joined at one juncture by a Bristol Fighter, were attacked by five Albatri from *Jasta 11*. The Albatri singled out Lt Warre Gilchrist, who had been separated from the rest of the patrol by a close burst of Archie. 'Poppy' Pope and 2Lt Sillers saw Gilchrist spinning down, under attack from an enemy two-seater, but before they could go to his aid the Nieuports, the lone Bristol and two Sopwith Triplanes from Naval 8 were attacked by additional Albatri. Alexander Little, flying one of the triplanes – the other was flown by P A Johnson – fired at one Albatros that went down in an evasive spin. Little lost sight of this Albatros, being attacked by another, but when he next saw it it was diving steeply, a thousand feet from the ground. Little was now out of ammunition and he escorted the Bristol Fighter back to the lines.[14] On the way back Little saw a Nieuport below the clouds, going down into enemy territory. This was Warre Gilchrist who had been wounded and forced to land by Karl Allmenroder of *Jasta 11*.

Captain Crowe took a six strong patrol out from 56 Squadron at 5.30am. The SEs saw nothing for over an hour, other than a formation of Sopwith Pups being archied just to the south of Cambrai, but Crowe led the Flight north and sighted a pair of enemy two-seaters over Beaumont. Crowe went down to attack one two-seater, leaving the other SEs to tackle its companion. Catching up with the fleeing enemy over the railway junction to the north of Evin-Malmaison, Crowe opened fire from 100 yards before realising that he was being attacked by three hostile scouts.

Discretion being the better part of valour, Crowe put his nose down and dived for the lines, easily outdistancing the pursuit. Climbing back to 4,000 feet, he was then attacked by an Albatros, 'with a very yellow fuselage.' The enemy pilot overshot the SE in his first pass and Crowe found himself directly under the fuselage of the enemy scout. He pulled down his Lewis gun and fired an entire drum at point blank range. The Albatros went down to crash between Dourges and Courcelles.

After Crowe had left in pursuit of the two-seater, the rest of the Flight tackled the other. Rhys Davids and Lt Keith Muspratt attacked in turn: Muspratt from broadside on, Rhys Davids from below. The enemy machine went down with Rhys Davids on its tail firing bursts from both guns until he silenced the enemy gunner. Pouring smoke, the two-seater went down to crash by the side of the Lens to Douai road.[15]

The pilots of 24 Squadron claimed their first victory since exchanging their DH2s for the DH5. On patrol over Ligny at 11.45am five de Havillands were attacked by nine hostile scouts. Lt S Cockerell saw one on the tail of Lt H W Woollett and shot it down to crash near Ligny. This was the first victory claimed by a DH5.[16]

Forty-one Squadron lost a pilot shot down in flames and killed by anti-aircraft fire during the morning and FltSubLt de Roeper of Naval 6 was wounded in action.

May 26 was fine and warm with considerable heat haze. In the morning eight FE2ds of 20 Squadron set out to bomb Comines railway station and Houthem ammunition dump, escorted by six Sopwith Pups of 46 Squadron and ten Nieuports from 1 Squadron . The FEs and Nieuports crossed the lines ahead of the Pups and Lt Stewart Keith-Jopp, the rear man in the formation came under attack from two Albatros scouts. Keith-Jopp turned to meet the attack, expecting that the other Nieuports would follow, but they had gone down with the FEs to attack a formation of fourteen Albatri climbing to meet them. Keith-Jopp's Nieuport was hit in the fuel tank and petrol poured out over his feet. He switched off his engine, in case of fire, and spun away out of the fight, but on pulling out of his spin at 2,000 feet one of the Albatros pilots dived on the Nieuport and resumed his attack. Risking a fire, Keith-Jopp restarted his engine and dived west. He was 15 miles over enemy territory and still under attack but another Nieuport then appeared and drove off the persistent Albatros. Keith-Jopps' petrol ran out just before he crossed the front lines but he glided the last five miles to his aerodrome. On landing it was found that three bullets had gone between Keith-Jopp's legs and into the petrol tank; another two into the tank from the side, and ten rounds had torn a tyre off its wheel. The Nieuport had several other bullets through the cowling, wings and tailplane and a bullet had gone through Keith-Jopp's coat and into the seat. It was both an unlucky and lucky day for Keith-Jopp. Earlier, Lt Stewart MacIntosh had 'borrowed' Keith-Jopp's much prized personal Nieuport and had been shot down and taken POW by *Ltn* Paul Strähle of *Jasta 18* for his second victory over a pilot of 1 Squadron in two days.

Lieutenant J C C Piggott had been wounded in the main fight, but Lt P F Fullard claimed an Albatros out of control for his first victory of an eventual forty.

A 6.30pm patrol from 56 Squadron saw a great deal of fighting. Captain P Prothero forced down a two-seater and Edric Broadberry sent another down in a 'vertical spinning nose-dive for over 2,000 feet.' Rhys Davids attacked two Albatri and saw his tracers going straight into the pilot's cockpit of the second. The Albatros nose-dived vertically for a thousand feet before turning over onto its side. A large formation of 12 enemy scouts then appeared and circled the SEs, but the British scouts cleared west before an attack could develop. On returning to Vert Galant it was found that 2Lt J Toogood had not returned. Going low after one of the two-seaters he had been hit by a shell burst which had almost severed his right leg. He managed to land but his leg was later amputated.[17] Despite the fact that Toogood had been hit by anti-aircraft fire he was awarded to *Vzfw* Diess and *Uffz* Woidt of *Schusta 19*.

In the early afternoon *Ltn* Werner Voss of *Jasta 5* shot down 2Lt M G Cole of 54 Squadron for his 30th victory. Voss shot away the control wires of the Pup and wounded Cole in the thigh. Cole crashed near the British support trenches at Gouzeacourt but survived. He was the third pilot of 54 Squadron to be shot down by Voss.

There were two casualties in the evening. A 66 Squadron pilot, 2Lt C F Smith, was shot down and taken prisoner over Etaing and 2Lt A S (Gould) Lee of 46 Squadron was attacked by an enemy two-seater from below and wounded in the leg. The wound was only slight and Lee dived to attack the enemy machine, silencing the gunner. The enemy pilot dived away and outdistanced Lee, whose Vickers had jammed. Lee could now feel blood trickling down his leg inside his flying boot and decided he must land. It was now so dark that he had difficulty in finding his bearings but finally forced landed near Dickebusch Lake. The Pup scraped over the edge of the lake, landed ten yards from its edge and ran for another dozen yards before dropping into a shell hole. Lee cracked his head on the butt of his Vickers gun in the crash and was helped out of his machine by some gunners. Taken to a dugout he was given a stiff whisky and asked if he had broken any bones. He replied that he hadn't but that he was wounded in the leg; it was now smarting painfully and he could feel blood pouring down into his boot. Gingerly taking off his sheepskin flying boot Lee found that his 'wound' was a small insignificant graze about two inches long which had scarcely drawn blood. 'It shows what imagination will do. I would have put money on my boot being soaked in gore.'

The following day B Flight of 56 Squadron were in action with four two-seaters working over the lines above Plouvain. Lts Leonard Barlow and Arthur Rhys Davids dived to attack these, Barlow shooting the port wings off one at 3,000 feet. The enemy two-seater spun down 'like an arrow,' its starboard wings breaking away from the fuselage a thousand feet lower. The remainder of the machine crashed just north of Plouvain and burst into flames, killing *Uffz* Max Hofmeier *and Ltn d R* Adam Wolff of *Fl Abt (A)288*. Barlow climbed back into the fight and sent another two-seater down to crash within half a mile of the first.

Rhys Davids gained no result from his attacks on the two-seaters but later, aided by a Sopwith Pup, hit an Albatros in the engine, forcing the pilot to land. Rhys Davids later reformed with the other SEs, but broke away to attack a pair of two-seaters east of Lens. He forced one of these down, firing all the time and finally left it gliding down with a stationary propeller. Rhys Davids was now very low, the wrong side of the lines, and opening up his engine he 'flew full out over houses at 500 feet, avoiding intense AA fire easily by dodging, but was much hit by machine gun fire from the ground.'

Over Lens the engine of the SE stopped. Rhys Davids pumped up enough pressure in his emergency tank to restart it for only a few moments before the pump broke away from its mounting under his furious pumping. The SE glided a short way before crash landing in a shell hole a mile east of Bully-Grenay. Rhys Davids was unhurt.

Lieutenant E A Lloyd failed to return from this patrol; he had been shot down and taken POW by *Ltn* Altmaier of *Jasta 33*.

An evening patrol from 56 Squadron saw a great deal of fighting, claiming three scouts and a two-seater sent down out of control.

There were two additional casualties during the day's fighting. Captain N Cauldwell of 46 Squadron was wounded and Lt S S Hume was shot down and taken POW during a combat east of Hermies.

The weather on May 28 was fine in the morning but became cloudy towards the evening. Major A J L Scott, 60 Squadron's CO, was out early, flying a solo patrol.[18] A patrol of SEs from 56 Squadron were also in Scott's area and two of their number had gone down to attack a pair of two-seaters working at 4,000 feet, the rest of the patrol staying up to engage two formations of scouts, between 13 or 15 in number, which were at their level. Suddenly, a Nieuport, coming from the direction of Douai, dived into the enemy scouts, got in a good burst 'at very close range ' then zoomed up and joined the SEs. This was Major Scott. The SEs and Scott then attacked the enemy formation and a fierce fight developed. Major Scott shot down one of the enemy scouts; Keith Muspratt sent one down out of control, and Leonard Barlow forced another to land, firing at it while it was on the ground. Despite the fierceness of the fighting these were the only positive results. Scott's Nieuport had been considerably shot about and he was forced to land behind the British lines. Scott telephoned his squadron, then borrowed a horse from an artillery ammunition column to get to the nearest road, where he rendezvoused with the squadron car which had been sent to fetch him. The reason for Scott's haste was that he was anxious to shave and change out of his flying clothes before an inspection of 60 Squadron by General Allenby, GOC of Third army, and the Brigade and Wing Commanders, due at 9.00am.

After the inspection, Lt Keith Caldwell took a patrol of four Nieuports out at 11.00am. They joined up with a Bristol Fighter and chased a formation of nine Albatros scouts towards Lens. At the beginning of the fight Lt Gunner had gun jams, the engine of Lt Jenkins' Nieuport began to run badly, and both left the fight. The Bristol Fighter had also disappeared and Caldwell and 2Lt R U Phalen were alone.

The odds were too great: Phalen was shot down and killed by *Ltn* Kurt Schuhmann of *Jasta 5*, but Caldwell managed to extricate himself from the fight and later attacked a pair of two-seaters. While he was fighting these he was in turn attacked by three Albatros scouts flown by *Ltn* Voss, Könnecke and Schuhmann. Caldwell later wrote in his logbook: 'Attacked 2 2-seaters near Lens at 7,500 and was attacked by 3 scouts from behind. One with streamers was hot stuff and I couldn't shake him off properly until at 800 feet I got on his tail and drove him down to 500 feet. My petrol tank, flying wires, aileron controls, struts and main spar were shot though, so came home after a brief scrap with the other 2 scouts who were pretty dud. Phalen missing from this show.' In the margin by the entry Caldwell wrote 'Voss.'

Forty Squadron were in action during the evening. Bond wrote home next morning:

'I think I got two Huns last night. It was on the last patrol again; it is becoming a regular thing to meet all the Huns just about sunset.' Bond was leading a patrol of six Nieuports and they had crossed the lines at 11,000 feet when he saw five enemy scouts about two miles to the east. Bond manoeuvred to approach these with the sun behind the patrol 'as the sun is absolutely blinding at sunset when you're in the sky.' Bond got close to one of the enemy and fired 30 rounds into it, but the enemy pilot, followed by his companions, turned east and dived away. One of the patrol, however, watched the scout shot at by Bond for some minutes and saw it 'falling and fluttering about right to the ground, quite out of control.'

Twenty minutes later, six miles behind the German lines, a formation of red Albatri was seen below the Nieuports. Bond again got the sun behind the patrol before taking the Nieuports down. Bond fired at one scout, finishing off his Lewis gun drum, and zoomed away to replace it. Having done so he looked around and saw the scout he had fired at stall, and fall away sideways, sometimes spinning, then diving. Bond dived back into the fight and fired at the nearest enemy scout, but his gun jammed after only one shot. As Bond reached up to clear the stoppage, 'I heard the horrid noise of a Hun's double gun just behind me. I hadn't chosen the nearest Hun after all, but had passed one; and now he was on my tail. I spun; the horrid noise stopped, so I stopped spinning. Instantly the horrid noise started again. I spun again. Once more the noise stopped and gently I eased my machine out of the spin and the dive. But the Hun was still there. When I heard the noise a third time I simply shut off the engine and *fell* down. I had started scrapping at 12,000. I ventured to pull out level at 7,000.'[19]

The enemy scout had been taken off Bond's tail by a British scout from another squadron, who shot it down. Bond's Nieuport had taken no hits: 'I didn't stay still long enough, I suppose.' Bond recorded that out of the seven red scouts another squadron had claimed two, he was awarded two out of control, and Steve Godfrey had claimed another out of

control. Lt W E Bassett also claimed a two-seater during the evening so it was a good day for 40 Squadron.

Casualties for the fighter squadrons were Lt G M Wilkinson of 56 Squadron, who was slightly wounded by AA fire but managed to bring his badly damaged SE5 back to Vert Galant; a pilot of 66 Squadron, Lt R M Roberts was shot down and taken POW; and 2Lt A M Wray of 29 Squadron was wounded in the knee.

There were low clouds and mist for the next three days and there was little flying. Fifty-Four Squadron lost Lt F W Kantel on May 30, shot down and taken POW by pilots from *Jasta 6* but there were no other casualties in the fighter squadrons for the month.

On May 31 the main artillery bombardment for the battle of Messines began and the main air fighting would begin to move to the north.

NOTES

1. Schäfer scored another five victories before he was shot down and killed on the evening of June 5 in a fight with the FE2bs of 20 Squadron.
2. *War In The Air*, the official history, gives eight balloons attacked, four of them destroyed with the remainder damaged.
3. *Scarlet and Khaki*, T B Marson, Jonathan Cape, 1931.
4. Cyril Crowe, one of Ball's fellow pilots, related to the author that sitting in the latrines during the gas attacks at the battle of Loos in September 1915 – when the British had used gas for the first time – he had personally told God that as he permitted such atrocities he had no further use for Him.
5. Both 24 and 32 Squadron were issued with the DH5 in the middle of May, but the unfortunate pilots of 41 Squadron were to soldier on with the FE8 until July 1917. Both their fellow FE8 squadrons had been re-equipped with Nieuports in the previous March.
6. During the morning Fry had flown a forty minute mock combat with a captured Albatros scout which was being taken round the squadrons by an experienced pilot, 'so that they (the pilots) would know what they were up against.'
7. *An Airman's Wife*, Herbert Jenkins Ltd., London 1918. In his letters home, later published as An Airmans Wife, Bond gave his fellow pilots in 40 Squadron psuedonymns.
8. The Douglass Whetton collection.
9. The German victory lists credit both *Ltn* Göring and *Ltn* A Heldmann with Sopwith Triplanes on May 10. Göring's claim is too late to have been Crundall; Heldmann's too early. A third triplane was credited to *Flakbatterie Grossherzog u Roester*. Some authorities have given this *Flakbatterie* credit for Crundall, but its claim is for a *Dreidecker*, fourteen kilometres miles from Ostend. Bethune is approximately 50 miles from Ostend.
10. William Mays Fry served in France from November 1914 until the end of the conflict; first with the infantry, then transferring to the RFC. Over sixty years later, through no wish of his own, he became embroiled in the controversy over the award of the Victoria Cross to William Bishop. During a hearing in the Canadian Senate on this subject, and with appalling ignorance

of Fry's service record, a senator publicly accused him of LMP (lack of moral fibre) cowardice. Such is the judgement of lesser men.
11. Some authorities give Noth as having been wounded by Fry's fire and later dying of his wounds, but Fry made no mention of this, either in his autobiography or during many talks with the author. There also exists a photograph of Noth standing by his Albatros after capture, obviously unharmed.
12. op.cit
13. Lewis Morgan, whose favourite expression was 'jolly old patrols,' later recovered from his wounds and flew with a false leg. He was killed in a flying accident in England in 1918, flying an SE5a. He is buried in Padstow, Cornwall.
14. Little went on leave the next day. While he was away a fellow pilot of Naval 8, Reggie Soar, flew Little's personal triplane, 'Blimp' while his own was being overhauled. He commented: 'I found I was overshooting until looking at the speed I saw I was coming in at 80 instead of 50/60 knots. I later found out that Little had his seat moved forward a bit so that he could dive faster, the crazy clown.'
15. This two-seater was possibly from *Schusta 24b*. *Uffz* Miltner and *Vzfw* Wens both killed in action.
16. Cockerell had joined 24 Squadron in early 1916 as a sergeant pilot and gained two victories before being wounded in October 1916. On recovery he rejoined the Squadron as a Lieutenant and gained another three victories while flying the DH2. His victory on May 25 was his only victory while flying a DH5. He returned to France in 1918 as a pilot with 151 Squadron and shot down a Gotha on the night of August 2 1918 for a total of eight victories. H W Woollett survived the war with 43 victories.
17. Toogood was imprisoned in Bavaria but repatriated to England on April 2 1918.
18. In his combat report of this action, under the heading 'Duty,' Major Scott wrote: 'Recreational.'
19. Ibid.

CHAPTER ELEVEN

NEW OBJECTIVES

At a conference in Paris the first week of May the Allied High Command had decided to transfer the main theatre of operations northwards, to the British front in Flanders. The disastrous failure of the French spring offensive on the Aisne, with its consequent loss of morale and mutinies in the French armies, was to throw the bulk of the summer fighting onto the British armies: a summer that was to witness, in the words of the British Prime Minister, Lloyd George, 'a profligate wastage of some of our finest young manhood.'

The eventual objective of the planned British offensive in Flanders was to clear the German forces from Belgian coast and turn the flank of the German defence system, but as a preliminary to the main offensive it was essential that the group of hills forming the Messines-Wytschaete ridge were in British hands.[1] These hills afforded the German forces direct observation over the whole of the area in which preparations for the main offensives would be made. In the north, from the ruins of Wytschaete, the highest point of the ridge, the whole British trench system to the east of Ypres and the town itself were under direct observation. At the southern end of the ridge, at Messines, the positions on the River Douve were in distinct danger of being enfiladed and the valley of the Lys taken by the enemy.

The British front at Ypres was held by the British Second Army under General Plumer who had been planning the operation for the attack on the Messines Ridge for over a year. Haig and his commanders decided that the capture of the Messines Ridge should be a separate and distinct operation; that the aim should be seizure of the main German positions in one day.

The 11th Army Wing of Plumer's Second Army comprised three single-seater fighter squadrons: Nos 1, 41 and 46. For the battle of Messines, five additional fighter squadrons were moved into the area. On May 14, Naval 10 (Sopwith Triplanes) moved to Droglandt aerodrome and Naval 1 (Sopwith Triplanes) flew into Bailleul (Asylum Ground) aerodrome on June 1, sharing the field with 1 Squadron. Both these Naval squadrons came under the direct orders of 11th Wing RFC. In addition, on May 31 HQ 9th Wing moved north for the coming battle, its three single-seater fighter squadrons, Nos. 19 Squadron (Spad) 66 Squadron (Sopwith Pup) and 56 Squadron (SE5a) all moving base to Estrée Blanche aerodrome.[2] In addition, First Army, on the immediate right of Second Army, received 23 Squadron (Spads), transferred from Fifth Army, and the patrols of 40 Squadron (Nieuports) were extended to cover the Ypres area.

General Sixt von Armin's Fourth Army held the line from the river Douvre to the sea, his 4th Corps defending the immediate area of the Messines Ridge. The German high command, well aware of the coming battle, appreciated the importance of artillery and observation, and reinforced the air power of the Fourth Army. The artillery and observation *Flieger Abteilungen* were increased from ten to nineteen and the *Jagdstaffeln* from four to nine. With the addition of some *Schutzstaffeln* this gave the *Luftstreitkräfte* a force of approximately 300 aeroplanes, half of which were fighters, from Messines to the sea. The strength of the RFC for the same area was 500 aeroplanes, augmented by a few French and Belgian squadrons, but 300 of these aeroplanes, just over half of which were fighters, were employed over the ten-mile front for the attack at Messines. The official history, War in The Air, states that 'It may be assumed that that the Allied aircraft outnumbered the enemy by about two to one along this stretch of the front generally, and that the disproportion was a little greater in the Messines area.'[3] Throughout the coming battles in Flanders the German High Command continued to reinforce its air power. In his memoirs *Deutschlands Krieg in der Luft*, *General* von Hoeppner later wrote: 'Because of their number and their sporting audacity, the English continued to be our most dangerous adversaries, and, as before, the major part of the German air strength was concentrated against them.'

Artillery supremacy was of utmost importance during the coming battle and, as always, the task of the fighter squadrons was to deny the enemy his eyes by the destruction of his artillery spotting and observation aeroplanes. To this end the objective of the British air offensive was the domination both of the immediate battle area and the enemy balloon line, some 10,000 yards from the British front line trenches. These were to be the main patrol areas of the fighter squadrons, the intention being to both deny the air space to enemy aeroplanes and give freedom of interference to the artillery aeroplanes of the Corps squadrons. It was realised, however, that standing patrols of fighters, even throughout the entire hours of daylight, could not guarantee that enemy observation aeroplanes would not evade them and a system of wireless interception was used. This system, which had first been used in October 1916, consisted of numerous army wireless stations, know as compass stations. These plotted the movements of the enemy aeroplanes throughout the day, not only passing on this information to forward ground stations, which laid out a series of strip panels to direct the fighters, but also keeping a record of the overall trend of enemy air activity. At the time it was it envisaged that fighters in the near future would be fitted with wireless receiving sets and that the information could be transmitted direct to the airborne fighters. [4]

In addition to patrols over the immediate battle area, fighter patrols were also to be flown as far east as a line Lille-Roulers-Menin; with the fighter squadrons of 9th Wing patrolling an even wider area: Houthulst Forest, Roulers, Menin and Quesnoy.

Above Messines

June 1 was fine and warm. The fighter squadrons of 9th Wing were fully occupied in moving into their new base, and 40 Squadron opened the day's fighting. Capt W T L Allcocks and Lts A E Godfrey and W E Bassett, caught an LVG working east of Arras. The three Nieuports succeeded in driving the enemy machine east but Bassett was attacking from underneath when the observer stood up and fired down at him, hitting him in the hip joint. Bassett managed to return to Bruay and made a good landing, but he was badly wounded and had lost a lot of blood.

After the action with the LVG, Godfrey turned his attention to an Aviatik which he sent spinning down into the cloud cover.

Capt Allcock was in action with an LVG, which he sent down in a dive, but he was then attacked by a DFW. Allcock reversed the position, got on the tail of the DFW and fired the remainder of his Lewis gun drum. The enemy two-seater dived away east.

The triplanes of Naval 10 had some success during the morning. The Squadron was attached to 11th Army Wing and was now operating from Droglandt aerodrome, situated some 13 or 14 miles behind Ypres. FltSubLt R Collishaw led B Flight – L E V Reid, L J E Sharman, L G E Nash and L W M Alexander – to the area of Menin. The *Jagdstaffeln* seemed to be out in force and the Flight were in action on three separate occasions during the 2 1/2 hours they were out. Over Menin at 16,000 feet Collishaw spotted three Albatros D IIIs flying two thousand feet below and took the Flight down to attack them.

In his first attack Collishaw had a gun jam and while he attempted to clear it the fighting went down to 8,000 feet. His jam cleared, Collishaw got onto the tail of one Albatros, painted in a mottled effect, and carrying a large letter 'L' on the side of its fuselage, and saw his tracers going straight into it. The Albatros went down out of control, bursting into flames before it hit the ground just south of Wervicq. Gerry Nash had also sent one of the Albatri down in a spin. The triplanes then reformed and began to return to Droglandt, but east of Armentières they attacked three more enemy aircraft. One of these was a two-seater, which was attacked by Ellis Reid, who hit both the pilot and observer with his fire. The two-seater went down in a near vertical dive and Collishaw was of the opinion that it could not have pulled out before crashing. [5]

Sgt G P Olley of 1 Squadron also claimed a two-seater out of control and nine others were also reported to have been driven down during the day.

Forty-One Squadron lost 2Lt P C S O'Longan killed in action in the day's fighting. The Squadron Commander of Naval 6, C D Breese, was slightly wounded, and 29 Squadron had Lt E A Stewardson taken POW.

At 3.57am on the morning of June 2 Lt. W Bishop of 60 Squadron left the ground alone with the intention of attacking a German aerodrome. It was not yet full light and heavily overcast. Bishop flew steadily east until he was sure he was in enemy territory, but when he came down through the cloud and saw he was over an enemy aerodrome he had no idea of his location. The aerodrome appeared to be deserted and Bishop flew on towards the Cambrai area, finally locating another aerodrome where some Albatros scouts were preparing to take off. Bishop attacked these and shot down two from a height of fifty feet. Another pair of enemy scouts managed to gain a thousand feet in height and one attacked Bishop who outmanoeuvred it and shot it down to crash by its aerodrome.

The fourth Albatros then attacked Bishop who drove it down with a whole drum of Lewis. Bishop then returned with his Nieuport considerably shot about.[6]

Two Flights of Naval 10 were in action in the morning. Collishaw's Flight, on the way back from an Hostile Aircraft Patrol, in which they send down an enemy two-seater, joined up with 'C' Flight led by Flt SubLt L A C Dissette. Dissette's Flight were escorting a formation of FE2bs of 20 Squadron on a photo-reconnaissance and a group of enemy fighters attacked them. Collishaw sent one of the attackers down out of control, but Arthur Dissette was shot down and killed near Proven.

Naval 3 also had a morning casualty: FltSubLt W E Orchard was mortally wounded but managed to land his damaged Pup at the Advanced Landing Ground. He was lifted from the cockpit of his aeroplane and taken to a Casualty Clearing Station where he later died of his wounds.

Arthur Lee of 46 Squadron had his second lucky escape in three days. On the last day of May, during a combat with enemy scouts – the first time Lee had been in a fight – his Pup was shot up, with eight bullets holes in the fuselage only two feet behind the Lee's back: 'which is as close as I want them!' The Pups were extricated from this combat by the arrival of Sopwith Triplanes of Naval 10 who drove off the enemy fighters. Now, on June 2, Lee was on patrol with Capt C A Brewster-Joske when they dived on a DFW over Comines. Lee was so intent on sighting through his Aldis sight that he failed to see that Brewster-Joske had pulled out of his dive: he had seen a group of six or seven Albatri above them, the DFW was a decoy.

As Lee pulled out of his dive on the DFW the enemy scouts attacked him and one, with a yellow spinner, closed to within thirty yards and hit the instrument board of Lee's Pup, smashing the height indicator. Lee dived away as fast as he could with the hostile scouts taking turns in firing at him. Lee levelled out at 500 feet. He had dived from 12,000 feet and the Albatri had left him, thinking that he was certain to crash. On his return to La Gorgue it was found that Lee's Pup had 29 bullet holes: seventeen in the fuselage and the rest in the wings. The bullet that had smashed the height indicator had gone through the collar of Lee's flying coat.

Two Nieuports were lost during the day's fighting. Nineteen Squadron lost 2Lt F Barrie, who was hit by fire from *M.Flakzug 2*, crashed behind the German Lines and taken prisoner, and 2Lt H E Waters of 1 Squadron was also taken POW.

Naval 10 were extremely busy on June 3. Collishaw, Reid, Sharman and Alexander flew three Hostile Aircraft Patrols during the morning and afternoon and at seven in the evening Collishaw – newly promoted to Acting Flight Lieutenant –

took Reid and Alexander on an offensive patrol to Roubaix. Soon after takeoff they were joined by Nash, Holcroft and FitzGibbon, and flying between Lille and Roubaix they spotted five Albatros scouts below them. Collishaw led the six triplanes down to attack these, firing at one which went down out of control before bursting into flames.

Another Flight from Naval 10 had been out a little earlier in the evening. Flt SubLt Percy G McNeil, leading 'A' Flight, was shot down near Wervicq at 6.00pm after the Flight had been in combat with a large formation of enemy scouts.

Thirty-two Squadron, now almost completely re-equipped with the DH5, had their last DH2 casualty when Lt F J Martin was wounded in the shoulder. One of his companions on this Low Patrol, 2Lt C F H Ley, was also wounded. Martin was the last DH2 casualty in France. The only single-seater pusher type still in service in France, the hopelessly outdated FE8, showed that it could still show its teeth: Lt A W Hogg of 41 Squadron chased an enemy machine east, forced it to fight, and sent it down to crash.

The Sopwith Pups of 54 Squadron flew two escorts for FEs on the morning of June 4. On the first of these escorts the Pups were in combat with enemy scouts of *Jasta 5* near Le Catelet and Capt R G H Pixley, the Flight Commander was shot down and killed by Werner Voss for his 32nd victory.

Capt Crowe took out five SE5s on patrol from Estrée Blanche at 6.35am. The Flight dived to attack a hostile scout over Moorslede but the enemy pilot outmanoeuvred them and escaped east. This abortive action had the effect of splitting up the SE formation and its various members had several indecisive combats. Rhys Davids flew to the Ypres area in the hope of finding the other SEs and as he approached the town he was joined by Lt Thomas M Dickinson and two Sopwith Pups of 46 Squadron. Rhys Davids then spotted a strong formation of enemy machines in the distance, higher than the British scouts. Rhys Davids and his companions flew parallel to the front lines, climbing to close the height advantage held by the enemy, but before they were in a position to attack, the enemy scouts – later reported as being 'of the V Strut Albatros type' – were attacked by a Flight of ten Sopwith Triplanes from Naval 1, led by Flight Commander T F N Gerrard, and four Nieuports from 1 Squadron: Capt Tom F Hazell, the A Flight Commander, and Lts P F Fullard, W G Milliship and F F Sharpe. The two SEs and the Pups hurried into the fight, which had started just to the east of Moorslede, with the enemy scouts persistently edging eastwards.

The fighting drifted over the Roulers-Menin Road. Rhys Davids fired at several Albatri but was outnumbered and unable to press home any attack. During the fighting Rhys Davids saw an Albatros with a red spinner diving away from the fight with its propeller stationary, and Lt Dickinson's SE going down in a steep spiral with two Albatri on its tail. But he was unable to help as he was now alone in the middle of eleven Albatri and he dived for the safety of the British lines, throwing off the pursuit. Still alone, Rhys Davids flew north and attacked five hostile scouts which were attempting to prevent machines of the Corps squadrons from working, intermittently fighting these enemy scouts for three quarters of an hour until joined by Lt Barlow and a Sopwith Triplane. The British trio pressed home their attacks on the five Albatri but these were joined by another three. These enemy scouts were from *Jasta 28* led by *Ltn* Karl Emil Schäfer and appeared to be afraid of the Naval Triplane, keeping well clear of it.[7] Rhys Davids later wrote: 'All five HA, especially the leader (red fuselage, red, gray and black wings, V-Strut type struts, pilot wearing a grey fur flying hat) manoeuvred very well.' After a little indecisive skirmishing the German pilots cleared east.

Thomas Dickinson had been shot down in the first fight and a note from him was later dropped by the Germans. 'I have been wounded in both legs and am being well looked after.'[8]

It appears that before he was shot down Dickinson had accounted for one of the Albatri, which was on the tail of Fullard. FltSubLt L H Cockey of Naval 1 was wounded in the leg and FltCom Gerrard's machine was badly shot about, forcing him to land near Moorslede. A Spad from 19 Squadron was also in the action, Capt G Chadwick was wounded in the knee and forced landed near Dickebusch.

The afternoon saw the first recorded combat of a Sopwith Camel when FltCom A M Shook of Naval 4 attacked an enemy scout that dived away into the sea haze off the coast near Nieuport. Naval 4 were the first squadron to be equipped with the Sopwith Camel.

Ltn Georg Simon of *Jasta 11*, flying Albatros D III 2015/16 was forced to land behind the British Lines by Capt C M B Chapman of 29 Squadron. Simon's Albatros was given the number G 42 and was sent back to England for evaluation.

The weather continued fine and warm and June 5 saw a great deal of fighting in the air. In the morning a patrol of Sopwith 1 1/2 Strutters of 45 Squadron were attacked by five Albatros scouts. Additional German fighters joined in the action and the Sopwiths lost two machines with the crews killed, another forced to land with the crew wounded and taken prisoner, and two more forced to land on the British side, one with both the crew wounded. The German formation, flushed with success, then attacked a patrol of seven Pups from 46 Squadron. The Pups were joined by three Spads from 19 Squadron but nearly all the British pilots suffered gun jams. Second Lieutenant P W Willcox's Pup was badly shot about by three of the enemy scouts but he managed to return to La Gorgue. His controls were cut, he crashed heavily on landing

and was badly shaken. Nineteen Squadron also lost a pilot in the action: 2Lt C D Grierson was shot down and taken POW.

Naval 10 flew an early morning patrol over Menin and destroyed an enemy two-seater in flames, the whole Flight firing into the enemy machine. To the north west of Poelcappelle they caught another two-seater and Collishaw dived below it and sent it down in a spin, with Desmond FitzGibbon firing at it as it spun down.

Major Jack Scott, CO of 60 Squadron, was out alone in the morning. Scott liked to fly alone and this morning he caught an Albatros D III over Monchy at 9.30am. Scott sent this Albatros, flown by *Ltn* Oskar von Schickfuss und Neudorff of *Jasta 3*, down in the British lines. Neudorff was killed and his Albatros D III was given the number G 43.

A pilot from 54 Squadron, 2Lt B G Chalmers, was shot down and taken POW for the last fighter casualty of the morning.

The fighting flared up again in the afternoon and late evening. Six Nieuports from 40 Squadron, led by Capt W T L Allcock, took off at 7.22pm and crossed the lines. Two of the Nieuports dropped out with engine trouble but the remaining four carried on and spotted four enemy aircraft 2,000 feet below them. William Bond had seen another five, further east and above the Nieuports, but before he could draw his Flight Commander's attention to them Allcock began to dive on the first four. Bond followed Allcock down, got very close to one of the enemy scouts, firing thirty or forty rounds and almost colliding with it before the enemy pilot dived away. Bond dived after it, finished off his drum and zoomed away. Bond watched the enemy scout crash in some patches of swamp, climbed back to 11,000 feet and again dived into the enemy formation. Bond got a burst of 25 rounds into one of the Albatri but it dived away and Bond was attacked from above by two others. 'I could only dive for all I was worth. They followed me to the lines and by that time I had lost 7,000 feet. It was practically dark when I landed. I was the last one home. Allison (Allcock)[9] had not arrived and nothing has been heard of him since.'

Flight Commander Shook of Naval 4 was again in action at 7.30pm. Flying his newly issued Sopwith Camel he attacked 15 hostile aircraft, shooting one down to crash on the beach and another, a two-seater, out of control between Ostend and Nieuport. These were the first confirmed and firm victories to be scored in a Sopwith Camel.

The fine weather continued on June 6, but the weather deteriorated as the day progressed, with thunderstorms in the afternoon and evening. At La Gorgue, Lee commented in his diary: 'we've had a easy time, loafing around. Very nice too. There's been a terrific lot of gunfire up north.'

For Naval 10 it was a highly successful morning. In Collishaw's words, 'June 6 surpassed anything that Naval 10 had thus far experienced.' In the days before and after the opening of the offensive at Messines, the squadron had orders to carry out Offensive Patrols using two Flights, a total of ten Sopwith Triplanes. Collishaw was in command of such a formation in the morning and at 16,000 feet over Polygon Wood he saw an Albatros two-seater flying towards the British lines. In an attempt to alleviate recent losses in artillery two-seaters, the Germans had been providing them with a fighter escort and this Albatros was escorted by some 15 Albatros and Halberstadt scouts. The naval pilots attacked immediately and, in Collishaw's words. 'a real "donnybrook" ensued.' Collishaw shot down two Albatri in quick succession, both in flames, and saw the pilot of a third fall back in his cockpit before his aeroplanes turned over onto its back and went down out of control. In the meantime, Gerry Nash had dispatched the two-seater, firing long bursts into it until it went down and crashed. Reid had attacked one of the Halberstadts which was also seen to crash. John Page saw his fire hit an Albatros pilot in the back and his machine went down. Sharman, Alexander and J H Keens were each credited with enemy scout out of control in the fight, which had lasted for 35 minutes and had drifted down from 15,000 to 5,000 feet before its conclusion. Collishaw led two further patrols during the day, but saw no enemy aeroplanes.

C Flight of 56 Squadron, led by Capt G H Bowman, took off at 8.00am and crossed the lines with a formation of Sopwith Pups of 66 Squadron. A formation of triplanes of Naval 1 – which had earlier had been attacking German aerodromes – were in combat with some Albatri and the SEs and Pups joined the fight. Bowman attacked one Albatros, which went down in a slow spin, before noticing that 'Georgie' Hoidge of his Flight was alone and fighting with three of the Albatri. Bowman dived to assist Hoidge and sent one of his attackers down out of control. More Albatros scouts then appeared, above the SEs, and Bowman took the Flight back to the lines. Bowman later commented in his logbook 'very unpleasant.' The Flight had lost one of their number in the fighting: Lt H Hamer had been shot down and killed by *Vzfw* Francke of *Jasta 8*.

The Sopwith Pups of 54 Squadron and the Nieuports of Naval 6 took part in a large fight during the morning. Some 30 British machines and 40 German were involved. Three enemy machines were seen crashed during the fighting and another five were claimed as out of control. Fifty-four Squadron had two casualties: Major C E Sutcliffe and Lt E J Y Grevelink were both killed in action by pilots of *Jasta 12*, and FltLt F P Reeves of Naval 6 was shot down and killed.

The battle of Messines opened on June 7. Zero hour was 3.10am. As the time drew near one British battalion recorded. 'Deep silence rained everywhere. Dawn was just breaking. The nightingales in Rossignol Wood were still finishing their night's song, when suddenly Hell was let loose, and the greatest earthquake ever felt in Northern Europe, accompanied by the mightiest crash of sound ever heard by mortal man, broke the still, summer morn.'

The 'earthquake' at zero hour was caused by nineteen mines, a total of 400 tons of ammonal, having been exploded under the German front line trenches. Before the roar of the explosions had died away every British artillery gun along the front opened fire and the infantry went over the top. Further south at La Gorgue, Arthur Lee would later write in his memoirs.

'Then at 3.10am exactly, with no preliminary shelling at all, there came a most God-almighty roar, the deep blast of a terrible explosion. The sky lit up with a vivid red glare. The ground shook as if we were in an earthquake, in fact the hut seemed to jump off the ground. I've never heard such a stupendous noise before, like the thunderclap of doom. It seemed so close it could have come from just across the canal instead of a dozen miles away, as we were soon to discover. Then as the roar ended, a hurricane bombardment began, a continuous rapid throbbing of guns, thousands of them. The hut vibrated without pause, the ground shuddered. All hell had been let loose up north.'[10]

Part of the overall plan for air operations on June 7 were attacks by single fighters on German aerodromes. Lt Leonard Barlow of 56 Squadron took off alone at 3.20am, ten minutes after zero hour, on a Special, Mission: his objectives were the German aerodromes at Bisseghem and Reckhem.

Barlow crossed the Front Lines at 1,500 feet, A mile behind the lines he lost height to 200 feet and flew along the Ypres to Menin road to Gheluwe, where he left the road and made for the railway junction on the outskirts of Cambrai. Climbing a little to 400 feet, Barlow followed the canal to Bisseghem, quickly locating the enemy aerodrome which was hard by a mineral factory – Barlow ascertained this by reading the advertisements on the walls of the factory. The enemy aerodrome appeared to be deserted and Barlow twice flew along the line of sheds firing bursts from both his Vickers and Lewis guns. There was still no response from the ground. Barlow went down to 20 feet, gave the sheds a final burst and zoomed away. As he gained some height he saw a goods train on a branch line; he went down to 50 feet and opened fire. The train stopped in a cloud of steam and smoke, completely hiding the engine from view. Barlow twice flew along the length of the train, firing both guns, but tiring of this he flew on to Wevelgem, where he saw some troops in the main street of the town. Barlow attacked these and the enemy infantry fled into the houses lining the street.

After attacking some trucks in the railway junction, Barlow flew at fifty feet along the Menin road to Reckem aerodrome, where he attacked the sheds, going to below their level and zooming out at the end of his runs. This aerodrome also appeared to be deserted until a solitary gun opened up at the SE – Barlow noted the shooting was very bad. Barlow dived and silenced the gunner, then made another pass over the aerodrome and sheds. Now out of ammunition, Barlow returned. The left elevator of Barlow's SE5 was shot away as he recrossed the Front Line but he landed safely at 5.00am. For this action, and his aerial victories, Barlow was awarded a Military Cross.

While Barlow was out, Rhys Davids led a formation of five SEs to patrol the area of Ypres to Wervicq. The SEs attacked three hostile scouts over Westroosebeke and drove them down from 10,000 to 5,000 feet. Rhys Davids, after nearly colliding with one enemy scout, sent it down, first in a spin, then a steep spiral, then completely out of control. This was possibly *FlugzgObMt* Fritz Kuhn of *Marine-Feld Jagdstaffel 1* who was taken prisoner but later died of his wounds.

Another Flight from 56 Squadron took off at 8.00am. Below them the battle was going well with British troops having already gained their first objective, holding the 'Black Line' and the crest of the ridge, well beyond the village of Messines. After a short indecisive skirmish with eight enemy scouts, the SEs attacked a pair of two-seaters over Poelcappelle at 4,000 feet and Capt Edric Broadberry shot one down out of control. Another pair of two-seaters was then seen over Ledeghem and Broadberry shot one down to crash-land in a field not far from the village.

Capt P B Prothero went down to attack troops in shell holes before climbing again and attacking another two-seater. He was joined in this attack by John Turnbull but both SEs suffered gun jams, and Prothero had a misfiring engine, so they returned. 'C' Flight flew the last patrol of the day, taking off at 11.30am. Visibility was poor, with mist and low cloud and the patrol split up. Capt Bowman went down to ground level and strafed troops marching along the Menin road. Hoidge also attacked enemy ground troops and William Turner-Coles, flying higher, attacked four two-seaters, but without result.

Cecil Lewis also strafed ground troops but then went to the aid of an RE8 being attacked by two black and white tailed Albatri. Two Spads of 19 Squadron joined Lewis and the enemy scouts dived away, but Lewis dived after the nearest and fired 50 rounds from his Vickers. The Albatros continued to dive away and Lewis was attacked from the rear by its companion. Lewis outmanoeuvred this Albatros, fired 60 rounds into it from 30 yards range and it went down to crash 'straight into Wervicq.' This was confirmed by the Spad pilots, Captains Cairnes and Leacroft.[11]

Twenty-three Squadron lost three pilots on an early morning patrol. In a fight with elements of *Jagdstaffeln 28* and *10* in the Comines-Warneton area, 2Lt F W Illingworth was wounded and taken POW; and 2Lt G C Stead and 2Lt Count L T B diBalme were also taken prisoner.

During the last days of the battle of Arras the value of free ranging operations by the fighter squadrons had been realised and similar duties were now put into operation. Pilots were encouraged to roam freely over the general battlefield to attack targets of opportunity: groundstrafing columns of enemy troops, gun emplacements, and trenches. Further to the rear, they were to attack railway junctions, trains, motor transport, and reinforcements making for the lines. This was extremely hazardous work, reflected in the casualties during the first days of the battle.

It was also again essential that the enemy balloons were destroyed and after lunch 1 Squadron attacked those in the vicinity of Quesnoy. Lt F Sharpe destroyed his balloon in flames, but 2Lt W G Milliship was shot down and killed. During a patrol in the morning, Lts F Sharpe and L F Jenkin of the squadron had claimed an Albatros that crashed near Zandvoorde.

As a portent of things to come, Lt Edward Mannock of 40 Squadron gained his first victory over an enemy aeroplane – he had been credited with a balloon on May 1. After a shaky start in the Squadron, Mannock was now leading patrols, his Flight Commander, Capt A W Keen, being in hospital for five days with influenza. Mannock's diary: 'in the meantime I have led the flight parties. Many scraps, and I brought my first dead certain Hun down this morning – over Lille – north. Two Huns this morning for C Flight. One for Hall, Godfrey and Redler got one each also. Four today! The push on the Armentiere-Ypres sector commenced this morning. We escorted FEs over Lille on bomb dropping business – and we met Huns. My man gave me an easy mark. I was only ten yards away from him – on top so I couldn't miss. A beautifully coloured insect he was – red, blue, green and yellow. I let him have sixty rounds at that range, so there wasn't much left of him. I saw him go spinning and slipping down from fourteen thousand. Rough luck, but it's war, and they're Huns.'[12]

In a later patrol over the same area, 40 Squadron claimed another two victories but lost Lt J W Shaw taken POW.

Two FE8s of 41 Squadron were shot down while groundstrafing in the early morning. Capt H Jackson was hit by Archie, crashlanded west of the lines, but later died of his wounds. In a later patrol before lunch, 2Lt N B Hair was shot down and taken prisoner.

The pilots of 46 Squadron were still incensed by a command from Wing, received the previous day, calling for a more offensive spirit to be shown. Lee caustically commented in his dairy: 'What bally cheek! I wonder what more they expect from us fighters with only one gun, when every Hun fighter has two, and when we do practically all our fighting over Hun territory, anyway.'

After breakfast – 'a quick cup of tea and a boiled egg with chunks of bread and marge (you've got to have *something* in you at this time in the morning to keep your pecker up') – Capt K W McDonald led F Barrager, S W Williams, C W Odell and Lee on a patrol to the area of Ploegsteert Wood. From 13,000 feet the whole of the battle was spread below the Pups: 'a great mantle of smoke, greenish grey, with long fingers stretching easwards under a light wind.' Through the smoke, in a crescent shape over the distant Messines ridge, were the continuous flashes of hundred of shells bursting. The air was full of corps machines working over the lines, spotting for the artillery, but only three Albatros fighters were seen, five miles over the lines, which quickly dived away east as the Pups dived at them, firing from long range. Later patrols by the Squadron had better luck. In one combat Brewster-Joske shot down an Albtros near Comines but Lt A P Mitchell, who had only been with the squadron three days, was wounded, shot down and taken prisoner, possibly by *Offst* M Muller of *Jasta 28*.

During a morning Offensive Patrol, one of 46 Squadron's fellow Pup Squadrons, 66 Squadron, lost a pilot over Roulers, shot down and taken POW and another returned with a badly shot up machine.

The naval squadrons had been given the task of engaging the *Jagdstaffeln* further east of the battle lines and Naval 10 sent out two Flight of five triplanes in the early morning, to the area beyond Ypres. Near Lille the Flights saw a formation of six Albatri. Unusually, these were above the triplanes, and the pilots were unable to catch them, but another formation of a dozen Albatri was then seen. These were in a more favourable position below and the triplanes attacked them, Collishaw and Nash sending two down before the enemy machines cleared east. When the triplanes reformed it was found that Reid and Sharman were no longer with them, they had become separated in the general melée.

Making his way back to Droglandt, Reid attacked an Albatros two-seater, killed the pilot with his fire and it went down to crash. Sharman, also making his way back to base, was attacked by three Albatri, which fought him down from 10,000 to 500 feet. One Albatros was so low that it crashed evading Sharman's fire – Sharman nearly suffering a similar fate. Climbing to regain his height, Sharman was then attacked by another four enemy fighters but he evaded these and returned.

Naval 10 flew two more patrols during the day but the weather became very cloudy and they saw no action. The squadron lost one pilot during the day's fighting: Lt John Keens, a Canadian from Toronto, was shot in the left lung but managed to land his triplane behind the British lines. Keens survived his wound and the war. He was claimed by *Ltn* A Niederhoff of *Jasta 11*.

Naval 1, carrying out similar duties to Naval 10, lost a pilot, severely wounded and forced to land near Tenbrielen.

The system of barrage patrols flown by the fighters during the day was mainly successful but in the afternoon some *Jagdstaffeln* evaded them and attacked five RE8s of 6 Squadron, shooting down two to crash east of the lines – two pilots killed, an observer killed and another POW. The remaining RE8s managed to escape back to their aerodrome, but with five men wounded, one fatally.

In the ground fighting the British troops had obtained all their objectives. The Second Army had advanced two and a half miles on a ten-mile front and had captured a great number of men and guns. This success had been achieved against a natural position, which had been further strengthened by a formidable defence system that the enemy had considered impregnable. The taking of the Messines-Wytschaete Ridge was a notable success and has been described as a tactical masterpiece of its kind.

On June 8 of the gains of the previous day were consolidated. Air reconnaissance revealed heavy road traffic in the areas of Roulers, Menin, Comines, Warneton and Lille. There was a German counter attack at 7.00pm but this was broken up by British artillery.

A patrol from 1 Squadron were in the air by 5.25am. The Nieuports, led by Hazell, were attacked by five Albatri from *Jasta 27*, led by Hermann Göring the *Jasta Führer*. Hazell attacked an Albatros with a broad white band painted around its black fuselage behind the cockpit and his fire hit the enemy scout, which turned over before going down in a vertical dive. At some time during the fighting *Jasta 27* were joined by elements of *Jasta 8* and two Nieuports were shot down behind the German lines: Second Lt R S L Boote was taken POW by *Oblt* Voigt of *Jasta 8*; and an Australian, 2Lt F D Slee, was also taken prisoner. 2Lt E G Nuding's machine was badly shot about, he crashlanded behind the British lines and the Nieuport was wrecked.

In the 1930s, Göring, who claimed Slee, wrote a highly colourful account of the fight, describing Slee as a brilliant, dashing flyer, with five victories to his credit, who put up a tremendous fight before being finally shot down. In actual fact Slee had been with 1 Squadron for only four days, posted straight from flying school.

It was a bad day for 66 Squadron. In a fight over the Roulers area with *Jasta 8* the Pups of 2Lt A V Shirley and 2Lt A G Robertson collided and both pilots were killed. In addition,

Capt J D Latta was wounded in the action and Lt A B Thorne's Pup was badly shot about.

Although there are reports of the German pilots being extremely wary of fighting with the Sopwith Triplanes of the naval squadrons, Naval 1 and Naval 9 both had casualties during the day. Naval 1 lost two pilots: FltLt T G Culling and FltSubLt T R Swinburne, both killed, and FltSubLt H F Stackard of Naval 9 was also shot down and killed. Thomas Culling was a particular loss to Naval 1. He had scored three victories in April, another three in May, and had been awarded a DSC.

On a patrol over the Ypres Salient in the afternoon, Capt W I Bailey of 41 Squadron was wounded and forced to land near the front line. His FE8 was destroyed by enemy shellfire.

With the successful conclusion of the offensive at Messines, the RFC curtailed its activities. The heavy losses of April were still being felt and the corps needed to conserve its strength for the main offensive in Flanders. Trenchard wrote to his brigade commanders on June 10: 'I would ask that as far as possible you do your best to point out to your Armies that it is of the utmost importance that the Flying Corps should avoid wastage of pilots and machines for some little time. My reserve at present is dangerously low, in fact, in some cases it barely exists at all, and the supply from home is not coming forward sufficiently freely to enable us to continue fighting an offensive in the air continuously. It is just as impossible for the air forces to fight a continuous offensive as it is for the infantry, and as we have no reserve squadrons it is necessary to do everything to avoid losses. It is of the utmost importance, however, that the offensive spirit is maintained in the Flying Corps.'

It is difficult to reconcile the main request and thrust of Trenchard's memorandum with the contradictory last sentence. The continuous offensive policy that he had always advocated had led to the very losses of men and machines that now placed the RFC in such a vulnerable condition. Luckily, bad weather – low clouds and rain – from June 9 to the 19th of the month, favoured Trenchard's demands and the tempo of the airfighting slackened.

Although it was cloudy and misty on June 9 some patrols were flown. In the morning 40 Squadron flew a Line Patrol and were in a fight with some 13 enemy aircraft – Albatri and two-seaters. 2Lt J L Barlow, who had originally been attacking a balloon, shot down an Albatros D III and a C type in the fighting but his Nieuport was badly shot about and he was forced to land. Another patrol from the squadron, during the evening, led by William Bond, unsuccessfully attacked a two-seater flying east: 'I didn't tackle it well. I was afraid to go straight on to it, fearing the observer's gun and tried to get

underneath it. The Hun fired a signal light as usual and opened all out and walked away from me.'

Bond turned south and climbed; he knew the signal light was for enemy scouts in the area. A little later he saw five enemy scouts below the Nieuports. Bond let them pass then dived on the rearmost, but the enemy pilot saw him coming and closed up to his leader. Bond switched his attack to the leader, fired forty rounds into it and watched it go down. After a short skirmish the enemy scout broke off the action and dived east.

46 Squadron took off at dawn. Led by K W McDonald, the Sopwith Pups crossed the lines at 7,000 feet, as Arthur Lee later commented: 'a bad height for Pups to fight, a good height for archie.' As Lee had feared, the Pups were badly archied and it was over an hour before they saw any enemy aircraft. The Flight went to the aid of some FEs fighting eight Albatri. The FEs were in their usual defensive circle the gunners covering each other's tails; the enemy scouts making dive and zoom attacks. As they approached the fight Lee fired at an Albatros that was in his sights and hit it in the petrol tank. A long plume of vapour came out of the punctured tank, followed by a vivid flash, and the whole aeroplane was engulfed in a ball of red fire. Although he had fired at the Albatros, it was at long range, and Lee was convinced that it had been hit one of the gunners in the FEs. The Pups had opened fire too soon and the enemy scouts broke off the action and dived away. In his diary that night, Lee wrote: 'I keep thinking of the flamer today. The pilot jumped. He had a light yellow flying coat and it billowed out, momentarily checking his fall, like a parachute, so that the machine left him behind. Then he turned over and dived after it, alongside the column of black smoke. A horrid sight. I hope it wasn't me that hit him. I'd hate to get a flamer, it would be on my conscience.' Like many pilots, Arthur Lee dreaded the possibility of being shot down in flames. 'What a way to die, to be sizzled alive or jump and fall thousands of feet. I'd much prefer a bullet through the head and have done with it.'

A large patrol of eight Nieuports from 1 Squadron flew an Offensive Patrol in the evening and had combats with various formations of enemy machines. In one action Frank Sharpe crashed a two-seater, but was then attacked by three Albatri. 2Lt R Anderson dived to the aid of his Flight Commander but he was too late; Sharpe's Nieuport was already spinning down. Anderson was fought down to 700 feet and while changing a drum he lost sight of Sharpe, last seeing him flying very low and pursued by Albatri. Sharpe had been wounded, he crashed and was taken prisoner, claimed by *Oblt* Kurt-Bertram von Döring of *Jasta 4*. This was the second casualty for 1 Squadron during the day: in a morning patrol

2Lt W G Mussared had also been shot down and made POW, by *Ltn* R Franke of *Jasta 8*.

Lee's diary entry for June 9 shows that a fighter pilot's life also held other, more mundane activities than daily airfighting. 'Today has been hectic. Before the main breakfast, a three hour patrol, hit by archie, a brush with HA, and a sight of a Hun flamer. Plus orderly dog duties. Immediately after breakfast, rushed off in a Crossley to the field cashier at Hinges near Béthune, drew the pay money, rushed into Béthune, had lunch, did some shopping, roared back to La Gorgue, held pay parade, six francs down. Censored the men's letters, inspected their quarters and midday meal. After lunch, another three hour patrol, archied again, another (distant) brush with HA and go back just in time for dinner. I definitely earned my pay today.'

At 5am Collishaw of Naval 10 had taken off with two companions to patrol east of Ypres. As he recounts in his autobiography, *Air Command*, 'it very nearly saw the end of Collishaw.' The triplanes dived to attack a formation of Albatros D IIIs and while Collishaw was concentrating on one enemy scout, which he had out turned, another came down on his tail and 'a devastating stream of bullets smashed into my cockpit.' Collishaw was not hit, but his controls were shattered and he had no control of the triplane, which fell off onto one wing and went into a hair-raising series of cartwheels, wild swoops and dives. Collishaw recalled that at first he was terrified, but that this gave way to a 'dulled sort of resignation,' while he reflected 'wistfully' on how nice it would be to have a parachute. The action had started at 16,000 feet and the out of control triplane took 15 minutes to descend. Fortunately for Collishaw, just before hitting the ground the triplane 'took it into its mind to try one final swoop.' This saved Collishaw. The triplane hit the ground and 'folded into a mass of wreckage,' leaving Collishaw with no more than bruises and a determination that 'I would never, never again, let anyone come at me from out of the sun.'

Over the next four days, the fighter squadrons lost three pilots. Accurate AA fire shot the wings of the Nieuport of 2Lt R W L Anderson of 1 Squadron on June 11. On June 13 a patrol from 1 Squadron were in action with enemy fighters and 2Lt R S Davies was forced to land. Davies was injured in the crash and his Nieuport, B1522, was completely wrecked. B1522 was the Nieuport that Albert Ball had initially flown in 56 Squadron. After Ball's death it had been returned to 2ASD and reissued to 1 Squadron.

Just before noon Naval 4 had taken off to intercept a formation of 16 Gothas. Whether due to enemy action or structural failure one wing of Sopwith Camel C6362 broke off and it crashed at Neumunster, five miles north west of

Bruges. FltSubLt L F W Smith DSC was killed. Smith had a total of eight victories while serving in Naval 4 and was the first Sopwith Camel casualty in France.

The weather improved a little on June 14; the day was fair with fine intervals. A patrol from 56 Squadron took off at 7.30am but saw nothing for nearly two hours, finally chasing a formation of Albatri east before returning. Another patrol in the evening saw more action. Bowman, the Flight Commander, shot down a two-seater that was seen to crash by British AA batteries. Later in the patrol the SE5s were in action with several enemy scouts east of Roulers. Bowman claimed one scout, recording in his diary. 'Shot down EA scout which nearly fell on Major Sanday. Confirmed by him.' Spads of 19 and 23 Squadrons were in the combat and it was possibly in this action that Lt G S Buck claimed a 'German Nieuport' as crashed. Lt Harry Rogerson of 56 Squadron was shot down in the fight and taken prisoner, awarded to *Ltn* Kuppers of *Jasta 6* for his third victory.

During the evening FltSubLt L H Parker of Naval 10 was shot down and killed by *Vzfw* F Krebs of *Jasta 6* for his fourth victory.

Although there was haze and mist in the early morning of June 15 the day was fine and warm. Prothero, Gerald Maxwell and J S Turnbull of 56 Squadron caught a two-seater over Fort Carnot and sent it down in a slow right hand spiral until it hit the ground near the fort.

In the late evening, Captain Keen of 40 Squadron surprised a silver and green Albatros scout which was stalking a patrol of Nieuports from 60 Squadron. Keen shot this Albatros down in flames for his fourth victory.

The pilots of Naval 10 had a successful day. In the morning, six triplanes, led by Collishaw, first attacked a pair of hostile two-seaters over Lille. These attacks were frustrated by the enemy machines diving away east but twenty-five minutes later the triplanes attacked five Halberstadt scouts to the north of St Julien. Collishaw recorded that the German pilots 'were as keen for a scrap as we were.' In his first attack Collishaw sent one of the enemy machines down in a steep dive. Thinking that his fire had either hit the pilot or his engine, Collishaw followed, but another Halberstadt got on his tail and the Canadian had to take violent evasive action. The Sopwith Triplane could 'outmanoeuvre at that height anything the Germans were flying' and Collishaw quickly reversed the positions and got onto the Halberstadt's tail. After only 20 rounds Collishaw's gun jammed and he climbed away to clear it. Desmond FitzGibbon sent one of the Halberstadts down out of control but the remainder cleared to the east.

In the evening, two Flights from Naval 10 were in action with five enemy two-seaters over Menin and Collishaw sent one down in a series of dives and sideslips. A little later, over Moorslede, the triplanes saw several two-seaters escorted by ten to fifteen Albatros and Halberstadt scouts. The Naval pilots attacked from out of the sun, completely surprising the enemy formation. Collishaw sent one Albatros down in a spin then saw another attacking Reid. Collishaw drove this Albatros off, but then saw a Halberstadt attacking Alexander. Collishaw got on the tail of the Halberstadt and fired several long bursts. The starboard wings of the enemy scout folded up and it fell out of control, 'shedding bits and pieces.' Reid sent two of the enemy scouts down out of control and John Page claimed another. After the individual combat reports were studied and assessed by Brigade the triplanes were credited with having destroyed one enemy scout and another seven out of control.

Pilots of 1 Naval, 41 and 66 Squadrons also claimed victories during the day. Naval 3 returned to the Dunkirk Command of the RNAS on June 15 and moved to Furnes aerodrome in Belgium. Naval 3's place was taken by Naval 9, which flew into Flez, an aerodrome west of St.Quentin.

June 16 was very hot, both for weather and action. Crowe led B Flight of 56 Squadron off the ground at 8.00am. After a short skirmish with enemy scouts the Flight attacked a two-seater and Crowe shot it down to crash near Passchendaele. Kenneth Knaggs was slightly wounded during this patrol and sent to hospital. The second patrol flown by the squadron was heavily and accurately archied over Ypres. Edric Broadberry had all his aileron controls shot away, and the port topplane, main spar and balance cable, fuselage cross bracing wire and shackles, and a fuselage strut, were all damaged. Broadberry was, as the Squadron Record Book described it, 'obliged to return.' Broadberry was a superb pilot and managed to bring the damaged SE back safely.

During a morning patrol 2Lt W C Campbell of 1 Squadron destroyed an Albatros two-seater over Houthem at 9.00am. Ten minutes later he sent another down to crash, then turned his attentions to a third. Attacking this Albatros, Campbell ran out of ammunition. He returned to Bailleul, rearmed, returned to the same area, and found a 'large two-seater machine.' Campbell emptied two drums of Lewis into this aeroplane and it went down to crash for his third victory of the morning and his twelfth overall. Campbell would finish the war with twenty-three victories, including five balloons, winning an MC and Bar and a DSO.

The naval squadrons were also successful during the day's fighting. FltCom R J O Compston and FltSubLt R R Thornely from Naval 8 shot down a DFW CV from *Fl Abt (A) 211*. The DFW crashed behind the British lines. The pilot, *Vzfw* Helmuth Totsch was killed but the wounded observer, *Ltn* Karl Riegel was taken prisoner. The DFW was designated G 47.

Eight Nieuports set out from 60 Squadron in the evening, 'Grid' Caldwell leading 'B' Flight with William Fry leading 'C' Flight above. Caldwell's formation was attacked by five Albatros scouts, but 'C' Flight dived on the enemy scouts and drove them down through the lower Flight. Fry, Young, Rutherford and Lloyd followed two of the Albatri down from 11,000 to 3,000 feet. Young fired fifteen rounds and Fry forty at an Albatros that was on the tail of Lt Lloyd's Nieuport. During the fierce fighting, Lt D R C Lloyd was again seen going down with an enemy scout close behind and at 2,000 feet he collided with one of the enemy scouts, flown by *Vzfw* Robert Riessinger of *Jasta 12,* killing both pilots. *Ltn* Hermann Becker of the *Jasta* was wounded and shot down by Caldwell.

The next day, June 17, was an unlucky day for 56 Squadron. Taking off at 8.00am the patrol first attacked three two-seaters over Lille. Bowman despatched one of these down out of control, its engine full on. Bowman and Hoidge then went down to attack some additional enemy two-seaters, but the rest of the Flight were slow to follow and were jumped by eight Albatri from *Jasta 6*. Lt Harry Spearpoint was shot down by *Vzfw* Krebs, and Lt William Turner-Coles was shared between the crew of the two-seater he was attacking – *Uffz* Heidingsfelder and *Ltn* Romberg from *Fl Abt (A) 292* – and *Ltn d R* Pollandt of *Jasta 6*. Both British pilots were taken POW. Turner-Coles was helped from the wreckage of his aeroplane by a German officer, taken to a dugout and given a strong coffee. Seventeen years later they were to meet again – on a train in Shanghai.

Cecil Lewis had seen the Albatri go down after C Flight and had stayed above the fight until he saw his opportunity. He dived on one of the Albatri, flown by Pollandt, and fired a double drum of Lewis into Pollandt's Albatros, which went down in a spin over Haubourdin. Max Pollandt had been wounded by Lewis' fire and crashed west of Lille.

In addition to the 56 Squadron casualties, 23 Squadron lost Capt A B Wright. The Spads had been attacking three two-seaters, two of which they sent down, one in flames, but Wright was wounded in the foot.

June 18 was a day of thunderstorms, but with clear intervals. Nieuports of 1 Squadron were in action with *Jasta 11* in the morning and lost 2Lt R S Lloyd, killed by *Ltn* Allmenroder, the only casualty of the day for the fighter squadrons.

Number 1 Squadron had another casualty the following day when 2Lt G C Atkins became seperated from his companions in heavy cloud. He was later reported to be a prisoner of war. Forty-one Squadron had two casualties: Lt L J MacLean was forced to land after combat with three enemy aeroplanes and Lt Hartridge was shot down, injured in the crash, and taken to hospital. Capt T Davidson of 23 Squadron was shot down by anti-aircraft fire east of Ypres in the morning and taken POW. June 20, a day of thunderstorms and heavy rain, saw very little war flying, but German anti-aircraft gunners claimed 2Lt A Hurley, also of 23 Squadron, who was wounded in the head.

• • •

On June 13 London had been attacked by a strong force of 17 Gothas causing casualties in the City and East End – 162 people were killed and 432 injured. Among the dead were 43 children and another 102 had been injured. In the words of the official history: 'This raid stirred the country' and there was a public outcry for a more effective defense against the raiders, should they return. The War Cabinet met in the afternoon of June 13; in its meeting the following day it decided that the long term solution should be the expansion of both the RFC and RNAS – to literally double the strength of the air services – but that in the interim a fighter squadron, or squadrons, should be brought back from France to give the raiders 'one of two sharp lessons'. It was finally decided that one fighter squadron in France should be transferred to England and that another squadron should be based near the French coast. These two squadrons could then carry out defensive patrols on both sides of the Straits of Dover. Haig was reluctant to lose even one squadron from France, but on June 21, 56 Squadron returned to England and 66 Squadron were moved to Calais. A jubilant Cecil Lewis commented: 'God bless the good old Gotha! Good old Jerry! Good old Lloyd George!'

A patrol of Sopwith Pups of 46 Squadron, led by A S Lee, approached an LVG during a morning patrol on June 21, but Lee was suspicious. The enemy crew had obviously seen the British scouts but it merely gradually turned to the east, in no apparent hurry. It was the bait in the classic booby trap. Lee looked up and round and spotted eight Albatros scouts at 8,000 feet above them. Lee fired a quick burst at the LVG, saw the Albatri beginning their diving attack and turned west. The enemy scouts turned away and Lee circled, saw that the LVG had resumed its work and attacked it again, firing a burst of a hundred rounds from 300 yards range. The LVG dived away east, the Albatri again began to come down, but the Pups dived for the safety of the British lines, happy to have spoiled the LVG's shoot. Another Flight of Pups had taken off the assist Lee's Flight and lost one of their number, 2Lt H A C Tonks who was shot down and killed by *Hptm* Hartmann of *Jasta 28*. A Nieuport of 1 Squadron was also lost in the morning. 2Lt T M McFerran was shot down and killed over Becelaere by *Ltn* Wewer of *Jasta 26*.

June 22 was a day of low clouds and rain and there was little war flying. The fighter squadrons had only one casualty on June 23, a Nieuport from 29 Squadron: 2Lt G T Harker was forced to land east of the lines and was captured.

June 24 was cloudy, but with large clear gaps between the clouds and a strong westerly wind. 2Lt D P Collis from 23 Squadron was shot up during a combat, forced to land and was injured. Capt W P Holt of 29 Squadron was in action with *Jasta 30* and was shot down near Beaumont by *Uffz* Heiligers. During an afternoon patrol, 2Lt T M Sturgess of 41 Squadron was seen to fire a green light and force land east of the lines. He was made POW.

It was a bad day for Naval 10. Two flights left at 7.00am to escort a pair of DH4s of 25 Squadron on a photo reconnaisance to Menin. Over Moorslede, 15 Albatri, some of which were from *Jasta 11,* attacked the DH4s, which were below their escort. Collishaw took the triplanes down into the fight, secured a position behind one of the red-nosed Albatri, closed the range to 25 yards and fired a burst of 40 rounds. One pair of wings broke away from its body and the Albatros went down to crash. Collishaw was then attacked by several of the enemy scouts, driven down to ground level and crossed the front lines at 15 feet. When the reports were made up, Sharman claimed to have shot the tailplane and wings off another of the Albatri and one of the DH4s claimed another down out of control. Despite these seemingly definite claims the Jagdstaffeln lost only two pilots: one injured in an accident and another shot down – probably by pilots of 23 Squadron – while attacking a balloon. This is not to necessarily dispute the claims by the naval pilots, both enemy pilots could have survived their crashes.

Two pilots from Naval 10 did not return from this action. FltSubLt A B Holcroft was shot down and taken POW by *Ltn* Karl Allmenröder of *Jasta 11* and FltSubLt R G Saunders was killed by *Ltn* Gisbert-Wilhelm Groos of the *Jasta* for his second victory.

Naval 10 lost another pilot to Karl Allmenröder the following day when he shot down FltSubLt Gerry Nash, who was taken POW. Despite the very bad weather – rain and snow – Naval 10 flew a patrol in the late afternoon and near Hollebeke were in combat with *Jasta 11*. The fight seemed to have ended without any positive result, but when the triplanes returned Gerry Nash was missing.

Allmenröder continued his running successes the next day – June 26 – when he shot down a Nieuport of 1 Squadron, flown by Lt C C Street, who was killed. Street was Allmenröder's 30th victory. A sergeant pilot from 1 Squadron claimed an Albatros out of control from this action but the *Jasta* reported no losses.

There were low clouds and high winds the next day; there was little flying until the evening. Nineteen Squadron lost Lt H M Lowe killed in action by *Oblt* Voigt of *Jasta 8* who claimed a Spad near Bixschoote. A Nieuport 23 of 29 Squadron – Lt J D J Bird, killed in action – was claimed by *Ltn* Nostitz and *Ltn* Knake of *Jasta 12,* and 60 Squadron lost Lt D C G Murray, wounded in action and taken POW by *Ltn* Kurt Wolff of *Jasta 11.*

The day ended badly for *Jasta 11.* In the morning, Karl Allmenröder was brought down and killed by British anti-aircraft fire over Zillebeke. Allmenröder crashed in No-Man's-Land and his body was brought into the German trenches that night.[13]

There was little flying on June 28. The next morning, 29 Squadron were in combat with elements of *Jasta 12* and *29.* The patrol of seven Nieuports were attacked by 25 hostile scouts flying in three formations, all coming from different directions and at varying heights. The enemy pilots in one formation appeared to be experienced, but the pilots of the other two showed 'little knowledge of fighting and manoeuvring.' The Nieuports were completely surrounded and split up, but fought their way back to the lines, claiming six of the enemy fighters down out of control and one destroyed, for the loss of one Nieuport: Lt V A Norvill, who was wounded and taken prisoner.

A patrol of A and B Flights from 60 Squadron were in action with eight enemy aircraft between Douai and Cambrai in the late afternoon. Capt W E Molesworth sent one down out of control but then lost contact with the other Nieuports. Returning alone he attacked four enemy scouts over Gavrelle, but these were joined by another five. Molesworth's Nieuport was hit twenty eight times: the petrol tank was holed, the propeller was hit, the cowling shot away, and the main spar in the upper starboard wing smashed. Despite this damage Molesworth managed to land in a clear space on the British side of the lines.

The weather was extremely bad on the last day of June, with low clouds and rain all day and there was no war flying.

Although the battle of Messines was subsidiary to the main battles in Flanders, planned to commence in late July, the airfighting over the battlefront had been fierce, intense, and hotly contested. The victory at Messines was due in no small part to the co-operation between the corps squadrons of the RFC and the artillery, but it had not been won without cost. The RFC had suffered over 200 casualties, 79 of which were from the fighter squadrons.

NOTES

1. It was also essential that the German U-Boat bases were cleared from the Belgian coast. The Royal Navy had warned Haig that with these still operational it might not be able to command the English Channel; as a consequence it might be impossible to continue the war in 1918.

2. The squadrons of 9th Wing continued to work over the Arras front to convince the enemy to believe that it remained the main battle area.

3. *War In The Air, Vol IV* (page 113), Oxford University Press, 1934.

4. The main reason that this expectation was not realised was that reception in the fighter would rely on transmissions of relatively high power, which was only possible at the cost of considerable interference with all other wireless communications in the area of the front line.

5. At this time the pilots of Naval 10, with the exception of two, were Canadians. Raymond Collishaw is famous for leading the 'Black Flight' of the Squadron but is at pains to point out in his autobiography that the Flights rarely flew at their full strength of five triplanes, that the majority of patrols were flown by two or three machines and it was not uncommon for a single machine to be sent up to intercept an enemy machine reported to be working over the lines.

6. During recent years the subject of Bishop's claim to have attacked a German aerodrome on the early morning of June 2 1917 – for which he was awarded a Victoria Cross – has led to a considerable amount of controversy. This book is not the place to review these arguments, but suffice it to be said that German records have no record of an attack on an aerodrome on June 2 1917 and noted Canadian aviation researcher, the late Philip Markham, who carried out an extensive review of Bishop's account of the event, concluded: 'There is not a shred of evidence to support Bishop's claims.'

7. Karl Emil Schäfer was killed in the afternoon during a combat with FE2ds of 20 Squadron.

8. Dickinson was awarded to *Vzfw* Wittekind of *Jasta 28* for his first victory.

9. Allcock had been shot down and killed, possibly by *Vzfw* Reiss of *Jasta 3* for his second victory.

10. *No Parachute,* Arthur Gould Lee, Jarrolds, London 1969.

11. Possibly *Ltn* Ernst Wiessner of *Jasta 18.*

12. *The Personal Diary of Mick Mannock,* Frederick Oughton, Neville Spearman, London 1966.

13. In his autobiography *Air Command* Collishaw relates how on June 27 he had fired from long range at an Albatros with a red body, and a white spinner and tailplane. He did not see the effect of his fire, but after the war, learning that Allmenröder had been shot down from extreme range and had crashed between the lines in the area of Ypres, he summised that he had shot down the thirty victory German ace. However, the action in which Collishaw shot at the Albatros was in the afternoon and Allmenröder was shot down at 9.45am.

CHAPTER TWELVE

ABOVE FLANDERS FIELDS

The first objective of the attack in Flanders was the capture of the Passchendaele-Staden Ridge, then possession of the Roulers to Thourout railway, which would threaten the rear of the German defences to the north. When the Passchendaele-Staden Ridge had been taken it was intended that a landing should be made on the coast between Ostend and the Yser River, accompanied by an attack on the Nieuport Front. The task of capturing the Passchendaele-Staden Ridge, and subsequently the Roulers-Thourout railway, was given to the British Fifth Army, commanded by General Sir Hubert Gough. The British Fourth Army, commanded by General Sir Henry Rawlinson, was to control operations on the coast.

From the coast, facing east, the disposition of the Allied armies was: the British Fourth Army, the Belgium Army, the French First Army, the British Fifth Army, and lastly, the British Second Army.

The French First Army was to act as the left defensive flank of the British Fifth Army; the British Second Army, its right. Facing Gough's Fifth Army was the German Fourth Army, commanded by General Sixt von Armin, and from Chateau Wood in the north to Klein Zillebeke in the south, the German Sixth Army (General Otto von Below). Southwards from Zillebeke the remainder of the German Sixth Army faced General Sir Herbert Plumer's Second Army.

The strength of the RFC concentrated for the offensive was considerable. Early in June the headquarters of V Brigade RFC, commanded by Brigadier-General C A H Longcroft, had moved north to the HQ of the Fifth Army. The Twenty-Second (Army) Wing of the brigade comprised four single-seater fighters squadrons: Naval 10 (Sopwith Triplane) 23 Squadron (Spad) 29 Squadron (Nieuport) and 32 Squadron (DH5). The Army Wing also included 57 Squadron (DH4) as a bomber squadron.

The fighter strength of Ninth Wing, commanded by Lieutenant-Colonel C L N Newall, was four squadrons: 19 Squadron (Spad) 56 Squadron (SE5 and SE5a) 66 Squadron (Sopwith Pup) 70 Squadron (Sopwith Camel) and 27 Squadron (Martinsyde Scout); the wing also had 55 Squadron (DH4) as a bombing squadron, and a Special Duty Flight (BE 12a and BE2e).

I Brigade RFC had First (Corps) Wing of six squadrons (RE8 and Armstrong Whitworth FK8); its Tenth (Army) Wing had only two single-seater fighter squadrons, Naval 8 (Sopwith Triplane and Sopwith Camel) and 40 Squadron (Nieuport) The wing's three remaining squadrons were 43 Squadron (Sopwith 1 1/2 Strutter) 100 Squadron (FE2b) and 25 Squadron (DH4 and FE2b).

II Brigade RFC consisted of Second (Corps) Wing with three squadrons flying the RE8, and Eleventh (Army) Wing: 1 Squadron (Nieuport) 1 Naval (Sopwith Triplane) 45 Squadron (Sopwith Camel) and 20 Squadron (FE2d).

III Brigade RFC comprised Twelfth (Corps) Wing whose squadrons flew the BE2e; RE8 and the Morane Parasol. Its Thirteenth (Army) Wing had three single-seater squadrons: 24 Squadron (DH5) 41 Squadron (DH5) and 60 Squadron (Nieuport), the three remaining squadrons were equipped with the Bristol F2b, and the FE2b.

IV Brigade's Third (Corps) Wing had two squadrons equipped with the RE8 and its Fourteenth (Army) Wing comprised 6 Naval (Sopwith Camel) 9 Naval (Sopwith Camel and Triplane) and 54 Squadron (Sopwith Pup), 48 Squadron, flying the Bristol F2b, completed its strength.

The strength of RFC, from the Lys, north east of Armentières, (on the right flank of the Second Army) was 508 aeroplanes, of which 230 were single-seater fighters. To this must be added the 104 aeroplanes of the RNAS squadrons operating over the Belgian coast. The French strength was 200 aeroplanes, (100 single-seater fighters) and 40 Belgian aeroplanes.

Exact figures for the strength of the *Luftstreitkräfte* are difficult to access. The air strength of the German Fourth Army was doubled between the first week of June and the end of July, the beginning of the British offensive, and over 600 aeroplanes were available to *General* Sixt von Armin by July 31, 200 of which were fighters. The earlier grouping of some *jagdstaffeln* into *jagdgeschwader* was formalised with the establishment of *Jagdgeschwader* 1 on June 24. The new *jagdgeschwader* consisted of *Jagdstaffeln* 4,6,10 and 11 and was placed under the command of Manfred von Richthofen, the *Staffelführer* of *Jasta 11*. The role of the *jagdgeschwader* was 'for the purpose of winning and securing dominance in the air in crucial combat sectors. It remains directly under the command of the Fourth Army High Command. The individual sections of the *Geschwader* are to assemble at one airfield if possible.'[1]

The *Luftstreitkräfte* had some 600 aeroplanes between La Bassée and coast (not including the units of the coast itself (roughly 49 seaplanes and 14 fighters) the Allies approximately 840. Of these figures the Germans had 200 fighters, the Allies 350, giving the Allies a numerical supremacy of three and a half to two.

The planning of the offensive called for considerable co-operation between the Allied air forces, with the RFC in loose overall command. The air offensive was to commence on July 7 on the British Fifth and Second Army fronts and fully developed by July 8 onwards.

The first day of July was quiet, only a few trench reconnaissances by the Corps squadrons were flown. On July 2, 40 Squadron saw a good deal of action. Lionel Blaxland, on escort duty, shot down an Albatros that crashed near Thelus. Steve Godfrey attacked a pair of Albatros scouts north of Douai. These Albatri were unusually coloured, Godfrey reported them as having green and red top wings with the crosses composed of white dots. Godfrey sent one down out of control and Crole shot another down in flames.[2] Lt G B Crole of 40 Squadron also claimed an Albatros scout during the day. A patrol from 1 Squadron went to the aid of a formation of RE8s under attack and Lt L F Jenkin shot down one of the attackers, which fell in flames, the pilot and observer jumping clear of their aeroplane.

A force of ten Sopwith Triplanes from Naval 10, led by Collishaw and J E Sharman, took off at 10.00am on a Special Offensive Patrol. Over Poelcapelle they attacked a pair of Aviatik two-seaters. Collishaw shot down one of these, which was seen to crash by the other members of squadron, but his triplane had been hit in the engine and he was forced to return.

Robert Little of Naval 8 was flying a Special Mission on July 3 when he surprised three Albatros scouts west of Lens. A quick burst send one down through the clouds. Later, patrolling near Douai, Little saw a formation of Sopwith 1 1/2 Strutters of 43 Squadron and he joined them just before they came under attack from six Albatros D III, one of the enemy scouts attacking the rearmost Sopwith. Little drove this machine away and attacked another, which he drove down. Capt T S Wynn of 43 Squadron was wounded in the head during this attack.

The day saw the first fighter casualty of the month. A patrol from 1 Squadron had taken off at 10.00am to patrol the Ypres Salient. On their return they were attacked and Lt Tom Littler went down in a spin, his attacker following, still firing. Littler cashed on 42 Squadron's aerodrome and was killed. Littler's attacker, which flew away to the south, was seen to be a Sopwith Pup, flying the single streamer of a deputy flight commander and it was later established that it came from 46 Squadron.

An inquiry at 'the very highest level' found that the culprit was a Canadian pilot of 46 Squadron, Lt Lloyd Fleming. Fleming was posted to the Middle East and 46 Squadron was moved south to Bruay on July 6.[3]

A force of six Nieuports of 60 Squadron, led by 'Grid' Caldwell, were returning from a patrol in the evening when they attacked seven Albatros scouts near Graincourt, sending one down out of control. Regaining their height, the Nieuports next attacked five enemy scouts, driving them east. There was a strong westerly wind blowing, the Nieuports were at the end of their endurance and Caldwell, abandoning the chase, turned his command back towards base. However, as they again approached Graincourt, Caldwell sighted three Albatros scouts below them and led the Flight down. Caldwell later wrote: 'when leading a Nieuport Flight over the lines in a strong adverse wind, I dawdled too long, hoping for a quick shot at a Hun formation below us, left it too late, and we lost a fellow named Adam, brought down by a "zooming" Albatros from below. I was naturally very upset at this bad judgement on my part. We had a job extricating the others from a bad situation as I remember.' 'The others' were pilots of C Flight from the squadron, who were flying top cover for Caldwell's B Flight. They dived down into the fight and Lt F Soden claimed an Albatros as out of control. Lt A R Adam was wounded and taken POW but later died of his wounds. He was claimed by *Ltn* Ballik of *Jasta 12*.

July 4 was cloudy with some rain, but there was spasmodic fighting throughout the day. Pilots of 60 and 1 Squadrons were in action, but the combats were indecisive, although some enemy aeroplanes were claimed as driven down or out of control. Naval 8 were in action, and FltLt R R Soar claimed an out of control. Naval 10 were also in combat with enemy fighters during the day, but with no positive result. The German fighter formations being met were now considerably larger in number, Collishaw noting that on July 4 the naval triplanes tangled with a formation of 20 and another of 18 the following day.

The weather conditions were very unsettled on July 5 with low clouds and intermittent rain and there was little service flying.

During the afternoon 56 Squadron returned to Estrée Blanche. The Squadron had seen no action with the Gothas while in England and Haig had stipulated that it would be 'urgently required to be back (in France) by July 5.' Sixty-Six Squadron was withdrawn from Calais the next day, also returning to Estrée Blanche.[4]

The day was fine and warm on July 6 and there was a great deal of fighting in the air. Robert Little of Naval 8 crashed a DFW just north of Izel and on his way back to the lines engaged another that was attacking the British balloon lines. Little had a gun jam while tackling this two-seater and 'stunted around it' until some Nieuports came up and drove the enemy machine east.

The Spads of 23 Squadron were in action with *Jasta 36* in the morning, losing one of their number, 2Lt W H Clark, to *Ltn* Bülow of the *Jasta*. Capt R G Neville, leading the formation, attacked one Albatros, which broke up in mid-air, and claimed another as out of control. The Spads were out again in the afternoon, this time led by Capt W J C Kennedy-Cochran-Patrick, who fired from long range at one Albatros that was seen to crash by British AA gunners. A member of this patrol, an American from Norfolk, Virginia, Capt Clive Wilson Warman, who had been only a short time with 23 Squadron, strayed a little further north, caught an Albatros over Thourout and shot it down for his first victory of an eventual twelve, killing *Vzfw* Hermann Denkhaus of *Jasta 7*.

After shooting down his Albatros, Kennedy-Cochrane-Patrick, 2Lts G I D Marks and D U McGregor attacked an enemy two-seater, described as 'small', and drove it down, McGregor following it down and firing into it until it crashed. This victory was shared between the three pilots.

After the frustration of the previous two days, which had brought combats but no decisive victories, Naval 10 had a better day. The whole squadron flew patrols in the morning. Collishaw, newly promoted to acting Flight Commander, led B Flight – Reid, Alexander and FitzGibbon – off the ground at 10.30am. The triplanes were six miles northeast of Armentières when they saw half a dozen FEs of 20 Squadron under attack by over 30 German fighters. The initial attack on the FEs had been by eight Albatros scouts of *Jasta 11*, led by Manfred von Richthofen, but these had quickly been joined by other

jagdstaffeln, eager to get into the fight. The FE crews had formed their usual defensive circle and 'were putting up a tremendous show … their gunners blazing away at their attackers, driving them off each time they tried to break up the defensive formation.' The fight was 8,000 feet below the triplanes and after a 'quick look around' they went down into the fight.

As the opposing forces met they disintegrated into what Collishaw described as 'a wild dogfight.' Pilots were jockeying for position, trying to get their sights onto an opponent for a short burst, only having to immediately take evasive action on being attacked themselves. 'You might get in a good shot and see the hostile fighter fall off on one wing and go down but you would not be able to follow up your attack for a pair of his fellows would be on your tail. You might see, out of the corner of your eye, an enemy machine going down, hopelessly out of control, but you would perhaps have little time to determine which member of your flight had been responsible. Much of this sort of information came to light only after returning to base and listening to the accounts of other members of your flight.'

Collishaw got in several good bursts at enemy fighters, sending six down, seemingly out of control: 'but whether they recovered or not I have no idea for on not a single occasion did I have a chance to follow up to see if my victim kept on falling.'

Alexander and FitzGibbon took an Albatros off their flight commander's tail, Alexander closing to within 75 yards before firing 25 rounds into it, watching his tracers going into the enemy pilot's back and his machine going down out of control. Collishaw thought he saw this Albatros crash, but there were no *Jasta* losses.

The crews of the FEs gave a good account of themselves, sending down six enemy fighters. One of these was Manfred von Richthofen, who had been hit in the head. Richthofen was completely paralysed, the grazing bullet had affected his optic nerve, completely blinding him. As his body began to recover from shock, and his sight began to return, Richthofen managed to switch off his engine and land his Albatros. The German ace would not return to his command until July 25.[5]

Despite the fierceness of the fight and the odds against them the FEs lost only one machine, which was badly damaged and forced to land, the observer later dying of his wounds.

The airfighting continued in intensity on July 7. Crowe of 56 Squadron took out his Flight at 4.35am to patrol a line ten miles east of Ypres to the coast. A formation of silver Albatros D IIIs was seen over Staden and Rhys Davids, flying one of the new higher-powered 200hp SE5s, flew under them as bait. It was taken. As the Albatri dived on the lone SE the rest of the Flight went down on to them and 'furious fighting took place.' There were no decisive results from this action, the SE pilots experiencing a number of gun stoppages and the Albatri cleared east. The SEs then individually made for the agreed rendezvous over Ypres. Crowe and Rhys Davids, the first to arrive, found a group of four enemy two-seaters over the town. Once again gun stoppages robbed the British pilots of a result. On his way back to the lines Rhys Davids had a fight with two Albatri. Using only his Lewis gun – his Vickers was out of action with a broken pipe of its Constantinesco gear – he drove one down, leaving it diving away to the east. He was then attacked by the other, but his Lewis had now also stopped and he broke off the action and returned.

Capt Bowman took out the second patrol of the day from the squadron. While the Flight was fighting five enemy aeroplanes just to the north of Douai, Bowman saw another formation of five enemy scouts coming down into the fight. Bowman fired a red light and made for the lines, but only Lt Maybery saw the signal and followed him. Looking back, Bowman saw that Lts D S Wilkinson and R Jardine had been caught by the arriving enemy scouts and he and Maybery turned back to their aid. Bowman and Maybery each send an Albatros down out of control and Jardine got a good burst into another with both guns. The enemy scout went down in a spinning nosedive, its engine full on.

Cecil Lewis had been wounded in the initial action. While Lewis was attacking a scout on Bowman's tail, another got on the tail of his SE, the enemy pilot firing short bursts, the sure sign of an experienced pilot. Lewis felt 'a white hot rod flicking along the round of my back.' He threw the SE into an evasive spin and returned. On landing at Estrée Blanche Lewis found a long red furrow had been seared across his back. Lewis was posted to Home Establishment six days later. The last patrol of the day by 56 Squadron engaged three black-painted two-seaters, but gun stoppages again robbed them of any result.

Out of control victories were claimed by the other fighter squadrons during the day, but at the cost of a considerable number of casualties. A pilot of 41 Squadron – the squadron were still soldiering on in their obsolescent FE8s – was shot down by groundfire while attacking a balloon and taken POW; a pilot of 66 Squadron on patrol over Arras was forced to land after a combat and injured; and two other pilots from the squadron were wounded in action. A pilot of 1 Squadron was shot in the leg and later died of his wounds. The naval squadrons suffered the worst. Naval 1 lost three triplanes: FltSubLt D W Ramsay was killed by *Ltn* Krüger of *Jasta 4*; FltSubLt K H Millward was killed by *Ltn* Wolff of *Jasta* 11 and a Flight Commander, C A Eyre, was killed either by *Vzfw* Altemeier of *Jasta 24* or *Ltn* Niederhoff of *Jasta 11*. A Sopwith Pup from Naval 9 was lost when FltSubLt J C Tanner crash landed after a combat and died of his injuries. FltSubLt L L Lindsay of

Naval 3 had a lucky escape from drowning. Intercepting a force of 22 Gothas, which was returning from bombing London, the engine of his Pup failed and he was forced to land in the sea a mile south west of Nieuport. He was picked up by a British boat.

The resourceful crews of the FEs of 20 Squadron had again been in the thick of the fighting. In the evening they were fighting eight Albatros scouts when twelve more enemy scouts joined in. The FEs claimed one Albatros down in flames and two more out of control. The enemy broke off the fight and dived away east.

There was a violent thunderstorm during the late evening, and there was little war flying for the next two days.

It rained all day on July 10. The Allied air offensive, planned to open on July 8, was still further delayed because of the bad weather. But in the midst of the Allied preparations the Germans struck first with a pre-emptive strike. A heavy bombardment opened up at 5.30am on the positions of the XV Corps of the British Fourth Army, lasting, with only a short break at midday, until 7.00pm, destroying all the bridges across the River Yser. A quarter of an hour after the end of the bombardment the German infantry attacked and by noon the next day held positions of the eastern bank of the Yser from the coast to Nieuport. Only on the extreme right had the British line held. British casualties were heavy: in two days 3,000 men and 126 officers were lost.

The German forces made full use of smoke screens and these, aided by the low cloud, hampered the work of the RFC. The *jagdstaffeln* and *schutzstaffeln* made a considerable number of low level attacks on troops and artillery; British counter-battery work was made almost impossible by the enemy's use of smoke pots placed around their guns, starting a smoke screen around their positions whenever a British observation aeroplane appeared.

The adverse conditions cleared a little in the evening, the rain ceased, and there was some war flying. Major Scott, commanding officer of 60 Squadron, who had returned from leave three days before with the unwelcome news that he was to be promoted to the command of a Wing, was determined to get in as much flying as he could in his few remaining weeks in command of the squadron. Shortly before 8pm the klaxon horn went off at Filescamp Farm: British troops near Monchy-le-Preux were being attacked by twelve enemy aeroplanes. Some of the 60 Squadron pilots were playing tennis, but Soden, Bishop, Major Scott, and several others, rushed to their Nieuports and took off. Arriving over the area they found the enemy aeroplanes were at 1,000 feet, about to return to their base, and the Nieuports went down to attack them.

Bishop found himself sandwiched between two hostile aeroplanes, both shooting at him. Scott saw Bishop was in trouble, turned towards the nearest enemy and shot it down in flames. Bishop then turned on the other hostile and sent it down out of the fight. On returning to Filescamp Farm, Bishop looked for Scott to thank him for extricating him from a very dangerous position, only to find that Scott had returned at 8.35am after only thirty-five minutes in the air. Scott had been wounded in the action and his Nieuport so badly damaged that he had difficulty in returning to the aerodrome. Scott was taken from his shattered cockpit by his mechanics, blood running down the sleeve of his tunic, and rushed to hospital. He was not to return to 60 Squadron, taking command of 11 Wing on his recovery.

The Camels of Naval 4 were in action with four enemy scouts over Pervyse and FltSubLt E W Busby was shot down and killed over Ramscapelle, possibly by *Vzfw* Strasser of *Jasta 17.*

It was fine and sunny on July 11, although there were scattered clouds and it was misty at ground level. The Allied air offensive, which was to have started on July 8 but had been delayed by the bad weather, was finally begun and there was a great deal of airfighting.

Thirty-two Squadron, at long last re-equipped with the DH5 to replace their outclassed DH2s, were first in action. Unfortunately 2Lt K G Cruickshank joined a formation of Albatri from *Jasta 18,* thinking they were friendly scouts, and was shot down in flames by *Ltn* Runge of the *Jasta.* Forty minutes later, in a combat with Albatros scouts over Hooge, Lt St C C Tayler scored the squadron's first victory flying the DH5, claiming an Albatros out of control. This Albatros was probably that flown by *Oblt* Kurt Wolff, the *Staffelführer* of *Jasta 11,* who was wounded in the hand on the morning of July 11 and did not return to his command until September 11.

Sixty-six Squadron were in action in the morning, Capt John Andrews shooting down an Albatros two-seater over Henin Lietard for the last of his twelve victories. Andrews closed to within 75 yards and opened fire at point blank range. The observer collapsed over the side of the fuselage and the Albatros went down. This Albatros was possibly from *Fl Abt (A)235.* The enemy pilot *Uffz* Marczinski managed to land but his observer, *Ltn* Fischer was wounded.[6]

Capt Phillip Prothero led A Flight of 56 Squadron in its second patrol of the day at 6.05pm. A large formation of enemy machines – scouts and two-seaters – was seen over Houthulst Forest at 12,000 feet. The SE5s – Prothero, Maxwell, Broadberry Lewis and J S Turnbull – finally caught this formation over Staden. Prothero claimed a scout out of control from the fight. Broadberry sent an enemy scout sent down with dense smoke pouring out of its engine, and one of the two-seaters down in a spin. Turnbull's fire sent one of the two-

seaters down in a series of sideslips that developed into a vertical dive.

In the evening Naval 10 were in action with Albatros scouts and lost FltSubLt Raymond Kent, who was shot down and taken POW by *Ltn* Mohnicke of *Jasta 11* for his third victory. Fullard and C S Lavers, of 1 Squadron were also in action during the evening. They attacked a formation of Albatros scouts over the Comines area and each shot down an Albatros out of control. Fifteen minutes later Fullard claimed another over Verlinghem.

Pilots of 54, 23, 32 Squadrons and Naval 10 all claimed victories during the day.

July 12 was fine and saw the heaviest airfighting of the war to date. The fighting was continuous throughout the day, encompassing the entire front, but was particularly intense over the Fifth Army front. The fighter squadrons lost four pilots killed in action, another four wounded, two taken prisoner of war and four forced to land. Additional casualties in the Army and Corps squadrons were four killed, two wounded and four POW.

The naval squadrons were out early. Naval 1 fought seven Albatri at 9.10am over Quesnoy and FltSubLt R P Minfie sent one down. Naval 10 were also in action in the morning, over Polygon Wood. The triplanes went down to attack three Albatros scouts and Collishaw hit the pilot in one red-painted Albatros, who slumped over his controls as his machine went into a spin. Additional enemy scouts now appeared and the naval pilots were soon fighting up to 30 enemy machines. Collishaw saw that most of the Albatri were predominately red in colour – probably from *Jasta 11* – and that others were green and a mottled brown and yellow. FltSubLt Ellis Reid shot the port wings off an Albatros and sent another down out of control, which Collishaw saw crash on a house near Veldhoek. Collishaw then came under attack by six Albatri 'the pilots of which seemed determined to do away with me.' He extricated himself only 'after a good deal of difficulty' and recrossed the British lines. FltSubLt Charles Peger was lost in this fight, shot down by *Ltn* W Güttler of *Jasta 24.*

Naval 10 were out again a little later and John Sharman, who had claimed an Albatros out of control in the earlier fight, which was not allowed, claimed a second at 12.15pm over Polygon Wood. During this patrol FltSubLt John Allan was wounded in the leg by anti-aircraft fire and forced to land.

Just after 8.00am Capt Tom Hazell led a large formation of twelve Nieuports of 1 Squadron over the lines. In the space of the next thirty minutes they were in almost continuous combat with three different formations of enemy scouts. At 8.30am they attacked a group of ten and Hazell and 2Lt Roger Money-Kyrle attacked a scout with a black fuselage circled with yellow bands. Both the Nieuport pilots closed to very close range before firing and the Albatros went down, rolling over and over. Money-Kyrle had been wounded in the leg during the fight, the bullet breaking his shinbone, and crashed on landing back at Bailleul.

Just before 10.00am, over Polygon Wood, six DH5s of 32 Squadron were fighting 20 enemy scouts. Despite the heavy odds all the deHavilands returned safely and claimed two victories: 2Lt Stephen Walter had shot the wings off one Albatros[7] and Lt St Cyprian Tayler claimed another as out of control. Later in the day, at 12.25pm, Capt Arthur Coningham of the squadron destroyed an Albatros over Gheluvelt

Seven Nieuports of 29 Squadron fought with ten Albatros scouts over Zonnebeke at 10.20am. Capt Jones-Williams drove one down, but two Nieuports were lost in the fight: 2Lt H H Whytehead and 2Lt J W Fleming, both killed. The Nieuports were claimed by *Oblt* Dostler and Ltn Deilmann *of Jasta 6*. Dostler was to claim another 29 Squadron pilot later in the day, shooting down 2Lt H M Lewis to be taken POW at 7.45pm over the Zonnebeke to Roulers area.

Just after noon Captain Noel Webb of 70 Squadron was flying a practice flight in one of the Squadron's newly issued Sopwith Camels. An enemy two-seater, 17,000 feet over Bellevue, was pointed out to him by British anti-aircraft fire. Webb quickly climbed to the height of the enemy machine and his first burst hit the observer. Webb then forced the two-seater – an Albatros CX from *Fl Abt 18* – to force land on Bellevue aerodrome, where it turned over onto its back. The observer, *Ltn* Johannes Wollenhaupt, was unhurt and taken prisoner, but his pilot, *Ltn d R* Hans Böhm had been wounded and died of his wounds the next day. The Albatros. No.9289/16 was designated as G51.

Mannock of 40 Squadron was on patrol over the lines when he saw two enemy two-seaters over Avion. Mannock attacked one, a DFW, and his first shots killed the pilot and wounded the observer. The DFW went down and crashed in the British lines just south of Avion. Mannock landed at Bruay and went with a tender to the scene of the crash. He later wrote to a friend. 'I shot the pilot in three places and wounded the observer in the side. The machine was smashed to pieces and a little black and white dog which was with the observer (a Captain) was also killed. The observer escaped death, although the machine fell about nine thousand feet. The pilot was horribly mutilated.' Mannock felt physically ill at the sight of his work. That evening he confided his feelings to William MacLanachan, his particular friend in the Squadron MacLanachan replied that he would never like to see the smashed up body of a man he had killed. 'Neither would I,' Mannock replied 'It sickened me, but I wanted to see where

my shots had gone. Do you know, there were three neat little bullet holes right here,' Mannock pointed to the side of his head. The reason that he had gone to the crash site, Mannock explained, was that he had fired so often at enemy machines without result that he had begun to wonder if he was seeing the target correctly. 'No matter how much nausea it caused I *had* to find out – and this one down on our side was my only chance.' The DFW was from *Schusta 12*, crewed by *Vzfw* Reubelt (killed) and *Vzfw* Hermann Johann Böttcher. Two hours later, over Brebieres, MacLanachan sent another two-seater down out of control.

In the afternoon the fighting continued with no let up in intensity. Bishop of 60 Squadron attempted to intercept a high flying Aviatik, but at the enemy machine's height of 19,500feet over Vitry, his Nieuport stalled and 'fell out of the sky.' – not surprisingly, its service ceiling was 17,500 feet. Bishop had more success later when he fought a green and yellow Albatros and sent it down to crash near Vitry. He was then attacked by another enemy scout, but this was taken off his tail by Robert Little of Naval 8. Little was flying a lone patrol on a Sopwith Camel (N6378) and had met up with a Nieuport west of Douai. Seeing a fight in progress between Nieuports of 60 Squadron and six Albatros scouts in the area of Vitry, he and the Nieuport pilot hurried into the action. During the fighting Little saw Bishop's green and yellow Albatros crash near Vitry, took another Albatros off Bishop's tail, and he and the Canadian then attacked another enemy machine. After their first attacks the German pilot waved what they took to be a white handkerchief and they broke off the action. The German pilot then turned and dived away east. Little followed and fired a burst that he considered probably wounded the enemy pilot, but the Albatros dived to ground level and escaped across its own lines. Little then attacked another Albatros that was confirmed as having gone down out of control by Bishop and other pilots of 60 Squadron.[8]

Frank Soden had sent one of the Albatri down but was then attacked by a black Albatros whose fire badly so damaged his Nieuport that it was later struck off squadron strength.

Fifty-six Squadron had a very successful afternoon's fighting. B Flight left Estrée Blanche at 1.30pm and first attacked a pair of two-seaters over Roulers. Although robbed of an almost certain victory by gun jams, the machine attacked by Leonard Barlow was seen to go down as if hit in the engine. After this action – which included an enemy scout – Rhys Davids saw five enemy scouts, which he described as 'new type scouts … climb not very remarkable, but speed fairly good. Very small black crosses, square ended top plane.' These were flying west from Menin at 11,000 feet. Rhys Davids waited until they were over the lines before attacking, closing to 30 yards behind a green scout. The enemy pilot had failed to see the SE5 and a burst from both guns sent him down out of control over Roncq.

Rhys Davids then attacked a DFW C.V from *Fl Abt 7,* crewed by *Ltn* Eugen Mann and *Uffz* Albert Hahnel. Under Rhys Davids' fire Hahnet put his machine into a steep dive before flattening out over Ploegsteert Wood. As Rhys Davids followed the DFW down an enemy scout got on his tail, but this was attacked by Ian Henderson who sent it down over Zanvoorde. Rhys Davids, unaware of his narrow escape, followed the DFW down to 1,500 feet but had to break of the action with a badly running engine – it had probably lost pressure in the dive. Hahnel saw his chance, turned, flew southwest towards Ploegsteert, then turned east for the safety of his own lines. Unfortunately for Hahnel, Keith Muspratt of 56 Squadron then arrived and three times frustrated Hahnel's attempts to regain the German lines. *Ltn* Mann fired a few shots at Muspratt, but Hahnel gave up his attempt to regain the safety of the German trenches and put the DFW down near Armentières. It bounced once before crashing into a small pond. Hahnel and Mann were taken prisoner and their DFW No.799/17 given the number G 53.

The second patrol of the day by 56 Squadron, A Flight, left Estrée Blanche at 6.00pm. At 14,000 feet over Menin they were jumped by 15 Albatros scouts of *Jasta 6*. In their first pass the German pilots shot down Capt Broadberry, J S Turnbull and hit the engine of Lt Messervy's SE5. Messervy attempted to land near Poperinghe but the SE hit a barbed wire fence and overturned. John Turnbull, hit in both legs, force landed at Le Becque and was taken to a casualty clearing station.

Edric Broadberry, flying at the rear of the formation, was the first to be hit. 'There was suddenly a burst of machine gun bullets, which riddled my aircraft. The instrument panel in the cockpit was hit, there was a sharp burning pain in the calf of my right leg, the engine began to splutter and then completely petered out.' Looking back, Broadberry saw more enemy aircraft diving on the patrol. Realising that it was impossible for him to take any part in a fight, Broadberry put the SE into a vertical dive until he was within 2,000 feet from the ground, hoping that the enemy pilots would not follow him down. 'During the dive I found that a quantity of petrol was blown onto my clothing, presumably from the punctured pressurised main fuel tank as the pressure gauge registered zero. I therefore switched off the ignition to avoid the possibility of bursting into flames. When pulling out of the dive, at about 2,000 feet, I realised that I was about ten or twelve miles over the enemy side of the lines, and that I had not enough height to glide to our side, so I switched over to the gravity fuel tank which was housed in the centre section of the top plane and

switched on the ignition again. To my great relief the engine picked up and I was able to cross the lines on our side and managed to make a normal landing at Bailleul aerodrome.'[9] Inspection of the SE5 showed that one of the main spars of the port lower wing had been shot through, an aileron control cable had been severed and the main fuel tank had been holed, causing the engine to fail through lack of pressure. That the SE5 had withstood the stresses of the vertical dive by Broadberry is evidence of the great structural strength of the SE5.

Broadberry went into the Mess at Bailleul, where his leg 'started to hurt.' Taking off his flying boot he found it full of blood. He was given an anti-tetanus shot and taken to an Advanced Dressing Station. He was later taken to hospital at St Omer where found John Turnbull. Both were returned to England. Broadberry was one of 56 Squadron's most promising pilots; with the exception of the Canadian, Reginald Hoidge, he was scoring quicker and more often than anyone in the Squadron. Broadberry was the sixteenth victory of *Oblt* Eduard von Dostler, the *Staffelführer* of *Jasta 6* who had led the Albatri in the attack.[10]

The last patrol of the day flown by 56 Squadron took off at 7.00pm. An hour after taking off they were joined by a formation of Sopwith Pups from 66 Squadron, a number of Nieuports and some French Spads. Bowman fired a red light and took the allied force down to attack a formation of 25 enemy scouts that he had been watching for sometime. Bowman later recorded. 'A general fight ensued. The EA appeared to be flown by some remarkably good pilots and some remarkably bad pilots.'

Bowman sent one Albatros down east of Polygon Wood, following it down for 6,000 feet until two other enemy machines began to dive on him. Bowman dispersed these with bursts from his Lewis gun. A yellow Albatros and Hoidge flew head on towards each other. Hoidge commenced firing at 25 yards. A puff of smoke came out of the engine of the Albatros, its nose dropped and Hoidge zoomed over it. Hoidge then fought another Albatros, this one coloured black and white, which he drove down out of control into the mist over Menin. Richard Maybery attacked a scout that was fighting a Sopwith Pup. The enemy pilot spun away from Maybery's fire before flattening out at lower level. Maybery attacked him again, aided by a French Spad, but both were forced to break off the attack by other enemy scouts. Maybery avoided these and watched the scout going down in a slow left hand spiral. This was possibly *Ltn* Edwin Kreuzer of *Jasta 36*, who force landed, crashing his Albatros. *Vzfw* Maier of the *Jasta* was wounded in the fight, possibly the pilot of the yellow scout sent down by Hoidge.

This fight was the largest of the day in terms of aircraft involved, some 60 machines in all. Despite the numbers of aircraft involved, and the fierceness of the fighting, losses on both sides during the day were relatively low, an indication of how evenly matched were the fighter pilots of the antagonists. When equal numbers of fighters were in combat the results were more often than not indecisive.

July 13 was a fine but cloudy day. There was only a slight let up in the intensity of the fighting, but casualties among the fighter squadrons were fewer: one pilot killed and three taken prisoner of war.

Mannock of 40 squadron was one of the first pilots in action, adding to his success of the previous day by shooting down another DFW C type, this time over Sallaumines. An hour after this combat Mannock tackled another two-seater: 'but I held my fire a fraction too long, with the result that I had to bank away to prevent collision. Turned again and fired forty or fifty rounds into him, and he steered straight for Douai in a dead line. Probably wounded or the engine hit. I did feel mad.'

Naval 8 were in the process of exchanging their Sopwith Triplanes for Sopwith Camels, and FltLts P A Johnston and W L Jordan were flying two of the new Camels when they attacked an enemy two-seater during a morning patrol. Johnston sent this down for his fourth victory. An hour later Jordan shot down a Rumpler out of control east of Lens for the first of his eventual 37 victories, the two-seater falling onto a house near Montigny. Their fellow pilots in Naval 8, Robert Little and Reggie Soar also had a successful morning flying Camels. At 10.15am they caught an enemy two-seater over Lens and shot it down, sharing the victory. An hour and a quarter later Little shot down an Albatros over Croiselles for his 31st victory.

Pilots of 1 Squadron were also in action early. At 8.45am Capt Louis Jenkin shot down a DFW over Houthem for his fifteenth victory. This was possibly *Ltn* Peter von Ustinow and *Vzfw* Georg Fick of *Fl Abt (A)250* both killed in action over Hollebeke.

Twenty-nine Squadron tangled with *Jasta 6* again. A morning patrol were in combat at 9.50am over Gheluvelt and lost Lt A W B Miller (killed) and Lt F W Winterbottham taken prisoner. *Oblt* Dostler, *Ltn* Deilmann and *Ltn* Adam all claimed victories over the Nieuports.

Capt Kennedy-Cochran-Patrick had a narrow escape in the morning. While diving to attack an enemy machine there was a 'loud report' and the covering of the top wing of the Spad came away. Kennedy-Cochran-Patrick, considerably shaken, nevertheless managed to land near Ypres.

Major Sanday was watching three RE8s carrying out a photo-reconnaissance over Messines when he saw a high flying enemy Rumpler at 21,000 feet over Lille. Sanday managed to get up to the height of the enemy two-seater, which had not seen him and had come down to 18,000 feet. Sanday hit the crew with his fire and the Rumpler went down to crash.

In the evening Fullard led a large formation from 1 Squadron in the last squadron patrol of the day and they attacked a formation of six enemy scouts over Wervicq. Fullard fired half a drum at one scout, which went down smoking, but was then attacked by its companions. At this critical juncture his engine failed and he dived west. Luckily the enemy scouts did not follow him and Fullard was able to stretch his glide to land behind the British front line. The ground was pitted with a large number of shell holes and the Nieuport turned over into one on landing, leaving Fullard suspended above the filthy water. Nearby troops lost no time in looting both his automatic pistol and the aeroplane watch. 2Lt W C Smith had been wounded in the fight, shot down and taken prisoner.

Ian Henderson took B Flight of 56 Squadron out at 7.00pm. Two earlier patrols by the squadron had seen no action, but this patrol saw a great deal. Henderson took the Flight across the lines at 12,500 feet and over 20 enemy aeroplanes could be seen, 'stretching from the sea to Lille.' Henderson and Arthur Rhys Davids, flying newly issued 200hp SE5as, were flying above the rest of the patrol and Henderson attacked an enemy scout over Moorslede, opening fire at a 100 yards range. This scout went down in a cloud of smoke. Henderson then drove another down for 2,000 feet before he was attacked by five others and forced to dive west, outdistancing the enemy scouts by virtue of his superior speed. Henderson then regained his height and rejoined Rhys Davids who was fighting alone with eight Albatri. The two SE pilots drove one of these scouts down and the others retreated east. Henderson and Rhys Davids then attacked 11 enemy machines over Iseghem, but the fighting was hotly contested and Henderson was forced to spin away out of trouble. Coming out of his spin, Henderson found that an enemy pilot was still on his tail. Despite his taking violent evasive action, the German pilot stuck closely to Henderson, firing all the time. Luckily for Henderson the enemy pilot's marksmanship did not match his flying ability. Rhys Davids now appeared and shot at the persistent enemy pilot who side slipped away from Rhys Davids' fire, almost colliding with Henderson.

The remainder of the Flight had no positive success. Barlow dived on two Albatri which were attacking an FE and one went down out of control over Moorslede with smoke pouring from its engine. Barlow was then attacked by its companion but he outmanoeuvred it and fired at it with both guns. The Albatros turned over onto its back and went down in a flat spin. Barlow failed to see either of these machines crash as the light was now very bad.

During the day 70 Squadron lost three Sopwith 1 1/2 Stutters in combat with *Jasta 6*. One crew managed to force land their aeroplane – which had also been damaged by anti-aircraft fire – but one crew was killed and the other taken POW. These were the last casualties of the squadron while flying the Sopwith two-seater as they were re-equipped with Sopwith Camels by the end of the month, the first RFC Squadron to be so.

July 14 was cloudy with a very strong northwest wind. The activity in the air slackened off considerably, no doubt due to the weather, and the fighter squadrons lost only one pilot killed and another POW.

Early in the morning 40 Squadron were in action with four green Albatros scouts of *Jasta 29* east of Douai and lost Lt G Davis, shot down and taken POW by *Ltn* Erwin Böhme.

The Nieuport of Lt C S Lavers of 1 Squadron was a badly shot up in a combat, forcing him to crash land, and Lt S R P Walter of 32 Squadron had his fuel tank shot through and crash landed in a shell hole. The last casualty of the day was Lt W G Thompson of 41 Squadron who was shot down in flames north of Boursies by *Vzfw* Oefele of *Jasta 12* for his first victory.

Edward Crundall, who had been wounded on May 10, had rejoined Naval 8 at St Mont St Eloi aerodrome the previous day. Squadron Commander Bromet gave Crundall and Soar permission to fly to Auchel, where the squadron had once been based, to renew acquaintances with French lady friends in nearby Lozinghem. The girls were pleased to see them again, but Soar rather unkindly told them that Crundall had been wounded in the bottom, 'so they were inclined to smile at me and look away.' Crundall gives a vivid picture of how the fighter pilots relaxed during the heavy fighting in July 1917.

'As there is no flying this morning the pilots are amusing themselves in various ways. Johnson is flying a model aeroplane, which he built, and it goes quite a long way. Little made a submarine out of a piece of wood, to which he fitted metal fins. It is propelled by elastic and he is demonstrating it in the swimming pool… There are long intervals with nothing to do. This can become very boring unless there is something to occupy the mind. So I am setting myself the task of making a model Triplane. Booker has given me permission to do this in C Flight workshop lorry. My model will be made of thin sheet brass, to the scale of half an inch to the foot.

In the evening it was decided we needed something to drink so a supply of champagne was obtained from somewhere in the neighbourhood. The piano was played, songs were sung, and it developed into a merry evening. Quite a number had rather too much to drink and it affected them in various ways. Little was running around with the squadron dog, Titch, which went under the floorboards after a rat, and Little followed it there. Jordan was marching up and down the room in deep thought. He imagined he was "a naval captain of considerable authority" and was entitled to a specified part of the ship's deck while in port. He became quietly annoyed when anyone got in his way. "My man" he said, "Don't you realise who I am?", and then continued quietly on his way.

Jenner-Parson had crouched in the corner of the room. Suddenly a wild expression came into his eyes as he saw Thornley sitting on the window ledge peacefully smoking his pipe. He jumped into the air, dashed across the room, and butted Thornley through the open window. It all happened so suddenly. There was a surprised look on Thornley's face as he saw Jenner rushing towards him, and the next instant Thornley did a backwards somersault though the window. After that the party got very rough and one after the other were thrown into the swimming pool.'[11]

July 15 was a day of low clouds and rain. The squadrons of Ninth Wing did no flying at all, but the Corps squadrons were in action artillery spotting over the trenches and 60 Squadron and Naval 10 fought combats during the evening when the weather had improved a little.

Five Nieuports of 60 Squadron, led by Keith 'Grid' Caldwell, were patrolling over Douai when they sighted a formation of eight Albatri. These were from *Jasta 12*, flying in a 'stepped down vee formation' and supported by four white-tailed Albatri from *Jasta 30*. Caldwell had seen a number of Sopwith Pups – possibly from 54 Squadron – in the distance and he waited to see if they had seen the enemy scouts before he took the Nieuports down, but the Pup pilots flew straight on. Before Caldwell could make a decision whether or not to attack the Albatri, 2Lt G A H Parkes, contrary to orders, went down and attacked the rearmost of them. Parkes was to pay dearly for this. The Albatros he attacked flew under its companions, with Parkes following, and the leader of the formation, *Oblt* Adolf Ritter von Tutschek, the *Staffelführer* of *Jasta 12*, hit the Nieuport in the fuel tank, flying controls and dashboard instruments, and wounded Parkes in his left arm. Parkes turned west, in an attempt to reach the safety of the British lines, but there was a strong headwind and Tutschek – unimpeded by any of the 60 Squadron pilots who were now fully engaged with the other Albatri – attacked again, heading him off. Parkes landed on a disused aerodrome a mile to the west of Douai and attempted to set fire to his Nieuport, but Tutschek flew round the aeroplane, firing his guns, until troops arrived and took Parkes prisoner.[12]

In the fight with the other Albatri, one was driven down and seen to crash near Vitry at 7.50pm by British troops. Twenty-five minutes after the fight, on their way back to base, Caldwell, Sherwood and Jenkins fired at an Albatros D III which forced landed at Mouvres.[13/14]

The Camels of Naval 8 were also in action during the evening. The redoubtable Robert Little attacked six enemy scouts over Lens and shot one down out of control. FltSubLt E A Bennetts claimed to have shot down one of the enemy formation in flames, but the *jagdstaffeln* reported no such loss and it is possible that it was his fellow squadron pilot FltSublt F Bray that Bennetts saw going down in flames from the fight. Bray was claimed by *Oblt* Hans Bethge, the *Staffelführer* of *Jasta 30* for his ninth victory.

Lieutenant C S Lavers of 1 Squadron was forced to land for the second successive day when his fuel tank was holed during a combat over Menin. Lavers was unhurt.

The weather returned fine on July 16 and the airfighting resumed with increased intensity. At 8.30am Little caught two Aviatiks over Gavrelle and sent one down out of control, but the claim was not allowed. The Sopwith 1 1/2 Stutters of 45 Squadron were in action with hostile scouts at 9.30am over Polygon Wood and sent one down out of control and another in flames. The Squadron was to be re-equipped with Sopwith Camels during the last weeks of the month.

A morning patrol by 1 Squadron were in action south of Poelcappele with Albatros scouts at 7.30am and Sgt Gordon Olley was awarded one as destroyed.

In the evening an enemy scout was reported to be attacking balloons and David Langlands of 23 Squadron attacked it, forcing it to fly further west into British territory. The enemy pilot, *Vzfw* Ernst Clausnitzer of *Jasta 4* eventually gave in and landed south east of Poperinghe to be taken prisoner. His machine, an Albatros D.V (1162/17) was designated G56.

An evening patrol by 1 Squadron fought with eight Albatros scouts over Becelaere. Capt W Campbell tackled the leader of the enemy formation and shot it down, claiming two Albatri destroyed and one out of control from the fighting in the space of twenty minutes.

There was a large fight in the evening over Roulers. Bowman of 56 Squadron first attacked a hostile scout over the town, but then saw a formation of 15 Albatri coming from the north, with a height advantage of 2,000 feet over the SEs. Outnumbered, and at a tactical disadvantage, Bowman turned his force – Maybery, Wilkinson and Jardine – back to the Lines, but a strong westerly wind impeded the SEs. The enemy scouts were now joined by an additional six or seven others, and a fight became unavoidable. Bowman turned the SEs to meet the attack, firing a red Very Light to attract the attention of some Spads of 19 Squadron flying nearby. As the red flare died away the entire enemy force dived on the four SEs, forcing them down 10,000 feet – 14,000 feet to 4,000 feet – through sheer weight of numbers.

The enemy pilots employed dive and zoom tactics, avoiding any close range fighting, but Bowman, using the superior zoom of the SE5, several times got on to the tails of the enemy pilots as they turned away after their dives. Getting a good position on the tail of one, Bowman fired a long burst from both guns and the Albatros went down to crash at the eastern end of the peacetime racecourse in Polygon Wood. *Vzfw* Fritz Krebs of *Jasta 6* was killed.

Richard Maybery had gun stoppages, but he managed to clear these and following Bowman's example he too managed to get on the tails of several of the Albatri, closing to within 15 yards of one. The enemy pilot slumped forward in his seat under Maybery's fire and the Albatros went down in a vertical dive. Three more of the enemy scouts then drove Maybery down to 3,000 feet but he managed to shake them off, rejoin Bowman, and cross the Lines.

Robert Jardine had spun away from the first attack. Regaining his height he turned to meet the next attacks but had a gun stoppage in his Vickers gun. He spun away again, corrected the stoppage and climbed back into the fight. He attacked an Albatros head on and opened fire from fifty yards. The Albatros went down but the pilot recovered at 1,500 feet and flew east. Jardine chased after him, firing all the time and the Albatros went down and flew into the ground.[15] Jardine's SE had been hit in the oil tank by the return fire from the Albatros, the engine seized solid, and Jardine force landed at Dranoutre in a field of wheat. The SE5 turned completely over and the fuselage broke in two just behind the cockpit. Jardine was unhurt.

This combat had developed into a large-scale fight. While fighting the enemy scouts, Bowman's Flight was joined by C Flight, led by Henderson, some Spads of 23 Squadron and Sopwith Pups of 66 Squadron. With the exception of Jardine all the SEs returned safely to Estrée Blanche.

The first casualty for the fighter squadrons the next morning was 2Lt C T Felton of 54 Squadron. In a fight with *Jasta 17* at 6.30am, Felton was wounded, went down in a steep glide and crashed in Middelkerke Lake to be taken prisoner. Shortly after noon, 29 Squadron were in combat with Albatros scouts from *Jasta 8* in the area of Ypres and Lt P E Palmer was shot down and killed by *Ltn* Göttsch of the *Jasta*.

The last casualties of the day were two pilots of 70 Squadron flying their newly issued Sopwith Camels. In a large scale fight with between 25 to 30 Albatri in the Menin-Iseghem-Menin area, Lt W E Grossett was shot down and taken prisoner and Lt C S Workman crashed behind the British lines, seriously wounded, later dying in hospital. The Camels had initiated this action and had been joined by SE5s from 56 Squadron, DH5s from 32 Squadron, FEs from 20 Squadron and two formations of triplanes from Naval 1 and 10 Squadrons. The pilots of B Flight, 56 Squadron, were awarded an Albatros out of control from the action – the enemy machine had been fired at by so many of the Flight that it was impossible to award the victory to an individual pilot – and Capt Noel Webb of 70 Squadron wounded *Ltn* Karl Meyer of *Jasta 11* who crash landed his Albatros. Two additional Albatri were claimed as out of control by Lt E Gribben and 2Lt J C Smith of 70 Squadron.

Low clouds and rain brought a welcome respite on July 18; these conditions continued the next day, but July 20 saw a return of the fine weather and the day was fine and clear.

Two Flights of Naval 10, ten triplanes led by Collishaw and John Sharman, were in action just after 8.00am in the Menin area with over 20 enemy scouts, most of them described by Collishaw as being the older type of Albatros. Collishaw saw one enemy machine, fired at by Alexander, burst into flames – 'there was no question at all about its having been destroyed.' Collishaw and Reid each claimed an enemy machine sent down out of control during the fight.

A little later in the morning, at 8.30am, FltCom Charles Booker of Naval 8 caught a Rumpler two-seater that was attacking British artillery spotting machines and shot it down out of control over Thelus for his 19th victory.

After lunch Bishop of 60 Squadron scored his last victory when flying a Nieuport – the squadron was re-equipping with SE5s – when he claimed an Albatros out of control south east of Havrincourt.

The pilots of 56 Squadron saw a great deal of action during the evening patrols. C and A Flights took off just before 7.00pm and made for the area of Roulers. Both Flights saw three Albatros scouts over Westroosbeke and pushed them east of the lines until Bowman, commanding C Flight, gave up the chase. Maxwell of A Flight, flying a speedier 200hp SE5a, continued the pursuit, caught up with the enemy formation over Poelcapelle and fired ninety rounds into the rearmost Albatros, which stalled, sideslipped and went down. Three black and white Albatri then attacked Maxwell but he managed to shake them off, get on the tail of one, and send it down out of control. These two victories were confirmed by Eric Turnbull and Richard Maybery. Maxwell later attacked a two-seater but had trouble with both his guns and engine and the enemy machine escaped east.

After its unsuccessful chase, C Flight attacked a lone enemy scout over St Julien. In view of the odds the enemy pilot hurriedly put his aeroplane down on heavily shell-holed ground a 1,000 yards behind the German trenches north east of Wieltje. The SEs reformed, climbed to 14,000 feet, and sighted a formation of 15 enemy machines to the east of Ypres. One of the enemy pilots left his formation and flew below the SE formation in an attempt to bring them down. Bowman was too old a hand to be caught by such an obvious trick. He led the SEs down as if about to attack the lone scout, but as the

other enemy machines came down he led the SEs in a zoom to meet the attack. There was a sharp engagement, but having failed to surprise the British scouts the Albatri broke off their attacks and flew east. The SEs had become separated during the fighting and returned to base where it was found that Lts Messervy and Jardine had not returned. They had both been shot down and killed: *OflgM* Schönfelder of *Jasta 7* and *Ltn* Kroll of *Jasta 24* were both awarded victories over SE5s in the area and the time in question.

Robert Little led a patrol of four Camels from Naval 8 in the evening and shot down an LVG over Lens at 6.40pm. The enemy machine went down in a spin, the tailplane crumpled up, and it crashed between the Canal de la Hte Deule and a small wood. This LVG was possibly from *Schusta 5*.

A patrol from 1 Squadron was out early the next morning. William Campbell shot down an Albatros north of Polygon Wood and ten minutes later destroyed a balloon over Wervicq. In the evening a patrol from 56 Squadron took off at 6.30pm – Capt Prothero leading Maxwell, Rhys Davids and James McCudden. McCudden was back in France flying a refresher course with 66 Squadron, which was sharing the aerodrome with 56 Squadron at Estrée Blanche, and Major Blomfield, the CO of 56 Squadron, had asked him if he would like to fly a patrol in an SE5a.

Arriving over Houthulst Forest, Prothero took the SEs down to attack some Albatros scouts. McCudden, not used to the tremendous speed built up by the SE5 in a dive, was left behind, arriving only in time to see his companions 'put the draught up some V Strutters.' Prothero forced one enemy scout east; Maxwell drove another down but was attacked by two others and was forced to break off the action with engine trouble. While attacking two Albatri, Rhys Davids came under attack from another seven. The odds were too great. Rhys Davids later succinctly commented: 'I fled.'

Rhys Davids later joined up with Barlow and Cronyn of B Flight over the Ypres area and a large scale dogfight with formations of enemy scouts and two-seaters was started by Verschoyle Cronyn diving on a large green two-seater, which he sent down in a slow spiral, one wing down. McCudden had by now rejoined the SEs and shot at a silvery grey Albatros that was about to attack Rhys Davids. The enemy scout 'turned east and wobbled laterally,' then went down in a spin, with one wing right down, for 11,000 feet. Prothero was credited with a black and white Albatros from the initial fight; Rhys Davids was credited with another of the black and white scouts and Cronyn with the two-seater, which was 56 Squadron's 100th victory.

Naval 8 were out in the evening and Little saw an Albatros diving on a Spad over Oppy. Little attacked the Albatros – which took no notice of him whatsoever – and fired 200 rounds into it at close range, sending it down in a spin. Little climbed away and the pilot of the Spad, Lt C D Thompson of 19 Squadron, waved his thanks.

The Spads, reinforced by Nieuports of 60 and 40 Squadrons, plus some naval Camels, had been in a general fight with some Albatri. Capt F Sowery of the Squadron had shot down an Albatros –the first victory for a Spad 13 of the RFC – but 2Lt J G S Candy's machine had been badly shot about, forcing him to land at 18 Squadron's aerodrome.

The Albatri from this action were from *Jasta 12,* led by *Oblt* Adolf Ritter von Tutschek, who later recorded his view of the engagement. 'It was a beautiful evening, and see here! All at once there comes a whole group of some fifteen to twenty Nieuport and Sopwith single-seaters. Over Bullecourt we meet. I attack a Nieuport and am just about to get my guns talking when a second Nieuport comes up behind me. I jerk round and get behind him. Tommy waves to me and finally I shot him down on the Bapaume to Cambrai road.'[16] Tutschek was full of praise for the flying of the Nieuport pilot. 'That fellow flew and shot excellently. I was not an iota better than he in flying. He gave me twenty hits, thank God all in wood.'[17]

July 22 was a costly day for Naval 10. Eight triplanes took off from Droglandt at 7.25am: Sharman leading Page, Weir and Trapp; Collishaw leading Alexander, Ellis and FitzGibbon. Between Menin and Ypres two formations of Albatros scouts attacked the naval triplanes. John Sharman's Flight, flying considerably higher than Collishaw's, was attacked by one hostile formation, while the other formation went down on Collishaw. During the fighting, which had drifted down to a lower level, John Sharman's triplane was seen to break up in mid-air, possibly hit by a shell – either anti aircraft or artillery – and John Page was shot down, possibly by *Ltn* Brauneck of *Jasta 11.*

Little and Booker of Naval 8 were also out early. Little shot down a two-seater over Rouvroy at 6.20am and Booker an Albatros scout at 7.35am over Quiery la Motte. Roderic Dallas of Naval 1 completed the day's tally for the naval squadrons by shooting down an Albatros two-seater over Lille at 9.30am.

Campbell of 1 Squadron, possibly infected by 'balloonitis' after his successful attack on a balloon the previous day, shot down another west of Lille at 7.30am. Philip Fullard of 1 Squadron shot down two Albatros scouts during a morning patrol, one at 11.00am, the other ten minutes later: the first out of control, the second destroyed. Tom Hazell, of the squadron, claimed a DFW over Houthem at 8.20am, and Stephen Walter of 32 Squadron also scored in the morning: an Albatros over Comines at 8.35am. The day ended with Hazell claiming two Albatros scouts destroyed in the evening: the first at 7.00pm over Wervicq, the other twenty minutes later

over Houthem, and Little claimed an Albatros scout out of control over Lens at 7.45pm for Naval 8.

Despite these successes there were casualties. In addition to those suffered by Naval 10, Capt W Young of 19 Squadron was wounded and forced to land; a Spad from 23 Squadron was also forced to land; two pilots from 32 Squadron were shot down, one of whom was killed, and a pilot from 60 Squadron was wounded in the leg. Forty Squadron suffered a heavy loss when the popular William Bond was killed; his Nieuport receiving a direct hit from an anti-aircraft shell. MacLanachan, flying on Bond's left, later wrote: 'We had reached eight thousand feet when the first shells came up, right amongst us. My machine was blown completely over, and on regaining control I saw the Bond had disappeared. Pierces of aeroplane fabric were whirling crazily in the air amidst the huge black smoke balls of the Archie bursts. Incredulous I looked around for Bond, but he had gone; all that remained in the air were the stupid, dancing remnants of his planes. Although I had been anxiously awaiting that first salvo from the deadly Archie gunner, his accuracy struck terror into me. One of the four shells, clustered only forty or fifty feet apart, had found its target in our Flight Commander's machine.' Sadly there would be no more letters to 'Dearest Aimée'. She and Bond had been married a day short of six months.

The pilots of 56 Squadron had had no decisive combats on July 22, but the next day they saw a great deal of fighting. Weather conditions were poor in the morning, with a great deal of cloud, but a patrol from the squadron took off in the evening. The *Luftstreitkräfte* was out in some strength and there were large formations of enemy machines in the sky. Bowman, leading the Flight, estimated that one formation alone contained some 20 Albatros 'V' Strutters 'of the new type' – the DV – and 'any number of groups of three or four scattered all over the sky.' The German pilots followed their usual practice of dive and zoom attacks, driving the SEs to lower level, refusing to fight at close quarters. Hoidge, driven down by several enemy scouts later wrote. 'As there were only six SEs it was quite impossible to cope with the EA present. I counted about thirty-five and there were still several formations of three or four at about 17,000 feet. They were not overly brave, because they merely dived on us and zoomed away, and did not come down to our level although they outnumbered us by five to one.'

Richard Maybery separated from the other SEs, later engaged two Albatros scouts, fighting them down to 2,000 feet over Moorslede. One landed 'apparently OK,' but Maybery saw the other crash.

During the afternoon, 60 Squadron pilots scored their last victory flying their Nieuports, when W E Molesworth, A R Penny and F Parkes attacked a balloon over Recourt, forcing the ground crew to haul it down. By the end of the month the squadron would be completely re-equipped with the SE5.

Henry Woollett of 24 Squadron, flying the unliked DH5 that had replaced the squadron's DH2s, attacked a two-seater and an Albatros scout, destroying the two-seater north east of Havrincourt at 6.45pm and the scout five minutes later over Marcoing.

July 24 was generally fine but with a very heavy ground mist. There was little enemy activity during the day. Lt A B Hill of 29 Squadron attacked a two-seater from *Fl Abt 221* east of Ypres at 6.10am, but was shot down by the crew and taken prisoner. In the evening Lt H D Tapp of 70 Squadron was killed over Moorslede, possibly by *Oblt* von Althaus of *Jasta 10*. This was 70 Squadron's second loss of the day: *Ltn* Göring had wounded Lt G Budden in the morning, forcing him to land near Bailleul. During the evening's fighting, Naval 10 lost FltSubLt T C May. May's triplane was seen to break up in mid-air, but although the triplanes had been in action with enemy scouts over the general area of Polygon Wood – May was awarded to *Ltn* Dilthey of *Jasta 27* – the Naval 10 pilots who witnessed the break-up of May's machine were positive that it was not due to enemy action.

Low clouds, thunderstorms and heavy rain curtailed flying on July 25. There was only one fighter squadron casualty: 2Lt D Langlands of 23 Squadron was hit in the foot while groundstrafing.

July 25 was to have seen the opening of the battle of Ypres, but air observation, essential to British counter-battery work, had been so effective that the enemy had moved many of his guns to the safety of his back areas. Consequently the offensive was postponed until July 28 to give the Corps squadrons of the RFC sufficient time to locate the new positions of the German guns and to enable the army to move their own guns forward.

Weather conditions on the morning of July 26 were bad, with low cloud and mist, but improved towards the evening, which was fine and clear. The intense air fighting had been gradually wearing down the resistance of the *Luftstreitkräfte* – the official history states that the enemy pilots were showing little inclination to cross the Front Lines – but the tactics of the *jagdstaffeln* were still to concentrate their available strength, to fight in considerable numbers, and on the evening of July 26, over Polygon Wood, these tactics led to the biggest airfight yet seen in the war.

The fighting began just after 7.30pm. Over a hundred aeroplanes were involved at various heights. At the lowest level, 5,000 feet, German two-seaters were attempting to carry out their vital photo-reconnaissance work, protected by thirty Albatros scouts flying at between 5 and 8,000 feet. These Albatri were in combat with the DH5s of 32 Squadron, which

were attempting to attack the two-seaters. At varying heights of between 12,000-14,000 feet, ten Albatri were fighting with the Camels of 70 Squadron, the SE5s of 56 Squadron and the Spads of 19 Squadron. Higher still, at 17,000 feet, more Albatri were in combat with Sopwith Triplanes of the Naval 10.

Prothero, Henderson and Barlow from 56 Squadron were fully engaged with the ten Albatri in the middle layer of enemy aeroplanes. In the confusion of the fighting Henderson nearly collided with a Spad and was forced to pull out of his dive, choking his engine. Barlow, after fighting several enemy scouts, zoomed away to clear a gun stoppage. As he levelled out a red-nosed machine went spinning past him, too fast for him to ascertain its type – German or British – falling to pieces, already minus its starboard wings. Sloley of 56 Squadron also saw this machine, both sets of wings now gone, spinning down past some Spads of 19 Squadron. This was an Albatros from *Jasta 11*, flown by *Ltn* Otto Brauneck, shot down by Captain Webb of 70 Squadron for his ninth victory.

Possibly because of the confused nature of the fighting, and the numbers of aeroplanes involved, there were few conclusive results. The naval pilots, although fighting a number of combats, made no claims. 2Lt J C Smith of 70 Squadron and Barlow and Maxwell of 56 Squadron were all credited with enemy aeroplanes as driven down, but Philip Prothero, 56 Squadron's B Flight Commander had been shot down and killed by *Vzfw* Alfred Muth of *Jasta 27,* his SE5 last seen going down in pieces, its starboard wings broken off.[18]

Under the cover of the furious fighting, several German two-seater crews managed to cross the British Lines and carry out a vitally important reconnaissance of the Ypres area.

July 27 was fine and very hot. It had been decided to set a trap for the large formations of enemy scouts now being met. These formations which particularly active in the evenings and were causing problems for the British squadrons. Polygon Wood was to be the scene of the trap, the bait, the FE2ds of 20 Squadron.

The FEs left the ground at 6.15pm and made for the Menin area. The intention was to patrol this area until sufficient numbers of enemy aircraft had been attracted and to then lead them towards Polygon Wood, where large numbers of British and French fighters would be waiting. The plan was successful: large numbers of enemy scouts appeared, outnumbering the FEs by three to one. 'One party of about a dozen worked round to cut us off from the Lines, while another crowd of 10 or 12 proceeded to attack us in the rear.' As the task was to decoy the enemy scouts to the waiting British and French scouts, the crews of the FEs did not adopt their usual tactics of forming a defensive circle, but fought in formation, flying towards Polygon Wood.

Over Polygon Wood the Albatri were attacked by the squadrons of Ninth Wing and Triplanes from Naval 10 – nearly 60 Allied fighters. As in the previous day, the fighting was confused and fierce. The pilots from Naval 10 were attacked by six Albatri, but after a brief fight the German pilots dived to 8,000feet, followed by the naval pilots. Nick Carter, a Flight Commander, shot down one Albatros, which turned over onto its back before going down. Collishaw, flying a twin gun Triplane, dived on three of the enemy scouts and fired into one's cockpit at close range. The Albatros shed its wings and went straight down. Ellis Reid attacked another Albatros, which also broke up in mid-air. Reid then fought several short engagements with other scouts, finally driving one down to 4,000 feet, where he got on its tail and sent it down to crash. William Alexander saw an Albatros get on the tail of the triplane flown FltSubLt Gerald Roach, and shoot it down, killing Roach, who was flying his first patrol only having joined the squadron that morning.

Ten SE5s of 56 Squadron were in both the thick of the action and on its edges. From their combat reports it seems that the squadron's pilots were distracted from the main fight over Polygon Wood by several scattered formations of enemy scouts. Ian Henderson, Gerald Maxwell and Robert Sloley saw a great deal of fighting, but all suffered gun and engine troubles and gained no victories. C Flight, led by 'Beery' Bowman, had better luck. Fighting with nine Albatri, Reginald 'Georgie' Hoidge saw one on the tail of Trevor White's SE5. Before Hoidge could go to White's aid, the German pilot, flying an Albatros with black stripes, shot White down out of control.

Hoidge then closed to within ten yards of the black striped Albatros and shot it down to fall out of control four miles north east of Roulers.

White survived the crash. In 1967 he wrote: 'being intent on getting a "Gerry" and staying with him far too long, I was jumped. I was dead lucky with only a scalp wound, but my engine caught it, with the result that I had to land in a field near Iseghem'. Despite Hoidge's claim to have shot down White's attacker, White was awarded to *Ltn* Zeigler of *Jasta 26* for his second victory.

Bowman had an extremely hazardous time. He drove down one Albatros but was then attacked by two others. His Vickers gun had jammed and the enemy pilots forced him down to 4,000 feet. Luckily Richard Maybery then arrived and took the enemy scouts off his flight commander's tail. Bowman was now down to 3,000 feet, dangerously low over enemy territory, the sky swarming with enemy fighters, and he turned west and climbed to regain his height. He was almost immediately attacked by an Albatros, which he later described: 'seemed to be red all over and very well flown.' Bowman still had only had his top wing Lewis gun working and the enemy

pilot continuously made dive and zoom attacks on the SE, forcing Bowman down to 1,000 feet.

Bowman, was now too low to see any landmarks and turned west into the eye of the setting sun. The pilot of the red Albatros continued to dive and fire at the SE, zooming at the end of each pass before turning to dive again onto the tail of the SE. Each time the enemy pilot zoomed away, Bowman took the opportunity to flew due west for the safety of the British Lines. The German pilot noticed this and changed his tactics. After his next dive he stall turned at the top of his zoom and came down for a head-on attack. Bowman saw this change of tactics and on the next attack throttled back. The enemy pilot overshot and Bowman, zooming after him, pulled down his Lewis gun and fired 50 rounds into the Albatros from a range of 20 feet, the only chance the enemy pilot had given him for a shot. The Albatros dived vertically and crashed just west of Roulers.

Almost before he could catch his breath, Bowman was then attacked by another Albatros. His Lewis gun had stopped after firing at the red scout and Bowman, hard pressed, turned again for the British Lines, turning and diving almost to ground level in an attempt to avoid this new attacker. The enemy pilot suddenly stopped firing and Bowman, who had managed to get his Vickers gun working, turned to face him. The antagonists were now so low that in turning to evade Bowman's fire the enemy pilot flew smack into a tree on the edge of Houthulst Forest. Again turning west, Bowman was then attacked by three more Albatri. Bowman had had enough. He turned again for the lines, zooming and diving to avoid their fire. Luckily the enemy pilots gave up the chase at the lines and Bowman crossed them over the Yser Canal by Het Sas at only 50 feet. Bowman's combat report of these actions ends with a masterpiece of understatement. 'I then returned to the aerodrome as it was getting late.' But in his logbook he recorded: 'Never been so frightened in my life.'

At least one of Bowman's opponents in these actions was from *Jasta 24*. The *Staffelführer* of the *Jasta, Oblt* Heinrich Kroll, was forced to land after a 'Spad' had put a burst into the engine of his Albatros and 'crashed him (Kroll) into a tree near a wood, which he took to be Houthulst.' Kroll stated that he, 'pulled up over a row of trees, under a high tension cable, took some telephone wires with me and landed in an open field.'[19]

It had been a highly successful evening's fighting for the fighter squadrons of the RFC – the main fight had lasted over an hour. Fifty-six Squadron claimed two scouts destroyed by Bowman; a scout each out of control to Maybery and Hoidge; Lt T V Hunter of 66 Squadron was awarded a scout destroyed; 70 Squadron had two driven down by Captain Clive Collett and Lt W B Kellog of 19 Squadron was credited with an out of control. Naval 10 were awarded three crashed and three out of control. The FE2ds of 20 Squadron, so often depicted as 'easy meat' for the German fighter pilots, claimed six enemy machines: two in flames, one seen to break up in mid-air and three seen to crash. The British casualties were White from 56 Squadron, taken POW; Roach from Naval 10, who was killed, and a wounded pilot and observer from 20 Squadron, who had nevertheless managed to land their damaged FE.

Earlier in the evening, Little and R Macdonald of Naval 8 had destroyed a DFW from *FlAbt (A)240,* crewed by *Uffz* Jourgens and *Ltn* Koehler. The two Camels had cut the enemy machine off from its own lines and as it dived for their safety Little and Macdonald fired at it as it passed, hitting both pilot and observer. The DFW spun in and crashed just behind the front line German trenches The German infantry that gathered around the wreck were fired on by British artillery, killing several of their number. This DFW, shared with Macdonald, was Little's last victory while with Naval 8. He was posted to Home Establishment at the end of the month.

In other combats during the day's fighting, James Forman of Naval 6 had destroyed an Albatros in flames at ten minutes past five north east of Nieuport, possibly *VzflugzgMstr* Otto Brandt of *Marine-Feldjagdstaffel Nr 1.* Albert Godfrey of 40 Squadron claimed an Albatros out of control east of Arras at 4.25pm; Frederick Gibbs of 23 Squadron, who had earlier claimed an Albatros shot down over St Julian at 2.45pm, claimed a two-seater over Kezelberg at 7.50pm, sharing it with his fellow pilot from 23 Squadron, Roger Neville. Capt Clive Warman, also of 23 Squadron, claimed an Albatros over Menin between 8.15 and 8.20pm. Major Arthur Coningham of 32 Squadron, flying a DH5, claimed an Albatros two-seater north of Polygon Wood at 9.00am, possibly *Uffz* Hermann Brauer and *Uffz* Karl Hönig of *Schusta 28b,* and an Albatros scout east of Houthulst Wood at 8.25 that evening.

July 28 was to have been the opening day of the offensive, but this was again postponed, not only because of a heavy ground mist but because the French were having difficulty in bringing up their artillery. The misty conditions at ground level, which so effectively cancelled the ground attack, had no effect on the air operations; the fighting continued in its fierceness of the last few days and casualties were heavy.

The pilots of 1 Squadron were on a patrol in the morning and Fullard and Louis Jenkin were in combat with five two-seaters in the area of Wervicq just before 10.00am. Fullard claimed a two-seater just north of Wervicq, but over 20 enemy scouts then attacked the patrol and 2Lt G B Buxton was shot down and killed. Jenkin destroyed one of the scouts and ten minutes later shot down a two-seater over Zandvoorde. In the afternoon, Campbell of 1 Squadron added to his balloon victories, shooting down two within twenty minutes of each other: the first at 1.50pm over Westroosebeke; the second south east of Houthulst. These two balloons – he destroyed a total of five – were the last victories by Campbell while serving in 1 Squadron. In only three months with the Squadron, less a fortnight's leave, he had scored 23 victories and had been awarded the DSO and MC and Bar.

Jasta 11 lost *Ltn* Alfred Niederhoff in a combat with 29 Squadron over Gheluvelt at 11.00am. Shot down by either Capt Charles Cudemore or Sgt Hervey-Bathurst – both of who claimed an Albatros destroyed from the combat – Neiderhoff had scored five victories while serving with *Jasta 11.* On the debit side for the squadron, 21Lt J K Campbell had been shot down and killed. Three German pilots claimed victories for the place and time in question: *Ltn* Adam and *Vzfw* Küllmer of *Jasta 6,* and Ltn J Schmidt of *Jasta 3.*

Booker, McCrudden and Crundall of Naval 8 were on patrol in the morning over the Méricourt area when they were attacked by ten Albatri from *Jasta 12* led by Adolf von Tutschek. Tutschek attacked Eric Crundall, who in the excitement of the action accidentally knocked up his engine's blip switch, stopping his triplane's engine as he was in a climbing turn, near to a stall. The triplane flicked over into a spin and this undoubedly saved Crundall's life. Crundall had never been in a spinning nose dive before and wondered if he could recover from it, but as the German pilots were following him down he decided to continue the spin for as long as possible, hoping to persuade his opponents that he was finished. His ruse having succeeded, Crundall recovered near the ground and flew back over the trenches at low level, his machine riddled with bullets. Booker and McCrudden had managed to escape from the enemy pilots, but Tutschek was awarded Crundall for his 20th victory.

A morning patrol from 56 Squadron went to aid of some FE2ds being attacked over Menin, but gained no decisive results from the action. An evening patrol by the squadron, led by Bowman, had better luck. Flying over Dadizele they were attacked by ten enemy scouts and in the fighting Hoidge shot one down to crash at Beselare.

Hoidge, Maybery and Wilkinson were later in action over Roulers, where some Camels of 70 Squadron were fighting a patrol of Albatri. Hoidge saw an Albatros on the tail of a Camel, attempting to turn inside it. Hoidge cut across the circle and 30 rounds from his Vickers and 50 from his Lewis at a range of only 20 feet sent the Albatros down in a steep dive, finally breaking up in mid air 3,000 feet below the action. Wilkinson attacked another Albatros and its wings folded up under his fire. Noel Webb of 70 Squadron claimed two Albatros shot down during this fight. The first destroyed over Roulers; the second out of control ten minutes later east of Polygon Wood.[20] Two Camel pilots from 70 Squadron were lost during this action: 2Lt R C Hume was shot down and taken POW and 2Lt J C Smith was killed.

Bishop, Young and Soden of 60 Squadron, flying their newly issued SE5s, were on a Close Offensive Patrol at 6.10pm when they sighted three enemy two-seaters working over the Front Lines. Because of the high rate of engine failures – three in the past week – the pilots had been forbidden to cross the lines, but Bishop left the Flight under G C Young's leadership and attacked the enemy machines, sending one down in flames near Phalempin.

Although still flying Sopwith Pups – outgunned by the German Albatros D types – the pilots of 66 Squadron gave a good account of themselves during the day, scoring the Squadron's greatest number of victories in one day. In an evening patrol led by Capt Gordon Taylor the Pups attacked a formation of Albatros scouts east of Roulers. The fight took place at 14,000 feet and at this height the lighter wing loading of the Sopwith Pup gave it a distinct advantage in manoeuvrability over the German Albatros. In the fighting, Cap C C Sharp badly damaged one Albatros and Walbanke Ashby Pritt – known as 'The War Baby – shot another off the tail of 2Lt Huxley and saw it crash just east of Roulers. Thomas Hunter claimed another of the enemy scouts out of control, and Thomas Luke shot one down in flames. Gordon Taylor turned inside a silver painted Albatros, got in a good burst and was just about to fire again when another Pup, flown by Lt Boumphrey – whose nickname was 'The Ratter' – shot between Taylor and the enemy machine. Taylor pushed his stick forward and dived under the Albatros, narrowly escaping a collision. It took Taylor a few minutes to recover from this narrow escape, but 'suddenly I snapped back to the realities of my own situation and kept my machine firmly in a turn, till I could sort out the action around me.' Taylor could see Boumphrey's Pup was still there, but another Pup was in trouble. 'I went for this Hun and was drawing a very careful bead on him when I was attacked from behind.' Taylor's attacker was so close that he could hear the sound of the enemy pilot's Spandau guns above the noise of his Pup's engine. Taylor's reaction was instictive; he put the Pup in a tight turn, causing the Albatros to overshoot. 'I saw him, hauling up, tail on, climbing into the sky. Then he was suddenly obliterated by a flaming mass plunging down in front of me, trailing a column of black smoke and putrid smoke. It was another Albatros. Sammy Luke's Pup was following it down. Then I saw the other Hun coming back in, diving on him. I couldn't reach him, or do anything, in time. Futilely, I shouted, "Look out, Sammy! Look out! I saw the tracer cutting into the Pup. It suddenly reared up, pulled over and started to go down, west, towards our lines. The Hun did not follow. He turned away to the east and disappeared.'[21]

Luke had been wounded in the arm, landed behind the Lines and was taken to hospital, but 2Lt J B Hine had been shot down and taken POW.

At 7.50pm, Naval 10 were in action with enemy fighters over Dadizeele. Alexander attacked one scout that fell over onto its back and went down, then saw another machine falling in pieces. After this action, in a sky empty of any enemy aircraft, Ellis Reid was seen flying between Dadizeele and Roulers at 12,500 feet. The remainder of the triplanes returned to Droglandt, but Reid did not return and it was thought that he had probably been shot down by anti-aircraft fire. *KFlak 41*, claimed a *Dreidecker* over Armentières, which is a little too far south from the position in which Reid was last seen, and flying at 12,500 feet, rather high for a lucky shot from an anti-aircraft battery. Both *Oblt* Weigand of *Jasta 10* and *Ltn* Oskar von Bönigk claimed Sopwith single seaters in the area at the time of Reid's loss. Reid was the third loss for the naval squadrons during the day. At 5.10pm FltSubLt J H Forman of Naval 6 had been wounded in a combat over the sea.

It had been a day of heavy casualties for the fighter squadrons. In addition to those mentioned, 32 Squadron had lost 2Lt R G Ottey, killed in action over Polygon Wood and another pilot hit in the engine by AA fire and forced to land. In a combat over Bixshoote the Spad of Lt F B Best of 19 Squadron had been badly shot up and Best forced to land near Bailleul.

July 29 opened with a severe thunderstorm in the late morning, but before the storm broke Bowman and Hoidge took out a number of new pilots to show them the Lines. A formation of nine Albatri was seen over Roulers. Bowman, with three inexperienced pilots with him – Hoidge had earlier returned with engine trouble – had no intention of attacking the enemy formation, but he knew that the DH4s of 55 Squadron were due to bomb the German aerodrome at Wynghene, just to the north of the town. Offering the SEs as bait to the enemy pilots he drew them south to Wervicq, away from the route which would be flown by the bombers, finally diving the SEs back across the British lines over Armentières. The enemy pilots, who had unsuccessfully attempted to climb to the height of the SEs, and had become split up in the attempt, regrouped over Lille.

The storm broke later that morning, the suddenness of its onset causing the loss of two aeroplanes at Estrée Blanche: a Camel of 70 Squadron and a Spad of 19 Squadron.

Because of the weather conditions all the aerial fighting was in the morning, before the storm broke. Sgt A E Parry of 23 Squadron was shot down and taken prisoner at 6.55am over Hooge by *Ltn* A Heldmann of *Jasta 10*, and Lt F B Best of 19 Squadron, who had successfully forced landed after a combat the previous day, was shot down and killed at 9.30am over Poelcappelle by *Vzfw* Misch of *Jasta 29.*

Caldwell, Bishop and W H Gunner of 60 Squadron were on patrol at 7.00am over Beaumont when they saw an enemy two-seater. The British pilots were suspicious of this machine, suspecting it was a decoy and their suspicions were justified when four Albatri from *Jasta 12*, led by Adolf von Tutschek, attacked them from out of the sun. During the fighting the engine of Gunner's SE failed and Gunner attempted to break away from the action. Tutschek saw that the SE was in trouble and went after it. Despite both Caldwell's and Bishop's attempts to stop him, Tutschek's attack set the SE on fire. It crashed near Henin-Liétard and Gunner was killed.

The fight continued. Caldwell had jams in both guns, but seeing Bishop hard pressed by several of the enemy scouts, he climbed back into the fight, his mere presence forcing the enemy pilots to break off the action, allowing the SEs to return to Filescamp Farm. Gunner was Tutschek's 21st victory and the 100th victory for *Jasta 12.*

There were two other casualties during the morning: Lt H O McDonald of 70 Squadron was shot down and taken POW in a combat at 9.25am over Langemarck by Ltn Wendelmuth of *Jasta 8*, and FltSubLt V G Austin of Naval 1 was wounded by *Flak,* forced to land and taken POW.

Naval 4 lost one of their best pilots when FltCom Arnold Chadwick was forced to ditch in the sea off La Panne at 4.10pm and drowned before he could be rescued. Chadwick had scored eleven victories, including an Albatros two-seater destroyed on the early morning of May 25, following this with the destruction of a Gotha over the sea at 6.30pm, which he shared with his Flight.

British troops were now moving up and concentrating in the forward areas for the opening of the battle of Ypres. On July 30 the weather was still poor and there was little flying. Thirty-two Squadron, flying low over the front lines in the evening seems to have been the only squadron in action during the day. In a combat with enemy scouts, Capt Coningham was slightly wounded in the head but returned safely. 2Lt A W Gordon's DH5 was badly shot up and he crashlanded in a shell hole near Vlamertinghe. Gordon was injured in the crash and died of his injuries thirteen days later.

NOTES

1. *Jagd in Flanderns Himmel,* Knorr & Hirth GMBH, München, 1935.
2. These Albatri were from *Jasta 30. Ltn* Hans Forstmann of the *Jasta* was shot down and killed near the Douges Canal by Lt Crole. The *jagdstaffeln* also lost a pilot to anti-aircraft fire: *Ltn* Horst Hellinger of *Jasta 5* was shot down and killed while attacking a balloon near Hendecourt. Hellinger's Albatros was designated G.50.
3. Fleming later won the MC for his work in Palestine. He shot down several enemy machines and was considered one of the most successful pilots of the RFC in the Middle East.
4. While in England 56 Squadron had been under the orders of the 6th Brigade Horse Guards. When the Gothas again bombed London on July 6 the Brigade ordered the squadron to intercept the raiders, only to find that it had returned to France the previous day. After more argument Haig was ordered to return a fighter squadron to England. On July 10, 46 Squadron was ordered to Sutton's Farm aerodrome in Essex.
5. The credit for shooting down Richthofen was given to Capt D C Cunnell and his gunner, 2Lt A E Woodbridge. Six days later Cunnell was hit by anti-aircraft fire and killed. His gunner on this last occasion was Lt A G Bill, who managed to fly the FE back to base, although he was injured in the subsequent crash landing.
6. John Oliver Andrews is officially credited with 24 victories, but these include twelve that were driven down and forced to land.
7. Possibly *Vzfw* Linus Patermann of *Jasta 4*, killed over Gheluvelt.
8. Bishop's account of this action was very terse and Robert Little gained the impression that the Canadian begrudged him his victory. Whatever the truth of the matter the Australian thereafter treated Bishop with some reserve.
9. Letter to the author.
10. On August 21 Dostler was shot down and killed by 2Lt M A O'Callaghan, the gunner of an RE8 of 7 Squadron. The 27-year-old Bavarian's Albatros fell in flames and crashed in No Man's Land.
11. *Fighter Pilot on the Western Front,* Wing Commander E D Crundall, DFC, AFC, William Kimber, London 1975.

12. The Nieuport was repaired by the Germans and flown two days later.
13. Possibly *Ltn* Erich Schlegelmilch who was slightly wounded. He was later killed in action, on August 12 1917.
14. RFC losses for the day were usually made up at 6.00pm. A loss after this time, as in the case of Parkes, could sometimes be incorrectly entered as having taken place the following day and Caldwell's logbook entry gives this fight and the loss of Parkes to have taken place on July 14. However, German records of Tutschek's victory, the wounding of *Ltn* Schlegelmilch and the victory over Bray of Naval 8 by Bethge give July 15.
15. *Ltn* Hermann Göring of *Jasta 27* was the pilot forced down by Jardine, his Albatros badly damaged. It is tantalising to speculate on the change in history if Jardine's fire had been a little more accurate. There is a discrepancy in the German victory list for July 16. Göring was awarded an SE5 at 8.05am (GT) but no SE5s were lost in the morning.
16. Tutschek's victory has been stated as being 2Lt F W Rook of 40 Squadron, but his victory is timed at 7.30pm (German time, one hour ahead of British time) and Rook had not taken off until 6.50pm. Given this discrepancy in time, and that Rook's Nieuport fell in flames, this casts some doubt on Rook being von Tutschek's 17th victory.
17. Tutschek letter. *Over The Front* Journal. Spring 1989.
18. Prothero, a Scotsman, always insisted on wearing a kilt while flying. When he returned from a patrol his knees would be blue with cold, the hairs on his legs sticking out like bristles. This always puzzled the Canadian, Cronyn. 'One day I asked him why he so punished himself, to which he replied. 'You wouldna have me taken prisoner in disguise, would you now laddie?'
19. The only claim by a Spad pilot for the evening of July 27 was by Lt Warman of 23 Squadron, but Warman's claim was over Menin at 10,000 feet, over 12 miles south east of Houthulst Forest.
20. *Ltn* Gustav Nolte of *Jasta 18* and *Hptm* Gustav Stenzel of *Jasta 8* were both killed in action in the area on July 28.
21. *Sopwith Scout 7309*, Sir Gordon Taylor, Cassell, London 1968.

CHAPTER THIRTEEN

THE THIRD BATTLE OF YPRES

On July 28, the previous date scheduled for the start of the battle, the weather conditions – low ground mist – had not been propitious for ground operations; now, by a reversal of conditions, the weather was good for ground operations, but was extremely bad – low clouds and mist all day – for the air operations, both offensive and support.

The ground attacks went well. The initial objectives were the first three German trench positions and by 10.00am the first two of these had been taken. German resistance stiffened at the third line and their counterattacks were aided by low flying aeroplanes of the *schutzstaffeln*. There were low clouds at 500 to 800 feet over the battlefield the whole day and by the afternoon it was raining steadily. The weather conditions seriously handicapped the vital work of the Corps squadrons. Forced to fly low because of the rain and low clouds the pilots and observers found it almost impossible to report on the progress of the infantry, which again, as at Messines, were reluctant to disclose their positions to the enemy by flares, although called upon by Klaxon horns to do so. In order to ascertain the positions of the ground troops and the general progress of the battle the aeroplanes of the Corps squadrons were forced to fly low enough to distinguish the uniforms of the troops. This led to heavy casualties amongst the crews of the RE8s: two crew members were killed, five were wounded and thirty machines were made unserviceable due to battle damage. Despite the adverse conditions, however, a reasonably complete picture of the general progress of the battle emerged and instances were recorded where the artillery, informed of the positions of German machine gun posts holding up the attacks, was able to shell the posts and enable the infantry to take the positions.

The pilots of the Army squadrons were unable to carry out any high offensive patrols and carried out roving commis-sions in the German back areas, looking for targets of opportunity: infantry on the march or in concentrations; transport convoys; staff motor cars; machine gun and battery emplacements; railway junctions; enemy aerodromes. These last had been part of the general plan of attack on the first morning of the battle. The Army squadrons of 9th Wing had been specifically ordered to detail five machines to individually attack the German aerodromes of Marcke, Bisseghem, Heule, Abeelhock and Ingelmunster. 'Machines will start as early as possible in order to arrive at their respective objectives as soon as it is light enough for accurate shooting.' Another eight enemy aerodromes were detailed as targets for the fighters of 2nd and 5th Brigades and all aerodromes were later to be bombed again.

For the first time, bombs were carried by the single-seater fighters, usually four 25lb Cooper bombs mounted under the wings in hurriedly improvised racks, fitted the night before the operations. Many pilots were worried that the extra weight would seriously endanger the flying capabilities of their aeroplanes and doubted that they would return from the day's operations.

Richard Maybery of 56 Squadron was one pilot detailed to carry out an attack on a German aerodrome and he took off at 4.45am. Flying at only 300 feet, just below the thick clouds and low enough to have to fly through smoke from the artillery barrage, blotting out his view ahead, Maybery crossed the Lines over Ypres. Away from the immediate battle area the air was clearer and Maybery turned southwest over Wervicq, went down to 30 feet and flew along a secondary road to Gheluive. Now sure of his position he flew due east to Bisseghem. Confirming his position from Courtrai, he flew northeast towards his destination, the German aerodrome at Heule. Suddenly, concentrating on his navigation, he was attacked by two Albatri. Handicapped by weight of his bombs, he manoeuvred as violently as he could, firing shot bursts from his Lewis gun in an attempt to 'frighten them away' but the enemy pilots were persistent and he was forced to turn west. The Albatri finally left him at the Front Line and Maybery flew north, picked up the canalised river Lys at Comines, then retraced his earlier route.

Finally arriving over Heule aerodrome, Maybery zoomed for a little height and circled the field at 200 feet. Other than a lone individual lighting smoke flares at the end of the field the aerodrome was deserted. Maybery turned, flew along the line of sheds and dropped his first bomb, hitting the third shed from the end of the line. 'This caused immense excitement.' People began to appear and run about the sheds. Maybery turned again and dropped his second bomb, which exploded on the first shed in the line. Turning sharply, Maybery dropped his third bomb at the Heule end of the aerodrome. This went straight through the shed and failed to explode until it hit the ground inside. The SE5 rocked violently under this explosion, but Maybery again flew along the sheds to drop his last bomb. The ground defences now began to fire at the SE5 – a solitary machine gun from behind the sheds. Maybery pulled the bomb toggle, but there was no explosion; the bomb had failed to release. Looking down, Maybery saw that he was over Courtrai railway station and he pulled the bomb toggle again. This time he was successful and saw the bomb explode between a goods train and a shed. His bombs now gone, Maybery turned back towards the aerodrome. Another machine gun had now been manned and joined the first, firing at the SE5. Maybery could see only one gun and he fired at this, scattering the crew. The other gun crew wisely stopped firing. Maybery then strafed the southern most row of sheds, changed his Lewis gun drum and flew back across the enemy aerodrome from the west, his wheels actually running along the ground, firing into the sheds. Zooming over the sheds, Maybery flew on to his next target, the aerodrome of *Jasta 4* at Cuerne, and attacked the sheds and hangars with both guns. An Albatros, being wheeled out of a hangar was hastily wheeled back in again. Maybery left the immediate vicinity of the aerodrome and attacked two officers on horseback, bolting their horses, before turning west to return to Estrée Blanche. On the way back he was firing at a train on the Courtrai to Menin line when he saw a column of infantry, 200 strong, marching along the road to Menin. Maybery's first attack scattered the enemy troops to both sides of the road; he replaced his Lewis gun drum and attacked them again. After this attack he looked up and saw an enemy two-seater flying above him at 200 feet, just under the cloudbank. Maybery left the troops, zoomed up and opened fire from under the tail of the two-seater, unseen by the enemy gunner. The enemy machine went down in a steep left hand turn with Maybery following. As the enemy pilot straightened out

Maybery opened fire again, this time with his Vickers, and the two-seater went down to crash just north of the railway line on the outskirts of Wevelghem. Maybery circled the crash. Only one man got out, but a small crowd of troops began to collect around the wreckage. Maybery attacked these, who either ran or fell flat to escape his fire. Maybery turned to attack the troops again, but noticed a train coming from the direction of Menin and dived to attack it, but he was out of ammunition for his Lewis gun and his Vickers had jammed. He turned west, crossed the Lines just south of Messines and returned to Estrée Blanche.

Eric Turnbull of 56 Squadron had taken off 25 minutes after Maybery with orders to attack ground forces in the Ypres, Menin, Wervicq areas. Visibility was extremely poor and the only way Turnbull could locate the positions of the enemy guns firing at him was to fly down their tracer. Flying towards Ypres, Turnbull attacked a light transport wagon and several groups of enemy troops. Coming under very intense and accurate fire from the ground, and with a jam in his Lewis gun, Turnbull climbed into and above the cloud cover. He was unsuccessful in his attempt to clear the jam in his Lewis gun and he realised that he was now hopelessly lost. Taking a bearing on some balloons he flew west, but still unsure of his position landed at a bombing school to ask the way. He then flew to Boisdinghem aerodrome, refuelled and returned to Estrée Blanche. 'One memory is that at times I was so low that it was possible to smell cordite fumes and gas. On inspecting the machine after landing there were quite a number of bullet holes between the engine and the petrol tank. The Hun shooting was good. I was lucky.'

The pilots of all the fighter squadrons carried out low level attacks during the day. Louis Jenkin of 1 Squadron attacked Herseaux aerodrome, firing into the hangars and a line of parked Albatros scouts from 200 feet, setting one on fire before silencing a machine gun that was firing at him. Fullard shot down a balloon, then located an enemy aerodrome. A long line of Albatros scouts was standing on the ground in front of the hangars and Fullard flew along it firing a complete drum of Lewis gun ammunition into them. Firing into a column of motor lorries on the Roulers to Menin road Fullard's fire caused the first lorry to stop so suddenly that the next vehicle smashed into its back, causing the whole line to jam. Fullard then attacked another balloon, but this refused to burn, despite repeated attacks. After firing at a train, Fullard then became lost in the heavy cloud and on emerging from it found he was over the sea with very little fuel left. Fullard threw his Lewis gun drums, both full and empty, and his personal revolvers over the side in an attempt to lighten the Nieuport and was finally able to land safely at the aerodrome of Naval 2. Due to the worsening weather over the next few days, Fullard was stranded there until August 4. Other pilots from 1 Squadron also carried out low level attacks: Hazell fired at ground targets in the areas of Tenbrielen and the Wervicq to Becelaere road. William Campbell attacked Mouveaux aerodrome, the base of *FlAbt(A)204* and fired 300 rounds into a dozen two-seaters. Three enemy aeroplanes then attacked him and he was slightly wounded.

John Firth and V R S White of 45 Squadron attacked transport and cars on the Becelaere to Zonnebeke road from 500 feet. Charlwood and Ward chased an anti-aircraft gun mounted on a lorry and six other pilots attacked various ground targets.

Clive Warman of 23 Squadron shot down an Albatros, which crashed near Westroosebeke at 12.15pm and his fellow pilots shot at troops and field batteries near Polygon Wood. Pilots of 32, 29, 66 and 70 Squadrons all attacked ground targets over the battle area.

The naval pilots were also busy during the day. Nick Carter of Naval 10 led a patrol in the afternoon to attack ground targets, but over Menin the Flight was attacked by five enemy scouts. These forced the triplanes down into the thick cloud at 600 feet where it was raining hard. One pilot had engine trouble and failed to pull out until down to 800 feet, but he later attacked a column of troops and transport on the Menin road. FltSubLt J S de Wilde of Naval 1 went down to 400 feet to attack the enemy aerodrome at Coucou, firing into the hangars and FltSubLt C B Ridley attacked the hangars on Reckem aerodrome. From 200 feet, FltCom F H M Maynard attacked a convoy of motor transport, a quarter of a mile long, north of Menin, returning for more ammunition and going out again. FltSubLts E Anthony and A G A Spence went down to 400 feet and attacked German trenches and FltSubLt Everitt fired into some tents near Menin. Minifie fired into huts near Gheluwe, then flew up and down the Ypres to Menin road at 200 feet firing at infantry columns. Other pilots from the squadron fired into gun pits, huts and enemy rest camps.

All these attacks were carried out a very low altitude, in hazardous weather conditions and under heavy fire from the ground. The aeroplanes of the 2nd and 5th Brigades and those of 9th Wing flew a total of 396 hours 25 minutes in ground-strafing and bombing, fired 11,258 rounds – fifteen with revolvers, the fighting was so low – and two Very lights. Six enemy aeroplanes were claimed during the day and one balloon for the loss of three British aeroplanes. Three pilots and one observer were killed, two pilots and observers were taken prisoner and four pilots and observers were wounded. At the end of the day the 9th Wing diary recorded.

'The keenness and gallantry displayed by the pilots on these expeditions was magnificent and the results were excellent. Although the pilots did not mention it in their reports directly they emerged from the clouds on the enemy's side they were received by a very heavy fire from AA guns, MG and rifle fire, and showers of rockets and pistol lights were fired at them and several pilots flew into and just above the barrage – one pilot suffering from the effects of gas! The scheme of attaching bombs to Scout Machines was proved successful as the accounts show. All this work was carried out in weather which would be considered normally to be totally unfit for flying.'

No doubt to the relief of the hard pressed pilots of both the army and corps squadrons the weather then became so bad, with heavy and continuous rain for the next four days, that there was no war flying until August 4. These adverse conditions were extremely fortuitous for the German ground forces. Not only was British counter battery work made impossible due to lack of air observation, but it gave them time to recover and regroup from the first day's fighting, confirmed the main thrust of the attack, and enabled reinforcements to be brought up. Also, the heavy and continuous rain, exacerbated by both the British and German barrages, which had destroyed the drainage system, had turned the waterlogged ground of Flanders into a morass in which movement was scarcely possible. Conditions for the infantry were appalling, defying belief. Many wounded, and even able-bodied men, who fell from the wooden duckboards that had been laid to enable some movement over the sea of water and liquid mud, literally drowned to death. Haig's dispatch summed up the situation. 'The low-lying, clayey soil, torn by shells and sodden by rain, turned to a succession of vast muddy pools. The valleys of the choked and overflowing streams were speedily transformed into long stretches of bog, impassable except for a few well-defined tracks, which became marks for the enemy's artillery. To leave these tracks was to risk death by drowning, and in the course of the subsequent fighting on several occasions both men and pack animals were lost in this way. In these conditions operations of any magnitude became impossible and the resumption of our offensive was necessarily postponed until a period of fine weather should allow the ground to recover.' Months later, seeing the conditions for the first time, one British General burst into tears and cried: 'My God, did we really send men to fight in that?'

There was little flying on August 4, the low clouds and rain persisting, but some artillery work was undertaken by the Corps squadrons and one crew member was hit in the stomach, later dying of his wounds. The only fighter casualty was a pilot of 32 Squadron. Hit by AA fire, 2Lt L F C St Clair crash landed his DH5, but died of his wounds.

Sunday, August 5, dawned fine but still a little cloudy. The first casualties of the day for the fighter squadrons were two pilots of 29 Squadron, both wounded in combat with *Jasta 4* in the early afternoon. Mannock of 40 Squadron scored his fifth victory, an Albatros scout over at Avion just after 4.00pm. In the evening, the Camels of 70 Squadron and the SE5s of 56 Squadron were in combat over Houthulst Forest with 14 enemy scouts. These Albatri, possibly from *Jagdstaffeln 4* and *27*, were first seen being chased by Spads of a French *escadrille* as they were about to attack some British Spads from 19 Squadron. The 56 Squadron pilots claimed no victories from this action, but two pilots from 70 Squadron were wounded, one was shot down and made POW, the other landed, wounded, on the British side. Lt D A Page of 56 Squadron was forced to land with a badly shot up SE5. Clive Collett of 70 Squadron claimed an Albatros destroyed during the fighting.

At 8.00pm a patrol from 60 Squadron, in a combat with Albatri from *Jasta 12*, shot down *Ltn* Lehmann over Hendecourt, shared between Lts William Molesworth and Spenser Horn. William Bishop claimed a further two Albatri from the fight: one destroyed and another out of control.

August 6 was a day of thick fog and there was little flying. Only Bishop of 60 Squadron claimed a victory during the day, an Albatros scout over Brebières at 3.45pm.

The next day the fog failed to lift until the late afternoon and the only casualty for the fighter squadrons was a DH5 of 32 Squadron forced to land by AA fire. August 8 was again a day of low clouds, thick ground mist and haze and there was little service flying, but pilots of 54, 23 and 32 Squadrons carried out ground-strafing attacks. Although August 9 was still cloudy, with rainstorms, a great deal of flying was done and there were six casualties.

Naval 9 lost a pilot to *Vzfw* Julius Buckler of *Jasta 17* at 6.45am. Flt SubLt M G Woodhouse's Camel fell in flames south east of Nieuport. Another naval pilot was killed just after noon: FltSubLt K R Munro of Naval 8, last seen spinning down after a fight with *Jasta 24* over Polygon Wood, was killed. In an evening patrol by 29 Squadron Lt W B Wood and Sgt Harvey-Bathhurst attacked a two-seater. Wood sent this down out of control but Hervey-Bathhust was wounded in the leg by the observer. A little later, over Poelcappelle, 2Lt H B Billings of the squadron was shot down by *Ltn* Dostler of *Jasta 6*. Billings was taken prisoner but later died of his wounds.

Pilots of 60 Squadron fought eight Albatri over Cagnicourt at 9.00am: Molesworth destroyed one and Horn sent another down out of control. Bishop fought one Albatros that was skilfully flown and succeeded only in driving it down before attacking a two-seater, which he sent down to crash.

In early August, 40 Squadron were using a small clover field at Mazingarbe as an advanced landing ground. In the middle of the shell-torn countryside, about a mile and a half from the Front Line, the field was used both for strafing attacks on enemy trenches and balloons and to intercept any enemy aeroplanes working over the trenches, which could be seen from the field. Pilots flew from Mazingarbe on a purely voluntary basis. MacLanachan remembered: 'the clover was becoming rather long, and the sweet smell of the flowers brought back memories of my childhood. We frequently had tea or even dinner there, the latter consisting of tinned lobster. A whole tin of this delicacy, of which we had grown tired in the Mess, had been dumped at Mazingarbe, and anyone who felt hungry could always have a tin if he were prepared to take the risk of Ptomaine poisoning.'

On August 9 seven Nieuports took off from Mazingarbe to attack balloons in the La Bassee-Arras area, flying all the way to the targets at only 20 feet. Tudhope hit some telephone wires, luckily with no damage to his machine and fired at some German troops who were paddling in a small pool. MacLanachan flew over the houses of a small village – causing a soldier carrying a small bucket to drop it and dash for cover – before making for his allotted balloon. It was still at 1,500 feet and as he approached at ground level he decided to wait until it had been hauled down further. Passing close to the winches he could see that the anti-aircraft batteries were situated west of the balloon site. 'It was then a good idea came to me … if I attacked from the east they would not be able to fire at me for fear of hitting the gas bags themselves.' With this in mind, MacLanachan flew further east for a mile before turning, but as he did so he saw a long column of German troops, led by a number of mounted officers. This target was too good to miss. MacLanachan zoomed to three or four hundred feet and dived at the head of the column, stampeding the horses, several of which threw their riders and galloped off across the fields. The Nieuport was so low that its undercarriage hit one German officer on the head. Leaving the column in some disarray, MacLanachan flew back to the balloon, now nearly down to ground level, only having time to fire half a drum of Lewis into the balloon before breaking away to avoid a collision. There was a 'woof' and MacLanachan's Nieuport was surrounded by flaming onions, but the balloon had failed to catch fire and MacLanachan made two more attacks before it finally went down deflated and smoking. Only Sgt L A Herbert succeeded in flaming a balloon but three others were sent down deflated, with smoke coming from them. All the Nieuports were badly damaged but all returned safely. Clive Warman of 23 Squadron was more successful, destroying a balloon in the 5th Brigade area.

Fifty-six Squadron flew three offensive patrols during the day. Enemy aeroplanes were seen in the first two patrols and a great deal of manoeuvring for favourable positions took place; although there were several combats there were no decisive results. The last patrol left the ground a half past six and saw no enemy aeroplanes until a quarter to eight when Barlow, leading the Flight, saw eight Albatros scouts flying in and out of the cloud banks above Zonnebeke. Getting above the enemy scouts the SEs were joined by a Flight of Nieuports from 1 Squadron and the British fighters, using dive and zoom tactics, forced the Albatri down towards the Menin road. Gordon Ross-Soden, who had been with 56 Squadron for only a short time and was inexperienced, made the mistake of staying down at the Albatri's level and was attacked by one. Barlow saw Ross-Soden's predicament and dived at the Albatros, forcing it to break off its attacks, but Ross-Soden had been wounded in the knee. He managed to return to base, but was taken to hospital. Another pilot, Ian MacGregor, failed to return. He crashlanded at 5 Squadron's aerodrome at Acq, the SE turned over and MacGregor was taken to hospital.

Although the weather continued changeable the next day, with wind and rain, there were fine intervals and the general pattern of the previous day's fighting was continued. All the scout squadrons recorded combats and victories during the day and had casualties. Fifty-six Squadron lost a pilot, Capt William Fleming, to *Ltn* Stock of *Jasta 6* during a morning patrol; Capt A B Jarvis of 1 Squadron was killed and 2Lt L J F Henderson was taken prisoner after a fight with *Jasta 3*; 23 Squadron lost a pilot taken POW; 24, 32 and Squadrons each had a pilot killed.

Naval 10 were out early, Alexander shot at the pilot of an Albatros over Wervicq and was convinced he had killed or wounded him, the Albatros going down in a steep sideslip. Alexander was not awarded a victory over this Albatros, but three German pilots were reported as wounded in action during the day.

Booker and Crundall of Naval 8 were not detailed for a patrol during the day so they decided to shoot up German troop positions at Oppy Wood. Arriving at 1,000 feet they shut off their engines and dived vertically at the German trenches, firing all the time. In this type of dive the naval pilots left their engine throttles wide open but closed the petrol fine adjustment, shutting off the petrol flow. This left the engine off but the propeller still rotating. At the bottom of the dive, as they flattened out, the pilots opened the fine adjustment. This immediately gave the engine full power and enabled them to zoom away in an almost vertical climb. After several dives, Crundall opened his fine adjustment but the engine failed to start and Crundall was down to 100 feet, on the German side of the Lines, with no engine. Crundall used what reserve of speed he had from the dive to glide towards the British trenches. 'Everywhere the surface was pitted with shell holes, like a honeycomb, so I knew I could not avoid crashing the machine. I attempted the landing as slowly as possible, but directly the wheels touched the hopeless surface the Triplane's nose dropped into a large shell hole, with its tail pointing vertically upwards.' Crundall scrambled out of his machine into the shell hole but the German infantry were already firing at the triplane and bullet holes were appearing in the fuselage. Within two minutes the German artillery also opened fire on the crash. Crundall decided that he would have to wait until dark before making for the safety of the trenches, but after an hour someone called to him and asked if he were all right. 'I replied I was unhurt. The voice said "Do not move, we are coming to your assistance but it will take some time to get to you."[1] Crundall waited in the shell hole until a trench had been dug out to him and then crawled back into the British trenches. Crundall was later given a lift on a narrow gauge railway back to Arras where he got another lift back to his aerodrome at Mont St Eloi. A breakdown party went out to the crash that night but only the engine of Crundall's triplane 'Joan' was worth salvaging.

August 11 was a day of low clouds and rain. There was some fighting, but fewer casualties in the fighter squadrons, with only three pilots lost. Twenty-nine Squadron lost Lt C G Guy who was shot down, taken POW and later died of his wounds, and a pilot from 32 Squadron was wounded in the arm by groundfire.

Booker of Naval 8, Crundall's companion of the previous day, took off from Mont St Eloi at fifteen minutes past six in the evening with two other pilots on an offensive patrol. At 8.00pm they were in action with Albatri from *Jasta 12*. During the fight the *Staffelführer,* von Tutschek, was wounded in the shoulder, possibly by FltSubLt Gordon, and then hit by fire from Booker. Booker was then attacked by *Ltn* Schobinger, his triplane 'Maude' badly damaged and he was forced to land near Farbus. Booker was unhurt.[2]

After a morning of thunderstorms the afternoon was fine on August 12. There was a great deal of fighting in the air after the weather cleared, fighting particularly successful for 40 Squadron. In a morning patrol Major William Keen, the commanding officer, shot down a DFW north of Douai for his ninth victory and in the evening destroyed an Albatros over Lens. Mannock was on duty at Mazingarbe in the afternoon when it was reported that an enemy machine was crossing the Lines. Mannock took off and soon located the enemy machine, an all black Albatros D.V, its Maltese Cross markings out lined in white. The pilot, *Ltn* Joachim von Bertrab of *Jasta 30,* had been attacking British balloons and was flying back across the Lines when Mannock caught him. Mannock wrote in his diary on August 19.

'Plenty of scrapping the air and much glory ... Had a splendid fight with a single-seater Albatros scout last week on our side of the Lines and got him down. This proved to be Lieutenant von Bartrap (sic) Iron Cross, and had been flying for eighteen months. He came over for one of our balloons – near Neuville-St Vaast – and I cut him off going back. He didn't get the balloon either. The scrap took place at two thousand feet up, well within view of the whole front. And the cheers!. It took me five minutes to get him to go down, and I had to shoot him before he would land. I was very pleased that I did not kill him. Right arm broken by a bullet, left arm and left leg deep flesh wounds. His machine, a beauty with black crosses picked out in white lines – turned over on landing and was damaged. Two machine guns with one thousand rounds of ammunition against my single Lewis and three hundred rounds! I went up to the trenches to salve the 'bus' later, and had a great ovation from everyone. Even Generals congratulated me. He didn't hit me once.'

Bertrab's Albatros was wrecked in the forced landing but was designated G60.

The day was not so successful for 1 Squadron. In a morning combat with *Jasta 27* over Polygon Wood it lost two pilots: one was killed, the other taken POW. Nineteen Squadron also lost a pilot killed and another forced to land with a severely damaged Spad, and its companion Spad Squadron, 23 Squadron, also had a pilot killed. A DH5 of 32 Squadron was shot down, its pilot killed, and 40 Squadron had a pilot taken prisoner.

Twenty-three Squadron lost another pilot the next morning in a combat with *Jasta 26* over Frezenberg. The day was again cloudy with some rain, but there was a great deal of aerial fighting. Bowman of 56 Squadron took a Flight out at 7.45am and attacked six Albatri flying between Houthulst Forest and Roulers. Maybery took an Albatros with a red and black-banded fuselage and a yellow tail off the tail of an SE flown by Lt Ramage, but his Vickers gun then jammed. Maybery turned away to rectify the stoppage but was attacked by two Albatri. He failed to get his Vickers gun to work, but he fought the yellow tailed Albatros down to 2,000 feet, firing good bursts from his Lewis gun at close range. Feeling that he was now too low on the wrong side of the lines, Maybery broke off the action and climbed northwest. The pilot of the Albatros climbed with him and as they reached 11,000 feet Maybery turned to attack it, driving it off with bursts from his Lewis gun, his Vickers still not working. Maybery then climbed to 16,000 feet and flew to join what he thought were four SE5s. As they approached, however, he saw that they were Albatros scouts, with yellow tail leading, who outdistanced his *Jasta* companions, catching Maybery over Leke. Maybery turned to face the attack, outmanoeuvred the enemy pilot and drove him westwards, but while Maybery was changing a Lewis gun drum – his Vickers was still inoperative – the German pilot saw his chance and dived east for his own lines. Maybery, by now determined to force a conclusion with the enemy pilot, followed and fought him down to 500 feet, getting in good bursts of fire. The German pilot finally landed, 'apparently

OK,' east of St Pierre-Capelle and Maybery had to be content with a moral victory.

In the evening, flying alone, Bishop of 60 Squadron shot down two Albatros scouts in flames, five miles south of Douai. Despite these positive claims the *jagdstaffeln* reported no losses for the time and place.

Pilots of 40, 1, 23, 70, and 19 Squadrons all claimed victories during the day, making a total of eleven enemy machines, scouts and two-seaters.

The weather the next day, August 14, was again poor, with low clouds, high winds and rainstorms. Despite these conditions there was no appreciable let up in the amount of fighting in the air. The *jagdstaffeln* were extremely active in attempting to stop the corps aeroplanes from working over the trenches and a number of British balloons were also attacked.

Barlow took out a Flight from 56 Squadron in the morning and after an inconclusive fight with some scouts, Barlow shot down a two-seater to crash in a small wood north of Moorslede. Keith Muspratt attacked its companion, which went down in a steep dive, its engine smoking badly, to crash on the eastern edge of Houthulst Forest. These two-seaters were possibly from *FlAbt(A)224* and *Schusta 12* both of whom lost machines in the area. The second patrol of the day by the squadron had mixed success. Maxwell and Sloley attacked a green two-seater and sent it down out of control west of Roulers, but its escort of Albatri from *Jasta 6* then arrived and in the fighting Dudley Page was shot down, mortally wounded, and John Young was taken POW.

Naval 10 were in action over Houthulst Forest in the afternoon. FltLt Saint led the triplanes down to attack three Albatros scouts, but these proved to be bait in a trap and another five came down on the naval pilots. Saint got behind one red Albatros and an accurate burst from very close range sent in down in flames, but in the fighting FltSubLt S H Lloyd was shot down and killed by *Uffz* Karl Steudel of *Jasta 3*.

The *jagdstaffeln* lost two pilots during the day. *Ltn d Res* Alfred Hübner of *Jasta 4* was shot down and killed by Tom Hazell of 1 Squadron – Hazell claimed another Albatros out of control from the same fight – and *Ltn* Hans Wolff of *Jasta 11* was wounded in the thigh and crashed near Zillebeke Lake.

Other casualties in the fighter squadrons were Capt Tom Oliver of 29 Squadron, who was shot down over Nieuwkapelle, south west of Dixmude, by *Oblt* Ernst Weigand of *Jasta 10* for his second victory; a Camel pilot, FltSubLt M N Baron from Naval 9, killed in action, and a pilot of 23 Squadron wounded in the foot.

On August 15 Canadian troops attacked Hill 70 at Loos. This attack was made with the intention of drawing enemy forces away from Ypres. Sixteen Squadron was detailed to carry out artillery co-operation, photography and contact patrols; 10, 25, 43 and 27 Squadrons were to bomb troop positions, railway junctions and aerodromes prior to the attack. To support and protect the machines of these squadrons, 40 Squadron and Naval 8 were to carry out offensive patrols and escort work.

Patrols by 40 Squadron were flown from the advanced landing field at Mazingarbe. Six Nieuports were stationed there throughout the day and from an advanced anti-aircraft observation post on the high ground west of Loos, were informed by wireless of enemy air activity over the battle. This information – from an officer of an anti-aircraft battery – proved highly accurate At 9.30am, Capt Arthur Keen claimed two Albatros scouts over Lens during a morning action; Mannock and Robert Hall each claimed another over Lens at 12.15 and 12.50pm. *Ltn* Heinrich Brügman of *Jasta* 30 was shot down in this fight, dying of his wounds at 1.00pm in an ambulance taking him to hospital, the time of his death possibly making him Mannock's victory. In an evening patrol, again during a fight with *Jasta 30*, Gerard Crole claimed another Albatros scout east of La Bassée and Mannock shot down another, but in this patrol Capt W G Pender was shot down and killed by *Oblt* Bethge of the *Jasta*.

Casualties were heavy in the corps squadrons during the fighting. 43 Squadron had four crew members killed, another later died of his wounds and two others were also wounded.

In the Ypres area of operations, FltLt Richard Minifie of Naval 1 crashed an Albatros east of Ypres at 9.15am, and FltSubLt Strathy of Naval 6 attacked a two-seater that broke up in mid-air. Fullard of 1 Squadron destroyed an Albatros over Poelcapelle at 6.00pm and sent another down out of control ten minutes later; Bishop of 60 Squadron shot down an Albatros over Henin Lietard at 8.20pm for his forty-fifth victory claim. Pender of 40 Squadron was the only fighter pilot killed during the day's fighting, but Lt O D Hay of 66 Squadron was wounded, crash landed, and was taken to hospital.

The Ypres offensive recommenced on August 16 with the battle of Langemarck. Misty conditions and cloud hampered air observation and although these conditions improved during the afternoon, smoke from the battlefield, blown by the prevailing west wind, spread over the German back areas, screening enemy movements.

The fighter strength of the RFC II and V Brigades and those of headquarters Ninth Wing were employed, with the addition of the Naval squadrons at Dunkirk. The DH5s of 32 Squadron – two on each divisional front – were to patrol at low height, short of the barrage, and attack any enemy strong points and troops concentrations. In addition, two patrols, each of four aircraft, were to strafe enemy back areas over the whole of the Fifth Army front for six hours after the beginning of the

attack, breaking up any counter attacks with machine gun fire. These aeroplanes were also to protect the troops from attacks by low flying German aircraft. With the expiry of the six hours, attacks were to be switched to further east: to bomb and machine gun any concentration of troops building up along the roads to Langemarck. Attacks at first light on German aerodromes by single fighters of V brigade, similar to those carried out on July 31 were also ordered.

The Spads of 23 Squadron were detailed to attack the enemy aerodromes at Beveren and Ingelmunster. 2Lt Clive Warman, an American, born in Norfolk, Virginia, took off from La Lovie at 4.35am and attacked Beveren, dropping two 25lb Cooper bombs on a building. Flying past the aerodrome, Warman then returned and found a DFW taking off. Warman attacked this from 100 feet and shot it down to crash on the aerodrome, firing another burst into the wreckage. Approaching the battle lines on his way back to La Lovie he saw a German battery firing into the British positions and he flew along the line of guns firing at the crews. The guns fell silent. Warman circled the position for five minutes but the guns did not fire again. Climbing for more height, Warman then attacked a balloon over Passchendaele and shot it down in flames. 2Lt W Brookes attacked Ingelmunster aerodrome, three times flying up and down the line of hangars at 50 feet, dropping his bombs and machine gunning. Several machine gun posts opened fire at him but he silenced them with short bursts of fire. While returning to base, he attacked troops marching along the Roulers road, an enemy battery, and fired 50 rounds at a train, but in this last attack he was wounded in the leg.

The planned attack on Rumbeke aerodrome was unsuccessful – it was being patrolled by enemy two-seaters – and Lt Webster, who set out to bomb Abeele, lost his way and attacked buildings in the town.

The ground fighting was extremely confused and complicated by the dense smoke. The low flying aeroplanes of V Brigade were unable to completely co-ordinate their low level attacks with the advancing troops. The pilots of 32 Squadron attacked many machine gun emplacements, strong points and enemy trenches, but the majority of attacks on ground targets were carried out by pilots of 29 Squadron. Lt F W Wilson from the squadron flew up and down the main street of Zonnebeke, firing at troops, then attacked a railway siding on the outskirts of the town. 2Lts E Holdsworth and E S Meek attacked troops concentrating in Polygon Wood and on the peacetime racecourse, and ten other pilots from the squadron all carried out similar attacks on targets of opportunity. While attacking troops on the Westroosbeke to Menin road, 2Lt A Colin was attacked by an Albatros scout but he outmanoeuvred it and shot it down. Over Zonnebeke, 2Lts D F Hilton and J

Machaffie were attacked by three Albatri, but Hilton shot one down, which was seen going down through the British barrage, still falling.

Lt W S Mansell of 1 Squadron attacked Mouveaux aerodrome firing into the hangars and three machines standing in front of them. On his return he fired 80 rounds into a train on the Wasquehal to Lille line, going down to 200 feet in his attacks. Mouveaux was also attacked by FltSubLt R Minifie of Naval 1. After firing into the hangars he fired at troops in the square in Mouveaux village. Minifie had previous attacked the aerodrome at Chateau du Sart. Arriving there he found an enemy aeroplane at 1,000 feet and attacked it. Reports from other pilots at the end of the day confirmed that it had crashed.

Lt C L Morley of 66 Squadron took off in the dark and flew to Abeelhoek aerodrome. Coming out of the clouds he was fired at by anti-aircraft guns. The fire was very accurate and Morley went back up into the cloud cover. Coming down again he found himself over Harlebeke railway station and he dropped two bombs. Lt Pritt – the 'War Baby' – attacked the enemy aerodrome at Marcke, dropping a bomb into the middle of a group of aeroplanes on the field. Pritt's second bomb fell harmlessly on a road bordering the aerodrome, but the third fell close to the same group of machines. Pritt dropped his last bomb on Herlebout siding, which was packed with troops, but he then saw an Albatros taking off from the aerodrome, obviously with the intention of attacking him. Pritt went after the enemy machine and shot it down to crash into a row of houses to the north east of its aerodrome. Turning away, Pritt saw another Albatros taking off and he shot this one down in a sideslip to crash on the field. A machine gun then began to fire at the Pup and Pritt went down and silenced it.

Lt C J Crang of 70 Squadron attacked Bisseghem aerodrome. There were seven hangars on the aerodrome, but although he went down to 100 feet all his bombs missed them, so he went back over the aerodrome and machine-gunned them. The aerodrome seemed to be deserted, so Crang flew to the Courtrai to Ypres railway line and fired at a train standing in a siding. He then turned north and on the outskirts of Roulers saw Rumbeke aerodrome. Crang went down to 20 feet and fired into five hangars, setting one on fire, with a two-seater inside it. Turning away from this attack he saw another two-seater on the landing field and fired at it. Crang then fired at a locomotive on the Courtrai to Tourcoing railway line, but his Camel was badly shot up by groundfire, forcing him to crash land on his return to Estrée Blanche.

Bishop of 60 Squadron claimed two Albatros C type destroyed over Harnes at 7.00pm and an Albatros scout, also destroyed, over Carvin two minutes later. This brought Bishop's service with 60 Squadron to a close. He had claimed

47 victories and two balloons in his five months with the squadron, but in the words of the squadron's historian, Squadron Leader Joe Warne: 'many were claimed on solo sorties over the other side of the lines and not substantiated for that reason.'

The fighter squadrons of Ninth Wing – 56, 70 and 66 Squadrons – flew close offensive patrols over the battle area from dawn to dusk. 56 Squadron saw many enemy aircraft in large formations and had several indecisive skirmishes, but with no positive results. Capt Tom Hazell of 1 Squadron gained his twentieth victory, the last while with the squadron, shooting down an Albatros over Houthulst at 7.45pm.

Not surprisingly, for a day of continuous and hazardous groundstrafing, casualties were heavy. Nineteen Squadron had two pilots wounded in action – one of whom came down on the enemy side and was taken POW – and two Spads were badly shot up. Manfred von Richthofen shot down 2Lt W H T Williams of 29 Squadron for his fifty-eighth victory,[3] and *Ltn* Groos of *Jasta 11* shot down FltSubLt A T Gray over Hollebeke. Gray was taken prisoner but later died of his wounds. FltLt H J T Saint of Naval 10 was wounded in the side, but returned safely to base.

Flying an offensive patrol in the evening the Camels of 70 Squadron, led by Noel Webb, dived on two German scouts over Polygon Wood. These enemy scouts were from *Jasta 10* and Werner Voss shot down Webb for his thirty-seventh victory. Webb was the second casualty for 70 Squadron during the day: on a ground-strafing mission to attack Bisseghem aerodrome at first light, Lt A R Hudson had been shot down and taken prisoner.

The next two days saw the battle of Langemarck drawing to a conclusion, but the fighting in the air continued with growing intensity. On August 17, Alexander and G L Trapp of Naval 10 were in combat with six Albatros scouts over Ledeghem at 8.30am. Although Trapp drove one Albatros down, all the triplanes had gun stoppages and opportunities to score were frustrated. The pilots of 19 Squadron saw a good deal of action and in one patrol Capt Gordon-Kidd, Lt F Sowery and Lt J Manley each shot down an Albatros out of control, Sowery's victory crashing west of Roulers at 6.30am. Henry Woollett of 24 Squadron shot down an Albatros over Ribecourt at 8.10am; Charles Lavers from 1 Squadron sent a DFW down out of control over Tenbrielen at 10.15am, and Mannock of 40 Squadron crashed a DFW north east of Sallaumines thirty-five minutes later.

Bowman took out C Flight from 56 Squadron at 5.40am. The SEs crossed the Front Line over Polygon Wood and were immediately attacked by 12 Albatri from *Jasta 28* led by an all red machine. In the fierce fighting Richard Leighton and

David Wilkinson were shot down. Wilkinson crashed by the side of the canalised river Lys at Bousbecque, the twenty-third victory of *Offz-Stellv* Max Müller. Wilkinson was badly wounded and died of his crash ten days later.

Richard Leighton, his controls shot away, survived an uncontrolled fall of 12,000 feet. While a prisoner of war he wrote to his mother, Lady Leighton.

'I had a fight with several German machines at well over 12,000 feet and all my controls were shot away so I was absolutely helpless at 12,000 feet. I started to fall and was followed down by one of the German machines. I was shot through the top of the shoulder and the side of the forehead, the machine was shot all over too, and came down with a terrific crash in a paddock in the middle of a village eight kilometers behind the German Lines. My left arm was broken high up and my forehead badly cut in the crash.' Richard Leighton was credited to *Ltn* Groos of *Jasta 11* and survived the war with a silver plate in his head: a memento of 17 August 1917.

In a later patrol Barlow shot down two Albatros scouts over Menin. The Albatri had dived to attack a formation of naval triplanes which had been attacking their two-seaters and Barlow joined in the fight, sending down one enemy machine out of control before turning his attentions to another, attacking it head on. The Albatros began to smoke badly and the enemy pilot hurriedly lost height, but at 3,000 feet his machine was burning fiercely, finally crashing at Moorslede.

2Lt E H Lascelles of 66 Squadron sent an Albatros down in a spinning nosedive over Houthulst at 7.45pm. This was possibly *Ltn* Paul Strähle of *Jasta 18* who recorded in his diary: 'In a combat with a Spad (I think it was probably Capt Bishop, the English Richthofen) I suddenly spun vertically down at full throttle to escape his fire. The fuselage was completely vertical. I thought the wings would break off! All the controls were quite slack.' When Strähle recovered from the spin the 'Spad' was still with him and his fellow *Jasta* pilot, *Ltn* Veltjens, later reported him as having been shot down.

Additional casualties during the day for the fighter squadrons were two Sopwith Camels of Naval 8, which collided over Wingles while in combat with *Obln* Bethge of *Jasta 30*, killing both pilots; a pilot from Naval 6, killed over Zevecote; and FltSubLt R F P Abbot of Naval 3 was wounded in a combat with *Ltn* Meyer of *Jasta 7*. A Camel from 70 Squadron was also lost, the pilot, Lt A M T Glover, was last seen in a steep dive east of Ypres, and 66 Squadron lost 2Lt Pat O'Brien who was shot down and taken prisoner.[4]

As the ground fighting died down the next day, enemy air activity close to the Front Lines was less than on the previous days, the *jagdstaffeln* concentrating their efforts on intercepting the long distance bombing and photographic aircraft of the RFC. The majority of the combats against enemy scouts

were fought by these machines, but the fighter squadrons were not inactive. George Lloyd of 40 Squadron destroyed an Albatros C type over Fromelles in the morning, but 29 Squadron lost a pilot shot down, wounded and taken POW, and a pilot of 32 Squadron was killed while groundstafing.

Fifty-six Squadron saw a great deal of fighting during the day and lost a pilot: Capt H Rushworth. All three Flights were out in the morning. Gerald Maxwell, now the A Flight Commander, wounded the observer of a two-seater before it dived under the cover of eight Albatros scouts from *Jasta 18*, which attacked the SEs. Maxwell shot one black and white Albatros down out of control in a slow spiral, but was then forced to break off the action with engine trouble. This Albatros sent down by Maxwell was possibly *Ltn* Weinschenk, who was slightly wounded in the leg.

Harold Rushworth, Eric Turnbull and William Potts were attacking enemy two-seaters east of Houthulst Forest when an accurate burst of fire from one of the enemy gunners hit Rushworth's SE5 in the petrol tank and smashed the rudder bar, the last bullet wounding Rushworth in the foot. Rushworth forced landed and was taken prisoner.

James McCudden, leading B Flight in his first patrol as B Flight Commander of 56 Squadron, also attacked these two-seaters. All the Flight, with the exception of Keith Muspratt, had gun stoppages and the two-seaters escaped. McCudden's stoppages were so severe that he had to land at Bailleul to rectify them. Leaving Bailleul, McCudden teamed up with Barlow and attacked a formation of Albatri over Comines. One enemy scout climbed away from an attack by Barlow and came under fire from McCudden, who fired 20 rounds from each gun at very close range. The Albatros went down at 'great speed' in a vertical spiral.

Muspratt attacked a two-seater, closing to very close range (he estimated it as three yards) and saw his tracers going into the pilot and engine. The two-seater went vertically down, but the observer had hit Muspratt's SE in the exhaust pipe, a magneto and a centre section strut and he was forced to land, 'at Leslie's old squadron, covered in petrol.' Detailing this action in a letter home to his father and aunt, Muspratt ended: 'I heard from uncle Frank today, he seems bored with life'.

Casualties for the day for the fighter squadrons were light. In addition to Rushworth, a Camel from Naval 4 was shot down in the morning by *Ltn* Paul Billik of *Jasta 7*, killing the pilot, FltSubLt C Hodges; a DH5 from 32 Squadron was seen to spin in while groundstrafing, and the pilot, 2Lt T Kirkness, was killed. Major H A van Ryneveld of 45 Squadron was wounded in the head while attacking a two-seater and 29 Squadron had 2Lt W Stiles shot down wounded and taken POW.

On August 19 the *jagdstaffeln* still employed their tactics of keeping well east of the lines and patrolling in large formations. A DFW, attacked by a patrol from Naval 8, was shot down by FltLt Ronald Thornley, east of Lens, and in a later patrol Booker and Crundall each shot down an Albatros scout in a combat over Henin-Lietard.

Six Nieuports of 1 Squadron, led by Fullard, were escorting the FE2ds of 20 Squadron when they were attacked by six Albatri from *Jasta 28* over Wervicq. Fullard shot down one Albatros painted yellow with black stripes in the fight, which crashed near Menin. One of the FEs was shot down by *Ltn* Ernst Hess of *Jasta 28* and the crew, both wounded, were taken prisoner.

In a morning combat over Polygon Wood, 2Lt J W Gillespie of 70 Squadron was shot down and taken prisoner and 2Lt A M Epps was wounded in the arm.

In the afternoon, during the only patrol flown by 56 Squadron in the day, James McCudden shot down an Albatros painted with red and yellow stripes over Gheluvelt. The weather was very warm. Keith Muspratt wrote home: ' a ripping bath in the afternoon saved me from dissolving. The heat is appalling, but flying and washing give great relief. Rhys Davids is on leave, so I am all alone, but bearing up.'

Further south, the pilots of 24, 41 and 60 Squadrons were co-operating with infantry attacking enemy positions south of Vendhuille. All the pilots carried out attacks on German troops, trenches and transport. Luckily there were no casualties.

The next day Warman of 23 Squadron ended his run of victories when he was wounded in the shoulder during a combat. Clive Wilson Warman had been with the squadron since July 6, had scored 12 victories, and been awarded a DSO and MC.[5]

It was again a bad day for 70 Squadron. A Flight of Camels attacked *Jasta 5* over Douai and lost 2Lt H D Turner, shot down by *Offz-Stellv* Josef Mai for the first of his eventual 30 victories. An afternoon patrol from Naval 10 was returning to base when it was attacked by five enemy scouts, forcing the triplanes down into the clouds below them. Alexander climbed back out of the cloud, and followed three of the enemy machines to Roubaix where they turned to attack him. Alexander sent one down out of control and drove the others off. FltSubLt C H Weir had been shot down in the fight, crashed landed and was taken prisoner, but died of his injuries the next day.

In the evening, McCudden led a large patrol of eleven SE5s to patrol in the vicinity of Houthulst. At ten minutes to seven McCudden led the Flight down to attack a formation of Albatros scouts coming north from Zandvoorde. Singling out the leader of the enemy formation, McCudden closed to fifty yards and opened fire with both guns. A trickle of flames came out of the fuselage of the Albatros and it went down in a ver-

tical dive, which fanned the flames until the whole machine was burning fiercely. The Albatros finally crashed in a small copse south east of Polygon Wood, killing *Vzfw* Karl-Josef Oehler of *Jasta 24,* and starting a large fire, which was still burning when the SE5s flew back to base. Ten minutes after this combat McCudden shot down another Albatros, which fell out of control over Polygon Wood and was confirmed by Lt Johnston. Barlow also shot at an Albatros, which spun for fifteen turns before it was lost to sight, still going down. The pilots of 56 Squadron were credited with two scouts destroyed and three out of control from this action.

The *Luftstreitkräfte* was very active until the evening of the following day, August 21, the s*chusta and jagdstaffeln* concentrating on attacking the British trenches and artillery machines of the corps squadrons. There were many combats and the corps squadron suffered heavy casualties, but the losses of the fighter squadrons were relatively light.

Two Sopwith Pups of 54 Squadron were hit by Archie in the morning: 2Lt T L Tebbit's Pup was hit in the undercarriage by two large pieces of shell fragments and Tebitt crashed on landing. The Pup flown by Lt F J Morse was also badly damaged but both Pups were repairable in the squadron workshops.

Walbanke Pritt of 66 Squadron was returning to base with a badly running engine when he saw a Aviatik two-seater working over the Lines south west of Roulers. Never one to miss an opportunity and despite his engine trouble, Pritt dived on the enemy machine and sent it down out of control.

The Sopwith 1 1/2 Strutters of 45 Squadron were returning from a mission when two Sopwith Triplanes from Naval 1 dived under the patrol from out of the clouds, pursued by several DFW two-seaters. The Sopwiths immediately went into their usual defensive circle and the first triplane climbed back to their height and joined them. The second triplane pilot was harder pressed; before he could climb back to the protection of the two-seaters, he was attacked by a DFW. The pilot of one of the 1 1/2 Strutters, Capt Norman Macmillan, saw his danger and swung out of the circle. 'I got in a few shots before my bus stalled and the nose flopped down again. As we stalled I kicked on rudder and shoved the stick hard across in a skidding turn and shouted down the tube to Morris: "Hun above us, shoot!" Morris, Macmillan's gunner, opened fire at fifty yards range and the DFW flew straight into the stream of bullets from his Lewis gun, raking the fuselage from nose to tail. Macmillan then lost sight of the enemy machine, but as he rejoined his leader he looked down and saw a camouflaged aeroplane falling out of control two thousand feet below them. 'It fell almost vertically, nosedown. And, as it fell, it developed a curious, uneven flicking turn – the certain sign of an aeroplane absolutely out of control.' Macmillan spiralled down to watch the end of the falling machine, but before it crashed, 'a tiny licking flame appeared from the middle of its fuselage, followed by a trail of smoke. Its end was sudden. It fell in a headlong dive and crashed sickeningly nose first into the ground.'[6] Intent on watching the end of the DFW, Macmillan and Morris were then attacked by another, but they managed to drive it off and return.

On landing, Macmillan found that the other pilots had seen only a British machine go down, had not seen the DFW he had followed down, and were of the opinion that he and Morris had shot down a naval triplane, an opinion reinforced by a telephone call from Naval 1 to say that they had lost a new pilot close to the position of the fight. There was also a message from British artillery that an aeroplane was down near the position. Even before the message from Naval 1, Macmillan, positive that Morris and he could not have shot down a friendly machine, had left for the scene of the crash. Locating the wreckage, partly buried in the soft soil beside a road, he found it *was* a Sopwith Triplane, but Macmillan's confidence that Morris had not shot down a triplane was justified. The DFW they had shot down had crashed in flames and the wreckage of the triplane showed no evidence of fire. Macmillan, wanting to leave no room for doubt, went up to the nearby front line trenches, where the infantry confirmed that an enemy machine had crashed within a minute of the triplane, an almost identical distance behind the German Front Line as the triplane behind the British. Macmillan returned to St Marie Cappel to find that during his absence an AA battery had also confirmed the crash of the DFW.[7]

This combat took place in the morning, at approximately 11.35am, and the naval pilot killed was FltSubLt F C Lewis of Naval 1. The naval triplanes had been fighting four enemy two-seaters and FltLt Everitt, out of ammunition, had returned to report that Lewis had been shot down by an enemy aircraft. Lewis has been credited to *Hptm* Hartmann of *Jasta 28,* but Hartmann's victory was at 6.35pm (BT) and at Terhand, a small hamlet between Dadizele and Becelaere, nearly ten miles from Lewis' crash east of Ploegsteert Wood. Although the position is just possible the time is not. Hartmann's victim was FltSubLt C Lowther of Naval 10, last seen going down over Menin at 6.40pm (BT), the only naval triplane lost in the evening. Lowther has been credited to *Ltn* Hess of *Jasta 28,* but his claim was for a 'Sopwith' between Ypres and Frezenberg at 9.50am (GT). Sixty-Six Squadron lost two pilots in the area at this time: Lt W R Keast who died of wounds and Lt P H Raney, killed in action.

In an evening patrol the Nieuports of 1 Squadron were in a fight with *Jasta 26* over Polygon Wood and *Ltn* Fritz Loerzer shot down 2Lt C A Moody.

August 22 was a day of bright sunshine and very warm. The *Luftstreitkräfte* was still active in some force, although not as much as the previous two days; the RFC communiqué records that the German pilots seemed disinclined to fight near the Lines.

The Canadian, Capt Albert Earl Godfrey, of 40 Squadron, scored his fourteenth and last victory at 10.40am, shooting down an enemy two-seater over Hullock. He was to leave 40 Squadron in early September, posted to Home Establishment. Godfrey, known in 40 Squadron as 'Steve', was vividly described by Bond in his letters home. 'He's my right hand man on patrol and is wonderfully reliable. He's a Canadian and talks violently and nasally – when he does talk, which is rare. Usually he is very quiet. But when he is excited – say, when he comes back from a scrap – nothing holds him. His language, all unconsciously is lurid. As it generally happens that the Odd Man[8] is waiting to hear all about it, the result is thrilling.

"Anything doing?" says the Odd Man. "Why, Christ almighty, I should say there was", shouts Grahaeme.[9] He still has his helmet on, and as he can't hear well he thinks he has to shout. He goes on – "The sky's stiff with bloody Huns". The Odd Man does not continue for the moment, but just looks more thoughtful. Someone else, less sensitive to blasphemy, goes on with the interrogation until the Odd Man, forgetting his feelings in the excitement of the story, chips in again.

"Did you get one down?"

"Jesus, yes. There were three of the red b-s and I was diving on one when I heard someone popping at me with his bloody double gun. Hell, I said. There's another damned Hun on my tail, so I yanked up the old bus and got on the devil's tail and just pumped blue hell into him! Christ – away he went spinning to hell and gone."

'No comment from the Odd Man.

It isn't only on these occasions that Grahaeme's mode of expression is unusual. At breakfast this morning the Odd Man was seated next to him and said.

"Out for more Huns today, Grahaeme?"

"Jesus, yes" said Grahaeme fervently and quite gravely. "Well, that's the right spirit anyway" commented to Odd Man in the stifled silence.'

The pilots of A Flight, 56 Squadron, had a successful morning's fighting. The sky over Houthulst Forest was swarming with enemy aeroplanes, Robert Sloley counted 25 enemy scouts at various heights from 14,000 to 5,000 feet flying over the forest. The SEs went down to attack a formation of Albatri from *Jasta 18*, one of the lower formations. Maxwell almost immediately shot down *Oblt* Harald Auffarth, who dived away from the fight, his Albatros badly shot about by Maxwell's fire. William Potts sent another of the Albatri down in a vertical dive and Charles Jeffs, in his first action since joining the squadron, emptied an entire drum of Lewis into an Albatros which went down to crash near Gheluvelt, possibly either *Oblt* Berthold or *Ltn* Schober. Maxwell wrote in his diary: 'Splendid scrap. About forty Huns over Ypres.'[10]

The Sopwith Camels of 70 Squadron were also in action over the area. Clive Collett and Lt Bickerton each claimed an Albatros scout out of control, Collett's falling over Gheluwe at 8.50am.

Richard Maybery took off on a solo mission before lunch. While over Armentières he saw four enemy two-seaters climbing for height over Marcq. Maybery attacked the first of these, his fire hitting the observer who fell forwards onto the fuselage decking, his hands hanging over the side of the fuselage. Maybery attempted to zoom and attack again but his engine had been hit by the observer's fire and refused to pick up. Maybery turned for the lines leaving the two-seater gliding down towards Menin. The German lists give a *Ltn de Res* Heinrich Lüders of *Fl Abt 26*, killed over Wevelghem on August 22.

A large patrol of 12 SE5s from 56 Squadron took off from Estrée Blanche in the evening. Arriving over Ypres, McCudden saw Bowman and C Flight, plus Eric Turnbull and Sloley, fighting with three Albatri over the eastern edge of Houthulst Forest. McCudden knew that Bowman's force would have no difficulty in containing the three Albatri and flew to attack four DFWs which he had seen making for the Front Lines. McCudden flew east to cut off any possibility of retreat for the DFWs, waiting until they were over Ypres before attacking them. McCudden badly damaged the leader of the enemy formation, which went down. Muspratt closed to within ten yards of another and fired a burst of 50 rounds, causing the DFW to serve to the left then go into a steep spin, increasing in speed as it fell. This DFW finally crashed behind the British lines, west of Zonnebeke by the St. Julien to Ypres road. McCudden wryly commented. 'I have never seen anything so funny as that old Hun going round and round for over two minutes. I bet the pilot and observer had a sick headache after that.' McCudden's amusement was ill placed. *Ltn* Albert Wolluhn and *Fl* Otto Koch of *FlAbt (A) 210* were both killed in the crash.

Verschoyle Cronyn also shot down one of the two-seaters, but his SE5 was hit in the engine and radiator he was forced to land at Bailleul aerodrome. Muspratt's DFW crashed behind the British Lines and was designated G65. Cronyn's crashed 80 yards behind the German trenches, but was confirmed by British batteries and pilots from other squadrons.

After fighting with Bowman and his Flight, the three Albatri had made off east and the SEs became split up. Bowman had a fight with another trio of Albatros scouts, forcing one down by continual dive and zoom attacks. Maybery attacked five other scouts over Houthulst Forest and shot a green painted Albatros down in a vertical dive to crash at Viekavenhock. This was possibly *Ltn d Res* Ludwig Luer of *Jasta 27* who survived the crash.

The two-seaters shot down by Muspratt and Cronyn made B Flight the first Flight of the squadron to score fifty victories. Before the day's fighting A Flight had 46 victories, B Flight 48 and C Flight 47. After detailing his part in the day's events, Muspratt summed up the mood of the squadron that night in a letter home. 'We are wildly bucked with life and I am all over myself. I am going to try to see the machine I got tomorrow.'[11]

Other pilots were successful during the day: Capt James Pearson of 32 Squadron shot down an Albatros scout over Bellewarde Lake at 5.30am; Capt Gerald Gibbs, 23 Squadron, shot down a DFW over Wervicq at 6.45am; Maclanachan of 40 Squadron, an Albatros scout from a patrol of seven, down out of control at 10.10am in the vicinity of Douai. 2Lt R L Graham, 19 Squadron, claimed a two-seater north of Houthulst Forest, and 2Lt H Rothery of 29 Squadron a balloon in the same area. FltLt Norman Macgregor from Naval 6 claimed an Albatros destroyed north of St Pierre Capelle at 9.45am for the naval squadrons. In the evening, Capt Fullard of 1 Squadron shot down a DFW over Poelcapelle at 6.35pm.

On the debit side, Lt H A Kennedy of 40 Squadron was killed in a fight over Dourges. The squadron had been ordered to attack German aerodromes in the evening and Mannock took out ten Nieuports. He later recorded in a diary entry.

'We met trouble halfway through the programme in the shape of seven Huns coming home east. I saw them first and had first blood. Got a lovely burst into the first machine from about twenty-five yards range. He immediately went over on his side and went down in a beautiful wide spiral. I hadn't time to observe him hit Mother Earth, as things were happening. A glorious mix up for about two minutes. One of my boys got another one soon, and they got poor old Kennedy. We finished up by driving them to ground to the safety of their anti-aircraft guns, but we ought to have got the lot. It was really a disappointing show.'

The weather began to change the next day, August 23. There was a strong westerly wind and frequent rainstorms throughout the day. Enemy activity in the air was consequently very slight. There was little fighting, but the Spads of 19 Squadron were in combat near Dixmude with *Jasta 10* and Werner Voss wounded Capt A L Gordon-Kidd in the thigh. Gordon-Kid managed to return and land his badly damaged Spad but died of his wounds four days later.

The pilots of 45 Squadron claimed their last victories while flying the Sopwith 1 1/2 Strutter. The Squadron was to be completely re-equipped with Sopwith Camels by the end of the month.

Low clouds, wind and strong rain stopped all war flying on August 24. A few patrols were flown the following day, despite the weather still being poor.

A patrol of DH5s from 24 Squadron fought with two Albatros C types at 6.00am. Capt Bernard Beanlands and Lt 2Lt W B Ives shot one down over Bellenglise for a shared victory and within minutes Beanlands shot down its companion. Ground observers reported that one enemy machine fell out of control, but the other fell in flames. The day seems to have been one of mixed fortunes for the squadrons flying the DH5. Flying a low patrol, two pilots of 32 Squadron attacked a DFW working over the Lines and shot it down in flames near Polygon Wood, but one pilot's machine was hit by groundfire and he crashed landed amongst shell holes. A DH5 pilot from 41 Squadron was also lost: Capt J S deL Bush was last seen flying southeast over Sorel-le-Grand. He was shot down by *Offstv* Joseph Mai of *Jasta 5* for his second victory and later died of his wounds in captivity.

Capt Norman Macmillan flew his first patrol in one of 45 Squadron's newly issued Camels in the evening. After joining a Flight of DH5s, Macmillan left them over Houthulst Forest and flew to the southeast, but was surprised by a formation of Albatros scouts that came at him from out of the evening haze. Macmillan fired at two of the enemy scouts and one went down. Macmillan had no time to watch it further, but ground batteries later confirmed that it had crashed. This was the first Camel victory for 45 Squadron.

Despite the weather, three offensive patrols were flown by 70 Squadron during the day. In an evening fight over Houthulst, 2Lt O C Bridgeman was wounded by *Obltn* Göring of *Jasta 27*. Bridgeman returned but was taken to hospital.

The triplanes of Naval 10 took off at 6.20am to patrol the Menin,Courtrai, Wervicq area. To the east of Courtrai a formation of enemy machines was seen, with another formation a little to the south of the town. FltLt Saint and C Flight attacked the lower formation, driving one of the enemy machines down, but these were decoys and they dived away east as the other enemy formation, with the morning sun behind them, came down on the naval triplanes, forcing them to retreat to the west. FltSubLt A D M Lewis of A Flight, flying only his second patrol with the Flight, was shot down and taken prisoner by *Ltn* Hans-Georg von der Osten of *Jasta 11*.

Naval 10 had better fortune during an evening patrol when Fitzgibbon shot down an enemy scout out of control north of Polygon Wood for his fifth victory.

August 26 was a day of mixed fortunes for the British Spad squadrons. Led by Capt John Leacroft, four Spads of 19 Squadron took off at 5.40am to attack the German aerodromes

at Bisseghem and Marke. On their way to the targets the British scouts engaged a pair of DFW two-seaters and their attacks wounded or killed the observers, one of the DFWs going down to crash near Moorsele. A number of Albatros scouts then appeared and attacked the Spads. Leacroft shot down one of these which was seen to crash near the aerodrome, but 2Lt Coningsby Williams was shot down and killed by Manfred von Richthofen for his 59th victory. Slightly earlier, Lt F E Barker had shot down an Albatros in flames, but although wounded in the thigh had managed to crash land his machine west of the lines and was taken to hospital.[12]

A little further to the west of these actions the Spads of 23 Squadron were fighting with Albatros scouts, 2Lt O'Grady and Capt D U McGregor each shooting down an Albatros out of control, and in the evening Capt Baker of the squadron shot down a DFW, seen to crash north of Zonnebeke. Capt Spenser Horn of 60 Squadron, flying a lone patrol saw an enemy two-seater firing red and green lights and he shot it down out of control over Gillemont Farm at 7.15am.

The wet weather had made any main ground attack in the Ypres area impossible, but minor attacks of a local nature were carried out on other fronts, in particular on the 3rd Army front. On August 26 the British infantry attacked Cologne Farm Hill on the front of III Corps and twelve DH5s of 24 and 41 Squadrons attacked infantry in trenches and motor transport on the roads in support of the attack.

Rain and strong winds interfered with operations the next day and the only action appears to be that fought by the Camels of 45 Squadron with seven Albatri over Moorslede at 12.15pm in which Capt Arthur Harris shot one down out of control.[13]

During the day Naval 6 Squadron was disbanded, its Sopwith Camels and pilots being distributed between Naval 9 and 10.

The bad weather intensified the next day and there was no war flying for four days. On the last day of the month, although low clouds and rain interfered with operations until the evening, some combats were fought. Twelve SE5s from 56 Squadron – A and B Flights – took off at 6.00pm and made for the patrol area of Houthulst Forest to Gheluvelt. Maxwell, leading A Flight, spotted a formation of eight Albatri circling Moorslede at 12,000 feet, but it was an obvious trap: eight additional Albatri were at 16,000 feet, flying west to put the setting sun between themselves and the SE5s before attacking. Maxwell knew that McCudden and B Flight were nearby, would tackle these Albatri, and he led his Flight down on the lower formation. Maxwell attacked one of the enemy scouts, which spun away from his fire. Another got behind him and hit the SE5 in the tailplane. Maxwell had stoppages in both guns and he dived for the cover of the British AA batteries over Ypres, 'chased by a very good red-nosed EA who kept on my tail and fired a large number of rounds' Maxwell went down to 5,000 feet, where the persistent enemy pilot was taken off his tail by Geoffrey Wilkinson, who shot the red-nosed scout down out of control. This was confirmed by Lt Taylor of 66 Squadron.[14] Wilkinson was then attacked by *Ltn* Adam of *Jasta 6*, and his SE5 so badly damaged that on return to Estrée Blanche it was struck off squadron strength.

McCudden's Flight had gone to assistance of two French Spads that were fighting with a group of black and white Albatros scouts. Henry Coote fired at one Albatros that went down emitting black and blue smoke, but after a great deal of skirmishing the remainder of the Albatros made off east over Armentières.

On August 31 the 9th Wing War Diary recorded that the pilots of 70 Squadron reported meeting a new enemy machine, described as: 'a double "V" Strut Albatross (sic) single-seater. It is also reported that the enemy has a new tri-plane (sic) with a single "V" strut on each side; top plane being the longest, middle plane slightly shorter, and the bottom plane shorter than either.' The reference to the 'double "V" strut' Albatros is puzzling. The only new biplane fighter to enter service with the *jagdstaffeln* at this time was the Pfalz D III. The new 'tri-plane' was one of the first examples of the Fokker Triplane – the V 4, later redesignated the Dr 1.[15]

The almost continuous rain during the last weeks of August had turned the ground in the Ypres area into a sea of mud, making large scale ground attacks impossible. Plans were being made, however, for a resumption of the Ypres offensive as soon as the ground had dried sufficiently, and an extensive programme was being prepared for the squadrons of the RFC.

NOTES

1. Crundall. *Op.cit.*

2. Tutschek, who had twenty-three victories when he was wounded suffered a shattered shoulder and was not to return to action until February 1918.

3. Williams was extricated from his crash by German troops and taken to hospital, but his wounds were severe and he died six days later. He was nineteen years of age.

4. O'Brien escaped from captivity in November 1917 and made his way back to England. After the war he returned to his native America and became a successful film actor.

5. Warman was killed in a flying accident on 12 June 1919 while serving with No.1 Canadian Squadron.

6. *Into the Blue*, Norman Macmillan, Duckworth, London 1929.

7. The German records give a crew of *Fl Abt (A) 227* as killed at Bondues. Bondues is on the outskirts of Lille and may have been the location of a German hospital.

8. The 'Odd Man' was 40 Squadron's much-loved chaplain, Padre Keymer.

9. Grahaeme was Godfrey's pseudonym in *An Airman's Wife*. Godfrey never returned to France. He returned to Canada in April 1918 and served with the Canadian training brigade until the end of the war. At the beginning of World War II Godfrey was a Group Captain in the Royal Canadian Air Force, serving in England at the Imperial Defence College. He died on 1 January 1982.

10. Detailing this action in his diary, the *Staffelführer* of *Jasta 18,* Paul Strahle, mentions the 'loss' of three pilots, but all three were again in action a few days later.

11. The squadron was now the most successful fighter squadron in France. At about this time, Ninth Wing totalled up the number of enemy aeroplanes brought down by its squadrons. Although 56 Squadron had been in France for only a third of the period in question, it had accounted for over 65% of the enemy machines brought down.

12. A message was received from the French on August 30, confirming Barker's victory.

13. Arthur Harris remained in the RAF after the war and in World War II was Air Officer Commanding Bomber Command from 1942 until 1945. Marshal of the Royal Air Force, Sir Arthur Harris, GCB, OBE, AFC, LL D died on 6 April 1984.

14. *Vzfw* Wilhelm Reiss of *Jasta 3*.

15. Air historians have long believed that only two Fokker Triplanes were at the Front in August 1917: F.1 102/17 to *Jasta 11* and F.1 103/17 to *Jasta 10*. Recent evidence, however, suggests the possibility that at least one additional triplane was at the Front in late August or early September.

CHAPTER FOURTEEN

EVENINGS ABOVE THE SALIENT

"The evenings were simply wonderful, as the fighting was usually very fierce and well-contested." — James McCudden

The amount of rainfall in northwest Europe during July and August 1917 was the worst for over 75 years. The first few days of September saw little improvement. A combination of low clouds, rain and mist seriously curtailed activity in the air. There were only two casualties on September 1: an RE8 of 6 Squadron and a Spad of 19 Squadron, flown by 2Lt E M Sant, which was seen going down in a spin near Houthulst Forest. Sant was taken POW. In this action the Spads had been fighting *Jasta 35b* and John Leacroft claimed an Albatros destroyed over Polygon Wood at 6.55am and another south east of Comines at 8.15am. Another Spad from 19 Squadron was lost the next day when 2Lt W A L Spenser was wounded, shot down and taken prisoner by *Ltn* Dilthey of *Jasta 27*.

Conditions on September 3 were 'fine and bright' and the airfighting resumed its usual intensity.

The pilots of 45 Squadron were now flying regular patrols a day in their Sopwith Camels, no doubt revelling in the superior performance of their new mounts after that of the Sopwith 1 1/2 Strutter. They had many old scores to settle with the *jagdstaffeln*. In the morning Norman Macmillan, now promoted to Captain and commanding A Flight, led an Offensive Patrol. Lt Shields turned back with engine trouble before reaching the Lines, and as the remaining three climbed hard to attack a formation of enemy aircraft, Lt R J Dawes dropped behind with a failing engine. Macmillan now had only Lt A T Heywood with him, but they attacked the enemy scouts over Dadizeele

Macmillan picked his opponent and opened fire from close range. The Albatros went down over Dadizeele, but although Macmillan was sure he had killed the pilot he failed to see the end of this machine. The other enemy scouts all dived away east and Macmillan, not wishing to lose height, let them go. Macmillan and Heywood then saw a pair of DFWs over

Comines, but these had seen the Camels and dived away east before they could be attacked. Macmillan then turned west. He could see no enemy aircraft, but Heywood broke formation and turned away, flying west towards the British Lines. Macmillan thought that Heywood probably had engine trouble, but as he could see no enemy aircraft, and as Heywood was making for base, thought it safe to leave him unescorted and flew north, where he saw a formation of RE8s under attack over Tenbreilen from three formations of Albatri. Macmillan dived to the assistance of the British two-seaters, shooting down one of the Albatri in flames. This was *Ltn* Heinrich Vollersten of *Jasta 36* who was killed at 10.40am (GT) over Tenbreilen.

On his return to Ste-Marie-Cappel, Macmillan found that Dawes and Shields had returned safely but Heywood was missing. After leaving Macmillan he had been shot down over Zandvoorde by Werner Voss for his thirty-ninth victory; the first while flying Fokker Triplane F.1 103/17.

Forty-six Squadron had returned to France from England on August 30, and were stationed at Ste-Marie-Cappel, sharing the aerodrome with 45 and 20 Squadrons. The 46 Squadron pilots were envious of 45 Squadron's Camels – Lee commented in a letter home: 'I sat in one – it's a little roomier than a Pup. And to see those *two* Vickers in front of me made my mouth water.'[1]

Forty-six Squadron's return to France started badly. On the morning of September 3, in its first patrol since returning, the squadron had four casualties. Five machines of A Flight were attacked by *Jasta 11* in the vicinity of Menin and Lt K W Macdonald and Lt Algernon Bird were shot down. Both pilots were taken prisoner, but Macdonald had been wounded and later died of his wounds. He was awarded to *Ltn* Mohnicke of *Jasta 11*. Bird was shot down by Richthofen, for his second victory while flying Fokker Triplane F.1 102/17. Bird's Pup was considerably shot about in the fight, but he fired at ground troops on his way down and deliberately crashed his Pup into a tree. Lt R S Asher's Pup had also been badly shot about and he came down in the Front Line trenches. The patrol later reported that one of the enemy scouts was a triplane painted red, but this was discounted at the time by the 46 Squadron pilots. Unaware of the existence of the new Fokker Triplanes at the Front they considered that it must have been a captured naval triplane.

The second patrol by 46 Squadron, taking off at 9.00am, fared little better. Going to the aid of some FEs from 20 Squadron being attacked by 12 Albatri, they lost two of their number despite the assistance of some Bristol Fighters which had joined in the fight. Lt F R Barrager was wounded but managed to land his damaged Pup at La Lovie, 23 Squadron's aerodrome, but Lt S W Williams had been shot down and made POW by *Ltn* Fruhner of *Jasta 26.*

Arthur Lee was due to fly in the next squadron patrol at 11.30am. 'The knowledge of what had hit the other patrols wasn't awfully inspiring.' The five Pups climbed steeply eastwards and as they approached the Lines they could see fifty or sixty aeroplanes 'milling around at different levels, like flocks of starlings assembling.'

Five hundred feet above the Pups, some Camels were in combat with several Albatri. It was the first time that Lee had seen Camels in action and he was astounded by their ability to turn in almost their own length. An Albatros came down from the fight, trailing vapour before bursting into flames and disintegrating. The Pups could not climb up into the fight, but climbed through various formations of enemy machines, which made no attempt to attack them and were too scattered for the Pups to attack in formation. Reaching 14,000 feet – a good height for the Pup, with its light wing loading, to fight – they saw a group of seven Albatros D Vs a thousand feet below and went down to attack them.

Lee attacked an Albatros with a blue fuselage and mauve wings, getting onto its tail, but he was fired at by another that had got behind him, hitting the Pup in a centre section strut. Lee half rolled away and the Albatros, this one coloured grey and green, passed under the Pup. Lee made to follow but his engine suddenly stopped. With no power and in the middle of the fight, Lee put the Pup into steep dive, hoping none of the Albatri would follow him. Levelling out 2,000 feet below the action, Lee glanced back up and saw that a formation of Camels had joined in the fight and the Albatri were fully occupied. Lee had 11,000 feet in height and was on the right side of the lines, but there was a strong smell of petrol and he made for the nearest aerodrome he knew, 46 Squadron's old aerodrome at La Gorgue. On landing, Lee found that the aerodrome was now occupied by 35 Squadron, whose mechanics soon repaired a broken petrol pipe.

Flying his second patrol of an eventful day, Lee's engine again cut out during a fight with some enemy scouts. He again had ample height, but as he approached the lines a close burst of anti-aircraft fire threw the Pup on its side. Lee, choking and coughing from the fumes of the burst, put the Pup in a steep dive and glided west. Luckily he met a patrol of Pups from 66 Squadron and they escorted him to the safety of the British lines.

The Sopwith Camels seen fighting the Albatri were from 45 Squadron. Arthur Harris destroyed an Albatros over Dadizeele – possibly the one seen by Lee – and O L McMaking and W C Moore each claimed an Albatros out of control from the fighting. A little earlier in the day, Matthew Frew had also claimed an Albatros out of control, over Zandvoorde.

A patrol in the evening from 56 Squadron were in action with enemy scouts over Noordschote. The A Flight commander, Gerald Maxwell, led the SE5s down to attack six Albatri and Eric Turnbull attacked one that he followed down, losing sight of it just north of Houthulst Forest, still going down.

C Flight of 56 Squadron were also out, attacking a formation of eight Albatri above the Ypres-Comines Canal, and Maybery shot one Albatros down in a steep dive to crash by the village of Houthem. McCudden and Rhys Davids had taken off together but became separated soon after leaving Estrée Blanche. Rhys Davids joined in the fight between C Flight and the eight Albatri, saw one on the fringe of the fight and shot it down. But this was the same Albatros – possibly from *Jasta 4* – shot down by Maybery and he and Rhys Davids shared the victory.

McCudden, with Potts and Jeffs of A Flight, attempted to attack three Albatri over Poelcapelle, but as he got up to their height his engine 'choked' and he found himself directly under an enemy scout, whose pilot was looking down at the SE5. Suddenly, McCudden saw tracers going into the enemy scout, which burst into flames and fell so close to the SE – within fifty feet – that McCudden distinctly heard 'the roar of it as it passed me'. Neither Jeffs or Potts, nor any other allied pilot, claimed this Albatros and the German lists give no loss in the area or for the time in question: an illustration of the unreliability of available German records.

The naval squadrons were successful in the evening's fighting: FltLt J Hunter of Naval 4 shot down an Albatros out of control for the first of his eventual 12 claims, and FltCom J S Fall scored his first victory with Naval 9, an Albatros destroyed over Pervyse at 6.30pm.

Other victories during the day were an Albatros out of control south east of Comines at 8.30am for Captain John Leacroft of 19 Squadron; an Albatros out of control over

Poelcapelle at 7.15am for Capt Cudemore of 29 Squadron, and Captain Hunter of 66 Squadron claimed an Albatros north east of Menin at 11.35am. William Mansell of 1 Squadron destroyed an Albatros in a fight over Gheluwe at 6.50pm for his fourth victory, but 2Lt L C Pickstone was shot down and killed in the fighting by *Ltn* Adam of *Jasta 6.*

The naval squadrons lost two pilots during the day: FltSubLt N D Hall of Naval 3 was taken POW in the morning, and Naval 1, in a fight with *Jasta 11* at 9.30am lost FltSubLt G Scott, shot down and killed.

September 4 was bright and clear all day. The airfighting followed the pattern of the previous day, but the RFC communiqué noted that although enemy fighters attacked the corps squadrons aeroplanes engaged on artillery work, they were 'less inclined than on the 3rd inst. to engage our scouts unless far east.'

Mannock had an eventful day. At 9.40am he had what he described in a diary entry as 'a beautiful running fight', with a DFW at 17,000 feet, chasing the two-seater from Bruay to east of Lens. The DFW finally got away, 'not withstanding the fact that I fired nearly three hundred rounds at close range. I saw the observer's head and arm lying over the side of the machine – he was dead apparently – but the pilot seemed alright (sic). He deserved to get away really as he must have been a brave Hun.' This fight had been watched from the advanced landing ground at Mazingarbe by 40 Squadron's mechanics and 'caused great excitement.' This DFW from *FltAbt (A) 211* force landed behind the German Lines. Contrary to Mannock's impression, it was the pilot, *Vzfw* Eddelbüttel, who was seriously wounded, but the observer *Ltn* Kuhm was unhurt.

Later in the morning, Mannock, Captain Keen and Sgt L A Herbert took off to find a DFW which had been reported as working over the lines. They found the two-seater east of Lens at 11.30am. Keen attacked first but broke away to change a Lewis gun drum and Mannock 'got quite close up and let him have a full drum, and he went nose down east.' Herbert had also fired at this DFW and although it was not seen to crash because of the ground mist, it was shared between him and Mannock.

Mannock was out again the afternoon and attacked another DFW that he shot down in flames at 4.30pm.

'I met this unfortunate DFW at about ten thousand feet over Avion coming southwest, and I was travelling southeast. I couldn't recognise the black crosses readily (he was about three hundred yards away and about five hundred feet above me) so I turned my tail towards him and went in the same direction, thinking that if he were British, he wouldn't take any notice of me, and if a Hun, I felt sure he would put his nose down and have a shot (thinking I hadn't seen him). The ruse worked beautifully. His nose went down (pointing at me)

and I immediately whipped round, dived and "zoomed" up behind him, before you could say "knife". He tried to turn but he was much too slow for the Nieuport. I got in about fifty rounds in short bursts whilst on the turn, and he went down in flames, pieces of wing and tail, etc. dropping away from the wreck. It was a horrible sight and made me feel sick. He fell down in our own lines and I followed to the ground, although I didn't land. The boys gave me a great ovation.'

This 'unfortunate' DFW was from *FlAbt (A) 235*, the crew, *Uffz* Georg Frischkorn and *Ltn* Fritz Frech were both killed. The wreckage of the DFW CV was numbered G 68.

After the disastrous events of the previous day, September 4 saw an improvement in the fortunes of 46 Squadron, especially so for Arthur Lee. 'I've got a Hun at last! And all on my own. *And* confirmed.' Lee flew three patrols during the day, an indication of how hard the fighter squadrons were being worked. After seeing a Camel shoot down an Albatros in pieces over Ypres – 'he could easily have got away with it if he'd had a parachute[2]' – the Pups climbed to 16,000 feet. After an hour without seeing any more activity the patrol went down to 8,000 feet and caught a DFW, which they all attacked. 'He fell into a spin and we watched him flicking down for what seemed five minutes until he crashed into the middle of the marsh of shell holes south of Polygon Wood.'

Over Comines, the Pups split up and made their separate ways back to Ste.Marie Cappele. It was a lovely evening, very clear, with a pale blue sky and Lee flew to the north of Ypres, where he saw an RE8 being attacked by an Albatros. Seeing the Pup the enemy pilot made off east, but Lee followed him in a wide, sweeping curve that brought him right behind the enemy scout and 200 feet above. The Albatros was still flying east, but at half throttle and Lee, suspecting a trap, carefully searched the sky. There was nothing in sight. 'I came down closer and closer, holding my fire. My heart was pounding, and I was trembling uncontrollably, but my mind was calm and collected. I closed to ten yards, edged out of his slip-stream, drew nearer still until I saw that if I wasn't careful I'd hit his rudder. His machine was green and grey and looked very spick and span. He had a dark brown flying helmet, with a white goggle strap round the back of his head.'[3] Lee aimed carefully at the enemy pilot's shoulders as they showed above the cockpit fairing and gently pressed his trigger. At Lee's first shots the pilot's head jerked back and, as he clutched the joystick, pulling it involuntarily back, his Albatros reared up and stalled to the left before falling into a vertical dive, the engine full on. Lee followed and estimated that the Albatros would crash northeast of Polygon Wood, but a burst of fire alerted him that there *were* other enemy scouts about. Lee pulled up in a sharp turn and three Albatri shot past him, still diving. By the time the enemy scouts had pulled out, Lee was a quarter of a mile to their west and although they fired several long range bursts at the Pup they gave up the chase and flew east. On Lee's return, Archie telephoned to confirm his victory, the first of an eventual seven.

Patrols by 56 Squadron during the morning had seen no positive results, but a evening patrol at 5.30pm saw a combat with Albatros scouts over Houthulst Forest and Lt William Potts shot *Ltn* Gebhard Emberger of *Jasta 29* down in flames Sooner than burn to death, Emberger jumped from his blazing Albatros, hitting the ground on the southern edge of Houthulst Forest, close by the remains of his machine. Emberger's watch, stopped forever, showed the time of his death: six minutes fifty seconds past eight.

Potts then turned his attention to another Albatros and although he had only time for a short burst of ten rounds before having to zoom to avoid a collision, he wounded *Ltn* Siegfried von Lieres und Wilkau, also of *Jasta 29.*

Victories were also scored during the day by Louis Jenkin of 1 Squadron, who shot down a DFW over Polygon Wood at 4.00pm, and Lt F A Smith of 66 Squadron, nicknamed 'the long'un' also scored. The only casualties for the fighter squadrons were a Nieuport of 29 Squadron, the pilot killed, and two Pups of 66 Squadron, both pilots wounded and taken prisoner.

September 5 was very cloudy, but with bright intervals. The Camels of 45 Squadron were in action at 8.00am, attacking a formation of six DFW two-seaters escorted by a number of Albatri. The Camels were joined by naval triplanes and Spads and in the fierce fighting McMaking shot down an Albatros out of control over Comines.

A large formation of eleven SE5s from 56 Squadron – A and C Flights – took off from Estrée Blanche at 5.30pm, but gun and engine troubles reduced the number that reached the lines to nine. Southeast of Roulers, Maybery and Rhys Davids attacked eight Albatros scouts, joined in their attack by another SE5, eight Camels from 70 Squadron and seven Nieuports, plus some FEs and Bristol Fighters. Rhys Davids fired at one enemy scout, sending it down in a steep spiral with smoke pouring from its engine, then pulled down his Lewis gun and fired at another above him. This Albatros, which had a red fuselage circled with a black band, 'wobbled' and went down. Zooming away, Rhys Davids looked down and saw the fuselage and one wing of the Albatros spinning down very fast with the detached right wing falling slowly in small pieces. After shaking off an attack by three more Albatri, Rhys Davids turned for the lines, but saw an Albatros flying under a formation of FEs. This Albatros, coloured green with a yellow band around the fuselage, was flown by *Vzfw* Alfred Muth of *Jasta 27,* who manoeuvred well and put some shots into Rhys Davids' SE5. Rhys Davids eventually got above Muth, who half-rolled away,

with Rhys Davids following, firing continuous bursts. The Albatros dived very steeply and crashed in a small copse a mile north east of Poelcapelle. Muth was killed.

The pilots of 56 Squadron claimed six victories from the evening's fighting, a two-seater out of control, three Albatri out of control and one destroyed, and Clive Collett of 70 Squadron claimed an Albatros destroyed in the fight.

In the evening an offensive sweep near the coast was flown by Naval 8, and Harold Beamish and Leonard 'Tich' Rochford each shot down an Albatros scout. The scout shot down by Beamish was his third victory; that shot down by Rochford his fourth of an eventual 29 and his first victory flying a Sopwith Camel.

On the debit side for the fighter squadrons there were five casualties. Two Camels from 45 Squadron were shot down, their pilots killed, another Camel, this one from 70 Squadron, was shot down in the evening fight, the pilot taken POW, and a pilot of 32 Squadron was killed over Ypres.

Werner Voss, flying his Fokker Triplane, shot down Lt Charles Odell of 46 Squadron. The Pups were patrolling northeast of Ypres when a triplane approached them from behind. Odell took no notice of this machine, thinking it was a naval triplane, but was astounded to find it firing at him. Odell turned quickly but Voss' fire had been accurate, severely damaging his Pup and he was forced to break off the unequal combat and return. Voss, who had been joined by an Albatros in the fight with the Pup, had put holes in all the British scouts. Lee later wrote: 'The Triplane, which was painted red, had a stupendous performance, and when he decided he'd had enough he lifted up above everybody like a rocket. He was a pretty hot pilot, for he holed most of the Pups, but nobody could get a bead on him.'[4]

September 6 was a day of low clouds mist and rain, but there was some aerial fighting. In a combat with Albatros scouts in the early morning 23 Squadron lost a pilot wounded and taken prisoner for the only fighter casualty of the day. Victories were also few. The Camels of Naval 10 claimed two Albatros scouts out of control in a morning patrol over Dixmude, and Lt R Winnicott of 41 Squadron claimed the first DH5 victory for the squadron when he shot down an Albatros two-seater out of control over Masnières in the early afternoon.

A morning patrol by 56 Squadron was notable in that it saw the squadron's first sighting of the new German scouts: the Pfalz D III and the Fokker Triplane. The patrol, led by McCudden, engaged a formation of enemy machines over Houthulst Forest. The enemy formation included a Pfalz D.111 (described by the British pilots as a new type Fokker biplane) and two Fokker Triplanes. In the view of both later knowledge and the tactics employed by the pilots of the two triplanes, it seems unlikely that they were flown by either Voss or

Richthofen. Sloley fired a shot burst at the Pfalz, which flew under the cover of its *jasta* companions and as Sloley turned away one of the triplanes fired at him from long range. Sloley's combat report that this triplane pilot 'showed little determination in spite of a very favourable position', makes it extremely unlikely that it was flown by either Richthofen or Voss, especially not Voss. Later in the patrol, Jeffs had shot down an Albatros to crash just east of Poelcapelle railway station. This was possibly either *Vzfw* Klein of *Jasta 8*, or *Ltn* Diether Collin of *Jasta 22,* both wounded in action on September 6.[5]

There was no flying for the next two days, the low clouds and rain making any war flying impossible, but although there were low clouds and ground mist on September 9 there was a great deal of fighting.

Although a pilot of 23 Squadron was lost in the morning in a fight with *Jasta 11* over Zonnebeke, the majority of the fighting seems to have been in the afternoon and evening, A patrol from 70 Squadron, led by Clive Collett, took off sometime after 4.00pm and saw a great deal of action over the area of Houthulst Forest. The Camels attacked enemy two-seaters over Gheluvelt and Collett shot one down out of control at 5.05pm – which he shared with Lt Saward – and destroyed another north east of Houthulst Forest twenty minutes later. Collett then reformed his patrol and flew towards Roulers. Approaching the town, the Camels were jumped from behind by Albatri from *Jasta 27* and *Jasta 35b*. Collett got on the tail of one Albatros and fired into it from short range. The Albatros went down, followed by Collett, who saw that the enemy pilot was attempting to land. Collett went down to 40 feet and fired again at the Albatros, which crashed, turned over and burst into flames. The pilot, *Ltn* Karl Hammes of *Jasta 35b,* was badly wounded.[6] Collett was then attacked by three Albatri, slightly wounded in the hand, and returned. After his combat with the two-seater, shared with Collett, Lt N Saward was shot down and taken POW. Earlier in the patrol, 2Lt H Weightman of 70 Squadron, in a fight with two Albatri, had been severely wounded in the abdomen and crashed in the front line trenches at 4.45pm.

A patrol of 56 Squadron took off from Estrée Blanche. This was again a large patrol of eleven SE5s but once again their numbers were depleted before they reached the lines. McCudden and Barlow dropped out with engine trouble and Lt William Potts and Eric Turnbull were involved in a collision. Potts failed to notice a change of direction by the leader, and in taking action to avoid him Turnbull's tailskid hit the top starboard wing of Pott's SE5, breaking the trailing spar. Both pilots managed to return safely.

After losing Potts and Turnbull the SE5s saw a good deal of action. Rhys Davids had taken over the command of the

Flight after McCudden's departure and he led them down to attack six Albatri over Gheluvelt, driving them east. Rhys Davids then attacked a lone Albatros over Polygon Wood. He got behind the enemy scout without being seen, but both his guns stopped after only having fired a few shots. Rhys Davids, who had to pull up sharply to avoid a collision with the enemy scout, then managed to rectify his Lewis gun and rejoined the other SEs. The Flight then engaged a formation of Albatri east of Polygon Wood. Rhys Davids was attacked by three of the enemy scouts and with only one gun working retreated west, but Sloley then appeared, flying towards him, flew over the SE5, and fired at the first pursuing Albatros, which turned east. Sloley had a gun stoppage and let this scout go, but Rhys Davids turned back and attacked it, hitting the Albatros in the cockpit and centre section. With clouds of steam and boiling water pouring out of the top wing radiator, the Albatros went down to crash in the trees of Houthulst Forest.

After singly attacking three separate enemy two-seaters without success, Rhys Davids rejoined the other SEs and they attacked a formation of enemy machines over the Menin to Roulers road. The fight was a long one, but neither side obtained a positive victory, Rhys Davids only succeeding in forcing one of the enemy machines 'right down.'

In a fight with Albatros two-seaters during the day, 2Lt E Smith of 45 Squadron shot one down in flames and another out of control. Harry Reeves of 1 Squadron shot a Rumpler two-seater down out of control east of Polygon Wood at 10.35, and in the afternoon William Mansell, also of 1 Squadron, destroyed an Albatros over Becelaere at 2.40pm. In this last fight 2Lt W E le B Diamond was shot down by *Ltn* Julius Schmidt of *Jasta 3* and taken POW.

The pilots of the naval squadrons claimed no victories during the day, but Naval 1 lost a pilot killed over Langemarck.

Following the usual pattern of the month the weather next day, September 10, was cloudy in the morning with considerable ground mist, but improved during the afternoon. The usual large patrol of eleven SE5s – C and A Flights – was flown by 56 Squadron and on this occasion there were no problems with guns or engines and all the SEs reached the patrol area. Maxwell and A Flight had some indecisive fighting with enemy scouts, with no positive result, but C Flight, led by Bowman, had better luck. The Flight first attacked eight Albatri over the Menin-Roulers road and although Bowman was forced to break off his attack with carburettor trouble, Hoidge closed to within 30 yards of another Albatros and sent it down out of control. Pressure trouble had delayed Richard Maybery from taking off with the rest of C Flight and he eventually crossed the Front Lines alone, to the north of Ypres. Seeing some SEs below him, diving to attack enemy aircraft, Maybery joined them, but finding they were A Flight, turned

Lt Arthur Gordon Jones-Williams. While in 29 Squadron in April 1917 Jones-Williams scored eight victories.

FltLt Robert Alexander Little. Naval 8.

Right: Capt Tom Falcon Hazell in a Nieuport of 1 Squadron. Hazell scored 20 victories as a Flight Commander with 1 Squadron between March and August 1917 before returning to England. After serving as an instructor at the Central Flying School he returned to France in June 1918 as a Flight Commander with 24 Squadron, bringing his total victories to 43 by the end of the war.

Nieuport 17 B1522. Albert Ball flew this Nieuport in 56 Squadron in April/May 1917. It is seen here in Egypt in 1918.

This DFW from FlAbt 18 was brought down by R A Little of Naval 8 on 24 April 1917. Ltn Huppertz and Ltn Neumüller were taken prisoner.

Top: Capt G B A Baker (left). Major Hubert D Harvey-Kelly. 19 Squadron. Vert Galant. April 1917.

Bottom: Lt Richard Applin 19 Squadron. Applin was shot down and killed on 29 April 1917 by Manfred von Richthofen for his 49th victory.

Top: 40 Squadron pilots at Bruay in April 1917. On ground. Left: J L Barlow. I P R Napier. Middle row, Left: H B Redler. L B Blaxland. Edward 'Mick' Mannock at rear.

Bottom: 2Lt W N Hamilton. The only survivor from the patrol by Spads of 19 Squadron on 29 April 1917, when Major Harvey-Kelly, Richard Applin and Hamilton were shot down by Jasta 11. Harvey-Kelly and Applin were both killed but Hamilton was taken prisoner.

Top: Lionel B Blaxland 40 Squadron in a Sopwith Camel.

Bottom: In happier days. Maurice Alfred Kay standing behind his close friend Keith Knox Muspratt while training at the Central Flying School in 1916. Kay was KIA on 30 April 1917, 56 Squadron's first casualty.

Above: Capt W A Bond DSO MC+Bar. 40 Squadron.

Top center: Capt W R Gregory. 40 Squadron.

Top right: FltCom Robert John Orton Compston DSO+2Bars.DSC. Compston served in Naval 8 and 40 Squadron. He is credited with 25 victories.

Right: Pilots of 40 Squadron at Bruay in 1917. L to R: Pettigrew (shaving). William 'McScotch' MacLanachan. L B Blaxland. Steve Godfrey. A H T Kennedy.

Below: Nieuport B 1514 'A4' of 60 Squadron was shot down on 6 May 1917. 2Lt C W McKissock was taken POW.

Top: Capt W L Harrison MC+Bar. Harrison scored 11 victories with 40 Squadron, and another while a flight commander in 1 Squadron.

Bottom: Lt John Owen Leach, 56 Squadron. Leach was wounded in the leg on the evening of 7 May 1917. His leg was later amputated.

Top: Capt W E Nixon. 40 Squadron.

Bottom: Capt Henry Meintjes MC. A South African, 'Duke' Meintjes flew with 60 and 56 Squadrons. Meintjes scored four victories with 60 Squadron and another four with 56 Squadron before he was wounded in action on the evening of 7 May 1917.

Top: Lt Lewis Langharne Morgan. 40 Squadron. 'The Air Hog'.

Bottom: Cyril Marconi 'Billy' Crowe DFC. Crowe began flying as an observer in 3 Squadron in January 1915. After pilot training he flew BE2s in 18 and 16 Squadrons until April 1917 when he was posted to 56 Squadron as a flight commander. Crowe scored 14 victories with 56 Squadron. Crowe later commanded 60 and 85 Squadrons.

Right: The cross erected by the Germans on Albert Ball's grave at Annoeullin.

Far right: After the war Albert Ball's father erected this memorial stone on the site of his son's crash.

Below: Sopwith Pups of A Flight 66 Squadron on Vert Galant aerodrome in May 1917.

Bottom: 2Lt George Hadrill of 54 Squadron was wounded and forced to land on 9 May 1917 by Ltn Werner Voss for his 27th victory. Hadrill's Pup A6174, the top of its rudder damaged, is seen here on a German aerodrome. The aeroplane is the background is an Albatros CX.

Right: Another view of Hadrill's Sopwith Pup in German hands.

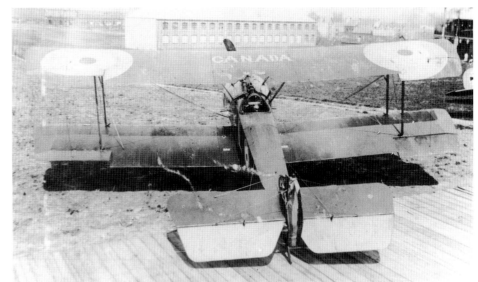

Below: FltLt Edward Duncan Crundall. Crundall flew Sopwith Triplanes with Naval 8, scoring three victories in April 1917. Crundall was wounded in the back by anti-aircraft fire on 10 May 1917 and did not return to France until 13 July 1917, rejoining Naval 8 and scoring another victory on 18 August. In October 1917 Crundall was posted to HE. After a spell in England, Crundall returned to France on 26 June 1918 as flight commander in 210 Squadron to fly Sopwith Camels. Crundall scored another four victories, but was sent to hospital on 30 August with a strained heart due to high flying.

Below center: Capt Horace Debenham. Debenham flew two tours with 46 Squadron, first as an observer, later as a pilot. After scoring four victories with 46 Squadron he was posted to 208 Squadron, adding one more victory to his total, a Pfalz DIII with a brown fuselage and yellow tail on 18 May 1918.

Below right: Major A W 'Keeno' Keen MC. Keen succeeded Dallas as CO of 40 Squadron in June 1918. He was injured in a flying accident on 15 August and died of his injuries on 12 September. Keen scored a total of 14 victories: One in 1916 with 70 Squadron; 11 as a flight commander with 40 Squadron in 1917, and two in 1918 as its commanding officer.

Right: This view of the cockpit of Sopwith Pup A 6174 shows to advantage the Aldis sight offset to port and the heavily padded end of the Vickers gun.

Two above: Although the quality of these two photographs is poor they are of great interest. They were taken surreptitiously by a member of 60 Squadron, the use or ownership of a camera being strictly forbidden. Ltn Georg Noth's Albatros D III. D 796/17 on Filescamp Farm aerodrome being examined by 60 Squadron personnel. The fuselage was coloured green with yellow spots. The tail unit was white, the Jasta B marking. Ltn Georg Noth of Jasta B was shot down by Lt Fry on 19 May 1917. Noth can just been seen under the tail of his Albatros.

Right: Lt James Pedraza Stephen. 46 Squadron.

Far right: Nieuport B 1642 '2' flown by Lt L L Morgan, 'The Air Hog' of 40 Squadron, after it had been hit by AA fire on 24 May 1917.

Below: After destroying a balloon in Nieuport A 6644 '6' Lt T H Lines of 1 Squadron was shot down by Flak and captured on 18 May 1917. This photograph shows the wing mountings of the Le Prieur rockets.

Right: B 1642 being taken away for scrap.

Right: Lt Anthony's Nieuport 17 A 6678 in German hands.

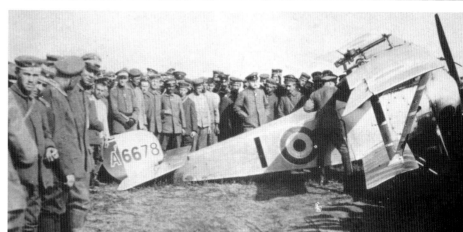

Below: Lt A E Godfrey. 25 and 40 Squadrons. Godfrey is credited with 14 victories.

Above: This Sopwith Pup A 7430 was shot down on 27 May 1917 by pilots of Jasta 33. The pilot, Lt S S Hume of 66 Squadron, was taken prisoner.

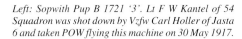

Left: Sopwith Pup B 1721 '3'. Lt F W Kantel of 54 Squadron was shot down by Vzfw Carl Holler of Jasta 6 and taken POW flying this machine on 30 May 1917.

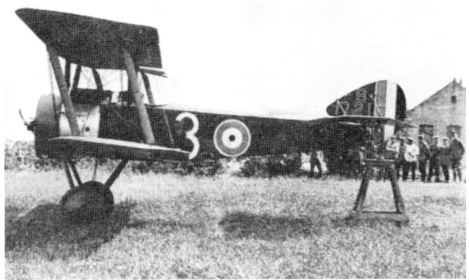

FltSubLt Ellis Vair Reid DSC. Naval 10. As with several other Naval 10 pilots, Reid first served with 3 Naval Wing. From 1 July until 28 July 1917, Reid scored 19 victories before he was shot down and killed by KFlak21 on 28 July 1917.

Left: Ltn Bernert of Jasta 6 poses by a captured Sopwith Pup in German markings. This is almost certainly Sopwith Pup B 1721 from 54 Squadron flown by Lt F W Kantel.

Left: FltCom John Edward Sharman. A Canadian from Manitoba, Sharman served with 3 Wing RNAS, flying Sopwith 1 1/2 Strutters on over 30 raids and claiming one victory: a Fokker E type on 25 February 1917. After the disbandment of 3 Wing, Sharman was one of the naval pilots to form the nucleus of Naval 10 Squadron flying Sopwith Triplanes. Sharman scored seven victories between 6 June and 12 July 1917, was made a flight commander in July and had won a DSC and a CdeG., but was shot down and killed on 22 July by anti-aircraft fire. A Bar to his DSC was awarded posthumously on 11 August 1917.

Above: Sgt Gordon Percy Olley MM. Olley first flew with 1 Squadron as a volunteer observer in 1916. After training as a pilot he rejoined the squadron in the early summer of 1917 to fly Nieuport Scouts, opening his scoring on 1 June 1917 with an enemy two-seater. By the October of 1917 Olley had brought his victory score to 10 and had been awarded an MM.

Top center: Major Thomas Francis Netterville Gerrard DSC, CdeG. 'Teddy' Gerrard first served with A Squadron 1 Naval Wing, claiming one victory in 1916. With the redesignation of the Wing to Naval 1 Squadron on 3 December 1916, equipped with Sopwith Triplanes, Gerrard scored another eight victories in the spring and early summer of 1917. Returning to France in the spring of 1918, Gerrard added one more victory to his total while flying with 208 Squadron before leaving to take command of 209 Squadron in June 1918. Gerrard died in a riding accident in 1921.

Top right: FltSubLt Percy Gordon McNeil flew with 3 Naval Wing, Naval 3, Naval 9 and Naval 10. He was credited with a victory with Naval 3 and a further two with Naval 10. McNeil was shot down and killed on 3 June 1917.

Above: Albatros D III 2015/16. This machine was flown by Ltn Georg Simon of Jasta 11 when he was shot down and taken prisoner by Capt Charles Chapman of 29 Squadron on 4 June 1917. In the original print the capture number G.42 is clearly discernible, marked on the rudder. The RFC report on this Albatros states: 'The body of the machine, including the streamlined cowl on the propeller boss, as far back as the pilot's seat, is painted red; thence for a distance of about 3 feet the fuselage is light green; thence to the end of the fuselage, red again. The planes are painted as follows. Top Plane: upper surface red in the centre, dark green on the outside portions. Lower surface light blue. Bottom planes: upper surface – inside portions next to the fuselage, red. Outside portions, dark green. Lower surface, light blue.' Below: Lt F Barrie of 19 Squadron was forced to land and taken POW by Flak on 2 June 1917 in Nieuport A 6675 '3'.

Above: Lt Leonard Monteagle Barlow MC. Barlow was credited with 20 victories while flying with 56 Squadron from April 1917 until 1 October 1917, when he was posted to HE. Barlow was killed in a flying accident in England on 5 February 1918.

Top center: Edward Mannock while training.

Top right: Lt R N Hall. 40 Squadron.

Right: Lt Thomas Dickinson's SE5 A 8920 down behind German lines. Dickinson of 56 Squadron was wounded and taken prisoner on 4 June 1917.

Right: Lt A P Mitchell of 46 Squadron was wounded and taken POW on 7 June 1917. His Sopwith Pup A 6157 '6' has been dismantled and loaded on a German lorry. Note the extra roundel carried on the centre section of the top wing and on the wheel covers.

Left: Offstv Paul Aue of Jasta 10 with his seventh victory, Spad B 1524 of 23 Squadron flown by 2Lt F W Illingworth who was wounded and taken prisoner on 7 June 1917.

Left: The officers' Mess of Naval 10 at Droglandt 1917.

Opposite
Top: Lt Harry Spearpoint's SE5 A 4862 marked C3 down behind the German lines. Spearpoint of 56 Squadron was taken prisoner on 17 June 1917.

Center: Lt William Turner-Coles of 56 Squadron miraculously escaped uninjured when he was brought down in enemy territory flying SE5 A 8922 on 17 June 1917.

Bottom: Another view of Turner-Coles crash.

Left: The wreckage of Rogerson's SE5a A 8919 B6 photographed on Moorseele aerodrome, the base of Fl Abt 33.

Above: Lt George Pollard Kay. 46 Squadron. Kay was injured in a flying accident on 27 June 1917 and died of his injuries the following day.

Top right: Harry Spearpoint's utter dejection after his capture is only too evident in this photograph. The German officer on the left is Ltn Hailer.

Right: The wreckage of Spearpoint's SE5 A 4862 in B Armee Flugpark 6.

Below: Capt T Davidson of 23 Squadron was flying this Spad 7 B3504 on 19 June 1917 when he was hit by Flak south east of Ypres. Davidson was taken prisoner.

Above: Lt Cecil 'Chaps' Marchant of 46 Squadron with Sopwith Pup A 7325 '1'. This Pup was allocated to 46 Squadron on 20 April 1917 and 2Lt N H Dimmock claimed an Albatros out of control while flying it on 5 June. It was badly damaged in a landing accident and returned to 2 ASD on 26 June 1917.

Top right: FltLt Gerald Ewart Nash. Another member of Collishaw's 'Black Flight' in Naval 10 Nash scored six victories between 21 May and 7 June 1917 before being shot down and taken prisoner on 25 June 1917 by Karl Allmenroder of Jasta 11 for his 30th victory.

Right: Lts W A Bishop, W E Molesworth and Graham C Young. 60 Squadron. Summer 1917.

Right: Major Frederick Sowery. While serving with 39 (Home Defence) Squadron, Sowery was awarded a DSO for shooting down Zeppelin L.32 on the night of 23/24 September 1916. In June 1917 Sowery was posted as a flight commander to 19 Squadron in France to fly Spads and was credited with 12 victories.

Far right: Capt Louis Fleming Jenkin. MC+Bar. Jenkin scored 22 victories while in 1 Squadron from May 1917 until 11 September when he was killed in action.

Right: In late June 1917, 56 Squadron were transferred to England for a brief period to combat the Gotha raids. The squadron was based at Bekesbourne in Kent and there were many reunions and social occasions with families and friends. This tea party took place on 5 July 1917. Around the improvised table of an aeroplane wheel on boxes are L to R: Ruth Eadon. Arthur Rhys Davids. Nasra Eadon. Maybery's mother and Richard Maybery. The girls were cousins of Maybery.

Below: FltLt Reginald Soar DSC. Soar first served with 5 Naval Wing, later transferring to Naval 8 to fly Sopwith Pups. He is credited with 12 victories, all gained while serving with Naval 8.

Below: Autumn 1917. Nieuports of 1 Squadron ready to leave on patrol from the Asylum aerodrome.

Above: Pilots of 56 Squadron on the aerodrome at Bekesbourne, June 1917. L to R: C A Lewis. G H Bowman. I H D Henderson. V P Cronyn. A P F Rhys Davids. The young girl is Thais Marson, the daughter of the squadron's recording officer, Capt T B Marson.

Above: Lt Phillip G Kelsey. 1 Squadron.

Top center: Major Alan John Lance Scott MC AFC. Scott flew Sopwith 1 1/2 Strutters with 43 Squadron before taking command of 60 Squadron in March 1917.

Top right: FltLt Richard Pearman Minifie DSC+2Bars. Another pilot from A Squadron 1 Naval Wing, Minifie began to score after it had been re-designated Naval 1 and equipped with Sopwith Triplanes, scoring 17 of his victories flying the type. When Naval 1 was re-equipped with Sopwith Camels in December 1917, Minifie added another four victories before he came down behind the German lines and was taken prisoner on 17 March 1918.

Right: Sopwith Pup B 1777 '4'. A presentation aeroplane, 'British Guiana No.2,' this Pup was issued to 46 Squadron on 10 July 1917. Lt A S G Lee scored five of his seven victories in this Pup and it carried his personal marking of Chu Chin Chow, a contemporary London stage show. Lee exchanged this Pup for a Sopwith Camel on 8 November 1917.

Right: Cheerful pilots of 1 Squadron in the summer of 1917. L to R: W V T Rooper. W W Rogers. P G Kelsey. P F Fullard. H G Reeves.

Above: Sopwith Triplane 'Peggy' of 1 Naval Squadron RNAS 1917.

Top right: Capt John Oliver Andrews MC+Bar. DSO. 24 Squadron 1916. Andrews scored seven of his 12 victories in 24 Squadron. In 1917 Andrew served in 66 Squadron, adding another five.

Right: The Sopwith Camel F.1. 'A buzzing hornet; a wild thing.' The Sopwith Camel is credited with having destroyed more enemy aeroplanes than any other type of fighter in service with the RFC/RAF in WW1.

Right: DFW C.V 799/17 of FlAbt 7 forced down behind British lines on 12 July 1917 by Lts Arthur Rhys Davids and Keith Muspratt of 56 Squadron. The crew, Uffz Albert Hahnel and Ltn Eugen Mann, were taken prisoner. This aeroplane was designated G53 in the British lists of captured aircraft.

Above: Capt Edric William Broadberry MC.

Top right: Capt R T C Hoidge in the cockpit of an SE5 of 56 Squadron at London Colney aerodrome, April 1917.

Right: Nieuport A 6680 of 40 Squadron starting out on patrol.

Above: Squadron Commander G R Bromet DSO. Bromet commanded Naval 8 in 1916-1917.

Right: This Nieuport 23 'BI' B1575 was shot down on 15 July 1917 by Oblt Tutschek Staffelführer of Jasta 12. Lt G A H Parkes of 60 Squadron was wounded and taken POW.

Left: This Albatros D.V No. 1162/17 was shot down on 16 July 1917 by 2Lt Langsland of 23 Squadron. The Pilot, Vzfw Clausnitzer of Jasta 4 was taken prisoner. The Albatros was designated G56.

Far left: Capt William Arthur Bond DSO.MC+Bar. Bond served in 40 Squadron in April 1917 and was credited with 5 victories before being killed when his Nieuport received a direct hit from anti-aircraft fire on 22 July 1917. Bond had married Aimée Constance Hardy on 23 January 1917 and after the war his wife published their letters as An Airman's Wife, dedicating it to 40 Squadron.

Left: Capt Phillip Bernard Prothero 56 Squadron. KIA 26 July 1917.

Opposite
Top: Pilots of B Flight 1 Squadron . Summer 1917. L to R: 2Lt R S Davies. Lt W V T Rooper. Capt W C Campbell. Lt W W Rogers. 2Lt P Wilson. 2Lt P G Kelsey.

Center: Camel B 3823 C5 of 70 Squadron was shot down on 28 July 1917 by Ltn Mohnicke of Jasta 11 for his 4th victory. Lt R C Hume was taken prisoner.

Bottom: Camel B 3823 packed up and being taken away.

Far left: Capt Geoffrey Hilton Bowman DSO. MC+Bar. DFC. CdeG. Bowman served in 29 and 56 Squadrons and later commanded 41 Squadron. 'Beery' Bowman was awarded two victories while flying DH2s in 29 Squadron, and as C Flight Commander in 56 Squadron took his victories to 24, adding a further eight victories while commanding 41 Squadron.

Left: Successful pilots were not known as 'aces' in the RFC/RAF; in the vernacular of the day a high-scoring pilot was known as a 'Star Turn.' Here are two 'Star Turns' of 1 Squadron. Left. Capt Philip Fletcher Fullard DSO. MC+Bar (40 victories). Right. Capt William Charles Campbell DSO. MC+Bar (23 victories in three months).

Right: Pilots of 56 and 66 Squadrons at Estrée Blanche aerodrome in the summer of 1917. L to R: Gerald Maxwell (56 Sqdn). W A Pritt (The 'War Baby' 66 Sqdn). T V Hunter (66 Sqdn). Eric Turnbull (56 Sqdn). E R Taylor (56 Sqdn). G M Wilkinson (56 Sqdn). unknown.

Above: Capt Richard Aveline Maybery MC. Maybery served in 56 Squadron from 17 June 1917 to 19 December, when he was KIA. He had scored 21 victories.

Top center: Capt Forster Herbert Martin Maynard. Maynard flew with Naval 1 in the spring and summer of 1917 and scored 6 victories.

Top right: FltCom Alfred Williams Carter DSC. 'Nick' Carter flew Sopwith Pups with Naval 3 in the spring of 1917, scoring five victories. On 2 July he was posted to Naval 10 to fly Sopwith Triplanes and in ten days added another four victories before going on leave to Canada on 15 August. On his return from Canada in January 1918 Carter rejoined Naval 10 in France, scoring one more victory before the squadron was renumbered 210 Squadron RAF on 1 April 1918. Between 10 April and 5 June 1918 Carter was awarded another seven victories, bringing his total to 17.

Right: Lt William MacLanachan. MacLanachan served with 40 Squadron in the summer and autumn of 1917 and was credited with seven victories.

Far right: Lt Walbanke Ashby Pritt. From this photograph, with possibly a wedge of toffee in one cheek, it is apparent why his fellow pilots in 66 Squadron nicknamed Pritt 'The War Baby'. Pritt was an aggressive pilot who revelled in attacking enemy airfields and and German staff cars. He was awarded an MC for his work with 66 Squadron and scored at least five victories. Pritt survived the war but was killed in a car accident between the wars.

Right: FltCom Charles Dawson Booker scored fourteen of his 23 victories in Naval 8 while flying this Sopwith Triplane N 5482 'Maude' from 7 April to 11 August 1917.

Right: Spad B 3507 of 19 Squadron. 2 Lt S L Nichols killed on 12 August 1917 by Oblt Eduard Ritter von Dostler Staffelführer of Jasta 6 for his 23rd victory.

Below: Albatros D III of Jasta 30 flown by Ltn Joachim von Bertrab. Bertrab was shot down and taken prisoner while flying this machine by Lt Edward Mannock of 40 Squadron on 12 August 1917.

Above: This Nieuport 27 was flown by both Edward Mannock and William 'McScotch' MacLanachan while in 40 Squadron in the summer and autumn of 1917. Mannock wrote on his copy of the photograph. 'A Perfect Lady. My only Love.'

Left: Offz-Stellv Max Müller of Jasta 28 leans on the wreckage of Lt David Stanley Wilkinson's SE5a A 8903 by the side of the canalised River Lys at Bousbecque. Wilkinson, who was the Bavarian pilot's 23rd victory, died of his wounds ten days later.

Below: Spad A 6634 of 19 Squadron. A T Shipwright POW on 16 August 1917. During the day 19 Squadron lost two pilots taken POW, another wounded, and two additional Spads badly damaged in combat.

Above: Three Flight Commanders 56 Squadron Estrée Blanche summer 1917. L to R: James MCudden. Ian Henderson (B Flt). Gerald Constable Maxwell (A Flt). This photograph was taken just before Henderson relinquished command of B Flight to McCudden on 15 August 1917.

Top center: Captain George Lawrence Lloyd. MC. AFC. 'Zulu' Lloyd served in 40 and 60 Squadrons. He is credited with eight victories.

Top right: Lt Richard Tihel Leighton. 56 Squadron. Leighton was shot down and made POW on 17 August 1917.

Right: Edward Mannock in his Nieuport. 40 Squadron, Bruay, summer 1917.

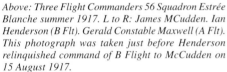

Right: Capt Norman MacMillan. MacMillan flew with 45 Squadron, initially in Sopwith 1 1/2 Strutters, scoring two victories, before the squadron was re-equipped with Sopwith Camels in July 1917. MacMillan claimed a further seven victories flying Camels in France before the squadron was moved to the Italian front in November 1917. On 1 January 1918 MacMillan shot down an Albatros D.III out of control, but was injured in an accident later in the month and returned to England on 28 January.

Far right: Lt H S Wolff 40 Squadron. Because of his smallness Wolff was nicknamed both 'Mighty Atom' and Little Samson' by his 40 Squadron compatriots.

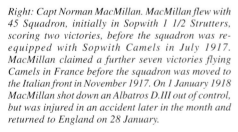

Right: The 'Odd Man'. The much-loved padre B W Keymer outside his Nissen hut 'Church of St Michael, The Flying Warrior.' 40 Squadron 1917-1918. Keymer died of pleurisy in 1924, leaving seven children, two of whom were killed in action serving with the RAF in World War II. Below right: The interior of the Church of St Michael.

Below: Capt Clive Franklyn Collett. A New Zealander, Collett flew with 70 Squadron as a flight commander from the summer to the early autumn of 1917, scoring 11 victories and winning an MC+Bar before being wounded on 9 September 1917. In 1916 Collett had been a test pilot and after recovering from his wound he resumed test flying. Collett was killed on 23 December 1917 while test flying Albatros DV 1162/ 17 (G56) over the Firth of Forth.

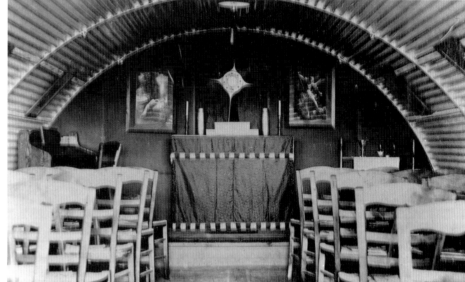

Right: L to R: Keith Knox Musprat. Arthur Percival Foley Rhys Davids. Maxwell Henry Coote. These three pilots were known collectively to 56 Squadron as 'The Children'. Rhys Davids and Muspratt had joined the RFC straight from school, Rhys Davids from Eton College, Muspratt from Sherborne School. Coote, slightly older than his companions, and also an ex-Etonian, was the only one of the three to survive the war. Rhys Davids was KIA on 27 October and Muspratt was killed while a test pilot in England on 16 March 1918.

Far right: 56 Squadron. Summer 1917. James McCudden B Flight Commander (centre) with two members of his Flight. On the left, Keith Knox Muspratt, right, Maxwell Henry Coote.

Above: Off Duty. Geoffrey 'Beery' Bowman with Major Blomfield in 56 Squadron's boat on the Lys Canal in the summer of 1917. Bowman, his ever present pipe firmly clenched, seems slightly unsure of the expertise at the tiller of his commanding officer, 'Dickie' Blomfield. Right: Herbert Charles, the engineering officer of 56 Squadron, seems happier with Richard Maybery at the tiller.

Right: Manfred von Richthofen (left) and Anthony Fokker sitting on the fuselage of Sopwith Pup B 1795, brought down by Richthofen for his 61st victory on 3 September 1917. The pilot, Lt A F Bird, was taken prisoner. Sitting on the fuselage with Richthofen is Anthony Fokker.

Below: C Flight 56 Squadron on Estrée Blanche aerodrome in the summer of 1917. The squadron marking, a small red dumbbell, can just be seen behind the identification letter on the fuselage. On 25 September this squadron marking was changed to an 18 inch wide white band, painted just in front of the tailplane.

Above: Nieuport B 6818 of 1 Squadron flown by P G Kelsey.

Right: Captain Gerald Joseph Constable Maxwell MC DFC. Maxwell flew with 56 Squadron in France from April 1917 until posted to HE on 21 October. He had scored 20 victories. After serving as a fighting instructor at the No.1 School of Aerial Fighting in Ayr, Scotland, Maxwell returned to 56 Squadron on a month's refresher course in June 1918 and gained a further six victories.

Far right: Lt Russell Winnicott served in 41 Squadron in the autumn of 1917, scoring ten victories before he was killed in a mid-air collision on 6 December 1917.

Right: Capt Raymond James Brownell MC. MM. Brownell served with the Australian artillery in both Gallipoli and France, where he won an MM, before transferring to the RFC in late 1916. He was posted to 45 Squadron in September 1917, flying in A Flight under the command of Capt MacMillan. Brownell scored five victories in France before the squadron moved to Italy, where he added a further seven.

Far right: Robert Leslie Chidlaw-Roberts. Childlaw-Roberts joined the RFC in May 1915 and flew for six months as an observer with 2 Squadron. After pilot training he served with 18 Squadron, flying FE2bs. In August 1917 he was posted to 60 Squadron, flying SE5as with the squadron until January 1918. Chidlaw-Roberts returned to France in the summer of 1918 as A Flight Commander in 40 Squadron. He is credited with 10 victories, all but one scored in 60 Squadron. Chidlaw-Roberts died in 1989.

Right: DH5 A 9435 'E' of 24 Squadron. 2Lt G P Robertson POW 10 September 1917.

Right: Nieuport 17 B1672 of 1 Squadron shot down behind the German lines on 15 September 1917 by Oblt Loerzer of Jasta 26 for his 7th victory. The pilot, E D Tyzack, was killed.

Below: SE5a A8918 was brought down behind German lines on 14 September 1917. The pilot, Lt H T Hammond of 60 Squadron was taken prisoner.

Above: Sopwith Camels of Naval 8 on Mont St Eloi aerodrome. May 1917.

Right: Sopwith Pup A 673 '5' of 46 Squadron after 2Lt L M Shadwell was forced to land by Ltn Schobinger of Jasta 12 on 16 September 1917.

Morning ablutions at Ste-Marie-Cappel. September 1917. Chidlaw-Roberts (left) and Keith Caldwell.

60 Squadron. C G Evans (shaving), H D Crompton, with squadron dog. John B Crompton. Autumn 1917.

An unknown photographer of 60 Squadron in the autumn of 1917 seemed to take a delight in photographing his fellow pilots while they were shaving. L to R: S L G 'Poppy' Pope, also known as 'The Cardinal'. G C 'Old' Young (shaving) and R L Chidlaw-Roberts.

Left: Relaxing in the autumn sunshine. Capt Keith 'Grid' Caldwell, outside his tent at Ste-Marie-Cappel, September 1917.

Above: Kennedy-Cochran-Patrick in cap, Keith 'Grid' Caldwell in profile nearest camera. Robert Chidlaw-Roberts, far right, intent on reading his mail from home.

Top right: Capt. Ronald Sykes DFC. Sykes served with Naval 9, Naval 3 and 201 Squadrons. He is credited with six victories.

Right: This Nieuport 27 was visiting from 1 Squadron, when photographed on 56 Squadron's aerodrome at Estrée Blanche by James McCudden. Capt R C Southam of 1 Squadron was KIA in this Nieuport on 9 January 1918.

Right: DH5 A 9197. Presentation Aeroplane 'New South Wales. No.15. The Upper Hunter.' This DH5 served with 68 Squadron.

Above: On 21 September 1917 the Nieuports of Lts R D G McKergow and MacHaffie of 29 Squadron collided in mid air. Both pilots were killed. The wreckage of Nieuport B 3634, flown by McKergow, is in the foreground.

Top right: 'Star Turns' of C Flight 56 Squadron in September 1917. L to R: Reginald Theodore Carlos 'Georgie' Hoidge. G H 'Beery' Bowman (Flight Commander) Richard Aveline Maybery. On 6 September Bowman had inadvertently burnt his left leg on the hot exhaust pipe of his SE5a and his leg was still bandaged when this photograph was taken.

Right: James McCudden took this atmospheric shot of Gerald Maxwell taxying out in his SE5a at Estrée Blanche in the late summer of 1917.

Right: Lt Arthur Foley Rhys Davids in the cockpit of his SE5 at Bekesbourne, England. July 1917.

away in search of his own Flight, finally finding them over Houthulst Forest in combat with the eight Albatri. Maybery dived to join in the fight, but a Nieuport suddenly appeared, nearly colliding with him, and in swerving away Maybery choked his engine. Bowman, his engine now running better, was attacking an enemy scout when the Nieuport attacked him from the rear. Bowman turned and got underneath his attacker, but when he saw it was a Nieuport he turned away. Bowman, who had now lost a great deal of height and had a stoppage in his Lewis, was forced back to the lines by the enemy scouts.

Maybery succeeded in restarting his engine and attacked three scouts east of Zonnebeke. The highest Albatros was coloured red and green and Maybery drove it down. Although his engine was still not running satisfactorily, Maybery next attacked four more enemy scouts before coming under attack from another three. The odds were too great and he turned west to escape them, but on looking back he saw that Hoidge had arrived at the scene of the fight and was being hard-pressed by the enemy pilots. Seeing Maybery returning, the enemy pilots sheered off and flew east. Maybery flew on to the vicinity of Houthulst Forest where he attacked two red-nosed Albatri. Closing onto the tail of one of these he fired both guns and the Albatros went down in a steep dive with its engine full on. As Maybery followed, still firing, the enemy scout broke up, the left wing breaking clean away from the fuselage, the rest of the machine finally hitting the ground just southeast of the Forest.[7]

Macmillan, leading five Camels of 45 Squadron, attacked two DFWs over Houthulst Forest. The DFWs were escorted by five Albatri and Macmillan and Brownell went down to tackle the two-seaters, leaving the other three Camels to fight the Albatri. Macmillan killed the observer in one of the DFWs and it went down, but as it did so it came into the sights of Brownell, on Macmillan's left, and he instinctively pressed his triggers. The DFW finally burst into flames and crashed. Brownell was a new pilot and Macmillan awarded him the victory, but both are credited with a DFW on the evening of September 10. Raymond Brownell, a Tasmanian, was to score an eventual 12 victories. An Albatros from the escort was shot down, claimed by Lt E A Smith.

At 6.00pm, a Flight of Sopwith Pups of Naval 3 forced a DFW from *FlAbt(A) 293* down over Furnes. The crew, *Vzfw* Eckhardt and *Ltn* Gilge, were taken POW.

The Camels of 70 Squadron, flying to their patrol area in the evening, saw a formation of enemy scouts flying below and dived to attack them. Lt L Wheeler attacked one of the enemy scouts, a triplane, which easily zoomed away from him. The triplane was flown by Werner Voss, the *Staffelführer* of *Jasta 10*, who quickly shot down 2Lt Arthur Smith Sisley in flames, the falling Camel almost colliding with 2Lt Bickerton,

fighting lower down. Voss then turned his attention to another Camel, flown by 2Lt O C Pearson, and shot it down to crash near Poelcapelle. Both pilots were killed.

The only other casualty of the day was a DH5 of 24 Squadron, shot down on the Third Army front, the pilot taken prisoner.

An evening patrol from Naval 8, led by FltLt R F Redpath, attacked a DFW returning from a reconnaissance flight over the British back areas. The whole Flight attacked this machine and forced the pilot to land in a field between Furnes and Adinkerke. The pilot was unhurt but the observer had been wounded and later died in hospital. The DFW was hardly damaged and after small repairs, with the German crosses replaced by British roundels, it was flown was by the naval pilots. Not surprisingly, this DFW was not given a G number by the RFC, being exclusively the property of the RNAS.

Casualties were heavy for the fighter squadrons on September 11. The morning was fine, with some sunshine and morning patrols were possible.

The first patrol of the day flown by 1 Squadron was led by Louis Jenkin, who dived on a green Albatros with grey wings and sent it down out of control. In the second patrol by the squadron, Lt W Mansell's Nieuport received a direct hit by Archie over Houthem, blowing off its right hand pair of wings. The third patrol of the day was to see a further loss when Louis Jenkin, the B Flight Commander and a leading pilot of the squadron with twenty-three victories, was shot down and killed. Jenkin and his Flight attacked a pair of two-seaters escorted by seven scouts over Westroosebeke. The Nieuports drove the enemy formation east, but one attacked Jenkin from behind. Although this machine was driven off, Jenkin was later seen low down, but seemingly under control. Jenkin, who has no known grave, was claimed by *Oblt* Otto Schmidt, the *Staffelführer* of *Jasta 29* for his eighth victory.

The pilots of 45 Squadron gained two victories in a morning patrol. Matthew Frew and Henry Moody both shot down enemy machines at 9.20am: Frew an Albatros out of control over Kortewilde for his ninth victory; Moody a DFW over Westroosebeke for his second. Earlier in the patrol, 2Lt E B Denison had been shot down and taken prisoner during a fight with enemy scouts over Roulers.

In the afternoon, Macmillan took out a Flight of seven Camels on a North Offensive Patrol. East of Langemarck, a number of enemy aircraft were seen, over twenty in number and including several of the new Fokker Triplanes. Despite the odds, Macmillan decided to attack these machines and rocking his wings in the signal to attack he led the Camels down on the enemy scouts. Macmillan first shot at one of the triplanes, which dived away under its *jasta* companions, but looking around Macmillan saw Oscar McMaking below him, under attack by another triplane. Macmillan dived to McMaking's assistance, firing a brief burst to distract the enemy pilot before his sights were on the enemy machine, a stratagem that usually worked. 'This fellow, however, was of a different breed. He looked round at me and I saw his black leather helmeted and begoggled face above his left shoulder as he swerved slightly to one side then looked ahead again and followed the Camel's tail.'

McMaking, who was an experienced pilot, took no evasive action to shake the triplane off his tail, the Camel continuing down in a steep dive, which gave Macmillan to believe that he had been wounded by the enemy pilot's first burst. Determined to avenge McMaking, Macmillan continued to dive after the triplane, firing short bursts, the enemy pilot looking round at him, coolly swerving to avoid his fire. 'He was a clever pilot.' Suddenly, an RE8 came between Macmillan and the enemy machine, its wings obliterating his sight of the enemy triplane. Macmillan could see the observer's horrified face staring up at him, only yards away. A collision seemed inevitable. Macmillan pulled the Camel's stick back into his stomach. 'I breathed man's shortest prayer: "My God"'. By some miracle the Camel missed the RE8, going up into an unintentional loop, falling out at the top. Macmillan blacked out. When he recovered the Camel was in an inverted spin, its engine had stopped through lack of pressure, and it had lost considerable height.

Macmillan was awarded two Fokker triplanes out of control from this encounter, but Voss, the pilot of the triplane, returned safely to his aerodrome at Heule and was awarded McMaking as his 47th and penultimate victory.

Fifty-six Squadron had a considerable number of combats during the morning and evening but continual gun jams robbed them of any positive victories and only two machines were claimed as out of control. Mannock claimed a DFW over Thelus at 11.15am, and Alexander Pentland and Frederick Sowery of 19 Squadron each claimed a Rumpler: Pentland's south of Bousbecque at 1.15pm; Sowery's east of Quesnoy five minutes later. Naval 8 pilots who claimed victories were 'Tich' Rochford, an Albatros at 11.10am over Thorout for his fifth victory, and Ronald Thornely a two-seater for the last of his nine victories. A pilot from Naval 9 destroyed an Albatros over Leke in the evening. A patrol from 46 Squadron, led by Captain 'Nobby' Scott, all shot at a two-seater over the Scarpe in the morning. The two-seater went down out of control, and the victory was shared between the whole Flight.

At 10.00am over Houthulst, 70 Squadron lost a pilot killed over the forest by *Ltn* Böhning of *Jasta 36.*

Low clouds on September 12 curtailed flying and there were few combats. The RFC communiqué for the day mentions a number of combats during the day, but none of the claims

are shown in the victory scores of the pilots concerned and some of the combats reported are obviously from the previous day. The only casualty for the fighter squadrons was a Spad from 23 Squadron last seen going down over Linselles, the pilot, 2Lt S Dronsfield, taken prisoner, was claimed by *Ltn* Kroll of *Jasta 24.*

Low clouds wind and rain the next day again curtailed flying, but the naval squadrons lost two pilots: a Sopwith Triplane from Naval 1 was shot down over Menin, its pilot wounded and taken prisoner by *Ltn* Wüsthoff of *Jasta 4,* and Naval 10 lost a Camel in a fight over Roulers. The Camels were returning from a patrol when a group of Albatri made a hit and run attack on the rear of the formation, shooting down FltSubLt E Abbott, before zooming away. Abbott was wounded and taken POW by *Ltn* Bülow of *Jasta 36.*

September 14 was a day of heavy clouds and strong westerly winds, but there was a great deal of fighting. A patrol from 56 Squadron set off at 8.05am led by Geoffrey Bowman. Keeping a little to the south of their usual patrol area because of the thick clouds, Bowman kept west of the front lines. There was a strong westerly wind, putting the SE5s at a tactical disadvantage, pushing them further into enemy territory, and Bowman had no intention of fighting east of the lines.

Over Zandvoorde Bowman saw a group of eight Albatros scouts below the SE5s and he dived to attack them. The enemy scouts scattered under the attack and Bowman's opponent flew into the cloud. Bowman followed, came out of the cloud and saw the Albatros a hundred yards away, flying east. Keeping to the edge of the cloud, Bowman flew after the enemy scout and finally caught it over Menin. The enemy pilot was completely unaware of Bowman's presence and thirty rounds from Bowman's guns 'at very close range' sent the Albatros down to crash in a field a mile north east of the town. This was possibly *Ltn* Groos of *Jasta 11* who was slightly wounded on September 14.

The other members of Bowman's Flight had mixed success. Robert Sloley attacked one Albatros with a red nose and tail but the pilot spun away from his fire, flattened out further down and flew east. Sloley turned his attentions to another, this one painted grey with a blue tail, and closed to within thirty yards before firing a hundred rounds into it. The enemy machine stalled, fell over onto its right side and went down completely out of the control, the pilot either dead or wounded. 'Georgie' Hoidge had been shot down, an accurate burst from one of the enemy pilots hitting his SE5 in the engine, forcing Hoidge to land just north of Zillebeke Lake. Hoidge was unhurt.

The squadron flew an evening patrol, the customary eleven SE5s – the squadron seemed to have a compulsion to send out this *exact* number of machines each evening – left the ground at 5.00pm. B Flight were the first in action, over Roulers with seven Albatri from *Jasta 11*. McCudden attacked *Oblt* Weigand, slightly wounding him and hitting his Albatros in the engine. The Albatros began to vibrate badly and Weigand shut off his engine and went down in a flat spiral, but managed to land his damaged fighter. Rhys Davids picked out a solitary Albatros and sent it down in a steep spiral, smoke pouring from its engine. Maxwell and A Flight now arrived at the scene of the action and the remainder of the Albatri flew off east. The SE5s now joined forces and patrolled towards Menin. Over the town a strong force of twelve or fourteen enemy scouts was seen, flying 2,000 feet above the SE5s and McCudden and Rhys Davids flew under the enemy formation to tempt them down. The leader of the Albatri finally dived on Rhys Davids and they fought for some time, Rhys Davids noting that the Albatros was very smartly finished with a green fuselage and tail. The German was a skilled pilot, outmanoeuvred Rhys Davids and shot his SE5s through the petrol tank. Petrol poured out over Rhys Davids' and he zoomed away and shut off his engine. The enemy pilot made no attempt to follow him down and Rhys Davids finally switched over to his gravity tank and landed at Bailleul aerodrome.[8]

In this last engagement, Lt Norman Crow was shot down and killed by *Vzfw* Menckhoff of *Jasta 3* for his eleventh victory.

Naval 10 flew two uneventful patrols in the morning, but the afternoon patrol fought eight enemy scouts over Tenbrielen and three enemy machines were claimed as out of control.

Six SE5s, A Flight of 60 Squadron, led by Capt Robert Chidlaw-Roberts, took off at 3.10pm to fly a Northern Offensive Patrol, with Capt Keith 'Grid'Caldwell leading another Flight of four on a Southern Offensive Patrol. 2Lt Henry 'Bunny' Hammond, an Australian pilot of A Flight, had carburettor trouble, struggled to keep position and was last seen during a fight over Menin. Hammond was attacked by two Albatri, who hit his SE5 and he was forced to land behind the German trenches at La Bassée. Hammond was hurriedly bundled out of his SE5 by German troops and photographs were taken of his machine.

Chidlaw-Roberts claimed an Albatros out of control from the fight, but 'Poppy' Pope's SE5 was damaged and he crashed on landing back at Ste-Marie-Cappel.

A patrol of Camels from Naval 3 were in combat with two enemy scouts a mile north east of Leke in the late afternoon and FltCom J S T Fall shot one down to crash at 5.15pm.

Other than Crow and Hammond, the only other casualties during the day, were a Camel of 70 Squadron which was shot down west of Roulers in the morning by *Jasta 17*, the pilot taken prisoner; a Camel from Naval 9, which forced landed near Pervyse, it controls shot up; and a pilot from 54 Squadron wounded in action.

Despite low clouds and wind there was little let up in fighting on September 15. In the afternoon a Flight of Camels from Naval 10, led by Desmond Fitzgibbon, saw a formation of DH4s safely back to the Front Line before carrying on with their offensive patrol. At 4.30pm over Moorslede five Albatros scouts and a Fokker Triplane from *Jasta 11* attacked the British scouts and in the fighting Norman Macgregor shot down the triplane, which was flown by *Oblt* Kurt Wolff, the *Staffelführer* of *Jasta 11*. Macgregor only claimed the triplane as out of control, but Wolff, flying F.1 102/17, crashed by the small village of Nachtigall, north of Wervicq, and was killed. This was a bad blow for *Jasta 11*. *Jasta 11* was a part of *Jagdgeschwader Nr 1* and its adjutant Karl Bodenschatz, described the diminutive Kurt Wolff in its war diary: 'At first glance, you could only say a "delicate little flower." A slender thin little figure, a very young face, whose entire manner is one of extreme shyness. He looks as if you could tip him over backwards with one harsh word.'[9] Wolff had flown with *Jasta 11* since 5 November 1916 and had scored 33 victories before his death.

The pilots of the RFC fighter squadrons claimed four victories in the day. For 29 Squadron, Lt J D Payne destroyed an Albatros which was attacking a Camel; MacLanachan of 40 Squadron sent an Albatros down out of control south east of Vimy at five minutes past two, for his fifth victory; and King and Wilson of 70 Squadron each claimed Albatros scouts in a combat near Menin. In addition to Macgregor's victory over Wolff, two pilots of Naval 9 each drove down an enemy scout out of control.

Seventy Squadron had three casualties during the day. Two pilots were shot down and taken POW from the morning patrol, and another two pilots were lost in the afternoon: one taken prisoner and the other injured in a crash landing. Lt J Simpson of 32 Squadron was wounded in a combat and forced to land east of Zillebeke and the DH5 was abandoned.

September 16 was cloudy with bright intervals. The Spads of 19 Squadron were detailed for ground-strafing duties in the morning. Lts Pentland and Graham flew up and down the German trenches at 200 feet, firing at enemy troops, waved on by adjacent British infantry. Leaving the trenches, the Spads flew east, attacking troops and transport on the roads. Returning to Fienvillers, Pentland spotted a two-seater and shot it down out of control. Lts Dawson and Capt Sowery from the squadron were also groundstrafing in the morning, attacking troops and transport, Sowery firing into the enemy trenches from 100 feet before attacking a party of troops at the cross roads of La Croix-au-Bois.

In its second patrol of the day, 56 Squadron saw a considerable amount of fighting. In one of the later combats over Houthem, Leonard Barlow attacked an Albatros, firing both guns. Its propeller stopped and the enemy scout went down in a slow right hand spiral. Barlow suspected that the enemy pilot was still in control and dived at the Albatros again. The enemy pilot zoomed, but Barlow caught the Albatros at the top of the zoom and fired another long burst into it. This time there was no mistake. The Albatros, possibly either *Ltn* Wendler or *Ltn* Grutter of *Jasta 17* went down and crashed near Wervicq. This victory was confirmed by Lt Soden of 60 Squadron, who were also involved in the fighting, Chidlaw-Roberts killing *Ltn* Alfred Bauer of *Jasta 17*, shooting him down in flames over Houthem. 2Lt J A Hawtrey from the squadron was wounded, shot down and taken prisoner, but died of his wounds the following day.

A patrol from 46 Squadron set out to find a two-seater working over the Lines but were attacked by seven Albatri over St Quentin and 2Lt L Shadwell was shot down in the fighting and made POW. Additional victories were claimed by Lt H Maddocks of 54 Squadron and Leacroft of 19 Squadron. Naval 1 claimed an Albatros scout and Naval 9 a DFW destroyed.

Seventy Squadron lost another two Camels during the morning in fighting over Houthulst Forest. Both pilots were taken prisoner.

The weather was extremely bad during the next two days and there was little flying on the Ypres front – in fact the fighter squadrons of 9th Wing did no flying at all – but further south, in the Cambrai area, conditions were better and 41 Squadron lost two pilots on the 17th and an additional two the following day, all four killed in combat by pilots of *Jagdstaffeln 30, 12* and *37*.

The resumption of the offensive at Ypres was planned for September 20 and on September 19, the day preceding the attack, there was a great deal of air fighting.

Camels of 70 Squadron were ground-strafing in the morning, machine gunning and bombing attacking enemy troops and positions. In the afternoon the pilots of Naval 10 were also engaged in low level bombing and machine gunning. While four Camels stayed up to provide top cover, another four went down to drop bombs and machine gun troops and transport in Houthulst Forest and the surrounding areas.

A patrol from Naval 1 led by Capt Stanley Rosevear fought with enemy scouts in the morning and Rosevear destroyed an Albatros scout over Becelaere at 10.10am, with two other pilots of the patrol claiming another out of control. In an evening patrol FltLt Richard Minifie destroyed an Albatros scout over Westroosbeke at 6.00pm.

Before their ground-strafing activities in the afternoon, Naval 10 had flown a morning offensive patrol over Ypres and attacked a formation of eight enemy scouts over Hooge. In a fifteen minute fight Hugh Maund and Ralph Carroll both claimed enemy scouts driven down, and Norman Macgregor drove another down emitting a large amount of black smoke, but FltSubLt Edmond Grace was shot down and killed by *Ltn* Adam of *Jasta 6*.

Spads of 19 Squadron attacked six Albatri over Becelaere in the afternoon; John Leacroft claimed one out of control north of Roubaix at 3.35pm and another west of Moorslede twenty-five minutes later. The Nieuports of 1 Squadron were in action in the evening and the A Flight Commander, Capt William Rooper, shot down an Albatros in flames east of Poelcapelle.

Bored with the inactivity of the last two days – the squadron had flown no patrols – James McCudden took off from Estrée Blanche at 10.30am 'to look for two-seaters'. There was a strong westerly wind, with clouds at low level. McCudden climbed to 18,000 feet, flew east, and over Bois-deBiez saw an enemy two-seater. However, this machine was well to the east, and while he was considering if he could catch it, in view of the adverse wind, he saw a DFW, going west and less than 400 feet below him. McCudden attacked this DFW over Merville and the enemy pilot dived away, so abruptly that a small black box and some signal cartridges fell out of its cockpit.

Thirty five minutes later McCudden saw a Rumpler crossing the Lines over Armentières and he carefully stalked this machine, getting into the sun and waiting until it was west of the lines before attacking. McCudden opened fire, but his Lewis gun stopped with a double feed after firing only one round. McCudden switched to his Vickers, but after thirty rounds this also stopped. McCudden's aim had been good, however, and the Rumpler glided down, its propeller stopped, and trailing blue smoke. McCudden cleared the stoppage in his Vickers and dived after the two-seater. He could see the enemy observer slumped down in his cockpit, leaving his gun unmanned, and he attacked again. McCudden was determined to crash this Rumpler, if possible in the British Lines, but the strong westerly wind had pushed the combat eastwards and the Rumpler finally crashed near Radinghem, about a mile behind the German Lines. This Rumpler was possibly from *FlAbt (A) 292b* who had an observer killed on September 19 and a pilot and observer wounded.[10] This combat was the first example of McCudden's skill in stalking enemy two-seaters, a skill he was to bring to perfection in December.

While McCudden was fighting the two-seaters, Gerald Maxwell and Robert Sloley had taken off on a 'Special Mission' – a euphemism for looking for trouble. The two SE5s first attacked a two-seater: Maxwell from the rear, Sloley from the front. The enemy pilot returned Sloley's fire with his front gun but turned away when only 50 yards separated them. Sloley saw that Maxwell had attacked from the rear and had silenced the enemy observer with his first burst, but the pilot dived away east, too fast for the SE5s to catch. As Sloley and Maxwell began to return, Maxwell saw a number of British Archie bursts – distinguishable from German by its white bursts – south of Armentières. The British gunners were firing at another two-seater, and the SE5s quickly flew to the action. Sloley attacked this machine first. The enemy pilot changed direction and evaded Sloley, but came under attack from Maxwell. Maxwell fired the remainder of his Lewis gun ammunition before opening fire with his Vickers, but this stopped after 50 rounds with a stoppage and the two-seater escaped east.

In addition to FltSubLt Grace from Naval 10, Naval 1 lost one pilot killed and the other taken POW. Another pilot from the squadron was wounded in the back but returned to be taken to hospital. The RFC fighter squadrons had two casualties in the day's fighting. A pilot from 19 Squadron was wounded in the shoulder, his Spad badly shot about, and another Spad from the squadron was badly damaged and forced to land.

The Battle of the Menin Road Ridge

The ground attacks during August had cost the British army nearly 70,000 casualties, 15,000 of them killed. Gains of only 4,000 yards deep had been made, less at some points. The early onset of the autumn rains in August and the intense artillery fire from both antagonists had turned the battlefield into a quagmire, and the objective of driving the German forces from the slight but tactically important heights which commanded the battlefield had not been achieved. By the middle of September the battle had become a race against time; against the onset of the rains of late autumn. Haig was now desperate to gain control of the heights and transferred II Corps from General Gough's Fifth Army to the command of General Herbert Plumer's Second Army. Plumer's particular skill consisted of lengthy preparations to take limited objectives, a skill that he had demonstrated in his capture of the Messines Ridge in June 1917. There was now another ridge to take: the Gheluvelt Plateau, which sheltered the main concentration of German guns. Plumer planned for a battle divided into four definite stages of short duration, separated in time; each aimed at limited objectives. The first stage was for an advance of 1,500 yards, backed up by a concentration of artillery power unsurpassed by anything yet seen on the Western Front, the troops to move forward behind a creeping barrage of fearsome proportions.

Twelve single-seater fighter squadrons were involved in the battle, which began on September 20. Nos 1, 19, 45, 60 and Naval 1 of II Brigade; Nos 23,29,32,70 and Naval 10 of V Brigade; and Nos 56 and 66 of Ninth HQ Wing. The operational orders for the fighter squadrons of the RFC were similar to those of July 31. In addition to the defence of the corps aeroplanes working over the Lines, extensive ground-strafing of enemy troop positions, the reports of enemy counter attacks building up, and attacks on German aerodromes were the orders of the day, and special maps were supplied showing the German assembly points, bussing facilities, and the roads most likely to be used for bringing up reinforcements.

The II Corps sector of the Second Army extended east of the line of the artillery barrage, as far as the Roulers to Menin railway, and was divided into three sectors. Each of these sectors was to be patrolled continuously by pairs of fighters from zero hour, each pair to be relieved by another at two hourly intervals. These fighters were to fly at less than 500 feet, with orders to machine gun troops, transport and artillery batteries, and to watch for all counter attack movements. They were also to attack any low flying enemy aircraft seen. On their return each pair was to report all enemy movements seen to the Second Army Report Centre.

Rain set in on the night of September 19 and although it had ceased by dawn a heavy wet mist covered the battlefield. From 6.00am single-seater fighters from II Brigade, V Brigade and Ninth Wing were over the Front Lines, but little could be accomplished until the mist cleared at 8.00am. By the end of the day sixty seven 25lb bombs had been dropped and 28,000 rounds of ammunition had been fired at ground targets: troops in the Front Line trenches; on the march, forming and in billets; barges on canals; motor transport, both heavy and light; artillery batteries; machine gun emplacements and balloons. The dawn attacks on German aerodromes by single-seater fighters could not be made because of the early ground mist, but they were attacked during the day by pilots of 27 Squadron, flying individually or in pairs. *Jagd in Flanderns Himmel* records that bombs were dropped on the aerodromes of *Jasta 4* and *Jasta 11* from very low altitude, totally destroying three aeroplanes and damaging six others, five of them seriously. Sheds and a depot were also damaged. Personnel casualties were one non commissioned officer, an officer and three enlisted men of *Jasta 4* killed by bombs and another wounded by machine gun fire. A special detachment of an anti-aircraft machine gun unit, specifically ordered for the aerodrome defence, had a gunner wounded (who later died in hospital), two men badly wounded and two slightly.

Those pilots not employed on ground-strafing duties flew offensive patrols during the day and kept the *jagdstaffeln* from interfering with the all important work of the corps aeroplanes and low flying fighters. This was the most important work of the day. Concentrations of enemy troops were seen and reported, and artillery fire broke up these concentrations before counter attacks could be made.

Starting at 9.00am and finishing at 5.45pm, the pilots of 60 Squadron were primarily involved in offensive patrols, four pilots taking off every 75 minutes, but two pilots took off at 6.00am to bomb the German aerodromes at Bisseghem and Marcke. One returned with engine trouble and the other returned because the ground mist made the attack impossible. A second offensive patrol left the ground at 10.20am and attacked eight enemy scouts north of Zonnebeke three quarters of an hour later. Frank Soden fired at one Albatros and saw it fall from 1500 feet and hit the ground, but then had gun trouble and returned to base. 2Lt Robert Steele had engine failure, and in crash landing west of Zonnebeke, suffered concussion and facial injuries which put him into hospital and struck off squadron strength. Capt James Law (the son of Arthur Bonar Law the Chancellor of the Exchequer) returned safely to Ste-Marie-Cappele, but with his machine badly shot about, and in the 4.20pm patrol, although he claimed an Albatros down out of control, his SE5 was again badly damaged in the fighting. Law ran out of fuel on returning and landed just short of the aerodrome. Ian MacGregor, a Canadian, claimed a black and grey striped Albatros from the afternoon's fighting.

Three Nieuports from 1 Squadron were lost during the day. In the morning Lt C Gray landed at 40 Squadron's aerodrome to refuel. On returning to the lines he climbed to 1500 feet and was hit by groundfire, which stopped his engine and wounded him in the lung. Gray force landed and was taken POW. In the afternoon two more Nieuports of the squadron were shot down: 2Lt R Garratt was last seen over Gheluvelt after combat with enemy scouts, shot down by *Ltn* Runge of *Jasta 18,* and another member of the patrol, 2Lt F Chown, crashed west of the Lines and was killed.

Maxwell and Sloley took off at ten minutes to eleven, flew above the thick clouds to Armentières and attacked a two-seater and an Albatros over Wervicq. Deserting his charge, the Albatros pilot made off east and Maxwell sent the two-seater down in a vertical dive, black smoke pouring from its engine. Separated from Sloley, Maxwell climbed through the clouds, joined some SE5s from 60 Squadron, a Sopwith Camel and some Spads in a fight with seven black and white Albatri and succeeded in driving one down through the clouds. The enemy scouts then dived away east but later reformed over Moorslede, where they were seen by Sloley who fired a red Very light to attract the attention of a flight of Nieuports. Three of the Nieuports followed Sloley down in his attack on the Albatri and he send one down in a series of sideslips, tail first.

Pairs of pilots from Naval 10 carried out ground-strafing duties throughout the day, although only a few machines carried bombs. After dropping his bombs on troops at Vifwagen, FltSubLt J G Manuel attacked a two-seater, hit the pilot with his fire and forced him to land. Manuel went down to 200 feet and fired at the enemy machine on the ground: neither pilot nor observer got out. FltComm Saint, dropped a bomb on a building, but on landing it was found that one of his bombs had not released. After ground-strafing troops on the Poecapelle to Westroosebeke road, Macgregor fought with scattered formations of Albatri to the east of Houthulst Forest and saw an Albatros driven down through the clouds by an SE5.

FltSubLts H Broughall and A F MacDonald took off at 11.05am. Forty minutes after taking off MacDonald had an indecisive engagement with an enemy scout, then finished his patrol by firing at enemy transport from 400 feet. Broughall did not return. He was last seen over in the clouds north of Ypres. He had been shot down and made POW.

In the afternoon the naval pilots returned to normal offensive patrol duties, although some bombs were carried. Saint and Manuel dropped their bombs over Poecapelle before fighting with six scouts over Westroosebeke, but this engagement was indecisive: the enemy scouts had seen a Flight of four SE5s coming up and dived away east.

Mannock shot down a DFW from *FlAbt(A)240* over Hulloch at 5.35pm. The enemy machine crashed at Grenay. The pilot, *Uffz* Kalbreiher, was wounded, but the observer, *Ltn de Res* Arthur Beauchamp was killed. Hulloch is under four miles from Mazingarbe, the advanced landing ground; the pilots of 40 Squadron had not far to go to find the fighting.

Other claims were made by a number of pilots at the end of the day's fighting: eight machines and two balloons were claimed as destroyed, and 12 machines as out of control. In addition the infantry shot down a low flying enemy aeroplane in flames. Casualties, however, were heavy. In addition to those already mentioned, 32 Squadron had a pilot taken POW, one injured in a crash landing and one with a badly shot up DH5; 23 Squadron had a pilot who died of wounds; 29 Squadron had a pilot killed, as did 45 Squadron; 66 Squadron had a pilot taken POW and 70 Squadron had a pilot wounded. Naval 1 had one pilot taken POW and another wounded. FltSubLt Ronald Sykes of Naval 9 was shot down by *Uffz* Paul Baümer of *Jasta B* as his fifth victory. Sykes crashed near St Pierre Capelle, east of the Lines, but he evaded capture by swimming the Yser River and regained the British Lines.

The ground fighting had gone well, the success in no small part due to the successful co-operation with the RFC. By 1.45pm the infantry had secured all its objectives and only a small sector of the Gheluvelt Plateau remained in German hands. The barrage stopped and the infantry began to dig in to prepare for any counter attacks during the afternoon. At 3.00pm one began to threaten at the eastern edge of Polygon Wood, but was immediately the attention of a fierce artillery barrage. When the shelling stopped no German troops could be seen and not further movement was observed.

The battle for the Menin Road Ridge was a success. At the end of the day, on a front of eight miles between Zillebeke and Langemarck, Plummer's troops had achieved penetrations of at least 1,500 yards, secured the base for his next attack and dislocated the enemy defensive system. But the cost had been high. In the day's fighting and in the attacks over the next two days to capture the rest of the plateau, 20,000 men were casualties, 3,000 of them killed.

Early morning reconnaissance on September 21 showed that the enemy was pouring troops into the battle, reinforcements arriving at Menin and Roulers railway stations. In the evening, more troops were arriving by rail to Menin and transported to the Front line trenches by buses. These activities led to a great deal of bombing, both day and night, by aeroplanes of the corps squadrons. In the air over the battlefield itself the *Luftstreitkräfte* was active in the morning, but slackened its efforts in the afternoon and it was reported that the enemy aircraft met often refused combat.

On an early morning patrol, A Flight of 46 Squadron fought with seven Albatri of *Jasta 12* west of Douai. In a 'stiff fight' Percy Wilcox shot one scout down, which was seen to crash, and V A H Robeson and P W S Bulman each claimed an Albatros out of control, but the war babe, R S Asher was shot down and killed by *Uffz* Neckel of the *Jasta,* coming down a mile behind the German lines in Jigsaw Wood.

Another morning patrol by the squadron found an LVG west of the Lines. Using tactics worked out while they were in England, the Pup pilots each attacked this LVG and sent it down in a twisting dive, out of control. The Pups were then attacked by five Albatri, but these made off as two Bristol Fighters joined in the fight.

Two Flights from 56 Squadron – A and C Flights – took off just after 8.00am. Maxwell saw four two-seaters escorted by six scouts east of Armentières. The Flight dived on the scouts, which dived away east, leaving the two-seaters undefended. Maxwell got underneath one and fired 100 rounds of Vickers and a whole drum of Lewis into its underside from 15 yards range. The two-seater burst into flames and went down. As it neared the ground a wing detached and it finally crashed in a small wood near Verlinghem, killing *Uffz* Kurt Krause and *Uffz* Wilhelm Schieber of *Schusta 21.* As Maxwell pulled away from the stricken machine he saw an SE5 going down with its wings folded up. This was Lt William Potts who had been shot down by *Ltn* Haack and *Ltn* Klostermannn of

FltAbt (A) 227. Wilkinson had sent another of the two-seaters down in a slow spin, which was confirmed by Turnbull.

Ten SE5s – B and C Flights – left Estrée Blanche at 4.45pm. Both Flights saw a good deal of indecisive fighting and only Hoidge claimed a victory. Hoidge had arrived at a fight between some Pups of 66 Squadron, SE5s from 60 Squadron and several Albatri. Hoidge saw one of the enemy scouts on the tail of a 60 Squadron SE5, got very close to avoid hitting the SE5 and fired a whole drum of Lewis into the Albatros, which went down for 2,000 feet. It then turned over and fell for another 500 feet before breaking into pieces. This victory was confirmed by Pritt of 66 Squadron. Hoidge was then attacked by a 'double V Strutter' and having a stoppage in both guns retreated to the west. The pilots of 60 Squadron claimed six enemy scouts during the afternoon's fighting. Chidlaw-Roberts claimed two Albatri destroyed over Langemarck within minutes of each other, shared with Lt J O Whiting; Lt Ian Macgregor claimed another two destroyed, and two additional victories were claimed by the patrol as a whole. Two of the Albatri were confirmed as destroyed by British AA batteries.

Cronyn described the afternoon's fighting in his diary:

'I had never seen so many Huns before: there must have been about sixty altogether and only about ten were two-seaters. They were all very much afraid to attack us, and as the wind was very strong we didn't wish to go far over to attack them.' Cronyn finished the extract with the comment 'The Huns are very much more cautious now than they were three weeks ago.'

The reference by the pilots of 56 Squadron to a 'double V Strutter' is puzzling. McCudden had seen this machine earlier in the day, describing it as 'an Albatros with two bays to each wing, instead of the usual one. This machine was known as the double V strutter and supposed to be flown by Baron von Richthofen.' On August 31 Clive Collett of 70 Squadron had also reported this machine and had made a sketch of it for RFC HQ, showing a double pair of wing struts on each side of the fuselage and estimating that it was a little larger than the usual Albatros. The description of this aeroplane given by McCudden, Hoidge and Collett, all experienced pilots, fits no German aeroplane known to have been in service during late August and early September 1917.

Other victories claimed during the day were an Albatros scout to Leacroft of 19 Squadron at 9.50am over Dadizeele; Sgt Gordon Olley of 1 Squadron, who shot the right hand pair of wings off a DFW over Wervicq at 9.50am; one of a formation of four Albatros scouts attacked by Capt R S Lloyd and Lt A W Wood was seen to crash by AA; and a patrol of DH5s from 24 Squadron, aided by two Bristol Fighters of 11 Squadron, destroyed one scout and drove another down out of control. A patrol from 45 Squadron fought with twenty Albatri over Comines. 'Bunty' Frew stopped the engine of one and sent another down in flames, and the Canadian, Emerson Smith, claimed another out of control. Naval pilots also scored: Stearne Edwards and Oliver Redgate of Naval 9 shot down a DFW over Zarren at 5.00pm, and Howard Saint of Naval 10 shot down an Albatros over Wervicq during a morning patrol.

Casualties were three Spads from 19 Squadron, shot down in the morning by *Jasta 18* over Dadizeele, the pilots killed; a pilot from 45 Squadron taken POW; Capt John Law shot down and killed in a morning patrol by 60 Squadron east of Ypres; and a pilot of 70 Squadron wounded in action. Not all casualties were the result of combat. Two pilots of 29 Squadron were killed in a collision during an afternoon patrol.

During the day the pilots of 68 Squadron arrived in France, flying their DH5s into Baizieux aerodrome, west of Albert.

There were low clouds on September 22, but there was no let up in the fighting, either in the air or on the ground. An early patrol by 40 Squadron attacked a formation of four DFWs and four Albatri over Pont-a-Vendin, driving the two-seaters down before fighting the scouts. The South African 'Tud' Tudhope attacked an Albatros from close range and it went down to crash by the village.

A patrol from 45 Squadron were also out in the morning, Kenneth Montgomery shooting down an Albatros out of control over Tenbrielen at 8.55am. Six SE5s of 60 Squadron took off at 9.25am and an hour and twenty minutes later were in action over Zonnebeke with 11 Albatros scouts. Chidlaw-Roberts and Harold Hamersley attacked an Albatros painted green and black and sent it down over Zonnebeke, but Macgregor was wounded in the leg and Lt J Whiting was killed.

It was a good day for the pilots of 46 Squadron, still fighting on with their outclassed Sopwith Pups. Lee's diary, September 22: 'We ran the flag up on C Flight hangar this morning. We bagged four Huns! Naturally we are slightly brimming over.' The Flight had left the ground at 9.30am, the four Pups flying at 16,000 feet with four Bristol Fighters at 8,000 feet. Within half an hour the Pups found an Albatros C Type and 'Nobby' Scott, the Flight Commander, Charles Courtneidge and Arthur Lee all attacked in a steep dive, converging on the enemy machine, their combined fire killing the observer. The Albatros went down in a steep dive, going over the vertical.

The Pups regained their height and half an hour later attacked five Albatri, two of which fastened onto Lee's tail, taking it in turns to fire at him. 'I saw them both, one a pale blue, the other green-grey, in between bursts of rak-ak-ak and tracer flashing past my nose. For once I really had the gust up, I couldn't think how I could get away from them.' Lee, in evading fire from the green-grey scout with a half roll, nearly

collided with the blue Albatros, finding it directly below the Pup and on a identical course. Upside down, Lee could see straight into the cockpit of the enemy scout. The pilot, who was not wearing goggles, was looking up. 'He had a small moustache, like me. In fact, I might have been looking at myself! We were so close I could have reached down and shaken hands. Fatuous thing to flash into one's mind in a fight, but it did and the mind works fast. Then he'd pushed his nose down violently, and vanished.'

Lifting his goggles which had misted over with sweat from his forehead – 'the risk of collision frightens you more than the risk of bullets'– Lee came under attack from two more of the enemy scouts, but these were taken off his tail by Clarke and Courtneidge. Lee then attacked an Albatros that was going down onto the tail of one of the Bristols, getting behind the enemy scout and firing thirty rounds from close range. The Albatros jerked up behind the Bristol and spun away, falling for 4,000 feet without flattening out. This last Albatros was awarded to Lee as his fourth victory, confirmed by both the Bristol Fighter crew and Courtneidge, who was close to it as it spun down. Clarke was also awarded the blue Albatros and Courtneidge another, both confirmed by British AA. The Albatros C type was shared between Scott, Lee, and Courtneidge.

The close up view of the German pilot of the blue Albatros, almost his double, put Lee in a philosophical mood that night. He confided in his diary: 'It made me realise that the Hun pilots and observers are just the same types as we are in the RFC, all young, keen on flying, volunteers for the job. We'd probably get along together like a house on fire, yet all we're here for is to slay each other. It's daft when you think of it. And for whose benefit, when we're all done in, and the war's over.'

Capt Clive Brewster-Joske of 46 Squadron had also scored in the morning's patrols, sharing an Albatros out of control north of Brebières at 10.15am, with Lt R Ferrie. Capt William Rutherford of 60 Squadron destroyed a two-seater at 6.45pm over the Ypres/Roulers area and Lt H Dawson claimed an Albatros out of control.

There were thin layers of low cloud at various heights on September 23. The Camels of Naval 10 and Nieuports of 29 Squadron were all in action during the morning north east of Ypres. Capt Arthur Jones-Williams of 29 Squadron shot down an Albatros over Zonnebeke, but in the fighting 2Lt E Holdworth was killed by *Ltn* Walter von Bülow of *Jasta 36* and 2Lt H Rothery was wounded and shot down east of the lines, later dying of his wounds. Naval 10 caught a formation of ten scouts and five two-seaters coming west from Westroosebeke; after several indecisive combats in which the Camels were plagued with gun troubles, Saint and Alexander each claimed an Albatros driven down. Edward Bussell also claimed an Albatros from the fighting but his Camel was badly shot about and he crashed.

In the early afternoon William MacLanachan of 40 Squadron was returning from patrol over Henin Lietard when he saw three Albatros scouts coming from the southwest. The enemy scouts had a height advantage of a thousand feet over MacLanachan, and when they were within half a mile of him one flew to the right to get behind the Nieuport. The remaining two climbed for even more height. It was obvious to MacLanachan that the enemy pilots intended to attack him simultaneously. MacLanachan was flying a Nieuport 24 named 'The Silver Queen' which was equipped with a double Lewis gun on a Foster mounting on the top wing which enabled it to be pulled down and fired upwards. MacLanachan pulled down these Lewis guns in preparation for the attack and dived slightly to gain a little extra speed for any quick manoeuvre necessary.

The two enemy scouts to MacLanachan's front dived at him 'in a half-hearted manner,' firing their guns before they were within effective range. The Albatros pilot behind had also dived to attack the Nieuport and MacLanachan, now determined to make a fight for it, dived away east to come up under the enemy scouts. The enemy pilots had not foreseen that MacLanachan would turn to the east – perhaps thinking he would make a break for the safety of the British Lines – and the two attacking from the front overshot the Nieuport. MacLanachan put his machine into a tight turn, with vertical bank, and came out immediately below the third Albatros, whose pilot had lost sight of the Nieuport, with no idea where it was. MacLanachan opened fire with tracer and armour piercing bullets, straight up into the bottom of the yellow fuselage, concentrating his fire on the front of the enemy machine. The Albatros seemed to stagger and went down almost vertically.

The remaining two enemy pilots, who by their opening fire on the Nieuport before they were in effective range were probably inexperienced, made off to the northeast, one straggling well behind the other. MacLanachan dived 'helter-skelter' after this last Albatros, shot it down to crash in a field to the east of Lens, then contour chased back to Mazingarbe.

MacLanachan later wrote that on his return Mannock was annoyed that he had not been with him in the fight with the three Albatri, but Mannock's mock annoyance was no doubt later mollified when he shot down a two-seater in the evening patrol, the enemy machine crashing in flames near Oppy. It was Mannock's fourteenth and penultimate victory while serving in 40 Squadron. To celebrate their victories Mannock and MacLanachan went into Bethune, to The Queen of Sheba, a teashop they had found in a small side street, and consumed quantities of tea and cream cakes, a speciality of the house.

During the afternoon patrol, John Barlow from the squadron had been shot down. The Flight had dived on a formation of Albatri from *Jasta 12* over Arleux and in the fighting Barlow was shot down and killed by *Ltn* Becker of the *Jasta*, who claimed a Nieuport south-west of Oppy at 4.55pm (GT).

Weather conditions in the evening were similar to the morning, with one exception: although there were still layers of clouds at various heights there was now a main bank of cloud at 9,000 feet, a thousand feet thick, putting a ceiling over the entire Front. There was a great deal of activity in the evening sky, with all the aircraft, British and German, operating under this main bank of cloud.

C and B Flights of 56 Squadron left Estrée Blanche at 5.00pm. McCudden and B Flight were flying south from Houthulst Forest when McCudden spotted a DFW coming north from Houthem. McCudden made short work of this DFW, sending it down to crash northeast of Houthem, killing *Ltn* Gustav Rudolph and *Uffz* Rudolf Franke of *FlAbt 6*.

McCudden then turned the SE5s east. Under the heavy grey cloud at 9,000 feet, the visibility was very good. Away to the east McCudden could see 'clusters of little black specks, all moving swiftly, first in one direction and then another.' To the north were formations of Sopwith Pups and Camels, SE5s, Spads and Bristol Fighters, all protecting the RE8s of the corps squadrons working over the lines at lower heights.

At 6.25pm three SE5s of 60 Squadron, the remnants of A Flight, led by Capt 'Grid Caldwell, were returning from a patrol. Slightly behind Caldwell were Robert Chidlaw-Roberts and an Australian pilot, Harold Hamersley, who saw what he took to be a Nieuport, pursued by an Albatros, dive past the front of the SE5s. Hamersley dived at the Albatros, but the 'Nieuport' immediately turned and attacked him, hitting the SE5 with an extremely accurate burst of fire, shooting through the left hand bottom engine bearer; two of the top planes, the centre section, spars, ribs, rudder and top post. The water jacket on the right hand side of the engine was shot through; the propeller, CC gear, generator and oil pipes were all hit, and there were numerous hits in the fabric. Hamersley threw the SE into a spin to escape from this murderous fire, but the 'Nieuport', which Hamersley had seen too late was a Fokker Triplane, followed him down, firing all the time, and Hamersley was forced to dive inverted to escape. Chidlaw-Roberts, seeing that Hamersley was in trouble, dived to attack the triplane, but it barely paused in its pursuit of Hamesrsley: 'in seconds he was on my tail and had shot my rudder bar about. I retired from the fray and that was all I saw of it.' Caldwell was also about to go to Hamersley's aid, but McCudden and his Flight had now arrived and were tackling the triplane.

After shooting down the DFW McCudden and B Flight had been about to attack a formation of six Albatros scouts when McCudden saw an SE5 under attack from a triplane. 'The SE certainly looked very unhappy, so we changed our minds about attacking the V Strutters and went to the rescue of the unfortunate SE.' McCudden and Rhys Davids both dived at the enemy scout, McCudden from the right, Rhys Davids from the left, both getting behind the triplane together. The enemy pilot saw them coming and turned 'in a most disconcertingly quick manner, not a climbing or Immelmann turn, but a sort of flat half spin. By now the German triplane was in the middle of our formation and its handling was wonderful to behold. The pilot seemed to be firing at all of us simultaneously, and although I got behind him a second time I could hardly stay there for a second. His movements were so quick and uncertain that none of us could hold him in sight at all for any decisive time. I now got a good opportunity as he was coming towards me nose on, and slightly underneath, and had apparently not seen me. I dropped my nose, got him well in my sight, and pressed both triggers. As soon as I fired up came his nose at me, and I heard clack-clack-clack-clack, as his bullets passed close to me and through my wings. I distinctly noticed the red-yellow flashes from his parallel Spandau guns. As he flashed by me I caught a glimpse of a black head in the triplane with no hat on at all.'

The enemy pilot was now fighting four SE5s, but seemed undeterred by the odds and made no attempt to break off the combat. Cronyn, who had followed McCudden and Rhys Davids down in their initial attack, fired a burst at the triplane, intending to then zoom away, but his engine had lost pressure in his dive and his zoom, 'was but a feeble climb. I take my hat off to that Hun, as he was a most skilful pilot, but he did give me a rough passage. On seeing my feeble attempt, he whipped round in an extraordinary way, using no bank at all, but just throwing his tail behind him. He attacked me from the side, and I had the opportunity of observing that he was one of the very latest design, being a triplane. He was at very close quarters and could hardly miss me. The bullets ripped all around me.' Cronyn kept his head and turned under the triplane, pumping furiously to regain his engine pressure, hoping that his companions would take the triplane away from him. 'I do not know how many times I turned under him; I did not stop to count, but it seemed an eternity.' In desperation, Cronyn finally took even more violent evasive action, going down in a spin, and the triplane pilot left him.

Bowman, Maybery and Hoidge had also now arrived at the scene of the fight. The triplane pilot had been joined by a red-nosed Albatros and the two German pilots were now fighting five SE5s, the triplane pilot having already sent both Muspratt and Cronyn out of the fight, limping back to the lines.

Maybery fired several bursts at the triplane, but found the Albatros on his tail and climbed away, turning and diving back at the triplane, firing both guns until his Lewis stopped. Both enemy scouts now turned on him and he was only saved by the intervention of two other SE5s.

Hoidge, who a little earlier had shot down a green coloured Pfalz that had been attacking Maybery, put a fresh drum on his Lewis gun and climbed into the fight with the triplane, attacking it from the side as it was flying nose on to McCudden. 'I attacked him four or five times but I didn't see what happened after this. I never saw the red-nosed scout at all. The green man didn't get a chance to scrap.'

Although none of the British pilots saw it go, the red-nosed Albatros, which had co-operated magnificently with the triplane, had left the fight and the pilot of the triplane was now alone. McCudden noted that at one time the triplane was 'in the apex of a cone of tracer bullets from at least five machines simultaneously.' Maybery reported that 'he seemed invulnerable.' The fight was now down to 2,000 feet, a mile behind the German Front Line. Bowman later commented that the odds did not appear to daunt the enemy pilot in the slightest. 'At that altitude he had a much better rate of climb, or rather zoom, than we had and frequently he was the highest machine of the seven (sic) and could have turned away east and got away had he wished to, but he was not that type and always came down on us again. His machine was exceptionally manoeuvrable and he appeared to be able to take flying liberties with impunity.' Bowman had only one chance for a shot at the triplane. It was passing in front of him, slightly lower, and Bowman put the nose of his machine down to give the triplane a burst. 'To my amazment he kicked on full rudder, without bank, pulled his nose up slightly, gave me a burst while he was skidding sideways, and then kicked on opposite rudder before the results of this amazing stunt appeared to have any effect on the manoeuvrability of his machine.'

As the triplane pilot swerved away from his attack on Bowman he was momentarily flying straight and level. Rhys Davids got onto his tail and opened fire: a whole drum of Lewis and an equal amount of Vickers. 'He made no attempt to turn until I was so close to him I was certain we would collide. He passed my right wing by inches and went down. I zoomed. I saw him next, with his engine apparently off, gliding west. I dived again and got one shot out of my Vickers; however, I reloaded and kept in the dive, I got another good burst and the triplane did a slight right-hand turn still going down. I now overshot him (this was at 1,000 feet) zoomed and never saw him again.'

Both McCudden and Bowman witnessed the end of the triplane. Turning away to change a Lewis gun drum, McCudden looked down: 'he was very low, still being engaged by an SE5 marked 1, the pilot being Rhys Davids. I noticed that the triplane's movements were very erratic, and then I saw the triplane hit the ground and disappear into a thousand fragments, for it seemed to me that it literally went to powder.' Bowman reported: 'When near the ground the triplane turned over on its back and hit the ground in this position just our side of the lines.'

After turning away from the triplane, Rhys Davids saw a red-nosed Albatros a little to the south-east and attacked it, opening fire at 100 yards, holding down his triggers with a continuous burst, until at 30 yards from the Albatros his Lewis gun drum was expended and his Vickers stopped. Rhys Davids zoomed away and when he next saw the Albatros it was spiralling down, its engine stopped.[11]

At dinner that evening in the 56 Squadron Mess there was a great deal of speculation as to the identity of the German pilot who had put up such a fight. In 60 Squadron's Mess 'Grid' Caldwell was in little doubt. 'I for one felt it could only have been Voss as I had experienced him before. He was a terrific chap, and rated easily No.1 including Richthofen.' Twenty-five years later, in the middle of another war, Bowman recalled 'Our elation was not nearly as great as you might have imagined. It was an amazing show on the part of Voss. I remember at the time feeling rather sorry it had to end the way it did. Rhys Davids, I think, was genuinely upset.' McCudden wrote: 'As long as I live I shall never forget my admiration for that German pilot who singlehandedly fought seven of us for ten minutes, and who put some bullets through all our machines. His flying was wonderful, his courage magnificent, and in my opinion he is the bravest German airman whom it has been my privilege to see fight.[12]

Ltn Werner Voss, *Staffelführer* of *Jasta 10*, crashed at the site of Plum Farm just north of Frezenberg, very near the Front Line, and was buried by a Lt Kiegan: 'without a coffin and without military honours, in exactly the same manner as all soldiers are buried in battle'.

The fighter squadrons had two other casualties during the day's fighting. A pilot from Naval 3 had been wounded in action in the morning and a DH5 pilot from 32 Squadron had been shot down and taken prisoner in the evening.

September 24 was fine and warm, but misty, and enemy activity was below normal. The Camels of Naval 10 took off at 9.15am. No enemy aeroplanes appeared to be in the air and at 10.50am FltLt Fitzgibbon took the Flight down to attack ground targets. Fitzgibbon fired 200 rounds at a train waiting in a siding and Carroll fired into a gun pit in a corner of Houthulst Forest. FltSubLt B Foster failed to return from this patrol. He was seen crossing the lines but had been shot down and made POW, possibly by *Ltn* Kurt Wüsthoff of *Jasta 4*.

A later patrol by the squadron sighted a large formation of twin-engined bombers, escorted by scouts, flying west from Westroosebeke. The Camels joined forces with a Flight of Nieuports to attack this large formation, but the leader of the Nieuports fired a red Very light and the Nieuports dived away. The Naval pilots attacked the enemy force but suffered gun troubles and although four combats were fought, there were no decisive results. Fitzgibbon led another patrol in the afternoon. He had a fight with an enemy scout over Roulers but gun stoppages again forced him to break off the fight. Daly attacked an Albatros two-seater north east of Houthulst Forest and sent it down out of control, but FltSubLt Stratton was forced to land after his petrol tank had been hit in a combat with two enemy scouts.

An afternoon patrol by 70 Squadron fought with enemy scouts over Moorslede and although both Lts Lomas and Gould attacked an Albatros, sending it down out of control, 2Lt C Primeau's Camel was badly damaged in the fighting and he was forced to land near Hondschoote.

Fifty-six Squadron had a great deal of 'desultory fighting' during the morning and afternoon patrols, the enemy machines engaged all diving away to the east, but in the late afternoon Leonard Barlow led Rhys Davids and Lt D Reason across the Lines at 11,000 feet and with Sopwith Triplanes and Camels kept a number of enemy formations well east of the Lines. Flying towards Passchendaele the three SE5s sighted a pair of two-seaters flying southeast over Houthulst Forest, but as they dived to attack these, another pair was seen. These were returning from the British side of the lines having completed their mission of photographing the British back areas. It was imperative that these were destroyed before they could return with their information and the SEs switched their attacks.

Rhys Davids chased after one, opening fire from 100 yards with both guns, silencing the observer. The two-seater, from *FlAbt (A) 256,* crewed by *Ltn* Karl von Esmarch and *Ltn d Res* Hans Fleischer went down in a steep dive; at 4,000 feet smoke and flames began to appear and the fuselage was soon blazing furiously. As Rhys Davids zoomed away he saw a second two-seater spinning down very fast, finally flattening out at 4,000 feet before it crashed just south of the Houthulst Forest. This enemy machine was destroyed by Barlow. Rhys Davids was now at 4,000 feet and seeing six red-nosed Albatri diving towards him retreated under a formation of DH5s.

Ronald Keirstead of Naval 4 claimed an Albatros out of control south east of St Pierre Capelle and another destroyed at 6.10pm.

Sixty-Six Squadron lost a pilot killed over Dixmude and a pilot of Naval 8 was wounded in the thigh.

The *Luftstreitkräfte* was very active on September 25, but the fighter squadrons had only two casualties. A pilot from 19 Squadron was killed over Gheluvelt and Naval 10, in a combat over Ypres, had a pilot wounded. There were a great many combats during the day and the official history records that out of 32 enemy aircraft claimed as driven down 19 were seen to crash.

In the morning a Flight of Pups from 46 Squadron attacked a two-seater over Pelves. Wilcox and Thompson each fired 70 rounds at the enemy machine and it went down, followed by Bulman, who continued firing into it until it crashed. At 11.30am a patrol from 54 Squadron attacked a formation of Albatros scouts over Middelkerke. Oliver Stewart shot one down, which was seen to crash in the sea, and Henry Maddocks shot another down in flames. A quarter of an hour earlier, south of Ypres, the Spads of 23 Squadron had claimed a pair of two-seaters north of Wervicq. 2Lt R Smith attacked one, which evaded his attacks and escaped east, but he then attacked another and shot it down in flames. Capt Frederick Gibbs saw yet another two-seater flying west. Gibbs climbed to 20,000 feet before diving to attack this machine, following it down to 4,000 feet until it finally crashed. Mannock of 40 Squadron claimed a Rumpler crashed at 1.00pm but for some reason this was not allowed.

In the early afternoon Capt John Firth of 45 Squadron shot down an Albatros two-seater over Passchendaele at ten minutes to three for his third victory. Twenty minutes later Mannock shot down a Rumpler over Sallaumines for his 15th victory.[13] This was to be the last victory scored by Mannock in 1917 and his penultimate victory while serving in 40 Squadron.

At ten minutes past six in the evening a patrol of DH5s from 41 Squadron fought with ten Albatri over Proville. The DH5s gave a good account of themselves. Russell Winnicott crashed one Albatros; Meredith Thomas sent one down out of control and another crashed, and although 2Lts Anderson, Haight and Langford-Sainbury each drove an enemy scout down, these were not allowed, being indecisive.

The pilots of Naval 10, flying a late morning patrol, saw a number of enemy scouts and two-seaters between Houthulst Forest and Ypres. The eight Camels attacked these but all the combats were indecisive. One Camel was forced to land with engine trouble and A F MacDonald was wounded in the left buttock and forced to land south of Ypres, wrecking his Camel in the landing.

The pilots of 56 Squadron had seen no action in their first patrols of the day, but an evening patrol of B and C Flight was to see a remarkable display of aggressive fighting by Leonard Barlow. After unsuccessfully trying to lure eight Albatri down to attack Maybery flying below them as bait, Bowman attacked an enemy two-seater, firing 50 rounds at it before leaving it for Barlow to chase. Before Barlow could close the range, however, the two-seater dived steeply east and made off. Barlow regained his height and returned to the lines with

Bowman, where they were rejoined by Maybery who had had an indecisive combat with an enemy scout. After a brief skirmish with two more Albatri, Barlow went down to attack four scouts – described as being 'two ordinary V Strutters and two Fokker biplanes' – flying at 15,000 feet over Houlthulst Forest. These were two Albatros D Vs and two Pfalz D IIIs from *Jasta 10*. Barlow first attacked the Albatros flown by *Oblt* Weigand, firing a continuous burst until he was forced to zoom away to avoid a collision. The Albatros went down in pieces before bursting into flames. At the top of his zoom, Barlow turned to the right and attacked the Pfalz flown by *Uffz* Werkmeister. The Pfalz went down in a steep spiral, smoke pouring from it and crashed at Stampkot. The two remaining enemy pilots, having witnessed the destruction of their companions, dived away east, followed by Barlow, who had time for only one short burst at the Albatros before zooming away – he had seen more enemy scouts diving to attack him – but his aim had been good and the Albatros went down and was seen to crash by Bowman half a mile from the north-west corner of Houthulst Forest.[14]

Other victories were claimed during the day: at noon, in a combat with Albatros scouts over Goenberb, Capt John Crompton and Lt Graham Young of 60 Squadron shared an Albatros destroyed, and there was another success for the squadron in the evening when Lt William Jenkins destroyed a two-seater a mile east of Ypres at 3.40pm. Pilots of 70 Squadron claimed two enemy machines, which went down spinning, and a two-seater in flames. Capt Leacroft of 19 Squadron drove a two-seater down out of control over Menin at 10.00am, and in an evening patrol pilots of the squadron attacked two Albatros scouts south-east of Houthem at 6.15pm, Capt Oliver Bryson destroying one, his first victory for a month. Fifteen minutes later Capt William Rooper of 1 Squadron destroyed an Albatros east of Gheluvelt.

September 26 was very cloudy with fine intervals, but there was a heavy ground mist that interfered with the work of the corps squadrons. Gerald Maxwell, leading A Flight of 56 Squadron, observed a formation of eleven enemy machines, consisting of twin-engined AEG GIVs and DFW C Vs, escorted by eight scouts. After a while the escort flew east and the SE5s attacked the large formation, forcing them to jettison their bombs, but with no other positive result. Maxwell fired nearly 400 rounds into two of the twin-engined machines, driving them east. He later commented in his diary. 'Saw and attacked eleven Gothas over Lines east of Ypres. Got underneath one and fired a lot of rounds, but Gotha did not notice at all. Played soccer in the evening with men. Draw.'

Another ground attack was opened in the morning in an attempt to take Polygon Wood; by the end of a day of extremely fierce and costly fighting the main part of the wood was firmly in the hands of Allied troops. There was a return to ground-strafing by the fighter squadrons, despite the ground mist. Pentland of 19 Squadron crossed the Lines at 2,000 feet and attacked a two-seater harassing the corps aeroplanes, but was forced to retreat west by enemy scouts. Shaking these off, he returned to the Front Lines and fired at troops in the rear of the trenches before finding an ammunition dump, which he blew up with a 20lb Cooper bomb. Pentland was then again attacked by more enemy scouts and in an attempt to avoid these he dived into the barrage. A shell from the British guns hit the fuselage of his Spad, and although it failed to explode, severed most of his control wires. Pentland, hit in the face by a shrapnel splinter, managed to crash-land his damaged Spad just in front of the British Front Line trenches, breaking his leg and 'getting the gun in my face.' A stretcher was found and two of the infantry began to carry Pentland back, but a shell landed nearby, and wounded him in the thigh, killing one of his stretcher bearers and wounding the other.

Pilots from 45, 70 and 23 Squadrons plus 1 Naval ground-strafed enemy troops and positions throughout the day. The pilots of Naval 10 had been designated to attack enemy aerodromes. Saint failed to find his target of Ingelmuster aerodrome, but successfully locating the aerodrome at Rumbeke, dropped two bombs in front of the sheds and fired 400 rounds into the hangars. FltSubLt J G Manuel attacked Abeele aerodrome arriving over the field at 6.15am and dropping two bombs from 1500 feet. One bomb fell in the middle of the field, doing no damage, but the other fell into a row of machines lined up in front of the hangars, seriously damaging one of them. Manuel then came under fire from a machine gun of the aerodrome's defences, but he fired 50 rounds at it, effectively silencing it. On his way back to his aerodrome, Manuel fired at a party of 500 troops near Roulers, firing 200 rounds at them, but he lost his way to Droglandt and landed at La Panne. Two Flights from the squadron carried out an offensive and low patrol at 10.00am. An hour after takeoff the Camels were in a fight with several formations of Albatri over Westroosebeke and Passchendaele. In the ten minute engagement, both Daly and Fitzgibbon each shot down an Albatros out of control. Fifteen minutes later eight 'Gothas' were seen approaching the front lines east of Ypres. These were possibly another contingent from the same *staffel* of *Kagohl IV* earlier seen by 56 Squadron. The naval pilots attacked these machines but had no more success than their RFC counterparts.

After these actions the Camels attacked numerous ground targets, but Daly's machine was hit by anti-aircraft fire; he forced landed at Naval 4 Squadron, and was injured. Two more patrols went out – at 12.20pm and 3.35pm – but saw no enemy aeroplanes were seen and the pilots concentrated on attacking

ground targets. At 6.00pm C Flight was ordered to attack balloons between Becelaere and Poecapelle. Before the balloons were attacked a two-seater was attacked by Manuel south of Houthulst Forest, but with no result. The attacks on the balloons were also unsuccessful. Although 700 rounds were fired into them they did not ignite.

An offensive patrol by 45 Squadron were on patrol over Passchendaele in the morning. John Firth destroyed an Albatros at 11.30am, and Lt E D Clarke crashed an Albatros C type. Three two-seaters were claimed by the pilots of 19 Squadron: Lt R Strang shot down one, which was seen to crash by observers on the ground, and Leacroft and Jones each sent another down out of control. Capt H Ferriera of 29 Squadron claimed an Albatros scout out of control and Lts J Wilson and A Dalton of 70 Squadron shared in the victory of a two-seater. Douglas McGregor of 23 Squadron shot down an Albatros, which crashed west of St Julien at 4.30pm and the infantry of Second Army scored five rare victories over low flying enemy aircraft over Polygon Wood, two of which, an LVG and a Rumpler, fell in the British Lines and were given the G numbers G76 and G 77 respectively. The Rumpler was from *Kagohl IV/Kasta 24* and the crew, *Ltn* Feigell and *Vzfw* Marquel were both taken POW.

Casualties for the day were heavy. Three pilots were lost from 19 Squadron, two wounded and one killed; 23 Squadron had a pilot died of wounds; 24 Squadron a pilot taken POW; 29 Squadron a pilot killed and 32 Squadron a pilot taken POW. The Camel squadrons suffered heavily: 45 Squadron had a Camel badly shot up, although the pilot was uninjured, but another pilot was killed in a combat with five Albatri over Passchendaele. Seventy Squadron lost four pilots, ground-strafing at low level over Passchendaele, all taken POW, and another Camel was badly shot about. Naval 1 had a pilot killed and another wounded; one pilot was wounded and taken POW, and a Frenchman, flying one of their Sopwith Triplanes, was also killed. A pilot from Naval 9 was also taken prisoner.

The good weather continued on September 27. The ground fighting for remainder of Polygon Wood continued throughout the day and by the evening the entire wood was in Allied hands. The fighter squadrons had only one casualty during the day, a pilot from Naval 10. The squadron flew three patrols during the day. Visibility was poor on the first patrol at 8.15am, the Front covered with two thick layers of cloud at 1,000 and 2,000 feet, and nothing was seen. Conditions were better at 12.15pm and two Flights flew an offensive patrol from Houthulst to Roulers, turning south to Ledeghem. The Flight then intended to turn west to Polygon Wood, but over Ledeghem they saw a formation of DH4s under attack from six Albatri and they attacked the enemy scouts, driving them off. The Camels were later joined by eight Sopwith Triplanes from Naval 1 and the combined force attacked four enemy scouts. There were no positive results from this combat, but Alexander reported that one of the enemy scouts, in addition to its usual pair of guns firing through the propeller, had another gun mounted on its top wing. FltLt Fitzgibbon led the final patrol of the day, taking off at 2.50pm to fly the same patrol line as the previous Flight. At 4.00pm Curtis shot down an Albatros scout northeast of Dixmude, confirmed by FltSubLt Carroll, and ten minutes later six enemy scouts were attacked to the north east of Westroosebeke. Stanley Hamilton-Bowyer drove down one of these and Fitzgibbon shot another down in a cloud of smoke, but FltSubLt J S de Wilde was shot down and killed.

McCudden, testing a newly fitted engine in his SE5a, was at 13,000 feet over Houthulst Forest when he saw an LVG circling over the Forest, ranging for the artillery. While McCudden was manoeuvring for a favourable position to attack this LVG a French Spad suddenly dived at the enemy two-seater, whose pilot took effective evasive action, his gunner hitting the Spad which went down out of control. 'The Hun went off east a little and then came back, apparently very pleased at having shot the Spad down.' The LVG pilot, not having seen the SE5, came nearer and McCudden got just underneath the enemy machine, the position he favoured for fighting two-seaters, and fired a burst from both guns, turning sharply away at the last moment to avoid a collision. The German gunner was an old hand, experienced in fighting enemy scouts – he had already dispatched the French Spad – and knowing that McCudden would have to turn sooner or later he had held his gun in a central position, waiting to see which way the SE5 would go. As McCudden turned away the gunner fired four shots, that McCudden distinctly heard hit his machine. McCudden half rolled away, getting clear of the gunner's fire, but when he looked back he saw the LVG going down in flames to hit the ground just north of the Ypres to Poelcapelle Road. At 12,000 feet, the brave German gunner either fell or jumped from the blazing LVG and fell in the German Lines, but the pilot and machine fell in the British Lines.[15]

Barlow took off alone at 5.30pm to look for an enemy two-seater reported to be over St Omer. Barlow climbed hard for the lines, getting up to 18,000 feet with the intention of catching the enemy machine as it returned to the east, but he saw no sign of it. After patrolling for some time he went down to attack six Albatri 5,000 feet below him, opening fire on the rearmost of the enemy scouts from 100 yards range. The Albatros zoomed, then fell away out of control, but Barlow's Lewis gun then fell down its slide and hit him on the head. The SE5 went down in a spin. When Barlow recovered control he could see the Albatros still going down, but he came under

attack from its companions and he dived away to land at Bailleul aerodrome, still shaken by the blow to his head.

For some days the pilots of 40 Squadron had heard reports of a particularly audacious Albatros pilot. This pilot – flying a machine with a black and white striped tailplane – was single-handedly carrying out raids across the British lines, shooting down aircraft and attacking balloons. On September 19 he had shot down a Sopwith 1 1/2 Strutter, and an RE8 of 13 Squadron, chasing this last machine well over the British back areas to crash on the aerodrome of Naval 8 at Mont-St Eloi. Mannock was furious. This could not be allowed. Mannock, Tudhope and MacLanachan patrolled the area for two days in the hope of catching this Albatros pilot, but in the afternoon of September 24 he shot down a Martinsyde of 27 Squadron, which crashed in the German lines with a wounded pilot. The 40 Squadron pilots had again patrolled the area the next day, but the Albatros did not appear, and in morning and afternoon patrols on September 27 there was still no sign of the elusive Albatros. After the patrols had landed, however, the Albatros pilot destroyed a balloon south-west of Roulette at 5.05pm(GT), followed five minutes later by an RE8 of 9 Squadron which crashed in Farbus Wood. These last attacks convinced Mannock that they were well planned and timed to coincide with the meal times of the British fighter squadrons. 'That fellow won't come over this afternoon. He's going to come over this evening when we are at dinner – but we aren't going to have dinner until after we've got him. We'll sit here till dark.'

That evening, the three Nieuports left Mazingarbe, each with a definite patrol area to protect the British balloon line: Mannock patrolled between Souchez and Mazingarbe; Tudhope those balloons nearest the Scarpe, and MacLanachan between Mazingarbe and the La Bassée Canal. MacLanachan felt very nauseous and unwell – later found to be the result of excessive engine vibration caused by a loose propeller, and transmitted to the body of his Nieuport – and was about to return when he saw one of the southern balloons – either that at Neuville-St Vaast or Ablain-St Nazaire – burst into flames. MacLanachan, fearful for the safety of his own balloon flew around it until his headache became unbearable and he returned to Bruay. On landing, leaning against his Nieuport, struggling to contain his sickness, Major Tilney ran up to him. 'Come on Mac, Tud's got him down, jump into my car and come with us.'

After destroying the balloon the Albatros pilot had stayed to fire at the observer, floating down in his parachute. This was his undoing. The burning balloon had been seen by three Camels of Naval 8 returning from a patrol and FltCom Charles Booker led them down to attack the Albatros, his fire hitting the pilot in arm and splintering the V struts of his Albatros. At just this moment, however, Booker broke off the attack and spiralled down: his Camel had been hit by an unlucky shot from a British infantryman. The enemy pilot dived and fired at Booker, but came under attack from FltSubLt Thompson, who hit the Albatros in the engine before overshooting in a near vertical dive. The enemy pilot was now wounded and with a dead engine. He turned in an attempt to glide for the German lines, but was again attacked, this time by 'Tud' Tudhope.

Both Mannock and Tudhope had had to leave their patrol lines and return to Mazingarbe with dud engines, and this had enabled the Albatros pilot to make his successful attack. Tudhope's engine was missing on one cylinder, but as he taxied in, Mannock, who had seen the balloon going down in flames, rushed out and urged Tudhope to take off again. 'Look Tud … there you are … go hell for leather … you'll get him … go on … you'll get the blighter.' With his engine spluttering and coughing Tudhope took off again, arriving at the scene of the fight as the enemy pilot was already gliding down. Tudhope had had no time to gain any height and attacked the Albatros from below, shooting the heel off the pilot's right flying boot. Thompson was also attacking again and the Albatros, in the words of its pilot, 'was like a shrivelled leaf in the wind.' Tudhope reported: 'he glided down flatly and crashed, with his tail swinging up and over, nearly catching my undercarriage as I shot past.'

The Albatros, flown by *Oblt* Hans Waldhausen of *Jasta 37,* finally crashed at Souchez, turning over, and Waldhausen was extricated from his machine by some drivers of an ammunition column who had stopped their vehicles on an adjacent road. Some nearby troops, who had witnessed Waldhausen's attack on the descending observer, were in an ugly mood and surrounded him, brandishing their entrenching tools – there is one report that a Canadian had already blacked both Waldhausen's eyes – but Mannock appeared and held the angry crowd at bay with his Very pistol.[16]

Waldhausen was later taken by staff car to Carency, where he was interrogated, then taken to RF HQ at St Omer, arriving late that night.[17]

MacLanachan later recalled. 'There was great jubilation that night in the balloon section. Mick's and Tudhope's healths were drunk in the best of all beverages.'

Enemy activity in the air slackened considerably the next day, September 28, but there was still an appreciable amount of fighting.

C and A Flights of Naval 10 took off at 9.30am on an offensive patrol but visibility was bad, and although four enemy scouts were fought over Moorslede only FltCom Alexander and FltSubLt G L Trapp claimed victories. Alexander forced

an enemy machine to land and tip over onto its nose and Trapp's opponent was seen to crash. FltCom H Saint led six Camels on a special bombing raid at 2.27pm, escorted by Spads of 23 Squadron and 70 Squadron Camels. The force attacked Rumbeke aerodrome, arriving over the field at 3.05pm. All six naval pilots dropped their bombs on the aerodrome – which were seen to explode both behind and near to the hangars and sheds – and machine-gunned enemy machines on the ground. Although this raid appears to have been highly successful, with no losses, Saint's report that it had been carried out from a height of 2,000 to 3,000 feet was to have serious repercussions.

Saint took off at ten minutes past midnight to bomb a German aerodrome, but returned almost immediately because of the heavy ground mist. The reason for this unusual and aborted flight is inexplicable, but in view of later events in Naval 10 Saint was possibly attempting to prove a point.

McCudden and B Flight were in action early in the morning, taking off at 7.45am. The Flight attacked a formation of Albatri over Houthulst Forest, McCudden going down at a terrific speed, the other members of the Flight diving at 180mph to keep their leader in sight. McCudden picked out the Albatros on the left of the enemy formation and opened fire at 200 yards, holding down his triggers until the range closed to 50 yards. The left wings of the Albatros broke off and it went down, breaking into pieces at 9,000 feet, the enemy pilot, *Ltn* Herbert Pastor of *Jasta 29,* falling from his machine.

McCudden now attacked the leader of the enemy formation, but the pilot was very skilful and fought well. Circling for position, he and McCudden lost height, going down to 4,000 feet. The pilot of the Albatros, *Oblt* Otto Schmidt of *Jasta 29* outmanoeuvred McCudden, driving him down to 2,000 feet over the Forest, a mile behind the German lines. McCudden, with engine full on, dived to within a 1,000 feet of the ground, intending to contour chase back to the British lines. No Albatros pilot would risk diving his machine at this speed and Schmidt broke off the action and flew east.

Bowman and Hoidge took off at 11.00am on a 'Special Mission – a convenient official synonym for 'looking for trouble'. After an indecisive brush with seven enemy scouts Bowman flew towards Ypres and attacked three Albatri, sending one down in a vertical dive. Bowman was then attacked by three machines that he had taken to be friendly Nieuports, but which were, in fact, Siemens-Schucket D Is, an almost exact copy of the French Nieuport. After fighting with these machines for sometime, Bowman returned. He was sure that the Albatros he had sent down in a vertical dive was positively out of control, but it was not allowed as a victory.

The squadron flew another patrol in the afternoon A and C Flights taking off at 4.30pm. There were thick clouds east of the Lines, extending from 2 to 3,000 feet, with very few gaps. Bowman and Hoidge kept just above this cloudbank and at 5.20pm a pair of Albatri cautiously poked their noses into the clear sky. Bowman and Hoidge immediately attacked and both the enemy scouts went down – Bowman's in a vertical dive, Hoidge's in a spiral – before breaking up in mid air. Hoidge's victim fell on the edge of Houthulst Forest, a mile west of Westroosebeke. Bowman's logbook entry has the cryptic entry. 'Got one V Strutter. Broke up in air after 4,000 feet. First EA of mine to seen break up. Splendid.'[18]

In the late evening Lt Meredith Thomas was leading a patrol of DH5s of 41 Squadron when nine enemy scouts, in two formations of five and four, were seen over Bugnicourt at ten minutes past six. Thomas took the DH5s down and in the fight claimed one scout, which was seen to crash. Lts Weiss and Winnicott each claimed a scout out of control. All three victories were confirmed by the pilots and observers of Bristol Fighters of 11 Squadron, but 2Lt J Haigh had been shot down and taken prisoner of war by *Ltn* Neckel of *Jasta 12* for his second victory. Haigh was one of three casualties for the fighter squadrons during the day: a pilot of 32 Squadron was killed when his DH5 suffered a direct hit from an AA shell, and in First Army's sector to the south, a pilot of 43 Squadron was shot down and killed by *Ltn* Udet of *Jasta 37* for his 13th victory. During this combat with *Jasta 37,* Capt T Wynn of 43 Squadron, shot an Albatros down in flames, which was seen to crash by observers on the ground, but his Camel had been badly damaged in the fight – possibly by Udet, who was awarded two Camels from the engagement – and he forced landed near Wingles. These were 43 Squadron's first casualty and first victory since being re-equipped with Camels.

Pilots of Naval 9 and 70 Squadron all claimed victories during the day.

September 29 was cloudy with bright intervals but a thick ground mist meant that only a small amount of flying was done.

Maxwell led A Flight in the last patrol to be flown by 56 Squadron during the day. Patrolling over the Staden area, Maxwell saw two formations, totalling 20 enemy machines, over Houthulst Forest and at 6.00pm he led the SE5s down to attack them. Maxwell fired a complete drum of Lewis and 150 rounds of Vickers into one enemy scout before zooming away. This machine was seen to break up in mid air by Lt Young. The other members of the Flight had no positive result, only the scout attacked by Charles Jeffs going down in a manner to indicate that it was out of control. After this fight Lt Herbert Johnston attacked an Albatros with an entirely red fuselage and sent it down in a steep spiral out of control. All these victories were confirmed by three Bristol Fighters of 22 Squadron, which kept above the fight and prevented other enemy scouts from diving on the SE5s.

The close of the day was notable for the first successful attack at night by single-seater fighters. Two Camels from Naval 8 took off at 9.45pm: one to attack the balloon shed near Quiéry-la-Motte, the other to attack the enemy aerodrome at Douai. The attack on the balloon shed was highly successful and spectacular. After a hundred rounds of Vickers from thirty feet, the balloons inside the shed exploded in flames, lighting up the surrounding countryside. The other Camel pilot had failed to find Douai aerodrome, but seeing the fire of the burning balloon shed attacked the ground crews, who had ran from their billets, his aim considerably helped by the light of the fires.

The last day of September saw the German ground forces begin a series of counter attacks north of the Menin Road and after the relative hiatus of the previous day, the fighting in the air flared up again.

A patrol from 66 Squadron was chasing a two-seater during the morning patrol when they were attacked by *Jasta 18.* The Pups were no match for the Albatri, but Capt T Bayetto wounded one of the enemy pilots, who fell over the side of his cockpit, his Albatros going down pouring smoke. Pritt fired at another scout that also went down, but 2Lt J Warter was shot down in flames by *Oblt* Berthold, and Lt J Boumphrey went down in a slow spin to be taken POW by *Ltn* Runge. Capt Bayetto crashed on his return Estrée Blanche and was injured.

The DH5s of 41 Squadron were on patrol with Bristol Fighters in the afternoon. At 4.00pm, over Eterpigny, they attacked a formation of seven Albatri and drove one down out of control. Half an hour later five Albatri were seen approaching about 150 feet below the DH5s and Winnicott dived and attacked the first, sending it down in a fast spin. 2Lt Whitehead also claimed an out of control from this fight, but had to force land on the way back to base. 2Lt G Gillings had been wounded in the face, but managed to land at Candas and was taken to hospital.

C Flight, 46 Squadron had a productive afternoon. 'Nobby' Scott led Odell, Armitage and Lee on an OP and a pair of DFW two-seaters was seen south west of Douai. As the Pups were about to dive on these DFWs, five Albatri dived on them from out of the sun. It was the classic decoy trap. 'We were instantly in a mad dog-fight, and while we were still whizzing round each other, two Bristols and a DH5 rushed up and joined in.'

Lee, circling tightly, endeavouring to get behind a green and yellow Albatros, realised that the enemy pilot was no novice and had to work hard to keep inside the turn of the Albatros. But at the height at which the fight was being fought, a Pup could turn inside an Albatros and Lee finally got behind the enemy machine and gave it a burst of 20 rounds at 50 yards range. Lee could see his tracer hitting the cockpit area of the enemy scout but it flew on, seemingly not hit. Lee was about to correct his aim when a stream of tracer flashing past him from behind forced him to skid off to the left. An Albatros shot by on Lee's right, pursued by Capt Scott, who shot it down out of control. As Lee pulled back into the fight a Bristol Fighter flew right in front of him, forcing Lee to frantically pull his Pup up to avoid a collision. The Pup stalled and spun down. Regaining control below the fight, Lee saw the decoy DFWs, 2,000 feet below him. Lee made for the rearmost two-seater, dark brown and dirty yellow in colour, diving underneath it as the enemy observer opened fire at the Pup. Zooming under the impetus of his dive, Lee opened fire with a long burst into the underside of the DFW, which reared up, went over sideways onto its back and went down. Lee followed it down to 3,000 feet, firing occasional short bursts, and saw a piece of the cowling detach from the nose section. Lee then lost sight of the enemy machine but estimated that it would crash just east of Jigsaw Wood.

Lee was now well below the general fight and as he climbed back into it an Albatros went spinning down past him with Scott on its tail. Scott left the enemy scout and he and Lee climbed to rejoin the rest of the patrol. Within minutes they found another two DFWs and they attacked these at once, all three Pups tackling the same machine. The enemy observer fired at both Lee and Armitage, who were nearest. Lee broke off as he was out of ammunition and saw Armitage also pulling out, breaking off the combat, giving the distress signal and turning for base. He had been wounded in the leg by the enemy observer. Escorted back to Filsecamp Farm by Lee and Scott, Armitage made a bumpy landing.

The pilots of all three Flights of 56 Squadron were anxious to score the squadron's 199th and 200th victory, but enemy territory was almost totally obscured by a thick ground mist and there no enemy aircraft were seen until it had cleared at around 9.00am. McCudden and his Flight had only one engagement, with five Albatri, but with no decisive result. Several lone missions were flown by individual pilots during the remainder of the morning and early afternoon, but enemy aircraft remained elusive and no claims were made.

The pilots of the evening patrol had better luck. C and A Flights took off at half past four and at 5.00pm Hoidge and Maybery of C Flight attacked six Pfalz D III over Roulers. Maybery sent one Pfalz down to crash just west of the town, but Hoidge had to break off his attack with jams in both guns. Clearing his guns, Hoidge rejoined Maybery and they attacked a two-seater over the eastern edge of Houthulst Forest, but they both had bad gun stoppages and broke off the action, the two-seater escaping east. Rectifying their guns, Maybery and Hoidge next chased, but failed to catch, a pair of two-seaters over the northern edge of the forest.

Maybery next attacked a two-seater just west of Menin, but after a short burst his Lewis gun stopped, the drum expended. Maybery turned away to replace the empty drum. In his eagerness, Maybery failed to correctly place the fresh drum on the gun and it fell off, hitting him on the head before bouncing over the edge of his cockpit. Maybery turned for home, having no more ammunition. Hoidge had attacked four Pfalz over east Houthulst, but his guns were still giving trouble and being low on petrol he returned, landing at Bailleul. The 200th victory was proving elusive.

Further south, Maxwell and A Flight had been in action with eight enemy scouts over Comines. Maxwell had sent one down out of control after firing a full drum of Lewis and almost 100 rounds of Vickers into the enemy scout; Jeffs had fired at another, which went straight down, but apparently under control.

When A Flight returned to Estrée Blanche, only Maybery had landed from C Flight and it was not until all the pilots had returned that the times of the victories could be compared. Maybery's was the first and Maxwell's half an hour later. When dusk fell the whole squadron assembled outside the sheds and at the order from Major Blomfield, the CO, the squadron's entire stock of Very lights was fired into the gathering darkness. Forty red, green and white lights lit up the countryside for miles around.

In addition to the casualties of 66 and 41 Squadrons, a pilot of 70 Squadron had been killed in action over Houthulst Forest in the morning, and a pilot of 46 Squadron had been fatally wounded, dying four days later.

At this time, the morale of pilots in the squadrons flying the DH5 was extremely low. Its performance was inferior to the already obsolescent Sopwith Pup, it was totally outclassed by the German fighters, and had been limited to a combat height of 9,000 feet. Its only positive attributes were its great structural strength and the ability to dive very steeply, which meant that it was primarily relegated to ground-strafing, an extremely hazardous duty which led to excessive casualties. In the two months from the beginning of the Ypres offensive on July 31 to the end of September, 32 Squadron lost 13 pilots in action, 41 Squadron lost six and 24 Squadron four. It was well known throughout the RFC how badly 32 Squadron had suffered on the Ypres Front. Writing of 41 Squadron, Canadian researcher Stewart Taylor has recorded: 'Some pilots were in near tears and completely frustrated with the aircraft's inability to handle the heavy operational traffic, especially low strafing missions over a battlefield bursting at the seams with both friendly and hostile fights.' In one squadron a Flight Commander had begun to drink himself to sleep 'in order to forget what the next day had in store.'

As with many of their fellow RFC pilots, the pilots of the naval squadrons were also questioning the value of ground-strafing and low-level raids on enemy aerodromes. In the view of many pilots the results achieved in relation to the cost in casualties were simply not worth it. Operational orders from staff officers at Wing, far removed from the reality of the position at the cutting edge of the fighting, were being questioned.[19]

The bombing raid on Rumbeke aerodrome by Naval 10 on September 28 is an illustration of this hardening attitude. The raid was successful, but on reading FltCom Saint's report, Lt-Col Holt, commanding officer of 22 (Army) Wing, was of the opinion that the value of the raid had been seriously weakened because it had not been carried out from a lower height. On September 30 Holt ordered that the raid be carried out again, with machines bombing from a lower height.

Redpath, acting commanding officer of Naval 10, asked Holt if the operation could be postponed until the following day, but on Holt's insistence that it be carried out that afternoon, bluntly informed Holt that 'his pilots weren't for it.' Holt did not directly order Redpath to undertake the raid, knowing that a refusal would have extremely serious consequences, but referred the matter to Trenchard the GOC. Trenchard realised that any disciplinary action against the naval officers concerned would possibly cause additional friction between the RFC and the RNAS – a relation that was never *without* friction – and that the attendant publicity would have an adverse effect on the morale of the RFC pilots, which he knew was already not good. On October 5 he quietly moved Naval 10 from the battlefront, transferring the squadron to Leffrinckhoucke aerodrome, where it came under the orders of IV Brigade.[20]

NOTES

1. *No Parachute*, Arthur Gould Lee.

2. Again, although this was a definite casualty, with a pilot certainly killed, and witnessed by pilots who had no personal interest, the German casualty lists give no loss for the time and place.

3. Ibid.

4. If the letter and diary extracts in *No Parachute* were not amended in the light of later knowledge, Lee's comment that the triplane was red is curious. There is no doubt that it was flown by Voss, whose triplane was predominately grey, with blue undersides.

5. In this combat report, Sloley described the triplane that fired at him as being yellow and brown, making it unlikely to have been either F1.102/17 or F1.103/17.

6. Hammes survived his wounds. After a successful career with the Viennese Opera between the wars, he was killed in action over Poland in 1939.

7. Both the Albatros D III and its later variant, the D V had a lower wing of narrow chord, influenced by the sesquiplane format of the French Nieuport. As in the Nieuport, this led to structural failures of the lower wing. This problem was not so apparent in the D III, but the uprating of the engine in the D V, and its overall increase in weight over the D III, imposed additional strains on the wing. Albatros pilots were cautioned not to dive their machines too steeply or for too long.

8. The German pilot was probably *Ltn* Julius Schmidt of *Jasta 3,* who claimed an SE5 shot down over de Ruiter at 7.00pm (GT).

9. *Jagd in Flanders Himmel*. Knorr and Hirth. Munchen 1935.

10. McCudden's autobiography, *Five Years In The Royal Flying Corps,* gives this machine as a DFW, but McCudden's log book states it was a Rumpler. McCudden's report from this action gives only an EA (enemy aircraft).

11. There is no evidence that this was the red-nosed Albatros that had fought with Voss. Both *Ltn* Wendelmuth of *Jasta 8* and *Ltn* Menckhoff of

Jasta 3 were in combat in the evening of September 23 and both forced landed in the area of the Voss fight: Wendelmuth in a field east of St Julien; Menckhoff north of Zonnebeke.

12. Voss is officially credited with 48 victories, but in his last fight he effectively forced five SE5s out of the uneven fight, badly damaging four.

13. From *FlAbt (A) 224w*. The observer, *Ltn d Res* Otto was killed. The pilot, *Vzfw* Karl Meckes died of his wounds two days later.

14. Werkmeister, who had joined *Jasta* 10 only two days before, was buried with Weingard in the churchyard of St Joseph's church on September 29.

15. This LVG was from *Schusta 27. Uffz* Gossler, the pilot, and his observer *Uffz* Weidermann were both killed. The wreckage was G.73.

16. After Booker had landed his damaged Camel among the shell holes surrounding Mazingarbe, Mannock, seeing he was unhurt, had grabbed a Very pistol and walked a mile to the scene of Waldhausen's crash.

17. Waldhausen, who had earned the rather fanciful sobriquet of The Eagle of Lens, later escaped, but he was quickly recaptured and spent the rest of the war in POW camp E4 at Oswestry.

18. *Ltn* Kurt Wissemann, *Jasta 3*, was killed over Westroosebeke on September 28. *Vzfw* Karl Menckhoff of *Jasta 3* crashed-landed.

19. Infantry officers, being ordered to mount attacks against positions which from their local knowledge they knew to have little or no chance of success, and at the cost of heavy and otherwise avoidable casualties, were asking identical questions.

20. I am indebted for these details to *A History of Naval 10 Squadron Royal Naval Air Service in World War One*, Mike Westrop, Schiffer Publishing Ltd., 2004.

CHAPTER FIFTEEN

WINTER OF DISCONTENT

The first day of October was sunny with no cloud. Capt William Rooper leading A Flight 1 Squadron, attacked DFW over Houthulst Forest at ten minutes past eleven. All the Flight shot at this DFW and were awarded it as being shot down out of control. 2Lt L Cummings attacked another two-seater, which from his description was a Junkers J I, an ungainly metal biplane just entering service with the *Luftstreitkräfte*. An armoured nose section of 5mm chrome-nickel sheet steel, which enclosed the engine and crew compartments, made these aeroplanes hard to bring down, but Cummings' attack was successful and the Junkers went down and crashed.

Just after noon, a patrol of Camels from 45 Squadron were in action with eight Albatros scouts over Quesnoy. Capt Raymond Brownell and Lt Emerson Smith both drove one down out of control. In an afternoon patrol Capt William Wright engaged an Albatros that was attacking an RE8 from 53 Squadron. Wright and the RE8 crew shot the enemy scout down in flames and it crashed in the British Lines at Hooge, killing *Ltn* Friedrich Cleiss of *Jasta 33*. The wreckage of his Albatros was designated G 78.

FltSubLt N M Macgregor led a patrol of Naval 10 into action with four enemy scouts east of Passchendaele at 2.15pm and FltSubLt W A Curtis claimed one scout out of control.

At Estrée Blanche, McCudden took off alone at 1.30pm to 'look for two-seaters.' After joining with Capt Keen of 40 Squadron in a long stalk of a high flying Rumpler – which climbed to 22,000 feet, easily out climbing the British scouts – McCudden spotted another, this one at only 18,000 feet, a 1,000 feet lower than the SE5. McCudden got into a good position to attack and wounded the observer with his first burst before his Vickers gun jammed. The Rumpler pilot dived away east. McCudden followed, changing his Lewis gun drum. Knowing he had nothing to fear from the observer's gun,

McCudden closed the range and fired a whole drum of Lewis into the fleeing two-seater. A thick cloud of brown smoke came out of the enemy machine. McCudden thought that it would burst into flames, but the enemy pilot merely steepened his dive, going east over Herlies at 9,000 feet, smoke still pouring from his machine. McCudden was satisfied that he had badly damaged this Rumpler, having fired nearly four hundred rounds at it from 75 yards, and turned away, having no more ammunition. McCudden had an excruciating headache for the remainder of the day, the legacy of an hour spent at high altitude without oxygen.

Headache or not, McCudden led his Flight in an afternoon patrol, taking off with A Flight at 4.30pm. A trio of two-seaters attacked over Becelaere, co-operated well and evaded the SE5s and McCudden and Rhys Davids, who had lost contact with the rest of the Flight, climbed back to 11,000 feet. To the west of Moorslede the two SE5s flew under seven Albatri of *Jasta 26* in an attempt to lure them nearer the Front Lines and under Maxwell's A Flight, which they knew were in the locality. The leader of the enemy formation, flying a black and white Pfalz, finally dived and attacked McCudden and Rhys Davids. Maxwell's Flight followed the Pfalz down and a furious fight developed: the SE5s reinforced by a formation of Bristol Fighters; the Pfalz formation by a large number of Albatri, bringing their number to nearly 20.

McCudden watched an SE5 circling inside four of the enemy scouts; before he could intervene an Albatros fastened onto the SE's tail and shot its wings off from 25 yards range. 'It was poor Sloley, who was, as usual, where the Huns were thickest.' Another SE5 was also in the thick of the action, fighting with four black and white Albatri. 'This SE was fighting magnificently and simply could be none other than Rhys Davids, for if one was ever over the Salient in the autumn of

1917 and saw an SE fighting like Hell amidst a heap of Huns, one would find nine times out of ten that the SE was flown by Rhys Davids.' McCudden and Maxwell dived to help Rhys Davids: 'for the next few minutes we fought like anything, but the Huns were all very good, and had not Maxwell and I gone to Rhys Davids' assistance when we did, I think the boy would have had a rather thin time.'

After shaking off the enemy scouts, McCudden and Rhys Davids attacked a pair of low flying two-seaters, but without success, Rhys Davids losing sight of his opponent against the chequered background of the fields below. Rhys Davids climbed to attack the other, but had used all his ammunition. Coming under attack by four Albatri, Rhys Davids escaped to the west.

Two enemy scouts were claimed from the large fight: one to B Flight and the other to Rhys Davids. Robert Sloley was a grievous loss to the squadron. He was a pilot of great promise and had scored six victories since joining the squadron in late July. He had been shot down by *Ltn* Danhuber of *Jasta 26*.

During the morning 29 Squadron's aerodrome at Poperinghe was bombed. Among the 14 casualties was Major C M B Chapman, who died of his wounds that evening.

In the evening an attempt was made by the pilots of 66 Squadron to bomb enemy aerodromes at night. The Pups took off at dusk, but returned because of a thick ground mist that made location of the aerodromes impossible. Night bombing was now an added duty for the single-seater fighter squadrons. It had been thought that single-seater scouts could not operate at night with safety, or with any hope of success, but on the night of September 3 two Sopwith Camel pilots of a Home Defence Squadron had attempted to intercept a raid on England. Although the attempt failed, both pilots returned safely, demonstrating that Camels could be safely flown at night. In France, that same night, two Camel pilots of 70 Squadron took off to intercept enemy aeroplanes that were bombing St Omer. This attempt was also unsuccessful, but Bristol Fighters also began to be used at night, and a defence scheme was worked out to intercept night flying enemy bombers, both in France and England.

The weather continued fine on October 2. Maxwell's diary recorded. 'Plenty of scrapping.' C and A Flights flew the first patrol by 56 Squadron in the morning, taking off at 10.00am. A pair of two-seaters flying low over Ploegsteert Wood evaded the SE5s but Maxwell later attacked another over Comines. Maxwell's Lewis gun was inoperative, but getting underneath the enemy machine he fired a long burst from his Vickers gun, hitting the observer who lay over the side of his cockpit, 'obviously dead.' The enemy machine glided east and Maxwell lost sight of it.

A few miles to the north of Maxwell's action, C Flight were in combat with three Albatros scouts over Moorslede. One of these was at the same height as the SE5s, its two companions slightly lower. Maybery dived at one of the lower Albatri and sent it down to crash half a mile west of St Pieter, killing *Ltn* Max Roemer of *Jasta 10*. The SE5s then attacked a trio of two-seaters, but these escaped by flying under the protection of their anti-aircraft guns and the SE5s were attacked by a formation of extremely skilled black and white Albatri.

Bowman twice went to the aid of Stanley Gardiner. Driving off the first of Gardiner's attackers – which had sent him down in a steep spiral – Bowman was attacked from behind by another of the enemy scouts. Bowman zoomed, the enemy pilot overshot the SE and dived away, followed by Bowman, who fired 40 rounds into it. The Albatros began to spiral down but Bowman could watch no longer as he could see that Gardiner was still in trouble, with another black and white Albatros following him down. Bowman drove this Albatros away then turned to locate his last opponent, but the Albatros was nowhere in sight. Bowman turned back to Gardiner. He could see the SE5 was not under full control and as he watched another Albatros attacked it. This Albatros was driven off by Richard Maybery, who had also seen that Gardiner was in trouble.

Hoidge attacked one Albatros, firing 50 rounds into it from close range. The enemy scout spun down, but Hoidge left it to attack another, which was firing at Lt John Gilbert. Hoidge drove off this scout, but Gilbert was 'going round very slowly' and Hoidge stayed with him until he force landed in a field near Poperinghe. Both Gardiner and Gilbert had been severely handled by the enemy scouts and were lucky to have escaped so lightly. Gardiner forced landed near Borre, the controls of his machine shot away, and Gilbert's SE5 had been hit in both petrol and oil tanks.

Patrols were also out in the morning from 1 Squadron. Capts H J Hamilton and G B Moore attacked a DFW over Comines at 11.05am and sent it down out of control for a shared victory. Just over an hour later, at 12.10pm, Sgt Olley and 2Lt R Sotham shared in sending down another DFW out of control east of Becelaere. Capt John Gibbs scored his last victory with 23 Squadron when he destroyed a Rumpler north of Wervicq at 11.15am.

C and B Flights from 56 Squadron were again in action in the afternoon, taking off at 4.30pm. Both Flights saw a great deal of action, but C Flight were in a bad tactical position from the onset, the enemy scouts having the advantage of height. Bowman's logbook carries the caustic comment: 'Driven out of sky twice.' All the combats were indecisive and no victories were claimed, but the patrols are of interest in that both Rhys Davids and Muspratt reported that the enemy formations included two Fokker Triplanes. Rhys Davids reported: saw two Fokker Triplanes with no dihedral, large extentions, Nieuport tail, Fokker rudder and Martinsyde shaped wings, engine probably rotary. Climb good.'[1]

Sixty-eight Squadron, which had flown its DH5s into Baizieux on September 21, was in action – the first to be fought by an Australian squadron – near St Quentin. Led by Capt W A McCloughry the DH5s attacked an enemy two-seater, which dived to ground level and escaped. Another two-seater was attacked later, but this also escaped, due to its superior speed over the DH5s. During this patrol 2Lt I C Agnew had engine failure, force landed and was taken POW, the first battle casualty of the Australian squadrons in France.

Ten Pups of 66 Squadron set out at dusk to bomb the enemy aerodromes of Cruyshautem and Waereghem, north west of Courtrai, the raid that had been aborted the night before. The attacks were carried out from low height and were successful, a bomb hitting a hangar at Waereghen and setting it on fire.

A pilot of 24 Squadron was wounded during the day for the only other casualty in the fighter squadrons.

Little flying was possible on October 3 due to the deteriorating weather, but 29 Squadron lost a pilot who force landed east of the Lines and was taken prisoner. The next day, although the weather was very bad for flying, fighting on the ground began again with an attack on the seven mile front between the Menin Road and the Ypres to Staden railway, with the objective of capturing the villages of Poelcappelle and Broodseinde on the Passchendaele Ridge. A minor attack was also mounted on a short front south of the Menin road to capture strong points.

The weather was appalling – heavy rain, clouds no higher than 400 feet and high winds – but co-operation with the corps squadrons during the attack was essential. An RE8 of 21 Squadron was forced to land by the strong winds and a pilot of 19 Squadron was killed in action.

The ground attacks were successful. By the evening all the objectives had been taken and consolidated, despite German counter attacks, which were repulsed with heavy losses to the enemy. It was seen as essential that the heights of the Passchendaele Ridge were taken before the onset of winter proper bought an end to the ground fighting until the spring, and the next ground attack was set for October 9.

The rain and clouds lifted a little on October 5 and some fighter squadrons flew offensive patrols. Rooper of 1 Squadron destroyed an Albatros scout at 9.55am over Zandvoorde for his last of eight victories while with the squadron. During an evening patrol Gordon Olley destroyed a two-seater west

of Roulers at 4.35pm and Guy Moore another at the same time over Houthulst. Philip Fullard destroyed a two-seater over Bousbecque at 4.45pm, his first victory since August 22.

Fifty-six Squadron flew a patrol in the morning and there was a great deal of fighting over the Menin to Roulers road and the hamlet of America. Charles Jeffs, chasing an Albatros down from the main action, became separated from the other SE5s and, low down, was jumped by three enemy scouts of *Jasta 26*. Pulling out only five or six hundred feet from the ground, Jeffs' engine lost pressure and stopped. 'The only thing I could do was to find a landing spot – which I did. I put her down into whatever was there – and it was a ploughed field. She bumped, bumped, about three times, went slip-bang down on her nose and crumpled up.'[2] Jeffs was catapulted out of his SE5 and while he lay on the ground the three enemy scouts dived and fired at him. Jeffs was claimed by *Oblt* Bruno Loerzer the *Staffelführer* of *Jasta 26* for his 13th victory.[3]

Early in the morning the pilots of 46 Squadron were shocked to hear that Lt E 'Armie' Armitage, who had been wounded in the calf on September 30, had died in the night of gangrene poisoning. Lee confided to his diary. 'What on earth could have caused a simple wound like this, under treatment by hospital staff within an hour of it happening, to go wrong so quickly. We could have taken it better if he'd been killed in a scrap.'

The bad weather persisted on October 6 and only a little flying was possible. Some idea of the conditions can be gained from the only casualty of the fighter squadrons during the day. A pilot from 23 Squadron on a WT patrol was last seen over Lille, *prior to a hailstorm*. He was wounded in action and taken POW.

Flying was only possible in the morning of October 7, heavy rain falling for the remainder of the day. George Lloyd of 40 Squadron was in action with a two-seater and its escort of three scouts at 7.45am over La Bassée. The two-seater escaped, but Lloyd destroyed one of its escorts for the last victory of 40 Squadron's Nieuports. The Squadron was to be completely re-equipped with the SE5a by October 17.

An offensive patrol from 1 Squadron led by Fullard first attacked a pair of DFWs over Wervicq – one of which he sent down out of control – and later attacked a formation of 13 Albatri over Menin, Guy Moore and William Rogers each shooting one of the enemy scouts down out of control over the town at 8.00am.[4] 2Lt M Peacock also claimed a scout as out of control during the morning's fighting.

Frederick Sowery of 19 Squadron led a patrol of three Spads to intercept enemy wireless machines reported to be spotting for the artillery over the Lines. They found one of these two-seaters, but were driven off by a large formation of enemy scouts. Sowery later returned to the area and engaged two enemy scouts attacking an RE8, destroying one, which crashed two miles east of Gheluvelt at five minutes past ten.

The heavy rain continued the next day and there was no war flying, but 28 Squadron, equipped with Sopwith Camels arrived in France and flew into St Omer, moving to Droglandt two days later.

In spite of the continuing rain on October 9, and against the advice of his army commanders, Gough and Plumer, Haig gave orders for the planned attack for the capture of the remainder of the Passchendaele Ridge, bounded on one side by Broodseinde and along the Goudberg Spur on the other. It has been argued that as Haig did not include taking the strategically important Westroosebeke (just north of Passchendaele) in his objectives, he was more interested in simply taking Passchendaele and killing Germans than in strategically important gains.

One of the few fighter squadrons that flew patrols during the day was 1 Squadron and it paid dearly with two casualties. Taking off at 12.40pm six Nieuports of the squadron engaged nine enemy scouts over Gheluwe. One of the enemy scouts attacking the Nieuport flown by Lt Wendell Rogers, was shot down out of control by Guy Moore, but 2Lt M A Peacock failed to return: he was last seen low down over Menin in combat with three enemy aircraft and he was shot down by *Ltn* Müller of *Jasta 11* and taken prisoner. The next patrol, taking off at 2.40pm, went to the aid of two RE8s of 6 Squadron under attack by enemy scouts from *Jasta 26* over Polygon Wood. Harry Reeves attacked *Ltn* Wagner of *Jasta 26*, who was firing at an RE8. Hit by either Reeves fire or the gunner of the RE8 (or both) Wagner's Albatros burst into flames and went down. At 2,500 feet Wagner jumped from his burning machine, which finally crashed by the wood. William Rooper was last seen low down over Polygon Wood, in combat with five enemy aircraft. There is some confusion over the exact details of Rooper's last fight. The casualty report merely states he crashed in the Front Line trenches, breaking his thigh, but he subsequently died and was buried in Bailleul cemetery.[5]

A Flight of Spads from 19 Squadron were in combat with two-seaters over Moorslede at 10.40am and Sowery claimed one as out of control. An Albatros scout destroyed over Lindeken at five minutes to four by Frank Hobson of 70 Squadron was the last claim of the day.

During the afternoon a party of pilots from 46 Squadron took a cross made from a propeller to the cemetery at Izel where Lt Armitage was buried. 'We erected it over his grave. Unlucky Armie.'

Owing to the rain, the only flying possible on October 10 was in the early morning and in the evening.

The Canadian, Francis Quigley of 70 Squadron, attacked an Albatros scout over Westroosebeke and shot it down in flames at five minutes past eight. Twenty minutes later Quigley was attacked over Houthulst Forest by six Albatri, but he managed to escape from these, shooting one down out of control as he did so. These were Quigley's first two victories of an eventual 33. In the evening, a patrol of eight Camels from the squadron had a fight with five enemy scouts. Lt Cook shot one down in flames and Capt C N Jones and Lt J Wilson sent another down out of control.

Twenty-nine Squadron lost two pilots wounded in an early morning patrol that took off at 5.35am. Both 2Lt C Hamilton and 2Lt G B Wigle were wounded during a combat, Wigle in the face.

A patrol of Camels from 45 Squadron attacked seven Albatri over Dadizeele at 2.30pm and Matthew Frew shot down two in quick succession for his 11th and 12th victories.

In the afternoon 56 Squadron was in a fight east of Ypres with 12 Albatri from *Jasta 26*, and lost Lt Geoffrey Wilkinson, shot down by *Ltn* Danhuber. Maxwell's diary: saw Wilkinson go down in pieces with a Hun on his tail.' It is possible that some of these enemy scouts were from *Jasta 18*. *Ltn* Paul Strähle of the *Jasta* recorded in his diary that the *Jasta* were in combat in the afternoon with SE5s, DH4s and triplanes. Other Albatri had joined in and shot down two British machines, one of which disintegrated in mid-air. *Oblt* Berthold of *Jasta 18* was severely wounded in the fighting, his right arm shattered, and *Ltn* Schober was forced to land with a bullet in his radiator.

A Deep Offensive Patrol by 41 Squadron, taking off at five minutes to three in the afternoon, lost 2Lt A W Edwards in a fight with *Jasta 12,* the second victory of *Ltn* Ewers. Edwards who had been severely wounded in the back, came down near Hendecourt and died on his way to hospital.

The low cloud and rain continued on October 11 but there was a great deal of fighting in the air. A large formation of 35 British aircraft flew a Deep Offensive Patrol, penetrating 12 miles east of the Front Lines: 11 Sopwith Pups of 46 Squadron, the remainder Bristol Fighters from 11 and DH5s from 41 Squadron. Despite the odds, six Albatros scouts attacked the Pups. 'They put up a very good show and we ought to have slaughtered them, but there were so many of us, all milling around at the same level, with no proper system of attack, that we got in each other's way, in fact one spent half the time dodging Bristols and DH5s.'

The Pups of 46 Squadron were the highest British formation and Capt C Brewster Joske led them down into the fight. Two of the Albatri went spinning down from the Pup's attack – one climbing back into the fight – but Lt A Allen who failed to pull out in time went down through the Albatri formation and was shot down and killed by *Ltn* Ewers of *Jasta 12*.[6]

Lee and Joske attacked an Albatros that was a little apart from the main fight. Both Pup pilots got to close range and each fired fifty rounds into the enemy scout. The Albatros jerked, a piece came off and it spun down. Lee and Joske both lost sight of this Albatros as it went down but as it did not climb back into the fight they claimed it as out of control.

Nine SE5s of 56 Squadron took off at 6.15am and attacked a mixed formation of Albatri and Pfalz –12 enemy scouts in all – at 7.20am. McCudden got onto the tail of a Pfalz but both his guns refused to fire. Both in frustration and to frighten the enemy pilot, McCudden fired his Very pistol at the Pfalz.

Additional Albatri now arrived at the scene of the fight and dived into the action in ones and twos from out of the morning sun. Rhys Davids attacked one of these arrivals. 'I sat on his tail firing both guns and he went down steeply south west with a lot of smoke coming out.'[7] Muspratt attacked a Pfalz, 'silver, like a Nieuport', but overshot and nearly collided with the enemy scout.[8]

The enemy machines finally cleared east and the SE5s returned to Estrée Blanche. Two of their number were missing. 2Lt Reginald Preston-Cobb had been shot down and killed by *Ltn* Hoyer of *Jasta 36* and Lt James Cunningham had been wounded in the back and force landed at Pont-de-Nieppe. Cunningham was taken to hospital but died of his wounds eight days later.

In the afternoon the pilots of 28 Squadron were flying their newly issued Sopwith Camels in a practice patrol when 2Lt W H Winter strayed from the formation and was last seen east of the Lines over Armentières. Winters was shot down and made POW by *Vzfw* Buckler of *Jasta 17* for his 17th victory. A Camel from Naval 9 was also lost during the day. FltSubLt N Black was last seen diving on the trenches by Zarren after a combat with three enemy scouts. Black crashed in the British lines and died of his wounds the next day.

The weather was again poor on October 12, with low clouds and rain, but there were some combats. 2Lt R Birkbeck of 1 Squadron shot down a two-seater, which crashed into a street in Comines; Camels of 45 Squadron fought with 20 enemy scouts and Lt Firth claimed one out of control – which was not allowed. 2Lt Crompton of 60 Squadron crashed an enemy scout, and 2Lt E Booth of 70 Squadron shot an Albatros down out of control south-east of Houthulst at 5.30pm.

The pilots of 66 Squadron flew at low level to attack troops, transport and gun positions. 2Lt G L Dore attacked an Albatros over Harlebeeke aerodrome, the base of *Jasta 18*. Strähle's diary recorded: 'two Sopwiths flew very low and one of them shot down an Albatros D III which glided in to land on our aerodrome.'

Flying a normal offensive patrol later in the morning the squadron lost three pilots, and two Pups were forced to land damaged after a fight at 12,000 feet over Ypres with *Jasta 36*. 2Lt M Newcomb was taken POW; 2Lt R Matthewson was also taken prisoner, but Lt A Nasmyth was shot down and killed. 2Lt Dore was wounded in the leg, but returned with his Pup badly shot up, and 2Lt F Gove also returned with a badly damaged machine. *Lts* Quandt, Haebler and Hoyer of *Jasta 36* were all awarded victories.

Casualties in the fighter squadrons were heavy. In addition to the 66 Squadron casualties, two pilots of 45 Squadron and a pilot from 19 Squadron were killed in action, and a pilot from 23 Squadron was wounded.

At 5.25am, the ground offensive had recommenced with an attack between the Ypres to Roulers railway and Houthulst Forest. Some progress was made but the flooded valleys to the west of the main ridge made further advance impossible, the troops floundering in the mud and impossible conditions. The tireless efforts of the pilots and observers of the corps squadrons had enabled artillery fire to be directed onto enemy positions; concentrations of troops were broken up, and enemy infantry were attacked throughout the day by low flying aircraft. There were no strong counter attacks: the British troops had made only little progress and the German command was unwilling to incur heavy casualties to retake the small amount of ground lost. Douglas Haig at last recognised that the hope of gaining more ground before the winter set in was futile, and although he kept up a limited amount of pressure on the Ypres front – partly to aid the French army in a forthcoming operation – he now turned his attentions to the next main offensive, to be launched in the Cambrai area in November.

The weather was to continue unsettled for over a week. On October 13 only one victory was claimed: a two-seater by Lt W Sherwood of 60 Squadron, but 54 Squadron lost two pilots killed and two more taken POW in a morning fight with elements of *Jagdstaffeln* 8, 10 and B over Zarren.

A patrol of DH5s of 68 Squadron were returning from patrol when Lt R McKenzie noticed that Lt D Morrison was lagging some distance behind the formation. McKenzie turned back to assist Morrison, but four Albatri from *Jasta 12* pounced on the straggler. McKenzie fired at one of the Albatri but had engine trouble and dived away. Morrison, badly wounded, crashlanded in No Mans Land. He was pulled from the wreckage of his machine by troops of the 13th London Regiment, but he died of his wounds soon afterwards. The German artillery shelled his DH5 to pieces. Morrison was the first victory of *Ltn* Staats of *Jasta 12*.

In the morning of October 14, six SE5s from 56 Squadron were detailed to escort the Martinsydes of 27 Squadron on a bombing raid to Ledeghem. After seeing the bombers back to the Lines, McCudden attacked six Albatri over Wervicq. The first Albatros spun away from McCudden's fire and his attack on another was frustrated by jams in both guns and by the skilful flying of the enemy pilot. McCudden was later attacked by a pair of Albatri over Zonnebeke. One broke off the action and flew east, but the other stayed and fought McCudden and Lt John Gilbert for sometime. The enemy pilot manoeuvred 'very well' and dived on Gilbert, but McCudden got on his tail and drove him down to 7,000 feet where the enemy pilot dived into a large cloud and escaped.

The pilots of Naval 10 broke a long spell of relative inactivity during the day. The first patrol, at 11.50am, engaged a formation of 14 Gothas and their escort flying north of Ypres. Fitzgibbon attacked two Gothas; the first over Langemarck, which he was forced to leave with stoppages in both guns; the second over Poelcappelle. Fitzgibbon fired all his ammunition at this second Gotha, from a range of 60 yards, without any appreciable effect on the enemy bomber. In a patrol over the same area in the afternoon, FltCom Saint led the Camels down on a formation of three enemy scouts that were attacking a French Spad. Two of the enemy scouts dived away from the fight, the odds no longer to their liking, but the third, coloured black and white, was shot down by the Spad and was seen to crash by FltSubLt Manuel.

Fullard and Olley each claimed two-seaters out of control during a morning patrol, and Leacroft of 19 Squadron shot down an Albatros over Becelaere at 4.20pm that was seen to crash by Sowery. In an earlier patrol by 19 Squadron, Lt C R Thompson had destroyed an Albatros, which crashed at Triez-Caillioux at 10.30am. A patrol of DH5s from 32 Squadron saw ten enemy scouts attacking an RE8 and went to its assistance, Lt W R Jones shooting one down in pierces to crash in the British Lines at Poelcappelle. The pilot, *Offstv* Weckbrodt, *of Jasta 26,* was killed and his Albatros designated G 79.

The only fighter casualty for the day was a pilot of 29 Squadron, shot down behind the British lines and killed, possibly the 'Camel' claimed by *Ltn* Böhme of *Jasta B* for his 19th victory.

Sixty-four Squadron equipped with DH5s, which had arrived in France the previous day, flew into Le Hameau aerodrome, sharing it with 46 Squadron.

An Albatros destroyed over Menin the next morning was the first combat victory for 84 Squadron. The Squadron, equipped with SE5s, had been in France since September 17 under the command of 9th Wing, and stationed at Estrée Blanche, but its first three weeks in France had been taken up with practice flying. October 15 was the first patrol flown, an escort for the DH4s of 25 Squadron that were bombing the enemy ammunition dump at Harlebeke. On the way back to the Lines, the formations were attacked by enemy scouts. 2Lt

E Krohn had engine trouble, was separated from the other SE5s, and on his way back to the Lines was continually attacked by enemy scouts. Despite his failing engine, Krohn managed to get several bursts into one of his attackers and the Albatros was seen to crash by the front line troops. Unfortunately the squadron also had its first casualty: 2Lt T Vernon-Lord had been shot down and taken prisoner.

Frederick Sowery, leading a Flight of 19 Squadron Spads, shot down an Albatros two-seater north east of Moorslede at 4.45pm for his 13th and last victory.[9]

Five Camels of 45 Squadron were on patrol over Houthulst Forest in the afternoon when they attacked a formation of enemy two-seaters. 2Lt K B Montgomery destroyed one of these, and the pilots watched it crash in the Forest at 4.50pm. Other victories in the day's fighting were a DFW destroyed over Comines at noon by Harry Reeves of 1 Squadron; Norman Macmillan of 45 Squadron a two-seater out of control over Houthulst Forest at 11.50am, and FltSubLt W Curtis of Naval 10 a two-seater down south east of Zarren at 1.45pm. FltSubLt Sutherland of Naval 10 was wounded in his left shoulder, but managed to return and land his Camel without damage.

No victories were claimed by the fighter squadrons on October 16, but there were four casualties. A Nieuport from 29 Squadron was forced down by *Ltn* Böhme of *Jasta B* and landed intact, the pilot, Lt F J Ortweiler taken POW; a Spad from 23 Squadron was shot through the petrol tank and forced to land, and a DH5 from 32 Squadron crashed landed in shell holes after a combat with enemy aircraft and was wrecked.

Enemy aircraft were both active and aggressive during the morning of October 17. Fullard scored three victories during the day: The first was a two-seater over Quesnoy at 9.45am; the second, a two-seater destroyed south east of Ledghem three quarters of an hour later; and in an afternoon patrol Fullard caught an Albatros scout over Moorslede, hitting the pilot and sending it down out of control at 2.25pm for his 34th victory.

The pilots of the naval squadrons were also in action. Richard Minifie and Stanley Rosevear of Naval 1 caught an LVG and an Albatros scout over Polygon Wood at 10.45am. Mifinie shot the LVG down in the British Lines south of Polygon Wood, killing the crew, *Ltn d res* Heinz Schuberth and *Uffz* Willi Keller from *Fl Abt 8*. The LVG was designated G 80. The Albatros also crashed south of Polygon Wood, destroyed by Rosevear.

It was an unlucky morning for *Fl Abt 8*. On patrol east of Ypres McCudden and B Flight saw a pair of LVGs over Bailleul. Seeing the SE5s approaching, one of the two-seaters made off to the east, followed by Muspratt and the rest of the Flight, but McCudden tackled the other, which had turned west in the hope of outclimbing the SE5s. After a burst from McCudden's Vickers gun the centre section of the LVG burst into flame. The enemy pilot turned left, his observer standing up in an attitude of 'abject dejection,' but the fire, after burning away most of the fabric of the LVG's rudder, went out. The enemy pilot glided northwards, with McCudden following, knowing that the LVG would have to land in the British lines, but Barlow and Muspratt now arrived and both shot at the LVG as it was going down, the enemy machine steepening its glide into a dive. Both wings of the LVG finally broke off and it crashed just south of Vlamertinghe. McCudden landed nearby and pushed his way through the Australian troops who had gathered around the remains of the LVG's observer, who had fallen out of his machine at 5,000 feet. 'He was a huge man named Ernst Hädrich and seeing that he was dead I went over to the other group of men, about a hundred yards away and there found the remains of machine and pilot.'[10]

McCudden's military and disciplined mind was horrified at the behaviour of the Australian troops, who in short time had stripped the LVG and its dead pilot of anything of value. After McCudden had returned to Estrée Blanche and expressed his disgust at the unedifying way in which the troops had behaved, Major Blomfield submitted an official report, pointing out that the troops had gone so far as to strip the dead observer of his clothing.

Other victories claimed from the day's fighting were a two-seater to Capt H M Ferreira of 29 Squadron, and another to 2Lt Herbert Drewitt of 23 Squadron, destroyed over Dixmude at 11.05am. The only loss for the fighter squadrons was a Sopwith Pup of 54 Squadron, which was shot up and forced to land. The pilot was uninjured.

There was less enemy activity over the Lines on October 18 although several large formations were seen and engaged over Roulers.

C Flight of 56 Squadron, joined in a fight with other SE5s – 84 Squadron were in the area as well as A Flight from 56 Squadron – and a number of Albatri. Bowman and Hoidge both made several attacks on one Albatros with a yellow tail, which both pilots noticed had an unusual form of armament. Bowman reported that it fired at right angles to its line of flight, and Hoidge stated that 'smoke came out in the shape of a fan in the vertical plane.' This Albatros repeatedly dived east on being attacked, but always returned to the scene of the action, and Hoidge fought it on and off for ten minutes until it finally flew away. It was noted that these Albatri had yellow noses and tails and that the tail of one was chequered like a draughts board. They were possibly from *Jasta 10*.

Leaving the Albatri diving away east, the Flight next attacked four enemy two-seaters, escorted by four scouts, one of which got onto the tail of Hoidge. Bowman shot this scout off his deputy flight commander's tail and another from the tail of Lt Gilbert's SE. Hoidge chased one of the two-seaters

to Comines and shot it down to crash between the River Leie and the road. Hoidge later attacked another two-seater, watching it go down in a vertical dive to within 500 feet of the ground before leaving it to go to the aid of John Gilbert, who was under attack from an Albatros. Hoidge drove off Gilbert's attacker. Whether from this attack or from another, Gilbert failed to return. He had been shot down and killed by *Ltn* Udet of *Jasta 37*. Geoffrey Shone also failed to return. He had been shot down in flames by *Vzfw* Kampe of *Jasta 27* and crashed behind the British lines at St Julien. Shone died of his wounds on No.27 Ambulance Train at 4.10pm the next day.

A formation from Naval 1 were in action east of Poelcappelle in the morning and FltLt Samuel Kinkead and FltSubLt James Forman claimed a DFW out of control at 10.30am. 2Lt James Payne closed the morning's victories with an Albatros out of control 2 miles north west of Menin at 11.05am for his fourth victory of an eventual 14.

In an afternoon patrol, FltLt Richard Minifie from Naval 1 attacked a Gotha north of Passchendaele at 2.30pm and fired 200 rounds into the bomber before it went vertically down and was lost to sight in the thick cloud. Capt 'Milford' Hyde and 2Lt M Gonne of 54 Squadron were on patrol over Leke at 2.30pm when they saw and attacked an Albatros, both sharing in its destruction.

At 3.30pm a Distant Offensive Patrol of DH5s from 41 Squadron attacked a formation of Albatri at 12,000 feet over Arleux. Lt Winnicott sent one of the enemy machines down in a flat spin and 2Lt R M Whitehead claimed another out of control, but 2Lt Gerald Huddart Swann was wounded, and while attempting to return crashed in the British Lines west of Havrincourt Wood. Swann was killed and the DH5 completely wrecked. Swann was awarded to *Uffz* Neckel of *Jasta 12* as his third victory. Winnicott's and Whitehead's victories were the last scored by 41 Squadron before it was re-equipped with SE5s in November.

Apart from those mentioned, other casualties were a pilot of 70 Squadron wounded in action; 84 Squadron had their second casualty when a pilot was shot down in a combat over Poelcappelle and taken prisoner; and a pilot of 24 Squadron was also taken prisoner from an early morning patrol.

There was no flying at all on October 19, due to both dense clouds and mist. It cleared the next day, but there was a thick haze at low height, which persisted throughout the day, hampering the work of the corps aeroplanes. Lt Frank Soden of 60 Squadron scored an unusual 'victory' while on a recreational flight. He saw a British balloon, which had broken away from its mooring, drifting east at 12,000 feet. First making sure that there were no observers in the basket, Soden fired into the balloon and it went down into a field, where it was surrounded by French and Portuguese troops. Soden landed alongside the balloon and persuaded the troops to carry it to a nearby road. His intention was that it could be picked up from there by the squadron's transport and its fabric used to line the pilots' huts. Winter was coming on! However, Soden's plan was frustrated by GHQ who insisted that the balloon be returned.

Earlier in the year, Lt Col Holt, commanding Twenty-second (Army) Wing, had put forward a plan to his squadron commanders for attacking enemy aerodromes. Not in the rather piecemeal way hitherto undertaken, with single or pairs of fighters, but with an overwhelming fighter force from the Wing, with the aim to destroy as many of the enemy machines on the ground as possible. The plan had not been carried out earlier in the year, enemy activity possibly not thought active enough to warrant it, but on the morning of October 20 a modified plan of the attack was carried out in a raid on Rumbeke aerodrome, south of Roulers, the base of *Jasta B*.

Forty-five fighters took part in the raid, taking off at 10.30am. Eleven Camels from 70 Squadron, each carrying two 25-lb bombs, were the bomber force, with eight Camels from the squadron flying as close escort. Nineteen Camels from 28 Squadron brought up the rear of the bombers to attack any enemy machines which managed to leave the ground, either before or during the attack, and seven Spads from 23 Squadron flew above the attack in a high offensive patrol to cover the whole operation.

The raid was a complete success. Coming in at 400 feet the first Camels dropped their bombs, some of which fell on enemy machines lined up in front of the hangars, blowing one of them to pieces; other bombs exploding near or on the hangars and sheds. Having dropped their bombs the Camels went down again and again, some to under 20 feet – the wheels of two of the Camels were said to have actually run along the ground, one sustaining a bent axle – flying over the aerodrome, machine gunning the personnel and machines. Above the strafing and bombing, the other pilots of 70 Squadron and those from 28 Squadron, flying in close escort, were in combat with a large number of enemy machines within sight of the aerodrome.

2Lt Koch fired 20 rounds at an Albatros from very close range, which went down out of control, before firing a longer burst of 80 rounds into another which force landed on the aerodrome. Koch then came under attack by three enemy scouts, but he went down to within 300 feet of the ground and contour chased back to the lines. 2Lt Booth fired 150 rounds into an Albatros that attempted to land in a field, but ran into a hedge and overturned. 2Lt J Michie attacked a two-seater, which was taking off from the aerodrome. The enemy machine turned, stalled and flew into the ground; Quigley shot at another two-seater that had managed to get into the air, but its

wings folded up under Quigley's fire. Pilots of 28 Squadron who were successful were 2Lt P G Mullholland, Lt J Mitchell and Capt William Barker, all of whom claimed enemy aircraft either seen to crash or break up in mid-air. Barker's victory was his first of an eventual 50.

On their way back to base the 70 Squadron pilots attacked targets of opportunity. Lt C Primeau and 2Lt F Hobson both attacked troop trains on the Menin to Roulers line, firing into the windows from a height of 50 feet, and Primeau also strafed another enemy aerodrome. Quigley fired on troops playing football and at horse transport on a road. Two Camels from 70 Squadron were lost. 2Lt F B Farquharson was shot down and made POW by *Ltn* Bassenge of *Jasta B*, and *Ltn* Kempf of *Jasta B* killed Cap J R Wilson over the Menin-Roulers Road. Returning to base an Indian pilot, Lt Singh Malik was attacked south west of Moorslede. His Camel was badly shot about, and Malik crash landed, overturning the Camel, but with no hurt to himself. These were the only casualties from the raid and for the entire day.

Naval 10 fought with nine Albatri northeast of Dixmude at 1.40pm. FltCom Saint shot down one, which was seen to crash near Praet Wood, and FltSubLt Manuel saw the Albatros that he had attacked land nearby.

Other victories were claimed during the day. Capt Macmillan, leading Lts E Clarke, R Brownell, and Davies, shot down an Albatros out of control at 12.40pm over Kastelhoek, all the Flight being credited; Minifie of Naval 1 claimed an Albatros at 11.00am south of Comines, and Rogers of 1 Squadron shot an Albatros down out of control over Linselles at 10.50am. Capts J Smith-Grant, Frederic Laurence and Lt Alfred Koch of 70 Squadron all claimed enemy machines down, either from the fights over the aerodrome at Rumbeke or while returning.

On October 21 the *Luftstreitkräfte* was both active and aggressive, but kept well east of the Front Line. Naval 10 were in action early, fighting Albatri over Nieuport, but there were no positive results from the fight. FltSubLt W N Fox was wounded in the leg but managed to return to Leffrinckoucke. A little later, at 11.00am, a patrol from Naval 1 found a two-seater south of Comines and FltSubLt Anthony Spence shot it down out of control. A patrol of Camels from 45 Squadron attacked four enemy two-seaters over Lille at 9.45am but were attacked themselves by seven Albatri, which came at them from out of the sun. The Camels fought these Albatri for some time. 2Lt Peter Carpenter shot one down in flames and Frew chased another, firing 300 rounds into it from very close range. The Albatros went down in an uncontrolled dive, its engine full on.

Over Menin at 10.20am a Flight of Spads from 19 Squadron led by John Leacroft saw two RE8s and some Spads –

possibly French – fighting 12 enemy scouts. Leacroft led his Flight into the fight and shot down an Albatros, which was seen to crash by British AA batteries. This was possibly *Vzfw* Bachmann of *Jasta 6* who was killed over Ypres at 11.20am(GT).

Naval 10 flew another patrol at 12.35pm and this time had better luck. Three two-seaters were seen coming towards the Lines over Dixmude at 1.30pm and all the Camels concentrated their attacks on one machine at the rear of the three, shooting it down in flames into the allied lines. Twenty minutes later FLtSubLt Paytner, flying on the outside of the Camel formation, was attacked by a lone Albatros, which perhaps had not seen the other Camels. Curtis turned back and shot this Albatros down, and it was later confirmed by the Belgian forces to have crashed.

The 46 Squadron pilots had a frustrating morning. They first attempted to attack two DFWs, flying at 12,000 feet, but the enemy pilots saw the Pups coming and dived away. Two more DFWs were seen later but these were protected by five Albatri, 3,000 feet above. Lee, leading the Pups, climbed up to the enemy scouts and attacked them – at that height he was confident that the Pups could out fly the Albatri – but when two Bristol Fighters appeared and attacked the DFWs the Albatros pilots tried to break off the action with the Pups to go to the aid of their two-seaters. Lee attacked one Albatros painted blue and grey and the usual circling for position began, each pilot attempting to turn inside his opponent to get in a burst of fire. At that height a Pup could easily out turn the heavier Albatros, and Lee soon got behind the enemy scout and opened fire. This seemed to have no effect, the Albatros pilot simply continued his turn before diving away, then climbing back into the fight, which continued for ten minutes, with no results for either side. The Albatri finally broke off the action and flew east. Lt Hurst had been hit in the engine and had to land at the advanced landing ground near Bapaume, but although the other Pups returned safely all had been shot about – Lee had eleven hits on his machine, including one in an interplane strut.

In the afternoon, Lee led a combined force of eight Pups and eight DH5s on a Deep Offensive Patrol, flying over 12 miles into German held territory. No enemy aeroplanes were seen and all sixteen machines returned safely.

Just before mid-day Ninth Wing HQ telephoned 56 Squadron to ask the squadron to intercept three enemy two-seaters that were flying south from Calais. McCudden, Rhys Davids and Muspratt took off and flew towards the coast. The SE5s failed to find the enemy machines, seeing only a DH4, which McCudden went to have a look at. Rhys Davids and Muspratt returned to Estrée Blanche and had a little joke with 'Grandpa' Marson, the squadron's recording officer, telling him that they

had left their flight commander carefully stalking a friendly DH4.

After his companions had left him, McCudden flew to the southeast and over Bethune he saw a Rumpler coming west from Givenchy. The Rumpler pilot was a 1,000 feet higher than the SE5, and seeing the threat he turned southeast. McCudden, however, knew that Rumpler pilots were not easily dissuaded from their duties and felt sure it would return; probably much higher, relying on its superior height to avoid a combat. McCudden went north. Although his engine was not running well he continued climbing, carefully hoarding his height. Over Armentières he could still see the Rumpler, 'a small speck against the herring-bone sky.' and he continued to climb, flying east, then south. Arriving over Don, McCudden was east of the Rumpler, which was now flying west, and he followed it until it had passed over La Basée. The Rumpler pilot, having seen the SE5 coming from the German back areas had concluded that it was a friendly scout, but he now realised his mistake and as McCudden closed at 18,000 feet over Bethune, he turned east again. It was too late. McCudden fired a long burst from both guns and the Rumpler went down, emitting clouds of steam, to crash near Mazingarbe. McCudden landed nearby and ran over to the wreckage of the Rumpler. The observer was dead but the pilot was alive. McCudden ordered some of the troops that had gathered around the crash to find a stretcher, but before one could be found the pilot died. For the second time in five days McCudden was brought face to face with the stark reality of his actions. 'I felt very sorry indeed, for shooting a man down in Hunland is a different thing from doing it in your own lines, where you can see the results of your work. Shooting Huns is very good fun while we have to do it, but at the same time it makes one think, as I say, when one views such an object as I was doing then.'[11]

This Rumpler was McCudden's 18th victory and the first example of an art he was to perfect: the stalking of high-flying Rumplers.

In an afternoon patrol 84 Squadron lost three pilots in a fight with enemy scouts over Roulers that lasted forty minutes. At 2.40pm, Capt Kenneth Leask had shot down a two-seater east of the Menin to Roulers Road, which sparked off the fight. Leask claimed an Albatros out of control over Roulers at 3.00pm and Lt Moloney claimed another, but 2Lts A Hempel, 2Lt F Yeomans and R B Steele were all shot down and taken prisoner, Steele, who had been wounded, dying of his wounds the next day. The victories were awarded to *Ltn* Kurt-Bertram von Döring of *Jasta 4* and *Ltn* Göring and *Ltn* Berkemeyer of *Jasta 27*.

In the morning, Laurence of 70 Squadron claimed an Albatros west of Roulers at 10.15am. Hamersley and Rutherford of 60 Squadron each claimed an Albatros during their patrols: Hamersley's at five minutes past one over Poecappelle, Rutherford's, which was shared with Soden, over Houthulst at 4.15pm. A patrol of eight Nieuports from 29 Squadron were also in action over Houthulst at 4.15pm, attacking seven enemy two-seaters. 2Lt James Payne shot down two of the enemy machines within minutes of each other, and assisted by Lts J M Leach and C Hamilton drove two more down out of control. During the day's fighting, pilots of 32 Squadron claimed two Albatros scouts between them.

It had been a day of varied success for the fighter squadrons. Victories had been claimed but not without cost. One pilot had been killed in action, three taken prisoner, one of whom died of his wounds, and two pilots were wounded. In addition, four aircraft were badly shot up and forced to land, with one pilot injured in landing.

The ground attacks resumed on October 22, again carried out in heavy rain, which cleared in the afternoon enabling some fighter squadrons to carry out low level attacks in the afternoon and evening on enemy troops, both in the trenches and the back areas. Two pilots from 45 Squadron attacked a concentration of enemy troops – two battalions strong – on the Staden to Houthulst road, eventually dispersing them. Payne of 29 Squadron was again in action. He outclimbed seven enemy aircraft over Menin then carried out dive and zoom attacks, sending one down in a vertical dive.

Despite the relative lack of enemy activity in the air, the fighter squadrons had three casualties. A pilot of 28 Squadron was hit by anti-aircraft fire and killed over Roulers, and two Pups of 54 Squadron collided while fighting with *Jasta 28* over St Pierre Capelle. Both Pups were awarded to *Ltn* Max Ritter von Müller of *Jasta 28*. Müller was a highly experienced pilot, the Pups were his 28th and 29th victories. A third Pup was awarded to *Ltn* Jannsen of the *Jasta*, but only two Pups were lost.

FltCom Richard M Munday of Naval 8 took off at dusk. Just after dark he dropped four bombs on the enemy aerodrome at Moncheaux, hitting four sheds – which were lit up – before machine-gunning the hangars from fifty feet. On the way back he finished his ammunition by firing into Cambrai railway station.

Rain and mist on October 23 prevented any patrols by the fighter squadrons, but conditions were better the next morning, and there was fighting throughout the day.

First in action were Fullard and Lt William Patrick of 1 Squadron, who attacked a two-seater at 2,000 feet over Moorslede at 6.25am. Fullard dived at the enemy machine from the front, holding his fire until a collision seemed inevitable. He then turned, closed to within ten yards of the enemy machine and fired the remainder of his Lewis gun drum into it. The two-seater went down in a steep left hand spiral, but

the enemy observer stuck by his gun and put an accurate burst into the Nieuport. One bullet hit the oil tank, another hit Fullard's goggles, while another went through his flying coat under his arm, but the most serious consequence of the observer's fire was a bullet which hit the Very cartridges in the Nieuport's cockpit, causing them to ignite and set fire to the fuselage. Fullard put the Nieuport into a steep sideslip, both to keep the flames away from the cockpit and hopefully to extinguish them. This was successful and the flames went out, but not before the Nieuport was very close to the ground and over German territory. Fullard returned to Bailleul, considerably shaken.

Nineteen Squadron were also out in the morning: Capts Leacroft and Huskinson and Lt Bryson attacked nine Albatros scouts over Menin and claimed three down out of control at 8.45am. There were more successes in the afternoon. Stanley Rosevear of Naval 1 scored his last victory flying a Sopwith Triplane when he shot down a two-seater at noon for his 8th victory. The enemy machine turned over, caught fire, and crashed near Comines. An hour and a half later his fellow Naval 1 pilot, Samuel Kinkead, destroyed another two-seater over the Comines-Wervicq area, firing 300 rounds at point blank range into the enemy machine that went down for 2,000 feet before its left hand wings broke off. This was Kinkead's seventh victory of an eventual 35.

James Payne of 29 Squadron again added to his score, shooting an Albatros scout down from a formation of five to crash two miles west of Roulers at 4.00pm. Lt J Womersley of 43 Squadron attacked a two-seater Aviatik over Lens, firing at it until within 800 feet from the ground. He was awarded it as out of control, confirmed by AA gunners. This was the first victory for 43 Squadron since being re-equipped with Sopwith Camels. At 2.10pm, over Menin, a patrol of five Camels from 45 Squadron were attacked from behind by seven Albatri. 2Lt T Williams quickly reversed the positions, getting behind one and firing from close range into its cockpit. The Albatros went down in a slow spin and crashed.

The Spad squadrons had a number of casualties. In a morning fight with *Jasta 36* two pilots were shot down, possibly by *Ltn* Bülow of the *Jasta*. Both were taken POW, but one died of his wounds four days later. In an afternoon patrol two more Spads were badly shot up. One pilot managed to return, but the other crashlanded so close to the front lines that his machine was unable to be salvaged. The Spads of 23 Squadron also fared badly in the day's fighting, losing a pilot killed and another, taken POW, who died of his wounds. Naval 1 lost a pilot killed in action and 54 and 24 Squadrons both had a pilot slightly wounded.

There was heavy rain and gale force winds on October 25 and only the corps squadrons of I and II Brigades did any flying at all. The strong winds having dried the ground a little it was decided that there would be an attack the next morning, from the Ypres to Roulers railway to beyond the village of Poelcappelle. During the night heavy rain set in which continued throughout the day, but the attack was not cancelled and at 5.45am the infantry began its assault. Undeterred by the rain the crews of the corps squadrons carried out their all-important tasks of artillery spotting and contact patrols, and the fighter squadrons of the army wings groundstrafed enemy troops, positions and transport throughout the day. There were only a few aerial victories reported. After firing on troops marching along the Ypres to Gheluwe road, 2Lt Eric Oliver of 19 Squadron attacked a two-seater south west of Gheluwe and shot it down out of control at 10.20am. 2Lt Frew and Montgomery of 45 Squadron attacked troops loading railway trucks, and troops and transport on roads, before sighting a pair of two-seaters south of Houthulst Forest at 10.20am. The Camels attacked these and shared in the destruction of one – named as a Junkers CL in Frew's victory awards. Lts Richard Hewat and de Pencier of 19 Squadron attacked troops in the main street of Moorslede, going down to 50 feet, flying along the street below the housetops. Lt de Pencier noted that he was flying below the church spire, but that Hewat was even lower. After this attack both pilots flew to Gheluwe, where Hewat saw a two-seater at 8,000 feet, just north of the town. Hewat attacked this machine and drove it down to 400 feet, but came under heavy fire from the ground, a bullet hitting him in the face, badly cutting one eye and his mouth and breaking his glasses (sic). Despite his wounds, Hewat returned to Bailleul. The two-seater was still seen to be going down at 200 feet and was credited to Hewat as out of control.

FltSubLt G Spence of Naval 1 was also in the Moorslede-Passchendaele area and shot down a two-seater at 10.10am.

A Flight of three Camels from 28 Squadron, Lts Fenton and Hardit Singh Malik led by Capt William Barker, were groundstrafing near Roulers. Fenton had dived to attack a convoy on the Roulers to Staden road, and Barker and Malik were following him down when they were attacked by four Albatri from *Jasta 18*. *Ltn* Strähle and Rahn dived after Malik, leaving *Ltn* Schober and *Offstv* Klein to engage Barker. Barker made a steep climbing turn, got into position behind the Albatros flown by Otto Schober, and shot it down in flames. Barker then attacked Klein, badly damaging his Albatros, and Klein was forced to land.

Strähle, chasing after Malik, later recorded in his diary: 'In a tough dogfight lasting over a quarter of an hour, sometimes only a few feet above the ground, I fought the enemy scout as far as Ichteghem where unfortunately I had to break off because my guns jammed. For me this fight was the hottest and most exciting that I had in my whole fighting career.

Apart from the good pilot, his machine was faster and more manoeuvrable than mine, to which must be added the low altitude, showers and rain. But for this I might have got him. Once I thought he would have to land, as he had a long trail of smoke, but it was not to be. I landed on the aerodrome at Ichteghem, where it was raining heavily. They could not tell me whether my adversary had landed. For the whole of the fight I had used full throttle, 1600 rpm, airspeed 125mph. Three times we were down to ground level! His machine had a 5 next to the cockade on the left upper wing.'[12]

Malik, wounded by Strähle's fire, fainted and crashed behind the British lines. Barker force landed near Arras and later returned to Droglandt. Fenton had been wounded in his ground attacks but had also returned to Droglandt.

While Malik was convalescing in hospital he read Barker's report of the fight. Barker had stated that he did not think Malik could have survived the fight with so many enemy scouts on his tail. Malik had made exactly the same comment about Barker's chances in his own report. 'The last I saw of Barker (Malik's report) of Malik (Barker's report) he was surrounded by Huns, fighting like hell, but I don't think there was the slightest chance of his getting away.'

There seems to have been only one victory recorded during the afternoon: a two-seater out of control east of Houthulst Forest at 5.05pm to Francis Williams of 29 Squadron.

Considering the dangerous nature of groundstrafing and the amount carried out during the day, casualties were light, only two in addition to those mentioned. In a combat over Kruistraat at 8.50am a pilot of 45 Squadron was shot down and taken prisoner by *Jasta 3* and another wounded in the arm.

Ironically from the point of view of ground operations, the weather on October 27 was fine. Operations on the ground were relatively quiet, with the main operations being by the artillery, but there was fierce and hotly contested fighting in the air as the *jagdstaffeln* and *schusta* made determined attacks on the allied troops and batteries.

Fullard was again in action in the morning, attacking a DFW northwest of Roulers at 9.40am. The enemy machine went down in a left hand spiral and crashed into trees lining a road. Thirty minutes later Fullard attacked a mixed formation of DFWs and AEG GIVs over Becelaere and shot down another DFW that was seen to crash by 2nd Army AA batteries.

The Camels of 45 Squadron saw an RE8 under attack by enemy scouts and went to its assistance. Frew attacked an Albatros at the rear of the enemy formation, which broke up under his fire, but he then saw a Camel, 3 to 4,000 feet below him, going down smoking under attack by three of the Albatri. Frew dived to the aid of the Camel and shot one of its attackers down in flames, to crash at Becelaere. However, Frew was too late to save his squadron companion, 2Lt C Phillips, who was shot down and killed, possibly by *Ltn* Kuke of *Jasta 33* who claimed a Sopwith single-seater at Dadizeele at 11.25(GT). John Firth shot down another of the Albatri, which crashed in flames northeast of Comines.

A patrol from 56 Squadron took off at 10.40am. A mile southwest of Roulers two formations of enemy fighters were seen: two Pfalz D.IIIs below the SE5 formation and six Albatri above them. Four of the SE5s, led by Bowman, dived on the two Pfalz, leaving the remainder of the Flight to deal with the Albatri above. Bowman forced one of the Pfalz down in a spiral but although he followed it down to 1,000 feet he could not get in a position to get in any more shots; to hit a spiralling aeroplane is extremely difficult. Bowman left the Pfalz and climbed back into the fight, but before he reached it the Albatri had all cleared east. Bowman reformed the SE5s and they climbed to 11,000 feet. Rhys Davids was not with the formation; he had last been seen diving east after the enemy scouts. Bowman and his Flight later outclimbed a formation of seven Albatri and attacked them two miles west of Iseghem. Bowman's opponent turned over onto its back then went down for a considerable distance before spinning. The other SE5s pilots were unlucky, the Albatri quickly scattering under the attack and diving away east.

Rhys Davids did not return. At first there was no anxiety, for as Bowman later recalled, 'it would have to be a damned good Hun to get RD.' But as the day progressed and there was still no word, it was obvious that Rhys Davids was down on the other side and he was posted as missing in action. He had been shot down and killed at Polterrjeberg by *Ltn* Gallwitz, acting *Staffelführer* of *Jasta B,* for his 4th victory.[13]

The loss of Rhys Davids was a great blow to 56 Squadron. He had been with the squadron since its arrival in France and was one of its finest pilots, with 25 victories to his credit. He was also well known and popular throughout the RFC in general and his loss was keenly felt.[14]

In its third patrol of the day, Naval 10 attacked six Albatros scouts of *Jasta 35* to the northeast of Dixmude at 1.20pm. Curtis attacked one scout that was eventually shot down by FltSubLt K Stratton, but FltSubLt G Morang was shot down in flames, possibly by *Vzfw* Knocke of the *Jasta,* who claimed a Camel at 2.30pm(GT) northwest of Dixmude.

A very large-scale fight developed over Roulers at 1.40pm. Thirteen Camels of 28 Squadron were fighting with 14 Albatros scouts when Camels from 70 Squadron also joined in the combat. Lt James Mitchell shot down one of the Albatri out of control before sending another down in flames, and 2Lt A Cooper claimed another Albatros out of control. Capt F H Laurence of 70 Squadron claimed an Albatros out of control and shared in the destruction of another with five other pilots

from his squadron. Seventy Squadron were in full squadron strength during the fight and lost a pilot killed, another taken prisoner and Capt Cedric Jones was wounded. Jones later recalled.

'The patrol had started off at 1.15pm. It was a full offensive patrol, led by the CO Major Nethersole, who climbed at full throttle and never did allow the rear formations to get into position. Consequently we were an easy target for the numerous hostile aircraft, as we were spread out all over the sky. I was soon separated from the patrol and found myself the attention of four Albatros scouts. Two were in my rear and slightly higher; one was lower, but also in my rear, while a yellow/green chap was almost on my tail. My pressure tank was shot through, the right gun jammed after a bullet had hit the ammunition box, I was wounded in the arm, and finally, soaked in petrol. Things began to look very bad indeed. Why the Hun didn't finish me off I do not know, for he had me cold. But I was fortunate and got down in one piece, and that evening I was on a hospital train on my way home.'[15]

It was an unlucky day for 60 Squadron. Two Flights, led by Capt F Selous took off at 12.50pm and were attacked by a large number of enemy scouts. In their first attack the enemy pilots shot down Lt William Sherwood, whose SE5 burst into flames and crashed on the German side between Moorslede and Dadizele.

In other combats, Herbert Drewitt of 23 Squadron; FltLt Minifie of Naval 1; Huskinson of 19 Squadron; and Capt A Fellows of 43 Squadron all claimed victories, but casualties had been heavy. A Spad pilot of 19 Squadron was wounded in action and taken POW. A pilot of 28 Squadron was also taken prisoner; a pilot of 43 Squadron was killed, another wounded, and a third forced to land; another Camel casualty was from 45 Squadron, with a pilot killed; a Pup of 54 Squadron was shot up and forced to land, and a pilot of Naval 1 was wounded in the arm.

During the day, 65 Squadron, equipped with Sopwith Camels, arrived in France and were stationed at La Lovie under the command of 11th Wing, II Brigade.

October 28 was still fine but there was a dense fog over the Front Lines and little work was possible by the corps squadrons.

It was again a bad day for 60 Squadron, two pilots, both Captains, were lost. C Flight from the squadron were in combat with Albatri in the vicinity of Westroosebeke at 9.30am and although Lt William Rutherford sent one down out of control and saw another also go down, Capt G Temperley, who had been posted to the squadron as a flight commander, was wounded in the foot and force landed near Poperinghe The SE5s managed to extricate themselves from the Albatri, but ten minutes later Capt John Caunter, possibly forced down low by the Albatri, was shot down and killed by small arms fire from the ground.

Bowman, leading C Flight, 56 Squadron, fell for the classic decoy trap on the morning patrol, although to give Bowman his due it was a trap with a difference. A single Pfalz D III was seen – the bait – flying below two Albatri. Bowman dived on the Pfalz, leaving the rest of the Flight to tackle the two Albatri. After a burst from Bowman's guns the Pfalz dived away, but Bowman did not follow: he had seen another fifteen enemy scouts diving on the rest of his Flight. The trap had been double baited. Bowman climbed back into the fight.

Richard Maybery, who had attacked one of the initial Albatri, had stoppages in both guns and as he climbed away to clear them he saw the additional Albatri coming down into the fight. One attacked Maybery, but the others stayed up. The Albatros, which had a tailplane painted in dark green and black stripes, overshot Maybery, who got in a good burst into it as it went by. The other Albatri now began to come down. Maybery dived to rejoin the other SE5s and they flew under a patrol of Bristol Fighters, causing the enemy scouts to sheer off and fly east. The black and green tailplaned Albatros was seen to crash near Dadizele by pilots of 2nd Brigade.

Apart from 60 Squadron's losses, the only other casualty for the fighter squadrons in the day was an SE5 from 84 Squadron whose pilot was taken POW.

The weather was fine and bright on October 29. A morning patrol by 56 Squadron saw a great deal of fighting. After an indecisive combat with enemy scouts, Muspratt, who had been leading the patrol, found himself alone. Undeterred, he continued to attack the enemy scouts: 'the EA split up and did not show much fight.' One of the Albatri, with a streamer on each elevator, dived away. Muspratt followed and fired a burst from his Vickers into it from very close range. The Albatros made a violent turn, the left hand side of its tailplane crumpled up and it went down through the clouds, where Muspratt lost sight of it.

Maxwell Coote, leading the Flight in Muspratt's absence, took them down to attack three Albatri. Coote picked his opponent, closed to within fifty yards and fired a long burst from both guns. The enemy scout turned over onto its back and 'floated' down inverted with periodical sideslips, disappearing into the clouds at 7,000 feet. This was confirmed by Lt Harry Slingsby. Muspratt then rejoined the patrol and they returned to Estrée Blanche.

Bowman took out the next patrol at 3.00pm. Over the Menin to Roulers road he saw a Spad attacking four enemy scouts. There was another formation of enemy scouts flying above the four and Bowman led the SE5s down to assist the Spad, flown by Lt Lovell Baker of 23 Squadron. Bowman

fired at a Pfalz, which stalled and fired up at him, and Bowman zoomed away to avoid a collision. Capt Phillip Cowan, who had joined the squadron two days before, and who had followed Bowman down, got a burst of 15 rounds into the Pfalz before it dived away under its *Jasta* companions. Bowman followed the Pfalz down and saw it crash just north of the railway line on the north side of Moorslede. The enemy scout attacked by Baker spun down past Bowman, but he was too preoccupied in watching his own Pfalz to see if Baker's also crashed. Although Bowman had seen only one Spad attacking the lower formation of enemy scouts, they had been taken into the fight by Capt J McAlery, who also claimed an Albatros out of control and witnessed Baker's Pfalz crash and burst into flames.

FltLt Kinkead of Naval 1 attacked an Albatros over Gheluveldt at 5.15pm. The light was bad and Kinkead closed to within 15 yards before opening fire. The Albatros went down out of control, possibly *Ltn d Res* Fritz Berkemeyer of *Jasta 27*, shot down in flames over Zandvoorde, although Kinkead made no mention of flames.

There were three casualties during the day. In a fight over Houthem at 11.35am a Nieuport from 1 Squadron was seen going down with seven enemy scouts on its tail. 2Lt A W Maclaughlin was shot down and killed, possibly by *Ltn* Buckler of *Jasta 17*.

A pilot from 43 Squadron was also killed in the morning. 2Lt C Harriman's Camel crashed behind the British Lines and was completely wrecked. The third casualty for the fighter squadrons was a DH5 of 41 Squadron. 2Lt Frederick Clark was last seen at 7.45am, flying west over Bullecourt. He was hit by fire from *Flakbatterie 711* and forced to land north of Noyelles to be taken prisoner.

On the morning of October 30 the ground offensive was resumed with the objective of capturing the village of Passchendaele. At 5.50am, when the troops began their attack, the sky was clear, but rain had set in by 10.00am. German aircraft took little interest in the ground fighting, made no attempts to molest the aeroplanes of the corps squadrons, and the patrols of the fighter squadrons – just over a hundred were flown – met with little opposition.

At 9.00am over Westroosebeke a patrol from 1 Squadron led by Fullard dived on three Albatros scouts sporting black fuselages with white bands – *Jasta 26*. Fullard singled out the leading Albatros and fired half a drum into it. The enemy scout went down to crash just north of Westroosebeke, but in the fighting the *staffelführer* of *Jasta 26*, *Oblt* Loerzer, killed 2Lt E Scott for his 20th victory.

Although the RFC communiqué for the day records that machines of 5th Brigade had 19 combats, only Lts D Hilton and D Robertson of 29 Squadron claimed victories, each claiming a two-seater down out of control, Hilton's victory being east of Houthulst Forest at 10.30am. Capt. J McAlery was the only other casualty, wounded in the foot.

In the ground fighting the Canadians had reached the outskirts of Passchendaele village, but the advance further to the north was frustrated by the swampy ground.

The next morning dawned bright and clear and there was a large amount of fighting in the air.

The first patrol from 56 Squadron saw a great deal of action – with both enemy two-seaters and scouts – but with no positive results, although Hoidge caused a two-seater to turn sharply to escape his fire and turn upside down. A shell bursting under the tail of his SE5 then distracted Hoidge's attention from the fate of this machine. A little later Maybery was attacking a two-seater when nine enemy scouts arrived. One came down to attack the Maybery who wisely retreated west. The Albatros pilot chased after him, but in doing so lost a great deal of height and Maybery led him under a naval triplane. The Albatros pilot saw his danger and turned east, but Maybery attacked him, pulling down his Lewis gun to fire upwards into the Albatros, which went down with smoke pouring from it. This was possibly *Uffz* Reinhold of *Jasta 24s* who was wounded in action over Houthulst at 10.45am.

B Flight from 56 Squadron was also in action. Keith Muspratt forced a two-seater down until both he and the enemy machine were under a 1,000 feet and the two-seater finally spiralled into the ground, hitting a row of trees near Stadenberg. Muspratt later wrote in a letter home. 'I was about three miles over and came back at great speed and nothing touched my machine at all.'

In the afternoon, Hoidge again took out A Flight, reinforced by SE5s from C Flight. Both Flights attacked a formation of eight enemy scouts a mile south west of Roulers and a furious fight developed. Hoidge and Lt Johnston each sent an Albatros down out of control, but Maybery had seen two other enemy formations approaching; breaking off his combat he zoomed away for extra height. The leader of the arriving enemy scouts dived into the lower fight. Maybery got behind him and opened fire from close range, but both his guns stopped after a few shots and the Albatros pilot dived away. The lower fight had now been broken off and Maybery was alone, the other SE5s no longer in sight, and he broke off the action. Later, while still alone, six enemy scouts passed under his SE5 and Maybery went down to attack them, firing at the leader flying a red and yellow Albatros. The enemy pilot turned under Maybery and evaded his fire. Maybery, who had zoomed away, dived again and attacked a black and light blue Albatros, whose pilot made the mistake of diving straight down. Maybery followed, fired a burst from both guns at 30 yards range and the Albatros continued down with its engine full on. Maybery, determined to finish this Albatros, followed it down, unwisely got below its Jasta companions, and they all dived to attack him. Maybery steepened his dive to get clear and saw the black and blue Albatros hit the ground in a large field, close by a hedge. Maybery was now very low and the pilot of the black and yellow Albatros hit his SE5 in the petrol tank, stopping the engine. Maybery went even lower, pursued both by the black and yellow Albatros and one other. With no engine, Maybery realised that he would have to land, and thinking it hardly judicious to land in the same field as his victim, the black and blue Albatros, looked for a more suitable spot. As he neared the ground, however, he remembered his emergency fuel tank, forgotten in the heat of the engagement. He turned it on, and his engine restarted. Putting the nose of his SE5 down even further, he contour chased back to the lines, crossing them between Messines and Ypres and landing at 1 Squadron's aerodrome at Bailleul.

There had been five casualties in the fighter squadrons. Lt H New of 3 Squadron had been shot down and killed for the squadron's first casualty on Sopwith Camels; two pilots of 23 Squadron had been shot down and taken prisoner in a fight with *Jasta 36;* one pilot of 84 Squadron had been killed in action and another, shot down wounded and made POW, later died of his wounds.

With the end of October the weather would deteriorate still further bringing a relative slackening to the fighting in the air, a welcome respite for the squadrons of the RFC.

NOTES
1. After the loss of Fokker Triplanes FI 102/17 and FI 103/17 in September, German records indicate that no other Fokker Triplanes arrived at the Front until *Jasta 11* received six 'about the middle of October.' In addition to the sightings by Rhys Davids and Muspratt on October 2 – and surely Rhys Davids would recognise the type after his long fight with Voss flying 103/17 ten days previously – combat reports in late September and early October of several allied pilots indicate that there were other Fokker Triplanes at the Front at the beginning of October or even at the end of September 1917.
2. Interview with author.
3. Loerzer, a close friend of Hermann Göring, had scored 44 victories by the end of the war. In the World War II he rose to the rank of *Generaloberst* in the *Luftwaffe*, and died in 1960.

4. *Ltn* Billik of *Jasta 7* was wounded in action during the day.
5. 1 Squadron had converted to Nieuports and started work as a scout squadron on February 15 1917. Reeves victory over Wagner brought the Squadron's total of victories shot down since that date to 200.
6. Allen was the last Sopwith Pup casualty of 46 Squadron before the squadron was re-equipped with Sopwith Camels.
7. This was Rhys Davids' 25th and last victory.
8. *Ltn* Bellen of *Jasta 10* was severely wounded on October 11.
9. Sowery was one of three brothers to fly in the war. On the night of 23 September 1916 he had destroyed Zeppelin L 32 and was awarded a DSO. Sowery remained in the RAF after the war, reached the rank of Group Captain and finally retired in 1940. He died in 1969.

10. The remains of the LVG, from *FlAbt 8,* were given the designation G 81. The crew were *Oblt* Ernst Hädich and *Flg* Heinrich Horstmann.

11. This Rumpler (G 84) was from *FlAbt 5,* crewed by *Ltn* Hans Laito and *Uffz* Richard Hiltweis.

12. Cross and Cockade International Journal, Vol 11, No.4.

13. Arthur Rhys Davids has no known grave and is commemorated on the Arras Memorial. Rhys Davids and his most famous opponent, Werner Voss, both lie in complete obscurity, a little under five miles apart.

14. For a full account of the life of Rhys Davids see *Brief Glory*, by Alex Revell, Kimber, London 1984.

15. Cross and Cockade International Journal, Vol 7 No.3.

CHAPTER SIXTEEN

CAMBRAI

The first day of November was a day of low clouds, mist and rain. There was to be very little flying by the fighter squadrons for eight days, but some victories were gained. In afternoon patrols, 60 Squadron claimed three victories. W J Rutherford and Soden attacked a two-seater over Moorslede at 1.45pm and shot it down out of control. Twenty-five minutes later they caught another over the same area and sent it down, also out of control. Lt Graham Young also claimed a victory – an Albatros out of control over Houthulst at 2.30pm.

November 3 saw an unfortunate casualty. Returning from an otherwise uneventful patrol, Capt E Bath of 1 Squadron was fired at by British troops and wounded in the foot.

On November 4, Henry Maddocks and 2Lt S J Schooley of 45 Squadron shared in the destruction of an Albatros north of Dixmude at 1.50pm, possibly *Ltn Kieckhafer* of *Jasta 29* who was slightly wounded but remained with the *Jasta*. This was the last victory for 54 squadron before their Sopwith Pups were replaced by Camels.

Naval 10 flew four patrols during the day but only the third, at 1.25pm, saw any decisive action, fighting seven enemy scouts to the northeast of Dixmude. William Curtis closed to close range and fired 150 rounds into one scout, driving it down before attacking another, which was later seen standing on its nose near the river Ijzer.

On patrol on the morning of November 5, 60 Squadron engaged six Albatri a mile north of Westroosebeke. Harold Hamersley attacked an Albatros with a yellow fuselage and sent it down to crash in a wood at 12.10pm. Twenty minutes earlier, John Firth of 45 Squadron had also claimed an Albatros out of control in a combat over Poelcappelle, but a member of the patrol, 2Lt R G Frith had been shot down and taken POW, possibly the victim of either *Vzfw* Bäumer of *Jasta B* or *Vzfw* Wüsthoff of *Jasta 4,* both of whom claimed a Camel at the time and place of the loss of Frith.

FltSubLt A Cameron of Naval 10 claimed an Albatros out of control northwest of Dixmude but his Camel was badly shot about in the combat and he forced landed at Droglandt.

Sixty Squadron pilots claimed more victories on November 6. Over Polygon Wood at 8.40am, Lt William Duncan, who had lost the rest of the patrol in the clouds, saw a DFW below him. Duncan went down to attack the enemy machine and although a burst from the observer's gun hit his SE5 in the oil pump, Duncan forced it down and it was seen to crash by pilots of 1 Squadron. Duncan attempted to fly back to his aerodrome, but his oil-starved engine finally seized and he was forced to land in a ploughed field. A little over an hour previously, over Zonnebeke at 7.30am, Soden and Rutherford of the squadron had had no difficulty in destroying a two-seater.

In the morning the Canadian troops had resumed their attacks, finally capturing Passchendaele and the high ground to the north and northwest of the village. Conditions over the battlefront were atrocious, with low clouds and mist severely hampering air support by the corps squadrons. Many of the fighter pilots, flying low over the fighting, had difficulty in seeing exactly where they were, but they constantly machine gunned the enemy infantry, firing over 11,000 rounds in the course of the day. 2Lt E Olivier of 19 Squadron, completely lost in the clouds, landed and asked a French labourer if there were any French or English troops about. 'No, only Germans,' was the answer. Olivier hurriedly took off again.

Four Sopwith Camel pilots from 3 Squadron were also victims of the atrocious conditions. The Flight became hopelessly lost. Realising that not only were they flying north, but that the strong westerly wind was also pushing them further east into German held territory, the four pilots landed to discover that they were near Namur, nearly 100 miles east of their patrol area and well behind the German Lines. One of the Camels had engine trouble and refused to restart, but the remaining three took off again, flying due west for friendly territory. The weather conditions had now worsened and after flying for sometime, and beginning to run out of fuel, they landed again, to find themselves near Rheims, over ninety miles south of Namur. All three pilots were taken prisoner. The pilot left behind at Namur, 2Lt T Bruce, burned his Camel, mingled with the local people, and went on the run, eventually escaping to Holland.

A pilot from 1 Squadron, 2Lt F Baker, was last seen over Passchendaele, flying west, but it was later found that he had been taken prisoner. No German pilot claimed him so Baker was also possibly a victim of the weather.

Three pilots were lost from 65 Squadron, the squadron's first combat casualties. In an early morning patrol, 2Lt Cutbill fell victim to either *Vzfw* Bäumer or *Ltn* Plange of *Jasta B,* before 8,00am, and a later patrol, flying over Ypres in the mist at 10.50am, were also attacked by *Jasta B: Ltn* Böhme and Bassenge both claiming Camels in the area and at the time. Other casualties were two pilots killed in action: one from 29 Squadron, the other from 19 Squadron.

The fighter squadrons had no casualties on November 7, but FltCom Richard Munday of Naval 8 shot down a balloon north of Meurchin, in the half light, at ten minutes past six, and Frank Gorringe of 70 Squadron shot down a two-seater south east of Houthulst Forest at 7.20am.[1]

The morning of November 8 was fine and there was a great deal of fighting during the day. Naval 8 scored early, at 8.20am, when Robert Compston destroyed an Albatros over Oppy for his eleventh victory. Albert Carter of 19 Squadron was also successful in a morning patrol, destroying a two-seater south of Gheluvelt at 9.25am for the third of his eventual 29 victories.

B Flight of 56 Squadron left Estrée Blanche at 8.45am. The Flight attacked six black and white Albatri over Moorslede and Lt Felix Cobbold was shot down in the fight and taken prisoner of war by *Ltn* Fritz Loerzer of *Jasta 26*. Henry Coote's SE5 was hit in the radiator and he was forced to land. Five minutes after the B Flight had taken off, C Flight left to patrol the area of Roulers-Menin. Bowman attacked a two-seater, escorted by an Albatros, but without success. The rest of the SE5s were slow in following him down and Lt Phillip Cowan was last seen over Comines under attack from an enemy scout. He was shot down and killed by *Ltn* Habler of *Jasta 26*.

Lt James Child of 45 Squadron destroyed a Junkers J I over Westroosebeke at 10.25am; at the same time 2Lt Peter Carpenter destroyed a two-seater south of Passchendaele. In an afternoon patrol by 45 Squadron, Lt Thomas Williams shot an Albatros down in flames over Westroosebeke at 4.05pm

and five minutes later he and Lt Firth each shot down an Albatros over Houthulst Forest.

The pilots of 60 Squadron also had a successful day. At 11.00am Capt Selous shot the wings off a two-seater from *Fl Abt (A) 202*, which crashed near Klein Zillebeke, killing the crew, *Vfzw* Willibald Steinicke and *Ltn* Horst Brassel, who were buried by troops of the 8th Battalion South Lancashire Regiment. 2Lt 'Poppy' Pope led an afternoon patrol from the squadron and shot down a two-seater over Gheluwe at 3.10pm, following this success twenty minutes later by shooting down another over Ypres, both victories being confirmed by ground observers. Capt Hamersley destroyed an Albatros at 3.40pm over Westroosebeke and Lt Rutherford drove another down out of control in the same action.

In the afternoon Capt William Molesworth of 29 Squadron was leading his Flight over Westroosebeke when he attacked a formation of 15 Albatri, shooting down the one at the rear of the formation to crash in flames east of the village at 3.15pm. Three quarters of an hour later he caught a pair of two-seaters over Houthulst Forest and shot one down, also in flames. Lt J G Coombe attacked the remaining two-seater and drove it down over Houthulst.

Other victories during the day were claimed by 2Lt Koch of 70 Squadron and Capt T Hunter of 66 Squadron. Capt R Child and Lt F Brown of 84 Squadron shared in a victory over an Albatros east of Poelcappelle, but two pilots from the squadron were lost in the fight: one killed and the other wounded and taken POW by *Jasta 36*. 2Lt E G Macleod of 46 Squadron scored the squadron's first Camel victory with an Albatros out of control over Cambrai.

A pilot of 19 Squadron was killed in action over Houthem and a pilot of 60 Squadron forced to land west of Poelcappelle, his SE5 badly shot up during a combat.

Weather conditions were again bad of November 9. Capt Albert Carter, leading a Flight of 19 Squadron Spads attacked five enemy scouts near Zuidhoek, and Lt Claude Thompson destroyed an Albatros at 10.00am. Half an hour later, over Zandvoorde, Carter saw an RE8 being attacked by an Albatros and he drove the enemy scout down out of control. Carter followed this success by driving a two-seater down south of Gheluvelt. Six other victories were claimed during the day by pilots of 1, 29 and 70 Squadrons. Two pilots were taken POW, one from 54 Squadron, the other from Naval 8. And two Nieuports of 29 Squadron were shot up, the pilots forced to land.

It rained all day of November 10 and there was little flying. No victories were recorded and the only casualty was a pilot of 24 Squadron whose DH5 was badly damaged by ground fire, forcing him to land behind the British lines.

On the ground the infantry attacked in heavy rain, extending their gains northwards of Passchendaele village. The fighting was extremely bitter for these last few acres of ground and lasted until late in the afternoon. As the last of the daylight faded the last shots of the bloody battles of Passchendaele of 1917 were fired. The carnage had been appalling. The British dead and missing numbered 80,000; the German, 50,000. Two hundred and thirty thousand British troops had been wounded and 113,000 German. The British had taken 14,000 prisoners and the Germans 37,000. In addition, 50,000 French troops were lost to the north of Ypres. The plan to liberate sections of the Belgian coast had long been abandoned. The sacrifices had been made for gains of just under an average depth of three miles on a seven-mile front.

A Camel pilot, Lt Guy Knocker, serving with 65 Squadron, gives an evocative picture of the Ypres Salient seen from the air during the winter of 1917.

'Between the ruins of Armentières in the south and Passchendaele in the north, lay a strip some 15 miles long and 10 miles broad of sheer and utter desolation. The water filled shell holes appeared to touch each other, like the cells in some monstrous honeycomb or like the hoofprints in a muddy farm gateway in a wet winter. Woods, field, roads, villages and even trenches were blotted out. Only the blur of what had once been Ploegsteert Wood and the Forest of Houthulst showed up dark against the muddy mosaic, and the Jew's harp of the Etang de Zillebeke shone with a metallic brightness when the light caught it. Sitting aloft in the cold, clean air, it was hard to believe that thousands of men were actually living in that abomination. In the morning after a fall of snow, you could always tell where there had been a "strafe" the night before because the shells had blackened and sullied the pure white of the ground. Sometimes in the evening, the jagged ruins of Ypres would flush with a warm, yellow light and away to the east, Menin and Roulers with their German fighter aerodromes showed up like menacing shadows. Kite balloons hung motionless along the Yser Canal and always, nearly always, the wind blew from the west … Such was the Salient and yet those who served there on the ground or in the air had a sort of wry affection for it and would later have a kind of pride at having fought there.'

Low clouds and rain interfered with activity in the air on November 11. Pope of 60 Squadron, destroyed an Albatros over Gheluwe in the afternoon, and Lts J Candy and A Rice of 19 Squadron claimed an Albatros out of control, also over Gheluwe, at 4.20pm. There was only one fighter casualty: a DH5 of 32 Squadron was badly shot about in combat and forced to land. The pilot was unhurt.

Naval 10 scored the first success on the morning of November 12. At 8.00am a patrol from the squadron sent a two-seater down out of control over Couckelaere, shared between FltLt G Trapp and FltSubLt A Beatie. In the afternoon a two-seater was seen over Forthem, but as the Camels dived to attack it Trapp's Camel was seen to break up and Trapp was killed.

At 12.20pm a patrol of Camels from 43 Squadron, led Major A Dore, attacked four Albatros scouts that were about to attack four British two-seaters east of Annay. Dore shot an Albatros down and Lt Cecil King, assisted by MacLanachan of 40 Squadron, shot down another.

Lt Phillip de Fontenay of 29 Squadron drove a two-seater down east of Houthulst Forest at 2,40pm, and in the late evening Francis Quigley of 70 Squadron shot down an Albatros east of Houthulst Forest for his fourth victory. Lt Oliver Bryson, of 19 Squadron also scored during the day: an Albatros out of control east of Gheluwe at 10.20am. FltSublt J H Forman and Kinkead scored for Naval 1 with a Pfalz D.III shot down in flames over Dixmude at 3.45pm.

Sixty four Squadron had four losses: Lt B Balfour crash landed his Camel after it had been hit in the fuel tank and badly damaged in a combat south of Armentières, possibly by *Ltn* Kroll of *Jasta 24*. Lt K S Morrison from the squadron was last seen after diving on an LVG over Quesnoy. He was apparently wounded by the observer and came down to be taken POW. Morrison was repatriated to Holland, in April 1918. Lt D Scott was killed when his Camel was hit by anti-aircraft fire, and Lt G Pitt was wounded during a patrol.

There were no fighter casualties on November 13. Pat Huskinson of 19 Squadron claimed a two-seater destroyed over Moorslede in the morning and during an afternoon patrol by the squadron Major A Carter and 2Lt Candy shared in the destruction of an Albatros scout north of Comines at 2.45pm. Williams of 45 Squadron destroyed a Junkers J I northwest of Westroosebeke at 11.55am and Henry Moody destroyed another, possibly from the same *Fl Abt*, northeast of Comines at 4.10pm. Bernard Beanlands of 24 Squadron shot down *Flgmt* Heinze of *Marine-Feldjagdstaffel 2* over Schoorbakke at 12.30pm. Heinze was taken POW and his Albatros D.III given the number G 89. An American pilot, D'Arcy Hilton of 29 Squadron, claimed an Albatros out of control north of Roulers at noon.

In the early afternoon, a Flight of Camels from Naval 9 caught a formation of Albatri over Pervyse and FltCom Joseph Fall and FltSubLt Arthur Wood shared in the destruction of one of the enemy scouts.

There was a thick ground mist on November 14 and there was no flying, but the next day saw a great deal of hotly contested fighting.

The pilots of 65 Squadron gained their first victories, but had their first casualty. In a fight with enemy scouts over

Dadizele at 7.40am Lts George Cox and Harry Symons each claimed an Albatros out of control, but 2Lt T Morgan was shot down and captured by *Vzfw* Esswein of *Jasta 26.*

A patrol of Camels from 45 Squadron were on patrol in the morning. A Rumpler was seen north east of Houthulst Forest at 9.10am and Peter Carpenter shot it down to crash. Twenty-five minutes later the Camels were endeavouring to attack a large formation of 15 enemy scouts, which seemed anxious to avoid a fight, when they were attacked by another seven Albatri which dived on them from out of the sun. In the fighting, 2Lt K Montgomery shot an Albatros down in flames, which broke into pieces as it went down to crash at Langemarck,[2] 2Lt E Hand sent another down out of control, which was seen to burst into flames lower down and crash at Poelcappelle by pilots of 32 Squadron. While these actions were being fought, another patrol from 45 Squadron, led by Capt Firth, were in action further south, fighting four Albatri near Comines, Firth shooting one down out of control east of the town for his last victory in France.

Major Carter and Eric Olivier of 19 Squadron shared in the destruction of an Albatros over Zandvoorde at 10.15am. Just before noon, Fullard, leading a patrol of 1 Squadron Nieuports, was just about to lead them down on a pair of two-seaters over Zandvoorde when they were attacked by eight Albatros scouts. Fullard shot one of the enemy scouts off a Nieuport's tail and the Albatros went down and crashed. Fullard then quickly engaged another Albatros, getting onto its tail and firing three quarters of a Lewis gun drum into it. One wing broke off the Albatros and it broke up in mid air. These were Fullard's last victories of his total of 40.[3] 2Lt Lumsden Cummings also claimed an Albatros out of control from this fight, but 2Lt C E Ogden's Nieuport was badly damaged and he was forced to land.

The *Luftstreitkräfte* suffered a heavy blow on November 15. *Ltn* Hans Ritter von Adam, the *Staffelführer* of *Jasta 6* and a 21-victory ace, was shot down and killed at 9.20am (German time, one hour ahead of British time) northwest of Kortewilde. Air historians have credited Adam to Lt Montgomery of 45 Squadron, but although the general area fits, the time of the 45 Squadron combat at 9.30am (BT) an hour later, does not. Other historians have given Lt G Cox of 65 Squadron as Adam's victor, but again, although the area is good the time – 7.40am (BT) – is still some forty minutes before Adam's crash. In his post war memoirs *An Airman Remembers,* Ltn Hans Schröder, a German air intelligence officer, compounds the confusion over Adam's loss. 'That was on November 15th, 1917. Three days later I had a talk with an English boy, who was shot down on his third flight. He was badly wounded, but he told me about his victory and the place and hour tallied exactly. I informed him who his victory was. "Oh, is that so"

he answered, and a gleam lit up his face. "He was an ass (sic)! Oh! I see" And a few hours later he was dead.'

Schröder's account begs two questions: why would a badly wounded pilot volunteer that he had shot down a German pilot – hardly the way to win any sympathy from his captors – and why was Schröder willing to accept that Adam had been brought down by a novice pilot. In addition, the young English pilot could not have been Cox, who was never a casualty and finished the war as a Captain with six victories, and there are no RFC casualties on or around November 18 that fit with Schröder's account. A further complication of Adam's death is that although the wreckage of his Albatros was quickly found, his body was not. Kortewilde itself was very near the front line trenches; north *west* of the village, the site of Adam's crash, would have been even nearer the front line fighting. Yet Schröder states that his comrades made a long and futile search,' before Adam's body was discovered, three days later, some distance from the wreckage, and under a bush, stripped naked of all his clothing.

The pilots of Naval 10 were also in action in the morning. A and C Flights attacked ten enemy aircraft near Keyem at 12.45pm. Curtis claimed one Albatros scout down out of control, and Manuel claimed another driven down and seen to crash. A quarter of an hour later FltSubLt A M Alexander attacked a two-seater west of Dixmude and wounded or killed the gunner, driving the enemy machine down until he lost sight of it in the cloud. Maund also attacked this two-seater, and at 4,000 feet saw it still falling out of control, very near the ground. Hall had attacked an Albatros and sent it down but then had engine trouble and force landed.

In a fight south east of Dixmude between a patrol of 24 Squadron and Albatri, four of the 24 Squadron pilots each claimed an Albatros out of control and another damaged.

Nineteen Squadron had a pilot wounded during the day and another forced to land. Twenty Nine Squadron had two pilots taken POW, one also being wounded, and a pilot of 70 Squadron was killed in action.

Very little flying was possible on November 16 owing to low clouds and mist. Although these conditions persisted until November 22, flying was resumed on November 18.

John Macrae of 23 Squadron was the first to claim a victory during the day: a two-seater south of Westroosebeke at 7.00am. Olivier of 19 Squadron shot down a two-seater over Passchendaele at 10.45am and in the afternoon his CO, Major Carter, shot down an Albatros C type at 3.30pm south of Passchendaele. Capt Harry Reeves, a flight commander in 1 Squadron, claimed a DFW out of control over Becelaere at 8.15am for his last of 13 victories, and Chidlaw-Roberts and Hamersley of 60 Squadron shared in the destruction of a DFW north west of Westroosebeke at 11.45am.

Fifty Six Squadron, which had been transferred to 13 Wing for the coming Cambrai offensive and stationed at Laviéville, flew its first patrol from its new base. McCudden, leading B Flight, took the SE5s from Albert 'up the main road to Bapaume.' The object of the patrol was to learn the disposition of the front line trenches, but while over Ronssoy McCudden saw a DFW C V flying west. Orders were not to cross the front lines, but the opportunity was too good to miss. McCudden got behind the DFW and opened fire with both guns. The DFW's engine stopped, the enemy gunner disappeared inside the fuselage and the enemy machine went down in a steep glide. The enemy pilot attempted a downwind landing, misjudged his speed, ran into a trench at high speed and crashed in a shower of chalky earth at Bellicourt, four miles behind the German Lines, completely wrecking the DFW. The time was 9.20am.

There were two casualties: a pilot of 19 Squadron was forced to land after a combat north of Ypres and 23 Squadron had a pilot killed over Passchendaele. 'Poppy' Pope of 60 Squadron, flying with Chidlaw-Roberts and Hamersley in the attack on the DFW in the morning, had his propeller smashed by a bullet from the observer's gun and was seen to crashland in a pond near St Julian by pilots of 23 Squadron. Pope was reported missing, but he had been pulled out of the 'pond' – a water-filled mine crater – by Canadian troops, who had taken him to a nearby pillbox which was being used as a battalion HQ. Being too busy to attend to Pope, they had passed him a china mug full of rum, which he promptly drank, much to the disgust of the Canadians whose rum ration it was. Pope then passed out. It was twenty-four hours before he telephoned the squadron to tell them he was safe, finally arriving back with his arms full of champagne. He had sustained a slight leg wound and was sent to hospital at Rouen.[4]

There was little flying the next day, November 19. Only four victories were claimed and only one casualty, a pilot of 32 Squadron wounded.

Cambrai – a missed opportunity

Haig, conscious of the failure of the Ypres offensives, the mutinies in the French army, and the generally unfavourable results of the year, now needed a successful offensive, however small, to set against the failures of the past months. Cambrai seemed to hold hope of this. The Third Army, under General Julian Byng was fresh and the country around Cambrai was hard, ideal for the use of tanks, which had become bogged down in the mud of Flanders. Haig had not the resources for a large scale offensive – these had been squandered in the Ypres battles. His objective at Cambrai was for a purely local success and he set a limit of 48 hours for the initial objectives to be taken. If these had not been achieved the offensive would

then be concluded. Allowing the success of the initial breakthrough, Cambrai was to be masked, not captured. Secondly – and this in Haig's view was the more important objective – Bourlon Ridge, the wood and Bourlon village were to be captured. Capture of the ridge was of particular importance as it would provide a superb view of the German back areas throughout the coming winter months.

The front of the attack at Cambrai was the six miles between the villages of Gonnelieu and Havrincourt. Zero hour was to be on the morning of Tuesday, November 20. To achieve complete surprise there was to be no preliminary bombardment. The tanks were to go over the top ahead of the infantry to cut wide access lanes through the enemy's wire, destroy machine gun emplacements and to spread 'general alarm.'

The part to be played by the fighter aircraft of the RFC was considerable. The fighter squadrons of the Thirteenth Army Wing, III Brigade, attached to the Third Army, were reinforced by five squadrons: Nos 3 (Camel), 56 (SE5a), 64 (DH5), 68 (DH5) and 84 (SE5a). The squadrons of I Brigade and 9th Wing were also to be employed in bombing, ground strafing and reconnaissance north of the battlefront.

On the eve of the attack the squadrons of 3rd Brigade alone consisted of 134 single-seater fighters against the 12 Albatros fighters of *Jasta 5*, the only *Jasta* stationed in the immediate area. With the addition of the fighter strength of Tenth Army Wing, I Brigade, and 9th Wing, the allied air forces had an overwhelming superiority in fighter aircraft.

The generally bad weather conditions during the Ypres battles had to a certain extent dictated the tasks undertaken by the fighter squadrons. Regardless of casualties, the value of ground attacks by low flying fighter aeroplanes, both over the battlefield and back areas, and on enemy aerodromes, had been realised. At Cambrai, four fighter squadrons were detailed for bombing and machine gun attacks against enemy troops and machine gun emplacements. As there was to be no counter-battery work, enemy artillery guns were also to be attacked, and detailed and comprehensive plans were drawn up. Camels were also to carry out low flying attacks on six enemy aerodromes. The fighter attacks on the German troops and transport were to begin on an extended front, forty-five minutes after zero hour, to deceive the enemy of the main point of the attack. To facilitate the work of the fighter squadrons, to obviate the pilots having to return to their aerodromes to refuel and rearm, an advanced landing ground was established at Bapaume with ample supplies of petrol, oil and ammunition.

The weather on the morning of November 20 was for once in favour of the British troops. There was very low cloud and a thick mist covered the battlefield. The troops began their attack at ten minutes past six, advancing behind the tanks in the thick mist. The surprise was almost complete – the questioning of prisoners captured the evening before had led the Germans commanders to expect an attack in the morning, but details were vague and there was little time to make detailed plans or warn their troops.

Although the weather conditions suited the ground operations it was very bad for flying, but the Camels of 3 and 46 Squadrons took off to bomb enemy aerodromes at Estourmel, Carnières and Caudry.[5]

At Estourmel, *Oblt* Richard Flashar, the *Staffelführer* of *Jasta 5* had been telephoned at 11pm the previous night, warned that an attack was imminent the next morning, and instructed to have his pilots ready to fly from 7am onwards. It was one of many such warnings, however, all of which had been false alarms, and knowing that in any case the weather would make flying impossible, even if the attack materialised, Flashar ignored the warning and went back to sleep.

Flashar was awakened just before dawn the next morning by the rattling of his window panes and the crash of artillery. This time HQ had been right and the attack was on! But when he and his pilots assembled on the aerodrome in rain and low mist it was obvious that it would be madness to fly. The telephone began to ring continuously, informing him that British tanks and troops were advancing and that British aeroplanes were flying over the battlefront. Why was his *Jasta* not flying? He tried to explain. Even if his pilots took off they would immediately be lost in the thick fog. It would be impossible to find the front lines. Many of his pilots would eventually be forced to land, damaging the only fighter aircraft available to the German Second Army. His objections were not accepted. British airmen were flying. He was ordered to start at once or face a court martial.

Thirty minutes later the pilots of *Jasta 5* were sitting in their cockpits, hoping the weather would improve, when three Camels of 3 Squadron suddenly appeared out of the fog, dropping their bombs and machine-gunning the aerodrome. Two German pilots managed to take off during the attack. *Offstv* Mai shot down one of the Camels and the remaining two hit trees in the fog, killing the pilots.

Camels and Pups of 46 Squadron had also been allocated German aerodromes to attack. Arthur Lee arrived over Estourmel aerodrome fifteen minutes after the attack by the 3 Squadron Camels: 'the German pilots were still angrily buzzing around their bombed aerodrome.' Lee had earlier been attacking batteries of 5.9 guns to the rear of Lateau Wood – his Flight's designated target. Flying extremely low, passing over the advancing tanks and troops, the Camels had reached the rear of the Hindenburg defence system. Here they had to climb a little in order to be able to drop their bombs, but they were immediately into the thick cloud, 'whirling blindly around at

50-100 feet, all but colliding, being shot at from below and trying to place bombs accurately.' Lee located a gun position and dropped his four bombs, one exploding between two of the guns, the others a few feet away. Ground fire splintered the centre section strut of Lee's Camel, fragments hitting him in the face and he dived at another gun, firing 100 rounds. A machine gun then opened fire at the Camel, but Lee located this and silenced it with one short burst. As Lee climbed away, a Camel suddenly appeared out of the mist, missing Lee by a matter of a few feet. This was too dangerous. He climbed to 300 feet, staying for only a moment before going down again, nearly hitting a tree. Suddenly there were no trees, only an open road and Lee flew along it 'trying to get my breath.' He next saw a transport column on the road and made several attacks, machine-gunning along its length, putting limbers and horses into the ditches – 'I'm sorry for the horses though.'

It was now that Lee found himself over Estourmel aerodrome. As he recognised the tents and sheds as those of an aerodrome he was attacked by two Albatri from behind. He fired a burst at one, but his guns jammed and he zoomed into the cloud. When he came out after fifteen minutes he was lost. He circled a large field, but came under attack from a group of German cavalry firing at him from the edge of the field. Lee attacked these, passed over them, and found they came from a sunken road full of transport, and he attacked along its length, stampeding horses and unseating riders. Realising that the road was most probably being used to bring reinforcements up to the fighting at Cambrai, Lee flew along it until he came upon a long line of lorries and marching troops. He machine-gunned these until he ran out of ammunition. Still lost, Lee decided to climb through the clouds. He had no idea of their height, but he came out into brilliant sunshine at 4,000 feet. Flying west for twenty minutes, Lee came down again. The air was clear, but he was still lost. Lee could see a chateau below him and he landed to find that he was near Creil, only thirty-five miles from Paris. He had drifted seventy miles south of the fighting around Cambrai. After more wanderings, Lee finally arrived back at Le Hameau the next afternoon to find he had been promoted to captain and given command of B Flight.

It had been a disastrous day for the low flying Camel and DH5 squadrons. Three Squadron had three pilots killed, two taken POW and three Camels badly shot up and forced to land. 46 Squadron had two pilots wounded and two Camels and a Pup badly shot up and forced to land. Sixty-four Squadron lost two pilots killed, three wounded – one taken POW – and three DH5s had been shot down by fire from the ground, one having a wing blown off. Its fellow DH5 Squadron, 68, lost a pilot taken POW, another died of wounds and four aircraft shot up and forced to land. Small wonder that many commanding officers of the fighter squadrons were reluctant to commit their pilots to ground strafing duties, seeing the gains as relatively unproductive against the possible loss of pilots with hard gained experience and of immense value to their squadron. An experienced and valuable flight commander, his hard won skills of no value at low height, could be shot down by a lucky machine gunner as easily as the most inexperienced member of the Flight. The RFC could ill afford the loss of such pilots.

Oliver Redgate of Naval 9 claimed an Albatros scout destroyed south of Pervyse at 3.00pm, and two enemy aeroplanes were claimed, both out of control, for the only victories on November 20. 2Lt A Cuffe of 32 Squadron claimed one, and the other was claimed by Capt William Mays Fry – now back in France with 23 Squadron as a flight commander – for his first victory since his return.

The ground attack had gone well. The troops had advanced four and a half miles, from Graincourt in the north to Masnières and Lateau Wood in the south, but there had been a delay at Flesquières village, where the tanks had come under heavy fire from field guns and suffered many casualties. The troops outflanked the village, but without the cover afforded by the tanks were held up by uncut wire and machine guns. Pilots of 64 Squadron had successfully bombed and machine-gunned the gun pits at Flesquières in their initial attacks, and on returning found no sign of the guns. They had been moved into the open country behind the ridge and were consequently harder to find. It was from these positions that they had inflicted the heavy tank casualties.

The ground offensive had been heavily dependent upon attacks on German strong points by low flying fighter aircraft, but these been frustrated by the adverse weather conditions during the day. If this support had been possible the situation at Flesquières may have been detected earlier and dealt with. This delay was to be crucial. At the end of the day's fighting it was too dark to allow the cavalry through and the tactically important Bourlon Ridge had not been taken. Casualties, however, for the ground gained, had been light.

Weather conditions the next day were even worse and there was no flying by the fighter squadrons – no doubt to the relief of the pilots. Despite the continuation of the bad weather, flying was resumed on November 22. It was essential that enemy movements were observed and attacked. The Camel and DH5 squadrons again carried out low level attacks on troops, transport and gun emplacements, but luckily there were fewer casualties than on the first day of the battle. Sixty Eight Squadron had a pilot killed and two forced to land, one being injured. Two pilots of 43 Squadron were captured, and a pilot of 3 Squadron was forced to land with a badly shot up Camel. A low patrol by 46 Squadron lost 2Lt T Atkinson, shot down while bombing Bourlon Wood.

A thick fog enveloped 46 Squadron's aerodrome, but assured by Wing that conditions were clearer over the front lines, Lee and 2Lt E G Macleod took off to bomb enemy positions in the wood. Macleod hit a tree on takeoff and crashed, dying of his injuries the next day. Lee flew down the Bapaume road, at one point nearly colliding with a chimneystack, then turned south. Finding conditions a little better here, Lee climbed to 1,500 feet. After firing at a hostile two-seater, which he left to some SE5s which had appeared, Lee went down to 400 feet and dropped his bombs on German batteries outside Bourlon Village, to the north of the wood. After dropping his bombs, Lee continued to attack troops and transport on the roads, finally circling over Fontaine where a fierce fight was taking place for possession of the village. Field grey and khaki were too intricately mixed for Lee to help the British troops. He flew over the village and attacked another group of enemy troops close to a large wood and canal. His guns jammed during this attack and while flying low across the field to rectify them a shell burst directly under his Camel. With his engine badly vibrating and his controls almost gone, Lee forced landed in the nearest field. Some rifle fire was coming from Fontaine, half a mile away, but a machine gun suddenly opened up on Lee from the woods bordering the field. Lee jumped from his Camel and sprinted for the shelter of a sunken road a hundred yards away. Lying in the safety of the road, Lee heard footsteps approaching. Not knowing whether this were friend or foe, he dropped into a 'funk hole.' The footsteps having passed, Lee looked out. It was a wounded Seaforth Highlander, his arm in a sling. Lee walked with the Highlander for a while, who told him that the British troops were being pushed out of Fontaine, German reinforcements having been brought up. A Tommy then appeared and asked Lee to have a few words with his officer, Captain Maxwell of the 9th Royal Scots. Maxwell had seen Lee come down, the machine gun opening up on him, and his sprint for the sunken road, and he and his men had laid bets on whether of not he would make it! Maxwell gave Lee a sip of whisky – 'I needed it' – promised to get a message through to his squadron by field telephone and gave him a runner to get him through to Cantaing village. From the village Lee could see the fighting around Fontaine and his Camel, which was now in the middle of No Man's Land. Later finding himself at an advanced dressing station, Lee helped as a stretcher-bearer, carrying a wounded Seaforth Highlander to a field hospital. The Highlander was heavy and Lee, encumbered by his flying kit, was finding it heavy going. Walking back through British reserve troops going up into the fighting, one approached him. 'Eh, look lads, a bleeding Jerry flier,' said one. 'Bleeding Jerry yourself!', Lee retorted. After a night's sleep in an Brigade Mess, Lee eventually made his way back to the squadron, finally arriving at 9.00pm the next evening, entering the Mess covered in mud, loaded down with souvenirs and too tired to eat.

Lee's experiences were typical of many pilots, but perhaps one of the more remarkable was that of Lt H Taylor of 68 Squadron. Shot down just behind the enemy lines, Taylor scrambled from the wreckage of his DH5. Getting down behind a small mound of earth he opened fire with his revolver at an advancing group of enemy troops, fifty yards away. His squadron companion, Capt G Wilson, saw Taylor's predicament and repeatedly dived on the German troops, scattering them in each attack, which enabled Taylor to each time make short runs back to some British troops. Here he picked up the rifle of a dead infantryman and he and the troops – who had lost their officer – held off the enemy troops. Wilson continued to attack these, but was hit by groundfire, a bullet shattering the tripex glass of his windscreen and flinging the fragments into his eyes. Wilson climbed away, waited until his eyes cleared, then flew back to Bapaume.

Taylor's little force had advanced too far from the main body of British troops, and after he had led them back Taylor left them to return to the advanced landing ground. On the way he found Capt J Bell's machine. Bell had earlier been hit in the chest by ground fire, but had managed to land his DH5 undamaged. With the aid of some troops, Taylor tried to start the DH5, but with no success and he eventually had to make his way back to Bapaume on foot.

Aerial victories were again few during the day. 2Lt L Herbert, of 40 Squadron, recently commissioned, and FltCom Compston, Naval 8, each claimed an enemy machine out of control, Compston's claim an LVG C V at 10.55am over Virty-en-Artois. Lts F G Huxley and Roy Phillipps of 68 Squadron each claimed victories during the fighting above Cambrai: Huxley, an Albatros scout – the first victory for the squadron – and Phillipps a two-seater.

The pilots of 84 Squadron fought several combats. In the first patrol of the day, led by Capt Kenneth Leask, two of the SE5s dropped out with various mechanical troubles. The remainder of the Flight carried on, but Peter Moloney lost touch with Leask in the clouds and was attacked by three Albatri from *Jasta 5*. Moloney was wounded in the backside by a bullet, and the flying wires, radiator and engine of his SE5 were all hit. Moloney managed to escape the Albatri by diving into a cloud, forced land by an AA battery, and was taken to 3rd Canadian Hospital where the bullet was removed.

In the second patrol flown by the squadron, Capt E Pennell, assisted by Lt Beauchamp-Proctor, shot down a balloon over Raillencourt at 8.50am, but in the attack Beauchamp Proctor's SE5 was hit by the balloon's defences and he force landed near Belle Eglise.

The third patrol took off at 10.55am and attacked four Albatros scouts over Bourlon Wood. James Child shot down an Albatros out of control, then turned his attentions to a DFW C V, which he forced down near Flesquières at 11.50am. This machine was from *Fl Abt (A) 269*. And its crew, *Flg* Elser and *Ltn de Res* Steiner volunteered the information that they were stationed at Busigny and had only been at the Front for a month. Their DFW was designated G 91.

Reports came in during the day that Bourlon Wood was strongly held by German forces, aided by low flying enemy aircraft, which were persistently attacking the British troops. Despite the fog at Lealvillers aerodrome making flying almost impossible, 41 Squadron was ordered by Wing to fly offensive patrols in the area of Bourlon Wood to deal with these German aircraft. Taking off, one pilot realised that visibility was so poor that it was useless to continue. Turning back to land he hit a tree, his machine burst into flames and he was killed. Another pilot turned back after twenty minutes. Coming in to land he collided with another SE5 taking off. Both pilots were killed. Lts Arkell and Cushney managed to reach the Cambrai area and were attacked by ten Albatros scouts. Arkell's SE5 was hit in the gravity tank and Cushney was wounded in the arm. Both pilots managed to return to the advanced landing ground at Bapaume, but the undercarriage of Cushney's badly shot up SE5, collapsed on landing and it was completely wrecked.

A later patrol had better luck, Lts L J Maclean, A Isbell and D H Jones driving down a DFW near Nierguies. Russell Winnicott attacked two Albatros scouts southwest of Cambrai, forcing one down, but then had engine trouble. He crashlanded east of Boursies in No Man's Land, and abandoned his SE5, which came under shellfire.

The weather had improved on November 23, the day was fine and clear. At 10.30am the British infantry began attacks on Bourlon Wood and the village of Fontaine-Notre-Dame, closely supported from 10.00am to dusk by low flying fighters of 3, 46, 64 and 68 Squadrons. Aerial fighting was also fierce over Bourlon Wood and Fontaine. On November 22, German air reinforcements had been moved into the area: four *jagdstaffeln* of *Jagdgeschwader Nr 1* – 4, 6, 10 and 11 – led by Manfred von Richthofen, plus *Jasta 15* from the German Seventh Army, were now operating over the fighting.

Flying from the advanced landing ground at Bapaume, which made repeated attacks possible, the pilots of the British fighters could see the results of their co-operation with the tanks and infantry at first hand. In the morning, the DH5s of 68 Squadron could see that an attack by three tanks in one corner of the wood was held up by a German battery of two guns. Lt F Huxley went down to 100 feet and dropped four 25lb bombs, silencing the enemy guns and allowing the tanks to continue their advance. On the left of the wood a German strong point held up the advance of the Royal Irish Rifles for a great deal of the morning. In the afternoon, Lt A Griggs, an American pilot serving with 68 Squadron, made repeated attacks on the position from 50 feet in an attempt to destroy it, but came under heavy fire and was shot down and killed. In addition to Griggs, the squadron had two other casualties. Lt S W Ayres was wounded by groundfire. He managed to land and taxi his DH5 on to a road, but later died of his wounds. Lt L Holden was attacked by enemy scouts but managed to land his badly damaged machine without injury.

Air activity reached its peak at 1.00pm: fifteen aircraft were over the wood and Fontaine village. One of these was Lt J A V Boddy of 64 Squadron. The DH5s of the squadron had left Izel-le-Hameau at twenty minutes to one. As they arrived over the wood it was evident that the battle was going well. Boddy later wrote.

'Above the gaunt shattered tress of the wood itself the scene was indescribable. Out of the fog of smoke and gas, artillery and contact machines loomed from every possible direction. Below there was an inferno of bursting shells and at the edge of the wood a row of tanks appeared to be held up by anti-tank fire. One was blazing furiously. In the hope of being able to help them I searched the wood for these batteries and did my best to silence them with bombs and machine gun fire.'

Boddy then selected another target: a trench filled with enemy troops. 'As I dived down I was treated to the thrilling spectacle of our men actually charging in and taking it at the point of the bayonet. Next I sprayed some reserves coming up from a village in the rear and then turned my attention to the support trenches behind Bourlon Wood which were too fully occupied to miss.'

Fate, however, was about to intervene. Above the smoke of the battle were the Albatros fighters of *Jagdgeschwader Nr 1*. Manfred von Richthofen, in his red Albatros, leading a fighting patrol from *Jagdstaffel 11*, a component of the *Jagdgeschwader*, had earlier taken off from its improvised base at Valenciennes. The aerodrome at Valenciennes, normally the home of a fighter training school, was only a short flight from the Front and the Albatros fighters arrived over Bourlon Wood shortly after 1.00pm. Looking down through the smoke and confusion of the battle below, Richthofen could see the DH5s darting through the shell bursts, seeking out their targets. With his height advantage they were easy prey. Selecting his first opponent he dived and fired, forcing the pilot of the DH5 to make a hasty emergency landing on the shattered ground in the wood. Richthofen's next victim was Boddy. Boddy was flying straight, trying to clear a gun jam, when the red Albatros swept down onto his tail and opened fire.

'What happened after that I am unable to say, but it seems that I was shot down and didn't regain consciousness until I reached a base hospital two or three days later. I do remember seeing some of the red machines from Richthofen's Circus a few thousand feet above, but there were some SE5s up there too, so I left it at that. Evidently one of them, and from the published list of his victories I believe it to have been the Baron himself, got through and on to my tail.'

Richthofen's fire was deadly in its accuracy, smashing into Boddy's aeroplane around the pilot's cockpit. 'A bullet fractured my skull, but subconsciously I must have kept control and tried to land – usually the DH5 being nose-heavy, dropped like a brick if you let go of the stick. I crashed between two trees in the north east corner of the wood and broke both my thighs, one being completely crushed by the engine. I was told afterwards by one of our own pilots, who had had a forced landing near the front line, that he had brought a rescue party out to me under heavy fire and that I was taken back to the dressing station in a tank. In this modest account of this stout effort, which won him the Military Cross, his own words were "I hailed a passing tank, put you in and wished you goodbye and good luck." I don't suppose he ever engaged a queerer conveyance for a friend.'[6]

The pilots of 46 Squadron were also ground-strafing over Bourlon Wood. The a Flight Commander, Capt Charles Courtneidge was wounded, but managed to land his badly shot about Camel at the advanced landing ground. 2Lt C Odell was attacked by enemy scouts, his Camel badly damaged and he crashlanded. Odell, who was unhurt, was claimed by *Vzfw* Rumey of *Jasta 5*. Lt H Robinson was also forced to land near Fontaine, his Camel badly shot about and Lt R Ferrie returned to Bapaume, his machine damaged but repairable. A bombing and machine gunning patrol over the wood later in the morning was also attacked by *Jasta 5* and *Vzfw* Könnecke claimed Lt S Hanafy who crashed behind the German Lines, later dying of his wounds.

Morning patrols by 60, 19 and 23 Squadrons resulted in three enemy aircraft shot down: Chidlaw-Roberts of 60 Squadron destroyed an Albatros west of Dadizeele at 10.10; Carter of 19 Squadron claimed an Albatros over Westroosebeke at 10.25; McKay of 23 Squadron shot down a DFW north of the Wervicq-Becelaere area at 11.20 for the last claim of the morning, and Frank Hobson of 70 Squadron destroyed an Albatros over Westroosebeke at 1.50pm. Only one pilot of the naval squadrons scored: FltCom F Banbury of Naval 9 claimed an Albatros scout out of control south of Dixmude at 12.20pm.[7]

The CO of 56 Squadron, Major Balcombe Brown, was one squadron commander who saw no sense in risking the lives of his pilots for no reason. The morning was overcast and Balcombe Brown took off at 10.00am to test the weather conditions nearer the Front Line. On his return he gave orders that Distant Offensive Patrols could be flown as long as conditions continued to improve. McCudden took B Flight off the ground at 10.40, led them across the Lines south of Bourlon Wood and attacked four Albatros scouts over Cambrai. The German flight commander was flying an Albatros with a red nose, a yellow fuselage and a green tail, with a large letter 'K' painted in white on its top wing. After a short skirmish the Albatri flew off east. This was the first appearance of 'Greentail' – as the Albatros was nicknamed by the pilots of 56 Squadron – an Albatros they were to be continually meeting over the next few months.

McCudden next saw a Bristol Fighter fighting with two Albatri over Marcoing and dived to its aid, getting behind one of the enemy scouts. McCudden's first burst hit the pilot. The Albatros went down in a vertical dive, its engine full on, the pilot's cap falling out, and hit the ground with 'a fearful whack' between Noyelles and Rumilly. This Albatros was possibly from *Jasta 5*, flown by *Vzfw* Karl Bey.

Maybery and C Flight were also in the area and he and Burdette Harmon attacked a two-seater. Maybery pulled away with gun jams but Harmon followed it down, firing from 50 yards. The enemy machine glided down, but crashed inverted.[8]

All the SE5s of B and C Flights returned to Estrée Blanche, with the exception of one, which landed at Bapaume with engine trouble. Balcombe Brown, flying a lone patrol, did not return. Attacking a two-seater, he had turned the wrong way and came under fire from the observer's gun. An accurate burst hit the SE5 in the petrol tank, blinding Balcombe Brown in a gush of petrol. Balcombe Brown switched to his emergency tank and landed at Lechelle.

The afternoon patrols saw a good deal of indecisive skirmishing and only Bowman claimed a victory: a brown coloured Albatros that crashed just to the northeast of Cambrai.[9]

In a morning fight with *Jasta 36* over the Dadizeele-Staden area, three Camels of 65 Squadron were lost: two pilots were killed and one taken POW. One Camel was credited to *Ltn* Bongartz of the *Jasta*. In the afternoon 65 Squadron were again in action with *Jasta 36*: Walter von Bülow, the *Staffelführer*, wounded 2Lt C Tiptaft who crashlanded his Camel in a shellhole.

Two pilots of 3 Squadron were killed during the day. They flew on a Line Patrol over Bourlon Wood in the morning and the casualty return seems to give some indication that they were killed in a collision. Lt David Rollo of 84 Squadron was wounded in the hand – squadron legend has it that he was thumbing his nose at the enemy – but landed at Agnez, otherwise unhurt.

Over the next two days the weather deteriorated and there was little flying. Fighting for the control of Bourlon Wood continued. It was taken in the afternoon of November 24, but regained by a German counter attack the following evening. Flying was restricted to the morning, a gale building up in the afternoon. The fighter squadrons had only one casualty on November 24: a pilot of 65 Squadron wounded.

A strong west wind and low clouds on November 25 made flying almost impossible. On November 26 the weather was a little better. B and C Flights of 56 Squadron took off in the morning to escort the DH4s of 49 Squadron on a bombing raid, but failed to find them. Enemy aircraft were seen but were too far east to engage. Twelve SE5s – the entire squadron strength – took off in the afternoon, again to escort 49 Squadron's DH4s, but the weather was so bad that the SE5s once again failed to find the bombers and split up to fly a normal patrol. McCudden took his Flight down over Bourlon village and fired into German positions before returning. Both Maybery and Bowman found visibility so bad – it was very dark under the cloud level – that they also returned.

The pilots of 29 Squadron had either better luck, were more persistent, or perhaps weather condition were better in the north. Attacking 12 enemy scouts in the area of Gulleghem, Capt James Payne claimed two out of control at 2.20pm and James Coombe claimed another at 2.30pm. Twenty minutes later, south east of Houthulst, William Molesworth shot down an Albatros for his ninth victory.

Lt H Taylor of 68 Squadron was at 1,500 feet over Bourlon Wood when he saw a DFW at the same height. The enemy pilot dived away but Taylor dived after him and opened fire from 200 yards. The DFW flew straight into the ground, 'where it stopped dead, without any run and with no signs of life.'

Five patrols from 84 Squadron were flown, but seven out of nineteen of the SE5s had to return with engine trouble. Despite this Lts J 'Swede' Larsen and William Brown claimed an Albatros over Fonsomme at 8.00am in one of the morning patrols.

On the Cambrai front, wind and rain stopped all flying on November 27, but further north a pilot of 29 Squadron was shot down and taken prisoner. The weather improved a little the next day, but was still poor over the front lines. Further north, in Flanders, conditions for flying were better and there was some fighting. A patrol at dawn by 65 Squadron lost 2Lt J Mackinnon, who was last seen in thick cloud over Zonnebeke. He was posted as missing and later found to have been killed. A pilot from 70 Squadron, 2Lt C H Brown, was wounded by gunfire from the ground, forced landed east of Becelaere behind enemy lines, but was seen to walk away from his Camel to a farm. A patrol of DH5s from 32 Squadron were in action with *Jasta 37* over Passchendaele in the early afternoon, and 2Lt D Francis was wounded, possibly by *Ltn* Udet.

Dawn on November 29 was fine. The German *Flieger Abteilung*, spotting for the guns, were more active than at any time since the Cambrai battle had begun and there were additional indications to show that the enemy was preparing a counter attack. Troops and transport were seen by air reconnaissance to be moving south, to the area of Cambrai. Further south, in the area of Vendhuille, the *jagdstaffeln* were flying low level patrols.

Haig was sure that the German attack would fall on the area of Bourlon. Confident that his reserves there were sufficient to contain them, the squadrons of I Brigade had been transferred from RFC headquarters and reverted to their work with the First Army. On November 28 the squadrons of 9th Wing had similarly been ordered to resume their normal work; which was for attacks against general strategic targets when no special ground operations were in progress.

At 7.00am on the morning of November 29, B and A Flights from 56 Squadron took off. McCudden took his Flight towards St Quentin and saw a DFW coming northwest over Bellincourt. McCudden attacked this DFW and after long a burst from both guns it fell to pieces, the wings floating down like so many pieces of paper, while the fuselage, with its heavy engine, went down like a misdirected arrow, finally hitting the ground south of Bellincourt, killing *Ltn d Res* Kurt Dettrich and *Ltn d Res* Manfred Hoettger of *Fl Abt (A) 202*.

Zooming away from the DFW, McCudden saw that Lt Fielding-Johnson was in trouble – the stabilising fin of his SE5 had broken during the dive, turning him upside down. McCudden escorted Fielding-Johnson back to the lines and flew back to the Cambrai area with the only remaining member of his Flight, Lt 'Jackie' Walkerdine. Arriving over the town they saw Maybery's Flight about to be attacked by two formations of enemy scouts. McCudden and Walkerdine dived to attack the lower group, but the Albatri scattered and flew east. Maybery and A Flight were then attacked from out of the sun by the higher formation of enemy scouts. Both sides lost a great deal of height in the fighting and Maybery, seeing that the other Albatri had returned and were about to join in the fight, fired a red light as a signal for his Flight to break off the fight. All the SE5s were fighting so fiercely, however, that his signal was not seen. Maybery found himself above the main fight and saw one of the enemy scouts about to attack an SE. Maybery dived and attacked this Albatros and it went down in a vertical dive.

Eric Turnbull had shot down an Albatros during the fighting. Firing a burst from broadside on at 75 yards he saw his tracer hitting the fuselage of the enemy scout, just behind the

pilot's cockpit. The Albatros turned over onto its side and went down in a slow spin. This Albatros D V 2082/17 was possibly that of *Offzstv Mai* of *Jasta 5,* who crashed on landing but was unhurt. Maybery made no claim for the Albatros he had sent down out of control, but Balcombe Brown noted on the bottom of Maybery's combat report: 'considering what a good shot he is and how modest his claims are, I, personally, an of the opinion that the EA was out of control.'

To offset these successes, Lt Alex Dodds had been taken prisoner. Attacked by *Ltn* Schubert of *Jasta 6* he was forced to land on the Jasta 5's aerodrome at Boistrancourt.

McCudden and his Flight were again in action in the afternoon, attacking three DFWs flying west from Douai. McCudden attacked one, Walkerdine another. McCudden's opponent began to glide down after his first burst. McCudden rectified stoppages in both guns and returned to the attack. After another burst from McCudden's guns the DFW did 'a terrific zoom,' its top wings folded up, meeting above the fuselage, and all four wings suddenly broke off. The DFW fell like a stone and McCudden saw the engine break loose. This DFW was from *Fl Abt 268(A)*, crewed by *Ltn d Res* Georg Dietrich and *Ltn* Deitrich Schenk, who were both killed. Turning away from the crash of the DFW McCudden realised that he was dangerously low over enemy territory. He opened his throttle to climb away, but the engine merely spluttered. The pressure gauge showed a reading of almost zero. Holding up the SE5 with one hand McCudden pumped furiously with other. Only a few feet from the ground the engine suddenly restarted. McCudden climbed a little, but was too low to locate any landmarks and flew west by the sun, passing over the barrels of German guns, taking his position from the direction in which their barrels were pointing. Eventually he passed over the British trenches, filled with waving troops, saw the remainder of his Flight and led them back to Estrée Blanche. Both the DFWs were confirmed by anti-aircraft batteries: McCudden's had crashed near Rouvroy; Walkerdine's at Neuvireuil.

At 10.50am, south east of Douai, Capt Loudon MacLean, leading B Flight of 41 Squadron, sighted eight Albatros scouts flying north west at 14,000 feet. Getting above the enemy scouts, MacLean led the SE5s down from out of the sun. Lt D A D I Macgregor got on the tail of one Albatros and fired from 40 yards range. The enemy machine turned over onto its back and went down through the clouds in a slow spin. The enemy scouts broke off the combat and flew east, chased by the 41 Squadron pilots, but without any further success.

Although fighting on the ground on the Cambrai front had been relatively quiet, there was some air fighting in the area. In the morning Lt R Howard of 68 Squadron fought a DFW at 400 feet over Cambrai, shooting the observer and forcing it to land. An afternoon patrol of four DH5s from the Squadron were attacked by eight Albatri over Bourlon Wood and the village of Fontaine. The Albatri made no attempt to attack the DH5s unless they tried to cross the Front Lines – each time they did so the enemy fighters attacked them. The DH5s were hampered by the weight of their bombs, but after dropping them, climbed to attack the Albatri, which flew east after a short skirmish. Lt Howard's DH5 was badly damaging in the fighting and he was forced to return.

Further north, a pilot of 19 Squadron was killed in the afternoon over Passchendaele, possibly by *Ltn* Bülow of *Jasta 36*.

The *Luftstreitkräfte* suffered a severe blow in the afternoon. The *Staffelführer of Jasta B, Oblt* Erwin Böhme, a 24 victory ace, was shot down in flames and killed by the crew of a 10 Squadron Armstrong Whitworth FK8. Böhme's Albatros crashed close by the HQ of the Second Battalion Royal Welch Fusiliers at Tyne Cot and Böhme was pulled from the wreckage by Llewelyn Evans, the Assistant Adjutant of the battalion.

Counterattack

On the morning of November 30, after a short but intense artillery bombardment – which cut British communications between HQ and the Front Lines – the German infantry began their assault between Masnières and Vendhuille, supported by low flying aircraft of the *Schutzstaffeln*.[10] These aircraft which came over in considerable numbers in front of the advancing troops 'caused many casualties and proved very demoralising.'

The German attack was a complete tactical surprise and quickly captured the villages of Gonnelieu, Villers-Guislain and later, Gouzeaucourt. The only good road to the Bourlon salient was threatened and the Third Army was in a serious position. Desperate resistance at Masnières gave time for a counter attack to be organised; Gouzeaucourt was recaptured at noon and progress made along the St Quentin ridge. The DH5s of 68 Squadron, whose duty was to attack the low flying enemy aircraft, greatly assisted this counter attack. Luckily there was only one casualty, a pilot shot down near the front line, who spent twenty-four hours in a shell hole under heavy fire until he could return to the squadron. Later in the morning a patrol from the squadron went out to attack enemy infantry, but this was prevented by the numerous low flying aircraft of the *Schusta*. Lt Taylor met four of these at 2,000 feet, flying directly towards him. Taylor waited until one of the enemy two-seaters filled his Aldis sight before firing a long burst at point blank range. The enemy machine turned sharply away, followed by Taylor, but seeing the remaining enemy aircraft coming to attack him he zoomed into the cloud cover.

Captain G Wilson had his petrol tank shot through by a shell splinter. He returned to the advanced landing ground, took off in another machine and returned to the battle. Over Gonnelieu village he saw a DFW at 1,600 feet and attacked it, silencing the gunner with his first burst. The enemy pilot turned east and Wilson chased the DFW to Bantouzelle, firing all the time, but with no visible effect. Wilson was then attacked by another DFW, but got underneath it and fired forty rounds. The DFW went down steeply, recovered, attempted to land, but turned over onto its back. Wilson had one bomb left and he dropped this on the DFW, blowing it to pieces. Wilson had now expended his ammunition and he made for home, but was attacked by another two-seater. Wilson's only option was bluff and he flew straight at the enemy machine. It turned away and flew east.

The pilots of 68 Squadron flew more patrols in the afternoon, most of them flying two or three sorties over the battlefront. They were also active over Bourlon Wood. They fired over 4,000 rounds and recorded thirty direct hits with bombs. In addition, their reports of the progress of the fighting were invaluable to the British artillery, blinded by the mist.

The German troops had also attacked in the area of Bourlon Wood, using similar tactics as further south, although not in such strength. It was in this sector of the front that the main force of the fighter squadrons of the RFC was concentrated. The Camel pilots of 3 Squadron and the DH5s of 64 Squadron flew back to the scene of the fighting time and time again, bombing and machine-gunning the advancing enemy infantry. During the day there were fifty or more aeroplanes of the RFC over the five-mile front from Moeuvres to Fontaine, this figure matched by those of the enemy. The official history quotes pilots as reporting: 'An absolute mêlée of aircraft around Bourlon Wood. The air was thick with DH5s, some SE5s, RE8s and Bristol Fighters.'[11]

In the afternoon, 41 Squadron were on patrol west of Bourlon Wood when they sighted two red-fuselaged Albatros scout flying at 2,000 feet over Inchy-en-Artois. Captain MacLean and D MacGregor at once attacked these Albatri, Maclean getting in a burst of 30 rounds into the nearest which went down in a spin and crashed. Maclean then turned to assist MacGregor, fighting the other Albatros, but had to do a climbing turn to avoid a collision. As he turned back he saw MacGregor going down in flames, to crash near Moeuvres, the Albatros flying off to the northeast. Russell Winnicott had also fired at one of the Albatri, zooming away into the clouds. Coming down again he also saw MacGregor's SE5 going down in flames.[12] Another Albatros was below him and Winnicott dived onto its tail and sent it down to crash near Fontaine. Fifteen minutes later Capt Meredith Thomas shot down an Albatros from a formation of six. It was seen to crash just east of Romilly, confirmed by Winnicott. Still in the same general area, Thomas Maclean, F H Taylor and Winnicott attacked a two-seater over Rumilly at 4.00pm shooting it down out of control, although it was not seen to crash.

The first patrol of the day flown by 56 Squadron took off at 9.55am. McCudden and B Flight crossed the Lines at 10.10am over Masnières. After an indecisive fight with some Albatri over Bourlon Wood, McCudden saw a pair of LVGs coming west over Fontaine. McCudden got behind the first and fired both guns. The LVG's engine immediately stopped, water poured from its radiator and it went down, gliding west. McCudden let it go. He knew the enemy machine must now land in British territory and the gunner had put a hole in the radiator of his SE5. McCudden put his SE5 down a mile from the LVG, which had finally landed at Havrincourt, but as the SE5 rolled to a stop its wheels ran into a small shell hole and it stood on its nose, breaking the propeller. McCudden clambered out, pulled down the SE's tail and ran to the LVG. The pilot, *Vzfw* Wilhelm Flohrig, was badly wounded and was having a tourniquet put on his arm – he later died on his way to hospital – but the observer, *Gefr* Eckerle was unhurt. The LVG C V. 9458/17, from *Fl Abt 19*, was brand new and was designated G94. McCudden telephoned Laviéville for a breakdown party to come out with a new radiator for his SE5 and to salvage the DFW.[13]

Bowman had led C Flight off the ground five minutes after B Flight. They had several indecisive combats with enemy two-seaters and scouts. Bowman attacked one Albatros, which went vertically down south of Bantouzelle, but was attacked by its companions and failed to see it crash. This was possibly *Ltn* Julius Buckler of *Jasta 17* who was seriously wounded in both arms and chest and who crashlanded near Vaucelles, close to Bantouzelle.

Richard Maybery took out A Flight at 11.00am. After indecisive combats with enemy scouts and two-seaters, Maybery and the Flight attacked sixteen enemy machines, including at least five two-seaters, over Bourlon Wood. As they came out of the clouds, directly above the enemy formation, the SE5s found they were too close to fire and the enemy machines scattered and dispersed. Later in the patrol, Maybery attacked a two-seater south of Rumilly. He opened fire from 30 yards, but both his guns jammed. The two-seater turned to the left and went down, Maybery following, desperately trying to clear his guns. The enemy pilot had been hit by Maybery's fire and Maybery could see the observer leaning over his pilot's shoulder, evidently trying to gain some measure of control over his machine. Maybery was powerless to interfere and it landed, 'apparently OK.'

Lt George Cawson was attacking another two-seater when his SE5 was hit by an accurate burst from the observer's gun. The wings of the SE5 folded up and Cawson was killed.[14]

More patrols were flown in the afternoon. Maybery, flying with Burdette Harmon and Indra Roy over Bourlon Wood, was twice chased back to the west by strong formations of enemy scouts, but returning a third time he saw six Albatri: five at 2,000 feet and one at his own level. Maybery attacked the single scout, which turned to meet his attack, but Maybery hit it with his first burst from 30 yards. The Albatros continued turning, engine full on, and crashed west of the wood. Its five *Jasta* companions made a half-hearted attack on Maybery but he dived away west.

Later, while Maybery was preparing to attack a formation of Albatri, an enemy scout suddenly dived out of the clouds and flattened out in front of him. The Albatros pilot had not seen the SE5 and Maybery got within twenty feet of him before opening fire with both guns. The Albatros dived a little, zoomed, then exploded into pieces.[15]

Bowman was delayed from taking off with his Flight. Flying alone, he attacked a Pfalz D III over Cantaing. A long burst from Bowman's guns sent the Pfalz down to crash by the canal at Cantaing, killing *Ltn* Friedrich Demandt of *Jasta 10*. Another Pfalz now attacked Bowman, who with both guns out of action was chased back to the lines, flying under a patrol of SE5s from 84 Squadron and a Camel from 46 Squadron flown by Lt G E Thompson. Intent on his chase of Bowman, the Pfalz pilot had not seen the other British scouts and was shot down by Thompson to crash in the British Lines, the first of the type to do so. This Pfalz was flown by *Ltn d Res* Hans Hofacker of *Jasta 3*. Hofacker was taken POW and his Pfalz designated G 93.

Bowman's Flight, under Capt Ronald Townsend, had attacked a pair of two-seaters a mile west of Lesdain, but before they could force a decision over these, they were attacked by six Albatri. Lt Maurice Mealing sent one of these down out of control, but three others attacked Ronald Townsend and shot him down, his SE5s bursting into flames at 1,000 feet, finally crashing at Le Pave.[16]

An early morning patrol from 46 Squadron, led by Lee, flew just below the cloud base at 2,000 feet. Lee could see that although there was wide spread shelling and a great deal of activity around Bourlon, there was even more on the southern flank. He took the Flight down to 800 feet and could plainly see where the German infantry had broken through the British defences to a depth of three to four miles. Isolated pockets of British troops, cut off by the advancing Germans, were firing distress rockets, but it was difficult to distinguish the enemy from the British troops and there was little the Camels could do in formation. Lee gave the signal for the Flight to split up and attack independently, then dived to 200 feet. From this height he found that the enemy infantry were too busy fighting to pay him much attention, but they were in small groups, none large enough to attack. Adding to the problem were a dozen or more enemy *Schusta* Halberstadts, bombing and machine-gunning the British troops. The low flying Halberstadts, were protected above by scores of Albatri and Pfalz, which were fighting fiercely with SE5s and Camels.

Lee attacked one Halberstadt, but the gunner was alert and Lee could see by his tracers that he was a good shot. The Halberstadt was too low for Lee to attack from below, so he left it and climbed to 4,000 feet, where he circled to see if he could asertain the extent of the German breakthrough. While Lee was circling a DFW suddenly appeared, its crew too intent on examining the ground to notice Lee's Camel. As the DFW went past him, Lee had time for only one quick deflection shot of fifty rounds from 200 yards; 'not expecting much, and was staggered when the machine suddenly dropped into a nose dive, engine on, and went down to hit the ground between Havrincourt and Flesquières.' Lee then came under attack by three enemy scouts and he dived away to land at Bapaume. While his Camel was being refuelled and rearmed, Lee telephoned Wing HQ and reported as best he could the situation on the ground. Two of Lee's Flight then arrived and as soon as they had been attended to by the groundcrews the three Camels took off again. Lee flew along the road to Lateau Wood, found a column of troops marching along it and dropped a bomb from 100 feet, so low that the explosion jerked up the tail of his Camel. Lee turned back and machine-gunned enemy troops, but they were now scattered along the sides of the road and began firing at him with rifles and machine guns. The targets were now dispersed, hard to hit and dangerous. Lee moved on and watched Robinson firing at a group of guns lining a hedge. Lee joined in this attack, dropped his remaining bombs and fired long bursts into the positions until he was low on ammunition. Both Camels then turned west, but Robinson's machine had been hit in the engine and he was forced to land a few miles short of Bapaume. When Lee landed again at Bapaume he found the aerodrome was now even busier, with DH5s from 64 and 68 Squadrons as well as the Camels of 3 and 46 Squadrons. The atmosphere was tense. 'Although there was an air of subdued excitement as we waited for our buses to be made ready, nobody spoke much. In fact there was an oppressive feeling. Almost everyone had been winged in the previous jobs, and I felt that people were inwardly asking, how long can my luck last out.'

Lee's third low level patrol of the day was a repetition of the first two and he finally flew back to Izel Le Hameau for lunch, where he learnt that the enemy had taken Gouzeaucourt

in the south and were being barely contained in the area of Bourlon. Lee took his Flight of four Camels out again after lunch. 'Personally, I hadn't much spirit for yet another job, but not a hint could I give of that, I was leading it!' Lee had been directed to attack a house on the edge of Bourlon village; the Camels attempted to seven times to cross the lines, but each time they were driven back by Albatri and Fokker Triplanes. 'Some had red colourings, which meant Richthofen's Circus, and it was no good trying to fight *them* with bombs on.' Lee finally took the Camels to the west, climbed to 4,000 feet and approached the target from another direction. His orders were to make four separate attacks, releasing a single bomb in each attack to make sure of hitting the house. Only R E Dusgate was now with Lee. The two Camels dived on the house, but were met with intense machine gun fire. Lee dropped one bomb and zoomed away in a climbing turn, glimpsing Dusgate for a brief moment, also climbing away. Lee's bomb had missed. Dusgate's four – Lee had instructed him to drop all four, then get away and rendezvous over Havrincourt – burst nearer. Lee felt sick at the prospect of diving again, this time with the machine gunners alert and waiting for him. He had to do it, he told himself, but only once. In a mood of fatalism, he dived, dropped his three remaining bombs from 100 feet and skidded away at twenty feet from the ground, where the gunners would find it hard to hit him. Whether or not he had hit the house, he no longer cared, he was no longer interested. One bullet had hit and broken the handle of his throttle control and another had smashed into his Very pistol cartridges, which luckily did not ignite.

Lee than flew to Havrincourt to find Dusgate, but an Albatros scout suddenly passed across his front, 200 feet below the Camel. Lee banked onto its tail and opened fire at 20 yards. The enemy scout reared up vertically in front of the Camel and Lee banked hard to avoid it, following it down until it crashed west of Bourlon village. As Lee flattened out his Camel was bracketed by shell bursts and hit in the engine, which stopped dead. Lee glided for the British lines, not sure, even at the moment of landing, if he had reached them, but as his Camel trundled to the edge of a trench and was pulled up by the parapet, Lee saw with relief that the tin helmets of the troops that appeared alongside his cockpit were British. After yet another long trudge through the back areas – including biscuits and tea at a YMCA at one o'clock in the morning – Lee arrived back at Izel at three in the morning after having been nine hours on the road. He would then have four hours sleep before he was due to lead another patrol in the morning. Dunsgate did not return. He had been wounded, shot down and taken prisoner. He died of his wounds in captivity on December 19.

The pilots of 84 Squadron flew six offensive patrols during the day. Capt Edward Pennell destroyed a DFW over Honnecourt at 10.00am and Capt James Child destroyed an Albatros scout at 12.30pm over Malincourt. Kenneth Leask destroyed another two-seater, which was seen to crash south east of Gouzeaucourt, and 2Lt C Travers also claimed a two-seater out of control.

Capt James Slater of 64 Squadron shot down a DFW over Bourlon Wood at 10.45am, and Edmund Tempest, also from 64 Squadron, shot down an Albatros north west of the wood in the afternoon. For both Slater and Tempest these were their last victories while flying DH5s, 64 Squadron would be re-equipped with SE5s during January and February of 1918.

On December 1 the battle on the ground continued with increased intensity The Guards, supported by tanks, captured Gonnelieu and completed the capture of Quentin ridge. There was still heavy fighting for Bourlon Wood, at Marcoing, and at Masnières, where the position of the British troops was so precarious that they withdrew to west of the village under cover of night. Mist and low cloud made flying almost impossible. German activity in the air was slight, and only British troops enjoyed the support of low flying aeroplanes during the fierce ground fighting of the day. Two DH5s of 68 Squadron were badly shot up while ground-strafing over Gouzeaucourt just after noon, but Lt R MacKenzie destroyed an Albatros scout north west of Viller-Guislain during the patrol, and Huxley shot down an Aviatik, which crashed and turned over onto its back. On his next patrol Huxley again saw the Aviatik, on the ground, surrounded by enemy troops, and he bombed it, blowing off its tail.

There were few combats in the air. Six Camels of 46 Squadron flew a low level patrol over the fighting at 800 feet in low cloud and mist, but saw nothing and after firing their ammunition into the enemy trenches, returned to Izel. One pilot of the patrol, 'Taffy' Hughes, lost touch with the formation; flying alone he attacked an Albatros over Cambrai and shot it down out of control.

On the afternoon of December 2 strong German attacks gained ground at La Vacquerie and west of Gonnelieu. In an afternoon ground-strafing mission by 46 Squadron, Arthur Lee was again shot down – for the third time since November 20. Diving on enemy trenches his Camel was hit – 'I felt the thud of a bullet' – and the engine stopped. Lee was at only a 100 feet, but he switched over to his gravity tank, the engine roared into life, and the Camel scraped over the parapet of a trench with only a few feet to spare. Landing at Izel he found that the bullet had hit an engine bearer, but his engine had stopped due to the failure of the pressure pump, either from the cold or the effect of his last dive on the trench. This narrow escape confirmed Lee's disapproval of trench strafing. Although he found

strafing the enemy back areas exhilarating, where it was possible to see the results of his attacks, to fly along a trench, with the enemy troops well dug in, was a terrifying prospect. The trenches were winding, full of machine-gun nests and rifles, all firing at the attacker as he zoomed away at the end of each dive: 'The strain of waiting for that one bullet with your name on it, knowing that you can't dodge it like you can Archie, is quite petrifying.' Lee considered, as did all fighter pilots, that ground-strafing was a suicidal job and that the 'staff types' who ordered it had no conception of the demands it made on the pilots. 'They ought to try it occasionally,' was Lee's succinct comment.

There were only two casualties for the fighter squadrons in the day, both in Flanders. Two pilots were shot down and taken prisoner: one from 19 Squadron, the other from 29 Squadron.

Although extremely cold, the weather was now generally fine, but with a thick ground mist. The wind was very strong on December 3. Patrols were flown, but although large formations of enemy machines were seen they were too far east to attack. The high wind caused many landing accidents on returning from these unproductive patrols. Four SE5s of 56 Squadron were lost in this way, with one pilot injured and taken to hospital.

Although there was still some local fighting, the battle-front at Cambrai gradually quietened. The result of the German gains since their counter attacks of November 30, meant that the British troops in the salient north of Flesquières were in danger of being overrun. The positions at Bourlon, fought for and captured with such sacrifice, were abandoned and the troops withdrawn to Flesquières Ridge. The withdrawal began on the night of December 4 and would be completed by the morning of December 7, effectively ending the battle of Cambrai.[17]

The weather was better on December 4, but there was thick cloud east of the lines. Bowman of 56 Squadron attacked a two-seater south of Moeuvres. The enemy pilot shut off his engine and glided south over the British Lines; each time he attempted to turn east, Bowman attacked again, forcing him back. After one such attack, Bowman turned away to change a drum of his Lewis gun – his Vickers was inoperative – and the enemy pilot saw his chance and dived for the enemy lines crossing them at 200 feet just south of Bourlon Wood.

On December 5 most of the air fighting seems to have been in Flanders. In the morning 2Lt Alexander Tyrrell and Capt W Pearson of 32 Squadron shared in forcing a two-seater down out of control over Becelaere, and FltCom Guy Price and Wilfred Sneath of Naval 8 shared an Albatros scout out of control over Wingles in the afternoon. Francis Quigley of 70 Squadron destroyed an enemy scout east of Westroosebeke at

1.45pm – possibly *Feldwebel* Hermann Seidel of *Jasta 26* – and John Macrae of 23 Squadron sent another Albatros down in the same area at 2.25pm. Capt Herbert Hamilton and 2Lt F J Williams of 29 Squadron shared an Albatros out of control east of Staden at 3.45pm.

In the afternoon an Albatros scout attacked the rearmost Camel of a patrol from Naval 10. FltLt W Curtis and FltSubLt F Hall both turned on this scout and shot it down in flames to crash between Keyem and Leke. This Albatros, described by the naval pilots as having a black fuselage and white tail, was possibly *Flgmstr* Ottomar Haggenmüller of *MFJ 1*, killed in action north of Dixmude. FltSubLt Rosevear of Naval 1 destroyed an Albatros east of Dixmude at 2.10pm for another victory for the naval squadrons.

McCudden took off alone at 11.00am. Visibility was good and he was certain that the high-flying Rumplers would be taking advantage of the conditions. McCudden climbed to 19,000 feet and over Havrincourt Wood saw a Rumpler coming west. The Rumpler, from *Fl Abt 45*, was well west of the British Lines and McCudden flew north, cutting off its retreat and finally attacking it over Boursies. After a long burst from McCudden's guns the Rumpler went down in a vertical dive; all four wings fell off at 16,000 feet and the wreckage fell in the British Lines at Hermies. The crew, *Ltn d Res* Fritz Pauly and *Ltn d Res* Ernst Sauter were both killed and the wreckage of the Rumpler designated G 95.[18]

There were six fighter casualties. A pilot from 70 Squadron had been killed; a pilot from 3 Squadron had been wounded and taken POW, and another wounded; 23 Squadron lost a pilot wounded and taken prisoner, and a pilot of 54 Squadron died of his wounds.

Maybery and Indra Roy took off on the morning of December 6 and were in combat with seven Albatri. Maybery's adversary was flying an aeroplane with a light blue tail. Maybery observed that the pilot was very skilled, but he finally hit the Albatros in the engine. Maybery was then attacked by two more Albatri and he lost sight of the blue tailed Albatros.

McCudden was also in the air, flying with Lt Edward Galley, and at 10.20am saw a Rumpler taking photographs over Vendelles. McCudden shot this Rumpler down with a short burst from both guns. A great deal of loose material fell out of it as it went down out of control, the observer hanging over the side of the fuselage. At 8,000 feet the Rumpler's right hand wings broke off and the wreckage fell in the British Lines near Holnon Wood, just north west of St Quentin. This Rumpler was from *Fl Abt 255*; its crew, *Uffz* Karl Pohlisch and *Ltn* Martin Becker were both killed.

In the afternoon, McCudden was in action with his Flight – plus Bowman and Maybery – with a formation of enemy scouts flying west over Fontaine-Notre-Dame. McCudden picked out an Albatros with a light blue tail and after a short burst from his guns it turned slowly over and went down in a vertical dive, petrol streaming from its fuselage. These Albatri all had red noses, and each had a different coloured tail: red, yellow, black and white striped. McCudden realised that these were the same Albatri that he had fought on November 23, and that 'Greentail' was with them. 'By Jove! They were a tough lot. We continued scrapping with them for half an hour, and they would not go down, although we were above them most of the time.' These Albatri were almost certainly from *Jasta 5*, although other *Jasta* may also have been present. During the fighting, Maurice Mealing sent an Albatros down out of control, but the *jagdstaffeln* reported no losses for the day.

In the late afternoon the German ground forces attacked Fontaine. Two patrols of DH5s from 68 Squadron were out, but it was too dark to observe the attack clearly and the pilots bombed the German reserve troops coming up from the rear. Huxley, having dropped his bombs, saw a pair of DFWs below him and shot one down in flames. This DFW was possibly from *Schusta 29b*, flown by *Uffz* Ulrich Hopfengärtner and *Gefr* Michael Höhne, killed over Rumaucourt, northwest of Fontaine. Two DH5s from the squadron were badly shot up in the afternoon, but these were to be the last patrols the squadron flew with the DH5: during the next few days the squadron was to be re-equipped with the SE5.

The only other casualties of the fighter squadrons during the day's fighting were two pilots killed further north: one from 65 Squadron, the other from 23 Squadron.

With the battle of Cambrai finally coming to an end on December 7, the fighter squadrons returned to their usual duties of offensive patrols. Relative to those suffered by the ground troops, the casualties of the fighter squadrons during the battle of Cambrai had been light, but the cost had still been high, both in pilots and aircraft lost and the mental strain that daily trench strafing imposed on those pilots who had survived. Arthur Lee commented on this: 'Even Thompson, and nobody in the squadron has more guts then him. He lives in the next cubicle to me, and last night, about midnight, I was awakened by awful screeching noises. It was Tommy. I took a torch and went into him. He was struggling and sweating and shouting, in the throes of a nightmare. The chaps in the other cubicles heard, and came in and we awakened him. He was very shamefaced. He'd just been shot down in flames, he said. Of course, this is the same sort of thing that Ferrie used to do in the cubicle behind me until he moved, and he's as stout as they make them. So it's not wind up. Just nervous strain.'

A few nights later Thompson reciprocated, waking Lee from *his* nightmare: 'I was diving into a black bottomless pit with hundreds of machine guns blasting up endlessly at me. I didn't like it a bit.'

From the commencement of the Cambrai offensive on November 20 to its close on December 7, the five squadrons which had almost exclusively flown ground support had lost 15 pilots killed; 16 wounded two wounded and taken prisoner; four who died of wounds, and eight taken POW. In addition, 29 aircraft had been badly shot up, many not repairable and struck off strength. The use of fighter aircraft as an offensive weapon against enemy troops and positions was extremely wasteful in the lives of highly skilled, experienced fighter pilots, pilots the RFC could ill afford to lose. This use of fighter aircraft would have to be curtailed to those of major offensives or defence emergencies.

Bad weather stopped nearly all flying until the afternoon of December 10, but Naval 10 flew an offensive patrol in the morning, taking off at 10.15. J G Clark and Macgregor attacked an Albatros west of Roulers and shot it down in flames. A Flight from Naval 9 were successful in the afternoon: FltSubLts, Wood, Redgate and Knott sharing in sending down a DFW in flames 4 miles east of Prevyse.

Lt Ian McDonald of 24 Squadron dived on a formation of enemy scouts which was attacking one of his patrol, closed to within close range of one and shot it down to crash south of Honnecourt for his last victory flying a DH5.

Patrols during the day by 56 Squadron saw a great deal of fighting. The squadron's pilots were now flying in pairs – 'fighting partners' – and ten SE5s took off in the afternoon. The SE5s had several combats with Albatros scouts: Bowman sent one down in a vertical dive and Capt Leslie Franklin claimed another out of control, but McCudden was forced to break off his attack by gun jams. After clearing his gun stoppages, McCudden joined up with his partner Galley and they attacked a two-seater over Havrincourt. The enemy machine zoomed and a great deal of smoke came out of its radiator, but the SE5s were chased away by several enemy scouts, which dived on them. Mealing fired a short burst at a balloon; although he only reported it being winched down later reports gave it as going down in flames.

The fighter squadrons did no flying on December 11, a day of low clouds and mist all day. McCudden took seven SE5s out in a morning patrol on December 12, but conditions had deteriorated – two of the pilots were lost in a snowstorm. The clouds were at 2,000 feet, the mist still thick, and the formation returned early, hoping conditions would improve in the afternoon.

McCudden took out six SE5s after lunch. After chasing away an Albatros that was firing into the British trenches, they attacked several Albatri over Moeuvres, but these made full use of the cloud cover to evade their attacks. The Flight then flew south and attacked a group of Pfalz strafing British troops near Villers-Guislain. The Flight succeeded in scattering these enemy scouts, but claimed no victories. Finally, a DFW was seen over Hermies, coming back from the British back areas. McCudden knew that if the SE5s were seen the enemy pilot would simply climb into the cloud cover and evade them, so he led the Flight above the clouds, then left them there while he went down to tackle the DFW. 'Now the Hun was for it, whichever way he went.'

The DFW crew stayed down to fight the single SE5 and proved more than a match for McCudden, who fought them for five minutes. 'EA put up a most determined and skillful fight and I was not able to use his blind spots for a single second. Moreover, enemy gunner was shooting very accurately and making splendid deflection, so that when I got down to 500 feet I left the EA, who then went north over Bourlon Wood.' McCudden later candidly admitted: 'The Hun was too good for me and shot me about a lot. Had I persisted he certainly would have got me for there was not a trick he did not know.'

A patrol from 1 Squadron, led by William Rogers, were patrolling the Ypres Salient in the early afternoon. Visibility was very poor and the Nieuports climbed through the low cloud, emerging into brilliant sunshine at 7,000 feet. To the east, 17 enemy aircraft were seen, flying west, and as they drew nearer the Nieuport pilots identified them as twin-engined Gothas. These machines, which had been attacking targets in the Ypres area during the summer, were formidable opponents. They carried a crew of four: two pilots, a bombadier/navigator in the nose – who was also a gunner – and a rear gunner. A great deal of thought had been given by its designer to the protection of the blind spots of the Gotha. The rear gunner could not only fire directly over his tailplane at an attacker diving from the top rear, but could also protect the vulnerable underside of his aeroplane by use of the so called 'Gotha Tunnel' in which the lower rear fuselage had been hollowed out, from the gunner's position back to the tail, which allowed him to shoot downwards at any fighter attacking from below. A technical report on the Gotha had recently been circulated amongst the fighter squadrons of the RFC and the Nieuport pilots were well aware of its formidable firepower.

Rogers flew to the rear and slightly above the enemy formation, his tiny Nieuport dwarfed by the sheer size of the Gothas' wingspan of nearly 80ft feet to that of the 26ft of his Nieuport. One of the Gothas had been slightly damaged by AA fire and turned back for its own lines. Rogers followed. Carefully keeping to a position directly behind its tail, he closed to 20 yards and fired a long burst from his Lewis gun. The enemy machine turned to the left and dived steeply, followed by Rogers. As it crossed the front lines at 4,000 feet a volume of black smoke came from the huge machine and it burst into flames. Two of the crew jumped from the blazing Gotha before it finally exploded, scattering the wreckage over both the British and German sides of the Front Line just to the north of Frelinghem. This Gotha G IV was from *Boghol 3*, flown by its *Kommandeur*, *Htpm* Rudolf Klein, who was killed with his crew, *Ltn* Werner Bülowius, *Ltn* Günther von der Nahmer and *Gefr* Michael Weber.[19]

Lts V Wigg and C Matthews of 65 Squadron were on patrol over Boesinghe and attacked two Albatros scouts. One was driven down out of control and then another sent down in flames to crash in the British lines. This was *Ltn d Res* Walter Börner of *Jasta 27*, who was killed. The wreckage of his Albatros was designated G98.

Twenty three Squadron were in action in the afternoon. Capt Alfred McKay shot an Albatros scout down out of control over Houthulst forest at 2.20pm and at 3.00pm William Mays Fry shot down another over Staden for his seventh victory.

A patrol of Camels from Naval 10 were in action east of Dixmude with six Albatros scouts from *Jasta 7*. No victories were claimed and FltSubLt J G Clark was shot down by *Ltn* Billik of the *Jasta* and taken prisoner, the only casualty of the day.

Other pilots claimed victories during the day. Quigley and Seth-Smith of 70 Squadron a scout each over Westroosebeke in the morning, and Capt Eric Hughes an Albatros scout over Cambrai at 10.20am.

There was little flying for the next two days, the weather being bad, with low cloud, mist and rain, but on December 13 a patrol from 46 Squadron had a brief skirmish with enemy scouts and 2Lt A L Clark was shot down and taken prisoner.

The weather improved on December 15 and there was a great deal of fighting.

Capt J Tudhope of 40 Squadron attacked a formation of Albatri over Douai in the afternoon and shot one down out of control at 3.10pm. In a later patrol by the squadron Lt R C Wade claimed a two-seater out of control. Philip de Fontenay and 2Lt FS Meek of 29 Squadron attacked a formation of enemy scouts escorting a two-seater and shared in a victory over one of the scouts. Major Carter and Lts E Blyth and Jennings of 19 Squadron attacked two-seaters over Comines. Carter closed to within 20 yards of one and shot it down in flames; Blyth and Jennings shot down another, which was seen to crash.

Richard Maybery led the first patrol from 56 Squadron in the morning and attacked six Albatri over Bourlon Wood. Maybery sent a red-nosed Albatros down in a spin, before attacking another, firing a long burst from his Vickers. An ob-

ject fell off the fuselage of the Albatros and it went into a slow left hand turn, nose dived for 2,000 feet, then flattened out. Lt Alfred Blenkiron claimed an Albatros out of control from this fight, which was confirmed by Eric Turnbull.

McCudden took off alone at 10.20am. He climbed steadily to 18,000 feet and saw an enemy two-seater over Gouzeaucourt, flying towards the British Lines. After waiting to see if this machine would come further over the British side, McCudden finally attacked, diving from 800 feet above it. McCudden badly misjudged both his own speed and that of the two-seater and had to quickly pull away to avoid a collision. While McCudden was turning for another attack the enemy pilot dived away to the east. Mindful of the strong westerly wind, McCudden let him go, climbed back to 16,000 feet and flew back to the Lines. When he arrived he found there were plenty of targets: 'the whole the sky seemed alive with Hun two-seaters.'

McCudden selected a Rumpler and attacked it just north of Gonnelieu at 11.05am. After thirty rounds from McCudden's guns, the enemy machine went down in a spiral dive for 5,000 feet and hit the ground half a mile east of Bois-de-Vaucelles. This was McCudden's twenty-second victory since joining 56 Squadron, bringing his total to twenty-seven.

The morning of December 16 was fine, but heavy snow fell in the afternoon, stopping all flying. More snow fell the next day, but a patrol from 1 Squadron attacked a mixed formation of scouts and two-seaters south west of Moorslede in the afternoon. A patrol of Camels from 65 Squadron joined in and the fighting drifted towards the front lines. Lt Philip Kelsey dived to the assistance of a 65 Squadron pilot being attacked by an Albatros and fought the enemy scout down to 3,000 feet where he got on its tail. A thirty round burst from Kelsey's gun at very close range sent the Albatros down in flames, both sets of wings broke off and the fuselage hit the ground south of Pilkem on the British side of the lines and was given the number G 100. The pilot, *Ltn* Karl-Heinrich Voss of *Marinefeldjasta 1* was killed. Rogers shared a two-seater out of control with Lt R C Sotham and 2Lt W D Patrick, and 2Lt L G Moore claimed another out of control.

The Spads of 19 Squadron were in action in the morning of December 18. Capt Oliver Bryson and Arthur Fairclough shot down an enemy two-seater over Comines at 10.35am, and in an afternoon patrol Fairclough destroyed an Albatros over Gheluvelt at 12.50pm. Major Carter, flying on this patrol, shot a Pfalz down over Gheluwe at 3.00pm and an Albatros in the same area thirty minutes later. Capt G Taylor, flying with Fairclough, also claimed an enemy machine out of control.

Frank Gorringe of 70 Squadron forced a two-seater down to crash in the British Lines at 12.45pm. This was a machine from *Fl Abt 8*, crewed by *Uffz* Walter Jumpelt and *Ltn d Res* Max Zachmann, both killed. The RFC communiqué gives this machine as being captured, but no G number was allocated, presumably because there was little left as the wreckage of the two-seater was seen to be burning on the ground.

A patrol from 23 Squadron led by Capt McKay was patrolling in the vicinity of Gheluvelt when a pair of two-seaters was seen. McKay led his Flight down to attack these, got unseen onto the tail of one and shot it down to crash at Gheluvelt. Twenty-five minutes later he shot down another two-seater, this one out of control, south of the village.

Five Nieuports from 1 Squadron, led by Rogers, attacked seven enemy scouts over Moorslede at 11.40am and Rogers shot one down. One of the Nieuports was under attack by an Albatros and 2Lt W Patrick closed to within ten yards and fired a burst of 50 rounds into it. The enemy machine went down vertically and was seen to crash by an anti-aircraft battery.

Led by their CO, Major Jack Cunningham, Camels of 65 Squadron were in action with Albatri over Roulers at 2.15. Lt Guy Knocker later wrote: 'OP at 2pm. led by Major Cunningham … the whole squadron. Great scrap with Albatri over Roulers. Sage shot down in flames and 2 missing from C Flight (Cowan and Cameron). The CO and Gilmour got two Huns each and Brembridge and I one between us. I shot it off Bill's (Lt Bremridge. Author) tail and he followed it down and finished it off. The CO never saw this episode! Dived on four two-seaters later but they got away.'

2Lt R H Cowan and 2Lt I D Cameron were both taken prisoner and 2Lt D M Sage was killed. The two Albatri credited to Capt John Gilmour were his fourth and fifth victories of an eventual 39.

During November the RFC in France had lost the services of two Sopwith Camel squadrons, Nos 28 and 66, which had been transferred to Italy, followed on December 18 by 45 Squadron. A new Camel Squadron, 71 Squadron, flew into St Omer on December 18, moving to Bruay on December 22. On 19 January 1918 the squadron was renumbered as 4 Squadron Australian Flying Corps.

December 19 was a day of mist and haze, making air operations difficult. Frank Gorringe and Francis Quigley of 70 Squadron were in action at 9.45am, sharing in the destruction of an Albatros scout over 20.Q 27. Leading his Flight in a late morning patrol, Capt Frank Hobson saw three two-seater Albatros C types over Stadenberg at 12.35pm. Hobson sent one down in flames, then attacked another. He failed to see the result of this second attack, coming under fire from the remaining enemy machine, but pilots of his Flight saw it go down in flames.

A patrol from 40 Squadron, led by Capt John Tudhope, engaged four enemy scouts over Lens and Tudhope shot one down out of control at 10.55am. Capt Gwilwyn Lewis, who had been posted in to the squadron on December 10 as a flight commander, shot down an Albatros over the same area at 1.00pm for his 3rd victory. Lewis was pleased that he had been posted to 40 Squadron. He wrote home: 'They are a very good bunch of fellows and Major Tilney is at their head … There is one particularly bright Flight Commander here with a bar to his MC. He is the only Flight Commander here at present. The others have gone home.' This 'bright' Flight Commander was Capt Edward 'Mick' Mannock, referred to in a later letter as 'an expert Hun strafer. Someone said he had got 17 Huns. Anyway he strafes about on his own, and seems to enjoy himself fairly well. I believe he will be going home soon though. He is an excellent fellow.'[20]

The pilots of 19 Squadron also had a successful day. Lt Fairclough claimed a two-seater east Hooglede at five minutes past eight in a morning patrol; out again later in the morning he shared with Capt Bryson in the destruction of another, west of Passchendaele at 11.30am. During an afternoon patrol, Major Carter and 2Lt H Galer each drove down an Albatros scout in a fight over Hollebeke at 3.45pm.

McCudden attacked a two-seater over Pontruet. The enemy machine went down, one wing low, but it was not seen to crash by observers on the ground and Balcombe Brown ruled it as indecisive.

An afternoon patrol by 56 Squadron of B and A Flights were in action with 14 Albatri east of Bourlon Wood at 1.00pm. Maybery and A Flight tackled the lower formation of eight, while McCudden and B Flight stayed up to prevent the higher formation of six from interfering. Eric Turnbull of A Flight saw an Albatros going down in flames with Maybery on its tail. Alfred Blenkiron fired at his opponent from close range; the Albatros rolled over onto its back and went down with black smoke pouring from its fuselage under the pilot's seat. Blenkiron was then attacked head on by another of the enemy scouts whose fire hit his SE5 in the propeller, luckily without doing any serious damage. Blenkiron climbed to rejoin the other SE5s and dived on another three enemy scouts that were climbing to attack them. In his report, Blenkiron stated that he knocked six inches off the tail of one of these machines, although quite how he did this is not made clear. Turnbull then saw B Flight about to attack another formation of enemy scouts and dived to join in the fight.

As McCudden turned away from one of the Albatri, Turnbull got a good burst into it. The enemy pilot spun down, but flattened out after falling for 3,000 feet and flew east. McCudden had been fighting a brown Pfalz and 'Greentail,' but the enemy pilots co-operated well and McCudden had to be content that his attacks prevented them from climbing back into the main fight above.

After the SE5s had landed back at Laviéville it was realised that Richard Maybery had last been seen following down the burning Albatros. He failed to appear or telephone by nightfall and was posted as missing. Maybery's loss was a great blow to 56 Squadron. He had joined the squadron in the first week of June, had scored 21 victories, was an excellent flight commander, and was extremely popular with all ranks. His loss was all the more tragic because he was coming to end of his tour in France and was due to be posted home in a few short weeks. Bowman, who had left on leave five days before the loss of Maybery, recalled in 1968: 'Richard was tired and I asked him to take my leave. I was still fresh, didn't need it, and was only going to Paris anyway. He wouldn't hear of it and I never saw him again.' Maybery was the only casualty of the fighter squadrons on December 19.[21]

Thick ground mist and fog stopped all flying for the next two days. The weather improved on December 22. It was cloudy, but conditions were gradually clearing as the morning wore on.

A patrol from 29 Squadron, led by Capt Payne, attacked four Albatros scouts over Staden at ten minutes to eleven and Payne claimed one down out of control. In the afternoon a Flight of seven Spads from 19 Squadron attacked eight Albatri south of Quesnoy at 2.20pm and all the Flight shared in the destruction of one enemy scout in flames. The Camels of 70 Squadron were also in action, attacking six enemy scouts over Westroosebeke at 1.50pm. Hobson destroyed an Albatros from the formation and later in the patrol 2Lt G Elliott shot down a two-seater which was last seen burning on the ground.

McCudden had taken off alone at 11.00am. Flying south at 17,000 feet, McCudden saw a pair of DFWs crossing the lines over Maissemy and as they passed over Holnon Wood, a thousand feet below him, he went down and attacked the nearest from 100 yards. McCudden's fire stopped the DFW's engine and he left it gliding down behind the British lines, still under partial control, and turned to attack its companion. The DFW crew put up a stiff fight for their lives and after chasing them as far as St Quentin, McCudden left them: looking back he had seen the first DFW had turned east and was gliding down to land on its own side of the lines. McCudden could not allow this and he turned back and fired a short burst from a range of 50 yards. The DFW C V from *Schusta 5* went down in a steep spiral and crashed half a mile behind the front line trenches to the south west of St Quentin.

It appears that this DFW was flying without an observer. McCudden's combat report comments on the non-appearance of one during the action and the G Report (104) names only *Uffz* Anton Bode, who was killed, as the pilot.

When McCudden landed back at Laviéville, his engine cowling had blown off and his windscreen was covered with blood. He thought at first that his nose was bleeding, but on inspecting his SE5 he found it was covered with blood from one of the DFWs.

McCudden flew another lone patrol in the afternoon. Although he attacked a two-seater east of Bapaume, the enemy machine had a height advantage, McCudden had carburettor trouble, and he was unable to gain a decision. He had better luck the next day.

Taking off alone at 10.55am, McCudden flew to west of St Quentin and almost immediately spotted a trio of two-seaters. These were above the SE5 and McCudden had to be content with driving them east, but while doing so he noticed an LVG cross the front lines just north of St Quentin at 17,000 feet. McCudden went after this LVG and caught up with it over Étreillers. The enemy pilot turned south, but McCudden got into his favourite attacking position and fired a burst from both guns. The LVG's engine stopped, water poured from its radiator, and it dived away east, the observer standing up and waving his right arm, apparently in surrender. McCudden held his fire and attempted to edge the enemy machine west, but it continued to glide towards its own lines. McCudden closed and fired a short burst. The LVG went into a steep dive and crashed behind the German lines, between the Canal de L'Oise a La Sambre and the road to Anguilcourt, The time was 11.25am.

McCudden regained his height and five minutes later saw a Rumpler south of Peronne. This Rumpler C V11 from *Fl Abt 23,* crewed by *Ltn* Otto Höring and *Ltn* Emil Tibussek was very high, at 18,200 feet, and it took McCudden, unseen, nearly fifteen minutes to climb to their height. When the Rumpler crew finally saw the danger the pilot tried to outclimb the SE5 but McCudden finally closed up and attacked them over Beauvois at 18,200 feet. Horing and Tibussek fought well, but at this height the SE5 was as fast as their machine and McCudden fought them down to 8,000 feet over Roupy, where a final burst from his guns shot the right hand wings off the Rumpler, the wreckage falling in the British Lines near Contescourt. (G 107).

Half an hour later, McCudden attacked two LVGs over Gouzeaucourt, but these co-operated well and McCudden, his petrol nearly exhausted, returned.

McCudden took off again at 1.55pm, leading his Flight on a normal patrol. Thirty-five minutes after take off McCudden saw a Rumpler coming west from over Metz-en-Couture. The Rumpler was at the same height as the SE5s, saw them and turned east, diving for it own lines, but McCudden caught it and a long burst from both guns sent it down to crash in the British lines northwest of Gouzeaucourt. This Rumpler (G 106) was from *Bogohl 7* and the crew were taken prisoner.[22] After crashing this Rumpler McCudden re-formed the patrol, crossed the Lines over Masnières, and attacked a formation of enemy scouts near Bourlon. These Albatri turned out to be led by 'Greentail.' The fight continued for sometime, going lower and lower over Bourlon Wood until the enemy pilots broke off the action and dived away to the east. Edward Galley's SE5 had been hit in the oil tank by one of the Albatri and he was forced to land at Bapaume, but the remainder of the Flight reformed over Flesquières. British anti-aircraft fire then pointed out an LVG coming west over Trescault and McCudden attacked it, a short burst putting the enemy machine up on one wingtip, with the observer holding on to a centre section strut and leaning into his pilot's cockpit. McCudden reported: 'The LVG then stalled and spun, and after that went down just like a leaf and took at least three minutes to crash. It landed on a light gauge train in a vertical dive and knocked some trucks off the line.' McCudden had followed the yellow-fuselaged LVG down: 'thousands of our Tommies rushing from everywhere to look at the fallen Hun. Having circled round for a while I flew back to the aerodrome feeling very satisfied, having totally destroyed four enemy two-seaters that day.'[23]

This was the first time an RFC pilot had destroyed four enemy machines in one day and McCudden received many telegrams from senior officers, including General Trenchard. That evening most of the 56 Squadron pilots went into Amiens for a celebratory dinner.

Arthur Lee took out B Flight of 46 Squadron and was impressed by the mantle of snow covering and effectively disguising the shell-pocked earth, the trenches showing up as black lines zigzagging across the almost unbroken white. A yellow-brown LVG brought Lee back to the realities of war and the Camels chased it until it landed on an aerodrome at La Brayelle. The enemy pilot, in his haste to land safely – or perhaps wounded by the fire from the Camels – crashed his machine. The machine gun defences of the aerodrome then forced the Camels to climb away and they returned, content to claim the LVG as driven down damaged. 'We enjoyed it all hugely, it was rather like having a hunt in the snow at Christmas.'

Other victories were claimed during the day. Frank Gorringe of 70 Squadron saw British anti-aircraft shells bursting over Ypres and went to investigate, finding a two-seater, which he shot down in flames north east of Hollebeke at 3.15pm. Capt John Steele a Flight Commander of 84 Squadron, claimed a two-seater out of control over St Quentin at 3.10pm, and another was claimed by two members of his

Flight: Capt E Pennell and 2Lt W Brown. There were no fighter casualties.

The weather was again bad, with dense fog for the next four days. On Christmas Day – the fourth of the war – there was snow and low cloud, but the next day it was fine and clear, with high cumuli. McCudden took off alone in the afternoon to look for enemy two-seaters. He saw one – east of Lens – and seven Albatri, but he made no attacks and returned to report that clouds were building up over the 3rd Army front.

The weather on December 27 was still bad for flying, with snowstorms and high winds. From the official communiqués it appears that only Naval 8 saw any action, claiming a DFW out of control over Henin-Lietard at 2.35pm, but Quigley, Hobson and Seth-Smith of 70 Squadron are credited with sharing a two-seater destroyed over Zarren at 10.50am.

The next day, December 28, the weather had improved and thirteen enemy aeroplanes were claimed.

FltCom G Price and FltSubLt H Day of Naval 8 shared in driving down a DFW over Vitry at 11.00am and FltSubLt William Jordon sent an Albatros down out of control over Mericourt twenty-five minutes later. A patrol from 70 Squadron were out in the morning and Lt George Howsam destroyed an Albatros two-seater over Zarren at 11.00am. Fifty minutes later the patrol attacked three enemy two-seaters over Ploegsteert. Gorringe destroyed one and Lt F Hobson dived after another, which had been forced down by Seth-Smith. This crashed, landing on its nose. Hobson fired into and it burst into flames.

Arthur Lee being too ill to lead the scheduled patrol, Lt H N C Robinson took his place. Three hours later he and 2Lt G D Lamburn burst into Lee's cubicle with the news that they had shot down a two-seater in flames three miles west of Havrincourt at noon. They had fired at it from long range – 300 yards – not expecting any result, but were delighted when it burst into flames and crashed.

McCudden had taken off alone in the morning. It was a beautifully clear, crisp winter's morning, but extremely cold, with 20 degrees of frost. McCudden climbed to 17,000 feet and as he approached the front lines saw a Rumpler coming from the direction of Bourlon Wood and slightly below him. McCudden closed to within 75 yards and fired a short burst from both guns. The Rumpler, from *Fl Abt 7*, went down in a right hand spiral; after it had fallen for a thousand feet its right hand wings broke off and it crashed in the British lines just north of Vélu Wood, killing the crew, *Uffz* Munz and *Ltn d Res* Rücker. The wreckage was numbered G 111.

Fifteen minutes later McCudden sighted another Rumpler going north over Haplincourt. A burst from McCudden's guns sent this Rumpler down in flames; it took two minutes to reach the ground, finally crashing near Flers, twenty miles behind the British lines, killing the crew *Ltn* Hans Mittag and *Uffz* Oskar Güntert from *Fl Abt 40*. The wreckage was designated G 112. McCudden had not followed this Rumpler down. He knew there were probably more two-seaters working in the clear conditions and he had no intention of having to regain any lost height in order to deal with them. His reasoning was correct: an LVG at 16,000 feet over Havrincourt was pointed out to him by British AA fire. As McCudden approached this LVG the AA gunners were still firing, but throwing caution to the winds, he attacked it, opening fire at long range, hoping this would cause the enemy pilot to dive steeply, making it difficult for his observer to man his gun and return fire. McCudden was right. The LVG dived steeply away, so steeply that McCudden estimated its speed to be 200 mph. McCudden dived after it, closed to 100 yards and opened fire with a long burst from both guns. The LVG burst into flames and broke up, the pieces falling near Havrincourt Wood. The crew, *Ltn* Walter Bergman and *Flg* Albert Weinrich, from *Fl Abt (A) 210*, were both killed. This LVG was numbered G 113.

British AA fire then pointed out another LVG over Lagnicourt. By the time McCudden caught up with this machine it was a long way east of the lines, but he closed to a hundred yards and fired a long burst from his Lewis gun. A small flicker of flame came out of the LVG's fuselage, but this almost at once went out and the enemy pilot dived steeply away, kicking his rudder in an attempt to throw McCudden off his aim. Steam was pouring out of the LVG's wing mounted radiator and McCudden could see the unfortunate observer leaning over the side of the fuselage in an attempt to escape the boiling water. McCudden had scant sympathy, writing later: 'I hope the water froze over him sold and gave him frostbite.'

McCudden was now running low on petrol and returned to Lavieville. Balcombe Brown thought that the last LVG may well have later crashed, but refused to allow it unless it was later confirmed to have done so by the AA batteries. McCudden was of the opinion that although badly damaged it was still under control when he left it and he was content with having positively destroyed three enemy machines, down in the British lines.

A future ace scored his first victory during the day. Lt George McElroy of 40 Squadron shot down a LVG at 11.20am over Drocourt-Vitry for the first of an eventual 47 victories. McElroy, an Irishman, was nicknamed 'McIrish' by Mannock to differentiate him from 'McScotch,' the Scot William MacLanachan.

There were two casualties for the fighter squadrons on December 28. A Nieuport of 1 Squadron was brought down by *Flak,* the pilot taken POW, and 23 Squadron lost one of its most experienced and successful pilots when the Canadian, Capt Alfred McKay, was shot down and killed over the Gheluvelt-Dadizeele area by the gunner of a two-seater he was attacking.

McCudden continued to cut a swath through the German *Flieger Abteilung* the next day. While leading his Flight on a morning patrol, three enemy two-seaters were seen coming west and the SE5s dived on them over Vaucelles Wood. The crew of the LVG attacked by McCudden proved to be both wily customers and experienced. McCudden drove them down from 13,500 feet to ground level, where the enemy pilot switched off his engine and made a pretence of landing in the British lines. Restarting his engine to clear a trench, the pilot changed his mind, decided to make a run for it and turned northeast. Flying only ten feet above the ground the LVG reached Havrincourt and the pilot turned due east for the safety of his own lines. Seeing this, McCudden dived after him and fired from close range. The LVG spun and crashed in the British lines, only 100 yards from the LVG that McCudden had shot down on November 23. McCudden circled the crash and watched the British troops helping the crew from their wrecked aeroplane. The pilot *Vzfw* Kurt Gerschel was mortally wounded, but his gunner, *Uffz* Lehnert was unhurt and taken POW. The LVG C V, from *Schusta 10*, was designated G 118.

McCudden climbed to rejoin his Flight, who had gained no positive result with the other two-seaters, all having suffered gun stoppages. After driving a formation of Albatri east from the vicinity of Bois-en-Vancelles, the Flight returned. Within forty minutes McCudden took off again. Flying alone he climbed to 18,000 feet. Visibility was very good and half an hour after taking off he attacked an LVG that was crossing the lines over Lagnicourt. Closing to within 100 yards, McCudden fired his usual short burst, hitting the enemy machine in the radiator. The enemy pilot dived steeply away and was too far east and too low for McCudden to attack again, anxious to preserve his height. It was nearly two hours, almost at the end of the endurance of the SE5, before McCudden saw another possible target: an LVG, this one over Gouzeaucourt at 15,000 feet. The enemy pilot saw McCudden coming and put his machine into a left hand turn, the gunner firing at the SE5 from long range, hoping to deter McCudden from attacking. McCudden knew that the strong wind was pushing the enemy machine west and was content to let the enemy pilot continue circling, knowing that he would have to eventually fly straight in order to reach his own lines. As the enemy pilot finally made his bid for safety, McCudden dived and fired, a long continuous burst, until the LVG first began to break up then burst into flames, the right hand pair of wings breaking off, the rest of the wreckage falling in the British lines north east of Épéhy. This LVG was from *Fl Abt 33* and its crew *Ltn d Res* Walter Dern and *Ltn d Res* Georg Müller were both killed.[24] McCudden returned to Lavieville, well pleased with his morning's work. 'I had a generous dinner, after which we listened to the gramophone for half an hour, and life again seemed full of cheer.'

The pilots of 19 Squadron had a successful morning's fighting. Engaging a formation of Albatri over Houthulst in actions between 10.10 and 10.25, Major Carter claimed one scout out of control; John Candy another; Arthur Fairclough claimed one as destroyed and another out of control; John de Pensier an Albatros out of control, and Patrick Huskinson claimed two more scouts out of control. All these victories were in the vicinity of Houthulst and Houthulst Forest, but 2Lt H E Galer had been shot down and taken prisoner by *Vzfw* Karl Menchhoff of *Jasta 3*.

Nineteen seventeen, the fourth year of the war, ended quietly. Little flying was possible for the last two days of the year. The weather was very bad with low cloud and mist.

War or no war, the New Year of 1918 was seen in in appropriate fashion. That adopted by 46 Squadron was no doubt typical of many RFC squadrons on the Western Front. At 11.55 the entire squadron gathered on the aerodrome, the officers with their Colt revolvers in one hand, their Very pistols in the other, Major Mealing, the CO, keeping an eye on his watch with a torch.

'Twelve o'clock! The Major fires a red Very light and instantly all the others go soaring up into the air. Then comes a fusillade of shots as the automatics are emptied, also upwards! Then hoots and catcalls followed by prolonged cheering. As it peters out we hear a similar din coming from 64 next door. We go into the Mess, drink toddy, sing *Auld Lang Syne,* yell "Cheerio 46!" and "Cherrio Chololovtich!" We're visited by some chaps from 64, go through it all again and eventually stagger off to bed. It's 1918, and we're all still alive!'[25]

NOTES

1. Munday made a speciality of shooting down balloons in the half-light. The balloon shot down on November 7 was the fourth since September 2. In January 1918 he would add the last to his tally of five.

2. This was *Ltn* Runge of *Jasta 18*. Strähle's diary gives that Runge was shot down in flames at Langemarck by an SE5. But Strähle was not flying in the patrol and there was no claim on November 15 by any SE5 pilot.

3. Philip Fletcher Fullard flew a remarkable eight months in France with 1 Squadron. He arrived at the end of April 1917 and scored his first victory, an Albatros scout, on May 26, shooting another down two days later. He scored another five victories in June, eight in July and 12 in August. On September 3, Fullard, fully confident of the strength of his Nieuport, decided to see how it would behave in a spin with the engine full on. The Nieuport had spun down at great speed for 12,000 feet when Fullard felt a sharp pain in his head and found he was totally blind. He managed to pull the Nieuport out of its spin and after a while his sight gradually improved until he could see the blurred utline of white objects with his left eye. Despite being in intense pain Fullard managed to land safely, but he was still completely blind in one eye and was sent to hospital in Boulogne. Lister, an eye specialist, diagnosed a burst blood vessel due to rapid alteration in pressure during the spin and advised rest. Fullard did not return to 1 Squadron until the beginning of October but immediately began to score again with 11 victories during the month. On November 17, in a football game against troops on rest near the aerodrome, Fullard sustained a compound fracture of his right leg. It was the end of his service flying in France. At the time of the accident Fullard had been in France for eight months and was probably due to be sent home, but it is interesting to speculate what his score might have been if he had flown during September. He had been scoring at the rate of 7.6 victories a month, which without the enforced rest would have brought his total score to approximately 50. Fullard's leg was slow to heal and he was not fully fit until September 1918, but if he had been fit enough to return to France to fly another tour in 1918 he would undoubtedly have been one of the most successful fighter pilots of the conflict, if not *the* most successful. Fullard had been recommended for the award of a Victoria Cross in late October, but this had been turned down by the Brigade Commander with the written comment that 'he should get more Huns.' Fullard finished the war with a DSO; an MC and bar. In November 1918 he was awarded the War medal of the Aero Club of America and in 1919 toured the States with other successful RFC/RAF pilots.

4. In the 1938 Warner film *Dawn Patrol*, starring Errol Flynn and David Niven, Niven's character, Scottie, returns to the squadron with his arms full of Champagne after having been given up for dead. Having seen the film, and meeting Niven at a party, Pope delighted in telling him: 'That was me!'

5. The CO of 46 Squadron, flying a test at first light had found the cloud base at fifty feet, but it was hoped conditions would be better at the front lines, the aerodrome at Izel le Hameau being only 100 feet above sea level.

6. Bourlon Wood was later recaptured in a German counter attack and Richthofen had A9299, the number of Boddy's DH5 – his sixty-second victory – cut from the rudder. During the thirties, in the Richthofen museum at Schweidnitz, the family home, it could still be seen, along with other Richthofen trophies of hunting and war. Happily, Boddy recovered from his injuries, but the afternoon of 23 November 1917 was the end of his war.During the attacks on Bourlon Wood on November 23, 64 Squadron lost a total of six DH5s. No pilots were killed but two were wounded, including Boddy. The pilot who placed Boddy in the tank was Lt. H T Fox Russell whose DH5 had had its tail blown off by an artillery shell.

7. Naval 10 had returned to the control of 4th Wing, Royal Naval Air Service on November 20. Naval 3 had been transferred to Walmer in Kent on November 4, leaving Naval 8 the only naval fighter squadron operating with the RFC during the battle of Cambrai.

8. This machine was possibly from *Fl Abt 225*. The observer *Ltn d Res* Erich Herold was killed, but the pilot was uninjured.

9. This was possibly *Ltn* Hans Wolff of *Jasta 11* who was wounded and crashlanded near Avnes-le-Sec.

10. The duties of the *Schutzstaffeln* (*Schusta*) were originally those of protection for the aircraft of the *Flieger Abteilung*, but during the battle of Arras they had also been used with advantage in attacking troops and trenches. As a result of this they ceased to be used in protective duties and were used as weapons of attack over the battlefield at any decisive point where German troops were either on the offensive, or to attack and break up any attacks by the allied armies. In March 1918, this change of role led to the *Schutzstaffeln* being renamed *Schlachtstaffeln(Schlasta)* and they were later grouped into *Schlachtgeschwader*.

11. *The War in The Air, Vol IV,* H A Jones, Oxford University Press, 1931.

12. D A D I MacGregor was the 63rd victory of Manfred von Richthofen.

13. Continuous shelling constantly interrupted the work of the salvage party and the partially dismantled LVG was later burnt as it was in danger of being overrun by the advancing German infantry. The rudder of this LVG was later displayed on the wall of the 56 Squadron Mess.

14. Cawson was awarded to *Vzfw* Voigt and *Vzfw* Kruse of *Schusta 12*.

15. This was most probably *Ltn* Johann von Senger of *Jasta 12*, killed over Bourlon Wood.

16. Townsend was credited to *Vzfw* Mai of *Jasta 5* for his fifth victory.

17. Post war German evaluation of the Cambrai battle regarded the initial British successes as a possible catastrophe for their forces and expressed astonishment at the British failure to exploit the advantages won.

18. Pieces of this Rumpler were still falling 20 minutes later and led to a erroneous claim by an AA battery which had been firing at another Rumpler. Parts of the wreckage of McCudden's Rumpler were given G 96.

19. British troops retrieved souvenirs from the wreckage of the Gotha and the squadron were given two of the crosses from its wings. Rogers took one home with him when he returned to Canada, where it is still. The other cross and two rudders were also given to 1 Squadron. Over the years the cross has been lost but the rudders are still in the squadron's museum.

20. Mannock was posted to Home Establishment on 2 January 1918, but in the short time they served together he and Lewis became firm friends. In a letter to his father Gwilym Lewis wrote: I told him to be sure to call on you if he had a chance. He is one of the finest personalities I have ever met, and a regular hero in this squadron. He loved fighting but hated killing – I believe it used to upset him for days after sometimes. He was originally in the ranks and I know you would like him if for no other reason than he is a most arrogant socialist!' *Wings over the Somme*, Wing Commander Gwilym H Lewis, DFC, William Kimber, 1976.

21. Maybery had been shot down by anti-aircraft fire, the first victory of *K-Flakbatterie 108* commanded by *Ltn* Thiel. Maybery crashed near the battery and was buried by Theil close by: 600 yards south of the village of Haynecourt by the side of the road to Sailly.

22. This crew were both given as captured, but are not in the German lists.

23. *Five Years in the RFC*, James McCudden, The Aeroplane and General Publishing Co., London 1918.

24. LVG C type. G 119.

25. *No Parachute*, Arthur Gould Lee, Jarrolds 1968.

CHAPTER SEVENTEEN

1918

Nineteen seventeen had been a year of mixed fortunes for the RFC. With the advent of the *jagdstaffeln* at the end of 1916, the pendulum of air superiority had swung firmly in favour of the *Luftstreitkräfte*, culminating in the heavy casualties in the battles of Arras in April and Messines in June. With the arrival of the SE5 in late April, and the Sopwith Camel in June, the fighter pilots of the RFC at last had fighter aeroplanes with which to contain and curtail the activities of the *jagdstaffeln*. However, an additional duty had been found for them – ground-strafing. This duty, considered by many pilots and squadron commanders to be of doubtful value in relation to the loss of experienced flight commanders and pilots, had again resulted in a high casualty rate, especially in the battle of Cambrai, where there had been little gain on the ground.[1]

By the end of 1917 the RFC had a formidable fighter force in France: 19 squadrons of single-seater fighters: five squadrons of the SE5a, six of Sopwith Camels, two of Nieuports, two of Spads and four of DH5s. Augmenting this force were six RNAS squadrons, equipped with Sopwith Camels. This superiority in numbers enjoyed by the fighter pilots of the RFC – a superiority that would increase still more in 1918 – resulted in the *jagdstaffeln* adopting tactics even more defensive in nature. The pendulum had swung once again, now firmly in favour of the RFC. However, these considerations were of little personal import to the pilots and observers of the RFC. They knew only too well that the New Year would bring a renewal of the heavy fighting; that they would see more of their comrades die in combat. For them, that was the only certainty.

January 1918 also saw changes in command. On January 2 the British Air Ministry was formed and the GOC of the RFC, Major-General Hugh Trenchard, knighted in the New Year's Honours List, was appointed Chief of Air Staff.

Trenchard's successor to the command of the RFC in France was Major-General John Maitland Salmond, who took up his command on January 18. 'Jack' Salmond was a popular replacement for 'Boom' Trenchard. Major Sholto Douglas, commanding 84 Squadron at the time of Salmond's appointment, remembered him with affection: 'The most sympathetic and human of all the senior officers whom I have ever known. He was always ready to listen to what we had to say, and we knew that there was no need for any hesitation in talking to him quite frankly about our problems.'[2]

Air activity slackened as winter set in over the Western Front. The battle of Cambrai had marked the end of the ground offensives until the spring of 1918 and the fighter squadrons now reverted to their original duties of offensive and defensive patrols. These patrols were now delimitated: the Camel squadrons fought nearer the front line trenches and at generally lower levels than the SE5 and Spad squadrons, which flew further into the enemy back areas, containing and destroying the enemy fighters before they could interfere with the activities of the corps squadrons working over the front line and its immediate rear areas.

The first victory of the New Year appears to have gone to 70 Squadron. On January 1 Capt Frank Gorringe and Lt C Smith attacked a two-seater and sent it down in flames east of Zandvoorde at 9.40am.

The Camels of Naval 8 were also on patrol in the morning. At 11.28am a Hannover C type two-seater was seen over Fampoux. FltCom Compston and his Flight attacked this two-seater, were joined by Mannock of 40 Squadron, and the British scouts shot it down in pieces, the fuselage finally crashing near Fampoux in the British lines. The crew, *Vzfw* Fritz Korbacher and *Ltn* Wilhelm Klein from *FltAbt (A) 288* were killed and the wreckage of the Hannover designated G 121.

This victory was shared between Compston, FltSubLt G K Cooper and Mannock. It was Mannock's 16th victory and his last while with 40 Squadron. Compston scored again in an afternoon patrol, shooting down an Albatros over Neuvireuil at 3.30pm, sharing the victory with FltSub A J Dixon.

Frank Soden of 60 Squadron scored his 12th victory, sharing with 2Lt J B Crompton in sending a DFW down out of control west of Roulers at 10.50am.

Three pilots from 56 Squadron flew lone missions, classified in the squadron record book as 'chasing EA.' McCudden chased two enemy two-seaters: the first saw him coming, diving away over its own lines, and in attacking the second both McCudden's guns froze and he was forced to break off the action and return.

Lt Alfred Blenkiron had better luck. Over Cambrai he saw a yellow fuselaged Albatros, with a black tail, 6,000 feet below him. Blenkiron attacked from out of the sun, forcing the enemy machine down to 4,000 feet. Blenkiron zoomed away and watched the Albatros crash between the railway line and Bourlon, the wings and fuselage breaking up, leaving the tail sticking up out of the wreckage. Blenkiron next attacked a two-seater but was in turn attacked by an enemy scout. Having lost the advantage of surprise, Blenkiron broke off the action and returned, confident that he could claim the Squadron's 250th victory. He was to be disappointed. Balcombe Brown refused to allow the yellow and black Albatros as there was no confirmation. Blenkiron offered to show him the crash, but Balcombe Brown refused. His reasons were two fold: even if he saw the crash there was no proof that it was Blenkiron who had shot the Albatros down; secondly, in view of the bad weather he refused to put two machines at risk merely to confirm a personal victory.

There was only one casualty for the fighter squadrons during the day: in the afternoon 2Lt A L Kidd of 46 Squadron was last seen east of Havrincourt. He was later reported to have been taken prisoner. Arthur Lee recorded that the day was very misty, 'much too thick for flying,' and Kidd may have become lost and landed behind the German lines.

January 2 saw little activity. There was a thick ground mist and low clouds at 400 feet were heavy with snow, but a patrol from Naval 8 were out, and FltCom Guy Price shot down an Albatros in flames over Cite St Auguste at 11.13am, killing *Ltn* Günther Auffarth of *Jasta 29*.

The weather changed dramatically on January 3, the day was fine and clear. In a morning patrol Henry Maddocks of 54 Squadron scored the first victory for the squadron since it had exchanged its Sopwith Pups for Camels, shooting down a DFW in flames east of St Quentin at 8.25am. A patrol from Naval 8 was also successful, Compston sharing with SubLts Jordon and Dennett in the destruction of a DFW over Arras at 10.05am.

An hour and a quarter later Compston scored his 19th victory, another DFW over Epinoy Wood.

More victories were claimed during the afternoon. Robert Chidlaw-Roberts and 2Lt C F Cunninham of 60 Squadron shared in a two-seater, shot down in flames over Comines-Menin at 12.40pm; Gorringe of 70 Squadron sent a two-seater down in flames north of Wervicq at 1.40pm, and five minutes later his squadron mate, Francis Quigley, sent a two-seater down out of control east of Moorslede for his 10th victory. A patrol from 29 Squadron, led by William Earle Molesworth, claimed three Albatros scouts out of control in a combat south of Moorslede, and Captain Rusby badly damaged an observation balloon. On the debit side, 2Lt C D Skinner returned wounded from the fight with the Albatri.

The pilots of 84 Squadron were now flying patrols in pairs. Taking off at 1.55pm, Lt Anthony Beauchamp Proctor and an American pilot, Lt Jens Larsen from Waltham, Massachusetts, attacked a pair of two-seaters three miles northeast of St Quentin. Proctor got into a good position on the tail of one and fired a drum of Lewis and 100 rounds of Vickers into it. The enemy machine went down to 3,000 feet, followed by Proctor, firing all the time, until he was forced to turn away by accurate and heavy anti-aircraft fire, the two-seater still going down in a vertical dive. This was the first victory for the young South African; he would survive the war with 54 victories and have been awarded a VC, DSO, DFC and MC and Bar. Larsen had disposed of the other two-seater, shooting it down in flames for his second victory of an eventual nine.

Naval 10 had two casualties in the day's fighting. At 1.45pm B Flight dived to attack an enemy two-seater, but were attacked by a group of Albatros scouts of *Jasta 30* which had dived through C Flight flying top cover. John Manuel had a stoppage in both guns, was forced down to 300 feet and chased to Ostend by three of the Albatri. He managed to evade the enemy scouts in the clouds and was able to land at Naval 3's aerodrome at Bray Dunes with his Camel considerably shot about. Two Camels were lost during the combat. FltSubLt F Booth of B Flight was shot down and killed and FltSubLt A G Beattie of C Flight was wounded in the ankle. While attempting to land Beattie lost control of his Camel, one wheel touching down first, tipping the Camel over onto its back. Beattie was taken prisoner. The Camels were awarded to *Vzfw* Oberländer and *Uffz* Liebert of *Jasta 30*.

Additional casualties were Lt R J G Stewart of 56 Squadron, who was shot down just behind the German front line trenches and taken prisoner by *Ltn* Hanstein of *Jasta 35,* and 3 Squadron had a pilot killed and another wounded.

The Canadian, Lt R L M Ferrie of 46 Squadron, was also killed. Leading his Flight back to the aerodrome after a combat his right wing suddenly folded back, then the left wing, and his Camel went down vertically. His Flight dived after him and could see him struggling to get clear of his harness straps, half-standing up. Horrified, they watched him trying to decide whether or not to jump; he didn't and he and the Camel were smashed 'to nothingness.' Arthur Lee wrote in his diary: 'I can't believe it. Little Ferrie, with his cheerful grin, one of the finest chaps in the squadron. God, imagine his last moments, seeing the ground rushing up at him, knowing he was a dead man, unable to move, unable to do anything but wait for it. A parachute could have saved him. There's no doubt about that. What the hell is wrong with those callous dolts at home that they won't give them to us.'[3]

The strain of the last months had at last taken its toll of Arthur Lee. An examination by the medical officer of the squadron found him to be run down physically and on New Year's Day he was ordered by Major Mealing not to fly anymore. Ferrie had taken over command of Lee's Flight, and perhaps his loss was the last straw. Lee was posted to Home Establishment on January 7.[4]

The weather continued fine on January 4. Most of the combats seem to have taken place in the morning. A patrol from 70 Squadron led by Gorringe attacked a two-seater east of Gheluvelt at 9.20am and Gorringe and Lt H Soulby shared in its destruction. Gorringe followed this success in an afternoon patrol, shooting down an Albatros scout in flames at 1.30pm over Passchendaele. William Jordon, leading a Flight of Camels from Naval 8 engaged a DFW over Oppy-Monchy at 11.30am and all four Camel pilots – Jordon, Johnstone, Dixon and Dennett – shared in its destruction, but FltSubLt A J Dixon was later shot down and killed.

Pilots from 1, 23 and 65 Squadrons were in combat with enemy scouts over Becelaere between 10.45 and 11.15am. John Gilmore of 65 Squadron, who had earlier shot down a two-seater over Roulers at 10.40am, sent an Albatros scout down out of control from the fight at 11.00am and ten minutes later destroyed another, which crashed south of Gheluvelt. Guy Knocker and the Canadian, Edward Eaton, both of 65 Squadron, also claimed enemy scouts out of control, but 2Lt Robert E Robb was shot down and killed, possibly by *Vzfw* Kampe of *Jasta 27*. Capt William Fry of 23 Squadron shot down an Albatros scout, that crashed east of Becelaere at 1.10am and 2Lt C Fowler, also from 23 Squadron, claimed an Albatros that fell in flames before breaking up in mid air. Capt Guy Moore of 1 Squadron attacked an Albatros with a red fuselage, white tail and black and white wingtips, and shot it down to crash south of Terhand at 11.05am for his last victory while flying Nieuports. The *jagdstaffeln* admitted to only one loss from this action: *Ltn* Graepel of *Jasta 28*, killed in action over Becelaere.

The only other casualty for the fighter squadrons was Capt F H B Selous of 60 Squadron. At 11.45am, east of Menin, Selous dived to attack a two-seater, well below him, and in the dive – estimated by the other pilots to be nearly 300mph – Selous' SE5 broke up in mid-air, its wings breaking away from the fuselage.[5]

Very little work was possible on January 5 owing to low clouds and mist, but some patrols were flown and Capt Michael Goone of 54 Squadron claimed a DFW, shot down over St Quentin-Marty at five minutes to four in the afternoon. The conditions were better the next day and there was considerable fighting. Capt Patrick Huskinson of 19 Squadron appears to have been the first to have scored, shooting down an Albatros over Houthulst Forest at 7.00am. This was Huskinson's seventh victory and his last flying a Spad VII. 19 Squadron were shortly withdrawn from the front to be re-equipped with the Sopwith 5F.1 Dolphin.

In the afternoon a patrol of Spads from 23 Squadron, led by William Fry, saw a large scale fight taking place over Passchendaele between Albatri and Sopwith Camels of 70 Squadron. 'We joined in just as the fight was breaking up, with several machines in sight going down out of control and at least one in flames.' The Spads then found five Albatros scouts from *Jasta B* flying west and Fry dived to attack the nearest, firing twenty rounds into it from behind. The Albatros rolled over, went down in a steep spiral and crashed in a shelled area south of Passchendaele. This was *Ltn* Walter von Bülow-Bothkamp, *Staffelfuhrer* of *Jasta B,* with 28 victories, who was killed. Although Bülow-Bothkamp's Albatros was designated G 123, little was left and nothing was salved.

The pilots of 70 Squadron claimed two Albatri from the initial action. Kemsley and Quigley shot down an Albatros that crashed at Stadenberg at 2.00pm, and fifteen minutes later Quigley and Gorringe destroyed another Albatros, which crashed east of Passchendaele.

The naval pilots were also in action during the morning. Compston and FltLt W L Jordon of Naval 8 attacked a Albatros over Quiery la Motte and shot it down out of control at 11.50am. FltCom Guy Price scored for the squadron again an hour later, destroying a two-seater over Oppy and in the afternoon, at 1.00pm, FltLt Harold Day destroyed another two-seater over Fresnoy. Capt James Payne of 29 Squadron scored his 13th and penultimate victory at 1.25pm, destroying an Albatros scout northeast of Staden. The only casualties in the day were a pilot of 29 Squadron who was wounded in action and a pilot from 60 Squadron who forced landed and was interned in Holland.

Very little flying was undertaken for the next two days, the weather being extremely bad, and on January 9, although the morning was fine it snowed in the afternoon. Before the snow began there were a few combats, although enemy activity was slight. Payne of 29 Squadron claimed a two-seater out of control and Lt Peverell of 70 Squadron forced a two-seater to land, which then turned over onto its nose. Capt Donald Patrick of 1 Squadron scored his fourth victory – his and 1 Squadron's last flying Nieuports – when he sent a DFW out of control over Comines at 10.25am, but two of the squadron's pilots were lost during the morning, both killed in action. A patrol of three SE5s from 41 Squadron, led by Capt Loudoun Maclean, caught a Rumpler east of Marcoing and drove it down out of control at 11.45am.

The SE5s of 56 Squadron were out in some force in the morning, ten crossing the lines, but only McCudden had decisive combats. He first attacked a pair of Hannovers at 12,000 feet over Bourlon Wood. Moisture had frozen over the lens of McCudden's Aldis sight, making it impossible to use and he was forced to aim by tracer. The Hannover went down in a spiral, with water or petrol streaming from it and McCudden last saw it at 500 feet, gliding down under control north of Raillencourt. McCudden drove off an Albatros scout from over Ribécourt before attacking an LVG over Graincourt, stopping its engine with a short burst from both guns. Although he was well east of the lines, the enemy pilot turned west and went down in a flat spiral glide. McCudden got under the tail of the LVG and fired another short burst from close range before having to turn away with a gun stoppage. The LVG continued to go down steeply and finally hit the ground in a flat glide, down wind. Balcombe Brown allowed this as a victory because of the steepness of the glide and the strong following wind and it was awarded to McCudden as his 38th victory and 56 Squadron's 250th. That evening McCudden received a telegram from General Salmond, congratulating him on leading the first Flight in the RFC to have brought down 100 enemy aircraft.

Another Camel squadron arrived in France during the day, 73 Squadron flying into St Omer before moving to Estrée Blanche three days later.

Strong winds, rain and cloud made flying almost impossible for the next two days, although Lt Harry Symons of 65 Squadron, while flying an engine test on the afternoon of January 10, saw two enemy scouts attacking an RE8 and shot one down out of control over Frelinghien.

January 13 was fine. Although visibility was 'indifferent' and there was a strong west wind, a great deal of flying was done. George McElroy and John Tudhope ended a drought of victories for 40 Squadron in the morning: McElroy shot down a Rumpler over Pont a Vendin at 9.20am and Tudhope a DFW in the same area an hour and thirty five minutes later. These successes were offset by the loss of 2Lt H E Davies, who was shot down by AA fire and taken prisoner.

Since 8 January 84 Squadron had been under orders to fly three successive patrols at intervals of two hours, commencing at 7.30am. In one of the morning patrols Capt Pennell drove a two-seater down out of control over Villers-Outreaux at 10.25am and forty minutes later, during another patrol, John Ralston claimed another two-seater, over Crevecoeur. A quarter of an hour later Lt Jack Sorsoleil claimed yet another two-seater, this one north west of Graincourt, and Lt H A Payne shot down the last victory for the squadron's day: an Albatros C type north west of Manières.

At 56 Squadron McCudden was the first to leave the ground, taking off alone at 8.40am. It was to be an unlucky day for three enemy two-seaters. McCudden glided out of the sun to attack the first, an LVG coming north over Bellenglise at 8,000 feet, closing to within fifty yards without being seen. A short burst from McCudden's guns sent the LVG down in a steep spiral glide, which steepened still further until it finally crashed east of Le Haucourt at 9.40am. McCudden then flew north and ten minutes later saw a pair of DFWs being shelled northeast of Ronssoy. McCudden attacked one of these – from *Bogohl 7* crewed by *Vzfw* Hans Rautenberg and *Ltn* Gerhard Besser – and it went down steeply, emitting smoke and water, to hit the ground in a vertical dive north of Vendhuile. McCudden then turned his attention to its companion, but the enemy crew put up a determined resistance and fought McCudden for five minutes. 'He knew every trick and worked the fight very skilfully over his lines.' As they were now east of the front lines and there were plenty of other enemy two-seaters in the area, McCudden gave this DFW crew best and left it.

At 10.00am, after again flying north, McCudden sighted two LVGs going west over Épéhy. McCudden closed to within 200 yards of one and opened fire with 200 rounds of Vickers. The LVG stalled, then went down in a vertical dive, the left hand wings broke off and it burst into flames, crashing in the British lines east of Lempire. This LVG was designated G 124, although little was left. After an indecisive fight with a DFW over Gonnelieu, McCudden returned. It is possible that this last DFW was also from *Bogohl 7* who had an observer, *Ltn d Res* Max Ritterman, killed over Gonnelieu.

The LVG shot down in the first of these actions was from *Fl Abt (A) 264*, crewed by a pilot named Notler – initial and rank unknown, possibly a *Vzfw* – and *Ltn d Res* Max Pappenheimer. Notler was unhurt in the crash but Pappenheimer was killed and his commanding officer later wrote to his parents.

'On January 13th, on a clear, cold winter day, your son had orders to observe and direct our batteries against enemy batteries, as always he did this with perfection. Afterwards he took photographs of the damaged enemy batteries. Shortly before turning for home he was intercepted by an English single-seater. After an exchange of machine gun fire, pilot Notler found your son dead in his seat. Pilot Notler came down at Le Haucourt, north of St Quentin. Your son was the best officer in our squadron. He had flown 288 times against the enemy and took photographs of 100 damaged enemy batteries, which is a record number.'

While the squadron had been grounded by the bad weather, McCudden had instructed his mechanics to fit the spinner of the LVG that he had shot down on November 30 to the nose of his SE5 and paint it a brilliant red. This patrol on January 13 was the first flown with the spinner in place, and having shot down three enemy two-seaters in the space of twenty minutes, McCudden was convinced it was bringing him luck.

Seventy-One Squadron, renumbered in January as 4 (Australian) Squadron had already had bad luck since arriving in France on December 18 1917. On January 6, C Flight were practising formation flying when two pilots collided, the wreckage of their falling machines hitting another Camel below them. All three pilots were killed. Now, on January 13, flying its first war patrol, the squadron had it first casualty when Lt W B Willmott, lagging behind the rest of the formation, was shot down and taken prisoner by *Ltn* Schuster of *Jasta 29.*

The Camels of 65 Squadron bombed the ammunition dump at Ledinghem. Guy Knocker's diary extract. 'Whole squadron, each machine carrying four 20lb bombs, bombing dump at Ledinghem. Thick and misty. Bombed from 8,000 feet. I don't think we hit anything much.'

The weather began to deteriorate the next day and there were very few combats, but Capt George Cox of 65 Squadron shot down a two-seater in flames over Westroosebeke at five minutes to twelve in the morning.

There was hardly any flying for the next three days, the weather conditions were bad, with low clouds mist and rain. On January 18 the weather began to clear and there were some combats. 2Lt A E Wylie of 65 Squadron is reported to have shot down an enemy machine over Westroosebeke, but was himself then shot down by *Ltn* Gallwitz of *Jasta B.* Lt W G Ivamy of 54 Squadron was also wounded in combat during the day.

The day was fine on January 19, with high cloud and good visibility. Most of the decisive fighting seems to have taken place in the morning.

A patrol from 54 Squadron fought seven Albatros scouts over Ramicourt at 9.15am. Capt K Shelton claimed one down out of control, but Lt Ohrt was shot down and made POW. Capt John Trollope of 43 Squadron scored the first of his eventual 18 victories, destroying a DFW over Vitry at 10.25am, but half an hour later in the patrol 2Lt C N Madeley was shot

down and killed, possibly by *Jasta 12.* A Canadian pilot with 70 Squadron, George Howsam, scored his second victory, shooting down an Albatros two-seater over Moorslede at 10.20am, and Frank Hobson of the squadron caught a two-seater over Warneton at forty minutes later and shot it down in flames. A patrol of Camels from Naval 8 were in combat with fourteen enemy scouts over Wingles at 11.25am. FltSubLts Johnstone, Dennett and Jordon all shared in an Albatros sent down out of control, and in an afternoon patrol Edward Johnstone claimed another Albatros out of control over Henin-Lietard at 3.00pm. McElroy and William Harrison of 40 Squadron caught a pair of DFWs over the Vitry area at noon. McElroy destroyed one over Vitry and Harrison the other east north east of Arras.

Five Camels from 65 Squadron were in action with 17 enemy scouts over Westroosebeke at 1.45pm and 2Lt E T Baker was shot down and killed, the possible victim of *Ltn* Gallwitz of *Jasta B.*

During the day the RFC suffered a heavy blow when the commander of I Brigade, Brigadier-General Gordon Shephard was killed in a flying accident. Shephard, the youngest brigade commander in the RFC and extremely popular with all ranks, flew as an independent observer of many of the actions flown by his squadrons. He also took an interest in the welfare of all the men under his command – particularly the recent arrivals – visiting the squadrons almost daily, flying his personal Nieuport. Coming in to land at Auchel his Nieuport stalled, spun in, and Shephard was killed.

During the day the order was received redesignating the Australian squadrons. Nos 68, 69 and 71 Squadrons were renumbered 2, 3 and 4 Squadrons, Australian Flying Corps.

A full squadron patrol, led by Geoffrey Bowman, was flown by 56 Squadron on the morning of January 20. At 10.15am Bowman went down alone to attack a pair of two-seaters over Bois de Cheneauz, leaving the rest of his Flight above to protect him from five Fokker Triplanes. Gun stoppages frustrated Bowman's attack and he zoomed to rejoin his Flight. The enemy triplanes did not attack and Bowman fired a Very light to wash out the squadron patrol.

McCudden was over Bourlon Wood at 9,000 feet and he attacked an LVG, opening fire from 100 yards. The LVG went down in a left hand spiral, smoking badly, and after falling for 4,000 feet its tailplane broke off and the wreckage fell between Raillencourt and Cambrai at 10.30am. This LVG was from *Fl Abt (A) 202,* crewed by *Uffz* Gustav Mosch and *Ltn* Friedrich Bracksiek, who were both killed.

There was little flying on January 21 and no combats were fought, but the following day there was a great deal of air fighting.

The naval pilots were in action in the late morning, FltCom Guy Price and Harold Day each claiming an Albatros out of control over Vitry at 11.20am. Kenneth Seth-Smith of 70 Squadron sent an Albatros scout down over Oostnieuwkerke at 10.35am, and in an afternoon patrol by the squadron Howsam shot a two-seater down in flames at 12.45pm over Westroosebeke. Howsam and Quigley shared in the destruction of an Albatros in flames north east of Houthulst Forest at 2.14am; sharing in another, out of control, six minutes later in the same area. Ten minutes later an Albatros dived on Quigley, but he turned to meet it, firing at it nose on. The enemy scout dived away, followed by Lt J Todd, firing into it until it crashed north east of the Forest. This scout was shared between Quigley and Todd. These successes were offset by the loss of 2Lt F W Dogherty, who was shot down and taken POW by *Ltn* Fruhner of *Jasta 26*. The only other casualty of the day was a Camel pilot of Naval 9 who was wounded by anti-aircraft fire and forced to land.

Capt Molesworth of 29 Squadron destroyed an Albatros north east of Staden at 12.35pm for his second of his five victories during the month.

Richard Mundy of Naval 8 took off in the dark at 7.00pm to attack an enemy balloon over Godault farm. He attacked twice from a height of 100 feet and on his second attack, closing to within thirty feet of the balloon, it burst into flames. This was the fifth and last balloon claimed by Munday, all but one destroyed at night.

Naval 10 were in action in the afternoon of January 23. FltCom William Alexander, a Canadian from Toronto, led ten Camels across the lines and at ten minutes to three a trio of two-seaters and a single scout were seen over Staden. These enemy machines dived away through the clouds, followed by some of the Camels. It was the classic decoy trap. Five additional Albatri were waiting below the cloud level. In the fighting FltCom Wilfred Curtis, also from Toronto, attacked one of the enemy two-seaters that was seen to break up in mid-air. Alexander fired up into the underside of an Albatros scout, which went down through the cloud, followed by Alexander, who saw that it was still falling, completely out of control. John Manuel saw FltSubLt R A Blyth under attack from an Albatros and dived to his assistance, but was forced to break away with stoppages in both guns. When next seen, Blyth's Camel and an Albatros were both going down out of control and crashed simultaneously near Staden. Blyth and the Albatros, flown by *Ltn* Gustav Wandelt of *Jasta 36,* had collided and both pilots were killed.

Naval 3 were also in action over the area, attacking four DFWs and three other enemy aircraft west of Zarren. This was very probably the same action as that of Naval 10. The Naval 3 pilots claimed no victories and FltSubLt Youens was shot down and made POW.[6]

January 24 was fine and there was a great deal of fighting. The naval squadrons were again in the forefront of the action, fighting with a formation of Albatri over Neuvireuil. William Jordon and Edward Johnstone of Naval 8 shared an Albatros out of control at 11.30am, both sharing another with FltSubLt R Johns a few minutes later. Flt SubLt James White destroyed another Albatros over Fresnes-Vitry at 11.40am – possibly *Uffz* Fritz Jacob of *Jasta 12* – and FltCom Guy Price crashed an Albatros over La Bassée at 12.25pm. FltSubLt Wilfred Sneath rounded off the day's victories for Naval 8 with an Albatros destroyed east of Lens at 3.00pm.

At 11.15am pilots of 70 Squadron were fighting with Albatros two-seaters over Westroosebeke. Howsam destroyed one over the village at 11.20am and Alfred Koch another, ten minutes later. Further south, another patrol of the squadron was in the Wervick area, Quigley crashing a two-seater south east of the village at 11.20am.

Capt Herbert Drewitt of 23 Squadron was leading his Flight on patrol in the vicinity of Comines when he saw a formation of six Albatros scout below them. Drewitt led the Spads down and attacked the enemy scouts, sending one down through the clouds in a spin.

A Flight of Nieuports of 29 Squadron, led by Capt Molesworth, attacked a formation of two-seaters north east of Roulers at noon. Molesworth closed to within 150 yards and fired a whole drum of Lewis into the nearest, which went down out of control. Molesworth then turned his attention to another, fired into it from a hundred yards and reported that a burst of smoke came out of it before it went down to crash. James Coombe of the patrol was also credited with another of the two-seaters as out of control. Half an hour later Philip de Fontenay of the squadron destroyed an Albatros scout north of Roulers.

Just after noon a patrol from 60 Squadron were attacked by *Jasta 6* over Becelaere. The enemy pilots came down from out of the sun and *Ltn* Mobius opened fire on Lt Clarks' SE5. Hearing the gunfire, Lt A W Morey turned sharply to the left and collided with Mobius, cutting the Albatros in half and losing both wings from the side of his SE5. The wreckage of both machines fell from 12,000 feet and both pilots were killed.

Capt O'Hara Wood scored the first victory for 4 Squadron AFC at 12.27pm, destroying a DFW over La Bassée, and McElroy of 40 Squadron claimed his fourth victory with a DFW out of control over the Oppy area at 12.50pm.

McCudden continued his private war with enemy two-seaters, catching a DFW over Monchy-le-Preux at 1.55pm. The enemy two-seater had been pointed out to him by British anti-aircraft bursts and McCudden closed to within 200 yards before opening fire. McCudden's shots evidently hit the enemy pilot because McCudden could see the observer leaning into the front cockpit to take control of his machine. In no danger from the rear gun, McCudden closed to within thirty yards and fired another burst into the DFW, which went down out of control, alternatively stalling and diving until finally spinning at 2,000 feet into the ground mist. This DFW was from *Fl Abt (A) 240*. The observer, *Lt d Res* Georg Palloks, later died of his wounds, but the pilot appears to have been uninjured.

The fighter squadrons had one other casualty for the day. Capt Harry Reeves, of 1 Squadron, about to be posted to Home Establishment after seven months with the squadron, was killed in a flying accident. The official casualty report records that he was flying an engine test in Nieuport B6774, but other reports state that he was stunting over the aerodrome. Pulling up into a climbing turn after a steep dive the lower left hand wing and interplane strut of the Nieuport broke away and it crashed on the north side of the aerodrome.

There was a thick mist on the morning of January 25 that failed to clear until the early afternoon. The day was then generally fine and there was a great deal of fighting.

Lt Geoffrey Bremridge of 65 Squadron destroyed a two-seater in flames over Warneton at 12.45pm, and during a patrol by 40 Squadron Lt J Hambley sent a two-seater down out of control: it was last seen at 3,000 feet still falling vertically. Lt Michael Gonne of 54 Squadron claimed an Albatros out of control over Grougis at 1.10pm and fifteen minutes later shot down a Rumpler in flames over Fieulaine, which he shared with Lts Kelly and Lawson.

The pilots of 56 Squadron had been unlucky in not being able to claim any victories for over a month. Since December 19, only McCudden had scored, the squadron victory lists showing his name for no less than sixteen consecutive victories. Their luck changed in the early afternoon of January 25. Capt Bowman and C Flight attacked five LVGs over Havrincourt. Getting onto the tail of one LVG, Bowman's first burst either killed or wounded the enemy observer, who fell back into his cockpit, leaving his gun unattended, pointing vertically upwards. Before Bowman could press home his advantage, however, an SE5 flown by Blenkiron dived between him and the enemy machine, forcing him to zoom away. Leaving Blenkiron to finish off this LVG, Bowman attacked another and shot it down to crash by the side of a quarry, a mile north west of Rumilly. After Blenkiron had seen the first LVG going down out of control southwest of Cambrai, he attacked another, but the crew were experienced and the pilot executed a series of tight turns, giving his gunner every chance

to make good shooting at Blenkiron. The fight continued, with Blenkiron and the LVG dropping lower and lower over the rooftops of Cambrai, until Bowman fired a red light to reform the Flight. Blenkiron left the LVG to make good its escape, the only one of the five to do so, Lt Douglas Woodman and Maurice Mealing having shot down the others.

B Flight, led by McCudden, also had some success, the Flight attacking a DFW over Graincourt. All the pilots made good shooting at this DFW and after a final burst from Trevor Durrant it went down out of control just south of Cambrai. After unsuccessfully attempting to lure 'Greentail' and his Flight into a fight, McCudden attacked a Rumpler flying west from St Quentin. After 200 rounds from McCudden's guns, the Rumpler, from *FlAbt(A) 225*, crewed by *Ltn* Schramm and *Ltn* Büscher, went down out of control over Urvillers at 2.40pm for McCudden's 44th victory. Both Schramm and Büscher had been wounded and Büscher later died of his wounds.

A little earlier in the afternoon Naval 8 had been in action with several Pfalz D III over Beaumont, and Jordon and Johnstone shared in the destruction of one at 1.15pm. Howsam of 70 Squadron saw an Albatros attacking an RE8. He dived to assist the British two-seater and forced the Albatros down to 1,000 feet until it turned over onto its back and went down north of Bixschoote at 3.25pm. This was possibly *Vzfw* Herbert Werner of *Jasta 26*. Harold Hamersley of 60 Squadron evened up the loss of Morey the previous day by destroying an Albatros. The Albatros, a white letter K on its black fuselage, crashed northeast of Staden.

It was a successful day for 84 Squadron. At 2.40pm a formation of enemy two-seaters was seen over Malincourt. Lt Hugh Saunders and Lt Edmund Krohn shot down one and Lts George Johnson and Charles Travers engaged another two, sending one down in flames. At approximately the same time, Lt Frank Taylor and 2Lt Henry Watson of 41 Squadron attacked a formation of eight Albatros scouts and shared in the destruction of one over Vitry, possibly *Ltn* Paland of *Jasta 20*, who was wounded in action. FltCom Miles Day of Naval 12 fought a Fokker Triplane over Staden at 3.25pm, finally sending it down out of control.

The fighter squadrons had only one casualty: FltSubLt J Carr of Naval 12 was shot down in flames at 2.15pm over Dixmude, but survived to become a prisoner of war.

The official RFC communiqué for January 26 records that enemy activity was slight and there were no combats. Thick mist made war flying impossible the next day.[7]

The weather was good on January 28. The naval squadrons appear to have been the first in action. A patrol from Naval 8 caught a two-seater from *Schusta 17* over La Bassée and Guy Price shot it down in flames, killing *Gefr* Ludwig Kneeb and his pilot, *Gefr* Wilhelm Walter. Half an hour later Jordon sent an Albatros down out of control over Beaumont-Drocourt for his 17th victory.

During the morning Leonard Rochford was leading B Flight of Naval 3, accompanied by three additional Camels from A Flight. At 11.00am he saw a pair of DFWs flying at 10,000 feet above Houthulst Forest. 'With Glen and Devereux I attacked one of them, firing at point blank range. The observer was either killed or wounded and the engine hit as the propeller ceased to revolve.' The DFW – possibly from *Fl Abt(A) 238* who had a crew member wounded in action – went down in a spin.

The Nieuports of 29 Squadron were also out. Philip de Fontenay shot down a two-seater out of control over Staden at noon and twenty minutes later the patrol was in action with enemy scouts south of Roulers. James Coombe claimed an Albatros out of control and Earl Meek sent down a Fokker Triplane.

During the relative inactivity of the past few days McCudden, using his expertise as an engine mechanic, had fitted a set of high compression pistons to the engine of his SE5a. These pistons were the type used in the Wolseley Viper engine, the Wolseley Company's redesigned version of the standard Hispano-Suiza that powered the SE5a. On the squadron's workshop test bench the re-pistoned engine gave considerably more revolutions per minute than the standard 200hp Hispano-Suiza and McCudden had high hopes that he could now catch the Maybach-powered high flying Rumpler C.VIIs.

A test flight in the morning showed that McCudden's hopes for the new engine were realised. As he opened the throttle he at once felt the extra power, and the rate of climb of the SE5a to 10,000 feet was vastly improved. Half an hour after landing from this test, McCudden took off again, anxious to try conclusions with the Rumplers. He stalked and caught one at 19,000 feet over Bellevue, but his guns gave serious trouble, robbing him of a victory. Despite this disappointment, McCudden was pleased with the increased performance of his SE5a: 'I knew that my machine was now a good deal more superior to anything the enemy had in the air, and I was very pleased that my experiment, of which I had entirely taken the responsibility, had proved an absolute success.'[8]

McCudden took his Flight out in the afternoon on a normal patrol and attacked a group of Albatri over Bourlon Wood. No decisive victories were scored but on returning it was realised that Lt Lester Williams was missing. He had last been seen in the fight with the Albatri and it was thought that he had been shot down by one of them – *Vzfw* Konnecke of *Jasta 5* was credited with an SE5 over Tilloy – but Williams had been shot

down by a two-seater from *Fl Abt (A) 233,* crewed by *Ltn* Schuppau and *Ltn* Schandva, and taken prisoner.

2Lt G Clapham of 54 Squadron dived on a formation of three Albatros scouts and shot one down, which was seen to crash, but 2Lt D Lawson was wounded in the fight. Additional out of control victories were claimed during the day by John Todd of 70 Squadron (a Fokker Triplane north west of Menin at 3.30pm) and Hutton and Wolff of 40 Squadron.

January 29 was fine but hazy. The Camels of 70 Squadron were in action with enemy scouts over Houthulst Forest at 11.10am, Quigley sending one down in flames to crash north east of the forest. Peverell also claimed another of the enemy scouts, out of control, and later, at 12.55pm over Moorslede, Seth-Smith claimed another. In afternoon patrols by the squadron, Frank Hobson claimed an Albatros out of control at 2.10pm west of Staden, and at 4.00pm, Alfred Koch claimed a two-seater out of control over Dadizeele. During these afternoon patrols by 70 Squadron Lt K M Rodger was wounded, shot down and taken prisoner near Poelcappelle by *Ltn* Bolle of *Jasta 28.*

FltCom Richard Munday was leading a patrol from Naval 8 in the area of Beaumont-Auby when he saw a group of five Albatros scouts below them. Munday attacked one at close range, firing 150 rounds. Munday's tracer was seen hitting the area of the enemy pilot's cockpit and the Albatros turned over and went down. FltSubLts Day and Johns each claimed an Albatros driven down during the fighting.

In the afternoon two patrols from 29 Squadron engaged fifteen enemy scouts east of Moorslede. Molesworth chased one of these east and sent it down in flames. Capt Earl Meek attacked another. After a burst of 50 rounds from 60 yards range, the Albatros zoomed, one wing crumpled, and it burst into flames. This was possibly *Ltn* Brecht of *Jasta 36*, killed in action over Passchendaele

At 7.00am an early morning victory had been awarded to Capt Patrick Huskinson of 19 Squadron: an Albatros out of control over Houthulst Forest for the squadron's last victory flying Spads before it was re-equipped with Sopwith Dolphins. 2Lt C J Howson achieved a similar distinction for 32 Squadron. At this time the squadron was receiving the SE5a, but flying one of the last of the DH5s, Howson destroyed an Albatros scout over Staden for the squadron's last victory on the type.

Pilots from 19, 65, 56 and 32 Squadrons all claimed out of control victories during the day. 2Lt A T Lindsay was credited with a balloon destroyed in flames, and FltSubLt J E Green of Naval 12 destroyed an enemy seaplane off Blankenberghe pier at 2.00pm.

There was one other casualty: 2Lt C L Van-der-Hoff of 3 Squadron was killed when his Camel broke up diving on an enemy two-seater over Bourlon Wood.

Although conditions were still hazy on January 30 there was a considerable amount of fighting.

McCudden took off alone at 9.45am. After two indecisive engagements – a Hannover two-seater over Bullecourt and five Albatri south of Venduille – he attacked four enemy scouts, three Albatri and a Pfalz, climbing for height over Anneux. McCudden dived behind and below one of the Albatri and fired a short burst from both guns from fifty yards. Pieces of wood flew off the fuselage of the enemy machine and it went vertically down, emitting smoke, completely out of control. This Albatros was from *Jasta 10* and *Vzfw* Adam Barth was killed in the crash.

The enemy pilots had still not realised they were under attack. McCudden flew on behind the Pfalz and fired another short burst from both guns. The Pfalz went down in a spiral, stalled – a sure sign the pilot was hit – sideslipped, then went down in a vertical dive out of control over Fontaine.[9] The remaining two enemy scouts flew off east.

Bowman and C Flight flew a patrol in the afternoon. At five minutes past two Bowman dived on an enemy scout over Gonnelieu and a long burst from both guns from 100 yards sent it down in a steep dive. Bowman left this Albatros, still going down, and went to the aid of his Flight who were fighting four Albatri over Wambaix. As Bowman hurried into the action he saw an Albatros fall in flames out of the fight, to crash half a mile from the village and continue to burn on the ground. This was *Obltn* Bruno Justinus, acting *Staffelführer* of *Jasta 35b,* who was thrown from his blazing Albatros as it hit the ground. German troops rushed to the scene to extinguish the flames from Justinus' flying coat, but mercifully he was already dead from gunshot wounds.

Bowman reformed the Flight and ten minutes later they were attacked by six Albatri, two of which had black tails. Bowman turned the SEs to meet the attack and fired both guns into one of the black-tailed Albatri from 30 yards. The enemy machine went down almost vertically and crashed by the side of a road. Although he was actually flying a Pfalz D III, this was probably *Ltn* Diemar of *Jasta 35b* who was forced to crashland near Premont.

McCudden and B Flight had seen the seven enemy scouts – which included 'Greentail'– attack C Flight and had joined in the fight, but the 56 Squadron pilots had no further success.[10]

At 11.45am, Capt Kenneth Leask, leading a Flight of 84 Squadron SE5s, attacked six enemy scouts and a two-seater over Villers Outreaux. Six additional enemy scouts joined in the fighting, but 84 Squadron lost no pilots in the action. Leask drove one enemy scout down out of control and Lt John Anthony McCudden, James McCudden's younger brother, claimed another out of control for his first victory as a fighter pilot.[11]

Leonard Rochford was leading his Flight on an Offensive Patrol in the Ypres-Roulers-Dixmude area when he saw six Albatros scouts, 2,000 feet below the Camels over Gheluvelt. The Naval 3 pilots attacked and Rochford, FltSubLts J A Glen and A B Ellwood shot down two out of control.

Out of control victories were claimed by pilots of 23, 29 and 43 Squadrons; there were no casualties.

There was no war flying on the last day of the month, a thick mist that lasted all day effectively grounded the antagonists.

NOTES

1. The *Luftstreitkräfte* had also used aircraft in attacks on ground troops and positions, but these had been carried out by the specialist *Schusta*, flying the fast and manoeuvrable Halberstadt CL II, armed with one or two forward firing machine guns for the pilot and another in the rear cockpit for the gunner, four or five 22lb bombs and anti-personnel hand grenades. The Halberstadts were also used in a more efficient way than the fighter aircraft of the RFC, being employed only at decisive points of attack, and with each flight – usually of four to six aircraft – having been given specific targets, with strict orders not to abandon these for others which the crews might consider more favourable.

2. *Years of Combat*, Sholto Douglas, Collins 1963.

3. *No Parachute*, Arthur Gould Lee.

4. Arthur Gould Lee was to have a distinguished career in the post war RAF, reaching the rank of Air Vice-Marshal. He died on 21 May 1975.

5. Selous, who was the son of the famous African hunter Frederick Selous, died on the first anniversary of his father's death in action in west Africa .

6. Wandelt was awarded two Camels during the afternoon; one was possibly Youens.

7. Some authorities give that 80 Squadron arrived in France during the day, flying their Sopwith Camels into Boisdinghem aerodrome. Others give the squadron arriving in France on January 22. In view of the weather conditions on January 27, the earlier date is the more likely.

8. *Five years in the Royal Flying Corps*, James McCudden.

9. This Pfalz pilot must have survived the crash as there were no other losses reported in the area.

10. The'Greentail' in this instance was almost certainly not the 'Greentail' which the pilots of 56 Squadron had been fighting since late November 1917, but a similarly marked Albatros from *Jasta 35b*. See McCudden's victory on 18 February 1918.

11. John McCudden had been awarded two victories while flying DH4s in 25 Squadron: an Albatros scout in October 1917 and an Albatros two-seater in November.

CHAPTER EIGHTEEN

FEBRUARY:
THE GATHERING STORM

After the costly battles of 1917, the British General Staff, their minds dominated for years by the problems of attack, began a comprehensive examination of the defensive role of their forces. In January 1917 a General Headquarters memorandum had outlined the change in principles, setting out a plan for defensive measures. Another paper was also issued in January, delineating the role of the RFC: the air offensive must be maintained; the first and most important duty of the RFC was to watch for any signs of an impending enemy offensive and to inform the army commanders concerned of the scope and time of the attack.

The bad weather had seriously hampered air observation during January, but it had become obvious that the German Army was preparing for a large-scale offensive to be opened in late March or early April. The preparations were extensive and far ranging, but by the beginning of February 1918 General Gough, commanding Fifth Army, was convinced that the main enemy attack would be made against the Third and Fifth Armies. Opposite the fronts of these armies, new enemy aerodromes, supply dumps, railway sidings and troop encampments had been observed: fourteen new aerodromes alone had been discovered east of the Forest of St Gobain, opposite the right of the Fifth Army. There was widespread and abnormal movement on the rail network on either flank of the Fifth Army, and the enemy was showing great activity in his forward areas.

A thick mist that persisted the entire day stopped all flying over the battlefronts on the first day of February, but conditions had improved the next day and a large amount of work was done by the Corps and Army squadrons of the RFC.

The pilots of Naval 8 were first in action. Over the Douai area FltCom Compston and FltSubLts Johns, Day and W F Crundall[1] shared in an enemy two-seater[2] shot down over Ostricourt at 11.30am and an Albatros scout three quarters of an hour later over Carvin.

McCudden took off at 10.30am. Ten minutes later he saw an LVG going northeast over Ruyaulcourt.

'I overtook EA and secured a firing position at 100 yards range and fired a long burst from both guns, after which EA went down vertically, then on its back, when the EA gunner fell out of EA and the machine finally crashed in our lines 1 mile E of Vélu, at Sheet 57G.J33. I returned at 10.50 to report weather.'

The LVG, No. 9775/17, was from *Bogohl 7* and designated G 130 in the captured aircraft lists. The crew, *Vzfw* Erich Szafranek and *Ltn* Werner von Kuczkowski were both killed.

At 12.45pm, Flt Com Miles Day of Naval 13 shot down a Rumpler, which fell in the British lines at Oostkerke, the crew, *Ltn d Res* Kohnke and *Ltn d Res* Molle from *Fl Abt (A) 231* were both killed.

Later in the afternoon, at 2.45pm, Capt Roy Chappell of 41 Squadron had shot down an Albatros, which fell at Erchin, when he was attacked by six enemy scouts. Chappell put his SE5 into an evasive spin; recovering, he saw an Albatros directly in front of him. The remaining five enemy scouts were still above, but Chappell fired into this machine and at 2,000 feet it was still spinning out of control. Lt Jones of the patrol also claimed an Albatros out of control from this fight, but the commanding officer of the squadron, Major Frederick James Powell had been wounded and shot down to be taken prisoner, possibly by *Ltn* Kühm of *Jasta 10*.

At 3.45pm, Capt Gorringe attacked a pair of two-seaters over Becelaere and destroyed one that was seen to crash by anti-aircraft gunners. A patrol from 54 Squadron saw a Camel under attack from an Albatros. Lt G C Cuthbertson attacked this Albatros and it broke up in mid-air, killing *Ltn* Tann from

Jasta 24. Capt K Shelton went down to within fifty feet of the ground to attack a balloon that had not been launched and it burst into flames.

An out of control victory was claimed by McElroy of 84 Squadron – a two-seater southeast of Habourdin at 3.30pm. James Child of the squadron attacked a DFW, his fire hitting the observer before Child was forced to break off the attack with gun trouble. This was Childs' last combat while with 84 Squadron: he was posted home three days later.

The weather continued fine on February 3. The Camels of 65 Squadron were on an Offensive Patrol at 10.15am and Guy Knocker was forced to land after a combat with enemy scouts.

'Chased about 17 Huns east of Lille and then dived on seven black and white Albatri south west of Roulers. Shot one down in a spin and was allowed him. Got bullet through sleeve of my Sidcot and longeron and main spar shot. Gilmour got a Hun. My original Camel written off.'[3]

At 10.45am 54 Squadron were in action over Honnecourt with five enemy scouts. In quick succession, Captain Henry Maddocks shot down two Albatri in flames from *Jasta 48*, killing *Ltn* Max Kersting and *Ltn* Karl Stock. Lt Cuthbertson also claimed an Albatros, which was seen by a member of the patrol to crash.

A patrol from 41 Squadron was on patrol north west of Douai at 10.10am and attacked an Albatros two-seater, which Capt Loudoun and Lt G A Lipsett sent down out of control. Later in the morning Compston of Naval 8 caught a DFW south east of Douai at 11.25am and shot it down out of control; an hour later, he shared with FltSublts W Crundall and E G Johnstone in the destruction of another DFW over Sallaumines.

Further north, a patrol from Naval 10 led by FltCom Alexander attacked five Albatros scouts over Rumbeke aerodrome at 3.15pm. The engine of Alexander's Camel lost pressure and he was forced to break off his attacks. FltLt W G R Hinchcliffe also lost his engine, going down to 400 feet above the enemy aerodrome and coming under attack by three of the Albatri before he managed to restart it. Hinchcliffe then attacked one of the enemy scouts, which went down out of control and crashed into a tree.[4] FltSubLt W H Wilmot was shot down and killed in this action.

Other out of control victories were claimed by Capt O'Hara-Wood of 2 Squadron AFC, Capt Horsley of 40 Squadron; FltCom Munday of Naval 8; 2Lt H Lewis of 32 Squadron and Capt Gilmour of 65 Squadron. There was one other casualty: FltCom R R Winter of Naval 9 was in combat with Fokker Triplanes of *Jasta 26* south east of Roulers at 2.00pm. He was seen to shoot down one of the triplanes, but the wings of his Camel then folded up and he was killed.

The only victories scored by the fighter squadrons on February 4 were by the pilots of 60 Squadron. The first success went to Lt William Duncan and 2Lt J O Priestley, when they shared in the destruction of an Albatros scout, shot down in flames over Ypres at 11.20am. Five minutes later, the patrol attacked a formation of Albatri over Zonnebeke, 2Lt Herbert Hegarty and Lt H D Crompton shooting one down in flames. The only casualty for the day was a pilot of 54 Squadron who was wounded in action.

The early afternoon of February 5 was highly successful for George McElroy. He first attacked a DFW at 12.40pm, closing to a 100 yards and firing a hundred rounds. Pieces fell from the enemy machine's tailplane and fuselage; it went down in a slow spin and crashed at Wingles. Twenty minutes later British anti-aircraft fire pointed out another DFW, north of La Bassée. McElroy closed with this machine and after 200 rounds it burst into flames.

At 12.45pm a patrol from Naval 8 led by FltCom Roderick McDonald attacked two Albatri over Pont à Vendin. All four Camel pilots – McDonald, Day, Sneath and Fowler – shared in the destruction of one of the enemy machines, but Harold Day, an experienced airfighter, with 12 victories, was diving to attack another Albatros when his Camel was seen to break up and he was killed.

Major Jack Cunningham, the CO of 65 Squadron, tackled an Albatros scout that was attacking one of his pilots, firing a burst of both guns from a range of 50 yards. The tailplane of the Albatros collapsed and it went down to crash at Beythem at 1.35pm.

Pilots of 29, 65, 60 and 70 Squadrons all claimed out of control victories, and Capt Gilmour was awarded a balloon, which went down with black smoke pouring from it after its occupants had taken to their parachutes.

There were two other casualties. A pilot from 65 Squadron was wounded in the head and 60 Squadron lost Lt Cyril Ball, the younger brother of Albert Ball. Ball had driven down an Albatros scout and was following it down when he was attacked by *Offstv* Esswein of *Jasta 26,* whose fire hit Ball's SE5a in the engine. Ball landed six miles behind the lines and was taken prisoner. After he was identified as the brother of Albert Ball he suffered a deal of inhumane treatment and was subjected to personal exhibition.

The weather began to deteriorate on February 6 and it appears that there was only one combat during the day by the fighter squadrons – a costly combat for 3 Squadron. In the afternoon a patrol from the squadron attacked six Albatros scouts in the vicinity of Remy. Capt Oliver Sutton collided with one of the Albatri, damaging his rudder, but he managed to return. The rest of the Flight later reported that 2Lts P Kent and A G D Alderson each shot down an Albatros – which were later reported by AA as being seen to crash – but both pilots were then themselves shot down: Kent falling in flames, and Alderson, claimed by *Ltn* H Becker of *Jasta 12*, taken prisoner.

Rain, strong winds and mist effectively stopped nearly all service flying for the next ten days. Although some work was done by the corps squadrons on February 9,10,11 and 12, in the main the fighter squadrons were grounded and there was only one casualty: 2Lt G A C Manley of 54 Squadron, shot down and taken POW on February 9.

The weather on February 16 was 'very fine' and visibility was good, and the air fighting recommenced with some fierceness. Most of the air fighting at this period seems to have taken place in the mornings and perhaps the explanation is that given by Gwilym Lewis in a letter home: … 'the Hun is seldom seen in the afternoon, when the sun is on our side of the Lines, and it is very often misty'

Geoffrey Bowman, now promoted to Major and commanding 41 Squadron, scored his 25th victory – the first in his new command – shooting down an LVG over Bantouzelle at 8.00am. At 9.40am, a patrol from 84 Squadron encountered a Rumpler over St Quentin, escorted by five Albatri. Anthony McCudden went for the Rumpler, shooting it down to crash near the town, and Jack Sorsoleil sent one of its escort down in flames. A little later in the morning another patrol from the squadron attacked four Albatros scouts over La Fère. The Flight Commander, Capt Federic Brown, and the American, Lens Larsen, each shot down an Albatros out of control, but the engine of Brown's SE5 then began to run badly with carburettor trouble and he made for home. On the way back, despite the trouble with his engine, Brown attacked an Albatros scout and a two-seater and shot both down: the scout out of control; the two-seater destroyed over La Fère at 11.00am. Another member of the patrol, the Canadian George Johnson, destroyed an Albatros south east of St Quentin at 11.15am.

While his brother was crashing a Rumpler, the elder McCudden was also in action – with another Rumpler. B and C Flights of 56 Squadron had taken off at 9.35am on an Offensive Patrol in conjunction with Bristol Fighters. While over Caudry, waiting for the Bristols to appear, McCudden saw a Rumpler getting its height over the town and dived to attack it. After a long burst the Rumpler went down in a vertical dive, all four wings breaking off, the wreckage falling south west of Caudry, the wings falling more slowly over a wide area. This Rumpler, which crashed at approximately 10.40am was from *Fl Abt (A)269*, crewed by *Uffz* Häicke and *Ltn* Düsterdieck.

Ten minutes later McCudden shot down a DFW from *Flt Abt (A)202*, which fell in flames before breaking up, the

wreckage crashing near Le Catelet, killing *Uffz* Fröhlich and *Ltn* E Karlowa. Just after sending this DFW down, McCudden felt bullets hitting his SE5 and looking up saw 'Greentail', whose long-range snipe hit McCudden's SE5 in one of its elevators, putting it out of action. McCudden's radiator had sprung a leak, the water had frozen over his windscreen and Aldis sight, and he decided to return, but as he re-crossed the Lines over Hargicourt he spotted another Rumpler. Despite his troubles, McCudden sent this Rumpler down in a steep dive, pouring smoke, and it was last seen by Fielding-Johnson the C Flight Commander, going down in a spiral dive, completely out of control. McCudden was delighted with Fielding-Johnson's confirmation as the Rumpler was his fiftieth victory – making him the first British pilot to achieve the half-century – but Balcombe Brown refused to credit the victory on Fielding-Johnson's confirmation alone. McCudden was extremely annoyed at Balcombe Brown's decision – justifiably so considering his past successes – and took off in another SE5 at 11.45am. By the time McCudden found a possible outlet for his anger – a Rumpler, west of the Lines – his anger had subsided and he stalked the Rumpler with his usual methodical calm, finally closing with it as it flew north west towards Douai. After a very short burst from both guns, the Rumpler dived steeply: … 'after going down 500 feet, every one of his four wings fell off and went fluttering down like a lot of waste paper, while the fuselage went down with that wobbling motion which a stick has when one sees it fall.' The Rumpler, from *Schusta 29b*, fell in the British Lines near Lagnicourt and was designated G 137. The crew, *Vzfw* Zeuch and *Gefr* Lechleiter were both killed. In the evening the AA batteries rang to confirm that the disputed Rumpler had crashed, making the machine from *Schusta 29b* McCudden's fifty-first victory.

In a morning combat with enemy scouts, Lewis and 'Pusher' Usher of 40 Squadron shared in a black Pfalz D III out of control over Lille. Lewis pulled down his top wing Lewis gun. 'Pressed the little trigger actuator and away spat that dear little specially-speeded-up gun of mine. I looked over my shoulder and there was the old Hun going down all over the place. Apparently Usher had had a shot just as I pulled round. Anyway, between us we had made him think of home!'[5]

It seems that RFC High Command had still learnt little from the lessons of the previous years. A long range German gun had been heavily shelling the British back areas. A number of RE8s – Lewis put it at 'about 30' – were sent to bomb the offending gun, 'in the daylight, which is of course a waste of time on the best occasions,' Gwilym Lewis commented in a letter home. Flying without observers in order to carry a heavier bomb load, four RE8s were brought down by *Jasta 46*. Lewis was disgusted. 'I simply couldn't believe my ears when I heard that such things were possible in 1918. It had happened on the Somme but I thought those days were over. We were simply furious. It is the biggest victory the Huns have had since I have been out here on this front.'[6]

On patrol over Mont Rouge at 11.30am, Lt Percy Clayson saw an Albatros scout, pointed out by Archie, diving on a ground target at Bailleul. Clayson got behind the enemy scout and shot it down to crash in a ploughed field, the enemy pilot, *Ltn* Bastgen of *Jasta 30,* getting out and walking around his crashed machine. The Albatros D V 4422/17 had a yellow fuselage with a black diagonal line running round it and was made G 134. Clayson had been with 1 Squadron since October 1917, but this was his first victory of an eventual 29. He was another of those pilots who found the Nieuport a difficult machine, but became successful flying the SE5.

Capt Harold Balfour, leading a patrol of Camels from 43 Squadron, attacked two formations of enemy scouts over Courrieres at 11.15. The first scout Balfour attacked went down out of control, but he destroyed the second, which crashed south of the village. Bailey saw an Albatros attacking an RE8 and shot it down in flames, and at 11.45, John Trollope destroyed a DFW over Vitry for his second victory.

John Ralston of 24 Squadron drove an Albatros scout down over Mont d'Origny, but while changing his Lewis gun drum he was attacked by another, whose fire badly damaged his SE5 and wounded Ralston. Despite his wound, Ralston managed to evade the Albatros and return to his aerodrome at Matigny. He was the only casualty of the day.

Three pilots from Naval 8 – Guy Price, and FltSubLts Sneath and Fowler – shared the credit for an Albatros down in flames over Pronville at 11.15. It was the last victory of the war for Guy Price. He had scored 12 victories since joining Naval 8 in December 1917.

Other out of control victories were scored by Major C Miles, CO of 43 Squadron; Capt G Thomson of 46 Squadron, shared with Lt H Debenham; James Hamilton of 29 Squadron, and George McElroy of 84 Squadron.

The fine weather continued the next day. Patrols from 43 Squadron were out early and Capt Balfour and Lts King and Grandy shared in an enemy two-seater out of control east of Pont à Vendin at 9.20am. 2Lt W Casson attacked another of the enemy machines: the left hand bottom wings crumpled up and it went down to crash.

During the morning the SE5s of 40 Squadron flew an escort for six DH4s bombing a German aerodrome. Six Pfalz D IIIs attempted to interfere with the bombers: George McElroy shot one down to crash and 2Lt R C Wade accounted for two others, all confirmed by the crews of the DH4s. On the way back to Bruay, McElroy shot a two-seater down in

flames four miles south east of Lens for his tenth victory: 'Some lad!' commented Gwilym Lewis.

McCudden took off alone at 9.50am and attacked a LVG escorted by a Hannover. Seeing McCudden approaching, the Hannover pilot hurriedly made off and McCudden attacked the LVG, which went down in a sideslip to disappear into the ground mist. The LVG was confirmed to have crashed by AA batteries and was McCudden's 52nd victory.

At 10.25am, Kenneth Junor of 56 Squadron took off, also alone. While looking for two-seaters over Bourlon Wood, Junor was attacked by an Albatros, but the enemy pilot missed in his first burst and dived away east. Junor followed and opened fire from 100 yards. The enemy machine went down in a steep left-hand spiral before bursting into flames and crashing in a field a mile east of Moeuvres. This victory was confirmed by Fielding-Johnson. *Vzfw* Klauke and *Ltn* Jablonski of *Fl Abt (A)263* were both lost over Bourlon Wood on February 17 and it is possible that Junor's reference to an Albatros scout was their Hannover. The Hannover CL IIIa was a reasonably new type being met by the pilots of the squadron at this time; they often referred to it as an Albatros scout. McCudden, writing of the type, commented: 'These machines are very deceptive and pilots are apt to mistake them for Albatros scouts until they get to close range, when up pops the Hun gunner from inside his office and makes rude noises at them with a thing which he pokes at them and spits flames and smoke and little bits of metal which hurt like anything if they hit them.'

A patrol by the squadron in the afternoon was in combat with Albatros scouts northwest of St Quentin. Fielding-Johnson, the C Flight Commander, sent one down out of control – which Balcombe Brown refused to allow as a victory – but Maurice Mealing followed his opponent down and saw it crash near Brancourt-le-Grand, confirmed by Capt Louis Jarvis.

The Australian fighter squadrons were out in some force during the day. Patrols from 4 Squadron had fights with several small formations of enemy machines over Lille. Lt Woolhouse of Capt Flockart's Flight shot down a two-seater from point blank range in one encounter, but Lt C Martin was killed when his Camel was hit by anti-aircraft fire.

Anthony McCudden fought a Fokker Dr.1 at 11.15am and shot it down to crash northeast of St Quentin, wounding *Ltn* Lübbert of *Jasta 11*.

Out of control victories were claimed by pilots of 3, 4 AFC, 43, 40, 29 and 84 Squadrons. The only other casualty was 2Lt D N Ross of 24 Squadron, whose SE5 broke up under the fire of *Uffz* Schweppe of *Jasta 35b*.

The next morning B Flight from Naval 10, led by FltCom John Manuel were in combat with five Albatros scouts over Menin. Manuel attacked one Albatros and after 100 rounds from close range it spun away and went down. Frederick Hall got onto the tail of one Albatros and fired 200 rounds into it, sending it down out of control. Hall followed this Albatros down to 8,000 feet before leaving it to attack another, which evaded his fire. FltSublt Ronald Burr was attacked by an Albatros, and although FltSubLt McKelvey successfully drove it off, Burr had been wounded and while returning from the patrol crashed on the British side of the lines, dying of his wounds two days later. Burr was possibly the 20th victory of *Ltn* Ernst Udet of *Jasta 37*.

McCudden took B Flight of 56 Squadron across the Lines over Moeuvres and at 9.40am saw four Albatros scouts of *Jasta 35b* flying north over Vitry-enArtois. Taking the SE5s down, McCudden attacked the leader of the enemy formation and fired a long burst into his machine. The Albatros flew straight for a brief moment, then burst into flames before turning over onto its side and going down, the pilot falling from his blazing machine after only a few hundred feet. As the Albatros went down, McCudden was gratified to see that it had a greentail and a white chevron on the top wing, which was also marked with a large letter K, and concluded that this was the same 'Greentail' which the pilots of the squadron had been fighting since November 1917 and which they believed had shot down Richard Maybery in December.

McCudden then flew on to the next Albatros, a blue-tailed machine, and shot it down to crash between Beaumont and Quiery-le-Motte, just east of the railway and only two and a half miles from the wreckage of the first Albatros, which hit the ground just north of Vitry-en-Artois, at Izel-les Equerchin. The pilot of the first Albatros was *Uffz* Julius Kaiser, whose body was found close by the village. The pilot of the blue-tailed machine was Uffz Joachim von Stein. McCudden's fire had wounded him in the shoulder and mouth, but he managed to land his badly damaged machine and was taken to Field Hospital No.204.[7]

The other SE5s had driven the remaining two Albatri east, without gaining any decisive result and McCudden, whose radiator had boiled dry, left the patrol and landed at 12 Squadron's aerodrome at Boiry St Martin.

A patrol from 60 Squadron, led by Capt Hamersley attacked four Fokker Triplanes north of Handzaeme at 12.40. Hamersley shot down one triplane which was seen to crash from 12,000 feet, and another was driven down to ground level by Lt C O Evans and Lt R B Clark to crash into a tree. Lt W M Kent claimed another as crashed.

The South African, Hugh 'Dingbat' Saunders took his Flight into action with Albatros scouts of *Jasta 5* over Beaurevoir at 11.00am and *Vzfw* Martin Klein was shot down and killed. Hans Joachim von Hippel recalled the action in the March 1963 edition of the *Jägerblatt*, the journal of the German Fighter Pilots' Association:

'I lost my left lower wing at 4,000 metres altitude after a combat at about the same moment that *Feldwebel* Martin Klein's aircraft (green tail and the letters K on his wings) past me into the depths far below with his wings stripped off. *Feldwebel* Klein had been shot through the head and his stripped fuselage fell past me at the same instant that I lost my lower left wing. I do not remember anyone shooting at me at that moment because I did not observe any SE5s behind me. However, since Klein was so close to me and without wings, it would indicate that he had been shot down from above and behind by an SE5 diving out of the sun. Our combat had started at 5,000 metres and I had started a dive down to 4,000 metres without any good reason. When I pulled my stick back and started to level off, my entire left wing became independent of the rest of the aeroplane. The strut did not break, but the mounting rivets on the fuselage as well as on the 'V' strut were ripped out so that the wing itself arrived complete and in one part on the ground. After I had landed and turned over, the wing was found, and eventually returned to *Jasta 5*. Upon losing my wings, I immediately turned off the ignition so that the motor could cool, and, in case of an impact, the plane would not start to burn. It was my desire to arrive on the ground as a reasonably good-looking body. Klein's machine came down about 1,000 metres from my own landing point, and despite his head wound, he had jumped from his Albatros before the impact and his body was lying close to the wreck. Klein had been with *Jasta 5* only a short time and did not have any air victories. Under both lower wings, was the letter K stencilled in white, and on both sides of his fuselage he carried a star as a personal insignia.'[8] The detached wing of Hippel's Albatros came down at Le Catelet, over ten miles from *Jasta 5's* aerodrome at Boistrancourt.

The pilots of 84 Squadron claimed four out of control victories in the morning of February 18. Percy Hobson and George Johnson each claimed an Albatros out of control over Beaurevoir at 11.00am and these would have been Klein and von Hippel. Hugh Saunders was also awarded an LVG out of control over Beaurevoir at the same time.

Just after noon, Frank Gorringe of 70 Squadron scored his last two victories of the war: two Albatros scouts destroyed over Houthulst at 12.15pm, bringing his total victories to fourteen. One of these Albatros scouts was possibly *Ltn* Willy Etzold *Jasta 26*, killed in action over Houthulst Forest. Gorringe would return to France as a flight commander in 210 Squadron RAF in October 1918.

Additional out of control victories were claimed by pilots of Naval 8, 2 (AFC) 40, 24, 29, 43, 70 and 84 Squadrons.

There were six additional casualties to those mentioned. Naval 8 lost a valuable pilot. The Irishman, FltCom Guy Price was making a low-level ground-strafing attack when he was shot down. Price had scored 12 victories since joining Naval 8 during the first week of December 1917 and his loss was a severe blow to the squadron. One of his fellow flight commanders, Robert Compston remembered him:

'Determination, pluck and the power to lead were the attributes of Price. Irish and impetuous, he gave much trouble to the enemy for, like Little, he never gave in. Scorning the Aldis telescopic sight for his guns, he would put his head over the side of the machine and watch his tracers bullets riddling the enemy; this gave him no small amount of satisfaction and I can see the sparkle in his eyes as he said to me one day: "sure I drilled him like a cullender till the blighter burst into flames". We presume he was killed while shooting down an enemy kite balloon and no doubt he was looking over the side watching his tracers bullets go into it when a bullet hit him in the head, so he died with the sparkle in his eyes, engine roaring, guns spurting flames in glorious action. Had he been told his time must come he would have asked for nothing better than to die like this.'[9]

Naval 8 also lost FltSubLt C R Walworth, who was shot down and killed near Arleux.[10]

Additional casualties to those mentioned were a pilot of 3 Squadron and another from 29 Squadron, both wounded in action, and a pilot from 70 Squadron shot down and taken POW.

The weather continued fine on February 19. The pilots of 24 Squadron were in action early. Lts Andrew Cowper, P A McDougall R Mark and Reuben Hammersley caught a Rumpler over Servais at 8.40am and shot it down in flames. Ten minutes later the patrol sighted a DFW and sent it down to crash at Bernot.

The SE5 squadrons were doing well. At 10.15 a patrol from 84 Squadron attacked a formation of two-seaters escorted by Albatros scouts over St Gobain Wood. Capt the Honourable Robert Grosvenor shot down two of the enemy two-seaters, within five minutes. The first crashed at St Gobain and the second went down out of control. The rest of the Flight had tackled the scouts. Jack Sorsoleil destroyed two: the first over St Gobain Wood at 10.15, the second a few minutes later just north of the wood; Anthony McCudden destroyed another, which crashed north of La Fère at 10.15 and five minutes later shared another scout with Jens Larsen, which went down out of control over Gobain Wood. Anthony Beauchamp Proctor also destroyed an Albatros, which crashed south east of La Fère to bring the total to seven enemy machines shot down.

2Lt Morley Kent, a Canadian pilot serving with 60 Squadron, saw a Spad and three Camels fighting some enemy scouts. Kent fired at one enemy machine from 400 yards – much further than the recommended range – but he hit the Albatros, flown by *Ltn* Hans von Puttkammer of *Jasta 3* and it went down to crash in the British lines at Hollebeke. Puttkammer was taken prisoner and his Albatros, No.4495/17, designated G 138.

Capt William Fielding-Johnson led C Flight of 56 Squadron off the ground at 11.10am. Forty minutes later the SE5s attacked four Hannovers over Rumaucourt, which had been pointed out to them by British AA fire. Fielding-Johnson sent one of the enemy machines down in a steep dive, but then had to break off the action with a gun stoppage, leaving his opponent still going down at 3,000 feet. At 12.40pm Louis Jarvis and Frank Billinge attacked another Hannover, the first burst of fire from Jarvis either killing or wounding the enemy observer. Billinge, coming in behind Jarvis, put another fifty rounds into the two-seater, which went down in a wide right hand spiral, doing well over 200mph and outstripping the SE5s. Both of these victories were confirmed by British AA batteries: the first to Fielding-Johnson; the second shared between Jarvis and Frank Billinge.

At 11.50am FltCom Alfred Carter of Naval 10 and Stanley Rosevear of Naval 1 shared in the destruction of an Albatros scout which went down in flames south of Zillebeke Lake.

Lt J Hewitt of 23 Squadron attacked an enemy two-seater, possibly from the same patrol as that attacked by 84 Squadron. Hewitt zoomed under the two-seater three times, firing bursts from both guns, before it finally went down to crash into a house in Crecy. Lts A Lindsay and N Clarke of 54 Squadron attacked five enemy scouts escorting a two-seater. Lindsay got behind one of the enemy machines and after a short burst it fell vertically to crash near Monceau. Clark followed his antagonist down for 8,000 feet, firing short bursts, until parts of the enemy machine broke off and it crashed close to Lindsay's victory.

In the late morning 80 Squadron lost two Camels, shot down while groundstrafing in the La Bassée area, possibly to pilots from *Jasta 30*. Both Camel pilots were killed. Another pilot from the squadron was wounded by groundfire.

There was a brief hiatus in the fine weather on February 20. In the morning the sky was overcast and there was a mist that turned to rain in the afternoon. The weather had cleared by the following morning and the day was fine and bright with good visibility.

A patrol from 60 Squadron were in action with Albatros scouts of *Jasta 27* at 9.00am over Houthulst Forest, and 2Lt W M Kent was shot down and killed by *Ltn* Klimke. *Oblt* Göring had singled out the SE5 flown by 2Lt George Craig, an American pilot. Craig put up a stout fight against the *Staffelfuhrer*, severely damaging Göring's Albatros before being fatally wounded. Both Kent and Craig were buried in the same grave at Moorsele.

A patrol from 2 Squadron AFC fought with ten Albatros scouts at 10.45am over Brebières. The Albatri, with silver bodies and red noses, were in two formations of six and four. Lt A G Clark, leading the patrol of four SE5s, reported. 'One hostile machine dived at me. I fired both guns, Vickers and Lewis, into the nose of this machine, getting a burst of fifty rounds into it at a range of forty yards. The machine fell over on its left wing and dropped vertically into an uncontrolled spin.'

Lt L Benjamin saw one of the Albatri diving across his front, at thirty yards. 'I had nothing to do,' he later reported, 'but to put my finger on my trigger and keep it there and the enemy got it fair in the middle.' The SE5s then climbed for height in order to attack again, and lost sight of the enemy machines for a brief moment until they were seen retreating east. The Australians saw one Albatros crash and another still going down out of control. During this combat Lt R Lang, a British pilot attached to the AFC was wounded, and 2Lt G C Logan was shot down and taken prisoner.

Five minutes later a patrol from 4 Squadron AFC attacked four two-seaters and their escort of six Albatri between Arras and Lens. Lt George Jones attacked one of the Albatri, which broke up under his fire, killing *Vzfw* Weber of *Jasta 46*. Lt S Adams chased after another, which was escaping to the north, and finally shot it down at Houbourdin, twenty miles north of the initial engagement. Lt A Couston was fighting a determined and skilfull enemy pilot – possibly *Ltn* Matthaei of *Jasta 46* – who pushed him north, finally forcing him to land and be taken prisoner near Wavrin.

At 1.47pm, James McCudden, flying alone, engaged a DFW at 9,000 feet over Acheville. The enemy pilot quickly dived away and McCudden had time for only six shots. They were sufficient: the DFW went down in flames and crashed on the railway line just south of Méricourt. McCudden's short burst had hit the enemy machine in the petrol tank: McCudden had a theory that the Germans were now using high grade petrol from Galicia and Roumania, which ignited more easily than the low grade petrol used by the British. The DFW was from *Fl Abt (A) 235*, crewed by *Vzfw* Erich Klingenberg and *Ltn* Karl Heger, who were both killed.

At 2.10pm, Archie bursts pointed out an enemy two-seater to Molesworth of 29 Squadron. Molesworth got in position behind the enemy machine and shot it down to crash in flames in the Allied lines between Hooge and Gheluvelt, killing the crew, *Ltn d Res* Kurt Niederländer and *Lt d Res* Emil Briese. This two-seater (given the number G 140) was from *Fl Abt (A) 238*.

Other claims included an Albatros out of control south of Honnecourt by George McElroy for his first victory since being transferred to 24 Squadron, and Capt Harry Symonds of 65 Squadron shot an Albatros down in flames three miles east of Dixmude. Richard Munday of Naval 8 claimed a two-seater out of control over Drocourt for his ninth and last victory of the war. The only other casualty was a pilot of 70 Squadron who was wounded in action by anti-aircraft fire.

For the next two days the weather was bad, with low clouds and rain. There were intervals of brighter weather on February 24 and there were a few combats, which resulted in some casualties. A pilot of 4 Squadron AFC, 2Lt W B Randell was last seen over La Bassée: he was shot down and taken prisoner. Capt C Sutton of 3 Squadron was wounded in action, and 2Lt Herbert of 40 Squadron was wounded when his SE5 was badly shot up in a combat.

The weather improved a little on February 26. It was generally fine, but with a strong west wind in the morning and during the afternoon squalls and rain set in.

Enemy aircraft were active along the whole of the Front. A morning patrol from 24 Squadron were in action with Fokker Triplanes east of Laon at 8.40am. Andrew Cowper destroyed one, which broke up in mid-air; Ian McDonald drove another down to 4,000 feet, firing short bursts from close range until it went down to crash. Twenty minutes later McDonald shared with Lts Dawe, Tubbs, Mark, Richardson and Poulter in the destruction of another triplane, which crashed at Samoussy.

At the same time as this action, Cowper attacked a Pfalz D III from *Jasta 15,* flown by *Vzfw* Hegeler. Hegeler had dived to 500 feet to evade Cowper's attacks and attempted to fly east, but Cowper kept to the east of him, heading him off and finally forcing him to land on 52 Squadron's aerodrome at Golancourt. Hegeler was taken prisoner and his Pfalz D III, 4184/17, was designated G.141. In the afternoon another patrol from 24 Squadron were in action, again with Fokker Triplanes, in the same area – Laon – as the morning. McElroy shot one down in flames to crash four miles east of Laon at 4.05pm, and Reuben Hammersley claimed an Abatros scout out of control in the same area. McElroy and Peter McDougall attacked another triplane. After a long fight of ten minutes it spun down and crashed east of Laon at 4.15pm. 2Lt C H Crosbee failed to return from this afternoon patrol.

While on patrol in the area of Becelaere at 11.00am, Molesworth attacked an enemy two-seater flying east. Molesworth fired two drums of Lewis into the enemy machine and it spun down to crash south east of the village. This two-seater was confirmed by pilots of 10 Squadron and was probably from *Fl Abt (A) 250*, crewed by *Uffz* Colsmann and *Ltn* Becka.

Lts A Dobie and Cecil King of 43 Squadron fought an enemy two-seater at 10.15am, driving it down from 12 to 6,000 feet before Dobie's fire sent it down to crash at Fresnoy. King was then engaged by three Albatros scouts and he went down to ground level to escape their attacks. While contour chasing west, King saw two Albatri just above him. He zoomed and attacked one of these, which went down and crashed.

James McCudden had a frustrating morning. He had been told the previous day by Lt-Col Playfair, commanding Thirteenth Wing, that he was to be shortly posted to Home Establishment and that he was to do no more flying for the remainder of his stay with 56 Squadron. McCudden had ignored Playfair's order; despite feeling extremely ill with a bad cold and sore throat had taken off alone at 9.35am. McCudden's first combat was with an LVG over Gonnelieu at 15,000ft. The enemy pilot fought superbly, half-rolling and Immelmann-turning his heavy aeroplane, which McCudden noticed was marked with a large number 6 on its top wing, in an identical manner to his own SE5. While McCudden was fighting with this LVG, three Albatros scouts attempted to attack him but were prevented from doing so by the arrival of three SE5s from 84 Squadron.

McCudden then flew north and attacked two Hannovers, but these were flown by experienced crews, who cooperated well and got in some good shooting at the SE5. These opponents were too dangerous and McCudden left them, flew north again and attacked a Rumpler from *Fl Abt 7* at 17,000 feet over Douai. This time McCudden made no mistake. He opened fire at 200 yards and continued firing until the Rumpler burst into flames and broke up, the wreckage falling east of Oppy, killing *Vzfw* Otto Kresse and *Ltn* Rudolph Binting.

McCudden then flew south and sighted a DFW escorted by a Hannover over Chérisy. As McCudden approached, the LVG made good its escape over the Lines, but the crew of the Hannover stayed to fight. McCudden was now feeling feverish and lightheaded, but he resolved to bring this Hannover down, whatever the cost. 'I now made an instant resolve. I had attacked many Hannovers before and had sent several down damaged, but I had never destroyed one, so I said to myself: "I am going to shoot down that Hannover or be shot down in the attempt."' McCudden got into his favourite position of behind and below, placed his sights on the fuselage of the enemy machine and fired both guns until it fell to pieces. As the wreckage went slowly down the enemy gunner fell out. 'I had no feeling for him for I knew he was dead, for I had fired three hundred rounds of ammunition at the Hannover at very close range, and I must have got 90 per cent hits.' This Hannover was McCudden's 57th and last victory. It was from *Fl Abt (A) 293*; the crew, *Uffz* Max Schwaier and *Ltn* Walter Jäger were both killed.

McCudden again flew north and saw a Rumpler above him, just about to cross the Front Lines. McCudden climbed to attack this machine, but before he did so another Rumpler flew across his nose and he switched his attack, opening fire at long range. Pieces fell off the Rumpler but it continued to glide down over the German lines, under control. McCudden had now used all his ammunition and he returned to Baizieux. 'But oh! as I flew back to the aerodrome I felt so ill that I thought I was dying. I just managed to stagger back as far as the aerodrome and land safely, and as I got out of my machine I was ready to drop. However, after I had rested and got warm, I was all right again.'

Despite the injunction that Squadron commanders were not to fly over the Lines, Geoffrey Bowman attacked a two-seater in the afternoon at ten minutes to two. His logbook entry is succinct: '1 crashed. 2.10. 17,000. Saw several EA our side of the Lines. Unable to engage them until 1.48 when saw an EA two seater over La Fère. Caught this machine over La Ferté. EA crashed in Berjaumont wood. Ran out of petrol and landed at Lechelle. Saw Alex. Lechelle to home.'

Lt J D de Pencier and 2Lt J L McLintock were in combat with Fokker Triplanes of *Jasta B* over Comines at 10.10am. J de Pencier sent a Fokker Triplane down out of control for the first victory for 19 Squadron's Sopwith Dolphins, but McLintock was shot down and killed by *Ltn* Plange of the *Jasta* for his third victory, although he incorrectly identified the Dolphin – a new type to the German fighter pilots – as a 'Spad.'

There were four other casualties during the day's fighting. Fifty-four Squadron lost two pilots shot down and captured; 40 Squadron had a pilot killed, and 23 Squadron lost a pilot shot down and captured by *Hptm* von Tutschek, the commanding officer of *Jagdgeschwader Nr.11,* for his twenty-fourth victory.

The sky was overcast all day on February 27 and there was rain in the afternoon. Enemy activity was slight and there were only a few combats. Lt G Howsam of 70 Squadron attacked a two-seater flying at 500 feet over Warneton at 11.05am and it went down to crash in the hedge of a field southeast of Comines. The only casualty of the day was FltCom M J G Day of Naval 13. Day was attacking six enemy seaplanes 24 miles north of Dunkirk when he was shot down in flames. He survived the crash, clinging on to the wreckage of his Camel, but drowned before help could reach him.

In the morning McCudden had flown to 84 Squadron. On reflection he had decided that the LVG he had fought the previous day – which had been marked with his number 6, and which he believed had been flying without an observer – had most probably been a decoy in order to trap him: a trap which had failed because of the intervention of the SE5s from 84 Squadron. After thanking the pilots concerned he stayed to lunch and again cautioned his young brother Anthony, whom he considered far too reckless.

The weather was bad the next day with only a few bright intervals. There were some combats. An afternoon patrol by 84 Squadron were in action south east of La Fère: they had attacked six Albatros scouts, but were then jumped by an additional twelve. The British pilots fought their way back to the lines, Beauchamp Proctor claiming one of the enemy scouts out of control, but Lt E Krohn was last seen being chased by three of the Albatri and he was shot down and killed over Gobain Woods. The pilots of *Jasta 12* claimed three SE5s from this fight and victories were awarded to *Ltn* Koch, *Ltn* Becker and *Vzfw* Neckel.

NOTES

1. Walter Crundall was the brother of Edward Crundall who had served in Naval 8 in 1916-1917.

2. Possibly from *Fl Abt (A)235*. Observer, *Ltn d Res* Seifert, wounded.

3. Cross and Cockade, U.S., Vol.12 No.4.

4. Hinchcliffe was flying a Camel marked, 'Allo! Lil Bird' in this combat.

5. *Wings over the Somme 1916-1918*, Gwilym H Lewis, Kimber 1976.

6. Ibid.

7. Kaiser was not the pilot of the greentailed Albatros that the pilots of 56 Squadron had been fighting since the morning of 23 November 1917. At the first sighting of 'Greentail' the only *jagdstaffel* in the squadron's area of operations was *Jasta 5*, based at Neuvilly. *Jagdgeschwader Nr.1* (*Jasta* 4, 6, 10 and 11) had moved into the area on November 22, but an examination of the War Diary of the *Jagdgeschwader*, shows that none of its pilots was in action on any of the days that pilots of 56 Squadron reported fights with Greentail and his Flight. It was recognised that Greentail was a highly experienced flight commander and all the available evidence points to the conclusion that Greentail was almost certainly *Vzfw* Otto Konnecke of *Jasta 5*, who survived the war with 35 victories. *Jasta 5's* Albatri are known to have had predominately greentails, but several of its pilots also flew machines with striped or chequered tailplanes.

8. Quoted in Cross and Cockade journal. Vol.6 No.4, Winter 1965.

9. *Naval Eight*, The Signal Press Ltd., 1931.

10. Some air historians have given Price and Walworth as having been shot down by *Ltn* Rumpel and *Vzfw* Küllmer of *Jasta 23*, but both these victories were too far north: Rumpel's victory at Givenchy, which is over 17 miles northwest of where Price was last seen and Küllmer's claim was at Bailleul, nearly thirty miles to the northwest.

CHAPTER NINETEEN

DIE KAISERSCHLACHT: THE IMPERIAL BATTLE

At the beginning of March 1918 it was realised that the imminent German offensive would fall on the British Third and Fifth Armies: in the north, one third of the attack would be on the front held by the Third Army; in the south the remaining two thirds would fall on almost the entire front of the Fifth Army. The scale of the planned German offensives in the spring of 1918 – *Die Kaiserschlacht* – was immense: reaching from just south of Arras in the north to La Fère in the south. Preparations for the attack were detailed and extensive, but were carried out only at night: during the day the *Luftstreitkräfte* flew over the immediate area of the coming attack to ensure that no abnormal activity was visible. Part of the detailed German deception plans, however, was not to increase the activities of the *Luftstreitkräfte* over the area, but to allow the corps aeroplanes of the RFC to operate normally: to do otherwise would alert the British to the exact location of the coming attack.

Some of the preparations, of course, could not be successfully hidden. Aerodromes were extremely difficult to hide and to overcome this a stratagem of concealment by sheer scale was employed. Hangars were erected evenly along the entire German front, thereby giving no indication of the exact position of the coming attack. Portable hangars would be erected only immediately before the opening of the offensive.

From the beginning of the month the duty of the RFC was to interfere with the German preparations. The work of the corps squadrons in co-operation with the artillery was of prime importance, both in general shelling and counter battery work. The observation and registration of the main enemy railheads, supply and detraining stations, all railway lines, bridges across the canals, ammunition dumps and all road access to the battle zone – all were of paramount importance. Thousands of aerial photographs, essential for the planning of the artillery programmes, needed to be taken before the threatened offensive began.

In the first days of the month the *Luftstreitkräfte* was relatively inactive: it was husbanding its available forces. For the first time in preparation for a coming battle on the Western Front, the concentration of these forces was greater than that of the RFC. The Third and Fifth Armies of the RFC had thirty-one squadrons on strength – a total of 579 serviceable aeroplanes, of which 261 were single-seater fighters. The German Second, Seventeenth and Eighteenth Armies had an air strength of 730 aeroplanes, 326 of which were single-seater fighters.[1]

During the first weeks of March the duties of the fighter squadrons of the Third Army were Close and Distant Patrols: Close Patrols were of the area between the front line trenches and a line running from north to south five miles on the German side; Distance Patrols covered the outer area of the Close Patrols, but extended to a line nine or ten miles further east. The fighters of the Fifth Army were to fly in Flights and their patrol line extended from just south of Marcoing, eight miles south of Cambrai, to Barisis in the south. The fighters of Ninth Wing, which moved to the Fifth Army on March 7, were given a patrol area stretching approximately from Cambrai to Le Catelet, the patrols therefore covering part of both army fronts.

There were low clouds throughout the day on March 1. There was little enemy activity, but a few combats were fought. Pilots of 1, 23, 24, 54, and 84 Squadrons claimed out of control victories, and although two Camels of 54 Squadron were shot up and forced to land, both pilots were unhurt.

Bad weather – days of low clouds, strong winds, mist and snow – then stopped all flying for the next three days and it was not until March 5 that air operations could be resumed, although these were on a small scale. Only Trollope and Usher of 43 Squadron claimed victories, east of La Bassée in the early afternoon. Usher's victory, an enemy scout, being seen by AA to burst into flames 2,000 feet from the ground. The only fighter casualty was a pilot of 24 Squadron, wounded, shot down and made POW, but who later died of his wounds.

The weather improved dramatically on March 6 and there was a great deal of aerial fighting.

A morning patrol from 4 Squadron AFC observed several Rumplers with an escort of six Albatri over Arras. Four of the Camels, led by Capt Flockhart, climbed to tackle the escort while three attacked the Rumplers. The Albatri attempted to escape to the east but Flockhart and Woolhouse shot one down, which crashed near the River Scarpe. Lt F J Scott chased one of the Rumplers as far as Lens before he managed to shoot it down. It crashed near the town and was confirmed by an observer from 5 Squadron.

Patrols from 24 Squadron were also out in the morning. McElroy destroyed an Albatros scout north east of Bellicourt at five minutes past seven; in a later patrol Capt Alfred Brown claimed an Albatros out of control at 10.15am over St Quentin and Herbert Richardson shot a Fokker Triplane down to crash at 10.55 between Fontaine and Croin.[2] During an afternoon patrol by the squadron, 2Lt D M Clementz collided with an Albatros scout from *Jasta 12* flown by *Ltn* Hans Staats at 1.20pm over Rony. Both machines fell in the Allied lines and the pilots were killed. The wreck of the Albatros was designated G.145. During this patrol, *Hptm* von Tutschek shot down 2Lt A P C Wigan at 1.45pm. Wigan came down near La Fère and was captured.

The pilots of 40 Squadron flew patrols throughout the day. William Harrison was the first to score, shooting down an Albatros northeast of La Bassée at noon. Patrols in the afternoon were also successful. In a fight with seven enemy scouts, northwest of Lens at twenty minutes past four, John Wallwork destroyed an Albatros; Harrison scored his second victory of the day five minutes later, another Albatros, and Ian Napier crashed an Albatros for his third victory. Observers on the ground confirmed these aircraft to have crashed: one north of Lens, one west of the town and the last just north of Mericourt. Capt R Tipton had also scored. He had attacked a Pfalz flown by *Gefr* Walther Conderert of *Jasta 52* and shot it down in the Allied lines. Conderert was killed and his Pfalz D IIIa., No.4236/17, was designated G.146.

2Lt Donald MacLaren of 46 Squadron began his highly successful career with the squadron by shooting down the first of his eventual 54 victories: a Hannover two-seater out of control east of Douai at 1.45pm.

Other victories in the day went to Lt Robert Owen, who shot down a scout, which was seen to crash east of the Bois du Biezat at noon by an AA battery, and Capt A H G Fellowes of

54 Squadron shot down and killed *Ltn* Bahr of *Jasta 11,* flying Fokker Dr.1 106/17. Out of control victories were also awarded to pilots of Naval 10, 24, 40, 41, 46, 54 and 56 Squadrons.

Casualties were relatively light. In addition to those mentioned, a pilot from 84 Squadron was taken prisoner and a pilot from 43 Squadron was wounded in action.

The day began fine on March 7 but there was mist in the afternoon. Several pilots flew Special Missions in mid-morning but returned to report that visibility was very bad and getting worse. Only the pilots of 23 Squadron appear to have seen any action, Capt J F Morris shooting down a Rumpler in flames.

The weather improved on March 8, although visibility was still reported to be 'indifferent.'

The SE5s of 56 Squadron were out in force at 9.00am. Lt Maurice Mealing lost touch with the other SEs soon after crossing the lines, a piece of burnt carbon having flown into his eye which took some time to remove. It was to be an eventful morning for Mealing. Half an hour after removing the offending particle he attacked a Rumpler. This escaped, but thirty minutes later Mealing saw another two-seater, escorted by three scouts, crossing the Lines over Gonnelieu. Mealing drove off the scouts before attacking the two-seater. A good burst from both Mealing's guns sent the enemy machine spinning down out of control at 1,000 feet over Villers-Outréaux.

After frustrating four attempts by enemy scouts to molest RE8s that were working over the lines, Mealing flew towards St Quentin, where he spotted another two-seater. A long burst caused smoke and flame to emit from the fuselage of the enemy machine and it went down over Homblières at 11.25am. Mealing was now nearly out of petrol and he landed at 84 Squadron's aerodrome for petrol and oil.

In the early morning, the two fighter squadrons of the AFC – 2 and 4 Squadrons – put every available machine into the air. As the Australian official historian rather colourfully put it: 'the sky over the Douai area was filled with these winged huntsmen waiting for the enemy to break cover from his aerodromes.' A large formation of 26 enemy scouts was seen over Lens. Lt R L Manuel had only four SE5s with him – two of which had reported engine trouble – and he wisely avoided contact with the enemy but returned to report their presence. At 10.00am 12 Camels left Brauy and four SE5s took off from Savy. The Australians wasted no time in attempting to locate the large enemy formations but flew to the vicinity of their aerodromes to await their return. Just to the west of Douai, Flockart's formation of Camels attacked a number of enemy scouts. Flockart and Woolhouse shot one down in flames and Lt G Nowland sent one down out of control before breaking off the action. A little to the north of this action, four SE5s led by Capt R W Howard, were in combat with a number of two-seaters, forcing one to land. Fifteen minutes later they shot down a two-seater out of control and an Albatros scout. As the SE5s turned for home they saw a black two-seater over Henin-Liètard. Diving to attack this machine the patrol were surprised by eight Albatri that dived at them from out of the sun. Howard saw the threat and quickly turned the SEs west, avoiding the enemy scouts which, their element of surprise gone, made off.

A patrol of Camels from Naval 3 caught an enemy two-seater over Torquesne at noon. Aubrey Ellwood, K MacLeod and C S Devereux all attacked this machine and it went down trailing yellow smoke, then burst into flames and crashed. This two-seater was possibly that of *Vzfw* Heinrich Traub and *Vzfw* Robert Blechmann of *Schusta 16*, both killed.

Capt Oliver Bryson of 19 Squadron scored his twelfth and last victory of the war by destroying an Albatros – its wings folded back before it went down in a spin – over Gheluvelt at 11.10am. This was possibly *OffStv* Willi Kampe of *Jasta 27*, killed in action over Gheluvelt at 12.08 (GT).

In a morning patrol by 24 Squadron, Andrew Cowper shot down a Rumpler at 8.00am, which crashed at Bellenglise. This machine was possibly from *Schusta 5* crewed by *Gefr* Walter Behm and *Gefr* Willi Sellenböhmer. Five minutes earlier, McElroy had caught a DFW east of St Quentin and shot it down out of control. A patrol by the squadron in the afternoon had further success. In a fight with Fokker Triplanes south east of La Fére at 3.00pm, Horace Barton and George McElroy each sent one down in flames.

Henry Woollett of 43 Squadron scored his sixth victory – his first in the New Year – by shooting an Albatros scout down in flames north east of La Bassée at 12.15pm. Fifteen minutes later, Capt Edmund Tempest of 64 Squadron shot down an Albatros over Graincourt.

The Camels of 70 Squadron fought with Albatros scouts over Roulers just after lunch. Both Francis Quigley and George Howsam claimed out of control victories, one of which was possibly *Ltn* Heinrich Minder of *Jasta 51*, killed in action over Rumbeke. On the debit side, 2Lt F G McNeil was killed in action during this combat.

Lt Jimmy Slater of 64 Squadron opened his score for 1918 with his fourth victory: a Pfalz D III shot down over Cambrai at 10.40am, but another member of the patrol, 2lt R H Topliss was wounded and shot down over Bourlon Wood by *Ltn* von Manteuffel-Szöge of *Jasta 35b* for his first victory. The only other casualty of the day was a pilot of Naval 12, shot down near Menin at 1.30pm by *Ltn* von Haebler of *Jasta 36*.

The intense fighting continued on March 9. The Camels of 70 Squadron were in action at 9.30am with Albatros scouts over the Menin-Roulers road. Lt Howsam destroyed one and sent another down out of control; Quigley shot an Albatros

down in flames at 9.30am and crashed another ten minutes later. Forty minutes later 65 Squadron were in action with Fokker Triplanes over Dadizeele. George Cox fired at one triplane, which stalled then went down in a spin before one of its wings folded up. This was possibly *Ltn* Max Naujock of *Jasta 36* who was killed in action over Moorslede. Lt G Bremridge also claimed a triplane out of control during the fighting. Guy Knocker was also in this fight. 'Our first experience of Fokker Triplanes. Five of them dived on the front lot. We went at four of them but did not get them. I shot at one diving on another Camel whereon all four transferred their attention to me. I faded away. Cox and Bremridge both got one today.'

Earlier in the morning, 23 Squadron had been in action south of Masnières at 9.15am, Capt James Fitz-Morris, 2Lt G W Poisley and Lt J MacRae sharing in the destruction of a Rumpler that crashed in a field near Walincourt.

Naval 3 were also in action, over Henin-Liétard, catching a DFW near the village at 11.20am. 'Glen and Adam went out in search of low flying EA and found a two-seater DFW near Henin-Liétard which they quickly shot down in flames.'[3]

Having settled into their new aerodrome at Bailleul the previous day 60 Squadron were on patrol in the Menin area when Harold Hamersley attacked a slate coloured Pfalz D III and shot it down to crash at Dadizeele at 11.35am. The last victory of the morning went to John Tudhope of 40 Squadron, with an Albatros shot down in flames over Pont a Vendin at 12.15pm, but the day was to end badly for the squadron. In an afternoon fight with Albatros scouts from *Jasta 52*, Capt R J Tipton was forced to land at Hersin fatally wounded, and while diving to the aid of a new pilot, Lt P La T Foster, the squadron's CO, Major Tilney, was attacked by *Ltn* Paul Billik of *Jasta 52*, who shot the wings off Tilney's SE5 at 12,000 feet. Foster had also been hit and went down to be taken prisoner. Gwilym Lewis, just back from leave, recalled. 'The Squadron were at the top of their glory before lunch, and at the bottom after. Seven Huns had been fetched down in the day. In the afternoon Tilney had broken up diving on a Hun. Tipton, who escaped from Turkey, got a bullet in his abdomen and died a few days later, like the hero he was. I never expect again to see a fellow lying halfway between life and death, knowing it, and yet showing such wonderful pluck.'

In the early afternoon – the intention was to catch the enemy pilots before they left on the afternoon patrols – bombing raids were carried out by sixty-one aircraft of Twenty-Second (Army) Wing on the German aerodromes at Bertry, Busigny and Escaufort. The Spads of 23 Squadron attacked Bertry aerodrome, with the SEs of 24 Squadron flying cover; the Camels of 54 Squadron and Bristol Fighters of 48 Squadron attacked Busigny and Escaufort, protected by the SE5s of

84 Squadron. The squadrons were led by their respective commanders and the operation was watched from above by the Wing Commander, Lt-Col F V Holt.

Fourteen bombs were dropped by the 23 Squadron pilots: four were seen to score direct hits on hangars and five burst amongst enemy machines lined up on the field. Twenty-two bombs were dropped on Busigny and Escaufort aerodrome by 54 Squadron from 500 feet and five direct hits were seen on hangars. The Bristol Fighters of 48 Squadron dropped thirty-two 25lb bombs from 400 feet and set two hangars on fire. All the aircraft returned to the lines at low altitude, strafing transport, troops – one group resting in an orchard – and a balloon that was hauled down smoking. There were no casualties and all the machines returned safely.

On a normal Offensive Patrol in the early afternoon, Patrick Huskinson of 19 Squadron destroyed a Pfalz D III southwest of Wervicq. Albatros scouts of *Jasta 57* were attacking RE8s when the 19 Squadron pilots intervened: 'a big dogfight ensued. I provided top cover and was attacked by several machines. *Ltn* Hafner was hit in the carburettor and radiator by a triplane (sic) causing him to force-land near Quesnoy with *Ballonzug 7*.[4]

Quigley added to his rapidly increasing score in the afternoon, shooting down two Albatros scouts over Quesnoy at ten minutes past one for his 22 and 23rd victories.

March 9 was a day of fiercely contested and hard fighting and over 23 out of control victories were claimed. Apart from those suffered by 40 Squadron, casualties were surprisingly light: an SE5 of 24 Squadron and a Sopwith Dolphin of 19 Squadron were both badly shot about, but both pilots were uninjured.

There was a slightly less fighting on March 10. Donald MacLaren of 43 Squadron, claimed an Albatros destroyed west of Graincourt at 7.30am, and the pilots of Naval 3 also scored during the morning. Rochford, leading his Flight on an Offensive Patrol had an indecisive fight with a DFW near Douai before attacking a formation of Albatros and Pfalz scouts over Lens. In the skirmishing which followed, Ellwood, W H Chisam and F J S Britnell claimed out of control victories over scouts and Arthur Whealy, leading C Flight, crashed another two miles east of Lens at 1.15pm. *Hptm* Hans Buddecke of *Jasta 18* was shot down and killed in this fight – probably Whealy's victory.

The Camels of 73 and 80 Squadrons were in action in the afternoon over Bohain, fighting Albatros scouts and Fokker Triplanes. Capt M Le Blanc-Smith destroyed a triplane over Bohain[5] at 2.15pm and his fellow squadron pilot, Lt G S Hodson another ten minutes later. St Cyprian Tayler of 80 Squadron crashed an Albatros over Bohain[6] and sent a second down out of control. 2Lt D Gardiner also claimed and out of

control victory from this action, but 2Lt C H Flere was shot down and made POW by *Vzfw* Hemer of *Jasta 6*.

SE5s of 84 Squadron were also in action during the afternoon. Edward Clear shot down a two-seater west of Estrees at 2.20pm – possibly from *Fl Abt (A)240* who had an observer wounded – and 2Lt W H Brown claimed another out of control.

For the second day running the pilots of 1 Squadron were detailed to attack balloons. The previous day they had been unsuccessful: Capt H J Hamilton's gun had jammed during his attack on a balloon near Lomme and the rest of his Flight had no better luck, the balloon going down in only a deflated state. It was a similarly disappointing story on March 10. Four balloons were attacked but all merely went down deflated, refusing to burn.

Lt Ronald St Clair McClintock of 64 Squadron scored the first of his eventual five victories at 1.50pm, shooting down an LVG over Marquion. McClintock had been with 64 Squadron since the previous July, but he was to leave the squadron in early April to take command of 3 Squadron.

Naval 10 flew patrols in the morning, which were indecisive, but a patrol in the afternoon resulted in a fight over Roulers at 3.45pm with enemy scouts and two-seaters. Alexander claimed a two-seater out of control and Hinchcliffe crashed another. Fifteeen minutes later six enemy scouts were engaged southeast of Dixmude and John Manuel and Mellings both claimed an Albatros shot down.

There were three other casualties during the day. The Camels of 3 Squadron were ground-stafing in the Marquion area in the morning: one pilot was wounded and taken prisoner and another wounded. Also in the morning, at about 9.50am, FltSubLt K D Campbell force landed his Camel behind the German lines and was taken prisoner.[7]

The air fighting continued in much the same vein on March 11. There were many combats during the day. Positive victories were claimed by Capt F E Brown and Lt Johnson of 84 Squadron, who shared in the destruction of an Albatros scout over Lavergies at 10.40am, and James Slater of 64 Squadron, shot down a Pfalz out of control over Cambrai at 11.30am; thirty minutes later he followed this with an Albatros in flames over Douai. At the same time, further north, Harrison of 40 Squadron destroyed a two-seater for his seventh victory, the enemy machine crashing west of La Bassée, near the canal. At 11.20am FltCom Frederick Armstrong of Naval 3 shot down an Albatros for his ninth victory, the enemy scout breaking up – its tail broke clean away from the fuselage – over Drocourt. Capt Thomas Sharpe of 73 Squadron shot down a Fokker Triplane three miles south west of Caudry at 1.55pm and fifty minutes later George Hodson, shot another triplane to pieces west of Bohain. 2Lt E R Varley of 23 Squadron attacked a pair of enemy scouts: one went down inverted and was seen to crash by British AA.

Quigley, Koch, Seth-Smith and Carlaw of 70 Squadron attacked a balloon over Menin at 12.30am, sending it down in flames, the observers still in the basket. The squadron were out again in the evening, attacking a formation of Pfalz D IIIs over Passchendaele at 5.00pm. Quigley and Koch shared in the destruction of one Pfalz and Quigley claimed two others out of control.

March 11 saw the first casualty for 56 Squadron since the end of January. At 12.45pm five SE5s hurried into a fight between Bristol Fighters of 48 Squadron and five Fokker Triplanes from *Jasta 11*. The fight lasted for nearly ten minutes before the triplanes dived away east. There were no positive results for the British pilots and Lt Douglas Woodman had been shot down by *Vzfw* Scholtz of the *Jasta,* crashing just in front of the British trenches.

Ten enemy aircraft were claimed as out of control by various pilots of the fighter squadrons. Other than Woodman the only other casualty was a pilot from 64 Squadron: 2Lt J Bell was wounded in combat but managed to land his badly damaged SE5 at 59 Squadron's aerodrome at Courcelles-le-Comte and was taken to hospital.

The morning of March 12 saw Harold Balfour of 43 Squadron score his final victory of the war: a Rumpler shot down in flames over Laventie at 10.45am. Peter McDougall of 24 Squadron also scored his last victory, a two-seater south east of St Quentin at 10.15am. McDougall was lucky; three quarters of an hour earlier he had been forced to land after his propeller had broken in half, shot through in a combat, possibly with elements of *Jasta 8,* the *Staffelführer, Oblt* Mettlich, being credited with shooting down 2Lt P J Nolan of the squadron. Nolan managed to land his badly damaged SE5 and was unhurt. Capt R F Drewitt, 23 Squadron went to the aid of an SE5 being attacked by an Albatros scout east of Bellenglise and shot it down to eventually crash by the canal. Capt J Morris of 43 Squadron was attacked by five enemy scouts, but he returned the attack, firing at the nearest scout until it went down and was confirmed to have crashed by a battery of the RFA

SE5s of 56 Squadron chased a pair of Albatros two-seaters from *Fl Abt (A)259* crossing the Lines over Ribécourt at 11.20am. Maurice Mealing shot one of these machines down to crash near the village. The pilot, *Ltn* Paul Heinemann was killed but the observer, *Ltn* Ludwig Roemmich, was unhurt and taken prisoner.

The Camels of 70 Squadron continued to add to their successes. At 12.45pm, in combat with Albatri from *Jasta 51* over the Menin area, John Aldred shot an Albatros that went down to crash between Menin and Wervicq, and Quigley claimed

two destroyed over Dadizeele and another out of control five minutes later. The *Jasta* lost *Flg* Georg Boit, killed in action.

The Australians were in action during the afternoon. A Flight of SE5s from 2 AFC Squadron, led by Capt R Howard, attacked six Albatros scouts escorting a two-seater over Wingles, north of Lens. Howard dived from out of the sun on the two-seater and the enemy formation quickly scattered. Lt A Rackett was on the tail of one of the Albatri and the enemy pilot, turning to escape his fire, gave Capt L H Holden an easy shot. Holden zoomed and fired up into the underside of the Albatros, which went down out of control before bursting into flames. Robert McKenzie had dived straight through the Albatri to attack the two-seater, shooting it down in flames after firing ninety rounds.

There were three casualties in the day's fighting: a pilot of 46 Squadron was shot down and killed and another taken prisoner during a morning fight over Moeuvres, and a pilot of 1 Squadron, Lt A H Fitzmaurice, was killed in action over Dixmude. Fitzmaurice was 1 Squadron's first casualty since December 28. Capt W Patrick had led six SEs from the squadron in a mid-morning patrol and just north of Staden, Denovan and Fitzmaurice had attacked a two-seater. This dived away and the two SEs were attacked by ten enemy scouts. Denovan took one off the tail of Fitzmaurice, but had to spin away from attacks by five others. Denovan contour chased back to the lines, his SE5 badly shot up, and landed with his ailerons shot away. Fitzmaurice did not return: he had been shot down and killed by pilots of *Jasta 46*.

A notable action took place on March 13. A bombing attack on Denain aerodome was carried out by DH4s of Nos 25 and 27 Squadrons. Eleven Bristol Fighters of 62 Squadron and two Flights of Camels from 73 Squadron were to protect the bombers: the Bristols by flying a patrol line of Cambrai to Le Cateau; the Camels from a patrol from Cambrai to Villers-Outreaux. How the pilots and observers of 62 Squadron viewed this duty can be imagined: they had flown the same line the previous day and had been severely mauled by Richthofen's *Jagdgeschwader 1*. Although one crew had claimed a Fokker Triplane out of control, six of the Bristols had been shot down: three crew had been killed, four taken prisoner and two wounded and taken prisoner.

On the morning of March 13, the *jagdstaffeln* were again out in some strength: thirty-five enemy scouts from *Jagdgeschwader 1* and *Jasta 56* – Fokker Triplanes and Albatri – were patrolling east of Cambrai as the Bristol Fighters and Camels came into the area.

Manfred von Richthofen, flying a Fokker Triplane, attacked the Bristol Fighters first, his fire hitting one in the engine. Seeing that the propeller of the British machine was only slowly revolving, Richthofen left the Bristol[8] going down and

Left: Capt James Thomas Byford McCudden VC. DSO+Bar. MC+Bar. MM. CdeG. James McCudden had a remarkable career in the RFC, rising on merit alone from a 2nd Class Air Mechanic in 1913 to a Major in 1918 - a considerable achievement in the class-conscious England of the time. After serving as a mechanic and observer in 3 Squadron, McCudden qualified as a pilot in 1916 and flew FE2bs with 20 Squadron in July 1916 until transferred to 29 Squadron to fly DH2s in August, where he scored five victories and gained a great deal of valuable experience. In August 1917, after flying Sopwith Pups with 66 Squadron for a month's refresher course, he was posted to 56 Squadron to command B Flight. A great tactician and a superb patrol leader, McCudden lost only four pilots of his Flight during the seven months he was with 56 Squadron. McCudden was posted to HE on 5 March 1918, having scored another 52 victories, and on 2 April 1918 was awarded a Victoria Cross 'for most conspicuous bravery, exceptional perseverance, keenness and devotion to duty.' Realising their importance, McCudden specialised in the destruction of German reconnaissance machines, which fell in the British back areas, and for this reason the majority of his 57 victories can be matched with German losses. On 9 July 1918 while flying back to France to take command of 60 Squadron, McCudden was killed in a flying accident. A sad end to a brilliant career. He was 23 years old. Chief Air Marshal Sir John Salmond later wrote: 'the secret of his remarkable success lay in the fact that he fought with his head as well as with his great heart.'

Pilots of 60 Squadron. Autumn 1917. L to R: R L Chidlaw-Roberts. H D Crompton. J B Crompton. F O Soden.

Ltn Werner Voss with Fokker Triplane FI 103/17. The cowling was painted yellow, the unit marking of Jasta 10, the face picked out in white.

Right: Pilots of 19 Squadron at Bailleul, September 1917. Irving. Fairclough. Capt Bryson. Olivier. Blake. Galer. Unknown.

Above: Pilots of 29 Squadron at Poperinghe aerodrome, September 1917. L to R. Capt A G Jones-Williams. Lt H M Ferreira. Lt C W Cudemore. Behind, with his hands on Jones-Williams shoulders, is Lt J Collier.

Top right: Lt H M Ferreira. 29 Squadron.

Right: FltSubLt Herbert Thompson of Naval 8. Thompson was also involved in the fight with Waldhausen.

Below: Oblt Hans Waldhausen, Staffelführer of Jasta 37 with his Albatros D.Va D2284/17. This machine had a black and white striped tailplane, the markings of Jasta 37, and Waldhausen's personal markings of a black half moon and star edged in white painted on both sides of the fuselage. Waldhausen was shot down in this Albatros and taken prisoner on 27 September 1917 by Lt Tudhope of 40 Squadron and FltCom Booker of Naval 8. The Albatros was given the designation G.75.

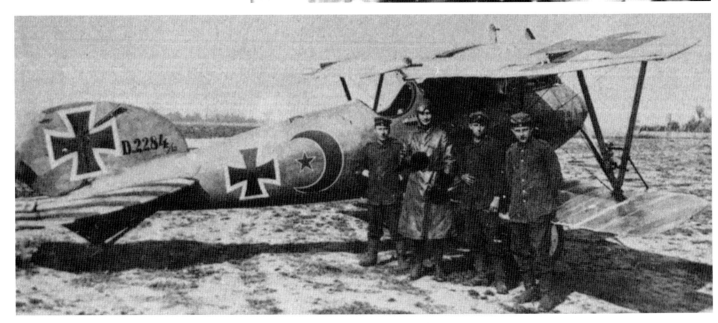

Right: This DH5 A 9276 of 41 Squadron was flown by 2Lt J L Haight on 28 September 1917 when he was wounded, shot down and taken POW.

60 Squadron. The officers' Mess at Baizieux. September 1918.

Right: Pfalz D.III 4114/17. The Pfalz D.III entered service with the jagdstaffeln in August 1917. The type was not popular with the pilots and was considered 'not of much account' by the pilots of the RFC, but at least one German pilot, Paul Bäumer of Jasta Boelcke, flew the Pfalz with great success.

H J T Saint. Naval 10. Saint served with Naval 10 from July 1917 until November, scoring seven victories.

Lt Robert Hugh Sloley, 56 Squadron, KIA 1 October 1917.

Lt Charles Jeffs after being shot down on 5 October 1917. On the left is his victor, Oblt Bruno Loerzer, Staffelführer of Jasta 26. Loerzer is wearing an English leather flying coat, much prized by German pilots.

Left: Capt Guy Borthwick Moore in the cockpit of a Nieuport Scout. A Canadian from Vancouver, Moore flew with 1 Squadron from August 1917 until the end of March 1918, winning an MC and scoring 10 victories. Moore was killed by anti-aircraft fire on 7 April 1918, his SE5a exploding in mid-air.

Left: Lt Wendal Rogers in a Nieuport of 1 Squadron. Rogers flew with 1 Squadron from the early summer of 1917 until the end of December. He is credited with nine victories.

Opposite
Top: German personnel examine the controls of SE5a B 574 of 84 Squadron. 2Lt Vernon-Lord was shot down and made POW on 15 October 1917 while flying this SE5a. He was the first combat loss for 84 Squadron.

Center left: Sopwith Pup B 1719. This Pup was first issued to 66 Squadron on 11 May 1917, but was shot up in combat and crashed on landing on 7 June. After repair it was issued to 46 Squadron on 28 June and marked '4'. 2Lt R L M Ferrie shot down an Albatros out of control on 16 September while flying this Pup, but it crashed on landing on 20 October 1917 and was struck off strength.

Center right: 60 Squadron pilots at Ste Marie Cappel. Autumn 1917. L to R: Lt H D Crompton. Capt R L Chidlaw-Roberts. Capt F O Soden. Sitting. 2Lt F W Clark.

Bottom left: Capt Matthew Brown Frew DSO+Bar. MC+Bar. 45 Squadron. Frew scored 16 victories with 45 Squadron on the Western Front, adding another seven victories when 45 Squadron was transferred to the Italian front in September 1917.

Bottom right: This Rumpler C.IV 8431/16 from FlAbt 5 was McCudden's 18th victory. Uffz Hiltweis and Ltn Laito were both killed.

Left: 2Lt M Newcomb of 66 Squadron was shot down and taken prisoner in Sopwith Pup A 635 'D' on 12 October 1917.

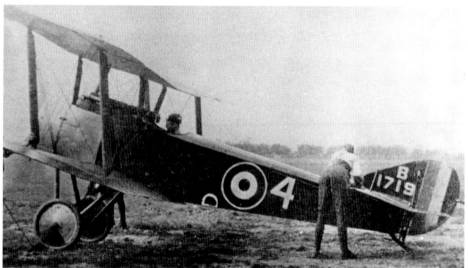

Above: L to R: Capt G A H Pidcock. Capt K M S G Leask. Unknown. Geoffrey Pidcock flew with 60, 44, 1 and 73 Squadrons, scoring six victories. Kenneth Leask flew with 42, 41 and 84 Squadrons and is credited with eight victories.

Right: Arthur Percival Foley Rhys Davids. DSO.MC+Bar. Rhys Davids joined the RFC straight from Eton and after training was posted to 56 Squadron, flying to France with the squadron on 7 April 1917. Rhys Davids scored 25 victories between May and October 1917. He was killed in action by Ltn Gallwitz of Jasta B on 27 October 1917. He was 20 years old.

Below: Sopwith Triplanes of Naval 1 on Bailleul aerodrome on 28 October 1917.

Right: The grim face of war. An SE5a of B Flight 56 Squadron. This SE5a was almost certainly a Martinsyde-built aeroplane and an examination of the 56 Squadron records points to strong possibility that the unfortunate pilot still lying under the wreckage of his aeroplane is Arthur Rhys Davids.

Right: Spad B 6776 of 19 Squadron in German hands. 2Lt S L Whitehouse WIA. POW 27 October 1917.

Below: Many squadrons had a group photograph taken just before leaving for France. This photograph of 65 Squadron was taken at Wye, Kent, in October 1917. Sitting, L to R: C F Keller. E G S Gordon. G M Cox. R S Morrison. A Rosenthal. H L Symons. V Wigg. G M Knocker. Standing, L to R: L Marshall. B Balfour. G Bremridge. G A Pitt. E H Cutbill. J A Cummingham (CO). L S Weedon (FltCom C Flight). T E Withington (Flt Com B Flight). W Harrison. D H Scott. W W Higgin (Flt Com A Flight) is not present. The aeroplane is a Sopwith Camel.

Right: Sopwith Camel B5178 in German hands after being shot down on 27 October 1917. Lt R A Cartledge of 28 Squadron was taken POW.

Right: A German officer tries the Lewis gun mounting in SE5a B 4876 'H'. 2Lt W E Watts of 84 Squadron was forced down in this machine while flying an escort duty to DH4s on the morning of 20 October 1917.

Below: This DH5 A 9474 of 41 Squadron was flown by 2Lt F S Clark who was WIA and taken POW on 29 October 1917. In the background is SE5a B 4876 of 2Lt W E Watts of 84 Squadron who was taken POW on 20 October 1917. Sopwith Camel B 6314, minus its engine, can just be seen behind the SE5a. This Camel was captured on 11 October 1917. 2Lt W H Winter of 28 Squadron took off from Droglandt on a practice flight, but became lost, landed behind German lines and was taken prisoner.

Above: These two SE5as in German hands were both from 84 Squadron. In the foreground is B 566 'J' flown by 2Lt A W Rush who was captured on 28 October 1917. Behind is B 544, the aircraft of 2Lt G R Gray. Gray was shot down wounded on 31 October 1917 and made POW but died of his wounds.

Top right: Major Rainsford Balcombe Brown (left) and Major Richard Graham Blomfield. This photograph was taken on 29 October 1917 when Blomfield was handing over command of 56 Squadron to Balcombe Brown. The sign on the door of the CO's office says 'Officer Commanding. Enter without knocking.'

Right: Lt Felix Cobbold's SE5a B 630 down behind German lines on 8 November 1917. Cobbold was wounded and taken prisoner by Ltn Fritz Loerzer of Jasta 26, the brother of Oblt Bruno Loerzer, the Staffelführer.

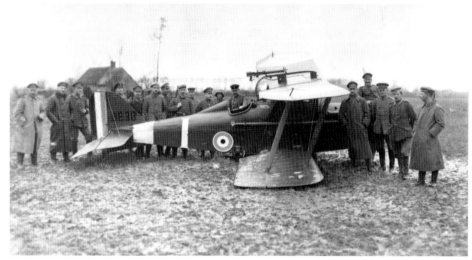

Right: FltSubLt Samuel Marcus Kinkead, while serving in Naval 1.

Far right: Capt Philip Fletcher Fullard. DSO. MC+Bar. Fullard scored 40 victories while serving with 1 Squadron in 1917.

Above: Lt Arthur Stanley Gould Lee MC. 46 Squadron.

Top right: This DFW CV 4977/16 of Fl Abt (A) 269 was shot down by Capt James Child of 84 Squadron on 22 November 1917. The crew, Ltn Steiner and Flgr Elser were taken prisoner. The DFW was designated G.91.

Right: SE5a B 4890 of 2Lt Alexander Dodds of 56 Squadron on the aerodrome of Jasta 5 at Boistrancourt after his capture on 29 November 1917.

Below: Lt L Kert of 29 Squadron was shot down in Nieuport B 3578 and taken prisoner on 27 November 1917.

Right: Ltn Schlömer (left) and Ltn Oppenhorst stand by SE5a B4890 on Boistrancourt aerodrome.

Right: Black and white striped Camels of A Flight (A W Carter Flt Com) Naval 10 on Teteghem aerodrome in late December 1917. B Flight (W M Alexander Flt Com) were marked with red and white stripes: C Flight (J G Manuel Flt Com) with blue and white stripes. Pilots had individual wheel markings.

Below: Wendel Rogers ready to start in a Nieuport of 1 Squadron in the winter of 1917-1918.

Right: A group of 46 Squadron pilots, autumn 1917. Back, L to R: N H Dimmock. C A Brewster-Joske. L M Shadwell. R S Asher. Front, L to R: Unknown. R L M Ferrie. H N C Robinson.

Right: Capt Richard Aveline Maybery in the cockpit of SE5a B506.

Below: FltSubLt F Booth of Naval 10 was flying this Camel B5658 on 3 January 1918 when he was shot down and killed west of Lille.

Bottom right: Capt John Ingles Gilmour DSO. MC+2Bars. Gilmour served in 27and 65 Squadrons before being posted to Italy to command 28 Squadron. Gilmour scored all but three of his 39 victories with 65 Squadron from December 1917 to July 1918 and was the squadron's top scorer.

Above: This Sopwith Camel B 2516 was being flown by Lt R L M Ferrie of 46 Squadron when he was killed on 3 January 1918. 46 Squadron carried out a great number of low bombing and strafing missions and four Cooper bombs can be clearly seen in their rack.

Top right: SE5a C 5329. 2Lt H E Davies of 84 Squadron survived this crash and was taken POW on 13 January 1918.

Right: C Flight 23 Squadron in February 1918. Left to right: Lt Keary. Lt Fielder. Capt W M Fry (Flight Commander). Lt Stinger. Lt Trudeau.

Right: A Sopwith Dolphin, the RAF's first multi-gun fighter. A departure from the Sopwith Company's usual conception of rotary-engined fighters, it had two fixed Vickers guns and two Lewis guns above the centre section.

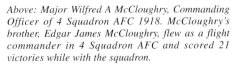

Top left: Another view of C 5329 after it had been righted by the Germans.

Above: Major Wilfred A McCloughry, Commanding Officer of 4 Squadron AFC 1918. McCloughry's brother, Edgar James McCloughry, flew as a flight commander in 4 Squadron AFC and scored 21 victories while with the squadron.

Left: McCudden's SE5a B 4891 '6'. McCudden had salvaged a spinner from an LVG which he had shot down on 30 November 1917, had it painted red and fitted to B 4891, claiming it added an extra 3mph to its speed.

Below: This photograph of SE5a B4897 shows the fine lines of the type. B4897 was issued to 60 Squadron on 26 November 1917 and was lost on 24 January 1918 when being flown by Lt A W Morey. Morey collided during combat over Becelaere with an Albatros flown by Ltn d R Martin Möbius of Jasta 7. Both pilots were killed.

Above: FltCom William Melville Alexander DSC. Alexander flew Sopwith Triplanes in Raymond Collishaw's 'Black Flight' of Naval 10 in the summer of 1917, scoring 12 victories before going home on leave to Canada from October until December 1917. Alexander rejoined Naval 10 in January 1918, and added a further 11 victories by the end of May. He was then posted to HE.

Top left: Colourfully marked Sopwith Camels of Naval 3 on Bray Dunes aerodrome, January-February 1918. The nearest Camel B6401, flown by both SqdnCom Lloyd Breadner and Leonard H Rochford, was decorated with a playing card on the top of the bottom wings; a crown motif on the top fuselage decking; red and white striped rising suns on the elevators and tailplane, and large white rings either side of the viewing panel on the top wing. Wheel covers were red with a white centre and rim.

Left: 'The Office.' The cockpit of an SE5a.

Below: A winter's start. Camels of Naval 8 in the winter of 1917-1918 at Mont St Eloi.

Above: Ltns Schuppau and Schandva of FlAbt (A) 233 pose by the wreckage of SE5a B 610 of 56 Squadron. This SE5a was flown by Lt Leslie Jansen Williams who was shot down by the German two-seater crew on 28 January 1918.

Top right: Lt R G McRae 24 Squadron. McRae was killed in a flying accident on 28 January 1918.

Right: Officers of 19 Squadron. This photograph was taken to mark the shooting down of 100 enemy aircraft in six months in 1917/1918. Front Row, L to R: Major A D Carter DSO. The CO. Major W D S Sanday DSO. MC. Capt P Huskinson. Lt Lord (standing). Middle Row, L to R: Lt A B Fairclough MC. Lt J D Hardman DFC. Lt H V Puckridge. Lt E Olivier. Capt John Leacroft MC. Lt G B Irving. Lt W E Reid. Back Row, L to R: Lt Ross (initials unknown). Lt F W Hainsby. Lt N W Hastings. Lt J A Aldridge. Lt E J Blythe. Lt M N Jennings MC. Lt C V Gardner. Lt W Jones.

Below: SE5as of C Flight 1 Squadron. Bailleul aerodrome, January-February 1918.

Above: Three pilots of 64 Squadron. L to R: Capt H T Fox-Russell. Capt Ronald St Clair McClintock. Victor W Thompson.

Top right: L to R: Lt S L E Pope. Lt H 'Splinter' Wood. Capt G L 'Zulu' Lloyd.

Right: The wreckage of LVG C.V 9775/17 being examined by RFC and army personnel. This LVG from Boghol 7, crewed by Ltn Werner von Kuczowski and Vzfw Erich Szafranek was shot down by James McCudden on 2 February 1918 for his 47th victory. Kuczowski and Szafranek were both killed. The LVG was designated G130.

Right: SE5a of 41 Squadron down behind the German lines. The squadron marking of a vertical white bar either side of the roundel gives that this aeroplane must have been brought down between late November 1917 when 41 Squadron were equipped with the SE5a and 22 March 1918 when the squadron marking was changed. This gives only two possibilities as to the identity of the pilot. Major F Powell, wounded and taken POW on 2 February 1918 in SE5a B 8273 or Lt A T Isell, wounded and taken POW on 21 March 1918 in SE5a B698. The possibility also exists that if the squadron was late in changing the squadron marking, then this could be either SE5a C1054 flown by 2Lt J P McCone or SE5a C 6399 of 2Lt D C Tucker. Both these pilots were killed in action on 24 March 1918.

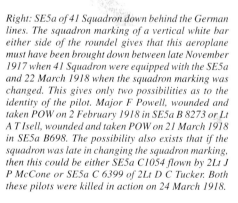

Right: Sopwith Camel B 5417 of 54 Squadron in German hands. The pilot, 2Lt G A C Manley was taken prisoner on 9 February 1918.

Right: Capt Percy Jack Clayson DFC. MC. in the cockpit of an SE5a of 1 Squadron. Clayson scored 29 victories, all while serving in 1 Squadron.

Below: A Hannover CL III C 9303. This two-seater type, with its later variant the CL IIIa, began to equip the schlachtstaffeln at the end of 1917. Known to the pilots of the RFC as 'Hannoveranas' these aeroplanes had plywood fuselages, were extremely strong and able to take a great deal of punishment.

Right: Pilots of 43 Squadron early 1918. Seated third from the left is Capt John Lightfoot Trollope. Trollope was the first RAF pilot to score six victories in one day.

Right: Capt Hugh William Lumsden Saunders. South African 'Dingbat' Saunders flew with 84 Squadron from November 1917 until the end of July 1918, scoring 15 victories. Saunders won an MC and DFC during the war and added a Bar to his DFC while serving in Iraq from 1920 to 1923. Saunders held several high commands during World War II and retired from the RAF in 1953 as Sir Hugh Saunders, CBE. KBE. MC. DFC+Bar. MM. A very approachable man, Hugh Saunders died on 8 May 1987.

Far right: Capt Jack Victor Sorsoleil. A Canadian from Toronto, Sorsoleil served with 84 Squadron scoring 14 victories.

Right: Capt Louis William Jarvis 56 Squadron in SE5a C 5430.

Above: Camel B 7230 'P' of 70 Squadron was damaged by anti-aircraft fire on 24 February 1918. The pilot, 2Lt J Todd, was unhurt.

Right and below: Two views of SE5a C 619 of 2 Squadron AFC. This SE5a was flown by Canadian 2Lt G C Logan who was shot down and taken POW on 21 February 1918 by OffzSt Jörke of Jasta 13 for his 10th victory.

Above: Vzfw Hegeler of Jasta 15 was forced down and captured in Pfalz D III 4184/17 by Lt A Cowper of 24 Squadron on 26 February 1918. The Pfalz was designated G 141.

Right: Pilots of 56 Squadron at Baizieux February-March 1918. Left to right: Douglas Woodman. Eugene Macdonald. B McPherson. H J Burden. C Parry. Only Woodman failed to survive the war, shot down and killed on 11 March 1918. Barclay McPherson was shot down and taken POW on 1 April 1918, the day the RAF was formed.

Below: Hptm Adolf Ritter von Tutschek poses with Spad B 6732, his 24th victory. The pilot, 2Lt D C Doyle of 23 Squadron, was shot down and taken prisoner on 26 February 1918.

Above: Capt William Mays Fry. Matigny, February 1918. Fry is wearing his favourite flying helmet made of leopard's fur.

Top right: Hptm Ritter von Tutschek, commanding officer of JG II, poses in SE5a C 1057 'C' after shooting down 2Lt P C Wigan of 24 Squadron on 6 March 1918 for his 26th and penultimate victory. Wigan was made POW.

Right: Major Donald Roderick MacLaren. DSO. MC+Bar. DFC. C de G. LdeH. A Canadian, Donald MacLaren joined 46 Squadron on 23 November 1917 and scored 54 victories with the squadron. On 9 October 1918 he broke his leg in a friendly wrestling match and was posted to HE in November.

Right: Some of the unsung heroes. Groundcrew of A Flight 56 Squadron early 1918. Back row. L to R: Fred Homer. Jock Allen. Corp E Clements. Jack Charles. Front Row L to R: Jack Cooper. Corp E Ellison. Arthur Moody. Shortly after this photograph was taken Cooper and Charles were both promoted to corporal and Ellison to sergeant.

Far right: Major L A Tilney MC. CO of 40 Squadron in 1917. Tilney was KIA on 9 March 1918.

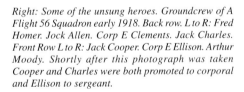

Above: James Alpheus Glen. A native of Ontario, Canada, Glen served with B Flight 3 Naval Squadron in the spring of 1917 until early August, scoring six victories. After a period of illness he rejoined 3 Naval in January 1918, had scored another nine victories by 11 April, and had won a DSC+Bar and the CdeG.

Top center: Roby Lewis Manuel flew with 2 Squadron AFC, scoring his first victory of an eventual 12 on 2 April 1918.

Top right: 2Lt Douglas Woodman. 56 Squadron. Woodman was shot down and killed on 11 March 1918 by Vzfw Scholz of Jasta 11.

Right: Leslie N Franklin of 56 Squadron in the cockpit of SE5a C 5303. Standing at the nose of the SE5a is Flt Sgt C Gibson, a C Flight rigger.

Right: Capt Henry Winslow Woollott DSO, MC+Bar, L'dH, CdeG avec palm. Woollett was awarded five victories while serving with 24 Squadron in 1917 before being posted to HE in August 1917. After a period as an instructor Woollett returned to France in March 1918, posted to 43 Squadron to fly Sopwith Camels. By 9 August Woollett had added another 30 victories to his score, including 11 balloons. On 12 April 1918 Woollett became the second RAF pilot to score six victories in one day. He is seen here in front of his Camel D 6402 in which he scored 23 of his victories. Insert is his personal marking of a dragon, carried underneath his cockpit.

Above: Pilots of 74 Squadron at London Colney. Edward Mannock, with pipe, is on the right.

Top center: Capt John Leacroft MC+Bar. Leacroft flew two tours with 19 Squadron, scoring 22 victories. This photograph was taken while Leacroft was a fighting instructor at No1 School of Aerial Fighting at Ayr, Scotland. The aeroplane is a Bristol M1C.

Top right: Capt Edmund Roger Tempest. MC. DFC. Tempest claimed 17 victories flying SE5as with 64 Squadron in 1917-1918.

Right: Pilots of 74 Squadron photographed at London Colney before leaving for France. Standing from L to R: Capt Benjamin Roxburgh-Smith. Capt Andrew Cameron Kiddie. Seated from the left: Capt Edward Mannock. Major Keith Logan Caldwell (Sqdn CO). Gerrard (Adj). Capt Wilfred Ernest Young.

Right: Sopwith Camel C 1576 '18' of 54 Squadron in German hands after 2Lt E B Lee was shot down and taken POW on 18 March 1918.

Above: Ltn Hans Kirschstein of Jasta 6 leans against his first victory, Sopwith Camel C 6720 of 54 Squadron. Capt F L Luxmoore was shot down and taken POW on 18 March 1918.

Right: Lt John Anthony McCudden MC. The younger brother of James McCudden, 'Jack' McCudden first flew DH4s with 25 Squadron in the late summer of 1917, scoring two victories. He was then transferred to 84 Squadron to fly SE5as and added another six victories until 18 March 1918 when he was shot down and killed by Ltn Hans Wolff of Jasta 11.

Far right: Capt Cecil 'Chaps' Marchant MC. 46 Squadron 1917. Marchant served in 46 Squadron from early 1917 until 14 June, when he was posted to HE. He returned to the squadron in March 1918 and was credited with nine victories until he was wounded in early June and sent to hospital.

Right: This SE5a B 8388 was crashed by Lt H V L Tubbs of 24 Squadron on the afternoon of 21st March 1918, the first day of the German offensive. The SE5a was badly shot up while ground-strafing and Tubbs was wounded.

Right: Major William Sholto Douglas MC. CO 84 Squadron, 8 August 1918 – 8 November 1918.

Far right: Capt Arthur Treloar Whealy DSC+Bar. DSO. Whealy joined C Flight Naval 3 in April 1917 to fly Sopwith Pups and scored three victories with the squadron before being posted to Naval 9 in May. After scoring two more victories flying Pups in Naval 9, Whealy scored his 6th and 7th victories flying a Sopwith Triplane and his 8th flying a Camel with the squadron. In early 1918 Whealy was back with Naval 3, flying Sopwith Camels, and between 17 February and 4 September 1918 increased his victories to 27.

Above and right: Two Camels of 70 Squadron abandoned on Marieux aerodrome during the German advance in March 1918. In the background can be seen the Albatros scouts of a Jasta which had taken over the aerodrome.

Right: Capt John Lightfoot Trollope MC+Bar. Trollope served in 70 and 43 Squadrons. He had scored 18 victories before he was shot down and taken prisoner on 28 March 1918.

Far right: John Trollope with his Sopwith Camel at La Gorgue.

Right: Sopwith Camel C 6724 'R' was shot down south of Bapaume on 25 March 1918. 2Lt G Miller of 80 Squadron was taken prisoner.

Below: Sopwith Camels of 4 Squadron AFC on Bruay aerodrome, 26 March 1918.

Right: Capt Francis Grainger Quigley DSO. MC+Bar. Quigley served in 70 Squadron from the summer of 1917 until wounded on 27 March 1918. He scored 33 victories, all with 70 Squadron. After instructing in his native Canada, Quigley was returning to England in October 1918, but contracted influenza on board ship and died in hospital in Liverpool on 20 October 1918.

Far right: Lt Ronald Adam. 73 Squadron. Adam was shot down on 7 April 1918, the sixth victory of Ltn Hans Kirschstein of Jasta 6. Adam served as a controller of fighter operations at Hornchurch during the Battle of Britain in 1940 and ended World War II as a wing commander. After the war Adam had a successful career as an actor in films and television. He died in March 1979.

Right: Pilots of 203 Squadron at Liettres, April 1918. L to R: E T Hayne. A T Whealy. H F Beamish. These three pilots served with Naval 3 until it was renumbered 203 Squadron on 1 April 1918. Capt Arthur Whealy scored 27 victories while flying with Naval 3 and Naval 9. Capt Edwin Hayne was credited with 15 victories flying with Naval 3, serving with the squadron from August 1917 until June 1918. Capt Harold Beamish flew with Naval 3 from April 1917 until May 1918, scoring 11 victories.

Right: Mechanics working on a SE5a of 32 Squadron on Humieres aerodrome on 6 April 1918. In the background are the Sopwith Camels of 73 Squadron.

Right: Edward David George Galley. Galley served as an observer in FE2bs with 22 Squadron until wounded on 24 March 1916. After training as a pilot he served with 56 Squadron from the end of November until 16 May 1918.

Far right: Major Keith Logan Caldwell MC. DFC+Bar. A charismatic leader and one of the great fighter pilots, New Zealander 'Grid' Caldwell served in France from July 1916 to the end of the war with 8, 60 and 74 Squadrons. He is credited with one victory while with 8 Squadron, seven with 60 Squadron and a further 16 while in command of 74 Squadron, bringing his total to 25.

Above: SE5as of B Flight of 74 Squadron on Clairmarais North Aerodrome. Spring 1918. The Squadron CO 'Grid' Caldwell in the nearest SE5a '2'.

Right: Officers of 74 Squadron in the summer of 1918. L to R standing: S T Stidolph. G R Hicks. L to R sitting: H Coverdale (armaments officer). F E Luff (USAS). F S Gordon. G W L G Gauld. H G Shoemaker (USAS).

Above: Officers of 40 Squadron, Brauy, April 1918. L to R: Capt W L Harrison MC. G A B Wheldon (equipment officer). Unknown. H S Cameron. C W Usher. J W Walwork. J H Tudhope. G H Lewis. Major R S Dallas DSO. DSC. (CO). Padre B W Keymer. L H Sutton.

Top right: Major Raymond-Barker. Raymond-Barker served in 6, 16, 48, and 11 Squadrons before being given command of 3 Squadron in September 1917. On 20 April 1918 Raymond-Barker was shot down in flames and killed by Manfred von Richthofen for his penultimate victory.

Right: The remains of Manfred von Richthofen's Fokker Triplane being examined by RAF officers at Poulainville.

Below: SE5a B 189 'S' of 40 Squadron, Bruay, spring 1918. This machine was flown by 2Lt W L Harrison, Lt R G Landis USAS and Capt J H Tudhope. Tudhope scored two victories while flying it: an Albatros on 10 April 1918 and a Fokker Triplane the next day.

Above: 'Tich' Rochford (right) and Lt R Stone in late April 1918. Stone later served in 201 Squadron and was killed by Fokker D VIIs while ground-strafing on 9 August 1918.

Top right: Lt Kenneth Charles Mills. Mills served in 1 Squadron from the spring of 1918 until 8 August when he was killed in action. Mills was credited with five victories.

Right: Pfalz D IIIa 8282/17 being inspected by cheerful RFC officers. The pilot, Flg Andreas Köhler of Jasta 35b, took off for a test flight in this machine on 24 April 1918, but became lost and was shot down by groundfire in the British lines near Vimy-Combles and taken prisoner.

OUT OF ACTION
British flying-men with a captured German aeroplane

Printed in England

Right: Capt Harry Alexander Rigby. Credited with six victories, Rigby served with 1 Squadron from February 1918 until 17 May when he was taken ill and returned to HE.

Far right: Lt John Todd. Todd served with 70 Squadron from January 1918 until July, claiming 18 victories. Todd was promoted to Captain and made a flight commander in late March 1918. He was awarded an MC and DFC.

Right: Major Rainsford Balcombe Brown. Balcombe Brown, commanding officer of 56 Squadron, was shot down and killed by Ltn Loewenhardt of Jasta 10 on 2 May 2 1918.

Far right: Capt William Roy Irwin 56 Squadron 1918.

Right: Major Raymond Collishaw, commanding officer of 203 Squadron, with Capt Arthur T Whealy in the cockpit of a Sopwith Camel.

Right: The Fokker Dr.1. The Fokker Triplane began to make its appearance at the Front in late August 1917. Although not fast, the Fokker Triplane was highly manoeuvrable, with a remarkable rate of climb and was ideally suited to the close in-fighting style of combat that was commonplace during the autumn of 1917 and the spring of 1918.

turned his attention to the Camels of 73 Squadron, already in combat with elements of his *staffeln*. During the fighting two Camels were shot down: Lt Elmer Heath, singled out by Richthofen, was wounded by his fire and crashed his Camel behind the German lines near Gonnelieu to be taken prisoner, and *Vzfw* Scholtz of *Jasta 11* was awarded 2Lt J N L Millett who was shot down in flames and killed.

Manfred's brother, Lothar, *Staffelführer* of *Jasta 11*, force landed from the fighting. Diving to attack a British machine the leading edge of the upper wing of his Fokker Triplane suffered a failure and the centre section of the wing broke away. Luckily, the ailerons were intact and Lothar was able to glide down under reasonable control, but nearing the ground he turned to avoid some high tension wires and stalled, hitting the ground with some force. Lothar was badly injured and did not return to active duty until July.[9]

Capt Orlebar and Lt George Hodson of 73 Squadron each claimed victories in the fight. Orlebar's victory was a Fokker Triplane (see note below) and Hodson's an Albatros, which was possibly that of *Ltn* Walter Bowien of *Jasta 56,* who was killed.

Northeast of St Quentin 84 Squadron were in action with *Jasta 8* over Remaucourt at ten minutes past ten. Capt C E Brown shot down one Albatros, which crashed at Homblières village and George Hodson's fire caused another enemy scout to break up in mid-air, the top and bottom left hand wings breaking away from the fuselage. These Albatri were flown by *Oblt* Konrad Mettlich and *Vzfw* Adolf Besenmüller. Mettlich was killed and Besenmüller died of his wounds the next day.

At half past twelve a formation of SE5s of 1 Squadron shot down a Pfalz D III over Weiltje, north east of Ypres, all nine pilots sharing in the victory. At the same time, further south, five Camels from 43 Squadron, led by Capt Woollett, attacked 12 enemy scouts that were attacking three Armstrong Whitworth FK8s over La Bassée. The Camel pilots claimed five enemy scouts destroyed and a further three out of control in the fighting: M F Peiler, King, Lomax and Lingham all claimed scouts crashed and Woollett was awarded two destroyed half an hour later over La Bassée. *Ltn* Häfner of *Jasta 57* and *Ltn* Kämmerer of *Jasta 20* were both killed over La Bassée during the day.

Just after noon seems to have been a busy time for the fighter squadrons. Fifty-four Squadron were also in action just before half past twelve, Capt F L Luxmoore and 2Lt J R Moore shooting a two-seater from *Fl Abt(A)220* down out of control over Mézières, wounding *Ltn* Schaue, but Moore's control were shot away by the return fire from Schaue and he was injured in the subsequent crash landing.

Other victories were claimed by Capt C C Taylor: an enemy scout which broke up in mid-air, and Capt D J Bell

shot down a Albatros two-seater, the left wings breaking off and the wreckage falling near Villers.

Additional casualties were a pilot of 80 Squadron who died of his wounds and during a combat with *Jasta 56* over La Fère at 10.30am, 2Lt E A Whitehead of 24 Squadron was killed when a wing of his SE5 broke off.

Low cloud mist and rain, prevented any flying in the morning of March 14, but conditions improved a little in the afternoon. There was little enemy activity and no combats took place, but the German aerodrome at Mont d'Origny was bombed by 24, 48 and 84 Squadrons. The SE5s of 24 Squadron bombed from heights of 100 to 2,000 feet dropping 12 bombs, setting one hangar on fire and damaging two others. The Bristols of 48 Squadron dropped 16 bombs at various targets and machine-gunned troops and transport. For some reason the pilots of 84 Squadron – other than 2Lt W H Brown – failed to find the enemy aerodrome and attacked barges on the canal at Bernot instead, scoring a direct hit on one.

On March 15 enemy aircraft were very active until noon, when the activity decreased dramatically: the *Luftstreitkräfte* was conserving its forces for the coming offensive, now only six days away.[10]

It was a highly successful morning for the fighter squadrons. At 8.15am, north of St Quentin, at Villeret, the SE5s of 84 Squadron were early in action, the Flight led by Capt Leask diving on a DFW that was crossing the lines. Leask lost air pressure in his dive. Beauchamp Proctor saw Leask continue his dive 'so I zoomed up underneath the enemy aircraft, opening fire at 200 yards, and, I believe, wounding the observer. I was now less than 100 yards from the enemy aircraft so opened fire with both guns. The enemy aircraft turned over on its side and began to spin slowly. Could see observer hanging over the side of cockpit. Spiralling down after enemy aircraft, saw it crash south of Villeret, about a mile our side of the lines.' This DFW was from *Fl Abt (A) 207* and was designated G 150. The crew, *Gefr* Johann Ommen and *Ltn* August Wagner were both killed. A later patrol by the squadron also had some success. Jens Larsen shot a Pfalz D III down north east of Ribemont at 9.20am; Edward Clear, an Albatros that crashed at Mesnil St Laurent, and Charles Travers shot another enemy scout down in flames.

Capt Drewitt and Lt G Macphee destroyed a DFW over Brissey at 10.15am. Ten minutes later, a pilot of 24 Squadron scored a notable victory. Capt Beanlands, leading a Flight of SE5s from 24 Squadron, had led them down to attack a Rumpler north of Premonte at 10.20am, all the Flight sharing in its destruction. Lt Herbert Redler, an experienced pilot with three victories with 40 Squadron in the spring and summer of 1917, then climbed to 16,000 feet, above the rest of the patrol, and five minutes later saw three Fokker Triplanes and a trio of

Albatros scouts going west a thousand feet below him. Redler dived out of the sun and attacked the highest of the three triplanes, putting forty rounds into it before pulling sharply away to avoid a collision. The triplane went into a spin and Redler watched it fall for 2,000 feet before having to dive away from the attentions of the remaining triplanes and Albatri, which had been completely surprised by his attack.

The pilot of the Fokker Triplane was *Hptm* Adolf Ritter von Tutschek, *Kommandeur* of *Jagdgeschwader Nr.II*. Under cover of darkness German troops later recovered Tutschek's body from the cockpit of his Fokker Triplane No.404/17.[11]

C Flight of 56 Squadron, led by William Fielding-Johnson, attacked ten Albatros scouts just north of Bourlon Wood at 10.30am. These Albatri were coloured yellow and orange and Mealing got on the tail of one, closed to within 40 yards and fired both guns. The Albatros turned over and went down. Mealing then engaged another, again attacking from behind. After only a few shots the Albatros stalled, hung almost stationary in front of Mealing's SE5, then went down, in a 'terrific spin.' Fielding-Johnson fired at this machine as it went past him, but he could spare no time to watch it fall any further as the fighting was extremely fierce. Two Albatri were definitely destroyed from this combat: one in flames, which was awarded to Fielding-Johnson and another, seen to spin into the ground and crash, awarded to Mealing. These Albatri were possibly from *Jasta 58* which lost *Vzfw* Wagner killed over Ecourt St Quentin.

After the enemy scouts had cleared east, the SE5s reformed, flew back to the Front Lines and engaged a Hannover southeast of Inchy. Mealing attacked first, a burst from both guns causing a small flicker of flame to emerge from the bottom left hand side of the Hannover's engine. Fielding-Johnson than attacked, firing a long burst from short range, and the enemy machine went into a steep dive to crash a mile west of Bourlon village, at Cagnicourt, killing *Uffz* Walter Seim and *Ltn d Res* Wilhelm Sommer of *Fl Abt (A) 293b*.

During a morning patrol, Capt William Patrick scored the last of his 7 victories while serving in 1 Squadron: an Albatros scout destroyed over Stadenberg at 10.10am. Twenty-five minutes later Francis Magoun and 2lt L Mawbey shared in the destruction of a DFW near Dadizeele.

Major Albert Carter, of 19 Squadron shot down two Pfalz D III within fifteen minutes. The first went down out of control south of Halluin at 11.15am; the second crashed in the same area fifteen minutes later. Huskinson and Hustings each claimed an Albatros out of control south east of Comines at 11.40am and John Leacroft was also awarded two Albatri down out of control: the first east of Tourcoing, the second at 11.50am east of Wervicq.

There were no casualties for the fighter squadrons on March 15.

March 16 was a fine day. Drewitt of 23 Squadron appears to have been the first to score, a two-seater from *Schlasta 6*, crewed by *Vzfw* Grief and *Vzfw* Zollinger, which fell in flames over Pontreut at 7.20am. Possibly in the same patrol, 2Lt E Varley of the squadron also shot down a two-seater, which went down smoking to finally crash north of Lehaucourt. Capt Douglas Bell of 3 Squadron attacked an Albatros over Cambrai at 9.15am and shot it down in a spin before it broke up in mid-air. He then saw a two-seater 2,000 feet below him. Bell dived, got below the enemy machine and shot its left wings off with a short burst of fire.

'Tich' Rochford of Naval 3 was leading his Flight over Gravelle when he spotted three Hannovers and led the Camels directly at them. Rochford, A Ellwood and J Glen shot one down in flames and Harry Chisam attacked another that was seen to crash at Hermies by an artillery observation post. *Fl Abt (A)205* lost *Sgt* Ahlert and *Ltn d Res* Olde killed.

George Thomson and Sydney Smith of 46 Squadron, shared a two-seater down out of control south of Brebieres at 11.30am and Thomson claimed another out of control. Half an hour later they shot another two-seater down in flames in the same area. Thomson claimed another out of control and again shared with Smith in yet another, out of control south of the village. At 10.40am Lt N Clark of 54 Squadron harassed a two-seater down to within 200 feet of the ground before it spun in and burst into flames. An Offensive Patrol from 84 Squadron, led by Capt F E Brown, found a LVG west of Serain. Johnson and Hobson shared in sending it down to crash near Outreaux. Pilots of 41 Squadron also claimed victories over two-seaters in the morning. Capt R Chappell attacked an LVG from a formation of three flying near Brebieres at 11.45am. Smoke and flame came out of the area of the LVG's cockpit and it went down to crash. In an evening patrol at 4.00pm over Bourlon, 2Lt D H Jones also shot down an LVG out of control. Herbert Richardson of 24 Squadron, claimed his eighth victory in the late afternoon: an Albatros scout crashed at Barisis at 4.30pm.

Louis Jarvis and 'Jackie' Walkerdine of 56 Squadron were each awarded an Albatros out of control from a fight in the morning – the Albatros awarded to Walkerdine went down in a series of stalls and dives, a sure sign that the pilot was unconscious or dead. The squadron had one casualty during the day. Diving to attack a pair of Halberstadts over Bourlon Wood, the wings of Lt Knagg's SE5 were seen to fold up, the rest of the machine breaking up. Knaggs was killed. Other casualties were a pilot of 4 Squadron AFC shot down and taken POW, and a pilot of 46 Squadron who was also taken prisoner.

The RFC communiqué for March 17 summed up the general situation: 'EA were very active and a considerable amount of fighting took place.' All the fighter squadrons on the active Front flew a great many patrols; victories were claimed, but casualties were light.

The Camels of 80 Squadron were active south of Cambrai. At 10.20am. Lt J Rodger dived on the Albatros at the rear of a the formation of four, sending it down out of control, and AA batteries later reported that it burst into flames before crashing. Additional enemy scouts then arrived at the fight and attacked the Camels. Capt Harold Whistler was fighting with one scout when three others attacked him from the rear. Whistler zoomed away, got behind his attackers and shot one down to crash in a wood. He later sent another Albatros down out of control. These two Albatri were the first of Whistler's eventual 23 victories with the squadron. Lt R A Preeston dived on one of the Albatri but was attacked by three others. He shook these off, climbed to 12,000 feet and found he had lost contact with the remaining Camels. He then came under attack from 12 enemy scouts and fired a short burst at one before spinning out of trouble. Preeston levelled out at 200 feet, but the enemy scouts were still with him and he was forced the whole way back to the British Lines in a running fight which was witnessed by 66 Division. It reported: 'one British scout put up a wonderful fight with eight EA and No.35 Squadron report one EA still falling out of control 300 feet from the ground at the same place and time. The EA was one of a large EA formation which were fighting a lone Camel.'

Preeston had been saved by his piloting skills, but two of his squadron comrades were not so fortunate: Capt St. C C Tayler and 2Lt Holt had both been shot down and killed during the fighting.

An hour later the SE5s of 64 Squadron were in combat over Douai with Pfalz D IIIs. Capt Edmund Tempest shot one down in flames near the town at 11.30am and five minutes later shot another down out of control over Biache, shared with the other members of his Flight. Two pilots from the squadron had their SEs badly shot up in the morning's fighting, but returned safely.

The commanding officer of 65 Squadron, Major Jack Cunningham, added to the success of the Camel squadrons by shooting down an Albatros, which crashed at Zuidhoek at 11.25am. Capt Trollope of 43 Squadron shot down an Albatros out of control over Maugne at 11.45am, following this three quarters of an hour later by shooting down another, in flames, four miles east of Armentières. The Camels of 3 Squadron were low bombing when they were attacked by enemy scouts, but Lt K V Peden shot down one of his attackers. In an Offensive Patrol by the squadron, 2Lt A Arlot also shot an enemy scout down in flames.

The SE5 squadrons were also seeing action. Three Flights of 84 Squadron were escorting the DH4s of Naval 5 on a bombing raid to Busigny aerodrome. Lt Charles Stubbs reported: 'We saw several large 'V' Strutters flying west. I attacked one on the same level as myself. After circling once, I got above and dived on him, firing with both guns. He nosed over, with myself following, seeing him eventually crash near Besquigny.' Beauchamp Proctor claimed two Albatri out of control in the fighting over Busigny and a Pfalz D III destroyed four miles to the west of the village, but his SE was hit in the engine and he had to return. Jack Sorsoleil destroyed another Pfalz a mile east of Maretz. Capt F E Brown also claimed two out of control victories. *Jasta 17* reported the loss of *Offstv* Adolf Schreder, killed over Busigny during the fighting and *Ltn* Steinhäuser of *Jasta 11* was wounded in the foot and force landed Briastre, *Jasta 3's* aerodrome. During an afternoon patrol by the squadron Edward Clear was attacking a Fokker Triplane when it collided with an Albatros and both machines went down in pieces. Capt F E Brown claimed a triplane out of control from this action. This was a good day for 84 Squadron with ten enemy aircraft shot down, bringing the squadron's overall score to 97.

The Sopwith Dolphins of 19 Squadron appear to have claimed the first victories of the afternoon. Just after noon, a patrol led by Capt Leacroft were in action with enemy scouts, possibly from *Jasta 28* and *Jasta 17*. Arthur Fairclough and Eric Olivier shared an Albatros in flames northeast of Menin at 12.15am, and ten minutes later Olivier, Leacroft and Huskinson each destroyed a Pfalz: Olivier and Huskinson over Roulers; Leacroft in flames over De Ruiter.

Lt N Clark of 54 Squadron added to his success of the previous day by shooting down a Rumpler, which caught fire in the pilot's cockpit and burst into flames as it hit the ground at 2.50pm. In the last patrol of the day, Andrew Cowper of 24 Squadron shot down a Pfalz southwest of Ramicourt at 6.20pm.

Other than the casualties already mentioned, two pilots of 23 Squadron were shot up, one with his prop shot off by AA fire, and another pilot from the squadron was killed in action over Bellicourt in the afternoon. Naval 1 lost a flight commander when R P Minifie was shot down over Houthulst Forest at 12.25pm and taken prisoner, possibly by *Vzfw* Ehmann of *Jasta 47* for his second victory.

The air fighting on March 18 increased still further in intensity and fierceness, literally dozens of action were fought.

The SE5s of 56 Squadron left the ground at 6.20am to escort the Camels of 3 Squadron which were detailed to carry out ground-strafing attacks in the Bullecourt area. As the Camels began their dives they were attacked by a mixed formation of ten Albatri and Pfalz scouts. The SE5s dived into the fight. Walkerdine crashed one Pfalz near Dartford Wood, northeast of Marquion and sent another down in a spin west of the town. Fielding-Johnson saw two Pfalz coming at him, slightly above. He attacked one of these and it crashed near Buissy. Chasing after another Pfalz, Fielding-Johnson caught it over Bois de Cocret and it spun into the ground north of the Marquion to Raillencourt road. Still not finished, Fielding-Johnson then attacked an Albatros, getting in a good burst with slight deflection. The enemy scout went down with smoke coming out of its fuselage. Fielding-Johnson did not wait to see the end of this Albatros, but turned to attack another Pfalz, which evaded his fire. Looking down Fielding-Johnson saw four Pfalz crashed and a fifth landing near the crash at Bois de Cocret. Fielding-Johnson dived to 1,000 feet to attack this Pfalz and fired a short burst. Zooming away, he saw an Albatros going vertically down over Dartford Wood. Fielding-Johnson was awarded two Pfalz destroyed, but not the Albatros as it was not seen to crash. Walkerdine was also awarded two Pfalz as crashed.

Capt Cyril Crowe took off alone at 10.20am. A two-seater flying at 19,000 feet was pointed out to him by British AA fire and getting underneath the enemy machine Crowe fired both guns. The two-seater went down in a spin for 5,000 feet before pulling out at 14,000 feet. Crowe's fire had either killed or wounded the observer and he drove the two-seater down for another 4,000 feet before he was forced to pull out by the steepness of his dive, losing sight of the two-seater when it was almost at ground level. Crowe then attacked a two-seater, over Inchy. This time he made no mistake: the enemy machine crashed near a lake north of Ecourt St Quentin. Crowe later attacked three two-seaters over Marquion, but these co-operated well and he failed to gain a decisive result. Crowe was credited with the first two-seater as out of control and the second as destroyed for his tenth and eleventh victories.

Earlier in the day a patrol from 23 Squadron had enemy aircraft flying east of Urvillers pointed out to them by AA fire. Lts E Varley and E A Richardson and Richardson shot an Albatros down to crash in the British lines at Essigny le Grand at 7.45am. This Albatros was from *Jasta 44s*, the pilot, *Uffz* Wilhelm Brinkmann, was made POW and his machine numbered G 151.

Woollett of 43 Squadron saw a two-seater east of La Bassée and followed it further east until he closed the range and fired over 90 rounds into it at 10.30am. The enemy machine spun down and hit the ground, exploding on impact with clouds of black smoke issuing from the wreck. Further north William Harrison of 40 Squadron also shot down a two-seater, which went down in flames over Courcelles at 10.25am for his eighth victory.

Molesworth was leading a patrol of Nieuports from 29 Squadron when they were attacked by a group of Pfalz D III from *Jasta 47*. Molesworth shot the leader of the enemy formation down to crash south east of Rumbeke. 2Lt F J Williams shot the wings off another, and Coombe, Davies and Wingate-Grey all claimed Pfalz as out of control, but 2Lt R E Neale and Lt L A Edens were both shot down and killed.

Just before mid-day another attack on the German aerodrome at Busigny was carried out by DH4s of 5 Naval, escorted by Camels of 54 Squadron and SE5s of 84 Squadron. The *jagdstaffenl* were waiting. Under the overall command of Manfred von Richthofen, upwards of fifty enemy fighters from *Jagdstaffeln* 3, 4, 5, 6, 10, 16b, 34b, 37, 47, 54 and 56 took to the air to meet the British formations. In the fierce fighting five Camels from 54 Squadron were shot down, with two pilots killed and three taken prisoner (one of these was 2Lt W G Ivamy, Richthofen's 66th victory). Two SE5s from 84 Squadron were lost. 2Lt H A Payne was killed and the younger brother of James McCudden, Anthony McCudden, was shot down and killed by *Ltn* Hans Joachim Wolff of *Jasta 11* for his first victory. The elder McCudden's fears for his younger brother had tragically been only too justified. Commenting later on his brother's death, James McCudden said: 'He was far too brave and headstrong to make a successful fighting pilot for he was in the habit of doing daily over the enemy lines the most hair raising things.'

One DH4 from Naval 5 was shot down, the crew both killed, and another returned with a wounded pilot. The pilots of 84 Squadron claimed seven victories. Lt W H Brown, Larsen, and Clear all claimed Fokker Triplanes, with Capt F E Brown, Capt Leask and Johnson, claiming Albatri. Two pilots of 54 Squadron, 2Lts Drysdale and E A Richardson both claimed enemy machines: Drysdale an Albatros out of control and Richardson a Fokker Triplane that broke up in flames. The *jagdstaffeln* admitted to only four aircraft lost. Max Holtzem of *Jasta 16b*, one of the German pilots involved in this fight – one of the biggest of the war – remembered: 'I followed an SE5 down and saw him land right side up so I flew home and rushed down with mechanics by truck to the plane. After a quick inspection I found the aircraft in condition to fly away except that in the excitement we forgot to paint out the British cockades. I made it to the *staffel* airfield at low altitude, being shot at from the ground by everyone with a loaded rifle. Instead of being credited with it, I got a reprimand. I had no witness to this victory and the SE5 was destroyed as there was no time to play with it.' This SE5 was possibly that of 2lt H A Payne.

On patrol over Roulers, Hamersley of 60 Squadron attacked several Albatri and shot one down to crash at Rumbeke at 12.50pm. At 12.55pm Capt Richard Howard of 2 Squadron AFC scored his last victory: a Rumpler in flames over Habourdin.

The Naval squadrons were also in action during the day. In a morning patrol, FltLt E T Hayne of Naval 3 shot down an Albatros out of control over Harbourdin at 11.05. Later in the morning a Rumpler over Haubourdin at 17,000 feet easily outpaced a patrol led by Rochford, but Hayne later attacked an enemy two-seater and fired 100 rounds at point blank range. The enemy machine dived under Hayne but was attacked by FlSubLt R C Berlyn. Berlyn's fire hit the observer, who was seen to collapse over his gun and the two-seater went down to crash by some houses about a mile east of Hénin-Liétard at 12.40pm. FltSubLt S Smith attacked five enemy scouts, firing 300 rounds into one and the patrol saw it go down to crash, but FltSubLt Allison was shot down and killed by *Ltn* Haebler of *Jasta 36*.

Naval 10 had an unproductive day. A patrol in the morning failed to lure a formation of eight Pfalz into combat. The second patrol of the day was attacked by eight Albatri southeast of Courtrai. The Camel pilots had no positive results from this fight and lost FltSubLt G T Steeves, who was shot down and taken prisoner, possibly by *Ltn* Thuy of *Jasta 28*.

The last positive victory of the day was at 2.15pm: Lt Frank Taylor of 41 Squadron destroyed a two-seater over Lecluse.

It rained for almost the entire day on March 19. The aeroplanes of the corps squadrons were active but the *jagdstaffeln* made no attempt to interfere with their work and the only casualty was a crewmember of an RE8 wounded by AA fire. There was no activity at all the next day. It was the quiet before the storm.

Operation Michael

On the morning of Thursday March 21 the most concentrated artillery bombardment the world had yet known opened on the forty-mile front between the River Scarpe in the north and the River Serre in the south. At 4.45am nearly 6,000 German guns opened fire. The sheer volume of noise numbed the mind and senses: the increase in volume by the answer of the 2,500 guns of the British artillery was hardly noticeable. Eugene Macdonald a pilot with 56 Squadron, stationed at Baizieux, recalled: 'Stewart Maxwell and I were awakened by a thunderous roar of guns. The noise was terrific and continuous, yet no shell appeared to land near us. People who heard our anti-aircraft guns and bombs dropping on London during the '39 war have some idea of noise, but it was peanuts compared with the roar, which seemed to continue endlessly, with which the Germans opened their advance.'[12]

The German guns continued their relentless bombardment for two hours, sometimes slackening as the guns moved to new target, but never ceasing. Countless tons of shells – some of gas – fell on the British front line positions and the general battle zone: artillery batteries and horse lines; wireless stations; communication trenches; casualty clearing stations; troop billets, all came under immense and accurate fire. The very air vibrated with shock and gas was everywhere, drenching whole areas, sending blinded and vomiting men to find what help they could from the first aid posts. The relentless fire switched from the front line infantry positions to the back areas, then back again. As daylight began to filter through it was clear that a thick mist lay over the battlefield, a mist shot through with a crimson, yellow-shot effervescence.

At 8.00am the German infantry began their attacks, advancing through the thick fog. Employing new tactics, the enemy storm troops, their rifles slung, using stick hand grenades, light machine guns and flame throwers, pushed forward, ignoring any strong points that could not be easily taken, leaving them to the following waves of support troops. By 10.00am the advance was general. Hidden by the fog, none of the schemes for checking the advance by cross fire from machine gun posts could be used. By noon the enemy forces had penetrated into the back area of the Fifth Army and infantry in the forward positions were often unaware of the extent of the advance until enemy troops appeared in their rear. German infantry suddenly appearing out of the fog a mere hundred yards away was the first indication many artillery batteries had of the closeness of the enemy troops.

The RFC had drawn up extensive plans to counter the coming offensive, but the fog made these – and those of the *Luftstreitkräfte* – impossible to implement. It was only on parts of the Third Army front that visibility was a little better and at 6.00am pilots of 46 Squadron began low flying attacks on enemy positions in the vicinity of Bourlon Wood, finding a group of artillery batteries, bombing and machine gunning them. At 11.00am the squadron's Camels were out again: German infantry was advancing in considerable force on Lagnicourt and attacks by the Camel pilots eased the pressure on the retreating British infantry. The pilots of 46 Squadron – the only squadron employed in low level flying on the Third Army front – continued these attacks on enemy troops and gun batteries throughout the day. Only one aerial victory was won: Alexander Vlasto of the squadron shot down an Albatros scout over Lagnicourt at 11.45am for his first victory.

On the Fifth Army front, it was not until mid-day that flying was possible – by both antagonists. As visibility improved towards mid-day, the high performance CL category aeroplanes of the *Schlachstaffeln* ranged over the whole of the battlefront, bombing with hand grenades and machine-gunning the front line British troops, harassing any reinforcements that were attempting to come up. On the Third and Fifth Army fronts the air fighting became confused and intense. All the fighter squadrons made low level attacks on the advancing enemy troops and flew offensive patrols at 2,000 feet in an attempt to protect the troops from the *Schlachstaffeln.*

By the afternoon, a great number of *jagdstaffeln* and *schlachstaffeln* aircraft were operating above the confusion of the battle on the ground. Any attempts by the *jagdstaffeln* pilots to attack the British corps aeroplanes working over the battlefield were frustrated by the RFC fighters and all the casualties suffered by the corps squadrons were the result of fire from the ground. The squadrons operating the RE8 had twelve aircraft badly damaged by ground fire, but miraculously had only three crewmembers wounded. The FK8 squadrons had five machines badly damaged, but only two crewmembers were lost.

On the Fifth Army front low level attacks were carried out throughout the day by squadrons of Twenty-Second Wing: Spads of 23 Squadron; the SE5as of 24, 84 Squadrons; 54 Squadron Camels, and the Bristol Fighters of 48 Squadron. Conditions were considerably clearer on the Third Army front and led to vicious and hotly contested air fighting.

The largest fight during the day was at 1.30pm over Bourlon Wood. Two Flights from 56 Squadron, led by Capts Mealing and Galley, left Baizieux at 12.50pm. B Flight, led by Galley, attacked fourteen enemy scouts – Albatri and Fokker Triplanes – over Inchy. Maurice Mealing, seeing another formation of eight enemy machines diving into the fight, also led his force down into the action. The 56 Squadron SEs, aided by two SEs from 64 Squadron, fought with these enemy machines for twenty minutes. Trevor Durrant sent one Albatros down in an inverted spin. The Canadian, Henry Burden, attacked another of the Albatri, following it down until it disappeared into the mist at ground level, but as Burden zoomed away he saw a large burst of flame and a column of smoke appear above the low mist. Edward Galley attacked a Fokker Triplane, flying streamers from its tailplane, which was on the tail of Mealing's SE5. Galley fired a burst of fifty rounds and the triplane pilot spun away. Mealing, hearing a machine gun firing above him, looked up. 'I saw a triplane firing at an SE5 about 20 yards above me, his wheels close to my centre section. I pulled down my Lewis and fired half a drum of ammunition right into his fuselage, just below the pilot's seat. He immediately went down out of control but I then had to turn and engage another EA.'

The fighting had gone down from 11,000 to 4,000 feet, the enemy scouts continually flying east before reforming to return to renew their attacks, but they finally broke off the action and flew east.

James Slater and Lt V W Thompson were the two 64 Squadron pilots involved with 56 Squadron in the fight with the large formations of enemy scouts. A little earlier, at 12.05pm, Slater had shot an Albatros down to crash at Inchy,

the enemy scout going down on its back and crashing near the village, and he and Thompson had also been successful in the later fight, sharing an Albatros and a Fokker Triplane out of control over Bourlon Wood.

The fighter squadrons of the Third Army were reinforced during the day by fighter squadrons from First Army: Nos 2 and 4 Squadrons AFC (SE5s and Camels) 40 (SE5s), 43 (Camels). 22 (Bristol Fighters) and Naval 3 (Camels).

'Tich' Rochford of Naval 3 led his Flight in a morning patrol at 10.30am. 'The fog had cleared and it was a sunny day, but visibility was poor and it was difficult to see the ground through the haze. After flying for about an hour I saw below us a large number of EA, among them a red triplane, near Douai. We attacked them and picking out an Albatros Scout I opened fire at close range and he went down out of control. I then had two more combats with Albatros Scouts, both with indecisive results. Jimmy Glen had helped me to shoot down this Albatros Scout out of control and Armstrong, with C Flight, got another one down in the same category.' In the afternoon, Rochford led a combination of B and A Flights on another patrol. Near Vaulx they intercepted an Albatros two-seater: 'Poor chap, he had not a hope of escaping us and we fell on him like a pack of bloodthirsty bloodhounds who had caught up with their prey. Nearly all of us took part in the attack and eventually the EA turned completely over and descended on its back in a flat spin until it hit the ground and was completely wrecked on our side of the lines.' This Albatros two-seater was possibly from *Fl Abt (A)228*, the crew *Vzfw* Weiss and *Lt d Res* Szajkowski were both killed.

The Camels of 4 Squadron AFC were also fighting over their new area. Despite the thick mist, two Flights left Bruay at 8.00am. Arthur Cobby and his Flight led the formation with J C Courtney's Flight slightly above and behind to guard their tails. Cobby reported that the country was so obscured by fog that after flying for forty minutes he, as leader of the whole formation of Camels, had no idea of their position.

'Every now and then we could see a captive balloon peeping through the mist. Finally I determined to follow this line north until near home, then strike across towards Bruay and endeavour to locate the aerodrome. At 9am we were flying north at about 4,000 feet, just above the balloons and fog, when three Albatros scouts came through the fog just below and to the left of us. They were followed by a straggling line of Pfalz and other scouts, and were flying on a line parallel to our own. Apparently they did not see us, for they made no attempt either to fight or avoid us. Rocking my machine fore and aft – the usual signal to follow the leader into action – I dived into the centre of the enemy formation. Courtney came down from above and joined in, and for about four minutes an all-in dogfight ensued. It was Richthofen's Circus again; all were red machines, except one yellow and black Albatros. The leaders first seen did not join in the fight; they were ahead in the fog.'

Cobby was credited with an Albatros out of control and another destroyed, both south of Brebières, and Lts Pflaum and Roberston each followed their opponents down through the ground mist to see them crash. Lt G Elwyn fought with a red scout for sometime but the enemy pilot hit his Camel in the engine and he was forced to land behind the British lines near Bapaume.

The Canadian Donald Maclaren of 46 Squadron scored three times during the afternoon. At 4.15pm he destroyed an enemy balloon over Biache St Vaast and fifteen minutes later attacked an LVG west of Douai, which crashed by the town. At 4.45pam Maclaren destroyed another LVG, east of Marquion.

The fighter squadrons suffered heavy casualties on the first day of the German offensive. While ground-strafing in the Vaulx-Vraucourt area, Camels of 3 Squadron were attacked by enemy scouts, most probably from *Jasta 35.* Hampered by their bombs, four Camels were shot up, badly damaged and forced to land, but only one pilot was wounded. In a combat near Bellicourt at 2.15pm, Lt H B Richardson of 24 Squadron claimed three Pfalz – one out of control and two others destroyed – but a pilot of the squadron was wounded and another forced to land. The pilots of 41 Squadron claimed three victories in the day's fighting, but lost 2Lt A T Isbell who was shot down and made prisoner, possibly by *Ltn* Schulze of *Jasta 48* who claimed an SE5 over Dury. Another SE5 casualty was a pilot from 29 Squadron who was wounded by groundfire and forced to return.

Forty-six Squadron, flying ground-strafing missions throughout the day, had five Camels badly damaged by fire from the ground, but only one pilot was wounded. A pilot from 73 Squadron had his Camel shot up by ground fire and crashed near Ham, and 2Lt C Coulson of 80 Squadron was shot down over St Quentin by *Oblt* Ritter von Greim *Kommandeur* of *Jagdgeschwader Nr.10.* Coulson was unhurt.

By the end of the day the German forces had made considerable gains on the Fifth Army front. Naval 5 had been shelled out of its aerodrome at Mons-en-Chaussée and moved at once to Champien. All the other squadrons with Fifth Army were ordered to move back to new aerodromes the next morning.

The fog persisted the next morning and there was no air fighting until the afternoon, when there was intense fighting on the Third Army front. The pilots of 46 Squadron again flew low level bombing missions throughout the day. Six Camels went out at 1.30pm, five at 4.20pm and five at 5.10pm. After dropping their bombs the pilots had several combats with

enemy machines. In the 1.30pm patrol, Horace Debenham claimed an Albatros out of control over Doignies at 1.30pm and a two-seater in the same area at 2.15pm; Maclaren sent a two-seater down out of control over Bullecourt at 2.00pm and an hour later shared another with Capt C J Marchant. The later patrols were also successful: Robinson destoyed an Albatros over Hendecourt at 5.30pm and half an hour later shared an LVG out of control over Bullecourt with 2Lt W Shorter. Capt George Thomson destroyed an Albatros scout over Bullecourt at 6.00pm and another out of control west of Boursies half an hour later for his 17th and 18th victories.

In the late afternoon the situation on the ground became serious opposite St Quentin. Low flying attacks on enemy troops were made by 24 and 84 Squadrons; from the evidence of German regimental histories these were extremely effectual. The pilots of 84 Squadron attacked troops by Holnon Wood. One enemy regiment reported that as they moved along the edge of the Wood, companies were hit by bombs, commenting: 'the way in which these airmen came down to 20 metres in order to throw their bombs.' One regiment suffered such heavy casualties from the bombing that it had to be relieved the following day. A battery of artillery, its gunners and horses were destroyed, and on the Third Army front a German division was held up. 'Under the heavy artillery and machine gun fire and frequent attacks by air squadrons the attack cannot go on,' says its history.

In the words of the British official history: 'There was a great amount of desultory air fighting in the afternoon and evening of the 22nd when large numbers of enemy aircraft were flying at all heights. Of the German low-flying aeroplanes which made attacks on the British infantry toll was taken: two were shot down by anti-aircraft fire and one by rifle or machine gun fire from the ground.'

The reference to the enemy machine brought down by rifle fire is an incident reported by Sholto Douglas, commanding 84 Squadron. In the afternoon, the enemy troops were uncomfortably near the squadron's aerodrome at Flez and Douglas was ordered to evacuate to Champien, just to the west of Roye. Douglas had all the squadron's stores and equipment loaded onto lorries, and after they had returned from their last patrols the SE5s were flown to Champien, leaving only Douglas's personal SE5 standing by. As a precaution, Douglas had earlier sent motorcyclists down each of the roads that converged on the aerodrome from the east, with instructions to return every hour and report on how far the German troops had advanced. One of the motorcyclists, a mechanic named A M Knight, reported that he had been attacked by an Albatros from a hundred feet. Knight had dived into a ditch, unslung his rifle, and fired at the enemy scout as it flew back over his position. To his astonishment the engine of the Albatros had stopped and the enemy pilot forced landed nearby. When Knight returned to Flez, Douglas was highly sceptical of his excited claim, but sent a Crossley tender to investigate. The Albatros was found exactly where Knight had reported, with a hole in its engine but no sign of the pilot. The Albatros was set on fire and Knight was given credit for an enemy aircraft destroyed. The squadron's history recorded the feat: 'believed to be the first instance of an RFC cyclist bringing down a Hun, a good but amusing show.'[13]

Typical of the intense air fighting during the day were the actions fought by 2 Squadron AFC in the early afternoon. Two Flights of eight SE5s – two had returned with engine trouble – dived on a mixed formation of enemy two-seaters and scouts north east of St Quentin. Henry Forrest attacked a two-seater from forty yards' range, sending it down in flames, and Robert McKenzie shot down an Albatros out of control over Omissy. The Australians then turned north and flew to the Bourlon Wood area. Five Fokker Triplanes were flying below them. Roy Phillipps singled out the leader and pushed it down for 2,000 feet, firing from close range until the triplane turned over onto its back, spun slowly down, then burst into flames and crashed at Sains les Marquion. The other triplanes had escaped into the low mist and the SE pilots flew to Bullecourt where they attacked a formation of Albatri. Forrest shot two of these down in quick succession and Capt L H Holden claimed a third. Shortly after this patrol had returned, another went out led by Richard Howard. In a fight north of St Quentin, Lt A R Rackett forced an Albatros down, but Howard was shot down over Vermand by either *Ltn* Böhning or *Ltn* Buchstett of *Jasta 79* and crashed near Epehy, mortally wounded.

It was a day of mixed fortunes for Naval 3. Rochford crashed an Albatros scout at Boursies at 12.30am and Aubery Ellwood shot down another out of control. Whealy of C Flight shot an Albatros down to crash in the British lines at 12.30pm and thirty minutes later the C Flight Commander, Frederick Armstrong, shot down another Albatros, also behind the British lines. Louis Bawlf claimed an Albatros out of control over Marquion at 12.30am and Edmond Pierce destroyed an Albatros scout over Boursies at 1.00pm. To offset these victories, FltSubLt L A Sands and Flt SubLt W A Moyle collided in mid-air north of St Quentin and were killed.

The pilots of 73 Squadron also saw a great deal of fighting. Although based considerably further south, at Champien south west of St Quentin, the squadron had been ordered to patrol the Third Army front between Marquion and Le Catelet. As the two Flights of Camels, led by Capts Augustus Orlebar and Thomas Sharpe, were flying over Ham at 2.30pm they attacked a large formation of Albatros scouts – possibly elements of *Jasta 68* and *Jasta 56*. Orlebar and Sharpe each shot down an Albatros: Orlebar's in flames over Ham and Sharpe's just to the north at Douchy. Orlebar also claimed an out of control victory during this combat, but was wounded in the leg and had to return, the only casualty of the afternoon.

Thirty minutes later, now northwest of St Quentin, the Camels attacked eight Albatros scouts, but these were joined by an additional twenty. There was a short, but fierce fight: one Albatros was destroyed and others were driven down. Separated during the combats, the Camels then re-formed and flew on to Roisel where they sighted five LVGs. Sharpe destroyed two, one over Roisel, the other north of the village.

March 22 had been a day of heavy fighting for the fighter squadrons, with no respite throughout the day. Twenty-one definite victories – aircraft in flames, breaking up, or seen to crash – had been awarded, and many out of control victories were also claimed. Two pilots had been killed, six wounded (one mortally) and two taken prisoner, one of whom later died of his wounds. In addition, five aircraft had been badly shot about in combat and were lost due to crashed or forced landings.

Saturday, March 23 was a fine day, but the ground mist persisted. The situation on the ground was desperate. The defences of the Fifth Army were disintegrating under the relentless German attacks. In the north, around the Flesquières Salient, where the edge of Fifth Army's V11 Corps met the flank of Third Army's V Corps, the position was rapidly becoming untenable.[14]

The pressure on the British ground forces was immense along the entire front, but north of the Bapaume to Cambrai road, in the centre of the Third Army front, air reconnaissance reported that despite the stubborn resistance of the IV and VI Corps of the Third Army, the enemy was continuing to attack and was threatening to break through at Mory and Beugny. The threat was so serious that the RFC fighter squadrons were called upon to extend their low level attacks. Two Flights of Camels from 3 Squadron were to begin attacks at dawn, attacks that were to be continued throughout the day and other squadrons were held in reserve should the situation deteriorate still further.

Despite the morning mist, in places extremely thick, 12 SE5s from 56 Squadron took off at 6.20am. There was no activity in the air, dense fog covering the enemy aerodromes. Mealing attacked a balloon over Noreuil, but although the observer jumped clear, Mealing's fire failed to set the balloon alight – it was possibly saturated by the early morning mist – and it merely crumpled and went slowly down. Mealing then saw a two-seater very low over Noreuil and took the Flight down to attack it, but the enemy pilot made a sharp turn, stalled, and crashed into the trenches between Lagnicourt and Noreuil before the SEs had fired a shot. Mealing reformed the Flight and led them to Queant. Arriving over the railway station at 7.40am the pilots could see that the junction was hive of activity: thousands of troops were detraining with their equipment and pack animals. The six SEs went down to 300 feet and attacked the station, firing 150 rounds each. The enemy troops scattered wildly for cover, many crawling under the trains. These attacks were pressed home with no little determination: Mealing's machine was hit in the main petrol tank and many other places, and Galley's SE, hit in a main fuselage strut, was unrepairable in the squadron and struck off strength.

Mealing took out another patrol at noon. His account of the patrol gives a graphic and typical picture of the actions during the day. Mealing's, and many other reports during March, give a clear impression that the pilots of the *jagdstaffel* were not anxious to enter into combat with the British scouts.

'Crossed Lines at 12.30 at 8,000 feet over Equancourt. 10 Camels were at 9,000 feet and A Flight was at 11,000 feet. Then saw about 7 Camels crossing very low by Bapaume-Cambrai road, so went above them and went after 10 EA scouts to the east of the Camels. EA went east hard. Watched Camels back to Lines as more EA were above us. Then climbed hard to reach two formations of EA but they climbed too. Triplanes remained above us and would not attack and Albatros scouts were too far east, although we got to their level. Lost touch with A Flight about middle of patrol and did not meet them again until the end, as we were further north.'

After the haze of the morning, the visibility was good in the afternoon and at 3.30pm the enemy made five infantry attacks from the direction of Vaulx-Vraucourt and another five from Beaumetz-lez-Cambrai. 46, 56 and 41 Squadrons were sent out to attack enemy troops and transport on the roads in the Bapaume-Cambrai area, in particular on the Vaulx-Vrancourt to Lagnicourt road.

Transferred from the First Army, the Camels of 4 Squadron AFC, had been concentrating their attacks on the village of Vaulx-Vraucourt and its converging roads since the morning. Twelve Camels, flying at less than 500 feet, found no lack of targets. Masses of troops were in the fields; the roads packed with marching bodies of men and their transport. One patrol of Camels, flying slightly above the other, intercepted an attack on the lower Flight by Albatros scouts and two, with little room to take evasive action, were shot down and seen to crash. The pilots of Naval 3, also from First Army, were in action in the area, but fighting above the battle, shooting down three Pfalz scouts.

On the Fifth Army front low flying attacks were carried out by 24 Squadron, which sent out four SE5s at two-hour intervals through out the day to bomb and machine gun targets along the St Quentin to Amiens road. 84 Squadron and 23 Squadron combined their ground-strafing attacks with normal offensive patrols. Flying north east of Ham, twelve SE5s of 84 Squadron surprised a large number of enemy troops in groups of 300 strong, advancing across fields near Viefville, and strafed these for twenty minutes until they had exhausted their ammunition. The pilots of 23 Squadron attacked mules and cavalry and scattered them throughout the fields.

March 23 saw more air fighting than the previous two days of the battle, but all the combats taking place at under 10,000 feet. The fighting had been at its most severe on the Third Army front, involving not only the six single-seater fighter squadrons of Thirteenth (Army) Wing, but the five single-seater fighter squadrons of the Tenth (Army) Wing of I Brigade. In addition the squadrons of Ninth (Day) Wing also fought over the threatened Third Army front. The official history records that thirty-nine German aeroplanes were claimed as destroyed along the whole of the British front, only three of which came down on the front of the Second Army, outside the area of the battle. On the Third and Fifth Army fronts the RFC fighter squadrons had three pilots wounded in action, three taken prisoner of war, and five aircraft badly damaged in action and forced to land.

Sunday, March 24, was a fine day. The situation on the ground, between Péronne and the Bapaume to Cambrai road, at the junction of the Third and Fifth Armies, became extremely critical in the morning. Air reconnaissance revealed that enemy troops had taken the village of Sailly-Saillisel and were advancing north and west of the village, threatening to drive a wedge between the two British armies. In the early afternoon, Combles fell and German troops were still advancing north to Lesboeufs. Under extreme difficulties the Third Army began to retreat in an attempt to establish a new line of defence. Sir Douglas Haig issued a special order of the day to all ranks of the British Army in France, calling for steadfastness and utmost exertion.

The fighting in the air followed the same general pattern of the previous days: low flying attacks with bombs and machine guns throughout the day. The *Schlachtstaffeln* were active above the battlefield, supporting their own troops and harassing the retreating British forces, but they did little to negate the attacks by low flying British fighters on their own troops. German regimental history accounts are full of reports of the effect the ground-strafing was having on their advance. A German regiment, passing through Morval reported: 'During the hot hours of the afternoon there was a pause, especially as the very active fighting and bombing squadrons of the enemy in the clear air imposed a very cautious advance on us.' Another regiment, advancing across the Bapaume to Péronne road, recorded: 'Hostile airmen, flying low, delay the march with machine-gun fire and bombs, especially on the Transloy to Lesboeufs road.'

In the afternoon German troops were seen to be massing in some strength for attacks at Béthencourt and Pargny and squadrons were at once sent out to attack them. The history of the German 12th Grenadier Regiment reported: 'During the advance one Company lost twelve killed and eight wounded by air bombs.' A bugler in the 8th Grenadier Regiment gave an evocative and graphic picture of the attacks on his Company. 'After we were moving forward towards the firing line after crossing the Somme, there suddenly appeared before us some twenty British aeroplanes which dived to a height of about 100 to 200 metres, and then, continuing to within 2-3 metres of the ground, attacked us with their machine-guns. At first we thought they intended to land; but we speedily saw the danger and opened a vigorous fire upon them. Several "Tommies" flew so low that the wheels of their aeroplanes touched the ground. My company commander, Leutnant Nocke, had to fling himself flat on the ground but for all that he was struck on the back by the wheels of one machine, thus being literally run over. Not far from me an aeroplane appeared at about one metre above the ground, making straight for me and for the moment I did not know in what direction to throw myself: the pilot seemed determined to run over me. At the last moment I was able to spring clear as the machine whizzed past me and through the firing line. It then turned, climbed a little, and sought to repeat the manoeuvre, whereupon it was hit by one of the companies firing on our left and brought down. In all, five enemy machines were shot in our Battalion's area.'

The squadrons of Fifth Army had been forced to evacuate their aerodromes on the first day of the German offensive; owing to the rapidity of the German advance it was now the turn of the Third Army squadrons. The squadrons had orders to pack up all their equipment and stand-by to evacuate their aerodromes at a moment's notice. These orders led to a certain amount of disorganisation in the squadrons concerned. When the evacuation orders did come, many pilots returning from patrol found their aerodromes deserted, the whole of the personnel gone. The squadrons of the First Army, detailed to fight over the Third and Fifth Army fronts had no such problem, operating from aerodromes to the north of the ground fighting. The aerodrome at Bruay, west of Lens, was extremely busy: as many as five squadrons' aircraft would be there, refuelling and rearming, pilots, anxious to return to the battle, working with their mechanics to check over machines, gun sights and ammunition, the last being particularly important – no pilot wanted gun jams to interfere with such vitally important work.

The air fighting had increased in fierceness and intensity, even more than the previous day, nearly all the combats now taking place at under 5,000 feet. An Australian pilot commented that the *jagdstaffeln* were to be seen, 'flying at a great height and well over their own side,' but they seemed 'indifferent about attacking or attempting to approach our Line. The great numbers of British machines evidently made them feel uncomfortable.' Despite this observation there were many combats. Some examples serve to give an overall view of the fighting above the ground-strafing.

While ground-strafing in the afternoon Captain Fitz-Morris of 23 Squadron caught a *Schlachtstaffel* two-seater and fought it down to within a hundred feet of the ground until it finally crashed it in flames at Canizy. Fifteen minutes later Fitz-Morris and his Flight were attacked by seven Pfalz D IIIs. One Pfalz was shot down to crash in the British Lines, shared between the Flight, but Fitz-Morris' Spad was badly shot about in the fight, his engine hit and he force landed. The two-seater was the last of Fitz-Morris' fourteen victories.

During the day's fighting, Captain John Trollope of 43 Squadron created a record by shooting down six enemy aeroplanes – the first pilot of the RFC to do so. Trollope reported:

'11am. Whilst leading my patrol east of Mercatel I saw three DFWs some way away trying to cross the line. I worked round east and attacked one, but was forced by gun jambs to break off. I corrected my guns and then attacked another DFW. I fired about 100 rounds at point blank range. Enemy aircraft went down in a spin and broke up about 1,000 feet below me. This was seen by Lieutenant Owen. I then attacked another DFW with Lieutenant Owen and after firing 75 rounds the machine burst into flames and fluttered down on fire. This was confirmed by Lieutenant Owen who also engaged it. I then saw an Albatros scout coming down on to one of our formations. I dived on him and fired about 100 rounds. Enemy aircraft fell completely out of control. This was seen to crash by Captain Woollett.'

The Camels of 43 Squadron were out again in the afternoon. Trollope was again successful.

'3.20pm. When I was leading my patrol over Sailly-Saillisel at about 6,000 feet, I saw four enemy aircraft two-seaters trying to interfere with RE8s. I dived down with my formation and attacked one enemy aircraft. I fired a shot burst at close range and the enemy machine fell to bits in the air. I saw two of my patrol engaging the other three two-seaters at close range and I saw two enemy aircraft go down completely out of control and crash. I gathered all my patrol and flew about looking for other enemy aircraft. I saw two pink two-seaters below me very close to the ground; I attacked each in turn from about 20 feet and they both nose-dived into the ground and I saw both crash. I climbed up and saw the rest of my patrol engaged by a large formation of enemy scouts. I got into the scrap and was forced to return through lack of ammunition.'[15]

Trollope later commented that after seeing the two-seaters crash: 'I then saw one of our fellows attacked by twelve Huns so I climbed up to him and let him get away but then ran out of ammunition and turned for home but not before being able to confirm that two enemy scouts attacked by Second Lieutenant Owen and Highton respectively, had crashed.'

The DFW in the morning, which had escaped by virtue of Trollope's gun stoppages, was attacked by Cecil King and 2Lt Owen and shot to pieces in mid-air. Captain Woollett had accounted for a fourth DFW that went down in flames south east of Arras. To add to the morning's successes, Lt Hector Daniel, separated from the other Camels, joined up with a patrol of Camels from Naval 3 and shot down an Albatros scout over Bullecourt.[16]

Thirty-one definite victories were claimed on March 24, and an additional 14 enemy machines out of control or forced down. The cost had been high. Six pilots had been killed,[17] four taken POW, two of whom died of their wounds, and two pilots wounded. Ten aeroplanes had been lost in forced landings and crashes.

The weather changed on March 25. There was a great deal of low cloud at 1,000 feet making sight of the ground impossible. All troops of the Fifth Army operating north of the River Somme, were to come under the orders of the Third Army Commander. The situation on the ground was still grave. The French Third Army, which had taken over the right flank of the British Fifth Army, had lost ground and there was an enemy advance towards Roye that threatened to drive a wedge between the British and French armies. The situation on the Third Army front was even more serious. Gaps had opened up in the defences and the enemy was advancing towards the Ancre. Vast concentrations of German troops were massing on both sides of the Cambrai road to the east of Bapaume, 10,000 German troops attacking between Bapaume and Ervillers, and by the afternoon the line was giving way between Montauban and Ervillers.

Maximum effort was again called for from the squadrons of the RFC. At 11.05am Major-General Salmond sent a message by hand to Lt-Col W R Freeman commanding Ninth Wing: 'I wish you as soon as you can after receipt of this to send out your scout squadrons and those of No.27, No.25 and No.62 Squadrons that are available on to the line Grévillers-Martinpuich-Maricourt. These squadrons will bomb and shoot up everything they can see on the enemy side of this line. Very low flying is essential. All risks to be taken. Urgent.'

In addition to the squadrons asked for by Salmond, ten squadrons (including corps squadrons) operating with the First Army, and two squadrons from V Brigade all made a concentrated effort to aid the hard-pressed squadrons of III Brigade working with the Third Army. All available aircraft – SE5s, Camels, Spads, Bristol Fighters, Sopwith Dolphins, DH4s and RE8s – were all to be flown at low height over the enemy troops, bombing and machine gunning. These duties were carried out with such grim determination that there can be no doubt that they had a great influence on the day's battles. A German regiment reached a camp at Bapaume in the early morning. 'The stay was not very pleasant because airmen bombed us causing heavy losses.' Another regiment, resting east of the Martinpuich-Bazentin-le-Petit road, reported: 'The strong activity of the airmen was most unpleasant. A squadron of about fifteen machines harassed us with bomb and machine-gun fire against which our machine-gun fire was powerless.' Advancing westwards in the early morning the 52nd Reserve Regiment reported: 'After only twenty minutes' marching the first hostile airmen flying low appear and seek to delay the advance with machine-gun fire. There were about twenty-five airmen over the Regiment.' Later, as the Regiment approached Thiepval: 'The English advance from Thiepval to counter attack. They are repulsed. This afternoon the hostile airmen are present in crowds. We count more than thirty above us at the same time.' The German regimental histories of the time are full of the eternal cry of the infantry – 'where are our airmen?'

During the low flying attacks in the area of Vaulx and Ervillers, 90,000 rounds of ammunition were fired at ground targets and an immense number of bombs dropped by the squadrons of the RFC in a supreme effort to aid the hard pressed ground forces.

The weather curtailed the air fighting in the upper air, but some combats took place: six positive victories were claimed by the single-seater fighter squadrons and two out of control. Casualties were heavy. Six pilots were killed, two wounded, and three aircraft were lost by the fighter squadrons. To put these figures into perspective, the two-seater squadrons engaged in low level work lost two pilots killed, ten wounded, two taken prisoner and lost ten aircraft.[18]

By the evening of March 25 it had become clear that the enemy was now about to concentrate his main attack on the Third Army front, opposite the V and VII Corps. German troops were massing in some considerable numbers west of Bapaume and on the morning of March 26 every available machine of Ninth Wing was ordered to attack this concentration and attempt to disorganise and break it up before an attack could develop. Maximum effort was again called for. All squadrons with the First Army again took part in the low flying operations throughout the day on the Third Army front, reinforced by four squadrons from Second Army and three squadrons from the Fifth Army: a total of 27 squadrons to fly low level operations. The fighter squadrons of Thirteenth (Army) Wing were to be used for offensive patrols over the front.

The Camels of 54 Squadron were in the air by 6.00am, attacking troops and transport in the Pozières area, and eleven pilots of 84 Squadron flew up and down the Bapaume to Albert road, continuously strafing enemy troops and transport. At the conclusion of their morning's work these two squadrons went back to operating in the Fifth Army area: a German attack was building towards Roye and threatening to cut off the British forces from the French and capturing Montdidier to cut the lateral railway communications. In the morning, while 84 Squadron had been ground-strafing further north, the Spad pilots from 23 Squadron and the Camels of 54 Squadron had been making low level attacks against enemy troops along the whole of the Fifth Army front, with pilots from 24 Squadron concentrating on the northern part. When air reconnaissance reported that the enemy had forced a gap in the defences at Roye, all squadrons were ordered to concentrate their efforts to stem the advance.

On March 26, the jagdstaffeln, conspicuous by their relative absence in the first days of the German offensive – 'there are many British but no German flying men up' was a common complaint of German regiments – made attempts to interfere with the low flying British aircraft attacking their troops. Although the commander of III Brigade, Brigadier-General J F A Higgins, reported that enemy air activity was 'slight, on the whole,' and his fighter squadrons reported little enemy activity encountered on offensive patrols, L E O Charleton, commanding V Brigade, reported that activity on his section of the front was 'normal.'

The pilots and observers of the corps and two-seater fighter aeroplanes working over the battle reported many combats with enemy fighters, claiming eight brought down – four to the DH4 crews of 18 Squadron; three to those of the Bristol Fighters of 22 Squadron and one to FK8s of 2 Squadron – but the offensive patrols of the fighter squadrons saw little action, only those from Tenth, Eleventh and Thirteenth Wings claiming ten victories: some of these were enemy scouts attacking low flying aeroplanes, but four were two-seaters, almost certainly Schlasta aircraft.

The combat reports of the fighter pilots of the RFC contain many references to the reluctance of the pilots of the jagdstaffeln to engage in combat. For example, on the morning of March 26, two Flights of SE5s from 56 Squadron attacked a formation of enemy scouts over Pozières, which immediately dived east 'at a great pace.' The SE5s then attacked a formation of Albatros scouts near Miraumont and the enemy machines

again dived away east without staying to fight. A third enemy formation was later driven east from over Albert. Several reasons have been put forward for this reluctance by the pilots of the jagdstaffeln to engage with the RFC fighters. That the success and rapidity of the German advance found the aerodromes of the jagdstaffeln ten or twenty miles behind the fighting and that the liaison with the ground forces had therefore broken down has been sited. This is hard to justify. The German offensive was meticulously planned and such an eventuality would surely have been considered. Also, many perfectly good aerodromes had been evacuated by the RFC Squadrons – in the example quoted above the pilots of 56 Squadron reported that German fighters were occupying the old RFC advanced landing ground at Bapaume. Supply difficulties have also been put forward. But the squadrons of the RFC had been forced to move back to new aerodromes with all the logistical supply problems entailed. Whatever the reasons, the failure of the jagdstaffeln to effectively interfere with the work of the low flying aeroplanes of both the Corps and fighter squadrons, work which had a significant effect on the outcome of the offensive, reflects badly on the jagdstaffeln and led many of their troops to feel betrayed.

On the Fifth Army front only 24 Squadron pilots saw any action, four pilots claiming a victory each. Over the Third Army ground fighting, seven positive victories were claimed and six out of control. Casualties were again heavy for the fighter squadrons, with five pilots killed; three wounded; three taken POW and six aeroplanes shot up, badly damaged.

On March 27 the main work over the Third Army front was again low level flying against enemy troops. The whole area east of Albert was thick with German infantry and low level attacks against them were made at first light. Pilots from 4 AFC, 19, and 40 squadrons all flew continuous attacks throughout the day and German regimental histories again give ample testimony of the effectiveness of these attacks, making many references to their considerable losses and the difficulties the attacks imposed on their advance.

At 8.30am, south of the Somme, the enemy began to attack the British Fifth Army and the French armies. The mistaken withdrawal of the right of the Third Army the previous afternoon had left the flank of the Fifth Army exposed and the German infantry crossed the Somme and took the left of the Fifth Army in the rear. The troops of Fifth Army fought all day and gave little ground, but on their right the French divisions were outfought and enemy troops captured Mondidier.

In the words of the official history, the conduct of the troops of the Fifth Army on March 27, grey with utter weariness, having been involved in continuous and fierce fighting since the start of the German offensive, 'was magnificent.' The resistance of the exhausted troops was considerably strengthened by the assistance given by the squadrons of the RFC. The fighter squadrons of I, II and III Brigades: 16 squadrons of single-seater fighters, plus the two-seater fighters and corps squadrons – and the fighter squadrons of Ninth Wing – made continuous attacks, especially on those enemy troops which had crossed behind the Fifth Army's left flank. There was little fighting in the upper air, the *Luftstreitkräfte* being active against the low flying aircraft of the RFC, but some victories were claimed.

The day had started with low cloud and rain, but it brightened near mid-day. Crowe and Billinge took out strong Flights of SE5s of 56 Squadron and at 12.45pm over Albert attacked eight enemy scouts. The fight was short but fierce, but the only result was an Albatros sent down in a flat glide. Half an hour later the SEs attacked six Albatri east of Bray. Jarvis and 'Jackie' Walkerdine both attacked one of the enemy scouts, which stalled, turned over and went down to crash in a ploughed field. Hank Burden closed to close range, firing continuously at another enemy scout until he had expended his Lewis gun drum and his Vickers jammed. The Albatros went down in a series of spirals and stalls until the enemy pilot managed to regain control close the ground and attempted to land downwind. The Albatros hit the middle of a road and bounced into an adjoining field.

Pilots of A Flight had gone down to attack enemy transport on the roads around Contelmaison and La Boiselle, finishing their ammunition on troops and transport around Suzanne and a battery at Fricourt. An evening patrol by the squadron – ten SE5s – were attacking ground targets three miles east of Morlancourt when they were attacked by seven Fokker Triplanes from *Jasta B*. Lt Stewart Maxwell was almost immediately shot down in flames by *Ltn* Vallendor but the remaining SEs turned to meet the attack. Crowe was diving on transport by Méaulte when the attack began.

I suddenly heard a machine gun behind me and discovered an enemy triplane on my tail. This was about 6.15. I immediately did a left hand climbing turn and had a most interesting scrap at 4,000 feet that lasted about four minutes. Triplane could turn quicker than 200hp SE, which manoeuvre he used considerably, but SE invariably managed to keep above him. It was impossible to keep sights on Triplane for more than a few seconds. I fired half a drum of Lewis and about 70 to 100 rounds of Vickers. Eventually Triplane dived east all out. I chased him as far as Contalmaison down to about 1,000 feet and left him.'

There was intense ground fighting at Albert in the afternoon and just in front of the infantry a formation of low flying Camels of 4 Squadron AFC fought with German scouts. Capt Roy Phillipps shot down a Fokker Triplane in flames

and forced a Pfalz D III to land behind the British positions – possibly *Gefr* Sielemann of *Jasta 57*. Lt E R Jeffree destroyed two Fokker triplanes that were attacking the British trenches and Lt T Hosking of 2 Squadron AFC fired 200 rounds at another triplane that rolled over and burst into flames.

Casualties were again heavy in the fighter squadrons. Eight pilots were killed and another eight wounded; three were taken POW, two of them wounded, and an additional six aircraft were shot up and made crash or forced landings.

On the morning of March 28 the German army launched a series of attacks at Arras, similar to the beginning of its offensive on March 21. This time, however, there was no fog, and British artillery fire, ranged by the aeroplanes of the corps squadrons, caused heavy losses to the attacking troops. More attacks in the afternoon, north of the Scarpe, were also repulsed. These attacks were on the extreme right of the First Army and on the left of the Third. The fighter squadrons of Tenth (Army) Wing – 2 and 4 Squadrons AFC, 3 Naval 40 and 43 Squadrons, plus 1 Squadron from Eleventh (Army) Wing – all concentrated on low flying attacks around Arras, continuing throughout the day. In the afternoon, pilots of 40 Squadron found the main Arras to Cambrai road and its side roads full of enemy troops and transport and attacked from 300 feet. Gwilym Lewis of the squadron wrote home:

'We all carried four nice little bombs, and found all sorts of nice funny things to drop them on. At least everything is spoilt at the time by being so frightened, but really there is quite a lot of humour in seeing rows of fat Huns walking along a long straight road, laying nice little eggs on them, and then shooting them up with a couple of guns, and seeing them run in all directions, and pretty fast too. It's funny enough when one sits in a nice comfortable hut, but it doesn't seem funny when the clouds are at 2,000, when the air is swarming with our machines and you feel frightened to move, when Archie starts pitching them all over you and machine guns crack from below. The only thing which didn't add to the humour of the show was the Hun Flying Corps; that seems to be resting!'

There was very little air fighting in the upper air on March 28. The day was one of high wind, with rain in the afternoon. Large enemy formations were seen over the Third Army front during the day, but these were flying higher than previously and avoided combat. Only five enemy machines were claimed by the fighter squadrons, but casualties were again high. Four pilots were killed in action; six taken prisoner (one of whom died of his wounds); four pilots were wounded and an additional three aeroplanes were badly shot up.

It had been a disastrous day for 43 Squadron. Two Flights, each of five Camels, led by Trollope and Cecil King, left Avesnes-le-Comte just after 8am to fly an Offensive Patrol in the Albert area. Just after 9.00am, four miles southeast of

Albert, a large force of 20 enemy fighters from *Jasta 4* and *Jasta 11* of *JG 1,* and *Jasta 5* and *Jasta 56* were seen. The German fighters attempted to attack some nearby Bristol Fighters, but these evaded the attack by climbing into the cloud cover. King's Flight was too far east to intervene, but Trollope took his five Camels to attack the enemy fighters.

In the fierce fighting Trollope first shot down a triplane in pieces, then an Albatros in flames. Trollope later wrote: 'I then "policed" the patrol and one Triplane went down in pieces (I think by Owen) and then two more Albatros scouts went down out of control and crashed. I do not know who got them but think Adam and Prier. The Huns then split up and ran for it. It was short but damned hot. Everyone fought well. The formation joined up OK and joined Bristol Fighters two miles west of Peronne, King still very far to the left. Two balloons appeared. I got one in flames, Owen got his, but it did not burst into flames, it simply went down deflated. Very hot machine gun fire from the ground and my aileron controls were cut. I waggled to and fro, (fore and aft I mean), and managed to get going west, but someone followed me, I don't know who. I was going west for about 15 seconds only when 3 EA came out of the clouds and came for me and in the first burst my wrist was almost blown off. I tried to reach the clouds but just as I was getting into them the main tank was shot through. It was 2,500 feet when my gravity tank picked up and they were still firing at me the whole time and I could only keep straight. I kept on and on till my engine was hit and the revs dropped to 1,000. I still kept on, both my front flying wires on both sides were shot away. This upset the stability and she started turning north slightly and then my gravity tank was shot through and that finished me. As soon as my engine stopped I got into a floppy spiral and finally at 150 feet into a spinning nosedive from which I did not recover. How I wasn't killed beats me. I cannot say what happened to the machine that followed me back. I finally crashed 200 yards behind their outpost line near Dernacourt, south west of Albert.'[19]

2Lts R Owen, C Maasdorp, H Adams and W Prior had all been shot down. Adams was killed, but Owen, Prier, and Trollope survived as prisoners of war; Maasdorp was also a prisoner, but died of his wounds. Lt Cecil King, who had been climbing into the fight in an attempt to come to the aid of Trollope's Flight, was also wounded, but claimed an Albatros, which went down four miles east of the Albert to Bray road. This was possibly *Ltn* Hans-Georg von der Osten of *Jasta 4* who was wounded in action.

It is hard to determine who shot down the 43 Squadron Camels, but the claims of Rautter of *Jasta 4* and *Ltn* Heims of *Jasta 56* are nearest for both time and place. Rumey (*Jasta 5*) Billik (*Jasta 52*) Werner (*Jasta 14*) and Koch (*Jasta 32*) all claimed Camels during the day's fighting but all are out, either in time or location, or both.

March 28 saw the turn of the tide in the battle, an ebbing of the German advance. By the evening, the British troops south of the Somme had withdrawn to the Amiens defence line, from Mezières to Ignaucourt and Hamel. General Sir Hubert Gough and the staff of the Fifth Army were removed from their duties – unfairly, as later evidence was to show[20] – and command of the British troops south of the Somme was given firstly to the staff of the Fourth Army, then in reserve, then to General Sir H S Rawlinson when he returned from his duties as representative at the Supreme War Council at Versailles.

On the morning of March 29 the greater part of the British line south of the Somme was held by reserves which had been hurriedly assembled under Brigadier-General G Carey on March 25, the 1st Cavalry Division and the remainder of the Fifth Army troops which had not been withdrawn. German troops were seen to be beginning to assemble south of the River Luce, but the weather was stormy, with high winds and no attacks from the air were possible. During the afternoon, however, the weather improved a little and low flying attacks were carried out. There was little aerial fighting by the fighter squadrons: only four victories were claimed by pilots of 4 AFC, 1, 32 and 43 Squadrons and casualties were appreciably lighter, with only three pilots wounded, but safe. One wounded pilot tried to land on a German aerodrome, but crashed and later died of his injuries. Three aircraft were badly damaged.

The enemy made a series of determined attacks in the valley of the Luce on the morning of March 30. The corps squadrons, and the fighters of 2 Squadron AFC, 65, 24, 84, 23 and 54 Squadrons, plus the two-seat Bristol Fighters of 48 Squadron, all attacked these troops. The fighting was intense in the area of Moreuil Wood. The regimental history of the German 122nd Regiment recorded:

'The French and British flying men circle over Moreuil Wood and join in the battle, attacking with bombs and machine-gun fire. A pair of British aviators pass at such low height over the wood than one expects them to hit the tree tops. They have dropped their bombs and used their machine-guns, and now, flying at the speed of arrows, attack our batteries. One bomb, dropped from a negligible height places the whole staff of the 1st Battalion *hors de combat*. Moreuil Wood is Hell.'

South of the Somme the *Schlasta* were active, attacking the British infantry. 2Lt E Clear of 84 Squadron attacked four of these fast two-seaters and shot one down to crash. Lts W J A Duncan and J Griffith of 60 Squadron shot down a LVG. At 10.35am over Mametz Wood Harold Hamersley also shot down an LVG and forty minutes later, in a fight with Albatri over

Fricourt, he claimed an Albatros out of control and destroyed another, which crashed into the roof of a house in Hem and burst into flames. Walter Copeland and 2Lt H Hegarty each shot down an Albatros scout in this fight: Copeland's victory was seen to crash in the centre of Boire village, Hegarty's at Theux.

Further north, in a fight south east of Arras, Arthur Cobby of 4 Squadron AFC destroyed a Pfalz D.III for his third victory. The enemy machine, which had been attacking a 4 Squadron Camel, spun away, one wing breaking off, and crashed.

Casualties were few. Three pilots wounded and one taken POW. Two aircraft were badly damaged.

The British troops held fast against the attacks and by the end of the day the line was little changed.

The next day the German forces attacked between Démuin and Moreuil, and the French held positions at Montdidier. The enemy troops made some progress, but strong and determined counter attacks partially restored the positions.

March 31 was notable in that the air fighting reverted to the upper air. The operational orders for the fighter squadrons of Ninth Wing stated implicitly: 'all efforts will be concentrated on attacking hostile machines and not on ground targets as of late. The concentration of force at such hours as the enemy is likely to be active will be aimed at, rather than continuous but weak patrols throughout the day ... Patrols will work at height if the weather is fine, but even if they are forced by the weather to work at low altitude, their objectives will be the enemy's machines and not ground targets.' The importance of large patrols to counter those now being flown by the *jagdstaffeln* had been realised.

Weather conditions were bad, the day overcast with showers of rain throughout the day. Large formations of enemy scouts were seen intermittently over the whole of the front, but these kept well to the east. On the whole of the British front there were only three combats, but the *Schlasta* were active over the fighting. Lt George Hodson of 73 Squadron shot an Albatros down in flames at 10.00am over Abancourt and 2Lt R Crowden crashed an enemy scout at Warfusee for the only claims by the pilots of the fighter squadrons during the day.

The impetus of the German advances had now finally stopped. Michael had spent itself and its immediate successor, Mars, the attack on Arras on March 28, had failed. There was to be a hiatus in the German offensives until April 9.

The failure of the attack at Arras on March 28 had led to *General* Ludendorff to cancel the next plan of attack, to take the high ground around Lens. He now decided to next attack on the plain of the Lys between La Bassée and Armentières, the sector that had once been considered as the main operation of the German spring offensive and for which all the preparatory work had been carried out. Allied air reconnaissance on the last day of March had shown a considerable movement northward of the German forces whose attacks had failed to take Arras, but the British General Staff found to hard to believe that Ludendorff would fail to exploit the ground won by the offensive at Amiens, ground which had almost achieved objectives of vitally strategic importance. They saw the concentration on the La Bassée front as the prelude to a subsidiary attack to draw reserves away from the next attack at Amiens. The German 2nd Army and the right wing of the 18th did, in fact, attack at Albert and south of the Somme towards Amiens, but these attacks were indecisive. Ludendorff later wrote, 'It was an established fact that the enemy's resistance was beyond our strength. We must not get drawn into a battle of exhaustion.'[21]

NOTES

1. In the winter of 1917, in preparation for the arrival of American forces on the Western Front, an expansion of the *Luftstreitkräfte* had been ordered – the *Amerikaprogramm*. By February 1918, the number of *jagdstaffeln* had been increased to 81 and two new *jagdgeschwader* had been formed, *Jagdgeschwader Nr.2 and Nr.3*. The strength of each *Flieger Abteilungen* was also increased, to nine aeroplanes, and during March 1918 the *Schutzstaffeln* (*Schusta*) were renamed *Schlachtstaffeln* (*Schlasta*) and grouped into *Schlachtgeschwadern*. These *Schlachtgeschwadern,* of four to six *Schlasta,* were used in an offensive role in supporting attacking infantry.

2. The RFC communiqué also credits McElroy with another Albatros shot down in flames in this action, but this is not reflected in his victory list for the day.

3. *I Chose the Sky*, Leonard Rochford.

4. Diary of Paul Strähle, *Jasta 57*, quoted in Cross and Cockade, Great B.,Vol.11 No.4. Strähle's diary quotes that the *Jasta* was attacked by triplanes, but no British triplanes were in service in March 1918.

5. Possibly *Uffz* Beschow of *Jasta 6*, wounded in action.

6. Probably *Ltn* Wilhelm Gürke of *Jasta 5*, killed in action over Honnecourt.

7. Campbell's Camel was later flown in combat by *Oblt* Otto Kissenberth, *Staffelführer* of *Jasta 23*. Kissenberth, who scored his last victory flying the Camel, crashed and was severely injured while flying it on 29 May 1918.

8. This Bristol was then attacked by pilots from *Jasta 56*. *Ltn* Heins and *Ltn* Schleiff of the *Jasta* were both awarded Bristols from the morning's fighting. Richthofen wrongly identified it in his combat report as a DH4.

9. Whether the failure of the triplane's wing was structural or due to enemy fire is unknown. Capt Orlebar of 73 Squadron claimed a Fokker Triplane that broke up under his fire while attacking a Bristol Fighter. The observer of the Bristol Fighter, Capt Claye, also fired at the triplane, claiming that its top wing 'fell off ' under his fire before his gun jammed.

10. The original opening date of the offensive had been planed for March 14, but Crown Prince Rupprecht, commanding the army group which would be responsible for two thirds of the troops in the attack had asked for more time to prepare.

11. Tutschek had flown as a fighter pilot since January 1917. He was seriously wounded in the August of that year and did not return to the Front until February 1918. At the time of his death he had 27 victories.

12. E R M Macdonald. Letter to the author.

13. Two German pilots are reported to have been forced to land by groundfire in the area. *Ltn* Zwiters of *Jasta 62*,who came down north west of Ham and *Vzfw* Dettmering, west of Ham. Both were taken prisoner.

14. The salient was the anchor point of the British defence system. Its evacuation early on Sunday morning, March 24, began the wholesale retreat of the British forces.

15. Writing home to his mother that evening, Trollope began his letter: 'This has been the most wonderful day of my life.'

16. An American pilot, George Whiting – immediately nicknamed 'Fishy' – had recently joined 43 Squadron. He recalled that at first he was closely watched to see if he ate his peas with his knife or perhaps had a bow and arrow secreted about his person. 'But this was soon resolved and I never hope to find myself in better company.' Whiting was allocated to Trollope's Flight. 'I still remember him with admiration and affection; he was a truly great man.'

17. One of these was Maurice Mealing of 56 Squadron who was last seen chasing enemy two-seaters over Le Transloy. Mealing was claimed by *Uffz* Zeter and *Ltn* Tegeder of *Fl Abt(A) 245.*

18. A particular loss was that of FltCom Frederick Armstrong of Naval 3. Armstrong was a very experienced pilot with thirteen victories, who had been flying with Naval 3 since the first week of April 1917. On March 25 he was groundstrafing south of Ervillers when his Camel was seen to go down in flames. Experience gave very little protection in the dangerous duty of low flying attacks.

19. Trollope was repatriated three months after his capture. He never flew again. His shattered hand was amputated in a German hospital – without anaesthetics, none were available – and post war, after thirty-nine operations, his arm was finally removed at the shoulder, 'which stopped me playing golf.' A bullet in his back was so near to his spine that over the next forty years no surgeon was prepared to take the risk of removing it. His multiple wounds and injuries stayed with him for the remainder of his life and although he was often in great pain his wife proudly testified, 'I never *once* heard a word of complaint.' In World War II Trollope rejoined the RAF and rose to the rank of Wing Commander.

20. Two brothers, friends of my family, both fought with the Fifth Army in March 1918. Both were immensely proud of being in Gough's command and, in direct contrast to their views of Haig, always spoke with warm affection and admiration of 'our' general.

21. On April 4 he took the 'extremely difficult' decision to abandon the attack on Amiens for good: 'Strategically we had not achieved what the events of the 23rd, 24th and 25th had encouraged us to hope for. That we had also failed to take Amiens was especially disappointing.' *My War Memories, General* Erich von Ludendorff.

CHAPTER TWENTY

THE ROYAL AIR FORCE

On the first day of April the RFC and the RNAS were officially amalgamated to become the Royal Air Force. The change made little difference to the hard pressed pilots and observers; their day was much the same as any other, marked only by heavy casualties – forty-eight aeroplanes crashed or missing.

On April 1 the fine weather and good visibility led to a great deal of air fighting, both at high and low levels. The *Schlachtstaffeln* were extremely active south of the Somme, attacking the British troops and large formations of enemy scouts were patrolling at height.

The SE5s of 64 Squadron were in action early. James Slater led his Flight over the Lines and attacked a formation of eight enemy scouts, selecting a Pfalz as his opponent. After a short burst from Slater's guns at a range of 200 feet, the enemy machine went down in flames and smoke to crash at Maricourt.

Albatros scouts of *Jasta 56* were attacking British troops in the vicinity of Gentelles when they were attacked by a patrol of SE5s from 60 Squadron. Lt William Duncan saw one of the enemy machines break off the action and fly west. It was extremely unusual for an enemy pilot to fly west on breaking away from an engagement and, although he suspected it was a decoy, Duncan nevertheless chased after the Albatros. The enemy pilot, *Vzfw* Weimar, attempted to escape by turning east, but Duncan forced him to land behind the British lines at Gentelles. Weimar, wounded in the back, was taken POW and his Albatros D.V 5734/17 given the number G159.

The immediate changes brought about by the amalgamation of the RFC and RNAS were felt chiefly by the former naval pilots. The naval squadrons were all renumbered by having 200 added to their number: Naval 3 becoming 203 Squadron RAF; Naval 8, 208 Squadron RAF and so on. On a more personal level their ranks were changed to army ranks. In common with their RFC counterparts, they now became Majors, Captains and Lieutenants. Former Naval Flight Commander Leonard 'Tich' Rochford recalled: 'When I rose from my bunk – I mean camp bed – on the morning of April 1st, I was Captain Rochford, commanding B Flight, 203 Squadron Royal Air Force.'

An old friend of Rochford had returned to active duty in France towards the end of March: Robert Little had been posted to Naval 3 as the C Flight Commander, but now, like Rochford, was a Captain in the Royal Air Force. Little's old friends noticed a difference in his attitude. Earlier, he had been a tactical fighter, always willing to break off a combat if he thought it had little chance of success, but he now seemed more aggressive, with a complete disregard of danger. On the afternoon of April 1 Little scored his first victory since joining 203 Squadron. Picking out the rear machine in a formation of Fokker Triplanes, Little fired 200 rounds into it a close range. The enemy machine went into a steep dive, the left-hand wings broke off and it was seen to crash three miles east of Oppy at 2.00pm.

The fighter squadrons of Ninth Wing and V Brigade worked at low altitude throughout the day, but their orders stressed that they were to attack low flying enemy machines as a first priority, with ground targets a secondary option. German regimental histories again give testimony to the success of these ground attacks. 'Numerous airmen attack with machine-gun and bombs and cause our line considerable casualties.'

Eight positive victories were claimed during the day, plus one balloon, but casualties were high. Five pilots had been killed, four wounded and three taken prisoner. The corps squadrons had fared no better, with four crew killed and nine wounded. The official history records that thirty-eight aeroplanes were lost. Twelve of these were severely damaged by ground fire, but the remainder were struck off strength as a result of forced landings due to engine failure, the history commenting that the high percentage of casualties due to accidents reflected both the strain under which the pilots were operating and the unsuitability of the new, temporary aerodromes occupied in the retreat. It was an inauspicious beginning for the RAF.

At a conference at Doullens on March 26 – the crucial day in the German offensive – General Foch had been appointed to co-ordinate the efforts of the Allied forces on the Western Front. On April 2, Royal Air Force headquarters received Foch's instructions for the employment of its forces. The instructions for the use of fighter squadrons stated that the first duty should be 'to assist the troops on the ground by incessant attacks, with bombs and machine-gun, on columns, concentrations, or bivouacs. Air fighting is not to be sought except so far as necessary for the fulfilment of this duty.' Although it was recognised that Foch's plans were well conceived and with strategic insight, it contained a flaw: the failure to concentrate the Allied air forces at any vital area of the ground fighting. Although the *Luftstreitkräfte* had fewer aeroplanes available overall, this was negated by the concentration of its strength where it was most needed. On April 2 the German air strength opposing the British forces on the Arras front was 822 German aircraft against 645 of the RAF. The French had 2,000 aircraft with no more than 367 German aircraft opposing them. Although the *Luftstreitkräfte* was outnumbered along the whole of the Western Front by nearly 3 to 1, on the active battlefront it enjoyed a numerical superiority of almost thirty per cent.

The general pattern of airfighting continued on April 2. Nine victories were claimed by the fighter squadrons, but there were fewer casualties, with only one pilot killed, two wounded and one taken POW. The weather began to deteriorate on April 3, but although flying was restricted during the day there was a large air fight over the enemy's advanced landing ground at Rosières, with 84 Squadron SE5s and 65 Squadron Camels fighting with over thirty enemy fighters – Albatri and Pfalz – which had come down from height to attack the British scouts flying at 1,500 feet and engaged in ground strafing. By some accounts the fighting lasted for over an hour and six enemy aircraft were claimed, with no loss to the British fighters, and the 84 Squadron Record Book records that the British pilots were 'left in possession of the sky.'

It was obvious from this combat, and other sightings of large formations of enemy aircraft flying at height, that the *jagdstaffeln* were now operating in larger numbers than before. An order issued on the evening of April 3 for operations on the next day by the fighter squadrons of Ninth Wing stated:

'Enemy aircraft have been very active today on the Fifth Army front, flying in massed formations at high altitudes. A large number of them were destroyed by the Fifth Brigade. Officer Commanding Ninth Wing will detail all available machines as offensive patrols tomorrow. Patrols will consist of not less than two squadrons to patrol continuously the line Bray-sur-Somme to Caix between the hours of 11am and 40m. At least a quarter of an hour overlap will be allowed for between patrols. Formations must be rigidly maintained. The whole object of these patrols is to seek out and destroy enemy formations.' These orders marked a new stage in the development of air fighting tactics; large formations of two or three fighter squadrons, working together in mutual support and to a prearranged plan, became commonplace.

There were low clouds and heavy rain the next day. The German army attacked south of the Somme, but ground strafing and bombing was only possible in the afternoon when the bad weather eased a little. On April 5 weather conditions were very bad, with low clouds mist and rain all day and there was no flying. The day saw the final failure of the German attacks on the ground; although there were still outbursts of local activity the German offensive on the Somme had come to an end.

Despite the low clouds and rain on April 6 a great deal of flying took place, with enemy aircraft very active. A Flight from 84 Squadron, led by Lt Jens Larsen, attacked an LVG from *Fl Abt (A)205*, crewed by *Uffz* Drexler and *Ltn* Kalfeken. Larsen's fire wounded Kalfeken, and the LVG went down to crash behind the British lines north of Hangard. Drexler and Kalfeken were made POWs and their machine was designated G166. All the Flight shared in this victory, Larsen's last in 84 Squadron.

Little was leading his Flight on patrol in the area of Lens and attacked a DFW two-seater. The enemy pilot dived into the cover of the clouds, but as he emerged Little pursued him, firing all the time. The LVG down in flames to crash northeast of Lens at 12.30pm. This LVG was possibly from *Fl Abt (A) 268*, both the crew were killed.

Despite the deteriorating weather conditions – low clouds and mist, with bad visibility – enemy air activity increased during the afternoon and there were many combats. Stanley Rosevear of 201 Squadron added to the ex-naval squadrons' scores during an early afternoon patrol. His Flight was attacked by a formation of Fokker Triplanes over Mericourt at 1.15pm. Rosevear fired a burst from point blank range into one triplane, which went down to crash in a ploughed field and Lt Anthony Spence shot another down to crash for his penultimate victory with 201 Squadron.

Banks of 43 Squadron, who seems to have rejoiced in the Christian names of Charles Chaplin, was attacked by a formation of Albatri over Guillaucourt in the late afternoon. He was forced down, but got good bursts into one of the enemy scouts, following it down to within fifty feet of the ground. The Albatros crashed and turned over, but Banks' Camel was hit in both petrol tanks by groundfire. With an elevator wire also severed, Banks managed to recross the Front Lines and land at Senslis, two miles behind the British lines.

A patrol of all three Flights from 56 Squadron, which left the ground at 5.40pm, is typical of the actions fought during the day. The weather conditions had been bad at takeoff and worsened rapidly with thick clouds and rain coming in from the southwest. All the Flights returned because of the conditions, but Trevor Durrant had become separated from the other SE5s in the heavy cloud and as he was flying alone south of Lamotte he sighted a single Albatros scout. Durrant dived to attack this Albatros, but before he could come within range he was jumped by four Fokker Triplanes. Durrant easily evaded these attacks by the superior speed of his SE5 and flew towards Guillaucourt where he had been told enemy two-seaters were operating. He sighted one over the village, flying south, but the enemy pilot escaped by diving into the cloud cover. At 6.45pm Durrant finally found a pair of two-seaters flying north from Lamotte. Durrant attacked one of these causing a large flash to come from the enemy machine, but as he followed it down he heard machine gun fire. Looking round Durrant saw four Fokker Triplanes firing at him from long range in the hope of forcing him to break off his attack on the two-seater. Durrant again evaded these triplanes, flying a circular course back to the scene of the action, where he saw the enemy two-seater on the ground, its tail sticking up out of the wreckage. The persistent triplanes again appeared. Durrant went down to 1,000 feet and contour chased back to the Front Lines. The enemy two-seater had crashed between the River Somme and Lamotte and was confirmed by Captain Jarvis.

Thirteen victories had been claimed during the day, but at heavy cost. Six pilots were killed, four wounded and six taken prisoner. Forty-three Squadron, flying ground-strafing missions in the afternoon, lost five pilots to *Jasta* 11. Two pilots were killed, and three taken prisoner, one severely wounded and another who later died of his wounds. Capt Sydney Smith from 46 Squadron was also shot down, in flames, crashing near a small wood northeast of Villers-Bretonneux. Smith was Manfred von Richthofen's 76th victory.

The weather was very changeable on Sunday, April 7. The clouds were at various heights and there were occasional showers of rain. At 11.15am the SE5s of 32 Squadron were on patrol in the vicinity of Lamotte and attacked a mixed formation of Fokker Triplanes and Albatros scouts. Walter Tyrrell claimed a Fokker Triplane destroyed at 11.15am, and an Albatros five minutes later, both of which crashed northeast of Lamotte.

Ten minutes later, Tyrrell sent an Albatros scout down out of control in the same area.

Three Flights of Camels from 73 Squadron took off from their aerodrome at Beauvois, a temporary base of canvas hangars and tents, hastily thrown up after the Allied retreat from the Somme eleven days previously, the squadron having been forced to move three times during the last seven days. The Flights had been told that large groups of enemy fighters were expected to be operating at midday and, aided by formations of SE5s flying 2,000 feet higher, they were to find and attack them. At 10.30am the Camels were circling for more height over Amiens. Flying in B Flight, led by Captain Maurice Le Blanc Smith, was Lt Ronald Adam who had joined the squadron five days previously. From 15,000 feet Adam could plainly see the whole of the Somme battlefields below him, the long straight road from Amiens to St Quentin plainly visible. Adam's Camel was brand new, he had collected it from the pool the previous evening, but the small, strut mounted propeller, which supplied air pressure to the main petrol tank, now stuck fast and the engine began to intermittently lose revolutions, forcing Adam to work furiously at the hand pressure pump in his cockpit. It was intensely cold at 15,000 feet, making the pump stiff, and encumbered by his heavy flying clothing Adam was soon gasping with exhaustion as he followed Le Blanc Smith over the Lines.

'It was approaching midday. The northern banks of clouds were a long way off and the formation floated in a patch of cloudless sky. "Archie" had ceased his attentions for the moment and I had time to think of, and appreciate, the intense cold from which I had always suffered so much acute discomfort. Le Blanc was going down, losing height and outdistancing me. I watched him idly as I put the nose of my Camel down to follow him. Something white flashed across the green and brown of the earth, and I caught a glimpse of a machine. I stared at it stupidly for a moment, watching it and Le Blanc circling round one another. Then, suddenly the air was filled with German Fokker Triplanes with great black crosses painted on their wings. Somehow I seemed to be just above many of them and lost sight of my companions.

My guns had been loaded as I left the aerodrome; singling out an enemy Fokker in front of me and slightly below me, I dived on him. He turned upside down in a half roll and disappeared. Immediately another Fokker Triplane flashed into view – a very lovely shot. Strung to the highest pitch of excitement, I pressed the triggers – and nothing happened. The enemy half rolled and went under. Giving a hasty glance at my guns, I pulled the Camel up and over in an Immelmann turn. The enemy was gone below. Once more I dived, getting a momentary sighting, and I attempted to fire. Oh, my guns! There were no signs of a jam and it could only be that the gun gears were improperly adjusted and my guns were useless to me. I turned in despair, and weaponless. I knew that I would have to manoeuvre amongst the enemy and keep my height above them.

At that point I heard an ominous staccato rattle. I turned to find a triplane coming in towards me broadside on and the smoke of tracer bullets trailing before my engine. Up and up I went into another Immelmann turn. Then my engine failed. In the rush and excitement I had forgotten my pressure pump and, with a few dismal splutters, the noise of the engine died away. There was nothing to do but go down into the swarming mass below. The first enemy machine was behind me; he was firing furiously but too excitedly. Two additional Fokker Triplanes came from behind and from either angle. The pressure was too far gone to get it at once by pumping – there was nothing to do but continue to lose height. I went down in a horrible, dizzy corkscrew drop. At 8,000 feet I straightened out and began pumping again, but once more I was furiously attacked. Down again, down through a little patch of cotton wool cloud, down, while my enemies pursued me.

Again an effort to get pressure; again a ripping and spattering of bullets through my wings and over my shoulders into the instrument board; again a stupendous drop. At 2,000 feet from the ground I straightened out for the last time. I was as good as dead or captured if I could not restart my engine. I pumped furiously and was sick with disappointment and despair as, once again, bullets cracked their way past me. Still, let them come and pump, pump, pump!'

Although he was unaware of it, Ronald Adam was now flying north, towards the advanced landing ground of *JG 1* at Harbonnieres. Close behind him was *Ltn* Hans Kirschstein, a member of *Jagdstaffel 6*, intent on making Adam his sixth victory. Adam, pumping furiously, at last succeeded in getting his pressure up. The Camel's engine coughed once or twice, then caught with a full blooded roar. Adam, with a sigh of relief, turned for the safety of the British lines, but at that moment Kirschstein fired again and one of his bullets hit Adam's petrol tank and the pressure again dropped, finally stopping his engine.

'True, I had a gravity tank which did not need pressure. I had not turned it on before because it only held half and hour's petrol, but I sought its aid now. Nothing happened and way below I saw Richthofen's aerodrome, with machines and mechanics out in front of the sheds. In a last despairing effort I pointed the nose of my machine at them and pressed the useless triggers. I shouted with mad laughter as the mechanics scattered and fell about in fear of me. Then a complete insanity seemed to take hold of me. "Better dead than captured!" I thought, while the Fokker Triplane behind was firing into my machine. Suddenly I saw a railway line below and put the nose straight down until the speed indicator needle stuck fast, unable to register more.

I just remember hitting the ties of the railway line. There was a colossal crash and a series of complete somersaults. When I came to I was dangling upside down in what was left of my Sopwith Camel. The Germans had thrown an old sack over me in the thought that I was dead. A German soldier happened to peek under the cloth at me and was greatly astonished when I peered back at him. *"Nich tot. Nich Verwundet"* ("Not dead? Not wounded?"), he asked. He pulled me out of the wreckage and stood me upright. I fell over several times and was finally taken to a small hut near Proyart.'

That evening, while Adam was still in the hut, an orderly came in, clicked his heels in salute and announced. *"Freiherr von Richthofen's compliments. You are his 79th victory."*[1] However, from the combat reports of von Richthofen and Kirschstein, and their reports of where their respective victories fell, it seems more likely that Ronald Adam was in fact Hans Kirschstein's sixth victory.

Adam was taken away to prisoner of war camp and ended his war at the notorious POW camp of Holzminden. He returned to England in December 1918, just before his twenty-second birthday. Ronald Adam was the luckiest of the trio who had fought that day in the skies above St.Quentin. Manfred von Richthofen had lived only another fourteen days and Hans Kirschstein died in a flying accident on 17 July 1918, with twenty-seven aerial victories to his credit and holding Germany's highest award for bravery, the *Pour Le Merité*.[2]

In addition to Adam, 73 Squadron also lost 2Lt Albert Gallie, but during the fight 2Lt Owen Baldwin of the squadron shot down one of the Fokker Triplanes, seen to crash south of Cerisy, which is just north of the Amiens to St Quentin Road. This was probably *Ltn* Gussmann of *Jasta 11* who was slightly wounded in the right calf.

A patrol of Camels from 203 Squadron led by Robert Little fared better in a fight with Fokker Triplanes at 1.00pm south east of Violaines. The Camels were attacked by ten enemy triplanes and Little shot one down out of control. The triplane went down through the clouds but was later seen on the ground about a mile southwest of Violaines.

George McElroy and Ian McDonald of 24 Squadron both had a successful day. In the morning, at 10.40am, McElroy sent an Albatros scout down out of control over Warfusee and twenty minutes later attacked three two-seaters east of Marcelcave. McElroy attacked the nearest from under its tail and the enemy machine went down to crash three miles east of the village. Fifteen minutes later, flying through the clouds at 3,000 feet, McElroy saw three SE5s being attacked by five

Fokker Triplanes. He got on the tail of one triplane closed to within point blank range and fired twenty rounds into it. The triplane spun down to crash north of Moreuil Wood.

Ian McDonald was in the vicinity of Moreuil Wood in the afternoon and shot down a two-seater that crashed, smoking, in a field near Moreuil.

It rained for almost the entire day on April 8 and there was very little flying. There were no combats; the only victory claimed was a balloon shot down east of Boyelles by Capt Bell of 3 Squadron. Capt Cyril Ridley of 201 Squadron had attacked this balloon first, firing 150 rounds into it, but his fire was ineffective and Bell then attacked and sent it down in flames.

Georgette: The Battle of the Lys

Air reconnaissance on April 6 and 7 had shown that the enemy was making preparations for an offensive northwards from the La Bassée Canal, on the left of the British First Army and the right flank of the Second Army. On the morning of April 7 crews of the corps squadrons reported that the main roads north of Aubers were full of enemy transport, ground observers could see that ammunition in large quantities was being carried into the German support trenches, and evening air reconnaissance revealed a significant increase in rail movements. There was considerable activity by the *Luftstreitkräfte* over the general area and an absence of enemy artillery fire.

On the night of April 7-8, German artillery opened an intense bombardment, mainly of mustard gas, saturating the areas on the flanks of the coming offensive, and on the morning of April 9 the German Sixth Army opened its attack between La Bassée and Armentières.

The RAF fighter squadrons working with the First Army were those of the Tenth (Army) Wing of I Brigade. Two of these fighter squadrons had been sent to reinforce the Third Army during the German March offensive, but on 1 April 210 Squadron and 19 Squadron were transferred to the Wing. The next day 208 Squadron was also added to its strength and on April 9, the morning of the German attack, the Wing had six fighter squadrons on it strength: 4 Squadron AFC, 203, 208 and 210 Squadrons (Camel); 40 Squadron (SE5a) and 19 Squadron (Sopwith Dolphin). When it became obvious that an attack was imminent, Major-General Salmond reinforced First Army air strength with 22 Squadron (Bristol Fighter) from Third Army and 41 Squadron (SE5as) from the General Headquarters reserve. Once the attack began, 46 Squadron (Camel) and 64 Squadron (SE5a) were to also moved to I Brigade. Other fighter squadrons were also detailed to work over the area of the attack from Ninth (Day) Wing – 32 Squadron (SE5a) 73 Squadron (Camel) and 79 Squadron (Dolphin).

The German artillery opened a bombardment at 4.05am on the morning of April 9 and the main infantry attack was launched at 8.45am, extending from the La Bassée Canal to Bois Grenier. The centre of the front of the attack, held by the Portuguese 2nd Division, was quickly overrun by masses of German infantry – seven divisions – the Line broke and the Portuguese division ceased to exist as a fighting unit.

To add to the general confusion, the countryside was blanketed in a thick fog, effectively grounding all aircraft. Stationed at La Gorgue, 208 Squadron, commanded by Major Christopher Draper, was directly in the path of the rapidly advancing German troops. Portuguese troops were falling back past the aerodrome, their grey uniforms adding to the confusion, and shells were falling in the general area. Behind La Gorgue British troops were hastily attempting to organise a line of defence along the River Lys, but to Draper there seemed to be nothing between his squadron and the German infantry but the retreating Portuguese troops and French civilians 'I had a squadron of Camels, grounded by fog. What could I do? *I burnt the ruddy lot!*'

In his report to the Officer Commanding 10th Wing RAF the next day, Draper was more official in his language, reminiscent of the reports of his naval officer ancestors in the Napoleonic war.

208 Squadron Royal Air Force In the Field, 10th April 1918

'Sir,

With reference to the destruction of the 16 machines of this Squadron, I have the honour to submit the following report:

At about 04.00 hours on the morning of the 9th we were aroused by the sound of very heavy gunfire, which increased in intensity towards dawn. There was considerable hostile shelling of Merville, La Gorgue and the surrounding districts. A large number of French civilians were passing through our camp to the west, followed by considerable numbers of Portuguese troops in open order, without rifles or equipment and apparently unofficered. By 07.00 hours the shelling became very intense, but owing to the fog it was impossible to ascertain definitely where the shells were falling. I gave orders for the machines to be removed from the hangars and spread out over the aerodrome in case of concentrated shelling of the hangars.'

After detailing his orders for the officers and men to pack all the general gear and stores as quickly as possible, Draper related how then he received a message from an RFC cyclist that German troops were in Laventie. Laventie was barely four miles from the aerodrome and Draper sent one of his own despatch riders with orders to get as far up the line as he could and report on the immediate position. The rider returned to report that the enemy had taken Laventie and were now just east of Estaires, even closer to the aerodrome. Draper telephoned XV Corps HQ on the only telephone line still operative and asked if they could confirm this. HQ could not, but the GOC asked Draper if he would carry out a reconnaissance. Draper refused: 'quite definitely, it was impossible to see across the aerodrome through the fog.'

Draper realised that he would have to act on his own initiative to save the Camels falling into enemy hands:

'After careful deliberation with my Flight Commanders, I decided I was not justified in risking personnel by flying the aircraft away in the fog, though the majority volunteered to try. We collected the machines in one bunch in the middle of the aerodrome, the idea being for everyone to withdraw, leaving one officer with a motor-cycle to stand by until the last moment, with orders to destroy the machines if necessary.'

The line to Corps HQ was now dead and when a passing British officer told Draper that he had come under machine gun fire from La Gorgue, Draper decided to set fire to the 16 Camels and follow the rest of the squadron, which had left for Serny:

'I fully realised the gravity of the decision I had to make, but being unable to communicate with any reliable authority, I had to act on my own. If there had been British troops in the area I should have left the machines for them to destroy, in accordance with orders, but I felt it extremely improbable that a panic stricken number of Portuguese would carry this out, even if they had received orders to do so. An ammunition column which had been parked alongside our hangars had gone. The machines were then destroyed and the rest of us moved off at 11.30 hours.

I have described the events as nearly as possible in the order in which they occurred. The times I have given are only approximate. The only things left behind were an Austin lighting set and some petrol and oil. The Squadron packed and moved in under three hours.

I have the honour to be, Sir,
Your obedient servant.
C Draper, Major.'

Draper was fully justified in his decision to burn the Camels. German troops overran the aerodrome that afternoon. Draper reformed 208 Squadron at Serny, where he found three other squadrons who had also been forced to evacuate their aerodromes. Within 48 hours 208 Squadron was completely re-equipped with 20 new Sopwith Camels. Draper's only regret was that they were Clerget-engined machines 'from the old RFC network … considered inferior to our late BR.1-engined machines. Up to the formation of the RAF the aircraft supplied by the Navy from Dunkirk were, in finish, workmanship and performance superior to anything supplied by the RFC. While the RFC had Camels from ten different contractors, ours were mainly of Sopwith's own manufacture.' However, Draper later admitted that the 'inferior Camels may have been a mixed blessing because the BR1 engine was giving trouble, traced to the products of an individual British firm.[3]

Although the fog had lifted by 2.00pm, visibility was still poor, with clouds down to 1,000 feet. Despite the fact that many RAF squadrons had to evacuate their aerodromes by the threat of the German advance – four fighter squadrons were forced to move – many low-level attacks were carried out by the single-seater fighters. From 2.30pm, flying at overlapping intervals, twenty Camels of 203 Squadron, plus a further 15 from 210 and five from 4 Squadron AFC, and seven SE5s of 40 Squadron attacked the advancing German infantry. Rochford's Flight from 203 Squadron were ground-strafing near the La Bassée Canal, and two of the Flight aided Little in shooting down an Albatros two-seater, which crashed near Givenchy at 2.10pm.

Gwilym Lewis gives a slightly different picture of 40 Squadron's activities during the day. The squadron was based at Bruay, east of Lens, and subsequently a little removed from the battles of March, further south. 'The war was being slowly lost down south, but we had given up watching the show, so what did we care? We looked after our own little show which was really quite a respectable little affair.' On April 9, however, 40 Squadron were in the path of the German advance. 'Then suddenly everything was spoilt; the blank German started disturbing the peace north of the canal! In no way could he have annoyed us more. We couldn't have the Huns playing any silly little monkey tricks on our little patch. Unfortunately the day commenced with a thick fog. It was impossible to see across our tennis court, and all we knew was that the Portuguese Army were all in a sort of marathon competition; no one knew much except that the Huns were being very nasty. Towards the close of evening a few of us managed to get up with four little bombs. It was absolutely filthy, but I could just clamber through the mist and spread a few eggs in the neighbourhood of La Bassée, and shoot a few rounds at odds and ends.'[4]

Despite the casual tone of Gwilym Lewis in relating the effects of ground-strafing, it was highly effective. The regimental history the German 202nd Reserve Regiment, attacking in the region of Festubert, recorded. 'The battalions all suffered severely during their approach march from the British low-flying aircraft which attacked them savagely with machine-gun fire and bombs. The German pilots were unable to do much in view of the British air supremacy.'

The fighter squadrons claimed four enemy two-seaters destroyed during the day, but only one scout, an Albatros in flames south of La Bassée. Casualties were light: a pilot from 40 Squadron was killed while ground-strafing; a pilot from 1 Squadron was taken prisoner and another wounded, and a pilot of 4 Squadron AFC returned with a badly shot up Camel.

Fog again made flying difficult the next day. After an initial bombardment the German Fourth Army attacked the British Second Army, further north above Armentières, and by noon Ploegsteert and a great deal of Messines were in enemy hands. The enemy also renewed his original attacks of the previous day, spreading out fanwise from the positions gained by the previous evening. Clouds were again at 1,000 feet for most of the day and although the fog of the early morning had cleared a little by midday it returned after 2.00pm. The fighter squadrons were again engaged in low flying attacks on the advancing enemy troops, columns and transport.

Gwilym Lewis reported the day's attacks in a little less casual tone, commenting that since the days of the Somme offensive the enemy had learnt, 'a thing or two. They saw this machine gunning was quite good sport for two or more players, and now they have nests of those beastly machine guns waiting for us, and they simply wipe years off one's life at a flash! At the end of the first day or so we left Bion missing, and Carnegie wounded but OK. Bion heard his brother was killed two or three days before.'[5]

The *schlachtstaffeln* and *jagdstaffeln* were again active over the battlefronts and the British fighter pilots claimed four enemy scouts destroyed and a two-seater for the loss of one pilot killed, three wounded and five taken POW.[5] No fewer than four enemy aircraft were captured during the day. Three two-seaters (G 161,162 and 164) and a Fokker Triplane 419/ 17 of *Jasta 19*, (G163) flown by *Ltn* Göttsch, who was killed by an RE8 crew from 52 Squadron.[6]

The bad weather continued on April 11; again it was not until the late afternoon that conditions improved sufficiently for flying. At dawn the ground battles were 'fiercely renewed' along the entire front. The British flanks held firm, but the German troops, although suffering heavy casualties, pushed resolutely forward, the defending troops becoming strung out and isolated. By the evening enemy troops were in possession of Merville, Nieppe and the whole of Messines.

After midday the mist and rain cleared and there was a great deal of flying by both the antagonists. Although the fighter squadrons concentrated once again on low level at-tacks, there were also many combats in the upper air between massed formations of fighters. A patrol from 40 Squadron were out in the afternoon and as soon as they crossed the front lines they were attacked by eight Fokker Triplanes. Tudhope shot one down north east of Lens for his tenth and last victory; Gwilym Lewis shot at another until his guns jammed, but he cleared these and a few minutes later 'found one of these stupid little things by itself and shot it down, confirmed by archie.'

Forty Squadron had received a new commanding officer on the formation of the RAF: Major Roderic Dallas, ex RNAS. Relations between the RFC and the RNAS had not always been cordial, but Dallas was immediately popular. He had scored 23 victories, mainly with Naval 1, before the formation of the RAF and his posting to command 40 Squadron, where he was promptly nicknamed 'The Admiral'. 'Our new CO, Dallas, is a splendid lad. Tall, good looking, a wonderful specimen of manhood, very reserved and charming; a veritable flapper's idol!' Dallas was flying alone on the evening of April 11 and destroyed a DFW two-seater over La Bassée, his first of nine victories while commanding 40 Squadron.

Another ex-naval pilot continued his successes during the day. At 2.30pm Little's Flight attacked three enemy two-seaters over Bac St Maur but were themselves attacked by a formation of Albatri. Little shot one Albatros down in a spin and followed it down to see it crash near Neuve Eglise.

In the fighting over the northern battles, the pilots of the fighter squadrons fought a great many combats, claiming fourteen enemy aircraft destroyed, but the fighter squadrons remaining further south also saw considerable action. At 5.30pm all three Flights of 56 Squadron took off on a combined Offensive Patrol. Four of the SE5s were forced to return with engine troubles, but an hour after taking off the eight SE5s attacked three enemy scouts and a pair of two-seaters at 6,000 feet over Aveluy. A Canadian pilot, Kenneth Junor, attacked one of the Albatri – a white circle around a small black cross on top of its wings – firing an entire drum of Lewis gun ammunition and 150 rounds of Vickers into it from 200 yards. Puffs of smoke and a quantity of water came out of the enemy machine and it went down in a steep dive to crash just west of the village. The remaining enemy scouts then dived away east and the SE5s reformed under the leadership of Edward Galley. Galley had seen a formation of six Albatros scouts with black and white tailplanes, led by an all red Fokker Triplane, manoeuvring into a favourable position to attack the SE5s, but the SE5s outclimbed the enemy force and attacked it west of Pozières.

Trevor Durrant attacked one of the black and white tailed Albatri and shot it down in flames near Ovillers. Louis Jarvis sent a Pfalz – its black crosses on its top wings enclosed in white circles – and sent it down smoking to crash near Bécourt.

The all red Fokker Triplane had stayed above the mêlée, possibly to pick off any straggler, but Kenneth Junor climbed to its height and 'chased it off'. 'Jackie' Walkerdine and an Albatros flew head on towards each other and the enemy pilot's fire hit Walkerdine's engine, two bullets coming through his windshield and grazing his forehead. Walkerdine managed to land bewteen Beauval and Doullens and was taken to No.3 Canadian Stationary Hospital.[7]

Casualties for the fighter squadrons on April 11 were relatively light. Two pilots had been killed; one wounded; two pilots were taken POW, one of whom was wounded, and two aircraft were badly shot up but with both pilots safe. To put these casualties in perspective, however, the corps squadrons flying RE8s suffered heavy casualties, all but three due to ground fire: three crew were killed, 12 wounded, two taken POW and three aircraft either returned or force landed badly damaged. Two FK8s were forced to land – one by friendly fire – and one crewmember wounded.

The weather was fine all day on April 12, with excellent visibility. It was a critical day for the British Armies. Reinforcements were on their way, but until they arrived the continuing German attacks had to be held and contained. In the morning, Haig issued his to be famous 'backs to the wall' order, exhorting the exhausted troops to hold their positions to the last man, causing the caustic comment from one war-weary fighter pilot to wonder where Haig expected the troops would find such a wall, and conjuring up visions of half a dozen British generals, all that was left of the British Armies, standing with swords drawn in a bed of wall flowers, their backs against the wall of their chateau, behind a barricade of empty champagne and whiskey bottles, ready to repulse the last attack by Ludendorff and his staff – all that was left of the German Armies – and encouraging each other with nostalgic memories of the playing fields of Eton. Unfair, perhaps, but understandable.

The weather being fine, the RAF flew and fought from dawn to dusk, flying a record number of hours, dropping a record number of bombs, and taking hundreds of photographs. High offensive patrols were flown above the battle to prevent the *jagdstaffeln* from interfering with the work of the corps squadrons, but a great many combats were fought at lower levels. Enemy aircraft were extremely active over the ground fighting, especially north of La Bassée and Hangard. The clear visibility gave the observation balloons, so often hampered by poor weather, a panorama of the fighting below them and the observers were able to give a great deal of information on the movements of enemy troops. The crews of the corps squadrons engaged on contact duties reported on the progress of the battle, literally hour by hour, with unparalleled clearness and

detail and were able to call down counter artillery fire with great effect.

The main thrust of the RAF fighting was in stemming the advance of the enemy forces towards Hazebrouck and in the early morning a great number of low flying attacks were carried out in the area. Towards 9.00am, however, the attacks were concentrated in the vicinity of Merville. From 6.00am to 7.00pm one hundred and thirty seven aircraft of I Brigade appeared in continuous waves and relentlessly bombed and machine-gunned the German troops and transport. The fighter squadrons of II Brigade also concentrated their efforts on the area of Hazebrouck, the SE5s of 1 Squadron dropping a hundred and twenty five 25lb bombs and firing over 5,000 rounds of ammunition.

Airfighting was continuous and fierce, the crews of the *schlachtstaffeln* showing great bravery in their determination to support their troops on the ground. While the RAF fighters were engaged in attacking these aircraft, the *jagdstaffel* occasionally evaded them to reconnoitre the British back areas. Offensive patrols from the fighters of I, II and IX Brigades flew at heights upward from 3,000 feet, with additional fighters from IX Brigade flying higher still. Combats between large formations were common, formations of between fifteen and twenty enemy scouts – Albatri and Pfalz – were in evidence particularly in the Merville area.

All the fighter squadrons saw a great deal of action in the day and many positive and out of control victories were claimed, 43, 24 and 74 Squadrons being particularly successful.

At 10.30am a patrol of Camels from 43 Squadron, led by Henry Woollett, attacked eight enemy machines of just south east of La Gorgue. Woollett quickly shot an Albatros down in flames to crash west of La Gorgue and then attacked a two-seater, which crashed north east of the village. In the same action, Lt 'Daisy' Hector Daniel, a South African pilot, destroyed two Albatri, and Lt Geoffrey Bailey claimed two victories: an Albatros destroyed and another out of control. Ten minutes after these combats, Woollett regained his height, got on the tail of another Albatros and fired 40 rounds into it. The enemy machine burst into flames went down in pieces. A little later, at 11.15am, another Flight from the squadron were in a combat with Pfalz and Albatri over Bois du Biez. Capt Banks destroyed one of the Albatri and Capt Cecil King, recovered from his wound on March 28, destroyed a Pfalz.

Patrols from 43 Squadron were out again in the evening. Woollett led the Camels down on 13 enemy machines just north of La Gorgue and fired thirty rounds into an Albatros flying east. Under Woollett's fire the enemy scout turned over onto its back before falling to pieces. Woollett then tackled another of the enemy scouts, which spun down and crashed northeast of La Gorgue. Daniel destroyed another Albatros scout for his third victory of the day, and flying back to the front lines Woollett saw another Albatros flying east at 2,000 feet and sent it down to crash northeast of La Gorgue. The squadron had shot down 13 enemy machines in the day's fighting with two casualties from the early patrol: Lt Dean, shot down and taken prisoner and an American pilot, Lt G H Kissell, killed in action.

The pilots of 74 Squadron were also successful during the day. The squadron had arrived in France on March 30, under the command of New Zealander, Major Keith Logan 'Grid' Caldwell flying SE5as. The squadron had worked up to strength at London Colney and Caldwell had been particularly lucky in having three experienced flight commanders. Capt Wilfred Young (B Flight) had served in 19 Squadron as a flight commander in the summer of 1917, scoring three victories before he was wounded in action on July 22; Capt W J Cairns (C Flight) had also served in 19 Squadron, also claiming three victories with the squadron before being posted to Home Establishment as an instructor. Capt Edward 'Mick' Mannock, who had served in 40 Squadron in 1917, claiming 15 victories, was given command of A Flight.

Before moving to Clairmarais North aerodrome on 11 April, 74 Squadron had exchanged aerodromes with 29 Squadron, based at La Lovie, the day before. One of the 29 Squadron pilots was heard to remark that the pilots of 74 were a ragtime crown, with no discipline, but with a cracker of a commanding officer. The Welshman, James Ira Jones, in C Flight, 74 Squadron, and destined to become a very successful fighter pilot, recalled that the squadron had dispensed with the strict and meaningless forms of discipline: 'The "yes, sir, no sir, three bags full, sir" 'We're a fighting squadron. We've come out to fight, and by our achievements as fighters we want to be judged, not by whether we wear breeches and puttees or slacks.'

The pilots of 74 Squadron were impatient to get into the fighting and Caldwell rang Wing every day for permission to begin patrols, but each day permission was refused. On April 12, however, the squadron flew its first patrol, C Flight taking off at 6.00am led by Capt Cairnes. The Flight was soon in trouble. Soon after crossing the lines they were attacked by a formation of Albatri from *Jasta 7* led by *Ltn* Josef Jacobs, the *staffelführer,* flying his personal Fokker Triplane. Cairnes had turned to the left as the enemy machines attacked, the rest of the Flight following him, but Jones, flying at the rear of the formation, became separated from the other SEs and was attacked by Jacobs. Jones was in a perilous position. It was his first combat and Jacobs was an experienced pilot with 13 victories, who had been flying in combat since February 1916.

But Jones remembered the advice given him by Mannock on the subject of fighting Fokker Triplanes. 'Don't ever attempt to dogfight a triplane on anything like equal terms as regards height, otherwise he will get on your tail and stay there until he shoots you down.' Jones followed Mannocks' advice, turning tightly with full throttle, his control column hard into his stomach, and again on Mannock's advice, 'praying hard.' Jacobs was firing in short bursts, the sure sign of an experienced pilot, but Jones kept his nerve, continued to turn as tightly as possible and took some comfort from the realisation that the triplane's fire was passing behind his tail. The antagonists were so close that Jones could see that, like himself, the enemy pilot was not wearing a flying helmet and that he had a small square face with a puggish little nose – a fair description of Jacobs. 'He was flying superbly. He seemed to slither round me.'

As Jones continued to circle he could see the Forêt de Nieppe, about five miles away in Allied territory, and he made up his mind that when he was eventually forced to make a break for safety he would do so for the forest. Taking his chance when Jacobs next zoomed to get above him, Jones obeyed additional instructions from Mannock. 'I put on full bottom rudder. My machine did a turn of a spin and when I came out of it I found my machine was facing east instead of west. Another spot of bottom rudder turned her round westward, and there in front, a few miles away was my landmark, the Forêt de Nieppe. But between me and my objective were half a dozen Huns, black and red Huns, light blue and dark blue Huns, grey and yellow Huns, hungry and angry Huns, just waiting for me to come their way.'

Despite his smallness, Jones was a Rugby player. Looking neither to the left nor right, he flew straight through the centre of the enemy machines – 'as I had often done through a rugger scrum when cornered – I went for home like Hell, kicking my rudder from side to side to make shooting more difficult for the enemy and praying hard.' When Jones finally landed back at Clairmarais no bullet holes were found in his SE5. 'Grid and Mick gave me a good pat on the back, which pleased me as much as getting away from the Huns.'

Mannock and A Flight, delighted that C Flight had not scored the first victory for the squadron, took off at 8.25am. When they returned an hour and a half later 'we knew they had been up to some dirty work. They were all firing Very lights of all colours and diving and zooming at the sheds where we stood waiting their arrival.'

Mannock and the Flight had attacked a formation of Albatros scouts at 13,000 feet over Merville and he and Lt Henry Dolan had each destroyed an Albatros for 74 Squadron's first victories. Later in the day Mannock took his Flight out again. All the Flight attacked a black and yellow Albatros scout, without result until Mannock closed to close range and sent it down to crash at Bois de Phalempin at 2.40pm. When making out his report, Mannock insisted that all the Flight should share in this victory, knowing full well the confidence this would inspire in his pilots.

In a late evening patrol, Caldwell and Wilfred Young each shot down an Albatros; Caldwell's crashed in a field alongside a balloon company south-east of Deulemont at 7.35pm; Young's west of Armentières five minutes later.

Ira Jones gained some satisfaction from the day in C Flight's last patrol, forcing a two-seater to land in a field a quarter of a mile south-east of Roulers. Mannock was angry at Jones for having followed the enemy machine down so low – 'it must never be done he says.'

A Special Mission of seven Camels of 210 Squadron set out at 1.15pm with an escort of five SE5s from 40 Squadron to attack enemy balloons. The Camels crossed the lines at 6,000 feet, their escort a thousand feet higher, then dived to attack the balloons, tethered at 2,000 feet. All the observers took to their parachutes but one was killed. One balloon burst into in flames and the others were deflated and hauled down. Later in the day 40 Squadron pilots were in action over Bethune at 5.30pm with a large formation of enemy scouts, claiming four Pfalz. Flying alone at 7.25pm Major Dallas destroyed an Albatros east of Estaires for his 25th.victory.

April 12 was a highly successful day for the fighter squadrons of the RAF. Forty-three enemy aircraft were claimed as destroyed and another 25 driven down out of control. The cost was relatively light. Seven pilots had been killed, two wounded and two taken prisoner. In addition six aeroplanes had been damaged by enemy action.

Low clouds and mist prevented much flying on April 13 and no combats were fought. The impetus of the German Sixth Army began to slacken, although the German Fourth Army continued its advance. The next day low clouds and mist again covered the whole of the Front. Only machines of I Brigade did any flying, reconnoitring and attacking enemy troops. Major Dallas attacked a convoy of ten lorries on a road near Bailleul, causing one to burst into flames, but he was hit in the foot by return fire and was forced to return. There was no activity by the *Luftstreitkräfte* during the entire day.

The bad weather continued on April 15 and there were no combats, but groundfire forced down two Camels of 54 Squadron, wounding one pilot. 208 Squadron also lost two Camels to groundfire with both pilots wounded.

On April 16 the mist and low cloud turned to continuous rain and only a small amount of flying was done. Enemy air activity was still below normal and only one victory was claimed: Capt Gilmour of 65 Squadron shot down a two-seater in flames over Bois de Hangard at 5.40pm. The fighter squadrons had four casualties: a pilot of 1 Squadron was shot down and taken prisoner by groundfire while ground-strafing and another was wounded. Flying at 4,000 feet over Domart, Lt B Balfour of 65 Squadron was hit by anti-aircraft fire and killed, and a pilot from 23 Squadron, on a practice flight to view the Lines, was also hit by Archie, forced to land near the lines, but was uninjured.

The weather was better the next morning, but after 11.00am the low mist and clouds returned. Enemy air activity was slight during the morning and practically ceased after the weather closed in. There were few combats and only two victories were claimed. It was a bad day for 54 Squadron, which flew three patrols during the day. In the first patrol of the day, which left at 6.00am, Lt C C Lloyd was shot down and killed by *Ltn* Legel of *Jasta 52*. On the second patrol, two Camels were badly shot up, but both pilots were uninjured. The third patrol, which took off at 12.15pm, were in combat with five Albatri from *Jasta 57*. The *Jasta* had just attacked British two-seaters working over the Lines, *Ltn* Jensen shooting down one and *Ltn* Strähle sending down an RE8 to crash beside the Berquin to Strazeele road – possibly from 4 Squadron – when they were attacked by the Camels. Strähle's Albatros was hit in the radiator and one gun but he zoomed above his attackers and shot down a Camel to crash at Outtersteene, killing Lt T Howe. 'The remaining Camels seemed to have had enough, but they came back and made quite a scrap of it. I think my red nose made quite an impression on them.' *Uffz* Meyer of the *Jasta* also claimed a Camel from this fight, shot down at Hazebrouck, but no other Camel was lost at this time, from 54 or any other Squadron. Strähle's diary also claims that *Vzfw* Wieprich of the *Jasta* lost his way and strayed over the aerodrome of an SE5 squadron, where he was attacked by five SE5s. Wieprich evaded them in the clouds and claims to have shot down one of his pursuers north of Hazebrouck, but no SE5s were lost during the day and the *Abschüsse* (German victory lists) awards only a DH4 to Wieprich.

During the next two days the weather was bad. On April 18 the German army attacked towards Bethune but was repulsed with heavy losses. The fighting took place in heavy rain, but although this restricted flying, aircraft of I Brigade attacked enemy troops. There was only one casualty: an SE5 of 1 Squadron was shot up and forced to land but the pilot was unhurt. On April 19th the low clouds and continuous rain of the previous day deteriorated still further, with strong winds and snow and hail storms.

The early morning of April 20 was fine but as the day wore on it became cloudy and very overcast, keeping the air fighting at lower levels. There were some combats in the morning. Lt Kenneth Junor of 56 Squadron took off alone to look for enemy two-seaters. This was in response to a request from

Wing that single machines should be sent up to attack German reconnaissance machines 'as McCudden used to do.' At five minutes past ten, Junor saw a machine crossing the lines over Aveluy. Junor was uncertain whether or not this aircraft was hostile, but British Archie bursts around it confirmed it was hostile – a Rumpler. As Junor got in position for an attack the enemy pilot dived steeply for the safety of his own lines, so steeply that Junor could see that the enemy observer was unable to use his gun. McCudden had often commented on this, recommending that it was a good time to make an attack, and Junor closed to very close range and fired 150 rounds into the hostile machine. The top right hand wing of the Rumpler broke off, followed almost immediately by the remaining three, and the fuselage went down to crash south west of Puisieux, bursting into flames as it hit the ground, killing *Ofstv* Max Hoffmann and *Ltn d Res* Max Trancre of *Fl Abt (A) 263*.

Lts C S Bowen and J R Moore of 54 Squadron each shot down a Rumpler during the day. Ira Jones of 74 Squadron, sharing Clairmarais aerodrome with 54 Squadron, considered 'this cancels their losses. But Mick says that two for two is not good arithmetic.'

In a morning patrol, George Foster and Ian McDonald of 24 Squadron each shot down a Pfalz in a combat south of Morcourt at 10.00am, and a patrol of Camels from 46 Squadron destroyed an Albatros scout over Harnes, shared between Cecil Marchant and 2Lt M Freehill for the last of the morning's victories. Only one positive victory was claimed during the afternoon. In a fight between the Camels of 3 Squadron and Fokker Triplanes from *Jasta 11* over Villers Bretonneaux, Capt Douglas Bell of 3 Squadron shot down one of the triplanes to crash north east of the town at ten minutes to six for the penultimate of his twenty victories, but in the course of the combat Manfred von Richthofen shot down two of the Camels for his 79th and 80th victories.

The first of the Camels to fall under Richthofen's guns was flown by the commanding officer of 3 Squadron, Major Richard Raymond-Barker, his Camel crashing in flames near the forest of Hamel. Richthofen then attacked and shot down 2Lt David Lewis. Bell had earlier chased a triplane off the tail of Lewis' Camel and Lewis had seen Major Raymond-Barker's Camel burst into flames under Richthofen's fire. Lewis, seeing a blue triplane below him, dived to attack it, but his fire had no discernible effect and he was attacked from behind by Richthofen. Lewis immediately put his machine into a tight turn, but at this height – 9,000 feet – the Fokker Triplane could equal the turning radius of the Camel. Lewis had only one chance to get his sights on Richthofen, who quickly reversed the positions. Try as he could, Lewis could not shake Richthofen off his tail: 'I felt he was so much my master that

he would get me sooner or later.' In 1934 Lewis recalled his last combat:

'His first burst shattered the compass in front of my face, the liquid there from fogging my goggles. Of which, however, I was relieved when a bullet severed the elastic from the frame, and they went over the side. My position was not improved, however, for my eyes filled with water caused by the rush of wind. Flying and landing wires struck by the bullets folded up before my eyes, and struts splintered before that withering fire. I do no think Richthofen was more than 50 feet from me all this time, for I could plainly see his begoggled and helmeted face, and his machine guns.

Next I heard the sound of flames, and the stream of bullets ceased. I turned round to find my machine was on fire. The petrol tank was alight.' In an attempt to keep the flames away from him, Lewis put the Camel into a vertical dive, but the flames intermittently overtook the speed of the diving Camel and were blown back into his face.

'When about five hundred feet from the ground the flames seemed to have subsided, so I pulled the control back to gain a horizontal position and was horrified to find that the machine would not answer the elevators. I held the stick back instinctively, I suppose, and then noticed that the aeroplane was slowly attaining the desired position, and I thought I should be able to land on an even keel. This was not to be, however. I hit the ground at terrific speed, but was hurled from the machine unhurt, except for minor burns and bruises which kept me in Cambrai hospital for six weeks. I later saw that not a stitch of fabric was left between my seat and the tail, but noticed that a few strips of the material left on my elevators had saved me. The back of my Sidcot suit was in charred strips and my helmet crumpled up when I took it off. I also had one bullet through my trouser leg and one through my sleeve. Major Barker's machine was burning fiercely not far from me, so I went over to see if I could pull his body out, but was hopelessly beaten by the flames. A German officer assured me that they would decently bury his remains. Richthofen came down to within 200 feet and waved at me, although I foolishly imagined at first that he was going to make sure of me. I returned his greeting. I was told that I was to see and talk to him that evening, but did not have the honour of meeting him. I was, of course, a prisoner for the rest of the war.'[8]

The weather was fine on April 21 and the general visibility was good. In the morning the *Luftstreitkräfte* suffered a severe blow when Manfred von Richthofen was shot down behind the British lines at Corbie.

Fifteen Camels of 209 Squadron took off from their aerodrome at Bertangles at 9.35am on a High offensive Patrol. Fifty minutes after takeoff, Capt Oliver Le Boutillier, the

American leader of B Flight attacked a pair of Albatros two-seaters over Beaucourt and, together with two of his Flight, shot one down in flames. The Camels then flew northwards.

Early in the morning, fog had covered Cappy, the aerodrome of *JG 1*, but it began to clear by 10.30am and two *Ketten* (chain, ie. Flight) of Fokker Triplanes left the ground, Richthofen leading the first, *Ltn* Hans Weiss the second. The triplanes climbed for height and made for the front lines.

Arriving over the area of Hamel, the triplanes saw seven Camels below them, with another seven above. Albatri of *Jasta 5* were also in the area, some little way off, over Sailly-le Sec, but these hurried to join the triplanes and a fight began.

Francis Mellersh of A Flight shot down a blue-tailed triplane to crash by side of the River Somme at Cerisy, but was attacked by two triplanes and only avoided them by spinning down to within fifty feet of the ground. Lt W J Mackenzie was attacked by a triplane and wounded in the back, but despite the pain of his wound he fought the enemy machine down before having to finally break off the action and fly back to Bertangles.

Flying in Capt Arthur Brown's Flight was an old school friend of Brown, Lt Wilfrid 'Wop' May, a Canadian from Edmonton Alberta. May had joined 209 Squadron only a short time before and on the morning of April 21 was in his first combat. May had been instructed by Brown that in the event of the Camels going down to attack any enemy machines he was to stay above and keep out of the fighting. May initially obeyed Brown's orders, letting one enemy machine pass below him, but when a second appeared May went down to attack it. May's fire missed the enemy machine and it dived away. May followed it and found himself in the middle of the main fight, with machines, both enemy and friendly, coming at him from all sides. May spun down out of the fight, levelled off and flew west, but was attacked from behind by Richthofen. In an attempt to escape Richthofen's fire May spun down to almost ground level then contoured chased west, but Richthofen was still behind him, firing continually. May later recounted: 'the only thing that saved me was my poor flying. I didn't know what I was doing myself and I don't suppose that Richthofen could figure out what I was going to do.'

As May crossed the British lines, Richthofen was close behind him. May followed the curve of the River Somme by the village of Corbie, but Richthofen cut off the curve and came over the hill, back onto May's tail. 'I was a sitting duck. I was too low down between the banks to make a turn away from him. I felt he had me cold and I was in such a state of mind at this time that I had to restrain myself from pushing my stick forward into the river as I knew I had had it.'

Looking down from the main fight, Brown saw May's danger and dived to assist him, getting behind the red triplane and opening fire: 'dived on a pure red triplane which was firing on Lt May. I got a long burst into him and he went down vertical and was observed to crash by Lieutenant Mellersh and Lieutenant May. I fired on two more but did not get them.'

After spinning down to 50 feet to escape from the triplanes which were attacking him, Mellersh was returning to the British lines with a failing engine. 'Whilst so returning I saw a bright red triplane crashed quite close to me and in looking up saw I saw Capt Brown's machine.' Later, both Le Boutillier and May claim to have seen the triplane crash after Brown's attack, although May's later statement in a letter written in 1950, that he saw the triplane 'do a spin and half and hit the ground,' is not substantiated, either by his combat report, in which he merely stated that 'I observed it crash into the ground', or by other eyes witnesses who stated that the red triplane hit the ground in a flat approach, wiping off the undercarriage.

In his low level pursuit of May, Richthofen had passed over Australian infantry, many of whom fired at the triplane and later claimed to have brought it down, but officially the credit was given to Roy Brown.[9]

German propaganda had made much of Richthofen's success and his invincibility in the air. His loss was a blow, not only to the morale of the German forces in France – Ludendorff had famously described him as being worth a thousand bayonets – but to the German public. The shock felt by the German public at Richthofen's death was one of the reasons why successful British pilots were not given similar publicity in the British Press.

Robert Little had an interesting afternoon. Little's own account, which he pinned on the squadron notice board, gives an evocative picture of his afternoon's fighting.

'After having a forced landing near Lillers I left the ground at 2.30pm and while coming home I saw an enemy aircraft on our side of the lines. So I climbed up and attacked it, and drove it east when I saw twelve enemy scouts to the west of me. I then steered west and when near our lines I attacked the last man in the formation, firing a long burst at very close range, about 20 yards. The enemy aircraft went down out of control. I watched it go down about 1,000 feet, when I was dived on by six enemy scouts which drove me under and down to the eleven enemy scouts below. I then spun and when coming out was fired at by the enemy scouts. They hit my petrol tank and then my machine went out of control and began to dive. The enemy aircraft were firing at me all the time. I had only rudder control and the machine was diving so fast I put it into a spin when about 100 feet from the ground. The machine flattened out with a jerk which broke the fuselage just behind my seat and the tail began to drop off the machine. I carried on straight for sometime, losing speed from 150 knots to 60 knots when I dived to the ground. I undid my belt before hitting the ground and was thrown over the top plane clear of the machine. The enemy scouts still fired at me when I was on the ground, and I fired back at them with my revolver, and our soldiers opened fire on them with Lewis guns. I did not see if the enemy aircraft I fired at crashed or not. I crashed at 3.30pm north of the Forest of Nieppe.'[10]

One pilot of the squadron, Ronald Sykes, added a little local colour to Little's account. 'When his machine broke up under him at about ground level and he was thrown clear into a super soft manure heap he was so annoyed that he blazed away at the Hun who had followed him down.' Sykes was in the 203 Squadron Mess when Little came back late from his adventure. 'I remember I made a rather tactless remark about his manure sodden clothes, not realising that he must have been bruised, sore and in no mood for humour. He told me that at the first opportunity he would take me over the Lines and give me a lesson in being brave – and he did.'[11]

The fighter squadrons claimed eight victories on April 21, and one balloon. Casualties were fairly light, with four pilots killed and three wounded.

The air fighting followed the general pattern for the rest of the month, with occasional days when little flying was possible due to the inclement weather.

On April 25 thirteen divisions of the German army reopened the offensive on the Lys by attacking the British and French forces between Bailleul and the Ypres-Comines Canal. The objective was to capture the positions held by the French at Kemmel Hill, which would give observation over the whole of the northern plain, making the position of the British Army in the Ypres salient untenable.

The fighter squadrons of II Brigade carried out ground-strafing attacks on the enemy troops, and although the 1st Army front was relatively quiet, the fighter squadrons also continued to attack enemy troops and transport.

In the early morning the aircraft of the *Schlachtstaffeln* were very active over the fighting in the area between Bailleul and Kemmel, attacking British troops and interfering with the work of the corps squadrons, but the weather then deteriorated until after 5.00m, when conditions improved, and there were several combats.

The SE5s of 84 Squadron fought 18 Pfalz and Albatri east of Wiencourt at 5.00pm. One of the Pfalz broke up under fire from Robert Grosvenor. The A Flight Commander, Jack Sorsoleil, shot down an Albatros out of control and within five minutes destroyed a Pfalz in flames. Edward Clear shot down another of the Pfalz, which crashed on the railway line near Hangard for his tenth victory. Roy Manzer was awarded an Albatros, which crashed east of Abancourt, and Hugh

Saunders a Pfalz out of control. On his way back to Bertangles, Clear attacked a two-seater that he sent down to crash south of Hangard Wood. The Pfalz in this fight were from *Jasta 34*, who lost *Uffz* Meyer killed – most probably Grosvenor's first victory, he was awarded another two Pfalz as out of control – and *Oblt* Dieterle wounded.

On the way home, no doubt elated with their successes, the SE5s attacked a balloon, forcing its observers to jump to safety. The only casualty of the fight with the Pfalz and Albatri was Capt Lister-Kaye. His SE5 was hit in the engine and in his forced landing Lister-Kaye hit a pole and was injured.

A patrol from 64 Squadron attacked a formation of seven Albatros scouts at 6.00pm. John Gilmour dived on the last machine in the formation and shot it down to crash north of Lamotte. Fighting with Fokker Triplanes and Pfalz, Kenneth Mills of 1 Squadron became separated from the rest of the SE5s and was attacked by four enemy scouts. Mills outmanoeuvred one of these – a Fokker Triplane – and sent it down with black smoke pouring from it to crash between Becelaere and Dadizeele at 6.45pm. Lts Clark, Bateman and Nesbitt of the squadron were all awarded out of control victories from the fight with the Pfalz, which were probably from *Jasta 36,* which had three pilots slightly wounded. A pilot of *Jasta 35b,* Andreas Köhler, was wounded by groundfire, landed behind the British lines and was taken prisoner. His Pfalz D III No. 8282/17, was designated G/IV Brigade/4.[12]

Casualties were light on April 25 with only one pilot killed, one wounded and three aircraft damaged – one in combat and one while ground-strafing.

There was thick mist all day of April 26. The *Schlasta* were again active over Kemmel and two were shot down by groundfire, one falling in the British lines, a Halberstadt from *Schlasta 14*, crewed by *Uffz* Kammrath and *Vzfw* Bremer, who were taken prisoner.

The thick mist persisted the following day. Enemy activity in the air was slight and there was only one combat: a patrol of Camels from 209 Squadron attacked a formation of enemy scouts over Villers Brettoneaux at 2.45pm and Lts O W Redgate, R M Foster and M S Taylor destroyed an Albatros for a shared victory.

On April 28, dreadful weather – low clouds mist and rain – again stopped nearly all flying and there was only one indecisive combat. The next day the weather had cleared a little and despite low clouds, mist and bad visibility, there was some airfighting.

The first victory of the day went to Capt Harry Rigby of 1 Squadron. Rigby attacked a pair of Albatros two-seaters over Wytschaete at 6.45am, firing continuously at one until he was so close that he almost collided with the enemy machine. The lower wing of the Albatros folded up and it went down in a spin.

A patrol from 40 Squadron was also out in the early morning and caught a DFW near Bruay. Capt Ian Napier – 'Naps' to everyone in the squadron – and Lts Learoyd and Sutton kept between the hostile machine and the lines, cutting off its escape to the east. Napier then attacked from behind and below and either killed or wounded the observer with a burst of a full drum of Lewis. As Napier zoomed away to change his drum, Sutton fired a burst from both guns, followed by Learoyd who fired a long burst from his Lewis gun and short bursts from his Vickers until the DFW went down and forced landed behind the British lines, west of Bethune at 7.20am. This DFW CV 7823/17, was from *Fl Abt 7*, crewed by *Hptm* Launer and *Ltn d Res* Heidelmehr and was designated G/I Brigade/1.

Mannock took his Flight over the lines and found ten enemy scouts over Dickebusch, south east of Ypres. Mannock attacked these from the east. Closing to within 20 yards of the Fokker Triplane of *Ltn* Vortmann of *Jasta B*, Mannock shot it down in flames. Henry Dolan attacked an Albatros and sent it down in pieces south of Dickebusch Lake. Clive Glynn saw a triplane approaching from above and behind, about to attack him, but Glynn zoomed and turned to face the attack, firing both guns, possibly killing the pilot because both Mannock and Dolan saw the triplane dive vertically into the ground. This Fokker Triplane was possibly from *Jasta 36* who had *Ltn* Bongartz severely wounded in action.

On their way back to the Lines, the Flight sighted an LVG engaged on artillery co-operation. Mannock led the patrol down to attack it, but pulled away with jams in both guns. Dolan and Ben Roxburgh-Smith – known to the squadron as 'Dad' because of his advanced age of 34 – both then dived after the two-seater, but nearly collided as Dolan swerved across the front of Roxburgh-Smith, 'putting him clean off apart from frightening the life out of him.' The pilot of the LVG flew well, turning his machine in a tight bank to give his observer a good field of fire, but 'Dad' got under his tail and wounded the enemy gunner. The enemy pilot then shut off his engine, and went down, followed by Roxburgh-Smith, firing all the time, and finally crashed in a shell hole close to Dickebusch Lake at 11.50am.

The Camels of 65 Squadron had also been in action during the morning, with Capt John Gilmour shooting down a Pfalz over Hamel at 10.30am for his 19th victory.

Capt John Manuel of 210 Squadron was leading a Flight of Camels in the early afternoon when they attacked a formation of Albatri north east of Hollebeke. Manuel was credited with one as destroyed at 2.45pm.

While on a practise flight in the late evening, Lts Todd and Chapman of 70 Squadron had a DFW over Villers-Bretonneux pointed out to them by British AA fire. Getting to the east of the enemy machine the two 70 Squadron pilots attacked, firing over 400 rounds at it as it attempted to escape back to its own lines. Hugh Saunders and Carl Falkenberg of 84 Squadron then appeared and by continuous attacks forced the DFW to land in the British lines, south east of St Gratien to the north of the Amiens to Albert road.[13]

There were only two casualties during the day. While attacking enemy troops from low level, 2Lt F Smith of 46 Squadron was killed when his Camel was hit by return machine gun fire from the ground and was seen to spin into the ground; and a pilot of 210 Squadron was killed by anti-aircraft fire.

On the morning of 29 April 54 Squadron had left the aerodrome at Clairmarais North, which it shared with 74 Squadron, and were sent out of the fighting to Caffiers, an aerodrome on the coast, for a well-deserved rest. The pilots of 74 Squadron were sorry to see them go; 'We got on so well together. But who couldn't get on with a squadron commanded by Maxwell.'[14]

Fifty-four Squadron were replaced by 4 Squadron AFC. After a welcome party thrown by 74 Squadron, Jones, a teetotaller, commented. 'If they can fight as well as they can knock back cocktails the Hun is in for a fine time. Richardson, Toronto's cocktail wizard, mixes what Grid has named the "74 Viper". By all accounts, it is the goods. A couple are guaranteed to blow your head off. These Aussies make them appear to be made of milk and water.'

The weather was bad on the last day of the month with low clouds mist and rain, but Dolan and Mannock shot down an Halberstadt CL II from *Schlasta* 28b. The crew, *Vzfw* Speer and *Uffz* Zimmermann being taken prisoner. The Halberstadt came down in the British lines and Mannock and Dolan took a lorry and a trailer with some mechanics out to the scene of the crash. When they arrived the area was being shelled with mustard gas, but with the aid of some infantry they got the remains of the Halberstadt onto the trailer. However, as they were leaving the trailer took a direct hit from a shell, killing two of the troops and demolishing the rest of the Halberstadt. The lorry carrying the squadron mechanics and Dolan and Mannock was not hit and got safely away.

'Grid' Caldwell had witnessed the fight with the Halberstadt and later wrote:

'The Hun crashed but not badly and most people would have been content with this – but not Mick Mannock, who dived half a dozen times at the machine, spraying bullets at the pilot and observer, who were still showing signs of life. I witnessed this business and flew alongside to Mick, yelling at the top of my voice (which was rather useless) and warning him to stop. On being questioned as to his wild behaviour after we had landed, he heatedly replied, "the swines are better dead – no prisoners for me."'[15]

The support given to the ground troops by the RAF during the battle of Lys had been considerable, but limited by the bad weather. On April 21, however, the critical day of the battle, the RAF was able to put its full weight into operations. As in the battles of the Somme in late March, the *Luftstreitkräfte* had begun well, but had become less effective as the battle progressed and had lost air superiority as RAF reinforcements arrived. This led to complaints from German troops on the ground that their air force was not protecting them from attack from the air. *General* von Hoeppner, commanding the *Luftstreitkräfte*, later wrote in his post war book, *Deutschlands Krieg in der Luftstreitkräfte,* that the failure of the *Schlachtstaffeln* to give this support was due to the rapid advance on the ground; that it was difficult to find suitable advanced landing grounds in the devastated area of the battlefield and that all telephonic communication between the ground troops and the *Flieger Abteilungen* was lost, adversely affecting the efficiency of artillery observation.

Noted air historian of the *Luftstreitkräfte*, Alex Imrie, has written that the failure of the German air service was due to four main reasons: the number of operational units was insufficient; that the failure of the *jagdstaffeln* to contain the fighter squadrons of the RFC/RAF at high level over the German lines showed an operational weakness; the lack of day bombing aircraft, and the failure to realise the difficulties of moving operational aerodromes forward.

These difficulties may well be valid, but the furthest limit of the German advance was still only a few minutes further flying time for the *jagdstaffeln*. Despite this they kept to the upper air, and failed to defend both their troops and the units of the *Schlachtstaffeln* from the effective low level attacks by British fighters. The defensive tactics employed by the *jagdstaffeln*, their reluctance to fight other than over their own territory was in direct contrast to the offensive policy of the RFC/RAF fighter pilots, costly though it was.

During the fighting in March and April the fighter squadrons had lost 528 aircraft, 130 of which were classified as missing, and the losses of *matériel* during the retreats, destroyed before being abandoned, had also been high.

By the last day of April the last great German offensive against the British armies had ended in failure. From March 21 to the end of April, 140 divisions had been employed in the attacks against the British and French armies. The Allies had finally stood firm, but at heavy cost: nearly 250,000 men had been killed, wounded or missing and 80,000 had been taken prisoner. German losses were numerically equally devastating, but time was running out for Germany. In April almost 120,000 American troops had arrived in France, followed by an additional 220,000 in May and 275,000 in June. The German High Command knew full well that it would lose the war if it failed to find a quick and drastic solution to end hostilities by force of arms before the American armies could enter the conflict in overwhelming numbers.

NOTES

1. Cross and Cockade, Autumn 1972, Douglass Whetton.
2. After the war Adam became a chartered accountant, a profession he hated. At the end of 1931 he took charge of the Embassy theatre, Hampstead, London, presenting nearly 150 plays during the next seven years. At the outbreak of World War II Adam was recalled to the RAF and was a controller of fighter operations at Hornchurch during the Battle of Britain, later going as fighter controller to 11 Group. He finished the war as a Wing Commander and wrote three novels based on his experiences during the conflict. In the 1946 New Year's Honours List Ronald Adam was awarded an OBE and returned to his great love – the theatre. He was an unspectacular but busy actor, appearing on stage and in over 150 films, in one of which he played the Prime Minister of Great Britain. He entered the television age, appearing in plays and commercials, thinking the latter "great fun". Ronald Adam OBE died in March 1979.
3. The AR1 engine, designed by W O Bentley, was the first production aero-engine to use aluminium as an air-cooled cylinder material. The AR1 was later renamed the BR1 (Bentley Rotary)
4. *Wings over the Somme, 1916-1918,* Wing Commander Gwilym Lewis, Kimber, 1976.
5. Ibid. Lt R E Bion was killed in action on April 9.
6. Additional fighter squadrons from II Brigade had been moved into the battle area on April 10: 1 Squadron (SE5a) 29 Squadron (Nieuports) and 54 Squadron (Camel). A Bristol Fighter squadron, No.20, had also been deployed.
7. Walkerdine survived the war. When he died in 1966 his flying helmet, that he had been wearing on April 11 1918, was cremated with him.
8. *Popular Flying*, May 1934.
9. In the 86 years since his death, who killed Manfred von Richthofen has been the subject of seemingly endless debate: Roy Brown, and two Australian Lewis gunners have all been credited. The discussion is outside the scope of this book, and the truth will never be known, but it should be taken into account that literally dozens of Australian infantrymen were firing with both rifles and machine guns at the triplane as it flew past. Many, by their upbringing and way of life in Australia, were expert and instinctive deflection marksmen, who could knock over a running rabbit or hare from long range. A man sitting in the cockpit of a triplane would have been a relatively easy shot.
10. Little's victory was possibly *Vzfw* Kaufmann of *Jasta 47* who was severely wounded on April 21 and died of his wounds the next day.
11. Cross and Cockade, Great Britain, Vol.7 No. 1, 1976, Douglass Whetton.
12. The allocation of a G number to captured German aircraft had ceased in late March 1918 and each brigade now independently reported enemy aircraft down in their areas and allocated numbers.
13. Some authorities give this as DFW C V, No.9746/17, designated G/V Bgd/5 and the crew, *Uffz* Krug and *Ltn* Adler of *Fl Abt(A) 218* taken prisoner, Krug being wounded. But the German casualty lists give Krug and Adler as being killed on April 25 and the V Brigade/5 report gives their machine as an Albatros two-seater.
14. Major Reginald Stuart Maxwell.
15. This side of Mannock's nature, an almost pathological hatred of Germans, so at variance with his usual quiet and kindly nature, was incomprehensible to his family and those who knew him well, and startled his fellow pilots. As a civilian, Mannock had been interned in Turkey at the outbreak of war and he and his fellow internees had been extremely badly treated. Mannock blamed Germany for the war and his first biographer, Ira Jones, felt that his hatred was intensified by the fear that Germany might win the war; an understandable fear in the March and April of 1918 when the German offensives were going so well.

MAY 1918:
GAINS AND LOSSES

In May 1918, Spring was slow in coming. Low clouds, mist and rain on the first day curtailed nearly all flying and there were no combats. Although the visibility was still bad on the morning of the following day, general conditions were fine. There was little enemy air activity but some combats were fought, the fighter pilots returning with some relief to their normal high-level offensive patrols.

Nine SE5s from 56 took off from Valheureux at 10.30am. Just under an hour later the SEs attacked a mixed formation of seven Pfalz and three Fokker Triplanes flying northeast from Bray-sur-Somme. Henry Burden shot at a Pfalz, following it down from ten to six thousand feet firing over 200 rounds into it until it went into a spin and disappeared into the clouds emitting a great deal of thick black and gray smoke.

Louis Jarvis attacked one of the triplanes; after twenty rounds it went straight down, turning over onto its back before entering the clouds. Jarvis dived below the clouds in time to watch the triplane emerge, still on its back, to crash at Martinpuich. Climbing back into the fight, Jarvis took a snap shot at a Pfalz, which spun away from his fire, then fired at another until both his guns stopped. Cyril Parry then attacked this Pfalz, turning onto its tail and firing a long burst. The Pfalz went down almost vertically and disappeared into the cloud cover. Trevor Durrant, who had gun stoppages at the beginning of the fight, had now cleared them and attacked a Pfalz from behind, firing a long burst into it from a range of 30 yards. The enemy machine reared up in front of Durrant's SE5, stalled, and fell out of control into the clouds. These Pfalz and triplanes were from *Jasta 10*: *Ltn* Weiss was killed in action over Mericourt and *Ltn* Stoy was lightly wounded over Peronne.

These successes were offset by the loss of the squadron's commanding officer, Major Rainsford Balcombe Brown. He had taken off with Capt Edward Atkinson on a Special Mission – official speak for 'looking for trouble.' Both Balcombe Brown and Atkinson were on the outskirts of the fight with the Pfalz and triplanes and Balcombe Brown was shot down by *Ltn* Erich Loewenhardt, the *Staffelführer* of *Jasta 10*, who claimed an SE5 at Montauban at 12.30pm (German time) the time and location of Balcombe Brown's loss.

The Camels of 65 Squadron also had a successful morning. Capt Gilmour's Flight found eight enemy two-seaters in the Bapaume area. Gilmour shot one down in flames almost at once, which crashed near Miraumont Wood, and Tom Williams chased another south and destroyed it in flames over Villers-Bretonneaux. 2Lt Scott-Kerr disposed of another of the two-seaters that was seen by Australian troops to crash into Monument Wood. Ten minutes after these combats, at 12.05pm, Gilmour crashed another two-seater behind the British lines near the south edge corner of Bois l'Abbe. In the afternoon a flight commander with the squadron, Capt Lewis Whitehead, shot down a two-seater for his second victory since December 1916, when he was flying with 60 Squadron, and his first since joining 65 Squadron.

Major Dallas, who had been recuperating since his wounding on April 14, was now out of hospital, back with 40 Squadron, and by the end of April 'has been able to hobble on a couple of sticks.' By May 2, Dallas had started to fly again and he took off after lunch and flew to the German aerodrome at La Brayelle, north of Douai. Arriving at low height over the hangars, Dallas first fired on them to attract attention before dropping a parcel of a pair of boots, containing the message. 'If you won't come up here and fight, herewith one pair of boots for work on the ground – pilots for the use of.' Waiting until a party of men had collected around the parcel to examine it, Dallas dived and dropped two bombs on the group, then fired on the hangars and ground personnel before leaving. Returning to Bruay, Dallas saw an Albatros scout and shot it down to crash at Brebières for his 26th victory.

Additional victories were scored during the day by pilots of 19 Squadron – Capt John Leacroft scored the last of his 22 victories with a Pfalz destroyed south of Armentières – and 4 AFC, 209, and 1 Squadrons for the loss of four pilots killed, two taken prisoner and one aeroplane struck off strength.

May 3 was a fine day with excellent visibility and there was a great deal of fighting in the air. Lewis Whitehead of 65 Squadron was again successful. At 6.45am he and 2Lt Crane attacked a pair of Hannover two-seaters, shooting one down to crash inside the British lines at Heilly. The Hannover CL II, No.13282/17, was from *Schlasta 31b*, the pilot, *Vzfw* Peez had been wounded and the gunner, *Gefr* Lang, killed. The Hannover was designated G/V Brigade/6.

The second patrol of the day from 56 Squadron, led by Trevor Durrant, attacked a pair of Rumplers going west over Albert. Durrant attacked one of the enemy machines that went down to crash south of Pozières. A quarter of an hour later another Rumpler was seen low down – 1,000 feet – over Aveluy Wood. Diving to attack this machine, Durrant fired only a short burst before both guns stopped, but the Rumpler went down with the gunner hanging over the side of the fuselage, his gun vertical. Atkinson and Irwin both fired at the falling Rumpler, which finally crashed at Montauban-de-Picarde. This last Rumpler was possibly from *Fl Abt (A)235*, crewed by *Flg* Paul and *Ltn* Lydorf, both killed.

A morning patrol from 203 Squadron attacked an enemy two-seater in the Lens area. Whealy closed to 150 yards before firing and the enemy machine dived away, Whealy followed it down, closed to within a 100 yards and fired a long burst. The two-seater steepened its dive until vertical and crashed into a house a mile from Lens. Twenty-five minutes later Lts Beamish and Hayne fought with Fokker Triplanes over Neuve-Eglise and claimed two down out of control.

Lt Walter Tyrrell of 32 Squadron saw a great deal of action in the morning. At noon he fought with two Fokker Triplanes, sending both down out of control over Frelinghem, but was then attacked by a pair of two-seaters. Tyrrell quickly got on the tail of one, an LVG with a large number 2 painted on the fuselage, and fired a short burst of fifty rounds into it. The enemy pilot turned west, and Tyrrell prevented him from turning east with short bursts of fire until the enemy pilot finally landed the LVG in the British lines about a mile from Poperinghe.[1]

Other claims during the morning's fighting were a Rumpler destroyed over Mercatel by a patrol from 64 Squadron; Capt Cyril Lowe and Lt Ronald March shared in a Fokker Triplane out of control over Marcelcave at 11.45am – possibly *Ltn* Just of *Jasta 11* who was wounded in action – and a Fokker Triplane crashed at Meteren by Lt Eric Cummings of 2 Squadron AFC. Following the triplane down to watch it crash, Cummings was attacked by four others who shot away his elevator controls, hit the SE5 in the petrol and oil tanks and shattered the instrument board. The SE5 was almost uncontrollable, but Cummings managed to keep it from spinning and crashed near the British front lines. His lap belt broke on impact and Cummings was thrown from his machine into a nearby shell hole. He was later rescued by fellow Australians who had also seen the triplane crash.

At 12.30pm a patrol from 73 Squadron were in combat with a mixed formation of triplanes and Albatri over Ploegstreet and Lt William Stephenson shot one of the triplanes down to crash into Ploegsteert Wood.

Also at 12.30pm, south of Bailleul, Camels of 46 Squadron found an LVG and the Canadian flight commander, Capt Donald MacLaren, shot it down in flames. Thirty minutes later the Flight attacked two Halberstadts north west of Don. MacLaren and Lt Victor Yeates both fired at one of the Halberstadts until the right hand wings broke away and it went down to crash.

There then seems to have been a slight slackening of enemy air activity until later in the afternoon. At 4.45pm Edmund Tempest of 64 Squadron added to the squadron's success of the morning by destroying a Pfalz D III over Vitry-en-Artois. At half past six Mannock and his Flight caught an LVG south of Merville and Mannock shot it down for his twenty-second victory, shared with his Flight. The LVG was from *Fl Abt (A) 32* and the crew, *Uffz* Schöning and *Ltn d Res* Beuttler, were both killed.

Capt Ian McDonald of 24 Squadron claimed the second Fokker triplane for the squadron during the day, shooting one down over Le Quesnel at 6.35pm. Fifteen minutes later, Capt Ian Napier of 40 Squadron had a DFW two-seater pointed out to him by British AA fire over Merville. Napier wounded the enemy observer in his first attack and continued his attacks until the DFW went down to crash.

For a day of considerable fighting the casualties of the fighter squadrons had been extremely light. Only one pilot had been killed and three taken prisoner, one of whom later died of his wounds.

The weather for the next two days was bad, with heavy mist, low clouds and showers of rain. Despite the weather there were some combats on May 4. No positive victories were claimed by the fighter squadrons, but 4 Squadron AFC lost a pilot killed in action in the evening and a pilot from 24 Squadron was wounded and taken POW.

There were no combats on May 5, but although the weather conditions remained poor on May 6 there was some fighting.

The bad weather persisted in the morning, enemy activity was slight, and it appears that the only victories claimed were by 74 Squadron.

Mannock's patrol were in combat with Fokker Triplanes over Gheluvelt at 9.20am and Mannock shot down *Ltn* Derlin of *Jasta 20* who crashed in Ploegsteert Wood and was killed. There was a little more enemy activity in the evening and MacLaren's Flight from 46 Squadron shot down a DFW of *Fl Abt 14*, crewed by *Ltn* Jünemann and *Ltn* Bath, in the British lines. Other victories were claimed by W J Duncan and J S Griffith of 60 Squadron, who shared in the destruction of an Albatros scout over Guillaucourt at 7.15pm; and Lt Henry Biziou of 87 Squadron claimed the first of his eight victories with a DFW shot down over Aveluy Wood. Three Sopwith Dolphin pilots of 87 Squadron shared in the squadron's first victory: a Rumpler sent down out of control over Gheluvelt at 5.40pm.

Only one pilot was reported missing during the day, but two SE5s from 1 Squadron and a Camel from 210 Squadron were shot up and damaged in forced landings.

It rained practically all day on May 7 and there was no enemy activity until the afternoon. 'Grid' Caldwell was out with Roxburgh-Smith and shot down a Fokker Triplane out of control from 11,000 feet. Later in the patrol, at 7,000 feet, he and Roxburgh-Smith shared in the destruction of a Fokker Triplane north east of Ypres at 3.20pm.[2] Kenneth Mills of 1 Squadron claimed his fifth and last victory: a two-seater a mile east of Kemmel at 4.45pm.

May 8 was a bad day for 74 Squadron. Two Flights took off: the first at 7.05, the second ten minutes later. After dropping their bombs on Menin, the SE5s were between Ypres and Menin when B Flight were attacked by Fokker Triplanes from *Jasta 26*. The leader of the enemy triplanes had seen the SE5s and carefully positioned his force to attack from a height advantage of a thousand feet, finally diving on the SE5s over Gheluvelt.

C Flight of 74 Squadron were still at 16,000 feet. They had seen the impending attack developing but were powerless to climb into the fight in time to come to the aid of their fellow Flight. Jones later wrote: 'The fight soon developed into the usual dogfight. It was a grim business we witnessed. We were beneath the battle, just circling round and round, looking upwards at our pals fighting for their lives. We could do nothing to help. Nothing! Nothing but look on in a state of anger and helplessness. It was a terrible feeling. May I never have to endure it again.'

Within a minute of the fight starting, Lt P J Stuart-Smith fell in flames, passing quite close to the SE5s of C Flight on the way down. Lt R E Bright was the next to fall, his SE5 burning fiercely. Next, Lt J R Piggott came spinning past C

Flight with a triplane in close pursuit. C Flight attacked the triplane, forcing it to leave Piggott who glided down towards the British lines.[3] The SE5 of Capt William Young, the B Flight Commander, had been badly shot about, and he managed to land at Marie Capelle, but Andrew Kiddie was the only member of the patrol who returned to Clairmarais.

Unfortunately, there was more to come. As C Flight arrived back over the aerodrome, Lt Skeddon half rolled off the top of a loop, both wings collapsed, and the SE5 spun into the ground and burst into flames. Ira Jones, a particular friend of Skeddon – they were sharing a hut – was so sickened by the sight that he could not bring himself to land, to have to taxi past the blazing wreckage, and flew on to Clairmarais south aerodrome, overshot in his approach and crashed, the SE5 going over onto its back.

Ira Jones was determined to avenge his friend and ordered another SE5 to be made ready. 'I ate a little more breakfast. Then I proceeded to my hut, where I had a damned good cry. I took care no one knew I was being so childish by locking the door.' He took off later, dropped his bombs at the nearest part of the German lines, flew for a while without seeing any enemy aircraft on which to vent his anger and grief, and returned. Another squadron patrol in the afternoon saw a few Albatros and Pfalz, 'but they were all in a yellow mood and would not fight.'

In the evening, after packing Skeddon's kit, Jones went out again. This time he was lucky. 'At 6.25pm I spotted a two-seater coming towards Bailleul from the direction of Armentières at about 4,000 feet. I was then at 3,000 feet, over Hazebrouck. The sun was behind me, nice and large. I climbed quickly to 8,000 feet towards Merville, then back towards Bailleul. Hun archie warned the enemy of my approach by sending up a series of puffs. Apparently he did not see it. It would not have mattered if he had done. I had made up my mind to get him, even if I had to ram the sod.'

Jones closed to point blank range before opening fire. Almost at once there was a glow from the fuselage of the enemy machine and it went down to crash near Nieppe, bursting into flames as it hit the ground. It was Jones' first victory.

Lts Claydon, Hendrie and Tyrrell of 32 Squadron all claimed victories during the day; Seymour of 40 Squadron shot down a scout to crash at Virty-en-Artois; two pilots of 206 Squadron shared a scout in flames and two pilots of 208 Squadron, G A Cox and E G Johnstone, each claimed a scout crashed.

In a morning fight east of Kemmel 1 Squadron lost two pilots shot down wounded and taken prisoner, and an SE5 badly shot about and forced to land. A pilot from 43 Squadron was shot down and killed, and a pilot of 208 Squadron was killed in action.

The weather was generally fine on May 9 and there was a great deal of fighting. Fifteen decisive victories were claimed for the loss of two pilots killed and two taken prisoner.

A patrol from 64 Squadron, which included the American, Charles Bissonette, and Thomas Rose, fought with a variety of enemy aircraft over the Boiry area at 10.40am and Bissonette claimed a Halberstadt two-seater and a Pfalz D III out of control in the fighting. Rose attacked a Rumpler from under its tail and sent it down to crash, bursting into flames as it hit the ground. This was possibly a machine from *Fl Abt (A) 210* that was lost in the general area.

During a morning patrol by 46 Squadron, two Fokker Triplanes dived on the Camels, got on the tail of Lt R McConnell's machine and shot both spars and a centre section wire. McConnell put his Camel into a spin and Lt H Dodson attacked one of the triplanes, firing 150 rounds into it from close range. The enemy machine went down in a spin for a thousand feet, temporarily recovered, then spun again, repeating this several times until the pilot crashed badly while attempting to land.

The Camels of 203 and 210 Squadrons were also out in the morning. At 11.30am 203 Squadron were in the La Bassée area and fought with Fokker Triplanes and Pfalz: Capt Whealy shot down a Pfalz D III which crashed a mile east of Herlies; Capt Beamish crashed a triplane, which crashed in the same vicinity and Capt Oliver Le Boutillier shot down another of the triplanes, flown by *Ltn* Janzen of *Jasta 6* who crashed on landing but was unhurt. Further north, Capt Alfred Carter of 210 Squadron, closed to within 15 yards of a Rumpler at 11.45am over Bailleul before opening fire. The Rumpler went down, followed by Carter, who fired another 100 rounds into it. Capt E Arnold and Lt Frederick Hall also fired at the enemy machine as it went down and all three pilots shared in the victory.

Gilmour of 65 Squadron dived on a pair of enemy two-seaters northeast of Albert at 1.00pm. A short burst at one sent it down in a vertical dive to crash north east of Aubercourt. A *Ltn* Teitz from *Fl Abt 40* was killed in the Bapaume-Albert area on May 9.

It was a good day for the Camel squadrons. At 3.10pm Cap Henry Woollett led his Flight from 43 Squadron down to attack a formation of Albatri. The enemy scouts flew east but the Camels pursued them, caught them south of La Gorgue and Woollett shot one down. Geoffrey Bailey chased another Albatros and sent it down out of control south of Nieppe Forest. While chasing the Albatros, Woollett had seen a balloon to the northeast of La Gorgue and he shot this down in flames. No one got out. To the south, nine enemy scouts attacked a patrol from 4 Squadron AFC. Fire from one of the enemy pilots hit the petrol tank of Lt Schafer's Camel and he dived

away, followed by two of the enemy machines, one of which broke up in mid-air and crashed east of St Eloi, bursting into flames on hitting the ground.

A Flight from 2 Squadron AFC, 4 AFC Squadron's fellow Australians, attacked fifteen enemy scouts east of Bapaume at 5.50pm. Lt J Adam, a Canadian attached to the squadron, attacked a Pfalz D III that rolled over onto its side. Lt Francis Smith then attacked the Pfalz and fired ninety rounds into it. The enemy machine went down and crashed near Marcoing.

Two Flights from 24 Squadron were patrolling in the Albert area. To the east, flying at 3,000 feet below, them a formation of enemy scouts was flying west. B Flight went down to attack the enemy machines, C Flight waiting for a moment to make sure there were no other enemy scouts above them. In a furious fight, which lasted for between 15 and 20 minutes, Capt Cyril Lowe sent a blue and red Albatros down out of control over Hangard Wood and drove another down damaged. An American pilot from Ohio, William Lambert, fired at a light blue Albatros that was fighting with Lt Hellett. Lambert fired 100 rounds at close range into this machine and he and Hellet watched it go down to crash in a field to the southeast of Corbie. Lambert then saw an SE5 on the tail of an Albatros, but another Albatros coming in from above and behind it. Lambert flew to attack this Albatros but it turned away, leaving the pilot of the SE5, Lt J Daley, to send the Albatros he was chasing down through the thin cloud, flatten out and crash into some trees.

May 10 was fine but very misty, especially in the north, but there was a little enemy activity, mainly in the south. In the morning 56 Squadron were in combat with fourteen Albatri in the area of Villers-Bretonneux and Lt Harmon was shot down by *Vzfw* Fritz Rumey of *Jasta 5*, his SE5 going down and breaking up 'like a burst feather pillow.' Hank Burden attacked a green and white Albatros following it down until it burst into flames and crashed to the south of the River Somme. All the SE5s of A Flight were shot about in this action – Cyril Parry, leading the Flight in the flight commander's absence – was convinced that he had lost them all.

A patrol of Camels from 65 Squadron were in the area of the 56 Squadron fight and at the same time. Gilmour's Flight of six Camels attacked a single enemy scout and sent it spinning down into the haze at low level. It was later confirmed by an AA battery to have crashed.

In the afternoon, a Flight of SE5s from 84 Squadron saw a Rumpler two-seater climbing for height over the River Somme. The South African, Beauchamp Proctor, carefully stalked this Rumpler and finally attacked it south east of Bray at 2.10pm, his first burst of 50 rounds killing or wounding the enemy observer, who disappeared into his cockpit leaving his gun unattended. Beauchamp Proctor closed the distance. After another burst from his guns the Rumpler went down in a vertical dive to 4,000 feet where it was lost in the ground haze. However, another pilot of the squadron saw it crash by the River Somme, to the southeast of Bray-sur-Somme and Beauchamp Proctor was awarded it for his twelfth victory.

Another South African, Samuel Kinkead, scored for 201 Squadron at 7.30pm, shooting down an Albatros from a formation of three to crash northeast of Villers-Bretonneux.

The Camels of 80 Squadron left the ground at 5.00pm to patrol the Villers-Bretonneux area and were attacked by elements of *Jasta 11* and *Jasta 36*. Capt O Bridgeman claimed a Fokker Triplane in flames from the fight, but three of the Camel pilots were shot down and killed, another was wounded, shot down and taken prisoner and the fifth crash landed his badly damaged Camel and was injured. Two other pilots were forced to land with badly shot about machines.

There was a thick mist all day on May 11, with only one short, clear interval. In the evening Mannock shot a Pfalz D III down in flames northeast of Armentières at 5.40pm, killing *Ltn d Res* Aeckerle of *Jasta 47w*. Capt William Mays Fry was credited with a Fokker Triplane, shot down over Bray-sur-Somme for his last victory of a total of 11, and his only victory flying Sopwith Dolphins with 79 Squadron. Camels of 210 Squadron were in action with upwards of 30 enemy scouts over Aremuntières at 7.25pm and Capt William Alexander broke his month-long drought of victories by shooting down an Albatros scout in flames. The Australian squadrons were again in action, Lt H G Watson of 4 Squadron AFC shooting down a Pfalz D III which broke up in the air at five minutes past six northeast of Armentières, but the squadron lost Lt O Barry in the fighting, shot down in flames.[4] Another Australian, Harry Rigby, flying in 1 Squadron, had just earlier shot down an Albatros over Bailleul at 5.15pm for his last victory of six. The squadron had been in a fight with enemy scouts and Lt C Pelletier had been shot down in flames and killed. Additional casualties during the day were a pilot of 41 Squadron, who was wounded and a pilot from 213 Squadron, killed in action.

There were low clouds all day on May 12 but 74 Squadron saw a great deal of fighting and lost one of their most promising pilots, Henry Dolan, who had scored seven victories since the squadron had begun operations.

The SE5s took off at 5.30pm, flying in three layers about half a mile apart. At 6.15pm Mannock sighted a formation of enemy scouts – Albatri and Pfalz – and manoeuvred for a quarter of an hour until his Flight was in a favourable position to attack. When the enemy scouts were over Wulverghem, Mannock took his Flight down onto them, joined almost immediately by the other Flights. Mannock shot down a Pfalz at the rear of the enemy formation, which sideslipped away and

collided with another enemy scout. Ira Jones fired at an Albatros which was on the tail of Roxburgh-Smith's SE5. The enemy machine reared up almost vertically in front of Jones, nearly colliding with his SE, before spinning away inverted. Looking down to follow the fall of this Albatros, Jones saw Dolan's SE5 going down in a spin to crash near Wulverghem, but he was attacked by a yellow Albatros that hit his SE5 in the petrol tank. Jones dived away out of the fight and landed at Proven aerodrome.

Mannock had claimed three Pfalz destroyed in the fight; Roxburgh-Smith had crashed another; the B Flight Commander, Capt Wilfred Young had destroyed another Pfalz, and Jones was awarded an Albatros as out of control. Wilfred Giles had shot at an Albatros that had turned over onto its back, but the pilot had regained control close to the ground. Seeing this Glies had dived from 5,000 feet and fired another burst into it. The Albatros made off east but was later seen to have crashed by another pilot. It was good arithmetic in Mannock's terms, but the squadron keenly felt the loss of Henry Dolan. He had not only shown great promise but was a very popular member of the squadron. However, as was common in the Messes of the RFC and RAF, the loss of Dolan – any casualty – was not allowed to effect morale by dwelling on the loss. Ira Jones returned from Proven at midnight to find his fellow pilots at a party in full swing in 1 Squadron's Mess. 'My appearance brought forth much whooping and halloing. I was carried shoulder high round the Mess to the strains of "Men of Harlech" on the gramophone. Rox then thumped the piano, while the rest of the company sang themselves hoarse. Wine was flowing freely. Clarke, Owen and Clayson of Number 1 were very full out, while our lads showed no trace of morbidness.'

May 13 started fine but rain set in later. Early in the morning, an FK8 of 2 Squadron was followed back to its aerodrome by a hostile two-seater and attacked over the field. The observer of the British two-seater, Lt Jennings, fired a burst at the enemy machine and Capt Napier of 40 Squadron also fired at it. After another burst from Jennings, the two-seater stalled and went down to crash near Lacouture.

Trevor Durrant of 56 Squadron scored his last victory, shooting down an LVG to crash on the railway line southwest of Beaucourt. This victory was confirmed by an AA battery.

On May 14, the delayed spring came in with a rush and for the next ten days the weather was fine, with good visibility. A great number of combats were fought, with large numbers of aircraft involved. Some fights stand out. On May 15, 29 Squadron scored its first victory since exchanging its Nieuports for SE5s when Capt Reginald Rusby attacked one of a pair of two-seaters. After a burst of a 100 rounds two large bursts of flames were seen to come out of the pilot's cockpit and the enemy machine went down in flames south east of Merris. Casualties for the day included two pilots of 209 Squadron killed and another wounded in a fight with some enemy scouts which were attacking DH4s. Capt Oliver Redgate of the squadron destroyed an Albatros over Pozières for his 16th and last victory, but he was wounded in the fighting.

On May 16, 56 Squadron lost one of its most popular and promising pilots when Capt Trevor Durrant was shot down and killed by *Ltn d Res* Kirschstein of *Jasta 6*. Only that morning Durrant had been promoted to Captain, given command of B Flight, and was leading his first patrol as a flight commander.

The SE5s were two Flights strong when they crossed the lines over Albert at 13,000 feet, with Durrant leading B Flight three to four thousand feet above C Flight, led by Capt Jarvis. Forty minutes after crossing the lines a formation of Fokker Triplanes was seen northeast of Le Sars. Eugene Macdonald, flying with B Flight recalled: 'The bottom Flight had not enough height to attack the first group of Huns observed. Captain Jarvis turned towards our Lines, still climbing to gain the necessary height. The top Flight kept station until we were separated by a thick layer of cloud. Captain Durrant must have assumed that the bottom Flight would turn east again, having gained height, and we, the top Flight, turned east, still climbing.'

Durrant, thinking that they were supported by C Flight, took his Flight down to attack the triplanes, but these were flying a very open and loose formation and the SEs were forced to split up in their dives and pick out individual opponents.

Macdonald got a good burst into his selected opponent but was attacked by two of the triplanes and forced to dive, then zoom away. As he did so he saw a machine going down in flames.

'When I looked round I found myself alone. I climbed to about 16,000 feet and thought that I had outclimbed all the triplanes. I was taken by surprise to find one slightly above me, in fact I did not see him until there was a sharp crack and my engine appeared to be hit and cut out, emitting black smoke. I had not the slightest chance to take offensive action. I turned over on my back and spun down a short distance and came out of the spin in a spiral in order to offer a more elusive target. I had throttled back immediately my engine cut out. I could have dived away at 230mph, without engine, but I was scared of going on fire. I glimpsed the triplane several times in my spiral descent, but he did not attack again. I can only assume that he considered me as finished. He may have spotted Sopwith Camels approaching and I did not see him again.'

As soon as the Camels had passed him Macdonald put his SE5 into a glide and made for the British Lines, finally landing in a field of growing corn a foot high. The field had a small hut in one corner and two mechanics came out to assist Macdonald. He had landed on an aerodrome about to be occupied by 3 Squadron AFC. The CO gave him a drink – 'much needed' – and telephoned 56 Squadron. Macdonald arrived back at the squadron that night. 'The new CO and some of the pilots were sitting around at a table outside. I made a brief report, stating that Capt Durrant had gone down in flames. I felt very bitter about this tragic patrol. Trevor Durrant was a very dear friend of mine. He has held a place in my memory for the last 50 years as the finest Englishman I ever knew.'[5]

Two days later Durrant was buried near where he fell, south of Contalmaison.[6]

May 17 was a day of mixed fortunes for 74 Squadron. In a morning patrol Capt Cairns led his Flight down to attack some Hannover enemy two-seaters, but a formation of enemy scouts attacked the SE5s. Jones recorded: 'The enemies were Pfalz scouts, well-flown and aggressive. Quite a change to find Huns who will fight, I thought.' Jones fired a few shots at a light green Pfalz, then zoomed away to give Nixon the chance of a shot. 'What the devil actually happened, I don't know; but when I had finished my zoom and steadied myself to look for Nicky on the Hun's tail, I saw to my horror quite the reverse picture. The Hun was pumping lead into Nicky, who was diving in a straight line away from him. Before I could help, my dear old machine with my mascot and poor old Nicky was enveloped in flames. Why have we no parachutes, for God's sake. A fine fellow had gone west through forgetting the golden rule of air fighting: never dive away if a Hun is on your tail. Turn, old boy. Turn!'[7]

Jones went after the Pfalz that had shot down Nixon, but the pilot dived away below the fight. Jones, knowing it would be dangerous to get below the main fight, pulled out and first attacked a green and black Pfalz, then one painted yellow and black.

Jones then spotted a silver Hannover two-seater. 'This poor hoot was easy money, and I made no mistake about him. I think I must have conked the pilot, for he went into a vertical dive immediately after my first burst, which was from under his tail at a range of about 50 yards.'[8] Smoke then came out of the Hannover and it burst into flames.

Mannock had destroyed a Pfalz D III in the morning, and an Albatros in the afternoon, both in flames, for his 29th and 30th victories, but Lt L Barton's SE5 was hit by archie and went down in flames in the afternoon patrol. In the evening another new pilot crashed on landing and was taken to hospital.

The SE5s of 84 Squadron were escorting a formation of DH4s when Capt H Smith saw that several enemy scouts were about to attack them. Smith dived on the nearest enemy, fired a great number of rounds and followed it down to see it crash near Rosieres. As Smith zoomed to regain his height, he was attacked by a triplane, one bullet hitting him in the right ankle and another his petrol tank, stopping his engine. Smith made for the British lines, kicking his rudder as he went, and eventually crossed the enemy lines at 100 feet over Villers-Bretonneux and crashed in No Man's Land. Getting out of the wreckage of his SE5, Smith was hit again, this time in his left ankle, and his left arm was badly broken by a machine gun bullet. Despite his wounds, Smith managed to roll into a small depression and was finally pulled into a sap-head by Australian troops, one of whom was badly wounded in the rescue.

Rochford of 203 Squadron shot down a Pfalz during a morning patrol, his Flight shot down another in flames, and a Flight led by Harold Beamish shot down an an Albatros south of Merville, but the squadron lost two pilots killed in the morning's fighting.

On May 18, Major Dallas, flying alone, saw a Rumpler climbing for height over its own lines. Dallas was unable to get up to the height of the enemy machine so shadowed it for almost an hour, waiting for it to loose height. A Camel, flying west, passed under the Rumpler, and the enemy pilot, mistaking the Camel for Dallas and thinking that he had abandoned any hope of attacking, began to lose height. Dallas seized his chance and fired a whole drum of Lewis in the Rumpler, which went down in flames and crashed near Lille at noon.

A patrol from 65 Squadron, led by John Gilmour, attacked a formation of 12 enemy scouts east of Bray-sur-Somme. Gilmour's opponent broke up under his fire and ten minutes later, at 10.30am, he crashed a two-seater in flames east of Lamotte, but two of the 65 Squadron pilots had been shot down and taken prisoner in the fight with the enemy scouts.

Ira Jones confided in his diary – officially, strictly forbidden to be kept – ' I got a Hun and a half for lunch today.' The Flight had taken off at midday and Jones had attacked an Albatros two-seater. His account gives an interesting picture of the technicalities of fighting in the air. After trying a deflection shot, which had no effect, the Albatros dived away. 'He continued to dive. I followed from beneath so that, because of the rush of wind, his observer could not operate his guns. Though he gained a little on me as I turned under him, I soon caught up again. My SE was diving full out, doing about 180mph. Once I got to within a hundred yards, I throttled back my engine and adjusted the speed of my machine to his. I then took deliberate aim, just in front of his nose, and straddled him. I continued firing on a long burst until I got right up to him by slightly opening my throttle. Soon the ominous streak of smoke appeared, and next the small flames. Finally a sort of explosion took place and the whole machine disintegrated in a flaming mass. I felt quite sick at the horrible sight.'[9]

As Jones crossed the lines on his way back to the aerodrome, British Archie pointed out another two-seater, circling in the middle of the bursts. Jones made to attack, but the AA batteries would not stop firing and he had to wait, keeping east of the enemy machine, knowing that sooner or later the enemy pilot would have to make a break for the safety of his own lines. When he finally did so Jones fired white Very lights requesting the batteries to stop firing. 'They kindly obliged, so I got on with my job.'

Jones attacked the enemy two-seater head on, opening fire at 400 yards. As the distance closed to 100 yards, Jones dived below the enemy machine, and turned quickly to get on its tail, now a hundred yards away. Jones closed to within 30 yards, slightly below his opponent, and opened fire with his top wing Lewis gun. Suddenly, Jones realised that bullets were hitting his SE5. 'Where were they coming from? We were still over our lines and I knew there could not be a Hun on my tail. Such happenings were now only fairy tales and relics of the past.' As he again closed the distance, Jones could see that a machine gun was 'peeping' through a hole in the bottom of the enemy machine's fuselage. Slightly startled by this, Jones zoomed above the enemy machine and dived on it, opening fire with his Vickers gun. The enemy observer quickly abandoned his downward firing gun and started to fire upwards with his top gun. Jones quickly dived below again, repeating this manoeuvre two or three times until, noticing that the lower gun was no longer firing at him, he stayed below, weaving from side to side. The enemy observer pointed his top gun down over the side of the fuselage and continued to fire at the SE, his pilot swerving from side to side to give him a good shot. 'He was a good pilot, I kept firing short bursts in order to tantalise him, often only taking pot-shots without proper aim.' This rattled the enemy pilot and he suddenly tilted his machine very steeply. For the moment Jones thought that the observer had thrown some sort of an object at him, possibly his gun, and slithered quickly to one side, looking to see what it was. 'To my amazement I saw the body of the observer, falling with arms outstretched and legs wide apart, and going down in a series of tumbling circles. It was a horrifying sight. He fell in the trenches near Meteren.'

While Jones watched the body of the observer falling, the pilot of the two-seater made good his escape, diving for his own lines. Jones chased after him as far as Armentières, but the enemy pilot had gained too large a lead; after firing a burst at long range, exhausting his remaining ammunition, Jones left him and returned.

Thirteen victories were claimed on May 19. James Slater of 64 Squadron, now a very experienced flight commander, led his Flight in an attack on a formation of Albatri and Pfalz east of Oppy, shooting down an Albatros over the village and a Pfalz D III five minutes later over Brebières for his 18th and 19th victories.

Anthony Beauchamp Proctor of 84 Squadron had a very successful day. In a morning patrol he drove a two-seater down out of control at Vauvillers at 9.45am and a quarter of an hour later destroyed an Albatros over Wiencourt. In an evening patrol he shot down *Ltn* Weber of *Jasta 46*, who was captured, and the Flight shared in two more victories: two Albatri destroyed south east of Villers-Bretonneux, one of whom was *Ltn* Witt of *Jasta 46,* who was killed.

Amongst the casualties during the day was 'the happy Canadian', Major Albert Carter of 19 Squadron, who was shot down and taken prisoner by *Ltn* Billik of *Jasta 62*. Carter, a native of Pointe de Bute, New Bruswick, was a professional soldier who had been commissioned in 1911. Serving with the infantry as a Major he had been wounded, and on recovery had transferred to the RFC, gaining his wings in the summer of 1917. Carter joined 19 Squadron that autumn, flying Spads, and was made a flight commander in November. At the beginning of January 1918 he had scored 15 victories and was awarded a DSO.[10]

The weather continued fine on May 20. Enemy aircraft were mainly inactive, but in the morning Capt Cyril Lowe and Lt Ronald Mark of 24 Squadron were in action with enemy scouts. Diving to attack one, the canvas on the right-hand top wing of Marks's SE5 began to break away. Under attack from another enemy scout, Mark broke off the action and dived west, but saw that Capt Lowe was going down with an enemy machine on his tail. Mark turned back and attacked this scout. The pilot abandoned his attack on Lowe and turned on Mark. Lowe saw this, turned back and fired 60 rounds into the enemy scout, which went down to land. On his return, Mark crashlanded at 84 Squadron's aerodrome. The SE5 burst into flames on impact, but Mark was unhurt.

MacLaren of 46 Squadron shot down a DFW north east of La Bassée in the evening – possibly *Ltn d Res* Meyer and *Ltn d Res* Röseler of *Fl Abt 7* who were both killed – and five minutes later he followed up this victory by flaming two balloons in quick succession south of Steenwerck.

'Mick' Mannock was now a superb formation leader and seemingly invincible as a fighter pilot. Ira Jones gave a graphic picture of Mannock at work in his diary entry for May 21.

'Mick cracked four Huns today! It sends a thrill through me as I write it. It has taken me seven weeks to do this.'

'In his first fight, which commenced at 12,000 feet, there were six Pfalz scouts flying east from the direction of Kemmel Hill. He shot one to pieces after firing a long burst from directly behind and above; another, he crashed. It spun into the ground after a deflection shot. Then Mick had a fine set-to with a

silver bird while his patrol looked on. It was a wonderful sight. First they waltzed round, with Mick tight on the bright lad's tail. Then the Pfalz half-rolled, falling a few hundred feet below him.

Mick did the same, firing as soon as he got his enemy in line. The Hun looped. Mick looped too, coming out behind and above the other, firing short bursts. The Pfalz spun. Mick spun also, firing as he did so. This shooting seemed to me a waste of ammunition. The Hun finally pulled out. Mick, who was now down to 4,000 feet, did the same. The Hun started twisting and turning, a sure sign of the "wind-up" and Mick administered the *coup de grace* with a burst from directly behind at about 25 yards range. The Hun went down, obviously out of control, and crashed.

This really was a remarkable exhibition of cruel, calculated Hun-strafing. I felt sorry for the Hun. He put up as fine a show of defensive fighting as I've ever seen.'

After they had landed Jones asked Mannock why he had fired while he and the Pfalz were both spinning. 'To intensify his wind-up', Mannock replied.

Mannock was awarded three Pfalz destroyed from this fight; his fourth victory, mentioned by Jones, was a Hannover two-seater, shot down over La Coureene in the morning patrol.

'Grid' Caldwell and William Young of the squadron had also claimed Pfalz during the fight. The Pfalz had been attacking British balloons when Caldwell first saw them. Attacking one Pfalz, Caldwell was attacked from behind by another, painted all black. After some jockeying for position, the Pfalz made a break for its own lines, with Caldwell in pursuit, overtaking it over the trenches near Ypres. The Pfalz was now down to within fifty feet of the ground and it zoomed and dived for about a mile, followed by Caldwell, firing all the time, until it finally crashed two miles west of Ypres.

The next day, 74 Squadron continued its success: Ira Jones shot down two Pfalz and Mannock another for his 36th victory. Little of 203 claimed his last victories during the day, shooting down an Albatros two-seater over St Leger at 11.40am and a DFW over Morchies five minutes later.

May 23 was fine in the morning, but in the afternoon the sky became overcast and a high wind sprang up. Patrols from 60 Squadron were out very early, Captain James Belgrave and Lt A Saunders sharing in the destruction of an Albatros over Fricourt at 5.50am, possibly flown by *Ltn* Angermund of *Jasta 76*, wounded in action.[11]

Caldwell was leading a Flight of three SE5s at 7.35pm when he saw four enemy aircraft – Pfalz D IIIs: two with silver wings, red tails and noses; two also with red tails and noses, but with black wings. Caldwell signalled the three SEs to follow him and dived to attack the Pfalz. Caldwell fought one Pfalz down from 9,000 to 6,000 feet and the enemy scout turned over onto its back and went down in a spin. Caldwell was then attacked by 'a lot of EA'. Unseen by Caldwell, these had come between him and the British lines. Caldwell's logbook carries the succinct comment: 'Chased home by 15 Pfalz'.

The fine weather finally broke on May 24 and it rained throughout the day. The commander of 2nd Army, General Plumer, made a surprise visit to 74 Squadron during the day, no doubt having heard of their successes. He praised the pilots on their fighting prowess, but looked somewhat startled by their casual form of dress. Plumer asked Caldwell to introduce him to Mannock, who ambled forward 'with no hat or collar, no Sam Browne, long hair and muffled, looking like a typical bushranger.' A startled Plumer stretched out his hand. Mannock took it in his own, rather dirty hand, and gave it a strong squeeze 'in his usual hearty manner'. Looking on, Ira Jones saw Plumer's face twitch and he thought the General was about to give a yell, but Plumer merely congratulated Mannock on his recent DSO. 'We expected that, sir.' Mannock replied. Plumer gave a slight puzzled smile. 'He went away wondering what sort of fellow this Mannock could be. I don't blame him.'[12]

Weather conditions were better the next day: the day was still overcast, with low cloud, and there were bright intervals, but enemy activity was very slight. In an evening patrol Capt Alfred Leitch of 65 Squadron scored his fourth victory, shooting down *Vzfw* Koller of *Jasta 76b* in the British lines. Koller was uninjured, was taken prisoner, and his Albatros No.7221/17 was designated G/III Brigade/7.

The Canadian, Frederick McCall, scored his first victory since joining 41 Squadron. McCall had served in 13 Squadron, flying RE8s, but was an aggressive pilot and had scored three victories while flying the two-seaters. He had been awarded an MC in January 1918 and a Bar in April. After two weeks leave he had then been posted to 41 Squadron to fly SE5s. He was to survive the war with 35 victories.

May 26 was very cloudy with poor visibility. Enemy activity in the air was again slight, but there were some combats. Ira Jones was in combat with Albatri. He had emptied his Lewis gun drum, had a stoppage in his Vickers, and was attacked from behind by an Albatros with a black tail and green fuselage. Luckily for Jones, Mannock saw his predicament and shot the Albatros off his tail. The last patrol by the squadron was typical of the type of fighting now becoming commonplace. Thirty SE5s and Bristol Fighters fought with over forty enemy aircraft for ten minutes. Friend and foe were in constant danger of collision, aircraft missing each other by the narrowest of margins. Jones and a Bristol Fighter attacked one Pfalz simultaneously and sent it down to crash by the railway line a mile east of Ploegstreet Wood. Jones made no claim: 'It was impossible to say whose bullets did the trick.'

On May 18, Ira Jones had commented in his diary. 'The Hun, by the way, has been very gutless of late. Day after day we patrol far over his lines The further over we go, the further east his fighters go. Can't make them fight at any price. I often wonder if they are trying to make us run out of petrol. It is very annoying to spot the devils and not be able to make them scrap. They've obviously got the wind up about something. The result of this listlessness on their part is to encourage us to shoot down the two-seaters who are co-operating with Fritz on the ground. These are the very people they are supposed to protect!'

The *jagdstaffel* had no doubt been ordered to conserve their strength for the coming German offensive, to commence on May 27, but this strategy cost the *Flieger Abteilungen* and *Schlachtstaffeln* many casualties.

The Aisne

In the battles of March and April the British infantry divisions engaged had suffered so many casualties that it was decided that five divisions should change places with French divisions on part of the front near Rheims. No threat was perceived on this quiet sector – its main feature, the Chemin des Dames, was known colloquially by its German occupants as the sanatorium of the west – and it would give the depleted British divisions time to rest and the opportunity to train their replacements. Only one squadron of the RAF was stationed in the sector, 52 Squadron (RE8), but the French Six and Tenth armies, holding the sector, had a strong air presence, with the Tenth Army employing 14 Escadrilles of fighters and observation aircraft, with an additional 24 fighter escadrilles stationed around Clermont, behind the front of the neighbouring Third Army.

The German Seventh Army, which was to make the assault had considerable air strength: *Jagdgeschwadern I* and *III* (each comprising four *jagdstaffeln,* a total strength of approximately 50 fighter aircraft); five additional *jagdstaffeln*; 14 *schlachtstaffeln*, in three groups; 23 *Flieger Abteilungen* and two *bombengeschwader.*

The RE8s of 52 Squadron made reconnaissance flights over the enemy areas, but the area was thickly wooded and it was not until the late evening of May 23 and the mornings of the 23 and 24 that clouds of dust were reported on the roads leading to the front. These observations did not appear to have aroused any particular interest, but they were in fact enemy heavy artillery moving into the area.[13] The French reconnaissance aircraft failed to discover the concentration by the German Seventh Army and when the blow fell on in the early morning of May 24, it came as an almost complete surprise.

The attack opened with one of the greatest bombardments of the war. Over 1,000 German heavy guns opened fire at 1.00am and the assault troops began to advance on the Chemin des Dames, between Rhiems and Soissons at 3.40am. The *Luftstreitkräfte* enjoyed complete command of the air over the battlefront and the advancing German infantry were supported by the *schlachtstaffeln,* making continuous attacks with bombs, hand grenades and machine guns on the retreating Allied troops. The French aerodrome at Fismes was heavily shelled as the day wore on and was eventually evacuated.[14] The aerodrome at Fismes, occupied by 52 Squadron, became untenable – one RE8 was destroyed by shellfire, and there were personnel casualties – and the squadron moved back to Cramaille aerodrome, already crowded with French aircraft. The aerodrome was bombed from dusk until dawn and ten French aircraft were destroyed by fire. The RE8s, were dispersed in the open and none were hit, but the squadron lost an observer in the retreat, taken prisoner wounded, and a pilot and observer shot down and killed by enemy aircraft.

The German infantry crossed the Aisne during the day and by nightfall had advanced over 12 miles into allied territory.

Further north, the weather was fine but very cloudy, and visibility was poor. James Slater of 64 Squadron shot down an Albatros over Cagnicourt at 10.55am for his 21st victory. Major Bishop, commanding 85 Squadron (SE5), which had arrived in France on May 22, scored his 48th victory and his squadron's first, destroying a two-seater east of Passchendaele at 4.32pm.

At 7.15pm, east of Estaires, William Claxton of 41 Squadron scored the first of his eventual 37 victories: a Fokker triplane sent down out of control. At 8.20pm, Major Dallas, leading a patrol from 40 Squadron took the SE5s down on a formation of eight Pfalz D IIIs over Hantay. Dallas shot down one of the Pfalz for his 32nd and last victory, and Gwilym Lewis shot down *Vzfw* Schiebler of *Jasta 30* in flames for his 10th.

Set against the successes of the day the RAF lost two of its most experienced and valued pilots. Captain Douglas Bell, and Lts W Hubbard and L Hamilton of 3 Squadron left at 12.10pm to intercept an enemy two-seater engaged in artillery observation near Thiepval. In his attack, Bell was hit by return fire from the enemy observer, crashed behind the enemy lines and was taken prisoner, but later died of his wounds. The enemy two-seater was sent down out of control and credited to all three Camel pilots. It was Bell's 20th victory.

A further blow to the RAF came that night. Collishaw the CO being on leave, Robert Little was in temporary command of 203 Squadron. Ronald Sykes remembers that the pilots were in the Mess drinking with the colonel from Wing when reports came in that German aircraft were bombing St Omer. Little took off at 10.30pm, leaving instructions with Sykes that flares were to lit on the aerodrome when he returned. When Little did not return that night there was no fear for his safety, it being thought that he had landed at another aerodrome, but at 5.00am the next morning his body was found at Noeux, about 30 miles away.

What exactly happened on Little's last flight will never be known, but it appears that he had been wounded in the groin, possibly by return fire from the German bomber he was attacking, and had crashed on landing, his Camel lying upside down and halfway across a hedge. The matron of the hospital where Little was taken later wrote to Mrs Little and told her that he had been wounded in both thighs and had died from loss of blood. Little had also suffered a fracture of the skull and ankle in the crash and it was obvious that even if he had been found in time the severity of his wounds would have prevented his recovery. Little was the most successful Australian fighter pilot of the war, with 47 enemy aircraft destroyed or out of control and many more forced to land or driven down.[15]

On May 28, Captain Hugh Saunders, leading A Flight from 84 Squadron, engaged eight enemy scouts over Warfusée and shot one down out of control at 9.20am. Lt Roy Manzer fired at an Albatros and sent it down out of control but was attacked by one of its companions from behind. Taking evasive action, Manzer hit the right hand top wing of the Albatros, the impact turning his SE5 upside down. On recovery, Manzer saw the Albatros going down minus it right hand wings and claimed it for his fourth victory

Mannock and Clements of 74 Squadron took off after tea 'for a bit of fun.' Flying to cut off a pair of enemy machines over Ploegstreet Wood, 'Clem' Clements saw a large formation of enemy machines getting into a favourable position to attack the two SE5s. Mannock had also seen the large formation but had gone down to take a snap shot at the two isolated scouts. Seeing that he would not make it in time before the large formation came down on him, Mannock turned west and dived underneath the formation, drawing them away from Clements. 'Clem says it was a rotten sight to see one SE being attacked by such a bunch. Had it been anyone else but Mick he would have been anxious about his safety. But we all believe no Hun will ever shoot Mick down.'[16]

One of the enemy scouts, a Pfalz, got very close to Mannock who suddenly went down on his back, spinning from 8 to 4,000 feet, seemingly out of control. The Pfalz pilot followed the SE down but pulled out at 5,000 feet to watch the crash. Mannock pulled out at 4,000 feet and dived for the British lines. The Pfalz pilot dived after the SE, but flew under Clements who attacked him. The enemy pilot turned to meet Clement's attack, 'a stout Hun this, a breed we don't often meet.' The rest of the enemy formation now dived to attack the two SEs, but Mannock and Clements dived towards the British lines over Ypres and the enemy scouts left them, coming under fire from British anti-aircraft batteries.

May 29 was cloudy for most of the day but cleared towards the evening. Mannock shot down an Albatros two-seater in flames north east of Armentiéres at 7.25pm and his Flight then joined forces with some SE5s from 85 Squadron, led by Capt Spenser 'Nigger' Horn. At 8.00pm the SE5s saw a dozen enemy scouts coming from the direction of Roubaix. In the fight which followed – which Jones described as 'a glorious and as frightening a dogfight as I've ever been in' – Mannock shot down a two Albatros scouts coloured slate-blue, and Clements shot down another for his first unshared victory.

The next day the weather was fine again, with good visibility. At 2.50pm a patrol of Camels from 43 Squadron attacked a formation of Albatros scouts, possibly from *Jasta 76*, over Combles. Geoffrey Bailey destroyed two, and Lts H C Daniel and Daly one each, but Lt P Bruce was killed during the action. Major William Bishop, flying alone, destroyed an enemy two-seater and an Albatros scout over Roulers at 3.45pm and at 7.50pm crashed another Albatros scout 5 miles north of Armentières. The Australian, Arthur Cobby shot down an Albatros in flames over Estaires at 4.40pm and within ten minutes destroyed a balloon for his 8th victory.

Ira Jones shot down an LVG in flames east of Bailleul at five minutes three in the afternoon, and in an evening patrol crashed a Halberstadt at 8.35pm southeast of Bois de Biez, the enemy machine crashing into the trees in flames.

Another blow to the RAF was the loss of Capt Edwin Benbow of 85 Squadron. Benbow had taken his Flight off the ground at five minutes to seven in the evening and forty minutes later they were combat with Albatri from *Jasta 51* over Nieppe Wood. In the fierce fighting Benbow was shot down by *Oblt* Gandert the *Staffelführer* of the *Jasta* for his third victory. Benbow had served with 40 Squadron in 1916 and 1917, and had scored eight victories before returning to England for a rest, later becoming an instructor. Benbow had returned to France as a flight commander in 85 Squadron on May 22 and his early death robbed the squadron of a highly experienced pilot.

Late in the evening of May 31, at 7.40pm, James Slater, leading a patrol from 64 Squadron, led his Flight down into a fight with eleven enemy scouts over La Bassée. It was to be 64 Squadron's most successful evening. In the fighting the 64 Squadron pilots claimed four of the enemy shot down: Slater claimed two Pfalz destroyed, Capt E D Atkinson, and Lts Lloyd-Evans and Farrow each destroyed a Pfalz. With the addition of a Pfalz shot down out of control east of Merris at 6.20am that morning by Edward Atkinson, the squadron's score for the day stood at six.

Seventy-Four Squadron flew patrols during the day. These yielded no positive results but Jones and Giles decided to fly a special mission after tea. At 7.10pm the two SEs saw 12 enemy scouts flying west from Menin at 10,000 feet. Jones and Giles climbed to the northeast, getting between the enemy scouts and Menin and attacked them east of Ploegstreet Wood. Jones fired at the scout in the rear of the enemy formation, but the enemy pilot half rolled and dived away from his attack. Jones then attacked the leader, closing to 75 yards from above and behind before opening fire. The enemy scout turned over onto its back and went down vertically, its wings folded up.

After an indecisive combat with some Pfalz, Jones saw another three just below him. These were attempting to climb to his height and Jones half rolled and fired a burst into the nearest, which went down in a spin over Comines. Giles had also dived to attack these Pfalz, but his engine had choked during the dive and a Pfalz had got on his tail, forcing him to dive away. Jones saw his predicament, fired at the Pfalz from long range and it left Giles and flew east.

By the evening of May 30 the German troops had penetrated as far as the Marne, but the sting had gone out of their attacks and the worst of the fighting was over. There was still some fighting, some of it very heavy, but by June 6 the French Sixth Army had been reinforced by nearly thirty divisions and the battle was over.

Casualties in the single-seater fighter squadrons had been heavy in May. Ninety-eight pilots had been killed, wounded or taken prisoner; in addition nearly fifty aeroplanes had been damaged, many struck off strength. With the good weather in June bringing even more intense fighting, there would be little change.

NOTES

1. G/II Brigade/7. LVG C V. No.3263/18 from *Fl Abt(A)266. Uffz* Nievitecki and *Uffz* Prieh both captured.

2. These victories are given in the lists as claimed on May 6, but Caldwell's logbook entry for May 7 clearly gives: '1 Triplane out of control. 1 Triplane out of control with Roxburgh-Smith, confirmed by AA.'

3. Two days later, the squadron received news that Piggott survived his crash landing and was being looked after by Australian troops.

4. Watson had been born in New Zealand, but was living in Sydney on the outbreak of war.

5. Letter to author.

6. Durrant now lies in Danzig Alley, the British military cemetary at Memetz, five miles east of Albert.

7. *Tiger Squadron*, Wing Commander Ira 'Taffy' Jones, W H Allen, 1954.

8. Ibid.

9. Ibid.

10. Carter was killed in a flying accident in 1919 while test flying a Fokker D VII. The Fokker broke up in mid-air and Carter was killed. The Fokker D VII was an extremely strong aeroplane, but many German pilots had

sabotaged their D VIIs when handing them over to the Allies. It may well be that Carter met his death in one of these aircraft.

11. The German lists give Angermund as being wounded at 9.50 (German Time), but there is little doubt that he was the pilot involved in the 60 Squadron action. Possibly either the German time, or the British time for the action, is incorrect.

12. Ibid.

13. The GOC of the British IX Corps was uneasy about the possibility of a German attack, but the representations that he made to the HQ of the French Sixth Army were rejected.

14. The aerodrome was overrun by the German forces on May 28: all its aircraft, fuel supplies and hangars were captured intact.

15. Robert Alexander Little, DSC+ and DSO+, Croix de Guerre, lies today in the British cemetery at Wavans. The cemetery is lonely, tiny by comparison with many in France – only thirty or so graves, some of them German – but Little lies with his great contemporary, Major James Thomas Byford McCudden VC, DSO+MC+, MM, and Croix de Guerre.

16. Ibid.

CHAPTER TWENTY-TWO

THE BATTLE OF THE MATZ

June opened badly for the RAF, in particular 40 Squadron. Early in the morning, Major Roderic Dallas took off with a squadron patrol to bomb ground targets in the Merville area. Having returned from the bombing, Dallas took off alone at 10.10am to look for enemy two-seaters. He saw none and was returning to Bruay when he was attacked by two Fokker Triplanes from *Jasta 14*. The enemy pilots had flown across the lines to attack British balloons and dived on the lone SE5 from the west. To be attacked by enemy scouts from the west was unusual and Dallas was possibly watching the eastern sky when the triplanes attacked. Whatever the reason, Dallas was taken completely by surprise and was shot down by the *Staffelführer*, *Ltn* Werner, for his sixth victory. After paying tribute to the positive effect on the morale of 40 Squadron under the leadership of Dallas, Gwilym Lewis summed up the shock felt by the squadron. 'We simply couldn't believe our ears when we first got the news, but all the same it was true. It wasn't a matter of admiring the "old fool"; we simply adored him.'

In the afternoon there was another blow: Jones wrote in his diary: 'Poor old Cairns was shot down this afternoon. No doubt he is dead. One of his wings came off.'

Ira Jones had led the early morning patrol from 74 Squadron. The day was grey but cloudless and there was a crisp bite to the dawn air. After dropping their bombs and engaging in an indecisive fight with two Albatros scouts, Jones saw a Pfalz D III returning from attacking British balloons. Jones made a flank attack on this Pfalz and shot it down in a spin to crash a mile and a half south east of Dickebusch Lake.

Landing from this patrol Jones found that B Flight, led by Wilfred Young, had also been out and Young had shot down two Hannover two-seaters. Jones was going on leave the next

day and Caldwell suggested that he should not fly for the rest of the day, but Mannock, who was to lead the afternoon patrol, teased Jones that if he flew on the patrol he would be sure to be shot down. Jones took a bet of 100 francs that he would return, knowing full well that in a patrol led by Mannock little harm could come to him. Jones later wrote: 'The flight with Mick in the afternoon turned out to be the hottest dog fight I've been in for a few days.'

Mannock led a combined force of ten SE5s from A and C Flights, and at 13,000 feet, in a cloudless sky over Estaires, they fought seven Pfalz D III with dark fuselages and white tails. In the ten minutes fight, Mannock destroyed two of the Pfalz and sent another down out of control, but *Ltn* Billik of *Jasta 52* got on the tail of Cairnes' SE5 and shot its wings off from 25 yards range.[1] That night Jones wrote: 'Cairnes was a great gentleman, and we are all very cut up. As I write this, just before packing to go home, there are tears in my eyes. I cannot imagine why we have no parachutes.'[2]

In this bad day for the RAF, only nine positive victories were claimed by the fighter squadrons, plus two balloons. Additional casualties were two pilots killed and two more taken POW.

For the next four days, although the weather was generally fine, enemy activity in the air was below normal. On June 2 only one victory was claimed but three pilots were killed in action. Two victories were claimed the following day for the cost of one pilot wounded. On June 4, Bishop shot down an Albatros in flames, which fell into the sea three miles of the coast at Nieuport at 11.28am, and another out of control over Leffingckoucke nine minutes later. There were no casualties. On June 5, a balloon was the only victory, but three pilots were killed and two wounded.

The Battle of Matz

During the last days of May and the early days of June it was evident that the Germans would mount another attack. There were indications that this would come from those German armies which had been fighting on the Aisne, and that the thrust would be towards Compiègne. On June 7, Foch telegramed British General HQ to say that there were strong indications of an impending attack on the Montdidier-Noyon front. The *Luftstreitkräfte* had been very active over this front, which no doubt explains the relative lack of activity over the British sectors in the north. Foch requested that there should be a concentration of British air strength – both bombing and fighting squadrons – over the Nesle-Roye sector, in addition to the RAF squadrons all ready operating with the French. Two days later the British HQ informed Foch that the air strength of the British Fourth Army had been increased by eight fighter squadrons, three day bomber squadrons and four night bombing squadrons. The fighter squadrons of IX Brigade, already working with the French, 32, 73, 2 AFC, 43 and 80 Squadrons, moved south on June 3.

The German attack began at 3.20am on June 9, between Montdidier and Noyon. The German forces had eleven divisions in the front line with another seven in support; the French with eight forward divisions and four in support. In the centre of the attack, along the Matz, the enemy made some progress, adding to this two days later, but the French army was well prepared and counterattacked on June 11, taking back much of the ground and convincing the enemy that nothing could be gained by prolonging the battle. The maximum penetration by the German forces had been six miles; it had captured guns and taken prisoners, but these successes were small in comparison to the offensives in the previous three months.

The fighter squadrons of IX Brigade were used in groundstrafing attacks during the battle. Ground targets were plentiful and the low flying aircraft caused many casualties. To aid the French counter attack on June 11, the French requested that the German balloon line be attacked. Seven balloons were up and were fiercely defended by the *jagdstaffeln*. The pilots of 73 Squadron were groundstrafing throughout the day and were in combat with both the *jagdstaffeln* and *schlachtstaffeln*. Three Fokker D.VIIs were claimed and a two-seater, but two American pilots, attached to the squadron, Lts J I Carpenter and C W Douglas, were shot down and killed by enemy fighters. Another American, Lt Lt J Ackerman, claimed a Fokker D.VII, but his Camel was shot about and Ackerman was wounded. Three other Camels were badly damaged in the fighting, one by anti-aircraft fire.

During the fighting in the south the northern sectors had been quiet but not completely inactive. On June 6 enemy air activity increased and was 'considerable.' Patrols from 1

Squadron were in combat over the Ploegsteert area at 7.30am and Percy Clayson shot down two Pfalz in flames. One of these Pfalz was *Vzfw* Heller of *Jasta 40* who was killed; the other possibly *Ltn* Derlin of *Jasta 20*, also killed over Ploegsteert. At 6.00pm the SE5s of 29 Squadron were in action with Pfalz and the new Fokker D.VIIs over Estaires. Lt A Reed destroyed a Pfalz D.III north west of Estaires, and Lts B R Rolfe and C H Largesse both shot down Fokker D.VIIs. Rolfe's victory was *Ltn* Mendel of *Jasta 18,* who was killed; that of Largesse, *Ltn d Res* Hans Schultz of *Jasta 18,* who was taken prisoner.[3]

The weather was generally fine on the morning of June 7. Capt Cyril Parry of 56 Squadron took his Flight off the ground at 8.20am and crossed the Front Lines at 11,000 feet over Albert. The squadron was going through a fallow period in respect of definite victories. It had fought a considerable number of combats, but the last positive victory had been on May 13. June 7 was to bring a change in luck. Parry saw three two-seaters: one over Fricourt at 3,000 feet, and two over Grévillers, all flying west.

Parry attacked the pair, getting under the tail of the first and opening fire. After a short burst the enemy machine went down out of control. Parry followed, firing half a drum of Lewis and a number of rounds from his Vickers. The two-seater burst into flames and crashed south east of Achiet-le-Petit, killing *Uffz* Kersten and *Gefr* Mertens of *Fl Abt (A) 211.*

Twenty-five minutes later Parry attacked another pair of two-seaters in the same area. Closing to within 30 yards of the first, Parry killed or wounded the observer, who slumped down over his gun, and the enemy machine went down to crash northeast of Grévillers. Parry then attacked its companion, firing the remainder of his ammunition into it from 20 yards. The observer collapsed over the side of his cockpit and the enemy pilot dived away. Eugene Macdonald then attacked and the two-seater crashlanded by the side of the other. Parry, Macdonald and Boger followed this two-seater down to within 300 feet of the ground and were considerably shot about by small arms fire, but all three SE5s returned safely. One of the last two-seaters was possibly that of *Fl Abt (A) 263,* who had *Ltn d Res* Toepfer killed in action on June 7.

That night the pilots went into Le Touquet to celebrate Parry's victories. For the first time in his life Parry was slightly drunk and was knocked down the stairs of the hotel by a burly MP!

On June 13, a patrol of SE5s from 60 Squadron – Capt James Belgrave and Lts Duncan, Gordon and Lewis – sent a hostile two-seater down out of control east of Albert. Belgrave followed this machine down into the mist. His SE5 was hit by groundfire and crashed, killing Belgrave.[4]

During the action, Lewis had engine failure and he force landed in enemy held territory between Albaincourt and Chaulnes, smashing undercarriage of his SE5.

Henry Gordon, on his first flight over the Lines, saw Lewis crash, landed nearby and ran to the crash to see if he could help. German troops then appeared and opened fire. Gordon ran back to his SE5, calling for Lewis to follow, but Lewis walked towards the enemy troops to distract them and give Gordon a chance to take off unmolested. Gordon circled the scene: Lewis was surrounded by the enemy troops.

During May the activities of the German night bombers had caused a great deal of damage. On the night of May 19 two Ordnance Depots had been attacked and 20 officers and men were killed and 78 wounded. On the night of May 20 the bombers attacked again, bombing the depot at Blarges from 10.15pm until 4.00am the following morning. At the beginning of the attack a hangar containing cordite was hit by an incendiary bomb and set alight. The flames guided successive waves of German aircraft to the target and the whole depot was soon burning out of control. Ammunition began to explode and the whole area became an inferno. The explosions continued throughout the day and 6,000 tons of ammunition were destroyed. That night the bombers returned, bombing the depot at Saigneville. The attack was again successful: 5,600 tons of ammunition were destroyed, including sixty nine million rounds of small arms ammunition.

To deal with these attacks the first night fighter squadron of the RAF, 151 Squadron, was formed from Flights of the Home Defence Squadrons in England. The first Flight of 151 Squadron, equipped with Sopwith Camels, arrived in France on June 16, the remainder of the squadron arriving on June 19 and stationed on the coast at Marquise before moving to Fontaine-sur-Maye, west of Doullens on June 23.

On June 16 Mannock scored his penultimate victory with 74 Squadron. Ira Jones, just back from leave, wrote: 'Giles and I went to church service and Communion in No.1 Hangar this morning … While I was in church, Mick was killing Huns over Zillebeke – a couple of black Pfalz.' The SE5s had attacked these Pfalz and Mannock had shot down two, three miles south of Zillebeke Lake, the first destroyed, the second out of control.

Gerald Maxwell, who had returned to 56 Squadron on June 11 for a refresher course, was flying in a squadron patrol when the cowling of his SE5s came loose. On his way back to Valheureux, Maxwell was attacked by a two-seater near Hamelincourt. Maxwell, at a disadvantage with his loose cowling, nevertheless fought this enemy machine for sometime, finally putting a good burst into it that caused the enemy pilot to dive away east. This was possibly a machine from *Fl Abt 2* who had *Oblt* Schacht wounded in action over

Frémicourt. Maxwell then landed at 85 Squadron aerodrome, had the cowling secured and took off again. Over Arras he saw another two-seater, just over the Front Line and east him. Maxwell dived on this machine, firing both guns. Smoke and flames came out of the enemy machine and it went down to crash near Wancourt at 7.35am, killing *Vzfw* Jockwer and *Ltn d Res* Spack of *Fl Abt (A) 284*. On landing at Valheureux Maxwell found that both two-seaters had been confirmed as crashed by British AA batteries.

The day was fine on June 17 with just a few clouds at 10,000 feet. In the morning Mannock shot down a silver coloured Halberstadt over Armentières for his last victory with 74 Squadron. Roxburgh-Smith shot down a lone Fokker D.VII in an afternoon patrol. The enemy machine was first seen at 19,000 feet. Mannock and Roxburgh-Smith flew below it to lure it down under the other SE5s but the enemy pilot was too cautious and refused the bait. Mannock then flew in front of the Fokker and slightly below it, tempting the enemy pilot to come down to his level. 'It was laughable to watch Mick's machine swinging from side to side (he was kicking his rudder) as he pulled the Hun's leg. Occasionally he would pump handle his controls and the machine would bounce about like a bucking bronco. Very funny it was. I could imagine Mick roaring with laughter.' Roxburgh-Smith had meanwhile been closing the distance and when he finally opened fire the Fokker went down on its back. Ira Jones followed it down, but the enemy machine flicked over, went down in a near vertical dive, came out lower down and continued with a gigantic zoom, ending again on its back, the pilot either dead or unconscious.

In the morning, the SE5s of 84 Squadron were flying an escort for the DH4s of 205 Squadron when a Fokker Triplane joined the British formation, mistaking them for friendly machines. Capt Jack Sorsoleil was the first to attack the triplane, which stalled, then did a half spin before diving. Sorsoleil turned away with gun trouble, but Lt Matthews followed the enemy machine down and saw it flatten out and dive away to the east. Matthews dived, got behind the triplane, and fired a long burst from both guns. The triplane was now at 1,000 feet and began to glide down, but Lt Carl Falkenberg dived vertically and fired both guns at it. It fell over onto its back and went down out of control in a series of stalls.

At midday a patrol from 24 Squadron fought with *Jasta 15* flying their newly issued Fokker D.VIIs.[5] An American pilot, William Lambert from Ohio, shot down two of the enemy machines, his fire smashing the tailplane of one and sending another down in flames, both crashing at Villers-Bretonneux. One of these Fokkers was flown by *Ltn* Schafer who managed to safely land his damaged fighter. The other brightly painted Fokkers – red noses, Prussian blue and white tailplanes – scattered under the attack and dived away east, but *Ltn* Kurt

Wüsthoff, the *staffelführer,* was separated from his *Jasta* and dived away from an attack by an SE5 flown by Lt J H Southey. Wüsthoff spun down, then recovered and made for the safety of his own lines, but Ian McDonald, Horace Barton and George Johnson, chased after him and forced him to land in the British lines at Cachy. Wüsthoff had been badly wounded and was taken to hospital, where he was later visited by Major Robeson, the CO, of 24 Squadron.[6]

The pilots of 85 Squadron made claims for five aircraft destroyed during the day. In an early morning patrol, Lt Alex Cunnigham-Reid destroyed a two-seater at 6.45am east of Bailleul and Lts Canning, Springs and Grider shared in another. Flying alone, Bishop claimed a two-seater in flames over Staden at 10.25am, another over Sailly-sur-Lys twenty-five minutes later, and an Albatros scout destroyed over Laventie at 10.55am.

At 8.20am, in a fight with *Jasta 7* over Dickebusch, two pilots of 210 Squadron were shot down. The eight Camels had come under attack from the *Jasta* south east of Zillebeke. The *Staffelführer,* Josef Jacobs, flying his black Fokker triplane pushed one Camel down, but turned away as an Albatros flown by *Uffz* Eigenbrodt also attacked it. The pilot, 2Lt C Strickland, wounded by Eigenbrodt's fire, crashlanded behind the British Lines. 2Lt K Campbell was shot down by *Ltn* Hillmann, his Camel disintegrating in mid-air. Another Camel was claimed by *Uffz* Mertens, but 210 Squadron lost only two aircraft.

The weather became overcast in the afternoon of June 18. At 9.10am Cyril Parry of 56 Squadron led his Flight into an action that was to win him a DFC. Seeing enemy scouts about to land on their aerodrome at Suzanne, Parry took his Flight down to attack them.

Parry opened fire at one Albatros from 200 yards and the enemy pilot immediately dived and landed a mile from the aerodrome. Attacked by other Albatri from above him, Parry could not follow this Albatros down but watched Burden attack another of the enemy scouts, sending it down out of control. Parry then fired a red light, signalling the SE5s to reform, intending to lead them in a strafing run over the enemy aerodrome, but they were all too busy fighting with the remaining Albatri. Parry dived back into the fight, shooting an Albatros off the tail of Mulroy's SE5. This Albatros went down in a vertical dive and was seen to crash by Burden. Parry then saw another Albatros about to attack Lt Molyneux, but he shot at it and succeeded in driving it off. As he turned away, Parry saw that two Albatri were taking off from Suzanne aerodrome. He dived to attack these, going down to 400 feet but was forced to break away with gun stoppages.

The Canadian, Henry Burden, shot at one Albatros which dived to 1,000 feet before breaking up under his fire, and on the way back to the lines he attacked two balloons, which were

pulled down. Burden landed at 85 Squadron's aerodrome to visit Bishop, his brother-in-law, met the American pilots Larry Callahan and Elliot White Springs and learnt that the third member of the triumvirate, John McGavock Grider had been shot down and killed that morning. Burden's diary records that Bishop was shortly returning to England with 'sixty seven Huns to his credit.'

As a result of the fight over Suzanne, Major Euan Gilchrist, commanding 56 Squadron, recommended Parry for a decoration, for showing 'exceptional skill and dash as a patrol leader,' adding that the moral effect of the attack on the enemy aerodrome must have been very great as a number people had gathered on the aerodrome to watch the fight.[7]

At 8.00am the Camels of 54 Squadron left on a bombing raid and were attacked by *Jasta 7* north Armentières. *Oberflm* Schoenfelder forced 2Lt J Connolly to land in a field close by the Ypres to Comines railway. Connolly was later taken to the aerodrome of *Jasta 7* and introduced to Schoenfelder who gave him a tour of the aerodrome and its machines.

Uttz Mertens and *Ltn* Nebgen each claimed a Camel from this fight but only Connolly was lost. *Ltn* Hillmann, described by Jacobs as one of his best pilots, and who had killed 2Lt Campbell of 210 Squadron the previous day, was shot down and killed in the fight, possibly by Lt M Burger of 54 Squadron.

The DH4s of 205 Squadron flew another bombing raid in the morning. At 10.50am they were being chased back to the Lines by 15 enemy scouts, but their escort, again the SE5s of 84 Squadron, intervened, Capt Walter Southey and Capt John Ralston leading the SE5s down on the enemy machines. In the general fighting, Lt Manzer saw a blue triplane of the edge of the combat and dived on it, but both his guns jammed and he half rolled under the enemy machine. After circling around each other for a few minutes, Manzer succeeded in putting a burst of 50 rounds into the side of the triplane and its struts collapsed, sending it down out of control in a vertical dive. Both Ralston and Southey each claimed a Fokker D.VII out of control from the fight.

The next day the weather over the whole Front was extremely bad, with drizzling rain and clouds down to 800 feet. Caldwell washed out the day's patrols, but sent a Flight out to ascertain conditions nearer the Front Line. The SE5s, led by Jones, patrolled from Ypres to the Forest of Nieppe, but after an hour gave it up as hopeless and returned. An hour after landing, 'Nigger' Horn of 85 Squadron telephoned to tell Caldwell that Bishop had just shot down four enemy aircraft.

Bishop was to return to England the next day and determined to win more victories he had taken off in the heavy drizzle. Over Ploegsteert he sighted three Pfalz with black and white tails, which turned away as Bishop came down behind them. As Bishop manoeuvred for a favourable position, two additional Pfalz came down on him from above. Bishop hurriedly opened fire from 120 yards at one of the initial Pfalz and killed the pilot. The Pfalz turned over and went down. The two remaining Pfalz began to climb into the clouds, but collided and broke up in midair, the wreckage falling beside that of the first Pfalz, burning on the ground.

The two Pfalz who had been above Bishop now climbed away, but one gave Bishop an easy shot from fifty yards and he sent it down to crash. Bishop turned away from the scene of the fight and made to return, but an enemy two-seater loomed up out of the mist. Bishop got underneath this machine and opened fire. One wheel came off under Bishop's fire before the two-seater went down to crash, bursting into flames as it hit the ground.

The incredulous pilots of 74 Squadron went to St Omer to read Bishop's account of the fight. They could not understand why a formation of enemy aircraft was flying in such bad weather – the German pilots were generally known not to fly in unfavourable weather conditions – and why, being in the same area, they had not seen the enemy aircraft. 'Luck of the game,' I suppose, commented Ira Jones. Jones was later asked by the Colonel why they had not helped Bishop, but exonerated them from any failure because of the appalling weather conditions.

Conditions improved towards the late evening. *Uffz* Eigenbrodt and *Uffz* Mertens of *Jasta 7* took off to attack British balloons near Hazebrouck. The two *Jasta 7* pilots had sent one balloon down smoking badly, and were circling around the other when the anti-aircraft bursts around them alerted a Flight of SE5s of 74 Squadron and the Camels of 4 Squadron AFC. Mertens went down to attack the remaining balloon, but Eigenbrodt saw the approaching British fighters and dived away to the east. The combined force of SE5s and Camels attacked Mertens. Some of the SE5 pilots pulled away from the fight: the sky was full of fighters, all trying to shoot down the lone Pfalz, and there was a serious danger of collision. Finally, Capt Arthur Cobby of 4 Squadron AFC got behind the Pfalz and from a range of 30 yards shot it down to crash in the British Lines at Bailleul at 6.45pm.[8] Max Mertens was killed in the crash and his body was later placed in one of 74 Squadron's hangars at Clairmarais, where he was found to be unshaven, with no collar or tie, and wearing a very shabby and worn Swallow-tailed Beaufort dress coat, and breeches, also in poor condition. There was much speculation amongst the Allied pilots as to the reason for this strange attire, the general opinion being that the morning being unfit for flying the pilots of the *Jasta* had spent it drinking.

For the next seven days the weather conditions remained poor. There were few combats. In the evening of June 21,

Jacobs had a long fight with a Camel from 210 Squadron flown by Lt R C Carr. After twenty minutes Carr broke off the action, but *Ltn* Schoenfelder attacked him from above, shot the Camel about, and Carr force landed near Menin. Carr was unwounded and later told Jacobs that he had intended to shoot them both down, one after the other!

In the evening of June 25 the Camels of 54 Squadron were on patrol over the Forest of Nieppe when they were attacked by enemy scouts. In the fight, Jacobs of *Jasta 7* was attacked by Lt O J Jones-Lloyd, in Jacob's own words, 'involving me in a very difficult dogfight.' Forced down by Jones-Lloyd, Jacobs was saved by the intervention of *Ltn* Degelow of *Jasta 40,* who forced Jones-Lloyd to leave Jacobs. Climbing back into the fight, Jacobs joined Degelow in an attack on Jones-Lloyd and his Camel went down in flames to crash by the side of the Wervicq to Menin road. Luckily, Jones-Lloyd survived the crash to be taken prisoner. Fifty Four Squadron lost another pilot in the fighting: Lt W H Stubbs was wounded and taken prisoner but later died of his wounds.

Jasta 7 were in action the next day, again with Sopwith Camels. The pilots of 210 Squadron were dropping bombs on Bac St Maur when they were attacked by the *Jasta*. Jacobs was fighting three of the Camels when he saw a Fokker D.VII going down past him – 'the right wing exploding into a thousand pieces. He crashed vertically and I recognised the Fokker of "Wasserman" by its golden star.'[9] Jacobs then shot down Lt C Boothman, who crashed into the castle gardens of Hennis. Jacobs later went to the scene of the crash but there was little left of the Camel, only a small amount of debris with Boothman's body lying next to them.

Capt Coombes and Lts Sanderson and Unger shared in the destruction of three Fokker DVIIs and two out of control. Schönfelder was awarded to an American pilot with the squadron, Lt Kenneth Unger, for the first of his eventual 14 victories. Twenty-five minutes later in this patrol, the Camels were in combat with Pfalz D IIIs west of Armentières and claimed three out of control.

June 27 was a fine day and there was a great deal of fighting. In the morning 84 Squadron fought with a large number of enemy scouts, the largest fight it had yet had.

The SE5s left the ground at 8.15am in squadron strength, the Flights led by Capts Ralston and Sorsoleil, with Sorsoleil's Flight flying top cover. Ralston saw AA bursts in the vicinity of Morlancourt and flying to investigate found an LVG two-seater. Ralston had seen several small formations of enemy scouts in the area and he waited for a favourable opportunity to attack the LVG. When the SE5s finally went down, all firing at the two-seater, they chased it for nearly 12 miles behind the lines, but were constantly harassed by enemy scouts. Eventually the SE5s turned on their attackers, but more joined them and almost 40 enemy scouts arrived to join in the action.

John Ralston shot down a Pfalz, which crashed near Villers-Bretonneux, but came under attack from so many enemy scouts that he had to dive to 50 feet and contour chase towards the distant lines. The enemy pilots were persistent, however, and he had to turn to fight them off. His SE5 was hit in the petrol tank, spraying him with fuel and his engine caught alight. Ralston force landed as quickly as he could, coming down near Cauchy. Within thirty seconds of landing the SE5 blew up and was totally destroyed by fire, but Ralston was unhurt.

Sorsoleil had taken his Flight down into the fight. At 3,000 feet he shot down a Pfalz that broke up and fell over Villers-Bretonneux, and 2Lt William Nel claimed an Albatros out of control. The SE5s were finally forced to break off the action, both by the overwhelming odds and lack of fuel and ammunition. All the SE5s were badly shot about in this action but surprisingly the squadron had only one loss: Lt D B Jones was badly wounded and died of his wounds six days later.

In the evening six SE5s of 56 Squadron took off on patrol. Gerald Maxwell, still flying with the squadron, led two SE5s, and Capt Cyril Crowe another two. The SE5s led by Crowe saw no enemy aeroplanes, but Maxwell's trio had better luck, attacking three Fokker D VIIs from behind and below at 16,000 feet over Morcourt. These D.VIIs were the first of the type to be seen by the squadron and Maxwell attacked one that 'wobbled a bit and dived, pursued by Lts Parry and Irwin.' Maxwell, who had zoomed away to change his Lewis gun drum, then saw that three Fokker Triplanes were preparing to go down after Parry and Irwin and he attacked them from out of the sun. 'Got on one EA's tail without him seeing me. I got to about ten yards range, so close I could see his face and goggles, and fired both guns.' The triplane, which had a black and white check marking round its fuselage, went down in a sideslip before turning over onto its side and slowly spinning down.

There were seven pilots killed during the day's fighting and another four were taken POW, three of whom died of their wounds. Worthy of note is a combat fought by Capt E B Drake of 209 Squadron with a Pfalz D.III. Drake shot this Pfalz down in flames and the pilot, *Ltn* Steinbrecher of *Jasta 46,* was seen to parachute from his burning aeroplane, reputedly the first German pilot to do so.

June 28 was again a fine day. It started badly for 56 Squadron. The first patrol went out at 3.45am, and over Miraumont at 4.45am, Lt Allan Garrett's SE5 was hit by anti-aircraft fire. Garrett was slightly wounded and went down to be taken POW. It was a lucky day for the German gunners. In a later patrol Lt Hollerans' machine was also hit, a near burst smashing a foot off the leading edge of the lower right hand wing and carrying away the top wing Lewis gun, part of which hit Holleran on the head.

In the evening, Maxwell led a large patrol of eleven machines in the last patrol of the day. An hour after taking off the SE5s were in action with a large group of enemy scouts – Fokker D VIIs, Albatri and Pfalz D.IIIs – at 12,000 feet over Dompierre. It was the largest fight the squadron had been in for sometime. Maxwell shot down one of the Fokker D VIIs; its right wings broke off and it crashed near Dompeirre. Crowe shot down a Pfalz, fighting until his ammunition ran out; Holleran was also credited with a Pfalz, but on landing it was found that his SE5 had been hit in a longeron, there were three or four bullet holes through the engine cowling and numerous holes in the wings. Even more potentially serious, Holleran's ammunition had been hit and was still smoking after he had landed. William Irwin had been forced down by two of the Albatri but at 2,000 feet had managed to outmanoeuvre them. He got on the tail of one and a drum of Lewis and 200 rounds of Vickers sent it down in a vertical dive, engine full on, to crash in a wood near Dompierre. Irwin was then chased back across the lines at 200 feet by other enemy scouts. Tom Hazen had been shot through the radiator and had forced landed at Harponville, but the only other loss was Lt Harry Austin, who was shot down by *Ltn d Res* Thuy of *Jasta 28* and taken prisoner.

Capt Cobby of 4 Squadron AFC claimed three victories during the day's fighting: an LVG east of Outtersteen at five minutes to three; a Pfalz D.III in flames ten minutes later south east of Estaires, and in a evening patrol he destroyed an Halberstadt over Wytschaete at 6.40pm.

There were few combats the next day and only one fighter pilot was shot down and taken prisoner.

The last day of the month was again fine with good visibility. The fine weather brought the *Luftstreitkräfte* out in force, but although there were many combats they were mainly indecisive and only a few victories were claimed by the fighter squadrons.

Major Arthur Keen of 40 Squadron attacked three Fokker Triplanes over Beauchamps at 12.40pm. One turned sharply in order to get on the tail of Keen's SE5, but Keen looped and came out 100 feet above the enemy machine. Keen dived, and although he managed to get off only ten shots before overshooting, the Fokker went down in a flat spin. Keen dived after it and fired several bursts until the triplane broke up in midair, its wings falling off.

Further north the Camels of 204 Squadron were in action with Fokker D VIIs of *Marine-Feld Jasta 1* and lost two pilots killed, possibly by *Ltnz* Thone of the *Jasta*.

Hostile balloons were shot down during the day. A patrol from 40 Squadron, Lts Whitten and Strange, led by Capt

George McElroy, shared in the destruction of one over Annay at 10.45am, and Lt Archie Buchanan of 210 Squadron destroyed another north east of Estaires at 11.10am for the first of his seven victories.

June had been a bad month for the fighter squadrons. Casualties were again heavy. Eighty-eight pilots had been killed, wounded or taken prisoner, and July was to see the loss of three of the RAF's finest pilots.

NOTES

1. Billik is credited with bringing down several other successful RAF pilots. John Malone of Naval 3 (10 victories); Major Tilney, the CO of 40 Squadron; Major A D Carter of 19 Squadron (29 victories) and Capt Arthur Claydon of 32 Squadron (7 victories).

2. Ibid.

3. The Fokker D.VII, No.368/18, was the first of the type to be captured. It was designated G/II Brigade/14.

4. Belgrave was an experienced fighter pilot. He had scored six victories flying Sopwith 1 1/2 Strutters with 45 Squadron in 1917, had joined 60 Squadron in April 1918, and was given command of B Flight on June 4. Belgrave had gained another 12 victories while with 60 Squadron, bringing his total to 18.

5. The Fokker D.VII entered service with the *jagdstaffeln* in April 1918, the finest fighter to be used by the *Luftstreitkräfte* in the war. It was strong, fast, manoeuvrable, and easy to fly, with the apparent facility to transform a poor pilot into a good one, and a good pilot into an exceptional one. At first the Mercedes-engined Fokkers gave the fighter pilots of the RAF little trouble, but re-engined with the BMW III engine, which vastly improved its performance, it became an extremely formidable opponent and was arguably the finest fighter aeroplane to see service with any of the combatants on the Western Front in the airwar of 1914-1918. Its reputation was such that it was specifically named in the terms of the Armistice designating specific items of equipment that were to be surrendered: *'In erster alle apparate D.VII.'* – 'especially all first-line D VII aircraft.'

6. Wüsthoff was flying *Ltn* Hantelmann's Fokker D.VII when he was shot down. The Fokker D.VII, No. 382/18, with a large skull and crossbones on the blue fuselage, was designated G/V Brigade/17. Kurt Wüsthoff had 27 victories at the time of his capture.

7. Signing a book belonging to the author, Cyril Parry added to his signature. 'An also ran in a stable of good horses.' It was the quality of these 'also rans' which made the strength of RAF in 1918 so formidable.

8. Merten's Pfalz D.III was designated G/II Brigade/16.

9. "Wasserman" was *Oberflm* Kurt Schönfelder.

CHAPTER TWENTY-THREE

THE LAST GERMAN OFFENSIVE

Enemy aircraft were very active in the morning of July 1. The weather was fine and visibility good.

A patrol SE5s from 56 Squadron took off at 5.10am and were patrolling the Suzanne to Bapaume area when British anti-aircraft bursts over Aveluy Wood pointed out an enemy two-seater. Capt Walter Copeland attacked this machine but both his guns jammed and as he turned away he was attacked by a bright red Fokker Triplane. As Copeland dived away from the triplane it was attacked by Gerald Maxwell, who got underneath it and fired from close range. The enemy pilot dived on Maxwell, firing as he came and Maxwell had to take violent evasive action to escape his fire. The triplane then dived away to the east, followed by Maxwell, who got on its tail and opened fire again, sending the triplane down in a steep dive. 'Billy' Crowe then appeared, chased after the triplane and opened fire at point blank range. 'The Triplane fell to pieces in my Aldis sight. I was then about 3,500 feet over Thiepval.'[1]

Crowe then saw a formation of Fokker D VIIs flying east, with one a good two miles behind the others. Crowe chased after this machine, 'he was very fast,' and opened fire at 200 yards, holding down his triggers as he gradually overhauled the Fokker. The enemy pilot made no attempt to evade Crowe's fire and the Fokker finally crashed north of Albert.

Ten SE5s of 24 Squadron left Conteville at 7.10am; Capt Selwyn leading the five machines of the bottom Flight with the other five flying top cover. The patrol area was between Amiens and Chaulnes at between 15 and 16,000 feet, and over Caix they saw enemy aircraft 2,000 feet below them – a mixed group of Albatri and Fokker D VIIs. Selwyn led the SE5s south until the sun was at their backs before going down to attack the first Flight of five D VIIs. The Fokkers – four with red fuselages and green wings, the fifth a dirty grey-green all over – scattered under the attack and the SE5 pilots each picked an opponent. The fighting went down into the other enemy machines below, increasing the number of enemy aircraft to twenty, but the odds were made a little more even by the top Flight of SE5s, led by Tom Hazell – with the appropriate second Christian name of Falcon – coming down into the fight.

The American, William Lambert, shot at an Albatros from fifty yards but with no result, then saw two SE5s, one flying a streamer – 'either Lowe or Hazell.' – after a DVII with green wings. The Fokker went down in a spin under their combined fire. An Albatros then attacked Lambert from one side, but he had no difficulty in evading this attack: full throttle, a climb for two hundred feet and a tight left hand turn put Lambert's SE5, C1084, dead on the tail of the enemy scout. 'This manoeuvre surprises me but 1084 just about acts on her own.' Lambert opened fire with both guns from fifty yards, until his Lewis gun drum was expended, then continued firing his Vickers until the enemy scout dived vertically for several thousand feet before flattening out and flying east.

Lambert then pulled down his Lewis gun in order to put on a fresh drum, but as he lifted the drum off he swung his arm out too far into the slipstream, with the drum broadside on, and the force of the wind slapped his arm back against the rear of his cockpit, snatching the drum out of his hand. For a few seconds, with no feeling in his hand and arm, Lambert feared that his arm was broken – he later found a large bruise on it – but feeling gradually returned and he was able to snap a fresh drum into place.

The enemy scouts having cleared east, the SE5s reformed and made their way back to the lines. Passing over Warfusee at 5,000 ft, three balloons were seen two thousand feet below them and three of the SE5s dived to attack. John Daley destroyed his balloon in flames and the remaining two were hastily winched down. The ground fire around the balloons was intense and Capt W Selwyn returned with a badly shot about SE5.

This combat, between large numbers of opposing aircraft, was typical of many of the fights that were now becoming commonplace: not only of the numbers of aircraft involved, but of how often the results were indecisive.

The Sopwith Dolphins of 23 Squadron lost two pilots in a fight over Hangest late in the morning with *Jasta 62*. An American pilot, James Pearson, destroyed an Albatros at 11.35am and sent another down out of control five minutes later for his third and fourth victories, but his fellow American, Lt C Sherwood was shot down and killed and Capt H Puckridge was shot down and taken prisoner.

The two Australian fighter squadrons, Nos 2 and 4 Squadrons AFC were now based on the same aerodrome at Reclinghem, south west of Aire and were in keen rivalry for the number of enemy aircraft brought down. Ten Camels from 4 Squadron AFC were in action in the afternoon of July 1, dropping bombs on Estaires, when they were attacked by Pfalz D IIIs. Three of the enemy machines dived to attack Capt Edgar McCloughry but two collided, one losing a wing, the other going down in a slow spiral. The third Pfalz attacked McCloughry but the Australian out manoeuvred it and it dived away to the east. McCloughry then attacked the Pfalz that had survived the collision, still spiralling down, and shot it down in flames south of Estaires at 4.45pm. Neither of these Pfalz pilots is given as lost in the German lists, but there can be little doubt that the pilot of the first must have been killed.

Stationed at Bertangles, 65 Squadron was working with the Australian forces. James Gilmour, the squadron's most successful pilot, was leading his patrol in the afternoon and attacked Fokker D.VIIs over Bray at 7.10pm. Gilmour shot down two of these, the first in flames south east of the village, the second out of control in the same area. Half an hour later, over Foucaucourt, the SE5s were attacked by nearly 40 enemy scouts – Fokker D VIIs, Pfalz D IIIs and Albatri – and in the fighting Gilmour shot a D VII down in flames and a Pfalz out of control. On his way back to the lines Gilmour was attacked by four Albatros scouts, but he got on the tail of the leader and shot it down in flames south east of Lamotte. Lt E F Peacock and Lt H Browne each claimed a Fokker D VII from the evening's fighting, but Lt H Borden had been shot down and killed by *Ltn* Rumey of *Jasta 5* for his 28th victory.

Although a little cloudy, the fine weather continued on July 2. The RAF communiqué gives that enemy activity was less than the previous day, but there seems to have been large formations of enemy fighters over the Villers-Bretonneux area in the morning.

A patrol of SE5s from 60 Squadron, led by Capt Alfred Saunders, had been joined by Major 'Casey' Joseph Callaghan, the CO of 87 Squadron, flying a Sopwith Dolphin, and were flying over the Bayonvillers area when they sighted a LVG and an Halberstadt escorted by six Pfalz D IIIs. As the enemy formation passed over Villers-Bretonneux, Saunders led the SE5s and the Dolphin down to attack it from a height advantage of 7,000 feet. Saunders opened fire on the rearmost Pfalz and it went down. Saunders then attacked a Pfalz on the left of the formation. Turning quickly to the right to avoid Saunder's fire, the enemy pilot collided with his leader and both machines went down to crash into the Bois de Pierret. An American pilot with the squadron, Lt F K Read USAS, was wounded in the combat but managed to return and land his SE5 at Flesselles, the aerodrome of 3 Squadron AFC. Read was taken to hospital.

Major Callaghan had become separated from the SE5s, ran into a large formation of enemy fighters near Albert, and was shot down in flames by *Ltn* Büchner of *Jasta 13* over Contay. Although 87 Squadron had been in France for two months, arriving in France on April 24, Callaghan, the commanding officer, was their first casualty.

At 11.10am, over Ploegsteert Wood. Percy Clayson of 1 Squadron attacked an Hannover C type. The hostile machine went into a steep dive, the observer's map fell out, followed by the observer, who managed to cling hold of his gun mounting and straddle the fuselage, but the Hannover burst into flames and crashed into the wood.

July 3 was a windy day, with a great deal of cloud and there were few combats, enemy aircraft keeping well east. Ira Jones, writing of this period, comments on the lack of opportunity for fighting. An influenza epidemic had also incapacitated many squadrons. 'Half the squadron has been laid up with 'flu. This epidemic appears to have spread to most of the squadrons around. Grid, Spiers, Birch, Richardson and Roxburgh have had it worse than the others. I don't expect they will be fit to fly for at least a fortnight.' As a consequence, those pilots who were still fit had to fly three or four patrols a day. Jones commented. 'Its not so bad if we can break the monotony with a fight, but often we can't get near a Hun. They are not very brave, on the whole, considering they are fighting on their own side of the lines. They have everything in their favour except height, and I take damned good care they don't get that.'[2]

The day was fine on July 4 and there was a strong west wind. The wind condition was unfavourable for the British fighters, encouraging the pilots of the *jagdstaffeln* to fight, and there was a large fight in the morning between ten SE5s from 24 Squadron and twenty hostile scouts – 14 Fokker D VIIs, two Pfalz D.IIIs and four Albatros scouts.

The pilots of the squadron had been groundstrafing the day before and they took off at 8.00am to continue these attacks on July 4. Hazell, leading the SE5s, crossed the River Somme at 2,000 feet, the town of Amiens on their right, and made towards their targets. There were no enemy aircraft in sight. Anti-aircraft fire was now becoming intense, and as A Flight went down to 1,000 feet machine gun fire also became fierce and the British scouts scattered to avoid it, giving the German gunners a more difficult target. Daley and Lambert went down to attack guns firing at them from woods south of Cerisy, flying east over the woods at 300 feet before turning back, dropping a hundred feet, and bombing and machine gunning the enemy positions. After another run back across the woods, dropping their remaining bombs, they could see Archie bursts over Hamel, showing the other SE5s were strafing in that area and Lambert and Daley flew to rejoin them. Reforming, the SE5s began to climb out of the immediate range of Archie, which at 2,000 feet was heavy and accurate.

Glancing towards the sun, Lambert saw flashes of light from the wings of enemy aircraft, 7,000 to 8,000 higher, and two or three miles to the east of the British fighters. As the enemy aircraft began to come down out of the sun, the SE5s climbed to meet the attack, but as they reached 3,500 feet the enemy formation was upon them.

Lambert, slightly higher than the other SE5s, saw that the attack was led by five Fokker D VIIs flying in line abreast, 50 yards apart, a tactic he had not seen before, with the remaining enemy fighters spread out fan-wise behind them: Fokker D VIIs, Pfalz D IIIs and Albatri, all painted in different colours, and a pair with all white wings. The front five D VIIs pulled up in a climbing turn, came back down in the rear of the SE5s formation and a furious and confused fight began.

Lambert found an Albatros below him and took a snap shot at it, but it dived away. He then saw a Fokker 100 feet below him and half a mile away and dived towards it, opening fire at 50 yards. Hearing Lamberts' fire, the enemy pilot twisted round in his seat and put his machine into an evasive spin, flattening out at ground level and flying south. Two other Fokkers were now coming in to attack Lambert. He was in no mood to tackle these on his own and flew towards some nearby SE5s. Another SE5 dived past, an Albatros on its tail. Lambert tried a quick deflection shot to take the enemy pilot off the SE5's tail, but he turned and attacked Lambert and they fought for a few minutes, until a short burst from Lambert's guns forced the enemy pilot to dive away. As Lambert watched the Albatros go down he came under attack from above by a light blue and silver Pfalz D III and two Fokker D VIIs, their bullets hitting his SE5. Lambert was at 1,500 feet, but another SE5 was lower still, firing up at the Pfalz, which fell away in a spin.

The D VIIs were still coming down on Lambert and he dived and zoomed, coming out above one of his pursuers, the Fokker only 20 yards away and right in his sights. Lambert fired 100 rounds from his Vickers into the enemy machine, hitting the pilot and the Fokker went down to crash. 'How did 1084 get into position for such a perfect shot? I do not know. I must have blacked out for an instance.'

The other Fokker was now 50 yards in front and slightly below Lambert and he dived onto it, closed the distance to 20 yards and fired his Vickers, which stopped after firing one shot. But it was enough. From only 800 feet the enemy machine hit the ground near Warfusee and burst into flames. 'One bullet may have done the job but I doubt it. That would have been a rare shot. More likely the pilot was paralysed with fear and could not move.'

Lambert was now at 500 feet, dangerously low, and he could see the remains of four aircraft burning on the ground, but whether British or German it was impossible to tell. In the distance, SE5s and enemy scouts were still fighting at low level. Clearing the stoppage in his Vickers, Lambert flew towards them and got on the tail of a yellow Pfalz, but before he could close the distance another SE5 came down and fired into the Pfalz, hitting the pilot. Lambert saw the enemy pilot jerk back, almost upright, then slump down into his cockpit and the Pfalz went down and hit the ground in a burst of flame. Lambert then climbed to 1,500 feet, where six SE5s were fighting eight or ten enemy scouts, and got behind a Fokker D VII that was attacking one of the SE5s. After short bursts from both Lambert's guns the Fokker went down in a series of jerks before landing and rolling into a shell hole. Another Fokker then attacked Lambert and they fought for a while, each trying to gain an advantageous position for a shot, until the enemy pilot finally dived away then pulled out and flew east. After several other brushes with Fokkers and Albatri, Lambert checked the time. 'Holy smoke! This affair has lasted only fifteen minutes. How could all that action take place in such a short time.'

The SE5s reformed. All were present. Anti-aircraft fire again began to come up at them from a small patch of woods south of Hamel. What would Hazell do? Take them down to ground-strafe again or take them home. Hazell went down to 500 feet, followed by the other SE5s, and attacked horse drawn artillery on the road through the remains of Lamotte. Lambert could not bring himself to fire on the horses. 'They suffered enough without any more from me. I just could not do it,' and with Daley on his right wing tip went down to fire at guns in the woods.

The SE5s all returned safely at 10.00am and the pilots went into the squadron office to make out their reports. 'The office was in an uproar. Everyone whooping, shouting and yelling at the same time. Yes, a regular madhouse and understandably so. We had been through a tough and vicious fight both on the ground and in the air. That ground action had been terrible. We had survived the thousands of rounds of ammunition sent up at us only by the will of the Almighty.'[3]

Hazell was awarded a Fokker D VII out of control; Lambert two Fokkers destroyed; Selwyn an Albatros crashed; Lts Barton, G B Foster and C M G Farrell each claimed enemy aircraft damaged, and Lt T Hellet had attacked a two-seater and killed or wounded the observer.

The ground-strafing attacks on July 4, carried out by 24 Squadron – and other fighter squadrons, 23, 41 and 209 Squadrons – throughout the day were in support of an attack on the village of Hamel by Australian and American troops. Under the talented Australian, Lieutenant General John Monash, the offensive was a complete success. With close support from 9 Squadron RAF, 3 Squadron AFC, and 8 Squadron RAF, all the objectives were taken in ninety minutes with only light casualties.

In addition to their ground-strafing duties, the pilots of 41 Squadron fought with enemy scouts and two-seaters during the day. In the morning patrols, Lt Stanley Puffer shot down a balloon in flames over Mericourt at 6.55am, and Lt Henry Watson shot down an LVG out of control over Bayonvillers at 7.10am. The afternoon patrols fought with enemy scouts over the Proyart area. Capt William Claxton claimed a Fokker Triplane over Proyart at 1.30pm and destroyed a Pfalz D III east of Harbonnières thirty minutes later. In the general fighting over Proyart, Capt Frederick McCall and Lt Ernest Davis shared in two Fokker D VIIs out of control.

The Camels of 54 Squadron claimed two Hannovers out of control over Harbonnières in the afternoon, but lost a pilot killed by a Fokker D VII in the evening. The ex-naval squadrons claimed only one victory during the day – a Fokker D VII out of control over Foucaucourt to Capt C Ridley for the last of his eleven victories – but 203 Squadron lost a pilot shot down and taken POW east of Ypres and 209 Squadron had a pilot wounded, another killed in a fight with Fokker D VIIs, and two Camels badly shot about by groundfire.

The morning of July 5 was very cloudy, and enemy activity was slight until the evening. Maxwell took a patrol from 56 Squadron out at 7.00pm. The patrol saw nothing for an hour and a half, when a Fokker D VII came out of the clouds over Dompierre. The enemy pilot had not seen the three SE5s and Maxwell immediately attacked, firing 70 rounds of Vickers and a whole drum of Lewis into the enemy scout. The Fokker went down and was seen to burst into flames and crash by pilots of 41 Squadron who were on patrol in the vicinity. This Fokker D VII was the last of Gerald Maxwell's 26 victories, all scored with 56 Squadron. Casualties for the fighter squadrons for the day were light, with only two pilots wounded in action.

On July 5, after two weeks leave in England, Edward Mannock returned to France to take command of 85 Squadron. Morale in 85 Squadron was low, with the pilots in need of leadership. The squadron's previous commanding officer, William Bishop, had left his pilots to fend for themselves, seldom if ever leading patrols, almost always flying alone to increase his personal score of victories. He appears to have made no attempt to instil any patrol or Flight tactics into his pilots, and patrols were flown on an *ad lib* basis, often led by inexperienced pilots. The squadron had lost one of its flight commanders, Capt Edwin Benbow, who had been shot down and killed eight days after arriving in France on May 22, and by July 6 had had another pilot killed, two taken prisoner and two injured. One of the flight commanders, Spenser 'Nigger' Horn, tried alone to organise the squadron into a more efficient force – his fellow flight commanders, Capt Malcolm McGregor, and Benbow's replacement, Capt Arthur Randall, were relatively inexperienced – but it had been an uphill task.[4]

Mannock was a supreme tactician and a patrol leader *par excellence*. As soon as he arrived he began to coach his pilots to fight as a team and within a very short period of time had transformed the squadron. Ira Jones, who visited Mannock for the day on July 25, recorded the change. 'The squadron (85) is very full out. Everyone says they much prefer Mick to Bishop as a CO. Mick leads all the squadron patrols and produces the Hun on a plate. Bishop rarely did this. He was an individualist, and most of his victories were on lone patrols.'

Two days after his arrival at the squadron, Mannock led a squadron patrol. He briefed the pilots before takeoff. He would lead three SE5s in the bottom Flight as a decoy, with Randall leading another three machines in the first layer above, and Horn leading another three in the top layer.

The twelve SE5s left the ground at 7.30pm. Fifty minutes later ten black and red Fokker D VIIs went down to attack Mannock and the bottom Flight. Randall and Horn then took their Flights down, sandwiching the enemy scouts, and the fight went down to 2,000 feet. Mannock destroyed one of the Fokkers and sent another down out of control; Horn also destroyed one and another out of control, and Lt Walter Longton destroyed one of the enemy scouts for his first victory. The only cost to the squadron was Capt Randall, who was forced to land at St Marie Capelle, unhurt, but with a badly shot about SE5, and one pilot who had had his hand grazed by a bullet.

The pilots of 85 Squadron were full of enthusiasm for the new tactics and sense of purpose that Mannock had given them, and Mannock himself was comfortable in his role as a teacher, even though it restricted his own successes to the extent that he scored no additional personal victories for another week.

On the morning of July 7, Gwilym Lewis of 40 Squadron, an old friend of Mannock, had scored the last of his 12 victories with an LVG shot down and captured near Lens, sharing it with Lt I F Hind. This was a machine from *Fl Abt 13,* given the designation G/I Brigade/9. The pilot, *Gef* Weber, was taken prisoner, wounded in both legs. There is no official record as to the fate of the observer, but Lewis wrote that he was unhurt.

The morning of July 8 was overcast and thunderstorms developed in the afternoon. Despite the adverse conditions, some combats were fought and there were some casualties for little gain. Capt Arthur Claydon, a flight commander in 32 squadron, with seven victories, was shot down and killed by *Ltn* Billik of *Jasta 52* in a fight with the *Jasta* in the Arras vicinity, and Lt H Burry was shot down and taken prisoner. A pilot of 2 Squadron AFC was wounded; a pilot of 73 Squadron was killed over Pont À Vendin and a pilot of 208 Squadron taken prisoner.

The thunderous conditions had cleared the next morning, giving way to intermittent showers. During the first days of the month the Camels of 4 Squadron AFC had been extremely active in ground operations, the machine gunning and bombing of the enemy positions in the Lys valley between Merville and La Bassée becoming a daily routine. These low flying operations were carried out with the SE5s of 2 Squadron AFC flying top cover, but the Camel pilots had also been active in the higher air. Released from strafing duties on the afternoon of July 1, Arthur Cobby had shot down a balloon over Bac St Maur at 3.35pm and twenty-five minutes later attacked four Fokker Triplanes, shooting down one to crash north east of La Bassée. In the late evening of July 9, Cobby scored again, shooting down an AGO two-seater north east of La Bassée for his 21st victory, before attacking balloons in the vicinity. Cobby's Camel was badly shot about in these attacks and he crashed near Gravelin.

During the morning of July 10 news began to filter through to the squadrons that James McCudden was dead. Ira Jones recorded in his diary entry for the day. 'The great McCudden is dead. What a blow! He was on his way to take over 60 Squadron. They say he did a climbing turn off the ground, stalled and crashed. I can't believe it. Not McCudden, surely! He was one of the finest pilots in the corps.'

Flying from England to take command of 60 Squadron, McCudden had taken off from the Royal Aircraft Factory at Farnborough shortly after 1.00pm, flying a brand new SE5a. He made a brief stop somewhere in France – probably at Hesdin – to telephone the commanding officer of 13 Wing, Lt-Col P Playfair, to say that he would arrive at Boffles, 60 Squadron's aerodrome, at about 6.00pm.

The afternoon was hazy, with poor visibilty. At 5.30pm, as McCudden approached the airfield at Auxi-le-Chateau, only

a short distance from Boffles, he may well have thought that he had arrived at his destination, but as he lost height he realised that the aircraft on the aerodrome were RE8s and Armstrong Whitworth FK8s, not the SE5s of 60 Squadron. Now not sure of his position, McCudden landed near the hangars and beckoned to two airmen standing nearby to ask where he was. The airmen told him, indicated the direction of Boffles, and helped him to turn the SE5. McCudden taxied to the far end of the airfield, turned into the wind, and took off in a steep climbing turn. As the SE5 came over the wood bordering the aerodrome, the engine 'choked' and it stalled, crashing into the trees. McCudden was thrown out of the aeroplane and was found lying unconscious under one of the wings. He was quickly taken to No.21 Casualty Clearing Station, situated on the aerodrome, where it was found that he had a fractured skull. McCudden never regained consciousness and died at 8.00pm.

On the afternoon of July 10 the pilots of 56 and 60 Squadrons attended McCudden's funeral at Wavans. The ceremony angered many who were there. Burden commented in his dairy: 'It was poorly arranged and rushed through.' Paul Winslow, an American pilot with 56 Squadron, recorded: 'All 60 were there, together with General Salmond, and some members of other squadrons. The ceremony made my blood boil – all in Latin, mumbled so that even if one knew the language, he couldn't have heard it. Nothing human in it at all, and far from impressive. Richthofen – an enemy – had a far better funeral, and if anyone deserved a real memorial, it was McCudden.' Winslow's reference to Richthofen is ironic, the enemy ace having been buried with full military honours: a cortege, a firing party, a full platoon of infantry, three volleys and the last post.

The airfighting followed the same general pattern for the next four days, with bad weather on the July 11,12,13 and 14, limiting the amount of flying possible. On July 15 the weather had improved only a little, but in the morning 'Grid' Caldwell led a squadron patrol to an enemy aerodrome near Roulers. Caldwell, as Jones observed, 'totally ignoring tactics,' circled the hostile aerodrome until a formation of enemy scouts returned from patrol and attacked the British scouts. In the fight which followed upwards of forty machines were involved – 'diving and firing like madmen at one another; zooming, turning, twisting diving and firing again and again.' Caldwell shot down a Fokker D VII, which dived away and broke up in midair, everyone, friend and foe, flying 'all out' to miss the falling pieces and each other.

The fighting then broke off except for a few isolated combats. Ira Jones commented: 'As so often happens in these fights, as soon as some catastrophe happens which is obvious to all, the remainder of the party breaks away. The fight fizzles out with a couple of toughs having a final go at each other in a private war.'

The squadron had lost two pilots in the fight: 2Lt R H Gray had been shot down and taken prisoner – Ira Jones, now promoted to Captain, saw him go down with several Fokker D VIIs on his tail – and the South African, Lt Percy Howe failed to return. 'Swazi', as Howe was nicknamed, had been wounded in the fight, had fainted from loss of blood, and had crashed while trying to get back to the aerodrome. News came later that he was safe, in a field hospital at Hazebrouck.

In the evening, Arthur Cobby and Herbert Watson of 4 Squadron AFC were on patrol over La Bassée at 6,000 feet when five Pfalz D IIIs were seen, flying from Bailleul towards Armentières. The two Camels climbed through the clouds and flew towards the Pfalz, hidden below. Coming down through the clouds when they judged they had would be above the enemy scouts, they found themselves just above and to the east of the Pfalz. A formation of Fokker Triplanes was in close proximity to the Pfalz, but undeterred by the odds, Cobby and Watson attacked the Pfalz. Watson claimed only one Pfalz out of control, but Cobby destroyed two: one in flames, the other in pieces, the wings of the enemy scout breaking away from the fuselage.

The Fokker Triplanes then came down and attcked the two Camels, but Cobby and Watson dived into the cloud cover, coming out close to the ground and contour chased home. Cobby's victories were awarded as over Armentières at 7.25pm.

Beginning with an artillery bombardment at midnight on July 14, the final German offensive in the west opened at dawn on July 15, the enemy troops attacking to each side of the cathedral city of Reims. In early hours of July 13, General Foch had sent a telegram to General Sir Douglas Haig, requesting that squadrons of the RAF be moved south to help meet the threat of the now imminent German attack. Flying through rainstorms the next day, nine squadrons of the RAF had flown south to reinforce the French. The single-seater fighter squadrons in the move were 32, 43, 54, 73, and 80 Squadrons.

Patrolling over the new front in the early afternoon of July 15, the Camels of 43 and 54 Squadron were attacked over Dormans by *Jasta B* and *Jasta 10*. 2Lt T Babbitt of 43 Squadron was shot down and killed by *Ltn* Bolle the *Staffelführer* of *Jasta B* and 54 also lost two pilots killed in the action: 2Lt M B Lewis, and Sgt P H Williams, who was awarded to *Ltn* Löwenhardt of *Jasta 10* for his 36th victory. The *Luftstreitkräfte* was very active over the battlefront; in their evening patrols the next day 54 Squadron had two more pilots killed in combat and another badly wounded.

On July 16, Wing ordered a bombing raid on the German aerodrome at Faucaucourt. The Sopwith Camels of 65 and 209 Squadrons, were to carry out the low level bombing, escorted by the Sopwith Dolphins of 23 Squadron and the SE5s of 24 and 84 Squadrons. Orders from Wing were to carry out 'the destruction of hangars and machines and the infliction of as many casualties as possible.'

The aerodrome at Faucaucourt was situated on the long straight road running due east from Amiens to St Quentin, and was less than thirty miles away from the British aerodrome at Bertangles, where all the attacking squadrons were based, with the exception of 24 Squadron, based a little further to the north at Conteville. The escorting fighters were stepped upwards to a height of 18,000 feet, the 15 SE5s from 84 Squadron led by the squadron CO, Major Sholto Douglas.

Arriving over the enemy aerodrome, the Camels of 65 and 209 went down to within 500 feet of the ground, dropping their bombs and shooting up the hangars, buildings and enemy machines. Douglas, from his vantage point of above the attacks, saw two direct hits on hangars, six on various huts and buildings and a Fokker D VII demolished by a direct hit. A hundred 25lb Cooper bombs were dropped and over 8,000 rounds fired by the attacking Camels of the two squadrons.

Major Douglas kept a sharp lookout for any enemy fighters that might attack the low flying Camels, but none appeared, and on reflection Douglas decided that the timing of the raid was the reason. 'It was deliberately staged at an hour when all the Germans, being the methodical people that they are, would be at their lunch; and that apparently included the German fighter pilots.'[5]

There were no casualties amongst the attacking aircraft and on their return the pilots of one of the escort squadrons shot down two balloons.

There were low clouds on the morning of July 17 and although these later cleared there were thunderstorms in the evening. The Australian fighter pilots were again ground-strafing in the morning, three Camels of 4 Squadron AFC bombing the railway station at Armentières at 4.00am and two others attacking enemy lines of supply at Estaires and shooting down a balloon. Leonard Taplin of the squadron, out alone, looking for his companions, was attacked by four Pfalz scouts, but he evaded these and later attacked a pair of Albatros two-seaters south west of Estaires. The first of these dived away but the other stayed to fight. Taplin first killed the enemy observer, then continued firing into the Albatros until it went down to crash. This victory was the first for Taplin of an eventual twelve.

The Australians were again successful in the afternoon. Capt Adrian Cole, from Melbourne, was leading a patrol of five SE5s from 2 Squadron AFC when they sighted a formation of six Fokker Triplanes near Armentières. The enemy pilots refused combat, but Cole took his Flight to the east, cutting off their retreat, and attacked them from slightly above. Cole dived on the leader of the enemy formation and it fell away on its back. Lt C Stone followed the triplane down and after firing a hundred rounds into it the enemy machine went down in flames from 17,000 feet, killing *Ltn* Franke of *Jasta 30*.

An evocative picture of the conditions of the evening of July 17 is given in the diary of Joseph Jacobs, *Staffelführer* of *Jasta 7*. Skirting the edge of a thundercloud, Jacobs first attacked two British fighters, then switched his attacks to the last machine in a larger formation. 'In the chase that followed I could not get him. I now flew full speed towards home in order to escape the thunderstorm. There was lightning everywhere and everywhere one could see planes racing home.'[6] *Jasta 56* reported that Jacobs had shot down one of the Camels on fire, and he was credited with it as his 23rd victory, but no Camels were lost on July 17.

On July 18, the advance of the German forces on the front at Reims was halted by a counter attack by French and American troops, supported by British and Italian forces, and in the following two days over six miles of lost ground had been retaken. More importantly the Germans abandoned Soissons, the vital rail centre on which depended all their operations in the sector. During the counterattack the RAF flew ground-strafing missions and 32 Squadron lost two pilots, one killed and the other taken POW.

With refreshing candour, Gwilym Lewis wrote home during the day: 'My weak little self is at last satisfied, and I have got the DFC. I therefore see no reason for staying in this dangerous country any longer and have applied to go home.'

The day was fine on July 19. In the morning 15 Camels of 209 Squadron attacked the enemy aerodrome at Cappy. A hangar was seen to receive a direct hit and casualties were inflicted on the personnel manning the German ground defence emplacements. The Camels went down to 100 feet in carrying out the attacks – Lt Cedric Edwards actually landing on the enemy aerodrome. On the way back to their aerodrome the Camels attacked troops and transport, and arriving at the front line trenches went down to fifty feet and shot at enemy troops, one pilot seeing a group of four men fall as they ran for the shelter of a dugout.

The SE5s of 74 Squadron left the ground at 8.00am to escort the Bristol Fighters of 20 Squadron in a bombing raid on Courtrai. After bombing their objective the returning Bristols were attacked by enemy scouts. Jacobs was fighting the Bristols with his *Kette* when the SE5s of 74 Squadron came down from height and attacked him. After fighting indecisively with several SE5s and Bristols, Jacobs singled out the SE5 flown by Lt A M Roberts, an American pilot. Jacobs kept to

within 30 yards of the SE5, firing continuously, and it went down to land in German held territory. 'He glided very slowly across a road, pulled his plane up a little and turned over on its head. He jumped out immediately and ran into a deserted trench, followed by some soldiers.'

After he had landed, Jacobs went by car to the scene. 'It was a brand new SE5a with an American 1st Lieutenant as pilot … He had been three months at the front and was astonished at the speed of my triplane. As a person he was very nice and spoke a lot about English pilots. He much regretted the death of Richthofen. He gave me his zippered map case.'[7]

During the fight, Jones had seen Roberts go down, but not his ultimate landing. 'Roberts was seen to pounce on a Fokker biplane and shoot it up good and hearty, then follow it down beneath the general engagement. Fatal. He was pounced upon by a biplane and a triplane. When last seen he was fighting for dear life. I hope he's not killed. He deserves a better fate.'[8]

Roxburgh-Smith had attacked two Fokker D VIIs which were chasing a lone SE5 back to the lines, a lucky long range shot in an attempt to distract one of the Fokkers, sending it down to crash. The remaining Fokker pilot persisted in his pursuit of the SE5, flown by 2Lt L A Richardson, and before turning away to fight Roxburgh-Smith had wounded Richardson in the arm. Richardson flew west, landed his machine in a cornfield behind the British lines and was taken to hospital.

After leaving Richardson, the enemy pilot fought with Roxburgh-Smith before spinning away. 'This is a favourite stunt of theirs,' commented Jones. Since they always fight over their own territory, I suppose it's the right thing to do when they decide they are beaten. They run away to fight another day.'[8]

Roxburgh-Smith visited Richardson in the hospital that afternoon. Richardson, known as the squadron's cocktail king was cheerful. 'No wonder … he is off to Blighty tonight.'

Later in the morning Capt Sidney Carlin, who had joined 74 Squadron on May 26, and had already shot down two enemy aircraft, shot down the first of the five balloons he was to destroy. While serving in the infantry in 1916, Carlin had been seriously wounded, losing a leg. Recovering, he transferred to the RFC and became an instructor at the Central Flying School before being posted to 74 Squadron. Carlin, known throughout the RAF as 'Timbertoes', was later to be involved in an incident with his squadron commander that nearly cost Keith Caldwell his life.

The morning of July 20 was fine, but there were thunderstorms again in the afternoon and evening. In the morning Caldwell led two Flights of SE5s in attacks on enemy balloons. One Flight stayed up as cover, while the other went down to attack balloons south west of Armentières, and Carlin destroyed one two miles south west of the town. The balloon attacks completed, the SE5s flew a normal Offensive Patrol and over Menin were attacked by enemy scouts from *Jagdstaffeln 7, 20* and *40,* a patrol of Camels from 70 Squadron joining in the fight. Jacobs, flying his black triplane, was attacked by four of the Camels, but some Fokker D VIIs of *Jasta 20* came to his aid and he was able to concentrate on a single opponent: by the streamers which Jacobs noted, a flight commander. *Uffz* Böhme of *Jasta 7* then joined his commander and Jacobs temporarily pulled away until he saw that Böhme was 'overwhelmed' by the Camel pilot. Jacobs went back into the fight, but had a gun stoppage and had to again break away.

Two pilots of *Jasta 20*, the *Staffelführer Ltn* Busse, and *Ltn* Dazur, both claimed Sopwith Camels from this fight, as did *Uffz* Hüttenrauch of *Jasta 7,* and according to Jacobs' diary, pilots of Jasta 40 also claimed one British scout, but 70 Squadron lost only two pilots shot down and taken prisoner. Seventy Four Squadron had no casualties from the action.

In an evening patrol over Lestrem, Capt Rochford and Lt W Sidebottom of 203 Squadron attacked a two-seater and shot it down to crash near the village. On the same patrol, a new pilot, Lt A Rudge, shot down an LVG that crashed near Merville. Collishaw, the commanding officer, had been out alone in the morning and had scored his 48th and 49th victories: a DFW south east of Merville at 11.00am and another, forty minutes later, out of control over Miraumont.

July 21 was a day of high winds and low clouds. The only activity by the aircraft of the *Luftstreitkräfte* was in the south, over the French front. Capt Ernest Salter of 54 Squadron had a successful day. Patrolling east of Dravegny in the afternoon, he attacked a pair of Halbertstadt two-seaters, shooting one down at 3.55pm and the other five minutes later, the first crashing near Dravegny, the second 5 miles east of Chery. Salter took his Flight out again at 6.00pm. An hour and a quarter after take off the Camels fought with *Jasta 11* over Fère at 13,000 feet. Salter claimed a Fokker D VII down in flames over Fere en Tardenois, but three Camels were shot down in the fighting. 2Lt B Fisher and Lt F Dougall were killed, and although Lt R Cuffe managed to return to 54 Squadron's aerodrome at Touquin he crashed on landing and was killed.

A patrol of Camels from 73 Squadron were also in action during the evening. Leaving the ground at 6.45pm, with the commanding officer Major R H Freeman flying as a member of the patrol, the Camels later fought with Fokker Triplanes of *Jasta 26*, west of Belleau – the whole Flight sharing in the destruction of a triplane, possibly *OfStv* Esswein of the *Jasta 26*. After the fight Major Freeman was last seen flying north from Belleau, apparently OK, but he failed to return and was later reported missing, shot down and killed by *Ltn* Bülow of *Jasta 36.*

July 22 was a day of exceptionally fine weather and there was a great deal of fighting in the air, at all heights. The day began badly for 'Tich' Rochford of 203 Squadron. The evening before he had walked over to 64 Squadron's Mess to visit his great friend Jimmy Slater, who was a flight commander in the squadron. One thing led to another and after a few drinks Tich finally got to bed at midnight. 'I soon fell asleep.' He was not best pleased to be woken three hours later by his CO, Raymond Collishaw, carrying a hurricane lamp and accompanied by a sentry. For several days Collishaw and Rochford had been discussing a plan for a dawn attack on the German aerodrome at Dorignies, near Douai, and Collishaw now announced that today was the day. After his night with Slater, Rochford felt more like going back to sleep than attacking a German aerodrome, but he pulled himself together, got up, dressed, and went to join Collishaw in the Mess.

Collishaw took off first, Rochford following almost immediately. Dawn was just breaking on a beautiful cloudless day, lighting up the eastern sky, the first rays of the sun reflected in the waters of the River Scarpe and the Lens to La Bassée Canal. Rochford was momentarily distracted by the beauty of the morning, but he concentrated on the job in hand as Dorignies came into sight. He went down to 5,000 feet, throttled his engine back and dived towards the aerodrome at 150mph. Levelling out at 200 feet, Rochford fired all his ammunition into the hangars and other buildings, dropping three of his bombs on the men's living quarters and the fourth on a hangar, which caught fire. Rochford then flew back to Le Hameau, landing safely, shortly followed by Collishaw.

Collishaw had arrived at the enemy aerodrome a few minutes after Rochford, had watched Rochford's attack and seen the results. Three enemy aircraft were now being wheeled from the hangars and Collishaw made several strafing runs over them, dropping his four bombs on the aerodrome buildings. Climbing away from his last run, Collishaw saw a two-seater coming in to land. 'It was obviously a machine that had been out on a night reconnaissance patrol and the pilot and observer must have wondered what was going on.' The two-seater was at 800 feet. Collishaw dived, opened fire from close range, and it went down to crash on the field, near a row of hangars, and burst into flames.

After having his Camel refuelled, Collishaw took off again and flew back to Dorignies to ascertain the amount of damage he and Rochford had done. This time he found the Germans were awake and he was attacked by three Albatros scouts as he neared the aerodrome, forcing him back towards the Front Lines. One Albatros got in front of its companions; Collishaw turned back and shot it down near the River Scarpe, where it was seen to crash by British anti-aircraft batteries.

It was the beginning of a productive day for 203 Squadron. At 9.00am Rochford took his Flight out on an offensive patrol. Thirty-five minutes later the Camels were at 17,000 feet over Festubert. Below them, an Armstrong Whitworth FK8 was under attack from two Fokker D VIIs. The Camels dived to the aid of the FK8, and Rochford shot one of the Fokkers down out of control, the observer of the British two-seater destroying the other. The five Camels then climbed to regain their height, but at 9,000 feet saw a distant patrol of five Fokker D.VIIs. These enemy machines were a long way east of the lines and the Camels climbed, both to gain more height and get between the Fokkers and the sun.

When the Camels had reached 17,000 feet, with the sun at their backs, they were in an advantageous position to attack. Their numbers had been reduced by one, Lt Y E S Kirkpatrick having returned with engine trouble, but as the enemy machines arrived over Carvin, Rochford led the Camels down.

Rochford held his fire until he almost collided with the leading Fokker, a short burst sending it down out of control. William Sidebottom shot down another, which was seen to crash, and a third went down out of control after being attacked by Lt Stone. Rochford watched the Fokker attacked by Lt Arthur Rudge burst into flames under his fire, but the last of the Fokkers was nowhere to be seen and the Camels reformed. Flying back to the aerodrome Rochford saw that one of the Camels was missing: Arthur Rudge,was later reported shot down and killed by *Vzfw* Wiehle of *Jasta 43*.[9]

Despite the loss of Rudge, it had been a productive day for 203 Squadron. In addition to the six victories mentioned, Capt Louis Bawlf, a Canadian from Winnipeg, had destroyed a DFW over Bauvin at 6.45am.

Forty Squadron were in action in the morning with Fokker D VIIs over Carvin. Reed Landis an American pilot destroyed one of the D VIIs, but Lt Indra La Roy was shot down in flames and killed. Nineteen years old, Indra Lal Roy was one of two young Indian pilots serving with the RAF.[10]

An early morning patrol by 60 Squadron were in combat with enemy scouts over Aveluy Wood at 5.40am. Captain Doyle, a flight commander, scored the first of his eventual nine victories, shooting down a Pfalz D III out of control over the wood, but Lt J MacVicker was shot down and killed by *Ltn* Koch of *Jasta 32*.

In the south, in a fight with Fokker D VIIs over Bazoches, Lt G L Graham of 73 Squadron claimed one out of control and another destroyed, and Lt William Stephenson claimed a Fokker Triplane destroyed and a D VII down in flames, but Lt W Kidder was wounded, shot down and taken prisoner.

There were no combats of July 23, high winds and rain keeping the airforces on the ground, but the weather had improved a little the next day, although there was still a strong wind.

A morning patrol from 84 Squadron led by John Ralston surprised a formation of seven Fokker D VIIs over Abancourt at 11.15am. The SE5s made dive and zoom attacks from 4,000 feet and in the first pass Ralston, Norman Mawle and William Nel each shot down a D VII. In an evening patrol, led by Capt Hugh Saunders, nine enemy scouts were seen over Peronne. Saunders' guns jammed in his first attack, but the American, George Vaughan, flying as a wing man to Saunders, shot down a Fokker D VII, east of Bray. A Canadian pilot, Carl Falkenberg, attacked a Fokker D VII, the rear of its fuselage painted white, and sent it down out of control, but a torrential rainstorm then stopped the fight, and the SE5s returned.

After the fight, in the clouds and rain, and separated from the other SE5s, Capt Southey was completely lost. The light was now so bad that Southey could see none of his instruments. Thinking he was flying west – in the bad light he mistook the moon for the sun – he flew for ten minutes until he crossed the River Somme. Thinking this was the River Hallue, Southey glided down to land, but as he touched down he was met by a hail of machinegun fire and flaming onions. Southey hurriedly took off again, managed to switch on the lights in his cockpit, and with their aid found the Amiens to Foucaucourt Road. Flying along the road at 300 feet, Southey finally landed back at Bertangles.

The pilots of 85 Squadron also saw action during the morning. B and C Flights Flights were out, flying in two layers, B Flight flying below, and at 10.35am six enemy aircraft were seen over Armentières. B Flight decoyed the enemy force towards the British lines and Capt Malcolm McGregor took C Flight down from out of the sun.

McGregor destroyed two Fokker D VIIs, the first out of control, the second crashed, both south east of Kemmel. Capt Arthur Randall crashed another D VII by Neuve Eglise; Orville Ralston shot down a green and black Fokker D VII, which crashed north west of Armentières, and Lt Walter Longton shot down a Pfalz with a yellow fuselage and tail to crash south east of Kemmel. These enemy aircraft were from *Jasta 43*, which had three pilots forced to land, with one, *Ltn* Friedrich Jakobs, wounded.

The weather was fine on July 25, with only scattered showers during the day. Capt A B Yuille of 151 Squadron was flying a night patrol and at 12.45am saw a Gotha. Yuille closed to within thirty yards and fired 50 rounds into the enemy machine, which flew on, seemingly undamaged. Yuille closed again and fired another burst into the Gotha, but his Camel was caught in the backwash of the enemy machine as it dived away and Yuille was forced to break off the attack. Regaining control of his Camel, Yuille made another attack but lost the Gotha in the dark. It was later confirmed that this machine had crash landed in the British trenches, hit in both engines and with one of the crew wounded. Although the pilots of 151 Squadron had engaged several night flying German bombers in July, this was the first decisive result for the squadron.

Rochford took his Flight out at 6.30am and attacked two Fokker D VIIs over La Bassée at 12,000 feet. Rochford and Sidebottom each accounted for an enemy scout, both seen to crash, but Lt C F Brown was wounded in the fight, shot down and taken prisoner, and later died of his wounds.

Still fighting on the southern part of the Front, 73 Squadron flew an escort for DH9s of 107 Squadron on a bombing raid. Returning from the raid, the deHavillands and their escorting Camels were attacked by 40 enemy scouts and there was a running fight back to the lines. Having seen the bombers safely across, with no loss, the 73 Squadron pilots went back. Stephenson destroyed a Fokker D VII with a blue fuselage and red tail; Lt Emile John Lussier, a French-Canadian pilot, sent one Fokker down out of control then attacked another. After firing over 700 rounds into this Fokker, which had a black and white chequered top wing, it went down to crash in a wood south of Villers. Gavin Graham shot another of the enemy machines down to crash into a wood east of Courmont. To offset these success, three of the Camels were lost: Lts W A Armstrong and R F Lewis had been shot down and killed and Lt K Laurie shot down and taken prisoner. Lt A V Gallie was also hit and his petrol tank set on fire. Gallie sideslipped, both to keep the flames away from his cockpit and in the hope that they would go out, which they did after falling for 3,000 feet, and Gallie was able to return to base. After the fight, on the way back to the lines, Stephenson and Lt Cooper attacked an LVG two-seater over Cohan and shot it down.

Forty Three and 32 Squadrons were also still fighting on the French Front in the south. In an evening patrol, 43 Squadron lost a pilot killed and two pilots taken POW – one of whom later died of his wounds – in a fight with *Jasta B* over Soissons, and 32 Squadron had a pilot shot down and taken prisoner by *Jasta 27* in a combat over Fismes.

During the day, the pilots of 64 Squadron claimed four victories, all Fokker D VIIs, in the general area of Neuve Chapelle. With only two pilots taken POW, casualties in July had been light up to the previous day, when the squadron had lost one of its most successful pilots, Capt Philip Burge, a flight commander with 11 victories, but on July 25 it lost two pilots, one taken prisoner, the other dying of his wounds.

The weather was cloudy on July 26, with frequent rainstorms. There was little enemy activity, but it was a tragic day for the RAF, with the loss of one of its most admired and charismatic pilots.

Weather conditions being bad, Major Mick Mannock had washed out the squadron patrols, but he took off at 5.10am with Lt Donald Inglis, a young New Zealander. Inglis had yet to score a victory and the previous evening Mannock had promised to take him out in the morning to show him how it was done. At 5.30am, at 5,000 feet over Merville, Mannock spotted an enemy two-seater, low down over the lines. With Inglis following, Mannock went down to attack the enemy machine and shot the enemy observer, leaving Inglis an easy shot for his first victory. Following instructions, Inglis came up underneath the two-seater and fired, hitting the petrol tank and almost colliding with the enemy machine before pulling away. The two-seater went down in flames and crashed at La Cix Marmuse. The two SE5s were now very low over German territory, but Mannock twice circled the burning wreckage on the ground – a most unusual thing for him to do and against all his teaching – before turning for the British lines. Groundfire now began to come up at the two SE5s, and as Inglis followed his leader he realised for the first time just how low they were. Suddenly, a small flicker of flame came out of the side of Mannock's machine, rapidly growing larger, watched by the horrified Inglis. The nose of Mannock's SE5 dropped, it turned twice in a slow right hand turn and hit the ground in flames, just south of La Pierre-au-Beure, a little over a mile from Pacaut Wood. Inglis circled the crash, was hit by groundfire in his petrol tank, and finally turned away to make a forced landing behind the front line British trenches. Inglis was helped out of his machine by Welsh troops, who sat him down on a fire step. His nerves were shattered. All he could say was: 'the sods have killed my Major.'

Ira Jones wrote in his diary: 'Mick is dead. Everyone is stunned. No one can believe it. I can write no more today. It is too terrible. Just off with Grid to 85 to cheer the lads up.' The next morning Jones and Caldwell flew over the area, but there was nothing to see and intense groundfire forced them to abandon their search. Jones wrote: 'I can now realise how the Hun airforce felt when they heard that Boelcke or Richthofen was killed. Mick's death is a terrible blow. We in 74 knew him better than anyone. I have a deep aching void in my breast. I keep on repeating to myself: "it can't be true. Mick cannot be dead." Yet I know he is.'[11]

Low clouds and rain stopped all flying the next day and on July 28, although it was fine in the morning, it became overcast as the day wore on and there were a few combats. The Australian fighter squadrons were engaged in their usual ground-strafing activities, a patrol from 4 Squadron AFC shooting up a train in the station at Estaires, and scoring a direct hit with a bomb from 500 feet. Waiting over the enemy balloon lines until the light improved, McCloughry glided down onto a balloon and shot it down in flames, following the burning mass down to within fifty feet of the ground. Flying northwards along the River Lys, McCloughry shot up eight transport wagons near Sailly, the drivers jumping off their wagons and the horses careering away over the adjacent fields. 'This sort of stunt', one pilot observed, 'gives you a first rate appetite for breakfast and tones you up for the day.'

Another pilot, Lt G S Jones-Evans, after dropping his bombs on a train leaving the station at Armentières, was attacked by a yellow LVG. He shot this LVG down, but was attacked by another on his way back. Jones-Evans destroyed this second two-seater, but the fight had gone down very low and Jones-Evans was hit in the foot by machine gun fire from the ground. Although faint from loss of blood, Jones-Evans turned west and made for St Pol, where he crashed on trying to land and had to crawl for a mile before he found assistance. An English pilot with the squadron, 2Lt A McCulloch, was not so lucky: he was shot down by groundfire and taken prisoner.

In the south, 73 Squadron also had a casualty: In an afternoon fight over Fère-en-Tardenois with Fokker D VIIs of *Jasta 10*, William Stephenson was shot down and taken prisoner by *Ltn* Grassmann of the *Jasta* for his third victory.

Visibility was poor on July 29. There were a few combats. In a morning patrol by 84 Squadron, Capt Hugh 'Dingbat' Saunders, shot down an LVG from a formation of four north of Bois de Tailles, for the last of his 15 victories, the pilots of his Flight shooting down another two. In the evening, Capt Owen Baldwin and Lt Gavin Graham were leading patrols from 73 Squadron and fought with Fokker D VIIs north of Soissons. Baldwin sent one Fokker down in flames and another out of control, and Robert Chandler shot the wings off another, but 2Lt E Cotton was shot down and killed by *Ltn* Büchner of *Jasta 13*.

Eighty Four Squadron were again in action on July 30. In the morning, enemy aircraft were very active over the northern sector of the Front, and a patrol led by Lt Norman Mawle saw seven enemy scouts attacking a British two-seater over Wiencourt. Mawle led the SE5s down with the sun at their backs and attacked the enemy scouts – Fokker D VIIs and Pfalz – and his opponent went down in a series of stalls south of Warvillers. Mawle then put his machine into a spin to escape attack by three Fokker D VIIs, and on pulling out saw that two of them had collided. William Nel had also sent a D VII down out of control. The remaining enemy machines cleared east.

It was an eventful day for 74 Squadron. Ira Jones took a patrol out at noon to look for high-flying reconnaissance machines. These usually crossed the lines at 20,000 feet to photograph and reconnoitre the British back areas and Jones and his Flight sighted one between Calais and Cassel as it was returning from its mission. The SE5s were at 18,000 feet, the enemy machine three thousand feet lower, but it was a long way off and Jones was uncertain of its nationality. As he approached the two-seater, Jones could see the observer standing up, manning his gun but not firing. Jones decided it was a French machine, but the observer suddenly began to fire at the SE5, hitting the rear bay outer wing strut, and Jones felt a 'very definite bump on my backside.' Jones got behind and below the two-seater, a Rumpler, and opened fire, but the enemy pilot dived steeply away. Jones did not follow, worried his wing would come off, and left the Rumpler to his two companions, Lts Harold Shoemaker and Gauld, who dived after the enemy machine and shot it down in flames. Deciding that his wing was all right, Jones continued the patrol and later shot down an LVG over Estaires. Returning to Clairmarais, Jones' SE5 collapsed on landing. The Rumpler gunner had made good shooting: two of the wing struts were badly shot about and Jones' seat cushion had seven bullet holes in it.[12] Inspecting the damage, Caldwell told Jones that he had been a fool to carry on with such a large hole in the wing strut, but Jones commented. 'I can see him coming back in such circumstances. Not Likely!'

Jones was still shaken by the death of Mannock – he was flying four times a day and sleeping very badly: 'got out of bed seven times last night. Always being shot down in flames. Very trying.' – and he confided in his diary that he had now got to the stage where he was indifferent to being killed. 'We only die once and what is good enough for my pals is good enough for me. One must expect to be killed in a war.'[13]

In the afternoon, Jones went out again, flying Shoemaker's SE5. A Rumpler was crossing the British lines at 18,000 feet over Meteren and Jones chased it to a mile east of Armentières before giving up the pursuit, the enemy machine being too fast for the SE5. Jones had gone down to 14,000 feet in the chase and was attacked by eight black Fokker DVIIs. He had no alternative but to stay and fight.

The enemy pilots were all keen to shoot down the SE5, so eager that Jones was convinced that at times they were firing at each other. Jones got a snap shot at one Fokker, which spun away, got on the tail of another with a red ring round its fuselage, and fired another burst. The Fokker went down 'all wobbly like' but Jones could watch no longer, being under constant attack. Looking up he saw a formation of ten additional aircraft coming down into the fight. '"Thank God." I said. "Here come the boys." They were the boys all right. Unfortunately they all wore black crosses.'

Jones decided that enough was enough and made a break for the safety of the British lines, 'like a scared rabbit among bracken,' finally crossing the trenches low over Bailleul.

The weather was fine on the last day of the month and there was a great deal of air fighting. Enemy aircraft were very active over Aubers Ridge. As usual the Australian squadrons were in the thick of the action. Capt Edgar McCloughry of 4 Squadron AFC crashed an LVG over Wavrin at 9.30am and a little later in the morning 2 Squadron and 4 Squadron AFC fought several actions. Taking off at 10.00am, Capt Roy Phillipps of 2 Squadron AFC took his SE5s up to 19,000 feet, the Camels of 4 Squadron AFC, led by Capt Elwyn King, flying at 8,000 feet. Phillipp's formation, from their considerable height advantage, were the first to see enemy aircraft: eight LVG two-seaters three miles east of Lavantie escorted by eight Fokker D VIIs, a thousand feet below the SE5 formation.

Phillipps and three other SE5s went down to attack the escort, which dived away east, leaving their charges. Lt F Follett dived after one of the Fokkers and fired 60 rounds into it from very close range. The enemy machine emitted a cloud of black smoke and went down. Lt T Baker sent another Fokker down out of control for the first of his eventual 12 victories. Lt Eric Cummings attacked one of the LVGs and on his third attack the LVG turned over onto its side, its cockpit on fire. The other LVGs fought Cummings off, but on returning to the lines he attacked four others, shooting one down over Merville.

Just after this fight had ended, seven Camels from 4 Squadron AFC and six SE5s from 2 Squadron AFC crossed the lines near Nieppe Forest and met seven Fokker D VIIs flying at 8,000 feet over Estaires, possibly the same Fokkers which had earlier deserted the LVGs. From a slight height advantage the Camels and SE5s dived to attack the enemy formation. Capt Leonard Taplin, leading the Camels, shot down a Fokker that crashed south of Lestrem, and sent another down out of control. Lt T R Edols, shot down another of the enemy machines, which crashed close by Taplin's victory. Cole's SE5s now arrived, plus King's Camels and some Bristol Fighters, and the remaining enemy scouts were driven east. McCloughry scored again in an evening patrol, shooting down a Fokker D VII east of Estaires at 8.35pm.

To offset these successes, the RAF suffered its third heavy blow of the month. Capt George McElroy, know to all as 'MacIrish,' the senior flight commander of 40 Squadron, took off alone at 8.15am to look for enemy two-seaters. He failed to return. There was no news of McElroy until the middle of August, when the Germans dropped a note to say that he had been shot down and killed by anti-aircraft fire after shooting down a Hannover two-seater over Laventie, and that he was buried nearby at Rue des Mont.

McElroy, who was a protégé of Mannock while they were both in 40 Squadron, had 47 victories at the time of his death. It was ironic that both McElroy and Mannock were killed by groundfire after following enemy aircraft down too low over German held territory. Not to do so was a cardinal rule of both, which they emphasised hard and often to new pilots, but it was a rule they both broke, with fatal consequences.

These three great pilots – James McCudden, Edward Mannock and George McElroy, all killed in July 1918 – had between them shot down over 165 enemy aircraft, but the true loss to the RAF lay not in the number of their victories, but in their leadership, teaching and example. In the last four months of the war they would be sorely missed.

NOTES

1. Possibly *Vzfw* Georg Schalk of *Jasta 34b*, killed in action over Albert.
2. *Tiger Squadron,* Wing Commander Ira Jones, W H Allen, 1954.
3. *Combat Report*, Bill Lambert, William Kimber, 1973.
4. An example of this was a patrol flown by Springs, Callahan and Grider – all inexperienced pilots – on June 17. At 4.30am, the day being very foggy, Horn decided to wash out any patrols, and went back to bed, but instructed Springs that if the fog lifted he was to take two pilots on a 'safety first patrol.' The weather having cleared by 6.00am, Springs Grider and Larry Callahan took off and went ten miles over the lines to shoot down an enemy two-seater in flames south of Merris. The three SE5s had gone down low to catch the two-seater and came under heavy machine gun fire from the ground. When they returned, elated at the victory, Horn was furious, saying that he had sent them out on a 'safe and sane' patrol and not to win the war before breakfast. He gave Springs a dressing down, pointing out that by the law of averages they should all have been killed.
5. *Years of Combat*, Sholto Douglas Marshal of the Royal Air Force Lord Douglas of Kirtleside, Collins, 1963.
6. Cross and Cockade International, Vol.25 No.3, 1994.
7. Ibid.
8. *Tiger Squadron*, Jones.
9. Arthur Rudge, who had been at preparatory school with Rochford, had been transferred to 209 Squadron from 66 Squadron, which had been fighting in Italy. On the Italian Front pilots could roam deep over enemy territory with little risk of meeting overwhelming numbers of enemy aircraft. Rochford suspected that Rudge had wandered too far over the lines during the fight with the Fokkers.
10. Roy was born in Calcutta but was at school in England at the outbreak of war. He had joined 56 Squadron in October 1917, but had crashed an SE5 in November and had been returned to England for further training. He was then pronounced unfit for flying but he managed to have this decision overturned and he was posted to 40 Squadron on June 19. Flying in George McElroy's Flight, Roy claimed ten victories between 6 and 19 July.
11. Edward 'Mick' Mannock VC, MC and Bar, DSO and two bars, has no known grave.
12. The SE5a, D6895, named 'Zanzibar No. 21', was a presentation machine from the government of Zanzibar. 'I have shot down twelve Huns with it. A pilot gets very fond of his machine, like a dog. I'm really quite sad about it.'
13. Ibid.

CHAPTER TWENTY-FOUR

AMIENS:
THE BEGINNING OF THE END

In preparation for the role to be played by the RAF in the coming Allied offensives, due to begin on August 8, an intensive bombing and close support role had been planned. An element of this programme was low level bombing attacks on German aerodromes by fighter aircraft – one example being the attack on Foucaucourt aerodrome on July 16. 13th Wing had planned a similar raid on Epinoy aerodrome, the home of *Jagdstaffeln 23b* and *35b*, both Bavarian units, to be undertaken by the Camels of 3 Squadron and the SE5s of 56 Squadron, with top cover in ascending steps of 1,000 feet by the SE5s of 60 Squadron and the Sopwith Dolphins of 87 Squadron. Still higher, the Bristol Fighters of 11 Squadron were to photograph the results of the attack and protect any stragglers. The formations had set out on July 30, and had reached the target, but the overall leader, Capt H le R Wallace of 3 Squadron, had decided that the weather conditions were unfavourable, that the low cloud over the target held the danger of collisions, and aborted the raid. The formations broke up and returned to their aerodromes.

Major Euan Gilchrist, the commanding officer of 56 Squadron was furious. Roderic Hill, visiting the squadron, wrote in his diary. 'Gilly came back livid.' Gilchrist had served as a fighter pilot in 60 Squadron and was worried about the new role of low level bombing of defended aerodromes his pilots were expected to undertake.

In the early hours of August 1, two night flying Camels from 151 Squadron flew over the enemy aerodromes at Estrées and Guizancourt. Capt Cockerell arrived over Estrées just as an enemy machine was landing, and dropped a bomb, which was seen to land only 50 yards from it. He then attacked another machine, also coming in to land, but all the aerodrome lights were extinguished and he failed to see the result of his attack. Cockerell dropped his remaining bombs on the aero-

drome and returned. Capt Haynes also attacked three enemy machines – reported to be Gothas – over Estrées. He first bombed the seachlights on the aerodrome, putting them out, then attacked one of the enemy machines, but lost it in the darkness. His guns had jammed in this attack and he returned.

The raid on Epinoy aerodrome, aborted on July 30, was carried out in the morning, the squadrons taking off as before, flying to form up over the rendezvous point – 1,000 feet over Arras. The SE5s of 56 Squadron were flying in groups of three and Gilchrist, leading Lts Molyneux and Winslow had trouble with his engine: the water temperature climbed to over 100 degrees and it was vibrating badly. Gilchrist signalled Molyneux and Winslow to carry on climbing without him and they joined three SE5s led by Burden. However, Gilchrist's engine got no worse, and the oil pressure was normal. In view of his misgivings about the operation and its hazardous nature he had no intention of letting his pilots fly it without him, so he joined the Camels at 11,000 feet and the SE5s formed up around him over Arras.

The Camels and SE5s then lost height. Over Marquion they were down to 2,000 feet, only three miles from the enemy aerodromes, which straddled the road at Epinoy. Gilchrist led the SE5s to the northeastern end of the aerodrome and at two minutes to noon attacked along the length of the hangars and sheds from 200 feet.

Gilchrist scored a direct hit on a workshed, setting it on fire. Boger flying on Gilchrist's left had been detailed to attack enemy gun positions – the raid had been meticulously planned with all the pilots given specific targets – and he shot at the crews as they ran out of their billets to man the aerodrome defences. Gilchrist later commented: 'He was as usual most determined and cool … he undoubtedly saved those coming afterwards from any machine gun fire'.

The scene over the aerodrome was one of utter confusion. Many of the SE5 pilots had to pull out of their initial attacks because of Camels flying across their path, but they pressed home their attacks with great determination, each pilot bombing their individual allocated targets that had been marked with letters on their maps. The Canadian, 'Hank' Burden, missed his first target, a large shed, but hit a smaller one on the edge of the field and set it on fire. He then dropped his remaining bombs and concentrated on strafing the enemy machines standing in front of the hangars. He set two alight himself, and reported that another machine – a black one – hit by another pilot, burst into flames. In his last dive, from 300 feet to ground level, Burden attacked another black-painted machine, standing a little apart from the others, and it burst into flames. Burden then climbed away from the action and made for home, firing a drum of Lewis gun ammunition into an enemy boat towing several barges on the Sensée Canal north of Epinoy.

Gilchrist attacked a Pfalz standing outside a hangar, setting it on fire, but his engine was now running so badly that he could not climb to a safe height and he flew home to Valheureux at 2,000 feet along the Arras to Cambrai road.

The American, Paul Winslow, later wrote. 'The great bomb raid came off today, most successfully to say the least.' Winslow had seen Gilchrist's bombs hit a shed and a patrol dump, setting both on fire, before destroying his own target, a hangar. 'The whole aerodrome was ablaze, as was the other across the road – No.3 had done their work also. Then we started, men running in and out, all over the place.' Winslow dived on his assigned target, the men's billets, and fired 400 rounds into them. 'It was war, but it was hell, also very funny. I actually laughed at the antics on the ground.' There was no return fire from the defences of the aerodrome, the biggest danger to the attackers was of collision. 'We stayed ten minutes and I doubt that there were many men or machines left. Coming home, Archie got my aileron and scared me to death. Even the General was in a Camel watching from above. It was the greatest experience I have ever had, and I shall never forget it. We celebrated by going over to 40 Squadron and seeing Landis and Andy and singing.'

Sixty-five machines took part in this raid, a great deal of damage was done and there were no losses. Brigadier-General Longcroft, commanding officer of 3rd Brigade – the 'general' referred to by Winslow – observed the whole operation and wrote to the commanding officer of 13 Wing, LtCol Playfair, asking for his congratulations to conveyed to all who took part; in particular the groundcrews of the squadrons. He pointed out that not a single machine had suffered engine failure during the operation and he considered that the complete success of the raid was to a great extent due to 'the excellent work of the WOs, NCOs and men.'

In his memoirs, *Wings of War*, Rudolf Stark, the *Staffelführer* of *Jasta 35b*, recounts how he and his pilots were relaxing in their Mess after lunch before the afternoon patrols:

'Suddenly we hear a roar and a crash; the next moment bombs come down and machine guns begin to fire. We rush out to see the air full of a wild medley of English machines. About twenty of them have come down to a thousand metres to drop their bombs, while a good way below them some thirty scouts are peppering our hangars with machine guns and hand grenades.' The German pilots could do nothing but keep under cover and watch the attack. Stark went on: 'One of *Jagdstaffel 23*'s hangars went up in flames and burnt to the ground with seven machines inside it. The bullets rained like hail on the roofs. The English were most amazingly impertinent and hardly knew how to find outlets for their arrogance. We had a huge notice board at the entrance to the aerodrome – about seven metres long and two metres high – which warned other troops that they were forbidden to enter. One of the fellows up above hit on the idea of knocking it over, and pounded away at its thick wooden posts until his bullets cut right through them.'

Stark and his pilots could only look on, their only hope that a neighbouring *Jasta* they had telephoned for help would arrive. 'But the storm vanished as quickly as it came. Up went a Very light as a signal and off went all the machines and vanished in the west.' Stark recorded that two large sheds and a tent were demolished, eleven aircraft were destroyed, and all but three of the remainder were badly damaged. 'It was a great day for the English. The raid hit us very hard in view of the difficulty in getting replacements.'[1]

During the night of August 1, Camels of 151 Squadron again raided Estrées and Guizancourt aerodromes. Major Christopher Brand, the CO of the squadron, was the first to arrive over Goizancourt and stayed for forty minutes, dropping his bombs on hangars and attacking a large enemy machine, which was landing. Brand later dropped two more bombs on another machine as it was landing and made circuits of the aerodrome, machinegunning the hangars and searchlights before returning. Shortly after Brand had left, Capt Stanley Cockerell arrived over the enemy field. The hangars were lit up by searchlights – possibly to aid either returning machines or to light up repair work. Cockerell first dropped his bombs on the hangars then extinguished the searchlights with machine gun fire. A Gotha pilot, coming in to land, realising that an enemy aircraft was active over his aerodrome, put out all his lights, but Cockerell attacked the Gotha and it crashed about two miles from the aerodrome.

On August 2 the pilots of 74 Squadron were on standby in pairs to take off and intercept German artillery spotting machines reported to be working over the lines. Ira Jones and Frederick Hunt succeeded only in driving their target away, but later, William Gauld and Frederick Gordon – Grid Caldwell's brother-in-law – shot down an LVG north of Poperinghe. The LVG CVI No.1534/18 from *Fl Abt (A) 268* came down in the Belgian lines, and the crew, *Vzfw* Daron and *Ltn* Molitor were both captured. The LVG was later designated G/II Brigade/21.

As was the custom with any enemy machine brought down in Allied lines, 74 Squadron went out in a lorry to claim their prize and bring back trophies. On arriving at the scene of the crash, Gordon and Gauld, accompanied by Ira Jones, found that the Belgians were reluctant to give up the LVG, having already packed it up to take away. The 74 Squadron pilots pointed out that they had shot it down, therefore it was theirs. The Belgians contested this. A little private war then commenced, but after an offensive action – mostly vocal – the 74 Squadron pilots won their case.

Having loaded the LVG onto the squadron lorry, the three pilots went to the nearby hospital where the wounded German crew had been taken. The enemy pilot – 'a nice lad of eighteen, with very fair hair and complexion'- told them that in their first attack Gauld and Gordon had wounded him in the arm. His observer had bandaged the wound with his handkerchief to stop the bleeding and they had carried on. In their second attack the SE5s had partially shot away his controls. As a result he could not turn and had to land. Jones, Gordon and Gauld gave the boy some cigarettes and money before they left, but gave the observer nothing. 'He was a nasty piece of work.' Jones, being told the observer could speak some English, approached to ask if there was anything they could do for him. The observer's reply was to spit in Jones' face. Jones did nothing. 'As he was wounded, I could not retaliate in any way.'

The enemy observer's reaction was perhaps understandable. After the LVG had landed he had tried to run away, but Gauld had fired at him, wounding him in the shoulder. Later, recounting the story in the squadron Mess, George Gauld remarked to Jones. 'I wish I had killed the sod.' Jones replied. 'If he could have shot as well with his guns as with his mouth, you and Freddie wouldn't be here.' As the joke was on me, the whole Mess roared.'

There was little enemy activity for the next five days, the weather being generally bad, but there were a few combats. On August 3 a patrol of 46 Squadron Camels led by Lt Roy McConnell attacked five Fokker D VIIs east of Lens. Lt Cyril Sawyer shot down one for the first of his six victories, McConnell's opponent broke up in mid air and Victor Yeates destroyed a third.[2]

On August 4 Ira Jones destroyed a Hannover C type west of Estaires for his 33rd victory – he had destroyed an LVG the previous evening for his 32nd.

There was little flying on August 5, the weather was stormy, with low clouds wind and rain, and although the next day was little better, and enemy activity was 'slight', Ira Jones shot down two Fokker D VIIs in flames over Sailly sur la Lys. Jones had left the ground alone and climbed towards Roulers. At 7.30am he spotted a formation of nine enemy scouts climbing for their height after taking off from their aerodrome. Jones got behind the enemy formation and joined it as last man. 'When I was 100 yards off, I pressed my triggers. Nothing happened! I have forgotten to pull up the charging handle of my Constantinesco.' Jones zoomed away, fully expecting that he had now been seen by the enemy scouts. 'Not a bit of it. The Huns were just ahead, still in the same peaceful formation.'

Jones now decided to wait until the enemy formation was nearer to the British Front Lines before attacking, and he shadowed the enemy scouts, keeping 500 feet above and directly behind the last machine. He had time to observe that they were Fokker D VIIs, with black fuselages and different coloured tails. 'They all looked half asleep. Not even the leader had a single look behind him.'

Over Merville, two of the Fokkers went down to attack an RE8 of 4 Squadron working over the lines. Jones dived after them and opened fire from 200 yards. The two Fokkers, who were flying very close together, turned sharply and collided. Jones fired into the entangled wreckage and it burst into flames. The other Fokkers then came down on Jones, but he easily evaded them and crossed the Lines over Meteren, joining up with the RE8. 'The old RE wagged his tail with joy.'

Coming in to land, reaction set in and Jones crashed, the SE5 turning over. Jones was unhurt and he hurried to change into uniform – King George V was to inspect the squadron. During the inspection the King asked Ira Jones his opinion of the German pilots and their machines, laughing out loud on Jones' reply that one Britisher was worth three of the enemy.[3]

The day was fine on August 7, but there was a heavy ground mist and visibility was poor. Capt Cobby and Lt N C Trescowthick of 4 Squadron AFC flew a Special Mission in the morning. Cobby caught an enemy two-seater over Lestrem and shot it down at 12.35am, killing *Uffz* Konz and Uffz Tegmeier of *Schlasta 13*. Ten minutes later the Camels attacked a formation of five Pflaz D III southeast of Armentières. Cobby destroyed one Pflaz and Trescowthick shot down two: one broke up in mid-air under his fire and the other fell in flames.

Major Brand and Lt D'Urban Armstrong of 151 Squadron took off that night and flew to the enemy aerodrome at Estrées. An enemy bomber was coming in to land and Armstrong followed it for sometime before opening fire. The enemy machine burst into flames and crashed. Both Camels then bombed the hangars before returning.

August 8: The Black Day in the German Army

At 4.20am on the morning of August 8 the Amiens offensive opened with an overwhelming artillery barrage: two thousand guns opened fire along a twenty mile front from Morlancourt and La Neuville. Quickly following the barrage, infantry, tanks, armoured cars and armed lorries advanced through a heavy ground mist, meeting little opposition.

The employment of the RAF squadrons during the battle had been laid out by Major-General Salmond on August 1. At daybreak the bomber squadrons were to attack enemy aerodromes, supported by fighters. At the conclusion of these attacks the fighter squadrons were to stand by, ready to operate over the army front if enemy air activity became a threat. In the evening the day bomber squadrons were to bomb the railway stations at Péronne and Chaulnes, again with the support of the fighter squadrons. The fighter squadrons of Third Army were also to stand by, ready to give help if the *Luftstreitkräfte* became unduly active over the battlefront.

On the eve of the battle, Allied air superiority was overwhelming. The British Brigades had available 800 aircraft, of which 376 were fighters. The French also transferred squadrons from the Champagne front, adding another 432 fighters, with the French First Army also deploying 180 fighters. Against the Allied fighter strength of 988 fighters, the German Second and Eighteenth Army (part) had a total of 365 aircraft, of which 140 were fighters.

The programme for the air work over the battlefront was hampered by mist in the early morning, but this cleared by 9.00am and there was a great deal of fighting, the skies over the battle filled with aircraft. There were innumerable actions and combats, but a few will give a picture of the day's events.

The initial ground-strafing patrols from 84 Squadron went out at 8.30am. The pilots, flying in pairs, shot up and bombed troops and transport in the area between the River Somme and Villers-Bretonneux, causing great confusion and many casualties. Lt Norman Mawle shot down a balloon, setting it on fire only 25 feet from the ground. He then turned his attention to an anti-tank gun. The crew attempted to limber up the gun, but Mawles' fire scattered the horses and the gun overturned into a ditch. Mawle was hit in the wrist and twice wounded in the stomach during these attacks, but he managed to return to Bertangles. Beauchamp Proctor attacked enemy guns that were holding up the advance of British tanks. The squadron flew normal offensive patrols later in the day, Beauchamp Proctor shooting down a balloon in flames at 2.40pm In an evening patrol, the SE5s ran into a formation of

Fokker D VIIs north of Foucaucourt and Sidney Highwood shot one down out of control.

At 8.30am Capt Tom Williams and 2Lt F Niseroi of 65 Squadron shared in a two-seater out of control north of Entineham, and Williams later bombed a train, which was seen to break in half. On patrol at 12.25am over Proyart Capt Eric Brookes' Flight fought with Fokker D.VIIs, forcing two to land in the British Lines: the pilots, *Vzfw* Walgenbach of *Jasta 42* and *Uffz* Löhr of *Jasta 44s* were taken prisoner. But casualties for 65 Squadron were heavy: the A Flight Commander, Eric Brookes, was killed, two pilots were wounded while ground-strafing, another shot down and taken POW, and four pilots were forced to land with badly shot up Camels, including the commanding officer, Major H C Champion de Crespigny.

The American, Reed Landis of 40 Squadron, scored three victories during the day: a Fokker Triplane in flames west of Douai at 10.35am, and ten minutes later over Vitry he crashed a DFW two-seater. Turning away from the DFW he attacked a balloon south of the town and shot it down in flames. In the same patrol Capt Ivan Hind sent a Fokker D VII down in a spin, Don Murman destroyed a Fokker D VII over Don and Gilbert Strange sent another down out of control.

Patrols from 60 Squadron were in action by mid-day. Alfred Saunders and Alex Beck attacked an enemy scout at 15,000 feet over Rosières. Saunders overshot in his attack, but Beck sent the enemy machine down in a spin and it crashed in a field by the side of the Amiens to Roye road. Saunders and Beck were uncertain as to the type of this enemy aircraft – 'a Fokker biplane, I think' – but Beck was credited with a Fokker D VII. Beck was then forced to land at Senlis with engine trouble, but Saunders carried on and attacked a two-seater with a white tail, which went down through the clouds out of control, possibly a machine from *Fl Abt (A) 241* which lost a crew killed over Rosières during the day. Other pilots of the squadron claimed victories during the day's fighting. John Doyle and Robert Whitney shared in the destruction of an Hannover two-seater over Foucaucourt at 4.40pm, Doyle destroying another fifteen minutes later over Estrées, with Whitney and Lt F Clark sharing another in flames in the same action, but 2Lt J G 'Shorty' Hall was shot down and killed in an evening fight south of Foucaucourt.

Although 56 Squadron was under command of Third Army, it had been ordered to assist over the Fourth Army front. Two Flights took off at 4.00am but saw no enemy aircraft, one Flight being forced to land at Bertangles by the low clouds and heavy rain. Conditions were better in the evening and eight SE5s left the ground at 6.40pm, crossing the lines south of Villers-Bretonneux. The 56 Squadron SE5s, plus two formations of Bristol Fighters and SE5s from 24 Squadron attacked a large number of Fokker D VIIs and Pfalz D IIIs – possibly elements of *Jagdstaffen 36, 26* and *27* – northeast of Chaulnes. Roy Irwin and Tommy Herbert were each awarded a Fokker D VII from the fight, but Boger was driven down to within 20 feet of the ground by three of the enemy scouts and returned with his SE5 'shot to bits.'

After shooting at a Fokker, which burst into flames, Herbert was wounded in the knee by another and forced to land behind the British lines. Faint with loss of blood, Herbert got to within ten feet of the ground, southwest of Amiens, but fainted as the SE5 hit the ground. He was extricated from the wreck by Canadian troops, but he came round to find himself on a stretcher being carried by German prisoners of war. Not unnaturally he concluded that he had been taken prisoner.

Tom Hazell of 24 Squadron was awarded a Fokker D VII out of control and another destroyed in the fight, and later shot down a DFW over Rosières, which was captured, but Lt F Beauchamp of the squadron was shot down and taken prisoner. *Jasta 36* had two pilots forced to land: *Ltn* Gutsche and *Ltn* Waldheim.

In the morning, Lt W A Rollason of 209 Squadron was an unexpected reinforcement for the cavalry. While ground-strafing in the Beaucourt area, his Camel was badly damaged by groundfire, forcing him to land opposite some British cavalry outposts. Rollason grabbed a rifle and joined in the fighting until a horse was found for him, enabling him to return to his aerodrome at Bertangles.

About 10.30am, two pilots of 201 Squadron were looking for targets in the area of Harbonnières. Seeing three trains loading ammunition, they attacked from 100 feet, each dropping four 25lb Cooper bombs. A nearby squadron of the 5th Dragoon Guards saw the train on fire and galloped to the scene. Two of the trains steamed away, but the third failed to move and was captured by the dragoons. The two Camel pilots later forced an enemy two-seater to land before attacking a wood near Proyart, which was 'swarming with troops'. The Camels strafed this wood for an hour and caused many casualties.

Another indication of the confused nature of the fighting on the ground was the experience of a pilot from 24 Squadron. After dropping his bombs on enemy infantry, he saw eight stationary British armoured cars, held up by an anti-tank gun. He made three attacks on this gun, silencing it, but later had his main petrol tank hit. Thinking the ground below him had been cleared of enemy troops, he landed, but a party of Germans ran towards him. The pilot fired his revolver into one German at twenty yards range, halting the others, before switching over to his gravity tank and taking off. Flying a short distance he saw a group of British cavalry. He landed, told them the position of the enemy troops, and the cavalry galloped forward and captured them. There were many such actions throughout the day.

About midday pilots reported that the roads leading to the Somme crossings were crowded with the retreating enemy troops and transport. It was realised that if the bridges could be destroyed, the German forces west of the River Somme would be trapped, compressed within a pocket of land: the result of the abrupt change of course the Somme takes at Péronne. To close the escape routes across the bridges would cause utter confusion, presenting countless targets of opportunity for low flying aircraft and artillery, and the German Army on the Somme would face utter disaster. In consequence, all bombing operations scheduled for the afternoon were cancelled and attacks on the bridges ordered 'for as long as weather and light permits.' These orders led to a conflict that the official history was to call 'as dramatic as any in the war in the air.'

The bridges at Voyennes, Pithon and Offoy were attacked by DH9s of 27 Squadron and the Camels of 73 Squadron. The bridge at Brie by the Camels of 54 Squadron, the DH9s of 107 Squadron and the DH4s of 205 Squadron, some pilots flying as many as three sorties during the rest of the day. Camels of 43 Squadron and SE5s of 1 Squadron, with DH9s of 98 Squadron, bombed the road and railway bridges at Péronne. The bridge at Bethencourt was attacked twice, by SE5s of 32 Squadron and DH9s of 49 Squadron. A total of 205 attacks were made on the bridges during the afternoon, and twelve tons of bombs were dropped.

These attacks on the bridges were not made without cost – both to the RAF and the *Luftstreitkräfte* – and were the scene of fierce and intense fighting. German air reinforcements had now arrived on the battlefront, including *Jagdgeswader Nr.1*, and the pilots of the *jagdstaffeln*, conscious of the seriousness of the situation, 'for the first time in the war, stayed to fight without calculation.'[4] The only way to negate their numerical inferiority was to spend as little time as possible on the ground and many of the enemy pilots flew ten hours during afternoon and evening.

Both attacks on the bridges at Voyennes, Pithon and Offoy were broken up by enemy fighters: 27 Squadron lost two crews shot down and taken prisoner and another machine badly damaged; 73 Squadron also lost two pilots taken POW.

In the first attack on the bridge at Bethencourt by 12 SE5s and ten DH9s, German fighters attacked the formation before the target could be reached and only four DH9s and three SE5s got through to bomb the bridge. In the second attack, German fighters appeared again, intercepting seven DH9s and eleven SE5s at 1,000 feet as they were diving on their target and only one bomb was seen to explode on the bridge.

The attacks on the bridge at Brie were made in heavy rainstorms. 54 Squadron lost two pilots, one wounded, the other taken prisoner, and 107 Squadron lost a crew killed.

In the morning, acting under the original orders of the day, the DH9s of 98 Squadron, escorted by the Camels of 43 Squadron, had bombed enemy airfields. 98 Squadron lost a crew taken prisoner and a 43 Squadron Camel was badly shot up. In the afternoon, with the attacks switched to the bridge at Péronne, again with 43 Squadron, and with the addition of the SE5s of 1 Squadron, 98 Squadron lost a crew wounded and taken prisoner, but claimed two Pfalz D IIIs shot down from the defending fighters. 43 Squadron lost a pilot killed and another wounded and taken prisoner; 1 Squadron also lost a pilot killed, with another wounded and taken prisoner.

At the end of the day, total casualties for the RAF were forty-five aircraft lost and fifty-two more wrecked or damaged and struck off strength. Of these 97 aircraft, 70 were from the bombers and fighters attacking the bridges over the Somme.[5]

Personnel casualties during the day were the worst for many months. In the fighter squadrons, 11 pilots were killed, 12 wounded, 18 taken prisoners of war, five of whom were wounded – two later dying – and 17 aircraft were badly shot up, damaged and forced to land.

The *Luftstreitkräfte* also sustained heavy and insupportable casualties, described by the *füchterliche Verluste* as 'terrible'. Over the next few days, *Jagdgeschwader Nr.1* alone was reduced to from 50 aeroplanes to eleven. The casualties were in quality as well as quantity: *Ltn* Billik (31 victories) shot down and taken prisoner; *Obltn* Löwenhardt (54 victories) killed; *Hptm* Berthold (44 victories) commanding officer *of Jagdgeschwader Nr.II,* shot down and wounded; Ltn Pippart (22 victories), *Staffelführer* of *Jasta 19* killed; Thom (37 victories) was severely wounded, and Lothar von Richthofen was also seriously wounded, putting him out of the war.

Jagdgeschwader Nr.1 – the Richthofen Circus – the elite of the *Luftstreitkräfte* had been fought almost to destruction. Reduced to one *jagdstaffel*, it was withdrawn from the battle. For the first time the German *jagdstaffeln* had tempered their hitherto successful defensive policy with that lack of caution that the pilots of the RFC/RAF had always shown, and their losses were severe.

August 8 was the final turning point of the war; a day referred to by Ludendorff as 'the black day in the German Army in the history of the war … it put the decline of our fighting power beyond all doubt. The war must be ended.'

The bridges were bombed again during the night, but although the attacks continued the next day, there was a change in tactics. Casualty figures for the attacks on the bridges on August 8 had shown a waste of low flying aircraft of approximately 23 per cent and a new approach was needed.

Orders for operations on August 9, drawn up on the evening of August 8 by IX Brigade HQ, stated:

'It is reported that during the day's operations, enemy aircraft scouts molested our bombers by diving on them from the clouds and prevented them from carrying out their missions effectively. Wing Commanders will, therefore, detail scouts for close protection of bombers to insure that the latter are not interfered with by enemy aircraft while trying to destroy the bridges. This is sole duty of these scouts who will not, therefore, carry bombs.'[6]

The first attacks were carried out at 5.00am on the morning of August 9. The DH9s of 27 Squadron set out to bomb the bridges at Voyennes, with an escort of Camels from 73 Squadron. Half an hour later, the DH9s of 49 Squadron left the ground to attack the bridges at Falvy and Bethencourt, also escorted by Camels of 73 Squadron. The bombers had orders to attack the bridges from 500 feet or lower.

The tactic of close escort by the fighters was new and there had been no opportunity to practice the necessary co-operation between the fighter and bomber crews. The Camels of 73 Squadron failed to find either of the DH9 formations and over their targets the bombers met with 20-30 enemy fighters, which successfully frustrated the attacks on the bridges. The Official History states that more than half the bombs were aimed at 'other targets', but this was more probably a case of jettisoning the encumbrance of the bomb loads by the hard-pressed crews. In the running fight back to the lines, four enemy aircraft were claimed as shot down by crews of 49 Squadron, but two crew members were wounded.

Six DH9s of 98 Squadron, escorted by five Camels of 43 Squadron, attacked the bridge at Feuillères, but met with heavy opposition from enemy fighters and made no hits on the bridge. A DH9 was shot down, the crew taken prisoner. The Camels made no claims nor had any casualties.

The bridge at Brie was attacked by the DH9s of 107 Squadron, escorted by the Camels of 54 Squadron. Orders were for three raids, commencing at 4.30am, in intervals of thirty minutes. The first formation, which left the ground at 5.00am, met 12 Fokker D VIIs over the target area. One Fokker was shot down in flames by a crew of 107 Squadron, and one DH9 was brought down. In the second raid, 107 Squadron lost three DH9s, their crews killed, and four crew taken prisoners, three later dying of their wounds. The third attack, by five DH9s with four Camels of 54 Squadron as close escort, was also met over the target, by 25 enemy fighters. One DH9 crew claimed three enemy scouts shot down, two destroyed and one out of control, but the pilot was wounded, fainted from loss of blood and the observer crashlanded the badly damaged DH9. The escorting Camels lost two pilots killed. Again, no hits were made on the bridge.

Brie bridge was also attacked throughout the day, by the DH4s of 205 Squadron. The attack in the morning was from 11,000 feet, in the afternoon from 2,000 feet. A hit was made on the west end of Brie bridge and another on transport crossing it, but caused only slight damage. The bridge at St Christ was also attacked during the day – from 5,000 feet – and in the evening the squadron again bombed both bridges from 12,000 feet. There were no positive results. These raids were carried out without fighter escort and with no losses. The DH4 was considerably faster than the DH9, and although they were in the vicinity of the attacks the German fighter pilots made no attempt to intercept the bombers.

In an attempt to resolve the unsuccessful escorts of the morning, an elaborate plan had been drawn up for the escort of the afternoon and evening raids on the bridges. Fifty fighters were detailed to fly close escort for the bombers with an additional 74 fighters on patrol immediately above the clouds, but the fighters again failed to find and protect the bombers.[7] The attacks were again without result, no bridges were hit, and in the evening a DH9 of 107 Squadron was shot down, the crew both killed, by Lothar von Richthofen for his second victory from 107 Squadron during the day.

Reinforcements for the *jagdstaffeln* had now arrived and were active over the battlefront. The fighter squadrons of V Brigade were now flying less low level attacks, seeking out the enemy fighters above the battlefield and there were many combats at 2,000 feet or lower.

During the day, 60 Squadron had been detailed to attack enemy balloons. In the morning, two balloons were driven down and John Doyle and Robert Whitney repeated their success of the previous day, sharing in the destruction of an Hannover two-seater over Croisilles. Two Fokker D VIIs were claimed by Gordon Duncan from a fight over the Nesles/Chaulnes area during a patrol in the afternoon.

The pilots of 29 Squadron fought many combats during the day. In the morning patrols, Arthur Reed shot down a Halberstadt in flames south east of Bailleul at 8.00am, and Henry Rath, shot down a DFW out of control over Steenwerck at 10.15am. In the afternoon, Francis Davies destroyed a Hannover two-seater west of Laventie at 5.35pm, and Thomas Harrison a Halberstadt east of Merville at 6.30pm.

The ground offensive had gone well. By nightfall, the British troops had reached the outskirts of Lihons and Proyart. North of the Somme, the line Chipilly-Morlancourt-Dernancourt had been gained and on the British right the French First Army had reached almost to Roye. But the British advance now began to slow: the difficult ground of the old Somme battles had been reached and the fighter squadrons of Fourth Army were having to cease their ground-strafing work – now so vital to the success of the ground battle – and fly high offensive patrols in an attempt to contain the fresh German fighters in the area of the battle. The German ground forces were also being reinforced; sixteen fresh divisions would have reached the front by the evening of August 11.

The bridges over the Somme were bombed during the night of August 9/10, but attacks by the day bombers of IX Brigade were discontinued on August 10 and only two raids were carried out during the day by DH4s of 205 Squadron. On the second of these, in the afternoon, on the bridges at St Christ and Brie, the bombers were attacked by 14 enemy fighters. One enemy fighter was claimed as brought down and an observer of a DH4 was fatally wounded.

On the morning of August 10, bombing attacks were switched to the important rail centres of Peronne and Equancourt and the railway network between Bapaume and Epéhy. Twelve DH9s from 27 and 49 Squadrons, escorted by SE5s from 32 Squadron and Bristol Fighters of 62 Squadron, took off in the late morning to attack the stations at Peronne and Equancourt and were met by fifteen Fokker D VIIs over the targets. Three pilots of 32 Squadron were casualties during the fight: one pilot was killed, another shot down and taken prisoner and another forced to leave the fight with a badly shot up SE5.

Two Flights of SE5s from 56 Squadron had seen the attack by the Fokkers and joined in the fight. William Irwin shot down one Fokker, which turned over onto its back and went down 'like a falling leaf.' Irwin then attacked three more enemy scouts below him, firing 150 rounds into the highest from close range. The Fokker burst into flames, half rolled and went down burning and smoking into the clouds. Irwin was then attacked by the two remaining Fokkers and he spun away into the cloud cover. 'When I climbed out again the fight was over.'

The top Flight from 56 Squadron had not been so lucky. William Boger had taken Paul Winslow and Herbert Flintoft down into the fight, and Winslow was the only member of the Flight to return to Valheureux. Flintoft was shot down by the Fokkers – which he described as having fuselages painted in yellow and black diamonds, from the cockpit area to the rear their tailplanes, with the pattern repeated on the top wings – and came down near some enemy artillery. 'Apart from a few bruises, I was unhurt, but well and truly in the bag.' Boger had been shot down and killed, possibly by either *Ltn* Veltjens or *Ltn* Borck of *Jasta 15*.

Although this patrol ended badly for 56 Squadron, another morning patrol by the squadron had some success. It attacked six Fokker D VIIs north of Suzanne and Hank Burden shot one down to crash north of the village, and a second which spun down and crashed by the river, east of Suzanne. The remaining Fokkers having spun down and flown east, Burden reformed the SE5s. Twenty-five minutes later, six more D VIIs were seen, low down, with another 15 higher, over Puzeaux. Burden took the SE5s to the east and attacked the Fokkers from out of the sun. Burden selected the top Fokker, got on its tail and held his fire until within 50 yards, the enemy pilot unaware that he was about to be attacked. Burden fired a long burst from his Vickers gun and a whole drum of Lewis. The top left wing of the Fokker folded back before the entire aircraft broke up, and Burden had to hurriedly pull out to avoid ramming the wreckage. The squadron had one casualty in this fight: Lt Herbert Allen had been shot down by *Uffz* Lohrmann of *Jasta 42.*

Although shaken by its losses, the squadron consolidated its successes of the morning by another five victories in an evening patrol. Burden's first victory was a Fokker D VII that crashed near Morchain; his second another D VII that dived into a field near Cizancourt. Irwin sent another of the enemy machines down to crash at Roye and Stenning and Winslow were each awarded a Fokker as out of control.

That night a spectacular victory was won by Capt A B Yuille of 151 Squadron. The pilots of 56 Squadron at Valheureux had a grandstand view. They had been woken up by the distinctive drone of an enemy night flying bomber and went out onto the aerodrome. It was a clear starlit light and the enemy bomber, a giant Zeppelin Staaken R XIV of *Reisenflugzeugabteilungen 501* was held in the cone of several searchlights. Paul Winslow wrote.

'Of course, by that time everything that could possibly reach him was being diligently fired in his direction. The row was terrific. Suddenly a red light flared out of the air about a mile away and the guns instantly ceased firing. For a few seconds the only audible sound was the drone of the Hun's engines. Then the nose of a Camel showed in the light just under the Gotha's (sic) tail and we could see his streams of flaming bullets as he fired his burst. The scout fell away and immediately little tongues of flame showed in Fritz's cockpit. They seemed to die down for a moment then burst out in an enormous glare and the Gotha (sic) turned over to one side then nosed down and plunged to earth, a single ball of fire. We could see the men dropping off as he came down. He still had a bomb on when he crashed and this exploded shortly afterwards, doing a great deal of damage to the remains of the bus and killing and wounding about fifty American soldiers who had rushed over to get souvenirs. Every soldier in twenty miles had seen the whole thing and the air fairly hummed with cheering.'[8]

On August 10, the concentration of British single-seater fighters in the battle area represented 70 per cent of the fighter strength of the RAF on the Western Front – 480 fighters. The Allied strength in the air was now overwhelming and the air fighting became less intense, with notably fewer casualties.

German resistance on the ground was also stiffening, and on August 11 Haig ordered an indefinite postponement of operations, effectively stopping the battle. The British and French armies had advanced twelve miles into German held territory, nearly 30,000 prisoners had been taken and over 400 guns captured. The German armies in France had been dealt a blow from which they would never recover.

To some extent the full effectiveness of the RAF had been squandered by the attacks on the Somme bridges and their casualties had risen alarmingly during the attacks. There is little doubt that if the squadrons had been allowed to continue their highly effective tactics during the first day of the battle, air power would have played a larger, more valuable part in the Battle of Amiens. The battle was a victory of great promise, but it was not unflawed.

The pattern of airfighting of the last two days of the battle continued over the remainder of August, with large formations of enemy fighters now being met. Victories were claimed but many fights were indecisive, as was often the case between evenly matched formations. Many German pilots were now seen to be taking to their parachutes to escape from crippled or burning aeroplanes. Combats are too numerous to detail, but some distinctive actions during the period are worth recording. August 12 saw the most successful day for the pilots of 29 Squadron for sometime, with eleven victories claimed during the day's fighting. The day started when two Flights of SE5s attacked eight Fokker D VIIs and a Pfalz D III over Ploegsteert. Capt Guy Wareing shot down the Pfalz, and five of the Fokkers were awarded to Lts W Dougan, E C Hoy, C G Ross and C J Venter. Later in the patrol, Tom Harrison destroyed a balloon in flames east of Estaires. In an evening patrol, Capt Lagesse attacked the leader of a formation of Fokker D VIIs and shot it down. The South African, Cristoffel Johannes Venter, shot down a Fokker, which burst into flames, the pilot taking to his parachute, and another South African pilot, Edgar Amm, destroyed another Fokker, also in flames. Lt Sydney Brown, an American pilot from Brooklyn, New York, attacked the remaining Fokker. Brown closed to extremely close range and his fire hit the outer wing struts of the enemy machine. The struts were destroyed and the whole enemy machine fell to pieces in mid air.

On August 12 the Australian squadrons were moved south to assist in the battle and soon made their arrival felt. On August 16 the enemy aerodome at Haubourdin was attacked by Bristol Fighters of 88 Squadron, the SE5s of 92 Squadron and 2 Squadron AFC, and the Camels of 4 Squadron AFC. Sixty-five machines took part in the raid, bombing and machine gunning. Three large hangars containing aircraft were hit and burnt out, and two aircraft standing outside the hangars were also set alight. Several additional hangars were hit, fires were started in huts and what was believed to be the officers' Mess was set alight. The attacking aircraft then turned their attentions to the railway station at Haubourdin, machinegunning embarking troops. Two staff cars were fired at; one of which ran up a steep bank and overturned, the other driving into a ditch. A train was stopped by machinegun fire and bombs. All the attacking machines returned safely.

On August 13 an attack was made on the enemy aerodrome at Varssenaere. The DH9s of 211 and 218 Squadrons, plus fifty Sopwith Camels from 210, 213 Squadrons, and the United Sates 17th Pursuit Squadron, attacked just after dawn, with the Camels of 204 Squadron flying at 5,000 feet as top cover. The attack was a complete surprise. Many enemy aircraft, valuable replacements for the *Luftstreitkräfte* were destroyed, and a great deal of damage inflicted on the infrastructure of the airfield. All the Allied machines returned safely.

During the pause in operations on the ground, from August 12 to 20, there were serious differences of opinion between Haig and Marshal Foch. On the afternoon of August 10, Foch ordered that the British Fourth Army, under General Rawlinson, was to push on to the Somme and establish bridgeheads over it south of Péronne. Rawlinson flatly refused. The momentum of his Army's attack had run out, German resistance was stiffening, and casualties were rising. The Fourth Army had reached the old front line of February 1917, a labyrinth of old trenches and a sea of shell holes, which were ideal enemy machine gun posts. The entire area over which his troops would have to fight was a maze of old barbed wire entanglements, many of them uncut, and the ground was covered with a heavy growth of thistle and brambles. Progress here would be tedious, slow, and incur heavy casualties for little gain. It was also evident that the German Army was preparing to fall back on the formidable defences of the Hindenburg Line, some thirty miles at the rear. When Haig told Rawlinson that the attack was the wish of Foch, he replied: 'Are you commanding the British Army or is Marshal Foch?'

A direct order from Foch that the British Fourth Army should mount an attack on Roye-Chaulnes positions took Haig to the HQ of the Marshal on August 15, where he made it clear that he had no intention of obeying such an order, which would involve massive loss of life for very little result. Instead, he proposed that the British Third and First Armies attack northwards, between Albert and Arras. The ground was more suitable for tanks and the thrust would turn the line of the Somme south of Péronne and force the enemy to fall back to the Hindenburg Line. The Germans, Haig pointed out, were already in a salient, threatened from the south, and did not seem prepared to meet an attack on its northern flank. Foch finally agreed – with bad grace, he withdrew the French First

Army from the command of Haig – and the next offensive undertaken by the British armies was on August 23: the battle of Bapaume.

For the air support of the Third and First Armies, which were to carry out the attack, it was only necessary to strengthen the III Brigade of the RAF. Those squadrons already active north of the Somme would stay, reinforced by four fighter squadrons. The single-seater fighter squadrons employed over the battle were: Nos 1, 56, and 60 Squadrons (SE5s); 87 Squadron (Sopwith Dolphins) and Nos 3, 54, 73, 201 Squadrons (Camels) plus two U.S. squadrons, Nos 17 and 148 – also equipped with Camels – which had been working with the RAF. In addition, the fighters of I Brigade, First Army, on the left flank of the battle, were also to operate over the area of the attack, flying high offensive patrols.

On August 17, as part of the preparation of the coming offensive, the enemy aerodrome at Lomme was bombed by 2 and 4 Squadrons AFC and 92 and 88 Squadrons. Some pilots were so low over the enemy field that several of their machines were damaged by the explosions of their own bombs. Direct hits were seen on hangars, sheds and huts. Two enemy aircraft, coming into land at the nearby aerodrome of Haubourdin – which had been attacked the previous day – crashlanded without being attacked. The aerodrome defences at Lomme were much stronger than at Haubourdin and a Camel pilot of 4 Squadron AFC was shot down and killed. Photographs taken of the raid showed that two huts were burning fiercely and that the wind direction would in all probability spread the fire to others.

During the day the RAF lost one of its most redoubtable fighter pilots: the Canadian, William Claxton a Flight Commander in 41 Squadron, who had scored ten victories since the beginning of the month, bringing his total to 37. Claxton, his fellow Canadian, Frederick McCall, and Lt T M Alexander, were involved in a fight with a large number of enemy scouts south of Ypres and in the fighting Claxton was wounded in the head, crashed behind the German lines and was taken prisoner.[9] McCall managed to extricate himself from the fight and returned but was immediately posted to Home Establishment.[10] Alexander had been shot down and killed.

An impression of the type and scale of the actions fought during August can be gained from the experiences of a patrol flown by 56 Squadron on the morning of August 19. The patrol had taken off at 7.00am, crossing the lines north of Arras twenty five minutes later. At 7.45am the patrol was passing over Frémicourt when a formation of seven Fokker D VIIs was seen to be passing under the SE5s, but as Owen Holleran, leading the patrol, made to attack these, he saw another formation of 15 enemy scouts approaching. Turning away from these, Holleran saw a third formation – 20 Fokker D VIIs and Triplanes – diving on his formation from the west. 'There was nothing for it so we ran. They pushed us very hard.'

Running for the lines, Holleran saw a Flight of SE5s of 92 Squadron approaching and fired two red Very lights to attract their help; the leader fired a red light in reply, but flew straight on. 'By this time the Huns were firing at us, so I opened full out and cleared away.' Holleran then reformed the SE5s and recrossed the lines northeast of Arras, where he saw a pair of Hannover two-seaters and an LVG working over the lines. Holleran first attacked the LVG, but turned away, leaving it to the other SE5s, and attacked the Hannovers. 'Was so angry over being chased across half France I dove on them, firing indiscriminately at both. Each one apparently thought he was my target so did a quick turn to give his back gun a crack at me. They collided at about 2,000 feet and fell near Biache on the Scarpe.'

Thomas 'Bill' Hazen, a particular friend of Holleran, failed to return. During the running fight he had been shot down and killed by *Vzfw* Mai of *Jasta 5*.

The preliminary fighting to the battle of Bapaume was an attack on August 21 to capture the Arras to Albert railway. To support this attack, three fighter squadrons of Third Brigade were allocated to attack ground targets, one squadron to each Corps front: 60 Squadron to VI Corps; 3 Squadron to IV Corps and 56 Squadron to V Corps. Beginning at 30 minutes after zero hour, the squadrons were to send their aircraft out in pairs at intervals of thirty minutes. Top cover was to be flown by the two American fighter squadrons, Nos 17 and 148, and by 87 and 11 Squadrons.[11] These plans were negated by the weather on the morning of the attack. A light rain had fallen the previous evening, continuing for some hours after dawn on August 21, followed by a ground mist, and the squadrons did not leave the ground until 11.00am.

The pilots of 60 Squadron seemed to have ignored the orders to fly in pairs and flew patrols of four SE5s throughout the day. In the first of the ground-strafing attacks, Lt Stephen Keen was shot down by groundfire and suffered a fractured skull in his crash. He was pulled from the wreckage of his SE5 by British troops and taken to No.3 CCS but died without recovering consciousness. The next patrol from the squadron attacked targets in the area of St Leger and Sapignies. Lt F E Smith strafed troops and transport on the Ervillers to Sapignies road, but his SE5 was so badly damaged by groundfire that on his return it was struck off strength.

In addition to ground targets, 3 Squadron were ordered to attack the enemy balloon lines. The squadron lost three pilots during the day. One pilot was wounded in the knee but managed to return to the aerodrome, another pilot was wounded, and Lt L McIntyre, who was last seen diving steeply to attack a balloon

near Bapaume, failed to return and was later found to have been killed.

Ground-strafing in pairs during the day, 56 Squadron lost two pilots. Burden bombed an old sugar refinery, bombed and machine gunned troops in the vicinity and later attacked troops in shell holes and trenches near Miraumont. Holleran dropped two of his bombs on German bivouac lines in a wood near Fricourt and his remaining two on German machine gun teams near Contalmaison. He returned to report that visibility was poor and that there was little movement of troops and transport.

John Blair and Noel Bishop were the next pair to take off. Blair dropped one bomb on a balloon site near Le Sars and three more on other targets. Bishop, on his first flight over the lines, dropped his bombs on an anti-aircraft battery but was hit in the chest by fire from a machine gun and forced to return, landing at 52 Squadron's aerodrome at Izel-le-Hameau. As with the other fighter squadrons, this pattern of attacks was repeated throughout the day, all the pilots flying two patrols. Lt Robert Ellis of the USAS, attached to the squadron, had been forced to land in the German lines, south east of Bapaume. 'We are very worried about him because we have been strafing that area all day and have done a tremendous lot of damage, and we assume that the Germans in that area are peevish.'[12]

A similar pattern of attacks by the fighter squadrons continued on the following day, August 22, but from midday normal Close Offensive patrols were also flown. Burden's Flight left the ground at noon and attacked five Fokker D VIIs over Péronne. Burden tackled the rearmost Fokker, which had yellow and black stripes on its tailplane, and it spun, momentarily recovered, then spun again, finally crashing a mile north west of Péronne. This was Burden's last of 15 victories.

At nightfall, four Camels from 151 Squadron bombed the German aerodromes at Moislains and Offoy setting fire to hangars and sheds at Offoy. Capt Yuille and Lt C R Knight of the squadron were on patrol when searchlights lit up a Friedrichshafen G III bomber. Yuille attacked first and fired two short bursts before overshooting. Knight then attacked and fired 100 rounds into the enemy bomber, which burst into flames and crashed in the British trenches, killing the three man crew. This Friedrichshafen G III No.378/17 was from *Bogohl VI/8* and was designated G/I Brigade/13.

The ground attacks in the day had gone well, Albert had been recaptured, and the Front Line had been pushed forward to beyond the village of Méaulte. The way was now clear for the main attack to begin on the morning of August 23. This offensive, the battle of Bapaume, was seen to be a crucial opportunity to finally bring the war to a conclusion. In a telegram to his army commanders, Haig pointed out the necessity of 'bold and resolute action' to take full advantage of the defeats and continuous attacks which had weakened the German army and sapped its morale; that it no longer had the means to deliver counter attacks, nor the numbers to defeat the extended attacks which were now to take place against it. 'Risks which a month ago would have been criminal to incur, ought now to be incurred as a duty.'

Bapaume: Prelude to Victory

At 4.45am on the morning of August 23 the battle opened along the entire front, from Arras to Soissons. The greater part of the fighting took place on the thirty-three miles of the British front, from just north of St Quentin in the south to Mercatel in the north, where the Hindenburg Line joined the old Arras-Vimy defence system of 1916. The three French armies made only little progress, but on the British Fourth Army front, south of the Somme, the 32nd British and 1st Australian Divisions, commanded by the Australian, Lt-General John Monash, fighting in great heat, forced the enemy to evacuate the bend in the Somme. In the north, the British Third Army attacked from Epéhy to Inchy. Fighting against numerically superior German forces – seven divisions – General Byng's troops decimated many German regiments and took a large number prisoners. The German forces, especially the machine gunners, fought with their customary courage and skill, but there were ever increasing signs of a decline in the morale of the enemy troops. The Third Army troops took all their objectives.

The RAF brigades mainly involved in the offensive were III Brigade, working with Third Army, the V Brigade with Fourth Army and the HQ IX Brigade. The work of the fighter squadrons was again low level attacks, the attention of all pilots drawn to the importance of taking action against anti-tank guns, which had held up tanks in the fighting at Amiens earlier in the month.[13]

The SE5s of 56 Squadron left the ground at 5.15am as escort to the Camels of 3 Squadron which were to attack ground targets. The Camels went 'well over' the enemy lines, attacking troops and transport and 'smashing up the German supports.' Holleran was flying in the escort and his diary records: 'Saw a formation of 11 Fokker biplanes who escorted us all the way down from in front of Arras to well south of Bapaume, trying to get a chance at the Camels. We and the Bristols (the Bristol Fighters of 11 Squadron were also part of the escort – Author.) finally started east after them and they went home.'

During the day, young Noel Bishop, who had been hit in the chest while ground-strafing two days previously, returned to the squadron. The bullet had knocked the wind out of him, convincing him that he had been killed. Two machineguns were firing at him from a shell hole and considering it unsportsmanlike to fire at a man already dead, Bishop dropped

all four of his Cooper bombs on them. The SE5 was so low that the explosions of his bombs almost brought it down, but the effort of regaining control confirmed to Bishop that he was still alive, and although extremely dizzy he made for home. Holleran wrote of Bishop's return:

'On the way home he got very sick and dizzy and overshot the aerodrome, going nearly twenty miles north before he found a place to land. He came down and enquired where he was, without mentioning having been hit. A flight commander of that place went to show him on the map and when he turned back to explain something he found the kid huddled upon the floor in a dead faint. He had had rather a strenuous day of it.'[14] Hank Burden's diary entry, commenting on Bishop's return, reads: 'Bishop got back from hospital today … was mad because someone had stolen the bullet that had lodged between his ribs.'[15]

Despite his first comment, Lt Albert McManus, flying with 3 Squadron later made light of the hazardous duty of ground-strafing in his diary. 'We've been having a perfectly perfect hell of a time. I dropped 25 pounds of TNT onto a Hun truck and it ceased to be a useful article forthwith. Another time I found some general's car hitting the high spots for some eastern point, so I went down to see if the buxom general was subject to lead poisoning. He was. I lent him about 200 rounds and was watching his car end its career in a large ditch when I heard the beloved rat-tac-tac of a Fokker. Oh yes, I was the target and I'll bet he wonders even now where I went. I must have done a good 250mph crossing the lines.'[16]

Patrols from 60 Squadron were ground-strafing during the day, but also flew normal offensive patrols. In the morning, Capt John Doyle, the senior flight commander of the squadron, and 2Lt M D Sinclair, caught a pair of DFWs over Croisilles: one dark-coloured, the other orange. Doyle shot down the dark-coloured DFW to crash at 9.55am, and 2Lt M D Sinclair sent the other down out of control.

In the north, Keith Caldwell had returned to 74 Squadron on August 20 from 14 days leave. He wasted no time in getting back into the fighting. Flying a patrol on the day of his return, he saw no action, but on August 23 he was leading a late evening patrol of SE5s southeast of Houthulst at 7,000 feet when he saw six Fokker D VIIs to the north. Caldwell and Roxburgh-Smith dived to attack the enemy formation, Caldwell picking out the enemy leader, who dived away to the east through the thin layer of cloud. Caldwell followed, fired a burst at close range and hit the Fokker in the petrol tank, the vapour streaming out. The enemy machine turned over and dived to the northwest. Caldwell dived after it and at 4,500 feet closed to within 50 yards and fired a full drum of Lewis. The enemy pilot never pulled out of his dive and hit the ground east of the forest at 7.27pm. Ben Roxburgh-Smith shot down two of the enemy formation in flames, both machines crashing at Passchendaele.

Escorted by the Bristol Fighters of 22 Squadron, the SE5s of 64 Squadron and the Camels of 209 Squadron bombed the enemy aerodrome at Cantin. The SE5s attacked first: the nearby railway station was crowded with troops and they dropped four bombs on the station before machinegunning the infantry. Both squadrons then attacked the airfield, setting five sheds on fire, completely destroying another and scoring a direct hit on a larger shed, which burst into flames. The SE5s and Camels then went back to the station and bombed a train standing in a siding. Before returning, the squadrons machinegunned the roads leading to the airfield. An LVG two-seater, that inadvertently wandered into the middle of the British scouts, was shot down and crashed near the aerodrome by Dudley Lloyd-Evans of 64 Squadron for his fourth victory. All the attackers returned safely.

The fighter squadrons on the Third Army front were ground-strafing throughout the day, but remarkably there were only two casualties, both from the U.S. 17th Pursuit Squadron. Lt M L Campbell was shot down and killed by fire from the ground over Warlencourt and Lt R D Williams, although wounded in the back and his Camel holed in the petrol tank, returned, his finger in the holed tank, to crash land at 3 Squadron's aerodrome. Williams was taken to hospital.

The casualties suffered by the low flying fighters of the RAF was high, both in pilots and machines. Burden wrote that the 56 Squadron pilots were flying 'in all kind of machines' so many of the squadron's SE5s having been badly damaged in the ground-strafing attacks. But allied air strength was overwhelming. Karl Bodenschatz, the adjutant of the Richthofen *Jagdgeschwader* wrote: 'The German *Luftwaffe* is choking to death under the weight of enemy strength in the air. There is little left that can be done.'

The night flying Camels of 151 Squadron were again successful on the night of August 23/24. Lt W Aitken saw a Gotha trapped by seachlights, but as he went into the attack, the enemy pilot threw off the beams and the gunners opened fire on the Camel. Aitken closed to 40 yards and fired 80 rounds at the enemy bomber, which dived away. Aitken tried to follow, lost the Gotha in the darkness, but it crashed in the British trenches at Puchevillers at 12.35am, killing one member of the three man crew, but with the remaining two taken prisoner. The wreckage of the Gotha G Vb, from *Bogohl III/17*, was classified G/III Bgd/11.

Forty minutes later, Lt C R W Knight shot down a Friedrichshafen in flames to crash north of Doullens. The three-man crew, from *Bogohl III/18* were all killed. This enemy

machine fell in the 1st Brigade area and was classified G/I Brigade/13.

By the end of the day, the Australian Corps south of the Somme had taken Herleville, Chuignolles and Chuignes, capturing over 2,000 prisoners; north of the Somme they had taken the high ground south and east of Albert. Further north the Third Army had gained much ground, had taken 5,000 prisoners and a great many guns.

The Third and Fourth Armies gave the enemy no respite, attacking again at 1.00am on August 24. The weather was bad in the morning, with low clouds, but cleared up in the afternoon. The fighter squadrons were again engaged in low level work but in addition six enemy balloons were destroyed. In one of these balloon attacks, H A Hamilton of the U.S. 17th Pursuit Squadron was seen to destroy his balloon, but was then hit by fire from the ground. Hamilton crashed four miles north of Bapaume and was killed. In the afternoon, another pilot of the squadron, 2Lt G T Wise, was shot down and killed by *Obltn* Greim of *Jasta 34*, and Lt M K Curtis of U.S. 148th Pursuit Squadron, was shot down and taken POW.

During the night *Schlachtstaffel 16* bombed Bertangles aerodrome, the home of 84, 209 and 48 Squadrons. The commanding officer of 48 Squadron, Keith Park, had invited all the squadrons to a cinema show in one of his squadron's hangars and the film had been under way for sometime when a bomb fell on an adjacent hangar, setting it alight. The fire lit up the target for more enemy bombers. They set more hangars alight, dropped anti-personnel bombs and machine-gunned the field. Major Sholto Douglas, in the front row of the cinema when the first bomb had exploded, had thrown himself under the piano, but not wanting to be caught in a burning hangar ran out and took shelter in a trench. From the trench he saw that one of his squadron's hangars was also ablaze and he gathered a party of men to push the SE5s out of the hangars. Most of the machines were successfully pulled to safety, but the roof of one hangar fell on one SE5 and broke its back.

Fifteen personnel of 48 Squadron were wounded in the raid, two fatally; a pilot of 84 Squadron, Alex Matthews, was killed and another seriously wounded; ten Bristol Fighters were completely destroyed and a great deal of damage done to stores, offices and huts. The extent of these losses was greater than any suffered by the RFC/RAF in a bombing raid throughout the entire war. Forty Eight Squadron was withdrawn to Boisdinghem to be re-equipped, but was back in action only two days later.

The attack on Bertangles was not allowed to go unpunished. On August 25, Etreux, the home of *Bombengeschwader Nr.1* was bombed by 27 and 49 Squadrons, and the aerodrome of *Bombengeschwader Nr.4* at Mont d'Origny was attacked by 98 and 107 Squadrons, with further support over the enemy aerodromes by the FE2bs of 62 Squadron. SE5s from 32 and 40 Squadrons were given orders to fly offensive patrols in St Quentin-Marcoing area to stop any interference from the *jagdstaffeln,* then to escort the bombers home. These raids were not a success. Conditions were very bad, the day was oppressive with thunderclouds – on their way home the DH9s of 49 Squadron had to fly through a heavy thunderstorm – and only eight of the 24 DH9s of 98 Squadron reached the target, many suffering engine problems and having to return. The Camels of 43 Squadron, detailed to escort the bombers, lost sight of them in the heavy clouds, and 32 Squadron were attacked by Fokker D VIIs, shooting down two, one pilot escaping by parachute. On its return flight, 49 Squadron was attacked by enemy scouts from *Jasta 35.* An enemy scout was claimed as shot down in flames, but two crews were lost: one killed, the other taken prisoner, and an additional two crew members were wounded.

Although these retaliatory raids had inflicted little damage, the pilots of 84 Squadron gained some compensation for the death of Alex Matthews. Burden's diary entry reads: 'This morning the whole of 84 Squadron went up to 21,000 feet and waited for the photographic Rumplers to come and get pictures of the damage. They got their pictures and then were both shot down in flames.'

In the day's fighting the long career of the Australian, Captain Alexander Augustus Norman Dudley Pentland finally came to a close. Pentland had flown BE2cs with 16 Squadron in June 1916 and only a few days after his arrival had shot down a Fokker E type. Later in the year he had joined 29 Squadron to fly DH2s, but had broken his leg playing rugby. Posted to 19 Squadron to fly Spads, he had scored nine victories, but was injured in a crash after his Spad had been hit by an anti-aircraft shell. In 1918 he returned to France as a flight commander with the newly formed 87 Squadron, flying Sopwith Dolphins. By August 25 Pentland had scored another 13 victories, bringing his total to 23, but after shooting down a DFW and a Fokker on the morning of August 25, he had been wounded in the foot, possibly by a pilot *of Jasta 57,* ending his war.

The night of August 25 saw another success for the night fighters of 151 Squadron. Lt C R W Knight shot down a Friedrichshafen, which exploded on hitting the ground.

The day was overcast with rainstorms on August 26. In the north the British First Army opened the Battle of the Scarpe with an attack eastwards from Arras. The Army was reinforced for the battle with 8 and 73 Squadrons – both specialising in attacking anti-tank guns – and the fighter squadrons of I Brigade were strengthened: Nos. 40, 54, 64, 208 and 209 squadrons were all involved in the battle. The Bristol Fighters

of 22 Squadron were also added to the strength. It was intended that 40 Squadron and 22 Squadron were to fly offensive patrol during the day, while the remainder of the force attacked ground targets and enemy aerodromes. In the event the attacks on the enemy aerodromes were abandoned because of the poor weather conditions, but the ground-strafing missions were flown, despite the strong southwest wind, low clouds and rain.

Eighteen Camels of 209 Squadron took off in a rainstorm at 7.20am and attacked troops, transport and machinegun emplacements. Three Camels were shot down by fire from the ground – with one pilot killed and another injured – and a fourth Camel returned badly damaged. The SE5s of 64 Squadron left at 8.00am, were relieved by the Camels of 54 Squadron at 10.00am and then by Camels of 208 Squadron at 10.00am. The squadrons followed this pattern throughout the day, flying from Le Hameau. Major B E Smythies, the commanding officer of 64 Squadron, was responsible for the co-ordination of these fighter attacks and new tactics were employed. Each patrol was given specific targets to attack, which had been reported by wireless messages from the observers of the corps squadrons, and Smythies also flew over the battlefield during the day to make personal assessments of the situation. A total of 553, bombs – 25lb Coopers – were dropped, and a staggering 26,000 rounds of machine gun ammunition were fired on ground targets. The cost was slight: one pilot was killed, three pilots wounded, and four aircraft were struck off strength as unsalvageable. There was no opposition from the *Luftstreitkräfte;* the patrols from 22 and 40 Squadrons reported no enemy activity in the air until the evening, when 40 Squadron had a brief indecisive fight with Fokker D VIIs over the Scarpe, with one claimed as out of control.

The American pilots of U.S. 17th Pursuit Squadron fighter had a disastrous day. At 5.25pm a patrol saw a pilot from U.S. 148th Pursuit Squadron under attack by enemy scouts and went down to his aid. The enemy scouts were elements of *Jagdstaffeln 27, B,* and *17,* and the inexperienced Americans had little chance against the highly experienced German pilots. Six pilots were lost: two were killed, and four were shot down and taken prisoner, three of whom were wounded, one fatally. The pilot of U.S. 148th Pursuit Squadron was also shot down and killed.

The Camels of 209 Squadron lost heavily while ground-strafing during the day. Five Camels were badly shot up, three being struck off strength, one pilot was injured, another wounded, and Lt L Belloc was killed when he was hit by groundfire and crashed into trees near Remy.

On August 27 the German forces fighting on the Scarpe desperately defended their positions, but the Canadian troops pressed determinedly on, supported by the low flying squadrons of the RAF, with the fighter squadrons operating at squadron strength. Between 5.15am and 7.30am, 66 pilots flew ground-strafing attacks, including twelve pilots from 73 Squadron who attacked anti-tank guns in the narrow area from the River Scarpe to the Arras to Cambrai road. From 7.30am until 5.00pm, two Flights from each of the single-seater fighter squadrons flew consecutively at hourly intervals, and from 5.00pm onwards, in spite of the low clouds and rain, the squadrons again flew in full squadron strength, bombing and machine gunning the enemy troops, artillery and transport. The single-seater fighter squadrons dropped a total of 646 Cooper bombs and fired 47,570 rounds of ammunition at ground targets in the battle area. German prisoners reported that against these constant low flying attacks it was impossible to reform beaten troops.

Enemy balloons were also attacked and brought down. A Flight from 84 Squadron led by Beauchamp Proctor took off in the early morning with orders to destroy balloons on the Australian front. The whole Flight shared in the destruction of the first balloon over Flaucourt at 8.40am, but was chased back to the lines by its guard of eight enemy scouts. The enemy pilots having left the SE5s at the front lines, Beauchamp Proctor flew into the cloud cover, navigated by compass to the position of another balloon he had noted over Mount St Quentin, and shot it down for his 42nd victory.[17]

The low clouds and rainstorms persisted on August 28 and there was a heavy ground mist that hampered low-level flying. Only a few enemy aircraft were seen, but four balloons were shot down by pilots of *Jagdstaffeln 65* and *18*. After recording that he and Burden had flown low level attacks seven times during the day, Holleran's diary entry for the day reads:

'A message came in the afternoon reporting that Fritz was ground-strafing our lines. Everyone in camp immediately rushed for their machines and up to the lines, each man on his own. We wandered about for an hour but there were no Huns there and we came back. Heard about dinnertime that the message had been caused by a lone Hun who sneaked over in the clouds and shot a kite balloon down. He repeated the performance about two hours later and then General Longcroft got peevish and turned about 100 Camels out on a fifty mile front. It is rumoured that they bagged nine of the Boche's gas bags.'

By the end of the day the Canadian troops were established on the western edges of Boiry-Notre-Dame and Rémy, hard against the Hindenburg Line. In the south the Australian troops had captured Mont St Quentin, threatening the crossings over the Somme, and the enemy was forced to abandon Bapaume. Ludendorff sanctioned a general withdrawal of his Second, Eighteenth and Ninth Armies.

On the morning of August 29 the airmen woke to that most welcome sound in their existence. Holleran again:

'Rain all day and no flying. I hope it stays so for three or four days because all the whole crowd are getting nervous. Our line is going forward beautifully but Fritz is fighting hard in spots. Nothing to compare with his previous resistance, however. I am beginning to agree with the others that this is the beginning of the end.'

Holleran's diary entry for August 29 is hard to understand, the RAF Communiqué for the day gives that the weather had improved over that of the previous day, was 'fair, but cloudy' and in the morning the day bombers of IX Brigade attempted to attack the railway stations at Cambrai, Valenciennes and Somain. The raid on Somain by 12 DH9s of 98 Squadron, escorted by 15 Camels of 43 Squadron, was frustrated by enemy fighters. As the formation approached the target area it was attacked by 20 enemy machines and the DH9s jettisoned their bombs. In the running fight back to the lines, the DH9s claimed two enemy fighters shot down, but a pilot and two observers were wounded and another observer killed. The pilots of 43 Squadron fought hard to protect their charges, claiming two Fokker D VIIs as destroyed, but lost six Camels. One pilot was killed, four were taken prisoner and a Camel returned badly shot up.[18]

The enemy fighters in this action were from *Jagdstaffeln 57, 32* and *26*, with *Jasta 57*, led by the *Staffelführer* Paul Strähle, leading the attack. Strähle claimed two Camels, one of which, flown by Sgt A C Harbour, he chased down to ground level until it finally crashed landed south of Brebières. Harbour was taken prisoner. *Vzfw* Knobel of the *Jasta* also chased a Camel down to ground level, but the pilot, Lt Charles Chaplin Banks, out manoeuvred Knobel, shot through the Fokker's *Höhensteuerkabel* (elevator control cable) and it crashed, bursting into flames as it hit the ground. Knobel was severely burnt.

On August 30 the DH9s of 98 Squadron attacked the railway junction at Valenciennes, this time escorted by the SE5s of 1 Squadron. The bombers hit the railway sidings with twenty 112lb bombs, and 16 enemy fighters that attempted to interfere were driven off by the escorting SE5s. Strähle and *Jasta 57* were again in the action, but were too low to successfully tackle the DH9s.[19]

Harold Kullberg of 1 Squadron dived on three Fokkers that were attacking a DH9. One Fokker spun away under Kullberg's fire, but it wings broke off as it pulled out lower down. The two remaining Fokkers continued to harass the DH9, but Kullberg attacked one, which went down and was seen to crash.[20]

On the last day of August the weather finally did clamp down, with low clouds and rain. Despite these conditions there was some flying by the fighter squadrons. In the early afternoon, 64 Squadron lost a pilot shot down in flames and killed. In the late evening, the Sopwith Dolphins of 23 Squadron were in combat with enemy scouts over Peronne and lost a pilot shot down, fatally wounded and taken prisoner, two other pilots wounded, and two Dolphins badly shot about and forced to land. Ground-strafing during the day, 24, 40, 60, 70, 84, 85, 203, squadrons and the U.S. 148 Pursuit Squadron, all had machines damaged and forced to land.

On the last three days of August all the fighter squadrons had continued their low level work, but on a reduced scale. There had also been many combats with enemy aircraft – too numerous to mention here – both at low and high levels: in the period from August 26 – the beginning of the battle of the Scarpe – until the end of the month, nearly 30 enemy aircraft were claimed as having been brought down.

The fighter squadrons of the RAF made a tremendous effort during the August offensives, but the cost had been heavy. From the opening of the Battle of Amiens on August 8, to the end of the month, 72 pilots had been killed in action; 53 wounded, and 62 – many of them wounded – taken prisoners of war. The *matériel* cost was also high. No less than 79 aircraft had been forced to land, shot up and badly damaged. The

majority of these casualties had been incurred during ground-strafing, illustrating the high cost of supporting the ground forces.

At the beginning of August 1918 the *Luftstreitkräfte* had faced increasing logistical problems. Alex Imrie, foremost historian of the *Luftstreitkräfte,* has written: 'the shortage of personnel and the continuingly worsening raw material position placed the German Army Air Service in a critical position.'[21] To negate the overwhelming superiority of the RAF in numbers of fighters, the *Jagdgeschwader* flew in large formations, concentrating their attacks where and when they chose to fight. By these tactics the fighters of the *Jagdgeschwader* often outnumbered the opposing fighters of the RAF and were able to inflict heavy losses, with correspondingly few losses of their own. However, the RAF could absorb these losses, the *Luftstreitkräfte* could not. Despite this it fought on. Imrie again: 'the German Army Air Service continued to fight until the end of the war without any weakening of morale, and the standard of skill displayed by the aircrews was just as high in the last few months of 1918 as at any time during the four years' struggle ... The *Fliegertruppe* never lost its fighting spirit.'[22]

NOTES

1. *Wings of War*, Rudolf Stark, John Hamilton Ltd., 1933. Stark's use of the terms 'impertinent' and 'arrogance' in describing the bravery and audacity of the British pilots during the attack is strange, but perhaps is the result of poor translation in the English edition of his book. Certainly no *Jasta* pilot could conceive that his aeroplane would be encumbered with bombs to carry out such attacks, which were left to the crews of the *schlachstaffeln* and *bombenstaffeln*.

2. Victor Yeates was the author of *Winged Victory*, a semi-autobiographical novel of his time with 46 Squadron. *Winged Victory* was first published by Jonathon Cape in 1934 and has been reprinted many times. It is a classic of World War I aviation literature and is highly recommended reading.

3. In the 1930s, at a dinner attended by many old flyers, German and British, Jones, sitting next to Hermann Göring, was asked if they had ever fought each other over the Western Front. Jones replied that they had not, otherwise Göring would not be present at the dinner. In recent years, in certain quarters, it has become fashionable to laugh at Ira Jones and his admittedly, rather naive patriotism. But his record speaks for itself.

4. *War in the Air, Vol 6*, H A Jones Oxford Press,' 1937.

5. The attacks on the bridges were a costly failure. Some of the bridges were damaged but not sufficiently to make them unusable. The bombing failed in its object and had little or no effect on the battle.

6. Ibid.

7. There is an interesting parallel here. Twenty-two years later, in the Battle of Britain, the German fighter pilots of the *Luftwaffe*, tied by Göring's orders to fly close escort with their bombers, failed to stop the attacks by the fighters of the RAF, even with the advantage – unknown in 1918 – of radio communication.

8. Paul Winslow's diary. Author's collection.

9. Cranial surgery by a skilful German surgeon saved Claxton's life. Claxton returned to Canada after the war and died in 1967.

10. This was possibly because of exhaustion and nerves. McCall had been involved in a great deal of fighting since January 1918 and had scored 35 victories.

11. Normally, SE5s were used to provide top cover for Camels when the latter were involved in low level attacks, the Camels being more manoeuvrable than the SE5. This plan, using Camels for top cover, is a curious reversal of roles.

12. Holleran's diary. Author's collection. Ellis sustained a cut head, a broken wrist, smashed shinbone and a strained back.

13. On August 8 a single anti-tank gun had disabled eight tanks in quick succession, effectively stopping the advance of the infantry in the area

14. Ibid.

15. Noel Bishop was to be killed in action on September 16 by *Ltn* Marcard of *Jasta 26*.

16. Cross and Cockade, Vol.20 No.3, 1979.

17. Beauchamp Proctor would destroy another four balloons in September and three more in October. From his total of 54 victories, 16 would be balloons, including three shared.

18. These were the last casualties for 43 Squadron while flying Camels. Within four days the Squadron was completely re-equipped with the Sopwith Snipe.

19. Strähle's diary entry for the day has the enigmatic comment: 'If our *Staffel* had been given a free hand in the fighting we could have guaranteed at least five victories over the English.'

20. *Gefr* Tegtmeyer of *Jasta 57* was forced to land with a badly damaged Fokker D VII. 'It took a long time before the craft could be repaired and restored to serviceable condition and used for flying again.'

21. *Pictorial History of the German Army Air Service, 1914-1918*, Alex Imrie, Ian Allan 1971.

22. Ibid.

CHAPTER TWENTY-FIVE

FINAL BATTLES: BLOODY SEPTEMBER

Having captured the key position of Mont St Quentin the previous day, the Australians entered Péronne of September 1, an action that Rawlinson, the Army Commander, considered to be the finest single feat of the whole war.

On the first day of the month the weather was generally fine but with a high wind. Enemy aircraft were active over the lines and there were some combats. A patrol from 32 Squadron were on patrol in the Cambrai area when they were attacked by *Jasta 36*. Lt E V Klingman and 2Lt J O Donaldson, both American pilots attached to the squadron, were shot down and taken prisoner. Lt A Sandys-Winsch was wounded in the fighting but managed to return to the squadron's base at La Bellevue.

As usual, the Australian fighter squadrons were in the thick of the action during the day. Elwyn King and Leonard Taplin of 4 Squadron AFC each destroyed a balloon in the early morning on the Aubers Ridge and dropped bombs on the railway station at Don. Their squadron compatriots, Norman Trescowthick and Thomas Barkell attacked an anti-aircraft battery nearby, bombing and machinegunning the enemy position until it was out of action. This was a 'flaming onions' battery, heartily detested by all pilots and destroying one brought a great deal of satisfaction. Pilots of 29 and 74 Squadrons also destroyed enemy balloons during the day.

The next offensive was to be an attack by the First and Third Armies astride the Arras to Cambai road against the Drocourt-Quéant switch line. The fighter squadrons of I Brigade – 54, 208, 64 and 209 Squadrons – were detailed to leave the ground at dawn in squadron strength. The ground-strafing plans had now reached a degree of sophistication, pilots no longer being given carte blanche to attack any targets of opportunity. Targets were now carefully assigned in advance to give maximum support to the attacking troops. For the three

hours after zero hour, the fortified villages of Saudemont, Ecourt St Quentin and Rumancourt were to be attacked, and the Cambrai to Arras road, from north of Villers les Cagnicourt eastwards to the Canal du Nord. Pilots were also to attack any enemy balloons seen. From zero plus three hours until zero plus six hours, attacks were to be made on the Canal du Nord villages of Palleul, Sauchy-Cauchy and Marquion. In addition, two or three aircraft were to attack the Cantin to Aubigny au Bac railway. Offensive patrols were also to be flown.

The attack on the Drocourt-Quéant switch line opened at 5.00am. It was a remarkable success. By noon the whole of the defence system had been taken, from the western outskirts of Cagnicourt to Étaing. The low bombing attacks by the fighter squadrons had begun at 5.45am by 17 Camels of 54 Squadron. The attacks by the squadrons continued at the staggered, prearranged times throughout the day – there was some overlapping – and at one time in the morning there were ninety aircraft bombing and strafing enemy troops, batteries and transport in front of the attacking Canadians. Eight tons of bombs were dropped and nearly 50,000 rounds of machine gun ammunition were fired, but five of the low flying aircraft were shot down.

Enemy fighters managed to penetrate the fighter screen being flown by the offensive patrols of the fighter squadrons not involved in low flying duties. In addition to the losses incurred from ground fire – one pilot killed, two wounded, three taken POW and two aircraft badly damaged – four pilots were killed, six taken POW and one wounded by the jagdstaffeln.

At 9.30am there was a large and bitterly contested fight over Marquion in which Camels, SE5s and Bristol Fighters fought with a large formation of enemy scouts. Honours were even, with three enemy aircraft shot down for the loss of three

British machines. Two and a half hours later, ten SE5s from 64 Squadron and four Bristol Fighters of 22 Squadron observed 15 enemy fighters flying in two layers, the bottom layer attacking the ground troops. The SE5s and Bristol Fighters attacked the enemy formations and were joined by nine Camels of the U.S. 148 Pursuit Squadron. More enemy scouts arrived to join the fight and several two-seater RE8s became involved. The combat became intense and confused. Elliott White Springs, who had earlier flown with 85 Squadron, but was now a flight commander in 148 Pursuit Squadron, reported:

'At 11.45am with three machines, I attacked four Fokker biplanes on the Arras-Cambrai road about four miles southwest of Haucourt. Three more came down out of the clouds and we were forced to withdraw. Seven more enemy aircraft came up from the northeast, and after some manoeuvring I attacked another enemy aircraft southeast of the road, but we, in turn, were attacked by a large number. Succeeded in drawing enemy aircraft closer to our lines and went in again. Our top flight attacked from above us and a dogfight ensued. We were badly outnumbered. Took one enemy aircraft off the tail of a Camel and was, in turn, attacked from above. Saw one enemy aircraft attack an RE8 and attacked him. Assisted by a Bristol attacked another enemy aircraft very low. We succeeded in preventing enemy aircraft from attacking RE8s and eventually drove them all east. Enemy aircraft finally disappeared in clouds over Cambrai. Very heavy clouds at 4-5,000 feet, but visibility good underneath. Fokker pilots very good, but poor shots. About 25 enemy aircraft seen.'

Five enemy aircraft were claimed from this combat, three by the pilots of 148 Squadron, but four pilots from the squadron were shot down and taken prisoner. Two other Camels of the squadron which managed to return where so badly shot about that they were struck off strength. Sgt Cowlishaw and Capt William Farrow of 64 Squadron claimed two of the enemy scouts: Cowlishaw's in flames and Farrow's out of control.

During the day an attack was carried out on the enemy aerodrome at Linselles by 29, 41 70 and 74 Squadrons. Twenty-nine and 74 Squadrons attacked first, dropping 91 Cooper bombs from between 2 and 6,000, then stayed above while 41 and 70 Squadrons went down to within 50 feet of the ground, dropping 113 bombs. The pilots also machine gunned the hangars and silenced a machinegun emplacement that had opened fire on them. Two hangars were seen to be completely gutted by fire and two others appeared damaged. All the attacking aircraft returned safely.

The jagdstaffeln of *Jagdgeschwader Nr III* were very active on September 3, fighting in large, concentrated formations, and claimed 26 victories during the day's fighting. Many of the German pilots in the *Jagdgeschwader* were veteran com-

bat pilots, flying the superb BMW- powered Fokker D VII and the new Pfalz D XII.[1] These factors made them formidable opponents for the allied fighter pilots, many of whom were novice pilots in the rapidly expanding RAF.

The activities of the *Jagdgeschwader* made considerable impact on the ground fighting: at one time 30 *Schlachtstaffeln* aircraft had complete control of the air over the battlefront, harassing the attacking Canadian troops and shooting down four of the corps aircraft working in support. It was not until the evening that the pilots of 64 Squadron came back into the action, coming down to 300 feet over the Palluel to Oisy le Verger road, bombing and machinegunning the enemy troops until they 'scattered in all directions.'

During the night of September 2/3 the German forces fell back rapidly along the right flank of First Army and along the entire front of Third Army. An early morning reconnaissance on September 3 revealed that there were no enemy troops west of the Canal du Nord and that the enemy was destroying the bridges over the canal. It was clear that the Germans intended to make a stand along the eastern bank of the Canal du Nord; it would take a strong attack to dislodge them and the operations on the First Army front were halted. Further south, the German forces withdrew from the eastern bank of the River Somme and the British Fourth Army and the French First Army crossed the river on September 5.

During the enemy's retirement it was constantly harassed by the low flying aircraft of the fighter squadrons, but in addition enemy aircraft were fought wherever they could be found and brought to combat. On the morning of September 3, a patrol from 56 Squadron attacked a force of 12 Fokker D VIIs flying in two layers over Etaign. Capt Harold Molyneux attacked the top formation of seven; William Irwin the bottom layer of five. The Fokker attacked by Molyneux gave 'a violent jerk' upwards and went over onto its back before going down in a spin. Irwin's opponent stalled, turned over and went down to crash south of Rumancourt. Turning away, Irwin saw a Fokker on the tail of Alfred Vickers' SE5. Irwin closed to point blank range and fired 150 rounds into the enemy machine, which went down in a spin before bursting into flames at 6,000 feet, the blazing wreckage finally hitting the ground west of Haynecourt, killing *Vzfw* Skworz of *Jasta 36*. Irwin had been too late to save Vickers, however, who was later reported killed. Henry Chubb claimed another of the Fokkers in flames from this action and Molyneux was awarded another as being out of control.

On the morning of September 4 the day bombers of IX Brigade attacked the railway stations at Douai, Denain and Cambrai. The bombers were escorted by SE5s of 32 Squadron and Bristol Fighters of 62 Squadron, but the formations were attacked by a large force of enemy fighters. Two pilots from 32 Squadron were shot down and killed, and 62 Squadron lost a crew. Lt F Hale of 32 Squadron claimed a Fokker in flames and crews of 62 Squadron claimed three enemy scouts out of control and another destroyed.

The day was disastrous for 70 Squadron. Twelve Camels took off at 7.20am to fly a patrol in the Douai area. Nearly thirty Fokker D VIIs of *Jagdstaffeln 26* and *27* – elements of *Jagdgeschwader Nr III* – had been fighting the DH4s of 18 Squadron, and had shot one down, and wounded the observer in another, before the Camels arrived. In the ensuing fight the Clerget-engined Camels were completely outclassed by the BMW-powered Fokker D VIIs and suffered severely at the hands of the German pilots. Three pilots were killed and four were shot down and taken prisoner. Another pilot returned, fatally wounded in the stomach, and two other Camels were badly damaged. Only Capt Kenneth Watson claimed a victory: one of the Fokkers down in flames.

One of those taken prisoner was Bill Rochford, brother of 'Tich' Rochford of 203 Squadron who at this time had 26 victories. When he returned home after the war, Bill Rochford explained that his engine had been hit in the fight and he had force landed in a field. Taken to a local prison, he met Capt Henry Forman, who had led the ill-fated patrol. Rochford and Forman managed to escape during the night and were on the run for several days before they were recaptured and taken to a POW camp.

At noon, Major Gilchrist led 12 SE5s from 56 Squadron, escorted by ten Bristol Fighters, to bomb the enemy aerodrome at Noyelles. The machines formed up over Arras and set course for Cambrai and Noyelles, but as they crossed the lines they saw dozens of enemy scouts to the east. Gilchrist fired a white light, washing out the raid – it would be impossible to fight impeded by the weight of their bombs – and the SE5s dropped their bombs on various targets. Gilchrist was chased back to the lines by the Fokker D VIIs but later joined with some SE5s from 60 Squadron and helped them drive away a formation of D VIIs flying over the outskirts of Cambrai. Gilchrist then flew to Noyelles, saw two balloons at 3,000 feet and attacked one. The observer jumped clear and the balloon slowly deflated and went down.

Eleven balloons were brought down during the day. Tom Hazell of 24 Squadron destroyed two in the space of five minutes. One fell on its winch and burned for twenty minutes. The observer escaped by parachute, but was attacked by Lt E Crossen, who collapsed the parachute. There was no room for chivalry; the observer may well have had information that he would report. Stopping him doing so might well save many lives. These two balloons were Hazell's 38th and 39th victories, and were the last of five he had destroyed since 21st of August.

On patrol in the morning, David Hughes of 3 Squadron was chased back to the British lines by three Fokker D VIIs. When Hughes reached the lines, two of the enemy machines turned back and Hughes attacked the other, wounding the pilot, Flg Wagner of *Jasta 79b*. Wagner's Fokker D VII was designated G/III Bgd/19.

With a pause in the ground operations, the troops being rested as much as possible, an operational order from RAF HQ informed its various brigadiers to adopt a similar policy for the squadrons of the RAF, 'which has now been working at high pressure for many months.' The fighter squadrons were ordered to cease low flying work. However, 'Should the enemy adopt an aggressive policy in the air, it will, of course, be necessary to continue a vigorous offensive, but, provided he keeps well back at a distance behind his lines, the policy of seeking out and destroying his machines will be less actively pursued and offensive patrol work will be restricted to keeping back his artillery and reconnaissance machines and enabling ours to do their work.'

In addition, the last paragraph of these orders emphasised the need for rest. 'To carry out the above policy the GOC wished brigadiers to reduce the number of fighting squadrons working over the lines to a minimum each day, and to take individual squadrons definitely off this work for a day, or more at a time, during which they will carry out training only.'

The weather was good on September 5, although a little hazy. The Luftstreitkräfte was very active, the jagdstaffeln flying in their now customary large formations.

Lt Frederick Gillet, who had been flying Sopwith Dolphins with 79 Squadron since the beginning of April, seems to have been slow in beginning to score, not claiming his first victory, a balloon, until August 3, but after destroying a Fokker D VII fifteen days later, he began to score with increasing frequency and by the end of the war his score stood at 20. In an evening patrol led by Capt Frederick Lord, an American from Wisconsin, the Dolphins attacked a formation of Fokker D VIIs. Gillet shot down one of the Fokkers, which burst into flames on hitting the ground and Lord's opponent turned over onto its back, the pilot falling out.

The day was an eventful one for 'Grid' Caldwell with an experience he would never forget. On an early morning patrol south of Cambrai he and 'Timbertoes' Carlin attacked a group of enemy scouts, each going for the same opponent. Carlin was slightly above Caldwell in the dive on the enemy scouts, failed to see his CO's SE5, and hit it on the tip of its top wing with his undercarriage. Carlin thought he had hit the German machine and returned to the aerodrome unaware that the collision had been with Caldwell.

Falling in a dive after the impact, with Caldwell fighting to regain control, the SE5 fell for 2,000 feet before Caldwell

Lt Charles Arthur Bissonette. 24 and 64 Squadrons. Bissonette scored four victories with 64 Squadron in 1918.

2Lt Eugene Ronald Macdonald. 56 Squadron. January to July 1918.

Trevor Durrant. 56 Squadron. Durrant was KIA on 16th May 1918, the day he had been made a Flight Commander.

This Sopwith Camel D 6402 'S' was flown by Capt Henry Woollett of 43 Squadron. Included in Woollett's 35 victories were 11 balloons and the bizarre markings of this Camel were intended as special camouflage for attacks on balloons. He was persuaded to remove these markings by members of his Flight who considered the Camel could be mistaken for an enemy machine.

Right: Capt Samuel Marcus Kinkead. DFC+Bar. DSC+Bar. A South African, Kinkead served with 3 Naval Wing, 1 Naval, and 201 Squadron. He was credited with 35 victories. Post-war, Kinkead flew in Russia with 47 Squadron, where he was awarded a DSO and is thought to have scored another ten victories. A member of the 1928 RAF Schneider Trophy Team, Kinkead was killed in practice on 12 March 1928 while flying Supermarine S5.

Right: Lt Ernest Owens. 1 Squadron 1918.

Bottom left: Major Albert Desbrisay Carter. DSO+Bar. Carter flew Spads and Sopwith Dolphins with 19 Squadron, scoring 29 victories before he was shot down and taken prisoner on 19 May 1918. Carter was killed in 1919 test flying a Fokker D VII, which broke up in mid-air.

Bottom center: Capt Edward 'Mick' Mannock VC. DSO+2Bars. MC+Bar. 40, 74, 85 Squadrons. This photograph was taken in the early summer of 1918 while Mannock was a flight commander in 74 Squadron.

Bottom right: 'Little Samson' Henry Wolff in the cockpit of his SE5a in 40 Squadron. 1918.

Above: Capt Frederick McCall, 41 Squadron, with the squadron dogs.

Top center: The Long and Short of it. Lt Henry S Wolff, 'Little Samson', standing under the arm of Capt Oswald 'Shorty' Horsley. 40 Squadron. Bruay 1918.

Top right: Capt Douglas John Bell MC+Bar. Bell served in 27 Squadron in the spring of 1917 flying Martinsyde G.100s and scored three victories. After serving in 78 (Home Defence) Squadron he was posted back to France in early 1918 as a flight commander with 3 Squadron, flying Sopwith Camels. Bell scored another 17 victories before he was shot down and taken prisoner on 27 May 1918. He later died of his wounds.

Right: This captured Sopwith Camel was remarked in German markings and flown by Oblt Otto Kissenberth, Staffelführer of Jasta 23b. Kissenberth is thought to have scored at least one victory while flying this Camel, but while flying it on 29 May 1918 he crashed and was seriously injured.

Below: Gwilym Lewis in his SE5a 'The Artful Dodger' while a flight commander in 40 Squadron, summer 1918. The interplane struts, letter 'K' and radiator shutters were painted black and white. The nickname 'The Artful Dodger' was painted on the lower front plate of the nose radiator.

Above: FltCom Robert Alexander Little DSO+Bar. DSC+Bar. CdeG. Little flew with 1 Naval Wing, 8 Naval and 203 Squadrons and is credited with 47 victories, the most successful Australian fighter pilot of the war. He was KIA on 27 May 1918.

Top center: Capt James Anderson Slater. Slater flew with 1 Squadron for a short period in 1917, scoring two victories. By November 1917 he was a flight commander in 64 Squadron and flew DH5s with the squadron, scoring one victory on the type before the squadron was re-equipped with SE5as in January 1918. From early March to the last day of May 1918 Slater scored another 21 victories, bring his total to 24 and winning an MC+Bar and a DFC. Jimmy Slater was extremely popular throughout the RFC and RAF and stayed in the RAF after the war. Slater was killed in a flying accident while instructing at the Central Flying School on 26 November 1926, the day before his 29th birthday.

Top right: 40 Squadron 1918. L to R: Capt James Riddle. Capt Gwilyn Hugh Lewis DFC.

Right: Major Dallas, commanding officer of 40 Squadron, in an unusually camouflaged SE5a D 3511. Although officially credited with 32 victories, an evaluation of claims made by Dallas shows a total of 56. This photograph was taken on 28 May 1918, only three days before Dallas was shot down and killed by three Fokker Triplanes of Jasta 14.

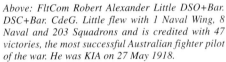

Right: The grave of Major R S Dallas.

Far right: Capt James Dacres Belgrave MC in the cockpit of Sopwith Pup '5' of 61 Squadron. Belgrave first flew Sopwith 1 1/2 Strutter two-seaters in 45 Squadron, claiming six victories while flying with various observers. After service with 61 Squadron on Home Defence duties he was posted to 60 Squadron in April 1918 as a flight commander, scoring another 12 victories before he was shot down and killed on 13 June 1918 while attacking an enemy two-seater.

Right: This Fokker Triplane Dr I 583/17 was shot down by SE5as of B and C Flights of 1 Squadron on 9 June 1918, the credit being awarded to Lt J C Bateman of the squadron. The pilot Gefr Reinhold Preiss of Jasta 14 was taken prisoner. The colours of the horizontal bands along the fuselage were in black and white, the unit marking of Jasta 14. The vertical bands around the fuselage were in red and white, the personal colours of Preiss.

Far right: Major Christopher Joseph Quintin-Brand. 'Flossie' Brand first flew in France with 1 Squadron in 1917, scoring seven victories flying Nieuport Scouts. He took 151 Squadron to France as its CO in June 1918 to act as a night fighter squadron flying Sopwith Camels and added another five victories to his score, all German night flying bombers, three of which came down in Allied Lines and were captured.

Right: Ltn Josef Jacobs (centre) with pilots of Jasta 7. Jacobs favoured the Fokker Triplane, flying the type after it had been withdrawn from general service. He survived the war with 48 victories.

Below: Kurt Wüsthoff, Staffelführer of Jasta 15, was flying this red and blue Fokker D.VII when he was shot down and taken prisoner by a Flight of SE5as of 24 Squadron on 17 June 1918. The captured Fokker, usually flown by Ltn Georg Hantelmann of Jasta 15, was designated G/5Brigade/17.

Above: Capt A H Cobby DSO. DFC. Cobby flew with 4 Squadron AFC from March 1918 until 4 September, scoring 29 victories. He retired from the RAAF in 1946 as Air Commodore Arthur Henry Cobby CBE. DSO. DFC. GM.

Top center: Capt Cyril Parry 56 Squadron. At the end of his service with 56 Squadron Parry was due to be posted to Home Establishment but he chose to be transferred to 60 Squadron, knowing it was to be commanded by his friend and mentor James McCudden. Parry was seriously injured in a flying accident on the afternoon of July 29 1918, effectively ending his war. Parry is wearing a DFC ribbon in its original form of horizontal stripes.

Top right: Happier Days. Capt Edric Broadberry MC (right) with John Seymour Turnbull in England in 1918. Broadberry and Turnbull were both wounded and shot down on 12 July 1917. John Turnbull was killed in action on 17 June 1918 while serving in 41 Squadron.

Right: Henry 'Hank' Burden puts the finishing touches to naming his SE5a 'Maybe'.

Far right: Major William Bishop VC. DSO+Bar. MC. DFC. CC. L d'H. CdeG. Photograph taken while Bishop was commanding 85 Squadron. The pilot on the left is the American Larry Callaghan.

Right: Pilots of A Flight, 4 Squadron AFC on Clairmarais aerodrome 16 June 1918. L to R: J S M Browne. C R Burton. C S Scobie. R G Smallwood. A H Cobby (flight commander). R King. R F McRae. A H Lockley. W A Armstrong.

Above: Pilots of C Flight 4 Squadron AFC on Clairmarais aerodrome 16 June 1918. L to R: R C Nelson. E C Crosse. E J McCloughry. E V Culverwell. V G M Sheppard. R H Youdale. J C F Wilkinson.

Right: 2Lt R G Carr of 210 Squadron was flying Sopwith Camel B 7227 when he was shot down and taken POW by Oberflugmeister Kurt Schönfelder of Jasta 7 on 21 June 1918. Carr escaped from captivity on 1 July 1918, which would suggest that he was uninjured in the crash. The remains of Carr's Camel is shown here piled up to be taken away for scrap.

Right: Four pilots of 4 Squadron AFC. Capt H G Watson (14 victories). Capt E J K McCloughry (21 victories). Major W A McCloughry MC (CO). Capt A H Cobby (29 victories).

Left: Pilots of B Flight 4 Squadron AFC. Clairmarais, 16 June 1918. Front Row, L to R: J H Weingarth. O B Ramsey. H G Watson. H F Davison. F I Tanner. Back Row, L to R: J W Milner. R Sly. Unknown. R Moore. A T Heller.

Above: 85 Squadron. St Omer June 1918. L to R: J D Canning. G B A Baker. G C Dixon. J W Warner. Seated L to R: A S Cunningham-Reid. J A Egan.

Above: Lt John Edgcombe Doyle on leave in 1917 with his mother and his sisters, Constance and Kathleen.

Left: The Fokker D VII entered service with the jagdstaffeln in April 1918. Strong, fast, manoeuvrable and easy to fly, it was the finest fighter aeroplane produced by the Germans in the First World War. When re-engined with the BMW IIIa it was an extremely formidable opponent and arguably the best fighter aeroplane to see front line service with any of the combatants. By the end of hostilities the Fokker D VII equipped 41 jagdstaffeln. This photograph shows Karl Thom of Jasta 21 in his personally marked aeroplane.

Opposite
Top: Pilots of 85 Squadron at St Omer on 21 June 1918. L to R: Cushing (adjutant). J Dymond. A H R Daniel. J D Canning. M C McGregor. L K Callahan USAS. E W Springs USAS. S B Horn. A C Randall. Baker. A S Cunningham-Reid. W H Longton. Rosie. D Curruthers. D C Inglis. E C Brown. G D Brewster. Unknown. A Abbott. G C Dixon. Note assortment of pets and mascots. Major William Bishop relinquished command of 85 Squadron on 19 June 1918 and was succeeded by Major Edward Mannock on 5 July 1918.

Bottom: 1 Squadron at Clarmarais aerodrome 3 July 1918. L to R: D Knight USAS. Newman. Henderson. P S Crossley. Unknown. F R Knapp. W A Smart. Capt Sison. Unknown. J I T Jones (74 Squadron). E E Owen. Moody. P J Clayson. C S T Lavers. Simpson. Padre Banks. J C Bateman. W M Chowne. E M Forsyth. H A Kullberg.

Above: 85 Squadron pilots relaxing in the sun, summer 1918. L to R: D J Trapp. George C Dixon. Lawrence K Callahan USAS. D C Inglis.

Above: Capts Gwilym Lewis DFC (left) and George (McIrish) McElroy. DFC+Bar. MC+2Bars. 40 Squadron. Summer 1918. Lewis survived the war with 12 victories. McElroy served with both 24 and 40 Squadrons and scored 47 victories before he was shot down and killed on 31 July 1918.

Top center: Capt William Carpenter Lambert DFC. Lambert, an American from Ohio, was posted to 24 Squadron in March 1918 and served with the squadron until 19 August, scoring 18 victories.

Top right: Three pilots of 24 Squadron. 1918 L to R: Lt J E A R Daley. Capt I D R MacDonald MC.DFC and Lt W J Miller. John Daley claimed six victories with 24 Squadron before he was killed in a forced landing on 3 July 1918, dying of his injuries five days later. Miller was KIA on 17 September 1918. Ian McDonald served with 24 Squadron from July 1917 until 21 June 1918, scoring 20 victories.

Right: SE5a D 6940 was a presentation aeroplane Parish of Inch No.2 issued to 29 Squadron in July 1918. Pilots of the squadron destroyed three aircraft and two balloons in this aeroplane.

Below: Major Joseph Creuss Callaghan flew this Sopwith Dolphin while commanding 87 Squadron in the spring and early summer of 1918. Callaghan was KIA on 2 July 1918.

Right: Major Joseph Creuss Callaghan. The commanding officer of 87 Squadron, Callahan was the squadron's first casualty when he was shot down in flames on 2 July 1918.

Far right: Capt Cyril Ridley DSC. Ridley served in 1 Naval, which became 201 Squadron on the formation of the RAF on 1 April 1918. He was awarded 11 victories while with the squadron.

Right: Pilots of 65 Squadron in the summer of 1918. L to R: Capt A G Jones-Williams. Capt M A Newman. Major H C Champion de Crespigny (CO). Unknown. Capt C L Morley.

Below: Capt W Selwyn in SE5a C 8840 'V' of 24 Squadron.

Right: Sopwith Camel B6418. Capt Cyril Ridley of 201 Squadron scored two of his 11 victories in this machine.

Right: This SE5a D 6933 was flown by Lt John C Rorison while serving in 85 Squadron in July 1918. It was later crashed by Lt D Benzies and returned to 2ASD for repair.

Right: Lt Arthur Clunie Randall. 'Snowy' Randall flew DH2s with 32 Squadron in January-March 1917, scoring two victories. He joined 85 Squadron as a flight commander in the summer of 1918, scoring a further eight victories and winning a DFC.

Far right: Visiting his old squadron on 12-13 June 1918, James McCudden proudly poses with the ribbon of his two month old Victoria Cross under his wings. He had just under a month to live.

Above: James McCudden's grave at Wavans cemetery. July 1918.

Top right: Capt Benjamin Roxburgh-Smith DFC+Bar. CdeG. Roxburgh-Smith served in 60 and 74 Squadrons, but scored all his 22 victories while serving with 74 Squadron in 1918.

Right: 74 Squadron outside the officer's Mess at Clairmarais North, early July 1918. Front Row, L to R: R Spiers (Adj). A C Kiddie (South Africa). G W Gauld (Canada). L Harrison (South Africa). F J Hunt (England). J Venter (South Africa. 29 Sqdn). S Carlin (England). H Coverdale (England). Middle Row, L to R: W E Berdgett. C B Glynn (England). P F C Howe (South Africa). H G Clements (England). C H Matthiessen (USAS). B Roxburgh-Smith (England). J Adamson (England). R H Gray (New Zealand). H C Goudie (Canada). S T Stidolph (New Zealand). F S Gordon (New Zealand). Padre Banks. Extreme Rear, L to R: L A Richardson (Canada). F E Luff (USAS). H G Shoemaker (USAS).

Below: SE5as of B Flight 24 Squadron on Conteville aerodrome, July 1918.

Above: Capt Sidney Carlin. Carlin won the DCM in August 1915 while serving in the ranks of the Royal Engineers, was later commissioned and seriously wounded in 1916, losing a leg. After recovering from his wounds, Carlin transferred to the RFC, learnt to fly, despite his wooden leg, and was an instructor at the Central Flying School before joining 74 Squadron in France on 26 May 1918. Inevitably nicknamed 'Timbertoes', Carlin scored 10 victories with 74 Squadron before being shot down on 21 September 1918 and taken POW. Carlin was killed in 1941 while serving in World War II.

Top right: Squadron Commander Raymond Collishaw DSO+Bar. DFC. DSC. in the cockpit of a Sopwith Camel. Collishaw served first with 3 Wing RNAS flying Sopwith 1 1/2 Strutters, before being posted to Naval 3 in February 1917 to fly Sopwith Pups. In April 1917 Collishaw joined Naval 10 as a Flight Commander, flying Sopwith triplanes. As a flight commander, Collishaw had the cowlings and wheel covers of his flight's triplanes painted black and each pilot's machine was given a 'black' name – Collishaw taking 'Black Maria' – and the famous 'Black Flight' was born. Collishaw went on leave to his native Canada in July 1917, returning to France in November to take command of 13 Naval. In January 1918 he took command of Naval 3 Squadron, flying Sopwith Camels, and led the squadron until October, when he was promoted to Lt-Colonel and posted to HE to assist in the setting up of the RCAF. He was awarded 59 victories during his service in France, from early 1916 to September 1918. After the war, Collishaw flew in south Russia with the White Russian forces and scored an additional victory while commanding 47 Squadron. In World War II Collishaw commanded 201 Group in the Western Desert and No.12 Group Fighter Command in England. He retired with the rank of Air Vice-Marshal in 1943 with a CBE and OBE. His autobiography, Air Command, was published in 1973.

Right: SE5as of 85 Squadron at St Omer 21 June 1918.The pilot of the nearest aeroplane is Capt S B 'Nigger' Horn. The serial numbers have been censored, but the first three aeroplanes are C 1904, D6851 and C1931.

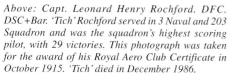

Above: Capt. Leonard Henry Rochford. DFC. DSC+Bar. 'Tich' Rochford served in 3 Naval and 203 Squadron and was the squadron's highest scoring pilot, with 29 victories. This photograph was taken for the award of his Royal Aero Club Certificate in October 1915. 'Tich' died in December 1986.

Top center: Indra Lal Roy. After a brief period with 56 Squadron 'Laddie' Roy was posted to 40 Squadron. Between 6 and 19 July 1918 Roy scored 10 victories and was awarded a DFC before being shot down in flames on 22 July 1918.

Top right: Lt George Augustus Vaughan USAS. Vaughan served with 84 Squadron, scoring seven victories before he was posted to 17 U.S. Pursuit Squadron, where he destroyed another six enemy aircraft.

Right: B Flight 40 Squadron. Taken just before the Flight Commander Gwilym Lewis went home on 25 July 1918. L to R: Donald Murman (The Baron). Paul Burwell USAS. Gerry Middleton. Gwilym Lewis. Ivan Hind (Deputy Flight Commander. KIA 12 August 1918). Don (Bolo) Poler USAS. W V Trubshaw.

Right: Sopwith Camel D 9398. Lt R F Lewis of 73 Squadron, KIA on 25 July 1918.

Above: Capt Edward 'Mick' Mannock. VC. DSO+2Bars. MC+Bar. Mannock was one of the great patrol leaders and tacticians of the RFC/RAF. He served in 40 and 74 Squadrons, before taking command of 85 Squadron in June 1918. The number of Mannock's victories is debatable, but the official total is 63. He was KIA on 26 July 1918.

Top center: Major 'Grid' Caldwell (left) and James Ira Thomas 'Taffy' Jones in 74 Squadron 1918.

Top right: Capt George E H 'McIrish' McElroy MC+2Bars.DFC+Bar. McElroy flew with 40 Squadron from the end of 1917 until February 1918, scoring 11 victories. He was then posted as a flight commander to 24 Squadron and added a further 16 victories. On 7 April 1918 he crashed on landing. After recovery he was posted back to 40 Squadron and again began to score rapidly, bringing his total to 47 before he was KIA on 31 July 1918.

Right: This DFW CV 342/18 (possibly from FlAbt(A) 232, crewed by Ltn de R Bolgihn and Uffz Neuendirf) was forced down by Lt H D Barton of 24 Squadron on 26 July 1918. Lt J H Southey is sitting on the fuselage.

Right: Lt William Samuel Stephenson MC. DFC. Stephenson was credited with 12 victories while flying with 73 Squadron in 1918. He was wounded, shot down and taken prisoner on 28 July 1918.

Top: Capt Owen John Frederick Scholte 60 Squadron. Owen Scholte was killed in a car accident on 29 July 1918.

Bottom: Captain Hazel LeRoy Wallace DFC. Wallace served in Naval 9, 201 and 3 Squadrons. He is credited with 14 victories.

Top: Major Euan James Leslie Warren Gilchrist. Gilchrist commanded 56 Squadron from May 2, 1918 until the end of the war.

Bottom: Lt Frederick Stanley Gordon. 74 Squadron. Gordon scored eight victories while serving with 74 Squadron.

Top: Lt Paul Winslow USAS. Winslow served in 56 Squadron RAF from June 29 1918 until September 12 1918, when he was transferred to the AEF.

Bottom: The grave of Capt G E H McElroy at Laventie. 1918.

Above: Henry Burden sent home this photograph of his SE5a C 1096. Burden sketched the details of his personal colour scheme around its edge.

Top right: Major Wilfred Ernest Young. Young served in 6, 19 and 74 Squadrons before being given command of 1 Squadron in August 1918.

Above left: Capt James Ira Thomas Jones DFC+Bar. MC. DSO. MM. Russian Medal of St George. A qualified wireless operator, 'Taffy' Jones served in 10 Squadron in 1915 as a 1st Class Air Mechanic on wireless duties. While on ground duties as a wireless operator in May 1916 he rescued two wounded gunners whose battery was under fire and was awarded a Military Medal and the Russian Medal of St George. At the end of May 1917, after flying as an observer with 10 Squadron since January 1916, he was posted to HE to train as a pilot. Jones returned to France with the newly-formed 74 Squadron on 30 March 1918 as a member of Capt W J Cairns' C Flight. By 31 May, Jones had scored 15 victories and was awarded an MC. In June, Jones was promoted to flight commander, and a further 17 victories by 2 August resulted in the award of a DFC, followed by a DSO on 25 August. Jones claimed the last of his 37 victories on 7 August 1918 and made no further claims although he continued to serve with 74 Squadron until the end of the war, and was awarded a Bar to his DFC in September. After the war, Jones remained in the RAF and served in north Russia until he was placed on the Reserve in 1936. A great admirer of Mick Mannock, Ira Jones wrote Mannock's biography, King of Air Fighters, in 1934; An Airfighter's Scrapbook in 1938 and Tiger Squadron The Story of 74 Squadron in Two World Wars in 1954. On 30 August 1960, Ira Jones died after a fall from a ladder. A bizarre end for a pilot. He was 65.

Above right: New Zealander Lt Frederick Stanley Gordon stands by his SE5a 'Z' of 74 Squadron. 1918.

Left: Lts Hugh Saunders and Cecil Thompson of 84 Squadron. August 1918.

Above: Standing in front of his Camel 'Waacall', 'Tich' Rochford shares a joke with King George V during the King's inspection of 203 Squadron at Izel-leHameau on 8 August 1918.

Left: Lt Cecil Robert Thompson DFC in the cockpit of his SE5a 'Chum'. Thompson served in 84 Squadron from April 1918 until 15 September when he was wounded. He is credited with six victories.

Below: The 56 Squadron baseball team. Summer 1918. L to R: H T Flintoft. R H Ellis USAS. W R Irwin. A P Thompson. T D Hazen. P S Winslow USAS. H J Burden. T J Herbert USAS. W O Boger.

Above: Capt Alexander Beck. Beck joined 60 Squadron at the end of July 1917 but after three weeks with the squadron, and having flown 13 patrols, his parents discovered that he was in France, informed the authorities that he was under age and had him posted to HE. Having reached the required age, Beck rejoined 60 Squadron in March 1918, became a flight commander, won a DFC, and served until the end of the war, scoring 11 victories.

Above: Capt Chidlaw-Roberts returned to France in the summer of 1918 as a flight commander in 40 Squadron. He took this photograph of three pilots of his Flight. L to R: 'Shorty' (surname unknown). A B Dunn. A S Underhill.

Top right: Capt A B Yuille of 151 Squadron.

Right: Zeppelin Staaken R.XIV R 43 of Reisenflug-zeugabteilungen 501 shot down in flames by Captain A B Yuille of 151 Squadron on the night of 10-11 August 1918.

Below: Sopwith Camels of B and C Flights 201 Squadron in August 1918. The three machines on the left are B Flight aeroplanes with the squadron marking further left of the roundel than ordered. Note chequered tailplane of Camel S F 6022.

Right: The wreckage of Zeppelin Staaken R 43 at Talmas.

Right: This Fokker D VII was shot down on 12 August 1918 by Capt F R McCall of 41 Squadron. The pilot, Gefr Johann Janizsewski of Jasta 75 was killed. The wreckage was designated G/5Brigade/24.

Bottom left: Capt Cristoffel Johannes Venter DFC+Bar. A South African, Venter joined 29 Squadron in May 1918 and scored 16 victories in three months before being shot down and made POW on 18 August 1918.

Bottom center: Capt Camille Henri Raoul Lagesse. DFC+Bar. Belgian CdeG. Lagesse flew with 29 Squadron from May until October1918, scoring 20 victories.

Bottom right: Major Arthur William ('Keeno') Keen MC. Keen flew with 70 and 40 Squadrons, serving with 40 Squadron as a Flight Commander in 1917 before rejoining the squadron as commanding officer in June 1918. Keen was injured in a flying accident on 15 August 1918, was severely burned and later died of his injuries.

Right: Capt Frederick Robert Gordon McCall MC+Bar. DSO. DFC. 41 Squadron. After scoring three victories flying two-seater RE8s with 13 Squadron in 1918, McCall was posted to 41 Squadron to fly SE5a's in late April 1918. Between 25 May and 17 August, McCall was awarded another 32 victories. On 17 August McCall and Claxton, his friend and fellow Canadian in 41 Squadron, were heavily outnumbered in a combat with enemy scouts and Claxton was wounded, shot down and taken POW. Immediately after this combat McCall was invalided to HE.

Far right: Capt William Gordon Claxton. 41 Squadron. A Canadian, Claxton served with 41 Squadron from the end of May 1918 until the middle of August, scoring 37 victories. Claxton was seriously wounded, shot down and taken prisoner on 17 August.

Right: This Fokker D.VII, Nickchen IV, was shot down by Capt McCall of 41 Squadron on 12 August 1918. The pilot, Ofstv Blumenthal of Jasta 53 was taken prisoner and his Fokker designated G/5Brigade/20.

Right: Lts J L Turner, R G Robinson and A F Diamond in front of an SE5a of 29 Squadron at Oudezeele. 18 August 1918.

Above: SE5as of 29 Squadron starting on an Offensive Patrol at 4.15pm on 18 August 1918 from Oudezeele aerodrome. It was a good day for the patrol leader, Lt Arthur Reed. He had shot down a balloon in a morning patrol and in this patrol he shot down a pair of Halberstadt two-seaters. Reed, a South African, scored a total of 19 victories and was awarded a DFC+Bar.

Right: Capt Charles Gordon Ross flew with 29 Squadron from the spring of 1918 until the end of the war, scoring 20 victories and winning a DFC+Bar.

Far right: Major Charles Dawson Booker DSC. CdeG. Booker served with 8 Naval, 1 Naval (later 201 Squadron RAF). He was awarded 29 victories, his first flying a Sopwith Pup, then 21 flying Sopwith Triplanes, followed by his last seven flying Sopwith Camels. Booker was KIA on 13 August 1918.

Right: Major Keith Rodney Park CO 48 Squadron. Park remained in the RAF after the war and retired as Air Vice Marshal Sir Keith Park GCB. KBE. MC. DFC. DCL. Park was AOC 11 Group in 1940 and with Hugh Dowding CIC of Fighter Command was the architect of victory over the Luftwaffe in the Battle of Britain.

Far right: Capt Alexander Augustus Norman Dudley Pentland. An Australian, 'Jerry' Pentland served with the 12th Australian Light Horse in Egypt and Gallipoli before transferring to the RFC in February 1916. Pentland first flew BEs with 16 Squadron, claiming one victory in June 1916. By the summer of 1917 he was flying Spads with 19 Squadron and flew with the squadron until the autumn, scoring nine victories and winning an MC. On 26 September 1917 he was injured in the face by an artillery shell and crashed. Pentland returned to France as a flight commander with 87 Squadron when it flew its Sopwith Dolphins to St Omer on 24 April 1918. Between 7 May and 25 August, Pentland added a further 23 victories to his score and was awarded a DFC before being wounded in the foot on 25 August 1918.

Above: L to R: Duerson Knight USAS. Possibly Grady Russell Touchstone USAS. Roland H Ritter USAS. Knight and Ritter both served in 1 Squadron in 1918, Knight scoring 10 victories with the squadron. Ritter served a month with 56 Squadron until he was sent to hospital on 14 June 1918. He joined 1 Squadron in July 1918 and was shot down and killed on 24 August 1918.

Top right: SE5a B 875 'M' of 40 Squadron. This SE5a was issued to the squadron on 8 June 1918 and crashed on the aerodrome on 13 August 1918 by 2Lt D F Murman.

Right: 84 Squadron pilots 1918. L to R: Lt Simpson. Capt Sidney William Highwood (16 victories DFC and Bar) Capt Anthony Beauchamp Proctor (54 victories). VC. DSO. DFC. MC and Bar). Lt Joseph E Boudwin USAS.

Right: A Flight, 60 Squadron, summer 1918. Standing, L to R: Sgt Scammel. Corporals: Barrett. Carmen. Wormald. Warrant Officers: Edwards. Robinson. Morris. Corporals: Hutcheson. Nash. Haworth. Duncan. Bird. Seated, L to R: Sgt Haslins. Lt B S Johnston. H S Stuart-Smith. J W Rayner. J E Doyle. S A Thomson. Of the pilots in this photograph, S Thomson was KIA on 5 September, Capt John Doyle was shot down and taken POW on 7 September and Stuart-Smith was KIA on 15 September.

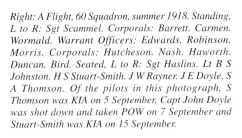

Above: SE5as of A Flight 24 Squadron on Cappy aerodrome in September 1918.

Right: Capt Tom Falcon Hazell DSO. DSC+Bar. Hazell served in 1, 24, and 203 Squadrons. He is credited with 43 victories.

Far right: Capt John Edgcombe Doyle. 56 and 60 Squadrons. John Doyle scored nine victories while serving with 60 Squadron in the summer and early autumn of 1918. He was shot down and taken POW on 5 September 1918.

Right: This brief impersonal postcard dated 20 December 1918 was the first news that John Doyle's mother received that he had lost his right leg and had been repatriated to England.

Far right: Lt Laurence Grant Bowen. KIA 15 September 1918.

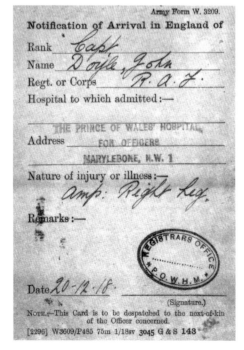

Above: Sopwith Camels of 201 Squadron on Baizieux aerodrome in September 1918.

Right: Capt D'Urban Victor Armstrong. A South African, Armstrong served in 60, 78, 39 and 151 Squadrons. In November 1916 he scored one victory while serving in 60 Squadron, but as a night fighter pilot with 151 Squadron in 1918 he scored another four victories, all at night. Armstrong was known throughout the RAF for his brilliant aerobatic flying of the notoriously difficult Sopwith Camel, but he was killed while stunting on 13 November 1918.

Far right: 2Lt Leslie Norman Hollinghurst. 'Holly' Hollinghurst served with 87 Squadron flying Sopwith Dolphins from April 1918 until the end of the war, claiming 11 victories.

Right: Fighting instructors at Turnberry in the autumn of 1918. L to R: R W Chappell (11 victories) H W L Saunders (15 victories). Sorsoleil (14 victories). A B Yuill (two victories, at night). P C Clayson (29 victories).

Right: This Pfalz DXII 2486/18 was flown by Ltn Paul Vogel of Jasta 23b who was shot down on 15 September 1918 after a combat with the SE5as of 1 Squadron and Bristol Fighters of 62 Squadron. Vogel was awarded to Douglas Cameron of 1 Squadron for his first victory. This photograph was taken at No.2 Aeroplane Supply Depot. Despite the fact that the Pfalz DXII was a new type and would have been of utmost interest to RAF intelligence, infantry souvenir hunters had reduced the Pfalz to this state within ten minutes of Vogel crashlanding.

Above: Three Captains of 213 Squadron 1918. L to R: Capt John E Greene (15 victories) of 213 Squadron. Capt Leonard H Slatter (seven victories) and Capt George C MacKay (18 victories).

Top right: Capt Duncan Grinnell-Milne. 56 Squadron's last commanding officer.

Right: Officers of 203 Squadron line up in front of the squadron's Sopwith Camels on Le Hameau aerodrome in July 1918. Raymond Collishaw, the squadron commander, seated in the centre, still wears his RNAS uniform. Immediately on Collishaw's left is Capt L H 'Tich' Rochford. Second on Collishaw's right is Capt Arthur Whealy.

Right: Duncan Grinnell-Milne's sketch of his near crash on 28 September 1918.

Above: SE5as of A Flight 2 Squadron AFC near Lille in October 1918. The nearest machine D379 was crashed shortly after this photograph was taken. Returning from a patrol, Lt Lionel Armstrong made several loops before landing normally, but as the SE5 came to a stop the fuselage collapsed. Armstrong was unhurt.

Right: Flight Commanders of 29 Squadron. Capt Earle Stanley Meek. Capt William Earle Molesworth MC+Bar. Capt Herbert James Hamilton MC. Winter 1918.

Right: Capt Clive Beverley Glynn. 74 Squadron. Glynn was awarded eight victories with 74 Squadron.

Far right: Major Arthur Holroyd O'Hara Wood. O'Hara Wood had been flying in France since 1916 and was appointed CO of 46 Squadron on 21 July 1918. On the morning of 4 October 1918, flying in a squadron patrol, O'Hara Wood collided with Lt L L Saunders at 14,000 feet and both pilots were killed.

Above: This Camel of 208 Squadron was crashed behind the allied lines near Cherisy on 4 October 1918 by 2Lt E Munro.

Top right: Capt Anthony Frederick Weatherby Beauchamp Proctor VC. DSO. MC+Bar. DFC. Beauchamp Proctor served in 84 Squadron from January 1918 until 8 October 1918 and scored 54 victories.

Right: Lt E H Barksdale USAS. 41 Squadron RAF 1918.

Right: 41 Squadron pilots on the former German aerodrome at Halluim in November 1918. L to R: Unknown. Capt E J Stephens. Lt N E Ohman. Lt G J Farnworth. Capt F O Soden.

Right: The Sopwith Snipe entered service with the RAF in September 1918. The Snipe was flown by 43 and 208 Squadrons RAF and 4 Squadron AFC.

Lt Kenneth Russell Unger. An American from Newark, New Jersey, Unger flew Sopwith Camels with 210 Squadron from 8 June 1918 until the end of the war. Unger scored 14 victories with 210 Squadron and won a DFC.

Major William Barker's Sopwith Snipe E8012 after the fight on 27 October 1918 which resulted in the award of Barker's VC.

Lt-Col Louis A Strange DSO. MC. DFC. Wing Commander Eightieth Wing, 1918.

Major G H Bowman, commanding 41 Squadron, sitting on the wheel of Fokker D VII 4043/18. Ltn Adolf Auer of Jasta 40 was flying this machine when he was wounded and brought down on 28 October 1918 by Lt Frank Soden of 41 Squadron.

Above: Pilots of 41 Squadron with Auer's Fokker DVII. Capt W A Shields. N Ohman. Unknown. F McGrath. M O'Rorke. B E Harmer. Unknown. Squadron's padre. Major G H Bowman (CO) and Byng the squadron dog.

Top right: Capt Joseph Leonard Maries White. DFC+Bar. CdeG. Canadian 'John' White, flew with 65 Squadron from April 1918 until the end of hostilities and claimed 22 victories. White was killed in a flying accident in 1925.

Right: Capt A G Jones-Williams in his immaculate Camel F3991 'Peggy'. 65 Squadron late 1918.

Gascoyne's flying helmet and the shattered windscreen of his SE5a after the incident of 9 November 1918.

Lt James V Gascoyne. DFC. 92 Squadron 1918.

This group of airfighters scored 138 aerial victories between them. L to R: Capt Beauchamp Proctor (54 victories). Major S E Parker. Major F Holliday (17 victories). Capt Gerald Constable Maxwell (27 victories) and Major Philip Fullard (40 victories) These pilots toured the United States in 1919 to promote the sale of Victory Bonds. This photograph was taken en route on board the Northland by another distinguished pilot on the tour, Capt Henry Woollett (35 victories).

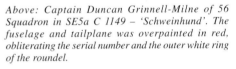

Above: Captain Duncan Grinnell-Milne of 56 Squadron in SE5a C 1149 – 'Schweinhund'. The fuselage and tailplane was overpainted in red, obliterating the serial number and the outer white ring of the roundel.

Left: Capt James Milne Robb DFC adjusting the top gun of his SE5a in 92 Squadron. Robb scored one victory flying DH2s with 32 Squadron in January 1917 and added another six while flying SE5as with 92 Squadron in 1918. Robb remained in the RAF after the war, served in World War II and retired in 1951 as Air Chief Marshal Sir James Robb, KBE. GCB. DSO. DFC.

Below: Armistice Day 11 November 1918. Three Flight Commanders of 41 Squadron. L to R: Capts Frank Soden. Eric Stephens. William Shields.

Bottom left: Pilots of 1 Squadron photographed shortly after the end of the war. Fifth from the left is Capt. R T C Hoidge, sixth is the Squadron CO Major W E Young (wearing socks), seventh is Capt C S T Lavers, eighth is Capt L W Jarvis, ninth is Lt F Magoun.

managed to convert the dive into a flat spin. George Hicks had followed the stricken SE5 down and at 5,000 feet was astonished to see Caldwell climb out onto the lower left wing, holding onto the centre section strut with his left hand and manipulating the control column with his right. Caldwell waved to Hicks, which Hicks took to be a farewell wave. Rather than watch his CO fall to certain death, Hicks turned away.

Caldwell, however, was not resigned to die – or be taken prisoner. At only 500 feet from the ground, with the position seemingly hopeless, Caldwell, using all his considerable skill, managed to regain enough control to turn SE5 towards the British trenches and just cleared the front lines. As the SE5 was about to hit the ground, Caldwell jumped clear, turned a couple of somersaults and came to a stop near a dugout. Watched with no little astonishment by the spellbound infantry, Caldwell stood up, walked towards them and asked to be taken to a telephone.

Caldwell's logbook entry of the incident reads: 'Carlin and I collided in the air, both got down. Very lucky still.'

On 5 September 1918, John Doyle, a senior Flight Commander with 60 Squadron, was looking forward to going home on leave the following day. He had been flying in France since March and in the last six months had done more than his share of fighting. Since joining 60 Squadron from 56 Squadron in July, Doyle had accounted for nine enemy aeroplanes and shared in the destruction of four observation balloons. His leave would be followed by a home posting, and with the war developing as it was Doyle had every reason to believe that he would survive the conflict without injury.

In the morning Major Clarke, 60 Squadron's Commanding Officer, called Doyle into the squadron office. '57 Squadron are doing a bomb raid east of Cambrai this afternoon. Its about thirty-five miles over and they want an escort. Take ten machines. You might as well fly over to lunch with them, then you can fix up the details'. This seemed a pleasant and uneventful way of passing his last day in France and Doyle flew to 57 Squadron's aerodrome for lunch and discussed the proposed raid. There were practically no details to arrange. Five DH4 bombers were to carry out the raid and Doyle agreed to rendezvous with them at 13,000 feet over Doullens.

At half past two, Doyle and his Flight met the bombers and he whole formation headed east. The heavily loaded bombers climbed slower than the fighters, but at the altitude at which the formation was flying as it approached its objective Doyle knew that once the DH4s had released their bombs they would be faster than the SE5s on the return trip.

'So I wanted a bit of height up my sleeve, so to speak. When they laid their eggs I was about four thousand feet above them. They headed west, but I flew on a little way so that when I did turn I could see them over the leading edge of my lower plane, which meant that I was some way behind them. It was a good strategic position as it turned out, because the pilots of four Fokker biplanes, which I presently noticed climbing up under the "Fours" were quite unaware of the presence of my escort.

Most British pilots have had experience of the various traps the Germans used to set so skilfully in order to lure unsuspecting airmen to their doom. This was the first occasion, however, as far as I was concerned, when the position was reversed. I was ideally placed. But, I decided I must not be in too great a hurry. I must wait till they were nibbling at the bait with their attention thus fully occupied.

So I closed my radiator shutter and rocked my machine slowly to attract the attention of my patrol. I wound my tail wheel forward and held the bus up with the stick while I watched the Fokkers' progress with interest. The way they could overhaul the "Fours" was an education.

Then I saw some tracer leave the leading Fokker. It was long range shooting but I knew I could not further delay matters. And at that moment a red Very light curved into the sky from one of the "Fours". This was clearly my summons, but I hoped it would not cause the Huns to look round.

I let my stick forward and my bus dropped from under me. I looked back. With one exception my patrol appeared to be unaware that I was diving for they remained above. The exception, Lt. Rayner, was close on my right. Soon we were down behind the Fokkers and rushing at them. We had the two rear machines respectively of that formation of five in our sights. It was essential in this, our first dive, that we should make certain of our men before the cat was out of the bag, and so we held our fire until the last possible minute, then opened up simultaneously. I can clearly recall being aware that tracer left Rayner's guns at the same instant that I pressed my own triggers. I was also aware of a sheet of flame in the right-hand Fokker's cockpit. My own target shot up vertically and stalled.

We were now below the level of the "Fours" for the Fokkers were still climbing up to them. My intention had been to get in my first burst and then zoom up to take stock of the situation. But I had been very close to my man when he reared up and I had to shoot my stick forward to pass below him. I was still travelling very fast and that put me in a dive again. I got the leader in my sight and let go another burst, This time the Fokker did a flick left turn and dived in a southerly direction. I did some rapid – and it seems faulty – thinking.

There were fifteen of us Britishers in the sky. We had accounted for two of the Jerries for certain. I thought I had another but wanted to make sure. Already I had turned south and was diving after my man. I had forgotten about my leave for the moment. There were two more Fokkers about, but, thought I, they will be well marked. I got in another burst and held it while I tried to close up, but the only result was that my man went into a still steeper dive, always flying straight. So I knew I had got him.

But the laugh was on me also, for a burst of close range stuff crashed into my SE at that moment. I think one's brain works at extra speed on such occasions. On looking back, at any rate, that is the impression I get. A result is a slowing up of the action, and so I will give my recollections in slow motion.

A bullet cracked past just clear of the cockpit; a second went through the instrument board into the tank; the third struck my head just behind the ear and cut the buckle of my chin strap, which fell slowly down. Two more cracks and then a terrific concussion. I was pressed against the side of the cockpit, unable to move, while the 'plane fell headlong, turning on its axis as it did so. Still I was pinned against the side. Petrol was pouring on to me and I managed to depress the switch.

Obviously something had broken; but what? I looked along each wing but could see nothing wrong. The twisting, patterned landscape ahead was growing in size ominously. I looked round at my tail, which seemed intact. But full left rudder was on! I must have been falling at over two hundred miles an hour, so the strain on tail and fuselage can be imagined. I looked into the cockpit for the first time and realised the trouble.

Naturally, as the aeroplane was standing on its nose all my weight was on the rudder bar. But it was my left leg which was carrying most of the weight, my right flying boot being folded back, but with the foot still in the stirrup. The cause of the machine's strange behaviour was instantly clear. That concussion I had experienced had been due to a bullet smashing my shinbone and at the same time paralysing the nerve. I grabbed the boot and dragged it out of the stirrup then pulled with my left leg and the aeroplane responded immediately. I looked up past my tail and got a head-on impression of two Fokkers diving after me. Instinct warned me that there was an ominous meaning in the speed with which they were following me down. They were not, I surmised, solicitous for my welfare! The ground was near but I dived again to maintain my lead and flattening out hurriedly made a landing of sorts in what appeared to be a park.

When the SE had stopped bouncing and come to a rest, I threw off my belt and stood on the seat. A burst of fire from the leading Fokker spattered around me, but I was not hit. When this had stopped I jumped to the ground, tried to take a step and of course fell. There was another long burst of firing from above and I lay without moving. Bullets seemed to be smacking into the grass in a circle round my body but again I was not touched.

Two German Tommies had approached me as near as seemed advisable, and when the firing ceased I got up and hopped over to them. I thought it would be healthier there, and it was. I showed them the condition of my leg by flapping it at them and they helped me away and presently laid me on the ground, where I was soon surrounded by a little crowd of sympathetic French women and children. Then a German in flying kit joined the group and I knew he must be one of the Fokker pilots. There was a fierce altercation between him and the crowd. The German was trying to drown all other voices by the power of his own.

I discovered he had been questioned as to why he had fired at a prisoner, and his reply was that I had killed his friend. I learnt later that three Fokkers had been brought down, but that was only partial compensation for that leave. The head wound was superficial – so at least I always stoutly maintain – but for three days gangrene crept up my leg, and then it was amputated high up. It was touch and go for me by that time. But I had several narrow squeaks on that trip, of which two bullets in the petrol tank were not the least. Still, all's well that ends well. Now I have to do my flying with one leg.'[2]

The Fokkers John Doyle described so vividly were from *Jasta 4, Ltn.* Egon Koepsch of the *Jasta* claiming a victory at the time and place of the action with 60 Squadron. The Fokker shot down by the 60 Squadron pilots – the friend given by Koepsch as killed – was possibly *Ltn* Joachim von Winterfield of Jasta 4, who was killed when his parachute failed to open.

It was a bad day for 4 Squadron AFC. In the afternoon five Camels from the squadron, led by Norman Trescowthick, took off to take part with other squadrons in a combined sweep over the Douai area. The formations failed to find each other and Trescowthick's patrol was attacked by three formations of Fokker D VIIs over Brebières. The Fokkers heavily outnumbered the Australians, had the advantage of height, and attacked simultaneously from two directions.

Trescowthick, seeing the Camels were badly outnumbered, signalled his pilots to break off the action, and dived away. The other Camels either did not see the signal or it was already too late to avoid the attack and all four were shot down. Leonard Taplin was wounded taken prisoner, but the other three pilots were all killed.

Taplin later recalled. 'We had to fight. No signal to avoid action could have had any effect. The escape of one machine (Trescowthick) was due to the Germans attention being centred on us four.'

When the Camels had failed to find the other squadrons. Taplin had climbed a thousand feet above the formation, uneasy at the situation. He had seen the two formations of Fokkers, 12 to 15 in number, attack the Camels below him, and seen

Trescowthick dive away, unseen by the attacking Fokkers. Another large formation of machines was coming into the uneven fight. Taplin at first thought these were British machines, but they were additional Fokkers.

From his height advantage above his companions, Taplin dived on the leader of the enemy fighters, a Fokker with a red and white tailplane, and put a burst into its radiator. Its engine hit, the Fokker went down in a glide. This attack had put Taplin into the middle of the enemy machines and one fired up at him, a bullet hitting his right hand and smashing his wrist. 'My Camel immediately stalled, and half-rolled itself, and, to conform with poetic justice, came out of the stall right on the tail of my attacker, who was recovering from his own stall. I was now under control with my left hand and easily shot this German down.' At this stage of the fight Taplin saw Lockley's machine going down out of control past his Camel, and both Eddie and Carter going down in flames.

Another Fokker then got in a burst at close range, smashing the breech and cocking handle of one of Taplin's guns, a steel splinter hitting him in the nose. Dazed by this fresh injury, Taplin spun down to 1,000 feet, fought with two Fokkers which had followed him down, shot one down – the other making off – then went down to 100 feet and started for home. With only one hand, Taplin could not properly control his badly shot up engine to gain any height and after flying for several miles he was shot down by groundfire, crashing a few hundred yards behind the enemy trenches to be taken prisoner.

On September 7, Guy Waring of 29 Squadron attacked a balloon over Gheluvelt at 6.55am. As the balloon went down in flames a number of people run out of a hut, and one began firing at Waring with a rifle. Waring dived and machinegunned the rifleman, who collapsed. Meanwhile, Capt Lagesse attacked two of the balloon's machine gun emplacements and put them out of action.

The pilots of 84 Squadron had been extremely active over the last few days, ground-strafing and shooting down balloons – three had been destroyed since September 4 – and on September 7 a patrol led by Beauchamp Proctor destroyed another four. The SE5s had been bombing St Quentin and returning to the British lines Beauchamp Proctor had seen the line of enemy balloons between Cambrai and St Quentin. Lts Sidney Highwood, L Corse – an American pilot – F Christiani, and Capt Beauchamp Proctor each shot down a balloon in flames.

The weather began to deteriorate the next day. It was overcast, rainy and few enemy aircraft were seen. The following day was one of low clouds, strong winds and heavy rainstorms. These conditions continued for the next four days and it was not until September 14 that enemy aircraft were again active over the front and combats were reported.

The night of September 13/14 saw more successes for the night flying Camels of 151 Squadron. Lt E P Mackay saw a Friedrichshafen G III bomber, caught in a cone of British searchlights at 9,000 feet, just north of Péronne. A burst of 50 rounds from Mackay at close range caused an explosion of signal flares in the rear cockpit of the bomber and it went down to a forced landing in the British lines. The crew, from Bogohl 1/1 were taken prisoner and their machine designated G/III Brigade/21.

Capt W Haynes of the squadron saw a Gotha at 7,000 feet, also held in a cone of British searchlights. Haynes closed to underneath the tail of the enemy machine and fired two bursts of 30 rounds. The bomber burst into flames and crashed near Manancourt. Twenty-five minutes later, Haynes attacked a Friedrichshafen, hitting it with two bursts of fifty rounds. The enemy machine went down in a slow spiral but Haynes lost sight of it and it was not confirmed as crashed. Another unconfirmed claim was made by Lt A V Blenkiron, who earlier in the year had served with 56 Squadron. Blenkiron attacked an AEG bomber over the Bapaume area, but although it went down after several bursts from Blenkiron's guns it was not seen to crash.

In the morning of September 14, Edgar McCloughry of 4 Squadron AFC shot up the enemy aerodrome at Ennetières, going down to within 200 feet of the ground and destroying two LVG two-seaters from a line of five standing outside the hangars. He also scored a direct hit on a hangar with one of his bombs.

Enemy balloons again suffered at the hands of 84 Squadron pilots: Southey and Highwood each destroyed a balloon in flames and the one attacked by 2Lt C Rees broke away from its moorings and drifted away to the east, rapidly gaining height as it did so. Capt Camille Henri Raoul Lagesse of 29 Squadron – whose surname was rather rudely corrupted by his friends to 'large arse' – also shot down a balloon in flames for his 10th victory.[3]

On September 15 the weather was fine; enemy air activity greatly increased.

An early patrol from 56 Squadron left Valheureux aerodrome at 6.30am – A Flight flying top cover for B Flight. Conditions were bad, with poor visibility and both Flight Commanders washed out their patrols. During the early part of the patrol Roy Irwin had seen a lone DFW working just behind the Front Lines. After washing out his patrol, he flew east, cutting of the retreat of the DFW and attacked it from out of the cloud cover at 3,000 feet over Bourlon. It was a case of the 'bitter bit'. After firing only twenty rounds into the enemy two-seater, Irwin felt 'the shock of a bullet in my side' and looking over his shoulder saw several Fokker D VIIs diving onto his tail. Irwin dived away and the enemy scouts followed him only as far as the Front Lines, where they left him, contenting themselves with shooting down a British balloon in flames. Irwin landed at the advanced landing ground at Bapaume, had his wound dressed, then flew back to Valheureux, where he was sent off to hospital.

The weather improved considerably as the day had worn on and in the late morning the German fighter pilots made determined attacks on the First and Third Army Front balloons, shooting down six and damaging another four. As a reply, it was decided to attack enemy aerodromes on the army front concerned and 56 Squadron had been allocated Estourmel, southeast of Cambrai. Holleran was packing Irwin's kit, when Major Gilchrist came into the hut to tell him that the squadron was to take off before tea to bomb the enemy aerodrome.

The SE5s, led by Gilchrist, crossed the lines east of Havrincourt Wood at 3.20pm, and flew straight to the target. Gilchrist went down to 70 feet and dropped his four bombs on a large shed. He then half rolled and dropped another two bombs on a line of sheds, before firing at a Hannover two-seater in the middle of the field. Five men standing around the enemy machine all ran away, one limping badly. Gilchrist fired at more men and saw three fall before firing into the hangars on the south end of the aerodrome. Selecting another Hannover that was standing outside one of the hangars, Gilchrist went down until his wheels were running along the ground. A machine gun opened up and hit the SE5 in the centre section and the right hand cylinder block of the engine. Gilchrist silenced the machine gun then 'hedge-hopped' home, shooting at five wagonloads of hay on the way.

All the pilots pressed home their attacks and inflicted a great deal of damage. On his way home, Vyvyan Hervey saw four or five men up a telephone pole – 'a sort of terminal or junction of wires. Fired at them – they all fell to the ground.'

Capt Owen Holleran had been hit by ground fire and shot down. On his way back he had attacked troops, transport and a train, killing the crew. Flying west, only 20 feet above the ground, he saw a machine gun nest east of Ribecourt and fired the last of his ammunition at it. Passing over the village, the British trenches only a 1,000 yards in front, a shell burst under the right wing of the SE5, and Holleran was struggling to get it back under control when the petrol tank exploded. Holleran's next remembrance is of standing on one foot alongside the SE5, surrounded by enemy troops.

The popular American, Larry Bowen, also failed to return from the raid. He had gone down low over the village of Estourmel and had seen a train unloading munitions on the outskirts. Bowen had attacked the train, setting it on fire, the munitions exploding, but as he turned away he was hit by machine gun fire from the ground and killed.

There had been many combats during the day. In the morning, Capt Donald MacLaren of 46 Squadron shot down a Fokker D VII out of control north of Gouzeaucourt for his 46th victory, and the Camels of 73 Squadron made nine claims. Capt Owen Baldwin's patrol attacked a formation of Fokker D VIIs over Cambrai at 11.00am; Baldwin destroyed one and claimed another out of control. Ten minutes later, over La Folie, Baldwin destroyed an enemy two-seater. His fourth and fifth victories for the day were two Fokker D VIIs in an evening patrol: one destroyed south of Gouy sous Bellone at 6.15pm, the other out of control in the same fight.

Pilots of 41 Squadron fought with Fokker D VIIs over Houthem at 4.45pm. Capt William Shields shot one down for his 14th victory, and Frank Soden destroyed a balloon over Beaucamps for his 20th victory. Fifteen minutes later, Capt Robert Foster of 209 Squadron claimed two Fokker D VIIs destroyed over Ecoust St Quentin at 5.00pm.

In the course of the day, four balloons were destroyed in flames. One each to Capt Beauchamp Proctor, 84 Squadron; Capt H A Whistler, 80 Squadron; Lt M Ward, 70 Squadron; and Capt F Soden, 41 Squadron.

There had been many casualties. In addition to those already mentioned, four pilots had been killed, two wounded, three taken POW, and seven aircraft had been forced down badly damaged.

Enemy aircraft were very active the next day, numbers of German reconnaissance machines flying over the back area of the Third Army. There were many combats, some indecisive, but eight German aeroplanes were claimed as destroyed and four British fell behind the enemy lines.

On the night of September 15/16 Major Brand of 151 Squadron attacked a Friedrichshafen bomber at 8,000 feet. Brand's fire evidently hit the enemy bomber in an oil sump and his Camel was smothered in oil, forcing Brand to break off the fight. Another pilot from the squadron, Lt F Broome attacked a four-engined Zeppelin Staaken RVI of *Riesenflugzeug Abteilung 500*, caught in a cone of searchlights. Broome fired over 500 rounds into the giant bomber before it finally burst into flames and fell in the British lines to be designated G/III Brigade/24. Only one member of the crew of seven is listed as surviving the crash to be taken prisoner.

The Camels of 4 Squadron AFC were out at dawn, flying in pairs, and Herbert Watson and Elwyn King attacked three black Fokker D VIIs north west of Lille at 4,000 feet. King destroyed one, with two bursts at close range, and Watson sent another down out of control, both enemy machines going down over Le Quesnoy. An hour later, the SE5s of 2 Squadron AFC, flying above the Camels of 4 Squadron AFC, attacked a formation of fifteen enemy scouts – Fokker D VIIs and Fokker Triplanes over Lille. In the melée that followed, the Australian pilots claimed five of the enemy scouts shot down, one in flames, for no loss. Capt Roby Manuel was leading his Flight back to base when British anti-aircraft bursts pointed out an enemy machine over La Bassée at 9,000 feet. Manuel chased this enemy machine – a Fokker D VII – a long way into the British back areas, as far as Cassel, before shooting it down to crash 1 1/2 miles south of Droglandt.[4]

At 8.35am the SE5s of 29 Squadron were in combat with Jasta 7 south of Linselles. Joseph Jacobs and his pilots had attacked three Camels – joined by four more – but although the Jasta succeeded in driving the British scouts back to the lines in a running fight, no victories were claimed. As the German scouts returned to the Front Lines, Jacobs saw seven SE5s climbing from the direction of Ypres. The German scouts having been split up in chasing the Camels, they were driven to the east by the SE5s from 29 Squadron – there were actually three Flights out, 14 SE5s – and there were many individual combats. Camille Largesse, Lts Amm, and Dougan and Capt Hoy, all claimed Fokker D VIIs from the fighting, Hoy claiming two. During the fight *Jasta 7* were reinforced by nine Fokker D VIIs, six diving into the fight over Comines and another three later coming down from 13,000 feet.

Jacobs was attacked by one of 29 Squadron's flight commanders. Jacobs' guns had jammed and the SE5 pilot, 'who flew brilliantly,' pushed Jacobs down to ground level. Luckily for Jacobs, two Fokker pilots had seen his predicament and came to his aid, driving off the SE5. Gaining some altitude, Jacobs cleared his gun jams and attacked a lone SE5. This was 2Lt P 'Jack' Fleming of 29 Squadron who later recalled that Jacobs came at him head-on, his tracer bullets passing through the left hand bay of his SE5's wings. Fleming could not return Jacobs' fire – earlier in the action his top wing Lewis gun had been hit and put out of action and he had a cross feed in his Vickers gun. As the distance closed, Jacobs dived under the SE5 and although he had no guns, Fleming half rolled to come down on the triplane's tail. But the fight was now within four hundred feet of the ground and Fleming made several tight, vertical turns before flattening out and making for the British lines. He had momentarily lost sight of the triplane, but as he straightened out Jacobs came at him from broadside on, his fire hitting the SE5 in the engine. Fleming crashed, the SE5 turning upside down on impact. Fleming was taken under guard to Iseghem and while there was visited by Jacobs and taken out for a coffee.

Half an hour after these series of actions, Lt A Diamond of 29 Squadron claimed a Fokker D VII crashed west of Perenchies – making six Fokker D VIIs claimed by the squadron – and later shot down a balloon in flames. Lts Edgar Davies and Claude Wilson attacked two Fokker Triplanes in the vicinity of the enemy aerodrome at Loos. Wilson's opponent

crashed north of the aerodrome and five minutes later Davies shot his down into some trees east of Lille.[5]

Jasta 7 claimed four SE5s from these combats, but only Fleming was lost.

At five minutes to six in the evening, the SE5s of 56 Squadron were flying at 13,000 feet over Havrincourt Wood as top cover for the Camels of 3 Squadron when the Camels were attacked by seven Fokker D VIIs, diving on them from the northeast. Capt Molyneux of 56 Squadron tackled one of the Fokkers, that was attacking a Camel, firing a short burst from close range. A large piece of the Fokker's top left hand wing broke off and it spun for 100 feet before all its wings collapsed and broke away from the fuselage.

Several additional enemy scouts had now joined in the fighting. Hervey, aided by a Camel sent another of the Fokkers down out of control, but Noel Bishop of the squadron was shot down and killed – the left wings of his SE5 'buckled' – by *Ltn* Marcard of *Jasta 26*.

An American pilot of 1 Squadron, Capt Howard Kullberg, from Massachusetts, shot down a Fokker D VII in flames over Valenciennes at 10.30am for his last victory, its five Jasta companions chasing him back to the Lines and wounding him in the leg. Kullberg was taken to hospital.[6]

Among the many combats during the day, too numerous to detail here, was one fought by a large force of Camels from 46, and 203 Squadrons, and SE5s from 85 Squadron. A Flight of Camels from 46 Squadron claimed a Fokker D VII in flames over Cambrai and Donald Maclaren of the squadron claimed another out of control. This last was possibly *Ltn* Stark *Staffelführer* of *Jasta 35b* who was lightly wounded in the leg. Capt Cyril Crowe of 85 Squadron claimed a Fokker D VII from the fight, crashed at Sauchy-Cauchy at 6.45.[7]

The fine weather continued on September 17 and enemy activity was 'normal' along the front. Soon after dawn, the enemy aerodrome at Emerchicourt was attacked by 64 and 209 Squadrons. Ninety-one bombs were dropped, hits were observed on hangars and huts and two fires were started in the living quarters and a nearby farm. A train was also attacked and damaged by a direct hit. Returning from the raid, Lt H Hayes saw a convoy of about 40 guns and wagons led by a staff car. Hayes attacked the column, the car overturning into a ditch and bursting into flames.

Jasta 36 lost three aircraft in the raid – a Fokker D VII, a Fokker Triplane and a Fokker D VIII. The attackers lost two aircraft: a pilot from 209 Squadron was killed and a pilot from 64 Squadron was shot down and taken prisoner.

Caldwell was leading five SE5s on patrol north west of Courtrai in the evening. Seven enemy scouts were seen, flying at 15,000 feet, but the enemy machines lost height, going down to 13,000 feet, and Caldwell sensed a trap. Looking up, he saw an additional six Fokker D VIIs coming in at a greater height than the SE5s. Two miles further east, however, Caldwell also saw a lone SE5 of his squadron being driven down by three enemy scouts and immediately took his Flight to its the aid, attacking the highest Fokker at 10,000 feet. Intent on the other SE5 – Lt Fred Hunt – the enemy pilot failed to see Caldwell and a short burst sent the Fokker D VII down to crash north west of Courtrai for Caldwell's 20th victory. The other two Fokkers had driven Hunt down to 7,000 feet, but Caldwell attacked the nearest, firing 100 rounds from 50 yards range. The Fokker fell sideways and dived away to the southwest. Caldwell did not stay to watch this machine go down, but immediately dived on Hunt's last attacker, which spun away from his fire.[8]

Caldwell shepherded Hunt back to the lines, but they were followed by four of the Fokkers. Although both his guns had jammed in his last attack – the Lewis with a broken extractor and the Vickers with a No.3 Stoppage – Caldwell turned to face the nearest enemy machine. He later wrote. 'I could only frighten it away.' As a later historian was to write, 'What superb confidence he must have possessed and an inversely low opinion of his opponent.'

Again, there were many similar combats throughout the day and although victories were claimed, casualties were heavy. Five pilots were killed, one wounded and five taken prisoner.

The night was overcast and very cloudy, but the pilots of 151 Squadron were in action. At ten minutes to nine, Lt E P Mackay shot down an AEG G V from *Bogohl4/Bosta19* that fell in the British lines and was designated G/V Brigade/27. The three-man crew were taken prisoner. Major Brand attacked a Friedrichshafen G III at twenty minutes to eleven. The enemy bomber began to go down in flames, but one of its bombs exploded, breaking it apart in mid-air, killing all the crew. The wreckage was given the number G/III Brigade/22. Captain D'Urban Armstrong also claimed at twenty minutes to eleven, shooting down a Friedrichshafen G III in flames to crash at Flétre, east of Bapaume. This machine, from Bogohl6/Bosta 5, was designated G/III Brigade/23. All three crewmembers were killed.

The battle of Havrincourt and Epéhy opened the next morning, September 18, the British Fourth and Third Armies attacking along the seven-mile front from Holnon to Gouzeaucourt, the French First Army attacking south of Holnon. The attack took place in heavy rain; enemy air activity was less and there were correspondingly fewer combats, but 46 Squadron lost a pilot killed; 92 Squadron had a pilot taken prisoner and 40 Squadron a pilot wounded.

The fighting on the ground went well and all the objectives necessary for the coming assault on the Hindenburg Line were taken.

There was little flying on September 19. The day was one of low clouds, high wind and rain, and there was hardly any enemy activity in the air.

These weather conditions continued the following day, but during the bright intervals the *jagdstaffeln* were active over the battlefront in some force and there was a great deal of fighting.

In the very early morning there was a large dogfight southeast of Cambrai between the Camels of 201 Squadron, the SE5s of 60 Squadron and a number of Fokker D VIIs. The SE5s had taken off before first light, using the flames from their exhausts to keep together. A new pilot, 2 Lt Fred Battle was very short and was sitting with an extra cushion on his seat to improve his view. In view of later events this proved to be fortunate.

Over the Havrincourt to Marcoing road the SE5s were attacked by a large number of Fokker D VIIs, which dived on them from the rear. Capt B McEntegart, leading the SE5 formation, had seen a patrol of Camels from 201 Squadron flying below them and he dived to bring his Flight and the attacking enemy scouts down to their level. But the Fokkers were too fast and opened fire before the SE5s could reach the Camels, wounding Lt George Caswell who forced landed to be taken prisoner. Fred Battle had also been wounded, hit in the backside and thigh, but the extra cushion saved him from more serious injury and he was able fly into the nearby cloud, go down to ground level and return to make a forced landing on Fremicourt aerodrome.

The Camel pilots of 201 Squadron had seen the Fokkers, which turned east after their attack on the SE5s, their pilots no doubt conscious that the strong west wind would give them an advantage in any fight that developed. Ronald Sykes, flying with the Camels, wrote:

'Our Flight of five Camels met 12 Fokkers at 5,000 feet SE of Cambrai and chased them east, well into enemy territory. Then they turned and must have opened the throttles of new, more powerful engines; to our surprise they easily climbed above us and we had to turn west into the misty air under a cloud. They came through the cloud and started a dogfight. In the streamers of mist, recognition was difficult but I fired into several "black crosses" as they crossed close ahead. A Camel was on my right and I heard the kak-ak-ak of guns very close behind and turned a sharp 45 degrees levelled up and looked round again; a misty shape just astern was starting to go down in flames. I dived below the mist to identify it but all I could see was the top of a column of black smoke so I zoomed up and joined a formation of three dim shapes but had the shock of my young life when I got close and saw their black crosses. They had not seen me so I fired into the nearest one and then pulled up and changed direction in the cloud and dived down into clear air. Could see three Camels a long way off going west and no Fokkers but I felt there could be a lot of them above me in the streamers of mist. Did a lot of evasive action to avoid being a sitting target. Then Archie started and I knew the Fokkers had gone and it was safe for me to fly for the other three Camels that were in clear air towards the Line. It was Lt Mills who had been shot down and much later, when the infantry advanced through the area, we found his shallow grave beside the remains of the Camel near Seranvillers.'[9]

Asked about the performance of these Fokkers, British intelligence reported that they belonged to a 'circus' and had the 185hp BMW engine which normally only used full throttle at high altitude. Sykes wrote: 'We did not meet them again. The Fokkers we usually meet have 160hp Mercedes engines and a performance similar to our Bentley Camels except that we can turn quicker. They (Fokkers) always appear to treat a close "V" formation of 5 Camels with respect but they often fly in an untidy bunch of about 12 which seems to include trainees.'

Later in the morning, on the Fourth Army front, seven Bristol Fighters from 20 Squadron and eleven SE5s of 84 Squadron were attacked by enemy scouts near Mont d'Origny. The fight was a long one, lasting over half an hour, going down from 14,000 feet to 1,500 feet. The Bristol Fighter crews claimed six enemy machines shot down, the SE5 pilots a further two, but a Bristol Fighter was shot down in flames, killing the crew.

There were innumerable combats throughout the day, ranging from the area of the coast to the extreme south of the British front, the pilots of the RAF fighting under the disadvantage of the strong westerly wind, which often pushed the fighting deeper into enemy territory.

That night the Camels of 151 Squadron again shot down German night flying bombers. It was a bright, moonlit night and Broome easily saw an AEG from *Bogohl4/Bosta19* flying at 7,000 feet north west of St Quentin. Broome closed to 200 yards and fired 100 rounds into the enemy machine, which went down in flames to crash near Tincourt, the bombs exploding as it hit the ground at 9.35pm. Capt A Mitchell also claimed an AEG destroyed and Major Brand a DFW.

The weather conditions persisted on September 21 with strong winds and cloud. Enemy activity during the day was reported to be 'slight' and most combats took place in the evening.

An evening patrol from 84 Squadron saw four Fokker D VIIs stalking a patrol of SE5s from 24 Squadron northeast of St Quentin. The 84 Squadron SE5s dived on the enemy scouts from a three thousand feet height advantage and claimed two Fokkers from the action. Further north, at 6.10pm over Don, a Flight of 41 Squadron SE5s was in action with Fokker D VIIs. Two of the Fokkers attacked by Capt William Shields collided. Shields was awarded them for his 15th and 16th victories.

In a fight with Fokker D VIIs over Lille at 6.00pm, 74 Squadron lost a great character, one of its most popular pilots. Caldwell was leading the patrol and intercepted ten Fokkers at 18,000 feet. In the fierce fighting, Caldwell and Roxburgh-Smith each claimed a Fokker out of control, and Capt Clive Glynn and Lt Fred Hunt each destroyed a Fokker, but Sidney 'Timbertoes' Carlin was shot down and crashed between the lines. Carlin made a brave attempt to reach the British trenches, but physically handicapped as he was the German troops stopped him before he got very far and took him prisoner.

Many years later Caldwell recalled:

'I remember this fight well and how badly it turned out to be. Previously we had noticed a Hun patrol of 10 to 12 Fokkers come up to the lines just before dark, and after we had set off for home, so I thought I would organise a surprise for them. I took four of our best chaps well behind the lines at 20,000 feet and then flew towards the lines and there, sure enough, were our enemy Fokkers. Our surprise failed, however, because they saw us coming and spread out in climbing turns (obviously old hands) In the dog fight that followed we did reasonably well for a start, but when another EA formation came in from the north, 10 or 12 strong, we were in dire trouble. I saw Carlin's SE going down with explosive ammunition hitting it, but I could not help as I was in the centre of several persistent Huns. We had to do just what we could to save ourselves. Glynn and Hunt of our five were forced down on our side of the line and only Roxburgh-Smith and I returned to the aerodrome at Clairmarais. It was a sad ending to what we had planned would be a successful venture.'

During the night three enemy bombers were shot down by 151 Squadron, the Camels patrolling in the Gouzeaucourt area.[10] At 9.26pm Major Brand attacked an enemy machine – reports differ whether it was a Friedrichshafen or an AEG – which zoomed before falling over onto its back and going down. Brand failed to see the end of this machine but it was later confirmed to have crashed by British troops. Ten minutes later Brand joined with Lt J H Summers in attacking a machine described as an 'AEG type.' After the Camels' attack the bomber went down to crash a little to the south of Brand's first success of the night. At 9.35pm, Lt A Mitchell caught another enemy bomber, north of Péronne, and shot it down, bringing the squadron's tally to three for the night in the space of fifteen minutes. Only one of these German aircraft appears to have been given a G number, G/III Brigade/25, an AEG, but III Brigade RAF list the wreckage of two other bombers as being found later. These were identified as an LVG CV and a Friedrichshafen G IIIa, the first classified as G/III Brigade/26, found on September 27; the latter, found on September 28, as G/III Brigade/27. The German lists give two crews killed from *Bogohl 7/Bosta 23* and a pilot from *Bogohl 7* as wounded.

The *jagdstaffeln* were now flying patrols in ever increasing numbers, both to offset the numerical superiority of the RAF fighters and to concentrate their available forces for maximum effect. Shortages were now becoming serious – the jagdstaffeln were allowed only 150 litres per day for each serviceable aeroplane, and replacement fighter aircraft were also becoming scarce. Writing in his diary on September 2, *Ltn* Raesch of *Jasta 43* had recorded:

'We still do not have machines and are lazing around. There isn't much to do except visit the different *staffeln*. Today *Ltn der Res* Marwitz and Eggers visited us and there is a lot of shoptalk with the complaint that our *Jagdgruppe* is not expertly led. The British are superior to us, not only in number, but in their tactics and organisation. The *staffel* should fly in echelons, and there should be more staffeln in the air at the same time in order that they can help each other.' In an earlier entry Raesch had commented that Marwitz's *Jasta 30* also had no machines and were unable to fly.

Those *jagdstaffeln* that were able were now flying patrols of 20 to 40 machines. Acknowledging this, on September 22 Brigadier-General Longcroft, commanding III Brigade, issued instructions for the tactical employment of the RAF fighters. After commenting on the numbers of German fighters now being met by the smaller numerical patrols of the RAF, Longcroft went on: 'This system makes the work of our small patrols difficult, as either they are not in sufficient strength to attack the enemy or no enemy are found in the air to attack.' As a solution Longcroft ordered that offensive patrols should consist of two or more fighter squadrons, working together whenever possible, each patrol to consist of an SE5 or Sopwith Dolphin squadron above, with one or more Camel squadrons below. The squadrons should also be divided into sub-formations, working at varying heights. The squadrons above should be responsible for keeping in close touch with the squadron immediately below, with the leader of the lowest squadron being the leader of the whole patrol.

The primary object of the patrol was to find and attack enemy formations, with the lowest formation being responsible for initiating any attack. If enemy activity was slight, then the Camels were to carry bombs with a view to attacking enemy aerodromes. The aerodromes to be attacked would be allocated to the Camel squadrons – photographs would be supplied – and while the Camels were bombing and machine-gunning these targets the SE5s and Dolphins would stay above to frustrate any attempt by enemy fighters to interfere.

The duties of the various sub-formations were also laid out in detail. The top sub-formation would be responsible for watching the upper air to make sure that the lower formations were not surprised. The lowest formation was responsible for seeking out enemy machines and for initiating attacks on them. The intermediate formations were to ensure that no enemy aircraft could dive below them without being attacked.

These new tactics were well thought out, with the possible exception that it was more likely that the higher formations, rather than the lower, would have been better placed to see enemy aircraft at a distance.

Weather conditions were again bad on September 22, with low clouds and rainstorms. Enemy aircraft were numerous in the morning, but decreased as the day wore on.

During the last few days the two Australian fighter squadrons had been bombing German billets and railway stations between Armentières and La Bassée with no interference from enemy fighters, but on the morning of September 22 this changed and the Australians again suffered badly at the hands of the German fighter pilots. Three Camels from 4 Squadron AFC were just about to bomb the station at Armentières when 13 Fokker D VIIs dived on them from out of the cloud cover. Only one of the Camels returned. Of the other two, one was forced to land in the British lines and the last was chased back to the lines by several of the enemy scouts and finally crashed landed in the British lines at Neuve Eglise.

Later in the morning the U.S. 17 Pursuit Squadron – still working with the RAF – and the Dolphins of 87 Squadron, were in combat with enemy fighters, possibly machines from Jasta 34 and JG III. The American pilots claimed three Fokkers, but lost a pilot killed and another shot down and taken prisoner. Capt Henry Biziou of 87 Squadron claimed two Fokker D VIIs from the fight, both destroyed.

Fifty-six Squadron suffered its seventh casualty for the month when John Gunn was seen going down over Hamel with one wing of his SE5 shot away by anti-aircraft fire. Gunn survived the crash to be taken prisoner – miraculously uninjured.

The day was overcast with rain and strong winds on September 23. There were some combats, and casualties, in the morning: 3 Squadron lost a pilot killed, shot down in flames. In the evening there were two large fights, both involving the Dolphins of 87 Squadron and Fokker D VIIs in the general area of Cambrai. The first fight was with 14 red and black Fokker D VIIs and the British pilots claimed a Fokker destroyed and two others out of control for no losses. In the second fight, possibly with the same enemy formation, Capt Leslie Hollinghurst destroyed a D VII over Bourlon Wood at 6.10pm, the enemy pilot baling out, but Lt Goodman was wounded and force landed his damaged Dolphin near Sailly.

The weather on September 24 was good, although there were some clouds. Enemy aircraft were out in force and there were many fights during the day.

The first action appears to have been flown by 4 Squadron AFC. An enemy machine was reported to be reconnoitring the British back area behind Ypres. Preparations for the coming attack on the Hindenburg Line were underway and Fifth Army HQ requested that this enemy machine be dealt with. Two pairs of Camels from 4 Squadron AFC took off and found the enemy machine near Lens, a Halberstadt, flying at 3,000 feet. Lt George Jones attacked from underneath the enemy machine, forcing it down to ground level, his fire hitting the observer, who half fell out of his cockpit, hanging over the side of the fuselage. Jones zoomed above the enemy two-seater, now only 80 feet above the ground, and fired a final burst at point blank range. The Halberstadt, from *Fl Abt 19*, went down and crashed just east of the town, killing both its crew.

A little earlier than this action, Edgar McCloughry had first bombed a train, wrecking the rear half. He then engaged a DFW two-seater at 6.25am and shot it down to crash east of Lille. Ten minutes later he was attacked by seven Fokker D VIIs and although he succeeded in destroying one, which broke up in mid air over Lille, he was wounded in the foot and thigh and crash landed near St Venant, only half conscious. It was the end of McCloughry's war: he had scored his first victory – a balloon – on June 12, and had won 21 victories by the morning of September 24.

The SE5s of 40 Squadron were in action with Fokker D VIIs of *Jasta 58* over Cambrai at 7.00am. Capt G 'Ben' Strange – the brother of LtCol Louis Strange, now commanding Eightieth Wing RAF – shot one of the Fokkers down in flames, but was then shot down and killed by *Ltn* Demisch of the *Jasta*. Demisch was himself then shot down, most probably by Lt G S Smith of 40 Squadron. Demisch was seriously wounded and died of his wounds the following day.

Later in the morning, the American pilots of the U.S. 148th Pursuit Squadron – like their fellow countrymen in the U.S. 17th Pursuit Squadron, also working with the RAF – were heavily outnumbered in a fight with over 40 Fokker D VIIs over Bourlon Wood. Although the American pilots claimed seven enemy machines shot down, three Camels were lost, all crashing in the British lines, luckily with no injuries to the pilots.

Two Flights of SE5s from 56 Squadron took off at 7.30am and three quarters of an hour later attacked a group of Fokker D VIIs. Henry Chubb got on the tail of the nearest Fokker and shot it down to crash near Sailly. Harold Molyneux opened fire at 75 yards and saw smoke coming out of the fuselage of

his opponent, which went down to crash just south of the Arras to Cambrai road. The Fokker D VIIs finally dived away to the east, the SE5s finally leaving them at 8,000 feet over Cambrai.

The SE5s then reformed and returned to the area of Bourlon Wood, where they were attacked by three Fokker D VIIs that came down on them from out of the bright morning sun. Two of the Fokkers carried on in their dives, but one stayed to fight with Frank Sedore, firing at his SE5 from close range. Cyril Stenning attacked this Fokker, and drove it away, but Sedore had been wounded in the foot. Although he managed to return to Valheureux, Sedore was taken to hospital and struck off the strength of the squadron.

A Flight of SE5s from 84 Squadron led by Beauchamp Proctor took off at 8.45am to attack balloons, with other SE5s from the squadron flying top cover. Each member of the Beauchamp Proctor's Flight selected a balloon and attacked at a prearranged signal. Three balloons went down in flames, while the Fokkers guarding the balloons were kept busy by SE5s above. One of these Fokker pilots, more daring – or conscientious – than the others, dived to attack the higher SE5s and was shot down by William Nel, the Fokker D VII crashing at Estrees-Gouy for the South African's 7th and last victory. In the afternoon 84 Squadron repeated the success of the morning. Carl Falkenberg took his Flight above the clouds along the line of enemy balloons before diving on them. Falkenberg shot one balloon down in flames and Lts S Highwood and F Cristiani each destroyed another, bringing the squadron's total for the day to six.

On the coast the Camels of 210 and 213 Squadrons fought with the Marine Jagdstaffeln in the early afternoon, claiming ten victories for one casualty: Capt Solomon Joseph of 210 Squadron, who was slightly wounded.

Over the Cambrai area 32 Squadron joined in a running fight from the town between Bristol Fighters, DH9s and Fokker D VIIs. Capt Alvin Callender, leading 32 Squadron's SE5s, flew east and engaged seven of the Fokkers from the direction of Le Cateau. Callender attacked the leading Fokker, flying a streamer, and shot it down to crash north of Bourlon Wood at 5.10pm. Five minutes later, flying below a fight between DH9s and several enemy scouts, Callender climbed into the action and attacked one of the Fokkers, which was last seen going down in a steep spiral over Havrincourt. In the initial fight over Cambrai, other pilots of 32 Squadron claimed Fokkers out of control.

Over Zillebeke at 5.15pm, SE5s from 41 Squadron were in action with Fokker D VIIs. Capt William Shields shot down one D VII in flames over Comines, and 2Lt Telfer claimed another as out of control, but Capt C Crawford from the squadron was shot down and taken prisoner.

Later in the evening, at 6.20pm, 15 SE5s from 2 Squadron AFC were flying at 15,000 feet over Haubourdin and attacked 11 Fokker D VIIs; five at the same height as the SE5s, with another six below. The Australian pilots claimed six Fokkers from the fight, completely dispersing the enemy formation, but were then attacked from above by three Pfalz D XII scouts. The SE5s went down under this attack to join Capt R Manuel's lower Flight. Eric Simonson got on the tail of one Pfalz and it turned over onto its back under his fire. Francis Smith – who that morning had shared with Capt Manuel in the destruction of an Albatros two-seater – fired more bursts into the Pfalz that went down vertically from 3,000 feet. Both the remaining Pfalz were destroyed: James Wellwood sent one down to crash northwest of Haubourdin, near the enemy aerodrome, and Adrian Cole shot down the other, which crashed near Pérenchies.

Jasta 7 had taken off in the afternoon, Jacobs, flying his all black Fokker Triplane with the Jasta marking of a white rudder, leading seven Fokker D VIIs. Flying towards Ypres the German formation met three Camels from 204 Squadron, 'who were above us and showed signs of aggression.' Jacobs 'turned a little' and the Camels flew towards Sweveghem with the intention of getting behind Jacobs and cutting off any retreat. 'I immediately brought the highest one under fire. Right away he went down steeply. Now we got cranked up. He again attacked and when he went down in a crash dive he was pounced on by my Staffel who forced him right down to the ground. The fellow resisted until the last moment and refused to land until he suddenly somersaulted into the old crater field near Moorslede. The pilot, a Lt Warburton was taken prisoner unharmed. That night I visited the aircraft which had been completely destroyed. The fellow had terrific luck. He was fortunate to be alive.'[11]

Warburton had been part of three Flights of Camels from 204 Squadron that had taken off at 5.00pm to patrol between Ostend and Dixmude. No enemy aircraft were seen during the patrol and the Camels had recrossed the lines and were making for home when A Flight were attracted by Archie bursts over La Panne. Capt T Nash took his Flight to investigate and found two formations of enemy fighters, fourteen in all. Nash attacked the lower of these two formations over Pervyse, but as the fight drifted towards Westende seven additional enemy machines were seen diving to join in. Three Camels, including Warburton, had left the other two Camels and flown to engage some more enemy aircraft northeast of Dixmude. These flew south and were reinforced by another nine, but were attacked by the three Camels flown by Warburton, William Craig and P F Lt Cormack. Craig, from Smith's Falls, Ontario, later described the enemy machines as being one Fokker Triplane and eight or nine Fokker D VIIs, all black with white mark-

ings and white tailplanes, and claims to have shot the triplane down in flames, confirmed by Cormack. Ground observers of the fight described Jacobs and his pilots as having attacked 'full out.' Outnumbering the Camels and added by a strong westerly wind, they drove the British fighters back over the lines as far as the aerodrome at Bray Dunes, where the enemy machines did a 'belligerent roll' before heading back to their own lines.

Camels of 213 Squadron also appear to have been in action at this time and over the same area, claiming one Fokker D VII out of control, but losing two pilots killed and another taken POW.

Despite high winds and violent rainstorms as the day ended, Major Hugh Champion de Crespigny, CO of 65 Squadron, and Lt Maurice Newham took off in the darkness at 10.00pm to bomb the enemy aerodrome at Gontrode. Their Camels had been 'specially fitted out for the raid' – probably with extra capacity fuel tanks – and in spite of the weather conditions both pilots found their target, went down to 200 feet and scored direct hits with four 25lb Cooper bombs on a Zeppelin shed. They then attacked another large hangar, which was lit up, and circled around the hostile aerodrome for twenty minutes, machinegunning any lights they could see and other targets of opportunity. Returning to the lines at low height, the two pilots shot at any targets that loomed up out of the darkness. Major de Crespigny and Newham were both awarded a Distinguished Flying Cross for this raid.

The concentration of available German aircraft to specific areas was now giving RAF pilots a contrasting picture of the effort of the *Luftstreitkräfte*. Those RAF fighters meeting these concentrations found themselves fighting seemingly ever increasing numbers of enemy fighters. Others met with little opposition, many pilots commenting on the lack of enemy activity on the air. Reginald Hoidge, who flew with 56 Squadron in 1917, now flying as a flight commander with 1 Squadron, wrote: 'There weren't many Huns in the sky, they were pretty well thinned out.'

On September 25 the weather was poor in the morning, overcast and with rain, but conditions cleared a little in the afternoon and although enemy activity was described as 'slight' in the RAF Communiqués, there were a few combats.

A patrol of SE5s from 64 Squadron caught an enemy two-seater from Fl Abt (A)207 at 5.40pm and shot it down out of control over La Terrieres, just south of Honnecourt, killing the crew.

At 6.30pm Major Geoffrey Bowman, commanding officer of 41 Squadron, shot down a DFW northeast of Ypres. Archie bursts had pointed out the enemy two-seater and Bowman attacked, firing 40 rounds from both guns at close range. The enemy machine burst into flames. Bowman left the enemy machine and turned back to the lines, but on looking back saw the flames had died down, that the DFW had turned north, flying nose down, and was 'not burning very well.' Bowman turned back and fired a burst from long range at the DFW. This appeared to have no effect and Bowman's combat report states that owing to bad visibility he did not see the DFW crash, although 'EA burnt slowly all the way down.' His log-book entry for the fight is more definite. 'Attacked DFW at 5,000 feet northeast of Ypres. EA caught fire and hit the ground north of Houthulst Forest.' This DFW was Bowman's 30th victory.[12]

The last action fought on September 25 was by Lt T Bloomfield of 151 Squadron who shot down an AEG of Bogohl 6 over Arras at 11.00pm. The burning machine hit the ground between Montenescourt and Agny, south west of the town, killing all four of the crew.

The weather was fine on September 26. The Camels of 65 and 204 Squadrons left the ground at 8.25am to fly an escort for the DH4s of 202 Squadron. Over Blankenberghe the formation was attacked by enemy fighters. 204 Squadron claimed two enemy aircraft destroyed and four out of control, but lost two pilots killed, one of whom was the Canadian, William Craig. 65 Squadron made no claims and lost a pilot shot down and taken prisoner.

In the afternoon, eleven SE5s from 40 Squadron and 14 Camels from 203 Squadron, escorted by the Bristol Fighters of 22 Squadron, attacked the German aerodrome at Lieu St Amand, nine miles north east of Cambrai. Collishaw wrote:

'We reached the German field shortly before 1 o'clock in the afternoon and the SE5as went in first, dropping their bombs on hangars and adjacent buildings, several of which were set on fire. We followed them in, setting fire to three hangars and getting direct hits on a fourth. After getting rid of our bombs both the SE5as and our Camels did a thorough strafing job, everyone taking great delight in using a hapless DFW two-seater parked in the open for target practice. In all we dropped 88 bombs on the field and fired almost 8,500 rounds of ammunition at ground targets. We were not allowed to carry out the attack unmolested for some Fokker D VIIs got off the field and about 15 or more from another aerodrome put in an appearance and attacked us. With two of my Camel pilots I attacked one of the enemy scouts, getting 70 rounds away and the Fokker went down, bursting into flames as it hit the ground. Before leaving I got another which crashed about two miles from the aerodrome. I still had ammunition left and on my way home one of my pilots, Lt D H Woodhouse, joined me with shooting up bodies of infantry and cavalry. All in all, it was a most successful affair. In addition to the damage and casualties that resulted from our ground attack, 203 Squadron destroyed five enemy machines in the aerial fighting and 22

Squadron accounted for two more. We lost one Camel which was hit by ground fire from the aerodrome but its pilot was able to land safely and survived as a POW.'

Although Collishaw only mentions one pilot lost, two other Camels were shot up by the German fighters, both force landing in the British front line, the pilots uninjured.

Pilots of 29, 65, and 80 Squadrons were all in action during the day. Capt Ernest Hoy of 29 Squadron was in combat with enemy scouts when his radiator was shot up and he force landed in the trenches, luckily unhurt. A pilot from 65 Squadron was shot down and taken POW and a pilot from 80 Squadron shot down and killed.

The Battle of the Canal du Nord

The British, French and American armies were now hard against the last of the organised defence line of the German armies – the Hindenburg Line. The British were to attack on the St Quentin to Cambrai front in the direction of Maubeuge; the French to attack west of Argonne, in support of the American army, whose objectives were towards Mézières. In Flanders, the Belgium Army and the British Second Army would attack towards Ghent.

On the evening of September 26 the British Fourth, Third and First Armies held a line running from Selency, through Gricourt and Pontruet, then east of Villaret and Lempire to Villers Guislain and Gouzeaucourt. The line then ran northwards towards Havrincourt and Moeuvres, then along the western side of the Canal du Nord. The main attack was to be on the front of the Fourth Army, but the German defences here were extremely strong – 'fortress like' – and a prolonged artillery bombardment was essential. So that the artillery of the Fourth Army could get into position to bombard these German positions in preparation for its attack, the northern defences would first have to be taken in the early stages of the offensive by the Third and First Armies.

On the morning of September 27 the British First and Third Armies attacked on thirteen miles of the front between Gouzeaucourt and Sauchy-Lesrée, in the direction of Cambrai. The plan for operations in the air were similar to those of earlier offensives. After completing their first offensive patrols, five fighter squadrons of I Brigade, 40, 54, 64, 203 and 209 Squadrons were to be concentrated on the aerodrome at Le Hameau, under the orders of Major B Smythies of 64 Squadron. The main objectives of the squadrons were low level attacks on the crossings of the Sensée and de L'Escaut Canals, to harass any enemy troops, guns and transport retreating east, especially along the road and valley between Wasnes au Bac and Bantigny. Other offensive patrols of I Brigade were to be flown by 19 Squadron (Sopwith Dolphins) and 22 Squadron (Bristol Fighters) to prevent the jagdstaffeln interfering with the work of the low flying aircraft and the day bombers. The squadrons were also to attack and destroy any enemy balloons seen.

The pilots of Third Army were given a less fixed role, with only 201 Squadron making low level attacks. Unlike the pilots of I Brigade they were given no specific ground targets, but were to generally assist the attacking troops, paying particular attention to any strong points of enemy resistance that might be holding up their progress.

The pilots of 3 and 56 Squadrons were to leave the ground at dawn, firstly to attack enemy balloons, then to fly offensive patrols. At 7.30am, the U.S. 148th Pursuit Squadron and 60 Squadron were to fly offensive patrols, but firstly the Camels of the American pilots were to carry bombs, fly below the screen of 60 Squadron and attack any suitable targets, paying particular attention to any enemy concentrations which might be approaching the crossings of the Canal de l'Escaut. An hour later, the pilots U.S. 17 Pursuit Squadron, with the Dolphins of 87 Squadron flying top cover, were to fly a similar mission. Above the general concentration the Bristol Fighters of 11 Squadron were to fly offensive patrols at maximum strength.

On the First Army front the ground-strafing activities of the fighter squadrons under Major Smythies, were extensive. Seven hundred 25lb Cooper bombs were dropped and 26,000 rounds of machine gun ammunition were fired. The main targets were the enemy troops and transport on or around the bridges across the Sensée and Schelde Canals.

The low flying single-seater fighters on the Third Army front roamed more freely over the battlefield, shooting at any targets of opportunity seen, co-ordinating their attacks with the advancing infantry and tanks, but in the afternoon they were allocated more specific targets, the fortified villages of Gonnelieu and Cantaing, which were holding up the advance.

In the battle of Cambrai in 1917 there had been many tank casualties by German anti-tank guns, but the lessons had been learnt. The pilots of 73 Squadron who specialised in attacking anti-tank guns, were extremely active over the fighting. Capt William Hubbard of the squadron was particularly successful in aiding his fellow Canadians on the ground. Flying very low, he silenced many anti-tank guns, in a number of instances chasing the gun crews away from their guns until they could be captured by the tanks. Out of sixteen tanks working with the Canadian Corps, fifteen successfully crossed the Canal du Nord near Moeuvres, and only three were put out of action in the day's fighting, one by a mine, the others by shell fire.

There was also fighting in the upper air. The Sopwith Dolphins of 19 Squadron fought with Fokker D VIIs and Pfalz D XIIs over Cambrai, Lewis Ray of the squadron claiming one D VII destroyed and two out of control north west of the town, before destroying a balloon in flames five minutes later.

The pilots of 3 Squadron also attacked balloons, George Riley of the squadron destroying three. A pair of LVG two-seaters was also shot down, but the Camels were then attacked by Fokker D VIIs and lost two pilots, one killed, the other taken prisoner.

The morning patrol by two Flights of 56 Squadron were flying top cover for the Camels of 3 Squadron when Henry Chubb, leading the lower Flight of SE5s, observed a number of Fokker D VIIs flying south under them. Getting the morning sun behind the Flight, Chubb led them down to attack the enemy formation, shooting down the rearmost Fokker with a burst of 50 rounds at close range to crash north of Cambrai. Zooming away to remedy a gun stoppage, Chubb saw Jack Pouchet send another of the enemy scouts down to crash north east of the town. William Clarkson attacked another of the Fokkers, which stalled and went down out of control, before zooming to join the top layer of SE5s. Cyril Stenning and Ivan Awde also claimed Fokkers from this fight, Stenning's to crash northeast of Cambrai, Awde's spinning down on its back. George Mackenzie failed to return from this fight. He had been shot down and killed *Ltn* Baümer of *Jasta B*.

Duncan Grinnell-Milne, in his first patrol since joining 56 Squadron, had the unpleasant and unnerving experience of reliving the circumstances that had led to his capture nearly three years previously. In the fight with the Fokkers a shot had hit the engine of Grinnell-Milne's SE5 and thick oily smoke was pouring from the starboard exhaust pipe. Grinnell-Milne made for the British lines, anxiously watching the revolution counter of his engine wavering slowly downwards. The altimeter showed plenty of height – 14,000 feet – but it was 15 miles to the safety of the British lines. Exactly the same thing had happened before, in December 1915, over the identical course. 'A bit of history, unimportant to anyone save myself, was repeating itself.'

At 3,000 feet the engine finally stopped and Grinnell-Milne switched off, the noise of the bombardment below now menacingly loud. Stretching the glide of his SE5 as best he could, Grinnell-Milne finally crashlanded in a field full of shell holes near Quéant, about a mile and a half behind the British front line positions.[13]

At 9.30am, a morning patrol by 32 Squadron attacked a formation of Fokker D VIIs over Emerchicourt, north of Cambrai. George Lawson of the squadron shot one D VII down in flames and another out of control. During his attack on the second Fokker, the undercarriage of Lawson's SE5 hit the enemy aircraft's top wing and it spun down. An American pilot, Bogart Rogers, shot another of the Fokkers down in flames and two other pilots claimed out of control victories.

The Camel squadrons fought many combats. At ten minutes to noon, 65 Squadron fought with Fokker D VIIs over Ghistelles, claiming four victories but losing a pilot killed. After mid day, 54 Squadron, fighting with enemy scouts northwest of Cambrai, had one pilot killed and another had his Camel badly damaged. The Camel pilots were now having difficulty fighting the excellent Fokker D VII, but 43 Squadron, now equipped with the replacement for the Camel, the Sopwith Snipe, were more successful, Capt Charles Banks and Capt Cecil King sharing in the destruction of a Fokker D VII over Cambrai that morning for the first Snipe victory.

The Sopwith Dolphins of 19 Squadron were again in action during the afternoon. Flying an escort for the DH4s of 18 Squadron the formation was attacked by ten enemy scouts over Bapaume and Capt Cecil Gardner, a flight commander of 19 Squadron was badly wounded. Gardner managed to return and land his damaged Dolphin, but he died of his wounds three days later.

The SE5s of 32 Squadron also flew in the afternoon. In a fight with Fokker D VIIs over Cambrai at 5.20pm, Capt Frank Hale, an American from Arkansas, claimed three D VIIs, one destroyed and two out of control, but 2Lt C Cawley was shot down and taken prisoner.

The jagdstaffeln lost two experienced pilots during the day. Ltn Strähle, *Staffelführer* of *Jasta 57*, with 15 victories, was wounded in the head in a fight with DH4s; and Ltn Fritz Rumey of Jasta 5, with 45 victories, was killed when his parachute failed to open after he bailed out of his damaged Fokker during a fight with SE5s over Awoingt.

The ground offensive had gone well. By the end of the day the British troops were across the Canal du Nord and were close to the Schelde canal, to the south of Cambrai. Ten thousand prisoners had been taken and 200 guns captured.

The weather was bad the next day with low clouds and rain during the morning. The ground offensive continued. The troops advancing towards the Schelde canal were held up by stubbon resistance near the villages of Cantaing and Fontaine Notre Dame, but by 10.00am this had been overcome and air reconnaissance showed that the enemy had retreated to a line east of the canal, blowing up the crossings as they retreated.

On the First Army front the low flying attacks were only carried out by the three Camel squadrons, Nos 54, 203 and 209; the SE5 squadrons, 40 and 64, were employed on offensive patrols with orders that they were to attack and destroy enemy balloons.

Despite the RAF communiqué for the day stating that enemy aircraft were only active in the afternoon and evening the fighter squadrons suffered an exceptional high number of casualties in the morning, although some may have been due to the bad weather. A patrol of SE5s from 29 Squadron left the ground at 6.50am and lost three pilots, all last seen going east in the rain. All three pilots were taken prisoner, and another was forced to land after being hit by anti-aircraft fire. Leaving the ground at 8.30am, 41 Squadron lost six aircraft in a combat over Moorslede – possibly with *Jasta 7*. Five pilots were shot down and taken prisoner, one dying of his wounds, and another SE5 was badly damaged and forced to land at Quaedypre. On the northern part of the front, a patrol from 65 Squadron, which left the ground at 6.55am, lost no less than seven pilots: four were taken prisoner, one was interned in Holland; one was killed, and the seventh was forced to land by anti-aircraft fire. 64 Squadron had a pilot killed in the morning, his patrol leaving at 8.05am, and 70 Squadron had three casualties when a low flying patrol, which had left the ground at 8.00am, was attacked by enemy fighters in the Ypres area. A Sopwith Dolphin of 79 Squadron was lost while ground-strafing near Staden, the pilot taken prisoner; a Camel pilot from 203 Squadron was shot down and killed in a combat with 16 Fokker D VIIs over Ham; a pilot of 209 Squadron was shot down and killed after low bombing near Epinoy, and two pilots from 213 Squadron were shot down and made POW, another returning with the fuel tank of his Camel shot up.

In the early afternoon, Camels of 204 Squadron were in combat with Fokker D VIIs over Wercken at 12.30pm, Adrian Tonks claiming a Fokker D VII destroyed and another out of control for the last of his 12 victories. An afternoon patrol by 29 Squadron had better luck than in the morning. Capt Charles Ross shot down a Fokker D VII in flames south of Menin at 5.10pm, and destroyed another twenty minutes later over the Menin to Gheluvelt road, but the patrol lost Capt Ernest Hoy, an experienced pilot with 13 victories, who was shot down east of Ypres and taken POW by *Ltn* Raesch of *Jasta 43*. A pilot from 70 Squadron was lost in the afternoon, last seen circling north of Gheluwe, the pilot later reported to have died of wounds, and a pilot of 87 Squadron was taken prisoner.

The pilots of 56 Squadron were ground-strafing during the day. Capt Johnny Speaks was wounded: his SE5s was hit in thirty places and his cheek grazed by a bullet. Grinnell-Milne wrote off his second SE5 in two days. Attacking a group of transport and troops, one of his bombs hit a hidden ammunition dump and the resulting explosion blew off the right hand tailplane and elevator of his SE5. 'Something kicked at the tail of my SE lifting it up as if it were paper, throwing the nose down in an almost vertical dive, out of control.' The stricken SE5 hit the ground, the control column rigid in Grinnell-Milne's hand.

'There was a ghastly noise of breaking and splintering, I was flung forward against the safety belt, my head hit the windscreen; but the machine quivered, bounced, and went on – minus her undercarriage. There must have been a slight fall in the ground just at that point, for had it been level or sloping up I would have crashed irremediably and fatally. As it was the machine seemed to stagger forward, her speed reduced almost to stalling point; gradually her nose came up until she hovered along a few feet from the ground. She could still fly; by some tiny fraction of time and distance she had missed stopping altogether.'[14]

The SE5 was badly damaged: the tailplane, although still attached to the rear of the fuselage, was held by only a single bracing wire and was trailing out behind the aeroplane. The undercarriage was gone and the tip of one blade of the propeller had snapped off on impact, causing the engine to vibrate with a nerve-shattering shudder. However, gingerly working the controls, Grinnell-Milne found that the SE5 would still fly, an indication of the great strength of the type. Grinnell-Milne levelled out at 100 feet and found the best flying speed to be 80mph. To maintain this speed it was necessary to run the vibrating engine at three quarters throttle, but Grinnell-Milne was again determined to escape capture for the second time and he gradually brought the nose of the SE5 round until he was heading north west. Slowly losing height until the SE5s was down to 20 feet, Grinnell-Milne recognised Bourlon village ahead. He knew that the village had been attacked that morning by British troops, but had they taken it? Realising that he could see faces not backs, in the trenches under his wings, Grinnell-Milne got his flying speed to below 80mph and switched off his engine. The SE5 slithered along the ground, hit the rim of a shell crater and turned over onto its back. Grinnell-Milne came round to find himself being pulled from the wreckage by a pair of British tommies. Apart from a nosebleed he was unhurt.

The Hindenburg Line

On Sunday, September 29, after two days of preliminary bombardment, the British Fourth Army began its attack on the formidable defences of the Hindenburg Line.

The previous evening, Brigadier-General Charlton, commanding V Brigade RAF, which would be working with the Fourth Army, had issued a memorandum to 22nd Wing on the objectives of the coming battle, asking that it be communicated to all officers. Charlton emphasised that the attack, if successful, would have wide and far-reaching results, and could be well decisive on the war on the Western Front. He stressed that the destruction of the enemy balloons was of utmost importance, and that low flying attacks would be ordered by the Central Information Bureau system, machines being directed to the localities where targets of major importance were known to exist. Particular attention was to be paid to the importance of destroying any enemy gun battery encountered in the open: 'it will be justifiable to leave all in order to attack it.'

The importance of offensive patrols was also emphasised. The pilots of the fighter squadrons of V Brigade – 23, 24, 80, 84, 210, and 209 Squadrons – were warned that the battle area was from Honnecourt to St Quentin; that they should not fly outside these limits, and on no account were they to fly so far east that it would give enemy aircraft an opportunity to pass them unseen.

The Sopwith Dolphins of 87 Squadron were first in action on September 29, in a combat near Cambrai at 7.30am. Leslie Hollinghurst claimed a Fokker D VII out of control over Estourmel for his tenth and penultimate victory, but Lt R MacDonald was shot down and taken prisoner southwest of the town.

At 10.10am, in accordance with their orders, the pilots of 84 Squadron attacked enemy balloons along the front. Capt Sidney Highwood, who had seven balloons to his credit, was chosen to lead the Flight to attack the balloons, with two Flights above to protect them from any enemy fighters protecting the balloons. Five balloons were despatched in flames, Highwood sending down two; Lts Millar, J G Coots and Christiani each destroying others. A formation of Fokker D VIIs which attempted to intervene was attacked by the higher formation of SE5s: Carl Falkenberg crashed one at Beaurevoir for his 16th victory, but 2Lt D C Rees was shot down and killed in the fighting.

Other squadrons were also successful against balloons during the day, particularly 29 Squadron. Guy Waring of the squadron destroyed two, and Lts E Amm and E Davies one each. William Shields of 41 Squadron destroyed a balloon south east of Comines for the first of his five balloon victories. Capt Charles Cudemore of 64 Squadron attacked four Fokker D VIIs which were protecting his intended balloon target, shooting down one out of control and destroying another, which crashed inside the British lines and burst into flames, killing *Ltn* Hoffmann of *Jasta B*.

In the morning, 1 Squadron flew an escort for the DH9s of 98 Squadron, bombing the enemy aerodrome at Montigny. The formations were attacked by enemy fighters and although the SE5 pilots claimed two Fokker D VIIs, Lt L N Elworthy was shot down and made POW. No bombers were lost.

Low flying took its inevitable toll. A 29 Squadron pilot, Lt R G Robertson, was brought down by groundfire in the morning, and in the afternoon another pilot from the squadron, Capt Holme, was also hit by groundfire. His SE5 was badly damaged, and Holme just managed to crash land in shell hole close by the British front line positions. Two pilots from 46 Squadron were shot down and taken prisoner; two Camel pilots from 80 Squadron were killed; and a pilot from 204 Squadron and another from 209 were also killed, all while ground-strafing.

There were also casualties due to combats with enemy aircraft. A Camel of 3 Squadron, ground-strafing in the Third Army area, was shot up by a Fokker D VII, badly damaged and crashed, luckily with no injury to the pilot; a Dolphin of 87 Squadron was lost, the pilot taken prisoner; and 2Lt J F Stafford, an American pilot with 210 Squadron, last seen diving on 15 enemy aircraft over Zarren, was later reported killed.

The fighting on the ground had been generally unsatisfactory. After some resistance the western end of the Le Tronquoy tunnel had been taken and the Schelde canal had been crossed at Bellenglise, but the German defences were intricate and formidable, unsuitable for tanks, and the enemy troops resisted stubbornly. The 27th and 30th American Divisions, which had attacked with IX Corps, had broken through the Hindenburg Line between Bellicourt and Vendhuille. Pushing rapidly forwards, the American troops lost touch with the Australian Divisions behind them. 'Eager to exploit their success, and no doubt confused and deceived by the smoke and mist which made it difficult to be sure that the numerous entrances to the canal tunnel had all been found and blocked, the Americans would seemed to have pushed on without misgivings. Many of the enemy troops, who had stayed quiet in the honeycombed tunnel during the bombardment, came from their hiding places and cut off those Americans who had passed on. When the smoke and mist began to clear, some of the advanced elements, realising for the first time the precariousness of their position, fought their way back again, but many of them, nearly all belonging to the 27th American division were isolated.'[15]

The uncertainly as to the whereabouts of the American troops made it impossible to order artillery support for the advance of the Australian Divisions, and it was only after heavy fighting that a line was eventually established east of Nauroy and Bellicourt and west of Bony-Knoll. Another cause for the unsatisfactory outcome of the day was the lack of air support caused by the poor weather conditions in the morning. In the afternoon there was a slight improvement but heavy rain set in at 5.00pm.

Despite the rainstorms during the night, Le Tronquoy and whole of the canal defences were captured. The morning of September 30 was overcast with occasional rain, again hampering air work. Attempts to locate the cut off American troops in order to drop supplies to them by parachute were unsuccessful.

September 1918 had been a bad month for the RAF, with the largest number of casualties since Bloody April of 1917. Despite the shortage of aircraft, fuel and experienced pilots, the jagdstaffeln had fought superbly well and would continue to do so until the end of the conflict.

As always, the vast majority of the air fighting had taken place over German held territory. The number of pilots taken prisoner, alone bears mute testimony to that. The casualties in the single-seater fighter squadrons were 82 pilots killed in action, 26 wounded and 82 taken prisoner. In addition, 55 aircraft had been lost, 27 in combat with enemy aircraft; 28 from ground fire. Little would change in the penultimate month's fighting, some days seeing the heaviest and most intense air fighting of the war.

NOTES

1. At this time the *Luftstreitkräfte* had 828 Fokker D VIIs and 168 Pflaz D XIIs in service on the Western Front.

2. "My Most Thrilling Flight", John Doyle, *Popular Flying*, April 1936.

3. Lagesse was to score an additional ten victories by the middle of October, but was then sent home, physically and mentally exhausted after 426 hours of war flying. Lagesse was awarded a DFC and Bar and the Belgian Croix de Guerre.

4. Some sources give this pilot as having been *Gefr* Brandt of Jasta 51, but Brandt was killed over Le Quesnoy, much further south.

5. These two victories are given in the British lists as Fokker D VIIs.

6. Kullberg had flown with 1 Squadron since May, had scored 19 victories and had been awarded a DFC and bar. While he was in hospital he was found to have a camera – possibly while his kit was being packed. Officially, cameras were not allowed and Kullberg was arrested for having one in his possession.

7. Cyril Crowe had taken command of 60 Squadron after McCudden's death in July. On July 29, returning from a late night party at 41 Squadron's aerodrome at Conteville, Crowe was driving a car which struck a tree, killing two pilots. Crowe was court-martialled and demoted to the rank of Captain for one month, joining 85 Squadron as a flight commander. On his reinstatement to Major he was given command of the Squadron.

8. Possibly Sgt Hans Popp of *Jasta* 77b. killed. G/II Brigade/22.

9. Author's collection.

10. On September 14, with the Allied armies now advancing, 151 Squadron had been relieved of its duty of defending Abbeville and was now operating over the forward areas of the British First, Third and Fourth Armies, aided by a searchlight barrier system.

11. The day after this combat, Jacobs and *Jasta* 7 entertained Warburton at St Marguerite aerodrome. Jacobs' diary commented on the occasion: 'He is Lt Warburton from London. This was his first aerial combat as he had only been at the Front a short time. In civilian life he had never worked but he is a very well educated person.

12. The British lists give this machine as a Rumpler.

13. Duncan Grinnell-Milne had been captured in December 1915 while flying with 16 Squadron, the engine of his BE2c failing on a long reconnaissance. After escaping three times, being recaptured each time, Grinnell-Milne finally escaped into Holland in April 1918. Grinnell-Milne wrote two classic books of his experiences in World War I, *An Escaper's Log*, and *Wind In The Wires*.

14. *Wind in the Wires*, Duncan Grinnell-Milne, Hurst & Blackett, 1933.

15. *War in the Air*, H A Jones, OUP 1937.

CHAPTER TWENTY-SIX

PRELUDE TO VICTORY

The bitter struggle of four long years was now coming to an end. In the fighting since the middle of July 1918 to the end of September, the German armies had lost 250,000 men taken prisoner, almost 4,000 guns and 25,000 machine guns. The *Reichstag* party leaders were informed that the war was lost, 'that every twenty four hours can only make the situation worse.' Ludendorff informed them that a peace offer must be made, 'at once.' On September 28 Crown Prince Rupprecht had recorded: 'the troops will no longer stand up to a serious attack.'

To the men still involved in the day-to-day fighting, these events were unknown; the end of the war seemed as remote as ever. Even Allied generals viewed with dread the seeming inevitability of spring and summer offensives in 1919. Although the Allied offensives of August and September had been largely successful, they did not appear to have broken the spirit or fighting capacity of the German forces and the Allied forces had met with stiff resistance in the advances during the last days of September. But the German troops *were* demoralised, both by their recent defeats on the ground and the constant attacks from the air. In the front line, just north of Cambrai, the 61st Infantry Regiment reported: 'there was little cover. It was important to burrow into the ground quickly and to be seen as little as possible because numerous enemy aircraft soon fired on any unit that was incautious.' Moving up to Eswars for a purely local counter attack, the 176th Infantry Regiment was bombed on the way, losing 25 men from the remaining small remnants of the regiment. Fighting to hold Tilloy, the 119th Reserve regiment bitterly recorded: 'during the entire day enemy aircraft were cavorting above the positions without any hindrance.'[1]

Suddenly, in October 1918, the German Army began to crumble in the first stages of its eventual disintegration.

The fine weather returned on October 1. Enemy aerial activity was described as 'moderate,' but the squadrons of the RAF were active all day, bombing the all important rail links supplying the German forces. Two attempts were made in the morning to bomb the vital junction at Aulnoye, where the railway line from Mézières and Hirson link with the main line to Maubeuge, Namur and hence, to Germany. Both these raids were disastrous.

The first attempt was made by twenty DH9s and two DH4s escorted by SE5s. Seven of the DH9s were forced to turn back with various engine troubles. Twenty-six bombs were dropped on the junction and sidings from 11,000 feet, but there were only four apparent hits. The second attempt was equally unsuccessful. Twenty-nine DH9s from the other two bomber squadrons in the HQ Wing set out at 8.00am, escorted by 15 SE5s. Fifteen DH9s turned back with engine troubles before they had even reached the lines and another pilot returned ill. Two of the DH9s returning with engine trouble crashed, one blown up by its bombs.

As the depleted formation of DH9s crossed the lines they were attacked by large numbers of enemy fighters, forced to jettison their bombs and retreat under the cover of the fighters. Another attempt in the afternoon was more successful. Of the twenty-one DH9s which set out only three returned with engine trouble; the remaining eighteen bombed the junction, exploding an ammunition train standing in a siding.

The Dolphins of 19 Squadron were in action east of Cambrai at 8.50 am, Capt Philip DeL'Haye shooting a Pfalz D III down out of control for the last of his nine victories, but 2Lt D Laird was wounded, his Dolphin badly damaged, and he was forced to land.

Both the Australian fighter squadrons were out. The Camels of 4 Squadron AFC, flying in pairs, covered by the SE5s of 2 Squadron AFC above, bombed and shot up ground targets along the Aubers Ridge: railway stations, trains, gun batteries, troops and transport. Throughout the day and the days following the Australian pilots ceaselessly strafed anything that moved in the Wavrin/Armentières area.

Eighty Four Squadron were in action over Fontaine, south of St Quentin, with 30 Fokker D VIIs and three two-seaters. The Fokkers were reported to all have different coloured tails: white, black, blue, red and yellow. Beauchamp Proctor shot down a blue-tailed D VII, which crashed south east of Fontaine at 4.05pm; his second victory was another D VII that went down in flames southeast of Ramicourt thirty five minutes later. Falkenberg, Highwood and Miller from the squadron were ground-strafing in the Estrées area, attacking troops and transport. Falkenberg saw British tanks and infantry advancing towards Estrées, German infantry falling back in front of them, and took his Flight down to attack the retreating troops. Highwood and Miller attacked another concentration of enemy troops that were attempting a counterattack, machinegunning the enemy force until they had expended their ammunition.

Further north, in Flanders, 74 Squadron were fighting in support of the Belgian Army. Capt Clive Glynn and his Flight were in action with Fokker D VIIs over Roulers and Glynn claimed two enemy machines: one crashed, the other destroyed in flames, both at 2.00pm, but Lt A M Sanderson was killed in the fighting.

In the evening the Camels of 210 Squadron, also fighting in Flanders, lost two pilots killed to the *Marine jagdstaffeln* and 213 Squadron had four Camels shot up and forced to land during the afternoon's combats.

The weather was fine the next morning, but clouded over with rain in the afternoon. The fighter squadrons continued to ground-strafe, attack balloons, and fly offensive patrols.

As usual the Australian fighter pilots from 4 Squadron AFC were out early, attacking the railway station at Don, the enemy aerodrome at Houplin – which they attacked from 700 feet – and a train, fired on as it was pulling out of Haubourdin station, stopped in a cloud of steam.

The fighter squadrons also took their toll of enemy observation balloons during the morning: Frederick Gillet of 79 Squadron destroyed one in flames west of Roulers at 7.10am; at 8.30am the diminutive Beauchamp Proctor of 84 Squadron destroyed another over Selvigny for his 50th victory – his 14th balloon – and Maurice Newnham of 65 Squadron sent another down in flames north west of Courtrai at 9.20am.

The Camel pilots of 73 Squadron destroyed enemy guns with bombs, attacked machine gun nests and strafed enemy troops and transport, causing many casualties.

Towards noon, ten Camels of 54 Squadron were returning from low bombing when they saw a British two-seater under attack from Fokker D VIIs of *Jasta 1*. The Camels attacked the enemy scouts and shot two down: *Ltn* Raven von Barnekow was only lightly wounded and remained with the *Jasta,* but *Vzfw* Belz was wounded, came down in the British lines, and was taken prisoner.[2] One pilot from 54 Squadron, 2Lt W Densham, was killed in the fight. *Rittmeister* von Döring, *Staffelführer* of *Jasta 1* claimed a Camel at 11.25am over Cambrai, and von Barnkow claimed another at 11.30am. Each was awarded a victory. *Uffz* Borm of the *Jasta* was also awarded an SE5 over Cambrai at 11.30am, but no SE5 was lost in the area during the day.

In the afternoon a patrol of 29 Squadron SE5s attacked eight Fokker D VIIs over Roulers. Capt Lagesse destroyed one at 3.20pm for his 12th victory; Charles Ross shot down another northeast of the town; Thomas Harrison's victory was west of Roulers, and Edgar Davies scored his third victory with another Fokker crashed, also west of the town.

Beauchamp Proctor scored his 52nd and 53rd victories during the morning of October 3: a Fokker D VII over Mont d'Origny at 10.25am and a balloon in flames over the same area an hour and twenty minutes later.

Ten SE5s from 56 Squadron took off after lunch to attack ground targets in the vicinity of Beauvois to Nergnies. Major Gilchrist and Grinnell-Milne left the formation to attack enemy balloons south of Caudry. The remaining eight SE5s crossed the lines south of Cambrai and split into pairs. Two pilots attacked Beauvois; two others attacked trains on the railway line near Cattenièrs; another pair, Wambaix. The seventh pilot – his partner had returned with engine trouble – attacked Niergnies.

Gilchrist found that no balloons were up, but he found one on the ground south of Caudry and dived at it, opening fire from 400 feet. Looking back, he was so intent on watching the balloon burning, that the SE5 hit the ground and 'bounced up.' Gilchrist then spotted a car – 'looked like a Ford' – and attacked it as it went west up a hill on the Fontaine to Cattenièrs road. After a burst of 50 rounds, the car swerved off the road.

Grinnell-Milne, attacking his balloon, had his usual trouble with groundfire. His SE5 was hit in the main petrol tank and he was forced to switch to the gravity tank and return, landing at 5 Squadron's aerodrome near Inchy. Two hours later he took off again, but was again forced to land, this time near 102 Squadron's aerodrome. He returned to Valheureux the next day, but by now the squadron's recording officer knew better than to post him missing at such short notice.

In the late afternoon, 70 Squadron Camels were in an action with Fokker D VIIs over Roulers at 5.10pm. Walter

Carlaw claimed two enemy machines destroyed during the fight and Lts M Ward and G Smith shared a Fokker D VII.

October 4 was fine but overcast. Enemy air activity in the morning was more than in the previous days, but slackened off in the afternoon. The duties of the fighter squadrons were unchanged, ground-strafing and offensive patrols. One patrol of note was reported by William Bland of 65 Squadron. Fighting with several Fokker D VIIs, he was driven down to within a 100 feet of the ground. He managed to destroy one of his attackers and send another down out of control, but the fighting had gone so close to the ground that enemy troops threw stones at him!

Only one patrol was flown by 56 Squadron during the day, eight SE5s leaving Valheureux at 12.30pm. The patrol saw a formation of 15 Fokker D VIIs, but these climbed away into the clouds, avoiding combat. Robert Caldwell had left the other SE5s, flown south from Caudry and saw three balloons near Bohain. Caldwell dived on the nearest balloon, but the machine gun fire and Archie from its defences were so heavy that he was forced to zoom away. He flew a little way to the east, turned and attacked again. This time the balloon went down and burst into flames at 4,000 feet. The remaining two balloons were quickly winched down, and as Caldwell climbed away he was again heavily Archied.

Caldwell then went down to ground level and flew east, looking for targets. He first saw a convoy of four double gun limbers, each drawn by eight mules and attended by large numbers of enemy troops. Caldwell fired over 100 rounds at the limbers, overturning two in a ditch, the mule teams running loose. Flying on, he next saw a party of 500 infantry marching in fours. Caldwell attacked these, firing 150 rounds at very close range, scattering the enemy column in panic. On the way back to the lines, Caldwell attacked three enemy gun batteries before finally landing. These types of attacks were typical of the many hundreds carried out by the fighter pilots during the last two months of the war.

On October 5 the weather was fair in the morning, but deteriorated in the afternoon, with low cloud. On the Flanders Front in the north, operations on the ground had been suspended. On October 1 the British Second Army had taken the left bank of the Lys, southwards from Comines, and the Belgian army had reached a line Moorslede-Staden-Dixmude. The area of the battles had been devastated by earlier fighting and it had become necessary to halt the advance while lines of communication and supply were established.

The German Armies in France and Belgium were now in an increasingly desperate position. Along the 250 miles of the Western Front the final battles of the war were approaching a climax. In the north, Lille was threatened; in the south, St Quentin had fallen, Cambrai had been outflanked, and a great part of the Hindenburg Line had been taken. The Allied armies were pressing relentlessly forwards, threatening the German positions along the River Meuse from Verdun to Mezières, the flank of their retreat back into Germany.

In a morning operation on the Flanders Front on October 5, Roxburgh-Smith shot down two enemy machines in quick succession at 9.30am, three miles south west of Roulers. Nine enemy fighters had been attacking British two-seaters when the 74 Squadron SE5s intervened. The first machine attacked by Roxburgh-Smith went down in a spin, the second, a triplane, burst into flames as it hit the ground. Roxburgh-Smith then attacked three of the remaining enemy scouts, firing at one in the centre of the enemy formation. The top wing of the Fokker D VII crumpled up under Roxburgh-Smith's fire and it went down to crash. Roxburgh-Smith was credited with two Fokker D VIIs destroyed in this combat. Lt F Bond of the squadron was shot down and taken prisoner in the fighting.

Pilots of 56 were again ground-strafing and attacking balloons in the day. Ivan Awde destroyed his balloon, but was wounded and came down in the German lines to be taken prisoner. Awde had managed to land his SE5 and had crawled out of his cockpit onto the ground before losing consciousness from the pain of his wound. 'The first thing I remember was seeing my machine sitting a few yards away, with a German officer in the cockpit working the controls and probably taking the shells out of the Vickers.'

Jack Pouchet also failed to return. He had reformed with the other SE5s but on the way back to the lines he was seen to dive slightly and begin to glide west as if hit in the engine, before suddenly falling out of control to crash just behind the German front line. The squadron never learnt the details of Pouchet's loss, but he had been killed in the crash and later buried by a Royal Field Artillery ammunition column that had found his body.

During this patrol, Johnny Speaks and Grinnell-Milne both destroyed balloons in flames before attacking troops, transport and railway stations, Grinnell-Milne for once returning safely and on time to Valheureux.

Beauchamp-Proctor and Lt A Hill of 84 Squadron both attacked a balloon while returning at low height from ground-strafing. Both pilots fired first at the basket – no observer was seen to jump out – and then at the balloon, which fell in flames onto some enemy troops on the ground below.

A total of seven balloons was destroyed in the day: another three falling to pilots of 29 Squadron, and one to a pilot of 4 Squadron AFC. This last was from a Flight of Camels from 4 Squadron AFC that had been low flying. The Camels had dropped a dozen 25lb Cooper bombs from a low height on a train standing in the railway station at Avelin, scoring a direct hit on one truck, which exploded, wrecking another two. They had then bombed an enemy aerodrome in the locality, shooting up the sheds and hangars before attacking troops, guns, and horse transport.

The weather was bad on October 6 and there were no decisive combats. Conditions were little better the next day, and although enemy activity in the air was described as being only 'slight' there were some combats.

In the north, a Flight of five SE5s from 29 Squadron were on patrol over Staden at 8.45am. Capt Lagesse and Lt T Harrison shot a LVG two-seater down to crash between Staden and Roulers, but a formation of SE5s from another squadron – possibly 74 Squadron – was then seen under attack from enemy fighters and Lageese took his Flight down into the fight. Singling out a Fokker D VII, Lagesse shot it down in flames. The enemy pilot parachuted out of his burning aircraft but his parachute and clothes were on fire and he fell to his death near Staden. Edgar Davies of the squadron claimed another D VII, which crashed east of Courtrai. Shortly after the fight with the Fokkers, Lagesse saw a Rumpler south east of Houthulst Forest and shot it down in the British lines.

A little further east, over Litchtervelde, the Camels of 70 Squadron were also in action at 8.45am. Oscar Heron dived on a formation of 15 Fokker D VIIs and quickly shot one down to crash before turning to attack another, which was on the tail of a Camel. Heron shot this D VII down in flames to crash at Litchtervelde. Walter Carlaw also claimed two Fokkers from this fight: one destroyed, the other out of control.

During the day the enemy aerodrome at Escarmain was attacked by 65 Squadron. The target proved very difficult to find – there were thick clouds at 4,000 feet and layers of mist and cloud at 300 feet – but despite these conditions forty five 25lb Cooper bombs were dropped and direct hits were made on a hangar, setting it on fire. Other hangars were seen to contain Fokker D VIIs and these were also bombed and machinegunned.

A large-scale raid was organised by 80th Wing to attack all roads and railway stations on the perimeter of Lille. The two fighter squadrons of the AFC took part, with DH9s from 103 Squadron and Bristol Fighters of 88 Squadron. A great deal of damage was done. Nine Camels of 4 Squadron AFC attacked Avelin railway station, dropping 34 bombs and firing 3,000 rounds into the crowded station yard. The SE5 pilots of 2 Squadron AFC attacked Annappes and Lille railway stations from 200 feet, dropping 71 bombs, hitting several trains full of troops. Some of the troops ran from the trains to take shelter in a house, but this was destroyed by bombs. Near Annappes the courtyard of a farmhouse was seen to be packed with cars and horse transport and this was also heavily bombed. Some of the fighters bombed from so low a height that their machines were hit by fragments of their own bombs.

On the early morning of October 8, the second battle of Le Cateau opened on the seventeen-mile front from south of Cambrai to Sequehart, with the French attacking on a four mile front on the British right flank. In the words of the official history: 'although the German troops fought with the courage of despair. Their resistance was vain. What had been left of the Hindenburg defence system was captured and the Germans moved back in some confusion.'

At noon German columns were reported to be converging on Clery, and in the afternoon the Camels of 208 Squadron were sent to attack these columns, shooting and bombing the marching troops, causing utter confusion and many casualties.

The low clouds and rain in the morning of October 8, cleared in the afternoon and the *Luftstreitkräfte* was active over the battlefront. It was essential that the work of the corps aeroplanes of the RAF was not interred with and the fighter squadrons of Fourth Army were detailed to fly offensive patrols to ensure this. The length of the Fourth Army front was only eight miles, with nine fighter squadrons to guard it, but there were masses of cloud formations at 2,000 feet, and aided by these, plus the superiority of speed and climb of the BMW-engined Fokker D VIIs, the German fighter pilots managed to evade many of the RAF fighter formations and attack the low flying aeroplanes of the corps squadrons.

Twenty Nine Squadron were active after lunch, Lagesse and his Flight attacking six Fokker D VIIs south east of Roulers at 1.30pm. Lagesse shot down one of these enemy machines, and Edgar Amm another out of control. Just under an hour later the Flight attacked another six Fokkers north of the town. In this combat, Lagesse destroyed a Fokker, Edgar Amm another, and Lts Murray, Murphy and D M Layton shared in the destruction of another in flames. At 4.25pm the Camels of 70 Squadron were in action with Fokker D VIIs north east of Menin. Frederick Gillet destroyed two: one north east of the town, the other over Gulleghem, south of Roulers.

The official communiqué for the day recorded. 'Low-flying scouts of 3rd Brigade consistently bombed and shot up enemy transport and troops throughout the day to a depth of 12 miles beyond the line, causing considerable confusion and greatly hampering the enemy's movements, both in bringing up local reinforcements and in the general trend of guns and transport eastwards.'

During the morning the brilliant career of Anthony Beauchamp Proctor came to an end. Flying from their new base at Bouvincourt, west of St Quentin, 84 Squadron were flying a patrol at squadron strength when Beauchamp Proctor attacked a Rumpler north east of Mametz at 11.30am. The enemy two-seater went down to crash, bursting into flames as it hit the ground, but Beauchamp Proctor had followed it down too low and was wounded in the arm by ground fire. Despite his wound, Beauchamp Proctor unsuccessfully attacked a balloon on his way back to Bouvincourt, but finally landed safely.[3] Major Sholto Douglas, commanding officer of 84 Squadron, wrote of Beauchamp Proctor:

'The effect he had on the morale of the squadron was tremendous, and quite apart from his genial nature he seemed to excel in everything he did in the air. He was a very good formation leader, and at long range his eyesight was extraordinary keen. He seemed to be able to spot an enemy aircraft much further away than the rest of us. He also had great courage, and he had developed a particularly good sense of tactics; after he had sighted the Huns he would proceed to stalk them with the greatest skill and patience, eventually taking them unaware and with the advantages all on our side. He had been showing extraordinary zest for attacking the enemy at any height and under any conditions, and in a manner that had become the talk of the Air Force. He had only one spell of leave during the entire time that we had been in France – by then over a year – and he had always been most persistent in his wishes to remain with the squadron. For all his size, that little man had the guts of a lion. Immediately after Beauchamp Proctor was wounded and taken off flying I proceeded, with the help of a few stiff drinks, to work myself into a sufficiently inspired mood to sit down and do justice to the writing of a recommendation that he should be awarded a Victoria Cross.'[4]

On the night of October 8/9, the Canadians troops forced their way into Cambrai. The advance continued on the morning of October 9, the work of the RAF fighter squadrons again being mainly low level bombing and machine gunning. Reports came in during the morning that congested enemy columns were moving towards Le Cateau and every available aircraft of V Brigade was sent to attack them.

Fighting in the upper air was mainly on the Flanders front in the north, pilots of 70 Squadron claiming a LVG two-seater over Courtrai and five Fokker D VIIs destroyed, but on the southern sector Capt Alexander Beck of 60 Squadron shot down a LVG in flames over Bohain.[5]

One of the casualties during the day was Lt W E Bardgett of 74 Squadron, who was shot down and taken prisoner. Bardgett later wrote of his capture:

'Flying over the Lines at about 18,000 feet we set off to attack our late enemies (Bardgett was writing in 1936. – Author) who were flying at 16,000 feet. In the attack my engine failed. The result was that the Fokker I was attacking was on my tail in a matter of seconds, while I was endeavouring to get my engine going by means of an auxiliary hand pump. One burst from his guns and my controls were gone, or partly gone. It was too late now to do anything: engine "konked", controls partly gone! I had to be thankful that I hit the ground at an acute angle – the final result of it all was two clean bullet

wounds in the leg which I knew nothing about until I tried to walk, and a short stay in Germany.'

Bardgett recalled that during his three months with 74 Squadron the squadron were in almost daily combat with white-tailed, black Fokker D VIIs, led by a Fokker Triplane. These were *Jasta 7*, led by Jacobs. 'Our ratio of victories to losses in these aerial combats was unusually high and many decorations were won by the officers of 74 Squadron.'[6]

October 10 was a day of low clouds and rain. There was little flying and enemy activity in the air was minimal, but the fighter squadrons continued their low flying bombing and strafing attacks over the battle fronts.

In the afternoon a patrol of SE5s from 41 Squadron shot down a Fokker D VII. The squadron commander, 'Beery' Bowman, was flying as a member of the patrol and his logbook entry reads: 'Saw white AA near Zonnebeke and then saw Fokker shoot down one of our balloons in flames. Shot down EA with Soden, our side N. of Moorslede.' Writing home that evening, Frank Soden wrote:

'I got another Hun this evening and saw him crash the other side of the lines, so tomorrow we are sending up a party to collect what we can in the way of souvenirs. While I was on his tail firing, I saw him turn round and look at me. I am sorry he was killed, because he was a jolly "stout" fellow, and had just got one of our balloons.'[7]

The weather was deteriorating the next day, but the low flying by the fighter squadrons continued. A patrol of 92 Squadron dropped a total of 74 bombs on transport, troops and gun batteries. Lt J V Gascoyne went down to 20 feet to attack a column of guns and limbers passing through Molain, shooting up one limber that blocked the road. Again, these attacks are typical of the many carried out daily by the fighter squadrons during the last months of the war.

Low clouds mist and rain stopped practically all flying for the next two days and there were no decisive combats, but conditions were better on October 14: enemy aircraft activity was normal in the south, but intense over the northern part of the Front, where the British Second Army and the Belgium Army – with some French divisions – had reopened the offensive in Flanders. During the day's fighting 22 enemy aircraft were shot down by pilots of II Brigade working on the Front, a record for the number of machines brought down in one day by a single brigade.

The pilots of 29 Squadron were again in the thick of the fighting. A patrol of four SE5s from the squadron were attacked over the Roulers area by 20 Fokker D VIIs, flying in two formations. Henry Rath shot down one Fokker, which crashed east of the town at 8.35am and fifteen minutes later destroyed another east of Inglemunster. Capt Lagesee claimed two Fokkers from the fight: one crashed at Roulers and the other west of the town in the British lines, possibly G/II Brigade/ 31. The squadron's losses were a pilot killed and another wounded in the combat, plus another pilot who was wounded by anti-aircraft fire and forced to return.

In the past month, Major Caldwell had flown only to ascertain the position of the position of the enemy forces, which were retreating rapidly eastwards. Flying alone on one such patrol on the morning of October 14, Caldwell saw a single Fokker D VII below him at 15,000 feet. From his height advantage of 3,000 feet, Caldwell dived on the enemy scout and fired a burst of 50 rounds into it. Visibility was perfect and Caldwell could see his shots taking effect. The Fokker went down to crash at Ledeghem at 11.00am. Caldwell was flying again in the afternoon, part of a squadron patrol. Over Courtrai the SE5s attacked a formation of 15 Fokker D VIIs. Roxburgh-Smith shot one down out of control over the town at 3,00pm; twenty minutes later he destroyed a Fokker over Lauwe and another over Reckem. 2Lt S Stidolph shot down a D VII in flames east of Menin and 2Lt E Roesch claimed another out of control.

The Camel squadrons on the Flanders Front were low flying during the day and suffered heavy casualties. A Camel of 203 Squadron was hit by groundfire and the pilot injured in a crashlanding; 204 Squadron had a pilot wounded, and 210 Squadron had a pilot killed and another taken POW. 213 Squadron were particularly heavily hit. The squadron lost three pilots killed in a fight with Fokker D VIIs in a morning patrol, and in the afternoon, again in combat with Fokker D VIIs, had three pilots shot down and killed over the Pervyse/Thourout area.

Frank Soden scored two victories in the day. He wrote home on October 15:

'Yesterday I got two more Huns, one in the morning which crashed in Lille, and the other in the afternoon which is lying upside down, south east of a place called Inglemunster. The second one I got under rather funny circumstances. The Huns had just driven down one of our observation machines and made him land on the other side. While they were all flying around our machine on the ground and gloating over it, I dived on them and picked off the odd Hun, more by luck than good shooting. Moral: don't gloat.'

In the evening patrol Soden came close to being shot down. The letter continues, giving some indication of the disadvantage of having to fight while carrying bombs.

'I got into rather a mess yesterday evening. I dived on some Huns our side of the lines and missed in my first dive. As luck would have it a rather good Hun turned and charged me, and before I knew what was happening I was being driven down. I had a heavy load of bombs, which were a great handicap, and which I could not drop as I was over our side.

All I could do was to keep throwing my machine about to put him off his shot, which succeeded pretty well. Eventually I got a burst into him and he pushed off. There were several holes in my machine but only one of importance.'

Early in the morning of October 15, Major Bowman scored the last of his 32 victories: a Fokker D VII south of Lichtervelde. Bowman's logbook entry:

'While at 17,000 feet over Winkel saw white AA west of Roulers. Dived down to 7,000 feet and found ten Fokkers flying NE. Fired a long burst at top EA and his top plane came off (unreadable) but was unable to locate EA on the ground. Found later. Did not report it but Belgians did!!! Therefore: "Forbidden to leave the ground on any pretext whatsoever without permission of GOC2nd Bde."'

Standing orders were that no squadron commander was to fly over the lines to take part in the fighting. Caldwell, Gilchrist and Bowman were only three of the many fighting COs of the RAF who ignored this order. Bowman had been ground-strafing and bombing with his pilots since the beginning of the Allied offensives in August and during September he had gained three victories: a Rumpler in flames and a Fokker D VII out of control on September 16, followed by a DFW in flames on September 25. These victories came to the attention of Wing HQ and on September 27 the GOC II Brigade issued an order that Bowman was not to cross the Lines. Bowman was not the type to take such an order seriously for too long. His next victory was the Fokker D VII shared with Soden on October 10, but his victory on October 15 – reported by the Belgians – resulted in the order from the GOC quoted in his logbook. The unambiguity of the order – 'on any pretext whatsoever' – makes it clear that the GOC knew only too well the calibre of the man he was dealing with, leaving no loophole for Bowman to wriggle through. This order kept Bowman on the ground for thirteen days.

Low clouds mist and rain curtailed much of the flying for the next two days. On October 18 the weather lifted a little, but it was still overcast and misty. There were some combats and the fighter squadrons carried out low level attacks. The two Australian fighter squadrons, accompanied by 88 and 103 Squadrons, again co-operated in attacks, this time in the Tournai area. The formations were led by Capt Eric Cummings of 2 Squadron AFC, the SE5s attacking from heights of 50 to 1,000 feet. Four direct hits were obtained on trains in the vicinity of Tournai, the ammunition of an anti-aircraft battery was blown up and troops and transports machinegunned. Bombs were also dropped on the enemy aerodromes at Froyennes and Pont-a-Chin. Six hangars were set alight at Froyennes and three at Pont-a-Chin. A formation of Fokker D VIIs attempted to interfere in these attacks. One was destroyed by Gregory Blaxland of 2 Squadron AFC, and Frank Alberry of the squadron crashed another and drove a second down out of control.

Weather conditions deteriorated on October 19, with low clouds and very thick mist. There was little enemy activity in the air and no decisive combats were fought. Owing to the rapidity of the Allied advance, plus the bad weather, communications between the front line troops and various headquarters of the armies were repeatedly being broken and General Rawlinson was often uncertain of the exact positions of his troops. The pilots of 84 Squadron, who had been flying low level attacks, were familiar with the area over which the troops were advancing and Major Sholto Douglas devised a method by which to ascertain the positions of the retreating enemy troops. The British troops were known to be immediately in front of Le Cateau and Sholto Douglas took off and flew just above the treetops along the long straight road that runs north of St Quentin to Le Cateau. Visibility was down to about 400 yards with a cloud base at 300 feet, but Douglas flew east along each of the roads radiating out from Le Cateau until he was shot at from the ground. Marking these positions on his map he then contoured chased back to the aerodrome, 'with my map on my knee,' and handed it to the army intelligence people, who joined up the half a dozen points on the map to give a fairly accurate position of the German troops. Sholto Douglas repeated this operation several times over the following days and for this work and his leadership of 84 Squadron he was awarded a DFC.

There was again little flying on October 20 and no enemy aircraft were reported to be working over the battlefront. The low clouds and mist persisted the next day, but there was some flying. Bombers of the Independent Air Force were bombing Frankfurt, suffering heavy losses to the fighter pilots of the *jagdstaffeln*, but fighter operations on the battlefronts in France continued to harass the retreating German armies with low flying attacks with bombs and machine guns.

In the wake of the retreating enemy, pilots of 56 Squadron were now flying from an aerodrome at Lechelle, south east of Bapaume. The low clouds and mist in the morning of October 21 cleared towards noon and the squadron prepared to take off to resume ground-strafing operations. While the engines of the SE5s were being run up, the squadron dog, Eppy, who was very attached to Robert Caldwell, ran up to his machine, was hit by the propeller and badly injured. Caldwell shot Eppy to put him out of his pain and the pilots waited while a new propeller was fitted to Caldwell's SE5. When the squadron finally left the ground after this delay the weather had again deteriorated and seven of the SE5s lost touch with Gilchrist in the clouds and returned, only Gilchrist, Caldwell, Grinnell-Milne and Winkler (an American from Laural, Mississippi) carried on to cross the lines.

Gilchrist attacked an enemy aerodrome east of Avesnes, noting that there were two Halberstadt two-seaters with bright yellow fuselages, green tails and silver and black striped top wings parked in front of four hangars. Gilchrist dropped his bombs and fired 100 rounds into the hangars and Halberstadts, but the groundfire became so intense that he was forced to zoom into the cloud cover.

Caldwell dropped his bombs from a height of 50 feet on a large and active railway siding at Maubeuge, one bomb hitting a train, another starting a fire in a goods train. Grinnell-Milne dropped his bombs on enemy troops near Vendegies, but then had minor engine trouble and flew west through the clouds. Coming out of the clouds to ascertain his position, Grinnell-Milne almost ran into a Fokker biplane. 'I was so startled that I fired both guns at him. The Fokker dived and I followed him down to about 200 feet, firing 150 rounds, when I ceased to fire as he had entered the ground. I zoomed up, intending to attack another Fokker I had observed on my left, but then I saw that there were eight Fokkers in the act of half rolling on to my tail. I dove to earth closely pursued by several of the Fokkers, one of them came down to within 100 feet of the ground and pursued me for some distance, firing several hundred rounds, most of which I managed to dodge.'

On his way back to the lines, Caldwell had also shot down a Fokker D VII, out of control over Hauntmont. It is indicative of the type of work the squadron had been doing that these were the first aerial victories for nearly a month.

The American, Moses Winkler, failed to return. Last seen 12 miles east of Le Cateau at 1,500 feet, he had come down in enemy territory and been taken prisoner.

There was a slight improvement of the weather on October 23 and enemy aircraft were active over the Third and Fourth Army fronts. An attack was made on the front from the western face of Mormal Wood to Valenciennes, but the bad weather of the few last days had made counter battery work almost impossible and the attacking troops were heavily shelled with high explosive and gas.

There was some fighting in the upper air, but casualties were light: one pilot was killed in a mid air collision, another taken prisoner, and a pilot from 84 Squadron returned with a badly shot up machine. On the Flanders Front, however, the *Marine Jagdstaffeln* took a heavy toll of the Camels of 204 Squadron. In a fight with 12 enemy fighters over Termonde, five pilots were shot down and killed. Lt John Lightbody was attacked by three Fokker D VIIs that got behind him and drove him down to almost ground level. At 100 feet, Lightbody pulled out of his evasive spin and two of the pursuing Fokkers collided. The effect of these losses on the squadron can be imagined, but in an afternoon patrol Capt William Sidebottom redressed the balance, if only slightly, by destroying one Fokker D VII and sharing another out of control with Lt D Barbour.

Bad weather resulted in minimal enemy air activity over the southern part of the front for the next two days, enabling valuable work by the corps squadrons to be carried out. In the north, enemy aircraft were active on October 26. In the morning 29 Squadron had two pilots killed in a mid air collision while in combat with Fokker D VIIs over Tournai, and in the early afternoon 65 Squadron lost a pilot killed, possibly by *Ltn* Rumey of *Jasta 5.*

Later in the afternoon, 74 Squadron were in action with Fokker D VIIs east of Tournai. Lt J Ferrand of the squadron attacked a D VII which he followed down to 500 feet to see crash. As Ferrand was climbing west again he was attacked by seven enemy scouts. Ferrand dived through them, firing as he went, and saw the right hand wing of one crumple up and another fall out of control. Both these Fokkers were observed to crash by pilots of another squadron in the vicinity. One pilot of the squadron had been shot down in the fighting and taken POW.

Bowman, ignoring the order of October 15, took off alone at 1.00pm. 'Saw a white V put out by an advance patrol of our infantry who waved rifles etc to me. Landed to enquire what was wanted, but had to take off again owing to Huns opening MG fire on machine. On returning was told that white V meant lack of SAA so went out again with two sand bags of SAA and cigarettes. White V removed and infantry gone.'

The weather improved considerably on October 27. Despite their losses of four days previously the Camels of 204 Squadron were out in some force and attacked 30 to 40 Fokker D VIIs over St Denis Westrem at 9.10am. Robert Gordon destroyed one Fokker in flames and Lt Charles Allen Phillip shot another down out of control, its wings breaking off lower down. Lts Clappison and P King, shared in the destruction of another of the enemy scouts. But the Sopwith Camel was now outclassed by the Fokker D VII and 204 Squadron lost another five pilots in the fighting: three killed, one wounded and another taken prisoner.

Further south, over Mormal Wood, Major William Barker fought an action in the morning that would win him a Victoria Cross. Barker had been highly successful fighting in Italy, scoring 46 victories and winning a DSO and a second Bar to his MC. On being posted to Home Establishment on September 30, to take command of a school of aerial fighting, Barker had requested that he be allowed to fly a refresher course in France, arguing, quite rightly, that tactics in France would differ from those in Italy and that to do justice to his new post he should be up to date with the latest tactics. Barker was allocated a Sopwith Snipe and attached to 201 Squadron for ten days, arriving on October 17.

Barker flew three uneventful patrols with 201 Squadron. On the morning of October 27, his tour having ended, Barker took off to fly back to England. Wanting to have one last look at the fighting, Barker climbed to 21,000 feet over the Forest of Mormal and attacked a Rumpler, which broke up under his fire. A formation of Fokkers was flying below Barker and one of the enemy pilots pulled his Fokker up into a near stalling position – a manoeuvre much favoured by Fokker D VII pilots – and fired into the Snipe, wounding Barker in the right thigh. Barker threw the Snipe into an evasive spin, but on pulling out found himself in the middle of the large formation of enemy scouts. Barker fired at one, sending it down in flames, but was attacked by the Fokkers and wounded again, this time in his left thigh. Barker fainted and the Snipe fell into a spin. Barker recovered consciousness at 15,000 feet and regained control, only to find he was now in the middle of a lower formation of Fokker D VIIs. Despite his wounds, Barker got on the tail of one of the enemy scouts and shot it down in flames, but there was another Fokker on the tail of the Snipe and its fire shattered Barker's left elbow. Barker fainted with the pain of this fresh wound and the Snipe again fell into a spin, this time falling for 3,000 feet before the rush of air brought Barker round.

Barker was still surrounded by hostile fighters, his Snipe badly damaged, its engine smoking, and he determined to finish the unequal fight by ramming the nearest Fokker, flying straight at it, firing as he closed the distance. The Fokker broke up in mid air and Barker's Snipe was damaged further as he flew through the wreckage. To his surprise, Barker found in was in clear air, free of enemy fighters, and he dived for safety of the British lines. Flying under yet another formation of Fokkers, Barker crossed the trenches at treetop height and crashed into the barbed wire surrounding the site of an observation balloon. Barker was taken from the wreckage of his Snipe and rushed to hospital in Rouen. Ten days later he was well enough to ruefully admit. 'By Jove, I was a foolish boy, but anyhow, I taught them a lesson. The only thing which bucks me up is to look back and see them going down in flames.'

The fight had been witnessed by literally thousands of British and Canadian front line troops. 'The hoarse shout, or rather prolonged roar, which greeted the triumph of the British fighter, and which echoed across the battle front, was never matched on any occasion.'[8]

The Greatest Air Battles of the War

During the last few days of October 1918 there was a temporary lull in the ground fighting and the corps squadrons were able to work with the artillery in their shelling of the enemy back areas and lines of communications. The German retreat had opened up many vulnerable targets to Allied bombers and the German High Command concentrated its remaining air strength in a desperate effort to prevent the British bombers from reaching their objectives. In the north these were the network of railway lines through Namur and Liége, which were essential to the German armies for the withdrawal of their armies from Belgium and northern France. The improvement of the weather over the next three days saw some of the heaviest air fighting of the war as the pilots of the *jagdstaffeln* came out in large numbers, sometimes as many as fifty aircraft, in an attempt to prevent the bombers from reaching these the vital targets.

The attacks on the main railway centres of Namur, Manage, La Louvière and Mariembourg, were flown by the squadrons of IX Brigade, equipped with the DH9 and DH9a bombers. These attacks failed, largely because of the poor performance of the DH9 and the unreliability of its BHP engine. General Salmond wrote of the DH9 'its low ceiling and inferior performance oblige it to accept battle when, and where, the defending forces choose, with the practical result that raids tend to become restricted to those areas within which protection can be afforded by the daily offensive patrols of scout squadrons.'

The disparity of the performance of the DH9 and DH9a had an effect on the deployment of the fighter squadrons that were to protect them from interference from enemy fighters. The DH9a was fast, had a ceiling of 19,000 feet, bombed from 17,000 feet and was not escorted by fighters. The DH9 flew at 13,000 feet, was more vulnerable, and was given fighter escort. Over these important and vital targets, the combats between the *jagdstaffeln*, the bombers and their defending fighters, led to some of the most intense and fiercely contested fighting of the air war: beginning on October 28 and culminating on October 30 in the heaviest air fighting in a single day of the whole war.

In the morning of October 28, the DH9s of 27 and 49 Squadrons set out to bomb Manage and La Louvière, escorted by the SE5s of 32 Squadron. Over Mons the bombers and their escort were attacked by thirty Fokker D VIIs, the bombers jettisoning their bomb loads as the fight began. A DH9 was shot down, the crew taken prisoner, and the pilot of another wounded. Two enemy fighters were claimed as destroyed. Although the loses were light the raid had been abandoned and was a failure.

A raid attempted by the DH9s of 107 Squadron – escorted on the way to the target at Mariembourg by 43 Squadron Camels and on the return by SE5s of 1 Squadron – was also a failure. The DH9s were depleted by engine troubles and the bombs were dropped on the railway at Hirson. On the way back the British formations were attacked by Fokker D VIIs. An American pilot, Lt Nat Trembath was seen to destroy two of the enemy fighters, but was then shot down and taken POW.

Lt D Cameron also claimed a Fokker destroyed and two others were claimed as out of control. Trembath was the only loss.[9]

At 11.00am a formation of SE5s from 2 Squadron AFC flew as far east as Ath and Mons. There were many 'ragged' formations of enemy aircraft in the air, fighters and two-seaters of all types, and at 11.15am, over Peruwelz 12 Fokker D VIIs were seen attacking a formation of DH9s at 15,000 feet. The SE5 formation, led by Cap Adrian Cole immediately went to the aid of the British bombers. Cole attacked a Fokker on the tail of a DH9, firing 300 rounds into it from close range. The enemy machine went down in flames, the pilot escaping by parachute. The Australian pilots claimed two additional D VIIs in flames, another seen to crash and a third going down in a spin.

Capt Ronald Sykes was leading a patrol from 201 Squadron in the general area of Barker's action the previous day.

'High Offensive patrol (14,000 feet) 24 Fokkers in distance over Mormal Forest. Flew towards 12 Fokkers E of Valenciennes and we were attacked by 8 Fokkers over Le Quesnoy – they kept above us out of our range; we turned sharply in formation at each attack until they gave up and went off SE. Saw a Squadron of DH4s away to the east of Mormal returning from a raid so we flew towards them. They were under attack by EA but were flying straight and level at 12,000 feet, so we flew through their formation and took the Huns by surprise head-on. An Albatros DVa and a DH4 observer were exchanging machine gun fire so I fired into the starboard side of the Albatros engine where its curved exhaust pipe interfered with the German's view of me. Although my tracer was going in he did not seem to see me and we nearly collided, but at the last minute he did a sharp diving left turn which put me on his tail very close and still firing. Some of his Fokker friends then came down on me and I last saw the Albatros gliding down with an escort of Fokkers. My guns vibrate a lot and must spray out a cone of bullets, not hitting the spot I had my sights on; I ought to have knocked pieces off his engine and tail.

I then climbed up to join the other 4 Camels in a high dog-fight which ended with all the remaining EA dispersing as they got the chance to break off. By this time the DH4s were miles away over the lines so I led "A" Flight in a dive over Mormal Forest searching the ground to see if the Albatros had landed. We continued in a fast shallow dive on course for La Targette and after crossing the lines a newly crashed plane was noticed but it had British roundels. During a later discussion at our base we thought it was probably Major Barker's Snipe, as we later knew that it had crashed and at about that place.'[10]

In the afternoon, 2 Squadron AFC set out to bomb Lessines, escorted by ten Sopwith Snipes of 4 Squadron AFC led by Capt Elwyn King. In the neighbourhood of the target three formations of Fokker D VIIs were seen: 15 at 10,000 feet; two more formations of seven and four machines at 7,000 feet.

King and his Snipes were over Ath and attacked one formation of Fokkers, which were unaware of their presence until King shot down the leader with a burst of fire from a range of fifty feet. Major W A McCloughry, the CO of the squadron, shot another Fokker down to crash near Ath, and Palliser claimed two more, also crashed in the vicinity of Ath. Capt Tom Baker led his Flight of Snipes into the fight, shot one Fokker down out of control and destroyed another.

The SE5s had hurriedly dropped their bombs on the town and climbed into the fighting, but it was over before they had reached its height. Only one pilot was successful. Capt Eric Simonson attacked a single Fokker that had got below the others and was attacking a Snipe at 6,000 feet. The enemy machine went down and crashed 3 miles west of Lessines.

On their way back to their aerodrome, King's formation passed another formation of Snipes, led by Capt H Ross. Over Tournai 12 Fokker D VIIs attacked the Australians, possibly mistaking the Snipes for Camels. The Snipe pilots immediately climbed to meet the attack, throwing the enemy pilots into some confusion. One got below the Snipes and Ross fired 200 rounds into it from 50 yards, turning it over onto its back.

The Camels of 70 Squadron were in action at 11.40am with Fokker D VIIs over Quatres. Oscar Heron destroyed one of the Fokkers in flames; Lt B Parker claimed another, also in flames, and Lts R Watson and A Webster each crashed an enemy machine.

'Grid' Caldwell scored his penultimate victory of the war during the morning. Flying alone over at 16,000 feet northeast of Tournai he surprised a black and white tailed Fokker D VII which went down with engine full on to crash northeast of the town. Caldwell then saw a formation of Camels fighting Fokker D VIIs with red tails and hurried to join in the fight. The Camels were from 70 Squadron and the pilots claimed two Fokkers in flames, and two seen to crash. Caldwell had no luck in this fight and he climbed towards Roubaix, where he saw an enemy two-seater flying between the town and Tourcoing. This enemy machine had already been fired on by anti-aircraft batteries before being attacked by Gilbert Murlis-Green, the CO of 70 Squadron, who had started a fire in its cockpit. Caldwell got behind the enemy machine and opened fire, but his guns stopped after only ten shots. There was no sign of the enemy observer, other than his gun sticking up vertically – he had probably been wounded by Murlis-Green. Under attack from Caldwell, the enemy pilot turned west, but when he realised that Caldwell had stopped firing, changed his mind and turned

east, gliding down over his own lines at 50 feet, his propeller slowly turning.

Frank Soden had a highly successful day. He wrote home that night:

'I have been in luck's way again. The day before yesterday I got another balloon in flames, which is a very pleasing sight. We have cleaned up seven Hun balloons in the last three days on this front alone and this afternoon they came across and tried to shoot some of ours, but luckily we caught them at it before they did any damage. We got three out of five.

I got one on our side of the lines and he landed perfectly and held his hands up to me as I flew around. I then landed alongside of him and found that I had hit him twice in the right leg, both flesh wounds. I talked to him for sometime in a mixture of French, German and English and he seemed quite a good fellow. We shook hands and parted in quite good humour. Tomorrow we hope to have the machine on our aerodrome and fly it, as it is in perfect condition, barring a few bullet holes. I am dropping a message the other side of the Line tomorrow about "my prisoner." MY SCORE IS FIFTEEN NOW![11]

A patrol of Camels from 3 Squadron took off at 9.30am on the morning of October 29. An hour after takeoff they were attacked by Fokker D VIIs and lost two pilots killed.

A patrol of from 92 Squadron, led by Capt William Reed, were also on patrol in the morning. Keeping below the cloud layer at 5,000 feet they first sighted five enemy two-seaters. The patrol chased these machines east from over Marbaix. At 9.15am a formation of five Fokker D VIIs passed over the patrol and Lt Thomas Horry turned to attack them as they dived east, firing a long burst into the rearmost machine, which 'flopped down very steeply out of control.'

Another formation of Fokker D VIIs was later seen over Berlaincourt, but these refused combat and flew east. The SE5s then strafed enemy troops before regaining their height, climbing above the clouds over Mormal Forest. Over the northeast corner of the forest, a solitary Fokker D VII climbed up through the clouds. The enemy pilot had obviously not seen the SE5s in the bright sun and Reed went down and attacked him, firing a long burst from fairly close range. The Fokker turned over onto its back and went down through the clouds. Reed found a gap in the clouds and watched it until it was very near the ground, still falling out of control.

Still flying above the clouds, and keeping an eye on a formation of D VIIs, well to the east, Reed next saw a number of enemy machines through a gap in the clouds, went down to investigate, and found six Fokker D VIIs and an Halberstadt two-seater east of Le Quesnoy. Reed attacked two of the Fokkers in quick succession. The right hand machine stalled, then went down in a spin; the Fokker on the left also went down. Reed then attacked several Fokkers that were attacking some of his Flight, driving two off the tail of an SE5. Lt Earl Crabb also attacked both these machines, which turned away from his fire and flew east. Crabb closed to within 25 yards of one and fired a short burst into it. The Fokker stalled in front of Crabb's SE5, forcing him to turn away to avoid a collision, then went down tail first before diving vertically. Crabb could not watch the end of this machine as he was being attacked by other Fokkers.

While his companions were fighting with the Fokkers, Horry had tackled the Halberstadt flying below them. A long burst from both guns caused smoke to come out of the two-seater, but Horry came under attack from two Fokkers and was forced to turn away.

Reed now saw that the seven Fokkers seen earlier had begun to come down to assist the others and he reformed the SE5s, circling to assist any stragglers. Seeing the SE5s were now together, the seven Fokkers dived away to the east.

The most successful pilot of 92 Squadron was an American, Capt Oren Rose. Rose had just returned from leave and he wasted no time in adding to his victories. Flying with Lt J V Gascoyne in the afternoon, he and Gascoyne shared in the destruction of a Fokker D VII over Favril at 4.05pm. This Fokker was Rose's fourteenth victory and Gascoyne's third.

In the afternoon a patrol from 56 Squadron attempted to attack three Fokker D VIIs over Mormal Wood, but the enemy pilots had seen the SE5s in time and dived away east. Ten minutes later six Fokker D VIIs were seen crossing the lines to attack British balloons. Vyvyan Hervey dived and fired a burst from long range at the leader who turned away from the balloons and dived away east. The rest of the Flight dived on the other Fokkers, but Grinnell-Milne had seen three others above and zoomed to attack them, firing short bursts at each, forcing them to break off their attacks and clear east. More aircraft, including some Sopwith Snipes, now arrived at the scene of the fight – Johnny Speaks later put their number as 50, equally split between British and German. All the opposing aircraft were at different heights and there was a great deal of manoeuvring for advantageous positions, with little actual fighting, and after 20 minutes the German pilots were driven east by the SE5s and Snipes.

Grinnell-Milne and a Snipe both attacked a Fokker, which went down out of control, but Grinnell-Milne then noticed British anti-aircraft bursts firing at enemy machines attacking balloons in the vicinity of Le Cateau. Grinnell-Milne dived from 11,000 to 5,000 feet to investigate and found a Fokker, which immediately dived away out of range. Grinnell-Milne chased this enemy machine, firing shot bursts, and after crossing the canal south east of Bois l'Evéque at 4,000 feet saw that the Fokker was 'more or less out of control. I pursued

him for a few miles down to the ground, into which he dived. I was then forced to return as my radiator had been pierced by a bullet and there was no water left.'

A particularly unfortunate – or lucky – pilot, Lt T Stead was flying with 29 Squadron. He had been slightly wounded on October 14 and again on October 28. On October 29, Stead was again wounded, this time seriously. Both he and Lt R Lovemore were forced to land in the German lines, east of the River Scheldt. Stead was unconscious, pinned underneath his SE5, but Lovemore succeded in getting him out of the wreckage and carried him across the swamps to the river bank. On the bank, Lovemore met a British infantry officer, cut off from his unit, and together they swam the river, supporting Stead between them. Despite being under machine gun fire during the crossing, they managed to get the wounded Stead and themselves under cover on the opposite bank.

Major Brand gained the last victory of the war for 151 Squadron, attacking a Friedrichshafen G III caught in searchlights. The enemy machine burst into flames but continued to fly level for some time until the fuselage broke in two, the wreckage falling in the British lines south east of Etreux.

October 30 was a day of fiercely contested and concentrated fighting – the heaviest single day of air fighting in the entire war – with the German pilots grimly determined in their defensive efforts. Sixty-seven German aircraft were destroyed, with 41 British aircraft struck off strength at the end of the day's fighting.

The DH9s of 98 Squadron set off in the morning to bomb Mons, escorted by Sopwith Dolphins of 19 Squadron. After they had bombed the target the formations came under attack by large formations of enemy fighters from *JG III*. In a running fight the German pilots continually attacked the British aircraft all the way back to the lines. Ten enemy machines were claimed as destroyed, four of them in flames, but five of the escorting Dolphins were shot down, with one pilot killed and four taken prisoner. The crews of the DH9s claimed five of the attacking enemy machines, but had two crews killed; two crews taken prisoner, both with dead observers; a pilot and observer came back wounded, and two DH9s crashed on landing at base.

A patrol of 74 Squadron fought with enemy scouts over the Quaremont area at 8.30am. Frederick Hunt destroyed two Fokker D VIIs, one in flames; Andrew Kiddie crashed another, and Lts W Goudie and J Ferrand, each claimed a scout out of control. Frederick Gordon attacked a balloon over Quaremont, shooting it down in flames.

Pilots of 84 Squadron flew a patrol in squadron strength in the morning, taking off at 9.00am. Over the general area of Le Cateau the SE5s attacked nine Fokker D VIIs, the fighting splitting up into individual combats. Walter Southey and Hector

MacDonald each destroyed a Fokker at 9.30am; Southey's victory over the Forest de Nouvion; MacDonald's two miles west of Leunelle. Sidney Highwood crashed his opponent over the Forest de Le Chelles fifteen minutes later. Sgt J Tarver was wounded in the fighting, but managed to return safely to 84 Squadron's aerodrome at Bertry West. In the fighting, 2Lt H Thorn was seriously wounded over Etreux, crashed in the French lines, and died of his wounds the next day. An hour after these actions Charles Stubbs of the squadron caught a Halberstadt two-seater north of Mormal Wood and shot it down out of control.

At 9.20am, over Ghislain, 32 Squadron lost four pilots in fighting with elements of *Jasta B* and *Jasta 40*. One pilot was killed, another made POW and the American, Capt A Callender, later died of wounds.

A little later in the morning, Camels of 210 Squadron were in action with seven Fokker D VIIs, possibly from *Jasta 24*. At 11.20am Capt Solomon Joseph shot down a Fokker D VII over Rombies, east of Valenciennes, for the last of his 13 victories, and Kenneth Unger shot down another in flames 200 yards east of Rombies which was also his 13th victory, but Lt Archie Buchanan, who had scored seven victories with the squadron, was shot down and taken prisoner.

The pilots of 41 Squadron saw a great deal of fighting during the day. In a morning patrol William Shields shot down a Halberstadt over Mansart at 11.30am and fifteen minutes later destroyed a DFW north of the town. In the same patrol, Lt Malcolm MacLeod shot down a Halberstadt two-seater north west of Barisoeuil for his third victory. In a late afternoon patrol, MacLeod scored again, shooting down a Fokker D VII north of Beclers Lt B Harmer claiming another over the Bois de St Martin.

One of the enemy pilots shot down in this patrol parachuted from his Fokker. Soden saw him going down. 'I spiralled round him all the way down, and we waved to each other, and he tapped his leg to show that he was wounded. It took him about fifteen minutes to fall 10,000 feet and for once the wind did us a good turn and blew him over our side.'

In the morning patrols it had been seen that a large number of enemy aircraft were operating from an aerodrome at Rebaix, north of Ath, and all squadrons of Eightieth Wing were ordered to attack the aerodrome in the afternoon. Sixty-two aircraft, led by the Wing Commander, LtCol Louis Strange, attacked the enemy aerodrome at 2.30pm. The Camels of 54 Squadron, the SE5s of 2 Squadron AFC, and the DH9s of 103 Squadron, carried out the bombing, with top cover flown by the Snipes of 4 Squadron AFC and the Bristol Fighters of 88 Squadron. Bombing from as low as 20 feet, the attackers demolished five hangars, destroying eleven enemy machines, and systematically machinegunned targets on or around the airfield.

Motor transport was attacked, horses stampeded, trains and motorcars shot up, and many casualties inflicted on ground personnel. Louis Strange recalled:

'The lion's share of the damage was done by Major Nethersole and Lt Corey in a DH9 as they managed to drop a 230lb bomb between two hangars: it demolished one of them and destroyed two machines that were on the ground. Major Nethersole got his DSO, I remember, for the brilliant way he handled his DH9 squadron on that occasion. The German Air Force fought well, but the 80th Wing was in fine fettle. Our total bag of enemy aircraft for the day was thirty-two, for which record we were congratulated by General Salmond.

To show how little one knows of what happens in an airfight, I may say that until I got back I was blissfully unaware that I had shot down a Fokker. An observer in one of the DH9s, who recognised the machine I flew, reported and confirmed that I had got this enemy when he was sitting on the DH9's tail. Personally, I had no idea this Hun had crashed, although I thought I got a good burst on him; but I was more worried about the question whether I had any undercarriage left, because I hit the Fokker's wing hard with my wheels when I pulled out of my dive, having left it a bit late in my anxiety to make sure of him before he got the DH9. At the critical moment he banked suddenly, thus causing a collision from which I was lucky to get away unscathed. At any rate, I could find no sign of damage to the undercarriage when I landed.'[12]

The raid was not uncontested by the *jagdstaffeln*. The attackers had to fight their way to and from the target. On the way back the DH9s and Snipes were attacked by a large group of enemy fighters at 4,000 feet over Leuze. Capt Elwyn King and Lt H A Wilkinson attacked two Fokkers diving on a DH9, Wilkinson sending his opponent down in flames. The Fokker attacked by King went down, but King was unable to follow it as he was attacked by four more Fokkers. King zoomed through the diving enemy machines and found himself in front of a higher Fokker. This Fokker went over onto its back in order to avoid a collision with King and collided with another Fokker that was zooming after King. Both enemy machines fell to pieces. Norman Trescowthick shot down another of the D VIIs for his last victory of the war, and Thomas Baker damaged another so badly that it was still going down, tail first, at 2,000 feet. The Australians lost a pilot shot down and taken prisoner in the fighting, and an observer in a DH9 was killed.

On the way back from this raid, the fighters contour chased along roads, shooting up troops, transport – motorised and horse drawn – especially in the villages of Leuze and Ligne, and a staff car was shot up, ran into a ditch and overturned.

Thankfully, after a day of such heavy fighting, October 31 was a day of low clouds and mist and few enemy aircraft were seen.

NOTES

1. In face of all the evidence, many historians of the 1914-1918 war as a whole have given little credit or importance to the part played by the RAF in such important and vital areas as artillery co-operation, reconnaissance, bombing and ground attack. Even such an imminent historian as John Keegan in his recent book *The First World War*, devotes only two pages to the war in the air, quoting as an 'interesting study' a book full of inaccuracies. More extensive reading, even if only of the official history, *War In The Air* by H A Jones, would have given him a more balanced view of the vital role played by the RFC/RAF/RNAS in World War I.

2. Fokker D VII No. 5301/18. G/I Brigade/17.

3. Beauchamp Proctor had flown to France with 84 Squadron on 23 September 1917 and scored his first victory on January 3, 1918. On March 7 he shot down three enemy scouts to bring his score to nine and he was awarded an MC followed by a Bar in May. The diminutive South African – he was only 5'2" in height and flew an SE5 with special adjustments to the rudder bar and seat – was posted to Home Establishment for a rest on June 13 and in July he was awarded one of the first of the new DFCs. 'Proccy' rejoined 84 Squadron on August 6 and began to score two days later. By the time of his wounding on October 8 he had been awarded 54 victories. After two recommendations, he was awarded a DSO on November 2, followed by a Victoria Cross, gazetted on 30 November 1918. Beauchamp Proctor returned to South Africa in February 1920, but was back in England by the winter of 1921. On 21 July 1921, he was practising aerobatics in a Sopwith Snipe when he lost control attempting to roll off the top of a loop. Beauchamp Proctor was too low to regain control was killed in the crash.

4. *Years of Combat,* Sholto Douglas, Collins, London 1963.

5. Weather conditions curtailing flying for the next few days, Beck flew over to the site of the crashed LVG and removed the observer's gun and Very Light pistol from the wreckage.

6. *Popular Flying*, March 1936.

7. The "stout" fellow was *Ltn der Res* Johann Schäfer of *Jasta 16b*. Schäfer was not killed by Soden's attack. Writing home five days later, Soden confided: 'We have collected a lot of souvenirs off the Hun I got our side of the Lines a few days ago. He had a bullet through his chest and several in his tank I asked the Belgians if he was dead and they said "No, but Belge kick him finish; he was an officer."'

8. Barker was awarded his Victoria Cross by King George V on 30 November 1918. The war had been over for 19 days.

9. Trembath was the last pilot of 1 Squadron to be taken prisoner. He survived his crashlanding and was taken to hospital in Liége. Evidently recovered from his injuries, Trembath was released by the Germans on November 11, and walking through the town was confronted by a German officer who had deliberately crossed the pavement to obstruct his way. Trembath floored the officer with an uppercut to the jaw, but he got up and a fistfight developed until they were separated by Belgian civilians.

10. Letter in author's collection.

11. This pilot was *Ltn* Adolph Auer of *Jasta 40*. The Fokker D VII No.4043/18 was designated G/II Bgd/27.

12. *Recollections of an Airman,* L A Strange, John Hamilton 1935.

CHAPTER TWENTY-SEVEN

THE FINAL DAYS

The first day of November was fine, but visibility was poor. Enemy aircraft were fairly active during the day and there were some combats.

At 7.00am, Lt H C Hayes of 64 Squadron won the distinction of being the only member of the squadron to destroy a balloon, shooting one down north east of Valenciennes. Later in the morning, Kenneth Unger from 210 Squadron also shot down a balloon, over Estreaux at 12.10pm.

RAF fighters were now patrolling well east of Valenciennes and an afternoon patrol from 32 Squadron fought with Fokker D VIIs from *Jasta B* six miles east of the town. No victories were claimed but the squadron lost two pilots killed in the fight and another returned with a badly shot up SE5.

In the afternoon, 2Lt H Clappison of 204 Squadron claimed a Fokker D VII at 1.15pm over Soffeghem; an hour later Capts Ernest Davies and Eric Cummings of 2 Squadron AFC shot an LVG down out of control over Antoing at 2.15pm.

The fighter squadrons lost one other pilot killed and another wounded, but the day bombers lost three crews taken prisoner and a pilot and observer. A crew of a Bristol fighter were also both killed. The *jagdstaffeln* were still a force to be reckoned with.

November 2 was a day of low clouds, mist and rain, and there was little enemy activity in the air. Despite the adverse conditions the fighter squadrons continued to fly ground-strafing missions. Typical of these were those flown by the pilots of 64 Squadron who attacked a large number of targets from very low height. A transport convoy was seen near Quarouelle and two direct hits were made on its limbers. Another Flight from the squadron went out in the afternoon on a low reconnaissance mission, flying at 500 feet. The SE5s met with heavy fire from the ground, and Capt J Bell returned with his SE5

badly damaged, but valuable information had been brought back.

There were only two casualties for the fighter squadrons: a pilot wounded and another taken prisoner.

Two Flights from 56 Squadron took off on the morning of November 3. The engine of Grinnell-Milne's SE5 was giving trouble and unable to keep up he lost touch with the other SE5s in the top Flight. After ten minutes of coaxing he managed to persuade his engine to give its full revs, and seeing a formation of aircraft to the northeast he flew to rejoin them. As he drew nearer, however, he saw that they were not the SE5s, but a mixed forced of four Fokker D VIIs and four Siemens Schuckert D IVs, the last being the first of the type seen by the squadron. Luckily the enemy pilots made no move to attack him and Grinnell-Milne climbed into the cloud cover. Keeping just below the clouds and flying northeast from Valenciennes in an attempt to find the SE5s, Grinnell-Milne saw that four of the enemy scouts had flown off to protect a balloon, leaving the remaining four – three Fokkers and one Siemens. The nearest Fokker in the formation was 1,000 feet below Grinnell-Milne and he attacked it, sending it diving away towards a large column of smoke coming from a burning factory. Grinnell-Milne dived after the enemy machine. Afraid that the Fokker would disappear into the smoke before he could close the range, Grinnell-Milne opened fire from 400 yards, but the SE5 rapidly overtook the Fokker and another long burst caused several large pieces to fly off the centre section of its top wing. SE5 and Fokker were now down to 500 feet, flying through the black smoke and fumes of the burning factory, compounded by black smoke and flames now coming out of the Fokker. Grinnell-Milne later commented in his combat report: 'It was probably to put out these that he plunged into the water at approx. Sheet 44.R.28.' The 'water' was either the canal north of Condé or one of the lakes a little to the north of the town.

Johnny Speaks and Hervey took their Flights out in afternoon and Speaks shot down a Fokker D VII over Bavai. 'He dived absolutely straight and I fired 150 rounds into him, no deflection being necessary, continuing until I was 400 feet from the ground. The other Fokkers came down on us, but were too late to catch us.' This Fokker shot down by the American Johnny Speaks was 56 Squadron's last victory of the war.

The weather improved considerably on November 4: a misty morning later gave way to fine, clear conditions and many combats were fought in a day of heavy and fiercely contested fighting. Although they must have known the end was near, the pilots of *jagdstaffeln* were out in large numbers and fought with both bravery and grim determination.

Most of the fighting seems to have been in the morning. Camels of 80 Squadron took off at 6.00am and had a pilot return with a damaged machine after a fight over the Forest of Mormal. Another patrol left at 10.15am and was also in combat over the forest, losing a pilot killed in a fight with German fighters and with two other Camels badly shot about.

Capt Charles Cudemore of 64 Squadron, aided by a Flight of Camels from 208 Squadron, shot down a Pfalz out of control over Bavay at 7.50am for his fourteenth and penultimate victory of the war.

Sixty Five Squadron fought its largest battle of the war. A Canadian, Capt Joseph White, led a squadron patrol, which included Capt Maurice Newnham's Flight, and a number of Camels from 204 Squadron. Over Zohleghem at 8.50am the Camels met 40 Fokker D VIIs with chequered fuselages and yellow and green tails. The enemy formations were at 12,000 feet, above the Camels, and dived to attack them.

The fighting was furious. White out-turned a Fokker on his tail and fired a long burst into it from 20 feet. The enemy machine turned over onto its back and both its wings folded up. White then came under attack by another Fokker; he did two turns of an evasive spin and came out in a right hand turn on the tail of his opponent. The Fokker pilot attempted to climb away, but White fired a burst into his machine and it went down, bursting into flames 2,000 feet below the fight. After tackling several more Fokkers, White singled one out that he had seen taking shots at several Camels. The Fokker pilot flew straight at White, firing as the distance closed, but White saw his tracers were hitting the Fokker, which passed over his top wing. White turned quickly, got behind the Fokker, fired a short burst, and it erupted in flames. White then fired at another enemy machine, which spun away. White followed the spinning Fokker down to 500 feet, but was dived on by several more enemy machines. White's Camel had been badly

shot about in the fighting and he returned to Bisseghem through heavy fire from the ground.

Maurice Newnham shook off one of two Fokkers on his tail, got behind another unseen and fired a long burst into its cockpit. The enemy fighter stalled, then fell over onto its back, going down in a spin. This Fokker D VII appears to have been the leader of the enemy formation and Newnham watched it fall from 12,000 to 3,000 feet – where it continued down out of control – before zooming underneath another Fokker, firing short bursts. This machine did a half roll and Newnham got into position on its tail and fired 100 rounds into it from point blank range. The enemy pilot zoomed in front of the Camel, but Newnham stayed on his tail and continued firing. The enemy pilot slumped forwards in his seat and the Fokker went down in a vertical dive. Newnham followed this machine down to 7,000 feet, but was forced to turn away when more Fokkers attacked him from above.

From a range of ten yards, Lt W Allison fired into the cockpit of a Fokker on the tail of a Camel. The enemy machine went down emitting smoke and burst into flames lower down. In the extremely confused fighting, Allison fired at several other Fokkers without decisive results, but finally sent another down to crash.

Lt William Bland sent one of the Fokkers down in a flat spin, but was too busy fighting with other Fokkers to see whether or not it crashed. Fighting with these he fired five bursts into one from broadside on and followed it down to see it burst into flames at 4,000 feet.

All the 65 Squadron pilots were fully engaged in this fight, claiming 8 destroyed, six out of control and another driven down for the loss of two pilots: one wounded; another wounded and taken POW. Pilots of 204 Squadron claimed two enemy machines destroyed and five out of control, but lost one pilot killed.

The Australian squadrons were in action early in the morning. All three Flights of 2 Squadron AFC had left the ground at 7.00am to patrol east of Renaix. Ernest Davies shot down a LVG over Elleselles at 8.10am and immediately afterwards Gregory Blaxland's Flight saw seven Fokker D VIIs over Renaix. The enemy machines began to circle and lose height and the SE5s went down to attack them. James Wellwood shot one Fokker down to crash near the village of Tombelle and Lt C O Stone, who had been born in Chingford in Essex, but had emigrated to Australia with his family, crashed another.

Davies' Flight had now arrived at the scene of the action. Davies fired at one Fokker, which turned over onto its back, but his SE5 was then overturned by a close burst of Archie. Capt Eric Simonson, who had followed Davies into the fight, shot down a Fokker that crashed near Tombelle.

Two hours later, five Snipes of 4 Squadron AFC were in action with seven Fokker D VIIs near Tournai. Lt E A Cato, leading the Snipes, had first seen the enemy formation at 10,000 feet northeast of the town. A Flight of SE5s was in the vicinity. Cato joined forces with them and climbed for more height: the Snipes flying south of the Fokkers, the SE5s to the north. Reaching a height advantage of 5,000 feet the Snipes dived on the enemy machines. Cato shot one Fokker down out of control, but Lt C Rhodes was shot down and taken prisoner in the fight. Returning from this patrol the Snipes had another casualty: Lt E Goodson was shot down by Archie, crashed near the canal at Tournai and also taken prisoner.

Eleven SE5s of 56 Squadron were flying in two Flights just west of Bavai at 9,000 feet when they were attacked by nine Fokker D VIIs that dived on the seven machines of the top Flight. One of the Fokkers attacked Richard Shutes, who was flying below his Flight Commander, Vyvyan Hervey. Hervey saw Shutes' predicament, half rolled and fired a burst at full deflection at his attacker. The enemy pilot half rolled away from Hervey's fire and dived away to the east, but he had wounded Shutes in his attack.

Grinnell-Milne, leading the lower Flight of SE5s did not see this action and at the end of their patrol time Grinnell-Milne decided to attack an enemy balloon, manoeuvring into the clouds before attacking out of the sun. The crew of the balloon had seen the SE5s coming and had hauled the balloon down to 1,000 feet before they got within range. Grinnell-Milne and James Crawford opened fire at 3,000 feet but Grinnell-Milne guns stopped 'almost immediately' with faulty ammunition. Grinnell-Milne reloaded and returned to renew his attack, but his guns again stopped with the same fault after firing only a 100 rounds. Crawford had trouble with his Lewis gun, but although he fired 100 rounds from his Vickers into the balloon it was successfully hauled down without catching fire.

Richard Shutes managed to return, landed safely and was taken to hospital, but Lt Oliver Price had been shot down and killed by *Oblt* Bolle the *Staffelführer* of *Jasta B*.

Capt Shields and Lt Malcolm MacLeod attacked balloons in the late morning. Shields flamed one south of Gaillaix at 11.20am, and MacLeod destroyed another over Baugnies at the same time. Five minutes later the two SE5s attacked another balloon over Pipaix and shared in its destruction. Another balloon was destroyed by Lt R Lovemore, fully recovered from his swim across the Scheldt on October 29.

Three squadrons of 80th Wing took off at noon to harass the retreating German troops on the Leuze to Ath road and to attack the enemy aerodrome at Chapelle-á-Wattines, north of the road and just east of Leuze. The Snipes of 4 Squadron AFC flew in squadron strength to provide the escort for the SE5s of 2 Squadron AFC and the DH9s of 103 Squadron, which were to carry out the bombing attacks. As the SE5s went down to low level to begin their attacks on the enemy aerodrome, the leading machines were engaged by five Fokkers, with another formation appearing above. The SE5 pilots hastily dropped their bombs on the aerodrome and began to fight the Fokkers, shooting down five, which fell into the clouds of smoke from the burning hangars below.

Lt-Col Louis Strange, flying above the attack in his personal Camel, joined the DH9s in bombing the aerodrome and saw six hangars burning fiercely. Strange then flew a northerly circuit of the area, shooting up transport and troops at Grandmetz and Leuze railway station.

The Snipes escorted the DH9s back to the Lines, but then turned back to attack 12 Fokker D VIIs which had been following the formation. Elwyn King attacked the leader of the Fokkers, which stalled and went down on its back under his fire. In the general fighting that followed, King shot a Fokker down in flames, and George Jones shot down another, also in flames, which was attacking Lt H Wilkinson. The fighting only lasted two or three minutes but the Australians were roughly handled by the Fokkers from *JG III* and lost three pilots killed, including Capt Thomas Baker who had scored 12 victories since the end of July.[1]

During the day the ground offensive had opened at dawn with the last great British effort of the war, the Third, Fourth and First armies attacking on a thirty mile front from Oisy on the Sambre to Valenciennes. In places, German resistance was still determined. The British and Canadian troops attacking a lock on the Sambre Canal met with salvo after salvo from German machine gunners in houses by the lock and lost nearly 150 men before taking the positions, but by the end of the day the Allied forces, fighting through a network of village houses, hedges and orchards, finally reached their objectives and the Fourth Army bridgehead over the Sambre Canal was 15 miles long and more than two miles deep. The day's fighting finally broke the resistance of the German armies and during the night they fell back in full retreat.

The airfighting on November 4 saw the last combats between large numbers of opposing aircraft. For the next four days the weather was very bad with low clouds, mist and continuous rain, and no enemy aircraft were seen.

Rudolph Stark, *Staffelführer* of *Jasta 35*, had heard rumours that there were mutinies in the French armies, but 'that our own troops are nearly finished.' Letters from home had also brought news of mutinies and revolutions in Germany. On October 23, Stark had written:

'We are alone in a world that we do not understand – a world that is changing around us. We no longer believe in victory, but we still cherish hope.' On November 4, his *Jasta* having been again moved back, he wrote:

'No communiqués came through today. We have no idea what is happening at the front.'

Although the almost continuous rain curtailed to some extent the low flying attacks, giving the German armies some respite, the fighter squadrons continued to harass them, machine gunning and bombing from low heights. On November 9 the SE5s of 92 Squadron were ground-strafing enemy troops, when Lt J V Gascoyne narrowly escaped being killed in these last two days of the war.

'I was engaged in low flying attacks on troops and transport when I observed a big, fat German staff officer riding across a rather muddy ploughed field. On seeing me he dismounted and, still holding the reins, attempted to hide under the horse! This intrigued me, but I did not want to harm the horse, so I dived down, fired a few rounds from my guns to make a noise and then with engine at full throttle zoomed over the horse, which immediately went off in a mad gallop with the German still clinging to the reins. He soon released them, but he looked a sorry mess, covered with rich mud.' A little later, Gascoyne was flying at roof top height along a village street, looking for targets:

'I was silly enough to fly straight and level for a little too long. At the end of the road was the village church and a German sniper, in total disregard of any religious scruples he may have had, had taken up a position in the tower with his machine gun and he behaved rather unkindly to me by firing this dangerous weapon at my machine. One bullet passed through my windscreen and several others hit various parts of the SE. One in fact hit my engine switch, but fortunately did not affect its function. However, the same bullet which passed through the windscreen carried on and actually went through my close fitting helmet. Fortunately, the flight of the missile was in line with my goggles on my helmet and by hitting the adjusting slide was deflected outwards again. The result was a hard bang on the side of my head and a part of the metal slide was embedded in it. This was removed later by a doctor at a field hospital. Had I not been left handed, and thereby looking over the left side of my machine, I would probably have caught the bullet right in the middle of my forehead.'[2]

On November 9 aircraft of 80th Wing carried out an attack on the enemy aerodrome at Enghien. Major Reginald Maxwell the CO of 54 Squadron, led the formations: Camels of 54 Squadron; SE5s of 2 Squadron AFC; DH9s of 103 Squadron – all carrying bombs – escorted Snipes of 4 Squadron AFC, and Bristol Fighters of 88 Squadron. There were a great number of targets on the congested roads as the formations passed over Ath, but Maxwell continued on to Enghien. Here there was great congestion of troops and transport of all descriptions on the roads and trains on the lines and in the station. Two aerodromes were seen with machines standing in the open.

Lt Col Louis Strange was flying with 54 Squadron:

'As the detail on the ground grew larger and more distinct, we all realised that every bomb could be made to tell on the targets which offered themselves in all directions. Our first blow fell on five hangars, which we burnt. No fewer than ten machines were destroyed on the ground, after which we turned our attentions to the station. When we left it two long trains, that must have been loaded with something highly inflammable, were burning. They had been set on fire by one of 103's 112lb bombs, and the blaze was visible for a long time afterwards.

Then about two miles of motor and horse transport, guns etc, were mercilessly shot up and bombed by No.4 AFC, causing the utmost confusion and destruction; while 2 AFC and the Bristols of 88 found targets of all descriptions in camps and bivouacs round the town. A large proportion of the 130 bombs (a total of over two tons) dropped must have been direct hits on troops and transport. Major Maxwell and the little Camels of No.54 led us well that day.'[3]

The official history relates:

'On one aerodrome a hangar was completely destroyed and one machine completely wrecked, and bombs seen bursting among other machines which must have been badly damaged. On another aerodrome, one hangar and a machine on the aerodrome were destroyed in flames and direct hits obtained on machines and hangars. Three large bombs and many 25lb bombs were seen to burst on troops and transport on the main Ath-Eighien road between Bassilly and Enghien, which was particularly congested, others on the roads north and south of the main road, where there were many targets of troops, mechanical transport, and heavy transport. Lorries were seen to collide, one being set on fire, many others being destroyed by direct hits and others ditched. Horse transport was seen stampeding in all directions and in numerous cases troops endeavouring to get into houses for cover were shot at and many casualties caused. In the station and junction at Enghien, no less than twenty direct hits were observed on trains. One train was set on fire from end to end and was still burning furiously when the raid had left, sheds and buildings in the station catching fire from it. A direct hit was obtained between some mechanical transport where troops were entraining at a siding just east of Bassilly, and a 230lb bomb scored a direct hit on trains in Bassilly. Escorting machines of No.88 Squadron, meeting with no opposition, came down and joined in the destruction on the ground. The ground targets were so obvious and numerous that every pilot and observer kept firing until stoppages or lack of ammunition compelled him to cease. The damage done and the confusion caused was almost indescribable and impossible to give in detail. It must have been very great, everyone agreeing that such an opportunity had never before been met with.'[4]

There was no respite for the retreating German armies. The next day the SE5s of 2 Squadron AFC led a raid of over a hundred machines, the CO of the squadron, Major Murray-Jones, taking the formations past Enghien to Hal. No opposition from enemy fighters was expected and all the machines – they had been joined by SE5s of 85 Squadron – had been loaded to capacity with bombs. Two hundred and forty bombs were dropped and 16,000 rounds of ammunition fired at troops and transports moving eastwards in long columns. Louis Strange counted eight lorries burning and that the SE5s of 2 Squadron AFC looked just like huge hornets as they attacked a train steaming at full speed towards Brussels until a bomb on the engine derailed it as it was passing through a small station. Two bombing attacks on the railway station at Enghien were carried out, the DH9s of 103 Squadron bombing from as low as 500 feet. Three or four trains side by side were completely wrecked and two other trains set on fire, almost every bomb falling on the station or tracks.

On this, the penultimate day of the war, the last combats in the air were fought. Capt William Jenkins of 210 Squadron shot down a DFW two-seater over Merbes le Chateau at 8.40am, and later in the morning the SE5s of 84 Squadron were in combat with Fokker D VIIs at 10.00am. Capt Frank Taylor of the squadron scored the last of his ten victories, a Fokker destroyed southeast of Faynolle. Major Charles Pickthorn shot down another Fokker, east of Mutagne, but Lt A Rosenbleet, was shot down and taken prisoner – surely to spend the shortest time in captivity of any member of the RAF.[5]

The last victory of the morning was a LVG two-seater, shot down seven miles southeast of Ghent at 10.40am by a Flight of Camels from 213 Squadron led by Capt George Chisholme MacKay.

In the early afternoon William Jenkins of 210 Squadron scored again: a Fokker D VII sent down east of Binche at 1.15pm for his 12th and last victory. Thirty minutes later, a patrol of SE5s from 29 Squadron fought with Fokker D VIIs in the vicinity of Moorleghem. Capt Thomas Harrison and Lt Edgar Davies each destroyed a D VII over the town and Capt Charles Ross shot another down in flames north of Elene.

These victories of 29 Squadron appear to have been the last of the war for the RAF single-seater fighter pilots.

Two pilots of 92 Squadron had their aircraft shot up and forced to land, but the last fatalities of the war seem to have been Lt J E Pugh of 210 Squadron and two pilots from 46 Squadron. Pugh was last seen at 9.10am near Bois de Wauhu,

over Mons, flying east, and was later reported as killed. The two Camel pilots, 2Lt G E Dowler and 2Lt W G Coulthurst took off at 9.00am and were killed when their Camels collided, both machines falling in flames.

In the early hours of November 11, orders were received by all squadrons that hostilities would cease at 11.00am. The news of the end of the war seems to have been received with very little elation. Louis Strange was woken by an orderly at 2.00am with the order: 'Hostilities will cease from 11.00am today. No machines to cross east of the balloon lines.' Louis Strange recalled: 'I gave instructions for the message to be sent out to the squadrons. Then I turned over and went to sleep again, dimly wondering why I could not wake myself up enough to be enthusiastic about it, and what on earth were we going to do with ourselves in the morning without a war.'

James Gascoyne heard the momentous news in an even more mundane manner. He was shaken awake by his squadron commander, Arthur 'Mary' Coningham and flight commander, James Robb, asking, 'Have you got a job to go to?' it was his first intimation that the end of war was so imminent. 'I do not think anyone of us had any idea it was so near.'

Some pilots had regrets the conflict was finally over. Many had grown from youth to manhood in the last four years, four years in which their lives had been dominated by the war, influencing their every thought and action. They knew little else. Echoing Louis Strange's thoughts, Frank Soden wrote:

'It is very tame now that we have no Huns to go and scrap. This may sound bloodthirsty, but there is a kind of fascination in looking for trouble.'

The patrols flown on the morning of November 11 saw no enemy aircraft, but the ceasefire at 11.00am was not meticulously observed. Geoffrey Bowman entered in his logbook: 'Last patrol of the war 10.15 to 12.10. While flying at 500 feet over Enghien at 11.20 saw 100 Huns in a field. They opened fire with rifles, hitting the m/c in several places. Put down my nose to get away and found that my sights were on about fifty Huns along a ridge. Pulled both plugs, firing about 50 rounds. Could not miss. Armistice was supposed to commence at 11.00am, but it didn't.'

Soden wrote on November 12:

'Yesterday I had the distinction of being fired on half an hour after hostilities had ceased, a thing of which I am quite proud. As a matter of fact we were violating the Armistice and quite deserved what we got.'

Louis Strange observed a similar situation on the morning of November 11. Early in the morning he had driven to Grand Ennetières, the aerodrome of 4 Squadron AFC where his personal Camel was hangared, intending to fly for one last look at the lines.

'But when I got to the aerodrome I could not find a single serviceable machine on the ground. Even my own Camel was gone. The Flight sergeant said something about testing the guns for me; I forbore to press him but drove on to the other aerodromes, where I found the same state of affairs.

Strange had been worried that a further message might arrive from Brigade, to say that that of the early hours had been only a rumour, but just after 11.00am he received a confirmation message from Brigade to say that the Armistice had been signed; that the previous order was in force. Remembering the last sentence of the order that no patrols were to cross east of the balloon Lines, Strange talked to the pilots who had returned from the morning patrols.

'When I questioned several of the Australian pilots, they said they had not seen any balloons and asked most innocently how far east the balloon line was supposed to be. But I noticed that their bomb racks were empty.

At noon some belated Snipes and SE5s put in an appearance, and when asked to give an account of themselves the pilots said they thought it would be all right for them to go out and look for Smith, the man who had been missing since the Enghien raid. But their bomb racks were empty.' War-like habits die hard.

All the squadrons celebrated Armistice night. William Clarkson of 56 Squadron remembered:

'We had quite a do in the Mess. King and I were both teetotal. I was sitting next to the CO and they brought me Champagne. I asked the orderly to smuggle it away and bring me a soft drink. King sipped his and pulled a wry face. The CO saw me and went swoosh, and sent it flying across the room – quite in good humour – and that's what happened to the soft drink. And next morning someone had to patrol the lines! I had to take King.'

Soden wrote: 'The country round here was a wonderful sight the night the news of the Armistice came through. The whole sky was lit up with flares and bonfires for miles around.'

Those pilots who were ordered to fly Line Patrols on the morning of November 12 found that the air was strangely quiet. The long struggle of over four years was finally over.

In those tragic and bloody four years of war a new tradition had been born: that of the fighter squadrons of the RAF. The spirit, skills and panache of the fighter pilots had been refined in the crucible of air combat. Perhaps one of the finest, if least known tributes to that spirit was made by a young American pilot. In October 1918, after serving with the RFC and RAF, he was leaving the RAF to join his own country's air service. He wrote:

'Just a word about our training and experiences with the British as we are now leaving them for good. If only I could in a small way express my feelings for these young fellows I would be mighty glad. These English fellows are surely gallant fighters. We have gone through Hell many times with them, but they always come back laughing and having a big time off parade and duty. I never thought a man could die as easy for his country as these young fellows of the Royal Air Force. I'll swear by them and stand up for them anywhere, and if they ever have another war I want to fight with them in their Royal Air Force.'

NOTES

1. *Oblt* Karl Bolle, *Staffelführer* of *Jasta B* was awarded two of the Snipes, *Ltn* Bormann of the *Jasta* another.

2. Letter in author's collection. Gascoyne had entered the RFC as a direct recruit on 28 May 1913 (Number 719) As a 2nd Class Air Mechanic he had gone to France with 3 Squadron on 12 August 1914. After learning to fly and being commissioned, Gascoyne joined 92 Squadron on 15 August 1918. For his five victories over five enemy aircraft and his prominent part in the destruction of seven others, plus his low-level work during October and November 1918, Gascoyne was awarded a DFC.

3. *Recollections of an Airman*, L A Strange.

4. *War In the Air*, H A Jones.

5. Major Pickthorne had taken over command of 84 Squadron from Major Sholto Douglas on November 8.

APPENDICES

VICTORY CLAIMS
AND EVALUATIONS

In recent years a great deal of disparaging comments have been made regarding the victory claims of the fighter pilots of the RFC, RNAS and RAF. Because many of these claims – especially those for out of control victories – are not reflected in the German casualty lists, the pilots and observers have been accused of being at best mistaken, or at worst, liars. These accusations are not only simplistic, but show an ignorance of the overall picture of the air war over the Western Front in 1914-1918.

Articles have been published, illustrated with spurious statistical graphs, in an attempt to show that Allied pilots overclaimed by as much as 6:1.[1] These statistics are valueless, being based on a completely false assumption: that the information researchers have concerning German casualties is complete or even near complete. This is very far from the case.

The German casualty list on which these invalid conclusions are based are from *Verlustliste der Deutschen Luftstreitkräfte im Weltkreige* compiled by Major a.D Wilhelm Zickerick. *Unsere Luftstreitkräfte 1914-1918* by Walter von Eberhardt, a book of flying anecdotes, was published in 1930, and contained Zickerick's list. Other reference sources are *Den Toten zur Ehrung,* and a list of Bavarian airmen who were killed, *Ehrenbuch der K.B.Fliegertruppe,* although the majority of the entries in these last books are contained in Zickerick's *Verlustliste.* Both Zickerick's work and these books were compiled after the war from documents which were in themselves incomplete, were lacking in important details of information, and not only contain discrepancies, one to the other, in omissions and corrections, but also lack important details. The diaries, memoranda, and contemporary letters home by German pilots and observers, plus the few *Jasta* War diaries which are still extant – and even some British regimental histories – all contain references to men killed or wounded, and forced and crashed landings, which are not recorded in these books.

Categories of Victories

Victories in the RFC, RNAS and RAF were awarded on the basis of combat reports submitted either by pilots and/or a flight commander. After the squadron commander had commented on these, copies were sent to both Wing and Brigade. At Wing the reports were collated with additional information from independent witnesses to the individual claims: other pilots from the squadron who had taken part in the combat; pilots from other squadrons, either involved in the action or nearby; balloon observers, and witnesses on the ground, such as AA batteries, observation posts etc. With these reports to hand, Wing would then evaluate the victory claims and award or deny victories to individual pilots.

During the war the RFC, RNAS and RAF classified victory claims as:

1. **Destroyed**: where an enemy aircraft was seen to go down in flames, break up in mid air, or was seen to crash.
2. **Out of control**: where an enemy aircraft was seen to go down in a manner which suggested the pilot may have been hit or his machine damaged in the fighting, but was not seen to crash.
3. **Driven down and forced to land**. (This category was used in the early days but later seems to have been discontinued.)

Let us examine these categories.

Destroyed. Many victories claimed in this category are not reflected in the German lists. Although some pilots and observers may have been uninjured in forced or crashed landings and therefore would not be listed, many – especially in those cases where an aircraft was seen to break up in mid air or fall in flames from a considerable height – must have been either killed or seriously wounded.

Out of control. The victories claimed in this category are the main cause of the contention that allied pilots vastly overclaimed. This category has several scenarios, but let us first look at the definition of what constitutes a victory in an aerial, or indeed any fight.

An enemy pilot, out fought and out manoeuvred, spinning away out of trouble, is no less a victory than one killed or wounded. He has still been outfought, defeated, and forced to leave the fight.

Spinning away out of a fight was a common practice of both the antagonists, but here the German pilot had a distinct advantage over his opponent. The vast majority of the air fighting being behind the German lines, he could take this evasive action knowing that he could pull out, make for base, even crash or force land, and live to fight another day. Few allied pilots would follow him down. To do so would involve the risk of being low over enemy territory, with the every present threat of engine failure – exacerbated by the nearly always prevalent westerly wind blowing him deeper into enemy territory – and the lack of height making him easy prey to German fighters or ground defences. For these same reasons, the choice of spinning away out of trouble was not a course of action many Allied pilots chose if fighting at some distance behind enemy lines. It would almost invariably mean capture. Only if fighting reasonably near the front lines was this an option for Allied pilots. Then, as did their opponents, they spun down and contoured chased back across the front lines, confident that no German pilot would follow for the same reasons as their own when fighting over the enemy lines.

As stated, an out of control victory claim could have several outcomes:

1. The enemy pilot was wounded and no longer had control of his aeroplane, which may or may not have also been damaged.

In this instance, after he had either crashed or forced landed, the wounded pilot would be extracted from his aeroplane and taken first to a casualty clearing station, then to a hospital, either in a rear area or even in Germany. There are then two possibilities: the pilot either recovered or died of his injuries. If the latter, this could take place days, even weeks, from the scene of his wounding and crash, and both the date and location of his death would be given as such in the German lists. From this it can be seen that any attempt to match the loss of such a pilot with a victory claim by an allied pilot would be practically impossible. Additionally, for the reason given below, we have no information as to the ultimate fate of his aeroplane.

2. The enemy pilot was unwounded but his aeroplane was damaged and out of control, forcing him to either crash or force land.

It is here that the main difficulty arises in evaluating German losses against the claims of Allied pilots for out of control victories. As in the many occasions when RFC/RNAS/RAF aircrew were forced to land their damaged aeroplanes over German held territory, so there must have been a similar number of German aircrew who landed their damaged aircraft *on their own side of the lines.* These aircraft must have been listed, even if for no other reason than indenting for replacements, but to the best of our knowledge these records are no longer extant. The critical and highly relevant omission in our knowledge of German losses is that we have no official returns/reports of these German *aircraft.* Without them there is no possibility of accurately evaluating the validity – or not – of out of control victory claims.

German Victory Claims

In the main these are very accurate. This is hardly surprising as the evidence was there on the ground: a crashed aeroplane and a dead, wounded or captive pilot. In fact, because the details of British losses are available – and for all intents and purposes complete – it is possible to see that many successful German pilots had possibly higher victory scores than awarded.

All British casualties were the subject of a report on Army Form WW 3347. As can be seen from the illustration, this form gave a detailed report, not only of the fate of the pilot, but full details of his aeroplane. From these forms it is possible to evaluate many British losses: wounded Allied pilots and damaged aeroplanes – sometimes so badly that they were struck off the strength of the squadron – which were in fact victories that were not awarded to pilots of the German *jagdstaffeln* because they had no knowledge of them.

There can be no doubt that a similar picture to that of these British losses would emerge if equivalent losses of German *aircraft* were also available.

Finally, faced by the extreme discrepancies – alleged – of the German victory claims to those of the British, a little common sense is called for. Here were two Anglo-Saxon peoples, very alike in many ways, each respectful of the fighting capabilities of the other, each considering the other worthy opponents. Yet the victory claims of the *jagdstaffeln,* day after day, show large numbers of *verifiable* victories with only a bare minimum of losses, sometimes none at all. It is inconceivable that there should be such a vast difference in the successes and losses of evenly matched sides.

In conclusion. Of course, there was some overclaiming, by both sides. In the fierceness and intense confusion of fast-moving aerial combat, mistakes and false impressions were only too easily made, but not by any means to the extent put forward by the detractors of the airmen of the RFC, RNAS and RAF who fought so well and hard – and died – over the skies of France in the first war in the air.

NOTES

1. *Over the Front*. Journal of the League of WW1 Aviation Historians. Various issues.

Army Form W 3347.

ROYAL FLYING CORPS.

REPORT ON CASUALTIES TO PERSONNEL AND MACHINES

(WHEN FLYING).

INSTRUCTIONS : *To be rendered in duplicate by Squadrons to Wings.*
Wings to forward one copy to H.Q., R.F.C., through Brigades.

No. **56** Squadron   No. **9** Wing.   Date **May 12th** 1917.

Type and No. of Machine : **SE.5 No. A.4860.**

Engine No.: **150 h.p. Hispano Suiza, 10072. WD, No.10122.**

Pilot : **Lieut. A. J. Jessopp.**

Observer : **none.**

Duty : **Offensive patrol.**

Locality : **Ten miles east of the line La Bassee Canal to Vimy.**

Lewis guns carried, with gun Nos.: **23382.   VICKERS Gun No. A623.**

Camera (Yes or No) : **No.**

Wireless (Yes or No) : **No.**

Other appliances (bomb racks, etc.) : **2" Aldis sight No. 73069.**

Where brought down : **Over Lens.**

Short report as to fate of personnel and machine. Date and time of leaving aerodrome. Any reports, messages, or conjectures received, stating source :

Left Aerodrome at 6.30 pm. May 12th 1917, with SE.5 formation. Last seen by other members of formation to go down in a spin over Lens, and break up under H.A.A.

J. B. Marson
2/Lt. for *Major,*
Commanding No. **56** Squadron.

Remarks by Wing Commander as to whether machine is to be struck off, repaired in Squadron or recommended for transfer to A.D. for repair :

Struck off

Shlewall

Lieut.-Colonel,
Commanding No. **9** *Wing.*

6 42 26) W6180—778 15,000 9/16 HWV(P312)   Forms/W3347/1
12971—M1305 20,000 1/17

343

ORDER OF BATTLE OF RFC FIGHTER SQUADRONS FOR THE BATTLE OF THE SOMME, 1 JULY 1916

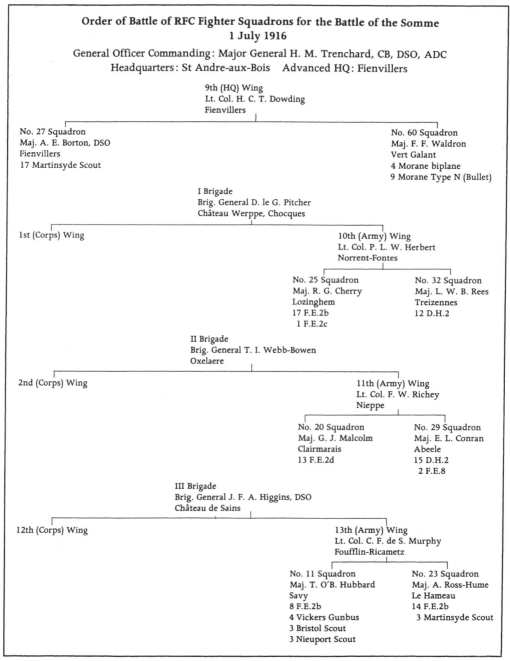

**Order of Battle of RFC Fighter Squadrons for the Battle of the Somme
1 July 1916**

General Officer Commanding: Major General H. M. Trenchard, CB, DSO, ADC
Headquarters: St Andre-aux-Bois   Advanced HQ: Fienvillers

9th (HQ) Wing
Lt. Col. H. C. T. Dowding
Fienvillers

No. 27 Squadron
Maj. A. E. Borton, DSO
Fienvillers
17 Martinsyde Scout

No. 60 Squadron
Maj. F. F. Waldron
Vert Galant
4 Morane biplane
9 Morane Type N (Bullet)

I Brigade
Brig. General D. le G. Pitcher
Château Werppe, Chocques

1st (Corps) Wing

10th (Army) Wing
Lt. Col. P. L. W. Herbert
Norrent-Fontes

No. 25 Squadron
Maj. R. G. Cherry
Lozinghem
17 F.E.2b
1 F.E.2c

No. 32 Squadron
Maj. L. W. B. Rees
Treizennes
12 D.H.2

II Brigade
Brig. General T. I. Webb-Bowen
Oxelaere

2nd (Corps) Wing

11th (Army) Wing
Lt. Col. F. W. Richey
Nieppe

No. 20 Squadron
Maj. G. J. Malcolm
Clairmarais
13 F.E.2d

No. 29 Squadron
Maj. E. L. Conran
Abeele
15 D.H.2
2 F.E.8

III Brigade
Brig. General J. F. A. Higgins, DSO
Château de Sains

12th (Corps) Wing

13th (Army) Wing
Lt. Col. C. F. de S. Murphy
Foufflin-Ricametz

No. 11 Squadron
Maj. T. O'B. Hubbard
Savy
8 F.E.2b
4 Vickers Gunbus
3 Bristol Scout
3 Nieuport Scout

No. 23 Squadron
Maj. A. Ross-Hume
Le Hameau
14 F.E.2b
3 Martinsyde Scout

```
                              IV Brigade
                              Brig. General E. B. Ashmore, CMG, MVO
                              Les Alençons
    ┌─────────────────────────────┴──────────────────────────────┐
3rd (Corps) Wing                                          14th (Army) Wing
                                                          Lt. Col. C. G. Hoare
                                                          Bertangles
                                                     ┌──────────┴──────────┐
                                            No. 22 Squadron          No. 24 Squadron
                                            Maj. R. B. Martyn         Maj. L. G. Hawker,
                                            Bertangles                VC, DSO
                                                                      Bertangles
                                            18 F.E.2b                 19 D.H.2
                                                                      3 Bristol Scout *
                                                                      2 Morane Scout *
*Attached from squadrons of 3rd (Corps) Wing
```

Dates of arrival of additional fighter squadrons during the battle.
No. 40 Squadron. Maj. R. Lorraine. 12 F.E.8 Treizennes. 10th Wing (I Brigade) A Flight, 2 August 1916. B and C Flights 25 August 1916.

No. 41 Squadron. Maj. J. H. A. Landon. 17 F.E.8. Abeele. 11th Wing (II Brigade) 21 October 1916.

8 Squadron, Royal Naval Air Service. Sqn. Commander G. R. Bromet. 6 Sopwith 1½ Strutter. 6 Sopwith Pup. 6 Nieuport Scout. Vert Galant. 22nd Wing (V Brigade). 26 October 1916.

BRITISH FIGHTER SQUADRON STRENGTH DURING THE MAJOR BATTLES OF 1917-1918

BRITISH FIGHTER SQUADRON STRENGTH DURING THE MAJOR BATTLES OF 1917–18

Battle of Ypres, 31 July 1917

General Officer Commanding the RFC in France:
Major-General H. M. Trenchard, CB, DSO, ADC

Headquarters 9th Wing, OC: Lt. Col. C. L. N. Newall

Squadron	Commanding Officer	Location
19 (Spad)	Maj. W. D. S. Sanday, DSO, MC	Estrée Blanche
56 (S.E.5a)	Maj. R. G. Blomfield	Estrée Blanche
66 (Pup)	Maj. G. L. P. Henderson, MC	Estrée Blanche
70 (Camel)	Maj. M. H. B. Nethersole	Estrée Blanche

10th (Army) Wing, OC: Lt. Col. W. R. Freeman, DSO, MC

Squadron	Commanding Officer	Location
8 Naval (Triplane/Camel)	Sqn. Cdr. G. R. Bromet	Mont St Eloi
40 (Nieuport 17)	Maj. L. A. Tilney	Bruay

11th (Army) Wing, OC: Lt. Col. A. J. L. Scott, MC

Squadron	Commanding Officer	Location
1 (Nieuport 17)	Maj. A. Barton Adams	Bailleul
1 Naval (Triplane)	Sqn. Cdr. R. S. Dallas, DSC	Bailleul
45 (Camel)	Maj. H. A. Van Ryneveld, MC	St Marie-Cappel

13th (Army) Wing, OC: Maj. C. T. MacLean, MC

Squadron	Commanding Officer	Location
24 (D.H.5)	Maj. A. G. Moore, MC	Baizieux
41 (D.H.5)	Maj. J. H. A. Landon, DSO	Lealvillers

Squadron	Commanding Officer	Location
60 (Nieuport/S.E.5)	Maj. W. J. C. Kennedy-Cochran-Patrick, DSO, MC	Le Hameau

14th (Army) Wing, OC: Lt. Col. R. P. Mills, MC

Squadron	Commanding Officer	Location
6 Naval (Camel)	Sqn. Cdr. C. D. Breese	Bray Dunes
9 Naval (Triplane/Camel)	Sqn. Cdr. H. Fawcett	Leffrinck-houcke
54 (Pup)	Maj. K. K. Horn	Leffrinck-houcke

22nd (Army) Wing, OC: Lt. Col. F. V. Holt, DSO

Squadron	Commanding Officer	Location
10 Naval (Triplane)	Sqn. Cdr. B. C. Bell, DSO, DSC	Droglandt
23 (Spad)	Maj. A. M. Wilkinson, DSO	La Lovie
29 (Nieuport 17)	Maj. C. M. B. Chapman, MC	Poperinghe
32 (D.H.5)	Maj. T. A. E. Cairnes, DSO	Droglandt

Battle of Cambrai, 20 November 1917

Headquarters 9th Wing, OC: Lt. Col. W. R. Freeman, DSO, MC
No single-seater fighter squadrons on strength.

10th (Army) Wing, OC: Lt. Col. R. B. Martyn, MC

Squadron	Commanding Officer	Location
8 Naval (Camel)	Sqn. Cdr. C. Draper	Mont St Eloi
40 (S.E.5a)	Maj. L. A. Tilney	Bruay
43 (Camel)	Maj. A. S. W. Dore	Auchel

Squadron	Commanding Officer	Location
11th (Army) Wing, OC: Lt. Col. A. J. L. Scott, MC		
1 (Nieuport 17)	Maj. A. Barton Adams	Bailleul
19 (Spad)	Maj. W. D. S. Sanday, DSO, MC	Bailleul
23 (Spad)	Maj. C. E. Bryant, DSO	La Lovie
29 (Nieuport 17)	Maj. C. H. Dixon, MC	Poperinghe
32 (D.H.5)	Maj. J. C. Russell	Droglandt
60 (S.E.5a)	Maj. W. J. C. Kennedy-Cochran-Patrick, DSO, MC	St Marie-Cappel
65 (Camel)	Maj. J. A. Cunningham	Bailleul
70 (Camel)	Maj. H. B. R. Grey-Edwards, MC	Poperinghe
13th (Army) Wing, OC: Lt. Col. G. F. Pretyman, DSO		
3 (Camel)	Maj. R. Raymond-Barker, MC	Warloy
41 (S.E.5a)	Maj. F. J. Powell, MC	Lealvillers
46 (Pup/Camel)	Maj. P. Babington, MC	Le Hameau
56 (S.E.5a)	Maj. R. Balcombe-Brown, MC	Laviéville
64 (D.H.5)	Maj. B. E. Smythies	Le Hameau
68 (D.H.5)	Maj. W. O. Watt	Baizieux
84 (S.E.5a)	Maj. W. S. Douglas, MC	Le Hameau
14th (Army) Wing, OC: Lt. Col. P. B. Joubert de la Ferté, DSO		
24 (D.H.5)	Maj. J. G. Swart, MC	Teteghem
54 (Pup)	Maj. K. K. Horn	Teteghem

German Offensive, 21 March 1918

General Officer Commanding the RFC in France:
Major-General J. M. Salmond, CMG, DSO

Headquarters 9th (Day) Wing, OC: Lt. Col. W. R. Freeman, DSO, MC

Squadron	Commanding Officer	Location
73 (Camel)	Maj. T. O'B. Hubbard, MC	Champien
79 (Dolphin)	Maj. M. W. Noel	Champien
80 (Camel)	Maj. V. D. Bell	Champien
10th (Army) Wing, OC: Lt. Col. C. T. Maclean, MC		
2 AFC (S.E.5a)	Maj. W. Sheldon	Savy

Squadron	Commanding Officer	Location
3 Naval (Camel)	Sqn. Cdr. R. Collishaw, DSO, DSC	Mont St Eloi
4 AFC (Camel)	Maj. W. A. McClaughry, MC	Bruay
40 (S.E.5a)	Maj. R. S. Dallas, DSC	Bruay
43 (Camel)	Maj. C. C. Miles, MC	La Gorgue
11th (Army) Wing, OC: Lt. Col. H. A. Van Ryneveld, MC		
1 (S.E.5a)	Maj. A. Barton Adams	Bailleul
19 (Dolphin)	Maj. E. R. Pretyman	Bailleul
29 (Nieuport)	Maj. C. H. Dixon, MC	La Lovie
32 (S.E.5a)	Maj. J. C. Russell	Bailleul
60 (S.E.5a)	Maj. B. F. Moore	Bailleul
65 (Camel)	Maj. J. A. Cunningham	Droglandt
13th (Army) Wing, OC: Lt. Col. P. H. L. Playfair, MC		
3 (Camel)	Maj. R. Raymond-Barker, MC	Warloy
41 (S.E.5a)	Maj. G. H. Bowman, MC	Lealvillers
46 (Camel)	Maj. R. H. S. Mealing	Le Hameau
56 (S.E.5a)	Maj. R. Balcombe-Brown, MC	Baizieux
64 (S.E.5a)	Maj. B. E. Smythies	Le Hameau
70 (Camel)	Maj. H. B. R. Grey-Edwards, MC	Marieux
22nd (Army) Wing, OC: Lt. Col. F. V. Holt, DSO		
23 (Spad)	Maj. C. E. Bryant, DSO	Matigny
24 (S.E.5a)	Maj. V. A. H. Robeson, MC	Matigny
54 (Camel)	Maj. R. S. Maxwell, MC	Flez
84 (S.E.5a)	Maj. W. S. Douglas, MC	Flez

Battle of Amiens, 8 August 1918

General Officer Commanding the RAF in France:
Major-General J. M. Salmond, CMG, CVO, DSO

Headquarters 9th Wing, OC: Lt. Col. A. V. Holt, DSO

Squadron	Commanding Officer	Location
32 (S.E.5a)	Maj. J. C. Russell	Bellevue

Squadron	Commanding Officer	Location	Squadron	Commanding Officer	Location
73 (Camel)	Maj. M. le Blanc-Smith, DFC	Bellevue	41 (S.E.5a)	Maj. G. H. Bowman, DSO, MC	Conteville
51st Wing, OC: Lt. Col. R. P. Mills, MC			65 (Camel)	Maj. H. V. Champion de Crespigny, MC	Bertangles
1 (S.E.5a)	Maj. W. E. Young, DFC	Fienvillers			
43 (Camel)	Maj. C. C. Miles, MC	Fienvillers	80 (Camel)	Maj. V. D. Bell	Vignacourt
54 (Camel)	Maj. R. S. Maxwell, MC	Fienvillers	84 (S.E.5a)	Maj. W. S. Douglas, MC	Bertangles
54th Wing, OC: Lt. Col. R. G. D. Small			201 (Camel)	Maj. C. D. Booker, DSC	Poulainville
151 (Camel)	Maj. J. C. Q. Brand, DSO, MC	Fontane-sur-Maye	209 (Camel)	Maj. J. O. Andrews, DSO, MC	Poulainville
10th (Army) Wing, OC: Lt. Col. C. T. Maclean, MC			**65th Wing, OC: Lt. Col. J. A. Cunningham, DFC**		
19 (Dolphin)	Maj. E. R. Pretyman	Savy	17 (American) (Camel)	Lt. E. B. Eckert	Petite Synthe
40 (S.E.5a)	Maj. A. W. Keen, MC	Bryas	148 (American) (Camel)	Lt. M. L. Newhall	Cappelle
64 (S.E.5a)	Maj. B. E. Smythies	Le Hameau	**80th (Army) Wing, OC: Lt. Col. L. A. Strange, MC**		
203 (Camel)	Maj. R. Collishaw, DSO, DSC, DFC	Filescamps Farm (Le Hameau)	2 (AFC) (S.E.5a)	Maj. A. Murray-Jones, MC, DFC	Reclinghem
208 (Camel)	Maj. C. Draper, DSC	Tramecourt	4 (AFC) (Camel)	Maj. W. A. McClaughry, MC	Reclinghem
11th (Army) Wing, OC: Lt. Col. H. A. Van Ryneveld, MC			46 (Camel)	Maj. A. H. O'Hara Wood	Serny
29 (S.E.5a)	Maj. C. H. Dixon, MC	Hooge Huys	92 (S.E.5a)	Maj. A. Coningham, DSO, MC	Serny
70 (Camel)	Maj. E. L. Foot, MC	Esquerdes	**61st Wing, OC: Lt. Col. E. Osmond**		
74 (S.E.5a)	Maj. K. L. Caldwell, MC	Clairmarais	204 (Camel)	Maj. E. W. Norton, DSC	Teteghem
79 (Dolphin)	Maj. A. R. Arnold, DFC	St Marie-Cappel	210 (Camel)	Maj. B. C. Bell, DSO, DSC	Eringhem
13th (Army) Wing, OC: Lt. Col. P. H. L. Playfair, MC			213 (Camel)	Maj. R. Grahame, DSO, DSC	Bergues
3 (Camel)	Maj. R. St Clair McClintock, MC	Valheureux			
56 (S.E.5a)	Maj. E. J. L. W. Gilchrist, MC	Valheureux			
60 (S.E.5a)	Maj. A. C. Clarke	Boffles			
87 (Dolphin)	Maj. C. J. W. Darwin	Rougefay			
22nd (Army) Wing, OC: Lt. Col. T. A. E. Cairnes, DSO					
23 (Dolphin)	Maj. C. E. Bryant, DSO	Bertangles			
24 (S.E.5a)	Maj. V. A. H. Robeson, MC	Conteville			

British Fighter Squadrons at 11 November 1918

S.E.5a: Nos. 1, 2 AFC, 24, 29, 32, 40, 41, 56, 60, 64, 74, 84, 85, 92, and 94.

Camel: Nos. 3, 45, 46, 54, 65, 70, 73, 80, 151, 152, 201, 203, 204, 208, 209, 210, and 213.

Dolphin: Nos. 19, 23, 79, and 87.

Snipe: Nos. 4 AFC, and 43.

BIBLIOGRAPHY

Bodenschatz. Karl, *Jagd in Flanderns Himmel.* Knorr and Hirth München 1935

Bond, Aimée Constance, *An Airman's Wife.* Herbert Jenkins Ltd 1928

Bowyer, Chaz, *Royal Flying Corps Communiqués 1917-1918.* Grub St. 1998

Bruce, Jack M, Page Gordan, Sturtivant Ray, *The Sopwith Pup.* Air Britain. 2002

Cole, Christopher ed. *Royal Flying Corps 1915-1916.* William Kimber 1969

Cole, Christopher ed. *Royal Air Force 1918.* William Kimber 1968

Collishaw, Raymond, Air-Vice Marshal and Dodds R V, *Air Command, A Fighter Pilot's Story.* William Kimber 1973

Cross and Cockade, Great Britain/International. Journals, 1970-2005

Cross and Cockade, America. Journals 1960-1985

Crundall, E O Wing Commander, *Fighter Pilot on the Western Front.* William Kimber 1975

Cutlack, F M, *The Australian Flying Corps.* Queensland Press 1984

Douglas, Sholto, Marshal of the Royal Air Force, Lord Douglas of Kirtleside, *Years of Combat.* Collins 1963

Eberhardt Walter von, *Unsere Luftstreitkräfte* 1914-1918

Franks, Norman, Bailey, Frank and Duiven Rick, *The Jasta Pilots.* Grub St 1996

Franks, Norman L R, Bailey Frank W and Guest, Russell, *Above The Lines.* Grub St 1993

Franks, Norman, O'Connor, Mike, *Number One in War and Peace.* Grub St 2000

Fry, Wing Commander William, *Air of Battle.* William Kimber 1974

Gannon R. *Jasta* Casualties. Unpublished lists

Gould Lee, Arthur, *No Parachute.* Jarrolds 1968

Grinnell-Milne, Duncan, *Wind In The Wires.* Aviation Bookshelf 1933

Henshaw, Trevor, *The Sky Their Battlefield.* Grub St 1995

Imrie, Alex, *Pictorial History of the German Air Service.* Ian Allan 1971

Jefford, C G, Wing Commander, *RAF Squadrons.* Airlife 1988

Jones, H A, *The War in the Air Vols 4-6.* Oxford University Press 1934-1937

Jones, Ira, *Tiger Squadron.* W H Allen 1954.

Jones, Ira, Flt Lt, *King Of Air Fighters.* Ivor Nicholson and Watson 1934

Lambert, Bill, *Combat Report.* William Kimber 1973

Lewis, Gwilym H Wing Commander, *Wings Over The Somme.* William Kimber 1976

MacMillan, Norman, *Into the Blue.* Duckworth 1929

McCudden, James T B, *Flying Fury.* John Hamilton 1930

McScotch, *Fighter Pilot.* Newnes 1936

Nachrichtenblätter der Luftstreitkräfte 1917 and 1918.

Popular Flying 1934-1938

Raleigh, W, *The War in the Air Vol 1.* Oxford. The Clarendon Press 1922.

Raleigh, W, Jones, H A, *The War in the Air Vol 2.* The Clarendon Press 1928

Revell, Alex, *High in the Empty Blue.* Flying Machine Press 1995

Revell, Alex, *Victoria Cross, World War One Airmen and their Aircraft.* Flying Machines Press 1997

Revell, Alex, *Brief Glory.* William Kimber 1984

Revell, Alex, *The Vivid Air.* William Kimber 1978

Rochford, Leonard H, *I Chose the* Sky. William Kimber 1997

Rogers, Les, *British Aviation Squadron Markings of World War 1 RFC.RAF.RNAS*. Schiffer Military History 2001

Stark, Rudolph, *Wings of War*. John Hamilton. 1933

Shores, Christopher, Franks, Norman L R and Guest, Russell, *Above The Trenches*. Grub St. 1990

Stewart, Oliver, *Words and Music for a Mechanical Man*. Faber and Faber 1927

Sturtivant, Ray, Page, Gordon, *The SE5 File*. Air Britain 1996

Sturtivant, Ray. Page, Gordon, The Camel File. Air Britain 1993

Taylor, Sir Gordon, *Sopwith Scout 7309*. Cassell 1968

Westrop, Mike, *A History of No.10 Squadron Royal Naval Air Service in World War One*. Schiffer Military History. 2004

Zickerick, Wilhelm, Major, *Verlustliste der Deutschschen Luftstreitkräfte im Weltkreige*.

GLOSSARY OF TERMS
AND ABBREVIATIONS

General Terms

COP   Close offensive patrol
DOP   Distant or deep offensive patrol
KIA   Killed in action
WIA   Wounded in action
DOW   Died of wounds.
DOI   Died of injuries
HE   Home Establishment
KiAcc   Killed in accident
InjAcc   Injured in accident
POW   Prisoner of war

Ranks British RFC/RAF

2Lt.   Second Lieutenant
Lt.   Lieutenant
Cap.   Captain
Maj.   Major
LtCol.   Lieutenant-Colonel

Ranks British RNAS

FltSubLt.   Flight Sub Lieutenant
FltLt.   Flight Lieutenant
FltCom.   Flight Commander
SqdnCom   Squadron Commander

Medals and awards

VC   Victoria Cross
DSO   Distinguished Service Order
MC   Military Cross
DFC   Distinguished Flying Cross
DSC   Distinguished Service Cross
AFC   Air Force Cross
MM   Military Medal
DFM   Distinguished Flying Medal
DSM   Distinguished Service medal
C de G   *Croix de Guerre.*
Ld'H   *Légion d' Honneur*

+ denotes a Bar to the award.

Ranks German		**British equivilant**
Flg.	*Flieger*	Private
Gfr.	*Gefreiter*	Private 1st Class.
Uffz.	*Unteroffizier*	Corporal
Vzfw.	*Vizefeldwebel*	Sergeant Major
Oberflm	*Oberflugmeister*	Senior NCO Marine Aviation.
Offstv.	*Offizierstellvertreter*	Warrant Officer
Ltn.	*Leutnant*	2nd Lieutenant
Ltn d Res	*Leutnant der Reserve*	2nd Lieutenant of the Reserve
Oblt	*Oberleutnant*	Lieutenant
Hptm.	*Hauptmann*	Captain
Ritt.	*Rittmeister*	Cavalry Captain
Obst.	*Oberst*	Colonel

Terms German

Bogohl	*Bombengeschwader*	Bombing squadron
FlAbt	*Fleiger Abteilung*	Field flying unit.
Fl(A)Abt	*Fleiger (A) Abteilung*	Field flying unit for artillery co-operation.
Flak	*Flugabwehrkanonen*	Anti aircraft gun/fire
	Flugmeldedienst	Unit for reporting enemy aerial activity
	Jagdgeschwader	Grouping of four *Jagdstaffeln*
Jasta	*Jagdstaffel*	Fighter squadron
KEK	*Kampfeinsitzer Kommandos*	Early temporary single seater fighter units
KG/KS Kagohl/Kasta	*Kampfgeschwader/Kampfstaffel*	Fighting Squadrons of Army High Command
	Luftstreitkräfte	Air Force
	Riesenflugzeug Abteilung	Squadron equipped with giant R category aeroplanes
Schusta	*Schutzstaffel*	Squadron for the protection of *Flieger Abteilung*
Schlasta	*Schlachtstaffel*	Renaming of Schusta in March 1918
	Staffelführer	Commanding officer of a *jagdstaffel*.

NAME INDEX

Bauer A. 148
Bauer E. 93
Baümer P. 150. 178, 179
Bawlf L. 232, 283
Bayetto T H. 27, 160
Beamish H F. 143, 257, 259, 262
Beanlands B. 138, 180, 225
Beatie. A. 180
Beattie A G. 203
Beauchamp A. 150
Beauchamp F. 291
Beauchamp-Proctor A. 185, 203, 216, 219, 225, 227, 259, 260, 263, 290, 300, 301fn., 307, 308, 313, 321, 322, 323, 324, 332fn.
Beck A. 290, 324, 332fn.
Becka. 217
Becker H. 106, 153, 213, 219
Becker M. 193
Behling A. 58fn.
Behm W. 222
Belgrave J. 263, 269, 274fn.
Below O Gen. 109
Bell B C. 56
Bell D J. 225, 226, 251, 265
Bell G. 10
Bell J. 185, 224, 333
Bellen G. 176fn.
Bell-Irving A. 17, 39
Bell-Irving M. 15
Bell-Irving R. 17
Belz. 321
Benbow E. 48, 54, 56, 58fn., 60, 266, 278
Benge A N. 47
Benjamin L. 217
Bennett S L. 76
Bennetts E A. 65, 118
Bentley W O. 255fn.
Berger. 70
Bergman W. 199
Berkemeyer F. 171, 175
Berkling. 57
Berlyn R C. 229
Bernert F O. 62, 65, 71
Berthold R. 40, 137, 160, 166, 292
Bertrab J von. 130, 131
Beschow. 239fn.
Besenmüller A. 225
Besser G. 205
Best F B. 124
Bethge H. 118, 125fn. 132, 134
Beuttler F. 257
Bevington R J. 61, 80fn.
Bey K. 187
Bickerton F H. 137, 145
Billik P. 78, 134, 176fn., 195, 222, 238, 263, 268, 274fn., 279, 292
Billinge F. 216, 237
Billings H B. 129
Binnie, A. 57, 66, 80fn.
Binting R. 218
Bion R E. 247, 255fn.

Birch R A. 276
Bird A. 140
Bird J D J. 108
Birkbeck R. 167
Berks N A. 60
Bishop N. 296, 297, 301fn., 309
Bishop W. 57, 60, 62, 63, 67, 69, 72, 74, 76, 79, 84, 98, 99, 108fn., 112, 113, 114, 119, 124, 125, 125fn., 129, 131, 132, 133, 134, 265, 266, 268, 271, 272, 278
Bissonette C. 259
Biziou H. 258, 312
Black C T. 57, 59
Black N. 167
Blair J. 296
Bland W. 322, 334
Blaxland G. 325, 334
Blaxland, L B. 55, 110
Blechmann R. 222
Blenkiron A V. 49, 195, 196, 203, 208 307
Blomfield R. 119, 161, 169
Bloomfield T. 315
Blume E. 49
Blyth E J. 195
Blyth R A. 207
Blythe H. 50
Boddy. 53
Boddy J A V. 186, 200fn.
Bode A. 197
Bodenschatz K. 147, 298, 349
Boelcke O. 17, 37, 39, 40-44, 46fn., 284
Boger W O. 269, 287, 291, 293
Böhm H. 114
Böhme E. 37, 40, 42, 4347, 50, 54, 117, 168, 179, 189
Böhme M. 53
Bohne. 36
Böhning H. 146, 232
Boit G. 224
Bolle K. 209, 280, 335, 338fn.
Bond A C. 349
Bond F. 322
Bond W. 70, 75, 82, 85, 86, 89, 92, 95, 96, 96fn., 100, 104, 120, 136
Bongartz H. 187, 254
Booker C D 64, 66, 71-73, 76, 78, 79, 89, 93, 117, 119, 120, 123, 130, 135, 158
Boote R S L. 103
Booth E. 167
Booth F. 203
Boothman C. 272
Borck H J. 293
Borden H. 276
Borm G. 3321
Börner W. 195
Böttcher J. 114
Boumphrey J. 124, 160
Bowen C S. 251
Bowen L. 308
Bower F. 54, 57
Bowien W. 225

Bowman G G. 92
Bowman G H. 20, 37, 101, 102, 105, 106, 112, 115, 118, 119, 120, 122, 124, 131, 133, 137, 144, 145, 146, 154, 155, 159, 160, 164, 169, 174, 175, 179, 187, 190, 192, 193, 194, 197, 206, 208, 210, 213, 218, 314, 315, 324, 325, 327, 337
Bowring J V. 39
Bowyer C. 349
Brabazon Rees L W. 21
Bracksiek F. 206
Braham. 53
Brand C. 288
Brandt O. 123
Bransby-Williams W D. 90
Brassel P. 179
Brauer H . 123
Brauneck O. 120, 121
Bray F. 118
Breadner L S. 65, 70, 82
Brecht K. 209
Breese C D. 98
Bremer. 253
Bremridge G. 208, 222
Bremridge W. 196
Brewis. J A G. 75, 80fn.
Brewster-Joske C A. 99, 103, 152, 166, 167
Bridgeman O C. 138, 260
Briese E. 217
Bright R E. 258
Brinkmann W. 228
Britnell F J S. 223
Broad H. 68, 90
Broadberry E. 84, 94, 102, 106, 113, 115
Bromet G. 43, 117
Brooke-Popham H R M. 10, 13
Brookes E. 290
Brookes W. 132
Broome F C. 308, 311
Brosius J. 80fn.
Broughall H. 150
Brown A. 221
Brown A R. 252
Brown C E. 225
Brown C F. 284
Brown C H. 187
Brown F E. 179, 213, 223, 226, 227, 228
Brown S M. 294
Brown W H. 187, 198, 223, 225, 228
Browne H. 276
Brownell R. 145, 163, 170
Browning S F. 83
Bruce J M. 349
Bruce P. 266
Bruce T. 179
Brügman H. 132
Bryson O. 156, 172, 180, 195, 196, 222
Buchanan A. 274, 331
Büchner F. 276, 285
Buchstett W. 232
Buck G S. 65, 105

Note: Ranks are omitted because of variance. Fn. denotes footnote.

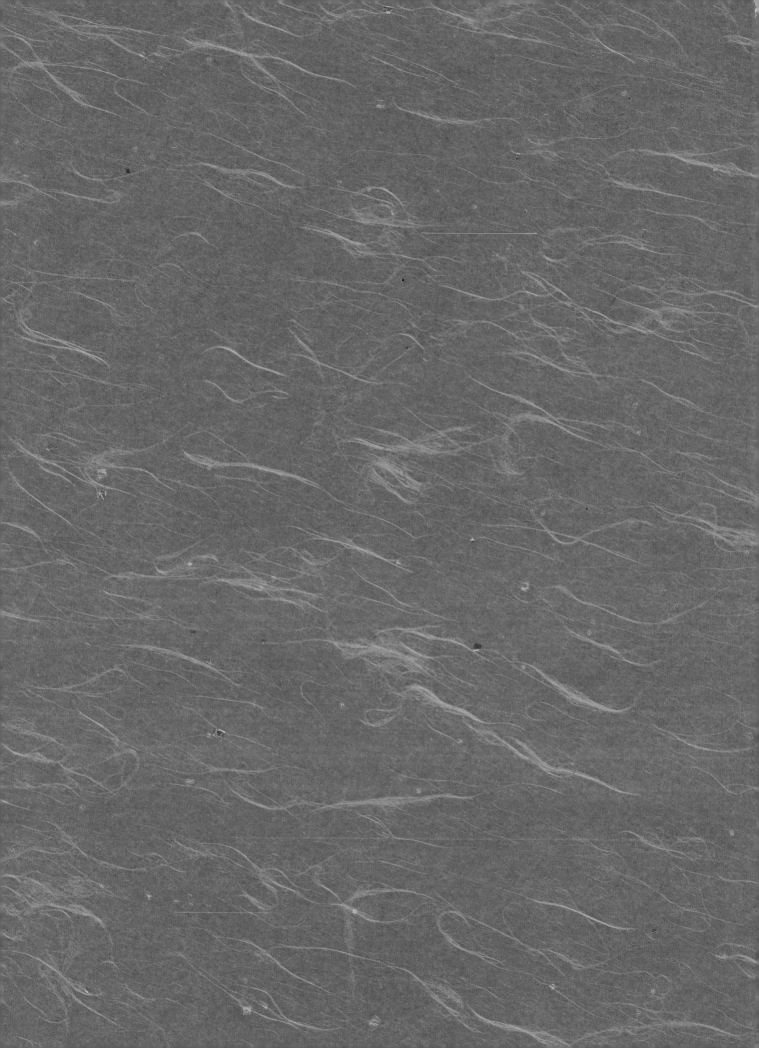